T H E
1988
Elias Baseball
Analyst

THE
1988
Elias Baseball
Analyst

Seymour Siwoff, Steve Hirdt
& Peter Hirdt

COLLIER BOOKS
Macmillan Publishing Company
New York
COLLIER MACMILLAN PUBLISHERS
London

Collier Books
Macmillan Publishing Company
866 Third Avenue, New York, NY 10022
Collier Macmillan Canada, Inc.

"The Library of Congress has cataloged this
serial publication as follows:".

The . . . Elias baseball analyst.—1985–   —New York:
  Collier Books, c1985–

    v.; 28 cm.

  Annual.
  Re-arrangement of material issued in a series of computerized reports called: The
Player analysis.
  Produced by the Elias Sports Bureau.
  Editors for 1985–   by S. Siwoff, S. Hirdt, and P. Hirdt.

  1. Baseball—United States—Statistics—Periodicals. 2. National League of Professional Baseball Clubs—Statistics—Periodicals. 3. Baseball—Statistics—
  1. Baseball—United States—Statistics—Periodicals. 2. National League of Periodicals. 4. Baseball—Miscellanea—Periodicals. I. Siwoff,   Seymour. II. Hirdt,
Steve. III. Hirdt, Peter. IV. Elias Sports Bureau. V. Player analysis. VI. Title:
Baseball analyst.
GV877.E44   85-643022
                     796.357′0973—dc19
                                           AACR 2   MARC-S

ISBN 0-02-044982-8

Macmillan books are available at special discounts
for bulk purchases for sales promotions, premiums,
fund-raising, or educational use. For details, contact:

  Special Sales Director
  Macmillan Publishing Company
  866 Third Avenue
  New York, NY 10022

10 9 8 7 6 5 4 3 2 1

Printed in the United States of America

Contents

I.   Introduction   3

II. Team Section   7

     American League
     Baltimore Orioles   11
     Boston Red Sox   18
     California Angels   25
     Chicago White Sox   32
     Cleveland Indians   39
     Detroit Tigers   46
     Kansas City Royals   53
     Milwaukee Brewers   60
     Minnesota Twins   67
     New York Yankees   74
     Oakland A's   81
     Seattle Mariners   88
     Texas Rangers   95
     Toronto Blue Jays   102

     National League
     Atlanta Braves   111
     Chicago Cubs   118
     Cincinnati Reds   125
     Houston Astros   132
     Los Angeles Dodgers   139
     Montreal Expos   146
     New York Mets   153
     Philadelphia Phillies   160
     Pittsburgh Pirates   167
     St. Louis Cardinals   171
     San Diego Padres   181
     San Francisco Giants   188

III. Batter Section   197
     American League Batters   201
     American League Teams   242

     National League Batters   249
     National League Teams   283

IV. Pitcher Section   287
     American League Pitchers   293
     American League Teams   325
     National League Pitchers   329
     National League Teams   358

V.   Rankings Section   363
     Batting Rankings   367
     Pitching Rankings   375

VI. Single Season and
     Career Leaders   385
     Batting Leaders   387
     Pitching Leaders   394

VII. Batter-Pitcher Matchups   401
     George Bell   405
     Eric Davis   406
     Andre Dawson   407
     Alan Trammell   409
     Steve Bedrosian   411
     Roger Clemens   413
     Frank Viola   414

VIII. Ballparks   419
     American League   420
     National League   427
     Ballpark Effects   433

ACKNOWLEDGEMENTS

Each year, it's our privilege to thank people who devote their time and energy to the preparation of the *Analyst*, but who do not receive commensurate credit. Someday, someone will invent a process whereby we can fit all of these names onto the cover, where they belong. For without them, the book simply would not exist.

First among equals is Tom Hirdt, who merely dedicates his autumns and winters to the production of the book. Tom has an uncanny knack of recognizing an interesting topic and rejecting a lousy one, and of chasing a lead that others would reject while leaving to others the pursuit of one that ends up on the cutting room floor. We only hope that the introduction of cable TV into his life this summer (yes, for those of you outside of New York, it's just reaching us here) will not lead to an overload of Atlanta Braves comments in the 1989 *Analyst*.

Christopher Thorn heads our computer department, which is only fitting. For a long time, he *was* our computer department. He has tolerated with good humor our ignorance of disk drives and megabytes longer that we've had a right to expect, and he has honored a couple of million of our requests to "Just let us have 20 more minutes before you back up that disk." Somehow, everything seems to get done, and although we're not quite sure how he manages it, Chris deserves the credit.

John Chymczuk and John Labombarda have done laborious research for each of the four editions of the *Analyst*, and we couldn't have done it without them. We hope that the toll has not been too great, although we must report that John L. has taken to wearing glasses lately. If you're ever in the loge level behind home plate at Shea Stadium, say hello to John C.; he's the only guy in the section who knows how many times a team that has outhomered its opponents over the course of a season by 50-or-more homers. When the Broadway musical version of the *Analyst* is produced, these guys will be the hardest to cast.

John and John were joined this year by a pair of rookies on the Elias team, Alex Stern and Chris Lasch. Rookie initiations at Elias are only slightly less onerous than they are on the Chicago Bears, but Alex and Chris never complained, regardless of how high we piled the work. Their solace is that you can be a rookie only once, and although neither hit 49 home runs or fashioned a 34-game hitting streak, they are the 1987 Rookies of the Year around our place.

In order to produce the quality that is expected of this book, a batter-by-batter description of every major-league game must be correctly computer-coded. John Chymczuk and Santo Labombarda were the stars of this operation. Santo is well-named, for his dedication to this seemingly endless task is indeed saintlike. Younger brother Frank Labombarda pitched in at crunch time, which around here is anytime after Larry Bowa holds his first clubhouse meeting. Thanks, coders.

Rocky Avakian spent part of last year on the disabled list, but he had his All-Star berth locked up by then. Rocky's performance at night is even better than Juan Berenguer's, and the Rock goes out there every night, year round. Just leave him a project at night, and it's done by morning. It'll be good to have him back at full speed in '88.

Bob Rosen's dedication to sports is tireless, as anyone who has seen him at Mets, Yankees, Knicks or Nets games can tell you. His documentation of anything that moves is legendary; so too, unfortunately, are his puns. Jay Chesler has the second-longest tenure of anyone at Elias, and his research, both long ago and current day, is the basis for much of the material in this book.

Andrew Serp, Anthony Sorrentino and Gil Traub have each made this a better book by applying their computer expertise and mathematical wizardry to baseball topics, instead of going into something more lucrative, like insider trading, for example. At least we've kept them on the right side of the law; the republic might be endangered if their brainpower were ever used for less noble pursuits.

Our outside computer experts are Larry Meisner and Dick Hata, who have made sure that our jobs have run promptly and smoothly. It's the last *Analyst* for Dick, who has retired, and will therefore be eligible for enshrinement in Cooperstown in five years. And, of course, Warren Bannerman is the granddaddy of all outside computer experts; it's not that Warren is old, he Rose Bowl.

ACKNOWLEDGEMENTS

Rick Wolff took over the editor's job at Macmillan just in time to be immersed in the infinite variety of details tangent to the *Analyst*. He weathered the storm well, and swears that he never once woke up in the middle of the night in a cold sweat mumbling incoherently about 'Late-Inning Pressure Situations.' He was capably assisted by David Blumenstein. Thanks, guys, now let's do it again.

David Frost and Paul Heacock did a terifec job copy edtng the ANALYST. Because this page was written last, its' the only one that they did'nt look at, but we're sure that its OKAY anyways.

We placed the design and look of the book in the hands of Casey Lee, Fred Richardson, Bob Keefe, Jackie Dickens and John Lynch, and they came through with a first-rate job. No author should be without such capable people.

Finally, the families of everyone involved in the project deserve a special salute, for without unending patience and understanding on their part, this book would never have been attempted, let alone completed.

THE
1988
Elias Baseball
Analyst

I
Introduction

INTRODUCTION

It's hard for us to believe, but here we are with our fourth annual edition of *The Elias Baseball Analyst*. We started in 1985, along with Vince Coleman, Teddy Higuera, Roger McDowell, and Ozzie Guillen, and we'd love to outlast all of them.

We are truly gratified with the response that the book has generated. To those of you who have purchased the book in past years, and especially to those who have written us with your appreciation or suggestions, we extend our thanks. To those who are coming aboard for the first time, a hearty welcome. We'll give you a brief background on what our book is about. (This year, we'll hold the backgrounding to three paragraphs; veteran readers can rejoin the group after that.)

The *Analyst* was created in 1985 from a series of computerized reports, called *The Player Analysis*, which we at the Elias Sports Bureau had designed in order to better evaluate the performance tendencies of major-league baseball players. And, you may ask, just what is the Elias Sports Bureau? Elias is a New York-based sports information company that, among other things, serves as the official statistician for major-league baseball, the National Football League and the National Basketball Association; and before you go looking for *Analysts* in those sports, sorry, but they don't exist, at least not yet. Our company has been the source of nearly all of the baseball statistics generated for the past seventy years.

The Player Analysis revealed to us, as early as 1975, what treasures had always been hidden below the surface of the ordinary statistics. It's rather commonplace now for us to observe writers and broadcasters as they refer to a player's batting average with runners in scoring position, or the batting average by a particular batter against a particular pitcher. But in 1975, when we first introduced those concepts and many others on a mass scale to the 26 major-league teams, they were regarded as the work of a group of revolutionaries.

For several years, the only exposure that these reports received was to the teams themselves. But in 1985 we wrapped the reports within two covers, added some essays and player comments, and sent the whole package out to the nation's bookstores, not knowing what to expect. What we found was that not only is baseball's popularity at an all-time high, but also that the interest in examining the performance of individual players and teams is also at a peak.

As the *Analyst* has become a familiar harbinger of spring, we have tried our best to keep it interesting and fresh. This year, we have restored some of the tables that appeared in the Team Section in the first two editions of the book, but which were dropped for space reasons in 1987. In addition, we have added pages within the Ballparks section that more clearly identify exactly which stadiums most greatly influence various facets of play, so that never again will you have to suffer in silence as someone refers to Fenway Park or the Metrodome as home-run havens when in fact they're not.

But our book is really all new every year, since each season gives us a unique backdrop of events, and putting events into perspective is what statistics do best. For example, picture yourself in the stands at Memorial Stadium last spring as Juan Nieves was throwing a no-hitter against the Orioles. If you had come to the game with a friend who knew nothing about baseball, that friend would likely consider the game to be boring, with not much going on. You, on the other hand, would be immersed in the drama while quickly trying to catch your friend up on the rarity of the event that was unfolding.

Determining the rarity or commonness of an event, and trying to determine the outcome of future events through past tendencies, is what this book is all about. Statistical information can be many things: interesting, trivial, dry, humorous, pointed, inconsequential. We hope that we hit the high notes and eliminate the low. Along the way, we'll pose and answer some questions that have intrigued us and that we hope will interest you. Do strikeout pitchers really win more games than finesse pitchers? See the White Sox essay. What all-time record received next to no attention last season, amid the trumpeting of more trivial performances? Take a quick look at the Astros essay. Which manager had his team attempt only one steal of third base all last season? It's not Tony LaRussa of the A's, but you'll find the answer in the Oakland essay anyway. How does the Twins' home-field advantage stack up against other teams, not only in baseball, but in all pro sports? We think you catch our drift.

There once was a time when baseball statistics were thought to be conversation-stoppers; now, people are recognizing that such information can be the life of the party. Where sports reporters once regarded the inclusion of statistics as an obligation, stories are now written with a single nugget of statistical information as the centerpiece. And without disparaging those who deal in 'trivia' (some of our best friends are trivial), baseball executives, the media and fans now realize that statistical information can be used for more than to fill the backs of bubblegum cards or the heads of trivia experts.

To all of you, veteran and rookie, who will ride with us, climb aboard. We feel that you'll find our book unlike any other, and we think that anyone who likes baseball will have an enjoyable time learning new things not only about the current crop of players, but also about the game itself.

Want to know who has hit 60 points higher with runners on base than with the bases empty over the past five years? Or why the Reds-Royals off-season trade should benefit both teams? Which pitcher Wade Boggs can't hit? Just keep turning the pages, and you'll have all the answers.

II
Team Section

Team Section

The Team Section consists of comments and statistics for each of the twenty-six major-league teams. The examples here, and in all of the section introductions, just happen to be taken from the 1985 season.

WON-LOST RECORD BY STARTING POSITION

BALTIMORE	83-78	C	1B	2B	3B	SS	LF	CF	RF	P	DH	Leadoff	Relief	Starts
Don Aase		·	·	·	·	·	·	·	·	·	·	·	26-28	·
Eric Bell		·	·	·	·	·	·	·	·	·	·	·	0-4	·
Mike Boddicker		·	·	·	·	·	·	·	·	13-19	·	·	·	13-19
Fritz Connally		·	1-0	·	12-15	·	·	·	·	·	1-0	·	·	14-15
Rich Dauer		·	·	32-31	4-4	·	·	·	·	·	·	·	·	36-35
Storm Davis		·	·	·	·	·	·	·	·	16-12	·	·	0-3	16-12
Rick Dempsey		57-56	·	·	·	·	·	·	·	·	·	·	·	57-56
Ken Dixon		·	·	·	·	·	·	·	·	10-8	·	·	2-14	10-8
Jim Dwyer		·	·	·	·	·	16-20	·	16-9	·	0-1	9-6	·	32-30
Mike Flanagan		·	·	·	·	·	·	·	·	7-8	·	·	·	7-8
Dan Ford		·	·	·	·	·	·	·	·	·	10-6	5-5	·	10-6
Wayne Gross		·	0-5	·	30-27	·	·	·	·	·	1-3	·	·	31-35
John Habyan		·	·	·	·	·	·	·	·	·	·	·	1-1	·
Brad Havens		·	·	·	·	·	·	·	·	0-1	·	·	2-5	0-1
Leo Hernandez		·	·	·	·	·	·	·	·	·	0-4	·	·	0-4
Phil Huffman		·	·	·	·	·	·	·	·	1-0	·	·	0-1	1-0
Lee Lacy		·	·	·	·	·	·	·	51-61	·	3-1	16-20	·	54-62
John Lowenstein		·	·	·	1-3	·	·	·	·	·	2-2	·	·	3-5

The first table following the team comments is the Won-Lost Record by Starting Position chart. This chart lists, for each player on a team, the team's won-lost record in games started by that player at each position, in the leadoff spot in the lineup, and in games in which a pitcher appeared in relief. (This last is included to give some insight into how the manager chose to use his relief staff.) The players are listed in alphabetical order.

Following this table is a series of eight charts detailing the performance of each player and pitcher on the team who played at least semiregularly. Included are all players who had at least 200 plate appearances in the season, all pitchers who faced at least 200 batters, and selected individuals who did not meet the standard but were still significant enough to merit inclusion.

Overall Batting Compared to Late Inning Pressure Situations

		BA	Rank	SA	Rank	OBA	Rank	HR %	Rank	BB %	Rank	SO %	Rank	RDI %	Rank
Rich Dauer	Overall	.202	155	.264	154	.275	148	0.96	129	8.55	73	2.99	1	.200	--
	Pressure	.118	--	.118	--	.118	--	0.00	--	0.00	--	0.00	--	.000	--
Rick Dempsey	Overall	.254	99	.406	88	.345	50	3.31	61	11.90	30	20.71	149	.318	48
	Pressure	.171	149	.293	124	.286	118	2.44	77	14.00	30	24.00	146	.286	--
Jim Dwyer	Overall	.249	106	.399	95	.353	36	3.00	73	13.50	16	11.31	50	.324	43
	Pressure	.344	13	.563	10	.500	2	3.13	56	23.81	2	14.29	82	.455	12
Wayne Gross	Overall	.235	134	.424	69	.369	17	5.07	17	17.42	2	18.18	133	.118	163
	Pressure	.184	143	.316	113	.225	149	2.63	69	5.00	124	20.00	133	.100	155
Lee Lacy	Overall	.293	22	.409	82	.343	52	1.83	105	7.22	103	17.59	124	.262	113
	Pressure	.297	40	.453	44	.378	33	4.69	38	10.81	56	16.22	100	.167	128
Fred Lynn	Overall	.263	78	.449	41	.339	63	5.13	15	10.43	40	19.69	140	.285	88
	Pressure	.231	104	.481	34	.333	73	7.69	11	13.33	35	23.33	143	.214	111
Eddie Murray	Overall	.297	16	.523	4	.383	6	5.32	24	12.41	24	10.04	42	.428	4
	Pressure	.333	15	.682	3	.400	23	9.09	4	10.67	57	8.00	23	.636	1
Floyd Rayford	Overall	.306	9	.521	5	.324	84	5.01	19	2.69	156	18.55	136	.214	143
	Pressure	.268	64	.585	8	.333	73	7.32	12	8.89	79	24.44	149	.250	87
Cal Ripken	Overall	.282	39	.469	25	.347	47	4.05	57	9.33	57	9.47	37	.378	9
	Pressure	.292	43	.528	23	.366	41	6.94	15	10.98	54	9.76	37	.250	87
Gary Roenicke	Overall	.218	151	.458	30	.342	57	6.67	4	16.06	4	13.14	77	.364	19
	Pressure	.043	--	.174	--	.185	--	4.35	--	14.81	--	14.81	--	.167	--
Larry Sheets	Overall	.262	81	.442	49	.323	90	5.18	14	7.76	92	14.40	98	.330	35
	Pressure	.235	102	.412	71	.291	116	5.88	25	7.27	101	20.00	133	.273	78
John Shelby	Overall	.283	38	.434	57	.307	121	3.41	60	3.27	154	20.56	147	.333	31
	Pressure	.200	130	.286	127	.222	150	0.00	113	2.78	143	25.00	150	.250	87
Alan Wiggins	Overall	.285	35	.349	130	.353	38	0.00	154	8.66	68	4.78	2	.339	29
	Pressure	.308	32	.346	94	.438	9	0.00	113	18.18	7	3.03	4	.400	22
Mike Young	Overall	.273	59	.513	11	.348	43	6.22	6	9.52	52	20.63	148	.293	73
	Pressure	.222	114	.426	56	.311	93	5.56	30	11.48	52	18.03	118	.333	55

Column Headings Information

BA	Batting Average
SA	Slugging Average
OBA	On-Base Average
HR%	Home Run Percentage (home runs per 100 at bats)
BB%	Base-on-Balls Percentage (bases on balls per 100 plate appearances)
SO%	Strikeout Percentage (strikeouts per 100 plate appearances)
RDI%	Percentage of Runners Driven In

Each chart provides a statistical breakdown of player performance in a selected category. For each category, the player's average or percentage is given, along with his ranking within the league. This enables us to see at a glance that while Jim Dwyer ranked 95th in the league in slugging overall in 1985, he ranked tenth in pressure situations (see below). Rankings in each category are listed for the 162 players and 145 pitchers with the most plate appearances or batters faced in the category (plus ties) in the American League, and the top 136 batters and 125 pitchers (plus ties) in the National League. If a player does not qualify under this standard, no ranking is listed. (For a more detailed description of the methods used in determining the number of qualifiers for a given category, see the introduction to the Leaders Section.)

The batter charts list breakdowns against left-handed and right-handed pitching, performance with bases empty and runners on base, and overall performance for the season compared with performance in pressure situations (all at bats occurring in the seventh inning or later with the score tied or the batter's team trailing by one, two, or three runs, or four runs with the bases loaded).

The final batter chart lists miscellaneous comparisons for each player, giving his batting average on grass fields and artificial turf; in home games and in road games; with runners in scoring position and with runners in scoring position and two out; on-base average leading off an inning; and the percentage of runners he drove in from third base with less than two out. (For players who played for more than one team in a league, all totals are combined. The "home" totals for Kevin Mitchell, for example, include all games played in San Diego when he was with the Padres, and all games played in San Francisco while he was with the Giants.)

On each chart, following the individual batter totals, are the team's averages for each category, and the team's ranking within the league. For purposes of comparison, the overall league average is also included.

The pitcher charts list breakdowns against left-handed and right-handed batters, performance with bases empty and runners on base, and overall performance for the season compared with performance in pressure situations (against all batters in the seventh inning or later with the score tied or the pitcher's team leading or trailing by one or two runs).

The final pitcher chart lists miscellaneous comparisons for each pitcher giving his opponents' batting average on grass fields and artificial turf; in home games and in road games; with runners in scoring position and with runners in scoring position and two out; and opponents' on-base average leading off an inning.

On each chart, following the individual pitcher statistics, are the team's averages for each category, and the team's ranking within the league. For purposes of comparison, the overall league average is also included.

For a detailed discussion of the use of opposing batters' records to examine pitching performance, see the introduction to the Pitcher Section.

American League

BALTIMORE ORIOLES

Remember the 1983 World Series? The Orioles defeating the Phillies, four games to one; Rick Dempsey getting five extra-base hits; Howard Cosell broadcasting a World Series for the last time (at least we *think* the last time).

Something strange may have been in the air during that Series. Maybe there was an unreported toxic spill along the Amtrak lines connecting the cities. But whatever the cause, a lot of people connected with that Series have experienced a reversal in professional fortunes over recent years.

Dempsey, the MVP of the Series, has taken the free-agent route from the Orioles to the Indians, has had his pitch-calling publicly derided by one of his own coaches, and last July served as Bo Jackson's personal tackling dummy as Bo honed the steamroller move he later used on Mike Harden and the Boz. Scott McGregor, who pitched the Series-clinching shutout in Game Five, spent part of last summer in the minor leagues. Only two of the nine players in the Phillies' starting lineup for Game One are still active in the majors. The opposing managers, Joe Altobelli of the Orioles and Paul Owens of the Phillies, have long since been removed from their commands.

Then there's Cosell, who left the broadcast booth, sport by sport, and took up with his old enemies in the print media. Earl Weaver was in the booth with Howard for that Series, but his own managerial comeback in 1985–86 served only to lower his all-time winning percentage. The city of Baltimore itself lost its football team overnight in the spring of 1984. Philadelphia's football team almost left later that year, and although the team stayed in town, no NFL team has been absent from the playoffs longer than the Eagles.

But the greatest misfortunes following the '83 Series beset the Orioles and the Phillies themselves. Not only has neither team been back to the World Series, but neither has won a divisional title, or even come close. In fact, in none of the four years since 1984 have either the Orioles or the Phillies finished less than 15 games out of first place.

Even given the recent volatility of baseball's standings, neither team could have anticipated such a colossal fall: at least 15 games behind in each of four years following a first-place finish. That had occurred to league or division pennant winners only five previous times in baseball history, and only once—to the Yankees following their 1964 American League championship—over the previous 50 years. (The other champions who fell apart in that manner are from baseball's Dark Ages: the 1904 Red Sox, the 1914 Athletics, the 1918 Red Sox, and the 1933 Senators.)

And in Baltimore's case, the team may not yet have hit bottom, as seen in its year-by-year record:

	W–L	Pct.	Pos.	GB	Runs Own	Runs Opp.
1983	98–64	.605	1st	—	799	652
1984	85–77	.525	5th	19	681	667
1985	83–78	.516	4th	16	818	764
1986	73–89	.451	7th	22.5	708	760
1987	67–95	.414	6th	31	729	880

In each of the past four seasons, the Orioles have played worse than they did the year before. Only one team in the past quarter-century has done that (the Tigers of 1972 through 1975), and should the Birds play less than .414 ball this year, they would match the modern major-league record of five consecutive declining seasons:

Dodgers		Athletics		Cubs	
1900:	.603	1931:	.704	1937:	.604
1901:	.581	1932:	.610	1938:	.586
1902:	.543	1933:	.523	1939:	.545
1903:	.515	1934:	.453	1940:	.487
1904:	.366	1935:	.389	1941:	.455
1905:	.316	1936:	.346	1942:	.442

The respected Roland Hemond has taken over the baseball operation in Baltimore, and his top priority has been to overhaul the player development system: scouts, minor-league instructors, farm teams. But it will be a couple of years until the effects of these changes are felt at the major-league level, so there's a good possibility that the Birds could indeed tie that record of five straight seasons with progressively lower winning percentages.

If the Orioles are to avoid that distinction, they must certainly get better pitching. Baltimore's 5.01 earned run average was not only the second-highest in the majors last season (Cleveland's was 5.28), but it was the second-highest in the majors in the last 25 years. It was a particular shock for an organization that has become so identified with first-rate pitching: In the sixties and seventies, Baltimore had the lowest earned run average in the American League 10 times in 20 years. And in the American League East, pitching has been the key to division titles. Since 1969, 14 of the 19 division titles have been won by the team allowing the fewest runs in the division.

But in 1987 only two starters, Mike Boddicker and rookie Eric Bell, started more than 16 games; the other spots in the rotation were split up among nine pitchers. The Orioles used six rookies among their 18 pitchers last season: Tony Arnold, Jeff Ballard, Bell, John Habyan, Jose Mesa, and Mark Williamson. These six combined to start more games (63) and pitch more innings (560 1/3) than rookies on any other major-league team. But they won only 27 games, lost 40, and had a cumulative earned run average of 5.20. In other words, they were only a little bit worse than the rest of the team's pitchers:

	W–L	Pct.	ERA
Baltimore rookies	27–40	.403	5.20
Baltimore veterans	40–55	.421	4.88

The Orioles got Doug Sisk from the Mets in an off-season trade. He'll join fellow National League refugee Tom Niedenfuer in the bullpen, but it's been three and one-half years since Sisk last demonstrated the consistency of a top reliever. The one thing that he may be able to accomplish, however, is keeping the ball in the yard. Sisk has allowed only 11 home runs in 412 1/3 innings in his major-league career, the lowest rate of home runs allowed by any active pitcher in the majors (minimum: 100 innings pitched). And considering that the Orioles hit 211 home runs last season only to find themselves outhomered by 15, Sisk could become a Balmer folk hero.

Diamond Vision Home Runs

There were 235 home runs hit at Memorial Stadium last season, the most at any ballpark in the majors. That brings to 614 the total hit there in the three seasons since the start of the 1985 season, also the most in the majors over that span. (1985 was the first season of play after the erection of a large DiamondVision board behind the right-center field fence.)

What we have here is baseball's version of "Which came first, the chicken or the egg?" Or, "It's not the heat, it's the humidity!" Are all those home runs being hit at Memorial Stadium because of the players who most frequently play there (the Orioles), or because of the ballpark itself?

If the home runs were chiefly attributable to the stadium alone, then you would see a dramatic difference between the rate of homers hit in the Orioles' home games and the rate in their road games. Here are the figures for the past three years:

	AB	HR	HR per 100 AB
Orioles Home Games	16,571	614	3.71
Orioles Road Games	16,678	543	3.26

The rate of homers at Memorial Stadium has been 13.8 percent higher than it has been on the road. At first glance, that seems like a large difference, but when we did the same computations for all 26 major-league stadiums over the past three years, we found that there were six stadiums that have influenced home runs even more than Memorial:

Wrigley Field	+39.7%
Kingdome	+30.4%
San Diego Stadium	+30.4%
Atlanta Stadium	+21.2%
Tiger Stadium	+17.2%
Anaheim Stadium	+15.4%
Memorial Stadium	+13.8%

Wrigley Field has increased home runs three times as much as has Memorial Stadium over the past three seasons; the Kingdome and San Diego/Jack Murphy Stadium have each boosted homers by more than twice as much as the Orioles' home field. Conclusion: Although environmental factors *have helped* the high home run output in Baltimore, the Orioles themselves are more responsible for the sheer volume of home runs that have been hit there in recent seasons.

What's most depressing to the Orioles is that their home-field advantage has eroded over recent seasons. Baltimore had the worst home record (31–51) in the majors last season. Even in home games in which the Orioles scored first—an advantage that produced a home-team winning percentage of .745 for other major-league teams—the Orioles still couldn't play .500 ball: They were 14–15.

But the most striking figures on the 1987 Orioles were their wildly divergent won-lost records against the East and the West. Against the seven teams from the West, Baltimore played .583 ball; but against the Big East, their won-lost percentage was .231.

Some statistics have underlying causes; others just exist. We're sometimes accused of going overboard on some of the performance breakdowns that we do. And although we try only to include such breakdowns as we think are important or interesting, occasionally there is something just so bizarre as to raise our curiosity.

For example, we're not very big proponents, generally, of breaking down player performance according to the opponent's division. We would feel more comfortable with such a breakdown if the teams that play in a particular division all play in small parks, or all play in domes, or all have home fields with artificial turf. Or if baseball aligned its divisions like British soccer, where teams are assigned to divisions according to skill level (no, Virginia, this is *not* how the American League teams have been divided). Now it's true that any team would rather win a game against a division rival than against an opponent from the other division, but that's a far cry from needless recitation of batting averages against East and West. There's nothing endemic to teams in the American League East, for instance, that makes them any different from teams in the West, and therefore subject to a special segregation of statistics.

Nevertheless (we love that word: It allows us to just sweep aside a logical argument with a single word), last year's Orioles had such an astounding performance breakdown against East and West teams that it demands examination. They were 49–35 against the West (a 94-win pace over a 162-game season), but only 18–60 against the East (a worse pace than the '62 Mets). With 31 fewer wins and 25 more losses against the East than the West, the Orioles' East record finished 28 "games behind" their West record.

There have been 478 team-years in the majors in the 19 years since the beginning of divisional play (19 years of 12 teams in the National League; eight years of 12 teams and eleven of 14 teams in the American). No other team among those 478 has ever behaved this way, playing so much better against one division that the other. Indeed, only one team (those 1983 Phillies) played even 20 games better against one division than against the other. Here are the largest such differences in baseball's divisional era:

	vs. Own Division		vs. Opp. Division		+/−.500
	W–L	Pct.	W–L	Pct.	Difference
1987 Orioles	18–60	.231	49–35	.583	28 games
1983 Phillies	60–30	.667	30–42	.417	21 games
1976 Dodgers	42–48	.467	50–22	.694	17 games
1980 Angels	40–38	.513	25–57	.305	17 games
1986 Indians	32–46	.410	52–32	.619	17 games

Of course, the Orioles' 28-game difference was due in greater measure to their terrible record against East teams than to success against the West. No team in history had ever been so bad against its own division; Baltimore won four fewer games against its own division than the previous record-holder, the 1979 Blue Jays. Here are the five worst records by a team against divisional opponents:

	W–L	Pct.
1987 Orioles	18–60	.231
1979 Blue Jays	22–56	.282
1974 Padres	27–63	.300
1970 White Sox	28–62	.311
1978 Blue Jays	28–61	.315

Every year, a cry goes up about the American League's so-called "balanced" schedule, which has teams playing divisional opponents 13 times each and non divisional foes 12 times apiece. Critics believe that a team should play significantly more games against opponents in its own division than against teams from the outside (as in the National League, where there is an 18/12 split.)

Teams in the American League East are among the most frequent critics, citing the need to develop intradivision rivalries. In recent years the cries have gotten louder as the most attractive American League teams have generally played in the East.

Suffice it to say that at least one A.L. East team is thankful that the American League has turned a deaf ear to the critics and has made no change in its scheduling pattern for 1988.

Let the others call for more games among the division rivals; the Birds think those inter-sectional games are just fine.

All My Children

Cal Ripken Sr.'s first year as manager was most notable for two incidents involving his children. On July 11, he installed son Billy as the team's regular second baseman, where the boy stayed until a season-ending injury on September 15. And on September 14, Cal Senior ended Cal Junior's streak of 8,243 consecutive innings by removing him in the eighth inning of a game in Toronto, with the Jays ahead, 17–3.

We commend both moves, and think that the old man can do more in each area. No, we're not advocating that Ripken press his two other children into service with the Orioles. Not that we doubt that 26-year-old Fred or 29-year-old Ellen could help the team. It's just that Rip's family has already done its share to help the organization.

What we mean is that the Orioles should open up some lineup positions to younger talent, as they did with Billy, who infused the team with some needed enthusiasm last summer. For one thing, this team needs some guys who can steal a base: The Orioles ranked last in the majors with 69 stolen bases last year, something that no Baltimore team had ever done since the team moved from St. Louis in 1954. In past years, the Orioles could always count on the Red Sox to match them, leadfoot for leadfoot, but since last spring, the Sox have added Ellis Burks, while the Orioles have rid themselves of Alan Wiggins, the only player on the team with more than 10 steals in 1987.

25-year-old infielder Pete Stanicek may be the guy to ignite the offense. He stole 77 bases in the minors in 1986, and had 37 last season, before being called up to the Orioles. He hit .270 with eight steals in 30 major-league games. Give the kid a shot.

On the matter of Cal Junior's ironman streaks, it's a case of one down, one to go. As we have said in the past (see the 1986 *Analyst*), there is a difference between achieving a record of will and a record of skill. Records of will are those achievements that can merely be extended by someone's will: in this case, the Ripkens' will to keep the consecutive-innings streak going. Thankfully, Papa finally came to realize that the streak could get in the way of the team's primary purpose, winning baseball games, and he ended it. Maybe he'll soon see that Cal Junior's other streak—927 consecutive games played, a streak that was still alive entering 1988—is yet another albatross, and that Junior is no different from 99 44/100 percent of other major-league players who, we are told, benefit from an occasional day off.

The whole matter reminds us of one baseball question that even we can't answer: Lou Gehrig played in 2,130 consecutive games. Why?

WON-LOST RECORD BY STARTING POSITION

BALTIMORE 67-95	C	1B	2B	3B	SS	LF	CF	RF	P	DH	Leadoff	Relief	Starts
Don Aase	.	.	.	.	.	.	.	.	.	.	.	4-3	.
Tony Arnold	.	.	.	.	.	.	.	.	.	.	.	3-24	.
Jeff Ballard	.	.	.	.	.	.	.	.	5-9	.	.	.	5-9
Eric Bell	.	.	.	.	.	.	.	.	12-17	.	.	1-3	12-17
Mike Boddicker	.	.	.	.	.	.	.	.	17-16	.	.	.	17-16
Rick Burleson	.	.	21-32	.	.	.	.	.	.	1-3	.	.	22-35
Doug Corbett	.	.	.	.	.	.	.	.	.	.	.	3-8	.
Luis DeLeon	.	.	.	.	.	.	.	.	.	.	.	3-8	.
Ken Dixon	.	.	.	.	.	.	.	.	6-9	.	.	10-9	6-9
Jim Dwyer	.	.	.	.	.	.	0-1	.	8-19	21-14	8-9	.	29-34
Mike Flanagan	.	.	.	.	.	.	.	.	8-8	.	.	.	8-8
Ken Gerhart	.	.	.	.	.	.	17-24	20-17	.	.	7-10	.	37-41
Rene Gonzales	.	.	6-9	.	.	.	.	.	.	.	.	.	6-9
Mike Griffin	.	.	.	.	.	.	.	.	3-3	.	.	4-13	3-3
Jackie Gutierrez	.	.	.	.	.	.	.	.	.	.	.	.	.
John Habyan	.	.	.	.	.	.	.	.	4-9	.	.	5-9	4-9
Mike Hart	.	.	.	.	.	.	8-16	.	.	.	0-2	.	8-16
Terry Kennedy	58-77	.	.	.	.	.	.	.	.	.	.	.	58-77
Mike Kinnunen	.	.	.	.	.	.	.	.	.	.	.	2-16	.
Ray Knight	.	1-4	.	51-77	.	.	.	.	.	7-6	.	.	59-87
Lee Lacy	.	.	.	.	.	.	0-1	27-34	.	1-1	8-8	.	28-36
Fred Lynn	.	.	.	.	.	.	.	38-58	.	0-7	.	.	38-65
Scott McGregor	.	.	.	.	.	.	.	.	4-11	.	.	1-10	4-11
Jose Mesa	.	.	.	.	.	.	.	.	1-4	.	.	1-0	1-4
Eddie Murray	.	65-91	.	.	.	.	.	.	.	1-3	.	.	66-94
Carl Nichols	3-4	.	.	.	.	.	.	.	.	.	.	.	3-4
Tom Niedenfuer	.	.	.	.	.	.	.	.	.	.	.	23-22	.
Jack O'Connor	.	.	.	.	.	.	.	.	.	.	.	9-20	.
Floyd Rayford	4-9	.	.	0-1	.	.	.	.	.	.	.	.	4-10
Billy Ripken	.	.	28-30	.	.	.	.	.	.	.	.	.	28-30
Cal Ripken	.	.	.	.	67-95	.	.	.	.	.	.	.	67-95
Dave Schmidt	.	.	.	.	.	.	.	.	7-7	.	.	11-10	7-7
Larry Sheets	.	1-0	.	.	.	.	24-42	.	25-30	3-3	.	.	53-75
John Shelby	.	.	.	.	.	.	.	0-1	3-4	.	.	.	3-5
Nelson Simmons	.	.	.	.	.	.	.	.	4-8	0-1	.	.	4-9
Pete Stanicek	.	.	5-12	1-1	.	.	.	.	.	1-8	7-21	.	7-21
Dave Van Gorder	2-5	.	.	.	.	.	.	.	.	.	.	.	2-5
Ron Washington	.	.	0-1	9-7	.	0-1	.	.	.	1-1	2-2	.	10-10
Alan Wiggins	.	.	13-20	.	.	2-0	.	.	.	19-17	33-32	.	34-37
Mark Williamson	.	.	.	.	.	.	.	.	0-2	.	.	22-37	0-2
Mike Young	.	.	.	.	.	.	24-27	1-2	.	12-31	2-11	.	37-60

Batting vs. Left and Right Handed Pitchers

		BA	Rank	SA	Rank	OBA	Rank	HR %	Rank	BB %	Rank	SO %	Rank
Rick Burleson	vs. Lefties	.195	151	.299	141	.279	138	0.00	145	8.89	79	14.44	81
	vs. Righties	.217	149	.326	145	.279	148	1.55	127	6.34	127	11.97	51
Jim Dwyer	vs. Lefties	.308	--	.538	--	.308	--	7.69	--	0.00	--	30.77	--
	vs. Righties	.272	69	.496	35	.375	31	6.14	22	13.81	13	19.78	131
Ken Gerhart	vs. Lefties	.240	109	.364	117	.272	142	3.10	83	4.35	147	17.39	102
	vs. Righties	.245	108	.503	29	.298	130	6.45	17	6.40	125	16.86	106
Terry Kennedy	vs. Lefties	.219	137	.339	130	.255	150	3.28	78	4.15	152	26.42	151
	vs. Righties	.267	79	.410	91	.323	91	3.65	76	7.58	101	17.13	109
Ray Knight	vs. Lefties	.218	138	.354	123	.293	126	3.88	61	9.17	70	14.85	87
	vs. Righties	.277	54	.384	108	.321	94	1.68	124	4.74	148	14.74	80
Lee Lacy	vs. Lefties	.237	114	.404	92	.306	114	2.56	96	9.20	69	13.79	75
	vs. Righties	.255	--	.392	--	.356	--	2.94	--	13.45	--	21.01	--
Fred Lynn	vs. Lefties	.224	133	.400	93	.297	120	4.00	58	9.42	63	20.29	126
	vs. Righties	.266	90	.528	21	.330	81	6.64	13	8.67	83	14.67	79
Eddie Murray	vs. Lefties	.271	74	.475	47	.336	76	4.98	35	9.02	76	13.52	71
	vs. Righties	.280	49	.479	42	.360	47	4.79	41	11.33	33	10.44	39
Billy Ripken	vs. Lefties	.348	8	.427	76	.392	25	1.12	132	7.22	114	7.22	11
	vs. Righties	.283	83	.338	139	.346	63	0.69	145	8.75	80	10.00	35
Cal Ripken	vs. Lefties	.242	106	.431	74	.311	106	3.32	76	9.66	60	7.56	16
	vs. Righties	.257	95	.438	68	.344	64	4.84	40	12.11	24	12.32	56
Larry Sheets	vs. Lefties	.303	36	.538	21	.348	66	6.90	10	5.16	144	14.19	79
	vs. Righties	.321	12	.574	10	.363	45	6.48	15	6.52	123	12.75	62
Alan Wiggins	vs. Lefties	.231	123	.246	155	.268	146	0.00	145	4.32	148	10.79	39
	vs. Righties	.233	130	.284	157	.318	99	0.57	150	10.84	44	9.36	31
Mike Young	vs. Lefties	.236	118	.354	124	.341	72	3.47	69	12.57	28	22.16	138
	vs. Righties	.242	115	.438	67	.318	97	5.02	36	10.20	52	22.04	143
Team Average	vs. Lefties	.243	14	.386	14	.302	14	3.26	6	7.46	14	15.74	7
	vs. Righties	.266	6	.437	3	.334	6	4.10	2	9.07	8	14.85	6
League Average	vs. Lefties	.265		.422		.333		3.29		8.94		15.64	
	vs. Righties	.265		.427		.334		3.43		8.94		15.26	

Batting with Runners on Base and Bases Empty

		BA	Rank	SA	Rank	OBA	Rank	HR %	Rank	BB %	Rank	SO %	Rank
Rick Burleson	Runners On	.188	159	.263	159	.286	142	0.00	150	9.28	85	8.25	22
	Bases Empty	.222	142	.349	131	.274	149	1.59	131	5.93	130	16.30	97
Jim Dwyer	Runners On	.194	158	.429	76	.339	86	7.14	4	17.21	9	24.59	153
	Bases Empty	.329	10	.545	19	.396	11	5.59	31	10.06	43	16.98	104
Ken Gerhart	Runners On	.205	154	.352	130	.227	161	3.28	78	2.99	161	14.93	93
	Bases Empty	.272	61	.506	31	.330	72	6.17	22	7.39	101	18.75	121
Terry Kennedy	Runners On	.239	128	.362	127	.308	123	2.75	93	9.13	88	18.26	95
	Bases Empty	.259	86	.401	95	.292	129	4.08	63	4.22	145	22.08	141
Ray Knight	Runners On	.286	59	.431	75	.336	88	3.05	86	6.71	124	14.84	92
	Bases Empty	.229	132	.322	142	.288	132	1.99	121	6.13	124	14.72	76
Lee Lacy	Runners On	.200	155	.333	141	.277	152	1.11	134	9.71	77	18.45	125
	Bases Empty	.268	67	.435	72	.353	47	3.57	80	11.58	23	15.79	87
Fred Lynn	Runners On	.256	102	.500	29	.352	67	6.41	12	13.19	31	18.68	128
	Bases Empty	.250	99	.479	44	.297	125	5.42	34	5.86	131	14.84	78
Eddie Murray	Runners On	.274	72	.486	42	.367	51	5.21	30	13.13	32	12.24	56
	Bases Empty	.279	51	.470	49	.337	56	4.55	51	8.08	79	10.86	37
Billy Ripken	Runners On	.323	21	.406	100	.359	59	2.08	109	5.77	135	5.77	11
	Bases Empty	.297	26	.348	132	.366	33	0.00	157	9.80	47	11.11	40
Cal Ripken	Runners On	.265	89	.498	34	.334	91	6.01	19	10.64	62	10.94	44
	Bases Empty	.240	115	.384	108	.332	64	2.93	94	11.86	21	10.57	33
Larry Sheets	Runners On	.298	44	.538	19	.326	104	6.25	14	4.02	155	15.18	95
	Bases Empty	.330	9	.582	9	.384	19	6.90	12	7.75	90	11.62	44
Alan Wiggins	Runners On	.233	131	.276	154	.280	147	0.00	150	6.11	133	9.92	32
	Bases Empty	.232	130	.263	160	.308	116	0.53	149	9.48	53	9.95	26
Mike Young	Runners On	.232	132	.413	93	.326	105	5.16	31	12.36	38	22.47	145
	Bases Empty	.245	108	.399	96	.329	75	3.85	72	10.26	39	21.79	140
Team Average	Runners On	.254	12	.422	10	.321	12	3.98	1	9.00	11	15.19	8
	Bases Empty	.260	8	.414	9	.323	9	3.64	6	8.06	9	15.18	5
League Average	Runners On	.271		.428		.343		3.25		9.68		14.87	
	Bases Empty	.260		.424		.326		3.49		8.34		15.79	

Overall Batting Compared to Late Inning Pressure Situations

		BA	Rank	SA	Rank	OBA	Rank	HR %	Rank	BB %	Rank	SO %	Rank	RDI %	Rank
Rick Burleson	Overall	.209	157	.316	152	.279	155	0.97	139	7.33	106	12.93	55	.240	--
	Pressure	.161	156	.226	151	.188	162	0.00	119	3.03	151	12.12	55	.250	91
Jim Dwyer	Overall	.274	65	.498	25	.371	30	6.22	10	13.17	16	20.28	133	.203	155
	Pressure	.242	105	.455	57	.375	46	6.06	27	17.50	9	20.00	112	.143	--
Ken Gerhart	Overall	.243	126	.440	69	.286	153	4.93	36	5.48	144	17.10	111	.229	147
	Pressure	.140	163	.163	164	.208	159	0.00	119	6.00	125	20.00	112	.333	51
Terry Kennedy	Overall	.250	112	.385	116	.299	135	3.52	80	6.38	129	20.40	135	.252	122
	Pressure	.233	118	.466	52	.309	113	6.85	18	9.76	75	21.95	121	.208	115
Ray Knight	Overall	.256	103	.373	123	.310	112	2.49	110	6.40	128	14.78	83	.244	128
	Pressure	.325	26	.425	75	.368	56	2.50	84	6.90	114	12.64	62	.379	35
Lee Lacy	Overall	.244	124	.399	106	.326	91	2.71	102	10.92	43	16.72	104	.309	60
	Pressure	.333	21	.485	41	.436	16	3.03	73	15.00	19	12.50	60	.429	--
Fred Lynn	Overall	.253	106	.487	31	.320	103	5.81	18	8.90	78	16.44	101	.277	93
	Pressure	.243	103	.400	87	.303	117	4.29	51	6.58	117	22.37	126	.118	146
Eddie Murray	Overall	.277	59	.477	41	.352	54	4.85	39	10.52	47	11.53	40	.305	64
	Pressure	.297	49	.484	43	.373	51	4.40	49	10.78	57	14.71	79	.455	11
Billy Ripken	Overall	.308	17	.372	126	.363	40	0.85	143	8.17	92	8.95	23	.283	--
	Pressure	.207	131	.207	156	.258	142	0.00	119	6.45	120	12.90	63	.167	--
Cal Ripken	Overall	.252	108	.436	74	.333	78	4.33	56	11.30	34	10.74	34	.339	30
	Pressure	.198	137	.264	144	.237	151	-1.10	118	5.15	135	14.43	74	.222	106
Larry Sheets	Overall	.316	12	.563	7	.358	47	6.61	8	6.10	134	13.19	57	.377	5
	Pressure	.282	66	.479	45	.303	117	5.63	35	2.63	154	17.11	93	.429	16
Alan Wiggins	Overall	.232	148	.268	159	.298	139	0.33	156	8.19	90	9.94	29	.188	159
	Pressure	.268	77	.268	143	.302	120	0.00	119	4.44	143	8.89	27	.000	--
Mike Young	Overall	.240	132	.405	100	.328	89	4.41	52	11.17	35	22.09	145	.220	151
	Pressure	.267	80	.500	31	.323	95	6.67	19	7.69	104	26.15	148	.300	72
Team Average	Overall	.258	12	.418	11	.322	13	3.78	3	8.47	11	15.18	6	.272	12
	Pressure	.248	13	.379	12	.304	14	3.28	5	7.19	13	17.04	9	.285	5
League Average	Overall	.265		.425		.333		3.38		8.94		15.38		.287	
	Pressure	.262		.405		.335		3.07		9.43		16.58		.280	

Additional Miscellaneous Batting Comparisons

	Grass Surface BA	Rank	Artificial Surface BA	Rank	Home Games BA	Rank	Road Games BA	Rank	Runners in Scoring Position BA	Rank	Runners in Scoring Pos and Two Outs BA	Rank	Leading Off Inning OBA	Rank	Runners on 3B with less than 2 Outs RDI %	Rank
Rick Burleson	.216	153	.171	--	.218	147	.198	152	.190	--	.158	--	.286	--	.500	--
Jim Dwyer	.254	107	.375	--	.238	124	.293	31	.167	154	.087	155	.468	1	.500	120
Ken Gerhart	.253	108	.196	145	.216	150	.267	72	.224	132	.240	95	.337	68	.500	120
Terry Kennedy	.241	126	.303	27	.213	153	.283	47	.244	111	.254	81	.344	60	.450	142
Ray Knight	.258	102	.244	99	.274	78	.239	117	.269	84	.271	61	.252	148	.273	162
Lee Lacy	.230	138	.317	18	.231	137	.258	87	.289	56	.364	7	.384	25	.636	50
Fred Lynn	.251	111	.267	70	.241	122	.263	80	.253	99	.171	143	.267	137	.522	118
Eddie Murray	.267	85	.330	10	.263	93	.289	36	.287	59	.203	125	.331	79	.680	31
Billy Ripken	.299	29	.351	--	.287	63	.328	7	.310	--	.316	--	.333	69	.667	--
Cal Ripken	.243	122	.301	29	.248	116	.255	92	.282	68	.254	82	.331	81	.707	24
Larry Sheets	.316	16	.310	22	.324	14	.307	23	.323	22	.306	35	.375	29	.607	66
Alan Wiggins	.251	110	.173	154	.231	137	.233	124	.213	138	.273	59	.246	153	.462	138
Mike Young	.242	123	.222	122	.237	126	.243	111	.143	160	.086	156	.310	101	.667	--
Team Average	.255	13	.272	2	.250	14	.265	5	.256	12	.229	12	.319	10	.532	13
League Average	.267		.261		.270		.260		.266		.247		.328		.581	

Pitching vs. Left and Right Handed Batters

		BA	Rank	SA	Rank	OBA	Rank	HR %	Rank	BB %	Rank	SO %	Rank
Tony Arnold	vs. Lefties	.351	--	.714	--	.407	--	6.49	--	9.20	--	6.90	--
	vs. Righties	.319	117	.449	94	.369	103	2.17	19	5.92	23	7.89	124
Jeff Ballard	vs. Lefties	.357	--	.571	--	.449	--	4.76	--	14.29	--	10.20	--
	vs. Righties	.341	121	.558	122	.406	124	5.22	116	10.07	97	7.91	123
Eric Bell	vs. Lefties	.326	--	.523	--	.389	--	4.65	--	9.47	--	11.58	--
	vs. Righties	.262	69	.490	109	.344	84	5.03	113	10.88	102	15.77	62
Mike Boddicker	vs. Lefties	.239	23	.416	60	.303	20	3.71	91	7.46	40	13.99	62
	vs. Righties	.260	66	.409	63	.330	65	2.98	62	9.18	85	18.60	40
Ken Dixon	vs. Lefties	.280	88	.556	123	.332	54	6.54	123	7.30	35	17.17	38
	vs. Righties	.302	108	.573	124	.333	69	7.56	124	4.22	7	21.52	24
Mike Griffin	vs. Lefties	.267	62	.467	97	.347	83	3.33	73	10.53	85	9.94	114
	vs. Righties	.271	84	.421	70	.346	86	2.86	55	9.38	92	15.63	63
John Habyan	vs. Lefties	.254	44	.441	81	.318	39	3.52	81	8.42	53	10.18	110
	vs. Righties	.241	40	.455	96	.301	38	5.88	122	7.69	54	16.83	52
Scott McGregor	vs. Lefties	.242	--	.339	--	.324	--	3.23	--	9.21	--	10.53	--
	vs. Righties	.344	122	.546	121	.403	121	4.61	105	8.83	76	9.78	117
Tom Niedenfuer	vs. Lefties	.306	111	.602	127	.370	107	7.41	127	9.17	66	14.17	61
	vs. Righties	.224	--	.378	--	.301	--	3.06	--	9.73	--	17.70	--
Jack O'Connor	vs. Lefties	.269	--	.538	--	.333	--	5.77	--	8.77	--	17.54	--
	vs. Righties	.260	66	.366	35	.347	88	1.63	12	12.41	114	15.86	61
Dave Schmidt	vs. Lefties	.313	115	.484	104	.358	93	3.23	68	6.47	23	12.50	81
	vs. Righties	.222	23	.352	28	.254	5	2.22	22	3.89	5	14.49	75
Mark Williamson	vs. Lefties	.271	71	.395	48	.338	68	2.38	35	8.44	54	13.92	65
	vs. Righties	.252	54	.380	48	.310	45	2.71	45	7.42	49	14.13	78
Team Average	vs. Lefties	.275	11	.469	13	.341	9	4.10	13	8.76	2	12.47	12
	vs. Righties	.277	12	.461	13	.342	12	3.97	13	8.68	10	14.75	11
League Average	vs. Lefties	.267		.427		.338		3.30		9.47		14.54	
	vs. Righties	.264		.424		.330		3.45		8.56		15.98	

Pitching with Runners on Base and Bases Empty

		BA	Rank	SA	Rank	OBA	Rank	HR %	Rank	BB %	Rank	SO %	Rank
Tony Arnold	Runners On	.299	99	.486	102	.372	105	2.80	58	9.60	73	8.00	120
	Bases Empty	.361	--	.602	--	.395	--	4.63	--	4.39	--	7.02	--
Jeff Ballard	Runners On	.339	119	.528	113	.414	123	4.72	102	11.72	104	6.90	127
	Bases Empty	.348	125	.585	126	.412	125	5.49	121	9.89	96	9.34	119
Eric Bell	Runners On	.305	106	.527	112	.400	118	5.02	107	13.73	116	14.08	75
	Bases Empty	.250	50	.475	103	.319	57	4.95	114	8.76	74	15.96	55
Mike Boddicker	Runners On	.245	35	.402	56	.321	45	3.02	69	9.71	77	16.27	45
	Bases Empty	.250	52	.421	68	.311	43	3.63	78	7.21	47	15.82	58
Ken Dixon	Runners On	.305	104	.552	117	.356	86	6.90	125	7.29	32	22.40	14
	Bases Empty	.283	101	.574	125	.317	51	7.17	126	4.68	14	17.27	44
Mike Griffin	Runners On	.281	87	.474	96	.351	78	2.96	66	9.62	74	10.90	107
	Bases Empty	.258	64	.419	65	.343	90	3.23	65	10.29	102	14.29	73
John Habyan	Runners On	.238	28	.397	53	.339	64	3.31	82	12.50	108	12.50	90
	Bases Empty	.253	55	.473	102	.294	25	5.14	117	5.50	24	13.27	86
Scott McGregor	Runners On	.353	124	.564	119	.404	120	5.77	118	8.70	55	9.78	111
	Bases Empty	.303	115	.463	100	.373	107	3.19	63	9.09	81	10.05	114
Tom Niedenfuer	Runners On	.266	68	.385	44	.341	67	1.83	22	10.24	85	17.32	33
	Bases Empty	.268	--	.619	--	.330	--	9.28	--	8.49	--	14.15	--
Dave Schmidt	Runners On	.261	60	.415	72	.300	19	2.42	41	5.45	8	14.09	74
	Bases Empty	.264	74	.407	56	.302	33	2.86	49	4.75	15	13.22	89
Mark Williamson	Runners On	.282	88	.385	43	.358	90	2.35	38	10.89	92	9.27	114
	Bases Empty	.243	38	.388	41	.290	20	2.75	45	5.15	19	18.38	34
Team Average	Runners On	.284	13	.455	12	.356	13	3.63	12	9.99	10	13.28	12
	Bases Empty	.271	12	.472	14	.330	10	4.31	14	7.71	1	14.31	11
League Average	Runners On	.271		.428		.343		3.25		9.68		14.87	
	Bases Empty	.260		.424		.326		3.49		8.34		15.79	

Overall Pitching Compared to Late Inning Pressure Situations

		BA	Rank	SA	Rank	OBA	Rank	HR %	Rank	BB %	Rank	SO %	Rank
Jeff Ballard	Overall	.344	127	.560	126	.413	127	5.15	120	10.70	103	8.26	124
	Pressure	.214	--	.286	--	.313	--	0.00	--	12.50	--	6.25	--
Eric Bell	Overall	.271	81	.495	116	.350	89	4.98	118	10.70	102	15.23	57
	Pressure	.205	17	.250	3	.286	24	0.00	1	10.20	74	14.29	70
Mike Boddicker	Overall	.248	35	.413	57	.315	39	3.40	81	8.21	54	16.00	48
	Pressure	.253	58	.379	59	.333	62	1.15	29	10.68	85	13.59	77
Ken Dixon	Overall	.292	106	.565	127	.333	68	7.06	127	5.74	14	19.36	23
	Pressure	.243	54	.430	81	.308	38	4.67	107	8.47	57	23.73	12
Mike Griffin	Overall	.269	78	.445	87	.347	82	3.10	63	9.97	93	12.69	87
	Pressure	.205	18	.256	6	.279	21	0.00	1	4.65	14	13.95	75
John Habyan	Overall	.248	37	.447	88	.311	33	4.51	104	8.11	52	12.98	84
	Pressure	.207	--	.483	--	.207	--	6.90	--	0.00	--	13.79	--
Scott McGregor	Overall	.326	121	.509	120	.388	122	4.36	102	8.91	72	9.92	115
	Pressure	.579	--	.789	--	.591	--	5.26	--	8.33	--	8.33	--
Tom Niedenfuer	Overall	.267	--	.495	--	.336	--	5.34	--	9.44	--	15.88	--
	Pressure	.262	66	.492	106	.326	56	5.38	115	9.03	61	18.75	34
Jack O'Connor	Overall	.263	--	.417	--	.343	--	2.86	--	11.39	--	16.34	--
	Pressure	.191	8	.298	19	.283	22	2.13	47	11.11	89	24.07	11
Dave Schmidt	Overall	.263	68	.411	53	.301	19	2.67	40	5.05	7	13.59	79
	Pressure	.313	112	.400	69	.353	78	0.00	1	5.88	24	8.24	116
Mark Williamson	Overall	.261	62	.387	34	.322	53	2.56	34	7.88	45	14.04	74
	Pressure	.318	114	.500	107	.394	111	4.04	95	10.48	79	11.79	100
Team Average	Overall	.277	12	.465	14	.341	11	4.02	14	8.71	8	13.86	12
	Pressure	.276	12	.447	12	.346	11	3.57	12	9.37	6	14.44	12
League Average	Overall	.265		.425		.333		3.38		8.94		15.38	
	Pressure	.262		.404		.337		2.99		9.73		16.42	

Additional Miscellaneous Pitching Comparisons

	Grass Surface		Artificial Surface		Home Games		Road Games		Runners in Scoring Position		Runners in Scoring Pos and Two Outs		Leading Off Inning	
	BA	Rank	BA	Rank	BA	Rank	BA	Rank	BA	Rank	BA	Rank	OBA	Rank
Tony Arnold	.314	113	.750	--	.306	--	.356	--	.300	100	.194	28	.298	--
Jeff Ballard	.348	127	.296	--	.351	126	.333	124	.397	128	.333	110	.456	127
Eric Bell	.279	89	.231	32	.281	99	.264	56	.309	107	.207	38	.337	73
Mike Boddicker	.257	56	.213	17	.241	43	.256	40	.234	35	.255	74	.319	51
Ken Dixon	.292	98	.292	96	.301	111	.280	83	.291	92	.339	115	.387	111
Mike Griffin	.269	76	.269	--	.251	55	.293	96	.275	79	.250	69	.347	84
John Habyan	.256	53	.171	5	.279	96	.217	8	.242	41	.208	40	.344	80
Scott McGregor	.348	126	.097	--	.335	125	.316	117	.368	125	.353	118	.424	124
Tom Niedenfuer	.259	60	.333	--	.268	--	.266	--	.256	62	.333	110	.300	--
Jack O'Connor	.237	15	.435	--	.246	50	.311	--	.302	--	.292	--	.390	--
Dave Schmidt	.257	57	.289	94	.253	59	.279	82	.236	38	.193	27	.231	6
Mark Williamson	.263	65	.246	49	.261	74	.261	49	.274	77	.318	106	.243	10
Team Average	.278	10	.270	8	.274	11	.279	12	.286	13	.267	13	.343	13
League Average	.267		.261		.260		.270		.266		.247		.328	

BOSTON RED SOX

Amid all the talk about the failure of any league champions to defend their titles successfully in nearly a decade, one explanation for the phenomenon has gone undocumented: Championship teams no longer dominate their opponents as they once did. And it stands to reason that teams that win their division or league titles by slimmer margins are less likely to repeat their success a year later.

The following table shows the average winning percentage and margin of victory (games ahead of the second-place teams) for all division and league champions in each decade during the 1900s. Notice that both figures have sunk to all-time lows in the 1980s:

Years	Pct.	Margin
1900–1909	.661	8.25
1910–1919	.647	8.97
1920–1929	.627	6.25
1930–1939	.641	7.75
1940–1949	.636	6.78
1950–1959	.627	5.97
1960–1969	.613	6.48
1970–1979	.596	6.46
1980–1987	.585	5.53

Of course, those figures don't fully explain what's happened recently. Even dominant champions like the 1986 New York Mets and the 1984 Detroit Tigers collapsed under the weight of their World Series victories. And the data above only partially explain why recent division winners have made such dramatic leaps in the standings to win their titles.

Division winners during the current decade, on average, have compiled winning percentages of just .522 and finished nearly 10 games out of first place in the seasons prior to their titles. The comparable figures for division and league champions in decades past:

Years	Pct.	Margin
1900–1909	.661	+ 1.88
1910–1919	.594	− 6.28
1920–1929	.584	− 4.05
1930–1939	.593	− 3.17
1940–1949	.583	− 6.15
1950–1959	.595	− 2.68
1960–1969	.548	− 8.14
1970–1979	.575	+ 0.55
1980–1987	.522	− 9.94

So two concurrent trends, somewhat related, have fused to ignite the volatility of the 1980s: a shrinking talent gap between the champions and their closest rivals, and increased upward mobility by the also-rans. Most of the results have been surprising. But some—particularly the inability of the 1986 Mets and the 1984 Tigers to repeat—have been stunning. A notable exception was the failure of the Boston Red Sox to defend their 1986 American League title successfully. Only the most loyal members of the BLOHARDS could have found last season's collapse anything other than inevitable.

Two factors combined to make Boston's defense of their 1986 championship a hopeless cause. First, the team that won the title two years ago was one of the league's oldest. Excluding pitchers, only two A.L. teams were older: California and Kansas City. And, second, the 1986 Sox lacked depth to an extraordinary degree for a pennant winner. With an aging roster of starting players unaided by an able supporting cast, the 1987 Sox were almost doomed to failure before The Wild Pitch of the previous October.

The following table summarizes those two key elements for the league champions of the past five seasons: an aging front line with inadequate reserves. The ages listed are the averages for all players weighted on each team, weighted by plate appearances for batters and the number of batters faced for pitchers. The home run and RBI figures for batters represent team totals for the reserves, excluding the players who batted most often throughout the season (the top eight for N.L. teams, nine for A.L. teams); the won-lost records for pitchers are those of the reserve starting pitchers, excluding the four winningest starters:

Year	Team	Batters			Pitchers			
		Age	HR	RBI	Age	W	L	Pct.
1987	Minnesota	28.1	34	159	32.0	11	16	.407
	St. Louis	28.8	25	170	28.5	16	12	.571
1986	Boston	31.3	8	72	28.2	14	22	.389
	New York	28.9	54	228	25.8	13	10	.565
1985	Kansas City	31.3	13	130	26.3	11	17	.393
	St. Louis	28.0	22	156	29.8	9	8	.529
1984	Detroit	28.8	40	190	30.2	12	12	.500
	San Diego	28.8	24	140	28.0	12	14	.462
1983	Baltimore	30.3	35	181	28.4	15	25	.375
	Philadelphia	32.8	30	213	31.1	9	17	.346

None of those teams relied as heavily on its starting lineup as the 1986 Red Sox, whose nine most frequent batters had a composite batting average *60 points higher than the rest of the team combined* (.219). But as you can see, that regular lineup was old even by comparison to other championship teams. And although the 1986 Boston pitching staff was relatively young, it was also shallow, especially by comparison to the other champs: The Red Sox' second-tier starters compiled the lowest winning percentage by those of a league champion since 1983. That combination of age and a lack of depth was fatal.

That's why what transpired in Boston last season was not only expected but, in truth, more encouraging than the events of the previous season. Because visible even through the rubble of the collapse of '87 was the growth of a nucleus of young talent. Those young players would certainly have stagnated at Pawtucket had the Sox not been eliminated from the 1987 pennant race before most of their fans had completed their therapy following the 1986 post-season disaster.

In fact, that's exactly what happened to the 1987 California Angels. The Angels team that lost to Boston in the 1986 A.L.C.S was even older than the Sox themselves. But because California remained in the pennant race throughout most of last season—despite an eventual last-place finish, the Angels were in second place as late as August 15, and still within three games on September 1—they made roster moves throughout the summer months that inhibited the development of their young players. Rookie second baseman Mark McLemore was supplanted by Johnny Ray for the September stretch drive; Tony Armas was signed to take over center field from Gary Pettis; Jerry Reuss, cut loose by two N.L. teams looking for a reliable fourth starter, found a home in Anaheim; and—horror of horrors—the Angels even found a spot for Bill Buckner.

Contrast the Angels' moves with those made by the Red Sox. After Boston fell 10 games out of the race before the end of April, John McNamara took the center field position from veteran Dave Henderson and handed it to rookie Ellis Burks. When that margin grew to 13½ games by the All-Star break, Mac switched Dwight Evans from right field to first base and Jim Rice from left field to designated hitter to open spots for Mike Greenwell and Todd Benzinger. In retrospect, McNamara used the luxury of a lost season to evaluate firsthand the progress of Burks, Greenwell, and Benzinger, and that of two other rookies as well, catcher John Marzano and DH Sam Horn.

Boston's own version of the junior achievement program was so extensive that by season's end, Red Sox rookies had strolled to the plate 1,829 times, more often than those of any other team since the 1982 Minnesota Twins (Brunansky, Gaetti, Hrbek, and Laudner, among others). And Boston's rookies were so successful that their composite statistics look flatteringly similar to a proportionate slice of the career statistics of a perennial All-Star, Cal Ripken:

Player	AB	R	H	2B	3B	HR	RBI	BB	BA	SA	OBA
Boston rookies	1657	265	458	95	10	69	268	134	.276	.471	.333
Ripken (pro-rated)	1639	268	463	90	10	68	244	168	.283	.475	.348
Ripken (actual)	3834	626	1084	211	23	160	570	394	.283	.475	.348

By season's end, the Sox had completely revamped their starting outfield with three rookies, strengthened an already solid infield with the addition of Evans, and found a rookie catcher in Marzano who appeared ready to supplant Rich Gedman. Those four rookies—Greenwell, Burks, Benzinger, and Marzano—started 28 games together, and Boston's 17–11 record promises that the spring of '88 will be nearly as exciting and infinitely more rewarding than the fall of '86.

Mr. Smith Goes to Boston...

Boston spent the entire 1987 season patching the holes that age had worn in the team fabric. Then, in one bold move last December, the Sox filled the gaping hole in their bullpen with the acquisition of Lee Smith. And if any post-stock market crash deal proved that a recession is indeed coming, it was the Filene's bargain-basement price that Boston paid: Calvin Schiraldi and Al Nipper.

Boston's recent bullpen problems have been enormous. Their starters pitched and won more complete games than those of any other team in the majors last season (37 wins in 47 CGs). But only two teams had poorer records than Boston in games in which they used their bullpen. Each team's record in "incomplete games":

Team	W	L	Pct.	Team	W	L	Pct.
Toronto	84	60	.583	St. Louis	85	67	.559
New York	79	64	.552	New York	78	68	.534
Detroit	71	58	.550	Montreal	76	70	.521
Milwaukee	73	61	.545	San Francisco	73	70	.510
Minnesota	77	69	.527	Cincinnati	77	78	.497
Oakland	70	74	.486	Philadelphia	69	80	.463
Chicago	59	74	.444	Chicago	66	84	.440
California	62	80	.437	Pittsburgh	59	78	.431
Texas	60	82	.423	Houston	64	85	.430
Kansas City	49	69	.415	Atlanta	55	90	.379
Seattle	49	74	.398	Los Angeles	49	84	.368
Baltimore	56	89	.386	San Diego	51	97	.345
Boston	41	74	.357				
Cleveland	46	92	.333				

Boston's relievers saved only 16 games last season; Smith had saved that many by June 16. In fact, Smith led the majors with 162 saves over the past five seasons—two more than the entire Red Sox bullpen—while pitching for a team with the fourth-lowest winning percentage in the National League. Moreover, Smith blew only 46 opportunities for saves during those five seasons. His percentage ranks third among pitchers with at least 50 saves since 1983. The top 10 among that group:

Player	Saves	Opp.	Pct.
Dan Quisenberry	146	181	.807
Steve Bedrosian	99	126	.786
Lee Smith	162	208	.779
Dave Smith	95	122	.779
Willie Hernandez	103	133	.774
Jeff Reardon	151	196	.770
Donnie Moore	79	103	.767
Al Holland	59	77	.766

Dave Righetti	137	181	.757
Tom Henke	77	102	.755

How does Smith's performance compare to some of the pretenders in the Boston bullpen during that same five-year period? Sit down, take a deep breath, and shield your eyes from these dismal figures:

Player	Saves	Opp.	Pct.
Wes Gardner	10	14	.714
Bob Stanley	81	118	.686
Mark Clear	15	23	.652
Calvin Schiraldi	15	23	.652
Steve Crawford	17	31	.548
Joe Sambito	12	32	.375

Smith has some other impressive numbers on his resume as well. He has struck out 478 batters since 1983, nearly 100 more than any other relief pitcher. (Willie Hernandez ranks second with 384.) And he has held opposing batters below the .200 mark with two outs and runners in scoring position four times during that five-year period.

But some questions arose over the winter regarding Smith's durability. He has pitched successively fewer innings in each of the past four seasons, and apparently that fact has caused some concern among those Red Sox fans who were seen pinching themselves shortly after the trade was announced. Rest easy, scouts. Smith was brought into 48 save situations last season. Only one pitcher in either league topped that total: Todd Worrell, who pitched for a team that won 20 more games than the Cubs, had one more save opportunity than Smith. Lee may not have missed many meals, but he's danced every dance as well.

It's also been reported that Smith isn't the same pitcher without a day of rest. And although he has pitched better with a day of rest than without one, the difference is only slight. Most teams would gladly accept that minor liability as part of the overall package. Smith's statistics for the past five seasons without a day of rest:

Year	G	W	L	GF	SV	IP	H	BB	SO	ERA
1983	21	1	4	19	11	32.2	24	13	34	1.93
1984	23	4	4	18	7	31.1	35	11	25	4.60
1985	20	0	2	18	13	27.1	27	11	26	3.95
1986	23	3	2	23	13	29.0	25	13	29	3.10
1987	17	1	3	17	13	19.2	20	6	21	2.29
No Rest	104	9	15	95	57	140.0	131	54	135	3.21
Rested	224	24	25	191	105	336.0	277	128	343	2.76

The concerns over this trade appear to be those of Bosox fans who can't believe their luck. As Red Sox GM Lou Gorman reportedly told Smith shortly after the deal was consummated, "People in Boston thought the trade was so good, it must be a joke." We think the joke's on the Cubs, because having lost only Schiraldi and Nipper, the Sox have made a steal if Smith is even half the pitcher in Boston that he was in Chicago.

WON-LOST RECORD BY STARTING POSITION

BOSTON 78-84	C	1B	2B	3B	SS	LF	CF	RF	P	DH	Leadoff	Relief	Starts
Marty Barrett	-	-	68-68	-	-	-	-	-	-	-	4-1	-	68-68
Don Baylor	-	-	-	-	-	-	-	-	-	43-47	-	-	43-47
Todd Benzinger	-	1-0	-	-	-	1-4	4-1	24-21	-	-	-	-	30-26
Wade Boggs	-	-	-	70-75	-	-	-	-	-	0-1	10-15	-	70-76
Tom Bolton	-	-	-	-	-	-	-	-	-	-	-	10-19	-
Oil Can Boyd	-	-	-	-	-	-	-	-	3-4	-	-	-	3-4
Bill Buckner	-	32-41	-	-	-	-	-	-	-	-	-	-	32-41
Ellis Burks	-	-	-	-	-	-	61-67	-	-	-	60-64	-	61-67
Roger Clemens	-	-	-	-	-	-	-	-	22-14	-	-	-	22-14
Steve Crawford	-	-	-	-	-	-	-	-	-	-	-	7-22	-
Pat Dodson	-	4-6	-	-	-	-	-	-	-	-	-	-	4-6
Dwight Evans	-	40-37	-	-	-	-	32-39	-	-	2-2	-	-	74-78
Wes Gardner	-	-	-	-	-	-	-	-	0-1	-	-	18-30	0-1
Rich Gedman	20-21	-	-	-	-	-	-	-	-	-	-	-	20-21
Mike Greenwell	-	-	-	-	-	32-29	-	13-14	-	6-9	-	-	51-52
Dave Henderson	-	-	-	-	-	0-2	12-15	8-8	-	-	3-3	-	20-25
Glenn Hoffman	-	-	-	5-9	-	-	-	-	-	-	-	-	5-9
Sam Horn	-	-	-	-	-	-	-	-	-	20-20	-	-	20-20
Bruce Hurst	-	-	-	-	-	-	-	-	17-16	-	-	-	17-16
John Leister	-	-	-	-	-	-	-	-	3-3	-	-	0-2	3-3
John Marzano	27-21	-	-	-	-	-	-	-	-	-	-	-	27-21
Al Nipper	-	-	-	-	-	-	-	-	13-17	-	-	-	13-17
Spike Owen	-	-	-	-	65-62	-	-	-	-	-	-	-	65-62
Jody Reed	-	-	0-2	-	2-4	-	-	-	-	-	1-1	-	2-6
Jim Rice	-	-	-	-	-	45-49	-	-	-	7-5	-	-	52-54
Ed Romero	-	1-0	10-14	8-9	6-9	-	-	-	-	-	-	-	25-32
Kevin Romine	-	-	-	-	-	-	1-1	1-2	-	-	-	-	2-3
Joe Sambito	-	-	-	-	-	-	-	-	-	-	-	10-37	-
Dave Sax	-	-	-	-	-	-	-	-	-	-	-	-	-
Calvin Schiraldi	-	-	-	-	-	-	-	-	0-1	-	-	23-38	0-1
Jeff Sellers	-	-	-	-	-	-	-	-	10-12	-	-	0-3	10-12
Danny Sheaffer	8-12	-	-	-	-	-	-	-	-	-	-	-	8-12
Bob Stanley	-	-	-	-	-	-	-	-	7-13	-	-	1-13	7-13
Marc Sullivan	23-30	-	-	-	-	-	-	-	-	-	-	-	23-30
Rob Woodward	-	-	-	-	-	-	-	-	3-3	-	-	0-3	3-3

Batting vs. Left and Right Handed Pitchers

		BA	Rank	SA	Rank	OBA	Rank	HR %	Rank	BB %	Rank	SO %	Rank
Marty Barrett	vs. Lefties	.347	9	.420	83	.412	14	1.33	124	10.23	50	2.27	1
	vs. Righties	.274	64	.325	146	.327	86	0.24	155	7.14	110	7.36	18
Todd Benzinger	vs. Lefties	.325	19	.450	64	.371	46	2.50	98	7.69	104	13.19	65
	vs. Righties	.252	102	.441	66	.329	83	4.20	58	9.26	67	17.90	117
Wade Boggs	vs. Lefties	.331	16	.544	19	.403	18	4.14	57	10.47	46	7.33	14
	vs. Righties	.377	1	.607	3	.484	1	4.45	48	17.86	5	7.14	15
Ellis Burks	vs. Lefties	.325	20	.483	40	.380	35	2.65	91	8.33	90	17.86	109
	vs. Righties	.253	101	.425	77	.303	126	3.93	68	6.16	132	15.53	92
Dwight Evans	vs. Lefties	.368	4	.688	1	.465	2	8.33	4	15.70	13	9.88	34
	vs. Righties	.282	45	.526	23	.400	13	5.54	28	16.29	10	16.70	103
Mike Greenwell	vs. Lefties	.378	2	.514	29	.420	11	1.35	123	4.94	145	7.41	15
	vs. Righties	.317	13	.583	6	.379	27	5.33	31	8.27	91	9.07	27
Dave Henderson	vs. Lefties	.258	93	.515	28	.319	94	6.06	20	8.33	90	23.61	146
	vs. Righties	.220	146	.364	125	.309	120	3.39	83	11.68	30	22.63	146
Sam Horn	vs. Lefties	.276	--	.655	--	.382	--	10.34	--	11.76	--	44.12	--
	vs. Righties	.279	53	.574	11	.350	58	8.53	2	9.09	72	27.97	156
Spike Owen	vs. Lefties	.321	21	.455	60	.393	24	1.49	115	10.60	45	9.27	29
	vs. Righties	.231	136	.294	156	.313	110	0.00	156	10.48	49	8.22	22
Jim Rice	vs. Lefties	.285	55	.398	97	.371	45	3.25	79	11.43	37	13.57	72
	vs. Righties	.274	63	.413	88	.351	56	3.20	86	9.09	72	18.18	122
Ed Romero	vs. Lefties	.153	162	.167	163	.225	161	0.00	145	8.75	82	11.25	47
	vs. Righties	.325	10	.350	134	.366	40	0.00	156	6.25	129	7.39	19
Team Average	vs. Lefties	.298	1	.444	2	.364	1	3.10	9	8.95	7	12.53	1
	vs. Righties	.271	5	.424	7	.347	3	3.12	10	9.76	2	13.15	1
League Average	vs. Lefties	.265		.422		.333		3.29		8.94		15.64	
	vs. Righties	.265		.427		.334		3.43		8.94		15.26	

Batting with Runners on Base and Bases Empty

		BA	Rank	SA	Rank	OBA	Rank	HR %	Rank	BB %	Rank	SO %	Rank
Marty Barrett	Runners On	.345	9	.417	86	.426	9	0.97	139	12.03	44	4.14	2
	Bases Empty	.263	76	.312	146	.301	122	0.28	156	5.11	138	7.26	10
Todd Benzinger	Runners On	.250	111	.481	43	.341	79	5.77	23	11.90	46	13.49	73
	Bases Empty	.303	23	.412	89	.346	50	1.68	129	5.51	135	18.90	123
Wade Boggs	Runners On	.358	4	.590	7	.480	2	4.80	41	20.07	4	5.35	8
	Bases Empty	.366	1	.587	8	.446	1	4.04	65	12.23	18	8.70	15
Ellis Burks	Runners On	.247	116	.461	58	.332	100	4.49	49	10.19	68	17.48	115
	Bases Empty	.284	43	.432	76	.320	92	3.16	88	5.00	140	15.50	85
Dwight Evans	Runners On	.324	18	.582	10	.450	4	6.25	14	18.96	5	13.76	77
	Bases Empty	.288	35	.558	16	.385	18	6.32	19	13.33	11	16.06	91
Mike Greenwell	Runners On	.359	3	.590	6	.405	16	4.27	52	6.61	126	8.95	25
	Bases Empty	.287	39	.545	20	.362	36	5.06	40	9.05	62	8.54	14
Dave Henderson	Runners On	.174	162	.349	131	.247	160	4.65	46	9.18	87	23.47	150
	Bases Empty	.286	--	.480	--	.369	--	4.08	--	11.71	--	22.52	--
John Marzano	Runners On	.267	87	.422	81	.333	92	3.33	75	6.73	123	20.19	139
	Bases Empty	.218	--	.372	--	.218	--	2.56	--	0.00	--	25.64	--
Spike Owen	Runners On	.280	62	.409	97	.352	66	0.54	147	10.36	65	6.76	16
	Bases Empty	.243	111	.295	150	.326	82	0.40	153	10.64	32	9.93	24
Jim Rice	Runners On	.274	71	.367	121	.356	62	1.86	113	9.72	76	16.19	103
	Bases Empty	.280	47	.455	61	.358	42	4.76	45	9.91	46	17.45	113
Ed Romero	Runners On	.274	74	.292	153	.301	127	0.00	150	4.39	153	6.14	12
	Bases Empty	.271	62	.295	151	.338	54	0.00	157	9.15	60	10.56	32
Team Average	Runners On	.289	2	.452	3	.373	1	3.30	6	11.15	1	12.47	1
	Bases Empty	.269	4	.412	10	.333	2	2.97	12	8.12	8	13.42	1
League Average	Runners On	.271		.428		.343		3.25		9.68		14.87	
	Bases Empty	.260		.424		.326		3.49		8.34		15.79	

Overall Batting Compared to Late Inning Pressure Situations

		BA	Rank	SA	Rank	OBA	Rank	HR %	Rank	BB %	Rank	SO %	Rank	RDI %	Rank
Marty Barrett	Overall	.293	29	.351	142	.351	56	0.54	152	7.99	96	5.96	5	.275	99
	Pressure	.273	72	.303	136	.385	36	0.00	119	15.00	19	5.00	4	.238	100
Todd Benzinger	Overall	.278	55	.444	66	.344	65	3.59	74	8.70	82	16.21	97	.305	63
	Pressure	.219	125	.313	130	.286	125	3.13	70	8.11	96	24.32	137	.188	122
Wade Boggs	Overall	.363	1	.588	3	.461	1	4.36	54	15.74	7	7.20	11	.344	26
	Pressure	.250	96	.355	106	.363	64	1.32	114	15.22	17	8.70	26	.333	51
Ellis Burks	Overall	.272	68	.441	68	.324	94	3.58	75	6.77	121	16.17	96	.234	139
	Pressure	.176	150	.250	145	.243	148	1.47	112	8.11	96	18.92	107	.227	104
Dwight Evans	Overall	.305	20	.569	5	.417	4	6.28	9	16.13	6	14.92	88	.358	17
	Pressure	.296	51	.469	50	.376	45	3.70	59	11.83	45	16.13	86	.207	116
Mike Greenwell	Overall	.328	6	.570	4	.386	19	4.61	48	7.68	104	8.77	21	.324	43
	Pressure	.328	25	.687	4	.392	34	7.46	11	8.11	38	10.81	38	.333	51
Dave Henderson	Overall	.234	145	.418	92	.313	109	4.35	55	10.53	46	22.97	149	.232	142
	Pressure	.214	126	.321	126	.290	124	3.57	61	9.38	79	28.13	154	.125	144
Sam Horn	Overall	.278	--	.589	--	.356	--	8.86	--	9.60	--	31.07	--	.296	70
	Pressure	.105	--	.263	--	.150	--	5.26	--	0.00	--	35.00	--	.375	38
John Marzano	Overall	.244	--	.399	--	.283	--	2.98	--	3.85	--	22.53	--	.317	49
	Pressure	.353	--	.412	--	.333	--	0.00	--	0.00	--	15.79	--	.333	--
Spike Owen	Overall	.259	95	.343	146	.337	72	0.46	154	10.52	48	8.53	18	.310	59
	Pressure	.237	114	.322	125	.328	90	1.69	105	11.59	47	4.35	2	.222	106
Jim Rice	Overall	.277	57	.408	97	.357	50	3.22	89	9.80	58	16.78	106	.293	73
	Pressure	.267	80	.333	118	.333	82	1.67	106	7.58	106	19.70	111	.318	68
Ed Romero	Overall	.272	69	.294	157	.322	97	0.00	161	7.03	111	8.59	19	.217	152
	Pressure	.425	6	.475	47	.429	17	0.00	119	2.38	155	9.52	29	.357	48
Team Average	Overall	.278	1	.430	4	.352	1	3.11	10	9.53	3	12.97	1	.297	4
	Pressure	.254	11	.364	13	.332	8	2.17	13	9.93	4	14.17	1	.254	10
League Average	Overall	.265		.425		.333		3.38		8.94		15.38		.287	
	Pressure	.262		.405		.335		3.07		9.43		16.58		.280	

Additional Miscellaneous Batting Comparisons

	Grass Surface BA	Rank	Artificial Surface BA	Rank	Home Games BA	Rank	Road Games BA	Rank	Runners in Scoring Position BA	Rank	Runners in Scoring Pos and Two Outs BA	Rank	Leading Off Inning OBA	Rank	Runners on 3B with less than 2 Outs RDI %	Rank
Marty Barrett	.292	39	.306	25	.292	55	.295	30	.300	42	.241	94	.296	119	.731	17
Todd Benzinger	.281	54	.250	--	.311	27	.248	102	.246	109	.346	14	.250	149	.500	120
Wade Boggs	.369	2	.333	7	.411	1	.312	19	.333	13	.291	48	.457	4	.750	9
Ellis Burks	.279	59	.239	107	.289	60	.258	86	.222	134	.129	152	.350	52	.588	86
Dwight Evans	.303	26	.313	20	.304	38	.306	25	.342	11	.313	29	.346	57	.549	103
Rich Gedman	.215	154	.143	--	.222	--	.180	--	.257	--	.188	--	.325	--	.500	--
Mike Greenwell	.305	23	.466	1	.327	12	.328	5	.317	32	.301	38	.392	18	.577	91
Dave Henderson	.226	144	.276	--	.234	131	.234	--	.154	159	.080	157	.375	29	.444	145
Sam Horn	.277	66	.294	--	.306	--	.256	--	.227	--	.231	101	.359	--	.600	71
John Marzano	.258	98	.118	--	.273	--	.213	--	.300	42	.282	53	.233	--	.714	--
Spike Owen	.257	103	.268	69	.263	92	.254	94	.320	25	.282	53	.309	102	.667	33
Jim Rice	.297	32	.189	148	.305	34	.252	95	.272	78	.203	125	.363	43	.750	9
Ed Romero	.285	49	.214	130	.296	49	.252	96	.250	102	.286	51	.308	105	.444	--
Marc Sullivan	.180	160	.111	--	.147	--	.188	--	.194	--	.227	--	.200	159	.167	--
Team Average	.280	3	.267	4	.294	1	.264	6	.286	2	.263	3	.343	2	.606	3
League Average	.267		.261		.270		.260		.266		.247		.328		.581	

Pitching vs. Left and Right Handed Batters

		BA	Rank	SA	Rank	OBA	Rank	HR %	Rank	BB %	Rank	SO %	Rank
Tom Bolton	vs. Lefties	.330	125	.423	66	.414	127	1.03	9	11.61	101	19.64	20
	vs. Righties	.331	119	.455	96	.384	116	2.60	40	8.00	61	15.43	66
Roger Clemens	vs. Lefties	.235	19	.332	12	.299	16	1.00	8	7.54	42	20.06	16
	vs. Righties	.235	33	.369	37	.290	25	2.88	56	6.68	33	24.90	11
Steve Crawford	vs. Lefties	.333	126	.538	119	.405	122	4.55	105	10.81	88	11.49	96
	vs. Righties	.297	106	.513	116	.369	102	4.43	102	9.09	82	14.77	71
Wes Gardner	vs. Lefties	.315	118	.549	121	.414	126	4.94	109	14.58	122	15.10	53
	vs. Righties	.249	51	.444	87	.306	41	4.76	110	6.70	34	19.62	33
Bruce Hurst	vs. Lefties	.248	36	.419	61	.333	57	3.10	62	10.81	88	21.62	9
	vs. Righties	.265	76	.435	80	.314	51	3.96	92	7.03	42	18.52	41
Al Nipper	vs. Lefties	.267	65	.471	100	.318	38	4.28	102	6.80	29	10.44	107
	vs. Righties	.303	109	.530	120	.375	108	4.42	101	9.32	90	12.60	98
Calvin Schiraldi	vs. Lefties	.282	91	.514	112	.392	122	6.34	122	15.61	124	18.50	27
	vs. Righties	.205	8	.345	17	.265	10	3.51	82	6.91	39	32.45	3
Jeff Sellers	vs. Lefties	.304	110	.436	76	.372	111	1.38	16	9.91	74	12.61	80
	vs. Righties	.292	105	.440	84	.364	99	2.40	30	9.76	95	19.86	32
Bob Stanley	vs. Lefties	.358	127	.522	113	.413	125	2.68	42	8.68	58	8.38	119
	vs. Righties	.287	100	.416	67	.314	50	2.84	54	3.80	3	11.40	108
Team Average	vs. Lefties	.287	14	.446	12	.353	14	2.75	4	9.14	5	14.90	7
	vs. Righties	.279	13	.455	12	.336	11	3.92	12	7.50	2	17.85	2
League Average	vs. Lefties	.267		.427		.338		3.30		9.47		14.54	
	vs. Righties	.264		.424		.330		3.45		8.56		15.98	

Pitching with Runners on Base and Bases Empty

		BA	Rank	SA	Rank	OBA	Rank	HR %	Rank	BB %	Rank	SO %	Rank
Tom Bolton	Runners On	.304	102	.370	30	.378	109	0.00	1	10.63	89	14.38	67
	Bases Empty	.362	--	.526	--	.417	--	4.31	--	7.87	--	20.47	--
Roger Clemens	Runners On	.205	6	.312	5	.289	12	2.03	26	9.66	75	22.09	16
	Bases Empty	.257	61	.374	30	.300	32	1.63	12	5.23	21	22.15	17
Steve Crawford	Runners On	.352	123	.634	128	.416	124	6.21	123	9.32	68	12.42	93
	Bases Empty	.276	93	.414	60	.356	101	2.76	46	10.43	103	14.11	74
Wes Gardner	Runners On	.276	79	.483	98	.357	88	5.17	110	10.84	91	13.30	81
	Bases Empty	.282	100	.503	113	.359	104	4.52	105	10.10	100	21.72	19
Bruce Hurst	Runners On	.272	76	.447	87	.315	34	3.61	86	6.27	19	16.54	40
	Bases Empty	.256	58	.423	72	.319	56	3.99	93	8.47	66	20.60	21
Al Nipper	Runners On	.278	82	.454	90	.350	77	3.87	89	10.09	83	10.39	109
	Bases Empty	.287	105	.528	120	.341	87	4.67	109	6.36	38	12.27	98
Calvin Schiraldi	Runners On	.247	40	.524	110	.316	37	7.65	128	9.23	66	27.69	2
	Bases Empty	.231	26	.301	6	.337	83	1.40	7	13.25	118	23.49	14
Jeff Sellers	Runners On	.311	109	.467	92	.360	94	1.64	15	7.39	35	17.25	34
	Bases Empty	.288	106	.414	59	.375	111	2.03	16	11.90	111	14.88	68
Bob Stanley	Runners On	.286	92	.429	77	.333	58	3.06	71	6.59	21	8.68	116
	Bases Empty	.354	127	.503	114	.392	119	2.48	29	5.85	30	11.11	104
Team Average	Runners On	.276	8	.450	11	.339	6	3.60	11	8.69	3	15.68	5
	Bases Empty	.288	14	.452	12	.348	13	3.21	5	7.88	6	17.21	4
League Average	Runners On	.271		.428		.343		3.25		9.68		14.87	
	Bases Empty	.260		.424		.326		3.49		8.34		15.79	

Overall Pitching Compared to Late Inning Pressure Situations

		BA	Rank	SA	Rank	OBA	Rank	HR %	Rank	BB %	Rank	SO %	Rank
Tom Bolton	Overall	.331	124	.442	83	.396	124	1.99	11	9.41	81	17.07	42
	Pressure	.500	--	.917	--	.571	--	8.33	--	13.33	--	20.00	--
Roger Clemens	Overall	.235	17	.348	9	.295	15	1.80	7	7.17	34	22.13	15
	Pressure	.262	67	.430	81	.336	69	4.67	107	9.84	71	18.85	33
Steve Crawford	Overall	.314	117	.524	121	.386	121	4.48	103	9.88	90	13.27	81
	Pressure	.261	--	.435	--	.393	--	4.35	--	17.86	--	14.29	--
Wes Gardner	Overall	.279	91	.493	115	.358	97	4.84	115	10.47	98	17.46	38
	Pressure	.285	89	.465	100	.377	103	4.17	98	12.87	106	19.88	27
Bruce Hurst	Overall	.262	66	.432	76	.317	42	3.84	90	7.59	39	18.98	25
	Pressure	.306	106	.561	122	.364	91	6.12	121	8.04	50	13.39	79
Al Nipper	Overall	.284	96	.498	117	.345	79	4.34	101	7.98	48	11.45	102
	Pressure	.292	93	.542	116	.314	41	6.25	122	3.77	7	15.09	62
Joe Sambito	Overall	.301	--	.536	--	.367	--	5.23	--	9.36	--	20.47	--
	Pressure	.279	84	.485	105	.372	100	4.41	102	12.50	101	22.50	18
Calvin Schiraldi	Overall	.240	26	.422	69	.326	59	4.79	114	11.08	109	25.76	4
	Pressure	.225	37	.391	65	.339	70	4.64	105	14.36	115	25.97	6
Jeff Sellers	Overall	.299	112	.438	8	.368	89	1.86	8	9.84	89	15.97	50
	Pressure	.355	123	.434	85	.398	116	0.00	1	6.98	36	12.79	85
Bob Stanley	Overall	.321	118	.468	105	.363	106	2.76	43	6.21	20	9.91	116
	Pressure	.384	126	.547	119	.438	125	2.33	53	8.91	60	7.92	118
Team Average	Overall	.282	14	.451	12	.344	12	3.39	7	8.25	3	16.50	4
	Pressure	.297	14	.480	14	.373	14	4.10	14	10.74	12	17.98	3
League Average	Overall	.265		.425		.333		3.38		8.94		15.38	
	Pressure	.262		.404		.337		2.99		9.73		16.42	

Additional Miscellaneous Pitching Comparisons

	Grass Surface		Artificial Surface		Home Games		Road Games		Runners in Scoring Position		Runners in Scoring Pos and Two Outs		Leading Off Inning	
	BA	Rank	BA	Rank	BA	Rank	BA	Rank	BA	Rank	BA	Rank	OBA	Rank
Tom Bolton	.338	125	.261	--	.373	--	.293	97	.278	81	.189	21	.298	37
Roger Clemens	.235	14	.236	39	.219	15	.256	39	.199	12	.200	32	.350	87
Steve Crawford	.306	111	.345	113	.301	112	.326	122	.349	121	.429	127	.397	119
Wes Gardner	.275	84	.293	98	.271	89	.288	89	.226	32	.208	40	.304	41
Bruce Hurst	.262	63	.266	74	.265	79	.259	43	.308	106	.260	80	.320	53
Al Nipper	.286	94	.270	80	.290	105	.279	80	.247	45	.219	48	.351	91
Calvin Schiraldi	.232	13	.263	71	.209	9	.271	70	.262	68	.222	49	.273	20
Jeff Sellers	.306	110	.270	81	.295	107	.302	106	.318	113	.308	104	.351	90
Bob Stanley	.305	108	.427	127	.299	110	.340	126	.290	90	.267	84	.445	126
Team Average	.282	14	.285	13	.279	13	.286	14	.269	8	.245	6	.355	14
League Average	.267		.261		.260		.270		.266		.247		.328	

CALIFORNIA ANGELS

Have you ever visited a racetrack, placed a perfecta wager on a couple of long shots, watched them break from the gate on top, and then recited a Hail Mary or two trying to keep them there all the way to the wire?

California Angels fans don't have to visit Santa Anita to experience that anxiety—they go through it nearly every season. The Angels have been the fastest starters in baseball for the past 10 years. They've led the American League West at the end of April five times since 1978, and trailed the division leader by one game or less in two other seasons during that time.

Unfortunately, things have seldom looked as good on Gene Autry's ranch in September as they did in April. In fact, for 10 consecutive seasons, the Angels have failed to fulfill their early-season promise, never once playing as well after April 30 as they did before—though it should be noted that they did hang to win three division titles. The following table indicates that the Angels have compiled by far the best April mark in the American League since 1978, but rank only seventh thereafter:

| | During April | | | After April 30 | | | | |
Team	W	L	Pct.	W	L	Pct.	Rank	Diff.
California	129	88	.594	663	686	.491	(7)	+.103
Detroit	104	83	.556	759	619	.551	(3)	+.005
Oakland	119	96	.553	604	748	.447	(11)	+.107
Milwaukee	101	86	.540	723	653	.525	(6)	+.015
Kansas City	96	87	.525	731	647	.530	(5)	−.006
Boston	100	95	.513	739	628	.541	(4)	−.028
New York	98	95	.508	786	584	.574	(1)	−.066
Baltimore	94	102	.480	757	605	.556	(2)	−.076
Texas	91	99	.479	646	724	.472	(10)	+.007
Toronto	94	104	.475	659	705	.483	(9)	−.008
Chicago	87	98	.470	675	699	.491	(8)	−.021
Minnesota	99	113	.467	618	736	.456	(13)	+.011
Cleveland	80	104	.435	629	742	.459	(12)	−.024
Seattle	91	133	.406	564	777	.421	(14)	−.014

You can analyze the details of those fast starts endlessly, but the simple fact is that California's early-season success has had more to do with the schedule than with the Angels themselves. Over the past 10 seasons, no American League team has played a softer schedule during the first month of the season than California has. To illustrate this fact, we borrowed the NFL's strength-of-schedule technique to compile the following table. The percentages listed represent the average end-of-season winning percentages of each team's April opponents for every season since 1978, weighted by the number of times they played:

Team	Pct.	Team	Pct.
Chicago	.536	Milwaukee	.497
Texas	.523	New York	.494
Cleveland	.518	Detroit	.486
Kansas City	.517	Seattle	.485
Boston	.508	Minnesota	.478
Toronto	.505	Oakland	.471
Baltimore	.504	California	.467

Those figures explain not only California's strong starts, but Oakland's as well. And in addition to easing into the season against the league's wimpiest opposition, the Angels and A's have played a predominantly home-bound schedule during April. Over the past 10 Aprils, California has played 15 more games at home than on the road. That margin is the fifth largest in the A.L. during that time, behind—surprise!—Oakland (30), Seattle (27), Texas (20), and Kansas City (17).

Clearly the schedule makers have tried to assign as many early-season games as possible west of the Mississippi, but one has to wonder whether that gives the West Coast teams an unfair advantage. Consider the following figures, which show the number of division leaders at the end of each month that went on to win their division titles:

	April	May	June	July	August
Winners	32	34	43	49	60
Percentage	44%	47%	60%	68%	83%

In other words, teams that led their divisions on the morning of May 1 won titles nearly half the time. But that doesn't prove that there's an inherent advantage to being in the role of chasee as opposed to being the chaser, except for the obvious edge of having the lead in the first place. It's simply an indication of the obvious: The best team overall is the one most likely to compile the best record in April, or in any other month for that matter.

Here's a more telling set of statistics that shows that championship teams play consistently well throughout the season, *but with a strong closing kick.* The month-by-month composite winning percentages of all division winners since 1969 (excluding the 1981 season):

Month	W	L	Pct.
April	820	554	.597

May	1095	809	.575
June	1184	828	.588
July	1217	838	.592
August	1234	868	.587
September	1246	770	.618
October	93	63	.596
Totals	6889	4730	.593

We think the month-by-month totals are the truest indication of when championships are won. Bill Russell, in his former role as commentator on NBA telecasts, often pointed out that teams that had erased large margins in a game were unlikely to win because they'd expended all their energy just catching up. But over a season-long baseball pennant race, that doesn't seem to be the case.

So when first-month leads are produced by easy April schedules like those assigned to California and Oakland for the past decade—facing soft opposition with a majority of the games at home—the downside might not be worth the risk. After all, if they're playing home games against lousy teams in April, they must be facing one hell of a tough schedule come crunch time. And September is when champions are made.

April Shower Power

Now that you know who the best April teams are—and why—we thought you might like to take a look at the best and worst individual players during the month of April. We've compiled composite statistics for the past six Aprils, but before we get to those, we'd first like to present for posterity's sake the remarkable April statistics of an otherwise unremarkable player.

Ken Reitz played third base in the National League for 11 seasons from 1972 through 1982, spending all but three of those years with the St. Louis Cardinals. Although Reitz's name was included on the 1988 Hall of Fame ballot, it surprised no one that he fell several hundred votes short of the 75 percent needed for election. After all, his career batting average was 107 points lower than Ty Cobb's; he hit 687 fewer home runs than Hank Aaron hit. But if they based the election only on his performances before May 1 of each year, you'd have to consider Reitz for a Cooperstown plaque. His nine Aprils in the majors approximated the number of at bats in a typical full season. And what a season it would have been:

Year	AB	H	2B	3B	HR	RBI	BA
1973	62	11	1	0	0	3	.177
1974	84	35	7	1	1	14	.417
1975	65	24	4	0	0	3	.369
1976	65	24	1	0	1	9	.369
1977	71	15	7	0	1	8	.211
1978	72	23	2	0	3	14	.319
1979	71	23	9	0	1	12	.324
1980	63	25	3	0	2	11	.397
1981	52	10	2	1	0	4	.192
Totals	605	190	36	2	9	78	.314

It's been nearly a decade since Reitz put on his last April

magic show, but there are some pretty good Reitz impersonators playing today. Kirby Puckett (.360), Tony Gwynn (.347), and Pat Tabler (.338) have the highest April batting averages over the past six seasons among players with at least 200 at bats. Bob Kearney (.188), Johnnie LeMaster (.197), and Bob Horner (.199) have the lowest. The following table lists the players with the largest differences between their April batting averages and those of later months:

Player	April	Diff.	Player	April	Diff.
Todd Cruz	.290	+.093	Bob Horner	.199	−.089
Candy Maldonado	.314	+.063	Ryne Sandberg	.227	−.070
Juan Bonilla	.295	+.062	Bill Doran	.217	−.068
Kirby Puckett	.360	+.054	Phil Bradley	.250	−.058
Pat Tabler	.338	+.048	Wade Boggs	.304	−.056
Tom Brookens	.278	+.044	Tony Fernandez	.253	−.055
Bobby Grich	.299	+.042	Terry Puhl	.229	−.055
Toby Harrah	.295	+.034	Bob Kearney	.188	−.054
Darryl Strawberry	.295	+.034	Bill Madlock	.241	−.053
Glenn Hubbard	.275	+.034	Alan Wiggins	.212	−.052

Dale Murphy leads the majors with 35 home runs since 1982 during the month of April. That's no shock, but the name of the American League leader is sure to surprise you: Brian Downing (with 30). Incidentally, Reggie Jackson is tied for second in the A.L. (22), and Doug DeCinces is tied for fourth (21), providing some further enlightenment on the Angels' early-season success.

Jack Morris is the only 20-game winner over the past six Aprils, and his total of 20 wins is six more than any other pitcher in the American League. But who would have guessed that the runner-up is Mike Smithson? Fernando Valenzuela leads the N.L. with 16 wins. The best ERA among pitchers with at least 75 innings belongs to Alejandro Pena (1.54); he's followed by ex-California starter Geoff Zahn (1.62), and Dwight Gooden (1.67). The highest ERAs are those of Matt Young (5.73), Dave Stewart (5.57), and Lary Sorensen (5.26).

The following table shows the pitchers with the largest ERA differences between April and the other months over the past six seasons, with at least 75 innings pitched during April:

Player	April	Diff.	Player	April	Diff.
Ray Burris	2.05	−2.44	Ron Darling	4.99	+1.81
Geoff Zahn	1.62	−2.28	Dave Stewart	5.57	+1.81
Alejandro Pena	1.54	−1.94	Matt Young	5.73	+1.62
Rick Honeycutt	2.18	−1.78	Jimmy Key	4.63	+1.57
Dennis Rasmussen	2.72	−1.68	Nolan Ryan	4.16	+1.12
John Butcher	3.14	−1.66	Jerry Koosman	4.95	+1.09
Mark Davis	2.63	−1.65	Mike LaCoss	4.71	+1.03
Mike Smithson	3.07	−1.56	Rick Rhoden	4.26	+0.89
Bruce Berenyi	2.71	−1.53	Charlie Hough	4.39	+0.86
Tommy John	2.95	−1.41	Mike Flanagan	4.68	+0.85

A Mockery of Mauch?

California led the American League with 70 sacrifice bunts last season. That's the sixth time in the past seven years that the Angels have led the A.L.; they missed by one when

Seattle led the league in 1984. Most baseball fans connect Gene Mauch's love of the sacrifice bunt with his alleged disdain for playing for the big inning. The story goes that Mauch will bunt and steal, scratch and squeeze for a single run, risking an out for the luxury of advancing his base runners, and often sacrificing a potentially big inning in the process.

Well, if you subscribe to that theory, here's your wake-up call. The following table compares the distribution of California's scoring over the past three seasons with the average of the other 13 American League teams. During that time, the Angels executed 260 sac bunts, more than twice as many as the average of the rest of the league (128), but they also scored roughly the same number of runs. More to the point, the distribution of California's scoring—that is, the number of innings of one run, two runs, and so on—was nearly identical to the league averages as well:

Team	Total Runs	Distribution of Scoring Innings									
		1	2	3	4	5	6	7	8	9	10
California	2288	683	309	162	66	27	13	1	1	1	0
Other teams	2276	677	317	141	67	29	12	4	2	1	1

One-run innings accounted for 29.9 percent of California's scoring, 29.7 percent of the rest of the league. In effect, no difference. And the Angels actually had more innings of three or more runs than the league average. Take that, Earl Weaver! Mauch's only apparent sacrifice—pardon the pun—was *very* big innings (seven runs or more), which most teams achieve only two or three times a season anyway.

So why hasn't Mauch's bunt-*philia* produced an abundance of one-run innings at the cost of big innings? Quite simply, we never should have expected it to in the first place. Big innings aren't suppressed by bunting and base stealing to nearly the extent that they are created by patient home run hitters.

We studied the last five American League seasons, and chose the 10 teams with the highest and lowest totals in each of four categories: sacrifice bunts, stolen base attempts, home runs, and walks. For each category, we compared the distribution of scoring by the teams with the most to that of the teams with the least. For instance, the following tables show the teams with the most and fewest sacrifice bunts ("SH" in the table), comparing the number of innings in which they scored only one run with those in which they scored three or more:

Year	Team	SH	1	3+	Year	Team	SH	1	3+
1985	Cal.	99	218	85	1985	Tor.	21	228	87
1986	Cal.	91	241	94	1986	K.C.	24	218	66
1987	Cal.	70	224	92	1986	Tor.	24	236	98
1983	Cal.	68	210	75	1984	Minn.	26	205	70
1984	Seat.	66	226	62	1985	Seat.	28	195	82
1984	Cal.	65	215	81	1983	Minn.	29	223	81
1984	N.Y.	64	205	89	1987	Tor.	30	236	101
1987	Milw.	63	220	111	1987	Balt.	31	203	82
1985	Oak.	63	222	89	1986	Tex.	31	222	78
1983	Milw.	61	221	88	1985	Balt.	31	205	97
	Totals	710	2202	866		Totals	275	2171	842

The first group had more than twice the number of sacrifice bunts as the second group, but the ratios of one-run innings to big innings (three runs or more) were nearly identical: 2.54 for the high-bunt group, 2.58 for the low-bunt group. That's right—the slight difference that did exist suggested that the teams with more bunts tended toward *fewer* one-run innings. We made similar studies of the other categories mentioned earlier, and here's what we found (the higher the ratio, the greater the emphasis on one-run innings at the cost of big innings):

Category	Team with the Most			Teams with the Fewest		
	1-Run	3+	Ratio	1-Run	3+	Ratio
Sacrifice bunts	2202	866	2.54	2171	842	2.58
Stolen base attempts	2269	836	2.71	2180	825	2.64
Home runs	2282	923	2.47	2105	706	2.98
Bases on balls	2524	991	2.55	2192	726	3.02

The differences for sac bunts and stolen base attempts—the two plays normally associated with one-run strategies—are trivial. But teams that don't hit many home runs had a much higher ratio of one-run innings than powerful teams. And the largest difference of all was found between teams that draw a lot of walks and those that seldom walk. Bases on balls, a category in which the Angels have led the American League in two of the past three years, are the truest indication of a big-inning team.

So let's get off Mauch's back. The statistics prove that his teams are no less likely to produce innings of three or more runs than anyone else's. To demean his style of managing with terms like "little ball" is not only to criticize him unfairly, but to betray an ignorance of the facts as well.

WON-LOST RECORD BY STARTING POSITION

CALIFORNIA 75-87	C	1B	2B	3B	SS	LF	CF	RF	P	DH	Leadoff	Relief	Starts
Tony Armas								8-11					8-11
Bob Boone	52-66												52-66
Bill Buckner		4-1								15-24			19-25
Dewayne Buice												32-25	
John Candelaria									12-8				12-8
Mike Cook									0-1			2-13	0-1
Doug DeCinces		0-3		59-59							1-1		59-62
Brian Downing						11-22				57-58	55-54		68-80
Jim Eppard									0-1				0-1
Jack Fimple	0-2												0-2
Chuck Finley									2-1			2-30	2-1
Willie Fraser									8-15			6-7	8-15
Miguel Garcia												0-1	
Bryan Harvey												0-3	
George Hendrick		3-4				11-16		5-3					19-23
Jack Howell			16-24	33-27				6-5			1-0		55-56
Ruppert Jones						11-13	1-1	3-10		1-0	4-8		16-24
Wally Joyner		67-78											67-78
Jack Lazorko									5-6			2-13	5-6
Gary Lucas												12-36	
Urbano Lugo									2-3			0-2	2-3
Kirk McCaskill									5-8			0-1	5-8
Mark McLemore			66-62								2-2		66-62
Darrell Miller	6-11					4-8		1-1					11-20
Greg Minton												27-14	
Donnie Moore												8-6	
Gary Pettis							55-53				9-16		55-53
Gus Polidor			0-3	0-4	15-16								15-23
Johnny Ray			9-20								0-1		9-21
Jerry Reuss									8-8			0-1	8-8
Mark Ryal		1-1		0-1	2-0			5-3		1-4	0-1		9-9
Dick Schofield		0-2		60-70						1-0	2-4		61-72
Don Sutton									15-19			1-0	15-19
Devon White						2-1	19-33	47-53			1-1		68-87
Tack Wilson						1-0							1-0
Mike Witt									18-18				18-18
Butch Wynegar	17-8												17-8

Batting vs. Left and Right Handed Pitchers

		BA	Rank	SA	Rank	OBA	Rank	HR %	Rank	BB %	Rank	SO %	Rank
Bob Boone	vs. Lefties	.284	57	.321	136	.333	78	0.00	145	7.24	113	5.26	3
	vs. Righties	.220	147	.306	152	.288	139	1.18	136	8.28	90	9.66	33
Bill Buckner	vs. Lefties	.261	90	.286	147	.272	143	0.00	145	2.38	158	8.73	25
	vs. Righties	.294	31	.391	101	.328	85	1.43	129	5.11	147	4.03	1
Doug DeCinces	vs. Lefties	.283	60	.459	56	.413	13	4.40	54	18.37	6	13.78	74
	vs. Righties	.207	157	.354	129	.292	134	3.06	92	10.18	53	17.96	120
Brian Downing	vs. Lefties	.299	40	.554	15	.432	7	6.21	15	18.47	5	15.77	93
	vs. Righties	.259	89	.456	55	.384	25	4.62	45	13.74	14	10.57	40
George Hendrick	vs. Lefties	.232	122	.384	102	.294	122	3.20	80	8.09	95	10.29	37
	vs. Righties	.270	--	.432	--	.325	--	2.70	--	7.50	--	10.00	--
Jack Howell	vs. Lefties	.123	163	.260	152	.200	163	1.37	120	8.75	82	31.25	162
	vs. Righties	.269	77	.500	30	.356	52	5.85	24	11.60	32	21.58	141
Ruppert Jones	vs. Lefties	.357	--	.643	--	.400	--	7.14	--	6.67	--	6.67	--
	vs. Righties	.236	126	.416	85	.310	117	3.93	66	9.60	63	18.69	125
Wally Joyner	vs. Lefties	.284	57	.478	42	.347	67	3.98	59	8.85	80	11.06	45
	vs. Righties	.287	40	.556	14	.376	30	7.16	8	12.18	23	9.13	28
Mark McLemore	vs. Lefties	.222	134	.294	144	.293	125	0.79	136	8.97	77	8.28	21
	vs. Righties	.241	118	.303	153	.317	102	0.65	148	9.89	58	16.95	107
Darrell Miller	vs. Lefties	.255	95	.400	93	.311	104	3.64	64	6.45	129	12.90	64
	vs. Righties	.226	--	.396	--	.295	--	3.77	--	8.06	--	8.06	--
Gary Pettis	vs. Lefties	.172	158	.250	154	.248	154	0.78	137	9.15	71	19.72	122
	vs. Righties	.226	143	.263	159	.327	87	0.00	156	12.75	20	31.37	159
Dick Schofield	vs. Lefties	.267	84	.379	107	.324	84	1.24	126	7.78	103	7.22	12
	vs. Righties	.242	114	.343	138	.296	131	2.20	110	6.55	121	14.25	75
Devon White	vs. Lefties	.246	103	.477	43	.296	121	5.53	25	6.05	133	16.74	98
	vs. Righties	.270	73	.427	76	.311	113	2.95	94	5.41	141	20.58	136
Team Average	vs. Lefties	.253	12	.399	13	.325	11	2.91	13	9.39	5	12.87	2
	vs. Righties	.252	14	.401	14	.326	12	3.17	9	9.35	4	15.56	9
League Average	vs. Lefties	.265		.422		.333		3.29		8.94		15.64	
	vs. Righties	.265		.427		.334		3.43		8.94		15.26	

Batting with Runners on Base and Bases Empty

		BA	Rank	SA	Rank	OBA	Rank	HR %	Rank	BB %	Rank	SO %	Rank
Bob Boone	Runners On	.264	92	.344	137	.309	121	0.00	150	5.73	136	6.77	17
	Bases Empty	.226	135	.288	157	.300	123	1.33	135	9.60	50	9.20	18
Bill Buckner	Runners On	.316	28	.421	82	.344	77	1.44	124	5.26	144	4.82	6
	Bases Empty	.262	80	.319	143	.289	131	0.77	143	3.70	151	5.56	5
Doug DeCinces	Runners On	.228	134	.365	124	.351	68	3.05	87	15.35	16	18.67	127
	Bases Empty	.238	119	.410	91	.325	83	3.91	69	11.42	24	14.53	72
Brian Downing	Runners On	.269	85	.407	98	.388	32	3.24	81	13.96	26	12.08	54
	Bases Empty	.274	57	.536	24	.407	6	6.27	21	16.05	4	12.33	55
George Hendrick	Runners On	.277	65	.506	25	.341	82	4.82	39	8.79	94	10.99	45
	Bases Empty	.203	--	.278	--	.259	--	1.27	--	7.06	--	9.41	--
Jack Howell	Runners On	.245	118	.454	64	.339	85	5.10	33	11.84	48	22.37	144
	Bases Empty	.245	109	.466	52	.325	84	5.14	38	10.60	34	23.67	144
Ruppert Jones	Runners On	.292	--	.528	--	.386	--	4.17	--	13.10	--	19.05	--
	Bases Empty	.217	148	.375	116	.271	152	4.17	61	6.98	106	17.05	106
Wally Joyner	Runners On	.308	33	.545	16	.399	19	4.89	37	13.85	28	9.85	29
	Bases Empty	.265	73	.513	28	.332	66	7.05	11	8.23	74	9.76	21
Mark McLemore	Runners On	.238	129	.316	147	.333	92	0.52	148	12.08	43	14.58	86
	Bases Empty	.233	125	.288	158	.290	130	0.83	141	7.34	102	14.29	71
Gary Pettis	Runners On	.177	161	.209	162	.278	149	0.00	150	12.15	41	29.28	158
	Bases Empty	.229	133	.292	154	.318	99	0.42	151	11.24	27	26.59	153
Dick Schofield	Runners On	.251	109	.349	132	.297	131	2.05	110	5.41	141	12.61	62
	Bases Empty	.250	99	.359	123	.311	110	1.76	125	8.09	77	11.33	42
Devon White	Runners On	.250	111	.397	103	.294	135	3.08	84	5.20	145	19.27	130
	Bases Empty	.274	56	.481	43	.317	102	4.32	59	5.96	127	19.51	128
Team Average	Runners On	.260	11	.398	13	.337	9	2.59	13	9.79	6	14.86	7
	Bases Empty	.246	13	.402	13	.317	13	3.48	9	9.01	4	14.56	3
League Average	Runners On	.271		.428		.343		3.25		9.68		14.87	
	Bases Empty	.260		.424		.326		3.49		8.34		15.79	

Overall Batting Compared to Late Inning Pressure Situations

		BA	Rank	SA	Rank	OBA	Rank	HR %	Rank	BB %	Rank	SO %	Rank	RDI %	Rank
Bob Boone	Overall	.242	128	.311	154	.304	126	0.77	145	7.92	100	8.14	17	.276	96
	Pressure	.182	146	.236	149	.274	136	1.82	103	8.82	85	10.29	36	.000	158
Bill Buckner	Overall	.286	40	.365	131	.314	107	1.07	138	4.42	153	5.22	3	.373	8
	Pressure	.270	75	.324	122	.316	104	0.00	119	6.33	122	5.06	5	.280	79
Doug DeCinces	Overall	.234	143	.391	113	.337	74	3.53	78	13.21	15	16.42	100	.273	103
	Pressure	.213	127	.344	114	.351	70	3.28	67	17.11	10	14.47	75	.167	133
Brian Downing	Overall	.272	71	.487	32	.400	8	5.11	32	15.25	8	12.23	49	.247	125
	Pressure	.244	100	.354	109	.364	61	2.44	87	15.00	19	12.00	52	.267	87
George Hendrick	Overall	.241	--	.395	--	.301	--	3.09	--	7.95	--	10.23	--	.295	71
	Pressure	.409	--	.818	--	.500	--	13.64	--	15.38	--	3.85	--	.556	3
Jack Howell	Overall	.245	121	.461	51	.331	81	5.12	31	11.15	37	23.09	150	.221	150
	Pressure	.253	95	.533	25	.349	74	6.67	19	12.79	36	26.74	151	.111	147
Ruppert Jones	Overall	.245	123	.432	77	.316	106	4.17	61	9.39	67	17.84	119	.289	--
	Pressure	.244	100	.366	101	.392	31	2.44	87	19.23	6	17.31	94	.636	1
Wally Joyner	Overall	.285	41	.528	17	.366	39	6.03	13	11.03	41	9.80	27	.373	7
	Pressure	.185	144	.326	121	.283	128	2.17	97	10.38	63	8.49	24	.324	66
Mark McLemore	Overall	.236	140	.300	156	.310	113	0.69	147	9.62	61	14.43	80	.259	115
	Pressure	.380	9	.451	60	.443	12	1.41	113	10.13	66	10.13	35	.389	32
Gary Pettis	Overall	.208	160	.259	160	.302	131	0.25	158	11.61	50	27.68	158	.152	162
	Pressure	.207	131	.224	154	.281	130	0.00	119	7.69	104	30.77	159	.222	106
Mark Ryal	Overall	.200	--	.410	--	.223	--	5.00	--	2.88	--	14.42	--	.286	--
	Pressure	.306	42	.639	6	.306	114	8.33	8	0.00	161	8.33	22	.417	20
Dick Schofield	Overall	.251	110	.355	137	.305	123	1.88	120	6.97	113	11.86	46	.252	121
	Pressure	.167	153	.182	163	.233	152	0.00	119	6.67	116	12.00	52	.100	153
Devon White	Overall	.263	87	.443	67	.306	120	3.76	69	5.60	142	19.40	131	.277	93
	Pressure	.229	121	.450	61	.276	134	6.42	23	5.17	134	23.28	131	.342	50
Butch Wynegar	Overall	.207	--	.228	--	.277	--	0.00	--	8.82	--	12.75	--	.207	--
	Pressure	.214	--	.286	--	.214	--	0.00	--	0.00	--	13.33	--	.100	153
Team Average	Overall	.252	14	.401	14	.326	11	3.09	11	9.36	6	14.70	4	.273	11
	Pressure	.245	14	.381	11	.323	12	3.13	8	9.55	6	15.16	2	.282	6
League Average	Overall	.265		.425		.333		3.38		8.94		15.38		.287	
	Pressure	.262		.405		.335		3.07		9.43		16.58		.280	

Additional Miscellaneous Batting Comparisons

	Grass Surface BA	Rank	Artificial Surface BA	Rank	Home Games BA	Rank	Road Games BA	Rank	Runners in Scoring Position BA	Rank	Runners in Scoring Pos and Two Outs BA	Rank	Leading Off Inning OBA	Rank	Runners on 3B with less than 2 Outs RDI %	Rank
Bob Boone	.249	114	.200	141	.242	120	.241	112	.271	81	.250	84	.248	152	.765	6
Bill Buckner	.275	71	.330	11	.303	39	.268	69	.302	39	.281	56	.344	59	.767	5
Doug DeCinces	.246	120	.177	153	.274	77	.194	156	.209	139	.226	107	.392	19	.444	145
Brian Downing	.272	76	.271	63	.279	70	.265	77	.215	137	.190	135	.433	6	.630	53
George Hendrick	.211	155	.379	--	.174	--	.290	34	.302	40	.304	36	.229	--	.545	104
Jack Howell	.247	119	.235	112	.270	85	.219	141	.175	152	.196	130	.353	51	.448	144
Ruppert Jones	.228	141	.324	--	.259	--	.234	123	.211	--	.176	--	.288	125	.667	--
Wally Joyner	.270	78	.366	5	.261	101	.315	17	.329	18	.224	108	.328	85	.755	8
Mark McLemore	.234	134	.243	101	.235	129	.236	121	.229	127	.186	136	.315	96	.750	9
Gary Pettis	.223	147	.123	161	.221	144	.195	155	.141	161	.053	161	.333	69	.444	145
Dick Schofield	.239	127	.312	21	.257	107	.243	110	.261	92	.246	90	.325	87	.500	120
Devon White	.267	86	.243	100	.248	115	.277	53	.253	100	.218	113	.324	90	.600	71
Team Average	.250	14	.264	7	.255	12	.250	13	.244	13	.208	14	.330	8	.603	5
League Average	.267		.261		.270		.260		.266		.247		.328		.581	

Pitching vs. Left and Right Handed Batters

		BA	Rank	SA	Rank	OBA	Rank	HR %	Rank	BB %	Rank	SO %	Rank
Dewayne Buice	vs. Lefties	.219	11	.349	16	.309	25	3.13	63	11.42	96	24.66	7
	vs. Righties	.208	13	.347	22	.264	9	2.78	51	6.30	28	23.11	14
John Candelaria	vs. Lefties	.338	--	.465	--	.377	--	2.82	--	6.41	--	20.51	--
	vs. Righties	.268	80	.440	85	.295	31	3.91	90	3.67	2	14.18	77
Chuck Finley	vs. Lefties	.259	53	.356	18	.299	15	0.74	6	5.56	10	20.14	14
	vs. Righties	.305	112	.445	91	.405	123	2.73	48	13.41	118	13.03	94
Willie Fraser	vs. Lefties	.250	40	.423	67	.331	53	3.70	89	10.00	77	11.89	92
	vs. Righties	.231	29	.406	60	.290	23	4.09	95	6.95	41	16.58	54
Jack Lazorko	vs. Lefties	.289	99	.553	122	.369	105	6.32	121	11.47	98	3.21	128
	vs. Righties	.216	16	.351	26	.277	15	3.27	73	7.06	44	17.84	45
Gary Lucas	vs. Lefties	.281	89	.448	87	.383	113	3.13	63	13.79	120	13.79	68
	vs. Righties	.219	20	.320	11	.298	34	2.25	23	9.31	89	13.73	83
Kirk McCaskill	vs. Lefties	.314	117	.532	116	.382	117	5.77	117	9.14	65	12.00	88
	vs. Righties	.254	57	.384	51	.342	81	3.62	85	11.32	106	22.01	22
Greg Minton	vs. Lefties	.268	66	.378	35	.338	70	2.36	33	9.72	72	6.94	124
	vs. Righties	.248	48	.295	4	.319	57	0.67	2	8.88	77	14.79	70
Jerry Reuss	vs. Lefties	.364	--	.530	--	.391	--	4.55	--	4.35	--	11.59	--
	vs. Righties	.318	116	.523	118	.354	95	4.69	109	4.68	13	9.70	118
Don Sutton	vs. Lefties	.233	17	.398	52	.286	10	4.34	103	6.02	16	11.53	95
	vs. Righties	.305	113	.518	117	.338	74	5.93	123	4.29	8	13.38	88
Mike Witt	vs. Lefties	.272	75	.463	93	.338	73	4.19	100	8.90	62	15.41	52
	vs. Righties	.248	46	.402	57	.300	36	2.73	48	6.65	32	21.21	25
Team Average	vs. Lefties	.270	8	.442	10	.337	7	3.93	12	8.97	3	13.33	11
	vs. Righties	.260	6	.421	8	.319	3	3.67	8	7.42	1	16.53	7
League Average	vs. Lefties	.267		.427		.338		3.30		9.47		14.54	
	vs. Righties	.264		.424		.330		3.45		8.56		15.98	

Pitching with Runners on Base and Bases Empty

		BA	Rank	SA	Rank	OBA	Rank	HR %	Rank	BB %	Rank	SO %	Rank
Dewayne Buice	Runners On	.251	44	.400	55	.318	41	2.86	63	8.00	41	22.50	12
	Bases Empty	.185	5	.309	8	.261	7	3.00	53	9.34	84	24.90	8
John Candelaria	Runners On	.331	117	.586	125	.355	84	5.92	121	4.76	4	15.34	55
	Bases Empty	.248	47	.360	24	.279	11	2.45	27	3.69	5	15.10	65
Chuck Finley	Runners On	.305	105	.439	84	.399	117	1.22	6	13.33	114	16.41	43
	Bases Empty	.272	89	.387	39	.338	85	2.62	36	8.10	61	14.76	69
Willie Fraser	Runners On	.243	33	.387	50	.296	17	3.17	75	6.65	23	15.82	51
	Bases Empty	.238	30	.435	82	.320	59	4.45	103	9.81	94	13.08	91
Jack Lazorko	Runners On	.284	90	.510	108	.363	95	5.81	119	11.05	98	13.26	82
	Bases Empty	.229	23	.400	48	.292	22	3.93	90	7.84	55	10.13	113
Gary Lucas	Runners On	.281	86	.414	69	.382	112	2.34	37	13.84	117	12.58	89
	Bases Empty	.205	9	.322	12	.280	12	2.74	44	8.07	59	14.91	67
Kirk McCaskill	Runners On	.295	96	.484	99	.374	108	5.74	117	11.27	100	14.79	62
	Bases Empty	.279	96	.448	94	.354	99	4.07	95	9.38	87	18.23	35
Greg Minton	Runners On	.252	47	.323	10	.326	52	0.79	3	9.40	70	12.08	97
	Bases Empty	.262	69	.342	16	.329	75	2.01	15	9.15	82	10.37	110
Jerry Reuss	Runners On	.353	125	.610	126	.382	113	5.88	120	4.70	3	12.08	97
	Bases Empty	.309	117	.469	101	.347	95	3.86	87	4.57	13	8.68	122
Don Sutton	Runners On	.291	95	.524	111	.322	48	6.18	122	3.70	1	12.12	94
	Bases Empty	.256	59	.419	65	.305	37	4.52	104	6.02	36	12.65	94
Mike Witt	Runners On	.247	39	.429	77	.314	32	4.60	99	8.97	63	17.95	28
	Bases Empty	.272	86	.440	87	.327	70	2.72	43	7.04	45	18.09	36
Team Average	Runners On	.280	10	.463	14	.342	7	4.29	14	8.58	2	15.52	7
	Bases Empty	.254	4	.406	4	.316	4	3.42	7	7.74	2	14.83	10
League Average	Runners On	.271		.428		.343		3.25		9.68		14.87	
	Bases Empty	.260		.424		.326		3.49		8.34		15.79	

Overall Pitching Compared to Late Inning Pressure Situations

		BA	Rank	SA	Rank	OBA	Rank	HR %	Rank	BB %	Rank	SO %	Rank
Dewayne Buice	Overall	.213	5	.348	10	.285	9	2.94	48	8.75	67	23.85	8
	Pressure	.224	35	.363	49	.295	31	2.45	57	8.70	58	23.19	14
John Candelaria	Overall	.279	90	.444	86	.308	28	3.74	87	4.11	3	15.20	58
	Pressure	.167	--	.167	--	.231	--	0.00	--	7.41	--	18.52	--
Chuck Finley	Overall	.287	102	.411	55	.367	110	1.97	10	10.62	101	15.56	54
	Pressure	.233	43	.329	29	.317	47	1.37	36	10.84	88	16.87	52
Willie Fraser	Overall	.240	27	.414	58	.310	31	3.90	92	8.47	70	14.25	70
	Pressure	.230	40	.361	48	.319	50	3.28	78	8.33	53	18.06	41
Jack Lazorko	Overall	.248	36	.439	81	.318	43	4.60	107	9.03	75	11.29	103
	Pressure	.203	15	.281	13	.261	9	1.56	38	6.94	34	8.33	115
Gary Lucas	Overall	.241	30	.365	19	.329	63	2.55	33	10.94	106	13.75	76
	Pressure	.217	27	.370	51	.365	95	3.26	77	18.33	123	13.33	80
Kirk McCaskill	Overall	.286	99	.463	100	.363	104	4.76	113	10.18	95	16.77	45
	Pressure	.500	--	.500	--	.556	--	0.00	--	11.11	--	0.00	--
Greg Minton	Overall	.257	55	.333	6	.328	61	1.45	5	9.27	79	11.18	105
	Pressure	.279	83	.350	42	.361	89	1.43	37	10.43	77	9.20	111
Donnie Moore	Overall	.259	--	.361	--	.339	--	1.85	--	10.66	--	13.93	--
	Pressure	.253	59	.337	35	.333	62	1.20	30	10.64	83	11.70	102
Jerry Reuss	Overall	.327	123	.525	122	.361	102	4.66	109	4.62	4	10.05	114
	Pressure	.429	--	.571	--	.409	--	0.00	--	0.00	--	8.70	--
Don Sutton	Overall	.269	77	.458	96	.311	35	5.14	119	5.16	10	12.45	94
	Pressure	.220	30	.463	97	.238	4	7.32	124	2.33	1	16.28	55
Mike Witt	Overall	.261	63	.435	79	.321	47	3.52	83	7.89	46	18.03	32
	Pressure	.260	65	.420	77	.331	61	3.82	90	9.46	67	12.84	83
Team Average	Overall	.264	7	.430	9	.327	4	3.79	11	8.10	2	15.13	8
	Pressure	.246	2	.377	3	.327	6	2.78	5	10.23	10	15.13	11
League Average	Overall	.265		.425		.333		3.38		8.94		15.13	
	Pressure	.262		.404		.337		2.99		9.73		16.42	

Additional Miscellaneous Pitching Comparisons

	Grass Surface		Artificial Surface		Home Games		Road Games		Runners in Scoring Position		Runners in Scoring Pos and Two Outs		Leading Off Inning	
	BA	Rank	BA	Rank	BA	Rank	BA	Rank	BA	Rank	BA	Rank	OBA	Rank
Dewayne Buice	.197	3	.321	106	.177	3	.248	32	.269	74	.281	95	.237	7
John Candelaria	.280	90	.276	85	.273	91	.290	91	.330	116	.341	116	.262	13
Chuck Finley	.270	78	.425	--	.278	95	.295	100	.297	97	.222	49	.378	106
Willie Fraser	.244	28	.222	22	.238	36	.242	28	.238	39	.225	54	.305	42
Jack Lazorko	.242	21	.282	90	.264	77	.228	12	.333	117	.333	110	.350	88
Gary Lucas	.231	10	.333	--	.192	6	.305	108	.308	103	.382	125	.348	86
Kirk McCaskill	.315	115	.200	9	.279	--	.290	90	.286	--	.222	--	.407	122
Greg Minton	.256	54	.263	--	.265	80	.248	34	.194	10	.171	11	.356	93
Jerry Reuss	.325	118	.364	--	.335	124	.317	118	.373	126	.379	--	.292	33
Don Sutton	.256	52	.331	108	.258	69	.279	79	.257	64	.153	5	.327	61
Mike Witt	.257	55	.284	92	.244	46	.282	84	.244	43	.229	58	.372	103
Team Average	.261	7	.281	12	.256	6	.273	7	.276	10	.259	12	.336	11
League Average	.267		.261		.260		.270		.266		.247		.328	

CHICAGO WHITE SOX

It was a comeback unlike any other in modern baseball history. For the first time ever, a team that had been more than 10 games behind entering the month of September came back to win the championship.

Before you think that you're on the wrong page, White Sox fans, let us assure you that, yes, this is the Sox essay. Then why are you reading about some other team, some "championship" team? Have our computer wires become crossed, or have our disk drives lost speed?

No, we *are* talking about the White Sox, and they *did* win a championship last year. True, it was not the American League West championship, but what they did early last autumn was to catch and surpass the crosstown Cubs, edging America's Daytime Team out by one-half game for Chicago's city championship. Or Chicago's City Championship, depending on how you feel about it.

It may not have meant much outside Cook County, but there once was a time when the Cubs and the White Sox met in an annual post-season "City Series" to determine the city champion. There were twenty-six such series from 1903 through 1942, with the White Sox winning 19 of them, but meetings between the teams are now confined to spring training or an occasional midseason exhibition game.

So until the Second City Series is resumed, regular-season records will have to suffice to determine the city's braggin' rights. And last year, those rights were won by the White Sox, who finished with a 77–85 record to the Cubs' 76–85 (with one game cancelled due to rain). And the White Sox did it in style. They spotted the Cubs a long lead, but then won 22 of 32 games, the best record in the major leagues, from September 1 until the end of the season, with 17 wins in their last 21 games:

	End of April	End of May	End of June	End of July	End of August	End of Season
Cubs	10–10	28–20	40–37	52–50	66–64	76–85
White Sox	6–12	20–25	27–46	41–59	55–75	77–85

How well did the White Sox play over the final five weeks? While a .688 percentage is nothing to sneeze at, neither is it an unreal pace for a team over a short period of time. But very few teams that have played as poorly as the Sox did through the first five months of a season have had such a rousing finish. We have listed here the best September/October records since 1900 among teams that had a won-lost percentage no higher than .450 on the morning of September

1. (The "Gain/Loss" column indicates the number of games that each team improved or declined in the year after the September surge.)

	Pre-Sept.		Sept./Oct.		Final	Next Yr.	Gain/
	W–L	Pct.	W–L	Pct.	W–L	W–L	Loss
1912 Indians	54–70	.435	21–8	.724	75–78	86–66	+11.5
1951 Athletics	53–77	.408	17–7	.708	70–84	79–75	+9
1980 Twins	57–75	.432	20–9	.690	77–84	41–68	−10
1987 White Sox	55–75	.423	22–10	.688	77–85		
1926 Braves	48–77	.384	18–9	.667	66–86	60–94	−7
1968 Dodgers	58–77	.430	18–9	.667	76–86	85–77	+9
1946 White Sox	57–71	.445	17–9	.654	74–80	70–84	−4
1909 Yankees	54–66	.450	20–11	.645	74–77	88–63	+14

Note that a great closing kick has been no sure indicator of success the next year. The last time that a team *that bad* finished its season *that good* was in 1980, when the Twins did it. But the hopes of Minnesota fans were dashed the next year when the Twins ended the strike-interrupted 1981 season with the worst record they had since moving to Minnesota.

Only four of the seven teams on the list bettered their record the next year; three did not. But it may be encouraging for Sox fans to observe that the four teams that improved their overall record the year after a big finish did so by large margins: Each gained at least nine games in the standings. In the American League West, where top and bottom were separated by only 10 games in 1987, nine games might be all that it takes for the White Sox to win a championship that extends beyond the city limits.

Strikeouts at a Premium

Who was responsible for Chicago's late-season rally? The pitching staff, it says here. The White Sox posted a collective 3.42 ERA from September 1 to season's end, second-best in the league (behind Toronto) during that stretch. For the season, the White Sox finished with the fourth-best ERA in the league, even though their pitchers struck out only 792 batters, the lowest total by any staff in the major leagues.

Strikeouts, as well as home runs, were at an all-time high in 1987. The two are not unrelated, of course, but subject to a logical connection. Talk of a juiced-up ball, whether accurate or not, invites batters to swing from the heels, which in turn produces more strikeouts. Here are the ever-rising figures for the major leagues in recent years:

	HR per Game	SO per Game
1984	1.55	10.69
1985	1.71	10.67
1986	1.81	11.75
1987	2.12	11.92

	W–L	Pct.	IP	ERA	SO/9
High	574–450	.561	8,599	3.60	8.11
Medium	1000–1034	.492	18,362.1	4.02	5.88
Low	528–618	.461	10,703.1	4.20	4.17

As strikeouts increase, we must constantly readjust the framework within which we interpret team and player statistics. Consider the example of the rate of strikeouts per nine innings. Thirty years ago, when the major-league average was 4.82 strikeouts per nine innings, pitchers who maintained an average of six per nine innings were considered "strikeout" pitchers. Today's pitchers with the same statistics are performing only at an average rate: The 1987 average for strikeouts per nine was 6.04 in the National League, 5.99 in the American.

Among the White Sox pitchers, only Jose DeLeon averaged better than six strikeouts per nine innings. Here are Chicago's pitchers who threw at least 50 innings in 1987, with their strikeout rates:

Jose DeLeon	6.68	Dave LaPoint	4.68
Bob James	5.67	Jim Winn	4.21
Ray Searage	5.34	Joel Davis	4.09
Bobby Thigpen	5.26	Bill Long	3.83
Floyd Bannister	4.88	Scott Nielsen	3.12
Richard Dotson	4.85		

There were 66 pitchers in the major leagues last season who pitched at least 50 innings and averaged seven-or-more strikeouts per nine innings. The White Sox were the only team that didn't have at least one such pitcher. But are strikeouts really all that important? After all, Tommy John, Mike Dunne, Lee Guetterman, and Ricky Horton each averaged less than four strikeouts per nine innings in 1987, and they combined for a record of 45–19. But a glance at some evidence suggests that these guys constitute the exception rather than the rule.

Let's break down all of last year's pitchers into three groups: those with high strikeout rates (seven or more per nine innings), those with medium strikeout rates (between five and seven per nine innings), and pitchers with low strikeout rates (five or fewer per nine innings). Here are the cumulative 1987 statistics for each group:

	W–L	Pct.	IP	ERA	SO/9
High	546–497	.523	9,048.2	3.95	8.28
Medium	981–968	.503	17,308.2	4.30	5.98
Low	578–640	.475	11,205	4.55	4.23

The chart shows a strong performance edge in both winning percentage and earned run average for high-strikeout pitchers over medium-strikeout pitchers. And the medium group has a similar edge over the low-strikeout group. Could this symmetry be just a one-year fluke? Let's repeat the study using the 1986 statistics:

These results are even more striking. In each of the past two seasons, despite individual exceptions such as John and Dunne, the group of all pitchers with high strikeout rates are better pitchers than the low-strikeout group, taking into account both winning percentage and earned run average.

Two years' evidence is suggestive, but not overwhelming. We're not ready to claim that having an entire staff full of strikeout pitchers will guarantee a pennant. The White Sox, for example, have led the American League in strikeouts only four times in their 87-year history, most recently in 1985, but they finished no higher than third in any of those seasons. But having a staff that finishes *last in the majors* in strikeouts is not what you want, either. No team whose pitchers finished last in the majors in strikeouts has ever won a league or division title.

Where does that leave the White Sox? Not in as bad shape as you might think. From last year's staff, Bannister, Dotson, and Nielsen have been traded, and James was not sent a contract last December. Rookies Jack McDowell and Melido Perez will get a chance to fill the vacant spots in the rotation, and each of them has impressive credentials.

The 22-year-old McDowell was Chicago's first-round selection in the 1987 amateur draft and the fifth player chosen overall. He won 35 of 48 decisions in three years at Stanford University, and pitched the Cardinal to a victory in the 1987 College World Series. After signing with the Sox, he pitched only six games in the minors before they called him up in September, where he was 3–0 with a 1.93 ERA in four starts. His combined pro pitching line for 1987, major and minor leagues, showed 44 strikeouts in 55 2/3 innings, a rate of 7.11 per nine innings. At Stanford, he fanned a school-record 337 in 392 2/3 innings, an average of 7.72 per nine.

Perez, just a month older than McDowell, was one of four pitchers acquired from the Royals in the Bannister deal. He was 12–8 with two minor-league teams last season, and fanned 177 batters in 198 innings. In his four seasons in the minors, Perez averaged 7.62 strikeouts per nine innings.

So regardless of whether or not the White Sox get any better in 1988, their pitching staff will certainly be younger. The last time that a pair of 22-year olds were in Chicago's rotation was in 1981, when Dotson and Britt Burns combined for a 19-14 mark in the strike year. That was when the Sox looked like they had their pitching staff lined up for the rest of the decade, with Dotson, Burns, Ross Baumgarten, LaMarr Hoyt, Steve Trout, and Dennis Lamp. Considering the troubles that befell that group of once-promising pitchers, maybe the pitching gods will see fit to cut the Sox a break this time around.

Say Goodbye to Comiskey

The White Sox say that Comiskey Park's days are numbered, and that they will be playing in a new stadium within a few years. Comiskey is the oldest stadium in the majors—

the first game there was played on July 1, 1910, seven months before Ronald Reagan was born—and its history should make it the subject of an entire book or a feature film rather than an essay. It's the source of some excellent trivia questions (our favorite: Who pitched the first World Series shutout at Comiskey?). But what we'll focus on here is the changing nature of the ballpark in terms of its effect on the games played there.

Throughout its history, Comiskey Park has been known as a pitcher's park. While that title has been bestowed too often, and sometimes indiscriminately, to several major league stadiums, it is literally true of Comiskey. According to accounts of how the stadium was constructed, credit (or blame) for the distant outfield fences belongs to Hall-of-Fame pitcher Big Ed Walsh, a 40-game winner for the 1908 Sox, who recommended such a configuration to team owner Charles Comiskey. When it opened, the foul-line distances were 362 feet, with 380 to the power alleys and 420 to center. In the dead-ball era, very few hitters challenged those fences, and they proved to be formidable to power hitters of later eras as well.

One result of the large outfield area was the tendency for games at Comiskey to be low-scoring affairs. Statistics from different eras show that through the dead ball, the lively ball, two World Wars, and Eddie Stanky, White Sox games at Comiskey Park featured fewer runs than their games in other parks (including Milwaukee's County Stadium, where the Sox played 20 "home" games in the late sixties):

	At Comiskey Park			At Other Parks			
	Games	Runs	Avg.	Games	Runs	Avg.	Diff.
1910–29	1494	12,332	8.25	1497	13,100	8.75	−5.7%
1930–49	1524	13,898	9.12	1542	14,384	9.33	−2.3%
1950–68	1496	11,156	7.46	1509	12,354	8.19	−8.9%
Totals	4514	37,386	8.28	4548	39,838	8.76	−5.4%

In 39 of Comiskey's first 59 seasons, there was a higher average of runs-per-game in Sox road games than in their home games. But then in 1969, the first year of baseball's divisional era, Sox management brought in the outfield fences, reducing the foul-line distances to 335 feet, 370 in the alleys, and 400 in center. For the next two years, run production at Comiskey Park soared:

	At Comiskey Park			At Other Parks			
	Games	Runs	Avg.	Games	Runs	Avg.	Diff.
1969	70	651	9.30	92	697	7.58	+22.8%
1970	84	815	9.70	78	640	8.21	+18.2%

The foul-line and power-alley distances were moved back slightly in 1971, and offensive totals declined. But they never fell back to the pre-1969 levels, so that in 13 of the last 19 years, there has been a higher average of runs scored in White Sox home games than in their road games:

	At Comiskey Park			At Other Parks			
	Games	Runs	Avg.	Games	Runs	Avg.	Diff.
1910–68	4514	37,386	8.28	4548	39,838	8.76	−5.4%
1969–87	*1491	13,176	8.84	1519	12,716	8.37	+5.6%

* Not including any forfeits on Disco Demolition Nights.

Still, reputations forged over decades are hard to erase, and Comiskey Park is still commonly called a "pitchers' park." But a glance at page 433 in the Ballparks section of this book reveals that over the past five seasons, Comiskey stands fourth among the 26 major-league stadiums when ranked by positive influence on run-scoring, behind only Wrigley Field, Atlanta Stadium, and Riverfront Stadium. It's still not a *home run* park, but the effects that The House That Walsh Built has on a game today are much different than they were back in Big Ed's day.

Oh yes, that trivia question. About the first World Series shutout at Comiskey Park. Hint: It was pitched by a Boston pitcher. Need more help? A Boston *Red Sox* pitcher.

What? How can the Sox play the Sox in the Series? Well, they can't, and despite some in baseball who would realign the leagues, hopefully they never will. But in 1918, when the Cubs won the National League pennant and faced the Red Sox in the Series, they rented Comiskey Park from the White Sox because its seating capacity was (and is) larger than that of Cubs Park, as Wrigley Field was then known. The World Series was played in early September that year, since the season had been curtailed due to the World War. And in the opening game, on September 5, the Cubs dropped a 1–0 decision to the man who, 15 years later, would hit the first All-Star Game home run in the same ballpark: Babe Ruth.

WON-LOST RECORD BY STARTING POSITION

CHICAGO 77-85	C	1B	2B	3B	SS	LF	CF	RF	P	DH	Leadoff	Relief	Starts
Neil Allen	·	·	·	·	·	·	·	·	1-9	·	·	0-5	1-9
Harold Baines	·	·	·	·	·	·	·	3-5	·	60-55	·	·	63-60
Floyd Bannister	·	·	·	·	·	·	·	·	19-15	·	·	·	19-15
Daryl Boston	·	·	·	·	·	22-20	16-23	·	·	0-1	14-22	·	38-44
Ivan Calderon	·	·	·	·	·	2-4	·	64-70	·	0-2	·	·	66-76
Ralph Citarella	·	·	·	·	·	·	·	·	·	·	·	2-3	·
Bryan Clark	·	·	·	·	·	·	·	·	·	·	·	2-9	
Joel Davis	·	·	·	·	·	·	·	3-6	·	·	·	0-4	3-6
Jose DeLeon	·	·	·	·	·	·	·	·	17-14	·	·	1-1	17-14
Richard Dotson	·	·	·	·	·	·	·	·	12-19	·	·	·	12-19
Carlton Fisk	51-51	2-4	·	·	·	2-0	·	·	·	1-6	·	·	56-61
Ozzie Guillen	·	·	·	·	68-78	·	·	·	·	·	33-22	·	68-78
Jerry Hairston	·	3-3	·	·	·	5-4	·	·	·	6-6	·	·	14-13
Ron Hassey	14-10	·	·	·	·	·	·	·	·	8-9	·	·	22-19
Donnie Hill	·	·	41-36	14-13	·	·	·	·	·	0-1	·	·	55-50
Tim Hulett	·	·	2-5	22-36	·	·	·	·	·	·	·	·	24-41
Bob James	·	·	·	·	·	·	·	·	·	·	·	20-23	·
Ron Karkovice	10-21	·	·	·	·	·	·	·	·	·	·	·	10-21
Pat Keedy	·	·	0-1	3-7	·	·	·	·	·	·	·	·	3-8
Dave LaPoint	·	·	·	·	·	·	·	·	6-6	·	·	1-1	6-6
Bill Lindsey	2-3	·	·	·	·	·	·	·	·	·	·	·	2-3
Bill Long	·	·	·	·	·	·	·	·	12-11	·	·	3-3	12-11
Steve Lyons	·	·	27-16	·	·	2-2	6-0	0-1	·	·	·	·	35-19
Fred Manrique	·	·	34-40	9-7	·	·	·	·	·	·	·	·	43-47
Jack McDowell	·	·	·	·	·	·	·	·	4-0	·	·	·	4-0
Joel McKeon	·	·	·	·	·	·	·	·	·	·	·	3-10	·
Scott Nielsen	·	·	·	·	·	·	·	2-5	·	·	·	4-8	2-5
John Pawlowski	·	·	·	·	·	·	·	·	·	·	·	1-1	
Adam Peterson	·	·	·	·	·	·	·	·	1-0	·	·	·	1-0
Gary Redus	·	·	·	·	·	42-48	4-8	9-8	·	0-1	22-34	·	55-65
Jerry Royster	·	·	0-3	11-13	·	2-7	·	·	·	0-4	8-5	·	13-27
Ray Searage	·	·	·	·	·	·	·	·	·	·	·	21-37	·
Bobby Thigpen	·	·	·	·	·	·	·	·	·	·	·	31-20	·
Greg Walker	·	72-78	·	·	·	·	·	·	·	2-0	·	·	74-78
Ken Williams	·	·	·	·	·	51-54	·	1-1	·	·	0-2	·	52-55
Jim Winn	·	·	·	·	·	·	·	·	·	·	·	20-36	·

Batting vs. Left and Right Handed Pitchers

		BA	Rank	SA	Rank	OBA	Rank	HR %	Rank	BB %	Rank	SO %	Rank
Harold Baines	vs. Lefties	.254	97	.409	89	.308	110	3.31	77	6.67	125	23.08	141
	vs. Righties	.315	15	.519	25	.376	29	4.32	53	9.19	68	10.31	37
Daryl Boston	vs. Lefties	.305	34	.373	111	.311	104	0.00	145	1.59	161	26.98	154
	vs. Righties	.248	103	.432	74	.306	124	3.60	78	7.84	94	16.67	101
Ivan Calderon	vs. Lefties	.279	64	.542	20	.360	53	6.84	11	11.21	40	18.69	114
	vs. Righties	.301	27	.517	26	.364	42	4.26	56	9.16	70	17.56	112
Carlton Fisk	vs. Lefties	.236	117	.451	63	.305	115	4.95	36	8.37	89	12.81	63
	vs. Righties	.268	78	.467	49	.332	79	5.15	34	7.21	108	15.08	87
Ozzie Guillen	vs. Lefties	.201	147	.238	156	.227	160	0.00	145	3.37	155	10.11	35
	vs. Righties	.311	18	.402	97	.334	78	0.51	153	3.76	155	7.98	21
Jerry Hairston	vs. Lefties	.254	96	.441	69	.375	39	3.39	71	15.07	15	17.81	107
	vs. Righties	.209	--	.388	--	.341	--	4.48	--	17.07	--	14.63	--
Ron Hassey	vs. Lefties	.000	--	.000	--	.200	--	0.00	--	15.00	--	10.00	--
	vs. Righties	.240	119	.380	116	.317	100	2.33	107	9.66	60	6.21	6
Donnie Hill	vs. Lefties	.262	88	.400	93	.319	94	3.85	71	8.22	93	8.90	27
	vs. Righties	.229	142	.354	130	.276	150	1.43	129	5.94	133	7.26	16
Tim Hulett	vs. Lefties	.247	102	.432	72	.265	149	4.94	37	2.38	158	15.48	92
	vs. Righties	.201	158	.302	154	.237	160	1.89	116	4.62	149	16.18	95
Steve Lyons	vs. Lefties	.320	--	.360	--	.320	--	0.00	--	0.00	--	23.08	--
	vs. Righties	.274	65	.363	126	.320	95	0.60	149	6.52	122	16.85	105
Fred Manrique	vs. Lefties	.299	42	.451	62	.361	52	1.39	118	8.13	94	21.25	132
	vs. Righties	.221	145	.279	158	.245	158	1.30	133	3.53	157	20.59	137
Gary Redus	vs. Lefties	.269	76	.473	48	.372	43	3.48	68	14.64	17	11.30	48
	vs. Righties	.212	154	.332	141	.295	132	1.82	119	10.79	45	20.00	132
Greg Walker	vs. Lefties	.238	112	.467	50	.324	85	6.19	18	9.21	68	20.92	130
	vs. Righties	.267	82	.463	51	.358	48	3.93	66	12.83	19	15.01	85
Ken Williams	vs. Lefties	.296	44	.503	32	.319	96	5.03	34	1.80	160	23.35	144
	vs. Righties	.272	70	.366	124	.310	116	1.29	134	2.83	159	17.81	114
Team Average	vs. Lefties	.250	13	.424	6	.313	13	3.82	2	7.95	12	17.74	14
	vs. Righties	.262	9	.411	13	.322	13	2.73	14	7.88	13	14.64	5
League Average	vs. Lefties	.265		.422		.333		3.29		8.94		15.64	
	vs. Righties	.265		.427		.334		3.43		8.94		15.26	

Batting with Runners on Base and Bases Empty

		BA	Rank	SA	Rank	OBA	Rank	HR %	Rank	BB %	Rank	SO %	Rank
Harold Baines	Runners On	.338	10	.616	2	.396	21	6.02	18	8.75	95	14.58	86
	Bases Empty	.260	84	.377	114	.318	98	2.42	110	7.96	83	14.97	80
Daryl Boston	Runners On	.213	149	.315	149	.280	148	1.57	121	8.84	92	17.69	117
	Bases Empty	.286	41	.486	41	.324	85	3.81	75	5.41	136	18.92	124
Ivan Calderon	Runners On	.263	93	.424	79	.331	101	3.53	65	9.76	73	19.86	137
	Bases Empty	.321	12	.617	4	.391	13	6.62	17	10.00	44	16.25	96
Carlton Fisk	Runners On	.231	133	.426	77	.300	129	5.13	32	7.59	108	19.64	135
	Bases Empty	.274	55	.486	40	.338	54	5.02	41	7.75	90	9.86	22
Ozzie Guillen	Runners On	.254	108	.316	148	.278	151	0.96	140	4.17	154	6.25	13
	Bases Empty	.293	30	.376	115	.319	97	0.00	157	3.30	153	10.16	30
Donnie Hill	Runners On	.247	117	.374	116	.301	128	1.72	118	7.61	107	7.61	20
	Bases Empty	.233	127	.364	120	.282	143	2.54	106	5.95	128	7.94	11
Tim Hulett	Runners On	.250	111	.348	134	.290	137	1.09	135	5.71	137	16.19	102
	Bases Empty	.196	159	.345	134	.217	161	4.05	64	2.63	160	15.79	87
Steve Lyons	Runners On	.310	32	.414	91	.351	70	1.15	133	6.12	132	12.24	57
	Bases Empty	.255	--	.321	--	.295	--	0.00	--	5.36	--	22.32	--
Fred Manrique	Runners On	.263	94	.364	125	.333	92	1.69	120	9.72	75	17.36	114
	Bases Empty	.256	92	.361	122	.280	144	1.11	138	2.69	159	23.66	143
Gary Redus	Runners On	.228	135	.327	145	.322	115	1.75	117	12.98	34	19.71	136
	Bases Empty	.240	117	.428	83	.332	65	2.96	92	12.14	20	14.16	68
Greg Walker	Runners On	.272	75	.506	26	.373	49	5.06	34	13.68	29	18.24	121
	Bases Empty	.243	112	.430	79	.322	89	4.53	53	9.57	52	16.23	95
Ken Williams	Runners On	.277	66	.435	74	.317	117	2.82	89	3.65	157	23.96	151
	Bases Empty	.285	42	.411	90	.311	109	2.80	95	1.35	162	16.67	101
Team Average	Runners On	.254	13	.406	12	.319	14	3.11	11	8.75	13	16.48	14
	Bases Empty	.260	7	.422	7	.319	12	3.13	11	7.26	12	15.20	6
League Average	Runners On	.271		.428		.343		3.25		9.68		14.87	
	Bases Empty	.260		.424		.326		3.49		8.34		15.79	

Overall Batting Compared to Late Inning Pressure Situations

		BA	Rank	SA	Rank	OBA	Rank	HR %	Rank	BB %	Rank	SO %	Rank	RDI %	Rank
Harold Baines	Overall	.293	31	.479	38	.352	51	3.96	67	8.30	87	14.80	85	.412	2
	Pressure	.310	38	.479	45	.380	41	2.82	78	10.13	66	11.39	46	.273	85
Daryl Boston	Overall	.258	97	.421	90	.307	119	2.97	93	6.78	120	18.43	122	.175	161
	Pressure	.196	139	.294	137	.255	146	0.00	119	7.14	109	25.00	141	.111	147
Ivan Calderon	Overall	.293	30	.526	18	.362	41	5.17	29	9.88	57	17.96	120	.273	104
	Pressure	.342	18	.468	51	.426	18	2.53	83	13.83	29	18.09	101	.304	71
Carlton Fisk	Overall	.256	104	.460	52	.321	98	5.07	33	7.68	103	14.17	77	.275	97
	Pressure	.233	118	.329	120	.325	93	2.74	79	10.71	59	26.19	149	.229	103
Ozzie Guillen	Overall	.279	54	.354	138	.303	129	0.36	155	3.64	159	8.61	20	.327	39
	Pressure	.258	91	.337	117	.280	132	1.12	117	2.08	157	7.29	10	.192	120
Jerry Hairston	Overall	.230	--	.413	--	.357	--	3.97	--	16.13	--	16.13	--	.361	--
	Pressure	.268	77	.415	81	.375	46	2.44	87	14.29	24	16.33	89	.286	75
Ron Hassey	Overall	.214	--	.338	--	.303	--	2.07	--	10.30	--	6.67	--	.170	--
	Pressure	.105	--	.158	--	.227	--	0.00	--	13.64	--	9.09	--	.000	158
Donnie Hill	Overall	.239	133	.368	130	.290	152	2.20	118	6.68	124	7.80	16	.254	119
	Pressure	.294	52	.451	59	.368	55	3.92	55	10.00	68	6.67	8	.333	51
Tim Hulett	Overall	.217	155	.346	144	.246	161	2.92	97	3.89	158	15.95	95	.286	83
	Pressure	.143	162	.200	157	.200	160	0.00	119	7.14	109	14.29	70	.364	43
Steve Lyons	Overall	.280	49	.363	132	.320	101	0.52	153	5.71	141	17.62	116	.273	105
	Pressure	.211	--	.211	--	.250	--	0.00	--	4.76	--	28.57	--	.250	--
Fred Manrique	Overall	.258	96	.362	133	.302	130	1.34	135	5.76	139	20.91	140	.286	83
	Pressure	.200	133	.200	157	.200	160	0.00	119	0.00	161	29.27	157	.125	144
Gary Redus	Overall	.236	138	.392	112	.328	87	2.53	108	12.45	21	16.25	98	.281	87
	Pressure	.284	63	.418	77	.372	52	2.99	75	12.66	38	17.72	97	.235	101
Greg Walker	Overall	.256	101	.465	48	.346	63	4.77	40	11.50	33	17.18	112	.299	69
	Pressure	.230	120	.378	100	.356	67	2.70	80	14.29	24	15.38	82	.219	112
Ken Williams	Overall	.281	47	.422	88	.314	108	2.81	99	2.42	161	20.05	132	.289	78
	Pressure	.229	122	.354	108	.269	139	2.08	101	1.92	158	34.62	164	.174	131
Team Average	Overall	.258	13	.415	12	.319	14	3.12	9	7.90	13	15.75	10	.288	8
	Pressure	.251	12	.361	14	.326	11	1.89	14	9.45	8	18.02	13	.224	14
League Average	Overall	.265		.425		.333		3.38		8.94		15.38		.287	
	Pressure	.262		.405		.335		3.07		9.43		16.58		.280	

Additional Miscellaneous Batting Comparisons

	Grass Surface		Artificial Surface		Home Games		Road Games		Runners in Scoring Position		Runners in Scoring Pos and Two Outs		Leading Off Inning		Runners on 3B with less than 2 Outs	
	BA	Rank	BA	Rank	BA	Rank	BA	Rank	BA	Rank	BA	Rank	OBA	Rank	RDI %	Rank
Harold Baines	.297	33	.269	66	.312	26	.274	57	.346	10	.333	16	.299	115	.714	19
Daryl Boston	.277	65	.122	--	.321	15	.195	154	.185	151	.156	146	.377	27	.417	151
Ivan Calderon	.302	28	.250	90	.315	21	.273	59	.272	77	.196	129	.364	41	.536	110
Carlton Fisk	.280	55	.098	162	.266	88	.246	103	.243	113	.204	124	.309	103	.630	53
Ozzie Guillen	.288	45	.211	133	.316	20	.244	107	.281	69	.283	52	.364	42	.711	22
Jerry Hairston	.213	--	.333	--	.259	--	.206	--	.241	--	.111	153	.353	--	.750	--
Donnie Hill	.248	117	.202	140	.254	109	.225	132	.241	115	.260	71	.296	120	.611	63
Tim Hulett	.191	158	.361	--	.161	162	.266	74	.254	98	.258	72	.213	156	.500	120
Steve Lyons	.284	51	.250	--	.280	68	.279	--	.333	13	.250	--	.260	144	.571	92
Fred Manrique	.276	68	.167	156	.305	35	.217	143	.288	58	.324	21	.200	159	.714	19
Gary Redus	.235	132	.238	109	.244	119	.228	131	.255	97	.319	25	.390	20	.565	94
Greg Walker	.262	95	.225	120	.249	114	.263	81	.245	110	.230	103	.377	28	.621	57
Ken Williams	.290	43	.217	129	.326	13	.237	119	.268	85	.269	63	.211	157	.556	99
Team Average	.264	6	.220	14	.274	5	.242	14	.257	10	.241	9	.328	9	.607	2
League Average	.267		.261		.270		.260		.266		.247		.328		.581	

Pitching vs. Left and Right Handed Batters

		BA	Rank	SA	Rank	OBA	Rank	HR %	Rank	BB %	Rank	SO %	Rank
Floyd Bannister	vs. Lefties	.240	25	.376	33	.314	36	2.40	37	10.00	77	12.86	76
	vs. Righties	.247	45	.434	79	.280	17	4.65	106	4.38	9	13.27	91
Joel Davis	vs. Lefties	.269	68	.471	101	.356	90	4.81	108	11.76	104	10.92	101
	vs. Righties	.259	--	.398	--	.347	--	1.85	--	12.10	--	9.68	--
Jose DeLeon	vs. Lefties	.254	45	.393	43	.351	87	3.27	70	12.77	112	13.85	66
	vs. Righties	.204	7	.346	18	.290	24	2.95	61	8.90	79	20.84	26
Richard Dotson	vs. Lefties	.251	43	.419	61	.326	49	3.49	80	9.98	76	13.10	73
	vs. Righties	.247	44	.377	43	.314	49	2.39	29	9.07	81	12.17	104
Bob James	vs. Lefties	.286	95	.560	125	.333	57	6.59	124	6.80	29	12.62	79
	vs. Righties	.233	--	.408	--	.311	--	3.33	--	7.41	--	15.56	--
Dave LaPoint	vs. Lefties	.225	--	.250	--	.311	--	0.00	--	10.87	--	13.04	--
	vs. Righties	.224	25	.347	20	.295	32	2.61	42	8.81	75	12.54	100
Bill Long	vs. Lefties	.279	85	.439	79	.307	23	2.91	55	3.58	2	10.74	103
	vs. Righties	.263	73	.429	73	.298	35	3.17	71	4.46	10	9.82	116
Scott Nielsen	vs. Lefties	.292	101	.408	57	.338	72	1.67	18	6.92	31	6.92	125
	vs. Righties	.320	118	.493	111	.387	117	4.67	107	9.47	94	8.28	122
Ray Searage	vs. Lefties	.302	--	.512	--	.375	--	3.49	--	9.38	--	13.54	--
	vs. Righties	.238	36	.437	81	.315	52	4.76	110	10.42	99	13.89	81
Bobby Thigpen	vs. Lefties	.277	83	.367	30	.340	77	2.26	30	8.21	51	12.82	77
	vs. Righties	.233	30	.377	45	.278	16	3.77	89	4.60	11	15.52	65
Jim Winn	vs. Lefties	.263	57	.336	14	.401	121	1.32	15	18.52	127	5.29	127
	vs. Righties	.278	92	.444	87	.381	113	4.04	93	11.59	108	14.59	74
Team Average	vs. Lefties	.268	7	.422	7	.341	10	3.35	8	9.77	11	12.02	13
	vs. Righties	.253	2	.412	6	.317	2	3.46	7	7.88	6	13.37	14
League Average	vs. Lefties	.267		.427		.338		3.30		9.47		14.54	
	vs. Righties	.264		.424		.330		3.45		8.56		15.98	

Pitching with Runners on Base and Bases Empty

		BA	Rank	SA	Rank	OBA	Rank	HR %	Rank	BB %	Rank	SO %	Rank
Floyd Bannister	Runners On	.248	42	.386	45	.287	10	3.27	79	5.36	7	13.10	83
	Bases Empty	.245	40	.448	93	.284	15	4.90	113	5.14	18	13.27	88
Joel Davis	Runners On	.315	--	.596	--	.392	--	5.62	--	11.65	--	5.83	--
	Bases Empty	.228	20	.317	10	.321	63	1.63	11	12.14	115	13.57	81
Jose DeLeon	Runners On	.234	24	.321	7	.336	62	1.28	8	13.07	113	16.53	41
	Bases Empty	.227	19	.404	54	.311	44	4.37	102	9.34	84	17.70	38
Richard Dotson	Runners On	.276	80	.429	79	.339	63	2.70	55	8.85	58	14.21	71
	Bases Empty	.230	25	.378	31	.307	39	3.16	62	10.06	99	11.57	102
Dave LaPoint	Runners On	.201	4	.291	3	.267	2	2.24	34	8.16	45	19.05	24
	Bases Empty	.241	35	.368	28	.320	58	2.30	22	9.79	93	7.73	127
Bill Long	Runners On	.323	114	.531	114	.363	96	3.98	90	5.98	17	7.17	126
	Bases Empty	.245	41	.383	36	.270	8	2.54	32	2.90	2	12.05	100
Scott Nielsen	Runners On	.390	128	.585	123	.438	127	4.88	105	8.70	55	7.25	125
	Bases Empty	.238	29	.347	20	.304	36	2.04	17	8.07	59	8.07	124
Ray Searage	Runners On	.314	112	.571	121	.393	115	5.71	116	11.38	102	15.45	54
	Bases Empty	.215	--	.364	--	.282	--	2.80	--	8.55	--	11.97	--
Bobby Thigpen	Runners On	.228	17	.323	9	.307	27	2.53	48	8.79	57	13.74	78
	Bases Empty	.281	98	.416	63	.316	50	3.37	70	4.28	10	14.44	71
Jim Winn	Runners On	.261	61	.335	13	.367	103	1.48	11	12.86	111	12.45	92
	Bases Empty	.286	102	.483	107	.420	126	4.76	111	17.13	124	7.73	126
Team Average	Runners On	.277	9	.426	7	.348	12	3.05	6	9.45	8	12.81	13
	Bases Empty	.246	2	.409	5	.312	3	3.68	9	8.09	7	12.79	14
League Average	Runners On	.271		.428		.343		3.25		9.68		14.87	
	Bases Empty	.260		.424		.326		3.49		8.34		15.79	

Overall Pitching Compared to Late Inning Pressure Situations

		BA	Rank	SA	Rank	OBA	Rank	HR %	Rank	BB %	Rank	SO %	Rank
Floyd Bannister	Overall	.246	33	.426	73	.285	7	4.33	100	5.22	11	13.21	82
	Pressure	.224	34	.408	73	.272	17	3.95	94	6.17	27	12.35	94
Jose DeLeon	Overall	.230	14	.370	23	.322	51	3.12	64	10.91	105	17.21	41
	Pressure	.253	60	.392	66	.359	85	2.53	59	12.77	103	12.77	87
Richard Dotson	Overall	.249	40	.399	45	.320	45	2.97	52	· 9.56	84	12.67	90
	Pressure	.299	102	.533	113	.330	60	5.61	118	4.46	10	12.50	89
Bob James	Overall	.256	--	.474	--	.321	--	4.74	--	7.14	--	14.29	--
	Pressure	.255	62	.451	92	.328	58	4.90	111	8.33	53	14.17	72
Dave LaPoint	Overall	.224	10	.334	7	.297	16	2.27	20	9.09	76	12.61	91
	Pressure	.267	--	.733	--	.267	--	13.33	--	0.00	--	6.67	--
Bill Long	Overall	.272	85	.434	78	.303	22	3.03	58	4.01	2	10.30	112
	Pressure	.272	78	.383	62	.314	43	1.23	32	5.75	22	17.24	48
Scott Nielsen	Overall	.307	116	.456	95	.366	109	3.33	76	8.36	58	7.69	126
	Pressure	.435	--	.696	--	.480	--	8.70	--	7.69	--	11.54	--
Ray Searage	Overall	.264	--	.467	--	.339	--	4.25	--	10.00	--	13.75	--
	Pressure	.280	85	.547	120	.360	88	5.33	114	11.63	94	12.79	85
Bobby Thigpen	Overall	.256	54	.372	24	.311	34	2.98	53	6.50	24	14.09	73
	Pressure	.239	50	.350	43	.299	33	3.05	73	6.88	33	13.30	81
Jim Winn	Overall	.271	83	.397	42	.390	123	2.86	45	14.69	123	10.43	109
	Pressure	.292	93	.438	87	.396	115	4.17	98	12.87	106	8.19	117
Team Average	Overall	.259	5	.416	7	.327	5	3.41	8	8.68	6	12.80	14
	Pressure	.275	11	.450	13	.347	12	4.06	13	9.13	3	12.24	14
League Average	Overall	.265		.425		.333		3.38		8.94		15.38	
	Pressure	.262		.404		.337		2.99		9.73		16.42	

Additional Miscellaneous Pitching Comparisons

	Grass Surface BA	Rank	Artificial Surface BA	Rank	Home Games BA	Rank	Road Games BA	Rank	Runners in Scoring Position BA	Rank	Runners in Scoring Pos and Two Outs BA	Rank	Leading Off Inning OBA	Rank
Floyd Bannister	.248	35	.237	40	.273	93	.227	11	.221	26	.190	24	.274	21
Joel Davis	.268	74	.000	--	.284	--	.240	--	.340	--	.400	--	.322	56
Jose DeLeon	.243	23	.181	6	.239	39	.222	10	.249	50	.278	90	.330	66
Richard Dotson	.246	31	.267	76	.259	70	.238	21	.291	93	.200	32	.296	34
Bob James	.243	26	.346	--	.252	56	.261	--	.205	16	.262	81	.375	--
Dave LaPoint	.232	12	.105	--	.249	52	.183	3	.185	7	.171	11	.310	43
Bill Long	.262	64	.333	109	.288	103	.260	48	.295	96	.250	69	.253	12
Scott Nielsen	.298	104	.375	--	.306	115	.309	114	.427	129	.361	121	.364	98
Ray Searage	.250	37	.344	--	.256	63	.277	--	.343	120	.273	88	.262	--
Bobby Thigpen	.265	71	.213	18	.269	87	.234	16	.225	30	.191	25	.380	109
Jim Winn	.265	68	.302	100	.281	98	.262	51	.276	80	.286	97	.405	121
Team Average	.259	5	.262	6	.270	10	.248	1	.279	12	.253	9	.319	4
League Average	.267		.261		.260		.270		.266		.247		.328	

CLEVELAND INDIANS

Over the past three seasons, the Cleveland Indians have taken their fans on a roller-coaster ride that was nearly unprecedented in modern major-league history. First, let's look at Cleveland's record during that time:

Year	W	L	Pct.	GB	Pos.
1985	60	102	.370	39.5	7th
1986	84	78	.519	11.5	5th
1987	61	101	.377	37	7th

Only one other team since 1900 wrapped a pair of last-place finishes around a winning season: the Washington Senators, from 1968 through 1970. And only one other team sandwiched two sub-.400 seasons around a winning season: the St. Louis Cardinals of 1916 through 1918.

What makes The Great Cleveland Tease of 1986 an especially cruel hoax for Indians fans is the fact that Cleveland hasn't finished within 10 games of a division or league title since 1959 (that is, if you discount the 1981 split-season when the Indians didn't have enough time to build a 10-game deficit in either half of the season). Only two teams have ever suffered through longer streaks without coming within 10 games of a title. The longest streaks in modern major-league history:

Team	Yrs.	From	To
Phil.-K.C.-Oak. Athletics	37	1932	1968
Philadelphia Phillies	33	1917	1949
Cleveland Indians	27	1960	1987
Chicago Cubs	23	1946	1968
St. Louis Browns	21	1923	1943
Boston Red Sox	19	1919	1937
St. Louis Cardinals	19	1902	1920
Houston Colt .45s/Astros	17	1962	1978
Boston Red Sox	16	1951	1966
Wash. Senators/Minn. Twins	16	1946	1961
Cincinnati Reds	16	1902	1917

Love Thy Enemy

What did the 1987 Cleveland Indians have in common with the 1962 New York Mets? Both had the worst records in the majors, and both had the highest ERAs as well. But a more unusual stigma also links the teams: Neither team won a season series against any of their opponents. Each of the teams managed to split one series—the '62 Mets took nine of 18 games from the Cubs; the '87 Indians won six of 12 against the Royals—and lost to every other opponent.

Over the past 25 years, few teams have failed to win a season series from at least one opponent. The reasons for that are simple. Years ago, the gap between the best and worst teams was greater than it is now, and with fewer teams to play, every team faced each of its opponents more often. But today, with American League teams playing series of no more than 13 games, it's more common for teams to win series against superior opponents than it was when teams faced each other 18 times a year. In fact, since the American League added a seventh team to each division in 1977, only one team besides the '87 Indians failed to win a series from any opponent: the 1982 Minnesota Twins.

Other similarities—and one significant difference—between that team and last season's Indians suggest that Cleveland will encounter a serious problem as it tries to build a contending team.

Like the Indians, the 1982 Twins had the highest ERA in either league. But each team had a promising left-handed starter developed within its own organization—Frank Viola for Minnesota, Greg Swindell for Cleveland. And both teams had several young hitters to provide a strong attack—Kent Hrbek, Tom Brunansky, and Gary Gaetti for the Twins; Joe Carter, Cory Snyder, Brook Jacoby, and Julio Franco for Cleveland.

That young lineup was the key to Minnesota's development from a last-place team to a World Series winner. Brunansky, Gaetti, and Hrbek all were rookies in 1982, giving the Twins a five-year period during which they could patiently build a pitching staff before having to worry about losing the heart of their starting lineup to free agency. This is one case in which the five-year plan worked.

The Twins acquired starting pitchers John Butcher and Mike Smithson prior to the 1984 season, and did so without sacrificing any of their best young talent. Then came a waiting game, during which Minnesota watched Hrbek, Brunansky, Gaetti, and Kirby Puckett develop into stars while its pitching staff labored without a reliable number-two starter to complement Viola. But when Bert Blyleven became available in 1986, Minnesota pounced on the opportunity, despite its lowly position in the standings at that time. The rest, as they say, is history.

Unfortunately, Cleveland doesn't have the luxury of five years to build its staff. Carter, Franco, Jacoby, and Snyder are indeed young—Jacoby, the oldest, was only 27 when the 1987 season ended. But all of them except Snyder had enough major-league service by the end of the '87 season to earn them the right to free agency when their contracts expired over the past winter.

As a result, the Indians will be under time pressure to build a respectable pitching staff that the Twins never felt during their own rebuilding period. As the *Analyst* went to press, it was uncertain how many of those three potential free agents would return to the shores of Lake Erie in 1988. Jacoby in particular seemed a likely candidate for parole; not only was he eligible to become a free agent, but his name was also mentioned in trade rumors throughout the winter.

Should Carter, Franco, or Jacoby depart—and with center fielder Brett Butler already gone to the Giants via free agency—the Tribe will place a heavy burden on the young shoulders of outfielder Dave Clark (.344, 26 HR, 69 RBI at Buffalo last season). The only other serious prospect likely to crack the Cleveland lineup over the next two years is Luis Medina, a power-hitting outfielder with limited range who'll probably play Triple-A ball in 1988.

On the other hand, the Indians have a leg up as they try to shape their starting rotation. For the first time in many years, Cleveland's organization has produced some pitching prospects of its own. Tom Candiotti's knuckleball guarantees him a spot; the leading contenders to fill the other spots are Swindell, Darrel Akerfelds, Tom Farrell, and Scott Bailes.

Should Swindell recover from the elbow problems that plagued him during 1987, the Indians may have their number-one starter for years to come. Akerfelds had a 10–3 record with Tacoma of the Pacific Coast League last season, and was reportedly sought over the past winter by the New York Mets, whose talent for judging young arms is unsurpassed. Farrell surprised everyone by winning nearly as many games in nine starts with the big team last season (5–1) as he did in almost three times that many appearances with Buffalo (6–12). Bailes has proven himself to be a useful if unspectacular starter in two seasons with Cleveland.

So despite the similarities between last season's Indians team and the 1982 Minnesota Twins, the time element that the Twins used to their advantage will work against Cleveland. It appears that with free agency looming as a major threat to the Indians' starting lineup, the likelihood of a turnaround in Cleveland might be measured by the depth of the owner's pockets.

So Much for the Agony of Defeat

In last year's *Analyst*, we published the results of a study that was prompted by Joe Carter's observation that teams tend to play better for a few days following a late-inning, come-from-behind victory. There were 102 games from 1982 through 1986 in which the winning team trailed by as many as five runs as late as the fifth inning; we've supplemented that data with 36 more such games from the 1987 season. We tracked the performance of each of those 138 teams over their next five games. Any carry-over effect from the comeback victory should have evaporated by the end of that period. Therefore, if teams did play better following those dramatic victories, their collective performances should have deteriorated over the course of that five-game period.

We found that the teams did indeed play better in the games immediately following each of the comeback victories than in any of the next four games. They also played much better during the early part of the five-game period than toward the end. But it wasn't that the teams raised their level of play right after the comeback victories; rather, they suffered a severe decline a few games later.

To support the theory that teams can ride an emotional wave to victory following dramatic wins, there should have been a marked improvement in the teams' composite record in the first game afterward *compared to their overall records for the entire season*. That wasn't the case: Over the past six seasons, the comeback teams compiled a .522 record immediately following their dramatic victories, compared to a composite winning percentage of .519 for the entire season.

But once again last season, the dismal results of games four and five were the real anomalies. We suggested in last year's edition that teams may stumble because they fail to translate the emotional lift of a come-from-behind win into victories. We think that explanation still merits consideration. The table below summarizes the results of the study:

	Game 1	Game 2	Game 3	Game 4	Game 5	Totals
1982	15–10	11–14	16–9	12–12	11–13	65–58
1983	10–7	8–9	8–9	10–7	9–8	45–40
1984	10–12	11–11	10–11	9–12	9–12	49–58
1985	7–12	9–10	9–10	12–7	6–13	43–52
1986	13–6	12–7	6–12	6–12	4–14	41–51
1987	17–19	15–21	21–15	13–23	19–17	85–95
Totals	72–66	66–72	70–66	62–73	58–77	328–354
	.522	.478	.515	.459	.430	.481

We did neglect one aspect of this subject last year: What happens to the teams that blow those big, late-inning leads? Clearly, the winning teams aren't able to capitalize on their emotional lift, but perhaps the losing teams suffer a letdown that translates into further losses.

The losing teams did play poorly immediately after the loss (.464 compared to an overall .494 mark), but not to such an extent that an explanation is warranted. Even the most unusual results—a record of 81–54 three games later—is within the normal range of expectations. A summary of the results:

	Game 1	Game 2	Game 3	Game 4	Game 5	Totals
1982	8–17	14–11	13–12	13–11	10–14	58–65
1983	9–8	9–8	10–6	7–9	4–12	39–43
1984	11–11	7–15	12–9	11–10	12–9	53–54
1985	12–7	10–9	12–7	6–13	10–9	50–45
1986	7–12	8–11	11–7	9–9	9–9	44–48
1987	17–19	20–16	23–13	16–20	15–21	91–89
Totals	64–74	68–70	81–54	62–72	60–75	335–344
	.464	.493	.600	.463	.444	.493

It's clear that Joe Carter's contention—namely, that dramatic comeback victories usually raise a team's level of play for a few games thereafter—doesn't hold water. Those teams many feel a lot better for a few days, but that euphoria is useless on the diamond. As to whether those games have *any* short-term effect at all on either of the teams involved, we can't say for sure. But it appears whatever effect there may be is slight.

Maybe, This Year a Loud Foul?

During his first two seasons in the majors, Cory Snyder has faced Roger Clemens nine times, and has struck out every time. Of course, both Snyder and Clemens have a natural inclination toward strikeouts; nevertheless, nine consecutive strikeouts is still an extraordinary event. In fact, only one other batter-pitcher combination produced as many as nine consecutive strikeouts during the 13 years we've been compiling the data.

The following table lists the only streaks of eight or more consecutive strikeouts since 1975; all are currently active except the Andujar-Sanderson and Cooper-Leonard streaks. (Yes, if J. R. returns, he can extend his streak against Matthews.)

Years	Batter	Pitcher	SO
1979–1980	Gary Matthews	J.R. Richard	9
1986–1987	Cory Snyder	Roger Clemens	9
1977	Cecil Cooper	Dennis Leonard	8
1978–1982	Bob Knepper	Tom Seaver	8
1979–1982	Joaquin Andujar	Scott Sanderson	8
1985–1986	John Russell	Mike Scott	8
1986–1987	Bruce Ruffin	Dwight Gooden	8

There are no active streaks of seven strikeouts that have been extended over the past two seasons. Those of six: Gary Pettis vs. Bert Blyleven; Rob Thompson vs. Nolan Ryan; Glenn Wilson vs. Tom Niedenfuer; and Doug DeCinces vs. Ron Davis.

Future confrontations between Snyder and Clemens are inevitable. But at least the Indians and their fans might not be forced to watch Gary Ward kick Ed Vande Berg around anymore.

Vande Berg made 55 relief appearances for Cleveland last season in utter anonymity. He didn't save a single game, and made 50 appearances before his first and only decision, a win on September 23 against Oakland. It's safe to assume that Vande Berg's phone wasn't ringing off the hook after his contract with the Indians expired at the end of the 1987 season.

But one man who'll be disappointed if his path never again crosses Vande Berg's is Ward, whose otherwise disappointing season was brightened by his five-for-five massacre of Cleveland's invisible man. That performance extended Ward's streak of consecutive hits against Vande Berg to eight in his last eight at bats, a streak dating back to June 16, 1984.

Ward is currently three hits short of the longest streak that any batter has amassed against a particular pitcher during the 13 years since we've compiled that information. The longest streaks since 1975, with asterisks marking current streaks:

Years	Batter	Pitcher	H
1975	George Brett	Ed Figueroa	11
1975–1977	Jim Rice	Rudy May	10
1975	Dick Allen	Doug Rau	8
1976–1977	Dave Parker	John Curtis	8
1977–1978	Chris Speier	Nino Espinosa	8
1977–1978	Robin Yount	Dave Lemanczyk	8
1979–1980	Pete Rose	Mike Krukow	8
1980–1981	Gene Richards	Mike Krukow	8
1980–1981	Ken Singleton	Dennis Eckersley	8
1980–1981	Bake McBride	Steve Rogers	8
1981	Tim Foli	Mike Krukow	8*
1982	Bob Brenly	John Candelaria	8
1981–1983	Warren Cromartie	Rick Camp	8
1982–1984	Tom Brunansky	Bruce Hurst	8
1984	Tony Gwynn	Mike LaCoss	8
1986	Rob Thompson	Doyle Alexander	8
1984–1987	Gary Ward	Ed Vande Berg	8*

There are no current streaks of seven consecutive hits among active major-league players. Those of six: Brian Downing vs. Charlie Leibrandt; Barry Bonds vs. Jimmy Jones; Dave Parker vs. Greg Maddux; Terry Harper vs. Rick Honeycutt; Keith Moreland vs. Fred Toliver; Tony Gwynn vs. Dave Smith; Terry Puhl vs. Dave LaPoint; George Hendrick vs. Cecilio Guante; and Craig Reynolds vs. Bert Blyleven.

WON-LOST RECORD BY STARTING POSITION

CLEVELAND 61-101	C	1B	2B	3B	SS	LF	CF	RF	P	DH	Leadoff	Relief	Starts
Darrel Akerfelds	·	·	·	·	·	·	·	·	6-7	·	·	0-3	6-7
Andy Allanson	20-27	·	·	·	·	·	·	·	·	·	·	·	20-27
Mike Armstrong	·	·	·	·	·	·	·	·	·	·	·	3-11	·
Scott Bailes	·	·	·	·	·	·	·	·	6-11	·	·	10-12	6-11
Chris Bando	23-42	·	·	·	·	·	·	·	·	·	·	·	23-42
Jay Bell	·	·	·	·	·	14-19	·	·	·	·	·	·	14-19
Tony Bernazard	·	·	27-50	·	·	·	·	·	·	·	6-16	·	27-50
Brett Butler	·	·	·	·	·	·	52-83	·	·	·	50-76	·	52-83
Ernie Camacho	·	·	·	·	·	·	·	·	·	·	·	2-13	·
Tom Candiotti	·	·	·	·	·	·	·	·	9-23	·	·	·	9-23
Steve Carlton	·	·	·	·	·	·	·	·	5-9	·	·	4-5	5-9
Joe Carter	·	35-45	·	·	·	14-25	2-9	2-8	·	1-3	·	·	54-90
Carmen Castillo	·	·	·	·	·	·	·	8-9	·	12-28	0-1	·	20-37
Dave Clark	·	·	·	·	·	1-0	·	4-7	·	4-6	·	·	9-13
Rick Dempsey	18-30	·	·	·	·	·	·	·	·	·	·	·	18-30
Brian Dorsett	0-2	·	·	·	·	·	·	·	·	·	·	·	0-2
Jamie Easterly	·	·	·	·	·	·	·	·	·	·	·	5-11	·
John Farrell	·	·	·	·	·	·	·	·	4-5	·	·	1-0	4-5
Julio Franco	·	·	3-5	·	41-69	·	·	·	·	2-6	4-5	·	46-80
Doug Frobel	·	·	·	·	·	0-1	·	0-2	·	1-3	·	·	1-6
Dave Gallagher	·	·	·	·	·	·	6-6	·	·	·	·	·	6-6
Don Gordon	·	·	·	·	·	·	·	·	·	·	·	5-16	·
Mel Hall	·	·	·	·	·	41-68	·	·	·	3-3	1-3	·	44-71
Tommy Hinzo	·	·	24-39	·	·	·	·	·	·	·	·	·	24-39
Mark Huismann	·	·	·	·	·	·	·	·	·	·	·	8-12	·
Brook Jacoby	·	4-2	·	53-89	·	·	·	·	·	0-4	·	·	57-95
Doug Jones	·	·	·	·	·	·	·	·	·	·	·	18-31	·
Jeff Kaiser	·	·	·	·	·	·	·	·	·	·	·	0-2	·
Phil Niekro	·	·	·	·	·	·	·	·	9-13	·	·	·	9-13
Otis Nixon	·	·	·	·	·	·	1-3	·	·	·	·	·	1-3
Junior Noboa	·	·	7-7	0-2	1-3	·	·	·	·	·	·	·	8-12
Casey Parsons	·	·	·	·	·	·	·	·	·	1-1	·	·	1-1
Reggie Ritter	·	·	·	·	·	·	·	·	·	·	·	4-10	·
Ken Schrom	·	·	·	·	·	·	·	·	11-18	·	·	0-3	11-18
Cory Snyder	·	·	·	·	5-10	5-7	·	47-75	·	·	·	·	57-92
Sammy Stewart	·	·	·	·	·	·	·	·	·	·	·	10-15	·
Greg Swindell	·	·	·	·	·	·	·	·	5-10	·	·	0-1	5-10
Pat Tabler	·	22-54	·	·	·	·	·	·	·	31-34	·	·	53-88
Andre Thornton	·	·	·	·	·	·	·	·	·	6-13	·	·	6-13
Ed Vande Berg	·	·	·	·	·	·	·	·	·	·	·	15-40	·
Tom Waddell	·	·	·	·	·	·	·	·	·	·	·	0-6	·
Eddie Williams	·	·	·	8-10	·	·	·	·	·	·	·	·	8-10
Frank Wills	·	·	·	·	·	·	·	·	·	·	·	2-4	·
Rich Yett	·	·	·	·	·	·	·	·	6-5	·	·	2-24	6-5

Batting vs. Left and Right Handed Pitchers

		BA	Rank	SA	Rank	OBA	Rank	HR %	Rank	BB %	Rank	SO %	Rank
Chris Bando	vs. Lefties	.176	--	.176	--	.208	--	0.00	--	3.57	--	10.71	--
	vs. Righties	.231	135	.381	113	.276	149	3.13	90	5.78	136	12.72	61
Brett Butler	vs. Lefties	.267	83	.342	128	.397	22	1.37	120	17.78	7	13.89	77
	vs. Righties	.306	21	.457	53	.400	12	1.86	117	13.47	17	6.85	11
Joe Carter	vs. Lefties	.248	99	.431	73	.287	133	4.58	45	4.27	150	17.07	99
	vs. Righties	.269	76	.497	34	.310	115	5.75	25	4.30	153	16.56	100
Carmen Castillo	vs. Lefties	.266	86	.516	26	.336	77	5.65	24	10.00	52	20.71	127
	vs. Righties	.229	--	.427	--	.240	--	4.17	--	1.98	--	22.77	--
Julio Franco	vs. Lefties	.308	32	.492	37	.389	26	3.08	84	12.08	32	14.09	78
	vs. Righties	.323	11	.405	93	.389	20	1.10	138	9.49	64	8.52	25
Mel Hall	vs. Lefties	.364	--	.515	--	.417	--	3.03	--	8.33	--	22.22	--
	vs. Righties	.274	61	.434	72	.301	129	3.76	73	3.60	156	12.71	60
Tommy Hinzo	vs. Lefties	.391	1	.547	18	.443	5	3.13	123	6.76	123	6.76	9
	vs. Righties	.223	144	.295	155	.245	159	0.52	152	2.43	161	20.39	135
Brook Jacoby	vs. Lefties	.261	89	.444	66	.382	32	3.52	66	16.47	10	11.76	50
	vs. Righties	.314	16	.575	9	.389	11	6.78	11	10.44	50	11.78	50
Cory Snyder	vs. Lefties	.221	135	.399	96	.271	144	3.07	85	6.78	122	31.07	161
	vs. Righties	.242	116	.478	43	.274	152	6.76	12	4.34	152	25.34	150
Pat Tabler	vs. Lefties	.366	5	.564	13	.412	14	3.49	67	6.95	120	6.42	8
	vs. Righties	.281	47	.383	111	.350	57	1.31	132	8.82	78	16.71	104
Team Average	vs. Lefties	.266	6	.421	9	.338	7	2.94	11	9.73	4	15.99	8
	vs. Righties	.262	7	.422	9	.318	14	3.48	7	7.17	14	15.63	10
League Average	vs. Lefties	.265		.422		.333		3.29		8.94		15.64	
	vs. Righties	.265		.427		.334		3.43		8.94		15.26	

Batting with Runners on Base and Bases Empty

		BA	Rank	SA	Rank	OBA	Rank	HR %	Rank	BB %	Rank	SO %	Rank
Chris Bando	Runners On	.225	--	.325	--	.262	--	2.50	--	4.44	--	12.22	--
	Bases Empty	.214	150	.336	139	.259	155	2.29	112	5.76	132	12.23	53
Brett Butler	Runners On	.303	37	.412	94	.432	7	1.21	130	18.27	6	8.17	21
	Bases Empty	.291	31	.431	77	.383	21	1.96	122	12.93	13	9.27	19
Joe Carter	Runners On	.241	125	.396	105	.278	149	3.63	63	4.00	156	17.54	116
	Bases Empty	.288	35	.568	13	.332	67	7.37	8	4.61	144	15.79	87
Carmen Castillo	Runners On	.213	148	.360	128	.267	155	2.25	106	7.84	104	19.61	133
	Bases Empty	.275	54	.557	17	.317	104	6.87	13	5.76	132	23.02	142
Julio Franco	Runners On	.278	63	.382	112	.365	54	1.89	111	11.65	52	10.04	35
	Bases Empty	.350	3	.463	55	.408	5	1.41	132	9.00	63	9.97	27
Mel Hall	Runners On	.271	76	.390	108	.308	124	2.38	102	5.36	142	13.39	71
	Bases Empty	.287	37	.476	48	.310	111	4.73	47	2.82	157	13.38	59
Tommy Hinzo	Runners On	.221	140	.265	157	.252	159	0.00	150	3.10	160	17.05	110
	Bases Empty	.299	25	.431	78	.331	69	2.08	120	3.97	146	16.56	100
Brook Jacoby	Runners On	.274	73	.393	106	.383	37	2.28	104	14.56	21	11.88	51
	Bases Empty	.318	14	.642	2	.390	15	8.41	4	10.31	38	11.70	47
Cory Snyder	Runners On	.216	146	.397	104	.266	156	4.31	51	6.64	125	26.17	156
	Bases Empty	.249	103	.496	36	.279	146	6.67	15	3.90	149	27.58	155
Pat Tabler	Runners On	.356	5	.459	60	.421	12	1.85	114	9.62	80	13.46	72
	Bases Empty	.261	81	.420	85	.317	103	2.12	116	6.86	107	13.73	62
Team Average	Runners On	.253	14	.373	14	.320	13	2.38	14	8.65	14	15.88	10
	Bases Empty	.271	2	.458	2	.327	6	4.05	2	7.26	13	15.61	7
League Average	Runners On	.271		.428		.343		3.25		9.68		14.87	
	Bases Empty	.260		.424		.326		3.49		8.34		15.79	

Overall Batting Compared to Late Inning Pressure Situations

		BA	Rank	SA	Rank	OBA	Rank	HR %	Rank	BB %	Rank	SO %	Rank	RDI %	Rank
Andy Allanson	Overall	.266	--	.364	--	.298	--	1.95	--	5.23	--	17.44	--	.255	116
	Pressure	.400	--	.400	--	.400	--	0.00	--	0.00	--	10.00	--	.167	--
Chris Bando	Overall	.218	154	.332	149	.260	159	2.37	114	5.24	145	12.23	48	.204	--
	Pressure	.182	--	.364	--	.280	--	4.55	--	11.11	--	7.41	--	.000	--
Brett Butler	Overall	.295	27	.425	86	.399	9	1.72	124	14.72	12	8.90	22	.290	77
	Pressure	.306	41	.500	31	.380	40	4.84	44	11.11	50	12.50	60	.583	2
Joe Carter	Overall	.264	85	.480	37	.304	125	5.44	24	4.29	155	16.69	103	.280	88
	Pressure	.241	110	.418	78	.318	103	5.06	41	7.87	103	17.98	98	.333	51
Carmen Castillo	Overall	.250	112	.477	42	.296	144	5.00	34	6.64	126	21.58	144	.227	148
	Pressure	.146	161	.244	147	.143	164	2.44	87	0.00	161	16.67	90	.111	147
Julio Franco	Overall	.319	11	.428	81	.389	12	1.62	127	10.18	55	10.00	30	.289	78
	Pressure	.379	10	.515	28	.447	10	1.52	110	11.84	44	11.84	50	.313	69
Mel Hall	Overall	.280	48	.439	71	.309	116	3.71	71	3.94	157	13.39	59	.331	35
	Pressure	.292	54	.458	55	.311	109	4.17	52	2.70	153	8.11	19	.200	117
Tommy Hinzo	Overall	.265	84	.358	136	.296	142	1.17	137	3.57	160	16.79	107	.232	142
	Pressure	.212	128	.333	118	.257	143	3.03	73	5.56	128	13.89	67	.000	--
Brook Jacoby	Overall	.300	23	.541	14	.387	18	5.93	15	12.10	24	11.77	43	.239	134
	Pressure	.267	79	.523	26	.323	96	6.98	17	6.45	120	11.83	49	.077	157
Cory Snyder	Overall	.236	139	.456	57	.273	156	5.72	20	5.04	148	26.99	156	.223	149
	Pressure	.278	68	.567	20	.283	129	7.78	9	1.09	160	25.00	141	.417	20
Pat Tabler	Overall	.307	18	.439	70	.369	36	1.99	119	8.25	88	13.59	62	.364	13
	Pressure	.321	28	.359	103	.400	26	0.00	119	10.99	55	14.29	70	.259	90
Andre Thornton	Overall	.118	--	.141	--	.206	--	0.00	--	10.31	--	25.77	--	.156	--
	Pressure	.000	--	.000	--	.118	--	0.00	--	11.76	--	35.29	--	.091	155
Team Average	Overall	.263	7	.422	9	.324	12	3.34	8	7.87	14	15.73	9	.266	13
	Pressure	.264	7	.431	4	.319	13	4.08	2	7.17	14	15.84	5	.242	12
League Average	Overall	.265		.425		.333		3.38		8.94		15.38		.287	
	Pressure	.262		.405		.335		3.07		9.43		16.58		.280	

Additional Miscellaneous Batting Comparisons

	Grass Surface		Artificial Surface		Home Games		Road Games		Runners in Scoring Position		Runners in Scoring Pos and Two Outs		Leading Off Inning		Runners on 3B with less than 2 Outs	
	BA	Rank	BA	Rank	BA	Rank	BA	Rank	BA	Rank	BA	Rank	OBA	Rank	RDI %	Rank
Andy Allanson	.287	47	.111	--	.200	--	.329	--	.098	163	.056	--	.282	--	.667	33
Chris Bando	.200	157	.293	--	.233	133	.204	151	.140	--	.250	--	.262	142	.429	--
Brett Butler	.320	13	.186	151	.337	7	.257	88	.322	23	.238	97	.408	12	.550	102
Joe Carter	.265	89	.253	89	.251	111	.275	56	.247	106	.223	109	.300	113	.531	112
Carmen Castillo	.250	112	.250	--	.314	24	.176	161	.233	125	.258	72	.320	93	.462	138
Rick Dempsey	.154	162	.333	--	.169	--	.186	--	.194	--	.143	--	.318	--	.364	157
Julio Franco	.304	25	.422	2	.310	28	.328	6	.250	102	.294	45	.406	15	.606	68
Mel Hall	.279	60	.290	42	.288	61	.274	58	.293	51	.232	100	.291	122	.633	52
Tommy Hinzo	.258	99	.295	38	.233	134	.291	33	.161	157	.077	158	.220	--	.615	58
Brook Jacoby	.294	36	.330	11	.279	70	.323	11	.221	135	.158	145	.388	21	.333	159
Cory Snyder	.236	131	.236	111	.214	152	.256	89	.191	147	.177	141	.333	69	.500	120
Pat Tabler	.319	15	.237	110	.333	10	.280	48	.383	3	.440	1	.252	147	.700	25
Team Average	.264	7	.260	9	.266	11	.260	7	.240	14	.217	13	.315	12	.549	12
League Average	.267		.261		.270		.260		.266		.247		.328		.581	

Pitching vs. Left and Right Handed Batters

		BA	Rank	SA	Rank	OBA	Rank	HR %	Rank	BB %	Rank	SO %	Rank
Darrel Akerfelds	vs. Lefties	.300	105	.613	128	.383	114	8.00	128	10.23	81	11.93	90
	vs. Righties	.267	79	.445	90	.365	100	4.11	96	11.70	110	12.28	102
Scott Bailes	vs. Lefties	.273	76	.394	46	.321	43	4.04	96	5.61	12	15.89	46
	vs. Righties	.302	107	.506	113	.367	100	4.35	100	9.23	88	10.81	110
Tom Candiotti	vs. Lefties	.237	22	.366	28	.319	41	3.09	61	10.96	91	10.07	112
	vs. Righties	.262	70	.447	93	.340	77	4.16	97	9.98	96	14.97	69
John Farrell	vs. Lefties	.271	71	.429	70	.360	96	2.14	26	11.73	102	7.41	123
	vs. Righties	.238	--	.373	--	.278	--	3.17	--	2.22	--	11.85	--
Don Gordon	vs. Lefties	.258	52	.404	56	.316	37	1.12	13	7.14	32	12.24	87
	vs. Righties	.291	--	.462	--	.349	--	3.42	--	6.15	--	8.46	--
Doug Jones	vs. Lefties	.270	69	.319	10	.312	28	0.54	3	5.88	14	19.61	21
	vs. Righties	.291	104	.389	53	.352	93	1.71	13	6.12	26	23.98	12
Ken Schrom	vs. Lefties	.316	120	.548	120	.363	99	5.26	114	7.46	39	8.29	120
	vs. Righties	.279	94	.465	102	.350	90	4.04	93	9.01	80	9.31	119
Greg Swindell	vs. Lefties	.309	--	.574	--	.333	--	5.88	--	4.17	--	18.06	--
	vs. Righties	.277	91	.445	89	.345	85	4.27	99	9.21	87	22.76	17
Ed Vande Berg	vs. Lefties	.279	86	.324	11	.322	44	0.00	1	6.16	18	12.33	86
	vs. Righties	.365	127	.591	126	.400	118	5.66	120	6.86	37	12.57	99
Rich Yett	vs. Lefties	.240	25	.377	34	.333	57	2.86	52	11.88	105	14.36	59
	vs. Righties	.273	85	.586	125	.358	98	8.08	125	10.87	100	13.04	93
Team Average	vs. Lefties	.275	10	.432	9	.345	12	3.14	6	9.31	8	11.93	14
	vs. Righties	.281	14	.472	14	.355	14	4.45	14	9.60	13	14.27	13
League Average	vs. Lefties	.267		.427		.338		3.30		9.47		14.54	
	vs. Righties	.264		.424		.330		3.45		8.56		15.98	

Pitching with Runners on Base and Bases Empty

		BA	Rank	SA	Rank	OBA	Rank	HR %	Rank	BB %	Rank	SO %	Rank
Darrel Akerfelds	Runners On	.248	41	.450	88	.344	72	4.65	101	10.90	94	14.10	73
	Bases Empty	.311	120	.593	127	.398	122	7.19	127	10.99	108	10.47	108
Scott Bailes	Runners On	.259	54	.388	51	.326	51	3.02	68	8.96	61	13.06	84
	Bases Empty	.329	122	.570	124	.389	118	5.43	119	8.13	62	10.60	107
Tom Candiotti	Runners On	.239	30	.366	23	.347	73	2.59	51	13.84	118	11.49	101
	Bases Empty	.256	60	.433	81	.317	53	4.31	101	7.92	57	13.27	87
John Farrell	Runners On	.257	52	.330	11	.317	39	0.92	4	5.69	14	8.94	115
	Bases Empty	.255	56	.452	95	.328	73	3.82	84	8.62	72	9.77	115
Doug Jones	Runners On	.312	110	.413	66	.372	106	1.59	14	8.18	47	18.18	27
	Bases Empty	.246	42	.287	5	.283	14	0.58	1	3.33	4	26.11	5
Ken Schrom	Runners On	.333	118	.544	115	.400	118	4.37	95	9.70	76	8.36	119
	Bases Empty	.274	91	.484	108	.326	68	4.89	112	7.07	46	9.09	121
Greg Swindell	Runners On	.306	107	.544	116	.360	92	5.63	115	7.69	38	17.58	29
	Bases Empty	.267	81	.415	62	.332	79	3.81	83	8.88	76	25.10	7
Ed Vande Berg	Runners On	.319	113	.429	80	.356	85	2.45	44	6.67	24	11.67	100
	Bases Empty	.333	124	.515	118	.376	112	3.79	82	6.38	39	13.48	82
Rich Yett	Runners On	.250	43	.500	105	.344	71	6.88	124	12.04	105	16.23	46
	Bases Empty	.263	70	.479	105	.349	97	4.69	110	10.79	105	11.62	101
Team Average	Runners On	.285	14	.449	10	.367	14	3.52	10	11.04	13	12.40	14
	Bases Empty	.273	13	.459	13	.337	12	4.20	13	8.09	8	14.05	13
League Average	Runners On	.271		.428		.343		3.25		9.68		14.87	
	Bases Empty	.260		.424		.326		3.49		8.34		15.79	

Overall Pitching Compared to Late Inning Pressure Situations

		BA	Rank	SA	Rank	OBA	Rank	HR %	Rank	BB %	Rank	SO %	Rank
Darrel Akerfelds	Overall	.284	97	.530	124	.374	115	6.08	125	10.95	107	12.10	97
	Pressure	.273	--	.273	--	.304	--	0.00	--	0.00	--	13.04	--
Scott Bailes	Overall	.296	108	.484	110	.358	99	4.29	99	8.53	63	11.80	99
	Pressure	.333	117	.440	88	.356	83	2.38	56	3.41	6	14.77	67
Tom Candiotti	Overall	.250	41	.406	50	.330	65	3.62	85	10.47	97	12.50	92
	Pressure	.245	55	.396	67	.350	74	3.77	88	12.80	104	12.80	84
John Farrell	Overall	.256	52	.402	48	.323	54	2.63	37	7.41	37	9.43	118
	Pressure	.308	--	.462	--	.400	--	3.85	--	12.90	--	9.68	--
Don Gordon	Overall	.277	--	.437	--	.335	--	2.43	--	6.58	--	10.09	--
	Pressure	.314	113	.543	118	.359	86	2.86	68	7.69	44	7.69	119
Mark Huismann	Overall	.251	--	.435	--	.298	--	3.66	--	5.66	--	17.92	--
	Pressure	.292	93	.542	116	.364	91	6.25	122	8.77	59	14.04	74
Doug Jones	Overall	.281	92	.353	13	.332	66	1.11	2	6.00	18	21.75	17
	Pressure	.293	96	.340	36	.363	90	0.67	21	8.05	51	22.41	19
Ken Schrom	Overall	.298	111	.508	119	.357	96	4.68	110	8.20	53	8.78	121
	Pressure	.267	70	.400	69	.333	62	2.22	50	9.62	69	3.85	126
Sammy Stewart	Overall	.234	--	.374	--	.362	--	3.74	--	16.15	--	19.23	--
	Pressure	.204	16	.347	41	.322	52	4.08	97	15.25	119	18.64	36
Greg Swindell	Overall	.283	94	.467	104	.343	77	4.55	105	8.39	59	22.00	16
	Pressure	.298	101	.456	93	.375	102	3.51	85	10.77	86	20.00	26
Ed Vande Berg	Overall	.325	119	.468	106	.364	108	3.05	60	6.54	25	12.46	93
	Pressure	.296	99	.370	52	.391	109	0.00	1	14.06	111	12.50	89
Rich Yett	Overall	.257	57	.488	113	.347	84	5.63	123	11.34	111	13.66	78
	Pressure	.241	52	.370	52	.359	87	3.70	87	14.93	117	14.93	66
Team Average	Overall	.279	13	.455	13	.351	14	3.90	13	9.48	13	13.28	13
	Pressure	.286	13	.406	9	.370	13	2.47	4	11.24	14	14.31	13
League Average	Overall	.265		.425		.333		3.38		8.94		15.38	
	Pressure	.262		.404		.337		2.99		9.73		16.42	

Additional Miscellaneous Pitching Comparisons

	Grass Surface		Artificial Surface		Home Games		Road Games		Runners in Scoring Position		Runners in Scoring Pos and Two Outs		Leading Off Inning	
	BA	Rank	BA	Rank	BA	Rank	BA	Rank	BA	Rank	BA	Rank	OBA	Rank
Darrel Akerfelds	.272	79	.357	117	.307	116	.266	60	.290	91	.143	3	.388	112
Scott Bailes	.304	107	.268	77	.319	120	.277	77	.248	46	.279	92	.392	114
Tom Candiotti	.243	26	.314	105	.243	45	.263	55	.267	73	.272	87	.312	45
John Farrell	.265	67	.179	--	.304	--	.230	13	.237	--	.278	90	.264	16
Don Gordon	.291	95	.185	--	.268	85	.291	--	.313	109	.240	--	.277	--
Mark Huismann	.273	--	.188	8	.200	--	.297	--	.291	--	.250	--	.370	--
Doug Jones	.292	100	.171	--	.296	108	.259	41	.314	111	.240	63	.338	74
Reggie Ritter	.227	--	.409	125	.231	--	.338	--	.286	--	.278	--	.346	--
Ken Schrom	.312	112	.169	3	.318	119	.262	54	.335	118	.304	102	.364	98
Greg Swindell	.274	82	.339	110	.256	61	.306	109	.275	78	.333	110	.321	54
Ed Vande Berg	.326	119	.318	--	.327	123	.323	120	.308	103	.265	83	.328	62
Rich Yett	.252	44	.281	88	.239	38	.271	71	.229	34	.222	49	.394	116
Team Average	.280	11	.270	9	.285	14	.272	6	.287	14	.271	14	.340	12
League Average	.267		.261		.260		.270		.266		.247		.328	

DETROIT TIGERS

It's unfortunate that so much of what happens between the covers of a good book gets forgotten in the wake of a spectacularly surprising climax. In most cases the climax would not be nearly as intriguing were it not for the intricate design that set it up. The same holds true of a baseball season. The Twins' unlikely success in post-season play probably wiped a lot of what happened earlier in 1987 out of our collective memory banks, especially for those of us who do not live in Detroit.

That's too bad, because the route that the Tigers took to win the American League East Division title was unique and worthy of extended consideration. The Tigers had to enact two comebacks to win their division title, one long-haul job and one short-termer, and it's difficult to determine which was more spectacular. Each of those comebacks ranks among the greatest in baseball history, but no team ever did both in a single season.

Just 18 games into the season, the Tigers already stood 10 games behind the division-leading Brewers. Now, we know that only one team in modern major-league history got off to a faster start than the Brewers (the 1918 Giants were 18–1); and we realize that even while Milwaukee was hot, very few observers felt that the Brewers were indeed the team to beat in that division. But neither were the Tigers playing well. Kirk Gibson started the season on the disabled list, the team had trouble scoring, and they would lose 19 of their first 30 games. These events might have perturbed a more flappable soul than George Lee Anderson, but rather than rant and rave, Sparky quieted the calls for his head, publicly extolled the virtues of both his hitters and his pitchers, and directed comeback number one.

The Tigers' largest deficit of the season was 11 games; they reached that point after only their 23rd game, a 3–2 loss in 13 innings at Oakland on the second day of May. By coming back to take the division, they became only the 14th team since 1900 that has overcome a double-digit deficit to win a league or division title. Those 14 are listed here, ranked according to the size of the deficit. (Ground rules: The information listed under the "largest deficit" column indicates the team's games behind after games played on a particular date. If the same deficit occurred more than once, the latest such date is used. Games behind are calculated at end of a day's play. To conform to official baseball rules, suspended games are calculated as of their original date. And savor the moment: This may be the only story you read in this election year that talks about "deficit" without blaming Reagan.)

	Final Record			Largest Deficit	
	W–L	Pct.	GA*	Date	GB
1914 Braves	94–59	.614	10.5	July 5	15
1978 Yankees	100–63	.613	1	July 19	14
1951 Giants	98–59	.624	1	Aug. 11	13
1973 Mets	82–79	.509	1.5	July 8	12.5
1911 Athletics	101–50	.669	13.5	May 19	12
1930 Cardinals	92–62	.597	2	Aug. 8	12
1964 Cardinals	93–69	.574	1	Aug. 23	11
1973 Reds	99–63	.611	3.5	June 30	11
1987 Tigers	98–64	.605	2	May 5	11
1935 Cubs	100–54	.649	4	July 5	10.5
1936 Giants	92–62	.597	5	July 16	10.5
1979 Reds	90–71	.559	1.5	July 4	10.5
1942 Cardinals	106–48	.688	2	Aug. 5	10
1969 Mets	100–62	.617	8	Aug. 14	10

* Games Ahead of second-place team.

The Tigers overcame the largest deficit of any division champion since Bucky Dent netted that Fenway fly ball in 1978, after his Yankees had spotted the Red Sox a 14-game lead. In fact, only six teams in this century have come from farther back to finish in first place. But in only one of those cases had the team in question fallen 10 or more games behind as early in the race as the Tigers did. That team was the 1914 Boston Braves, whose comeback victory (capped by a World Series triumph over Connie Mack's Athletics) was so legendary that 74 years later that team is still unmistakably identified merely by the phrase "Miracle Braves." Here's how the seasons of the Miracle Braves and the Miracle Tigers parallel each other:

	1914 Braves		1987 Tigers	
	W–L	GB	W–L	GB
After 10 Decisions	2–8	7.5	6–4	4.5
After 20 Decisions	4–16	9.5	8–12	10
After 30 Decisions	9–21	11	11–19	9.5
After 40 Decisions	12–28	13.5	19–21	7
After 50 Decisions	20–30	10	25–25	6.5
After 60 Decisions	25–35	11.5	33–27	5.5
After 70 Decisions	30–40	11.5	38–32	6
After 80 Decisions	37–43	10.5	45–35	5
After 90 Decisions	45–45	8	52–38	4
After 100 Decisions	54–46	3.5	59–41	2
After 110 Decisions	60–50	0.5	64–46	1.5
After 120 Decisions	68–52	+0	71–49	+.002
After 130 Decisions	75–55	+3.5	78–52	+1
After 140 Decisions	84–56	+7.5	84–56	+0
After 150 Decisions	92–58	+10.5	91–59	–0.5
After 154 Decisions	—		92–62	–3.5
Final Record	94–59	+10.5	98–64	+2
In First Place to Stay	Sept. 5		Oct. 2	
Largest Deficit	15 games, July 5		11 games, May 5	

The Tigers started their climb back into contention earlier in the season than did the Braves, who in 1914 went from 10 games behind to 10 games ahead in the span of exactly two months, July 30 to September 30. And the Braves won the pennant by 10½ games, compared to the Tigers' two-game margin. But they don't pay off extra based on how much you win by. These are the only two major-league teams since 1900 that played under .400 ball over the first 30 games of a season, but finished the season above the .600 mark. These two and the 1974 Pirates (who won the National League East with an unusually low percentage of .543) are the only teams to rebound from a sub-.400 first 30 games to a league or division championship.

Of course, a large deficit early in the season cuts both ways. While falling behind *that* far, *that* early means that a team has more time left in the season in which to fashion a comeback, a large early deficit could also lead to a team questioning its own ability more than on a team that went through at least a few good weeks before falling back.

So much for the long-haul comeback; let's flip ahead to the last week of September. In the interim, the Brewers had fallen out of the lead by mid-May, and the Yankees and Blue Jays took turns leading the division while the Tigers climbed up through the pack. After pulling to within a half-game of the lead on July 27, Detroit fell back, but finally reached the top spot on August 19. They held first place for 30 of the next 33 days before Toronto regained it on September 21.

But the Tigers had left in them a comeback that was at least the equal of, if not superior to, their earlier one. On the morning of Sunday, September 27, with eight games left to play, Detroit trailed the Blue Jays by three and one-half games, and the Tigers were reeling. The previous afternoon, they had blown a 9–4 lead at Toronto, losing the game in the bottom of the ninth on Juan Beniquez's pinch-hit three-run triple off Dickie Noles. It was their third straight loss to the division leaders.

Three and one-half games behind, eight games left. Never in the history of the American League had a team made up that much ground with so few games remaining. Such comebacks had been accomplished twice in the National League in this century. In each of those cases, a playoff series was necessary to determine the champion:

- On September 19, 1951, the Giants trailed the Dodgers by three and one-half with eight to play, and then, following a Brooklyn win and a New York loss the next day, the Giants fell to four and one-half behind with seven games remaining. The Giants won all seven of their remaining games, while the Dodgers went 4–6, to finish in a tie and force the three-game playoff eventually won by Bobby Thomson's home run.
- On September 22, 1962, after moving to California, the Giants trailed the Dodgers by four games with seven to play. But while the Giants went 5–2, the Dodgers lost six of seven. Again,

the Giants completed their comeback by winning the best-of-three playoff.

Propelled by Kirk Gibson's ninth-inning game-tying homer, the Tigers won that Sunday afternoon game, took five of seven after that, and won the pennant by two games over the Blue Jays, who dropped their last seven games. But despite the dramatics of the last week, and indeed, of the previous five months, the joy of winning the division title was short-lived, as the Tigers were eliminated by the Twins in five games in the playoffs.

Although both the 1951 and 1962 Giants lost their respective World Series to the Yankees, their regular-season comebacks (and the corresponding blown leads by the Dodgers) are still celebrated. This is especially true of the 1951 team, a group that has become the something of a barometer against which other comebacks are measured. If that's the case, then perhaps with the passage of time, what the Tigers achieved in winning their division title in 1987 will be accorded similar respect, and the team will be remembered for a season that is unique in baseball history for its two comebacks, rather than for losing a playoff series to a team that it was favored to beat.

Hitting Against Morris: Mission Impossible

Scene: a single telephone booth alongside a quiet rural road. A well-dressed man in a trench coat enters the booth, reaches below the ledge on which the phone rests, and removes a small cassette tape recorder. He places the recorder on the ledge, and switches it on.

"Good morning, Mr. Phelps. The photo that you are looking at is of Jack Morris, the ace right-hander of the Detroit Tigers. Mr. Morris has won 141 games during the 1980s, more than any other pitcher in the major leagues. He has won at least 15 games in every season since 1979, with the exception of the 1981 strike season, when he tied for the league lead with 14 wins.

"During his career, one of the few vulnerabilities that Mr. Morris has shown is to the home-run ball. He allowed 39 home runs last season, after allowing 40 the preceding year. We have arranged for you to meet Mr. Morris under conditions optimal to you, a power hitter. You will meet him only at either Tiger Stadium or the Kingdome, the two best home-run parks in baseball last year.

"Your assignment, if you choose to accept it, is to take Mr. Morris deep, go downtown, kiss that baby goodbye, and touch 'em all. As always, this tape will self-destruct in 5 seconds."

If the Mr. Phelps in question is James Phelps, leader of the Impossible Missions Force, hey, no problem. He's a can-do guy who would put Ollie North to shame. But if we're talking about Seattle designated hitter Ken Phelps, well, he might choose to go up in smoke along with the tape recording rather than to face Jack Morris again.

Despite their career tendencies and the ballparks in which they meet, Mr. Ken Phelps has never had a home run off Mr. Morris. But, hell, you can't have a home run off a guy if you've never even had a *hit* off him, and that's the real rub: Including an 0-for-6 performance last year, Phelps carries an 0-for-26 career mark against Morris into the 1988 season. The year-by-year tally:

	AB	H	BB	SO
1983	4	0	0	1
1984	4	0	0	3
1985	7	0	1	4
1986	5	0	2	4
1987	6	0	1	1
Totals	26	0	4	13

We've been charting these batter-pitcher matchups for every player in baseball over the last 13 years. And while there are a lot of batters throughout baseball who are dominated by particular pitchers, Phelps-Morris is among the very top.

Here is the list of the longest current streaks of consecutive hitless at bats by a particular batter against a particular pitcher in regular-season games, among all combinations of players who played in the majors in 1987. An asterisk marks those cases in which the streak encompasses the entire career of the player, and we have included players who are currently in different leagues.

Years	Batter	Pitcher	AB
1983–1987	Ken Phelps	Jack Morris	26*
1983–1987	Keith Moreland	Mike Krukow	25
1986–1987	Mel Hall	Jack Morris	22
1982–1985	Gary Matthews	Bryn Smith	22
1983–1985	Eddie Murray	Bob Ojeda	22
1983–1986	Dave Concepcion	Charles Hudson	21*
1985–1987	Kirk Gibson	Bret Saberhagen	21
1984–1987	Spike Owen	Tom Candiotti	21
1985–1987	Ryne Sandberg	Bryn Smith	21
1984–1987	Ozzie Virgil	Sid Fernandez	21*
1983–1987	Tom Brunansky	Doyle Alexander	20
1979–1985	Reggie Jackson	Aurelio Lopez	20
1980–1987	Garry Templeton	Tom Hume	20

Where does that 0-for-26 streak stand among the "all-time" leaders? With 1975 as the starting point, there have been only 11 longer streaks:

Years	Batter	Pitcher	AB
1976–1979	Butch Wynegar	Nolan Ryan	38
1975–1979	Larry Parrish	J.R. Richard	34
1983–1986	Glenn Hubbard	Fernando Valenzuela	34
1983–1986	Bill Doran	Mario Soto	33
1976–1981	Doug DeCinces	Dennis Eckersley	31
1979–1985	Larry Bowa	Jerry Reuss	30
1980–1982	Ivan DeJesus	Steve Rogers	27
1979–1984	Ivan DeJesus	Vern Ruhle	27
1979–1982	Dave Kingman	Don Robinson	27
1975–1978	Roger Metzger	Doug Rau	27
1978–1980	Ozzie Smith	Bob Forsch	27

Of course, even the most one-sided mastery does not guarantee perpetual success. Perhaps Phelps can take note of Tom Brunansky's streak of 20 consecutive hitless at bats against Doyle Alexander. As we said, these streaks count regular-season games only. But in last year's American League Championship Series, Brunansky broke loose with a vengeance, slamming a run-scoring double in Game One, and another double, this one knocking in two runs, in Game Five. Maybe if Phelps finally meets Morris under *post-season* conditions, he'll snap out of his funk, too.

WON-LOST RECORD BY STARTING POSITION

DETROIT 98-64	C	1B	2B	3B	SS	LF	CF	RF	P	DH	Leadoff	Relief	Starts
Doyle Alexander	·	·	·	·	·	·	·	·	11-0	·	·	·	11-0
Doug Baker	·	·	·	·	·	·	·	·	·	·	·	·	·
Bill Bean	·	·	·	·	·	2-2	9-5	1-1	·	·	1-2	·	12-8
Dave Bergman	·	20-18	·	·	·	2-0	·	1-0	·	·	0-2	·	23-18
Tom Brookens	·	·	2-3	70-40	5-6	·	·	·	·	·	4-4	·	77-49
Darnell Coles	·	3-2	·	13-18	·	1-0	·	5-0	·	0-2	·	·	22-22
Darrell Evans	·	63-35	·	·	·	·	·	·	·	20-18	·	·	83-53
Kirk Gibson	·	·	·	·	·	74-43	2-0	·	·	4-0	·	·	80-43
Johnny Grubb	·	·	·	·	·	9-7	·	3-4	·	5-2	·	·	17-13
Terry Harper	·	·	·	·	·	0-1	·	7-4	·	0-8	·	·	7-13
Mike Heath	34-20	0-1	·	·	·	·	1-0	3-8	·	·	·	·	38-29
Mike Henneman	·	·	·	·	·	·	·	·	·	·	·	37-18	·
Willie Hernandez	·	·	·	·	·	·	·	·	·	·	·	24-21	·
Larry Herndon	·	·	·	·	·	7-10	12-10	·	·	12-6	·	·	31-26
Bryan Kelly	·	·	·	·	·	·	·	·	·	·	·	0-5	·
Eric King	·	·	·	·	·	·	·	·	1-3	·	·	31-20	1-3
Chet Lemon	·	·	·	·	·	·	78-52	·	·	·	·	·	78-52
Dwight Lowry	4-2	·	·	·	·	·	·	·	·	·	·	·	4-2
Scott Lusader	·	·	·	·	·	·	·	9-2	·	·	·	·	9-2
Morris Madden	·	·	·	·	·	·	·	·	·	·	·	0-2	·
Bill Madlock	·	12-8	1-0	·	·	·	·	·	·	44-20	·	·	57-28
Orlando Mercado	0-8	·	·	·	·	·	·	·	·	·	·	·	0-8
Jack Morris	·	·	·	·	·	·	·	·	21-13	·	·	·	21-13
Jim Morrison	·	·	1-1	12-4	0-2	1-0	·	1-1	·	3-2	·	·	18-10
Matt Nokes	60-34	·	·	·	·	1-1	·	1-0	·	10-6	·	·	72-41
Dickie Noles	·	·	·	·	·	·	·	·	·	·	·	2-2	·
Dan Petry	·	·	·	·	·	·	·	·	·	13-8	·	2-7	13-8
Jeff M. Robinson	·	·	·	·	·	·	·	·	·	14-7	·	3-5	14-7
Pat Sheridan	·	·	·	·	·	·	8-7	54-32	·	·	5-6	·	62-39
Nate Snell	·	·	·	·	·	·	·	·	·	0-2	·	7-13	0-2
Frank Tanana	·	·	·	·	·	·	·	·	19-15	·	·	·	19-15
Walt Terrell	·	·	·	·	·	·	·	·	19-16	·	·	·	19-16
Mark Thurmond	·	·	·	·	·	·	·	·	·	·	·	20-28	·
Tim Tolman	·	·	·	·	·	1-0	·	1-2	·	·	·	·	2-2
Alan Trammell	·	·	·	·	93-54	·	·	·	·	·	·	·	93-54
Jim Walewander	·	·	4-5	2-2	0-2	·	·	·	·	·	0-1	·	6-9
Lou Whitaker	·	·	91-55	·	·	·	·	·	·	·	88-49	·	91-55

Batting vs. Left and Right Handed Pitchers

		BA	Rank	SA	Rank	OBA	Rank	HR %	Rank	BB %	Rank	SO %	Rank
Dave Bergman	vs. Lefties	.263	--	.263	--	.263	--	0.00	--	0.00	--	21.05	--
	vs. Righties	.275	58	.477	45	.390	18	3.92	69	15.96	11	10.11	36
Tom Brookens	vs. Lefties	.240	110	.422	79	.310	108	4.55	47	9.25	67	13.87	76
	vs. Righties	.241	117	.352	132	.287	142	2.07	112	5.36	143	12.30	54
Darnell Coles	vs. Lefties	.156	161	.273	151	.244	156	2.60	95	9.30	66	12.79	62
	vs. Righties	.208	--	.347	--	.284	--	2.78	--	8.43	--	14.46	--
Darrell Evans	vs. Lefties	.209	143	.338	132	.312	103	3.38	72	12.64	27	17.82	108
	vs. Righties	.276	56	.570	13	.406	8	8.26	3	17.93	4	12.18	53
Kirk Gibson	vs. Lefties	.268	80	.385	101	.374	41	2.23	105	13.21	23	23.58	145
	vs. Righties	.282	44	.549	16	.371	37	6.49	14	12.08	25	18.82	127
Terry Harper	vs. Lefties	.213	142	.410	87	.314	100	4.92	38	12.68	26	9.86	33
	vs. Righties	.000	--	.000	--	.000	--	0.00	--	0.00	--	33.33	--
Mike Heath	vs. Lefties	.302	37	.465	54	.356	55	3.14	81	6.86	121	8.57	23
	vs. Righties	.252	--	.378	--	.314	--	2.70	--	7.38	--	22.13	--
Larry Herndon	vs. Lefties	.373	3	.593	9	.426	10	4.52	49	9.90	54	11.88	53
	vs. Righties	.146	--	.250	--	.192	--	2.08	--	5.77	--	21.15	--
Chet Lemon	vs. Lefties	.272	72	.494	36	.382	33	4.44	51	15.09	14	12.26	55
	vs. Righties	.279	51	.472	46	.372	34	4.14	60	11.14	38	16.42	96
Bill Madlock	vs. Lefties	.278	65	.477	44	.323	87	4.64	43	5.92	134	15.38	90
	vs. Righties	.280	48	.446	62	.373	32	4.00	63	8.70	82	9.18	29
Matt Nokes	vs. Lefties	.207	146	.356	121	.278	139	4.60	44	8.08	96	23.23	142
	vs. Righties	.307	20	.578	8	.360	46	7.49	7	6.60	119	11.49	45
Pat Sheridan	vs. Lefties	.195	151	.234	157	.250	145	0.00	--	5.81	138	27.91	157
	vs. Righties	.273	67	.390	103	.344	68	1.74	121	10.08	57	17.05	108
Alan Trammell	vs. Lefties	.360	7	.575	12	.419	12	5.14	31	9.92	53	7.85	19
	vs. Righties	.334	4	.538	18	.393	15	4.44	49	8.45	87	6.57	10
Lou Whitaker	vs. Lefties	.217	140	.327	133	.279	136	1.77	112	7.60	108	18.80	115
	vs. Righties	.294	33	.487	38	.376	28	3.17	89	11.98	26	14.06	72
Team Average	vs. Lefties	.263	10	.420	10	.338	6	3.41	5	9.79	3	15.10	5
	vs. Righties	.276	2	.468	1	.355	1	4.30	1	10.32	1	13.65	2
League Average	vs. Lefties	.265		.422		.333		3.29		8.94		15.64	
	vs. Righties	.265		.427		.334		3.43		8.94		15.26	

Batting with Runners on Base and Bases Empty

		BA	Rank	SA	Rank	OBA	Rank	HR %	Rank	BB %	Rank	SO %	Rank
Dave Bergman	Runners On	.264	91	.389	110	.378	42	2.78	91	15.38	14	9.89	31
	Bases Empty	.280	48	.500	34	.379	22	4.00	66	13.79	8	12.07	51
Tom Brookens	Runners On	.242	123	.381	113	.298	130	3.26	80	6.97	120	15.57	98
	Bases Empty	.240	116	.371	117	.293	128	2.62	101	6.50	116	10.16	29
Darrell Evans	Runners On	.291	52	.556	13	.401	18	6.84	10	16.26	10	13.84	78
	Bases Empty	.226	134	.453	63	.359	40	6.79	14	16.56	2	13.75	63
Kirk Gibson	Runners On	.290	54	.462	57	.392	24	4.52	48	14.29	24	16.54	107
	Bases Empty	.267	71	.511	29	.354	45	5.26	36	10.93	28	24.17	146
Mike Heath	Runners On	.301	43	.451	67	.365	56	3.54	64	9.38	82	13.28	69
	Bases Empty	.268	68	.414	87	.320	94	2.55	105	5.33	137	14.79	77
Larry Herndon	Runners On	.302	41	.500	29	.365	56	5.66	25	11.11	57	15.08	94
	Bases Empty	.345	4	.538	22	.391	13	2.52	108	7.03	104	12.50	56
Chet Lemon	Runners On	.295	48	.498	35	.390	28	3.69	62	12.36	39	11.97	53
	Bases Empty	.261	82	.466	52	.364	34	4.74	46	12.93	14	17.35	109
Bill Madlock	Runners On	.306	35	.472	49	.388	30	4.17	55	7.30	114	10.11	37
	Bases Empty	.258	87	.451	64	.318	100	4.40	56	7.58	96	13.64	61
Matt Nokes	Runners On	.290	53	.465	55	.324	110	4.90	36	4.91	149	17.36	113
	Bases Empty	.287	38	.616	5	.366	32	9.26	2	9.05	61	9.88	23
Pat Sheridan	Runners On	.270	78	.367	122	.324	111	1.02	137	8.14	102	20.36	140
	Bases Empty	.249	104	.356	127	.329	73	1.78	124	10.32	37	17.86	117
Alan Trammell	Runners On	.322	22	.490	38	.388	30	3.36	73	10.23	66	7.31	19
	Bases Empty	.365	2	.612	6	.417	3	6.02	25	7.67	94	6.75	7
Lou Whitaker	Runners On	.207	153	.357	129	.282	145	3.29	77	9.80	72	16.33	105
	Bases Empty	.297	27	.465	54	.374	25	2.30	111	10.71	30	15.49	84
Team Average	Runners On	.273	6	.437	5	.348	5	3.72	2	10.18	3	14.14	4
	Bases Empty	.271	3	.463	1	.350	1	4.21	1	10.09	1	14.19	2
League Average	Runners On	.271		.428		.343		3.25		9.68		14.87	
	Bases Empty	.260		.424		.326		3.49		8.34		15.79	

Overall Batting Compared to Late Inning Pressure Situations

		BA	Rank	SA	Rank	OBA	Rank	HR %	Rank	BB %	Rank	SO %	Rank	RDI %	Rank
Dave Bergman	Overall	.273	66	.453	63	.379	24	3.49	81	14.49	13	11.11	36	.259	112
	Pressure	.259	89	.481	44	.323	96	7.41	13	9.68	76	19.35	110	.167	133
Tom Brookens	Overall	.241	129	.376	120	.295	146	2.93	96	6.73	122	12.86	54	.252	123
	Pressure	.275	69	.400	87	.310	110	2.50	84	4.65	141	13.95	68	.143	140
Darrell Evans	Overall	.257	100	.501	22	.379	23	6.81	6	16.42	5	13.79	71	.318	48
	Pressure	.270	76	.397	91	.370	54	3.17	69	12.16	41	8.11	19	.167	133
Kirk Gibson	Overall	.277	58	.489	30	.372	29	4.93	37	12.50	20	20.60	138	.320	46
	Pressure	.311	37	.578	15	.466	7	6.67	19	20.69	5	22.41	127	.222	106
Mike Heath	Overall	.281	46	.430	80	.339	70	2.96	94	7.07	110	14.14	76	.259	114
	Pressure	.150	159	.225	153	.222	155	0.00	119	8.70	87	17.39	95	.333	51
Larry Herndon	Overall	.324	8	.520	19	.378	26	4.00	65	9.06	74	13.78	67	.348	22
	Pressure	.394	8	.485	41	.444	11	0.00	119	8.33	91	16.67	90	.143	--
Chet Lemon	Overall	.277	60	.481	35	.376	28	4.26	59	12.66	19	14.83	86	.322	45
	Pressure	.130	164	.185	162	.217	158	0.00	119	10.00	68	21.67	120	.500	5
Bill Madlock	Overall	.279	51	.460	53	.351	57	4.29	57	7.45	105	11.97	47	.326	42
	Pressure	.448	2	.621	7	.500	3	3.45	65	8.11	96	5.41	6	.500	5
Jim Morrison	Overall	.205	--	.333	--	.221	--	3.42	--	1.64	--	21.31	--	.232	141
	Pressure	.000	--	.000	--	.100	--	0.00	--	0.00	--	10.00	--	.200	--
Matt Nokes	Overall	.289	36	.536	15	.345	64	6.94	5	6.89	115	13.78	67	.240	133
	Pressure	.241	108	.407	82	.268	140	5.56	36	3.51	149	15.79	83	.500	5
Pat Sheridan	Overall	.259	94	.361	134	.327	90	1.43	133	9.30	68	19.03	128	.262	111
	Pressure	.182	146	.273	142	.229	153	2.27	93	4.17	144	14.58	77	.091	155
Alan Trammell	Overall	.343	3	.551	9	.402	7	4.69	44	8.98	76	7.04	10	.302	67
	Pressure	.431	4	.615	8	.466	6	4.62	46	8.22	95	9.59	33	.407	26
Lou Whitaker	Overall	.265	83	.427	84	.341	68	2.65	103	10.38	51	15.79	93	.247	126
	Pressure	.290	55	.464	54	.319	101	2.90	77	4.00	146	22.67	129	.158	138
Team Average	Overall	.272	4	.451	1	.349	2	3.98	1	10.13	1	14.17	3	.284	9
	Pressure	.265	5	.407	8	.336	6	3.12	9	9.02	10	15.30	3	.251	11
League Average	Overall	.265		.425		.333		3.38		8.94		15.38		.287	
	Pressure	.262		.405		.335		3.07		9.43		16.58		.280	

Additional Miscellaneous Batting Comparisons

	Grass Surface BA	Rank	Artificial Surface BA	Rank	Home Games BA	Rank	Road Games BA	Rank	Runners in Scoring Position BA	Rank	Runners in Scoring Pos and Two Outs BA	Rank	Leading Off Inning OBA	Rank	Runners on 3B with less than 2 Outs RDI %	Rank
Dave Bergman	.278	61	.238	--	.306	--	.241	112	.209	139	.200	127	.308	105	.667	--
Tom Brookens	.254	106	.167	156	.226	140	.254	93	.234	123	.257	77	.307	108	.476	133
Darrell Evans	.255	104	.266	73	.248	117	.265	76	.286	60	.368	6	.328	84	.531	111
Kirk Gibson	.280	56	.265	74	.242	121	.312	21	.279	72	.255	80	.333	69	.655	43
Mike Heath	.291	41	.233	114	.297	48	.264	78	.275	74	.206	121	.362	45	.500	120
Larry Herndon	.308	21	.400	3	.313	25	.336	4	.284	67	.258	72	.465	--	.650	45
Chet Lemon	.276	69	.282	54	.260	102	.291	32	.320	27	.239	96	.325	88	.462	138
Bill Madlock	.278	62	.286	47	.270	84	.287	38	.267	86	.314	28	.414	11	.609	64
Jim Morrison	.193	--	.235	--	.098	--	.263	--	.150	--	.050	--	.292	--	.750	9
Matt Nokes	.309	20	.159	158	.308	30	.271	63	.234	122	.265	68	.394	17	.500	120
Pat Sheridan	.261	96	.239	107	.278	72	.244	109	.293	49	.281	54	.333	69	.560	96
Alan Trammell	.352	3	.297	36	.348	5	.339	3	.297	45	.301	38	.433	7	.587	89
Lou Whitaker	.263	94	.276	59	.261	97	.268	71	.161	156	.141	148	.406	14	.606	68
Team Average	.276	4	.245	10	.270	6	.273	1	.256	11	.246	7	.362	1	.569	10
League Average	.267		.261		.270		.260		.266		.247		.328		.581	

Pitching vs. Left and Right Handed Batters

		BA	Rank	SA	Rank	OBA	Rank	HR %	Rank	BB %	Rank	SO %	Rank
Doyle Alexander	vs. Lefties	.199	8	.258	2	.288	11	0.66	5	11.18	95	12.35	84
	vs. Righties	.204	6	.265	1	.237	3	1.23	8	4.12	6	13.53	86
Mike Henneman	vs. Lefties	.241	29	.412	59	.328	51	3.53	82	10.42	84	15.10	53
	vs. Righties	.234	32	.297	5	.273	14	1.04	6	4.83	15	22.22	21
Eric King	vs. Lefties	.240	27	.358	21	.332	55	2.18	27	11.74	103	17.80	32
	vs. Righties	.262	68	.430	74	.355	96	4.67	108	11.65	109	16.87	51
Jack Morris	vs. Lefties	.236	21	.441	80	.313	33	5.25	113	10.17	80	15.67	48
	vs. Righties	.218	18	.333	14	.269	12	2.38	28	6.39	29	22.75	18
Dan Petry	vs. Lefties	.272	73	.433	73	.367	102	3.15	66	12.96	114	13.62	70
	vs. Righties	.285	99	.491	110	.383	115	5.05	114	11.31	105	15.90	58
Jeff M. Robinson	vs. Lefties	.227	12	.397	51	.312	30	3.25	69	11.08	93	14.87	56
	vs. Righties	.304	110	.432	77	.375	109	3.08	68	7.51	52	20.16	30
Frank Tanana	vs. Lefties	.236	20	.364	26	.296	14	2.86	52	7.24	33	21.05	10
	vs. Righties	.260	65	.419	69	.304	39	3.27	74	5.83	21	14.77	72
Walt Terrell	vs. Lefties	.257	50	.419	63	.326	50	3.16	67	9.19	68	12.95	75
	vs. Righties	.280	95	.430	75	.340	78	3.18	72	8.59	72	14.12	79
Mark Thurmond	vs. Lefties	.275	78	.363	23	.330	52	1.10	12	8.74	60	9.71	115
	vs. Righties	.363	126	.525	119	.415	125	2.50	35	8.47	70	6.21	126
Team Average	vs. Lefties	.245	1	.407	5	.325	1	3.42	10	10.46	13	14.37	8
	vs. Righties	.265	8	.407	4	.326	5	3.06	4	7.77	4	16.56	6
League Average	vs. Lefties	.267		.427		.338		3.30		9.47		14.54	
	vs. Righties	.264		.424		.330		3.45		8.56		15.98	

Pitching with Runners on Base and Bases Empty

		BA	Rank	SA	Rank	OBA	Rank	HR %	Rank	BB %	Rank	SO %	Rank
Doyle Alexander	Runners On	.214	8	.291	4	.314	31	0.97	5	12.61	110	12.61	88
	Bases Empty	.195	6	.248	2	.235	2	0.95	5	4.98	17	13.12	90
Mike Henneman	Runners On	.210	7	.290	2	.284	6	1.70	17	9.05	65	18.59	25
	Bases Empty	.263	73	.409	57	.315	48	2.69	41	6.00	34	19.00	31
Eric King	Runners On	.260	59	.403	57	.365	98	3.06	71	13.98	120	17.37	31
	Bases Empty	.243	37	.385	38	.325	66	3.64	79	9.75	92	17.33	42
Jack Morris	Runners On	.225	14	.368	27	.305	23	3.30	81	10.26	86	16.71	39
	Bases Empty	.229	24	.403	53	.286	18	4.27	100	7.33	48	20.23	24
Dan Petry	Runners On	.275	78	.484	101	.366	101	5.04	109	10.97	95	13.87	77
	Bases Empty	.282	99	.443	89	.384	117	3.30	66	13.21	117	15.72	60
Jeff M. Robinson	Runners On	.350	122	.579	122	.437	98	4.57	98	12.45	107	14.59	65
	Bases Empty	.205	8	.306	7	.274	10	2.28	21	7.44	50	19.05	30
Frank Tanana	Runners On	.268	70	.367	25	.315	36	1.81	21	6.86	27	14.78	63
	Bases Empty	.248	46	.438	85	.294	23	4.10	96	5.50	25	16.51	48
Walt Terrell	Runners On	.256	51	.415	70	.331	57	2.85	62	10.51	88	14.32	68
	Bases Empty	.276	95	.431	78	.334	81	3.39	72	7.70	52	12.95	93
Mark Thurmond	Runners On	.314	111	.451	89	.359	91	1.96	24	7.60	37	7.60	124
	Bases Empty	.357	--	.490	--	.422	--	2.04	--	10.09	--	7.34	--
Team Average	Runners On	.265	5	.415	5	.344	9	3.05	5	10.57	12	14.52	10
	Bases Empty	.249	3	.401	2	.311	2	3.35	6	7.74	3	16.40	6
League Average	Runners On	.271		.428		.343		3.25		9.68		14.87	
	Bases Empty	.260		.424		.326		3.49		8.34		15.79	

Overall Pitching Compared to Late Inning Pressure Situations

		BA	Rank	SA	Rank	OBA	Rank	HR %	Rank	BB %	Rank	SO %	Rank
Doyle Alexander	Overall	.201	3	.262	1	.263	3	0.96	1	7.65	40	12.94	85
	Pressure	.207	19	.276	11	.303	35	0.00	1	11.76	98	11.76	101
Mike Henneman	Overall	.238	20	.351	12	.300	17	2.21	16	7.52	38	18.80	28
	Pressure	.177	4	.274	10	.250	6	1.77	42	7.20	39	21.60	21
Willie Hernandez	Overall	.276	--	.469	--	.340	--	4.17	--	9.22	--	13.82	--
	Pressure	.271	77	.448	91	.355	80	3.13	74	11.61	93	15.18	61
Eric King	Overall	.251	42	.393	41	.343	76	3.39	80	11.70	115	17.35	39
	Pressure	.267	73	.335	33	.353	79	1.24	34	11.29	90	16.67	54
Jack Morris	Overall	.228	11	.391	37	.293	11	3.92	93	8.45	61	18.89	26
	Pressure	.235	46	.434	84	.291	26	5.15	113	7.43	41	17.57	45
Dan Petry	Overall	.279	89	.463	101	.375	116	4.14	98	12.10	117	14.81	64
	Pressure	.294	97	.647	125	.400	118	8.82	126	12.20	100	12.20	96
Jeff M. Robinson	Overall	.262	64	.413	56	.340	73	3.17	68	9.49	82	17.22	40
	Pressure	.189	6	.270	9	.250	6	2.70	64	7.32	40	17.07	50
Nate Snell	Overall	.267	--	.438	--	.349	--	3.42	--	11.31	--	11.31	--
	Pressure	.190	7	.286	15	.261	9	0.00	1	8.33	53	14.58	68
Frank Tanana	Overall	.256	53	.410	52	.302	21	3.20	70	6.06	19	15.80	51
	Pressure	.273	79	.377	57	.291	28	0.00	1	2.50	2	15.00	63
Walt Terrell	Overall	.268	76	.424	71	.333	69	3.17	67	8.89	70	13.53	80
	Pressure	.303	104	.535	114	.364	91	6.06	120	9.09	62	10.00	106
Mark Thurmond	Overall	.331	124	.466	102	.384	119	1.99	11	8.57	64	7.50	127
	Pressure	.302	103	.465	99	.367	96	4.65	106	10.00	73	6.00	124
Team Average	Overall	.256	3	.407	3	.325	3	3.22	5	8.98	10	15.57	7
	Pressure	.251	5	.396	6	.323	3	2.95	8	9.34	5	15.16	10
League Average	Overall	.265		.425		.333		3.38		8.94		15.38	
	Pressure	.262		.404		.337		2.99		9.73		16.42	

Additional Miscellaneous Pitching Comparisons

	Grass Surface		Artificial Surface		Home Games		Road Games		Runners in Scoring Position		Runners in Scoring Pos and Two Outs		Leading Off Inning	
	BA	Rank	BA	Rank	BA	Rank	BA	Rank	BA	Rank	BA	Rank	OBA	Rank
Doyle Alexander	.191	2	.227	25	.221	18	.185	4	.189	--	.167	--	.264	15
Mike Henneman	.239	19	.230	30	.178	4	.290	92	.184	6	.170	10	.301	40
Willie Hernandez	.269	75	.353	--	.300	--	.262	53	.295	95	.290	99	.325	--
Eric King	.253	47	.229	29	.281	97	.221	9	.239	40	.224	53	.297	36
Jack Morris	.222	7	.266	74	.220	17	.239	22	.176	4	.082	1	.272	19
Dan Petry	.275	85	.293	97	.274	94	.283	86	.253	55	.225	55	.380	110
Jeff M. Robinson	.258	58	.277	87	.223	19	.295	99	.366	124	.364	122	.226	3
Frank Tanana	.253	48	.269	79	.228	24	.283	87	.251	51	.233	59	.319	50
Walt Terrell	.261	61	.312	103	.229	26	.315	116	.256	61	.189	22	.316	49
Mark Thurmond	.337	124	.125	--	.325	--	.336	125	.308	103	.326	109	.451	--
Team Average	.253	1	.272	10	.237	2	.275	9	.250	4	.219	1	.306	1
League Average	.267		.261		.260		.270		.266		.247		.328	

KANSAS CITY ROYALS

More than 100 years ago, Ralph Waldo Emerson said that the world would beat a path to the door of any man who could write a better book, preach a better sermon, or build a better mousetrap. If Ralphie-boy were alive today, he'd surely add to that list the ability to build a better lineup.

Anyone who's listened to radio call-in shows knows that nearly every baseball fan thinks he or she can put together a batting order that would produce more runs than the one his team's manager prefers: Move Boggs to the leadoff spot; protect Strawberry with a right-handed power hitter; switch Raines to the middle of the order; get Trammell out of the cleanup position; put speed at the top, a contact hitter behind him; and so on, and so on.

At first it seemed to us that this whole lineup business has been exaggerated. Bat Wade Boggs leadoff and you weaken the middle of the order; bat him third, and you lose the best leadoff hitter in the majors. But one thing's for certain: Even the staunchest advocates of the DH rule aren't about to allow Boggs to bat first *and* third. (That is right, isn't it guys?) No matter the batting order, you've got the same nine players; you just can't create a whole that's significantly greater than the sum of the parts.

On the other hand, 23 of the 40 division titles over the past 10 years were decided by three games or less, so even a *slight* improvement in a team's batting order could have enormous implications. So we decided to take an up–close–and–personal look at some of the most popular rules of lineup construction. We found that much of the conventional wisdom on the subject is invalid. And no team proves that point better than the Kansas City Royals.

Here's a typical Kansas City lineup from last season, composed of the batters with the most plate appearances in each of the nine batting slots. We've also built a lineup that's not so different, but one that conforms to the rules that do, in fact, maximize a team's scoring potential:

Actual Order	Proposed Order
Willie Wilson	Kevin Seitzer
Kevin Seitzer	George Brett
George Brett	Bo Jackson
Danny Tartabull	Danny Tartabull
Frank White	Steve Balboni
Bo Jackson	Frank White
Steve Balboni	Larry Owen
Angel Salazar	Angel Salazar
Larry Owen	Willie Wilson

Kansas City's batting order is built upon a commonly held assumption that it's best to cluster your strongest hitters together, maximizing the strength of the "heart of the order." The following tables show Kansas City's composite batting statistics for last season according to batting-order position:

Slot	AB	R	H	2B	3B	HR	RBI	BB	SO	BA	SA	OBA
1	701	112	202	23	15	9	46	35	103	.288	.402	.327
2	649	96	202	32	7	11	78	79	91	.311	.433	.390
3	628	91	178	27	4	26	107	84	74	.283	.463	.365
4	608	80	157	24	2	30	97	82	124	.258	.452	.344
5	609	83	159	35	5	21	94	64	126	.261	.438	.331
6	609	73	149	32	4	23	87	40	146	.245	.424	.295
7	580	70	136	25	2	31	75	56	161	.234	.445	.304
8	564	49	122	18	1	7	47	46	95	.216	.289	.276
9	551	58	138	23	0	10	46	37	114	.250	.347	.298

Notice that Kansas City's batting averages increase steadily from a low of .216 in the eighth slot to .311 in the 2d slot, and then, with only one minor exception, decrease steadily back down to that low. (Don't think of the lineup as a straight line, but as a continuous cycle with a starting point.) As a result, Kansas City's five highest batting averages are bunched together at the top of the order; their four lowest are clustered at the bottom. No team in baseball last season clustered its lineup according to batting average to a greater extent than the Royals. In fact, contrast the shape of K.C.'s batting order to that of the White Sox. Chicago created a series of peaks and valleys, alternating high marks in the eighth (Ken Williams), first (Ozzie Guillen), and third (Harold Baines) slots with horrible averages in the ninth (Ron Karkovice) and second (Gary Redus, Donnie Hill) positions:

	1st	2d	3d	4th	5th	6th	7th	8th	9th
Kansas City	.288	.311	.283	.258	.261	.245	.234	.216	.250
Chicago	.282	.223	.274	.264	.255	.272	.256	.282	.208

The Royals also had the majors' most clustered batting order according to on-base percentage, creating strength at the top of the order and a vacuum at the bottom with the "automatic outs" bunched together. On the other hand, few teams distributed their home run power throughout the order more than Kansas City: The seventh slot generated the most homers, but right behind it, the eighth slot produced the fewest. The fourth slot produced the second-highest total, but behind it the fifth slot ranked only fifth.

But here's the rub, unfortunately for the Royals, bunching

one's home-run hitters is an effective lineup strategy, bunching according to batting average and on-base average is counter-productive. That's just the opposite of their batting order last season.

Let's look at the proof. We used a complex statistical technique called serial correlation—having nothing to do with comparing Trix to Wheaties—to evaluate the extent to which teams clustered their batting orders according to a variety of categories. Last season, the three American League teams that bunched their lineups most according to batting average were Kansas City, Minnesota, and Boston. Now if "batting-average clustering" were the best way to maximize scoring potential, then those teams should have created a greater whole than the sum of their parts; that is, they should have scored more runs than the abilities of their individual players indicated.

We know how many runs each team scored, or "the whole"; the linear weights formula gives us a reliable estimate of "the sum of the parts." The linear weights formula evaluates the components of scoring—singles, doubles, triples, home runs, walks, stolen bases, and some things so obscure even Tim McCarver would have trouble explaining them—and projects the number of runs those factors *should* produce. But because it fails to account for the interaction of a team's batting order, teams with well-constructed lineups ought to outscore their linear weights projections consistently. Here's how the three teams with the most clustered batting averages fared in relation to their linear weights estimates:

Team	Runs	Weights	Diff.
Kansas City	715	750	−35
Minnesota	786	766	+20
Boston	842	827	+15
Totals	2343	2343	0

The three teams combined to score *exactly* the number of runs expected merely by evaluating their players individually. To put it in plain English, the batting orders they used failed to increase their scoring potential. And when we examined data from other seasons, we found that there was actually a slight *negative* bias for teams that had clustered their lineups according to batting average. From 1982 through 1987, teams that ranked among the top three in the American League each season in batting-average clustering scored 20 fewer runs than expected (an average of 1.1 per season). Those that clustered by on-base average also scored less than expected (by less than one run per season).

In contrast, when we examined the three teams in each season that bunched their players according to slugging average or home runs to the greatest degree, we found an advantage: *The 18 teams (three in each season since 1982) that most clustered their home run hitters scored an average of 3.8 more runs than expected; those clustered by slugging average scored 10.4 runs more than projected.*

We'll be the first to admit that those aren't earth-shaking differences. But there are two points to remember. First, it's often easy to demonstrate statistically that a trend exists, even if the effects are slight. The odds that 18 teams with clustered slugging averages would outscore their estimates by 10 runs per season merely by chance is 47 to one. Second, as we pointed out earlier, most division races are decided by three games or less, so an increase of 10 runs over the course of a season could affect the outcome of a pennant race.

We also looked at several specific lineup features to which many managers subscribe: leadoff hitters who draw lots of walks, or reach base often; second-slot hitters who rarely strike out; and batting the leading home run hitter in the cleanup spot. The reviews were mixed.

Walking to Victory

Over the past six seasons, 15 American League teams got more walks from the leadoff position than from any other slot in the lineup. On 17 others, the leadoff position ranked second in bases on balls. The complete breakdown of A.L. teams since 1982 according to where their leadoff hitters ranked on the team in walks:

1st	2d	3d	4th	5th	6th	7th	8th	9th
15	17	5	5	2	8	5	7	6

The teams whose leadoff batters ranked among the top four slots in walks scored an average of 9.9 runs more (relative to expectations) than the other teams. Among the starters in Kansas City's usual lineup, its leadoff hitter, Willie Wilson, had only the eighth-highest walks ratio. That probably cost the Royals about five runs.

Twenty A.L. teams had leadoff positions with the highest on-base averages of any slot in the batting order. They scored an average of 1.2 more runs than expected. (The advantage was much greater in the National League, raising the edge to 4.1 runs on a major-league-wide basis.) Wilson's on-base average was 79 points lower than Kevin Seitzer's, whom we consider Kansas City's best leadoff hitter.

The 12 teams whose second-slot batters had the fewest strikeouts scored an average of 4.7 more runs than expected. So in making out our Royals' lineup, we've moved George Brett, who struck out only once per 10.8 plate appearances last season, to the second spot.

The breakdown of the batting-order position that produced the most home runs on each American League team over the past six seasons:

1st	2d	3d	4th	5th	6th	7th	8th	9th
1	4	10	30	15	7	2	1	0

Nearly half the teams generated their highest home run totals from the cleanup position, but those 30 teams fell an average of 1.7 runs short of their expected totals. More surprising is the fact that the teams that had their highest totals from the fifth through eighth slots in the order performed 5.41 runs per season better than those with their highest totals earlier in the order. The Royals got this one right: Steve Balboni, whose average of one home run for every 16.1 at bats was the best ratio among the starters, batted seventh for Kansas City. We've moved him to fifth in our ideal lineup.

That proposed lineup incorporates all the concepts that we've studied: clustering according to slugging percentage and home runs; distribution of the highest batting averages throughout the order; batting the on-base average leader in the leadoff position; batting the best contact hitter in the second spot; and batting the best home run hitter lower than the cleanup slot.

How many runs would such a lineup add to Kansas City's production? Truthfully, probably no more than 10 to 15 compared to a typical American League batting order—but maybe as many as 20 more runs than the Royals managed with their poorly-constructed 1987 batting order. Not a huge total, we agree, but enough to make a difference in a tight pennant race? You bet.

The "DH" Factor

Incidentally, we'd be delinquent not to mention that the rules for constructing the most productive batting order differ between the two leagues on account of the designated hitter. It's particularly important to note that clustering of any type—whether by batting, slugging, or on-base average, or home runs—is detrimental to scoring in the National League. Teams that intermingle their best hitters with their worst fare much better in the N.L. than those that bunch their good hitters together.

The following table compares the three N.L. teams in each of the past six seasons with the most clustered batting orders to those with the least clustered (that is, the most evenly distributed). The differences (expressed in runs per season) aren't drastic, but they are significant:

	BA	SA	OBA	HR
Most clustered	−1.0	−7.8	−2.6	+0.3
Least clustered	+3.6	+5.3	+6.6	+4.0

Notice that the greatest gain is made by distributing the players with the highest on-base averages. This suggests that it's important *not* to bunch the so-called automatic outs together. Placing your weak hitters together in front of the pitcher is a poor strategy.

The leadoff hitter's walk potential is of lesser importance but his on-base potential is heightened in the National League; the ability of the second-place hitter to make contact is also of greater importance. And teams are at no disadvantage with their best home run hitters batting cleanup, although batting them any higher than that had disastrous effects, costing the teams an average of 15.5 runs per season. That effect is logical, considering that a home run hitter batting third in the National League has diminished RBI potential on account of the universally unproductive ninth position.

Building a Powerful Staff...

They've broken up that ol' gang. Over the past three seasons, Charlie Leibrandt, Danny Jackson, Bret Saberhagen, Mark Gubicza, and Bud Black started 427 of Kansas City's 486 games. No other major-league team had as stable a starting staff during that period. The last pitcher other than those five to start 20 games in one season for the Royals was Larry Gura in 1984, though it seems like ages ago.

All that will change in 1988, this year following the off-season trade that sent Jackson to Cincinnati for right-hander Ted Power in a deal that also exchanged Argenis Salazar for Kurt Stillwell. What makes this transaction particularly noteworthy is that for several seasons, the pitching-rich Royals were criticized for refusing to sacrifice one of their arms for a badly-needed piece of lumber. But the addition of Danny Tartabull last season and the rapid development of Kevin Seitzer and Bo "T.D." Jackson bolstered Kansas City's attack giving GM John Schuerholz several options.

Schuerholz has gambled that the Royals' bats will remain potent, dealing Danny Jackson not for a hitter, but for a pitcher who is arguably the most versatile in the majors. Power saved 27 games for Cincinnati 1985, but was promoted to the rotation in September 1986 when John Franco's emergence in the Reds' bullpen made Power more valuable as a starter. Ted compiled a 17–17 record during his time in the rotation. Over the past several years, only one other pitcher saved more than 10 games in a season and subsequently won as many as 10 games in one season as a starter. And that pitcher, Brian Fisher, had barely half the saves in his best season in relief (14 saves in 1985) as Power had in 1985. Given the uncertainty surrounding Dan Quisenberry's future as a reliable stopper, Power's flexibility gives Kansas City an edge that few pitchers could provide.

WON-LOST RECORD BY STARTING POSITION

KANSAS CITY 83-79	C	1B	2B	3B	SS	LF	CF	RF	P	DH	Leadoff	Relief	Starts
Rick Anderson	-	-	-	-	-	-	-	-	0-2	-	-	1-3	0-2
Steve Balboni	-	30-24	-	-	-	-	-	-	-	26-24	-	-	56-48
Juan Beniquez	-	2-3	-	3-2	-	7-7	0-1	2-1	-	7-5	4-2	-	21-19
Buddy Biancalana	-	-	2-3	-	3-4	-	-	-	-	-	-	-	5-7
Bud Black	-	-	-	-	-	-	-	-	11-7	-	-	5-6	11-7
Thad Bosley	-	-	-	-	-	5-0	-	3-4	-	5-7	-	-	13-11
George Brett	-	41-42	-	6-5	-	-	-	-	-	10-11	-	-	57-58
John Davis	-	-	-	-	-	-	-	-	-	-	-	13-14	-
Jim Eisenreich	-	-	-	-	-	-	-	-	-	11-14	-	-	11-14
Steve Farr	-	-	-	-	-	-	-	-	-	-	-	12-35	
Gene Garber	-	-	-	-	-	-	-	-	-	-	-	9-4	
Jerry Don Gleaton	-	-	-	-	-	-	-	-	-	-	-	18-30	
Mark Gubicza	-	-	-	-	-	-	-	-	15-20	-	-	-	15-20
Dave Gumpert	-	-	-	-	-	-	-	-	-	-	-	1-7	
Ed Hearn	3-2	-	-	-	-	-	-	-	-	-	-	-	3-2
Bo Jackson	-	-	-	-	-	42-47	11-4	2-1	-	0-1	-	-	55-53
Danny Jackson	-	-	-	-	-	-	-	-	12-22	-	-	1-1	12-22
Ross Jones	-	-	1-0	-	17-18	-	-	-	-	-	-	-	18-18
Charlie Leibrandt	-	-	-	-	-	-	-	-	21-14	-	-	-	21-14
Mike MacFarlane	2-5	-	-	-	-	-	-	-	-	-	-	-	2-5
Scotti Madison	3-0	1-0	-	-	-	-	-	-	-	-	-	-	4-0
Hal McRae	-	-	-	-	-	-	-	-	-	5-1	-	-	5-1
Jorge Orta	-	-	-	-	-	-	-	-	-	7-4	-	-	7-4
Larry Owen	27-32	-	-	-	-	-	-	-	-	-	-	-	27-32
Bill Pecota	-	-	3-3	4-3	17-9	-	-	-	-	-	-	-	24-15
Melido Perez	-	-	-	-	-	-	-	-	2-1	-	-	-	2-1
Jamie Quirk	48-40	-	-	-	-	-	-	-	-	-	-	-	48-40
Dan Quisenberry	-	-	-	-	-	-	-	-	-	-	-	23-24	
Bret Saberhagen	-	-	-	-	-	-	-	-	21-12	-	-	-	21-12
Argenis Salazar	-	-	-	-	46-48	-	-	-	-	-	2-3	-	46-48
Kevin Seitzer	-	9-10	-	70-69	-	2-0	-	-	-	1-0	-	-	82-79
Bob Shirley	-	-	-	-	-	-	-	-	-	-	-	0-3	
Lonnie Smith	-	-	-	-	-	14-17	-	-	-	5-9	5-0	-	19-26
Bob Stoddard	-	-	-	-	-	-	-	-	1-1	-	-	2-13	1-1
Danny Tartabull	-	-	-	-	-	-	-	76-73	-	4-2	-	-	80-75
Gary Thurman	-	-	-	-	-	13-8	3-1	-	-	-	2-0	-	16-9
Frank White	-	-	77-73	-	-	-	-	-	-	1-0	-	-	78-73
Willie Wilson	-	-	-	-	-	-	69-73	-	-	1-1	70-74	-	70-74

Batting vs. Left and Right Handed Pitchers

		BA	Rank	SA	Rank	OBA	Rank	HR %	Rank	BB %	Rank	SO %	Rank
Steve Balboni	vs. Lefties	.194	153	.379	108	.265	148	5.83	23	8.85	80	23.89	147
	vs. Righties	.212	153	.445	63	.276	151	6.36	19	7.69	100	22.44	145
Thad Bosley	vs. Lefties	.357	--	.429	--	.400	--	0.00	--	6.67	--	33.33	--
	vs. Righties	.270	74	.349	135	.309	120	0.79	141	5.84	134	15.33	89
George Brett	vs. Lefties	.268	77	.430	75	.317	97	4.70	41	7.32	111	13.41	69
	vs. Righties	.302	26	.532	19	.422	4	5.40	29	17.44	7	7.27	17
Bo Jackson	vs. Lefties	.248	100	.496	35	.315	98	6.19	17	8.06	98	37.10	163
	vs. Righties	.230	139	.438	69	.288	140	5.30	32	6.45	124	36.13	161
Larry Owen	vs. Lefties	.226	130	.419	84	.291	129	5.38	28	8.49	87	21.70	136
	vs. Righties	.141	--	.183	--	.218	--	0.00	--	8.54	--	34.15	--
Jamie Quirk	vs. Lefties	.235	--	.294	--	.316	--	0.00	--	5.26	--	21.05	--
	vs. Righties	.237	124	.348	136	.307	122	1.79	120	8.57	84	16.51	98
Argenis Salazar	vs. Lefties	.198	150	.286	147	.207	162	2.20	106	1.09	163	16.30	95
	vs. Righties	.208	156	.230	161	.224	162	0.00	156	2.08	162	12.92	63
Kevin Seitzer	vs. Lefties	.309	29	.434	71	.386	29	1.14	131	11.17	41	10.15	36
	vs. Righties	.328	8	.483	40	.404	10	2.79	98	10.98	40	12.31	55
Lonnie Smith	vs. Lefties	.280	--	.380	--	.390	--	0.00	--	15.25	--	13.56	--
	vs. Righties	.239	120	.350	133	.341	72	2.56	104	10.87	42	16.67	101
Danny Tartabull	vs. Lefties	.289	48	.503	31	.389	27	4.70	41	14.29	19	22.29	139
	vs. Righties	.316	14	.554	15	.390	19	6.24	20	10.98	41	19.72	130
Frank White	vs. Lefties	.284	56	.453	61	.352	62	3.38	72	9.09	72	10.91	43
	vs. Righties	.231	134	.381	114	.292	133	2.89	96	7.84	94	14.81	81
Willie Wilson	vs. Lefties	.241	107	.312	138	.270	145	0.59	143	3.91	153	19.55	121
	vs. Righties	.293	35	.402	94	.340	73	0.68	146	5.27	145	11.18	43
Team Average	vs. Lefties	.263	9	.416	11	.327	9	3.17	8	8.52	10	17.41	13
	vs. Righties	.262	8	.411	12	.328	10	3.01	12	8.54	11	16.68	12
League Average	vs. Lefties	.265		.422		.333		3.29		8.94		15.64	
	vs. Righties	.265		.427		.334		3.43		8.94		15.26	

Batting with Runners on Base and Bases Empty

		BA	Rank	SA	Rank	OBA	Rank	HR %	Rank	BB %	Rank	SO %	Rank
Steve Balboni	Runners On	.216	145	.442	70	.262	157	5.79	22	6.31	129	20.87	141
	Bases Empty	.199	158	.413	88	.283	140	6.63	16	9.59	51	24.66	148
George Brett	Runners On	.286	60	.437	73	.387	34	3.46	68	15.25	17	8.87	24
	Bases Empty	.296	28	.566	14	.389	16	7.14	9	12.83	15	9.73	20
Bo Jackson	Runners On	.207	152	.363	126	.258	158	3.35	74	6.15	131	38.46	162
	Bases Empty	.258	88	.530	26	.326	80	7.37	7	7.53	97	34.73	162
Jamie Quirk	Runners On	.284	61	.422	80	.351	72	1.72	118	8.82	93	14.71	91
	Bases Empty	.206	156	.294	152	.278	147	1.67	130	8.08	78	18.18	118
Argenis Salazar	Runners On	.200	155	.231	161	.211	162	0.77	144	1.42	162	12.77	64
	Bases Empty	.209	153	.257	161	.225	160	0.53	148	2.09	161	14.66	73
Kevin Seitzer	Runners On	.307	34	.470	50	.391	26	2.65	96	12.21	40	13.20	68
	Bases Empty	.334	8	.469	50	.405	8	2.12	115	10.19	40	10.66	34
Lonnie Smith	Runners On	.226	--	.283	--	.338	--	0.00	--	13.85	--	12.31	--
	Bases Empty	.263	77	.395	100	.364	35	2.63	100	11.36	25	17.42	111
Danny Tartabull	Runners On	.302	40	.517	22	.378	43	5.56	27	11.48	53	19.64	134
	Bases Empty	.316	16	.565	15	.402	9	6.12	23	12.20	19	21.13	136
Frank White	Runners On	.269	82	.417	88	.334	90	2.27	105	9.00	90	12.33	59
	Bases Empty	.224	139	.385	107	.284	139	3.68	77	7.41	100	15.12	81
Willie Wilson	Runners On	.271	77	.367	123	.318	116	0.00	150	5.05	146	11.01	46
	Bases Empty	.282	45	.382	110	.322	88	0.97	140	4.83	143	14.71	75
Team Average	Runners On	.264	10	.409	11	.329	11	2.66	12	8.89	12	15.98	12
	Bases Empty	.261	6	.415	8	.326	7	3.36	10	8.25	7	17.59	12
League Average	Runners On	.271		.428		.343		3.25		9.68		14.87	
	Bases Empty	.260		.424		.326		3.49		8.34		15.79	

Overall Batting Compared to Late Inning Pressure Situations

		BA	Rank	SA	Rank	OBA	Rank	HR %	Rank	BB %	Rank	SO %	Rank	RDI %	Rank
Steve Balboni	Overall	.207	159	.427	83	.273	157	6.22	11	8.00	95	22.82	148	.179	160
	Pressure	.197	138	.492	37	.219	157	9.84	3	3.13	150	26.56	150	.143	140
Thad Bosley	Overall	.279	--	.357	--	.318	--	0.71	--	5.92	--	17.11	--	.255	116
	Pressure	.313	34	.313	130	.395	30	0.00	119	13.16	33	18.42	104	.250	91
George Brett	Overall	.290	33	.496	28	.388	16	5.15	30	14.17	14	9.25	24	.338	31
	Pressure	.302	45	.472	48	.397	29	3.77	57	14.29	24	9.52	29	.421	18
Bo Jackson	Overall	.235	141	.455	61	.296	145	5.56	22	6.91	114	36.41	162	.194	158
	Pressure	.234	117	.319	129	.339	79	2.13	98	12.50	40	33.93	162	.133	142
Jamie Quirk	Overall	.236	137	.345	145	.307	118	1.69	126	8.38	85	16.77	105	.357	18
	Pressure	.333	21	.487	38	.381	39	0.00	119	4.76	139	14.29	70	.400	27
Argenis Salazar	Overall	.205	160	.246	161	.219	162	0.63	150	1.81	162	13.86	72	.209	154
	Pressure	.179	149	.214	155	.179	163	0.00	119	0.00	161	29.03	156	.000	158
Kevin Seitzer	Overall	.323	9	.470	46	.399	10	2.34	115	11.03	40	11.72	42	.312	55
	Pressure	.342	17	.447	63	.400	26	0.00	119	9.41	78	11.76	47	.333	51
Danny Tartabull	Overall	.309	15	.541	13	.390	11	5.84	17	11.84	28	20.39	134	.269	107
	Pressure	.274	70	.507	30	.312	107	5.48	38	5.19	133	22.08	122	.250	91
Frank White	Overall	.245	120	.400	104	.308	117	3.02	92	8.17	91	13.78	69	.280	89
	Pressure	.185	145	.308	133	.274	137	3.08	72	10.53	61	9.21	28	.174	131
Willie Wilson	Overall	.279	53	.377	119	.320	99	0.66	149	4.90	150	13.48	60	.231	144
	Pressure	.347	16	.500	31	.382	38	0.00	119	5.13	136	14.10	69	.211	114
Team Average	Overall	.262	8	.412	13	.328	10	3.06	12	8.53	10	16.87	12	.266	14
	Pressure	.265	6	.403	9	.329	9	2.33	12	8.58	11	17.95	12	.238	13
League Average	Overall	.265		.425		.333		3.38		8.94		15.38		.287	
	Pressure	.262		.405		.335		3.07		9.43		16.58		.280	

Additional Miscellaneous Batting Comparisons

	Grass Surface BA	Rank	Artificial Surface BA	Rank	Home Games BA	Rank	Road Games BA	Rank	Runners in Scoring Position BA	Rank	Runners in Scoring Pos and Two Outs BA	Rank	Leading Off Inning OBA	Rank	Runners on 3B with less than 2 Outs RDI %	Rank
Steve Balboni	.226	143	.196	146	.189	157	.224	133	.185	150	.172	142	.216	155	.320	161
Thad Bosley	.273	--	.284	49	.348	--	.245	104	.333	--	.333	--	.281	--	.667	--
George Brett	.325	9	.270	64	.268	86	.316	15	.319	28	.220	111	.333	69	.788	4
Jim Eisenreich	.167	--	.267	70	.302	--	.173	--	.219	--	.250	84	.105	--	1.000	--
Bo Jackson	.178	161	.272	62	.284	65	.186	159	.194	146	.250	84	.333	69	.350	158
Ross Jones	.178	--	.304	26	.313	--	.170	--	.172	--	.308	--	.375	--	.800	--
Larry Owen	.194	--	.186	150	.189	--	.189	157	.175	--	.250	84	.250	--	.429	--
Bill Pecota	.255	--	.287	46	.250	--	.303	--	.256	--	.167	--	.342	--	.600	--
Jamie Quirk	.281	--	.209	136	.218	149	.255	91	.271	80	.257	75	.263	141	.900	1
Argenis Salazar	.232	--	.184	152	.182	159	.222	139	.234	124	.190	134	.183	162	.500	120
Kevin Seitzer	.320	14	.325	14	.335	9	.311	22	.310	36	.364	7	.371	34	.472	135
Lonnie Smith	.263	--	.242	102	.259	--	.244	106	.111	--	.071	--	.273	134	.600	--
Danny Tartabull	.326	8	.298	35	.291	58	.327	8	.280	70	.192	132	.367	38	.563	95
Gary Thurman	.355	--	.260	79	.227	--	.378	--	.267	--	.143	--	.333	--	.500	--
Frank White	.227	142	.259	82	.273	79	.221	140	.259	95	.228	106	.277	133	.571	92
Willie Wilson	.252	109	.293	40	.296	51	.260	85	.247	107	.211	117	.349	54	.636	50
Team Average	.262	10	.263	8	.268	8	.257	9	.258	9	.234	11	.305	14	.578	9
League Average	.267		.261		.270		.260		.266		.247		.328		.581	

Pitching vs. Left and Right Handed Batters

		BA	Rank	SA	Rank	OBA	Rank	HR %	Rank	BB %	Rank	SO %	Rank
Bud Black	vs. Lefties	.231	14	.393	44	.278	9	3.42	77	6.35	20	15.08	55
	vs. Righties	.277	89	.444	86	.334	71	3.35	77	6.85	36	10.66	112
Steve Farr	vs. Lefties	.274	77	.432	72	.369	106	2.74	48	13.02	115	20.12	15
	vs. Righties	.269	81	.406	59	.339	75	2.36	27	9.21	86	22.59	19
Jerry Don Gleaton	vs. Lefties	.210	--	.306	--	.286	--	1.61	--	9.86	--	22.54	--
	vs. Righties	.219	21	.333	15	.336	73	2.63	44	15.11	120	20.14	31
Mark Gubicza	vs. Lefties	.260	55	.385	38	.350	84	1.95	24	12.10	108	13.95	64
	vs. Righties	.257	60	.383	50	.342	82	2.10	18	10.88	103	18.82	36
Danny Jackson	vs. Lefties	.280	87	.348	15	.333	57	0.62	4	7.91	46	25.42	6
	vs. Righties	.253	56	.368	36	.347	87	1.45	10	11.82	111	13.31	90
Charlie Leibrandt	vs. Lefties	.232	15	.310	9	.273	8	1.29	14	5.36	9	13.69	69
	vs. Righties	.257	59	.408	45	.314	48	2.71	45	7.67	53	15.11	68
Dan Quisenberry	vs. Lefties	.320	123	.466	96	.364	100	1.94	23	6.36	21	10.00	113
	vs. Righties	.253	--	.374	--	.279	--	1.01	--	2.86	--	5.71	--
Bret Saberhagen	vs. Lefties	.242	32	.391	41	.290	12	2.73	47	6.14	17	18.59	26
	vs. Righties	.263	74	.410	64	.298	33	2.81	53	3.85	4	12.15	105
Team Average	vs. Lefties	.261	5	.389	1	.329	3	2.13	1	9.27	7	16.11	4
	vs. Righties	.262	7	.404	3	.331	10	2.48	1	8.78	11	14.50	12
League Average	vs. Lefties	.267		.427		.338		3.30		9.47		14.54	
	vs. Righties	.264		.424		.330		3.45		8.56		15.98	

Pitching with Runners on Base and Bases Empty

		BA	Rank	SA	Rank	OBA	Rank	HR %	Rank	BB %	Rank	SO %	Rank
Bud Black	Runners On	.227	15	.353	18	.288	11	3.38	83	6.96	29	11.30	102
	Bases Empty	.295	110	.493	110	.346	94	3.36	69	6.55	42	12.07	99
Steve Farr	Runners On	.264	65	.381	38	.327	54	2.03	25	8.64	54	23.64	6
	Bases Empty	.280	97	.460	98	.380	115	3.11	58	13.30	119	19.15	29
Mark Gubicza	Runners On	.242	32	.376	34	.334	61	2.89	65	12.09	106	16.04	48
	Bases Empty	.271	85	.390	43	.356	102	1.36	6	11.19	109	16.01	54
Danny Jackson	Runners On	.265	66	.387	49	.344	70	1.80	20	9.91	82	14.98	59
	Bases Empty	.252	53	.345	18	.345	93	0.87	4	12.14	116	15.94	56
Charlie Leibrandt	Runners On	.246	37	.340	14	.322	47	1.66	16	10.12	84	13.49	79
	Bases Empty	.257	62	.425	74	.297	29	3.00	52	5.33	23	15.83	57
Bret Saberhagen	Runners On	.234	25	.361	21	.287	8	2.20	32	6.67	24	14.07	76
	Bases Empty	.263	72	.423	73	.298	31	3.10	57	4.04	8	16.49	49
Team Average	Runners On	.258	3	.384	1	.332	3	2.31	1	9.78	9	14.58	9
	Bases Empty	.264	9	.410	6	.329	9	2.38	1	8.30	11	15.52	9
League Average	Runners On	.271		.428		.343		3.25		9.68		14.87	
	Bases Empty	.260		.424		.326		3.49		8.34		15.79	

Overall Pitching Compared to Late Inning Pressure Situations

		BA	Rank	SA	Rank	OBA	Rank	HR %	Rank	BB %	Rank	SO %	Rank
Bud Black	Overall	.265	72	.432	75	.320	46	3.37	78	6.73	27	11.73	100
	Pressure	.308	107	.538	115	.386	107	2.56	61	11.36	91	20.45	24
John Davis	Overall	.195	--	.248	--	.315	--	0.00	--	14.36	--	13.26	--
	Pressure	.203	14	.253	5	.319	51	0.00	1	14.89	116	13.83	76
Steve Farr	Overall	.271	82	.416	60	.351	92	2.51	30	10.78	104	21.57	18
	Pressure	.327	116	.564	123	.395	112	5.45	116	10.48	80	16.94	51
Jerry Don Gleaton	Overall	.216	--	.324	--	.319	--	2.27	--	13.33	--	20.95	--
	Pressure	.226	38	.290	17	.327	57	1.08	27	12.84	105	19.27	31
Mark Gubicza	Overall	.259	60	.384	33	.347	83	2.02	13	11.58	113	16.02	47
	Pressure	.312	111	.441	89	.381	106	3.23	76	10.38	76	19.81	29
Danny Jackson	Overall	.258	59	.364	17	.345	80	1.30	3	11.11	110	15.49	56
	Pressure	.231	41	.308	22	.289	25	0.96	25	7.83	47	18.26	38
Charlie Leibrandt	Overall	.253	47	.392	40	.307	27	2.48	26	7.29	36	14.88	63
	Pressure	.237	47	.408	73	.314	43	2.63	63	10.47	78	16.28	55
Dan Quisenberry	Overall	.287	--	.421	--	.322	--	1.49	--	4.65	--	7.91	--
	Pressure	.310	110	.460	95	.341	72	2.30	51	3.26	5	6.52	123
Bret Saberhagen	Overall	.252	46	.400	46	.294	14	2.77	44	5.06	8	15.55	55
	Pressure	.288	92	.462	96	.324	54	3.85	91	4.42	9	14.16	73
Team Average	Overall	.261	6	.398	2	.330	6	2.35	1	8.96	9	15.10	9
	Pressure	.270	10	.406	10	.339	9	2.47	3	9.43	8	15.57	8
League Average	Overall	.265		.425		.333		3.38		8.94		15.38	
	Pressure	.262		.404		.337		2.99		9.73		16.42	

Additional Miscellaneous Pitching Comparisons

	Grass Surface BA	Rank	Artificial Surface BA	Rank	Home Games BA	Rank	Road Games BA	Rank	Runners in Scoring Position BA	Rank	Runners in Scoring Pos and Two Outs BA	Rank	Leading Off Inning OBA	Rank
Bud Black	.327	120	.234	35	.239	40	.291	94	.224	29	.241	65	.339	75
John Davis	.159	--	.221	21	.224	--	.171	--	.227	--	.364	--	.189	--
Steve Farr	.313	--	.251	56	.257	66	.284	88	.273	76	.214	45	.329	64
Jerry Don Gleaton	.227	--	.208	14	.183	--	.245	--	.255	58	.258	75	.308	--
Mark Gubicza	.258	59	.259	67	.258	67	.260	46	.211	20	.202	36	.357	94
Danny Jackson	.246	30	.265	73	.254	60	.262	52	.265	70	.239	62	.350	89
Charlie Leibrandt	.273	80	.241	44	.237	34	.267	63	.200	13	.214	45	.291	29
Melido Perez	.000	--	.375	120	.375	--	.000	--	.389	--	.200	--	.500	--
Dan Quisenberry	.352	--	.234	36	.228	--	.347	--	.353	122	.366	123	.179	--
Bret Saberhagen	.251	40	.253	58	.261	74	.242	30	.235	37	.194	30	.297	35
Bob Shirley	.291	--	.275	82	.341	--	.228	--	.262	--	.250	--	.324	--
Bob Stoddard	.286	--	.342	111	.342	--	.286	--	.245	--	.258	75	.282	--
Team Average	.270	8	.256	4	.258	7	.265	5	.247	3	.243	5	.319	5
League Average	.267		.261		.260		.270		.266		.247		.328	

MILWAUKEE BREWERS

All across America, 1987 was the season of the home run. Except, that is, in Milwaukee, where it was the season of the streak. Paul Molitor mounted the most serious challenge in nearly a decade to Joe DiMaggio's record of hitting safely in 56 consecutive games. But equally noteworthy were Milwaukee's 13-game winning streak to start the season, and the 12-game losing streak that started less than two weeks after its winning streak ended.

That 13-game winning streak clearly proclaimed to the rest of the American League that the Brewers had arrived. After all, of the 59 teams in modern major-league history that had streaks of at least 13 consecutive wins, only seven failed to finish the season within 10 games of a division or league title (none since the 1951 Chicago White Sox). And only one of those teams finished the season with a losing record (the 1942 Cleveland Indians).

But the suspicion that April winning streaks are less meaningful than those later in the season was supported by a study of the longest streaks since 1900. That study leaves no doubt that teams whose streaks occur late in the season are, on average, better than those whose streaks occur early.

The following table shows the composite records of the 260 teams that won at least 10 games in a row, classified according to the months in which their streaks began. The won-lost totals do not include the games during the streaks:

Month	No.	Avg. Length	Won	Lost	Pct.
April	37	11.2	2882	2494	.536
May	44	11.8	3511	2778	.558
June	34	11.7	2656	2179	.549
July	45	11.3	3596	2893	.554
August	57	11.4	4692	3441	.576
September	43	11.6	3530	2654	.570
Totals	260	11.5	20867	16439	.559

It's clear that as the season progresses, a long winning streak becomes an increasingly reliable sign of an excellent team. Teams that win 10 consecutive games after August 1 are likely to win at least 98 games by season's end (11.5 wins during a typical streak, plus .574 of their other games). But those clubs that win 10 in a row during April will, on average, barely hit the 90 mark.

Let's examine the question another way. There have been 59 streaks of at least 10 consecutive wins since the leagues split into divisions in 1969. They produced 22 divisional winners. Teams with streaks over the final two months of the season accounted for 36 percent of the streaks but 55 percent of the division winners:

	Division Winners	Division Losers
Month streak began		
April through July	10	28
August or September	12	9

For years, managers have recited *ad nauseum* the axiom that games in April are just as important as those in September, a truth that we hold to be self-evident. And although streaks of 10 wins may also be as important early in the season as late, it's nevertheless true that it takes a better team—one more likely to win a pennant—to piece those streaks together at crunch time.

Hey, Milwaukee—This Brew's for You!

Milwaukee's success last season demonstrated the value of hitting in the clutch. During the 13 seasons that we've compiled situational batting statistics, no team's hitting was as timely over the course of an entire season as that of the 1987 Brewers. Their .298 batting average with runners on base was the highest in either league during that entire time; only three teams beat Milwaukee's .298 mark with runners in scoring position; and only one topped their mark of .293 with two outs and runners on base (the 1975 Reds hit .294).

The timeliness of Milwaukee's hitting appears to have earned the Brewers a substantial reward last season. The following table compares their statistics to those of the four A.L. teams of the last five seasons with slugging and on-base averages within 10 points of Milwaukee's own, and batting averages within five points. Those three averages represent the building blocks of scoring; teams with similar averages generally produce similar scoring totals. But—and it's an important but—Milwaukee outscored the other teams by an average of 50 runs, despite having a lower slugging average than all of them, and a lower on-base average than all but one.

Year	Team	AB	R	H	2B	3B	HR	BB	BA	SLG	OBA
1982	California	5532	814	1518	268	26	186	613	.274	.433	.347
1983	Toronto	5581	795	1546	268	58	167	510	.277	.436	.338
1986	New York	5570	797	1512	275	23	188	645	.271	.430	.347
1987	Boston	5586	842	1554	273	26	174	606	.278	.430	.352
1987	Milwaukee	5625	862	1552	272	46	163	598	.276	.428	.346

The Brewers didn't just hit well with runners on, they also rose to the occasion in the late innings of close games, batting .308 in Late-Inning Pressure Situations, the third-highest mark we've ever recorded. That won't come as welcome news to all those Milwaukee daddies who vetoed their children's objections and left County Stadium early to beat the traffic. But the facts are there—Milwaukee stormed back to win seven games in which they trailed after the eighth inning, the highest total in the American League.

The following tables show the 10 players with the largest margins, both positive and negative, between their batting averages in Late-Inning Pressure Situations and in unpressured at bats over the past two seasons (with at least 100 LIP at bats during that time). Milwaukee and Detroit were the only teams to place two players in the top ten:

The Top 10	LIP	Unp.	Diff.	The Bottom 10	LIP	Unp.	Diff.
Rickey Henderson	.381	.257	.124	Roy Smalley	.152	.276	.124
Candy Maldonado	.351	.253	.098	Chet Lemon	.167	.280	.114
Benito Santiago	.369	.284	.085	Tim Flannery	.165	.278	.113
Cecil Cooper	.327	.245	.082	Dan Gladden	.167	.278	.111
Kirk Gibson	.339	.264	.076	Greg Brock	.190	.288	.098
Ray Knight	.338	.265	.073	Carney Lansford	.213	.298	.086
Darrell Evans	.311	.239	.072	Lonnie Smith	.208	.291	.083
Paul Molitor	.379	.309	.070	Dick Schofield	.182	.261	.079
Ivan Calderon	.343	.273	.070	Scott Fletcher	.228	.303	.075
Steve Sax	.365	.296	.069	Jose Oquendo	.235	.310	.075

The Clutch Hitter Lives

As in the past, we feel it's our duty to demonstrate that clutch hitting isn't simply a random trait of a player's profile. To most of us, of course, that's obvious, and has been as long as there have been baseball fans to notice it. Nevertheless, a small group of shrill pseudo-statisticians has used insufficient data and faulty methods to try to disprove the existence of the clutch hitter. But with four seasons of statistics now in the public domain in the four editions of the *Analyst*, there's no longer an excuse for anyone not to recognize this simple fact of baseball life. Here's the conclusive evidence.

We found 43 players who hit better in Late-Inning Pressure Situations than in unpressured at bats in both 1985 and 1986. Two examples:

	Cecil Cooper		Paul Molitor	
Year	LIP	Unp.	LIP	Unp.
1985	.356	.283	.312	.295
1986	.271	.256	.339	.272

We found 64 others with higher batting averages in unpressured at bats in both of those years. Another pair of examples:

	Greg Brock		Rick Manning	
Year	LIP	Unp.	LIP	Unp.
1985	.164	.265	.150	.233
1986	.058	.267	.240	.256

Incidentally, we restricted the groups to players with at

least 25 LIP at bats in each of the past three seasons. Then we checked to see how each of the players fared in Late-Inning Pressure Situations during the 1987 season. The theory is this: If players don't reproduce their clutch tendencies over a period of years, then the good clutch hitters of 1985 and 1986 should have hit no better in Late-Inning Pressure Situations last season than the poor clutch hitters of the two previous years. The results speak for themselves: The group of good clutch hitters was far better:

	Better in LIP in 1987	Worse in LIP in 1987	Pct. Better in 1987
Tendencies of 2 Prior Seasons			
Good in clutch in 1985 and 1986	21	22	.488
Poor in clutch in 1985 and 1986	24	40	.375

Maybe the confusion on this topic stems from the fact that a solid majority of players hits better in unpressured at bats than in Late-Inning Pressure Situations, since the clutch stats are heavily weighted by at bats against the best relief pitchers. As a result, a player who hits *as well* in Late-Inning Pressure Situations as in unpressured at bats is a good clutch hitter.

Or maybe the problem is that in any season, only about 10 players will bat even 100 times in LIP situations. When dealing in such small samples, there's no guarantee that you'll get an accurate reading on a player's ability. Even Wade Boggs and Don Mattingly go through slumps over such short periods. Nevertheless, when the clutch-hitting data is analyzed properly, the trends are undeniably apparent except to those who choose not to see.

We performed the same study as above on the three other sets of three years for which we have clutch-hitting statistics (1982–84, 1979–81, and 1976–78). For each set of three years, we divided the players into groups as above: (1) those who, in each of the first two seasons, hit better in LIP situations than overall; (2) those who hit better overall than in LIP in each of those seasons; and 3) and those who mixed one good clutch season with one poor one, or who failed to bat at least 25 times in LIP in one or both of those seasons. We then checked to see how each group fared in the third of the three years. *In every case, the good clutch hitters of the two previous years hit better in the clutch than either of the other groups*; in all but one case, the mixed group hit better in the clutch than the poor clutch hitters.

The plus and minus designations in the following table refer to the players' clutch tendencies in the third year:

	Good in Clutch in 1st 2 Years			Mixed in Clutch in 1st 2 Years			Poor in Clutch in 1st 2 Years		
Years	+	–	Pct.	+	–	Pct.	+	–	Pct.
1985–87	21	22	.488	98	113	.464	24	40	.375
1982–84	24	25	.490	95	132	.419	22	35	.386
1979–81	20	15	.571	83	87	.488	24	37	.393
1976–78	24	25	.490	96	114	.457	31	33	.484
Totals	89	87	.506	372	446	.455	101	145	.411

Even including the anomalous 1976-78 period, the good

clutch hitters of the first two seasons were 23 percent more likely to hit well in Late-Inning Pressure Situations (that is, better than their overall batting averages) in the third of the three years than the poor clutch hitters were. That, despite the fact that on an individual-player basis, we were often dealing with only 25 to 50 at bats.

The facts are here. Enough is enough.

Monitoring Molitor's Odds

Was Paul Molitor the unlikeliest player ever to challenge Joe DiMaggio's record of hitting safely in 56 consecutive games? Molitor was the ninth player in major-league history to hit in more than 35 straight games, but only the second who carried a career batting average below the .300 mark. The following table shows the odds that each of those streaks would occur at some point during the players' careers:

Year	Player	Streak	BA	Odds
1941	Joe DiMaggio	56	.325	271–1
1897	Willie Keeler	44	.345	3–1
1978	Pete Rose	44	.303	39–1
1894	Bill Dahlen	42	.274	2,442–1
1922	George Sisler	41	.340	2–1
1911	Ty Cobb	40	.367	1–14
1987	Paul Molitor	39	.297	50–1
1945	Tommy Holmes	37	.302	17–1
1894	Billy Hamilton	36	.344	3–5

Let's use DiMaggio's streak as an example of how we computed the odds. For the sake of simplicity, we assumed that the batters had four at bats per game. It follows that a player with a .325 batting average has a 79 percent chance of getting a hit in any game. That in turn suggests that there's roughly one chance in 456,000 to hit safely in 56 consecutive games *starting at a given point*. Since DiMaggio played in 1,736 games, he had 1,681 chances to start a 56-game streak, giving him one chance in 272 to do it at some point during his career. By that measure, only two of the streaks listed above were less likely than Molitor's.

Incidentally, we estimate that Cobb's chances of hitting in 50 consecutive games were 38 percent; in 57 consecutive games, 13 percent. And we estimate that even if Wade Boggs were to hit .350 for another 10 seasons, he'd have only one chance in 47 of breaking Joe D.'s mark.

A Designated Asterisk

Shortly before Molitor's streak was snapped last August, an article in *USA Today* suggested that if he were to break DiMaggio's record, the streak might merit an asterisk in the record book because Molitor had been exclusively a designated hitter during that time. But fifteen years of data on designated hitters clearly shows that if the alternative is playing the field, then sitting in the dugout for extended periods between at bats has a *detrimental* effect on a player's hitting. That shouldn't be too surprising; after all, for most everyday players, an occasional turn as designated hitter functions as an off day, and it's often intended to benefit him over the next few games.

Since the American League instituted the DH rule in 1973, 171 players accumulated at least 100 at bats as a designated hitter in the same season in which they batted at least 100 other times. More than 60 percent of those players—108 to be exact—hit better in the games in which they played the field.

As an extension of this basic study, we assigned to each of the 171 players the position he played most often during the season in question. For example, Molitor (who had 237 of his 465 at bats as a DH) played more games at third base last season than at any other position. The survey showed that outfielders suffered most when used as designated hitters, infielders (with first basemen comprising most of the infield sample) were at a lesser disadvantage, and catchers were an exception to the rule, thriving on days spent away from the wars behind the plate:

Position	Better as DH	Worse as DH
First Basemen	19	31
Second Basemen	1	2
Shortstops	0	2
Third Basemen	2	5
Outfielders	33	65
Catchers	8	3

When the players were divided by age group, another rule became apparent: that older players experienced a greater disadvantage when used as designated hitters than younger ones:

Age	Better as DH	Worse as DH
Up to 27 years	23	27
28 to 34 years	33	59
35 years and up	7	22

Younger players hit nearly as well as designated hitters as they did when playing the field. The strategic implications are noteworthy. Aging outfielders comprise a large segment of the DH population, but those are the same players whose hitting deteriorates the most when they aren't playing the field. Of course, using a regular first baseman or catcher for an occasional turns as a DH also affects a team's defense, and could limit a manager's strategic options in the late innings of close games. But maybe, in light of these figures, that's an alternative worth exploring. It just might be that a team's best choice for designated hitter would be an infielder or catcher not yet past his prime.

WON-LOST RECORD BY STARTING POSITION

MILWAUKEE 91-71	C	1B	2B	3B	SS	LF	CF	RF	P	DH	Leadoff	Relief	Starts
Jay Aldrich	·	·	·	·	·	·	·	·	·	·	·	11-20	·
Len Barker	·	·	·	·	·	·	·	·	8-3	·	·	·	8-3
Mike Birkbeck	·	·	·	·	·	·	·	·	5-5	·	·	·	5-5
Chris Bosio	·	·	·	·	·	·	·	·	10-9	·	·	12-15	10-9
Glenn Braggs	·	·	·	·	·	·	·	70-49	·	6-1	·	·	76-50
Greg Brock	·	82-56	·	·	·	·	·	·	·	·	·	·	82-56
Ray Burris	·	·	·	·	·	·	·	·	1-1	·	·	4-4	1-1
Juan Castillo	·	·	37-44	3-0	5-2	·	·	·	·	·	4-13	·	45-46
Mark Ciardi	·	·	·	·	·	·	·	·	1-2	·	·	1-0	1-2
Mark Clear	·	·	·	·	·	·	·	·	0-1	·	·	27-30	0-1
Cecil Cooper	·	·	·	·	·	·	·	·	·	31-31	·	·	31-31
Chuck Crim	·	·	·	·	·	·	·	·	1-4	·	·	27-21	1-4
Rob Deer	·	2-4	·	·	·	62-36	·	11-13	·	2-2	·	·	77-55
Mike Felder	·	·	·	·	·	26-28	7-6	·	·	1-0	11-16	·	34-34
Jim Gantner	·	·	34-17	6-19	·	·	·	·	·	·	0-1	·	40-36
Ted Higuera	·	·	·	·	·	·	·	·	22-13	·	·	·	22-13
John Henry Johnson	·	·	·	·	·	·	·	·	1-1	·	·	2-6	1-1
Steve Kiefer	·	·	1-0	13-10	·	·	·	·	·	·	·	·	14-10
Mark Knudson	·	·	·	·	·	·	·	·	4-4	·	·	2-5	4-4
Brad Komminsk	·	·	·	·	·	·	·	3-0	·	0-1	·	·	3-1
Alex Madrid	·	·	·	·	·	·	·	·	·	·	·	2-1	·
Rick Manning	·	·	·	·	·	1-5	·	7-9	·	·	1-2	·	8-14
Paul Mirabella	·	·	·	·	·	·	·	·	·	·	10-19	·	·
Paul Molitor	·	·	12-6	27-13	·	·	·	·	·	36-22	71-34	·	75-41
Juan Nieves	·	·	·	·	·	·	·	·	19-14	·	·	1-0	19-14
Charlie O'Brien	0-10	·	·	·	·	·	·	·	·	·	·	·	0-10
Jim Paciorek	·	4-5	·	5-5	·	2-2	·	·	·	0-2	1-0	·	11-14
Dan Plesac	·	·	·	·	·	·	·	·	·	·	·	37-20	·
Ernest Riles	·	·	36-23	8-8	·	·	·	·	·	·	1-1	·	44-31
Billy Jo Robidoux	·	2-5	·	·	·	·	·	·	·	8-2	·	·	10-7
Bill Schroeder	37-25	1-1	·	·	·	·	·	·	·	0-2	·	·	38-28
Steve Stanicek	·	·	·	·	·	·	·	·	·	0-1	·	·	0-1
Dave Stapleton	·	·	·	·	·	·	·	·	·	·	·	2-2	·
B.J. Surhoff	54-36	·	·	1-1	·	·	·	·	·	2-4	·	·	57-41
Dale Sveum	·	·	7-4	·	78-61	·	·	·	·	·	·	·	85-65
Bill Wegman	·	·	·	·	·	·	·	·	19-14	·	·	0-1	19-14
Robin Yount	·	·	·	·	·	·	84-65	·	·	5-3	2-4	·	89-68

Batting vs. Left and Right Handed Pitchers

		BA	Rank	SA	Rank	OBA	Rank	HR %	Rank	BB %	Rank	SO %	Rank
Glenn Braggs	vs. Lefties	.274	69	.393	100	.349	64	1.19	129	9.47	61	15.26	89
	vs. Righties	.267	80	.448	61	.324	89	3.26	84	7.73	96	17.87	115
Greg Brock	vs. Lefties	.287	51	.395	98	.351	63	1.91	110	7.95	99	12.50	56
	vs. Righties	.304	25	.456	57	.380	26	2.67	103	10.09	56	9.62	32
Juan Castillo	vs. Lefties	.217	139	.297	142	.229	159	0.72	140	1.39	162	19.44	119
	vs. Righties	.230	140	.322	148	.349	60	1.09	139	13.60	15	21.05	139
Cecil Cooper	vs. Lefties	.259	91	.358	120	.308	110	1.23	127	7.69	104	20.88	129
	vs. Righties	.243	113	.379	117	.285	143	2.96	93	5.59	140	17.88	116
Rob Deer	vs. Lefties	.257	94	.467	49	.394	23	5.26	29	18.62	4	25.53	149
	vs. Righties	.230	138	.450	59	.344	66	6.21	21	13.49	16	36.51	162
Mike Felder	vs. Lefties	.309	30	.372	112	.383	31	0.00	145	10.62	43	5.31	4
	vs. Righties	.246	106	.344	137	.303	125	1.03	140	7.44	104	7.91	20
Jim Gantner	vs. Lefties	.233	121	.279	150	.280	135	0.00	145	4.21	151	9.47	30
	vs. Righties	.291	38	.413	87	.355	54	2.23	109	7.46	103	6.47	9
Paul Molitor	vs. Lefties	.331	17	.476	45	.426	9	2.07	107	13.45	21	8.77	26
	vs. Righties	.363	2	.606	4	.443	2	4.06	62	12.40	21	14.02	70
Jim Paciorek	vs. Lefties	.221	136	.353	125	.276	141	2.94	88	7.89	100	17.11	100
	vs. Righties	.242	--	.303	--	.350	--	0.00	--	15.00	--	17.50	--
Ernest Riles	vs. Lefties	.175	157	.228	158	.250	152	0.00	145	8.96	78	26.87	153
	vs. Righties	.283	42	.384	109	.349	59	1.83	118	9.64	61	11.65	48
Bill Schroeder	vs. Lefties	.344	12	.550	17	.368	49	6.11	19	2.94	157	27.94	158
	vs. Righties	.319	--	.546	--	.391	--	5.04	--	8.96	--	13.43	--
B.J. Surhoff	vs. Lefties	.318	24	.424	78	.379	36	2.35	102	9.47	61	6.32	7
	vs. Righties	.294	34	.423	78	.342	70	1.61	126	7.71	98	6.86	12
Dale Sveum	vs. Lefties	.286	53	.535	22	.338	74	5.95	21	7.80	102	22.44	140
	vs. Righties	.234	128	.411	90	.284	144	4.00	63	6.30	128	22.83	147
Robin Yount	vs. Lefties	.272	73	.369	115	.336	75	1.03	134	9.09	72	12.73	60
	vs. Righties	.330	6	.527	22	.404	11	4.32	54	11.13	39	13.12	66
Team Average	vs. Lefties	.274	4	.410	12	.340	5	2.56	14	8.92	8	17.17	11
	vs. Righties	.277	1	.436	4	.349	2	3.06	11	9.61	3	15.92	11
League Average	vs. Lefties	.265		.422		.333		3.29		8.94		15.64	
	vs. Righties	.265		.427		.334		3.43		8.94		15.26	

Batting with Runners on Base and Bases Empty

		BA	Rank	SA	Rank	OBA	Rank	HR %	Rank	BB %	Rank	SO %	Rank
Glenn Braggs	Runners On	.267	86	.392	107	.332	98	1.29	127	8.61	97	16.48	106
	Bases Empty	.271	63	.462	56	.332	68	3.66	78	8.05	80	17.45	112
Greg Brock	Runners On	.347	8	.500	29	.416	14	2.67	95	9.93	70	10.93	43
	Bases Empty	.252	96	.378	113	.327	78	2.22	113	9.00	64	10.00	28
Juan Castillo	Runners On	.211	150	.305	152	.287	143	0.78	152	8.28	100	22.93	148
	Bases Empty	.233	126	.316	144	.312	107	1.04	139	9.30	56	18.60	120
Cecil Cooper	Runners On	.278	64	.407	98	.341	79	2.78	91	9.76	73	16.26	104
	Bases Empty	.225	136	.345	133	.252	157	2.11	117	3.40	152	21.09	135
Rob Deer	Runners On	.234	130	.443	69	.351	69	5.96	20	14.70	19	36.56	161
	Bases Empty	.243	113	.469	51	.369	29	5.86	28	15.68	5	29.27	160
Mike Felder	Runners On	.293	50	.414	91	.366	53	0.86	142	9.93	71	5.67	10
	Bases Empty	.249	105	.312	145	.305	119	0.58	147	7.49	99	8.02	12
Jim Gantner	Runners On	.226	139	.331	143	.287	140	2.42	99	6.34	127	9.15	27
	Bases Empty	.312	22	.404	94	.370	27	0.71	146	6.49	117	5.84	6
Paul Molitor	Runners On	.422	1	.681	1	.495	1	4.82	39	11.68	51	12.69	63
	Bases Empty	.314	18	.502	33	.406	7	2.68	98	13.33	11	12.17	52
Ernest Riles	Runners On	.269	84	.306	151	.316	118	0.75	145	7.10	117	12.26	58
	Bases Empty	.254	94	.394	101	.342	53	2.11	117	11.80	22	17.39	110
Bill Schroeder	Runners On	.348	7	.591	5	.390	27	6.96	9	4.84	150	20.16	138
	Bases Empty	.319	13	.511	30	.370	28	4.44	55	6.85	109	21.23	138
B.J. Surhoff	Runners On	.333	13	.467	54	.374	47	2.22	107	8.06	103	6.64	14
	Bases Empty	.270	65	.386	65	.329	75	1.40	133	8.12	76	6.84	8
Dale Sveum	Runners On	.276	67	.539	18	.322	114	5.76	24	6.99	119	19.49	131
	Bases Empty	.233	129	.384	109	.287	134	3.77	76	6.69	113	25.48	150
Robin Yount	Runners On	.376	2	.583	9	.448	5	4.14	57	11.95	45	11.66	50
	Bases Empty	.258	89	.391	102	.326	81	2.61	102	9.21	59	14.21	69
Team Average	Runners On	.298	1	.461	1	.365	2	3.27	7	9.41	9	15.93	11
	Bases Empty	.258	10	.400	14	.331	3	2.59	14	9.37	2	16.67	11
League Average	Runners On	.271		.428		.343		3.25		9.68		14.87	
	Bases Empty	.260		.424		.326		3.49		8.34		15.79	

Overall Batting Compared to Late Inning Pressure Situations

		BA	Rank	SA	Rank	OBA	Rank	HR %	Rank	BB %	Rank	SO %	Rank	RDI %	Rank
Glenn Braggs	Overall	.269	75	.430	79	.332	79	2.57	106	8.32	86	16.99	110	.309	61
	Pressure	.284	63	.388	95	.359	66	0.00	119	11.39	48	22.78	130	.321	67
Greg Brock	Overall	.299	24	.438	73	.371	32	2.44	112	9.47	66	10.47	32	.341	27
	Pressure	.290	55	.348	111	.372	52	0.00	119	11.25	49	7.50	12	.278	81
Juan Castillo	Overall	.224	149	.312	153	.302	133	0.93	140	8.87	79	20.43	136	.239	135
	Pressure	.265	83	.324	124	.342	77	0.00	119	10.00	68	15.00	80	.400	27
Cecil Cooper	Overall	.248	115	.372	125	.293	147	2.40	113	6.30	131	18.89	124	.357	18
	Pressure	.452	1	.613	9	.455	9	3.23	68	3.03	151	15.15	81	.385	33
Rob Deer	Overall	.238	135	.456	58	.360	43	5.91	16	15.19	9	32.86	161	.266	110
	Pressure	.308	39	.538	23	.438	15	5.77	32	15.63	15	28.13	154	.353	49
Mike Felder	Overall	.266	78	.353	139	.330	84	0.69	148	8.54	83	7.01	9	.305	64
	Pressure	.340	19	.362	102	.392	31	0.00	119	7.55	107	7.55	13	.375	38
Jim Gantner	Overall	.272	70	.370	128	.331	82	1.51	130	6.42	127	7.43	12	.278	92
	Pressure	.297	48	.324	122	.341	78	0.00	119	7.14	109	9.52	29	.250	91
Rick Manning	Overall	.228	--	.307	--	.299	--	0.00	--	9.30	--	13.95	--	.300	--
	Pressure	.286	59	.393	93	.323	96	0.00	119	6.06	124	12.12	55	.250	91
Paul Molitor	Overall	.353	2	.566	6	.438	4	3.44	83	12.73	18	12.36	50	.388	3
	Pressure	.426	5	.704	3	.483	4	7.41	13	9.84	73	18.03	99	.400	27
Ernest Riles	Overall	.261	90	.351	141	.329	85	1.45	132	9.49	65	14.87	87	.361	14
	Pressure	.286	59	.429	72	.302	120	0.00	119	2.22	156	13.33	66	.333	51
Bill Schroeder	Overall	.332	4	.548	11	.379	22	5.60	21	5.93	135	20.74	139	.271	106
	Pressure	.407	7	.778	1	.515	2	11.11	1	12.12	42	18.18	102	.417	20
B.J. Surhoff	Overall	.299	25	.423	87	.350	58	1.77	123	8.09	94	6.74	7	.355	20
	Pressure	.299	46	.448	62	.338	81	2.99	75	6.58	117	10.53	37	.379	35
Dale Sveum	Overall	.252	107	.454	62	.303	128	4.67	45	6.83	118	22.70	146	.328	37
	Pressure	.284	62	.568	17	.310	110	7.41	13	3.53	148	24.71	140	.333	51
Robin Yount	Overall	.312	13	.479	40	.384	20	3.31	88	10.51	49	13.00	56	.345	24
	Pressure	.298	47	.345	113	.354	68	1.19	116	9.00	84	11.00	40	.306	70
Team Average	Overall	.276	2	.428	8	.346	3	2.90	14	9.39	5	16.33	11	.315	1
	Pressure	.308	1	.445	1	.368	1	2.60	11	8.53	12	16.27	7	.340	2
League Average	Overall	.265		.425		.333		3.38		8.94		15.38		.287	
	Pressure	.262		.405		.335		3.07		9.43		16.58		.280	

Additional Miscellaneous Batting Comparisons

	Grass Surface		Artificial Surface		Home Games		Road Games		Runners in Scoring Position		Runners in Scoring Pos and Two Outs		Leading Off Inning		Runners on 3B with less than 2 Outs	
	BA	Rank	BA	Rank	BA	Rank	BA	Rank	BA	Rank	BA	Rank	OBA	Rank	RDI %	Rank
Glenn Braggs	.278	63	.226	119	.261	98	.278	52	.284	66	.256	79	.363	44	.667	33
Greg Brock	.303	27	.276	58	.300	43	.298	29	.325	20	.319	26	.313	99	.600	71
Juan Castillo	.229	140	.203	138	.262	95	.185	160	.189	149	.167	144	.318	95	.667	33
Cecil Cooper	.264	91	.167	--	.296	49	.211	147	.317	33	.292	47	.333	--	.800	3
Rob Deer	.236	130	.254	88	.228	139	.248	101	.260	94	.291	48	.361	47	.400	152
Mike Felder	.265	90	.278	--	.302	40	.239	116	.279	71	.278	58	.286	126	.722	18
Jim Gantner	.269	82	.286	47	.298	46	.250	98	.250	102	.195	131	.419	9	.667	--
Paul Molitor	.376	1	.197	144	.394	2	.312	20	.449	1	.400	2	.421	8	.600	71
Ernest Riles	.270	77	.188	--	.286	64	.238	118	.289	55	.364	7	.259	146	.765	6
Bill Schroeder	.332	5	.333	7	.350	4	.315	16	.352	9	.355	10	.333	69	.429	150
B.J. Surhoff	.306	22	.244	97	.314	23	.284	45	.321	24	.396	3	.300	113	.600	71
Dale Sveum	.261	97	.205	137	.261	99	.245	105	.290	54	.301	38	.289	123	.607	66
Robin Yount	.320	12	.269	65	.354	3	.272	61	.324	21	.313	30	.318	94	.600	71
Team Average	.284	1	.234	13	.293	2	.260	8	.298	1	.292	1	.331	6	.612	1
League Average	.267		.261		.270		.260		.266		.247		.328		.581	

Pitching vs. Left and Right Handed Batters

		BA	Rank	SA	Rank	OBA	Rank	HR %	Rank	BB %	Rank	SO %	Rank
Jay Aldrich	vs. Lefties	.282	92	.464	94	.336	65	4.55	105	7.38	37	8.20	121
	vs. Righties	.328	--	.459	--	.352	--	2.46	--	3.05	--	9.16	--
Len Barker	vs. Lefties	.360	128	.558	124	.433	128	2.33	31	9.18	67	10.20	109
	vs. Righties	.250	--	.402	--	.310	--	4.35	--	8.00	--	12.00	--
Mike Birkbeck	vs. Lefties	.267	62	.367	29	.323	47	2.22	29	8.08	47	11.11	99
	vs. Righties	.398	--	.684	--	.455	--	6.12	--	9.91	--	12.61	--
Chris Bosio	vs. Lefties	.264	58	.424	69	.322	45	3.09	60	7.73	45	20.36	13
	vs. Righties	.290	103	.405	58	.329	64	2.18	20	5.78	20	20.52	27
Mark Clear	vs. Lefties	.250	40	.464	95	.394	120	3.57	83	18.18	126	21.02	11
	vs. Righties	.229	27	.346	19	.333	69	2.61	43	12.50	115	23.91	13
Chuck Crim	vs. Lefties	.286	97	.436	77	.357	92	3.96	95	9.41	71	10.59	105
	vs. Righties	.249	52	.352	27	.292	28	2.20	21	5.10	18	9.86	115
Ted Higuera	vs. Lefties	.276	82	.393	42	.310	27	2.45	39	4.65	4	23.26	8
	vs. Righties	.234	31	.364	33	.300	37	2.45	33	8.66	73	21.93	23
Mark Knudson	vs. Lefties	.324	124	.453	89	.359	94	2.88	54	6.49	24	11.04	100
	vs. Righties	.339	--	.433	--	.356	--	2.36	--	2.99	--	6.72	--
Juan Nieves	vs. Lefties	.183	4	.286	6	.302	19	2.38	35	14.67	123	26.67	3
	vs. Righties	.280	96	.447	92	.358	97	3.34	76	10.88	101	17.15	49
Dan Plesac	vs. Lefties	.140	--	.281	--	.219	--	3.51	--	9.38	--	31.25	--
	vs. Righties	.230	28	.326	13	.288	21	2.51	36	6.51	30	26.44	8
Bill Wegman	vs. Lefties	.257	51	.420	65	.308	24	3.43	78	6.51	25	10.65	104
	vs. Righties	.274	87	.432	78	.311	47	3.77	88	4.68	14	11.24	109
Team Average	vs. Lefties	.271	9	.422	8	.339	8	3.10	5	9.11	4	15.60	6
	vs. Righties	.272	11	.411	5	.330	7	2.88	2	7.86	5	16.85	5
League Average	vs. Lefties	.267		.427		.338		3.30		9.47		14.54	
	vs. Righties	.264		.424		.330		3.45		8.56		15.98	

Pitching with Runners on Base and Bases Empty

		BA	Rank	SA	Rank	OBA	Rank	HR %	Rank	BB %	Rank	SO %	Rank
Jay Aldrich	Runners On	.327	116	.442	85	.371	104	2.88	64	6.72	26	6.72	128
	Bases Empty	.289	107	.477	104	.321	62	3.91	89	3.73	6	10.45	109
Chris Bosio	Runners On	.290	94	.406	60	.347	74	2.05	27	8.28	48	17.18	35
	Bases Empty	.266	78	.422	71	.309	40	3.13	60	5.64	27	23.04	15
Mark Clear	Runners On	.225	13	.375	32	.352	80	2.50	47	15.92	126	22.89	9
	Bases Empty	.256	57	.436	84	.377	113	3.76	81	14.47	121	22.01	18
Chuck Crim	Runners On	.259	55	.377	35	.331	56	2.63	53	9.23	66	10.77	108
	Bases Empty	.272	88	.401	50	.315	47	3.31	67	5.19	20	9.69	117
Ted Higuera	Runners On	.266	69	.383	41	.315	35	1.49	12	7.33	33	17.56	30
	Bases Empty	.223	16	.358	21	.292	21	3.11	59	8.52	67	25.39	6
Mark Knudson	Runners On	.310	108	.468	94	.333	58	4.76	103	4.96	6	7.80	123
	Bases Empty	.350	126	.421	69	.381	116	0.71	3	4.76	16	10.20	112
Juan Nieves	Runners On	.271	73	.418	74	.349	76	2.74	57	11.02	97	19.16	23
	Bases Empty	.258	63	.422	70	.348	96	3.51	77	11.93	112	18.52	32
Dan Plesac	Runners On	.252	46	.427	76	.310	29	4.90	106	7.55	36	25.79	4
	Bases Empty	.176	3	.216	1	.241	3	0.65	2	6.63	43	28.92	3
Bill Wegman	Runners On	.262	62	.443	86	.303	21	4.31	94	5.60	10	12.89	86
	Bases Empty	.267	80	.415	61	.314	45	3.15	61	5.72	28	9.71	116
Team Average	Runners On	.281	11	.428	8	.344	10	2.86	4	8.97	4	15.72	4
	Bases Empty	.264	11	.406	3	.325	6	3.05	3	7.81	4	16.92	5
League Average	Runners On	.271		.428		.343		3.25		9.68		14.87	
	Bases Empty	.260		.424		.326		3.49		8.34		15.79	

Overall Pitching Compared to Late Inning Pressure Situations

		BA	Rank	SA	Rank	OBA	Rank	HR %	Rank	BB %	Rank	SO %	Rank
Jay Aldrich	Overall	.306	115	.461	99	.344	78	3.45	82	5.14	9	8.70	122
	Pressure	.310	108	.310	23	.370	99	0.00	1	8.33	53	12.50	89
Chris Bosio	Overall	.276	86	.415	59	.326	58	2.66	39	6.81	28	20.44	20
	Pressure	.262	68	.381	60	.304	39	1.59	39	5.84	23	18.98	32
Mark Clear	Overall	.239	23	.403	49	.363	105	3.07	62	15.28	124	22.50	13
	Pressure	.235	45	.374	55	.393	110	2.61	62	21.19	124	19.87	28
Chuck Crim	Overall	.266	73	.390	36	.322	52	3.00	54	7.10	33	10.20	113
	Pressure	.267	70	.347	40	.325	55	2.00	46	7.88	49	12.12	97
Ted Higuera	Overall	.241	28	.368	22	.301	20	2.45	24	8.03	50	22.14	14
	Pressure	.194	10	.317	25	.233	2	2.88	69	4.73	15	20.27	25
Mark Knudson	Overall	.331	126	.444	85	.358	98	2.63	37	4.86	5	9.03	120
	Pressure	.300	--	.400	--	.323	--	0.00	--	3.13	--	9.38	--
Paul Mirabella	Overall	.268	--	.357	--	.351	--	0.00	--	12.03	--	10.53	--
	Pressure	.286	90	.343	37	.390	108	0.00	1	14.29	113	9.52	110
Juan Nieves	Overall	.264	69	.420	67	.348	86	3.18	69	11.53	112	18.80	27
	Pressure	.233	44	.467	102	.410	122	3.33	80	22.50	125	12.50	89
Dan Plesac	Overall	.213	4	.318	3	.275	6	2.70	42	7.08	32	27.38	3
	Pressure	.238	49	.355	46	.301	34	2.80	67	7.17	38	24.89	9
Bill Wegman	Overall	.265	71	.425	72	.310	30	3.58	84	5.67	13	10.92	106
	Pressure	.267	70	.373	54	.309	39	1.33	35	6.10	26	7.32	121
Team Average	Overall	.271	10	.415	6	.333	9	2.96	3	8.34	4	16.38	5
	Pressure	.248	3	.358	2	.321	2	2.19	2	9.41	7	17.33	6
League Average	Overall	.265		.425		.333		3.38		8.94		15.38	
	Pressure	.262		.404		.337		2.99		9.73		16.42	

Additional Miscellaneous Pitching Comparisons

	Grass Surface		Artificial Surface		Home Games		Road Games		Runners in Scoring Position		Runners in Scoring Pos and Two Outs		Leading Off Inning	
	BA	Rank	BA	Rank	BA	Rank	BA	Rank	BA	Rank	BA	Rank	OBA	Rank
Jay Aldrich	.303	106	.333	--	.333	--	.272	--	.313	109	.231	--	.245	--
Mike Birkbeck	.303	--	.411	126	.306	--	.377	--	.278	--	.348	--	.333	--
Chris Bosio	.284	93	.228	26	.283	100	.271	72	.281	84	.280	94	.343	78
Mark Clear	.252	43	.143	1	.236	31	.241	27	.193	9	.180	14	.378	107
Chuck Crim	.267	73	.263	71	.270	88	.262	50	.248	48	.194	28	.331	67
Ted Higuera	.246	32	.203	11	.241	42	.241	25	.305	102	.258	75	.301	39
Mark Knudson	.331	121	.000	--	.401	127	.256	38	.311	--	.333	--	.364	98
Juan Nieves	.266	72	.253	59	.288	104	.251	36	.258	65	.226	56	.346	83
Dan Plesac	.203	4	.275	--	.219	16	.208	6	.259	66	.250	69	.219	2
Bill Wegman	.265	70	.262	69	.249	53	.291	93	.253	53	.210	43	.322	56
Team Average	.274	9	.254	3	.278	12	.265	4	.278	11	.251	8	.329	8
League Average	.267		.261		.260		.270		.266		.247		.328	

MINNESOTA TWINS

"The worst team to ever to win a World Series."

"The only World Series winner not to win a single game on the road."

"The only team in baseball history to reach the World Series after being outscored during the regular season."

"The worst road team ever to win a league or division title."

The Twins and their home stadium have been called every name imaginable: lucky, unfair, ridiculous, a garbage bag. But though sticks and stones may break the Twins' bones (and would again bring down the Metrodome roof), names will never hurt them. Their World Series rings are all the proof they need of their standing as the champions of major league baseball for 1987.

Most every World Series or Super Bowl winner brings to its town a special feeling, at least for a few days, but unless you happen to live in that particular town in the year in question, it's not something that you usually come to recognize. Sure, you might see the obligatory we're-number-one/downtown parade/key-to-the-city stuff on the network news, but to paraphrase Spiro Agnew, if you've seen one civic demonstration you've seen them all.

But of all of those recent champions, the Twins' rags-to-riches story stands out as one of the most heartwarming sports stories of its particular year. The Twins' championship was such an unlikely event, and it came on the heels of so many defeats by teams and individuals representing Minnesota that nearly everyone has been mentioned as part of the backdrop to the story. A short list of those contributing to the drama would include Andy MacPhail, Jeff Reardon, George Mikan, Frank Viola, Calvin Griffith, Carl Pohlad, Kent Hrbek, Hubert Humphrey, Tom Kelly, Mary Tyler Moore, Ralph Houk, Bob Short, Darrell Evans, Kirby Puckett, Walter Mondale, Lee Weyer, Fran Tarkenton, and Gary Gaetti.

Metrodome bashing has been a popular pastime in recent years, but even the image of the Dome underwent a transformation in 1987. For one thing, all rational human beings have *finally* stopped referring to it as the "Homerdome," a misnomer that hasn't been deserved since the air conditioning was turned on in 1983. In addition, three weeks' worth of exposure to it during the playoffs and World Series changed a lot of people's opinions about the park itself. Instead of looking at it as yet another abhorrent bastardization of baseball architecture, even die-hard traditionalists came to view it as a cozy, ol'-time ballpark that happened to have a vinyl roof overhead and a tightly-strung tarpaulin for a right field fence. Sure, some fly balls might get lost in the white roof, and others might hit speakers, but there's something to be said for a modern major-league stadium that is so idiosyncratic that it couldn't be confused with any other. (Remember the words of Richie Hebner: "I stand at the plate in Philadelphia and I don't honestly know whether I'm in Pittsburgh, Cincinnati, St. Louis, or Philly. They all look alike.")

One of the Dome's more endearing characteristics is that it was built with asymmetric distances, and with varying heights and surfaces along the outfield, ahem, "wall." Part of the charm that Brooklyn fans recall about Ebbets Field had to do with the nature of the outfield barriers. The wall stood about 10 feet high in left field, while it was 20 feet in center field, where a screen stood atop the unpadded concrete wall. Right field was the real masterpiece: the 19-foot-high concrete wall was bent halfway up, so that the lower part of the wall was angled and the upper part was vertical. A 19-foot screen stood above it all, so that right fielders would have to plan to play balls that hit off angled concrete, vertical concrete, or a screen. The mastery of that wall, first by Dixie Walker and later by Carl Furillo, was a part of the romance of the ballpark.

Put the Twins in a few more post-season series and Tom Brunansky will be just as renowned for playing the right field barrier at the Metrodome: 23 feet of canvas with girders behind it, making caroms unpredictable to foreigners, but somewhat routine to Brunansky. How does he field ground balls that roll into the right field corner? "I just run to the 3," he said during last year's series, referring to the 327 figure painted on the wall. "The ball always seems to roll to that spot."

In the Cubs' essay in the *1987 Analyst*, we studied the degree to which every major league team's home-field edge differs. While, over a period of years, *every* team plays better at home than on the road, the difference between a team's winning percentage at home and its winning percentage on the road varies from team to team. The team with the largest gap between those figures may be said to use its home field to the greatest advantage.

Listed below are the home and road figures for all major league teams for the period from 1982 to 1987, the six years during which the Metrodome has been open for business. (The Metrodome is still the youngest stadium in the majors, even though some stadiums such as Montreal's Olympic and Baltimore's Memorial have undergone recent face-lifts.)

	Home Games		Road Games		
A.L.	W–L	Pct.	W–L	Pct.	Diff.
Minnesota	268–220	.549	175–308	.362	+187
Texas	247–236	.511	187–299	.385	+126
New York	294–190	.607	238–248	.490	+117
Oakland	254–232	.523	198–287	.408	+115
Kansas City	286–200	.588	217–268	.447	+111
Chicago	270–214	.558	223–264	.458	+100
Milwaukee	267–218	.551	220–263	.455	+96
Cleveland	236–248	.488	192–295	.394	+94
Toronto	289–195	.597	248–238	.510	+87
Seattle	237–252	.485	192–290	.398	+87
Detroit	295–192	.606	252–231	.522	+84
Boston	272–211	.563	235–252	.483	+80
California	261–224	.538	239–247	.492	+46
Baltimore	260–224	.537	240–246	.494	+43

	Home Games		Road Games		
N.L.	W–L	Pct.	W–L	Pct.	Diff.
Houston	275–212	.565	222–263	.458	+107
Chicago	255–227	.529	208–277	.429	+100
San Diego	262–224	.539	214–272	.440	+99
Philadelphia	273–212	.563	228–258	.469	+94
San Francisco	253–233	.521	214–272	.440	+81
Los Angeles	265–220	.546	234–253	.480	+66
New York	277–210	.569	244–241	.503	+66
Pittsburgh	237–248	.489	207–279	.426	+63
St. Louis	279–207	.574	251–234	.518	+56
Atlanta	241–244	.497	223–262	.460	+37
Cincinnati	240–246	.494	224–261	.462	+32
Montreal	253–232	.522	246–238	.508	+14

The Metrodome stands number one in the major leagues in providing its home team with a distinct home field advantage. While that may not come as a news flash to the Cardinals or their fans, we decided to check the other professional team sports to see how various stadiums and arenas compare with the Metrodome.

In doing the inter-sport comparisons, we realize that conditions are not identical from sport to sport. For one thing, there have been franchise shifts, and other stadium and arena changes, over the past six seasons. Moreover, the four sports differ quite widely not only in the number of games scheduled for each team, but also in the percentage of games that are won by the home team. Here are the home-team winning percentages over the past six regular seasons in each of the four sports (for the winter sports, the totals run from the 1981–82 season through 1986–87):

	Won	Lost	Tied	Pct.
NBA	3635	2023	0	.642
NHL	2667	1736	637	.592
NFL	692	534	6	.564
* Baseball	6846	5771	8	.543

* In baseball, tied games are not calculated in percentage; other sports count them as half-win, half-loss.

If all that you want to know is which team has had the best *home winning percentage* over the past six years, the answer is simple: the Boston Celtics, with a record of 215–31 (.874).

But NBA teams play only half the number of home games that baseball teams do, allowing for more extremes in terms of percentages. And, even more importantly, it is an intrinsic characteristic of the sport of basketball that more games are won by the home team than in any other sport.

To take these differences into account, we calculated the *average difference* in each sport between home and road winning percentage. In baseball, the average was 84 percentage points; in the NFL, 129 points; in hockey, 185 points; and in hoops, 286 points.

Simple so far, but here's where our computations enter the realm of Mr. Spock. To determine which team has the greatest home-field advantage (HFA), you must consider its record in relation not only to the average home-field advantage in its particular sport, but also with regard to the distribution of HFAs in that sport. For instance, in the NFL, the average HFA is 129 points, but the distribution is such that only one team in five can be expected to fall within 25 points of that average. NFL teams tend toward the extremes; the short season makes that possible. Seemingly huge differences are common, and thus, less significant.

But in baseball, nearly half the teams can be expected to fall within 25 points of the average home-field advantage (84 points), making extreme cases, like that of the Twins, all the more unusual.

We've consolidated those factors into a single value called a z-score, which represents the number of standard deviations between a particular team's home-field advantage and the average advantage for teams in its sport. (For example, the Twins' z-score of 2.95 is calculated by comparing their HFA of 187 points with the baseball average of 84 points, a difference that is 2.95 times baseball's standard deviation of 35 points.) And by that measure, the Twins have by far the most significant home-field advantage of any team in the four major team sports:

Team	League	Z-Score	Home	Road
Minnesota Twins	A.L.	2.95	.549	.362
Kansas City Chiefs	NFL	2.30	.605	.244
Portland Trail Blazers	NBA	1.84	.740	.346
Chicago Black Hawks	NHL	1.81	.629	.381
Philadelphia Flyers	NHL	1.76	.763	.517
St. Louis Blues	NHL	1.76	.598	.352
Denver Nuggets	NBA	1.70	.732	.346
Phoenix Suns	NBA	1.63	.687	.305
Seattle Seahawks	NFL	1.60	.733	.442
Houston Oilers	NFL	1.20	.409	.159
Tampa Bay Buccaneers	NFL	1.20	.364	.114
Texas Rangers	A.L.	1.20	.511	.385

The conclusion is worth repeating: Since its opening in 1982, the Metrodome has provided the Twins with the greatest home field advantage, *relative to their sport*, possessed by any team in any of the four major pro sports. So, Cardinal fans, perk up; although your guys couldn't come away with a win in the Metrodome, maybe it'll make you feel better that the Lakers, Canadiens, or Bears probably wouldn't have beaten the Twins, either!

Viola and Blyleven—The Twins' Advantage?

Among the many analyses of the Twins' World Series victory, one went like this:

"Of course, the Twins won the World Series. The rules of a short series were stacked in their favor, and against the Cardinals. Minnesota could start Viola or Blyleven a total of five times, while they hardly had to dip into their second-line pitchers at all. And the Cardinals, with a more balanced staff in which no pitcher won more than 11 games, didn't get to use that depth in the Series."

The analysis makes a good deal of sense. It's true that the top two pitchers on a staff can make five starts in a seven-game series (71 percent), while during the regular season they would not account for much more than 40 percent of their team's starts. But the application to the 1987 World Series was somewhat askew.

For one thing, while it is true that no Cardinals' pitcher won more than 11 games during the regular season, that figure is also somewhat spurious. John Tudor and Danny Cox were just as much (if not more) of a formidable one-two punch as were Frank Viola and Bert Blyleven. It's just that because both Tudor and Cox spent part of the season on the disabled list, their totals of starts and wins were short of what they would normally be. (Tudor was 10–2 in 16 starts. Tell us he wouldn't have won close to 20 games—thereby blowing apart that whole "no–12–game–winner" business—had he spent his time between starts in the bullpen, rather than in a dugout unprotected by a warning track.)

But beyond that, the fact that the Twins had a solid one-two starting punch, backed up by less-than-formidable depth in the three-four-five starting spots, is nothing new. First, here are the 1987 regular-season numbers for the Twins' two top starters, compared with their other starters:

	Won	Lost	Pct.
Viola and Blyleven	32	22	.593
All other starters	23	32	.418

Note that difference of 175 percentage points between the winning percentage of the top two and the rest of the guys. Let's look back at the 10 teams that have played in the last five World Series, looking at the differences in winning percentages between a team's top two starters and the rest of their starters.

(Aside to those interested: A team's "top two starters" were the top two starting pitchers on a team, when ranked according to the following criteria:

- the starter with the most wins; if tied, then
- the starter with the fewest losses; if tied, then
- the starter with the most starts; if tied, then
- the starter with the most innings; if tied, then
- the best record in the conference, then strength of schedule, then consultation with Danny Sheridan.)

The 10 teams in the World Series from 1982 to 1986:

	Top 2 Starters		Others		
	W–L	Pct.	W–L	Pct.	Diff.
1986 Red Sox	40–14	.741	37–42	.468	273
1985 Royals	37–15	.712	38–39	.494	218
1983 Phillies	34–22	.607	23–34	.404	203
1983 Orioles	34–15	.694	40–36	.526	168
1984 Padres	29–16	.644	37–35	.514	130
1985 Cardinals	42–20	.677	37–26	.587	90
1984 Tigers	37–19	.661	40–30	.571	90
1986 Mets	34–11	.756	44–22	.667	89
1982 Cardinals	30–19	.612	34–30	.531	81
1982 Brewers	35–19	.648	41–31	.569	79
Totals	352–170	.674	371–325	.533	141

The Twins' difference of 175 points is not that far above the average of 141 points for the 10 teams in our study. Moreover, three teams in the past four World Series have surpassed that 175-point difference, and another has almost matched it, with nary a word spoken. Did the 1986 Red Sox possess an "unfair" advantage with Clemens and Hurst? Or the 1985 Royals with Saberhagen and Leibrandt. Or the 1983 Phillies with Denny and Carlton? Why pick on the Twins?

If anything, the Twins' advantage in the series was twofold: first, the fact that it was the American League's turn to host the four home games; second, by clinching the division early and by eliminating Detroit in five games, the Twins could get their pitching set up so that Viola could be used three times, if needed.

Like we say, a mixture of lucky and good: the classic baseball formula for success.

WON-LOST RECORD BY STARTING POSITION

MINNESOTA 85-77	C	1B	2B	3B	SS	LF	CF	RF	P	DH	Leadoff	Relief	Starts
Allan Anderson	-	-	-	-	-	-	-	-	2-0	-	-	0-2	2-0
Keith Atherton	-	-	-	-	-	-	-	-	-	-	-	29-30	-
Don Baylor	-	-	-	-	-	-	-	-	-	7-7	-	-	7-7
Billy Beane	-	-	-	-	-	-	-	0-2	-	-	-	-	0-2
Juan Berenguer	-	-	-	-	-	-	-	-	4-2	-	-	20-21	4-2
Jeff Bittiger	-	-	-	-	-	-	-	-	1-0	-	-	1-1	1-0
Bert Blyleven	-	-	-	-	-	-	-	-	23-14	-	-	-	23-14
Tom Brunansky	-	-	-	-	-	30-23	-	39-45	-	11-6	-	-	80-74
Randy Bush	-	5-1	-	-	0-2	-	-	34-23	-	1-7	5-7	-	40-33
Sal Butera	14-26	-	-	-	-	-	-	-	-	-	-	-	14-26
Steve Carlton	-	-	-	-	-	-	-	-	1-6	-	-	0-2	1-6
Mark Davidson	-	-	-	-	-	6-5	5-5	12-7	-	-	1-0	-	23-17
George Frazier	-	-	-	-	-	-	-	-	-	-	-	21-33	-
Gary Gaetti	-	-	82-67	-	-	-	-	-	-	1-1	-	-	83-68
Greg Gagne	-	-	-	65-59	-	-	-	-	-	-	3-1	-	65-59
Dan Gladden	-	-	-	-	-	49-47	3-2	-	-	1-2	45-42	-	53-51
Kent Hrbek	-	69-66	-	-	-	-	-	-	-	-	-	-	69-66
Joe Klink	-	-	-	-	-	-	-	-	-	-	-	3-9	-
Gene Larkin	-	9-9	-	-	-	-	-	-	-	23-16	-	-	32-25
Tim Laudner	47-29	2-1	-	-	-	-	-	-	-	0-2	-	-	49-32
Steve Lombardozzi	-	-	65-62	-	-	-	-	-	-	-	3-5	-	65-62
Al Newman	-	-	19-13	1-2	20-18	-	-	-	-	-	27-20	-	42-33
Joe Niekro	-	-	-	-	-	-	-	-	6-12	2-0	-	-	6-12
Randy Niemann	-	-	-	-	-	-	-	-	-	-	-	1-0	-
Tom Nieto	19-17	-	-	-	-	-	-	-	-	-	-	2-4	19-17
Chris Pittaro	-	-	1-2	-	-	-	-	-	-	-	1-1	-	1-2
Mark Portugal	-	-	-	-	-	-	-	-	4-3	-	-	2-4	4-3
Kirby Puckett	-	-	-	-	-	77-70	-	-	-	4-4	0-1	-	81-74
Jeff Reardon	-	-	-	-	-	-	-	-	-	-	-	46-17	-
Mark Salas	5-5	-	-	-	-	-	-	-	-	-	-	-	5-5
Dan Schatzeder	-	-	-	-	-	-	-	-	0-1	-	-	10-19	0-1
Roy Smalley	-	-	-	2-8	-	-	-	-	-	35-32	-	-	37-40
Roy Smith	-	-	-	-	-	-	-	-	1-0	-	-	0-6	1-0
Mike Smithson	-	-	-	-	-	-	-	-	11-9	-	-	0-1	11-9
Les Straker	-	-	-	-	-	-	-	-	10-16	-	-	1-4	10-16
Frank Viola	-	-	-	-	-	-	-	-	22-14	-	-	-	22-14

Batting vs. Left and Right Handed Pitchers

		BA	Rank	SA	Rank	OBA	Rank	HR %	Rank	BB %	Rank	SO %	Rank
Don Baylor	vs. Lefties	.267	85	.407	90	.353	60	4.44	51	7.69	104	9.62	32
	vs. Righties	.233	129	.383	110	.363	43	3.95	65	10.61	47	14.15	74
Tom Brunansky	vs. Lefties	.228	129	.481	41	.321	90	6.33	13	12.50	29	10.87	41
	vs. Righties	.273	68	.492	36	.365	41	5.88	23	11.86	29	19.53	129
Randy Bush	vs. Lefties	.222	--	.222	--	.417	--	0.00	--	23.08	--	15.38	--
	vs. Righties	.254	100	.419	81	.346	62	3.87	71	11.90	27	13.99	69
Mark Davidson	vs. Lefties	.243	105	.291	145	.310	109	0.00	145	8.55	86	15.38	90
	vs. Righties	.319	--	.404	--	.346	--	2.13	--	5.77	--	15.38	--
Gary Gaetti	vs. Lefties	.235	120	.422	80	.287	132	4.22	56	6.63	126	16.02	94
	vs. Righties	.266	84	.510	28	.309	118	5.74	26	5.59	139	14.09	73
Greg Gagne	vs. Lefties	.266	87	.367	116	.294	122	0.00	145	4.29	149	20.00	123
	vs. Righties	.265	85	.456	56	.316	103	3.24	85	5.60	138	16.52	99
Dan Gladden	vs. Lefties	.258	92	.362	119	.307	112	1.23	128	6.25	131	10.80	40
	vs. Righties	.244	112	.360	127	.315	105	2.18	111	8.82	77	17.32	110
Kent Hrbek	vs. Lefties	.225	132	.370	114	.290	130	4.35	55	9.03	75	14.84	86
	vs. Righties	.310	19	.617	1	.426	3	8.26	4	17.03	9	9.00	26
Gene Larkin	vs. Lefties	.286	54	.377	109	.375	39	1.30	125	12.50	29	12.50	56
	vs. Righties	.256	97	.385	106	.322	92	1.92	115	8.05	92	11.49	46
Tim Laudner	vs. Lefties	.194	154	.449	65	.279	137	7.14	8	10.62	43	19.47	120
	vs. Righties	.189	159	.358	128	.236	161	4.74	42	5.39	142	28.43	157
Steve Lombardozzi	vs. Lefties	.288	50	.417	86	.333	78	1.44	116	5.88	135	11.11	46
	vs. Righties	.215	152	.321	149	.281	145	2.05	113	7.36	105	15.03	86
Al Newman	vs. Lefties	.319	22	.489	39	.407	16	0.00	145	12.73	25	10.91	43
	vs. Righties	.178	162	.221	162	.248	157	0.00	156	8.37	88	6.28	7
Kirby Puckett	vs. Lefties	.339	15	.627	5	.377	38	6.21	15	5.76	139	12.57	58
	vs. Righties	.329	7	.497	33	.363	44	3.80	72	4.40	151	14.05	71
Roy Smalley	vs. Lefties	.250	--	.375	--	.280	--	4.17	--	3.85	--	15.38	--
	vs. Righties	.277	55	.414	86	.357	50	2.46	106	10.87	42	14.91	82
Team Average	vs. Lefties	.266	5	.429	5	.326	10	3.06	10	8.10	11	14.09	3
	vs. Righties	.259	11	.430	6	.329	8	3.82	4	8.78	9	15.01	7
League Average	vs. Lefties	.265		.422		.333		3.29		8.94		15.64	
	vs. Righties	.265		.427		.334		3.43		8.94		15.26	

Batting with Runners on Base and Bases Empty

		BA	Rank	SA	Rank	OBA	Rank	HR %	Rank	BB %	Rank	SO %	Rank
Don Baylor	Runners On	.275	69	.440	72	.392	25	4.40	50	10.57	64	13.66	75
	Bases Empty	.218	145	.350	130	.329	74	3.88	70	8.75	70	11.67	46
Tom Brunansky	Runners On	.269	81	.502	28	.379	41	5.38	29	14.50	23	14.50	84
	Bases Empty	.252	95	.479	45	.330	71	6.47	18	10.14	42	18.84	122
Randy Bush	Runners On	.289	55	.453	65	.385	35	3.13	83	14.29	24	10.56	40
	Bases Empty	.224	138	.382	111	.319	96	4.24	60	10.64	32	17.02	105
Gary Gaetti	Runners On	.276	68	.481	45	.325	109	4.24	53	6.80	121	13.59	74
	Bases Empty	.239	118	.488	38	.282	142	6.31	20	5.02	139	15.67	86
Greg Gagne	Runners On	.250	111	.384	111	.292	136	1.16	132	5.64	138	18.46	126
	Bases Empty	.275	57	.460	57	.322	90	3.02	90	4.93	141	16.90	103
Dan Gladden	Runners On	.217	143	.311	150	.285	143	1.24	128	8.33	99	11.11	47
	Bases Empty	.267	70	.390	104	.328	77	2.17	114	7.62	95	17.22	108
Kent Hrbek	Runners On	.302	39	.556	13	.417	13	7.11	5	17.27	8	10.43	39
	Bases Empty	.270	64	.536	23	.361	38	7.14	9	12.50	16	10.76	35
Gene Larkin	Runners On	.259	99	.324	146	.344	76	0.00	150	11.20	55	12.80	65
	Bases Empty	.272	59	.432	74	.336	58	3.20	86	8.03	81	10.95	38
Tim Laudner	Runners On	.221	140	.487	40	.302	126	7.96	1	10.61	63	22.73	146
	Bases Empty	.171	161	.326	141	.216	162	4.00	66	4.86	142	27.03	154
Steve Lombardozzi	Runners On	.244	120	.369	118	.303	125	1.88	112	7.07	118	14.13	82
	Bases Empty	.235	124	.342	136	.295	126	1.84	123	6.78	111	13.56	60
Al Newman	Runners On	.241	126	.346	136	.277	153	0.00	150	4.73	151	4.73	4
	Bases Empty	.207	154	.270	159	.313	105	0.00	157	13.43	10	9.95	25
Kirby Puckett	Runners On	.319	26	.481	44	.355	64	2.81	90	5.81	134	14.52	85
	Bases Empty	.342	6	.578	10	.377	23	5.90	26	3.91	141	12.85	57
Roy Smalley	Runners On	.240	127	.376	115	.329	102	2.40	100	11.81	50	14.58	86
	Bases Empty	.299	24	.435	71	.368	31	2.72	97	9.31	55	15.20	82
Team Average	Runners On	.266	9	.430	9	.336	10	3.20	9	9.35	10	13.63	3
	Bases Empty	.258	11	.429	4	.323	10	3.90	4	8.00	10	15.62	8
League Average	Runners On	.271		.428		.343		3.25		9.68		14.87	
	Bases Empty	.260		.424		.326		3.49		8.34		15.79	

Overall Batting Compared to Late Inning Pressure Situations

		BA	Rank	SA	Rank	OBA	Rank	HR %	Rank	BB %	Rank	SO %	Rank	RDI %	Rank
Don Baylor	Overall	.245	122	.392	111	.360	44	4.12	62	9.64	60	12.63	52	.287	82
	Pressure	.246	97	.344	114	.351	70	1.64	107	10.81	56	12.16	57	.176	130
Tom Brunansky	Overall	.259	92	.489	29	.352	53	6.02	14	12.05	26	16.94	108	.327	40
	Pressure	.273	72	.545	22	.377	44	7.58	10	14.29	24	22.08	122	.154	139
Randy Bush	Overall	.253	105	.413	94	.349	61	3.75	70	12.32	22	14.04	74	.309	61
	Pressure	.243	102	.351	110	.364	61	0.00	119	13.33	31	22.22	124	.222	106
Gary Gaetti	Overall	.257	99	.485	33	.303	127	5.31	26	5.89	136	14.65	81	.327	38
	Pressure	.254	94	.492	36	.329	89	6.35	24	8.57	88	20.00	112	.375	38
Greg Gagne	Overall	.265	80	.430	78	.310	114	2.29	117	5.22	146	17.54	115	.238	137
	Pressure	.150	159	.250	145	.227	154	2.50	84	9.09	82	15.91	84	.250	--
Dan Gladden	Overall	.249	114	.361	135	.312	110	1.83	122	7.88	101	14.94	89	.236	138
	Pressure	.170	152	.321	127	.237	150	3.77	91	8.33	91	23.33	132	.286	75
Kent Hrbek	Overall	.285	42	.545	12	.389	13	7.13	4	14.84	11	10.60	33	.312	56
	Pressure	.358	14	.597	11	.384	37	5.97	29	5.48	130	6.85	9	.364	43
Gene Larkin	Overall	.266	79	.382	118	.340	69	1.72	125	9.54	63	11.83	45	.244	129
	Pressure	.359		.487	38	.419	20	0.00	119	9.30	81	16.28	88	.412	25
Tim Laudner	Overall	.191	162	.389	115	.252	160	5.56	22	7.26	108	25.24	152	.274	101
	Pressure	.194	140	.389	94	.275	135	5.56	36	10.00	68	32.50	160	.250	91
Steve Lombardozzi	Overall	.238	134	.352	140	.298	137	1.85	121	6.89	116	13.78	66	.230	145
	Pressure	.302	44	.465	53	.423	19	4.65	45	16.67	11	16.67	90	.444	13
Al Newman	Overall	.221	151	.303	155	.298	136	0.00	161	9.74	59	7.74	15	.274	102
	Pressure	.194	141	.226	151	.286	125	0.00	119	11.11	50	11.11	41	.286	--
Kirby Puckett	Overall	.332	5	.534	16	.367	37	4.49	49	4.79	151	13.62	65	.326	41
	Pressure	.324	27	.676	5	.365	60	8.82	5	5.41	131	12.16	57	.278	81
Roy Smalley	Overall	.275	63	.411	95	.352	54	2.59	105	10.34	52	14.94	90	.241	132
	Pressure	.152	158	.196	159	.220	156	0.00	119	8.00	101	16.00	85	.000	158
Team Average	Overall	.261	10	.430	5	.328	9	3.60	5	8.59	9	14.75	5	.291	6
	Pressure	.254	10	.432	3	.326	10	4.15	1	9.30	9	17.78	11	.279	7
League Average	Overall	.265		.425		.333		3.38		8.94		15.38		.287	
	Pressure	.262		.405		.335		3.07		9.43		16.58		.280	

Additional Miscellaneous Batting Comparisons

	Grass Surface BA	Rank	Artificial Surface BA	Rank	Home Games BA	Rank	Road Games BA	Rank	Runners in Scoring Position BA	Rank	Runners in Scoring Pos and Two Outs BA	Rank	Leading Off Inning OBA	Rank	Runners on 3B with less than 2 Outs RDI %	Rank
Don Baylor	.243	121	.250	90	.268	87	.224	134	.310	37	.308	31	.340	62	.552	101
Tom Brunansky	.218	152	.284	51	.300	44	.216	144	.295	48	.207	120	.314	97	.667	33
Randy Bush	.264	92	.244	98	.258	105	.248	100	.286	60	.242	91	.347	56	.600	71
Sal Butera	.100	--	.230	116	.286	--	.101	--	.200	--	.118	--	.286	--	.625	--
Mark Davidson	.288	--	.255	87	.256	--	.279	--	.321	--	.389	--	.351	--	.750	--
Gary Gaetti	.219	151	.279	55	.306	33	.205	150	.300	42	.326	19	.281	130	.538	108
Greg Gagne	.269	80	.263	75	.241	123	.289	37	.238	118	.211	117	.347	55	.500	120
Dan Gladden	.239	128	.256	86	.271	83	.230	127	.207	142	.205	123	.339	66	.591	85
Kent Hrbek	.299	29	.275	60	.295	52	.276	55	.235	121	.177	140	.354	50	.700	25
Gene Larkin	.263	--	.268	68	.295	53	.240	115	.229	128	.229	105	.333	69	.529	113
Tim Laudner	.220	--	.173	155	.172	161	.212	146	.227	130	.130	151	.250	149	.529	113
Steve Lombardozzi	.267	87	.221	124	.211	154	.265	75	.263	87	.267	65	.325	88	.467	137
Al Newman	.188	--	.246	96	.235	128	.208	149	.241	116	.257	75	.339	64	.692	30
Tom Nieto	.233	--	.187	149	.203	--	.196	--	.259	--	.154	--	.185	--	.500	--
Kirby Puckett	.336	4	.329	13	.301	42	.362	1	.291	52	.267	65	.462	3	.612	62
Roy Smalley	.277	64	.273	61	.271	82	.278	51	.224	133	.206	121	.384	25	.333	159
Team Average	.257	12	.264	6	.268	9	.255	11	.262	8	.240	10	.335	3	.583	8
League Average	.267		.261		.270		.260		.266		.247		.328		.581	

Pitching vs. Left and Right Handed Batters

		BA	Rank	SA	Rank	OBA	Rank	HR %	Rank	BB %	Rank	SO %	Rank
Keith Atherton	vs. Lefties	.265	61	.444	84	.339	75	3.70	89	9.39	70	15.47	50
	vs. Righties	.259	61	.401	56	.325	61	2.72	47	7.78	55	13.77	82
Juan Berenguer	vs. Lefties	.278	84	.462	91	.360	95	3.59	84	11.42	97	19.69	19
	vs. Righties	.193	3	.274	6	.257	6	1.02	5	8.22	63	27.40	7
Bert Blyleven	vs. Lefties	.234	18	.447	86	.313	31	5.77	116	9.76	73	18.24	29
	vs. Righties	.266	77	.416	66	.331	67	3.13	69	8.05	62	16.50	55
Steve Carlton	vs. Lefties	.257	48	.389	39	.336	64	1.77	20	10.08	79	14.73	57
	vs. Righties	.284	98	.478	105	.380	112	4.59	104	12.94	117	12.77	96
George Frazier	vs. Lefties	.249	39	.402	54	.345	81	2.96	57	12.94	113	15.92	45
	vs. Righties	.269	82	.392	54	.377	110	3.08	67	15.43	121	16.05	57
Joe Niekro	vs. Lefties	.288	98	.484	103	.367	103	3.59	85	10.86	90	11.71	93
	vs. Righties	.250	53	.347	20	.332	68	1.49	11	8.52	71	14.10	80
Mark Portugal	vs. Lefties	.255	46	.481	102	.339	74	5.66	115	11.57	100	19.01	23
	vs. Righties	.431	--	.792	--	.506	--	9.72	--	12.05	--	6.02	--
Jeff Reardon	vs. Lefties	.301	106	.532	116	.364	100	5.77	117	9.04	63	16.95	39
	vs. Righties	.158	1	.295	3	.231	2	3.42	81	7.50	51	33.13	2
Mike Smithson	vs. Lefties	.320	122	.593	126	.371	109	6.72	126	7.53	41	10.75	102
	vs. Righties	.239	38	.303	7	.326	62	0.00	1	7.91	58	10.70	111
Les Straker	vs. Lefties	.265	59	.489	106	.338	69	4.98	110	9.92	75	12.40	83
	vs. Righties	.248	47	.385	52	.308	43	3.05	66	7.85	57	10.58	113
Frank Viola	vs. Lefties	.245	34	.374	31	.305	22	3.07	59	6.78	27	19.77	18
	vs. Righties	.240	39	.379	46	.291	26	3.03	64	6.28	24	18.84	35
Team Average	vs. Lefties	.276	12	.485	14	.349	13	4.81	14	9.77	12	15.67	5
	vs. Righties	.257	4	.398	2	.326	6	2.96	3	8.50	9	16.20	8
League Average	vs. Lefties	.267		.427		.338		3.30		9.47		14.54	
	vs. Righties	.264		.424		.330		3.45		8.56		15.98	

Pitching with Runners on Base and Bases Empty

		BA	Rank	SA	Rank	OBA	Rank	HR %	Rank	BB %	Rank	SO %	Rank
Keith Atherton	Runners On	.251	45	.407	61	.323	49	2.40	39	8.38	50	15.18	57
	Bases Empty	.275	92	.444	90	.344	91	4.23	99	8.92	77	14.01	77
Juan Berenguer	Runners On	.266	67	.412	65	.343	69	2.26	35	11.17	99	22.82	10
	Bases Empty	.218	14	.346	19	.288	19	2.47	28	8.99	79	23.60	13
Bert Blyleven	Runners On	.247	38	.386	47	.322	46	3.15	74	9.40	71	16.74	37
	Bases Empty	.250	49	.462	99	.321	61	5.48	120	8.75	73	17.93	37
Steve Carlton	Runners On	.304	103	.498	104	.406	121	4.18	92	14.29	122	12.11	95
	Bases Empty	.258	66	.432	80	.342	89	3.95	91	10.78	104	14.02	76
George Frazier	Runners On	.272	75	.462	91	.342	68	4.43	96	10.99	96	14.66	64
	Bases Empty	.241	33	.326	13	.378	114	1.42	8	17.44	125	17.44	40
Joe Niekro	Runners On	.303	101	.474	97	.380	110	2.56	49	9.89	81	12.09	96
	Bases Empty	.247	45	.382	35	.330	76	2.65	40	9.69	91	13.35	84
Jeff Reardon	Runners On	.254	48	.500	105	.319	43	7.04	126	8.07	43	25.47	5
	Bases Empty	.213	12	.344	17	.284	16	2.50	31	8.52	69	23.86	12
Dan Schatzeder	Runners On	.342	120	.586	124	.380	111	5.41	112	6.61	22	16.53	42
	Bases Empty	.342	--	.487	--	.425	--	2.63	--	11.49	--	11.49	--
Mike Smithson	Runners On	.346	121	.617	127	.396	116	5.32	111	6.57	20	8.45	117
	Bases Empty	.241	32	.360	23	.317	52	2.77	47	8.54	70	12.46	95
Les Straker	Runners On	.233	23	.420	75	.307	26	4.57	97	9.73	78	12.06	99
	Bases Empty	.272	87	.456	96	.336	82	3.85	85	8.52	68	11.28	103
Frank Viola	Runners On	.232	21	.369	28	.287	8	3.01	67	6.91	28	19.75	22
	Bases Empty	.246	43	.384	37	.297	30	3.06	54	6.01	35	18.51	33
Team Average	Runners On	.274	7	.457	13	.343	8	3.93	13	9.18	5	15.67	6
	Bases Empty	.259	7	.423	8	.332	11	3.72	10	9.01	13	16.18	7
League Average	Runners On	.271		.428		.343		3.25		9.68		14.87	
	Bases Empty	.260		.424		.326		3.49		8.34		15.79	

Overall Pitching Compared to Late Inning Pressure Situations

		BA	Rank	SA	Rank	OBA	Rank	HR %	Rank	BB %	Rank	SO %	Rank
Keith Atherton	Overall	.262	65	.424	70	.332	67	3.24	73	8.62	65	14.66	66
	Pressure	.243	53	.412	75	.323	53	2.94	70	10.83	87	8.92	112
Juan Berenguer	Overall	.238	21	.374	28	.312	36	2.38	23	9.94	92	23.26	10
	Pressure	.211	22	.301	20	.291	27	0.81	22	10.56	81	21.13	22
Bert Blyleven	Overall	.249	38	.433	77	.321	48	4.59	106	9.00	74	17.47	37
	Pressure	.219	29	.333	30	.336	68	0.95	24	14.06	111	22.66	17
Steve Carlton	Overall	.279	88	.461	98	.372	114	4.05	98	12.41	118	13.13	83
	Pressure	.350	121	.517	110	.412	123	3.33	80	9.86	72	8.45	114
George Frazier	Overall	.258	58	.398	43	.359	100	3.01	55	14.05	120	15.98	49
	Pressure	.281	87	.337	34	.377	104	1.12	28	14.02	110	17.76	43
Joe Niekro	Overall	.270	80	.420	66	.351	90	2.61	35	9.77	87	12.82	86
	Pressure	.190	--	.286	--	.227	--	0.00	--	4.55	--	13.64	--
Jeff Reardon	Overall	.232	15	.417	61	.301	18	4.64	108	8.31	57	24.63	5
	Pressure	.245	46	.426	79	.315	46	4.63	104	9.09	62	25.21	7
Mike Smithson	Overall	.286	99	.469	107	.351	91	3.85	91	7.69	41	10.73	108
	Pressure	.292	--	.333	--	.393	--	0.00	--	10.71	--	3.57	--
Les Straker	Overall	.257	56	.443	84	.325	55	4.12	97	8.99	73	11.59	101
	Pressure	.359	124	.821	127	.395	113	10.26	127	6.98	36	6.98	122
Frank Viola	Overall	.241	29	.378	30	.293	13	3.04	59	6.36	22	19.00	24
	Pressure	.246	57	.316	24	.283	23	0.88	23	3.25	4	11.38	103
Team Average	Overall	.266	9	.438	10	.337	10	3.81	12	9.09	11	15.95	6
	Pressure	.249	4	.394	4	.329	7	2.81	6	10.24	11	17.27	7
League Average	Overall	.265		.425		.333		3.38		8.94		15.38	
	Pressure	.262		.404		.337		2.99		9.73		16.42	

Additional Miscellaneous Pitching Comparisons

	Grass Surface BA	Rank	Artificial Surface BA	Rank	Home Games BA	Rank	Road Games BA	Rank	Runners in Scoring Position BA	Rank	Runners in Scoring Pos and Two Outs BA	Rank	Leading Off Inning OBA	Rank
Allan Anderson	.417	--	.385	121	.385	--	.417	--	.438	--	.667	--	.615	--
Keith Atherton	.282	--	.249	51	.227	23	.292	95	.297	97	.333	110	.267	17
Juan Berenguer	.278	88	.211	15	.204	8	.278	78	.248	46	.241	66	.283	26
Bert Blyleven	.281	91	.236	38	.237	32	.266	62	.244	42	.240	64	.316	48
Steve Carlton	.292	100	.234	34	.266	82	.294	98	.294	94	.299	101	.346	82
George Frazier	.294	--	.231	33	.234	28	.279	81	.210	19	.204	37	.333	69
Joe Klink	.400	--	.328	107	.328	--	.400	--	.441	--	.438	--	.435	--
Joe Niekro	.255	49	.287	93	.260	72	.276	76	.309	108	.259	78	.340	76
Mark Portugal	.253	--	.402	124	.402	--	.253	--	.279	--	.263	--	.449	--
Jeff Reardon	.214	--	.243	47	.225	21	.239	24	.280	83	.353	118	.200	1
Dan Schatzeder	.287	--	.390	122	.397	--	.311	115	.339	--	.364	--	.333	--
Mike Smithson	.331	122	.261	68	.265	80	.302	105	.290	89	.264	82	.336	72
Les Straker	.243	25	.268	78	.256	62	.259	42	.215	22	.182	15	.331	68
Frank Viola	.238	17	.242	46	.245	49	.235	17	.214	21	.189	20	.292	30
Team Average	.280	12	.257	5	.253	4	.279	13	.264	6	.254	10	.325	7
League Average	.267		.261		.260		.270		.266		.247		.328	

NEW YORK YANKEES

Over the past winter, the most popular question in the New York newspapers that didn't concern either Donna Rice or Jessica Hahn was "Why would Steinbrenner hire Billy Martin again?"

Everyone seemed to have a different answer: Billy's already on the payroll . . . He puts fans in the seats . . . He's ideal for a quick fix . . . Billy's "better now" . . . Steinbrenner's lost his marbles. But almost no one suggested what we feel was the best reason of all for bringing Billy back for a fifth term as Yankees skipper—*that Billy Martin happens to be the best manager in the history of major-league baseball.*

Past readers of the *Analyst* will recall that in last year's edition we rated the managers of baseball's expansion era and that Martin topped the list. Since then, we've refined the system and expanded our survey to include all managers in modern major-league history. And when our computers stopped buzzing, Billy's name still came out on top.

We know what you're going to say: "You can't compare managers by their records. Guys like Earl Weaver, Joe McCarthy, and Al Lopez would have an unfair advantage because they managed good teams throughout their careers. Dick Williams, Gene Mauch, and Gil Hodges, to name a few, had to work with inferior talent." That's true, but we haven't rated the managers on their won-lost records alone. Each manager's value is determined by the difference between how many games his teams *actually* won and how many his teams *should* have won—that is, the number we expect they would have won with a typical manager. That figure—the number of games each team should have won—was determined by a complex mathematical model that analyzed each team's recent past. (That's all we'll say about it here. For those interested in the details, we've explained the system in detail at the end of this essay.)

It's clear that if the model can accurately determine the number of games a team would win with an average manager, then the manager's effect can be considered the difference between that total and the number of games that his team actually did win. Of course, in any season there are lots of events that alter a team's potential, events that our model knows nothing about. A major injury to a star player, the rapid development of young talent, and off-season trades (both good and bad) are all examples of influences that would warp our projection of the number of games a team should win.

But over the course of time, random events such as those tend to even out; good fortune balances bad. To ensure that

balance, we've considered only those managers with at least 1000 games of experience. Sorry, Davey; sorry, Petey: three or four seasons simply isn't enough time for us to assume with confidence that good luck hasn't been a major ingredient in your success. And incidentally, on those teams for which the luck always seems to be good—or bad—we'd suggest that those looking for the reason begin the search by knocking on the door to the manager's office.

But enough on *how* we rated the managers; let's take a look at the results. (Seasons prior to 1903 are not included.) The best 25 managers in major-league history:

Manager	Actual			Expected			Difference	
	W	L	Pct.	W	L	Pct.	Total	W/162G
Billy Martin	1218	990	.552	1116	1092	.506	101.53	7.45
Billy Southworth	1064	729	.593	993	800	.554	70.57	6.38
Sparky Anderson	1611	1185	.576	1520	1276	.544	90.90	5.27
Pat Moran	748	586	.561	706	628	.529	41.80	5.08
Fielder Jones	586	489	.545	554	521	.515	31.89	4.81
John McGraw	2633	1785	.596	2510	1908	.568	123.21	4.52
Paul Richards	923	901	.506	873	951	.479	50.17	4.46
Whitey Herzog	1084	914	.543	1030	968	.515	54.10	4.39
Bobby Cox	621	615	.502	588	648	.475	33.36	4.37
Earl Weaver	1480	1060	.583	1413	1127	.556	66.88	4.27
Steve O'Neill	1039	819	.559	990	868	.533	48.76	4.25
Joe McCarthy	2126	1335	.614	2035	1426	.588	90.51	4.24
Dick Williams	1548	1418	.522	1477	1489	.498	71.48	3.90
Danny Ozark	618	542	.533	591	569	.509	27.14	3.79
George Stallings	732	735	.499	703	764	.479	29.32	3.24
Danny Murtaugh	1115	950	.540	1075	990	.521	39.57	3.10
Herman Franks	605	521	.537	584	542	.518	21.29	3.06
Tris Speaker	616	520	.542	595	541	.524	21.03	3.00
Miller Huggins	1413	1134	.555	1367	1180	.537	46.45	2.95
Frank Chance	932	640	.593	908	664	.577	24.47	2.52
Leo Durocher	2010	1710	.540	1952	1768	.525	57.72	2.51
Harry Walker	630	604	.511	611	623	.495	18.77	2.46
Luke Sewell	606	644	.485	587	663	.470	18.62	2.41
Fred Hutchinson	830	827	.501	808	849	.488	21.51	2.10
Charlie Grimm	1287	1069	.546	1257	1099	.533	30.44	2.09

A year-by-year analysis of Martin's career not only illustrates how the system works, but also reinforces on a common-sense level the assertion that Billy might be the best of all time.

Year	Team	Actual Record			Expected Record			Diff.
		W	L	Pct.	W	L	Pct.	
1969	Minnesota	97	65	.599	82	80	.508	+14.8
1971	Detroit	91	71	.562	85	77	.522	+6.4
1972	Detroit	86	70	.551	83	73	.531	+3.2

1973	Detroit	76	67	.531	77	66	.538	−0.9
1973	Texas	9	14	.391	10	13	.425	−0.8
1974	Texas	84	76	.525	65	95	.409	+18.6
1975	Texas	44	51	.463	46	49	.485	−2.0
1975	New York	30	26	.536	29	27	.526	+0.6
1976	New York	97	62	.610	83	76	.520	+14.3
1977	New York	100	62	.617	91	71	.559	+9.5
1978	New York	52	42	.553	54	40	.570	−1.6
1979	New York	55	41	.573	55	41	.576	−0.3
1980	Oakland	83	79	.512	67	95	.412	+16.2
1981	Oakland	64	45	.587	53	56	.482	+11.4
1982	Oakland	68	94	.420	84	78	.517	−15.8
1983	New York	91	71	.562	79	83	.488	+11.9
1985	New York	91	54	.628	75	70	.516	+16.2
	Totals	1218	990	.552	1116	1092	.506	+101.5

Billy won at least 10 games more than expected seven times, failing to come within two games of his expected level only once. He won a division title in Minnesota with a team that had a losing record a year earlier. In his first full season with the Rangers, he won 84 games, 27 more than they had won the previous season *for Whitey Herzog, considered by some to be the best manager in baseball today, and rated by our system as the eighth best in major-league history.*

Martin led the Yankees to a league title in 1976 with a 97–62 record, 14 more wins than they'd accumulated in 1975, and a world championship the next season. In 1980, Martin joined the Oakland A's and took a team that had lost 108 games in 1979 to an 83–79 mark (16 games better than expected), and a year later, to a division title. Billy returned to the Yankees for single-season terms in 1983 and 1985. Lost amid the three-ring atmosphere that Martin's returns fueled was some of the best managing of his career: New York's records in those seasons (91–71 in 1983, 97–64 in 1985) were their two best of the past seven years.

How does Billy do it? Let's compare the first seasons of each of Martin's terms to his teams' previous seasons. (For example, his 1969 Minnesota team to its 1968 performance. By the way, we didn't include Martin's one-year term with the Yankees in 1985; his imprint on the 1984 team was too strong since he'd managed New York in 1983 as well.) Those teams allowed an average of 67 fewer runs in their first seasons under Martin's guidance than they had a year earlier.

But Billy's impact on the offense was even greater: His teams increased their own scoring by an average of 93 runs in just one season. But the difference was hardly attributable to the reputed aggressiveness of Martin's teams. He did increase stolen-bases by 39 percent, but runners caught stealing increased substantially as well (by 23 percent), so that Billy's teams' stolen base percentage was only slightly improved (from 61 percent to 64 percent). And as far as Billyball was concerned on the basepaths, his teams were only slightly more aggressive: For the three seasons for which we have such figures, his runners advanced two bases on singles only four percent more often than in the years before his arrivals. And for all the emphasis on Martin's strategic genius, he increased sacrifice bunts by only three percent. Billy had an enormous impact on his teams' production, but clearly not in the ways that most fans envision. And, oh yes, not to be overlooked—Billy increased complete games by 44 percent.

How Much is a Manager Worth?

Martin's particular genius has been turning around teams that have hit rock bottom. According to the study, Billy was worth 5.0 wins per 162 games for teams forecast to have winning seasons, but a remarkable 12.6 wins for the six teams he managed that were expected to play below the .500 mark (Texas 1973–75, Oakland 1980-81, and New York 1983). That raises the question as to whether managers like Earl Weaver—who in 17 years at the Orioles' helm never managed a team expected to lose half its games—might have fared better in our survey had they been given the chance to clean up someone else's mess. Or how Martin would have rated if he *hadn't* changed his address so often. Consider these lists of the top ten managers in expected winning and losing situations:

With Expected Winning Teams			With Expected Losing Teams		
Manager	Yrs.	W/162G	Manager	Yrs.	W/162G
Chuck Dressen	9	5.39	Bill McKechnie	8	8.04
Sparky Anderson	18	5.27	Clark Griffith	10	7.14
Billy Martin	11	5.00	Wilbert Robinson	8	5.44
Whitey Herzog	10	4.50	George Stallings	7	5.07
Billy Southworth	10	4.48	Paul Richards	7	4.42
Dick Williams	9	4.42	Fred Hutchinson	7	3.53
Earl Weaver	17	4.27	Dick Williams	11	3.47
Joe McCarthy	23	4.13	Gil Hodges	7	3.42
Miller Huggins	11	3.80	Jimmy Dykes	10	3.15
John McGraw	28	3.36	Bucky Harris	21	2.84

Once again, the analysis is limited to managers with at least 1000 games in each category. (That explains why Martin doesn't head the list of skippers with expected losing teams—he managed only 711 games under those circumstances.) The tables indicate that even considered on an equal basis, Weaver doesn't improve his standing significantly, moving from 10th place overall to seventh when compared only to other managers with expected winning teams. And they demonstrate that there are managers, unlike Martin, who have thrived with talented teams but, having inherited teams of inferior quality, have managed no better than their lesser players performed.

For example, Chuck Dressen, the best of all time with good teams, was so poor with inferior ones (costing them an average of four wins per 162 games) that he ranked only 38th overall among the 74 managers with 1000 games since 1903. Another manager who, like Dressen, did his best work with talented teams was Casey Stengel. During his first nine seasons as manager, for the Brooklyn Dodgers (1934–36) and Boston Braves (1938–43), Casey had a negative value of –4.9 wins per season. But during his 12 seasons with the Yankees (1949–60), during which New York won 10 American League titles and seven World Series, the Ol' Perfesser added 4.0 wins per season to his team's already lofty expectations. Then, with the Mets during their first four seasons, Stengel again had a negative impact (–6.4 wins).

Some other observations: Paul Richards and Earl Weaver

would have ranked second and fourth, respectively, on the all-time list had they not made unsuccessful comebacks, Richards with the 1976 White Sox following a 15-year absence from the dugouts, and Weaver with the Orioles in 1985 and 1986.

John McGraw won a total of 123 more games than expected over the course of his career, the largest overall number in major-league history. Incidentally, by that measure, which accounts for longevity as well as excellence, Bucky Harris, who didn't make the top 25 based on percentage, ranks ninth.

Branch Rickey, considered by many the most brilliant baseball administrator of all time, was a managerial disaster, costing his teams 3.65 wins per 162 games, the sixth-worst performance among the 1000-game managers. The lowest mark (–6.45) belongs to Jimmie Wilson, who managed Pittsburgh in the 1930s and the Boston Braves in the 1940s.

The values of unlisted current managers with at least 1000 games: Tony LaRussa (+1.59 wins per 162 games); Tommy Lasorda (+0.83); Gene Mauch (+0.77); John McNamara (–0.42); Don Zimmer (–0.66).

No Experience Required

The managerial database also proved useful in the analysis of some related topics. The most pertinent of these to the Yankees' situation was a study of managers making their major-league debuts without minor-league experience.

Last August, as the Yankees blew their Eastern Division lead and drifted steadily further away from first place, Steinbrenner commented that maybe he'd made a mistake hiring a manager—Piniella—who didn't have any minor-league experience. The early-success of Milwaukee's Tom Trebelhorn and Minnesota's Tom Kelly probably did little to change that conviction.

So to that end, we examined every first-year major-league manager of the past 40 years who made his debut at the start of a season. There were 88 of them; 69 had managed previously in the minors, the other 19 had not. We considered a manager to have a "plus value" if his team won more games than our model forecast, a "minus value" if it won fewer than projected:

	Plus	Minus
With minor-league experience	34	35
Without minor-league experience	11	8

That's right: In their first seasons, the managers *without* minor-league experience won more games than expected 11

of 19 times; those who had worked previously in the minors won more games than expected less than half the time.

Some of the novice first-timers presided over major turnarounds: Eddie Stanky (1952 Cardinals), Ted Williams (1969 Senators), Dick Howser (1980 Yankees), and George Bamberger (1978 Brewers). So is this solid *proof* that managers without minor-league experience are actually better than those with it? Not really, but these figures sure make it difficult to accept Steinbrenner's accusing finger pointed at Lou Piniella. And by the way, let's not forget that Cal Ripken and Larry Bowa, who both served minor-league apprenticeships, did a pretty good job balancing the debuts of Trebelhorn and Kelly.

How It Was Done...

A few words on how the mathematical model makes its forecast for how many games a team should win. Three factors are considered: a team's record in each of its two previous seasons; its pattern of progress, for better or for worse, during that period; and the volatility of the standings during the era in question.

The best leading indicator of a team's future performance is its most recent won-lost records. That needs no elaboration. But also crucial is the team's improvement or deterioration during that time. A team that improved its record in each of its past two seasons isn't nearly as likely to improve again as one that has declined for several consecutive seasons. Many baseball fans mistakenly judge a team that makes an unexpected leap in the standings one season to be a favorite for a division title the next. Last season's Cleveland Indians and Texas Rangers demonstrated that, under those conditions, a drop is much more likely. So each team's projection, based on its two most recent records, is colored by the shape of its development in the standings during that time.

A final ingredient is the year-to-year stability or volatility of the standings during the period in question. The 1980s have been a time of great change in baseball. It's been relatively common over the past few seasons for teams that finished near the bottom of the standings one season to contend for or win a title the next. But there have been eras (the 1950s, for example) when the standings changed very little from one year to the next. Consequently, the range of movement becomes a key factor in forecasting a team's performance.

Expansion teams, with no history to guide us, are evaluated on what little information exists: the average first-season marks of new teams, and the projected movement from year one to year two.

WON-LOST RECORD BY STARTING POSITION

NEW YORK 89-73	C	1B	2B	3B	SS	LF	CF	RF	P	DH	Leadoff	Relief	Starts
Neil Allen	·	·	·	·	·	·	·	·	0-1	·	·	2-5	0-1
Brad Arnsberg	·	·	·	·	·	·	·	·	1-1	·	·	0-4	1-1
Juan Bonilla	·	·	10-7	·	·	·	·	·	·	·	·	·	10-7
Rich Bordi	·	·	·	·	·	·	·	·	0-1	·	·	8-7	0-1
Jay Buhner	·	·	·	·	·	0-2	1-2	1-1	·	·	·	·	2-5
Rick Cerone	46-40	·	·	·	·	·	·	·	·	·	·	0-2	46-40
Pat Clements	·	·	·	·	·	·	·	·	·	·	·	27-28	·
Henry Cotto	·	·	·	·	·	2-6	14-11	·	·	·	2-3	·	16-17
Orestes Destrade	·	2-0	·	·	·	·	·	·	·	1-1	·	·	3-1
Mike Easler	·	·	·	·	·	10-3	·	1-0	·	15-14	·	·	26-17
Pete Filson	·	·	·	·	·	·	·	·	1-1	·	·	0-5	1-1
Bill Fulton	·	·	·	·	·	·	·	·	·	·	·	1-2	·
Cecilio Guante	·	·	·	·	·	·	·	·	·	·	·	13-13	·
Ron Guidry	·	·	·	·	·	·	·	·	7-10	·	·	3-2	7-10
Bill Gullickson	·	·	·	·	·	·	·	·	5-3	·	·	·	5-3
Rickey Henderson	·	·	·	·	·	17-16	23-13	·	·	10-14	49-41	·	50-43
Al Holland	·	·	·	·	·	·	·	·	·	·	·	0-3	·
Charles Hudson	·	·	·	·	·	·	·	·	7-9	·	·	8-11	7-9
Keith Hughes	·	·	·	·	·	·	·	·	·	·	·	·	·
Tommy John	·	·	·	·	·	·	·	·	22-11	·	·	·	22-11
Roberto Kelly	·	·	·	·	·	·	6-6	·	·	·	5-4	·	6-6
Ron Kittle	·	·	·	·	·	1-0	·	·	·	23-16	·	·	24-16
Al Leiter	·	·	·	·	·	·	·	2-2	·	·	·	·	2-2
Phil Lombardi	·	·	·	·	·	·	·	·	·	·	·	·	·
Don Mattingly	·	76-63	·	·	·	·	·	·	·	1-0	·	·	77-63
Bobby Meacham	·	·	5-12	·	24-21	·	·	·	·	·	1-0	·	29-33
Jeff Moronko	·	·	1-1	1-0	·	·	·	·	·	·	·	·	2-1
Joe Niekro	·	·	·	·	·	·	·	·	4-4	·	·	·	4-4
Mike Pagliarulo	·	·	·	77-61	·	·	·	·	·	·	·	·	77-61
Dan Pasqua	·	3-5	·	·	·	27-22	·	8-3	·	7-7	·	·	45-37
Willie Randolph	·	·	68-51	·	·	·	·	·	·	1-0	13-9	·	69-51
Dennis Rasmussen	·	·	·	·	·	·	·	·	15-10	·	·	0-1	15-10
Rick Rhoden	·	·	·	·	·	·	·	·	18-11	·	·	1-0	18-11
Dave Righetti	·	·	·	·	·	·	·	·	·	·	·	45-15	·
Jerry Royster	·	1-0	3-6	0-1	·	1-0	·	·	·	·	·	·	5-7
Lenn Sakata	·	·	1-1	7-5	·	·	·	·	·	·	·	·	8-6
Mark Salas	16-14	·	·	·	·	·	·	·	·	1-1	·	·	17-15
Bob Shirley	·	·	·	·	·	·	·	·	1-0	·	·	1-10	1-0
Joel Skinner	27-19	·	·	·	·	·	·	·	·	·	·	·	27-19
Tim Stoddard	·	·	·	·	·	·	·	·	·	·	·	31-26	·
Bob Tewksbury	·	·	·	·	·	·	·	·	2-4	·	·	0-2	2-4
Wayne Tolleson	·	·	1-0	·	61-47	·	·	·	·	·	·	·	62-47
Steve Trout	·	·	·	·	·	·	·	·	4-5	·	·	1-4	4-5
Randy Velarde	·	·	·	2-4	·	·	·	·	·	·	·	·	2-4
Gary Ward	·	8-5	·	·	·	30-23	13-12	2-3	·	20-13	1-1	·	73-56
Claudell Washington	·	·	·	·	·	1-1	32-29	0-1	·	5-4	18-15	·	38-35
Dave Winfield	·	·	·	·	·	·	·	77-65	·	5-3	·	·	82-68
Paul Zuvella	·	·	4-2	1-0	·	·	·	·	·	·	·	·	5-2

Batting vs. Left and Right Handed Pitchers

		BA	Rank	SA	Rank	OBA	Rank	HR %	Rank	BB %	Rank	SO %	Rank
Rick Cerone	vs. Lefties	.273	70	.341	129	.329	81	0.76	139	6.76	123	13.51	70
	vs. Righties	.217	148	.329	144	.313	112	1.97	114	11.17	36	14.53	76
Henry Cotto	vs. Lefties	.200	148	.325	135	.229	158	2.50	98	3.57	154	21.43	133
	vs. Righties	.275	--	.493	--	.315	--	4.35	--	4.11	--	23.29	--
Mike Easler	vs. Lefties	.190	--	.190	--	.333	--	0.00	--	14.81	--	33.33	--
	vs. Righties	.295	29	.418	83	.338	75	2.74	100	6.37	126	14.65	78
Rickey Henderson	vs. Lefties	.314	25	.585	10	.445	4	5.93	22	19.18	2	9.59	31
	vs. Righties	.279	52	.454	58	.412	6	4.17	59	17.69	6	12.93	64
Ron Kittle	vs. Lefties	.309	30	.553	16	.368	48	6.38	12	8.49	87	17.92	110
	vs. Righties	.231	--	.508	--	.239	--	9.23	--	1.49	--	25.37	--
Don Mattingly	vs. Lefties	.302	38	.523	25	.355	58	5.53	25	7.37	109	6.91	10
	vs. Righties	.341	3	.578	7	.391	16	5.14	35	8.47	86	5.57	5
Bobby Meacham	vs. Lefties	.306	33	.459	57	.379	36	3.53	65	10.42	47	16.67	97
	vs. Righties	.246	107	.373	119	.328	84	1.69	123	6.62	117	12.50	58
Mike Pagliarulo	vs. Lefties	.230	125	.355	122	.283	134	2.63	92	6.55	127	25.60	150
	vs. Righties	.235	107	.530	20	.314	107	7.57	6	10.14	54	16.43	97
Dan Pasqua	vs. Lefties	.164	160	.200	162	.246	155	0.00	145	9.68	58	30.65	160
	vs. Righties	.247	104	.468	48	.334	77	6.46	16	11.33	33	26.67	153
Willie Randolph	vs. Lefties	.331	18	.459	58	.467	1	2.26	104	20.00	1	4.12	2
	vs. Righties	.294	30	.396	100	.385	24	1.27	135	12.87	18	4.83	2
Jerry Royster	vs. Lefties	.269	75	.441	68	.325	83	3.45	70	8.07	97	11.80	52
	vs. Righties	.255	--	.431	--	.387	--	3.92	--	15.63	--	20.31	--
Mark Salas	vs. Lefties	.200	--	.200	--	.250	--	0.00	--	5.88	--	23.53	--
	vs. Righties	.255	98	.421	80	.329	82	4.14	60	8.54	85	11.59	47
Wayne Tolleson	vs. Lefties	.198	149	.208	161	.315	98	0.00	145	14.40	18	24.80	148
	vs. Righties	.230	137	.255	160	.302	127	0.41	154	9.12	71	14.96	83
Gary Ward	vs. Lefties	.279	63	.376	110	.321	91	2.03	108	5.74	140	13.40	68
	vs. Righties	.229	141	.389	105	.274	153	3.61	77	5.83	135	20.28	134

Batting vs. Left and Right Handed Pitchers

		BA	Rank	SA	Rank	OBA	Rank	HR %	Rank	BB %	Rank	SO %	Rank
Claudell Washington	vs. Lefties	.361	6	.475	46	.435	6	1.64	113	11.59	34	17.39	102
	vs. Righties	.259	90	.406	92	.311	114	3.19	87	7.04	112	15.56	93
Dave Winfield	vs. Lefties	.345	11	.621	7	.449	3	7.34	7	16.36	11	12.15	54
	vs. Righties	.244	111	.384	107	.314	108	3.52	81	9.30	66	15.87	94
Team Average	vs. Lefties	.276	3	.421	8	.354	2	3.25	7	10.56	1	15.37	6
	vs. Righties	.255	13	.416	11	.327	11	3.71	5	9.27	6	15.19	8
League Average	vs. Lefties	.265		.422		.333		3.29		8.94		15.64	
	vs. Righties	.265		.427		.334		3.43		8.94		15.26	

Batting with Runners on Base and Bases Empty

		BA	Rank	SA	Rank	OBA	Rank	HR %	Rank	BB %	Rank	SO %	Rank
Rick Cerone	Runners On	.198	157	.261	160	.295	133	0.90	141	10.22	67	13.87	79
	Bases Empty	.272	60	.382	112	.337	57	1.73	126	8.42	73	14.21	69
Rickey Henderson	Runners On	.244	121	.378	114	.423	11	3.36	72	23.72	2	12.18	55
	Bases Empty	.314	20	.556	18	.423	2	5.44	33	15.14	6	11.62	44
Don Mattingly	Runners On	.337	11	.591	4	.395	22	6.09	17	9.69	78	6.88	18
	Bases Empty	.317	15	.528	27	.361	37	4.48	54	6.45	118	5.16	3
Bobby Meacham	Runners On	.318	27	.412	95	.398	20	2.35	103	10.89	59	11.88	52
	Bases Empty	.237	121	.407	93	.313	106	2.54	106	6.11	125	16.03	90
Mike Pagliarulo	Runners On	.251	110	.512	24	.333	92	6.51	11	10.89	60	20.97	142
	Bases Empty	.221	143	.456	60	.284	137	5.86	27	7.78	88	17.66	116
Dan Pasqua	Runners On	.210	151	.399	102	.333	92	5.80	21	14.97	18	26.35	157
	Bases Empty	.250	99	.439	70	.308	117	5.00	42	7.69	93	28.21	159
Willie Randolph	Runners On	.326	16	.492	37	.430	8	2.67	94	15.74	12	3.83	1
	Bases Empty	.290	32	.359	125	.396	12	0.76	144	14.61	7	5.19	4
Jerry Royster	Runners On	.239	--	.328	--	.321	--	1.49	--	11.11	--	12.35	--
	Bases Empty	.279	50	.496	35	.354	46	4.65	49	9.72	49	15.28	83
Mark Salas	Runners On	.263	95	.475	47	.322	113	6.25	14	7.69	105	14.29	83
	Bases Empty	.238	--	.325	--	.322	--	1.25	--	8.89	--	11.11	--
Wayne Tolleson	Runners On	.256	103	.263	158	.340	84	0.00	150	10.90	58	16.67	108
	Bases Empty	.199	157	.227	162	.285	136	0.46	150	10.70	31	18.93	125
Gary Ward	Runners On	.287	56	.414	90	.326	106	2.46	98	5.64	139	14.66	90
	Bases Empty	.214	149	.358	126	.261	154	3.51	81	5.94	129	20.46	133
Claudell Washington	Runners On	.352	6	.541	17	.415	15	4.10	58	9.63	79	13.33	70
	Bases Empty	.232	130	.342	135	.284	138	2.11	119	6.86	107	17.65	115
Dave Winfield	Runners On	.320	25	.486	41	.403	17	3.86	60	12.62	37	12.96	67
	Bases Empty	.237	120	.434	73	.319	95	5.38	35	10.73	29	16.10	92
Team Average	Runners On	.275	5	.432	7	.356	3	3.62	4	10.92	2	14.32	6
	Bases Empty	.252	12	.407	12	.321	11	3.51	8	8.75	5	15.98	9
League Average	Runners On	.271		.428		.343		3.25		9.68		14.87	
	Bases Empty	.260		.424		.326		3.49		8.34		15.79	

Overall Batting Compared to Late Inning Pressure Situations

		BA	Rank	SA	Rank	OBA	Rank	HR %	Rank	BB %	Rank	SO %	Rank	RDI %	Rank
Rick Cerone	Overall	.243	126	.335	148	.320	102	1.41	134	9.17	70	14.07	75	.253	120
	Pressure	.200	133	.233	150	.314	106	0.00	119	13.51	30	10.81	38	.182	124
Henry Cotto	Overall	.235	--	.403	--	.269	--	3.36	--	3.82	--	22.29	--	.273	--
	Pressure	.056	--	.056	--	.150	--	0.00	--	5.00	--	25.00	--	.000	158
Rickey Henderson	Overall	.291	32	.497	26	.423	3	4.75	41	18.18	3	11.82	44	.200	157
	Pressure	.431	3	.725	2	.525	1	5.88	31	16.39	13	18.03	99	.364	43
Don Mattingly	Overall	.327	7	.559	8	.378	25	5.27	28	8.10	93	6.03	6	.376	6
	Pressure	.200	133	.308	133	.303	117	1.54	108	13.16	33	7.89	18	.250	91
Bobby Meacham	Overall	.271	73	.409	96	.349	60	2.46	111	8.19	89	14.22	79	.241	130
	Pressure	.333	--	.417	--	.429	--	0.00	--	13.79	--	20.69	--	1.000	--
Mike Pagliarulo	Overall	.234	144	.479	39	.305	124	6.13	12	9.11	73	19.07	129	.279	91
	Pressure	.188	143	.507	29	.278	133	10.14	2	11.11	50	12.35	59	.364	43
Dan Pasqua	Overall	.233	147	.421	89	.319	104	5.35	25	11.05	39	27.35	157	.241	130
	Pressure	.273	72	.568	16	.365	59	9.09	4	13.21	32	22.64	128	.417	20
Willie Randolph	Overall	.305	19	.414	93	.411	5	1.56	128	15.10	10	4.60	1	.360	15
	Pressure	.364	11	.436	69	.462	8	0.00	119	15.15	18	4.55	3	.440	14
Jerry Royster	Overall	.265	81	.439	72	.342	67	3.57	77	10.22	54	14.22	78	.422	--
	Pressure	.355	15	.452	58	.417	22	0.00	119	11.11	50	11.11	41	.364	43
Mark Salas	Overall	.250	--	.400	--	.322	--	3.75	--	8.29	--	12.71	--	.255	--
	Pressure	.250	--	.417	--	.357	--	4.17	--	10.34	--	20.69	--	.375	38
Wayne Tolleson	Overall	.221	152	.241	162	.306	122	0.29	157	10.78	45	18.05	121	.229	146
	Pressure	.340	19	.404	83	.392	31	2.13	98	7.55	107	18.87	106	.500	5
Gary Ward	Overall	.248	116	.384	117	.291	150	3.02	98	5.80	138	17.75	118	.315	51
	Pressure	.292	53	.538	23	.333	82	6.15	26	5.56	128	22.22	124	.333	51
Claudell Washington	Overall	.279	52	.420	91	.336	75	2.88	98	7.96	98	15.93	94	.372	9
	Pressure	.238	113	.238	148	.273	138	0.00	119	4.55	142	27.27	152	.333	--
Dave Winfield	Overall	.275	64	.457	55	.358	49	4.70	43	11.60	31	14.66	82	.368	12
	Pressure	.260	88	.416	80	.321	99	3.90	56	8.33	91	11.90	51	.550	4
Team Average	Overall	.262	9	.418	10	.336	5	3.56	6	9.71	2	15.25	7	.298	3
	Pressure	.271	2	.414	7	.350	4	3.39	4	10.20	3	16.71	8	.358	1
League Average	Overall	.265		.425		.333		3.38		8.94		15.38		.287	
	Pressure	.262		.405		.335		3.07		9.43		16.58		.280	

Additional Miscellaneous Batting Comparisons

	Grass Surface		Artificial Surface		Home Games		Road Games		Runners in Scoring Position		Runners in Scoring Pos and Two Outs		Leading Off Inning		Runners on 3B with less than 2 Outs	
	BA	Rank	BA	Rank	BA	Rank	BA	Rank	BA	Rank	BA	Rank	OBA	Rank	RDI %	Rank
Rick Cerone	.231	137	.310	23	.189	158	.301	26	.203	143	.219	112	.403	16	.667	33
Mike Easler	.291	40	.111	--	.356	--	.195	--	.295	47	.235	--	.381	--	.462	138
Rickey Henderson	.291	42	.290	42	.317	19	.269	67	.203	144	.136	149	.408	13	.389	153
Ron Kittle	.278	--	.273	--	.288	--	.267	--	.216	--	.353	--	.282	--	.385	154
Don Mattingly	.323	10	.347	6	.336	8	.318	13	.320	26	.242	91	.362	46	.696	29
Bobby Meacham	.274	74	.256	85	.280	69	.264	79	.286	60	.308	31	.286	126	.667	--
Mike Pagliarulo	.232	136	.241	103	.214	151	.251	97	.231	126	.150	147	.297	118	.700	25
Dan Pasqua	.234	133	.222	122	.277	74	.198	153	.197	145	.069	160	.299	116	.588	86
Willie Randolph	.294	37	.392	4	.292	54	.321	12	.316	34	.315	27	.387	22	.742	15
Jerry Royster	.268	84	.235	--	.273	80	.256	--	.294	--	.444	--	.419	9	.615	58
Mark Salas	.206	--	.412	--	.235	--	.266	--	.216	--	.200	--	.278	--	.600	71
Wayne Tolleson	.221	149	.220	125	.211	155	.228	130	.276	73	.212	116	.289	124	.526	115
Gary Ward	.249	115	.240	105	.282	67	.215	145	.286	60	.257	77	.286	126	.679	32
Claudell Washington	.275	73	.298	34	.299	45	.262	82	.362	6	.390	4	.206	158	.500	120
Dave Winfield	.277	67	.266	72	.283	66	.268	70	.355	8	.333	16	.303	112	.600	71
Team Average	.261	11	.269	3	.269	7	.255	10	.273	5	.244	8	.313	13	.604	4
League Average	.267		.261		.270		.260		.266		.247		.328		.581	

Pitching vs. Left and Right Handed Batters

		BA	Rank	SA	Rank	OBA	Rank	HR %	Rank	BB %	Rank	SO %	Rank
Neil Allen	vs. Lefties	.303	109	.485	105	.368	104	4.24	101	9.24	69	12.50	81
	vs. Righties	.353	125	.466	103	.436	126	0.75	3	12.03	113	12.03	106
Pat Clements	vs. Lefties	.167	--	.250	--	.255	--	1.19	--	8.33	--	21.88	--
	vs. Righties	.350	124	.455	96	.405	122	1.36	9	8.76	74	5.98	127
Ron Guidry	vs. Lefties	.302	--	.453	--	.362	--	3.49	--	7.37	--	20.00	--
	vs. Righties	.235	34	.409	62	.294	29	3.04	65	7.79	56	19.35	34
Bill Gullickson	vs. Lefties	.283	93	.528	115	.336	66	6.60	125	6.78	27	9.32	118
	vs. Righties	.211	--	.276	--	.238	--	0.00	--	3.75	--	21.25	--
Charles Hudson	vs. Lefties	.268	67	.424	68	.354	89	2.80	51	12.33	110	11.99	89
	vs. Righties	.217	17	.365	34	.270	13	3.72	86	6.02	24	18.62	39
Tommy John	vs. Lefties	.203	9	.260	3	.258	5	0.81	7	5.93	15	13.33	72
	vs. Righties	.305	114	.413	65	.351	92	1.79	15	5.85	22	6.75	125
Dennis Rasmussen	vs. Lefties	.313	113	.535	118	.370	108	5.05	111	8.26	52	17.43	34
	vs. Righties	.248	49	.497	112	.319	56	5.66	121	8.88	78	13.51	87
Rick Rhoden	vs. Lefties	.275	79	.455	90	.342	78	3.86	94	9.11	64	11.58	94
	vs. Righties	.259	62	.380	47	.311	46	2.47	34	6.70	35	16.76	53
Dave Righetti	vs. Lefties	.271	70	.396	49	.324	48	3.13	63	8.18	49	17.27	36
	vs. Righties	.259	63	.350	23	.348	89	2.26	24	11.33	107	18.77	38
Tim Stoddard	vs. Lefties	.276	98	.448	88	.340	76	4.14	97	8.81	61	11.32	97
	vs. Righties	.207	10	.351	25	.260	8	3.37	78	7.05	43	26.43	9
Steve Trout	vs. Lefties	.281	--	.406	--	.378	--	3.13	--	10.81	--	8.11	--
	vs. Righties	.273	85	.383	49	.401	119	1.95	17	17.65	125	12.83	95
Team Average	vs. Lefties	.266	6	.415	6	.335	6	3.16	7	9.25	6	13.52	9
	vs. Righties	.265	9	.419	7	.330	8	3.26	6	8.43	8	14.94	10
League Average	vs. Lefties	.267		.427		.338		3.30		9.47		14.54	
	vs. Righties	.264		.424		.330		3.45		8.56		15.98	

Pitching with Runners on Base and Bases Empty

		BA	Rank	SA	Rank	OBA	Rank	HR %	Rank	BB %	Rank	SO %	Rank
Neil Allen	Runners On	.359	126	.514	109	.443	128	2.82	59	12.87	112	9.36	113
	Bases Empty	.295	111	.442	88	.357	103	2.56	33	8.19	64	15.20	63
Pat Clements	Runners On	.298	98	.379	37	.364	97	0.62	2	9.47	72	11.05	106
	Bases Empty	.301	114	.420	67	.363	106	2.10	19	7.64	51	9.55	118
Ron Guidry	Runners On	.244	34	.386	48	.289	13	1.70	17	5.67	13	22.68	11
	Bases Empty	.250	50	.438	85	.318	54	4.04	94	9.03	80	17.39	41
Bill Gullickson	Runners On	.327	--	.418	--	.391	--	0.00	--	9.09	--	9.09	--
	Bases Empty	.220	15	.425	75	.250	6	5.51	122	3.79	7	16.67	47
Charles Hudson	Runners On	.236	26	.367	24	.290	15	3.06	70	7.39	34	15.95	49
	Bases Empty	.241	34	.407	55	.320	60	3.49	75	9.90	97	15.36	62
Tommy John	Runners On	.283	89	.368	26	.348	75	1.30	9	7.98	40	7.98	121
	Bases Empty	.291	109	.401	51	.326	69	1.86	13	4.21	9	7.76	125
Dennis Rasmussen	Runners On	.219	9	.405	59	.285	7	3.26	78	8.50	53	17.00	36
	Bases Empty	.286	102	.566	123	.355	100	7.00	125	8.95	78	12.37	96
Rick Rhoden	Runners On	.259	54	.399	54	.324	50	3.42	84	8.85	59	15.08	58
	Bases Empty	.274	90	.432	79	.329	74	3.07	55	7.41	49	13.29	85
Dave Righetti	Runners On	.279	83	.383	41	.356	87	2.49	46	11.30	101	16.74	38
	Bases Empty	.242	36	.335	15	.322	65	2.48	29	9.44	88	20.56	23
Tim Stoddard	Runners On	.230	19	.375	32	.302	20	3.29	80	9.88	80	19.77	21
	Bases Empty	.239	31	.403	52	.285	17	3.98	92	6.07	37	20.56	22
Team Average	Runners On	.268	6	.406	4	.336	4	2.73	2	9.34	7	14.72	8
	Bases Empty	.264	10	.427	10	.328	8	3.60	8	8.20	9	14.25	12
League Average	Runners On	.271		.428		.343		3.25		9.68		14.87	
	Bases Empty	.260		.424		.326		3.49		8.34		15.79	

Overall Pitching Compared to Late Inning Pressure Situations

		BA	Rank	SA	Rank	OBA	Rank	HR %	Rank	BB %	Rank	SO %	Rank
Neil Allen	Overall	.326	120	.477	109	.399	125	2.68	41	10.53	100	12.28	96
	Pressure	.316	--	.316	--	.435	--	0.00	--	16.67	--	8.33	--
Pat Clements	Overall	.299	113	.398	44	.364	107	1.32	4	8.65	66	10.37	110
	Pressure	.333	117	.457	94	.364	91	1.23	32	5.56	21	8.89	113
Cecilio Guante	Overall	.247	--	.441	--	.323	--	4.71	--	10.26	--	23.59	--
	Pressure	.200	12	.382	61	.267	12	5.45	116	6.67	31	25.00	8
Ron Guidry	Overall	.248	34	.417	62	.307	26	3.13	65	7.71	42	19.47	22
	Pressure	.304	105	.518	111	.339	70	3.57	86	5.00	17	15.00	63
Charles Hudson	Overall	.239	24	.391	38	.308	29	3.32	75	8.89	69	15.60	52
	Pressure	.222	32	.286	15	.269	14	1.59	39	5.88	24	13.24	82
Tommy John	Overall	.288	104	.387	35	.335	71	1.63	6	5.86	16	7.86	125
	Pressure	.297	100	.324	27	.333	62	0.00	1	5.00	17	2.50	127
Dennis Rasmussen	Overall	.260	61	.504	118	.328	62	5.56	122	8.77	68	14.19	71
	Pressure	.222	32	.389	64	.275	20	2.78	66	7.50	42	5.00	125
Rick Rhoden	Overall	.268	75	.419	65	.327	60	3.20	71	7.98	49	14.01	75
	Pressure	.192	9	.346	38	.236	3	3.85	91	5.26	20	12.28	95
Dave Righetti	Overall	.262	69	.362	16	.341	75	2.49	27	10.50	96	18.38	30
	Pressure	.264	69	.346	39	.347	73	1.97	45	11.67	96	18.67	35
Tim Stoddard	Overall	.235	18	.391	39	.293	10	3.68	86	7.77	44	20.21	21
	Pressure	.273	81	.406	72	.329	59	3.13	74	7.86	48	15.00	63
Team Average	Overall	.266	8	.418	8	.332	8	3.22	6	8.71	7	14.46	11
	Pressure	.267	9	.395	5	.324	4	2.94	7	7.95	1	15.27	9
League Average	Overall	.265		.425		.333		3.38		8.94		15.38	
	Pressure	.262		.404		.337		2.99		9.73		16.42	

Additional Miscellaneous Pitching Comparisons

	Grass Surface BA	Rank	Artificial Surface BA	Rank	Home Games BA	Rank	Road Games BA	Rank	Runners in Scoring Position BA	Rank	Runners in Scoring Pos and Two Outs BA	Rank	Leading Off Inning OBA	Rank
Neil Allen	.332	123	.250	--	.326	122	.325	121	.354	123	.267	84	.360	95
Pat Clements	.291	96	.348	114	.297	109	.301	104	.324	115	.347	117	.377	105
Cecilio Guante	.206	--	.448	--	.205	--	.328	--	.222	27	.250	--	.452	--
Ron Guidry	.251	39	.235	37	.224	20	.271	68	.265	69	.286	97	.262	13
Bill Gullickson	.253	46	.000	--	.238	37	.314	--	.406	--	.182	--	.288	--
Charles Hudson	.242	22	.215	19	.248	51	.231	15	.228	33	.172	13	.299	38
Tommy John	.295	103	.250	52	.304	114	.273	74	.260	67	.250	69	.323	59
Dennis Rasmussen	.262	62	.250	52	.252	56	.266	58	.198	11	.212	44	.363	97
Rick Rhoden	.241	20	.354	116	.265	78	.271	69	.218	24	.183	18	.311	44
Dave Righetti	.265	69	.250	52	.218	14	.306	110	.289	88	.292	100	.373	104
Tim Stoddard	.238	18	.211	--	.235	29	.236	18	.223	28	.191	25	.229	4
Steve Trout	.264	66	.750	--	.213	--	.321	119	.321	--	.250	--	.453	--
Team Average	.261	6	.290	14	.258	8	.273	8	.267	7	.254	11	.319	6
League Average	.267		.261		.260		.270		.266		.247		.328	

OAKLAND A'S

What does Tony LaRussa like to do more than any American League manager?

(a) Sit back for a quiet evening at home, browsing through the *Stanford Law Review*;

(b) Drive across the Bay Bridge to Ghiradelli Square for a plateful of guanchali at Modesto Lanzone;

(c) Have his baserunners steal third base.

Not knowing for sure about LaRussa's reading or eating habits, we come down squarely on the side of (c).

Stealing third base is an area that has fallen through the increasingly narrow cracks within the body of baseball statistics. Its regular practitioners are few, and to our knowledge no league-wide numbers had ever been compiled on this particular specialty. It has been a little like the dark side of the moon once was: Everyone knows that it's there, but no one's quite sure what an investigation would show.

In the case of the Athletics, the regular old 1987 statistics show that they attempted 203 stolen bases, the third-highest total in the American League behind Milwaukee (250) and Seattle (247). But when it came to stealing third base, we found that no team in the league did it as often as the A's, who were successful on 28 of 34 attempts at swiping third.

How does that rate of 82 percent stack up against the rest of the league? Is stealing third any easier, according to the percentages, than stealing second? What would your guess be?

Before you go on to the answer, consider these elements that are a part of the basic geometry of the game. The distance of a catcher's throw from home plate to second base is 127 feet, 3 3/8 inches. From home to third, of course, it's 90 feet. But the compensating factor is that without a fielder holding him on, a runner on second generally takes a bigger lead than a runner on first. In addition, most pitchers are more adept at a quick step-and-throw to first base than at a more cumbersome wheel-and-throw motion to second. And then there are the pitchers who don't even step as they throw to first.

Well, what's your answer? We use the honor system, so here are the figures from the 1987 season:

	American League			National League		
	SB	CS	Pct.	SB	CS	Pct.
Stealing 2nd Base	1553	671	.698	1668	644	.721
Stealing 3rd Base	173	82	.678	174	70	.713
Stealing Home	8	19	.296	9	43	.173
Totals	1734	772	.692	1851	757	.710

In terms of the overall percentages, stealing third base turns out to be a little bit harder than stealing second. (The figures for stealing home are distorted to a large degree by aborted suicide squeeze plays, in which the runner hung up between third and home is officially regarded as "caught stealing" if he broke from third on the pitch.) Which teams stole third most frequently, and which teams were best at it? That's where the A's come in.

	American League				National League		
	SB	CS	Pct.		SB	CS	Pct.
Seattle	11	1	.917	Houston	14	0	1.000
Kansas City	10	1	.909	Cincinnati	27	5	.844
Chicago	10	2	.833	San Diego	22	5	.815
Oakland	28	6	.824	Los Angeles	23	6	.793
Detroit	16	7	.696	St. Louis	31	10	.756
California	21	10	.677	Pittsburgh	15	5	.750
Boston	2	1	.667	New York	6	4	.600
New York	17	10	.630	Montreal	11	8	.579
Milwaukee	18	12	.600	Chicago	6	5	.545
Texas	16	11	.593	San Francisco	8	8	.500
Baltimore	10	8	.556	Atlanta	7	8	.467
Minnesota	11	9	.550	Philadelphia	4	6	.400
Cleveland	3	3	.500				
Toronto	0	1	.000				

LaRussa's men were successful 82 percent of the time, but there were two other facets to his stealing-third strategy that bear comment: the variety of players who were involved, and the fact that so many of the attempts came with two outs.

Teams with a lot of attempted steals of third base generally had a single player specialize in it. Of the Cardinals' total of 41 attempts, Vince Coleman (surprise!) was responsible for 29, including 24 successful steals of third, the most in the majors. Eric Davis of the Reds was 14 for 14, the most steals of third without being caught. Similarly, Paul Molitor (10 for 10), Tony Gwynn (10 for 10), and Devon White (8 for 11) all accounted for sizeable chunks of their team's total.

Oakland? Despite its league-leading 34 attempts, no one player had more than six. And which of the Oakland swifties stole third base most often? It was a tie between Mike Davis and that ol' speedster, Jose Canseco; each was a perfect 6 for 6. Alfredo Griffin was 4 for 6, Carney Lansford 3 for 5, with five other players involved in smaller doses.

Moreover, whoever fashioned the baseball adage that you should never make the first or third out of an inning at third base obviously doesn't have the manager of the Athletics as a disciple. LaRussa didn't fear making the third out at third, otherwise he wouldn't have allowed his base runners to try to steal third 15 times with two down, more than double the amount of such attempts by any other team in the league. These tables show the distribution of attempted steals of third according to the number of outs at the time:

	American League				National League		
	None Out	One Out	Two Out		None Out	One Out	Two Out
Oakland	3	16	15	Cincinnati	4	9	19
California	7	17	7	San Diego	1	11	15
Texas	8	14	5	St. Louis	10	21	10
Detroit	4	15	4	Houston	3	6	5
Chicago	1	8	3	Chicago	0	8	3
New York	3	21	3	Montreal	2	14	3
Cleveland	0	4	2	Pittsburgh	3	14	3
Kansas City	2	7	2	Atlanta	2	11	2
Boston	1	1	1	Los Angeles	3	24	2
Milwaukee	3	26	1	Philadelphia	2	6	2
Baltimore	4	14	0	New York	0	9	1
Minnesota	3	17	0	San Francisco	4	12	0
Seattle	3	9	0	Totals	34	145	65
Toronto	1	0	0				
Totals	43	169	43				

Besides breaking down stolen-base attempts according to a particular base and how many outs, we also looked at the breakdown against left- and right-handed pitchers. We found that while runners have a better success rate stealing second base against right-handed pitchers, that pattern is reversed when runners try to steal third base.

That difference certainly has a lot to do with the type of hitter (left-handed or right-handed) who can be expected to be at the plate against a particular type of pitcher. Since left-handed pitchers normally face right-handed batters, a catcher would more often have to throw around a hitter in an attempt to catch a runner stealing third. Similarly, against right-handed pitchers, a left-handed batter may momentarily obstruct the catcher's vision in the case of a runner stealing second, thereby helping the runner's chances. These totals include all stolen-base attempts last year in both leagues:

	Vs. Left-Handers			Vs. Right-Handers		
	SB	CS	Pct.	SB	CS	Pct.
Stealing 2nd Base	765	434	63.8	2456	881	73.6
Stealing 3rd Base	165	52	76.0	182	100	64.5
Stealing Home	4	24	14.3	13	38	25.5
Totals	934	510	64.7	2651	1019	72.2

But left-handed pitchers have an additional effect in thwarting base stealers, beyond those percentages: Fewer runners *try to steal* against lefties than against righties. The major-league rate of stolen base-attempts per nine innings is more than 20 percent higher against right-handers (1.30) than against left-handers (1.07).

So if you're watching the Athletics this season, look for the situation with an Oakland runner on second, even if he's not generally a threat to run, even if there are two out, and especially if a left-handed pitcher is on the mound. Then nudge the guy next to you in the stands, and show him this essay. Chances are that by the time he's through reading it, that runner will be on third.

Dave Parker: Cooperstown Bound?

How will history judge Dave Parker?

Parker, who makes his American League debut in 1988, has alternately thrilled and disappointed his fans throughout his major-league career. He commanded attention in the mid- to late '70s, when he batted over .300 for five straight seasons, including two batting championships, and capped that five-year span by batting .341 during post-season play as the Pirates won the world championship in 1979. His average season over those five years: .321, 23 homers, 98 RBI.

Next came his blue period, four more years in Pittsburgh in which he not only failed to average .300, 20 homers, or 80 RBI; he failed to reach any of those levels in any of those four seasons. But that was the least of his worries, as he spent a good deal of his time dodging batteries and bullets thrown from the stands, recovering from injuries, and battling to defend his reputation.

Free agency following the 1983 season had a therapeutic effect, and during his four years in Cincinnati, only one major leaguer drove in as many runs (Don Mattingly had 483 to Parker's 432). Traded to Oakland during the winter meetings, Parker brings to the American League a 15-year batting average of .297, with 273 home runs. Among active major leaguers, only Jim Rice has an average that high with as many home runs (.302, 364).

In assessing Parker's career, consider those numbers: he is 27 homers shy of 300, and three batting average points shy of .300. How many players in major-league history are in the 300/.300 Club? Glad you asked.

	HR	BA
Hank Aaron	755	.305
Joe DiMaggio	361	.325
Jimmie Foxx	534	.325
Lou Gehrig	493	.340
Hank Greenberg	331	.313
Rogers Hornsby	301	.358
Chuck Klein	300	.320
Willie Mays	660	.302
Johnny Mize	359	.312
Stan Musial	475	.331
Mel Ott	511	.304
Jim Rice	364	.302
Babe Ruth	714	.342
Al Simmons	307	.334
Ted Williams	521	.344

Except for Rice, who is still active, what do the other 14 club members have in common? A plaque in Cooperstown, N.Y.

Ah, some among you may be thinking, "Sure, Parker may

well hit 27 more home runs, but picking up those three points on his batting average may not be easy at his age (37 on June 9) and in that park (Oakland Coliseum, which has depressed batting averages more than any other stadium over the past five years). So he may never make that 300/.300 Club, and please don't give me that Hall-of-Fame junk."

Alright, maybe he won't see .300 again, so let's look through the Club's admission applications file to find players whose qualifications came up just short: guys who hit the 300 home runs, but whose batting average fell between .295 and .300. There are five such players in major-league history:

	HR	BA
Orlando Cepeda	379	.297
Al Kaline	399	.297
Mickey Mantle	536	.298
Eddie Murray	305	.296
Duke Snider	407	.295

Mantle, Snider, and Kaline are Hall of Famers, and Murray is still active. That leaves Cepeda as the only player in major league history with 300 or more home runs and a batting average of .295 or higher whose plaque is not in the Hall of Fame.

In assessing Parker's chances at eventual enshrinement, the fact that 18 of 19 retired players who have reached those statistical plateaus are in is about as strong a statistical harbinger as you can get. Even so, the Cepeda precedent is troubling: Cepeda, like Parker, is a past winner of the National League Most Valuable Player award. Cepeda, like Parker, was the best hitter on a world-champion team. Cepeda, like Parker, went to the American League late in his career. And unfortunately, Cepeda, like Parker, has seen his name linked to drugs.

In the 1985 Curtis Strong trial in Federal District Court in Pittsburgh, Parker testified that he used drugs during some of the years that he played in Pittsburgh, but that he has since stopped. How much the drug issue hurts a player's Hall of Fame chances is an open question. After all, we're not talking about a Supreme Court nominee here. Presumably, the American people hold a Judge Ginsberg to a higher standard of past conduct than the baseball writers do Cepeda, Parker, Ferguson Jenkins, and others. Nevertheless, the rules that guide the baseball writers who vote state that Hall of Famers are to be chosen not only on the basis of playing ability, but also on "integrity, sportsmanship, character, (and their contribution) to baseball in general."

The late Dick Young took the stance that he would never vote for a "druggie" for the Hall of Fame, but that strident position is likely to become less of a factor as younger writers qualify to be Hall-of-Fame electors (you must be a member of the writers' association for at least 10 years before you get to vote).

Ours is not to decide that question—after all, the Hall of Fame can enshrine anyone it wants—but we do have some other evidence that we believe should definitely be considered when the time comes to turn thumbs-up or thumbs-down on Parker. Our evidence relates to his on-field ability:

- Parker is the only player in the majors who has hit at least 60 points higher with runners on base than he has with the bases empty over the past five years (among players with 1,000 at bats in each category).
- Parker is the only player in the majors who has hit at least 50 points higher with runners on base than he has with the bases empty over the past 10 years (among players with 2,000 at bats in each category).
- Parker has batted over .340 with runners in scoring position in six of the 13 years that we have been monitoring these things.
- Since 1975, Parker has batted .344 with the bases loaded.

It's one of the frustrations of our job that while computers have now made us aware of these types of numbers for contemporary players, we don't have the same breakdowns for the great players of the past. It would be great to compare Parker's figures with those of Lou Gehrig, Ted Williams, or Willie Mays, but until the Elias archaeologists produce a major find in the way of reliable play-by-play scorecards from earlier eras, we'll be somewhat limited in our comparisons.

But Parker's outstanding performance in these clutch-hitting categories should play a part in the evaluation process among Hall of Fame voters. The same should be true for someone like Graig Nettles, a possible future nominee based on traditional statistics, who also has hit higher with runners on base than with the bases empty in each of the 13 seasons for which we have been keeping track.

As this type of material becomes available, let's hope that the voters take note of a player's performance in the clutch, and incorporate that factor into their vote. In earlier eras, there was no one in the clutch-hitting forest to hear the noise made by the falling trees. But now that we have our noise meters in place, the data is there for everyone to evaluate.

WON-LOST RECORD BY STARTING POSITION

OAKLAND 81-81	C	1B	2B	3B	SS	LF	CF	RF	P	DH	Leadoff	Relief	Starts
Joaquin Andujar	·	·	·	·	·	·	·	·	7-6	·	·	·	7-6
Tony Bernazard	·	·	27-28	·	·	·	·	·	·	1-2	8-9	·	28-30
Greg Cadaret	·	·	·	·	·	·	·	·	·	·	·	14-15	·
Jose Canseco	·	·	·	·	·	61-67	·	·	·	17-12	·	·	78-79
Bill Caudill	·	·	·	·	·	·	·	·	·	·	·	3-3	·
Ron Cey	·	3-2	·	2-1	·	·	·	·	·	14-11	·	·	19-14
Chris Codiroli	·	·	·	·	·	·	·	·	0-3	·	·	·	0-3
Mike Davis	·	·	·	·	·	·	·	57-52	·	4-8	4-11	·	61-60
Storm Davis	·	·	·	·	·	·	·	·	3-2	·	·	·	3-2
Dennis Eckersley	·	·	·	·	·	·	·	·	0-2	·	·	30-22	0-2
Mike Gallego	·	·	6-13	4-1	8-1	·	·	·	·	·	0-1	·	18-15
Alfredo Griffin	·	·	0-1	·	65-71	·	·	·	·	·	5-9	·	65-72
Moose Haas	·	·	·	·	·	·	·	·	6-3	·	·	·	6-3
Brian Harper	·	·	·	·	·	·	·	·	·	2-2	·	·	2-2
Steve Henderson	·	·	·	·	·	1-0	·	9-15	·	4-0	·	·	14-15
Rick Honeycutt	·	·	·	·	·	·	·	·	1-3	·	·	0-3	1-3
Jay Howell	·	·	·	·	·	·	·	·	·	·	·	25-11	·
Reggie Jackson	·	·	·	·	·	·	·	10-10	·	29-34	·	·	39-44
Stan Javier	·	2-1	·	·	·	3-1	14-15	0-3	·	·	1-1	·	19-20
Bill Krueger	·	·	·	·	·	·	·	·	·	·	·	1-8	·
Dennis Lamp	·	·	·	·	·	·	·	·	2-3	·	·	11-20	2-3
Carney Lansford	·	1-5	·	68-71	·	·	·	·	·	2-2	·	·	71-78
Gary Lavelle	·	·	·	·	·	·	·	·	·	·	·	1-5	·
Dave Leiper	·	·	·	·	·	·	·	·	·	·	·	22-23	·
Johnnie LeMaster	·	·	1-3	0-1	0-1	·	·	·	·	·	·	·	1-5
Mark McGwire	·	73-68	·	4-1	·	·	·	1-1	·	·	·	·	78-70
Dwayne Murphy	·	·	·	·	·	·	35-35	·	·	·	0-1	·	35-35
Gene Nelson	·	·	·	·	·	·	·	·	2-4	·	·	23-25	2-4
Rob Nelson	·	2-5	·	·	·	·	·	·	·	·	·	·	2-5
Steve Ontiveros	·	·	·	·	·	·	·	·	12-10	·	·	7-6	12-10
Dave Otto	·	·	·	·	·	·	·	·	·	·	·	0-3	·
Tony Phillips	·	·	47-36	3-4	4-4	·	·	·	·	·	13-7	·	54-44
Eric Plunk	·	·	·	·	·	·	·	·	5-6	·	·	12-9	5-6
Luis Polonia	·	·	·	·	·	16-13	32-31	3-0	·	6-2	50-42	·	57-46
Jose Rijo	·	·	·	·	·	·	·	·	3-11	·	·	0-7	3-11
Rick Rodriguez	·	·	·	·	·	·	·	·	·	·	·	4-11	·
Alejandro Sanchez	·	·	·	·	·	·	·	1-0	·	·	·	·	1-0
Matt Sinatro	·	·	·	·	·	·	·	·	·	·	·	·	·
Terry Steinbach	46-50	·	·	0-2	·	·	·	·	·	1-6	·	·	47-58
Dave Stewart	·	·	·	·	·	·	·	20-17	·	·	·	·	20-17
Mickey Tettleton	35-31	·	·	·	·	·	·	·	·	1-0	·	·	36-31
Dave Von Ohlen	·	·	·	·	·	·	·	·	·	·	·	1-3	·
Walter Weiss	·	·	·	4-4	·	·	·	·	·	·	·	·	4-4
Jerry Willard	·	·	·	·	·	·	·	·	·	·	0-2	·	0-2
Curt Young	·	·	·	·	·	·	·	·	20-11	·	·	·	20-11

Batting vs. Left and Right Handed Pitchers

		BA	Rank	SA	Rank	OBA	Rank	HR %	Rank	BB %	Rank	SO %	Rank
Tony Bernazard	vs. Lefties	.230	127	.381	104	.323	89	2.88	89	11.88	33	13.75	73
	vs. Righties	.258	91	.397	99	.324	89	2.72	101	8.72	81	13.80	67
Jose Canseco	vs. Lefties	.309	28	.618	8	.356	56	7.35	6	7.21	115	20.72	128
	vs. Righties	.232	133	.399	98	.288	141	3.76	74	7.25	107	23.67	149
Ron Cey	vs. Lefties	.237	116	.421	81	.372	44	3.95	60	17.02	8	27.66	156
	vs. Righties	.179	--	.321	--	.324	--	3.57	--	17.65	--	17.65	--
Mike Davis	vs. Lefties	.278	66	.500	33	.326	82	4.76	39	7.14	118	22.14	137
	vs. Righties	.261	88	.457	54	.319	96	4.35	51	7.86	93	15.48	91
Mike Gallego	vs. Lefties	.300	39	.467	50	.348	65	3.33	74	7.35	110	17.65	104
	vs. Righties	.203	--	.234	--	.292	--	0.00	--	9.33	--	12.00	--
Alfredo Griffin	vs. Lefties	.245	104	.309	140	.292	127	0.53	144	5.31	143	6.28	6
	vs. Righties	.275	58	.373	120	.315	104	0.65	147	5.12	146	8.43	24
Steve Henderson	vs. Lefties	.311	26	.467	50	.374	42	3.33	74	9.09	72	9.09	28
	vs. Righties	.208	--	.292	--	.296	--	0.00	--	11.11	--	37.04	--
Reggie Jackson	vs. Lefties	.292	--	.521	--	.333	--	4.17	--	3.92	--	29.41	--
	vs. Righties	.208	155	.382	112	.291	135	4.51	47	9.60	62	25.39	151
Stan Javier	vs. Lefties	.165	159	.212	160	.253	151	1.18	130	10.10	51	17.17	101
	vs. Righties	.212	--	.318	--	.307	--	1.52	--	11.69	--	20.78	--
Carney Lansford	vs. Lefties	.280	62	.440	70	.352	61	4.57	46	8.67	84	8.16	20
	vs. Righties	.293	36	.462	52	.372	35	2.90	95	9.89	59	6.44	8
Mark McGwire	vs. Lefties	.287	52	.626	6	.400	21	9.36	1	16.67	9	19.05	117
	vs. Righties	.290	49	.614	2	.355	55	8.55	1	8.35	89	21.11	140
Dwayne Murphy	vs. Lefties	.182	155	.288	146	.304	117	3.03	87	14.81	16	27.16	155
	vs. Righties	.255	99	.412	89	.421	5	3.92	69	22.66	1	19.21	128
Tony Phillips	vs. Lefties	.289	47	.383	103	.403	20	2.34	103	16.03	12	10.90	42
	vs. Righties	.215	151	.367	123	.302	128	2.79	99	11.23	35	20.70	138
Luis Polonia	vs. Lefties	.236	119	.326	134	.292	128	0.00	145	7.29	112	17.71	106
	vs. Righties	.301	28	.416	84	.347	61	1.16	137	6.70	116	12.60	59
Terry Steinbach	vs. Lefties	.292	45	.504	30	.359	54	3.65	63	7.84	101	14.38	80
	vs. Righties	.280	50	.441	65	.344	65	4.33	52	7.02	113	15.44	90
Mickey Tettleton	vs. Lefties	.214	141	.310	139	.323	88	2.38	101	14.14	20	19.19	118
	vs. Righties	.181	161	.331	143	.271	154	4.72	43	10.74	46	30.87	158
Team Average	vs. Lefties	.264	8	.435	3	.341	3	3.79	3	10.25	2	16.04	9
	vs. Righties	.258	12	.424	8	.329	9	3.52	6	9.13	7	17.38	14
League Average	vs. Lefties	.265		.422		.333		3.29		8.94		15.64	
	vs. Righties	.265		.427		.334		3.43		8.94		15.26	

Batting with Runners on Base and Bases Empty

		BA	Rank	SA	Rank	OBA	Rank	HR %	Rank	BB %	Rank	SO %	Rank
Tony Bernazard	Runners On	.245	119	.339	139	.345	75	1.56	122	13.30	30	14.59	89
	Bases Empty	.254	93	.425	84	.309	112	3.49	82	7.06	103	13.24	58
Jose Canseco	Runners On	.270	79	.460	59	.327	103	4.15	56	8.56	98	18.96	129
	Bases Empty	.246	107	.478	47	.294	127	5.57	32	6.04	126	26.10	152
Mike Davis	Runners On	.269	83	.453	66	.332	99	3.77	61	9.39	81	16.73	109
	Bases Empty	.262	79	.479	46	.311	108	4.96	43	6.29	122	17.55	114
Alfredo Griffin	Runners On	.321	24	.419	85	.346	73	1.40	126	3.36	158	6.72	15
	Bases Empty	.219	144	.294	153	.276	148	0.00	157	6.64	114	8.31	13
Reggie Jackson	Runners On	.217	144	.455	61	.289	138	6.99	8	8.18	101	23.27	149
	Bases Empty	.223	141	.363	121	.302	121	2.59	103	9.30	56	27.91	156
Carney Lansford	Runners On	.296	47	.465	56	.380	40	3.48	67	11.81	49	9.96	33
	Bases Empty	.284	44	.448	66	.356	44	3.40	83	7.78	89	4.72	1
Mark McGwire	Runners On	.302	42	.595	3	.383	36	7.02	6	11.85	47	19.51	132
	Bases Empty	.279	49	.635	3	.359	41	10.16	1	10.45	35	21.19	137
Dwayne Murphy	Runners On	.330	15	.500	29	.462	3	3.41	70	20.83	3	18.33	123
	Bases Empty	.168	162	.290	156	.335	59	3.82	74	20.12	1	23.78	145
Tony Phillips	Runners On	.287	58	.490	39	.382	38	4.20	54	13.95	27	13.95	80
	Bases Empty	.212	152	.301	148	.309	115	1.69	128	12.27	17	19.33	127
Luis Polonia	Runners On	.333	13	.444	68	.354	65	1.17	131	3.35	159	9.50	28
	Bases Empty	.258	90	.367	118	.324	86	0.76	145	8.97	65	16.21	94
Terry Steinbach	Runners On	.316	28	.503	27	.368	50	3.51	66	6.22	130	15.54	97
	Bases Empty	.259	85	.432	75	.335	61	4.55	51	8.16	75	14.69	74
Mickey Tettleton	Runners On	.218	142	.368	119	.346	74	4.60	47	16.07	11	24.11	152
	Bases Empty	.177	160	.290	155	.250	158	3.23	85	8.82	66	27.94	157
Team Average	Runners On	.283	3	.454	2	.355	4	3.61	5	10.00	5	15.50	9
	Bases Empty	.243	14	.409	11	.317	14	3.61	7	9.12	3	18.02	13
League Average	Runners On	.271		.428		.343		3.25		9.68		14.87	
	Bases Empty	.260		.424		.326		3.49		8.34		15.79	

Overall Batting Compared to Late Inning Pressure Situations

		BA	Rank	SA	Rank	OBA	Rank	HR %	Rank	BB %	Rank	SO %	Rank	RDI %	Rank
Tony Bernazard	Overall	.250	111	.393	110	.323	96	2.76	101	9.60	62	13.79	70	.234	140
	Pressure	.304	43	.518	27	.409	24	3.57	61	14.71	23	19.12	108	.300	72
Jose Canseco	Overall	.257	98	.470	44	.310	115	4.92	38	7.24	109	22.72	147	.300	68
	Pressure	.262	86	.440	65	.315	105	3.57	61	6.52	119	23.91	134	.455	11
Ron Cey	Overall	.221	--	.394	--	.359	--	3.85	--	17.19	--	25.00	--	.152	--
	Pressure	.471	--	.706	--	.526	--	5.88	--	10.53	--	5.26	--	.182	124
Mike Davis	Overall	.265	82	.468	47	.320	100	4.45	51	7.68	102	17.18	113	.303	66
	Pressure	.313	34	.578	14	.400	26	6.25	25	13.16	33	25.00	141	.400	27
Alfredo Griffin	Overall	.263	86	.348	143	.306	121	0.61	151	5.19	147	7.61	14	.339	29
	Pressure	.319	29	.348	111	.351	70	0.00	119	5.13	136	7.69	15	.500	5
Reggie Jackson	Overall	.220	153	.402	102	.297	141	4.46	50	8.82	81	25.94	154	.202	156
	Pressure	.212	128	.394	92	.257	143	4.55	47	5.71	127	25.71	147	.133	142
Stan Javier	Overall	.185	--	.258	--	.276	--	1.32	--	10.80	--	18.75	--	.135	--
	Pressure	.118	--	.118	--	.286	--	0.00	--	18.18	--	18.18	--	.111	147
Carney Lansford	Overall	.289	35	.455	60	.366	38	3.43	85	9.51	64	6.97	8	.336	32
	Pressure	.235	116	.383	98	.333	82	3.70	59	11.70	46	8.51	25	.333	51
Mark McGwire	Overall	.289	34	.618	1	.370	35	8.80	1	11.08	38	20.44	137	.282	85
	Pressure	.288	58	.600	10	.345	76	8.75	7	6.90	114	25.29	144	.105	152
Dwayne Murphy	Overall	.233	146	.374	121	.388	15	3.65	73	20.42	1	21.48	142	.348	22
	Pressure	.179	148	.282	140	.304	115	2.56	81	14.89	22	25.53	146	.200	117
Tony Phillips	Overall	.240	131	.372	124	.337	73	2.64	104	12.93	17	17.23	114	.293	72
	Pressure	.161	157	.304	135	.250	147	3.57	61	10.77	112	20.00	112	.190	121
Luis Polonia	Overall	.287	38	.398	108	.335	76	0.92	141	6.82	119	13.65	64	.351	21
	Pressure	.283	65	.321	127	.333	82	0.00	119	7.02	113	19.30	109	.280	79
Terry Steinbach	Overall	.284	43	.463	49	.349	59	4.09	63	7.31	107	15.07	91	.287	81
	Pressure	.262	85	.426	74	.338	80	4.92	42	8.82	85	16.18	87	.231	102
Mickey Tettleton	Overall	.194	161	.322	151	.292	148	3.79	68	12.10	24	26.21	155	.246	127
	Pressure	.217	--	.348	--	.321	--	4.35	--	13.79	--	27.59	--	.333	--
Team Average	Overall	.260	11	.428	7	.333	8	3.61	4	9.51	4	16.93	13	.289	7
	Pressure	.258	9	.415	6	.334	7	3.66	3	9.84	5	18.88	14	.295	4
League Average	Overall	.265		.425		.333		3.38		8.94		15.38		.287	
	Pressure	.262		.405		.335		3.07		9.43		16.58		.280	

Additional Miscellaneous Batting Comparisons

	Grass Surface		Artificial Surface		Home Games		Road Games		Runners in Scoring Position		Runners in Scoring Pos and Two Outs		Leading Off Inning		Runners on 3B with less than 2 Outs	
	BA	Rank	BA	Rank	BA	Rank	BA	Rank	BA	Rank	BA	Rank	OBA	Rank	RDI %	Rank
Tony Bernazard	.249	116	.258	84	.238	125	.261	84	.217	136	.183	137	.231	154	.500	120
Jose Canseco	.266	88	.210	135	.275	76	.241	114	.262	91	.273	59	.308	105	.468	136
Mike Davis	.275	70	.220	127	.261	100	.269	65	.260	93	.340	15	.339	63	.609	64
Mike Gallego	.250	--	.250	--	.247	--	.255	--	.242	--	.143	--	.333	--	.545	104
Alfredo Griffin	.258	101	.289	44	.236	127	.287	38	.286	60	.306	34	.268	136	.556	99
Reggie Jackson	.220	150	.224	121	.218	147	.222	138	.169	153	.133	150	.374	31	.368	156
Stan Javier	.186	159	.182	--	.264	89	.078	--	.167	154	.000	162	.333	--	.500	--
Carney Lansford	.286	48	.302	28	.288	62	.290	35	.333	13	.321	22	.349	53	.522	118
Mark McGwire	.288	46	.296	37	.277	73	.301	27	.291	53	.271	61	.365	39	.559	98
Dwayne Murphy	.225	145	.268	67	.178	160	.280	49	.333	13	.281	54	.369	35	.714	19
Tony Phillips	.248	118	.200	141	.251	110	.230	126	.275	75	.289	50	.280	131	.733	16
Luis Polonia	.292	38	.258	83	.258	104	.317	14	.333	13	.298	44	.322	91	.593	83
Terry Steinbach	.295	35	.220	125	.234	130	.324	10	.250	102	.191	133	.358	48	.647	46
Mickey Tettleton	.205	156	.150	160	.219	146	.170	162	.137	162	.182	138	.273	134	.545	104
Team Average	.263	9	.243	12	.251	13	.268	4	.262	7	.252	5	.331	5	.532	14
League Average	.267		.261		.270		.260		.266		.247		.328		.581	

Pitching vs. Left and Right Handed Batters

		BA	Rank	SA	Rank	OBA	Rank	HR %	Rank	BB %	Rank	SO %	Rank
Joaquin Andujar	vs. Lefties	.267	64	.397	50	.356	91	2.59	41	12.03	107	11.28	98
	vs. Righties	.271	--	.500	--	.341	--	6.78	--	7.58	--	12.88	--
Dennis Eckersley	vs. Lefties	.272	74	.429	71	.313	32	2.72	44	5.56	10	16.16	42
	vs. Righties	.196	4	.312	8	.220	1	2.40	30	2.29	1	30.92	4
Moose Haas	vs. Lefties	.307	112	.446	85	.336	67	2.97	58	4.63	3	6.48	126
	vs. Righties	.377	--	.681	--	.411	--	5.80	--	5.48	--	8.22	--
Dennis Lamp	vs. Lefties	.316	120	.379	36	.405	122	1.05	11	13.39	117	14.29	60
	vs. Righties	.333	120	.507	114	.365	101	2.90	58	4.67	12	13.33	89
Dave Leiper	vs. Lefties	.198	7	.354	17	.259	6	4.17	98	7.34	36	18.35	28
	vs. Righties	.291	--	.447	--	.351	--	1.94	--	8.70	--	11.30	--
Gene Nelson	vs. Lefties	.259	54	.393	45	.300	17	1.67	19	5.79	13	16.60	41
	vs. Righties	.239	37	.428	72	.307	42	3.29	75	7.38	48	18.82	37
Steve Ontiveros	vs. Lefties	.241	48	.400	53	.323	46	3.79	92	10.37	83	17.38	35
	vs. Righties	.242	42	.362	32	.287	18	2.73	50	5.05	17	12.62	97
Eric Plunk	vs. Lefties	.276	81	.365	27	.371	110	1.04	10	13.27	116	19.03	22
	vs. Righties	.228	26	.371	40	.353	94	3.59	84	15.53	122	22.82	16
Jose Rijo	vs. Lefties	.303	108	.491	108	.387	117	3.43	79	12.20	109	18.05	31
	vs. Righties	.308	115	.419	68	.370	105	2.33	26	8.47	69	15.87	60
Dave Stewart	vs. Lefties	.233	16	.357	19	.314	35	2.35	32	10.69	87	18.98	24
	vs. Righties	.223	24	.357	29	.294	30	2.58	39	7.98	60	18.07	43
Curt Young	vs. Lefties	.218	10	.361	22	.243	3	3.40	76	1.95	1	12.34	85
	vs. Righties	.260	64	.474	104	.304	40	5.29	118	6.08	25	15.58	64
Team Average	vs. Lefties	.258	4	.391	2	.330	4	2.50	2	9.51	10	16.45	2
	vs. Righties	.259	5	.430	10	.320	4	3.70	9	7.66	3	16.92	4
League Average	vs. Lefties	.267		.427		.338		3.30		9.47		14.54	
	vs. Righties	.264		.424		.330		3.45		8.56		15.98	

Pitching with Runners on Base and Bases Empty

		BA	Rank	SA	Rank	OBA	Rank	HR %	Rank	BB %	Rank	SO %	Rank
Joaquin Andujar	Runners On	.284	--	.547	--	.378	--	7.37	--	12.50	--	10.71	--
	Bases Empty	.259	67	.381	34	.327	71	2.88	50	7.84	55	13.07	92
Dennis Eckersley	Runners On	.198	2	.322	8	.245	1	2.82	61	5.64	12	22.05	17
	Bases Empty	.249	48	.389	42	.272	9	2.33	26	2.26	1	26.42	4
Dennis Lamp	Runners On	.362	127	.509	107	.412	122	2.59	50	8.96	61	13.43	80
	Bases Empty	.291	--	.402	--	.352	--	1.71	--	7.81	--	14.06	--
Gene Nelson	Runners On	.255	49	.435	83	.314	33	3.70	87	8.16	45	18.37	26
	Bases Empty	.244	39	.391	44	.295	26	1.50	9	5.26	22	17.19	45
Steve Ontiveros	Runners On	.259	49	.382	39	.319	42	3.07	73	7.78	39	14.40	66
	Bases Empty	.231	27	.380	33	.296	28	3.38	71	7.73	53	15.46	61
Eric Plunk	Runners On	.232	22	.341	15	.329	55	2.16	30	12.56	109	21.52	18
	Bases Empty	.276	93	.397	47	.397	121	2.30	22	16.27	123	20.10	25
Jose Rijo	Runners On	.279	84	.413	67	.365	100	2.33	36	11.44	103	19.90	20
	Bases Empty	.331	123	.497	111	.394	120	3.43	73	9.33	83	13.99	78
Dave Stewart	Runners On	.231	20	.348	16	.321	44	2.08	29	10.89	93	17.33	32
	Bases Empty	.227	18	.363	25	.296	27	2.69	42	8.58	71	19.45	26
Curt Young	Runners On	.260	58	.484	100	.292	16	5.42	113	4.32	2	12.62	87
	Bases Empty	.247	44	.435	83	.294	24	4.66	107	5.88	31	16.32	51
Team Average	Runners On	.262	4	.415	6	.332	2	3.19	8	9.33	6	16.06	3
	Bases Empty	.255	6	.410	7	.318	5	3.13	4	7.86	5	17.22	3
League Average	Runners On	.271		.428		.343		3.25		9.68		14.87	
	Bases Empty	.260		.424		.326		3.49		8.34		15.79	

Overall Pitching Compared to Late Inning Pressure Situations

		BA	Rank	SA	Rank	OBA	Rank	HR %	Rank	BB %	Rank	SO %	Rank
Joaquin Andujar	Overall	.269	79	.449	89	.348	87	4.70	111	9.81	88	12.08	98
	Pressure	.333	--	.733	--	.375	--	13.33	--	6.25	--	6.25	--
Greg Cadaret	Overall	.252	--	.401	--	.356	--	4.08	--	13.64	--	17.05	--
	Pressure	.225	36	.325	28	.333	62	2.50	58	14.00	109	18.00	42
Dennis Eckersley	Overall	.228	12	.362	15	.260	2	2.53	32	3.70	1	24.57	6
	Pressure	.239	51	.386	63	.270	16	3.41	82	4.28	8	26.74	4
Jay Howell	Overall	.277	--	.474	--	.355	--	3.47	--	10.50	--	17.50	--
	Pressure	.273	79	.421	78	.355	81	1.65	41	10.64	83	17.73	44
Dennis Lamp	Overall	.326	122	.455	93	.382	118	2.15	15	8.40	60	13.74	77
	Pressure	.263	--	.263	--	.391	--	0.00	--	16.67	--	16.67	--
Gary Lavelle	Overall	.308	--	.454	--	.405	--	1.54	--	14.01	--	14.65	--
	Pressure	.484	127	.645	124	.564	127	0.00	1	17.50	122	10.00	106
Dave Leiper	Overall	.246	--	.402	--	.306	--	3.02	--	8.04	--	14.73	--
	Pressure	.212	23	.333	30	.293	29	3.03	72	9.21	66	17.11	49
Gene Nelson	Overall	.249	39	.411	54	.304	23	2.49	28	6.60	26	17.74	36
	Pressure	.215	26	.364	50	.256	8	3.31	79	4.58	12	16.79	53
Steve Ontiveros	Overall	.242	31	.381	31	.305	24	3.26	74	7.75	43	15.04	59
	Pressure	.287	91	.414	76	.380	105	2.30	51	9.62	69	17.31	47
Eric Plunk	Overall	.253	48	.368	20	.362	103	2.23	18	14.35	122	20.83	19
	Pressure	.176	3	.284	14	.295	32	2.70	64	14.29	113	24.18	10
Jose Rijo	Overall	.305	114	.455	94	.379	117	2.88	46	10.41	96	17.01	43
	Pressure	.333	--	.722	--	.455	--	11.11	--	18.18	--	13.64	--
Dave Stewart	Overall	.229	14	.357	14	.306	25	2.45	24	9.52	83	18.59	29
	Pressure	.270	75	.443	90	.356	82	4.35	101	11.94	99	15.67	60
Curt Young	Overall	.252	45	.453	90	.293	12	4.93	117	5.31	12	14.98	62
	Pressure	.254	61	.397	68	.314	45	4.76	109	6.94	34	9.72	109
Team Average	Overall	.258	4	.412	4	.324	2	3.15	4	8.51	5	16.70	3
	Pressure	.252	6	.399	7	.325	5	3.39	11	9.30	4	17.89	4
League Average	Overall	.265		.425		.333		3.38		8.94		15.38	
	Pressure	.262		.404		.337		2.99		9.73		16.42	

Additional Miscellaneous Pitching Comparisons

	Grass Surface BA	Rank	Artificial Surface BA	Rank	Home Games BA	Rank	Road Games BA	Rank	Runners in Scoring Position BA	Rank	Runners in Scoring Pos and Two Outs BA	Rank	Leading Off Inning OBA	Rank
Joaquin Andujar	.269	77	.000	--	.256	65	.295	--	.268	--	.286	--	.400	120
Dennis Eckersley	.226	8	.240	43	.154	1	.300	102	.173	3	.167	8	.245	11
Jay Howell	.250	37	.476	--	.211	--	.330	123	.291	--	.400	--	.432	--
Dennis Lamp	.314	114	.385	--	.279	--	.364	127	.382	127	.441	128	.393	115
Gary Lavelle	.352	--	.276	86	.254	--	.365	--	.392	--	.360	120	.240	--
Dave Leiper	.231	11	.308	--	.167	--	.330	--	.286	--	.292	--	.310	--
Gene Nelson	.243	24	.284	91	.229	25	.273	73	.256	60	.224	52	.292	32
Steve Ontiveros	.256	51	.170	4	.245	48	.238	20	.218	25	.153	5	.281	24
Eric Plunk	.253	45	.257	65	.237	33	.269	67	.216	23	.260	79	.344	79
Jose Rijo	.293	102	.358	118	.304	113	.307	112	.297	99	.255	73	.330	65
Rick Rodriguez	.296	--	.390	123	.283	--	.388	--	.179	--	.118	--	.318	--
Dave Stewart	.229	9	.229	27	.215	12	.242	31	.226	31	.182	15	.289	28
Curt Young	.247	33	.275	83	.234	27	.265	57	.269	75	.207	38	.283	26
Team Average	.256	4	.273	11	.239	3	.278	10	.257	5	.229	2	.316	3
League Average	.267		.261		.260		.270		.266		.247		.328	

SEATTLE MARINERS

October baseball in the Kingdome? No, we're not about to predict a pennant in Seattle. But we don't think that the Mariners have nearly as far to go as it seems either.

Of course, the biggest knock against Seattle's chances is its streak of 10 consecutive seasons with losing records, a streak that comprises the team's entire history. Only 29 of the 213 division or league champions in modern major-league history have won their titles following losing seasons; and of those 29, just six had streaks of three or more losing seasons immediately preceding their championship seasons. Even more, only one of those was an American League team:

Year	Team	Seasons
1914	Boston Braves	11
1945	Chicago Cubs	5
1961	Cincinnati Reds	3
1967	Boston Red Sox	8
1969	New York Mets	7
1984	Chicago Cubs	6

But if you're still looking for reasons to be optimistic about the pennant chances of a team that's never even had a winning record, here are a few to consider:

- The 1987 American League West was by far the most tightly packed league or division in modern major-league history. The Texas Rangers and California Angels tied for last place, 10 games behind the Minnesota Twins. No other last-place team in modern major-league history finished within even 14 games of first place. It wouldn't take much to turn the division inside-out this season.
- Seattle finished in fourth place last season, but much closer to the division leader than most fourth-place clubs, seven games behind the Twins. During the era of divisional play, fourth-place teams finished an average of 16.3 games behind; only three finished closer than the 1987 Mariners (the 1972 New York Yankees, the 1973 Montreal Expos, and the 1979 Twins).
- Seattle manager Dick Williams, whose magic touch has reversed the fortunes of several teams over the past 20 years, has been particularly

effective in the third seasons of his recent managerial tenures. The following table shows how Williams's teams have progressed during his terms:

Team	Prior Year W–L	Pct.	First Year W–L	Pct.	Second Year W–L	Pct.	Third Year W–L	Pct.
Boston	72–90	.444	92–70	.568	86–76	.531	87–75	.537
Oakland	89–73	.549	101–60	.627	93–62	.600	94–68	.580
California	79–83	.488	68–94	.420	72–89	.447	76–86	.469
Montreal	55–107	.340	75–87	.463	76–86	.469	95–65	.594
San Diego	41–69	.373	81–81	.500	81–81	.500	92–70	.568
Seattle	74–88	.457	67–95	.414	78–84	.481	—	—
Averages		.439		.516		.509		.550

The only Williams team that failed to improve its record in his third year compared to his second was the 1973 Oakland A's, which merely won its third consecutive division title (all under Williams). The teams improved, on average, by 41 percentage points in Year 3 (six and one-half wins over a 162-game schedule).

On the negative side, the pattern of Seattle's progress is unlike that of most of Williams's teams. The averages in the table above indicate that Williams usually makes an immediate positive impact, followed by a second season during which the team treads water, consolidating the gains of the previous year. The Mariners' progress is, unfortunately, more similar to that of the California Angels, Williams's only failure. In both cases, he took over teams that weren't too far below the .500 mark before his arrival, but he failed to drag them across the line that separates losers from winners. Nevertheless, the gap between that line and a division title has traditionally been rather narrow in the A.L. West, so nothing that happens out there this season would shock us.

Still Looking for a New Platoon

Attention, major-league managers, the Elias Sports Bureau is looking for a few good men. Who among you is sharp enough, innovative enough, and courageous enough to accept our challenge? For the past two years, we've written about a little-known characteristic that can be used as the basis for platooning, a trait that has nearly as great an impact on individual batter-pitcher matchups as whether a player bats or throws left or right-handed. We know that old habits die hard in baseball, and that new ideas are flicked away like dirt off home plate. But the fact is that the same innovations that are treated like subversive plots at the time they're proposed are often embraced after their value is proven.

So we're offering this challenge to any major-league managers who find themselves 10 games out of first place this September, with no hope of recovery: Forget about writing lineups based on whether the opposing pitcher throws left- or right-handed. Name your starters according to whether he throws mostly ground balls or fly balls. Win a few games and you'll be hailed as an innovative genius; lose and you can use us as a reference on your resume.

The guidelines are akin to the lefty-righty rules, according to which matchups of similar types (a left-handed batter facing a southpaw pitcher, for example) favor pitchers, and meetings of dissimilar types (left-handed batters vs. right-handed pitchers, for example) favor batters. Ground out–fly out distributions work the same way: When similar types face each other (ground-ball pitchers vs. ground-ball hitters or fly-ball pitchers vs. fly-ball hitters), the pitcher has the advantage. When dissimilar types meet, the advantage swings to the batter.

We think that Seattle is a particularly fertile ground for the experiment for two reasons. First, Dick Williams is as tough as three-day-old stubble; he can handle the heat. Second, Seattle had the American League's most prolific collection of ground-ball hitters last season. Its team average of 1.29 ground outs per air out was the league's highest. With such an extreme bias toward ground-ball hitting, the Mariners have much to lose by continuing to ignore this strategy.

To prove our point, we found 30 pairs of batters with similar batting averages and at-bat totals last season (allowing margins of no more than five batting-average points, or 10 percent of a player's at bats). Each pair of players had to come from the same league, and hit from the same side of the plate to eliminate the lefty-righty bias. (We allowed matches of switch-hitters with left-handers.) But in each pair, one was a ground-ball hitter, the other a fly-ball hitter. The statistic that determines those tendencies is the ground outs-to-air outs ratio, noted for all pitchers and many batters in the individual player comments of this book's Batter and Pitcher sections. For example, the pairs that included Mariners players:

Ground-ballers	AB	H	BA	Fly-ballers	AB	H	BA
Harold Reynolds	530	146	.275	Kirk Gibson	487	135	.277
Phil Bradley	603	179	.297	Marty Barrett	559	164	.293
Jim Presley	575	142	.247	Cal Ripken	624	157	.252
Scott Bradley	342	95	.278	Mike Kingery	354	99	.280

The result was two groups of 30 players with nearly identical batting averages during the 1987 season; one group hit predominantly ground balls, and the other fly balls:

	AB	H	BA
Ground-ball hitters	14,594	3,973	.27224
Fly-ball hitters	14,493	3,934	.27144

We composed groups of 25 pairs of pitchers in the same way, so that we had two pitching groups nearly identical in terms of batting average attained by opposing hitters. Again, one threw mostly ground balls and the other mostly fly balls. The composite opponents' batting statistics of the two groups of pitchers:

	AB	H	BA
Ground-ball pitchers	12,026	3,104	.25811
Fly-ball pitchers	11,697	3,021	.25827

For each batter in the study, we compiled statistics for last season only against pitchers included in one of those groups. Those figures, with each ground-ball hitter listed across from the fly-ball hitter with whom he was paired:

Ground-ballers	Vs. GBP	Vs. FBP	Fly-ballers	Vs. GBP	Vs. FBP
Jesse Barfield	.192	.116	Joe Carter	.209	.387
Rafael Belliard	.286	.308	Luis Aguayo	.185	.167
Phil Bradley	.350	.200	Marty Barrett	.370	.356
Scott Bradley	.150	.158	Mike Kingery	.077	.524
Jerry Browne	.200	.346	Mike Davis	.370	.324
Bill Buckner	.294	.409	Mel Hall	.357	.227
Scott Fletcher	.296	.258	Carney Lansford	.250	.333
Tony Fernandez	.261	.294	Don Mattingly	.311	.273
Jim Gantner	.200	.091	Jim Dwyer	.444	.333
Ozzie Guillen	.313	.229	Wally Joyner	.278	.211
Billy Hatcher	.246	.373	Tim Wallach	.296	.259
Von Hayes	.194	.294	Darryl Strawberry	.375	.442
Dion James	.279	.390	Will Clark	.386	.300
Stan Jefferson	.190	.231	Franklin Stubbs	.233	.220
Steve Jeltz	.292	.233	Tim Flannery	.233	.270
Tracy Jones	.143	.375	Chris James	.196	.359
Shane Mack	.233	.227	Mike Diaz	.130	.143
Willie McGee	.254	.330	Mitch Webster	.348	.179
Mark McLemore	.125	.231	Donnie Hill	.310	.200
Dale Murphy	.279	.282	Mike Schmidt	.225	.321
Gerald Perry	.204	.203	Howard Johnson	.255	.308
Jim Presley	.143	.262	Cal Ripken	.304	.200
Harold Reynolds	.361	.372	Kirk Gibson	.333	.208
Steve Sax	.247	.338	Kevin McReynolds	.262	.179
Dale Sveum	.176	.350	Darrell Evans	.351	.167
Gary Ward	.162	.167	Frank White	.148	.267
Devon White	.300	.286	Ruben Sierra	.323	.200
Alan Wiggins	.150	.182	Dan Pasqua	.130	.308
Glenn Wilson	.188	.145	Keith Moreland	.314	.286
Dave Winfield	.279	.375	Ellis Burks	.257	.278

Remember that the batting averages for the batters listed above are drawn from a subset of their 1987 season totals that is too small to make the differences meaningful on an individual player basis. But the groups of batters and pitchers are large enough that *at the group level* the differences are attributable to their tendencies to hit or throw ground balls or fly balls. A summary of the data:

	Better Vs. GBP	Better Vs. FBP
Ground-ball hitters	10	20
Fly-ball hitters	18	12

A solid majority of batters in each group hit better against pitchers of the opposite type: on average, ground-ball hitters hit better against fly-ball pitchers and fly-ball hitters preferred ground-ball pitchers. Not every single batter followed the pattern—there are exceptions to every general rule. For example, if you look through the Batter Section, you'll also find lots of right-handed batters who hit better against right-handed pitchers last season than against southpaws. But a few exceptions don't invalidate established general principles.

The results won't surprise anyone who read the past two editions of the *Analyst*, in which we proved that the platoon differences between ground-ball and fly-ball groups are nearly as great as between left-handers and right-handers. But as far as we know, not a single major-league manager has acknowledged this bias, let alone used it as the basis for selecting starting lineups or pinch-hitters. Obviously any manager who claims that he goes "by the book" just hasn't been reading the right book.

And Batting Ninth...

During the past 15 years, the designated hitter has brought about many strategic changes. Some happened immediately, like a reduction in the number of pitching changes, pinch-hitters, and sacrifice bunts. Others have evolved over a period of time, like the development of the ninth spot in the batting order as the so-called "second leadoff spot."

The evolution has been slow, and not every team has embraced the principle of putting a player with the traditional leadoff characteristics—high on-base potential and speed—at the bottom of the order. In fact, the composite statistics of all ninth-place hitters in the American League last season still had the lowest batting and on-base averages of any position in the lineup (.239 and .297, respectively, compared to .274 and .348 for leadoff hitters).

But last season, the production of Seattle's ninth spot was the envy of most leadoff batters. (Harold Reynolds started 160 of Seattle's 162 games, all but three of them in the ninth spot.) The Mariners were one of three teams with a higher batting average from their ninth-place hitters (.283) than from their leadoff hitters (.275); and on those other two teams (Minnesota and Texas) that distinction resulted more from the deficiencies of their leadoff hitters than from the success of their ninth-place hitters.

The Mariners scored an average of 6.3 runs for every 10 innings in which its ninth-place hitter led off, higher than the average for any other batting-order position on the team except the second. And Reynolds played the role of table-setter well: The Mariners scored an average of 1.35 runs per inning in which its ninth-place hitter led off and reached base, a figure 21 percent higher than the corresponding mark on the 13 other American League teams (1.11). The composite statistics of Seattle's ninth spot compared to the averages of the other A.L. teams:

Team	AB	R	H	2B	3B	HR	RBI	BB	SB	BA	SLG	OBA
Seattle	555	75	158	35	8	2	39	39	59	.285	.387	.331
Others	556	67	131	25	3	11	59	45	5	.235	.349	.295

The bottom line on a strong bottom? Seattle's ninth-place hitters ranked fourth among the team's nine batting-order positions in on-base average last season. Over the past six seasons, the 17 American League teams whose ninth slots ranked among the team's top five positions in on-base average showed almost no effect compared to other teams that used more conventional (that is, weak) ninth-place hitters. Those 17 teams scored an average of 0.4 fewer runs per season than expected. Which is to say that the simple act of weakening or strengthening the ninth position in your batting order merely by rearranging the same nine hitters has no effect on a team's ultimate scoring potential.

(See the Kansas City Royals essay for a more detailed discussion of batting orders, including a description of how we determine the number of runs a team is expected to score.)

WON-LOST RECORD BY STARTING POSITION

SEATTLE 78-84	C	1B	2B	3B	SS	LF	CF	RF	P	DH	Leadoff	Relief	Starts
Scott Bankhead	·	·	·	·	·	·	·	·	12-13	·	·	1-1	12-13
Phil Bradley	·	·	·	·	·	77-81	·	·	·	·	·	·	77-81
Scott Bradley	36-41	·	·	3-2	·	·	·	·	1-1	·	·	·	40-44
Mickey Brantley	·	·	·	·	·	1-3	20-24	13-17	·	5-2	20-24	·	39-46
Mike Brown	·	·	·	·	·	·	·	·	·	·	·	0-1	·
Mike Campbell	·	·	·	·	·	·	·	·	5-4	·	·	·	5-4
John Christensen	·	·	·	·	·	·	15-14	·	·	3-0	·	·	18-14
Stan Clarke	·	·	·	·	·	·	·	·	·	·	·	4-18	·
Alvin Davis	·	74-83	·	·	·	·	·	·	·	·	·	·	74-83
Mario Diaz	·	·	·	3-3	·	·	·	·	·	·	·	·	3-3
Lee Guetterman	·	·	·	·	·	·	·	·	10-7	·	·	2-6	10-7
Dave Hengel	·	·	·	·	·	·	0-2	·	·	·	·	·	0-2
Mark Huismann	·	·	·	·	·	·	·	·	·	·	·	1-5	·
Bob Kearney	8-5	·	·	·	·	·	·	·	·	·	·	·	8-5
Mike Kingery	·	·	·	·	·	·	·	47-50	·	·	3-5	· ·	47-50
Mark Langston	·	·	·	·	·	·	·	·	21-14	·	·	·	21-14
Edgar Martinez	·	·	·	4-6	·	·	·	·	·	·	·	·	4-6
Gary Matthews	·	·	·	·	·	·	·	·	·	12-17	·	·	12-17
Rich Monteleone	·	·	·	·	·	·	·	·	·	·	·	0-3	·
Mike Moore	·	·	·	·	·	·	·	·	12-21	·	·	·	12-21
Mike Morgan	·	·	·	·	·	·	·	·	13-18	·	·	0-3	13-18
John Moses	·	2-0	·	·	·	·	42-45	2-1	·	·	35-37	·	46-46
Jerry Narron	2-0	·	·	·	·	·	·	·	·	·	·	·	2-0
Donell Nixon	·	·	·	·	·	·	16-15	·	·	3-2	18-17	·	19-17
Edwin Nunez	·	·	·	·	·	·	·	·	·	·	·	22-26	·
Clay Parker	·	·	·	·	·	·	·	·	1-0	·	·	0-2	1-0
Ken Phelps	·	1-0	·	·	·	·	·	·	·	48-56	·	·	49-56
Dennis Powell	·	·	·	·	·	·	·	·	1-2	·	·	5-8	1-2
Jim Presley	·	·	71-75	1-0	·	·	·	·	·	·	·	·	72-75
Rey Quinones	·	·	·	·	62-72	·	·	·	·	·	·	·	62-72
Domingo Ramos	·	·	2-1	0-1	12-9	·	·	·	·	·	·	·	14-11
Jerry Reed	·	·	·	·	·	·	·	·	0-1	·	·	16-22	0-1
Rich Renteria	·	·	·	·	·	·	·	·	·	1-0	·	·	1-0
Harold Reynolds	·	·	76-83	·	·	·	·	·	·	·	2-1	·	76-83
Steve Shields	·	·	·	·	·	·	·	·	·	·	·	7-13	·
Brick Smith	·	1-1	·	·	·	·	·	·	·	·	·	·	1-1
Roy Thomas	·	·	·	·	·	·	·	·	·	·	·	1-7	·
Mike Trujillo	·	·	·	·	·	·	·	·	3-4	·	·	6-15	3-4
Dave Valle	32-38	·	·	·	·	·	·	·	·	5-6	·	·	37-44
Jim Weaver	·	·	·	·	·	·	·	1-0	·	·	·	·	1-0
Bill Wilkinson	·	·	·	·	·	·	·	·	·	·	·	25-31	·

Batting vs. Left and Right Handed Pitchers

		BA	Rank	SA	Rank	OBA	Rank	HR %	Rank	BB %	Rank	SO %	Rank
Phil Bradley	vs. Lefties	.347	10	.642	3	.426	8	6.25	14	12.20	31	14.63	84
	vs. Righties	.276	57	.389	104	.371	36	0.70	144	11.87	28	17.91	118
Scott Bradley	vs. Lefties	.259	--	.352	--	.273	--	1.85	--	1.79	--	5.36	--
	vs. Righties	.281	46	.375	118	.317	101	1.39	131	4.52	150	4.84	3
Mickey Brantley	vs. Lefties	.283	59	.528	23	.324	85	5.51	27	5.88	135	10.29	37
	vs. Righties	.313	17	.482	41	.355	53	3.13	90	6.61	118	12.40	57
John Christensen	vs. Lefties	.229	128	.352	126	.302	118	1.90	111	9.40	64	14.53	83
	vs. Righties	.296	--	.333	--	.321	--	0.00	--	3.45	--	37.93	--
Alvin Davis	vs. Lefties	.240	108	.380	106	.301	119	2.40	100	8.30	92	16.59	96
	vs. Righties	.325	9	.591	5	.406	7	6.45	17	12.24	22	10.62	41
Mike Kingery	vs. Lefties	.179	--	.282	--	.200	--	2.56	--	2.44	--	19.51	--
	vs. Righties	.292	37	.470	47	.344	67	2.54	105	7.34	106	9.89	34
Gary Matthews	vs. Lefties	.239	111	.296	143	.341	71	1.41	117	13.41	22	14.63	84
	vs. Righties	.229	--	.354	--	.283	--	4.17	--	7.55	--	18.87	--
John Moses	vs. Lefties	.209	144	.256	153	.277	140	0.78	138	7.69	104	7.69	17
	vs. Righties	.264	87	.368	122	.313	109	0.77	143	6.21	131	13.10	65
Ken Phelps	vs. Lefties	.270	--	.622	--	.451	--	8.11	--	21.57	--	15.69	--
	vs. Righties	.258	93	.539	17	.405	9	8.14	5	18.50	3	17.96	119
Jim Presley	vs. Lefties	.268	78	.426	77	.310	107	2.63	92	5.88	135	20.10	125
	vs. Righties	.236	125	.436	70	.289	137	4.94	38	6.22	130	27.75	155
Rey Quinones	vs. Lefties	.290	46	.443	67	.345	69	3.05	86	6.99	119	13.29	66
	vs. Righties	.271	72	.380	115	.306	123	2.31	108	4.28	154	13.90	68
Harold Reynolds	vs. Lefties	.278	66	.370	113	.320	93	0.62	142	5.56	142	7.78	18
	vs. Righties	.274	60	.370	121	.327	88	0.00	156	7.18	109	4.95	4
Dave Valle	vs. Lefties	.304	35	.554	14	.340	73	4.73	40	5.66	141	11.32	49
	vs. Righties	.216	150	.335	140	.251	155	2.84	97	3.21	158	14.97	84
Team Average	vs. Lefties	.265	7	.422	7	.324	12	2.93	12	7.73	13	14.12	4
	vs. Righties	.275	3	.431	5	.340	4	2.92	13	8.32	12	14.01	3
League Average	vs. Lefties	.265		.422		.333		3.29		8.94		15.64	
	vs. Righties	.265		.427		.334		3.43		8.94		15.26	

Batting with Runners on Base and Bases Empty

		BA	Rank	SA	Rank	OBA	Rank	HR %	Rank	BB %	Rank	SO %	Rank
Phil Bradley	Runners On	.243	122	.348	133	.358	61	1.21	129	14.67	20	18.00	120
	Bases Empty	.334	7	.542	21	.409	4	3.09	89	9.95	45	16.17	93
Scott Bradley	Runners On	.241	124	.335	140	.289	139	1.76	116	5.29	143	4.76	5
	Bases Empty	.314	19	.407	92	.333	62	1.16	136	2.82	156	5.08	2
Mickey Brantley	Runners On	.323	20	.569	11	.359	60	5.38	28	6.34	127	11.27	49
	Bases Empty	.290	33	.457	59	.335	60	3.17	87	6.36	120	11.86	49
Alvin Davis	Runners On	.294	49	.550	15	.381	39	6.32	13	13.13	33	11.25	48
	Bases Empty	.296	29	.486	42	.360	39	3.86	71	8.77	69	14.04	67
Mike Kingery	Runners On	.298	45	.477	46	.341	81	2.65	97	7.43	111	9.14	26
	Bases Empty	.266	72	.429	82	.320	93	2.46	109	6.36	119	12.27	54
John Moses	Runners On	.270	80	.369	117	.325	107	1.42	125	7.27	115	10.30	38
	Bases Empty	.233	128	.309	147	.287	133	0.40	152	6.34	121	11.94	50
Ken Phelps	Runners On	.255	104	.516	23	.438	6	7.19	3	24.29	1	17.14	112
	Bases Empty	.263	78	.575	11	.383	20	8.94	3	13.55	9	18.22	119
Jim Presley	Runners On	.254	106	.474	48	.308	122	4.85	38	6.76	122	25.00	154
	Bases Empty	.241	114	.397	97	.285	135	3.58	79	5.52	134	25.46	149
Rey Quinones	Runners On	.316	30	.417	87	.367	52	2.14	108	7.51	109	9.86	30
	Bases Empty	.251	98	.385	106	.283	141	2.75	96	3.29	154	16.45	99
Harold Reynolds	Runners On	.259	98	.330	144	.296	132	0.00	150	5.04	147	4.20	3
	Bases Empty	.286	40	.396	99	.344	52	0.31	155	7.80	87	6.94	9
Dave Valle	Runners On	.297	46	.441	71	.338	87	3.45	69	5.63	140	12.50	60
	Bases Empty	.223	140	.430	80	.253	156	3.91	68	3.23	155	13.98	64
Team Average	Runners On	.272	7	.431	8	.343	8	3.18	10	9.56	8	13.33	2
	Bases Empty	.272	1	.427	5	.328	5	2.73	13	7.00	14	14.61	4
League Average	Runners On	.271		.428		.343		3.25		9.68		14.87	
	Bases Empty	.260		.424		.326		3.49		8.34		15.79	

Overall Batting Compared to Late Inning Pressure Situations

		BA	Rank	SA	Rank	OBA	Rank	HR %	Rank	BB %	Rank	SO %	Rank	RDI %	Rank
Phil Bradley	Overall	.297	26	.463	50	.387	17	2.32	116	11.97	27	16.95	109	.247	124
	Pressure	.308	39	.431	71	.366	57	1.54	108	8.45	90	25.35	145	.182	124
Scott Bradley	Overall	.278	56	.371	127	.310	111	1.46	131	4.10	156	4.92	2	.316	50
	Pressure	.333	21	.487	38	.366	58	2.56	81	4.76	139	9.52	29	.385	33
Mickey Brantley	Overall	.302	21	.499	24	.344	66	3.99	66	6.35	130	11.64	41	.370	11
	Pressure	.289	57	.400	87	.333	82	2.22	94	6.25	123	14.58	77	.182	124
John Christensen	Overall	.242	--	.348	--	.306	--	1.52	--	8.22	--	19.18	--	.171	--
	Pressure	.294	--	.412	--	.400	--	0.00	--	15.00	--	20.00	--	.250	91
Alvin Davis	Overall	.295	28	.516	20	.370	34	5.00	34	10.88	44	12.69	53	.280	89
	Pressure	.313	32	.567	18	.405	25	5.97	29	13.92	28	7.59	14	.222	106
Mike Kingery	Overall	.280	50	.449	65	.329	86	2.54	107	6.84	117	10.89	35	.313	53
	Pressure	.256	92	.442	64	.333	82	2.33	92	10.00	68	10.00	34	.267	87
John Moses	Overall	.246	119	.331	150	.301	134	0.77	146	6.70	123	11.32	39	.267	109
	Pressure	.222	123	.289	139	.255	145	0.00	119	3.92	147	11.76	47	.286	75
Ken Phelps	Overall	.259	93	.548	10	.410	6	8.13	2	18.87	2	17.69	117	.314	52
	Pressure	.167	153	.433	70	.375	46	6.67	19	25.00	2	30.00	158	.250	91
Jim Presley	Overall	.247	118	.433	76	.296	142	4.17	60	6.11	133	25.24	153	.274	100
	Pressure	.209	130	.403	85	.284	127	4.48	48	9.33	80	24.00	135	.261	89
Rey Quinones	Overall	.276	61	.397	109	.317	105	2.51	109	5.03	149	13.73	65	.289	80
	Pressure	.313	32	.567	18	.360	65	7.46	11	7.89	102	23.68	133	.421	18
Harold Reynolds	Overall	.275	62	.370	128	.325	92	0.19	160	6.68	125	5.82	4	.290	76
	Pressure	.274	70	.384	96	.325	94	0.00	119	7.14	109	8.33	22	.333	51
Dave Valle	Overall	.256	102	.435	75	.292	149	3.70	72	4.34	154	13.29	58	.333	34
	Pressure	.246	98	.456	56	.259	141	5.26	39	1.72	159	12.07	54	.167	133
Team Average	Overall	.272	3	.428	6	.335	6	2.92	13	8.14	12	14.04	2	.284	10
	Pressure	.268	4	.433	2	.337	5	3.24	6	9.47	7	17.77	10	.263	9
League Average	Overall	.265		.425		.333		3.38		8.94		15.38		.287	
	Pressure	.262		.405		.335		3.07		9.43		16.58		.280	

Additional Miscellaneous Batting Comparisons

	Grass Surface		Artificial Surface		Home Games		Road Games		Runners in Scoring Position		Runners in Scoring Pos and Two Outs		Leading Off Inning		Runners on 3B with less than 2 Outs	
	BA	Rank	BA	Rank	BA	Rank	BA	Rank	BA	Rank	BA	Rank	OBA	Rank	RDI %	Rank
Phil Bradley	.268	83	.315	19	.309	29	.284	43	.224	131	.241	93	.463	2	.595	82
Scott Bradley	.297	34	.262	76	.290	59	.269	67	.228	129	.214	114	.292	121	.708	23
Mickey Brantley	.329	6	.283	52	.321	17	.286	41	.376	5	.300	41	.322	92	.600	71
John Christensen	.278	--	.218	128	.246	--	.238	--	.229	--	.077	--	.308	--	.400	--
Alvin Davis	.305	24	.288	45	.307	31	.284	44	.256	96	.269	63	.371	33	.667	33
Mike Kingery	.250	112	.299	33	.305	37	.256	90	.319	29	.326	19	.385	24	.667	33
Gary Matthews	.274	--	.193	147	.222	--	.241	--	.237	--	.211	--	.250	--	.857	--
John Moses	.285	50	.227	118	.220	145	.278	50	.242	114	.235	98	.266	138	.700	25
Donell Nixon	.200	--	.292	41	.288	--	.212	--	.345	--	.250	--	.365	40	.400	--
Ken Phelps	.279	58	.246	93	.232	136	.286	42	.238	118	.213	115	.367	37	.500	120
Jim Presley	.258	100	.240	104	.257	106	.237	120	.269	83	.321	22	.260	145	.375	155
Rey Quinones	.241	125	.300	30	.330	11	.230	129	.304	38	.302	37	.311	100	.667	33
Domingo Ramos	.348	--	.300	31	.282	--	.375	--	.179	--	.176	--	.444	--	.600	--
Harold Reynolds	.320	11	.247	92	.233	132	.315	18	.243	112	.200	127	.329	83	.593	83
Dave Valle	.288	--	.239	106	.244	118	.271	64	.326	19	.326	18	.265	139	.600	71
Team Average	.281	2	.266	5	.274	4	.271	2	.266	6	.260	4	.331	7	.590	7
League Average	.267		.261		.270		.260		.266		.247		.328		.581	

Pitching vs. Left and Right Handed Batters

		BA	Rank	SA	Rank	OBA	Rank	HR %	Rank	BB %	Rank	SO %	Rank
Scott Bankhead	vs. Lefties	.299	104	.506	110	.332	56	3.66	86	4.82	5	12.75	78
	vs. Righties	.264	75	.558	123	.317	54	8.68	127	6.92	40	17.30	48
Mike Campbell	vs. Lefties	.248	35	.419	64	.344	80	4.76	107	13.60	118	16.00	44
	vs. Righties	.192	--	.372	--	.284	--	5.13	--	8.89	--	16.67	--
Lee Guetterman	vs. Lefties	.160	--	.213	--	.220	--	0.00	--	7.23	--	8.43	--
	vs. Righties	.288	101	.462	100	.341	80	3.57	83	7.25	46	8.75	120
Mark Langston	vs. Lefties	.197	6	.293	8	.265	7	2.72	45	8.54	55	25.61	5
	vs. Righties	.245	43	.399	55	.325	60	3.00	63	10.12	98	22.27	20
Mike Moore	vs. Lefties	.298	102	.463	92	.353	88	2.74	49	8.13	48	9.62	117
	vs. Righties	.282	97	.457	99	.341	79	3.76	87	8.39	68	13.67	84
Mike Morgan	vs. Lefties	.302	107	.468	99	.345	82	2.91	56	6.39	22	10.10	111
	vs. Righties	.289	102	.439	83	.335	72	3.16	70	5.33	19	8.72	121
Edwin Nunez	vs. Lefties	.286	95	.490	107	.343	79	5.10	112	7.41	38	15.74	47
	vs. Righties	.230	--	.338	--	.310	--	2.70	--	11.11	--	18.89	--
Jerry Reed	vs. Lefties	.263	56	.358	20	.320	42	2.19	28	7.28	34	11.92	91
	vs. Righties	.249	50	.370	39	.309	44	2.31	25	6.88	38	17.46	46
Mike Trujillo	vs. Lefties	.283	94	.442	82	.363	98	4.17	98	11.03	92	13.97	63
	vs. Righties	.271	83	.489	108	.331	66	5.26	117	7.43	50	11.49	107
Bill Wilkinson	vs. Lefties	.192	5	.394	47	.243	2	5.77	117	6.25	19	25.89	4
	vs. Righties	.241	41	.324	12	.289	22	1.18	7	7.33	47	23.04	15
Team Average	vs. Lefties	.278	13	.444	11	.333	5	3.37	9	7.72	1	13.39	10
	vs. Righties	.267	10	.436	11	.331	9	3.76	11	8.31	7	16.00	9
League Average	vs. Lefties	.267		.427		.338		3.30		9.47		14.54	
	vs. Righties	.264		.424		.330		3.45		8.56		15.98	

Pitching with Runners on Base and Bases Empty

		BA	Rank	SA	Rank	OBA	Rank	HR %	Rank	BB %	Rank	SO %	Rank
Scott Bankhead	Runners On	.324	115	.556	118	.360	93	4.83	104	5.63	11	14.29	69
	Bases Empty	.262	68	.516	119	.307	38	6.48	123	5.84	29	15.09	66
Mike Campbell	Runners On	.246	--	.406	--	.345	--	4.35	--	12.79	--	16.28	--
	Bases Empty	.211	11	.395	46	.302	35	5.26	118	10.85	107	16.28	52
Lee Guetterman	Runners On	.268	71	.408	62	.327	53	2.23	33	8.33	49	7.84	122
	Bases Empty	.265	76	.427	77	.315	49	3.46	74	6.45	40	9.32	120
Mark Langston	Runners On	.255	50	.404	58	.310	30	2.66	54	7.09	30	22.44	13
	Bases Empty	.225	17	.367	27	.321	63	3.19	63	12.11	114	22.98	16
Mike Moore	Runners On	.298	97	.432	82	.353	81	2.48	45	8.50	52	10.02	110
	Bases Empty	.287	104	.483	106	.344	92	3.68	80	8.02	58	12.30	97
Mike Morgan	Runners On	.279	85	.415	71	.317	40	2.44	43	4.94	5	8.40	118
	Bases Empty	.310	118	.487	109	.359	105	3.49	76	6.69	44	10.34	111
Jerry Reed	Runners On	.239	29	.362	22	.307	28	2.17	31	8.39	51	12.90	85
	Bases Empty	.267	82	.366	26	.319	55	2.33	25	5.95	33	16.76	46
Mike Trujillo	Runners On	.306	--	.531	--	.375	--	6.12	--	8.85	--	8.85	--
	Bases Empty	.258	64	.426	76	.327	72	3.87	88	9.36	86	15.20	63
Bill Wilkinson	Runners On	.277	81	.369	29	.306	25	1.54	13	5.48	9	23.29	7
	Bases Empty	.174	2	.333	14	.242	4	4.17	98	8.28	65	24.84	9
Team Average	Runners On	.282	12	.440	9	.338	5	3.15	7	7.83	1	13.86	11
	Bases Empty	.263	8	.439	11	.327	7	3.94	12	8.24	10	15.73	8
League Average	Runners On	.271		.428		.343		3.25		9.68		14.87	
	Bases Empty	.260		.424		.326		3.49		8.34		15.79	

Overall Pitching Compared to Late Inning Pressure Situations

		BA	Rank	SA	Rank	OBA	Rank	HR %	Rank	BB %	Rank	SO %	Rank
Scott Bankhead	Overall	.283	95	.530	123	.326	57	5.90	124	5.76	15	14.80	65
	Pressure	.357	--	.500	--	.379	--	3.57	--	3.45	--	17.24	--
Stan Clarke	Overall	.333	--	.591	--	.387	--	7.53	--	9.35	--	12.15	--
	Pressure	.346	120	.500	107	.438	125	3.85	91	15.15	118	12.12	97
Lee Guetterman	Overall	.267	74	.419	64	.320	44	2.96	50	7.25	35	8.70	122
	Pressure	.083	--	.083	--	.200	--	0.00	--	12.50	--	18.75	--
Mark Langston	Overall	.238	22	.383	32	.317	41	2.96	49	9.90	91	22.74	12
	Pressure	.238	48	.317	26	.274	19	0.99	26	4.63	13	19.44	30
Mike Moore	Overall	.292	107	.460	97	.348	85	3.16	66	8.24	55	11.27	104
	Pressure	.256	63	.463	97	.351	75	4.88	110	12.50	101	12.50	89
Mike Morgan	Overall	.296	109	.455	92	.340	74	3.02	56	5.90	17	9.47	117
	Pressure	.294	97	.500	107	.368	97	5.88	119	7.69	44	7.69	119
Edwin Nunez	Overall	.262	--	.424	--	.328	--	4.07	--	9.09	--	17.17	--
	Pressure	.345	119	.552	121	.406	121	4.60	103	10.58	82	14.42	69
Jerry Reed	Overall	.255	49	.365	18	.314	37	2.26	19	7.06	31	15.00	61
	Pressure	.214	--	.304	21	.267	12	1.79	43	6.61	30	15.70	59
Steve Shields	Overall	.333	--	.589	--	.382	--	5.43	--	8.33	--	15.28	--
	Pressure	.351	122	.649	126	.368	97	8.11	125	2.63	3	18.42	37
Mike Trujillo	Overall	.277	87	.466	103	.346	81	4.74	112	9.15	77	12.68	88
	Pressure	.270	76	.351	44	.317	47	0.00	1	4.76	16	14.29	70
Bill Wilkinson	Overall	.223	8	.350	11	.272	5	2.92	47	6.93	30	24.09	7
	Pressure	.201	13	.295	18	.263	11	2.16	49	7.79	46	27.27	3
Team Average	Overall	.272	11	.439	11	.332	7	3.60	9	8.06	1	14.90	10
	Pressure	.266	8	.402	8	.330	8	3.02	9	8.48	2	17.33	5
League Average	Overall	.265		.425		.333		3.38		8.94		15.38	
	Pressure	.262		.404		.337		2.99		9.73		16.42	

Additional Miscellaneous Pitching Comparisons

	Grass Surface		Artificial Surface		Home Games		Road Games		Runners in Scoring Position		Runners in Scoring Pos and Two Outs		Leading Off Inning	
	BA	Rank	BA	Rank	BA	Rank	BA	Rank	BA	Rank	BA	Rank	OBA	Rank
Scott Bankhead	.322	117	.256	64	.258	68	.306	111	.340	119	.315	105	.282	25
Mike Campbell	.214	--	.226	24	.225	22	.220	--	.244	--	.125	--	.315	47
Stan Clarke	.319	--	.348	114	.390	--	.288	--	.265	--	.143	--	.389	--
Lee Guetterman	.250	--	.276	84	.267	84	.266	61	.202	14	.149	4	.322	56
Mark Langston	.238	16	.239	42	.235	30	.241	26	.283	85	.238	61	.329	63
Mike Moore	.306	109	.281	89	.273	92	.308	113	.300	101	.271	86	.362	96
Mike Morgan	.291	97	.298	99	.291	106	.305	107	.244	43	.247	68	.366	101
Edwin Nunez	.345	--	.222	22	.228	--	.310	--	.283	--	.250	--	.300	--
Dennis Powell	.241	--	.257	66	.254	--	.246	--	.200	--	.267	--	.361	--
Jerry Reed	.290	--	.229	28	.242	44	.268	65	.210	18	.233	59	.278	22
Steve Shields	.321	--	.342	112	.350	--	.319	--	.348	--	.304	--	.417	--
Roy Thomas	.367	--	.255	63	.257	--	.333	--	.273	--	.231	--	.450	--
Mike Trujillo	.325	--	.254	62	.261	74	.296	101	.339	--	.238	--	.353	92
Bill Wilkinson	.167	--	.250	52	.272	90	.165	1	.253	55	.306	103	.271	18
Team Average	.281	13	.266	7	.265	9	.279	11	.273	9	.250	7	.336	9
League Average	.267		.261		.260		.270		.266		.247		.328	

TEXAS RANGERS

Was it the heat of the Arlington summer that sparked all the nastiness between the Texas Rangers and the American League umpires last season? The hostilities reached a climax in September when Rangers manager Bobby Valentine actually accused the umps of trying to "run [him] out of baseball" following an ejection by Ted Hendry, Valentine's fourteenth heave-ho of the season.

Whatever happened to peace, love, and understanding? Well, we'd like to encourage the spirit of *glasnost* between Valentine and the A.L. umpires. And we've got some valuable information that will help not only Valentine, but the rest of us as well, to get to know the men in blue a little better. Because after more than a century's worth of statistics on major-league baseball players, it's about time the umpires got their due.

In order to develop a statistical profile of each umpire, we accumulated the batting statistics in all games in which he worked home plate last season. Because no umpire worked as many as 40 games behind the plate, most of the figures told us more about the teams and pitchers in those games than they did about the umps themselves. Unfortunately, a comparative analysis of the past two seasons' statistics on National League umpires revealed that their "batting averages" and "home run ratios" bore little year-to-year relationship to each other; those stats were predominantly a function of the teams and pitchers in each umpire's games. But the strikeout-to-walk ratios were quite predictable from one season to the next; they had more to do with the tendencies of the umpires than those of the pitchers.

For that reason, we've chosen to publish only the strikeout-to-walk ratios for the 1987 season. To print anything else would only invite misinterpretation of the type that has already sprouted on a limited basis. We hope that, in time, baseball fans will identify Derryl Cousins and John Kibler as batters' umpires with small strike zones (based on their low ratios of strikeouts to walks) with the same confidence with which they label Pete Incaviglia a power hitter or Eddie Murray a great clutch hitter.

The following table lists the strikeout-to-walk ratios for umpires with at least 10 games behind the plate last season. (The won-lost records will be explained following the table.) Remember, high ratios suggest large strike zones, the sign of a pitchers' umpire; low ratios equal small strike zones, denoting batters' umps:

A.L. Umpires	SO/BB	W–L	N.L. Umpires	SO/BB	W–L
Larry Barnett	1.83	26–12	Greg Bonin	1.90	8–11
Nick Bremigan	1.68	29–8	Fred Brocklander	1.68	11–12
Joe Brinkman	1.69	20–17	Jerry Crawford	1.80	16–20
Al Clark	1.68	18–21	Gary Darling	1.63	9–2
Drew Coble	1.80	14–16	Bob Davidson	2.14	19–17
Terry Cooney	1.98	10–14	Gerry Davis	1.58	21–15
Derryl Cousins	1.37	22–16	Dana DeMuth	1.88	19–11
Don Denkinger	1.53	14–22	Bob Engel	2.59	16–20
Jim Evans	1.87	19–20	Bruce Froemming	1.66	23–13
Dale Ford	1.59	20–16	Eric Gregg	1.75	21–15
Rich Garcia	1.57	20–17	Tom Hallion	1.53	8–10
Ted Hendry	2.19	26–12	Doug Harvey	1.66	22–16
John Hirschbeck	1.84	18–18	John Kibler	1.53	19–19
Mark Johnson	1.59	11–14	Randy Marsh	1.76	16–22
Ken Kaiser	1.70	17–17	John McSherry	1.39	20–17
Greg Kosc	1.96	21–18	Ed Montague	1.80	20–17
Tim McClelland	1.77	27–10	Dave Pallone	2.07	21–17
Larry McCoy	2.00	19–18	Larry Poncino	1.32	7–7
Jim McKean	1.68	17–16	Frank Pulli	1.88	21–16
Durwood Merrill	1.79	23–13	Jim Quick	1.72	21–15
Dan Morrison	1.52	18–19	Dutch Rennert	1.91	16–21
Steve Palermo	1.70	23–14	Steve Rippley	1.88	15–15
Dave Phillips	1.84	20–17	Paul Runge	1.77	18–16
Rick Reed	1.59	21–16	Dick Stello	1.63	23–15
Mike Reilly	1.85	18–18	Terry Tata	1.69	24–13
Rocky Roe	1.71	18–20	Harry Wendelstedt	1.84	18–13
Dale Scott	1.82	15–13	Joe West	1.94	18–19
John Shulock	1.56	23–14	Lee Weyer	2.18	28–11
Tim Tschida	1.61	16–15	Billy Williams	1.45	10–9
Vic Voltaggio	1.77	13–16	Charlie Williams	1.61	17–20
Tim Welke	1.55	22–15			
Larry Young	1.82	16–15			

Now, about those won-lost records. We thought that major-league managers, armed with this new information about their buddies in blue, might be able to twist their pitching rotations in order to exploit the rotation of the umpires. For example, let's say that Bobby Valentine wants to start swing man Paul Kilgus during the current series. Kilgus's average of 3.12 walks per nine innings was the best among Texas' starters last season, indicating that he has good control. But Ted Hendry is working the plate tonight; his strikeout-to-walk ratio, the highest in the A.L. last season, indicates that he has a large strike zone. Wouldn't that benefit Bobby Witt, who walked 140 batters in 143 innings, more than it would Kilgus? After all, Don Denkinger will be behind the plate tomorrow night, and his 1.53 ratio suggests that he could squeeze Witt right out of the game, doesn't it?

This strategy makes a lot of sense to us, and it probably makes a lot of sense to you, too. But unfortunately, it's wrong.

Last season, the pitcher with better control (that is, the lower rate of bases on balls per nine innings) won only 14 of the 36 games that Denkinger worked behind the plate. (Note his 14–22 record in the table above). That, despite Denkinger's presumably small strike zone. On the other hand, the better control pitcher won 26 of the 38 games in which Hendry worked the plate, although Hendry's high ratio of strikeouts to walks suggested that control was less crucial when he umped.

Let's take a closer look at Witt's 1987 statistics. We've classified each A.L. umpire as having a large or small strike zone according to whether his strikeout-to-walk ratio was above (large) or below (small) the league average. You might think that Witt was dead meat when umps with small strike zones worked his games, but that was not the case:

Home-plate umpires	G	GS	W–L	IP	H	HR	BB	SO	ERA
Small strike zones	17	16	5–6	95.0	77	8	89	107	4.55
Large strike zones	9	9	3–4	48.0	37	2	51	53	5.63

We chose those extreme examples—examples that contradict conventional wisdom—in order to emphasize that pitchers cannot be strategically matched with umpires according to their control and the relative size of the home-plate umpire's strike zone.

The records in the following table represent the performance of the pitcher in each game who, among the two pitchers of decision, had better control (as measured by their ratios of walks to innings pitched for the entire season). The relative size of umpires' strike zones is deduced from the ratios of strikeouts to walks (above the league average indicates large zones, below the average indicates small zones):

	Home Plate Umpires With Large Zones			Home Plate Umpires With Small Zones		
	W	L	Pct.	W	L	Pct.
American League	288	234	.552	334	278	.546
National League	235	208	.530	291	237	.551
Major-league Totals	523	442	.542	625	515	.548

The major-league totals indicate that the pitcher with better control wins roughly 54 of every 100 games. But his winning percentage is only .006 higher when the home-plate umpire has a small strike zone than when the umpire has a large zone. It's going to be extremely difficult for managers or bettors to exploit such a narrow margin to a strategic advantage.

Pitching by Intimidation: Fact or Fantasy?

Let's move on to another topic close to the hearts of both the Rangers and the American League umpires—the effect of hitting a batter with a pitched ball.

Last season, Texas' pitchers hit 55 opposing batters with pitches, the highest total in either league. Let us make it clear that we aren't accusing the Rangers of any intentionally aggressive action—they also walked more batters (760) than any team since the 1971 Indians. Had Witt, Correa, and the rest of the staff actually aimed at opposing batters, we suspect that their major-league-leading total would have been somewhat lower.

But the incidence of bench-clearing brawls precipitated by pitches aimed at various parts of batters' bodies seemed to increase to such an extent last season that we thought John Ziegler had been hired as baseball's marketing director. Or was it just that no TV sports producer considered his highlights segment complete without tape of a basebrawl? Whatever the reason, the incidents prompted lots of tough talk from ex–big leaguers about pitchers needing to throw at batters in order to take control of the plate. Some even suggested that the home run increase of the past few seasons can be attributed to the growing reluctance of pitchers to intimidate opposing batters.

Do pitchers really gain an advantage over batters by hitting them with pitches? Our play-by-play database for the 12 seasons from 1975 through 1986 contained 2,554 instances of batters being hit by pitches that also met this criterion: the batter and pitcher involved had faced each other at least five times prior to the incident and five times subsequent to it. We limited the search to those cases in order to see if there were a difference between the batters' collective performance against those pitchers before and after being hit.

The following table shows the cumulative statistics for the five previous and five subsequent plate appearances in the 2,554 cases, for a grand total of 12,770 times at the plate both before and after:

	AB	H	2B	3B	HR	BB	SO	BA	SA	OBA
Before	11376	3137	504	84	315	1111	1685	.276	.418	.344
After	11400	3035	533	82	324	1069	1665	.266	.413	.332

The figures seem to indicate that the pitchers gained a slight advantage over the batters. But 10 batting-average points, even over more than 11,000 at bats, doesn't constitute conclusive evidence—such a result would occur 10 percent of the time merely by chance.

Another piece of information that we uncovered seems to indicate that the 10-point difference is, in fact, just that: a random event. Let's consider only the first plate appearances between the batters and pitchers immediately after the batsmen were hit. If the pitchers had truly intimidated the batters, the effect should have been greatest the very next time they faced each other. Those 2,554 meetings immediately following the HBPs produced a .276 batting average—exactly the same as the composite results *prior* to the batters being hit. And they yielded an even higher slugging average than before, the result of a higher home-run rate:

	AB	H	2B	3B	HR	BB	SO	BA	SA	OBA
Before	11376	3137	504	84	315	1111	1685	.276	.418	.344
After	2285	630	101	18	70	211	331	.276	.428	.337

Maybe some commentators, like Bill White and Don Drysdale, are correct when they claim that pitchers can gain an advantage over some batters through intimidation. But those former players might have overlooked the revenge factor that other batters have used to balance the scales after being hit.

Our files were chock-full of cases like that of Larry Parrish and Don Robinson. Parrish had only one hit in his previous six at bats against Robinson when the Pirates right-hander hit him with a pitch on April 7, 1979. Parrish didn't face Robinson again until June 27, but on that day he unleashed three months' worth of pent-up fury. Parrish hit a home run, a double, and a single in three at bats against Robinson that day. Parrish continued the assault when he next faced Robinson, eight weeks later, with doubles in each of his first two at bats.

Or consider the case of Bobby Murcer and Doug Rau. On June 26, 1976, Rau hit Murcer with a pitch for the second time that season. To that point in their careers, Murcer had only four hits in 18 at bats against Rau, and they were all singles. His next time up, Murcer tagged Rau for a home run, a ninth-inning game-winner. The next time Murcer faced Rau was five weeks later, but apparently Bobby didn't forget his bruises that quickly: He hit a two-run homer in the first inning. When Murcer returned to the plate in the second, Rau once again hit him with a pitch. Never mind that the bases were loaded—this was a point of honor, right? Murcer and Rau didn't meet again until September 21, when, after grounding out and striking out in his first two appearances, Murcer hit a game-tying, seventh-inning homer. Case closed.

We could go on and on with examples of batters who spanked opposing pitchers with barrages of extra-base hits after having been plunked with pitches. And by the same token, examples also exist to support the intimidation theory. For instance, Gary Redus had two singles, a walk, and a home run in his first five appearances against Danny Cox. Cox then hit him with a pitch, and Redus has gone hitless in 14 at bats against Cox since then. Cox plunked Ozzie Virgil in 1985 after Osvaldo climaxed a 4-for-8 streak against him with two home runs in three at bats. Virgil has two hits in 15 at bats versus Cox since then.

The point is that for every pitcher who intimidates a batter by hitting him, there's a batter who makes a pitcher pay a stiff price for the privilege of inflicting bodily harm. So, as George Gershwin once wrote, "Let's call the whole thing off." Get our pitch?

Knuckling Down on Knuckleballers

One of the unqualified joys of being a baseball fan is reading Roger Angell's romantic and enlightening pieces for *The New Yorker*. At about the time that the excitement of a new season begins to dull, and before the thrill of a pennant race or record chase begins, you can always count on Angell to fill the void with something provocative, sensitive, creative, and passionate.

Such was the case again last spring. Therein, Angell recounted a conversation with Phil Niekro, who described the apprehension that annually confronts all knuckleball pitchers in spring training. According to Niekro, the members of the limited fraternity of knuckleballers head to Florida or Arizona, to a man not knowing when or if they will rediscover the feel for their *raison d'etre*.

If that were the case, it followed that, as a general rule, the brothers Niekro and their soul mates might be much better pitchers during the second half of the season than the first half. But at the same time, we couldn't help noticing Charlie Hough's fast start. The Rangers' contribution to the Knuckleball Society of America even earned a trip to Oakland for the mid-season classic by compiling a 10–4 record through the All-Star break.

When Hough managed only an 8–9 mark during the second half of the season, we began to wonder whether Niekro's comments had any validity. So we took a look at Hough's career and those of 14 other knuckleballers, and found that grandpa Phil was absolutely correct; that Hough's 1987 season was atypical not only of knuckleball pitchers in general, but of the rest of his own career as well.

The following table shows the career won-lost records of those 15 pitchers before and after the All-Star break. (Tom Candiotti's records include only the past two years. He didn't throw the knuckleball until 1986.) For years in which two All-Star Games were played, we considered the first game to be the dividing line. Ten of the 15 pitchers had better records during the second half:

Player	First Half			Second Half		
	W	L	Pct.	W	L	Pct.
Gene Bearden	20	16	.556	25	22	.532
Tom Candiotti	10	15	.400	13	15	.464
Eddie Fisher	47	46	.505	38	24	.613
Freddie Fitzsimmons	104	70	.598	113	76	.598
Mickey Haefner	34	47	.420	44	44	.500
Charlie Hough	71	65	.522	78	63	.553
Dutch Leonard	92	85	.520	99	96	.508
Joe Niekro	113	105	.518	107	98	.522
Phil Niekro	170	155	.523	148	119	.554
Johnny Niggeling	28	31	.475	36	38	.486
Willie Ramsdell	16	22	.421	8	17	.320
Barney Schultz	10	11	.476	10	9	.526
Hoyt Wilhelm	62	69	.473	81	53	.604
Roger Wolff	30	34	.469	22	35	.386
Wilbur Wood	99	86	.535	65	69	.485
Totals	906	857	.514	887	778	.533

The difference isn't big, but it's significant in an era in which aging players are sold like mercenaries to the highest bidders during heated late-season pennant races. Contending teams looking for three or four good starts down the stretch might do best to ignore the full-season statistics on knuckleballers, and hope instead for a little second-half magic from those few remaining practitioners of one of baseball's dying arts.

WON-LOST RECORD BY STARTING POSITION

TEXAS 75-87	C	1B	2B	3B	SS	LF	CF	RF	P	DH	Leadoff	Relief	Starts
Scott Anderson	·	·	·	·	·	·	·	·	·	·	·	3-5	·
Bob Brower	·	·	·	·	·	10-12	27-28	0-2	·	1-1	19-24	·	38-43
Jerry Browne	·	·	57-62	·	·	·	·	·	·	·	42-40	·	57-62
Steve Buechele	·	·	6-10	46-48	·	·	·	·	·	·	·	·	52-58
Edwin Correa	·	·	·	·	·	·	·	·	7-8	·	·	·	7-8
Keith Creel	·	·	·	·	·	·	·	·	·	·	·	4-2	·
Cecil Espy	·	·	·	·	·	0-1	·	1-0	·	·	·	·	1-1
Scott Fletcher	·	·	·	·	68-79	·	·	·	·	·	2-2	·	68-79
Jose Guzman	·	·	·	·	·	·	·	·	12-18	·	·	4-3	12-18
Greg Harris	·	·	·	·	·	·	·	·	7-12	·	·	4-19	7-12
Dwayne Henry	·	·	·	·	·	·	·	·	·	·	·	1-4	·
Charlie Hough	·	·	·	·	·	·	·	·	22-18	·	·	·	22-18
Steve Howe	·	·	·	·	·	·	·	·	·	·	·	5-19	·
Pete Incaviglia	·	·	·	·	·	59-71	·	·	·	2-3	·	·	61-74
Mike Jeffcoat	·	·	·	·	·	·	·	·	1-1	·	·	·	1-1
Paul Kilgus	·	·	·	·	·	·	·	·	4-8	·	·	2-11	4-8
Jeff Kunkel	·	·	5-4	0-1	·	·	·	·	·	·	·	·	5-5
Mike Loynd	·	·	·	·	·	·	·	·	3-5	·	·	6-12	3-5
Bob Malloy	·	·	·	·	·	·	·	·	1-1	·	·	·	1-1
Mike Mason	·	·	·	·	·	·	·	·	4-2	·	·	0-2	4-2
Oddibe McDowell	·	·	·	·	·	·	48-58	·	·	·	10-17	·	48-58
Dave Meier	·	·	·	·	·	4-0	·	1-1	·	·	·	·	5-1
Ron Meridith	·	·	·	·	·	·	·	·	·	·	·	4-7	·
Gary Mielke	·	·	·	·	·	·	·	·	·	·	·	0-3	·
Dale Mohorcic	·	·	·	·	·	·	·	·	·	·	·	32-42	·
Pete O'Brien	·	68-79	·	·	·	·	·	·	·	·	·	·	68-79
Tom O'Malley	·	·	·	15-16	·	·	·	·	·	·	·	·	15-16
Tom Paciorek	·	5-2	·	·	·	2-3	·	0-2	·	0-1	·	·	7-8
Larry Parrish	·	·	·	11-17	·	·	·	·	·	57-61	·	·	68-78
Geno Petralli	21-28	0-1	·	2-4	·	·	·	·	·	·	·	·	23-33
Darrell Porter	1-0	·	·	·	·	·	·	·	·	14-15	·	·	15-15
Jeff Russell	·	·	·	·	·	·	·	·	1-1	·	·	17-33	1-1
Ruben Sierra	·	·	·	·	·	0-1	·	73-82	·	·	0-2	·	73-83
Don Slaught	26-29	·	·	·	·	·	·	·	·	0-4	·	·	26-33
Mike Stanley	27-30	·	2-5	·	·	·	·	·	·	1-2	·	·	30-37
Greg Tabor	·	·	1-2	·	·	·	·	·	·	·	·	·	1-2
Curtis Wilkerson	·	·	6-9	1-1	7-8	·	·	·	·	·	2-2	·	14-18
Mitch Williams	·	·	·	·	·	·	·	·	0-1	·	·	33-51	0-1
Bobby Witt	·	·	·	·	·	·	·	·	13-12	·	·	·	13-12

Batting vs. Left and Right Handed Pitchers

		BA	Rank	SA	Rank	OBA	Rank	HR %	Rank	BB %	Rank	SO %	Rank
Bob Brower	vs. Lefties	.273	70	.466	53	.355	57	4.55	47	11.22	39	19.02	116
	vs. Righties	.244	109	.433	73	.314	106	4.72	43	9.03	75	18.75	126
Jerry Browne	vs. Lefties	.311	27	.420	82	.403	19	0.84	135	12.77	24	5.67	5
	vs. Righties	.257	94	.310	150	.342	69	0.00	156	11.17	37	10.91	42
Steve Buechele	vs. Lefties	.288	49	.497	34	.333	78	4.52	49	6.22	132	14.51	82
	vs. Righties	.188	160	.306	151	.250	156	2.69	102	7.73	97	18.36	123
Scott Fletcher	vs. Lefties	.318	23	.409	88	.388	28	1.36	122	9.68	58	7.26	13
	vs. Righties	.269	75	.353	131	.341	71	0.54	151	8.81	79	11.43	44
Pete Incaviglia	vs. Lefties	.341	14	.632	4	.407	17	7.14	8	10.29	48	26.47	152
	vs. Righties	.232	132	.422	79	.290	136	4.28	55	7.52	102	31.75	160
Oddibe McDowell	vs. Lefties	.225	131	.352	127	.371	46	2.82	90	19.10	3	17.98	111
	vs. Righties	.244	110	.443	64	.313	111	3.57	79	9.09	72	22.19	144
Pete O'Brien	vs. Lefties	.247	101	.339	131	.294	124	1.61	114	6.47	128	14.93	88
	vs. Righties	.305	23	.514	27	.373	33	5.22	33	10.53	48	7.09	14
Larry Parrish	vs. Lefties	.268	78	.516	27	.346	68	7.37	5	10.28	49	28.04	159
	vs. Righties	.267	81	.466	50	.318	98	4.90	39	6.77	115	23.56	148
Geno Petralli	vs. Lefties	.267	--	.267	--	.353	--	0.00	--	11.76	--	17.65	--
	vs. Righties	.305	24	.497	32	.391	17	3.74	75	11.63	31	12.09	52
Darrell Porter	vs. Lefties	.250	--	.250	--	.250	--	0.00	--	0.00	--	37.50	--
	vs. Righties	.238	122	.434	71	.394	14	5.74	27	19.35	2	25.81	152
Ruben Sierra	vs. Lefties	.249	98	.456	59	.267	147	5.06	33	3.19	156	12.75	61
	vs. Righties	.271	71	.478	44	.321	93	4.43	50	6.97	114	18.43	124
Don Slaught	vs. Lefties	.237	115	.459	55	.313	102	4.44	51	9.33	65	18.67	113
	vs. Righties	.206	--	.333	--	.277	--	1.96	--	8.62	--	19.83	--
Mike Stanley	vs. Lefties	.283	61	.404	91	.354	59	2.02	109	9.73	56	17.70	105
	vs. Righties	.265	86	.402	96	.367	38	3.42	82	14.29	12	20.00	132
Team Average	vs. Lefties	.277	2	.454	1	.340	4	3.99	1	8.64	9	17.19	12
	vs. Righties	.260	10	.418	10	.330	7	3.22	8	9.30	5	17.36	13
League Average	vs. Lefties	.265		.422		.333		3.29		8.94		15.64	
	vs. Righties	.265		.427		.334		3.43		8.94		15.26	

Batting with Runners on Base and Bases Empty

		BA	Rank	SA	Rank	OBA	Rank	HR %	Rank	BB %	Rank	SO %	Rank
Bob Brower	Runners On	.336	12	.538	20	.424	10	5.04	35	12.84	35	15.54	96
	Bases Empty	.212	151	.397	98	.279	145	4.35	57	8.46	72	21.39	139
Jerry Browne	Runners On	.254	107	.333	141	.364	58	0.00	150	14.53	22	5.23	7
	Bases Empty	.278	52	.342	137	.356	43	0.32	154	10.17	41	11.58	43
Steve Buechele	Runners On	.228	136	.347	135	.281	146	1.80	115	7.41	112	15.87	99
	Bases Empty	.245	110	.444	68	.299	124	5.10	39	6.64	115	17.06	107
Scott Fletcher	Runners On	.322	23	.403	101	.377	44	0.42	149	7.35	113	8.46	23
	Bases Empty	.264	74	.355	128	.346	51	1.14	137	10.35	36	10.86	36
Pete Incaviglia	Runners On	.260	97	.455	61	.310	120	4.76	42	7.45	110	29.41	159
	Bases Empty	.281	46	.532	25	.351	48	5.76	29	9.42	54	30.19	161
Oddibe McDowell	Runners On	.228	136	.389	109	.325	108	2.40	101	12.69	36	22.84	147
	Bases Empty	.250	99	.454	62	.323	87	4.17	61	9.77	48	20.30	131
Pete O'Brien	Runners On	.310	31	.468	51	.374	48	3.23	82	10.73	61	10.03	34
	Bases Empty	.268	66	.449	65	.327	79	4.67	79	8.02	82	9.17	17
Larry Parrish	Runners On	.326	17	.589	8	.388	29	7.36	2	9.28	85	21.99	143
	Bases Empty	.217	147	.391	102	.273	150	4.35	57	6.83	110	27.95	158
Geno Petralli	Runners On	.258	100	.340	138	.376	45	1.03	136	15.38	14	13.68	76
	Bases Empty	.343	5	.610	7	.400	10	5.71	30	7.83	86	11.30	41
Ruben Sierra	Runners On	.266	88	.500	29	.295	134	4.75	43	4.91	148	15.90	100
	Bases Empty	.260	83	.440	69	.309	114	4.59	50	6.29	123	16.86	102
Don Slaught	Runners On	.186	160	.275	155	.272	154	0.98	138	9.32	84	17.80	118
	Bases Empty	.252	96	.504	32	.318	101	5.19	37	8.78	68	20.27	130
Mike Stanley	Runners On	.293	51	.455	61	.393	23	3.03	88	15.45	13	17.89	119
	Bases Empty	.256	91	.359	124	.331	70	2.56	104	9.23	58	20.00	129
Team Average	Runners On	.276	4	.437	6	.344	7	3.21	8	9.64	7	16.38	13
	Bases Empty	.258	9	.425	6	.325	8	3.70	5	8.63	6	18.03	14
League Average	Runners On	.271		.428		.343		3.25		9.68		14.87	
	Bases Empty	.260		.424		.326		3.49		8.34		15.79	

Overall Batting Compared to Late Inning Pressure Situations

		BA	Rank	SA	Rank	OBA	Rank	HR %	Rank	BB %	Rank	SO %	Rank	RDI %	Rank
Bob Brower	Overall	.261	91	.452	64	.338	71	4.62	47	10.32	53	18.91	125	.360	15
	Pressure	.162	155	.189	161	.304	115	0.00	119	16.67	11	20.83	119	.214	113
Jerry Browne	Overall	.271	74	.339	147	.358	45	0.22	159	11.60	32	9.51	25	.339	28
	Pressure	.333	21	.404	84	.479	5	0.00	119	21.05	4	3.95	1	.292	74
Steve Buechele	Overall	.237	136	.399	105	.290	151	3.58	76	7.00	102	16.50	102	.324	44
	Pressure	.267	80	.422	76	.377	43	2.22	94	12.73	37	14.55	76	.273	85
Scott Fletcher	Overall	.287	37	.374	122	.358	48	0.85	144	9.13	72	9.88	28	.329	36
	Pressure	.241	107	.289	138	.333	82	0.00	119	12.12	42	11.11	41	.275	84
Pete Incaviglia	Overall	.271	72	.497	27	.332	79	5.30	27	8.53	84	29.84	160	.290	74
	Pressure	.243	103	.500	31	.321	100	5.71	33	11.11	50	33.33	161	.167	133
Oddibe McDowell	Overall	.241	130	.428	82	.324	95	3.44	84	11.02	42	21.38	141	.277	95
	Pressure	.316	30	.439	67	.443	13	1.75	104	18.31	8	11.27	44	.438	15
Pete O'Brien	Overall	.286	39	.457	56	.348	62	4.04	64	9.25	69	9.56	26	.313	54
	Pressure	.297	49	.593	12	.363	63	8.79	6	9.80	74	7.84	17	.227	104
Tom O'Malley	Overall	.274	--	.368	--	.351	--	0.85	--	11.19	--	6.72	--	.297	--
	Pressure	.167	--	.278	--	.304	--	0.00	--	17.39	--	4.35	--	.111	147
Larry Parrish	Overall	.268	77	.483	34	.328	88	5.75	19	7.99	97	25.12	151	.344	25
	Pressure	.237	115	.355	106	.310	110	3.95	54	8.33	91	27.38	153	.368	42
Geno Petralli	Overall	.302	22	.480	36	.388	14	3.47	82	11.64	29	12.50	51	.318	47
	Pressure	.262	86	.381	99	.347	75	2.38	91	10.20	64	8.16	21	.278	81
Darrell Porter	Overall	.238	--	.423	--	.387	--	5.38	--	18.40	--	26.38	--	.277	--
	Pressure	.172	151	.310	132	.415	23	3.45	65	29.27	1	24.39	138	.429	16
Ruben Sierra	Overall	.263	88	.470	45	.302	132	4.67	46	5.60	142	16.38	99	.275	98
	Pressure	.242	106	.418	79	.281	130	4.40	49	5.21	132	17.71	96	.182	124
Don Slaught	Overall	.224	150	.405	99	.298	138	3.38	86	9.02	75	19.17	99	.076	163
	Pressure	.255	93	.383	97	.327	92	2.13	98	9.09	82	18.18	102	.000	158
Mike Stanley	Overall	.273	67	.403	101	.361	42	2.78	100	12.25	23	18.97	126	.371	10
	Pressure	.400	--	.600	--	.435	--	5.00	--	8.33	--	16.67	--	.800	--
Team Average	Overall	.266	6	.430	3	.333	7	3.49	7	9.07	7	17.30	14	.300	2
	Pressure	.258	8	.401	10	.353	2	3.14	7	12.23	1	16.06	6	.269	8
League Average	Overall	.265		.425		.333		3.38		8.94		15.38		.287	
	Pressure	.262		.405		.335		3.07		9.43		16.58		.280	

Additional Miscellaneous Batting Comparisons

	Grass Surface BA	Rank	Artificial Surface BA	Rank	Home Games BA	Rank	Road Games BA	Rank	Runners in Scoring Position BA	Rank	Runners in Scoring Pos and Two Outs BA	Rank	Leading Off Inning OBA	Rank	Runners on 3B with less than 2 Outs RDI %	Rank
Bob Brower	.283	53	.088	--	.297	47	.223	136	.302	41	.353	11	.303	111	.588	86
Jerry Browne	.275	72	.246	94	.306	32	.230	128	.289	56	.300	41	.330	82	.652	44
Steve Buechele	.233	135	.259	81	.250	112	.223	137	.247	108	.294	45	.264	140	.667	33
Scott Fletcher	.315	17	.152	159	.341	6	.236	122	.338	12	.348	13	.339	67	.630	53
Pete Incaviglia	.270	79	.279	56	.259	103	.283	46	.252	101	.230	104	.368	36	.606	68
Oddibe McDowell	.224	146	.319	15	.250	112	.232	125	.275	76	.267	65	.339	65	.524	117
Pete O'Brien	.284	52	.300	31	.272	81	.299	28	.270	82	.263	70	.331	80	.643	47
Larry Parrish	.269	81	.260	78	.264	91	.271	62	.356	7	.353	11	.278	132	.630	53
Geno Petralli	.313	18	.256	--	.319	18	.287	40	.293	49	.300	41	.448	5	.538	108
Darrell Porter	.248	--	.207	--	.242	--	.235	--	.257	--	.188	--	.440	--	.545	104
Ruben Sierra	.263	93	.262	77	.276	75	.250	98	.239	117	.253	83	.298	117	.560	96
Don Slaught	.222	148	.233	--	.256	108	.188	158	.161	157	.071	159	.333	69	.143	--
Mike Stanley	.290	44	.200	141	.321	16	.224	135	.296	46	.320	24	.314	98	.750	9
Team Average	.270	5	.243	11	.279	3	.253	12	.277	4	.279	2	.332	4	.597	6
League Average	.267		.261		.270		.260		.266		.247		.328		.581	

Pitching vs. Left and Right Handed Batters

		BA	Rank	SA	Rank	OBA	Rank	HR %	Rank	BB %	Rank	SO %	Rank
Edwin Correa	vs. Lefties	.243	33	.404	55	.350	85	3.68	88	13.66	119	18.63	25
	vs. Righties	.350	123	.692	127	.469	127	8.39	126	16.85	123	17.42	47
Jose Guzman	vs. Lefties	.240	28	.363	24	.300	18	2.70	43	7.57	43	16.04	43
	vs. Righties	.263	71	.483	106	.344	83	5.09	115	11.14	104	16.47	56
Greg Harris	vs. Lefties	.256	47	.363	25	.319	40	1.48	17	8.70	59	16.72	40
	vs. Righties	.304	111	.512	115	.377	110	4.84	112	9.09	82	16.97	50
Charlie Hough	vs. Lefties	.240	24	.375	32	.336	63	3.34	74	11.93	106	15.63	49
	vs. Righties	.207	12	.370	38	.288	19	3.39	80	8.33	65	20.44	28
Paul Kilgus	vs. Lefties	.250	--	.539	--	.313	--	7.89	--	8.43	--	13.25	--
	vs. Righties	.277	90	.431	76	.340	76	2.92	59	7.95	59	10.26	114
Mike Loynd	vs. Lefties	.313	116	.522	114	.392	119	5.97	120	11.11	94	10.46	106
	vs. Righties	.263	72	.454	95	.351	91	3.95	91	12.00	112	18.29	42
Dale Mohorcic	vs. Lefties	.298	103	.444	83	.335	72	3.31	72	4.85	6	9.70	116
	vs. Righties	.207	10	.313	9	.249	4	2.88	57	4.89	16	14.22	76
Jeff Russell	vs. Lefties	.291	100	.467	98	.362	97	3.85	93	10.63	86	13.04	74
	vs. Righties	.279	93	.373	42	.374	107	1.00	4	12.77	116	12.34	101
Mitch Williams	vs. Lefties	.146	1	.244	1	.309	26	2.44	38	16.34	125	32.68	1
	vs. Righties	.189	2	.298	6	.374	106	2.52	38	21.84	126	25.00	10
Bobby Witt	vs. Lefties	.229	13	.332	13	.387	115	2.05	25	19.79	128	19.79	17
	vs. Righties	.206	9	.316	10	.382	114	1.75	14	22.07	127	28.76	6
Team Average	vs. Lefties	.252	2	.403	4	.344	11	3.49	11	11.72	14	16.40	3
	vs. Righties	.254	3	.425	9	.350	13	3.74	10	12.04	14	17.96	1
League Average	vs. Lefties	.267		.427		.338		3.30		9.47		14.54	
	vs. Righties	.264		.424		.330		3.45		8.56		15.98	

Pitching with Runners on Base and Bases Empty

		BA	Rank	SA	Rank	OBA	Rank	HR %	Rank	BB %	Rank	SO %	Rank
Edwin Correa	Runners On	.271	72	.568	120	.425	125	7.63	127	20.78	127	14.29	69
	Bases Empty	.317	121	.540	121	.402	124	4.97	115	10.81	106	21.08	20
Jose Guzman	Runners On	.286	93	.470	95	.340	66	4.61	100	8.07	42	14.12	72
	Bases Empty	.229	22	.388	40	.310	41	3.35	68	10.13	101	17.64	39
Greg Harris	Runners On	.303	100	.498	103	.367	102	3.98	91	9.03	64	16.32	44
	Bases Empty	.263	71	.393	45	.334	80	2.60	35	8.80	75	17.30	43
Charlie Hough	Runners On	.205	5	.314	6	.305	24	2.62	52	10.67	90	20.55	19
	Bases Empty	.234	28	.410	58	.314	46	3.85	86	9.66	90	16.41	50
Paul Kilgus	Runners On	.229	18	.382	40	.284	5	3.18	76	5.85	16	11.11	104
	Bases Empty	.306	116	.513	117	.374	109	4.66	108	9.81	94	10.75	106
Mike Loynd	Runners On	.275	77	.415	73	.340	65	2.82	52	9.38	69	15.63	53
	Bases Empty	.299	112	.556	122	.399	123	6.94	124	13.69	120	13.69	80
Dale Mohorcic	Runners On	.222	10	.357	19	.270	3	3.78	88	6.25	18	11.06	105
	Bases Empty	.270	84	.379	32	.302	34	2.30	22	3.30	3	13.74	79
Jeff Russell	Runners On	.259	57	.378	36	.365	98	2.07	28	15.02	123	11.16	103
	Bases Empty	.311	119	.458	97	.373	107	2.63	38	8.13	63	14.35	72
Mitch Williams	Runners On	.180	1	.290	1	.373	107	2.73	56	22.18	128	25.81	3
	Bases Empty	.169	1	.270	3	.330	77	2.25	20	17.65	126	29.41	2
Bobby Witt	Runners On	.228	16	.331	12	.351	79	1.78	19	15.56	125	23.05	8
	Bases Empty	.209	10	.318	11	.420	127	2.09	18	26.38	127	24.54	10
Team Average	Runners On	.252	2	.404	3	.346	11	3.38	9	12.08	14	16.89	1
	Bases Empty	.254	5	.424	9	.348	14	3.83	11	11.73	14	17.58	2
League Average	Runners On	.271		.428		.343		3.25		9.68		14.87	
	Bases Empty	.260		.424		.326		3.49		8.34		15.79	

Overall Pitching Compared to Late Inning Pressure Situations

		BA	Rank	SA	Rank	OBA	Rank	HR %	Rank	BB %	Rank	SO %	Rank
Edwin Correa	Overall	.297	110	.552	125	.412	126	6.09	126	15.34	125	17.99	33
	Pressure	.429	--	.714	--	.429	--	7.14	--	0.00	--	21.43	--
Jose Guzman	Overall	.251	43	.420	68	.322	50	3.84	89	9.32	80	16.25	46
	Pressure	.259	64	.466	101	.306	37	3.45	83	6.45	29	20.97	23
Greg Harris	Overall	.281	93	.440	82	.349	88	3.22	72	8.90	71	16.85	44
	Pressure	.319	115	.528	112	.405	119	4.17	98	11.63	94	17.44	46
Charlie Hough	Overall	.223	9	.372	25	.311	32	3.37	77	10.07	94	18.12	31
	Pressure	.220	30	.374	56	.273	18	4.07	96	4.48	11	22.39	20
Steve Howe	Overall	.280	--	.398	--	.341	--	1.69	--	6.11	--	14.50	--
	Pressure	.277	82	.404	71	.358	84	2.13	47	9.09	62	12.73	88
Paul Kilgus	Overall	.271	83	.454	91	.334	70	4.00	94	8.05	51	10.91	107
	Pressure	.231	--	.654	--	.333	--	11.54	--	13.33	--	16.67	--
Mike Loynd	Overall	.287	111	.486	111	.370	113	4.90	116	11.59	114	14.63	67
	Pressure	.000	--	.000	--	.500	--	0.00	--	50.00	--	0.00	--
Dale Mohorcic	Overall	.245	32	.368	20	.285	8	3.06	61	4.87	6	12.31	95
	Pressure	.310	--	.473	104	.352	77	3.80	89	6.40	28	11.33	104
Jeff Russell	Overall	.285	98	.418	63	.369	112	2.35	22	11.76	116	12.67	89
	Pressure	.280	86	.378	58	.372	101	1.22	31	11.70	97	15.96	57
Mitch Williams	Overall	.175	1	.280	2	.353	93	2.49	29	20.04	126	27.51	2
	Pressure	.183	5	.278	12	.314	41	2.37	55	13.04	108	28.50	2
Bobby Witt	Overall	.219	6	.325	4	.385	120	1.92	9	20.80	127	23.77	9
	Pressure	.211	21	.263	7	.423	124	0.00	1	25.00	127	23.08	15
Team Average	Overall	.253	2	.415	5	.347	13	3.63	10	11.89	14	17.26	2
	Pressure	.261	7	.414	11	.346	10	3.22	10	10.11	9	18.89	2
League Average	Overall	.265		.425		.333		3.38		8.94		15.38	
	Pressure	.262		.404		.337		2.99		9.73		16.42	

Additional Miscellaneous Pitching Comparisons

	Grass Surface BA	Rank	Artificial Surface BA	Rank	Home Games BA	Rank	Road Games BA	Rank	Runners in Scoring Position BA	Rank	Runners in Scoring Pos and Two Outs BA	Rank	Leading Off Inning OBA	Rank
Edwin Correa	.321	116	.207	13	.317	117	.282	85	.253	54	.275	89	.395	117
Jose Guzman	.251	42	.247	50	.259	71	.242	29	.267	72	.200	32	.279	23
Greg Harris	.276	86	.312	104	.266	83	.300	103	.266	71	.210	42	.342	77
Charlie Hough	.219	5	.238	41	.238	35	.205	5	.188	8	.227	57	.312	46
Paul Kilgus	.276	87	.254	60	.269	86	.273	75	.253	55	.324	107	.368	102
Mike Loynd	.292	99	.250	--	.286	101	.289	--	.321	114	.324	107	.333	69
Dale Mohorcic	.246	29	.241	45	.253	58	.237	19	.257	63	.156	7	.292	30
Jeff Russell	.282	92	.302	101	.317	117	.260	47	.316	112	.400	126	.344	81
Mitch Williams	.176	1	.167	2	.181	5	.168	2	.162	1	.188	19	.379	108
Bobby Witt	.222	6	.200	9	.210	10	.230	14	.208	17	.111	2	.427	125
Team Average	.253	2	.253	2	.254	5	.251	2	.245	2	.236	4	.336	10
League Average	.267		.261		.260		.270		.266		.247		.328	

TORONTO BLUE JAYS

Over the past six seasons, no team has spent more time in first place in the A.L. East than the Toronto Blue Jays. But despite that division-leading total of 249 days holding at least a share of first place, Toronto has been in first place only once on the mornings after those seasons ended. The number of days each team has spent in first place since 1983:

Team	Days
Toronto	249
Detroit	247
Boston	172
Baltimore	138
New York	97
Milwaukee	55
Cleveland	22

Combine Toronto's failure to hold those division leads with their collapses in the 1985 American League Championship Series and during the final week of the 1987 season, and it's easy to understand why the Blue Jays have been made the butt of an endless series of cruel jokes involving apple orchards, fish bones, and automobile carburetors. But have the Blue Jays really been guilty of—pardon us while we clear our throats—melting in the heat of a pennant race? There—we didn't say *choke*.

The two most incriminating items in the indictment are the sudden-death endings to Toronto's 1985 and 1987 seasons. Three years ago, the Blue Jays coughed up the American League title to Kansas City after building a three-games-to-one lead in the A.L.C.S. Only six other teams in major-league history have lost a best-of-seven post-season series after leading by that margin. And last season, Detroit staged the greatest final-week comeback to win a division or league championship in American League history, and they did it at Toronto's expense.

But those are only two charges, involving just two weeks' worth of play. How many of us would relish the prospect of being judged by the two worst weeks of our own professional careers? A more reasonable test of the Blue Jays' tolerance for pressure is to examine their performance over the past five years, classifying each game according to the team's position in the standings at the time:

Position	W	L	Pct.
First place	127	96	.570
Second place	156	136	.534
Third or lower	176	118	.599
Totals	459	350	.567

The Blue Jays played their best baseball when the pressure was least—that is, when they weren't among the division's two leading teams. Keep in mind that the group of games played when Toronto led the A.L. East was weighted heavily with games from Toronto's best season during that period; conversely, nearly half of the "third-or-lower" group was drawn from the Jays' worst season in their last five. Specifically, when Toronto won the division title in 1985 with a 99–62 record, they were in first place for 149 days, and in third place or lower for only 20 days. But in 1986, when Toronto won only 86 games (its lowest total over the past five seasons), they were in third place or lower for 143 days.

That skew made it unlikely that Toronto would compile its best record when it was no higher than third in the A.L. East standings. Still, the Blue Jays played far better when they weren't among the division's top two teams than when they were. That seems to indicate that Toronto has problems handling pressure.

But we looked at the question in what we consider a more revealing way, and by that measure, Toronto looks as though it stings like a bee when those butterflies arrive. We examined only those games played after the All-Star break over the past five seasons, and classified them according to the margin by which Toronto led the division or trailed the leader. The Blue Jays played best when that margin was slimmest:

Position in standings	W	L	Pct.
Led by more than 2 games	42	32	.568
Small leads or deficits	73	49	.598
Trailed by more than 3 games	100	88	.532
Totals	215	169	.560

So take your pick. If you want to tell the one about why the Blue Jays can't start their cars on cold mornings, go right ahead. But there's also some pretty compelling evidence that suggests that the Blue Jays not only can tolerate the heat of a pennant race, but that they flourish under those conditions.

Ex-Terminating Henke

It's safe to assume that none of Toronto's players were terribly thrilled with the results of the final week of the 1987 season, during which the Blue Jays surrendered a three and one-half-game lead to Detroit. But probably none was more upset than Tom Henke, the American League leader in saves. Other than Tony Fernandez, who was sidelined by a fractured elbow, Henke was the only player on the Blue Jays' roster throughout the season who did not play during the final week of the season as Toronto's lead slowly slipped away.

Toronto manager Jimy Williams was sharply criticized for wasting Henke's talent during that final week. But no situation cried out more loudly or at greater length for the A.L.'s most overpowering stopper than the late innings of a nationally televised game in which the Blue Jays and Tigers needed 12 innings to determine which team would take a one-game lead into the season finale the next day.

Toronto starter Mike Flanagan pitched brilliantly in that game, but Jack Morris was just as effective for Detroit. And while everyone waited for Flanagan to receive a well-earned ovation as Williams called for his bullpen ace, Iron Mike just kept mowing down the Tigers' lineup. By the time Flanagan was finally relieved, he'd pitched 11 innings—his longest outing since August 15, 1979, when he tossed a 12-inning, complete-game victory over Chicago.

And when Williams did remove Flanagan from the game, who replaced him? Not Henke, but left-handed Harvard man Jeff Musselman. Within minutes, the Tigers were in sole possession of first place. Boola, boola, Jeff.

In one way, it's ironic that Williams allowed Flanagan to pitch 11 innings without calling for any of his relievers, let alone Henke. No American League manager made more pitching changes during the 1987 season than Williams (336), or allowed his relief pitchers to face fewer batters per outing (an average of 6.07). On the other hand, it was logical —to a fault—that the Jays' manager would keep the Terminator locked in the pen. Williams had developed a scheme in which he had four capable relievers—Henke, Mark Eichhorn, Musselman, and Jose Nunez—and four specific roles, one for each.

But the system that worked so well for Williams all season long paralyzed him when it counted most. Let's examine the roles that each pitcher assumed:

- Henke was the stopper, brought into games in the late innings to protect leads of all sizes. Williams preferred to bring Henke into the game at the start of an inning.
- Musselman was Henke's set-up man, used to protect leads in the seventh and eighth innings and turn them over to Henke. As the only southpaw among the group, Musselman was also used occasionally to face one or two left-handed batters.
- Eichhorn pitched in 89 games, but rarely entered when Toronto had a small lead: 56 of those appearances were made when Toronto was tied or behind, and another 17 when the Jays trailed by four runs or more.
- Nunez, also a part-time starter, was Toronto's

early-inning reliever, making 11 of his 28 entries in the sixth inning or earlier. He was rarely called on to protect a lead.

A summary follows of the situations in which each of those relievers entered games. A "+" margin indicates that Toronto led, a "−" that the Jays trailed; "SI" indicates that the pitcher started an inning, "ROB" that he entered with runners on base:

Player	Inning					Margin				
	1–6	7	8	9	Ex	+	0	−	SI	ROB
Henke	0	5	33	32	2	57	3	12	36	36
Musselman	18	19	18	6	6	34	14	19	19	40
Eichhorn	34	27	15	9	4	33	21	35	24	58
Nunez	11	6	3	5	3	2	5	21	5	19

It's interesting to note that Williams rarely called on Henke in tie games; in fact, the *last* of the three times that Henke entered a tied game was on April 25. But unless Williams was bound by contract not to use Henke in those situations, what possible excuse was there for using Musselman for Toronto's most important relief appearance of the season? We can only speculate that Henke was physically subpar for that final series, or that the game-tying, ninth-inning home run that he surrendered to Kirk Gibson in a key game the previous weekend had shattered Williams's confidence in him. Or simply that Williams is about as flexible as a cadaver lying on the frozen tundra of the Yukon.

"Rubber-Armed" Relievers

One possible explanation for Williams's reluctance to use Henke was that the manager might have considered Henke a liability coming off a week of inactivity. As we mentioned earlier, not only did Henke remain in the bullpen in the crucial Saturday game, he didn't pitch at all after allowing a costly home run to Gibson six days earlier.

A look at Henke's work coming off extended rests over the past three seasons provided one final irony to the situation: *During his three seasons with Toronto, Henke has been almost unhittable when he hasn't pitched over the previous five days.*

The following table classifies each of Henke's appearances for Toronto since 1985 according to the number of appearances he had made over the previous five days. Notice that his strikeout potential appears to have been unaffected; but the ratios of hits and earned runs that Henke allowed per nine innings rose steadily relative to the extent of his recent activity:

Last 5 days	G	SV	IP	H	ER	BB	SO	Per 9 Innings		
								ERA	Hits	SO
0 games	32	15	47.0	18	7	11	59	1.34	3.45	11.30
1 game	63	24	91.1	59	27	25	113	2.66	5.81	11.14
2 games	56	30	69.2	58	26	22	93	3.36	7.49	12.01
3 games	12	5	17.1	19	9	7	23	4.67	9.87	11.94
Totals	163	74	225.1	154	69	65	288	2.76	6.15	11.50

Henke's performance contradicts the commonly promoted theory that relief pitchers thrive on activity; that they should be forced into games in certain cases simply to prevent prolonged periods of inactivity.

Is that theory bogus, or is Henke an exception to the rule? Eight other pitchers saved at least 20 games last season (Jeff Reardon, Dave Righetti, and Dan Plesac in the American League; Steve Bedrosian, Lee Smith, Todd Worrell, John Franco, and Roger McDowell in the National League). Here's how they performed collectively according to the number of appearances they made over the previous five days:

								Per 9 Innings		
Last 5 days	G	SV	IP	H	ER	BB	SO	ERA	Hits	SO
0 games	152	69	209.0	191	82	74	198	3.53	8.22	8.53
1 game	201	96	264.1	238	91	91	247	3.10	8.10	8.41
2 games	161	89	225.0	208	74	82	197	2.96	8.32	7.88
3 + games	42	21	54.1	53	13	18	35	2.15	8.78	5.80
Totals	556	275	752.2	690	260	265	677	3.11	8.25	8.10

Unlike Henke's, these earned-run averages dropped steadily as recent activity increased. And although ERAs can be misleading for relief pitchers, we consider these reliable given the number of innings involved. Notice that the ratio of saves to appearances increases with activity until the three-game level. And if those figures are reliable indicators of a general trend, then the conventional wisdom about relief pitchers thriving on constant work is valid, and Henke is a notable exception to the rule.

Although many of the relievers whose statistics are represented in the previous table are, like Henke, high-strikeout pitchers, Henke's ratio of 12.3 strikeouts per nine innings last season was outstanding even among that group. That raised the question of whether extreme power pitchers were a collective exception to the activity rule. The following table includes the statistics of eight pitchers other than Henke who made at least 20 relief appearances last season with ratios of at least 10 strikeouts per nine innings (Scott Garrelts, Randy Myers, Dan Plesac, Joe Price, Calvin Schiraldi, Dave Smith, Lee Smith, and Mitch Williams):

								Per 9 Innings		
Last 5 days	G	SV	IP	H	ER	BB	SO	ERA	Hits	SO
0 games	123	30	163.2	133	70	81	193	3.85	7.31	10.61
1 game	173	47	254.2	182	80	110	294	2.83	6.43	10.39
2 games	120	27	157.2	115	54	87	178	3.08	6.56	10.16
3 + games	36	10	44.2	37	17	27	59	3.43	7.46	11.89
Totals	452	114	620.2	467	221	305	724	3.20	6.77	10.50

Well, it seemed like a good idea at the time, officer. But Henke is an exception even compared to these extreme power pitchers. It's generally true that relievers of all types don't perform at their peaks without at least some activity over the previous five days. But Henke is clearly an outstanding exception to that rule.

We don't think that either Williams or Henke himself were aware of the Terminator's enormous success following long rests. There were many instances during the season in which Henke was used on two days' rest in situations that did not require his special talent. For example, on April 29 Henke pitched the ninth inning with a seven-run lead. On May 9 he entered that game with an eight-run lead in the eighth. On July 31 he protected a five-run lead for the final inning. In those cases, as well as several others in which the Blue Jays held substantial leads, Henke was apparently used simply because he hadn't pitched for the past two days.

But if Williams knew of Henke's success after an extended rest—and we repeat, we don't think he did—it would explain the manager's reluctance to use his ace in losing situations during the early part of the final week of the season. But it would also make his failure of omission on that final Saturday all the more astounding.

The Best Outfield in Baseball

With the passing of each season, it becomes increasingly difficult to deny that Toronto's outfield of George Bell, Jesse Barfield, and Lloyd Moseby is the best outfield of the 1980s, and possibly one of the greatest of all time. And the selection of Bell as the Most Valuable Player in the American League last season suggests that we may not yet have seen the best that this group has to offer.

To put their accomplishments in perspective, we've compiled statistics for the starting outfielders in every game over the past three seasons. (Although Bell, Barfield, and Moseby were starting at least semiregularly for Toronto for several seasons before that, it's only since 1985 that they have all started together on an everyday basis.) When Toronto's outfielders are compared to those of the other American League teams, it's clear that no one has matched their performance.

The following table lists those statistics, with the teams ranked by batting average. But note that Toronto also leads the league in home runs, RBIs, and slugging average:

Team	AB	R	H	2B	3B	HR	RBI	BA	SA	OBA
Toronto	5587	904	1565	287	45	268	886	.280	.491	.345
Boston	5554	852	1551	288	32	212	853	.279	.457	.351
New York	5524	921	1526	272	28	218	803	.276	.454	.353
Minnesota	5572	756	1538	267	44	172	697	.276	.432	.333
Cleveland	5476	795	1505	248	49	166	668	.275	.429	.329
Seattle	5594	798	1531	302	54	153	688	.274	.429	.340
Milwaukee	5445	755	1457	245	58	159	729	.268	.421	.339
Baltimore	5349	755	1426	218	20	228	721	.267	.443	.331
Detroit	5182	732	1383	254	39	178	692	.267	.434	.342
Kansas City	5626	758	1487	242	75	126	543	.264	.401	.319
Chicago	5435	724	1426	268	35	146	644	.262	.405	.324
Texas	5464	802	1421	232	48	205	696	.260	.433	.319
Oakland	5382	799	1393	264	33	189	712	.259	.425	.331
California	5322	789	1337	242	35	167	680	.251	.404	.333

Shortly after the season ended, Barfield signed a two-year contract with Toronto. And although Bell and Moseby had contracts that expire at the end of the 1988 season, it's possible that as you read this , both will have signed deals that will keep them north of the border into the 1990s.

The prospect of several more seasons of Bell, Barfield, and Moseby roaming the plastic pasture of Exhibition Stadium together suggests that years from now, they will take their place alongside DiMaggio, Keller, and Henrich, Ruth, Meusel, and Combs, and the other great outfields in baseball history.

WON-LOST RECORD BY STARTING POSITION

TORONTO 96-66	C	1B	2B	3B	SS	LF	CF	RF	P	DH	Leadoff	Relief	Starts
Jesse Barfield	-	-	-	-	-	-	5-5	79-57	-	-	-	-	84-62
George Bell	-	-	-	-	-	89-58	-	-	-	5-2	-	-	94-60
Juan Beniquez	-	-	-	-	-	1-0	-	0-4	-	5-8	0-1	-	6-12
John Cerutti	-	-	-	-	-	-	-	-	13-8	-	-	11-12	13-8
Jim Clancy	-	-	-	-	-	-	-	-	22-15	-	-	-	22-15
Jeff DeWillis	5-5	-	-	-	-	-	-	-	-	-	-	-	5-5
Rob Ducey	-	-	-	-	-	2-2	2-2	2-0	-	-	-	-	6-4
Mark Eichhorn	-	-	-	-	-	-	-	-	-	-	-	48-41	-
Tony Fernandez	-	-	-	-	87-55	-	-	-	-	-	67-48	-	87-55
Cecil Fielder	-	7-8	-	-	-	-	-	-	-	15-19	-	-	22-27
Mike Flanagan	-	-	-	-	-	-	-	-	4-3	-	-	-	4-3
Don Gordon	-	-	-	-	-	-	-	-	-	-	-	1-4	-
Kelly Gruber	-	-	1-0	36-38	7-1	-	-	-	-	-	1-0	-	44-39
Tom Henke	-	-	-	-	-	-	-	-	-	-	-	52-20	-
Alexis Infante	-	-	-	-	-	-	-	-	-	-	-	-	-
Garth Iorg	-	-	43-32	5-4	-	-	-	-	-	0-1	-	-	48-37
Joe Johnson	-	-	-	-	-	-	-	-	8-6	-	-	-	8-6
Jimmy Key	-	-	-	-	-	-	-	-	24-12	-	-	-	24-12
Gary Lavelle	-	-	-	-	-	-	-	-	-	-	-	7-16	-
Rick Leach	-	-	-	-	-	4-5	-	15-5	13-5	-	-	-	32-15
Manny Lee	-	-	12-8	-	2-10	-	-	-	-	-	-	-	14-18
Nelson Liriano	-	-	22-14	-	-	-	-	-	-	-	22-14	-	22-14
Fred McGriff	-	8-4	-	-	-	-	-	-	-	50-26	-	-	58-30
Charlie Moore	14-20	-	-	-	-	0-1	-	-	-	-	-	-	14-21
Lloyd Moseby	-	-	-	-	-	-	89-59	-	-	-	1-2	-	89-59
Rance Mulliniks	-	-	-	55-24	-	-	-	-	-	8-5	-	-	63-29
Jeff Musselman	-	-	-	-	-	-	-	-	0-1	-	-	39-28	0-1
Greg Myers	0-2	-	-	-	-	-	-	-	-	-	-	-	0-2
Phil Niekro	-	-	-	-	-	-	-	-	0-3	-	-	-	0-3
Jose Nunez	-	-	-	-	-	-	-	-	5-4	-	-	8-20	5-4
Mike Sharperson	-	-	18-12	-	-	-	-	-	-	-	-	-	18-12
Matt Stark	2-1	-	-	-	-	-	-	-	-	-	-	-	2-1
Dave Stieb	-	-	-	-	-	-	-	-	19-12	-	-	0-2	19-12
Louis Thornton	-	-	-	-	-	-	-	-	-	-	-	-	-
Willie Upshaw	-	81-54	-	-	-	-	-	-	-	-	5-1	-	81-54
Duane Ward	-	-	-	-	-	-	-	-	1-0	-	-	6-5	1-0
David Wells	-	-	-	-	-	-	-	-	0-2	-	-	9-7	0-2
Ernie Whitt	75-38	-	-	-	-	-	-	-	-	-	-	-	75-38

Batting vs. Left and Right Handed Pitchers

		BA	Rank	SA	Rank	OBA	Rank	HR %	Rank	BB %	Rank	SO %	Rank
Jesse Barfield	vs. Lefties	.299	40	.525	24	.380	34	5.08	32	11.50	35	21.50	135
	vs. Righties	.247	105	.429	75	.309	119	4.60	46	7.71	99	21.59	142
George Bell	vs. Lefties	.343	13	.686	2	.385	30	9.14	2	6.38	130	13.30	67
	vs. Righties	.294	32	.572	12	.339	74	7.13	9	5.64	137	10.44	38
Juan Beniquez	vs. Lefties	.267	82	.491	38	.306	113	5.17	30	4.76	146	12.70	59
	vs. Righties	.237	123	.324	147	.289	137	1.44	128	6.58	120	15.13	88
Tony Fernandez	vs. Lefties	.297	43	.380	105	.367	50	1.04	133	9.72	57	8.33	22
	vs. Righties	.334	5	.448	60	.385	23	0.78	142	7.04	111	7.04	13
Cecil Fielder	vs. Lefties	.268	81	.582	11	.343	70	8.50	3	9.88	55	23.26	143
	vs. Righties	.273	--	.409	--	.360	--	4.55	--	12.00	--	32.00	--
Kelly Gruber	vs. Lefties	.230	125	.395	99	.289	131	2.63	92	7.19	117	20.96	131
	vs. Righties	.238	121	.402	95	.279	147	4.23	57	2.49	160	17.41	111
Garth Iorg	vs. Lefties	.181	156	.225	159	.238	157	0.72	140	7.19	116	11.76	50
	vs. Righties	.233	131	.331	142	.281	146	1.74	121	5.29	144	17.99	121
Rick Leach	vs. Lefties	.375	--	.563	--	.500	--	0.00	--	20.00	--	30.00	--
	vs. Righties	.274	66	.391	102	.358	49	1.68	125	10.29	51	9.31	30
Fred McGriff	vs. Lefties	.154	--	.346	--	.241	--	3.85	--	10.34	--	48.28	--
	vs. Righties	.257	96	.520	24	.388	22	7.06	10	17.43	8	27.52	154
Charlie Moore	vs. Lefties	.231	123	.363	118	.320	92	0.00	145	11.43	37	8.57	23
	vs. Righties	.125	--	.313	--	.222	--	6.25	--	5.00	--	15.00	--
Lloyd Moseby	vs. Lefties	.278	66	.419	85	.362	51	2.53	97	11.11	42	20.00	123
	vs. Righties	.284	41	.500	30	.357	51	5.33	30	10.11	55	17.75	113
Rance Mulliniks	vs. Lefties	.389	--	.667	--	.450	--	5.56	--	8.70	--	17.39	--
	vs. Righties	.306	22	.490	37	.367	39	3.18	88	9.17	69	14.61	77
Willie Upshaw	vs. Lefties	.208	145	.319	137	.305	116	1.39	118	11.45	36	18.07	112
	vs. Righties	.258	91	.418	82	.332	80	3.53	80	9.49	64	11.68	49
Ernie Whitt	vs. Lefties	.238	112	.286	147	.314	100	0.00	145	8.57	85	21.43	133
	vs. Righties	.274	62	.483	39	.337	76	4.96	37	8.96	76	8.25	23
Team Average	vs. Lefties	.261	11	.434	4	.331	8	3.56	4	9.15	6	17.14	10
	vs. Righties	.272	4	.451	2	.339	5	3.93	3	8.66	10	14.62	4
League Average	vs. Lefties	.265		.422		.333		3.29		8.94		15.64	
	vs. Righties	.265		.427		.334		3.43		8.94		15.26	

Batting with Runners on Base and Bases Empty

		BA	Rank	SA	Rank	OBA	Rank	HR %	Rank	BB %	Rank	SO %	Rank
Jesse Barfield	Runners On	.257	101	.410	96	.342	78	3.07	85	11.37	54	18.39	124
	Bases Empty	.267	69	.495	37	.321	91	6.08	24	6.76	112	24.23	147
George Bell	Runners On	.303	36	.563	12	.355	63	7.00	7	7.69	105	10.65	41
	Bases Empty	.313	21	.645	1	.349	49	8.39	5	3.95	147	11.85	48
Juan Beniquez	Runners On	.287	56	.467	52	.323	112	3.28	78	4.44	152	14.07	81
	Bases Empty	.218	146	.338	138	.273	151	3.01	91	6.99	105	13.99	66
Tony Fernandez	Runners On	.324	19	.419	84	.387	33	0.00	150	8.68	96	5.37	9
	Bases Empty	.321	11	.429	81	.375	24	1.36	134	7.50	98	8.75	16
Cecil Fielder	Runners On	.261	96	.420	83	.333	92	3.41	70	9.09	89	25.25	155
	Bases Empty	.276	--	.701	--	.357	--	12.64	--	11.22	--	23.47	--
Kelly Gruber	Runners On	.250	111	.368	120	.311	119	1.47	123	7.24	116	17.11	111
	Bases Empty	.224	137	.420	86	.264	153	4.88	44	2.78	158	20.37	132
Garth Iorg	Runners On	.215	147	.267	156	.283	144	0.74	146	8.86	91	10.76	42
	Bases Empty	.206	155	.297	149	.245	159	1.71	127	3.80	150	19.02	126
Rick Leach	Runners On	.361	--	.500	--	.466	--	2.78	--	14.77	--	11.36	--
	Bases Empty	.236	123	.350	129	.309	112	0.81	142	8.82	66	11.03	39
Nelson Liriano	Runners On	.226	--	.358	--	.317	--	3.77	--	11.29	--	8.06	--
	Bases Empty	.248	106	.333	140	.307	118	0.00	157	7.89	84	14.91	79
Fred McGriff	Runners On	.227	138	.414	89	.365	55	4.69	45	17.31	7	33.33	160
	Bases Empty	.263	75	.575	12	.385	17	8.38	6	16.50	3	26.00	151
Lloyd Moseby	Runners On	.274	70	.492	36	.340	83	5.64	26	9.33	83	16.00	101
	Bases Empty	.288	34	.457	58	.373	26	3.37	84	11.35	26	20.54	134
Rance Mulliniks	Runners On	.302	38	.519	21	.376	46	3.88	59	11.18	56	12.50	60
	Bases Empty	.315	17	.488	39	.368	30	2.96	93	7.73	92	16.36	98
Willie Upshaw	Runners On	.255	105	.425	78	.351	71	3.30	76	12.10	42	12.90	66
	Bases Empty	.237	122	.367	119	.304	120	2.67	99	8.51	71	13.98	65
Ernie Whitt	Runners On	.264	90	.467	53	.335	89	4.72	44	10.04	69	10.04	36
	Bases Empty	.274	57	.444	67	.333	62	3.85	72	7.84	85	10.20	31
Team Average	Runners On	.272	8	.447	4	.347	6	3.68	3	10.05	4	14.22	5
	Bases Empty	.267	5	.445	3	.328	4	3.91	3	7.85	11	16.34	10
League Average	Runners On	.271		.428		.343		3.25		9.68		14.87	
	Bases Empty	.260		.424		.326		3.49		8.34		15.79	

Overall Batting Compared to Late Inning Pressure Situations

		BA	Rank	SA	Rank	OBA	Rank	HR %	Rank	BB %	Rank	SO %	Rank	RDI %	Rank
Jesse Barfield	Overall	.263	89	.458	54	.331	83	4.75	42	8.87	80	21.56	143	.267	108
	Pressure	.281	67	.427	73	.349	73	3.13	70	8.49	89	20.75	118	.417	20
George Bell	Overall	.308	16	.605	2	.352	52	7.70	3	5.85	137	11.24	38	.335	33
	Pressure	.316	30	.547	21	.353	69	5.26	39	4.85	138	7.77	16	.286	75
Juan Beniquez	Overall	.251	109	.400	103	.297	140	3.14	90	5.76	140	14.03	73	.415	1
	Pressure	.244	99	.356	105	.292	123	2.22	94	4.17	144	18.75	105	.467	10
Tony Fernandez	Overall	.322	10	.426	85	.379	21	0.87	142	7.94	99	7.48	13	.385	4
	Pressure	.363	12	.500	31	.418	21	1.25	115	9.57	77	7.45	11	.378	37
Cecil Fielder	Overall	.269	--	.560	--	.345	--	8.00	--	10.15	--	24.37	--	.254	118
	Pressure	.259	89	.593	13	.375	46	7.41	13	15.63	15	34.38	163	.000	--
Kelly Gruber	Overall	.235	142	.399	107	.283	154	3.52	79	4.62	152	19.02	127	.239	135
	Pressure	.240	111	.440	66	.328	91	6.00	28	10.17	65	20.34	117	.333	51
Garth Iorg	Overall	.210	156	.284	158	.262	158	1.29	136	6.14	132	15.20	92	.281	86
	Pressure	.241	108	.278	141	.295	122	0.00	119	8.06	100	11.29	45	.471	9
Rick Leach	Overall	.282	45	.405	98	.371	33	1.54	129	11.16	36	11.16	37	.435	--
	Pressure	.286	59	.469	49	.375	46	4.08	53	10.71	59	14.29	70	.333	51
Nelson Liriano	Overall	.241	--	.342	--	.310	--	1.27	--	9.09	--	12.50	--	.176	--
	Pressure	.194	141	.194	160	.242	149	0.00	119	5.88	126	5.88	7	.143	--
Fred McGriff	Overall	.247	117	.505	21	.376	27	6.78	7	16.85	4	29.21	159	.212	153
	Pressure	.200	133	.400	87	.378	42	5.71	33	22.22	3	24.44	139	.182	124
Lloyd Moseby	Overall	.282	44	.473	43	.358	46	4.39	53	10.45	50	18.51	123	.312	57
	Pressure	.220	124	.402	86	.319	102	4.88	43	12.63	39	24.21	136	.200	117
Rance Mulliniks	Overall	.310	14	.500	23	.371	31	3.31	87	9.14	71	14.78	84	.290	75
	Pressure	.313	34	.438	68	.441	14	2.08	101	18.33	7	20.00	112	.333	51
Willie Upshaw	Overall	.244	125	.391	114	.324	93	2.93	95	10.05	56	13.52	61	.259	113
	Pressure	.263	84	.342	116	.391	35	0.00	119	16.13	14	12.90	63	.188	122
Ernie Whitt	Overall	.269	76	.455	59	.334	77	4.26	58	8.91	77	10.12	31	.311	58
	Pressure	.239	112	.358	104	.312	107	1.49	111	10.39	62	12.99	65	.400	27
Team Average	Overall	.269	5	.446	2	.336	4	3.82	2	8.82	8	15.41	8	.297	5
	Pressure	.268	3	.421	5	.351	3	2.94	10	10.95	2	15.84	4	.331	3
League Average	Overall	.265		.425		.333		3.38		8.94		15.38		.287	
	Pressure	.262		.405		.335		3.07		9.43		16.58		.280	

Additional Miscellaneous Batting Comparisons

	Grass Surface BA	Rank	Artificial Surface BA	Rank	Home Games BA	Rank	Road Games BA	Rank	Runners in Scoring Position BA	Rank	Runners in Scoring Pos and Two Outs BA	Rank	Leading Off Inning OBA	Rank	Runners on 3B with less than 2 Outs RDI %	Rank
Jesse Barfield	.230	139	.283	53	.305	36	.219	142	.235	120	.222	110	.286	126	.444	145
George Bell	.311	19	.306	24	.291	57	.325	9	.318	30	.250	84	.386	23	.641	48
Juan Beniquez	.275	--	.230	115	.232	135	.266	73	.318	30	.280	57	.304	109	.833	2
Tony Fernandez	.329	7	.318	17	.301	41	.344	2	.377	4	.375	5	.345	58	.613	61
Cecil Fielder	.148	--	.333	7	.344	--	.188	--	.208	141	.091	154	.298	--	.750	9
Kelly Gruber	.237	129	.233	113	.222	143	.244	108	.263	87	.211	117	.262	143	.476	133
Garth Iorg	.219	--	.203	139	.209	156	.210	148	.263	90	.308	31	.200	159	.579	90
Rick Leach	.258	--	.295	39	.264	90	.306	--	.436	2	.429	--	.304	109	.750	--
Manny Lee	.341	--	.213	132	.200	--	.311	--	.296	--	.214	--	.375	--	.571	--
Nelson Liriano	.204	--	.260	80	.263	94	.203	--	.250	--	.200	--	.344	61	.429	--
Fred McGriff	.274	75	.228	117	.223	142	.269	65	.191	147	.179	139	.357	49	.450	142
Charlie Moore	.220	--	.211	134	.224	--	.207	--	.182	--	.083	--	.303	--	.400	--
Lloyd Moseby	.279	57	.284	50	.292	56	.272	60	.315	35	.234	99	.328	86	.639	49
Rance Mulliniks	.298	31	.319	16	.315	22	.306	24	.284	65	.263	69	.373	32	.526	115
Mike Sharperson	.200	--	.214	130	.205	--	.212	--	.280	--	.231	--	.385	--	.667	--
Willie Upshaw	.242	124	.246	94	.225	141	.261	83	.263	89	.231	101	.250	149	.435	149
Ernie Whitt	.254	105	.279	57	.262	96	.276	54	.272	78	.250	84	.309	104	.615	58
Team Average	.263	8	.272	1	.268	10	.270	3	.284	3	.248	6	.318	11	.566	11
League Average	.267		.261		.270		.260		.266		.247		.328		.581	

Pitching vs. Left and Right Handed Batters

		BA	Rank	SA	Rank	OBA	Rank	HR %	Rank	BB %	Rank	SO %	Rank
John Cerutti	vs. Lefties	.248	37	.438	78	.313	34	4.38	104	8.61	56	17.22	37
	vs. Righties	.252	55	.489	107	.324	58	5.50	119	9.45	93	13.55	85
Jim Clancy	vs. Lefties	.281	90	.433	73	.335	61	2.36	33	7.59	44	17.72	33
	vs. Righties	.222	22	.361	30	.288	20	2.93	60	8.35	66	18.02	44
Mark Eichhorn	vs. Lefties	.257	49	.410	58	.350	86	3.28	71	11.52	99	13.82	67
	vs. Righties	.219	19	.351	24	.292	27	2.78	51	8.36	67	20.43	29
Mike Flanagan	vs. Lefties	.250	40	.270	4	.312	29	0.00	1	8.18	49	14.55	58
	vs. Righties	.267	78	.438	82	.327	63	2.60	41	8.25	64	15.13	67
Tom Henke	vs. Lefties	.172	3	.288	7	.225	1	1.84	22	6.63	26	32.60	2
	vs. Righties	.204	5	.371	40	.258	7	4.19	98	7.14	45	37.91	1
Joe Johnson	vs. Lefties	.265	60	.435	75	.303	21	2.72	45	5.16	7	10.32	108
	vs. Righties	.319	--	.555	--	.379	--	5.04	--	7.46	--	8.21	--
Jimmy Key	vs. Lefties	.248	38	.382	37	.290	13	2.55	40	5.29	8	20.59	12
	vs. Righties	.215	15	.336	16	.268	11	2.52	37	6.60	31	14.60	73
Jeff Musselman	vs. Lefties	.165	2	.275	5	.252	4	1.83	21	8.66	57	18.11	30
	vs. Righties	.275	88	.425	71	.402	120	2.42	32	16.93	124	12.20	103
Phil Niekro	vs. Lefties	.313	114	.507	111	.387	115	3.67	87	10.23	82	8.19	122
	vs. Righties	.256	58	.463	101	.325	59	4.47	103	9.09	82	13.09	92
Jose Nunez	vs. Lefties	.315	119	.503	109	.409	124	3.36	75	13.81	121	15.47	50
	vs. Righties	.213	14	.377	44	.317	53	3.38	79	13.41	119	28.86	5
Dave Stieb	vs. Lefties	.242	31	.390	40	.338	71	2.75	50	12.50	111	13.44	71
	vs. Righties	.237	35	.361	31	.319	55	1.87	16	9.32	90	15.89	59
Team Average	vs. Lefties	.254	3	.402	3	.326	2	2.66	3	9.39	9	17.22	1
	vs. Righties	.237	1	.391	1	.310	1	3.07	5	9.23	12	17.57	3
League Average	vs. Lefties	.267		.427		.338		3.30		9.47		14.54	
	vs. Righties	.264		.424		.330		3.45		8.56		15.98	

Pitching with Runners on Base and Bases Empty

		BA	Rank	SA	Rank	OBA	Rank	HR %	Rank	BB %	Rank	SO %	Rank
John Cerutti	Runners On	.222	11	.430	81	.290	14	5.43	114	8.87	60	14.92	60
	Bases Empty	.270	83	.506	115	.341	88	5.11	116	9.49	89	14.10	75
Jim Clancy	Runners On	.238	27	.374	31	.298	18	1.91	23	8.09	44	15.69	52
	Bases Empty	.266	79	.418	64	.325	67	3.08	56	7.83	54	19.33	27
Mark Eichhorn	Runners On	.240	31	.392	52	.354	82	3.43	85	14.23	121	16.21	47
	Bases Empty	.228	21	.360	22	.282	13	2.62	37	5.57	26	19.16	28
Mike Flanagan	Runners On	.262	63	.359	20	.304	22	1.27	7	5.79	15	15.83	50
	Bases Empty	.265	77	.444	91	.339	86	2.78	48	10.00	98	14.44	70
Tom Henke	Runners On	.201	3	.410	64	.275	4	5.04	108	9.82	79	31.90	1
	Bases Empty	.178	4	.272	4	.215	1	1.57	10	4.50	12	38.00	1
Joe Johnson	Runners On	.271	--	.448	--	.349	--	3.13	--	9.01	--	10.81	--
	Bases Empty	.300	113	.512	116	.331	78	4.12	97	4.49	11	8.43	123
Jimmy Key	Runners On	.263	64	.408	63	.316	37	2.42	42	7.26	31	15.32	56
	Bases Empty	.198	7	.310	9	.248	5	2.58	34	5.90	32	15.73	59
Jeff Musselman	Runners On	.223	12	.349	17	.333	58	2.41	40	13.37	115	14.85	61
	Bases Empty	.253	54	.400	48	.374	110	2.00	14	15.08	122	13.41	83
Phil Niekro	Runners On	.284	91	.468	93	.388	114	3.21	77	13.96	119	9.43	112
	Bases Empty	.290	108	.500	112	.338	84	4.57	106	6.53	41	11.08	105
Jose Nunez	Runners On	.246	36	.413	68	.358	89	4.19	93	15.09	124	22.17	15
	Bases Empty	.265	75	.444	91	.353	98	2.65	39	12.09	113	24.19	11
Dave Stieb	Runners On	.271	74	.386	46	.355	83	1.43	10	10.33	87	12.46	91
	Bases Empty	.217	13	.370	29	.311	42	2.96	51	11.52	110	16.09	53
Team Average	Runners On	.247	1	.395	2	.328	1	2.81	3	10.48	11	16.44	2
	Bases Empty	.241	1	.395	1	.308	1	2.98	2	8.40	12	18.18	1
League Average	Runners On	.271		.428		.343		3.25		9.68		14.87	
	Bases Empty	.260		.424		.326		3.49		8.34		15.79	

Overall Pitching Compared to Late Inning Pressure Situations

		BA	Rank	SA	Rank	OBA	Rank	HR %	Rank	BB %	Rank	SO %	Rank
John Cerutti	Overall	.251	44	.476	108	.321	49	5.24	121	9.25	78	14.42	69
	Pressure	.231	41	.436	86	.318	49	5.13	112	11.36	91	18.18	39
Jim Clancy	Overall	.255	50	.401	47	.314	38	2.61	36	7.94	47	17.86	34
	Pressure	.359	125	.469	103	.406	120	0.00	1	6.85	32	10.96	105
Mark Eichhorn	Overall	.234	16	.374	27	.315	40	2.97	51	9.63	85	17.78	35
	Pressure	.229	39	.353	45	.309	40	2.35	54	10.26	75	23.59	13
Mike Flanagan	Overall	.264	70	.408	51	.325	56	2.14	14	8.24	56	15.02	60
	Pressure	.284	88	.433	83	.351	76	2.99	71	9.46	67	13.51	78
Tom Henke	Overall	.188	2	.330	5	.242	1	3.03	57	6.89	29	35.26	1
	Pressure	.174	2	.269	8	.239	5	1.83	44	8.13	52	33.33	1
Joe Johnson	Overall	.289	105	.489	114	.338	72	3.76	88	6.23	21	9.34	119
	Pressure	.273	--	.545	--	.273	--	9.09	--	0.00	--	0.00	--
Jimmy Key	Overall	.221	7	.344	8	.272	4	2.52	31	6.39	23	15.59	53
	Pressure	.217	27	.357	47	.295	30	3.48	62	9.09	62	18.18	39
Jeff Musselman	Overall	.237	19	.373	26	.353	94	2.22	17	14.17	121	14.17	72
	Pressure	.268	74	.427	80	.398	117	2.55	60	15.66	120	12.12	97
Phil Niekro	Overall	.288	103	.487	112	.359	101	4.03	95	9.72	86	10.37	111
	Pressure	.195	11	.244	2	.333	62	0.00	1	15.69	121	9.80	108
Jose Nunez	Overall	.256	51	.430	74	.356	95	3.37	79	13.58	119	23.19	11
	Pressure	.212	23	.333	30	.395	113	0.00	1	22.73	126	15.91	58
Dave Stieb	Overall	.239	25	.377	29	.329	64	2.34	21	11.03	108	14.58	68
	Pressure	.056	1	.056	1	.105	1	0.00	1	5.13	19	23.08	15
David Wells	Overall	.311	--	.370	--	.374	--	0.00	--	9.09	--	24.24	--
	Pressure	.208	20	.250	3	.269	15	0.00	1	7.55	43	26.42	5
Team Average	Overall	.244	1	.395	1	.316	1	2.91	2	9.29	12	17.43	1
	Pressure	.231	1	.348	1	.317	1	1.98	1	10.85	13	20.99	1
League Average	Overall	.265		.425		.333		3.38		8.94		15.38	
	Pressure	.262		.404		.337		2.99		9.73		16.42	

Additional Miscellaneous Pitching Comparisons

	Grass Surface BA	Rank	Artificial Surface BA	Rank	Home Games BA	Rank	Road Games BA	Rank	Runners in Scoring Position BA	Rank	Runners in Scoring Pos and Two Outs BA	Rank	Leading Off Inning OBA	Rank
John Cerutti	.248	34	.254	61	.256	63	.248	32	.178	5	.182	15	.321	54
Jim Clancy	.274	83	.244	48	.251	54	.259	44	.253	52	.198	31	.347	85
Mark Eichhorn	.273	80	.212	16	.218	13	.251	35	.172	2	.167	8	.239	8
Mike Flanagan	.249	36	.289	95	.260	73	.268	66	.234	35	.190	23	.335	71
Tom Henke	.197	--	.182	7	.165	2	.213	7	.205	15	.214	45	.231	5
Joe Johnson	.253	--	.305	102	.286	101	.297	--	.298	--	.320	--	.389	113
Jimmy Key	.255	50	.203	12	.193	7	.259	45	.249	49	.200	32	.242	9
Jeff Musselman	.260	--	.218	20	.213	11	.256	37	.255	59	.279	93	.395	118
Phil Niekro	.299	105	.263	70	.320	121	.266	59	.288	87	.281	96	.324	60
Jose Nunez	.262	--	.252	57	.244	47	.267	64	.286	86	.370	124	.419	123
Dave Stieb	.251	41	.230	31	.240	41	.239	23	.280	82	.243	67	.320	52
David Wells	.250	--	.365	119	.321	--	.303	--	.220	--	.217	--	.500	--
Team Average	.255	3	.237	1	.233	1	.255	3	.242	1	.230	3	.315	2
League Average	.267		.261		.260		.270		.266		.247		.328	

National League

ATLANTA BRAVES

Six years ago, the Atlanta Braves won the Western Division title with a lineup of players too young ever to have seen Rhett kiss Scarlett, National League baseball in Milwaukee, or Phil Niekro without grey hair and wrinkles.

Ted Turner must have daydreamed of dynasties as he drooled over the thought of promising minor-league All Stars like Brad Komminsk and Gerald Perry joining established young hitters like Dale Murphy and Bob Horner to terrorize National League pitchers into the 1990s, but things deteriorated rapidly. Admiral Turner shipped out starting outfielder Brett Butler and blue-chip prospect Brook Jacoby in a panic during the 1983 pennant race. Even worse, Perry developed slowly and Komminsk not at all. Horner's absences from the starting lineup were measured in calendar pages until he finally jumped *sampan*. Murphy did win consecutive MVP awards early in the decade, but without a supporting cast he became a paper tiger. The Braves fell into a downward spiral as the team aged rapidly, posting the worst overall record in the N.L.'s Western Division since winning that title in 1982:

Team	W	L	Pct.
Houston	420	390	.518
Los Angeles	411	399	.507
Cincinnati	403	406	.498
San Diego	395	415	.487
San Francisco	380	430	.469
Atlanta	375	433	.464

During those five seasons, the Braves remained immune to the volatility that scrambled the major-league standings on an annual basis. Even perennial doormats like the Texas Rangers Cleveland Indians, and San Francisco Giants proved to be upwardly mobile, but over the past three years, the Braves became the first team since the New York Mets of 1978 through 1980 to finish below the .450 mark for three consecutive seasons. Braves fans can look to the strong and quick rebound of the Mets for consolation and inspiration, but without a Gooden or Strawberry on the horizon, it's difficult to tell whether the Braves are even headed in the right direction.

One ominous sign is the team's age. Despite the advantages of cosmetic surgery, most of us still age at the approximate rate of one year for every revolution of Pete Rose around the sun. But through the miracle of the free agent market, baseball teams are supposed to defy nature and mature by slightly less than a year for every revolution of the planet Pluto, shedding its skin like a snake and regenerating a new one that is faster, stronger, and hits with more power for a lower salary. But the Braves have aged just like the rest of us, adding dinosaurs like Ken Griffey, Ted Simmons, and Graig Nettles to compensate for the failure of prospects like Komminsk and Paul Runge and Paul Zuvella to make the big team. In fact, since winning the division title in 1982, the average age of the Braves' lineup has increased steadily from the second-youngest to the second-oldest in the league as its on-the-field performance eroded. The ages in the following table are weighted by plate appearances for batters and batters faced by pitchers, so that those who played more contribute more heavily to the team averages than occasional players do:

Atlanta Braves	1982	1983	1984	1985	1986	1987
Hitters' Age	27.0	27.9	28.0	28.5	30.1	29.9
Pitchers' Age	30.1	29.7	28.9	29.3	29.3	29.9
Winning Pct.	.549	.543	.494	.407	.447	.429

The only consolation appears to be that two of Atlanta's disappointing prospects of the mid-1980s finally made significant contributions to the team last season. Gerald Perry's potential became apparent when he succeeded Don Mattingly as the International League's All Star first baseman in 1983 but alas, he was still a Triple-A All Star three years later. Last season, Perry finally made it: He drove in 74 runs to rank second on the Braves to Murphy and stole more bases (42) than any Braves player since Hap Myers set a franchise record with 57 for the Boston Braves in 1913.

Albert Hall, who led the International League in stolen bases in 1982 but hung around Richmond long enough to do it again four years later, contributed a .284 batting average and 33 steals to Atlanta's hopeless cause last season. But now the bad news: Both players have reached an age (29) at which few players launch productive major-league careers, raising the question as to whether Atlanta has any foundation on which to build a winning team before the end of the decade.

Building on the Mound

It's often said that winning teams are built from a foundation of good pitching. Proponents of that theory point to the rapid development of the New York Mets from the worst expansion team in the history of baseball to world champions within eight years, a rise made possible by the emergence of a series of spectacular young pitchers: Tom Seaver, Jerry Koosman, Nolan Ryan, and Gary Gentry. A survey of perennially poor teams of the expansion era supports that theory.

We found ten teams since 1960 that had finished below the .450 level for three consecutive seasons, like the current Braves, but then posted consecutive winning seasons immediately thereafter. For example, the New York Mets of the early 1980s:

	1981	1982	1983	1984	1985
W–L	41–62	65–97	68–94	90–72	98–64
Pct.	.398	.401	.420	.556	.605

We contrasted the profile of that 10-team group with that of a group consisting of 21 other teams that failed to reach .450 for three seasons in a row, and then also failed to reach the .500 level in either of the next two seasons, like the Seattle Mariners of the late 1970s and early 1980's.

	1979	1980	1981	1982	1983
W–L	67–95	59–103	44–65	76–86	60–102
Pct.	.414	.364	.404	.469	.370

We found that the group that rebounded for winning seasons had stronger pitching during their losing seasons than did the group that continued to post losing records. We compared the league ranking in road-game scoring of each team to its rank in runs allowed in road games. (We excluded home games from consideration in order to eliminate the stadium bias of the teams' home fields. For example, if we'd included home games, Atlanta's hitting would nearly always appear superior to its pitching because Atlanta Stadium is such a good hitters' park.) In the table below, Group 1 includes the teams that rebounded, Group 2 includes those that didn't:

Comparison of Road-Game Ranks	Group 1	Group 2
Hitting better than pitching	2	11
Hitting and pitching equal	1	4
Pitching better than hitting	7	7

The table illustrates that teams with better pitching than hitting stand an even chance of turning things around quickly. Those whose pitching is only equal to or inferior to their hitting—and remember that since these are teams consistently near the bottom of their leagues, that offense can't be too powerful to begin with—stand little chance of getting off the mat.

The Braves ranked higher last season in road-game pitching (eighth) than road-game hitting (ninth), but by a narrow margin. That's not a raving endorsement of Atlanta's potential to rebound from its dismal recent performances, but things could be worse.

Graybeards at the Plate

We mentioned earlier that the Braves had the second-oldest lineup in the National League last season. Ken Griffey,

Graig Nettles, and Ted Simmons started a full season's worth of games among them last season, but they also formed the nucleus of baseball's oldest pinch-hitting corps, and one of its most successful. Despite a .225 batting average (eight points below the league average), Braves pinch-hitters drove in more runs (49) than those of any other team in the majors, with a total of 209 at bats, the second lowest amount in the National League.

Was experience a factor in the success of Atlanta's pinch-hitters? Well, you'd have a tough time convincing the Houston Astros of that; they had the second-oldest pinch-hitters in the majors last season. And Houston was the only team in the majors without a pinch-hit home run and its total of 21 pinch RBIs ranked last in the N.L.

Still, the question deserves further consideration, not only from a competitive standpoint but from an economic one as well. Older pinch-hitters are often high-salaried former stars. If their experience isn't an advantage in pinch-hitting situations, teams would be better off using younger players, presumably with lower salaries, in those roles.

First, let's look at the best and worst pinch-hitters of the past three seasons. The highest and lowest pinch-hit batting averages since 1985 among players with at least 50 at bats:

The Top 10	AB	H	BA	The Bottom 10	AB	H	BA
Ken Griffey	55	21	.382	Len Matuszek	67	8	.119
Jerry Mumphrey	74	26	.351	Scot Thompson	62	9	.145
Milt Thompson	55	19	.345	Carmen Castillo	59	9	.153
Larry Herndon	53	18	.340	Mickey Hatcher	59	9	.153
Candy Maldonado	75	25	.333	Tim Flannery	52	8	.154
Rance Mulliniks	58	19	.328	Ron Roenicke	82	13	.159
Denny Walling	69	22	.319	Terry Harper	67	11	.164
Thad Bosley	153	48	.314	Gerald Perry	60	10	.167
Juan Beniquez	66	20	.303	Rick Schu	54	9	.167
Jose Oquendo	53	16	.302	Gary Matthews	76	13	.171

Both groups are sprinkled with a mix of players, young and old. The group of the best pinch-hitters is slightly older (31.93 years old, on average, as of the end of the 1987 season) than the group of poor pinch-hitters (30.90). But the average age of all other pinch-hitters with at least 50 at bats over the past three seasons is considerably older than either group (33.50).

We performed one other test to determine if older players have an advantage over younger ones in the pressure situations on which the best pinch-hitters thrive. We divided the 78 players with at least 50 pinch at bats since 1985 into three groups according to their age, and compared their batting averages as pinch-hitters to their batting averages in other at bats. Good pinch-hitters are those with higher marks as pinch-hitters than otherwise; poor pinch-hitters are those who hit at least 60 points lower as pinch-hitters; average represents the in-between group:

	Good	Average	Poor
Born in 1953 or before	9	13	6
Born between 1954 and 1956	12	5	10
Born in 1957 or later	6	7	10

These variances aren't great enough to suggest that experience is a factor in a player's success or failure as a pinch-hitter. The only odd result—that only six of 28 older players hit poorly in the clutch—simply reflects the reality that aging players who couldn't cut it as pinch-hitters were most likely released before they could accumulate 50 at bats.

Today's Game Revisited

In last year's *Analyst*, we published the results of a study that proved that a player's recent performance (that is, over the past week or so) has no bearing on how he'll hit in today's game. The evidence showed that, in general, players are no likelier to have a good game coming off a hot week than they are when mired in a slump. It also demonstrated that two players of equal ability were equally likely to have a good game, even if one had hit well over the past few games and the other were slumping. We reexamined this question based on data from the 1987 season, and the results were the same. Players hit no better coming off hot streaks than off slumps.

A brief explanation of how the study works. For every player in the majors with at least 502 plate appearances, we compiled two sets of batting statistics. The first included all games played coming off hot streaks, defined as a series of five games over no more than seven days during which the player hit at least .400. The other set of stats included only those games prior to which the player had been in a slump, hitting .125 or less over five games within the past seven days. The comparisons for last season's qualifying Braves:

Player	Following Hot Streaks				Following Cold Streaks			
	Games	AB	H	BA	Games	AB	H	BA
Hubbard	7	18	1	.056	17	55	15	.273
James	34	132	36	.273	23	81	22	.272
Murphy	31	108	22	.204	22	78	20	.256
Oberkfell	8	32	8	.250	9	36	11	.306
Perry	14	55	12	.218	15	56	15	.268

Four of the five Atlanta players hit better coming off slumps than off hot streaks. When we compared the rest of the qualifying major leaguers, we found that a majority did likewise, corroborating the data we published last year for the previous three seasons:

	1984	1985	1986	1987	Total
Higher avg. after streaks	42	60	59	55	216
Higher avg. after slumps	65	59	60	73	257

We're not about to suggest that managers ought to sit players down *because* they're hot in favor of players in slumps. But we think that such a strategy makes no less sense than resting a player *because* he's slumping or keeping a hot one in the lineup when he ordinarily would be given a rest. The simple fact is that how a player has been hitting recently should have as little to do with who starts and who sits as does the day of the week. It just doesn't matter.

There are players who, in any given season, are streaky and there are those who hit consistently throughout the season, but we also suggested in the 1987 *Analyst* that streakiness is *not* a trait, like power, speed, or contact hitting, that players tend to reproduce in their hitting patterns year after year. In other words, the streaky hitters of one season are just as likely to be models of consistency a year later as they are to experience the peaks and valleys of the previous season.

We defined streaky players as those who hit better coming off hot streaks than off cold ones. Think about it: Players who usually hit well after a good series and poorly after a bad one are more likely to extend those streaks than those who don't. Conversely, we considered steady players to be those who hit well coming off a few poor games, nipping a potential slump in the bud, and who hit poorly after several good games.

We listed the names of all players who had qualified as streaky in each of the seasons from 1984 through 1986, and those of the players who qualified as steady in each of those seasons. We suggested that in 1987, the perennially streaky group might be just as consistent as the steady group.

Unfortunately, there weren't nearly enough players involved to make the results meaningful. Of the nine streaky players, three failed to play regularly enough to gather adequate information (Steve Garvey, Graig Nettles, and Rafael Ramirez). Among the other six, three were streaky last season, three were not. Among the 15 perennially steady players, only Juan Beniquez and Rich Gedman failed to provide sufficient data. Five of the remaining 13 were streaky, eight were steady. Those results hardly support our contention that streakiness isn't a recurring trait, but they don't invalidate it either. Those curious about the issue should check the more extensive research we published last year, and in the meantime, we'll keep an eye on 1988 for you.

WON-LOST RECORD BY STARTING POSITION

ATLANTA 69-92	C	1B	2B	3B	SS	LF	CF	RF	P	Leadoff	Relief	Starts
Jim Acker	-	-	-	-	-	-	-	-	-	-	26-42	-
Doyle Alexander	-	-	-	-	-	-	-	-	6-10	-	-	6-10
Paul Assenmacher	-	-	-	-	-	-	-	-	-	-	18-34	-
Terry Bell	-	-	-	-	-	-	-	-	-	-	-	-
Bruce Benedict	10-18	-	-	-	-	-	-	-	-	-	-	10-18
Jeff Blauser	-	-	-	20-30	-	-	-	-	-	-	-	20-30
Joe Boever	-	-	-	-	-	-	-	-	-	-	2-12	-
Chuck Cary	-	-	-	-	-	-	-	-	-	-	3-10	-
Marty Clary	-	-	-	-	-	-	-	-	0-1	-	1-5	0-1
Kevin Coffman	-	-	-	-	-	-	-	-	2-3	-	-	2-3
Trench Davis	-	-	-	-	-	-	-	-	-	-	-	-
Jeff Dedmon	-	-	-	-	-	-	-	-	1-2	-	16-34	1-2
Mike Fischlin	-	-	-	-	-	-	-	-	-	-	-	-
Ron Gant	-	-	9-10	-	-	-	-	-	-	2-0	-	9-10
Gene Garber	-	-	-	-	-	-	-	-	-	-	23-26	-
Tom Glavine	-	-	-	-	-	-	-	-	4-5	-	-	4-5
Ken Griffey	-	0-2	-	-	-	41-56	-	-	-	-	-	41-58
Albert Hall	-	-	-	-	-	-	30-35	-	-	28-35	-	30-35
Glenn Hubbard	-	-	58-78	-	-	-	-	-	-	-	-	58-78
Dion James	-	-	-	-	-	10-12	39-57	-	-	39-57	-	49-69
Rick Mahler	-	-	-	-	-	-	-	-	10-18	-	5-6	10-18
Larry McWilliams	-	-	-	-	-	-	-	-	1-1	-	0-7	1-1
Darryl Motley	-	-	-	-	-	1-0	-	-	-	-	-	1-0
Dale Murphy	-	-	-	-	-	-	69-90	-	-	-	-	69-90
Graig Nettles	-	2-3	-	6-14	-	-	-	-	-	-	-	8-17
Phil Niekro	-	-	-	-	-	-	-	-	0-1	-	-	0-1
Randy O'Neal	-	-	-	-	-	-	-	-	4-6	-	1-5	4-6
Ken Oberkfell	-	-	2-3	53-67	-	-	-	-	-	-	-	55-70
Ed Olwine	-	-	-	-	-	-	-	-	-	-	6-21	-
David Palmer	-	-	-	-	-	-	-	-	12-16	-	-	12-16
Gerald Perry	-	52-73	-	-	-	2-4	-	-	-	-	-	54-77
Charlie Puleo	-	-	-	-	-	-	-	-	5-11	-	5-14	5-11
Rafael Ramirez	-	-	-	4-7	13-16	-	-	-	-	-	-	17-23
Gary Roenicke	-	5-1	-	-	-	15-20	-	0-2	-	-	-	20-23
Paul Runge	-	-	0-1	6-3	1-1	-	-	-	-	-	-	7-5
Ted Simmons	9-5	10-13	-	0-1	-	-	-	-	-	-	-	19-19
Pete Smith	-	-	-	-	-	-	-	-	2-4	-	-	2-4
Zane Smith	-	-	-	-	-	-	-	-	22-14	-	-	22-14
Andres Thomas	-	-	-	-	35-45	-	-	-	-	-	-	35-45
Ozzie Virgil	50-69	-	-	-	-	-	-	-	-	-	-	50-69
Steve Ziem	-	-	-	-	-	-	-	-	-	-	0-2	-

Batting vs. Left and Right Handed Pitchers

		BA	Rank	SA	Rank	OBA	Rank	HR %	Rank	BB %	Rank	SO %	Rank
Jeff Blauser	vs. Lefties	.277	--	.511	--	.346	--	4.26	--	9.62	--	15.38	--
	vs. Righties	.229	117	.288	130	.321	89	0.00	126	9.63	59	19.26	110
Ken Griffey	vs. Lefties	.253	92	.345	107	.298	111	2.30	78	6.32	95	9.47	37
	vs. Righties	.295	30	.487	27	.374	25	3.85	37	11.24	32	12.64	49
Albert Hall	vs. Lefties	.287	52	.377	93	.358	47	0.82	109	9.49	50	11.68	51
	vs. Righties	.282	50	.435	50	.378	22	1.18	102	12.50	19	10.00	24
Glenn Hubbard	vs. Lefties	.288	49	.433	66	.419	12	1.92	85	18.32	6	9.16	35
	vs. Righties	.257	88	.366	96	.365	33	0.88	110	13.18	13	11.19	39
Dion James	vs. Lefties	.303	37	.438	65	.442	7	1.12	101	18.80	5	11.97	56
	vs. Righties	.314	13	.479	34	.386	19	2.22	76	10.50	44	10.72	32
Dale Murphy	vs. Lefties	.320	25	.653	2	.512	1	9.33	2	28.44	2	15.17	85
	vs. Righties	.286	41	.553	8	.376	23	7.21	6	11.41	30	21.58	121
Graig Nettles	vs. Lefties	.229	117	.313	117	.291	114	0.00	113	9.09	61	12.73	63
	vs. Righties	.202	130	.364	100	.295	105	3.88	36	11.64	25	12.33	46
Ken Oberkfell	vs. Lefties	.310	30	.415	77	.349	57	0.00	113	5.23	112	6.54	9
	vs. Righties	.268	77	.342	104	.340	63	0.82	114	9.69	57	4.60	2
Gerald Perry	vs. Lefties	.256	87	.480	38	.321	89	4.00	45	7.97	76	15.22	86
	vs. Righties	.275	65	.390	79	.331	75	1.72	88	8.19	80	9.29	20
Rafael Ramirez	vs. Lefties	.323	23	.400	86	.353	50	0.00	113	4.35	117	7.25	16
	vs. Righties	.228	118	.316	120	.270	129	0.88	111	4.00	129	8.80	16
Gary Roenicke	vs. Lefties	.205	127	.453	53	.329	79	6.84	12	15.38	13	11.19	49
	vs. Righties	.265	--	.441	--	.432	--	2.94	--	22.73	--	15.91	--
Ted Simmons	vs. Lefties	.264	78	.440	63	.306	103	3.30	58	6.12	99	16.33	95
	vs. Righties	.291	--	.337	--	.392	--	1.16	--	14.71	--	6.86	--
Andres Thomas	vs. Lefties	.229	113	.302	119	.260	129	1.04	105	3.00	132	8.00	23
	vs. Righties	.232	112	.316	120	.271	128	1.75	87	4.53	122	17.28	99
Ozzie Virgil	vs. Lefties	.218	122	.427	70	.328	80	6.36	15	12.50	26	15.63	89
	vs. Righties	.257	87	.486	30	.331	74	6.27	11	8.66	73	17.04	97
Team Average	vs. Lefties	.257	10	.412	7	.347	1	3.04	6	11.68	1	13.04	1
	vs. Righties	.259	7	.400	7	.335	4	2.70	6	9.71	2	13.54	1
League Average	vs. Lefties	.263		.409		.332		2.81		9.08		15.22	
	vs. Righties	.260		.401		.327		2.73		8.70		15.85	

Batting with Runners on Base and Bases Empty

		BA	Rank	SA	Rank	OBA	Rank	HR %	Rank	BB %	Rank	SO %	Rank
Ken Griffey	Runners On	.242	110	.342	109	.330	92	0.53	118	12.16	34	12.16	52
	Bases Empty	.325	9	.560	11	.384	19	6.22	16	8.30	57	11.79	44
Albert Hall	Runners On	.217	123	.272	130	.354	64	0.00	122	16.24	13	6.84	14
	Bases Empty	.315	17	.475	37	.377	24	1.50	98	8.64	53	12.73	52
Glenn Hubbard	Runners On	.277	76	.367	102	.423	11	1.13	103	18.61	6	12.12	51
	Bases Empty	.256	80	.391	80	.344	49	1.13	105	11.26	22	9.60	19
Dion James	Runners On	.318	19	.497	29	.415	16	2.31	74	14.15	23	12.26	54
	Bases Empty	.308	20	.458	47	.387	17	1.87	88	11.05	25	10.22	29
Dale Murphy	Runners On	.263	91	.521	14	.424	10	7.34	7	20.59	2	20.00	121
	Bases Empty	.322	13	.629	2	.411	7	8.14	6	12.75	9	19.26	109
Graig Nettles	Runners On	.253	102	.462	46	.352	66	4.40	28	13.89	27	13.89	79
	Bases Empty	.163	--	.233	--	.226	--	1.16	--	7.53	--	10.75	--
Ken Oberkfell	Runners On	.265	84	.341	110	.347	76	0.47	120	11.34	47	5.67	7
	Bases Empty	.290	37	.377	91	.339	55	0.67	116	6.27	98	4.70	1
Gerald Perry	Runners On	.280	71	.435	67	.336	83	2.85	52	7.94	95	9.39	27
	Bases Empty	.261	74	.390	81	.323	77	1.74	93	8.31	56	11.82	45
Rafael Ramirez	Runners On	.256	100	.329	116	.287	119	0.00	122	3.30	133	8.79	24
	Bases Empty	.268	68	.361	101	.311	89	1.03	107	4.85	116	7.77	11
Gary Roenicke	Runners On	.260	93	.479	34	.367	48	5.48	12	14.44	20	10.00	29
	Bases Empty	.179	--	.423	--	.340	--	6.41	--	19.59	--	14.43	--
Ted Simmons	Runners On	.362	3	.532	13	.431	7	3.19	47	11.93	38	12.84	59
	Bases Empty	.181	--	.229	--	.253	--	1.20	--	8.79	--	9.89	--
Andres Thomas	Runners On	.255	101	.350	105	.287	120	1.91	83	3.59	132	11.98	48
	Bases Empty	.210	125	.275	130	.250	131	1.20	103	4.55	122	17.05	94
Ozzie Virgil	Runners On	.247	104	.397	84	.326	100	3.61	41	8.64	85	13.64	73
	Bases Empty	.247	97	.532	21	.335	59	8.51	4	10.53	31	19.17	108
Team Average	Runners On	.255	10	.389	10	.347	6	2.54	6	11.73	1	13.24	1
	Bases Empty	.261	3	.415	4	.332	1	3.00	6	9.09	3	13.52	1
League Average	Runners On	.267		.410		.341		2.66		9.88		14.92	
	Bases Empty	.256		.399		.319		2.82		7.98		16.22	

Overall Batting Compared to Late Inning Pressure Situations

		BA	Rank	SA	Rank	OBA	Rank	HR %	Rank	BB %	Rank	SO %	Rank	RDI %	Rank
Ken Griffey	Overall	.286	46	.456	43	.358	43	3.51	48	10.20	47	11.97	46	.310	43
	Pressure	.228	103	.342	100	.247	127	1.27	97	2.44	131	15.85	72	.241	76
Albert Hall	Overall	.284	50	.411	75	.369	30	1.03	114	11.28	30	10.68	32	.278	70
	Pressure	.321	25	.482	30	.397	28	0.00	105	9.52	64	11.11	28	.235	78
Glenn Hubbard	Overall	.264	84	.381	92	.378	23	1.13	109	14.45	9	10.69	33	.277	74
	Pressure	.254	82	.352	92	.321	87	1.41	91	7.41	93	13.58	50	.214	87
Dion James	Overall	.312	12	.472	32	.397	16	2.02	86	12.20	21	10.98	38	.314	36
	Pressure	.268	66	.305	115	.362	52	0.00	105	11.22	45	9.18	18	.263	67
Dale Murphy	Overall	.295	25	.580	6	.417	7	7.77	4	16.59	5	19.62	122	.287	62
	Pressure	.241	88	.422	56	.394	30	4.82	22	19.23	7	24.04	121	.095	130
Graig Nettles	Overall	.209	129	.350	109	.294	119	2.82	64	10.95	35	12.44	51	.342	19
	Pressure	.250	83	.404	61	.333	73	3.85	35	11.67	40	15.00	62	.429	10
Ken Oberkfell	Overall	.280	61	.362	103	.342	63	0.59	119	8.48	70	5.12	3	.266	85
	Pressure	.224	108	.276	121	.294	101	0.00	105	9.20	69	8.05	14	.154	118
Gerald Perry	Overall	.270	77	.411	77	.329	77	2.25	81	8.14	80	10.68	31	.318	32
	Pressure	.289	47	.398	64	.326	82	1.20	100	5.62	112	16.85	82	.370	24
Rafael Ramirez	Overall	.263	--	.346	--	.300	--	0.56	--	4.12	--	8.25	--	.344	17
	Pressure	.206	122	.265	128	.282	109	0.00	105	5.00	115	5.00	2	.353	32
Gary Roenicke	Overall	.219	--	.450	--	.353	--	5.96	--	17.11	--	12.30	--	.333	22
	Pressure	.182	--	.318	--	.357	--	4.55	--	21.43	--	14.29	--	.167	--
Ted Simmons	Overall	.277	64	.390	88	.350	49	2.26	80	10.50	41	11.50	42	.324	30
	Pressure	.310	33	.381	74	.383	39	2.38	67	10.64	52	10.64	26	.222	83
Andres Thomas	Overall	.231	121	.312	125	.268	129	1.54	97	4.08	130	14.58	78	.284	65
	Pressure	.133	136	.133	138	.204	136	0.00	105	8.00	83	16.00	76	.125	--
Ozzie Virgil	Overall	.247	104	.471	33	.331	73	6.29	13	9.67	55	16.67	98	.273	77
	Pressure	.235	94	.456	39	.307	94	7.35	7	9.21	68	17.11	85	.400	15
Team Average	Overall	.258	9	.403	6	.339	3	2.80	6	10.29	1	13.39	1	.281	4
	Pressure	.240	11	.344	10	.320	9	1.88	10	9.88	5	15.02	2	.257	7
League Average	Overall	.261		.404		.328		2.75		8.83		15.64		.272	
	Pressure	.258		.385		.331		2.46		9.54		16.95		.261	

Additional Miscellaneous Batting Comparisons

	Grass Surface BA	Rank	Artificial Surface BA	Rank	Home Games BA	Rank	Road Games BA	Rank	Runners in Scoring Position BA	Rank	Runners in Scoring Pos and Two Outs BA	Rank	Leading Off Inning OBA	Rank	Runners on 3B with less than 2 Outs RDI %	Rank
Bruce Benedict	.135	136	.190	--	.180	--	.111	--	.286	--	.429	--	.314	--	.333	--
Jeff Blauser	.256	87	.208	--	.295	--	.195	--	.293	--	.294	--	.308	--	.300	137
Ken Griffey	.281	50	.307	25	.291	47	.278	47	.252	87	.234	79	.354	45	.625	47
Albert Hall	.283	47	.286	50	.294	42	.276	57	.262	78	.259	65	.423	9	.571	72
Glenn Hubbard	.269	70	.252	94	.252	98	.276	56	.273	66	.238	76	.386	22	.700	19
Dion James	.328	10	.257	85	.376	3	.253	86	.319	22	.286	42	.411	12	.630	45
Dale Murphy	.314	16	.245	103	.346	6	.249	93	.248	89	.228	86	.384	25	.636	40
Graig Nettles	.206	129	.222	--	.232	115	.189	135	.196	124	.259	65	.150	--	.588	63
Ken Oberkfell	.282	48	.273	67	.293	44	.265	74	.248	90	.217	92	.319	84	.680	23
Gerald Perry	.273	62	.262	81	.259	91	.281	42	.286	51	.273	51	.297	105	.537	85
Rafael Ramirez	.233	108	.340	--	.253	--	.271	--	.321	20	.304	29	.250	--	.636	40
Gary Roenicke	.230	111	.196	--	.288	--	.154	--	.283	53	.056	--	.378	--	.714	16
Ted Simmons	.258	84	.316	--	.278	--	.276	58	.423	2	.448	4	.156	--	.500	91
Andres Thomas	.248	95	.179	133	.259	92	.200	133	.258	83	.313	25	.274	119	.444	115
Ozzie Virgil	.252	91	.235	110	.258	93	.236	110	.264	76	.193	114	.321	82	.455	113
Team Average	.262	5	.248	12	.277	2	.240	12	.260	6	.239	7	.336	3	.571	2
League Average	.260		.261		.265		.256		.258		.241		.324		.554	

Pitching vs. Left and Right Handed Batters

		BA	Rank	SA	Rank	OBA	Rank	HR %	Rank	BB %	Rank	SO %	Rank
Jim Acker	vs. Lefties	.238	29	.329	21	.317	35	1.30	23	10.23	64	11.74	71
	vs. Righties	.271	80	.447	90	.358	97	4.02	92	10.57	97	16.30	61
Doyle Alexander	vs. Lefties	.303	96	.559	112	.348	68	7.11	112	6.17	13	9.69	92
	vs. Righties	.215	18	.338	20	.257	9	2.53	43	5.12	13	16.54	58
Paul Assenmacher	vs. Lefties	.177	--	.253	--	.261	--	1.27	--	8.99	--	19.10	--
	vs. Righties	.306	104	.556	110	.373	104	4.86	105	9.88	89	13.58	84
Jeff Dedmon	vs. Lefties	.222	11	.323	19	.311	30	2.53	69	11.96	88	7.61	106
	vs. Righties	.267	76	.409	62	.342	87	2.27	30	10.00	90	13.00	86
Gene Garber	vs. Lefties	.279	78	.380	48	.350	70	1.55	30	9.33	51	17.33	35
	vs. Righties	.338	110	.510	106	.391	109	3.31	72	8.24	70	12.94	88
Tom Glavine	vs. Lefties	.259	--	.333	--	.375	--	0.00	--	12.50	--	3.13	--
	vs. Righties	.282	93	.435	85	.387	107	2.94	56	14.08	110	9.22	107
Rick Mahler	vs. Lefties	.314	104	.469	96	.391	102	2.74	80	11.16	75	10.07	87
	vs. Righties	.246	42	.401	53	.314	52	3.72	82	8.67	80	12.50	95
David Palmer	vs. Lefties	.289	85	.449	85	.371	92	2.71	77	10.99	70	17.28	36
	vs. Righties	.270	79	.404	57	.332	74	2.96	59	7.21	46	14.75	74
Charlie Puleo	vs. Lefties	.285	81	.459	90	.347	66	3.66	102	9.09	45	15.64	42
	vs. Righties	.237	35	.315	13	.288	28	0.91	8	6.02	27	22.49	16
Zane Smith	vs. Lefties	.257	47	.314	15	.310	29	0.95	12	6.96	18	19.13	22
	vs. Righties	.267	75	.386	44	.336	80	2.20	29	9.02	84	11.74	101
Team Average	vs. Lefties	.288	11	.433	11	.362	10	2.84	12	10.25	9	12.78	10
	vs. Righties	.268	12	.413	10	.336	12	3.02	8	8.72	9	13.77	12
League Average	vs. Lefties	.268		.404		.341		2.34		9.74		14.31	
	vs. Righties	.255		.403		.319		3.05		8.16		16.61	

Pitching with Runners on Base and Bases Empty

		BA	Rank	SA	Rank	OBA	Rank	HR %	Rank	BB %	Rank	SO %	Rank
Jim Acker	Runners On	.251	40	.353	26	.333	52	1.45	21	10.00	63	14.17	64
	Bases Empty	.256	64	.413	75	.339	84	3.59	86	10.76	98	13.55	85
Doyle Alexander	Runners On	.300	99	.507	109	.337	61	6.00	112	6.10	6	14.02	67
	Bases Empty	.235	30	.409	73	.281	14	4.03	94	5.36	12	12.93	92
Paul Assenmacher	Runners On	.317	110	.545	112	.402	112	3.96	98	12.61	97	14.29	62
	Bases Empty	.213	10	.369	36	.273	6	3.28	82	6.82	37	16.67	44
Jeff Dedmon	Runners On	.268	67	.439	82	.349	79	3.05	75	11.86	90	10.31	98
	Bases Empty	.224	19	.300	7	.305	38	1.76	22	10.00	95	10.53	105
Gene Garber	Runners On	.286	92	.391	51	.359	91	2.48	56	9.90	61	15.10	58
	Bases Empty	.345	112	.529	110	.391	111	2.52	51	7.03	46	14.84	64
Rick Mahler	Runners On	.301	102	.456	90	.388	109	2.59	63	12.26	96	10.35	97
	Bases Empty	.270	81	.424	82	.332	77	3.63	88	8.30	67	11.83	96
David Palmer	Runners On	.284	88	.444	84	.370	98	3.45	87	10.19	66	16.88	42
	Bases Empty	.279	91	.416	79	.340	87	2.35	43	8.58	72	15.55	57
Charlie Puleo	Runners On	.285	91	.415	66	.329	43	2.90	71	7.47	17	16.18	48
	Bases Empty	.244	44	.372	43	.311	47	1.94	29	7.77	57	21.20	17
Zane Smith	Runners On	.276	76	.421	72	.346	73	3.32	84	9.47	54	11.89	84
	Bases Empty	.258	66	.345	20	.324	69	1.13	5	8.26	66	13.08	90
Team Average	Runners On	.290	12	.438	12	.367	12	3.06	11	10.65	9	13.17	12
	Bases Empty	.266	10	.408	8	.330	10	2.86	7	8.26	9	13.50	12
League Average	Runners On	.267		.410		.341		2.66		9.88		14.92	
	Bases Empty	.256		.399		.319		2.82		7.98		16.22	

Overall Pitching Compared to Late Inning Pressure Situations

		BA	Rank	SA	Rank	OBA	Rank	HR %	Rank	BB %	Rank	SO %	Rank
Jim Acker	Overall	.253	52	.384	49	.336	82	2.56	57	10.39	88	13.85	74
	Pressure	.296	89	.439	83	.382	93	2.55	63	11.01	78	10.57	89
Doyle Alexander	Overall	.257	57	.442	91	.300	16	4.69	110	5.61	7	13.31	79
	Pressure	.462	112	.885	112	.525	112	11.54	111	11.29	82	6.45	106
Paul Assenmacher	Overall	.260	64	.448	94	.333	75	3.59	96	9.56	75	15.54	55
	Pressure	.210	14	.321	19	.289	19	1.23	29	10.00	61	17.78	46
Jeff Dedmon	Overall	.246	46	.368	38	.327	61	2.40	41	10.94	101	10.42	74
	Pressure	.260	61	.365	48	.357	74	1.04	25	13.79	98	11.21	85
Gene Garber	Overall	.311	111	.450	97	.372	108	2.50	54	8.75	57	15.00	61
	Pressure	.314	96	.435	81	.378	90	1.93	47	9.13	56	15.35	60
Rick Mahler	Overall	.283	98	.437	89	.356	102	3.20	79	10.01	83	11.19	99
	Pressure	.347	105	.542	103	.434	105	4.17	91	12.79	89	8.14	103
Ed Olwine	Overall	.269	--	.452	--	.330	--	4.30	--	7.69	--	11.54	--
	Pressure	.250	46	.531	100	.265	9	6.25	102	2.86	5	11.43	82
David Palmer	Overall	.281	96	.429	83	.354	98	2.82	70	9.32	69	16.16	46
	Pressure	.208	--	.333	--	.296	--	4.17	--	11.11	--	11.11	--
Charlie Puleo	Overall	.262	65	.391	57	.319	41	2.37	46	7.63	25	18.89	25
	Pressure	.238	35	.333	26	.273	15	0.00	1	4.35	12	19.57	34
Zane Smith	Overall	.266	70	.377	42	.333	75	2.06	31	8.79	60	12.56	87
	Pressure	.309	94	.456	87	.329	49	2.94	73	1.41	3	9.86	96
Team Average	Overall	.276	12	.421	10	.347	11	2.95	8	9.36	9	13.35	12
	Pressure	.301	12	.456	12	.372	12	2.91	9	9.73	6	12.35	12
League Average	Overall	.261		.404		.328		2.75		8.83		15.64	
	Pressure	.260		.391		.337		2.47		10.04		17.14	

Additional Miscellaneous Pitching Comparisons

	Grass Surface		Artificial Surface		Home Games		Road Games		Runners in Scoring Position		Runners in Scoring Pos and Two Outs		Leading Off Inning	
	BA	Rank	BA	Rank	BA	Rank	BA	Rank	BA	Rank	BA	Rank	OBA	Rank
Jim Acker	.254	49	.252	46	.247	39	.261	52	.241	42	.290	91	.321	56
Doyle Alexander	.255	52	.266	--	.273	85	.234	23	.352	111	.359	110	.248	9
Paul Assenmacher	.269	67	.238	--	.288	--	.232	21	.343	110	.310	--	.321	--
Kevin Coffman	.313	107	.000	--	.382	--	.227	--	.200	--	.300	--	.393	--
Jeff Dedmon	.243	31	.253	--	.256	59	.235	24	.245	49	.352	107	.381	101
Gene Garber	.311	106	.311	--	.298	102	.330	107	.248	54	.279	85	.339	78
Tom Glavine	.289	96	.265	--	.266	--	.291	88	.304	98	.259	76	.321	--
Rick Mahler	.272	75	.323	106	.265	72	.305	102	.308	102	.299	95	.369	96
David Palmer	.279	80	.285	86	.306	105	.255	47	.267	75	.224	50	.329	68
Charlie Puleo	.258	57	.273	70	.245	37	.277	72	.264	72	.233	62	.344	83
Pete Smith	.288	93	.438	--	.265	--	.356	--	.400	--	.333	--	.394	--
Zane Smith	.271	73	.252	45	.309	108	.226	18	.286	84	.276	84	.304	38
Team Average	.276	10	.279	10	.285	12	.267	7	.284	12	.284	12	.337	10
League Average	.260		.261		.256		.265		.258		.241		.324	

CHICAGO CUBS

Baseball Statistical Riddle Number 173: How can a team hit 50 more home runs than it allows, and yet allow 81 more runs than it scores? Answer: Easy, if that team is the Cubs.

Each baseball season produces its share of anomalies, and the Cubs' home run riddle is a real cutie. For those of you who weren't paying attention, the Cubs clouted a team-record 209 home runs last season, while their pitchers allowed only 159, quite a moderate total in view of Wrigley Field and the Year of the Homer. But despite that head start of 50 runs, the Cubs wound up being outscored, 801 to 720, on their way to a last-place finish in the National League East.

Certainly it's no big deal when a Cubs team hits a lot of home runs, but that 50-homer margin over their opponents caught our eye. We looked back and found that only twice before in this century had the Cubs outhomered their opponents by that large a margin. Those instances came in 1929 and 1930, when Hack Wilson was in his heyday, but in each of those seasons, the Cubs translated their home run advantage into an overall scoring advantage and a winning record. Contrast those years with what happened in 1987:

	Own HR	Opp. HR	HR Diff.	Own Runs	Opp. Runs	Runs Diff.	W–L
1929 Cubs	171	111	+60	982	758	+224	98–54
1930 Cubs	140	77	+63	998	870	+128	90–64
1987 Cubs	209	159	+50	720	801	−81	75–86

Somewhere, the 1987 Cubs misplaced about 200 runs!

The magnitude of this disparity becomes apparent the farther you look back into baseball history. Not counting the '87 Cubs, there have been 70 major league teams that have outhomered their opponents in a given season by a margin of 50 or more. As you would expect, some of the greatest teams in baseball history are included among those 70 teams: the '27 Yankees, the '39 Yankees, the '61 Yankees, the '54 Indians, the '69 Orioles, the '84 Tigers. (The '27 Yankees, in fact, hit 158 home runs to their opponents' 42, a margin of 116 homers that is still the all-time record.) In all, 35 of the 70 teams won either the league or division title.

But of those 70, *none was outscored by as great a margin as the 1987 Cubs!* In fact, only one of those 70 other teams had been outscored *at all*: Led by Jimmie Foxx, the 1934 Philadelphia Athletics won the battle of home runs, 144 to 84, but lost the run-scoring war, 838 to 764.

How on earth did the Cubs manage to produce so little with so much?

To start, let's look at the home runs themselves. Did the Cubs usually hit them with no one on base? For a frame of reference, consider that 58.4 percent of all major league home runs last year were hit with the bases empty; in fact, the percentage was nearly exactly the same in each league: 58.5 percent in the N.L., 58.4 in the A.L. But the Cubs hit 64 percent of their 209 homers with the bases empty, the highest rate by any team in the National League, and the second-highest rate (to Cleveland's 69 percent) in the majors.

Of the 50 "additional" home runs that Chicago hit, 45 came with the bases empty. The result: Despite hitting 50 more homers than their opponents, the Cubs scored only 60 more runs on home runs than the opposition:

	HR	0-on	1-on	2-on	3-on	Runs on HR	Runs per HR
Cubs	209	134	55	14	6	310	1.48
Opponents	159	89	52	15	3	250	1.57

So excluding runs scored on homers, the Cubs were outscored 551 to 410 last season. Why?

Let's look at the other elements of offensive play. Here's a brief recap of the 1987 statistics:

	Runs	BA	2B	3B	HR	SB	BB	SO
Cubs	720	.264	244	33	209	109	504	1064
Opponents	801	.275	267	43	159	169	628	1024

Although Chicago had the edge in home runs, its opponents had the edge in batting average, doubles, triples, stolen bases, and walks—activities that not only put runners on base, but also move them along. Only one other team in the majors was outperformed in all five of those categories last season: the woebegone Orioles, who were outscored by 151 runs, and who finished with an even worse record than the Cubs. Excluding home runs, the Cubs had 1,791 runners reach base on hits, walks, and hit batters, while their opponents had 2,020 such runners.

Then, there was the matter of timely hitting. Despite their .264 overall average, the Cubs batted only .239 with runners in scoring position. That 25-point drop-off was big time: Not only was it the largest by any National League team last season (see chart in Mets' essay), but it was the largest in the majors. We've been keeping track of these statistics since 1975, and only twice in those 13 seasons has a team had as large a clutch falloff as the '87 Cubs:

	Overall	Scor. Pos.	Difference
1981 Mets	.248	.214	−34
1976 White Sox	.255	.227	−28
1987 Cubs	.264	.239	−25

Meanwhile, Chicago's opponents batted just as well with men in scoring position (.275) as they did overall.

Anyone familiar with this book and past *Analysts* recognizes the categories of information that we present for each player and team: performance with runners on base, with runners in scoring position, etc. But even these categories are consolidations of narrower categories. Actually, there are eight possible base situations in baseball: no runners on; runner on first; runner on second; runner on third; runners on first and second; runners on first and third; runners on second and third; and bases loaded.

To underscore how completely the Cubs were outhit last season, especially in key situations, consider these batting average figures for the Cubs and their opponents:

Bases Occupied	Cubs PA	BA	Opponents PA	BA
None	3484	.271	3364	.272
1st	1125	.276	1121	.285
2nd	526	.207	625	.290
3rd	181	.240	207	.257
1st–2nd	420	.251	459	.280
1st–3rd	201	.291	221	.259
2nd–3rd	126	.260	163	.271
Loaded	134	.225	151	.244

The Cubs' opponents batted more frequently than did the Cubs in every runners-on-base situation except "first base only," where the plate appearances were practically identical. And in only one situation (runners on first and third) did the Cubs outhit their opponents.

What we see is that the hidden power inherent in the effective combination of baserunners and timely hitting is more than enough to offset the more obvious sort of power, the kind generated by home runs. Granted, the statistical profile presented by the 1987 Cubs is unique in baseball history; and (rest easy, George Will), we may not see their like again in this century. But their lasting legacy will be the best example that we have yet seen of how home runs do not necessarily make or break a team.

The June Swoon and Other Facts of Life

Fool us once, shame on you; fool us twice, shame on us. It's an old proverb, but how should we feel after being fooled for the fifth time? We admit it, the Cubs fooled us again. You see, we're enamored of using the first 40 games—one quarter of the season—as a yardstick, in the belief that the 40-game mark is usually a strong indicator of how a particular team will perform that season.

In fact, this is not an unreasonable premise. Of the 725 teams since 1900 that played sub-.500 ball through the first 40 games, only 158 (22 percent) finished that season above .500, and only 11 have come back to win a league or division title.

But what of the reverse? How about teams that have a strong first 40 games; let's say, play .600 ball (or win 24 games) over the first forty. There have been 327 such teams since 1900, and only 21 of them have finished the season below the .500 mark. But there's an interesting breakdown of those 327 teams:

	.600 Ball In First 40 Games	Final Record Below .500	Rate
Cubs	22	5	22.7%
Other Teams	305	16	5.2%

A rule of thumb that applies very well to everyone else in the major leagues has as its exception the Cubs, whose rate of going the penthouse-to-outhouse route is four times that of all other major-league teams combined. No other team has teased its fans in that manner as frequently as the Cubs:

	After 40 Games		Final Record	
1917 Cubs	25–15	.625	74–80	.481
1920 Cubs	24–16	.600	75–79	.487
1973 Cubs	24–16	.600	77–84	.478
1985 Cubs	25–15	.625	77–84	.478
1987 Cubs	24–16	.600	76–85	.472

Only two National League teams and five in the American League, after enjoying a .600 percentage through 40 games, have finished the year with worse final records than the Cubs did last season. The two National League teams were the 1914 Reds, who had a 25–15 start but finished at 60–94 (.390), and the 1956 Pirates, who started 24–16 but wound up at 66–88 (.429). That Reds team, incidentally, is the only team ever to finish below .400 after winning at least 24 of their first 40 games.

Of course, injuries played a part in the Cubs' demise last season: Ryne Sandberg and Shawon Dunston went onto the disabled list, and Paul Noce and Mike Brumley, who filled in, batted a combined .218 for the season. But when *aren't* injuries a part of a team's troubles? In '85, it was the entire pitching staff that was disabled. Back in '73, Glenn Beckert went out with a heel injury in early August and couldn't play second base the rest of the season. As Roseanne Rosannadanna's father used to say, "It's always somethin'."

What happens to these teams the year after their 40-game tease? Not much good. Only five of the 20 teams came back to finish above the .500 mark the following year, and only one of them won a league or division pennant. The one? The Chicago Cubs, in 1918.

Game Winning RBI Reexamined

Andre Dawson's performance in 1987 included league-leading totals of 49 home runs, 137 runs batted in, and 353 total bases. He won the MVP award, with 269 points to Ozzie Smith's 193, despite the Cubs' last-place finish. Curiously, Ernie Banks had led the National League in the same three categories in 1958, when he was honored with the MVP Award despite playing for a fifth-place Cubs team.

Dawson also shared the National League lead in game-winning runs batted in (16) with Howard Johnson, Dave Parker and Tim Wallach.

Whenever the subject of baseball statistics is discussed in some detail on either television or radio, most notably on call-in shows, the subject of the game-winning RBI hovers over the discussion like Damocles's sword. We have avoided the topic in the first three *Analysts,* but we are still bombarded with questions about its significance.

For those of you who have been held behind enemy lines for the past eight years, the game-winning RBI is credited to the player who drives in the run that gives his team a lead that it never relinquishes. It's a simple enough definition (an important consideration for a mass-consumption category) since the particular run that determines the game-winning RBI is also the run that in most cases determines the pitcher of decision. But it upsets some fans that the first run driven across the plate in a 12–0 win is determined to be the game-winner, even though the same people don't give a hoot about awarding a win to a pitcher in a game in which he doesn't pitch particularly well.

We think that, if anything, not enough significant RBI are recognized. One problem with the game-winning RBI is that it is awarded in hindsight: only after the game is finished do you look back and say, "Aha, here it is." Indeed, the same is true of winning and losing pitchers. But this procedure ignores the dynamics of the game, and places artificial limits on recognition of a player's performance. We feel it's important that whenever a batter puts his team into the lead, it's essential to reward that effort—at any time of a game, regardless of whether or not, retrospectively, that particular run put his team in the lead to stay. So we went back through the 1987 season and counted up how many times each batter put his team into the lead at any time during a game; in other words, rather than counting "game-winners," we counted "go-aheads."

Here are the top 10 players in each league in three categories: total RBI, game-winning RBI, and go-aheads:

American League

Runs Batted In		Game-Winning RBI		Go-Aheads	
Bell, Tor.	134	Tartabull, K.C.	21	Tartabull, K.C.	34
Evans, Bos.	123	Canseco, Oak.	17	Ripken, Balt.	31
McGwire, Oak.	118	Fisk, Chi.	17	Bell, Tor.	30
Joyner, Cal.	117	Yount, Mil.	17	Sierra, Tex.	30
Mattingly, N.Y.	115	Bell, Tor.	16	Tabler, Clev.	30
Canseco, Oak.	113	Trammell, Det.	16	Trammell, Det.	30
Gaetti, Minn.	109	Boggs, Bos.	15	Boggs, Bos.	28
Sierra, Tex.	109	Gaetti, Minn.	14	Gaetti, Minn.	28
Carter, Clev.	106	McGwire, Oak.	14	McGwire, Oak.	28
Trammell, Det.	105	O'Brien, Tex.	14	Murray, Balt.	28
				Puckett, Minn.	28

Tim Wallach was the go-ahead champion of the majors, followed by Danny Tartabull and Dawson. Wallach put the Expos ahead 41 times during the 1987 season, but because most of the time the Expos relinquished the lead, he was credited with only 16 GW-RBI. The go-ahead column is especially valuable to measure the contributions of those who play for teams with poor pitching staffs: these guys knock in runs that put their team on top, only to go back into the field and see their pitchers blow the lead (and with it, the credit for the game-winning RBI). Baltimore's Cal Ripken lived that scenario in 1987; he lifted the Birds into the lead 31 times last year, but the pitchers give back that lead on 23 occasions, leaving him with only eight game-winners.

Another way to make the game-winning RBI more "meaningful" would be to consider only those that occur in the seventh inning or later. Or, to keep a separate tally for each: total game-winners and late-inning game-winners. But even though you can spin a number of variations off the same theme, well, the Rockies may crumble and Gibraltar may tumble, but the game-winning RBI is here to stay.

National League

Runs Batted In		Game-Winning RBI		Go-Aheads	
Dawson, Chi.	137	Dawson, Chi.	16	Wallach, Mtl.	41
Wallach, Mtl.	123	Johnson, N.Y.	16	Dawson, Chi.	32
Schmidt, Phil.	113	Parker, Cin.	16	Doran, Hou.	28
Clark, St.L.	106	Wallach, Mtl.	16	Hernandez, N.Y.	28
McGee, St.L.	105	Clark, St.L.	15	Clark, St.L.	27
Murphy, Atl.	105	Herr, St.L.	14	Davis, Hou.	27
Strawberry, N.Y.	104	Doran, Hou.	13	Johnson, N.Y.	25
Davis, Cin.	100	Hernandez, N.Y.	13	Maldonado, S.F.	25
Samuel, Phil.	100	Maldonado, S.F.	12	Schmidt, Phil.	25
Johnson, N.Y.	99	Perry, Atl.	12	Strawberry, N.Y.	25

WON-LOST RECORD BY STARTING POSITION

CHICAGO 76-85	C	1B	2B	3B	SS	LF	CF	RF	P	Leadoff	Relief	Starts
Jay Baller	·	·	·	·	·	·	·	·	·	·	6-17	·
Damon Berryhill	2-5	·	·	·	·	·	·	·	·	·	·	2-5
Mike Brumley	·	·	·	·	15-15	·	·	·	·	·	·	15-15
Jody Davis	60-59	·	·	·	·	·	·	·	·	·	·	60-59
Ron Davis	·	·	·	·	·	·	·	·	·	·	5-16	·
Andre Dawson	·	·	·	·	·	·	·	70-81	·	·	·	70-81
Brian Dayett	·	·	·	·	·	15-22	1-0	·	·	·	·	16-22
Bob Dernier	·	·	·	·	·	·	18-22	·	·	18-22	·	18-22
Frank DiPino	·	·	·	·	·	·	·	·	·	·	27-42	·
Shawon Dunston	·	·	·	·	·	43-49	·	·	·	·	·	43-49
Leon Durham	·	58-56	·	·	·	·	·	·	·	·	·	58-56
Drew Hall	·	·	·	·	·	·	·	·	·	·	4-17	·
Darrin Jackson	·	·	·	·	·	·	·	·	·	·	·	·
Les Lancaster	·	·	·	·	·	·	·	·	7-11	·	2-7	7-11
Ed Lynch	·	·	·	·	·	·	·	·	4-4	·	15-35	4-4
Greg Maddux	·	·	·	·	·	·	·	·	9-18	·	0-3	9-18
Dave Martinez	·	·	·	·	·	·	57-62	·	·	35-44	·	57-62
Mike Mason	·	·	·	·	·	·	·	·	3-1	·	3-10	3-1
Gary Matthews	·	·	·	·	·	2-0	·	·	·	·	·	2-0
Keith Moreland	·	·	·	74-75	·	·	·	·	·	·	·	74-75
Jamie Moyer	·	·	·	·	·	·	·	·	14-19	·	1-1	14-19
Jerry Mumphrey	·	·	·	·	·	31-38	·	4-3	·	·	·	35-41
Paul Noce	·	·	13-16	·	7-11	·	·	·	·	·	·	20-27
Dickie Noles	·	·	·	·	·	·	·	·	0-1	·	17-23	0-1
Rafael Palmeiro	·	5-8	·	·	17-17	·	·	·	·	·	·	22-25
Luis Quinones	·	·	0-1	·	10-10	·	·	·	·	·	·	10-11
Wade Rowdon	·	·	·	2-5	·	·	·	·	·	·	·	2-5
Ryne Sandberg	·	·	62-68	·	·	·	·	·	·	11-9	·	62-68
Scott Sanderson	·	·	·	·	·	·	·	·	10-12	·	5-5	10-12
Lee Smith	·	·	·	·	·	·	·	·	·	·	44-18	·
Jim Sundberg	14-21	·	·	·	·	·	·	·	·	·	·	14-21
Rick Sutcliffe	·	·	·	·	·	·	·	·	22-12	·	·	22-12
Bob Tewksbury	·	·	·	·	·	·	·	·	0-3	·	0-4	0-3
Manny Trillo	·	13-21	1-0	0-5	1-0	·	·	·	·	·	·	15-26
Steve Trout	·	·	·	·	·	·	·	·	7-4	·	·	7-4
Chico Walker	·	·	·	·	·	11-8	1-1	1-1	·	12-10	·	13-10

Batting vs. Left and Right Handed Pitchers

		BA	Rank	SA	Rank	OBA	Rank	HR %	Rank	BB %	Rank	SO %	Rank
Jody Davis	vs. Lefties	.252	94	.430	68	.325	83	4.67	30	9.17	60	15.83	90
	vs. Righties	.246	101	.414	64	.332	70	4.36	29	11.23	33	19.73	112
Andre Dawson	vs. Lefties	.298	40	.525	28	.348	58	6.38	14	6.45	93	14.19	77
	vs. Righties	.283	49	.581	7	.321	87	8.33	3	4.34	125	15.98	86
Brian Dayett	vs. Lefties	.331	19	.540	22	.391	22	4.03	44	9.42	53	13.77	70
	vs. Righties	.151	--	.245	--	.250	--	0.00	--	11.67	--	30.00	--
Bob Dernier	vs. Lefties	.340	11	.553	17	.408	16	4.96	25	9.49	49	7.59	19
	vs. Righties	.259	--	.362	--	.306	--	1.72	--	6.45	--	11.29	--
Shawon Dunston	vs. Lefties	.231	110	.321	114	.238	133	1.28	99	0.00	136	15.00	82
	vs. Righties	.250	95	.369	93	.276	123	1.49	94	3.58	131	20.07	116
Leon Durham	vs. Lefties	.257	85	.378	92	.286	119	2.70	72	3.90	124	24.68	134
	vs. Righties	.277	63	.540	13	.359	41	6.85	8	11.57	27	17.59	104
Dave Martinez	vs. Lefties	.261	--	.391	--	.320	--	4.35	--	8.00	--	32.00	--
	vs. Righties	.294	33	.420	61	.374	24	1.61	89	11.11	35	17.78	105
Keith Moreland	vs. Lefties	.295	44	.451	55	.362	48	2.46	75	10.56	43	10.56	43
	vs. Righties	.259	86	.469	38	.294	106	5.44	17	5.08	117	10.81	34
Jerry Mumphrey	vs. Lefties	.143	--	.286	--	.250	--	0.00	--	11.11	--	11.11	--
	vs. Righties	.338	4	.540	12	.404	11	4.30	30	10.09	54	13.65	63
Paul Noce	vs. Lefties	.148	136	.148	136	.193	136	0.00	113	5.26	111	31.58	136
	vs. Righties	.262	79	.437	49	.290	109	2.38	72	2.22	136	22.96	128
Rafael Palmeiro	vs. Lefties	.115	--	.231	--	.226	--	3.85	--	12.90	--	9.68	--
	vs. Righties	.297	26	.585	6	.352	50	6.67	9	7.51	91	10.80	33
Ryne Sandberg	vs. Lefties	.307	34	.439	64	.412	14	1.75	90	15.44	11	11.76	52
	vs. Righties	.291	38	.443	46	.353	48	3.42	50	8.43	75	13.97	70
Jim Sundberg	vs. Lefties	.261	--	.435	--	.414	--	4.35	--	20.69	--	24.14	--
	vs. Righties	.190	132	.276	132	.282	115	2.59	65	9.85	56	25.00	131
Manny Trillo	vs. Lefties	.298	40	.447	60	.362	42	4.26	38	9.43	51	16.98	98
	vs. Righties	.292	37	.442	47	.370	28	3.33	52	10.87	39	13.77	67
Team Average	vs. Lefties	.270	3	.418	5	.335	7	3.27	5	8.76	7	17.04	11
	vs. Righties	.263	5	.436	1	.323	9	3.88	1	7.94	11	17.21	10
League Average	vs. Lefties	.263		.409		.332		2.81		9.08		15.22	
	vs. Righties	.260		.401		.327		2.73		8.70		15.85	

Batting with Runners on Base and Bases Empty

		BA	Rank	SA	Rank	OBA	Rank	HR %	Rank	BB %	Rank	SO %	Rank
Jody Davis	Runners On	.205	130	.305	120	.292	117	2.11	80	11.06	54	16.59	98
	Bases Empty	.282	46	.508	27	.362	32	6.30	14	10.45	33	20.52	120
Andre Dawson	Runners On	.310	29	.597	6	.341	80	7.42	5	3.96	128	13.72	74
	Bases Empty	.264	71	.540	18	.314	88	8.36	5	5.69	107	17.37	96
Brian Dayett	Runners On	.295	48	.511	23	.357	60	3.41	43	9.18	77	23.47	133
	Bases Empty	.258	--	.393	--	.340	--	2.25	--	11.00	--	14.00	--
Bob Dernier	Runners On	.292	--	.369	--	.361	--	1.54	--	8.22	--	6.85	--
	Bases Empty	.328	7	.560	12	.388	16	5.22	26	8.84	50	9.52	17
Shawon Dunston	Runners On	.229	118	.336	112	.237	133	1.53	91	0.74	135	11.85	47
	Bases Empty	.256	79	.372	98	.286	111	1.40	100	4.02	126	23.21	129
Leon Durham	Runners On	.247	105	.429	69	.359	55	4.40	28	15.21	14	17.51	110
	Bases Empty	.292	35	.572	9	.338	56	7.39	9	6.55	87	19.64	112
Dave Martinez	Runners On	.278	73	.354	104	.372	42	0.63	117	13.04	32	22.28	129
	Bases Empty	.299	28	.452	48	.372	25	2.33	78	9.82	41	16.37	92
Keith Moreland	Runners On	.263	89	.458	48	.314	105	4.78	21	8.04	94	9.79	28
	Bases Empty	.269	67	.471	39	.305	92	4.81	31	4.88	114	11.59	42
Jerry Mumphrey	Runners On	.284	65	.410	74	.378	40	2.24	78	13.38	30	15.29	92
	Bases Empty	.371	2	.629	3	.418	3	5.71	20	7.41	67	12.17	47
Paul Noce	Runners On	.197	--	.310	--	.230	--	1.41	--	2.56	--	26.92	--
	Bases Empty	.248	94	.376	93	.281	118	1.83	90	3.51	130	24.56	134
Rafael Palmeiro	Runners On	.245	107	.479	35	.330	93	5.32	14	11.93	38	6.42	11
	Bases Empty	.299	26	.591	4	.341	52	7.09	11	5.19	112	14.07	68
Ryne Sandberg	Runners On	.285	62	.374	86	.362	52	1.87	86	10.25	63	13.52	68
	Bases Empty	.301	23	.489	31	.370	26	3.88	46	9.91	39	13.41	58
Manny Trillo	Runners On	.310	30	.452	53	.404	24	4.76	22	13.59	28	11.65	44
	Bases Empty	.285	43	.438	57	.340	53	3.08	59	7.80	61	17.73	102
Team Average	Runners On	.255	9	.399	9	.324	10	3.17	4	9.14	10	15.85	11
	Bases Empty	.271	1	.456	1	.327	4	4.17	1	7.35	9	18.20	10
League Average	Runners On	.267		.410		.341		2.66		9.88		14.92	
	Bases Empty	.256		.399		.319		2.82		7.98		16.22	

Overall Batting Compared to Late Inning Pressure Situations

		BA	Rank	SA	Rank	OBA	Rank	HR %	Rank	BB %	Rank	SO %	Rank	RDI %	Rank
Jody Davis	Overall	.248	103	.418	70	.331	73	4.44	29	10.72	37	18.76	112	.229	114
	Pressure	.316	28	.544	13	.381	40	7.02	9	7.94	84	22.22	117	.364	28
Andre Dawson	Overall	.287	42	.568	7	.328	80	7.89	2	4.83	127	15.56	86	.324	29
	Pressure	.274	60	.607	6	.307	93	10.71	2	4.55	117	15.91	74	.361	31
Brian Dayett	Overall	.277	--	.452	--	.348	--	2.82	--	10.10	--	18.69	--	.302	--
	Pressure	.226	--	.323	--	.250	--	0.00	--	3.13	--	28.13	--	.200	96
Bob Dernier	Overall	.317	10	.497	24	.379	22	4.02	37	8.64	67	8.64	13	.229	--
	Pressure	.389	4	.556	12	.463	4	5.56	15	12.20	38	12.20	33	.400	--
Shawon Dunston	Overall	.246	106	.358	105	.267	130	1.45	101	2.79	136	18.94	114	.211	119
	Pressure	.313	32	.391	69	.338	72	0.00	105	4.41	118	19.12	99	.182	105
Leon Durham	Overall	.273	69	.513	18	.348	53	6.15	14	10.37	43	18.70	110	.261	88
	Pressure	.255	80	.333	104	.309	92	1.96	76	7.27	95	18.18	89	.111	123
Dave Martinez	Overall	.292	35	.418	69	.372	28	1.74	92	10.96	33	18.46	109	.241	105
	Pressure	.371	10	.435	49	.409	21	0.00	105	5.97	107	20.90	107	.250	71
Gary Matthews	Overall	.262	--	.333	--	.326	--	0.00	--	8.70	--	23.91	--	.400	--
	Pressure	.125	--	.125	--	.176	--	0.00	--	5.88	--	29.41	--	.111	123
Keith Moreland	Overall	.266	80	.465	37	.309	103	4.80	20	6.35	112	10.75	34	.272	81
	Pressure	.236	93	.361	84	.276	115	2.78	53	5.26	113	13.16	44	.000	140
Jerry Mumphrey	Overall	.333	4	.534	12	.400	12	4.21	34	10.12	51	13.58	63	.308	46
	Pressure	.409	1	.636	4	.490	2	4.55	26	13.46	27	7.69	11	.333	36
Rafael Palmeiro	Overall	.276	66	.543	10	.336	67	6.33	12	8.20	79	10.66	29	.241	--
	Pressure	.343	14	.514	20	.410	19	2.86	48	10.26	58	20.51	104	.250	--
Ryne Sandberg	Overall	.294	26	.442	50	.367	33	3.06	61	10.05	52	13.46	61	.273	77
	Pressure	.297	41	.375	76	.416	16	1.56	88	16.88	12	12.99	43	.345	35
Jim Sundberg	Overall	.201	--	.302	--	.306	--	2.88	--	11.80	--	24.84	--	.191	--
	Pressure	.217	--	.348	--	.308	--	4.35	--	11.11	--	29.63	--	.222	83
Manny Trillo	Overall	.294	27	.444	47	.367	34	3.74	43	10.25	46	15.16	83	.246	103
	Pressure	.212	117	.404	61	.333	73	5.77	12	15.63	15	12.50	39	.313	48
Team Average	Overall	.264	5	.432	2	.326	9	3.74	1	8.13	10	17.17	10	.254	10
	Pressure	.282	1	.427	3	.344	2	3.49	1	8.48	11	18.35	11	.264	6
League Average	Overall	.261		.404		.328		2.75		8.83		15.64		.272	
	Pressure	.258		.385		.331		2.46		9.54		16.95		.261	

Additional Miscellaneous Batting Comparisons

	Grass Surface		Artificial Surface		Home Games		Road Games		Runners in Scoring Position		Runners in Scoring Pos and Two Outs		Leading Off Inning		Runners on 3B with less than 2 Outs	
	BA	Rank	BA	Rank	BA	Rank	BA	Rank	BA	Rank	BA	Rank	OBA	Rank	RDI %	Rank
Mike Brumley	.174	--	.257	--	.190	--	.217	--	.156	--	.091	--	.286	--	.545	79
Jody Davis	.257	86	.226	118	.256	94	.240	104	.200	121	.193	114	.371	32	.500	91
Andre Dawson	.305	24	.247	102	.332	13	.246	100	.328	14	.356	10	.290	111	.650	34
Brian Dayett	.265	76	.300	--	.228	--	.316	14	.283	--	.226	88	.282	--	.600	--
Bob Dernier	.307	20	.339	--	.313	22	.320	11	.267	--	.300	--	.318	85	.500	--
Shawon Dunston	.227	113	.283	52	.221	123	.273	63	.242	98	.323	17	.303	102	.294	139
Leon Durham	.272	65	.277	61	.297	41	.246	97	.204	119	.171	121	.325	78	.385	128
Dave Martinez	.288	39	.301	28	.281	63	.303	24	.277	64	.216	94	.353	46	.500	91
Keith Moreland	.287	41	.220	123	.290	49	.244	103	.228	110	.208	101	.290	110	.611	51
Jerry Mumphrey	.318	13	.372	1	.288	51	.379	1	.303	32	.289	37	.368	36	.643	37
Paul Noce	.221	118	.245	--	.234	113	.221	--	.154	--	.105	--	.321	82	.444	--
Rafael Palmeiro	.239	104	.342	9	.273	72	.278	48	.196	125	.200	108	.333	62	.625	--
Ryne Sandberg	.294	31	.295	36	.300	35	.289	36	.234	107	.212	97	.347	52	.500	91
Jim Sundberg	.194	133	.220	--	.206	--	.197	--	.179	--	.111	--	.323	--	.400	125
Manny Trillo	.340	4	.180	--	.348	5	.235	111	.292	46	.167	--	.391	17	.538	84
Chico Walker	.154	--	.275	--	.153	--	.261	--	.125	--	.077	--	.286	113	.714	--
Team Average	.266	4	.260	6	.273	3	.256	9	.239	11	.218	12	.319	8	.515	10
League Average	.260		.261		.265		.256		.258		.241		.324		.554	

Pitching vs. Left and Right Handed Batters

		BA	Rank	SA	Rank	OBA	Rank	HR %	Rank	BB %	Rank	SO %	Rank
Frank DiPino	vs. Lefties	.245	37	.340	27	.284	11	2.13	53	4.76	7	21.90	12
	vs. Righties	.256	58	.379	41	.346	91	2.46	41	12.18	104	15.97	64
Les Lancaster	vs. Lefties	.318	107	.481	102	.379	97	3.03	90	9.36	52	10.37	83
	vs. Righties	.215	17	.327	18	.280	21	2.39	37	8.24	72	16.85	53
Ed Lynch	vs. Lefties	.332	109	.534	111	.411	107	2.88	86	11.30	78	12.55	65
	vs. Righties	.262	67	.446	89	.324	68	4.72	104	8.11	63	19.31	35
Greg Maddux	vs. Lefties	.323	108	.487	104	.403	106	2.35	61	11.79	86	12.56	64
	vs. Righties	.259	63	.409	61	.336	79	3.28	71	9.00	83	16.72	54
Jamie Moyer	vs. Lefties	.222	12	.398	58	.336	53	4.63	109	13.74	103	11.45	76
	vs. Righties	.278	88	.433	81	.355	95	3.44	76	10.29	94	17.19	50
Dickie Noles	vs. Lefties	.291	87	.417	70	.359	78	0.79	5	9.72	56	10.42	82
	vs. Righties	.183	--	.242	--	.290	--	0.00	--	9.22	--	12.77	--
Scott Sanderson	vs. Lefties	.293	90	.472	98	.365	87	3.40	97	10.14	62	12.33	66
	vs. Righties	.249	48	.465	96	.289	29	4.90	106	4.89	10	22.93	13
Lee Smith	vs. Lefties	.270	63	.399	60	.360	79	1.69	36	12.20	91	22.93	10
	vs. Righties	.247	43	.308	11	.281	22	0.68	5	4.52	5	31.61	2
Rick Sutcliffe	vs. Lefties	.262	53	.420	72	.357	76	2.60	74	12.37	94	17.01	37
	vs. Righties	.240	37	.378	40	.299	34	2.86	52	7.91	59	17.44	46
Steve Trout	vs. Lefties	.310	--	.448	--	.375	--	0.00	--	6.25	--	18.75	--
	vs. Righties	.254	55	.327	17	.320	61	1.21	9	9.06	85	9.42	106
Team Average	vs. Lefties	.297	12	.464	12	.374	12	2.83	11	10.84	10	14.47	6
	vs. Righties	.259	9	.395	6	.330	11	2.90	6	9.27	12	17.58	5
League Average	vs. Lefties	.268		.404		.341		2.34		9.74		14.31	
	vs. Righties	.255		.403		.319		3.05		8.16		16.61	

Pitching with Runners on Base and Bases Empty

		BA	Rank	SA	Rank	OBA	Rank	HR %	Rank	BB %	Rank	SO %	Rank
Frank DiPino	Runners On	.264	59	.361	33	.341	67	1.39	20	10.92	77	17.24	37
	Bases Empty	.242	38	.373	44	.314	53	3.27	81	8.88	80	18.34	30
Les Lancaster	Runners On	.264	58	.423	73	.333	52	3.64	94	9.73	58	12.45	76
	Bases Empty	.271	84	.393	62	.330	76	2.03	30	8.10	64	14.33	70
Ed Lynch	Runners On	.286	92	.486	100	.373	99	3.81	95	12.15	94	13.36	72
	Bases Empty	.303	105	.489	103	.359	100	3.90	91	7.17	48	18.73	29
Greg Maddux	Runners On	.301	100	.486	101	.383	105	3.50	89	11.41	83	11.71	90
	Bases Empty	.289	96	.422	81	.364	102	2.13	33	9.78	91	16.85	42
Jamie Moyer	Runners On	.267	64	.446	85	.358	90	4.11	100	11.84	89	12.32	80
	Bases Empty	.274	86	.414	77	.348	98	3.22	79	9.90	93	19.79	26
Dickie Noles	Runners On	.248	35	.331	20	.338	63	0.83	11	9.72	57	6.94	112
	Bases Empty	.230	22	.333	15	.312	50	0.00	1	9.22	85	16.31	52
Scott Sanderson	Runners On	.250	38	.417	69	.328	40	3.07	77	10.53	71	17.29	35
	Bases Empty	.290	97	.504	106	.337	81	4.69	107	6.03	18	16.44	47
Lee Smith	Runners On	.253	43	.312	12	.339	65	0.00	1	11.22	81	28.06	2
	Bases Empty	.266	73	.409	72	.311	48	2.60	55	6.10	23	25.00	4
Rick Sutcliffe	Runners On	.265	61	.403	60	.361	95	2.06	40	13.08	102	15.74	51
	Bases Empty	.244	45	.401	68	.313	51	3.13	77	8.68	76	18.20	32
Steve Trout	Runners On	.252	42	.311	10	.305	15	0.84	13	7.58	18	9.09	106
	Bases Empty	.266	71	.361	28	.341	88	1.27	7	9.66	89	11.36	99
Team Average	Runners On	.279	11	.427	9	.359	11	2.80	8	10.99	12	14.32	7
	Bases Empty	.272	12	.423	10	.341	12	2.92	8	9.04	12	17.90	3
League Average	Runners On	.267		.410		.341		2.66		9.88		14.92	
	Bases Empty	.256		.399		.319		2.82		7.98		16.22	

Overall Pitching Compared to Late Inning Pressure Situations

		BA	Rank	SA	Rank	OBA	Rank	HR %	Rank	BB %	Rank	SO %	Rank
Jay Baller	Overall	.325	--	.496	--	.423	--	3.42	--	14.39	--	19.42	--
	Pressure	.211	16	.289	12	.388	96	2.63	65	22.00	111	24.00	14
Frank DiPino	Overall	.253	51	.367	37	.327	62	2.36	45	9.91	80	17.78	28
	Pressure	.224	25	.291	14	.293	21	1.49	40	8.44	39	19.48	36
Les Lancaster	Overall	.268	76	.406	64	.332	69	2.72	64	8.82	62	13.49	76
	Pressure	.235	33	.353	40	.333	53	2.94	73	12.82	90	5.13	108
Ed Lynch	Overall	.295	107	.488	109	.366	106	3.85	103	9.64	77	16.06	49
	Pressure	.364	107	.675	109	.430	104	6.49	104	8.89	48	10.00	95
Greg Maddux	Overall	.294	106	.452	99	.373	110	2.76	68	10.56	95	14.41	69
	Pressure	.274	73	.468	91	.348	69	4.84	94	10.14	64	15.94	58
Jamie Moyer	Overall	.271	81	.428	80	.353	97	3.61	98	10.79	98	16.35	44
	Pressure	.325	101	.578	104	.434	106	6.02	100	14.71	104	4.90	109
Dickie Noles	Overall	.239	18	.332	9	.325	54	0.40	1	9.47	72	11.58	96
	Pressure	.237	34	.290	13	.304	30	0.00	1	8.57	43	10.48	90
Scott Sanderson	Overall	.274	87	.469	106	.333	75	4.04	105	7.92	36	16.80	40
	Pressure	.230	29	.410	73	.304	31	4.92	96	8.45	40	18.31	42
Lee Smith	Overall	.259	62	.358	27	.326	57	1.23	7	8.89	63	26.67	4
	Pressure	.282	81	.387	63	.360	80	1.26	30	10.70	70	26.20	9
Rick Sutcliffe	Overall	.252	50	.402	60	.332	72	2.71	60	10.47	92	17.19	65
	Pressure	.250	46	.382	60	.363	82	1.32	35	14.13	100	17.39	47
Steve Trout	Overall	.260	63	.339	15	.326	56	1.08	4	8.77	59	10.39	105
	Pressure	.444	--	.556	--	.400	--	0.00	--	0.00	--	9.09	--
Team Average	Overall	.275	11	.425	11	.349	12	2.87	7	9.95	12	16.23	6
	Pressure	.271	10	.403	9	.357	11	2.52	7	11.30	9	16.86	8
League Average	Overall	.261		.404		.328		2.75		8.83		15.64	
	Pressure	.260		.391		.337		2.47		10.04		17.14	

Additional Miscellaneous Pitching Comparisons

	Grass Surface		Artificial Surface		Home Games		Road Games		Runners in Scoring Position		Runners in Scoring Pos and Two Outs		Leading Off Inning	
	BA	Rank	BA	Rank	BA	Rank	BA	Rank	BA	Rank	BA	Rank	OBA	Rank
Frank DiPino	.235	24	.300	--	.214	14	.294	91	.279	81	.261	77	.235	6
Drew Hall	.330	110	.256	--	.321	--	.288	--	.354	--	.368	--	.448	--
Les Lancaster	.251	44	.314	103	.255	55	.283	79	.235	35	.145	10	.353	88
Ed Lynch	.316	108	.240	25	.295	101	.294	93	.294	91	.222	48	.346	85
Greg Maddux	.287	90	.311	101	.275	88	.313	106	.305	99	.321	101	.290	18
Mike Mason	.302	101	.304	--	.308	--	.299	--	.315	--	.053	--	.526	--
Jamie Moyer	.269	68	.274	73	.259	64	.283	80	.299	93	.309	97	.367	94
Dickie Noles	.223	17	.272	--	.218	18	.267	57	.266	73	.270	80	.323	60
Scott Sanderson	.258	58	.318	105	.289	99	.264	53	.242	45	.155	16	.309	42
Lee Smith	.280	82	.217	13	.309	109	.215	12	.257	64	.185	25	.275	13
Rick Sutcliffe	.242	30	.280	81	.248	40	.257	48	.234	34	.282	87	.313	46
Steve Trout	.260	59	.261	--	.237	30	.310	--	.152	--	.194	--	.338	76
Team Average	.272	9	.283	11	.269	10	.281	12	.275	10	.252	8	.335	8
League Average	.260		.261		.256		.265		.258		.241		.324	

CINCINNATI REDS

We've heard Pete Rose called a lot of things during his quarter-century as a major-league player and manager; *patient* is not one of them. But in three full seasons as manager of the Cincinnati Reds, Rose has led his team to three consecutive second-place finishes, patiently allowing three different teams to pass through the revolving door to the National League West title—Los Angeles in 1985, Houston in 1986, and San Francisco last season—while his team laid the groundwork for an assault on the division title well into the 1990s.

If you eliminate the 1981 season from consideration, the Reds are only the 10th team in modern major-league history to finish second for three years running, and only the second to play runner-up to three consecutive different champions. The Giants of the late 1960s finished second for five straight seasons, under three different champions from 1967 through 1969 (the Dodgers, Cardinals, and Braves respectively). The 10 teams with three straight second-place finishes:

Team	Years	Next 3 Seasons		
New York Yankees	1933–1935	1	1	1
St. Louis Cardinals	1947–1949	5	3	3
Cleveland Indians	1951–1953	1	2	2
Chicago White Sox	1963–1965	4	4	8
San Francisco Giants	1965–1967	2	2	3
San Francisco Giants	1966–1968	2	3	1
San Francisco Giants	1967–1969	3	1	5
Baltimore Orioles	1975–1977	4	1	2
Pittsburgh Pirates	1976–1978	1	3	4
Cincinnati Reds	1985–1987	—	—	—

Although most of those teams won a division or league title shortly after their three-year apprenticeships as runners-up, none since the Yankees of the late 1930s has parlayed that experience into an extended period at the top of the heap. Still, even in the current baseball environment of constant upheaval among division champions, we think that what the Reds have accomplished during the past three seasons will pay off handsomely over the next few years.

Consider the sorry condition that Rose faced when he rejoined the Reds in August 1984 as player-manager: a fifth-place team, 21 games behind the division leader, following consecutive last-place finishes. To make matters worse, Dave Concepcion (36 years old at the time) and Dan Driessen (33) remained from the great Reds teams of a decade earlier; their presence and the absence of young talent combined to give Cincinnati one of the National league's oldest lineups. And

the moves that Rose's Reds made in his first year on the job only exacerbated that situation: Bo Diaz was 35 and Buddy Bell 33 when they joined Cincinnati in 1985. Of course, Pete also awarded himself the starting first base spot, making Cincinnati's 1985 starting lineup the oldest of any National League team since the 1983 Philadelphia Phillies, who won a pennant and then disintegrated.

Actually, Reds fans could hardly object to the developments, since their team had made a startling turnaround (1985 was the first of their three consecutive second-place finishes). But the Reds had gambled that their old-timers would survive until some promising minor leaguers reached Riverfront.

The gamble worked. Over the past three seasons, Cincinnati phased Rose, Driessen, and Concepcion out of its starting lineup, as well as Eddie Milner, Ron Oester, and, for the 1988 season, Dave Parker. Despite that loss of experience and talent, the Reds have maintained their position in the standings by adding to their lineup some of the most promising young players in the majors: Eric Davis, Kal Daniels, Barry Larkin, Tracy Jones, and Kurt Stillwell among them.

The following table shows how Cincinnati has managed to cut an average of three years per player from its starting lineup over the past two seasons without significantly harming its performance on the field. The ages are weighted by plate appearances, so that those who played regularly contribute a proportionately larger slice to the pie than part-timers:

Year	W	L	Pct.	Pos.	Age	Rank
1984	70	92	.432	5th	30.0	3d
1985	89	72	.553	2d	32.5	1st
1986	86	76	.531	2d	31.5	1st
1987	84	78	.519	2d	29.3	4th

So the Reds find themselves in an unusual position as the 1988 season begins. The team responded to three years of failure (from 1981 through 1983) with a highly successful rebuilding program, during which Cincinnati actually compiled the best overall record in its division. Parker's departure signals the end of that transition, but also raises the question of whether the Reds can absorb the loss of the National League's RBI leader over the past three seasons without an impact on the team's performance. Despite their consistency over the past three years, the Reds haven't given their fans a pennant race to speak of. (Cincinnati hasn't come closer than four games behind the division leader during any of the past three Septembers.) So if, after three seasons as bridesmaids, the Reds don't reach the altar themselves this year, it will be interesting to see if the team's fans can muster the same patience as its front office.

The Two-Headed MVP

Which of the three outfield positions was Cincinnati's most productive last season? Was it right field? Dave Parker hit 26 home runs and drove in 97 runs. Or how about center field? Eric Davis hit more home runs (37) with more RBIs (100) while batting 40 points higher than Parker (.293).

Actually, Cincinnati's left-field platoon of Kal Daniels against right-handed pitchers and Tracy Jones against left-handers accumulated better numbers than Parker or Davis. The following table compares the composite statistics of the Reds' starters at each of the three outfield positions last season. Davis accounted for 123 of the 162 games started in center, and Parker for 141 starts in right. Daniels started 93 games in left field, and Jones started 42:

Position	AB	R	H	HR	RBI	BA	SA	OBA
Left fielders	618	120	209	33	90	.338	.571	.422
Center fielders	613	134	172	40	119	.281	.543	.370
Right fielders	629	78	156	28	102	.248	.431	.305

No contest. Daniels and Jones put together a season that looks good even when compared with Davis and Parker, and great when judged against the league standard. Here's how Cincinnati's left-field platoon stacked up against the average of the starting left fielders for the other 11 National League teams:

	AB	R	H	HR	RBI	BA	SA	OBA
Reds left fielders	618	120	209	33	90	.338	.571	.422
Other N.L. teams	608	92	170	19	73	.279	.437	.350

Compared to the starters at each position on every N.L. club Cincinnati's left fielders matched up well against the best of the National League in almost every statistical category. They ranked second in batting average to San Diego's right fielders (predominantly Tony Gwynn); third in slugging average; third in on-base average; third in extra-base hits; seventh in runs; and ninth in home runs.

If that sounds like an MVP performance to you, you're absolutely right. The Daniels-Jones tandem compares favorably with both of last season's league MVPs, especially when you consider that Rose's decision to bat his left fielders in the leadoff position is partially responsible for their RBI deficit:

	AB	R	H	HR	RBI	BA	SA	OBA
Reds left fielders	618	120	209	33	90	.338	.571	.422
George Bell	610	111	188	47	134	.308	.604	.351
Andre Dawson	621	90	178	49	137	.286	.568	.327

The 1988 season will provide a stiff test for both Daniels and Jones. The loss of Parker will give both a shot at the full-time status that they've craved during their two previous seasons with Cincinnati.

But Jones hasn't hit right-handed pitchers with nearly the authority that he's shown against southpaws. His two-year batting average of .341 against left-handed pitchers ranks ninth in the majors during that period (minimum 200 at bats). But against right-handed pitchers, who accounted for 67 percent of all pitchers that batters faced in the National League last season, Jones has a career batting average of .258 with five home runs in 190 at bats.

Daniels has been nearly as feeble against left-handers as he's been overwhelming against righties. During his first two seasons in the majors, Daniels has hit .363 against right-handers. Only one player, Boston's Wade Boggs, had a higher mark during that time (minimum 400 at bats). But Daniels is on the far side of the Mendoza Line against southpaws, with a .194 batting average and only one home run in 108 at bats.

To approximate the effect of facing all types of pitching, we've compiled figures for hypothetical 600-plate appearance seasons for both Daniels and Jones. Their career statistics have been pro-rated for 196 plate appearances against lefties and 404 against righties, representing the average National League distribution for the 1987 season. Here's what the totals look like:

Player	AB	H	2B	3B	HR	RRF	BB	SO	BA	SA	OBA
Daniels	519	159	31	4	26	73	74	92	.306	.532	.397
Jones	555	158	23	3	14	40	34	59	.285	.413	.310

Daniels should fare better on an everyday basis than Jones, even if he never hits .200 against southpaws. The solid majority of right-handed pitchers guarantees his success, but presents an obstacle to Jones. Regardless, it appears that Cincinnati has two reliable starting outfielders with the potential to become outstanding players given the time to adjust. But in promoting Daniels and Jones to everyday status, the Reds will forfeit major-league baseball's undisputed M.V.P.—as in Most Valuable Platoon.

A Left-Handed Complement

Over a three-month period last year, the Reds made a pair of trades for pitchers with a notable common trait: both were left-handers who spent their entire careers in the American League.

Dennis Rasmussen was acquired from the Yankees in August for Bill Gullickson. (Actually, Rasmussen pitched 14 innings for San Diego in 1983, but has been an American Leaguer since then.) Danny Jackson was acquired from the Royals over the winter for Ted Power. Both trades involved a swap of right-handed starters for left-handers, and they brought to mind the recent success of American League southpaws who had migrated to the senior circuit.

Last season, Neal Heaton joined the Montreal Expos and posted a 13–10 record, far better than the mark of 8–15 he'd compiled a year earlier for the Cleveland Indians and Minnesota Twins. In 1986, Bob Ojeda was the winningest pitcher on the New York Mets' championship team, going 18–5 following a 9–11 season for the Boston Red Sox in 1985. And, of course, John Tudor has blossomed into one of baseball's top starters following his departure from the American League.

On the other hand, starting pitchers are rarely traded after good seasons. Did those turnarounds simply represent the pendulum swinging back after the mediocre seasons that prompted the trades? The following table lists all American League left-handers who made at least 15 starts in any of the past seven seasons (at least 10 in 1981) and then joined National League teams to start the next season:

Years	Player	Last AL Season	First NL Season
1981–1982	Ross Baumgarten	5–9	0–5
1981–1982	Dan Schatzeder	6–8	1–4
1982–1983	Steve Trout	6–9	10–14
1983–1984	Jerry Koosman	11–7	14–15
1983–1984	John Tudor	13–12	12–11
1984–1985	Ray Fontenot	8–9	6–10
1985–1986	Bob Ojeda	9–11	18–5
1986–1987	Neal Heaton	8–15	13–10

Those eight pitchers had a composite record of 66–80 in their final seasons in the American League, and raised that mark to the .500 level in their first National League seasons (74–74). How does that compare to right-handers who also switched from the American to the National League?

Eleven right-handed pitchers qualified according to the same criteria as those we established for the southpaws listed above (Joe Cowley, Storm Davis, Doug Drabek, and Tim Leary in 1987; Ray Burris in 1986; LaMarr Hoyt and Lary Sorensen in 1985; Chuck Rainey and Mike Torrez in 1983; Rich Gale and Ferguson Jenkins in 1982). A comparison of the totals by each group of pitchers in the seasons before and after they switched leagues:

From A.L. to N.L.	Before			After			
	W	L	Pct.	W	L	Pct.	Diff.
Left-handed pitchers	66	80	.452	74	74	.500	+.048
Right-handed pitchers	94	115	.450	84	113	.426	−.023

The two groups were nearly identical in the seasons prior to their trades. But right-handed pitchers declined by half the degree to which left-handers improved, suggesting that American League southpaws have a distinct advantage in their first seasons in the National League.

Although that trend has received some attention over the past few seasons—primarily due to the success of Tudor and Ojeda—few have noticed that right-handed pitchers have a corresponding edge travelling in the opposite direction. Three qualifying left-handers moved from the N.L. to the A.L. over the past six years: Vida Blue (in 1982), Bob Shirley (in 1983), and Tim Lollar (in 1985). Compare their results to those of 17 right-handers who made that journey (Doyle Alexander, Bill Caudill, Gaylord Perry, Lary Sorensen, and Ed Whitson in 1982; Doug Bird and Juan Eichelberger in 1983; Ray Burris, Phil Niekro, and Tom Seaver in 1984; Jeff Russell, Walt Terrell, and Whitson in 1985; Joaquin Andujar in 1986; Dennis Eckersley, Charles Hudson, and Rick Rhoden in 1987):

From N.L. to A.L.	Before			After			
	W	L	Pct.	W	L	Pct.	Diff.
Left-handed pitchers	27	32	.458	26	30	.464	−.007
Right-handed pitchers	160	184	.465	160	146	.523	+.058

Based on the results of past interleague trades involving starting pitchers, Rasmussen and Jackson are likely to satisfy both the Cincinnati front office and its fans. But don't be surprised if Ted Power contributes even more to Kansas City's chances than Cincinnati's two new southpaws contribute to the Reds'.

WON-LOST RECORD BY STARTING POSITION

CINCINNATI 84-78	C	1B	2B	3B	SS	LF	CF	RF	P	Leadoff	Relief	Starts
Buddy Bell	-	-	-	77-64	-	-	-	-	-	-	-	77-64
Tom Browning	-	-	-	-	-	-	-	-	18-13	-	0-1	18-13
Sal Butera	2-1	-	-	-	-	-	-	-	-	-	-	2-1
Dave Collins	-	-	-	-	-	6-2	0-1	-	-	6-2	-	6-3
Dave Concepcion	-	9-6	20-21	2-6	1-1	-	-	-	-	-	-	32-34
Kal Daniels	-	-	-	-	-	49-44	-	-	-	41-33	-	49-44
Eric Davis	-	-	-	-	-	1-3	65-58	-	-	-	-	66-61
Bo Diaz	67-63	-	-	-	-	-	-	-	-	-	-	67-63
Nick Esasky	-	45-47	-	-	-	-	-	-	-	-	-	45-47
John Franco	-	-	-	-	-	-	-	-	-	-	53-15	-
Terry Francona	-	21-20	-	-	-	-	-	0-1	-	-	-	21-21
Leo Garcia	-	-	-	-	-	-	2-2	-	-	2-2	-	2-2
Bill Gullickson	-	-	-	-	-	-	-	-	14-13	-	-	14-13
Guy Hoffman	-	-	-	-	-	-	-	-	10-12	-	4-10	10-12
Tom Hume	-	-	-	-	-	-	-	-	-	-	3-8	-
Tracy Jones	-	-	-	-	-	21-21	14-12	6-5	-	18-23	-	41-38
Bill Landrum	-	-	-	-	-	-	-	-	1-1	-	15-27	1-1
Barry Larkin	-	-	-	-	58-56	-	-	-	-	12-14	-	58-56
Lloyd McClendon	2-4	2-1	-	-	-	0-1	-	-	-	-	-	4-6
Terry McGriff	13-10	-	-	-	-	-	-	-	-	-	-	13-10
Jeff Montgomery	-	-	-	-	-	-	-	-	0-1	-	3-10	0-1
Rob Murphy	-	-	-	-	-	-	-	-	-	-	46-41	-
Paul O'Neill	-	1-1	-	-	-	7-7	3-4	4-5	-	-	0-1	15-17
Ron Oester	-	-	38-28	-	-	-	-	-	-	-	-	38-28
Pat Pacillo	-	-	-	-	-	-	-	-	4-3	-	3-2	4-3
Dave Parker	-	6-3	-	-	-	-	-	74-67	-	-	-	80-70
Pat Perry	-	-	-	-	-	-	-	-	-	-	6-6	-
Ted Power	-	-	-	-	-	-	-	-	18-16	-	-	18-16
Dennis Rasmussen	-	-	-	-	-	-	-	-	6-1	-	-	6-1
Jerry Reuss	-	-	-	-	-	-	-	-	0-7	-	-	0-7
Ron Robinson	-	-	-	-	-	-	-	-	10-8	-	17-13	10-8
Bill Scherrer	-	-	-	-	-	-	-	-	-	-	3-20	-
Mario Soto	-	-	-	-	-	-	-	-	3-3	-	-	3-3
Kurt Stillwell	-	-	14-20	5-8	25-21	-	-	-	-	5-3	-	44-49
Jeff Treadway	-	12-9	-	-	-	-	-	-	-	-	-	12-9
Max Venable	-	-	-	-	-	0-1	-	-	-	0-1	-	0-1
Frank Williams	-	-	-	-	-	-	-	-	-	-	41-44	-

Batting vs. Left and Right Handed Pitchers

		BA	Rank	SA	Rank	OBA	Rank	HR %	Rank	BB %	Rank	SO %	Rank
Buddy Bell	vs. Lefties	.261	82	.430	69	.367	38	4.93	26	14.46	18	7.23	15
	vs. Righties	.292	36	.424	57	.370	29	2.63	62	10.90	38	6.26	6
Dave Concepcion	vs. Lefties	.340	13	.420	73	.392	21	0.67	110	8.43	72	6.63	10
	vs. Righties	.295	31	.341	105	.361	38	0.00	126	9.66	58	8.97	17
Kal Daniels	vs. Lefties	.197	130	.289	122	.291	115	1.32	96	10.34	41	19.54	117
	vs. Righties	.370	2	.702	1	.464	1	8.56	2	14.87	8	13.12	59
Eric Davis	vs. Lefties	.340	12	.741	1	.440	9	11.56	1	15.43	12	20.57	122
	vs. Righties	.272	67	.526	18	.380	21	6.12	9	14.73	9	25.32	133
Bo Diaz	vs. Lefties	.355	6	.529	26	.383	30	2.90	69	4.64	116	13.25	68
	vs. Righties	.237	109	.380	87	.268	130	3.07	57	3.17	133	13.98	71
Nick Esasky	vs. Lefties	.253	93	.505	34	.370	35	6.59	13	15.74	10	20.37	121
	vs. Righties	.278	58	.537	14	.310	98	6.27	10	4.44	123	20.00	114
Terry Francona	vs. Lefties	.053	--	.053	--	.143	--	0.00	--	9.52	--	9.52	--
	vs. Righties	.245	102	.319	118	.279	119	1.60	90	4.04	127	5.05	3
Tracy Jones	vs. Lefties	.349	8	.521	29	.405	17	2.96	67	8.95	64	8.95	32
	vs. Righties	.237	110	.363	101	.265	131	2.63	62	3.00	134	11.50	41
Barry Larkin	vs. Lefties	.275	65	.450	57	.349	55	3.82	52	9.59	46	8.22	27
	vs. Righties	.231	115	.338	107	.288	112	2.27	74	6.43	105	11.70	42
Paul O'Neill	vs. Lefties	.091	--	.182	--	.167	--	0.00	--	8.33	--	25.00	--
	vs. Righties	.268	74	.510	23	.343	62	4.70	23	10.24	52	15.66	84
Ron Oester	vs. Lefties	.200	129	.217	134	.262	128	0.00	113	7.69	80	30.77	135
	vs. Righties	.271	69	.418	62	.335	67	1.13	105	8.67	72	15.82	85
Dave Parker	vs. Lefties	.239	105	.410	80	.285	121	3.90	48	4.07	120	20.36	120
	vs. Righties	.260	83	.445	45	.324	82	4.69	24	8.22	79	13.85	69
Kurt Stillwell	vs. Lefties	.227	116	.289	123	.286	119	0.00	113	5.71	104	15.24	87
	vs. Righties	.268	74	.403	69	.325	81	1.34	97	7.93	88	10.37	28
Team Average	vs. Lefties	.269	4	.426	4	.339	5	3.38	4	9.08	6	16.03	8
	vs. Righties	.265	3	.427	3	.326	7	3.49	3	7.97	10	14.54	2
League Average	vs. Lefties	.263		.409		.332		2.81		9.08		15.22	
	vs. Righties	.260		.401		.327		2.73		8.70		15.85	

Batting with Runners on Base and Bases Empty

		BA	Rank	SA	Rank	OBA	Rank	HR %	Rank	BB %	Rank	SO %	Rank
Buddy Bell	Runners On	.282	67	.454	52	.369	46	3.70	40	12.00	37	8.40	20
	Bases Empty	.284	44	.405	72	.369	27	2.94	62	11.82	16	5.19	4
Dave Concepcion	Runners On	.346	5	.392	86	.397	28	0.00	122	8.84		5.44	6
	Bases Empty	.295	33	.376	94	.360	33	0.67	117	9.15	45	9.76	23
Kal Daniels	Runners On	.307	33	.520	15	.429	8	3.94	35	16.77	11	13.55	70
	Bases Empty	.349	3	.668	1	.429	2	8.71	3	12.36	12	14.91	76
Eric Davis	Runners On	.286	60	.606	5	.410	21	7.39	6	17.93	8	25.90	136
	Bases Empty	.299	29	.583	5	.389	15	8.12	7	12.54	11	22.19	125
Bo Diaz	Runners On	.290	52	.512	22	.322	104	4.61	25	4.58	124	10.83	39
	Bases Empty	.254	83	.351	105	.283	116	1.79	91	2.76	135	16.21	90
Nick Esasky	Runners On	.297	46	.635	4	.367	47	8.11	3	10.12	65	20.24	124
	Bases Empty	.253	88	.449	50	.295	101	5.05	27	5.71	106	20.00	114
Terry Francona	Runners On	.202	131	.234	135	.250	130	1.06	106	4.95	120	3.96	4
	Bases Empty	.248	93	.345	108	.280	119	1.77	92	4.24	124	6.78	8
Tracy Jones	Runners On	.308	31	.415	72	.345	79	2.31	75	5.52	117	12.41	56
	Bases Empty	.279	52	.450	49	.327	71	3.06	60	6.12	102	8.98	15
Barry Larkin	Runners On	.290	53	.443	60	.354	45	3.28	45	8.06	93	6.16	10
	Bases Empty	.211	123	.320	114	.271	126	2.34	76	6.86	80	14.08	69
Ron Oester	Runners On	.266	80	.394	85	.350	73	0.92	113	11.20	51	17.60	111
	Bases Empty	.242	102	.344	109	.287	110	0.78	114	5.88	104	21.32	124
Dave Parker	Runners On	.281	70	.489	30	.350	72	5.40	13	8.83	83	15.77	94
	Bases Empty	.228	118	.383	88	.273	123	3.54	52	4.85	117	16.36	91
Kurt Stillwell	Runners On	.299	40	.459	47	.353	65	1.91	83	7.43	105	14.29	83
	Bases Empty	.231	112	.319	115	.291	108	0.42	126	7.36	70	9.69	20
Team Average	Runners On	.280	2	.457	1	.350	3	3.68	1	9.49	9	14.27	3
	Bases Empty	.256	6	.405	6	.314	9	3.29	5	7.38	8	15.52	6
League Average	Runners On	.267		.410		.341		2.66		9.88		14.92	
	Bases Empty	.256		.399		.319		2.82		7.98		16.22	

Overall Batting Compared to Late Inning Pressure Situations

		BA	Rank	SA	Rank	OBA	Rank	HR %	Rank	BB %	Rank	SO %	Rank	RDI %	Rank
Buddy Bell	Overall	.284	53	.425	62	.369	31	3.26	56	11.89	24	6.53	8	.251	94
	Pressure	.269	64	.433	51	.347	66	2.99	46	10.53	53	7.89	12	.222	83
Dave Concepcion	Overall	.319	8	.384	90	.377	24	0.36	129	9.00	61	7.72	10	.330	25
	Pressure	.372	9	.442	47	.426	11	0.00	105	8.33	78	10.42	24	.273	61
Kal Daniels	Overall	.334	3	.617	1	.429	4	7.07	6	13.95	11	14.42	74	.378	2
	Pressure	.373	8	.490	28	.522	1	1.96	76	22.06	3	14.71	60	.364	28
Eric Davis	Overall	.293	31	.593	3	.399	13	7.81	3	14.95	8	23.84	132	.324	28
	Pressure	.203	123	.492	26	.360	54	8.47	4	20.00	5	26.67	134	.296	59
Bo Diaz	Overall	.270	78	.421	66	.300	114	3.02	62	3.58	134	13.77	66	.359	7
	Pressure	.180	128	.262	129	.227	133	1.64	82	4.41	118	20.59	105	.167	111
Nick Esasky	Overall	.272	75	.529	13	.327	82	6.36	11	7.67	86	20.11	126	.250	95
	Pressure	.286	49	.429	53	.375	44	4.08	30	12.28	35	22.81	119	.250	71
Terry Francona	Overall	.227	124	.295	131	.266	132	1.45	100	4.57	128	5.48	5	.155	132
	Pressure	.229	102	.343	99	.270	120	2.86	48	5.26	113	5.26	3	.182	105
Tracy Jones	Overall	.290	38	.437	52	.333	70	2.79	65	5.90	120	10.26	23	.311	42
	Pressure	.278	59	.352	93	.322	84	1.85	79	3.39	123	15.25	64	.368	26
Barry Larkin	Overall	.244	108	.371	97	.306	108	2.73	67	7.38	92	10.66	29	.240	106
	Pressure	.246	86	.295	116	.258	124	1.64	82	1.56	136	15.63	67	.158	116
Paul O'Neill	Overall	.256	--	.488	--	.331	--	4.38	--	10.11	--	16.29	--	.304	49
	Pressure	.273	61	.576	10	.368	49	6.06	11	13.16	29	21.05	110	.368	26
Ron Oester	Overall	.253	95	.367	99	.317	95	0.84	118	8.43	73	19.54	119	.311	39
	Pressure	.257	76	.429	53	.278	113	2.86	48	2.63	127	15.79	69	.500	5
Dave Parker	Overall	.253	96	.433	56	.311	100	4.41	30	6.80	102	16.07	93	.264	87
	Pressure	.240	89	.347	95	.253	125	2.67	59	1.27	137	26.58	133	.192	99
Kurt Stillwell	Overall	.258	91	.375	95	.316	96	1.01	115	7.39	91	11.55	43	.250	95
	Pressure	.242	87	.274	124	.290	104	0.00	105	7.14	97	12.86	41	.273	61
Team Average	Overall	.266	2	.427	4	.330	6	3.45	3	8.30	8	14.98	5	.281	3
	Pressure	.253	9	.370	9	.320	10	2.49	7	8.56	10	17.48	8	.274	3
League Average	Overall	.261		.404		.328		2.75		8.83		15.64		.272	
	Pressure	.258		.385		.331		2.46		9.54		16.95		.261	

Additional Miscellaneous Batting Comparisons

	Grass Surface BA	Rank	Artificial Surface BA	Rank	Home Games BA	Rank	Road Games BA	Rank	Runners in Scoring Position BA	Rank	Runners in Scoring Pos and Two Outs BA	Rank	Leading Off Inning OBA	Rank	Runners on 3B with less than 2 Outs RDI %	Rank
Buddy Bell	.266	74	.292	38	.298	36	.269	67	.288	49	.312	26	.297	104	.474	106
Dave Collins	.353	--	.279	58	.239	--	.359	--	.353	--	.286	--	.400	--	.500	--
Dave Concepcion	.273	63	.337	11	.316	19	.322	10	.368	4	.310	27	.329	72	.500	91
Kal Daniels	.324	11	.341	10	.309	23	.358	2	.316	24	.161	123	.450	2	.810	5
Eric Davis	.306	21	.287	48	.280	66	.306	22	.280	57	.213	96	.442	3	.483	101
Bo Diaz	.245	99	.280	57	.306	25	.234	112	.320	21	.322	19	.315	91	.769	8
Nick Esasky	.292	33	.264	77	.246	105	.303	23	.280	56	.263	61	.296	106	.462	111
Terry Francona	.200	--	.236	108	.227	118	.227	115	.188	127	.115	130	.283	115	.500	--
Tracy Jones	.221	119	.321	17	.300	33	.281	40	.338	8	.289	37	.327	76	.591	62
Barry Larkin	.271	67	.235	111	.237	111	.253	88	.243	97	.190	116	.327	75	.500	91
Paul O'Neill	.379	--	.229	113	.253	97	.260	--	.298	39	.250	69	.281	--	.500	--
Ron Oester	.333	--	.226	117	.232	114	.277	54	.273	66	.318	23	.340	59	.438	116
Dave Parker	.208	128	.272	69	.282	62	.225	118	.244	96	.111	133	.302	103	.600	57
Kurt Stillwell	.225	114	.274	65	.260	88	.257	82	.271	69	.314	24	.333	62	.533	86
Team Average	.255	9	.270	1	.268	6	.263	2	.277	1	.237	8	.330	4	.552	9
League Average	.260		.261		.265		.256		.258		.241		.324		.554	

Pitching vs. Left and Right Handed Batters

		BA	Rank	SA	Rank	OBA	Rank	HR %	Rank	BB %	Rank	SO %	Rank
Tom Browning	vs. Lefties	.267	58	.431	75	.351	72	3.45	98	11.19	77	15.67	41
	vs. Righties	.287	98	.480	101	.340	84	3.89	88	7.00	40	14.61	76
John Franco	vs. Lefties	.239	--	.283	--	.280	--	0.00	--	5.77	--	21.15	--
	vs. Righties	.246	41	.356	27	.308	40	2.27	30	8.22	69	17.12	51
Bill Gullickson	vs. Lefties	.262	52	.479	101	.305	28	5.06	111	5.99	12	9.54	93
	vs. Righties	.272	81	.495	103	.311	44	5.18	107	5.14	14	16.31	60
Guy Hoffman	vs. Lefties	.307	98	.446	83	.388	101	1.98	46	11.11	73	14.53	46
	vs. Righties	.257	61	.449	91	.309	41	3.59	80	6.52	32	12.68	93
Tom Hume	vs. Lefties	.338	111	.490	106	.433	112	1.99	48	14.05	104	5.41	111
	vs. Righties	.226	26	.417	68	.309	42	4.17	95	8.76	81	11.86	100
Bill Landrum	vs. Lefties	.270	64	.380	50	.381	99	2.00	49	14.75	105	12.30	68
	vs. Righties	.308	105	.421	70	.377	105	0.75	7	10.39	95	17.53	45
Rob Murphy	vs. Lefties	.233	24	.308	13	.287	13	0.83	6	6.92	17	25.38	5
	vs. Righties	.242	38	.377	42	.302	36	2.31	35	8.07	61	23.16	12
Pat Pacillo	vs. Lefties	.258	48	.461	91	.362	83	4.49	108	13.08	99	11.21	77
	vs. Righties	.286	--	.508	--	.333	--	4.76	--	7.25	--	15.94	--
Pat Perry	vs. Lefties	.239	31	.370	40	.268	8	1.09	16	2.04	1	10.20	85
	vs. Righties	.190	5	.330	19	.277	20	3.00	61	10.18	91	12.83	91
Ted Power	vs. Lefties	.285	82	.440	79	.347	67	2.59	73	9.26	48	14.95	45
	vs. Righties	.247	44	.437	86	.302	37	4.56	100	6.55	33	15.05	72
Dennis Rasmussen	vs. Lefties	.111	--	.222	--	.200	--	0.00	--	9.09	--	27.27	--
	vs. Righties	.236	33	.385	43	.287	27	3.11	67	6.25	30	20.45	30
Ron Robinson	vs. Lefties	.292	89	.456	89	.341	59	1.82	41	7.49	23	9.77	91
	vs. Righties	.223	22	.370	34	.271	17	2.95	57	6.04	28	20.85	27
Mario Soto	vs. Lefties	.274	70	.452	88	.337	54	3.57	100	8.60	36	7.53	107
	vs. Righties	.289	--	.605	--	.357	--	10.53	--	8.89	--	8.89	--
Frank Williams	vs. Lefties	.235	26	.271	4	.318	38	0.00	1	10.94	67	13.02	59
	vs. Righties	.269	77	.427	77	.325	71	2.20	28	7.09	43	13.78	82
Team Average	vs. Lefties	.275	9	.424	9	.340	8	2.53	9	9.08	3	13.18	8
	vs. Righties	.263	10	.432	12	.318	7	3.36	10	7.12	2	15.82	8
League Average	vs. Lefties	.268		.404		.341		2.34		9.74		14.31	
	vs. Righties	.255		.403		.319		3.05		8.16		16.61	

Pitching with Runners on Base and Bases Empty

		BA	Rank	SA	Rank	OBA	Rank	HR %	Rank	BB %	Rank	SO %	Rank
Tom Browning	Runners On	.258	54	.426	75	.327	37	3.36	86	8.60	25	11.75	87
	Bases Empty	.302	104	.505	107	.353	99	4.15	95	7.01	45	17.19	41
John Franco	Runners On	.257	51	.321	17	.338	62	0.71	9	10.91	76	17.58	31
	Bases Empty	.235	31	.365	30	.274	7	2.94	71	5.03	10	17.88	38
Bill Gullickson	Runners On	.272	72	.494	105	.307	16	4.53	106	5.19	4	10.37	96
	Bases Empty	.264	70	.483	102	.308	43	5.47	109	5.84	17	14.25	73
Guy Hoffman	Runners On	.284	90	.534	111	.350	82	4.31	103	8.46	24	11.03	93
	Bases Empty	.254	62	.395	66	.305	37	2.70	61	6.55	32	14.36	69
Tom Hume	Runners On	.234	24	.392	53	.352	85	2.53	57	12.94	99	6.97	111
	Bases Empty	.323	110	.509	109	.388	110	3.73	89	9.55	88	10.67	104
Bill Landrum	Runners On	.296	98	.417	70	.390	110	0.87	16	13.29	104	15.38	56
	Bases Empty	.288	95	.390	61	.368	107	1.69	20	11.28	101	15.04	63
Rob Murphy	Runners On	.250	38	.336	21	.318	26	0.00	1	9.36	48	22.81	10
	Bases Empty	.232	24	.368	33	.283	15	3.07	74	6.56	33	24.59	6
Pat Perry	Runners On	.231	20	.423	74	.302	13	3.85	96	9.24	45	12.61	75
	Bases Empty	.191	5	.298	6	.259	4	1.60	16	6.83	38	11.71	98
Ted Power	Runners On	.267	64	.428	80	.332	51	3.52	90	9.16	40	16.28	64
	Bases Empty	.267	74	.446	88	.322	68	3.50	85	7.09	47	13.97	77
Ron Robinson	Runners On	.276	77	.448	87	.343	69	1.81	34	9.92	62	11.83	85
	Bases Empty	.243	42	.388	59	.279	13	2.79	64	4.52	8	18.09	54
Frank Williams	Runners On	.272	72	.383	41	.360	93	0.62	7	11.34	82	9.28	104
	Bases Empty	.243	40	.345	19	.294	25	1.70	21	6.75	35	16.67	44
Team Average	Runners On	.276	10	.433	11	.341	7	2.51	4	9.00	3	13.79	9
	Bases Empty	.262	8	.427	11	.315	4	3.45	12	6.95	2	15.67	7
League Average	Runners On	.267		.410		.341		2.66		9.88		14.92	
	Bases Empty	.256		.399		.319		2.82		7.98		16.22	

Overall Pitching Compared to Late Inning Pressure Situations

		BA	Rank	SA	Rank	OBA	Rank	HR %	Rank	BB %	Rank	SO %	Rank
Tom Browning	Overall	.284	99	.472	107	.342	87	3.81	101	7.71	29	14.79	64
	Pressure	.357	106	.536	101	.419	103	3.57	86	9.09	53	9.09	100
John Franco	Overall	.245	33	.345	21	.304	22	1.94	24	7.85	33	17.73	29
	Pressure	.234	31	.322	20	.313	40	1.46	38	10.21	65	16.60	55
Bill Gullickson	Overall	.267	73	.487	108	.308	26	5.12	111	5.59	6	12.75	85
	Pressure	.321	--	.393	--	.345	--	0.00	--	3.33	--	6.67	--
Guy Hoffman	Overall	.266	71	.449	95	.323	50	3.32	83	7.32	23	13.00	84
	Pressure	.219	21	.406	70	.219	3	3.13	79	0.00	1	24.24	13
Tom Hume	Overall	.279	92	.451	98	.369	107	3.13	78	11.35	104	8.71	109
	Pressure	.385	102	.538	102	.500	110	0.00	1	13.21	92	3.77	110
Bill Landrum	Overall	.292	105	.403	61	.379	112	1.29	9	12.32	108	15.22	58
	Pressure	.234	32	.281	10	.347	67	0.00	1	14.47	101	13.16	72
Rob Murphy	Overall	.239	20	.355	25	.297	14	1.84	23	7.71	28	23.86	6
	Pressure	.260	59	.394	66	.331	52	2.36	56	9.86	60	21.13	25
Pat Perry	Overall	.205	4	.342	17	.274	3	2.40	49	7.72	30	12.04	92
	Pressure	.189	7	.331	25	.275	17	2.36	56	8.97	49	10.34	93
Ted Power	Overall	.267	74	.439	90	.327	59	3.51	93	8.00	39	14.99	62
	Pressure	.293	87	.366	50	.383	95	0.00	1	10.42	67	10.42	92
Ron Robinson	Overall	.256	55	.411	69	.305	23	2.42	50	6.74	16	15.52	56
	Pressure	.295	88	.465	89	.359	79	3.88	90	9.46	57	16.22	57
Frank Williams	Overall	.254	54	.360	29	.322	48	1.26	8	8.74	56	13.45	77
	Pressure	.255	55	.357	42	.335	56	1.27	33	10.33	66	14.13	68
Team Average	Overall	.267	10	.429	12	.326	7	3.06	11	7.84	2	14.85	8
	Pressure	.257	6	.379	4	.331	4	2.03	4	9.61	5	15.39	10
League Average	Overall	.261		.404		.328		2.75		8.83		15.64	
	Pressure	.260		.391		.337		2.47		10.04		17.14	

Additional Miscellaneous Pitching Comparisons

	Grass Surface BA	Rank	Artificial Surface BA	Rank	Home Games BA	Rank	Road Games BA	Rank	Runners in Scoring Position BA	Rank	Runners in Scoring Pos and Two Outs BA	Rank	Leading Off Inning OBA	Rank
Tom Browning	.288	92	.282	83	.263	68	.308	104	.287	86	.225	55	.370	98
John Franco	.186	4	.274	74	.310	110	.190	5	.198	9	.298	94	.297	27
Bill Gullickson	.255	51	.271	67	.282	91	.253	42	.252	58	.243	67	.300	29
Guy Hoffman	.289	95	.255	49	.265	71	.267	57	.289	88	.281	86	.325	63
Tom Hume	.284	87	.277	76	.286	95	.267	59	.233	33	.140	7	.415	111
Bill Landrum	.269	--	.298	94	.292	100	.292	90	.371	112	.321	--	.393	107
Rob Murphy	.265	66	.230	17	.269	76	.202	7	.329	109	.231	60	.234	5
Pat Pacillo	.326	--	.245	33	.216	--	.364	--	.364	--	.400	--	.357	--
Pat Perry	.233	--	.198	7	.190	4	.223	17	.246	--	.107	3	.296	25
Ted Power	.244	33	.278	77	.287	96	.252	41	.277	80	.264	79	.319	53
Dennis Rasmussen	.269	--	.212	12	.189	--	.280	--	.231	--	.125	--	.298	--
Jerry Reuss	.000	--	.354	111	.339	112	.435	--	.390	--	.500	--	.306	--
Ron Robinson	.219	13	.270	65	.283	92	.227	19	.248	56	.197	30	.329	67
Frank Williams	.288	94	.242	28	.250	47	.260	51	.311	105	.351	106	.243	7
Team Average	.265	8	.268	8	.273	11	.262	5	.282	11	.264	11	.324	4
League Average	.260		.261		.256		.265		.258		.241		.324	

HOUSTON ASTROS

Baseball statistics are scrutinized today with a zeal that's often overwhelming. Unfortunately, the media have a tendency to exaggerate the importance of events that are best described as oddities while totally ignoring truly significant performances.

Sure, it's fun to watch Phil and Joe Niekro try to become the winningest brothers in big-league history; or to have a pool on which part of Don Baylor's anatomy will take the hit when he breaks Ron Hunt's record for being hit with pitches. But there's something wrong when most baseball fans can recite chapter and verse on Cal Ripken's consecutive–innings streak, while almost no one knows that last season, Nolan Ryan shattered one of baseball's most significant performance records.

At the age of 40, Ryan struck out an average of 11.48 batters for every nine innings he pitched, the highest mark in major-league history. Let's put that number in proper perspective. Until Herb Score did it in 1955, no pitcher had ever struck out one batter per inning over the course of an entire season—not Cy Young (whose best average was 5.83 per nine innings); not Christy Mathewson (6.57); not Walter Johnson (7.55); not even Bob Feller (8.44). (Incidentally, a pitcher needs one inning for every game his team played to qualify as is the case with ERA championships and, for that matter, all other ratios.)

Four years after Score struck out 245 batters in 227 innings for the 1955 Cleveland Indians, Sandy Koufax became the first of a select group of five pitchers to crack the 10-strikeout level. Those five pitchers have accounted for 13 seasons in double figures (see the table below). Ryan himself has done it five times, more than anyone else. But even among those 13 seasons, only two pitchers have exceeded 11.00 strikeouts per nine innings. Ryan's average of 11.48 last season was more than three-quarters of a strikeout per game higher than all but one other pitcher's in baseball history. That's the statistical equivalent of batting nearly .400 in today's environment, or of hitting 65 home runs.

The highest single-season averages in major-league history:

	National League			American League	
Year	Pitcher	SO/9	Year	Pitcher	SO/9
1987	Nolan Ryan	11.48	1965	Sam McDowell	10.71
1984	Dwight Gooden	11.39	1973	Nolan Ryan	10.57
1962	Sandy Koufax	10.57	1966	Sam McDowell	10.44
1965	Sandy Koufax	10.23	1972	Nolan Ryan	10.43

1959	Sandy Koufax	10.18	1976	Nolan Ryan	10.36
1960	Sandy Koufax	10.13	1977	Nolan Ryan	10.26
1986	Mike Scott	10.00	1978	Nolan Ryan	9.96
1978	J.R. Richard	9.92	1974	Nolan Ryan	9.92
1986	Nolan Ryan	9.81	1955	Herb Score	9.71
1984	Nolan Ryan	9.65	1956	Herb Score	9.51

Five years ago, Ryan became the all-time major-league strikeout leader, surpassing the career total of Walter Johnson, whose mark of 3,508 had stood since he retired following the 1927 season. Ryan held the record for a somewhat shorter period—41 days to be exact. And by the end of the 1983 season, Steve Carlton had taken a lead of 32 strikeouts. And although Ryan was two years younger than Lefty, most observers—ourselves included—felt that Carlton would eventually draw away with the all-time leadership. After all, Carlton was enjoying a renaissance of his own at the time, having led the National League in strikeouts in both 1982 and 1983, and had relentlessly narrowed the gap between Ryan and himself for a number of seasons before passing him. A statistical recap of their head-to-head battle:

	After 1979	After 1980	After 1981	After 1982	After 1983	After 1984	After 1985	After 1986	After 1987
Ryan	2909	3109	3249	3494	3677	3874	4083	4277	4547
Carlton	2683	2969	3148	3434	3709	3872	3920	4040	4131
margin	+226	+140	+101	+60	−32	+2	+163	+237	+416

Ryan now holds the biggest lead in career strikeouts since Bob Gibson moved to within 400 of Johnson's record shortly before his retirement in 1975. With Lefty nearing the end of the line yet again, it looks like Von Ryan's Express will steam ahead to even further glory.

Taking Care of First Things First

Houston's pitchers held their opponents to a .275 on-base average leading off innings last season. That was the 3rd-lowest mark in the 13 years we've compiled those figures. The 10 best since 1975:

Year	Team	PA	H	BB	HP	OBA
1975	Los Angeles	1476	280	98	8	.262
1981	Houston	992	203	59	2	.266
1987	Houston	1446	299	93	5	.275
1982	Los Angeles	1492	329	80	6	.278
1981	St. Louis	947	199	63	3	.280
1983	Toronto	1449	304	94	9	.281

1976	New York	1458	311	95	4	.281
1985	Los Angeles	1467	304	103	6	.282
1982	Houston	1452	296	102	11	.282
1978	Baltimore	1432	299	106	2	.284

Of the 10 individual major-league leaders in keeping leadoff hitters off base last season, three came from Houston's starting rotation. The 1987 leaders among pitchers with at least 162 leadoff batters faced:

Pitcher	PA	H	BB	HP	OBA
Scott, Hou.	251	51	7	0	.231
Welch, L.A.	259	47	13	0	.232
Key, Tor.	269	54	10	1	.242
Heaton, Mtl.	203	46	3	1	.248
Long, Chi. (AL)	178	39	5	1	.253
Alexander, Atl.-Det.	212	45	9	0	.255
Ryan, Hou.	219	38	19	1	.265
Morris, Det.	272	48	26	0	.272
Bannister, Chi. (AL)	237	50	15	0	.274
Darwin, Hou.	206	39	16	2	.277

Broadcasters often comment on the importance of keeping the leadoff batter off base. But did you know that a team that puts its leadoff batter on is *three times* more likely to score in that inning than one whose first batter is put out? Here are the National League averages for the 1987 season:

Leadoff Batter	Total Innings	Scoring Innings	Scoring Pct.	Total Runs	Avg. Runs
Reaches base	5,835	3,009	51.6%	5,568	0.95
Put out	11,604	1,934	16.7%	3,203	0.28

Not only are teams three times as likely to score when their leadoff batters reach base; it's also true that when they do score, they produce an average of 1.85 runs an inning, or 12 percent more than the scoring innings of teams whose leadoff batters are retired (1.66).

A final note: The sharp increase in scoring last season produced a corresponding rise in the importance of retiring the leadoff batter. The difference between teams whose leadoff batters reached base and those whose leadoff batters didn't—a figure, that like the overall N.L. scoring average, had remained fairly constant over the three previous seasons —rose to 0.68 runs per inning last season, up more than 4 percent over the 1986 average.

The following table illustrates that increase. "R/G" represents the league average for runs per game; "Yes" and "No" refer to the average number of runs scored in innings in which the leadoff batter did and did not reach base; "Diff." indicates the difference of those two figures:

Year	R/G	Yes	No	Diff.
1984	8.13	0.90	0.24	0.661
1985	8.13	0.89	0.24	0.655
1986	8.36	0.90	0.25	0.649
1987	9.03	0.95	0.28	0.678

A Question of Balance

Houston's attack made a sharp left turn at the All-Star break last season with the addition of third baseman Ken Caminiti and outfielder Gerald Young. Over the first half of the season, Houston batted 25 points higher against right-handed pitching than against left-handers. That's an unusually large margin; in fact, only one National League team had a bigger gap for the entire 1987 season (Montreal).

But Young and Caminiti, a pair of rookies who collectively hit more than 100 points higher against southpaws than against right-handers, more than neutralized Houston's disadvantage against left-handers:

	Vs. Left-Handers			Vs. Right-Handers			
	AB	H	BA	AB	H	BA	Diff.
1st half	1024	244	.238	1912	503	.263	− .025
2d half	966	245	.254	1583	394	.249	+ .005

The irony of Houston's sudden improvement against left-handers and its corresponding decline against right-handers is that Caminiti and Young, the players most responsible for the turnaround, are both switch hitters. And the results demonstrate the exaggerated benefit that's often attributed to the ability to hit from both sides of the plate.

The mere presence of switch hitters doesn't provide an inherent advantage, because so many players who hit both ways aren't nearly as good from one side of the plate as they are from the other. Caminiti, Young, and several other Astros are prime examples. The career batting statistics of Houston's switch-hitters (Ashby's figures are since 1975 only):

	Vs. Left-Handers			Vs. Right-Handers			
Player	AB	H	BA	AB	H	BA	Diff.
Ashby	1031	225	.218	2768	715	.258	.040
Bailey	331	79	.239	562	122	.217	.022
Bass	983	274	.279	1298	356	.274	.004
Biancalana	129	26	.202	421	87	.207	.005
Caminiti	100	31	.310	103	19	.184	.126
Doran	1052	295	.280	1881	515	.274	.007
Householder	448	122	.272	878	191	.218	.055
Young	105	41	.390	169	47	.278	.112

Notice that four of the eight players hit at least 40 points better from one side than from the other. Only three—Bass, Doran, and Young—have truly hit well both ways. And there are many other switch hitters around the majors with similar imbalances: Wally Backman (Mets), Stan Javier (Athletics), and Jerry Mumphrey (Cubs) all have career batting averages at least 50 points better from the left side than from the right; Jerry Browne (Rangers), Mariano Duncan (Dodgers), Mike Felder (Brewers), and Al Newman (Twins) have all hit at least 50 points better from the right side. None of those players can be considered legitimate switch hitters in the sense that managers must strategically acknowledge their ability to hit from either side of the plate.

Of course, there are also examples of switch hitters who hit well from both sides, but their number is probably less than you think. Of the 62 switch hitters who batted at least 100 times last season, only 12 have career batting averages of at least .270 against both left- and right-handed pitchers, including Bass, Doran, and Young, whose statistics are listed above. The career statistics of the other nine (since 1975 for Simmons):

Player	Vs. Left-Handers			Vs. Right-Handers		
	AB	H	BA	AB	H	BA
Tony Fernandez	676	200	.296	1420	434	.306
Tommy Herr	1276	346	.271	2396	662	.276
Willie McGee	1060	304	.287	2263	679	.300
Eddie Murray	1964	583	.297	4278	1267	.296
Tim Raines	1134	350	.309	2767	853	.308
Ted Simmons	2263	657	.290	3687	1031	.280
Garry Templeton	2133	601	.282	3938	1090	.277
Mookie Wilson	1158	318	.275	2242	631	.281
Willie Wilson	1808	541	.299	3710	1086	.293

The bottom line on switch hitting? Players who hit from both sides of the plate hit 28 points better, on average, from their good side than from their bad. That's a narrower margin than the corresponding figure for one-way hitters, but by only five points.

Each player, whether a switch-hitter or one-way hitter, must be evaluated on an individual basis. The statistics in the Batter Section of each edition of the *Analyst* provide a breakdown against left- and right-handed pitching that will prove useful in that regard. And those statistics suggest that if the 1987 season is a valid indication of the abilities of Young and Caminiti, Astros manager Hal Lanier may have no choice but to platoon them just like any other right-handed swingers who can't handle right-handed pitchers.

WON-LOST RECORD BY STARTING POSITION

HOUSTON 76-86	C	1B	2B	3B	SS	LF	CF	RF	P	Leadoff	Relief	Starts
Troy Afenir	1-4	·	·	·	·	·	·	·	·	·	·	1-4
Juan Agosto	·	·	·	·	·	·	·	·	·	·	8-19	·
Larry Andersen	·	·	·	·	·	·	·	·	·	·	31-36	·
Alan Ashby	54-51	·	·	·	·	·	·	·	·	·	·	54-51
Mark Bailey	5-9	·	·	·	·	·	·	·	·	·	·	5-9
Kevin Bass	·	·	·	·	·	·	·	73-81	·	·	·	73-81
Dale Berra	·	·	·	·	7-9	·	·	·	·	·	·	7-9
Buddy Biancalana	·	·	·	·	1-5	·	·	·	·	·	·	1-5
Ken Caminiti	·	·	·	19-32	·	·	·	·	·	·	·	19-32
Rocky Childress	·	·	·	·	·	·	·	·	·	·	8-24	·
Jose Cruz	·	·	·	·	·	43-46	·	·	·	·	·	43-46
Danny Darwin	·	·	·	·	·	·	·	·	18-12	·	2-1	18-12
Glenn Davis	·	70-80	·	·	·	·	·	·	·	·	·	70-80
Jim Deshaies	·	·	·	·	·	·	·	·	13-12	·	0-1	13-12
Bill Doran	·	·	76-86	·	·	·	·	·	·	16-14	·	76-86
Ty Gainey	·	·	·	·	·	2-1	·	·	·	·	·	2-1
Phil Garner	·	·	·	16-13	·	·	·	·	·	·	·	16-13
Billy Hatcher	·	·	·	·	·	18-24	49-44	1-3	·	35-37	·	68-71
Jeff Heathcock	·	·	·	·	·	·	·	·	1-1	·	7-10	1-1
Manny Hernandez	·	·	·	·	·	·	·	·	1-2	·	0-3	1-2
Paul Householder	·	·	·	·	·	·	0-1	·	·	·	·	0-1
Chuck Jackson	·	·	·	6-7	·	·	2-2	·	·	·	·	8-9
Charlie Kerfeld	·	·	·	·	·	·	·	·	·	·	7-14	·
Bob Knepper	·	·	·	·	·	·	·	·	12-19	·	0-2	12-19
Dave Lopes	·	·	·	·	·	1-4	·	·	·	1-0	·	1-4
Aurelio Lopez	·	·	·	·	·	·	·	·	·	·	10-16	·
Rob Mallicoat	·	·	·	·	·	·	·	·	0-1	·	0-3	0-1
Ron Mathis	·	·	·	·	·	·	·	·	·	·	2-6	·
Dave Meads	·	·	·	·	·	·	·	·	·	·	14-31	·
Jim Pankovits	·	·	1-0	·	0-5	·	·	·	·	·	·	1-5
Bert Pena	·	·	·	·	8-6	·	·	·	·	·	·	8-6
Terry Puhl	·	·	·	·	·	9-5	·	2-0	·	·	·	11-5
Craig Reynolds	·	·	·	·	50-58	·	·	·	·	·	·	50-58
Ronn Reynolds	13-17	·	·	·	·	·	·	·	·	·	·	13-17
Nolan Ryan	·	·	·	·	·	·	·	·	12-22	·	·	12-22
Mike Scott	·	·	·	·	·	·	·	·	19-17	·	·	19-17
Dave Smith	·	·	·	·	·	·	·	·	·	·	33-17	·
Julio Solano	·	·	·	·	·	·	·	·	·	·	3-8	·
Dickie Thon	·	·	·	·	10-8	·	·	·	·	·	·	10-8
Ty Waller	·	·	·	·	·	·	·	·	·	·	·	·
Denny Walling	·	6-6	·	34-34	·	3-1	·	0-2	·	·	·	43-43
Robbie Wine	3-5	·	·	·	·	·	·	·	·	·	·	3-5
Gerald Young	·	·	·	·	·	·	25-39	·	·	24-35	·	25-39

Batting vs. Left and Right Handed Pitchers

		BA	Rank	SA	Rank	OBA	Rank	HR %	Rank	BB %	Rank	SO %	Rank
Alan Ashby	vs. Lefties	.255	90	.277	127	.318	90	0.00	113	8.28	74	7.64	20
	vs. Righties	.306	16	.531	16	.394	18	5.71	15	12.76	15	13.79	68
Kevin Bass	vs. Lefties	.282	55	.507	33	.315	93	4.41	32	4.15	118	12.86	65
	vs. Righties	.285	44	.414	65	.361	40	2.47	69	10.41	50	11.14	38
Ken Caminiti	vs. Lefties	.310	29	.430	67	.349	56	2.00	82	5.56	107	17.59	101
	vs. Righties	.184	--	.243	--	.227	--	0.97	--	5.45	--	22.73	--
Jose Cruz	vs. Lefties	.227	117	.359	101	.270	126	3.13	61	5.84	101	18.25	108
	vs. Righties	.249	96	.422	58	.326	80	2.95	58	10.45	48	14.93	78
Glenn Davis	vs. Lefties	.244	101	.477	40	.323	85	5.18	20	9.22	59	13.82	72
	vs. Righties	.255	91	.449	43	.304	102	4.42	28	6.46	104	12.92	54
Bill Doran	vs. Lefties	.291	45	.417	74	.395	19	3.14	60	14.77	16	7.20	14
	vs. Righties	.279	57	.400	70	.348	55	2.24	75	9.45	61	9.89	23
Billy Hatcher	vs. Lefties	.277	61	.406	83	.335	73	1.98	83	7.46	83	12.72	62
	vs. Righties	.307	15	.420	60	.361	38	1.93	82	6.27	106	10.28	26
Jim Pankovits	vs. Lefties	.271	73	.375	95	.340	68	2.08	80	9.43	51	18.87	115
	vs. Righties	.077	--	.077	--	.143	--	0.00	--	7.14	--	21.43	--
Terry Puhl	vs. Lefties	.111	--	.111	--	.200	--	0.00	--	10.00	--	20.00	--
	vs. Righties	.239	108	.336	108	.301	103	1.77	86	8.06	84	11.29	40
Craig Reynolds	vs. Lefties	.140	--	.140	--	.196	--	0.00	--	6.38	--	21.28	--
	vs. Righties	.269	73	.375	90	.317	93	1.21	101	7.32	94	9.21	18
Dickie Thon	vs. Lefties	.196	131	.250	132	.348	59	1.79	87	18.84	4	14.49	78
	vs. Righties	.300	--	.400	--	.462	--	0.00	--	21.43	--	21.43	--
Denny Walling	vs. Lefties	.200	--	.314	--	.222	--	2.86	--	2.63	--	26.32	--
	vs. Righties	.293	34	.431	52	.370	27	1.38	96	11.45	29	8.13	14
Gerald Young	vs. Lefties	.390	3	.467	45	.425	11	0.95	107	5.31	110	10.62	44
	vs. Righties	.278	60	.325	115	.353	49	0.00	126	10.53	43	7.89	13
Team Average	vs. Lefties	.246	12	.363	12	.314	12	2.26	9	8.65	8	16.26	9
	vs. Righties	.257	9	.379	9	.321	10	2.20	9	8.50	8	14.63	3
League Average	vs. Lefties	.263		.409		.332		2.81		9.08		15.22	
	vs. Righties	.260		.401		.327		2.73		8.70		15.85	

Batting with Runners on Base and Bases Empty

		BA	Rank	SA	Rank	OBA	Rank	HR %	Rank	BB %	Rank	SO %	Rank
Alan Ashby	Runners On	.272	78	.400	79	.354	63	2.78	55	11.79	40	11.79	45
	Bases Empty	.301	23	.471	40	.379	23	4.37	36	10.64	28	11.49	40
Kevin Bass	Runners On	.282	69	.463	42	.350	70	3.86	37	9.86	70	13.61	72
	Bases Empty	.285	42	.438	58	.339	54	2.70	66	6.67	84	10.28	30
Ken Caminiti	Runners On	.237	113	.309	119	.272	127	1.03	109	4.76	122	21.90	128
	Bases Empty	.255	82	.358	102	.301	95	1.89	87	6.19	100	18.58	105
Jose Cruz	Runners On	.230	117	.348	107	.310	108	1.24	97	10.81	56	17.84	113
	Bases Empty	.250	89	.441	55	.305	93	4.41	34	7.27	71	14.55	72
Glenn Davis	Runners On	.248	103	.442	61	.327	97	3.96	33	10.06	67	13.84	78
	Bases Empty	.253	85	.473	38	.293	104	5.33	23	4.73	119	12.62	49
Bill Doran	Runners On	.316	20	.449	57	.385	35	2.73	58	10.07	66	6.71	13
	Bases Empty	.260	75	.377	92	.352	42	2.44	71	12.35	13	10.45	32
Billy Hatcher	Runners On	.314	21	.455	51	.370	45	2.62	61	8.97	80	11.21	41
	Bases Empty	.287	40	.394	77	.342	50	1.61	96	5.45	110	11.14	36
Craig Reynolds	Runners On	.209	126	.288	128	.267	128	1.23	99	8.38	89	12.04	50
	Bases Empty	.289	39	.393	78	.333	62	0.95	110	6.22	99	9.33	16
Denny Walling	Runners On	.232	115	.371	98	.306	109	2.65	60	10.29	60	10.29	33
	Bases Empty	.328	8	.460	45	.400	13	0.57	120	10.77	27	9.74	22
Gerald Young	Runners On	.346	5	.397	82	.411	20	0.00	122	11.11	52	10.00	29
	Bases Empty	.311	18	.372	96	.366	28	0.51	122	7.51	64	8.45	13
Team Average	Runners On	.252	12	.374	12	.323	11	2.26	8	9.59	8	15.06	8
	Bases Empty	.253	9	.372	9	.314	8	2.20	10	7.73	6	15.35	5
League Average	Runners On	.267		.410		.341		2.66		9.88		14.92	
	Bases Empty	.256		.399		.319		2.82		7.98		16.22	

Overall Batting Compared to Late Inning Pressure Situations

		BA	Rank	SA	Rank	OBA	Rank	HR %	Rank	BB %	Rank	SO %	Rank	RDI %	Rank
Alan Ashby	Overall	.288	41	.438	51	.367	32	3.63	46	11.19	31	11.63	44	.346	15
	Pressure	.329	19	.514	20	.385	36	5.71	13	8.64	74	13.58	50	.160	115
Kevin Bass	Overall	.284	52	.449	46	.344	58	3.21	59	8.10	81	11.77	45	.330	26
	Pressure	.313	31	.505	24	.364	50	4.04	33	7.27	95	11.82	31	.424	12
Ken Caminiti	Overall	.246	105	.335	118	.287	122	1.48	99	5.50	123	20.18	127	.275	75
	Pressure	.368	11	.500	25	.390	34	2.63	61	4.76	116	11.90	32	.235	78
Jose Cruz	Overall	.241	109	.400	82	.307	106	3.01	63	8.89	62	16.05	92	.232	111
	Pressure	.233	95	.384	71	.296	100	2.74	54	8.54	76	17.07	84	.235	78
Glenn Davis	Overall	.251	98	.458	42	.310	102	4.67	24	7.40	90	13.23	59	.275	76
	Pressure	.168	132	.326	110	.266	121	4.21	29	11.01	47	18.35	92	.205	95
Bill Doran	Overall	.283	54	.406	80	.365	35	2.56	69	11.40	28	8.90	15	.277	71
	Pressure	.309	34	.371	77	.393	31	1.03	104	12.39	34	7.08	10	.324	46
Billy Hatcher	Overall	.296	24	.415	72	.352	45	1.95	87	6.70	107	11.16	40	.307	47
	Pressure	.358	12	.531	18	.409	21	1.23	99	6.74	100	15.73	68	.348	33
Jim Pankovits	Overall	.230	--	.311	--	.299	--	1.64	--	8.96	--	19.40	--	.250	--
	Pressure	.231	--	.231	--	.259	--	0.00	--	3.70	--	25.93	--	.364	28
Terry Puhl	Overall	.230	--	.320	--	.293	--	1.64	--	8.21	--	11.94	--	.220	--
	Pressure	.286	49	.357	89	.375	44	0.00	105	12.24	37	12.24	36	.333	36
Craig Reynolds	Overall	.254	93	.348	111	.303	110	1.07	110	7.21	96	10.58	28	.183	128
	Pressure	.258	75	.306	113	.303	97	1.61	86	5.88	109	13.24	47	.000	140
Denny Walling	Overall	.283	55	.418	68	.356	44	1.54	98	10.54	39	10.00	21	.204	124
	Pressure	.282	52	.333	104	.391	32	0.00	105	14.89	20	12.77	40	.375	--
Gerald Young	Overall	.321	7	.380	94	.380	21	0.36	128	8.58	68	8.91	16	.236	--
	Pressure	.306	35	.367	80	.370	47	0.00	105	9.26	66	9.26	20	.308	55
Team Average	Overall	.253	11	.373	11	.318	11	2.22	9	8.55	7	15.22	7	.254	11
	Pressure	.276	3	.390	7	.343	3	2.10	8	8.99	9	14.86	1	.273	5
League Average	Overall	.261		.404		.328		2.75		8.83		15.64		.272	
	Pressure	.258		.385		.331		2.46		9.54		16.95		.261	

Additional Miscellaneous Batting Comparisons

	Grass Surface BA	Rank	Artificial Surface BA	Rank	Home Games BA	Rank	Road Games BA	Rank	Runners in Scoring Position BA	Rank	Runners in Scoring Pos and Two Outs BA	Rank	Leading Off Inning OBA	Rank	Runners on 3B with less than 2 Outs RDI %	Rank
Alan Ashby	.216	124	.313	20	.335	12	.237	109	.298	38	.302	30	.402	13	.607	53
Kevin Bass	.291	35	.281	55	.285	56	.283	39	.278	61	.247	73	.361	42	.667	25
Ken Caminiti	.237	--	.252	93	.267	79	.230	114	.246	93	.235	77	.306	--	.667	--
Jose Cruz	.190	134	.260	84	.267	79	.216	124	.239	104	.289	40	.277	117	.467	109
Glenn Davis	.269	70	.242	105	.249	104	.253	87	.245	95	.269	56	.291	108	.436	117
Bill Doran	.273	61	.288	47	.305	27	.264	75	.297	40	.250	69	.371	34	.629	46
Billy Hatcher	.275	58	.307	25	.305	26	.289	37	.321	18	.300	32	.371	33	.652	33
Terry Puhl	.313	--	.200	128	.197	--	.275	--	.250	--	.273	--	.280	--	.667	--
Craig Reynolds	.262	80	.250	96	.259	90	.249	95	.131	135	.093	134	.341	57	.684	22
Denny Walling	.255	88	.295	35	.288	51	.278	49	.219	113	.205	107	.381	28	.421	120
Gerald Young	.308	19	.328	13	.359	4	.279	45	.326	16	.250	69	.383	27	.667	25
Team Average	.244	11	.256	9	.263	8	.243	11	.247	10	.228	10	.323	7	.568	3
League Average	.260		.261		.265		.256		.258		.241		.324		.554	

Pitching vs. Left and Right Handed Batters

		BA	Rank	SA	Rank	OBA	Rank	HR %	Rank	BB %	Rank	SO %	Rank
Larry Andersen	vs. Lefties	.233	21	.344	30	.326	44	1.59	32	11.66	84	17.94	30
	vs. Righties	.260	66	.388	45	.313	49	2.04	23	6.91	39	24.88	9
Rocky Childress	vs. Lefties	.306	97	.506	107	.375	95	3.53	99	10.20	63	10.20	85
	vs. Righties	.217	--	.272	--	.275	--	1.09	--	7.77	--	15.53	--
Danny Darwin	vs. Lefties	.268	60	.434	77	.342	61	2.95	88	9.86	58	13.70	53
	vs. Righties	.224	25	.315	12	.283	23	1.60	15	6.71	35	18.47	39
Jim Deshaies	vs. Lefties	.263	54	.404	63	.345	65	2.02	50	11.40	81	13.16	58
	vs. Righties	.256	59	.431	80	.317	57	4.17	95	8.24	71	16.67	56
Bob Knepper	vs. Lefties	.282	80	.419	71	.317	36	2.56	72	4.00	3	13.60	54
	vs. Righties	.318	109	.518	109	.370	102	3.80	84	7.35	49	8.85	109
Dave Meads	vs. Lefties	.268	--	.411	--	.317	--	3.57	--	6.45	--	17.74	--
	vs. Righties	.344	111	.588	112	.395	110	4.58	101	8.16	64	14.29	79
Nolan Ryan	vs. Lefties	.211	7	.289	7	.300	21	1.49	28	11.16	75	29.10	3
	vs. Righties	.187	4	.295	7	.266	13	2.17	26	8.65	79	32.93	1
Mike Scott	vs. Lefties	.235	25	.335	25	.300	22	1.78	39	8.21	30	17.68	33
	vs. Righties	.196	8	.325	16	.258	10	2.93	55	7.33	48	29.78	3
Dave Smith	vs. Lefties	.204	6	.239	2	.297	19	0.00	1	11.63	83	19.38	21
	vs. Righties	.158	--	.218	--	.211	--	0.00	--	5.41	--	43.24	--
Team Average	vs. Lefties	.252	1	.376	2	.328	4	2.18	4	9.76	8	17.28	1
	vs. Righties	.249	3	.394	4	.309	2	2.87	5	7.75	3	19.54	1
League Average	vs. Lefties	.268		.404		.341		2.34		9.74		14.31	
	vs. Righties	.255		.403		.319		3.05		8.16		16.61	

Pitching with Runners on Base and Bases Empty

		BA	Rank	SA	Rank	OBA	Rank	HR %	Rank	BB %	Rank	SO %	Rank
Larry Andersen	Runners On	.240	27	.353	27	.338	64	1.80	33	12.62	98	17.48	33
	Bases Empty	.252	55	.376	49	.303	35	1.83	24	6.41	31	24.79	5
Danny Darwin	Runners On	.266	63	.355	29	.331	46	1.32	19	8.38	23	15.61	55
	Bases Empty	.232	23	.387	58	.300	31	2.93	70	8.21	65	16.43	48
Jim Deshaies	Runners On	.262	57	.457	93	.328	39	4.52	105	8.98	36	19.14	18
	Bases Empty	.254	63	.408	71	.319	63	3.35	84	8.67	75	14.03	76
Bob Knepper	Runners On	.330	113	.497	106	.383	106	2.61	64	7.80	21	8.67	108
	Bases Empty	.300	102	.506	108	.345	94	4.32	101	6.05	19	10.31	106
Nolan Ryan	Runners On	.215	10	.327	18	.295	12	2.31	49	10.03	64	26.93	3
	Bases Empty	.190	3	.269	2	.277	9	1.50	12	9.92	94	33.59	1
Mike Scott	Runners On	.264	60	.374	36	.347	75	2.13	45	10.70	74	21.67	11
	Bases Empty	.191	4	.307	10	.242	3	2.39	45	6.06	20	23.92	7
Dave Smith	Runners On	.204	6	.235	2	.307	17	0.00	1	11.97	91	26.50	6
	Bases Empty	.164	--	.224	--	.211	--	0.00	--	5.69	--	34.15	--
Team Average	Runners On	.272	8	.406	6	.344	10	2.51	3	9.74	6	16.88	1
	Bases Empty	.235	1	.373	3	.298	2	2.64	6	7.73	4	19.87	1
League Average	Runners On	.267		.410		.341		2.66		9.88		14.92	
	Bases Empty	.256		.399		.319		2.82		7.98		16.22	

Overall Pitching Compared to Late Inning Pressure Situations

		BA	Rank	SA	Rank	OBA	Rank	HR %	Rank	BB %	Rank	SO %	Rank
Juan Agosto	Overall	.248	--	.324	--	.313	--	0.95	--	8.47	--	5.08	--
	Pressure	.273	71	.382	61	.310	36	1.82	46	5.00	18	3.33	111
Larry Andersen	Overall	.247	40	.366	35	.319	42	1.82	22	9.32	70	21.36	12
	Pressure	.255	54	.365	49	.321	44	1.52	42	8.31	37	21.93	19
Rocky Childress	Overall	.260	--	.384	--	.323	--	2.26	--	8.96	--	12.94	--
	Pressure	.292	86	.396	67	.358	78	0.00	1	9.09	53	14.55	65
Danny Darwin	Overall	.246	37	.374	39	.313	42	2.27	39	8.28	43	16.09	48
	Pressure	.297	90	.422	78	.357	75	0.00	1	7.04	26	14.08	69
Jim Deshaies	Overall	.257	58	.427	78	.322	49	3.80	100	8.80	61	16.05	50
	Pressure	.308		.308		.308		0.00	--	0.00	--	20.00	--
Charlie Kerfeld	Overall	.309	--	.482	--	.421	--	2.73	--	15.33	--	12.41	--
	Pressure	.238	35	.500	96	.441	107	7.14	106	25.81	112	11.29	84
Bob Knepper	Overall	.313	112	.502	111	.362	104	3.60	97	6.82	18	9.60	108
	Pressure	.283	83	.358	45	.356	73	0.00	1	8.47	41	15.25	62
Aurelio Lopez	Overall	.273	--	.455	--	.333	--	4.20	--	7.32	--	12.80	--
	Pressure	.200	12	.350	38	.244	6	2.50	62	4.35	12	10.87	87
Dave Meads	Overall	.321	--	.535	--	.372	--	4.28	--	7.66	--	15.31	--
	Pressure	.260	60	.438	82	.325	47	2.74	68	7.41	30	24.69	11
Nolan Ryan	Overall	.200	3	.292	2	.284	6	1.82	21	9.97	81	30.93	1
	Pressure	.175	3	.190	2	.268	12	0.00	1	11.11	79	44.44	1
Mike Scott	Overall	.217	7	.331	8	.281	4	2.29	41	7.82	32	23.07	11
	Pressure	.253	52	.326	23	.270	14	1.05	26	2.97	6	30.69	3
Dave Smith	Overall	.182	--	.229	--	.257	--	0.00	--	8.75	--	30.42	--
	Pressure	.192	9	.233	5	.270	13	0.00	1	9.04	52	27.11	6
Team Average	Overall	.250	1	.386	3	.317	2	2.59	4	8.59	5	18.60	1
	Pressure	.248	3	.354	2	.316	2	1.39	1	8.36	2	20.99	1
League Average	Overall	.261		.404		.328		2.75		8.83		15.64	
	Pressure	.260		.391		.337		2.47		10.04		17.14	

Additional Miscellaneous Pitching Comparisons

	Grass Surface BA	Rank	Artificial Surface BA	Rank	Home Games BA	Rank	Road Games BA	Rank	Runners in Scoring Position BA	Rank	Runners in Scoring Pos and Two Outs BA	Rank	Leading Off Inning OBA	Rank
Larry Andersen	.238	25	.251	40	.244	35	.250	40	.252	59	.309	98	.295	23
Rocky Childress	.211	--	.297	92	.274	--	.250	--	.314	--	.318	--	.302	--
Danny Darwin	.213	9	.256	50	.248	43	.244	35	.237	38	.178	24	.277	15
Jim Deshaies	.283	85	.246	35	.215	15	.295	96	.248	55	.222	48	.281	16
Bob Knepper	.381	112	.290	88	.287	97	.342	108	.288	87	.333	103	.301	30
Aurelio Lopez	.351		.245	33	.216	--	.333	--	.433	--	.412	--	.189	--
Dave Meads	.426	--	.261	54	.278	--	.352	110	.375	--	.400	--	.370	--
Nolan Ryan	.209	8	.195	5	.192	5	.208	10	.191	7	.224	51	.265	11
Mike Scott	.283	86	.195	6	.196	7	.237	27	.241	40	.210	39	.231	3
Dave Smith	.259	--	.156	2	.172	3	.198	--	.209	17	.147	11	.240	--
Team Average	.278	11	.238	1	.233	1	.268	8	.260	9	.257	9	.275	1
League Average	.260		.261		.256		.265		.258		.241		.324	

LOS ANGELES DODGERS

If there's anything to be learned from the performance of the 1987 Dodgers, it's that a three-man pitching staff, however talented, does not a team make. Nor a division win. Nor a .500 record reach. Apparently the Dodgers agree, having sent Bob Welch to the Athletics in December in a three-team trade that brought them a left-handed reliever (Jesse Orosco from the Mets), a right-handed reliever (Jay Howell), and a starting shortstop (Alfredo Griffin).

Experience has taught us that the best remedy for the analytic fever that follows any major trade is patience. Will Orosco and Howell overcome the inconsistencies that greased their paths to Los Angeles? Toss a coin. Will Griffin reward GM Fred Claire's own strategic defense initiative by stabilizing the shakiest West Coast infield since the great San Francisco earthquake? Ask us in a year or two. But one thing is certain: The Welch trade will have an immediate impact on Tommy Lasorda's pitching strategy.

In recent years, especially last season, whenever one of his three thoroughbreds (Welch, Valenzuela, or Hershiser) took the mound, Lasorda was free to spend the early innings mugging for the dugout camera, talking on the phone to Sinatra, listening to Vin, working out on the Nautilus, or power-chowing a plateful of linguine, because the one thing Lasorda knew he *wouldn't* have to do was rumble out to the mound to replace his starting pitcher.

Even in 1987, the Year of the Homer, Lasorda let his starters go longer than did any other manager in the league. The average National League starter lasted only 6.02 innings last season, down from 6.18 in 1986 and 6.28 in 1985. Despite that trend, the Dodgers were one of only two National League teams whose starting pitchers collectively threw more innings than they did in either of the two preceding years:

Team	1985	1986	1987
Los Angeles	1074	1052.1	1075.2
Houston	1037.2	1019	1009.1
Pittsburgh	983.1	976	1009.1
New York	1091.2	1091.1	997
St. Louis	1066.1	1060.1	973.1
Chicago	970.2	947	965.2
Atlanta	900.1	982.2	958.1
Philadelphia	1019.2	982.1	952.1
San Francisco	992.2	984.1	944.1
Montreal	973	979.2	941.2
Cincinnati	1050.2	990.1	938.1
San Diego	1042.1	918.2	928.1

Lasorda's handling of his starters was so different from the rest of the league's managers that the gap between the number of innings pitched by L.A.'s starters and that of the second-place teams last season was greater than the margin between the second- and ninth-place teams. But it's not that the Dodgers are changing their stripes; rather, they have been running counter to the prevailing trend of a lighter work load for starting pitchers throughout this decade. Here are the figures for each of the seven seasons since Fernando became the darling of Lalaland. Totals are rounded off to the nearest inning for clarity:

	1981	1982	1983	1984	1985	1986	1987
Dodgers	714	1033	1064	1088	1074	1052	1076
*N.L. Average	653	1004	1000	990	1012	994	965
Difference	61	29	64	98	62	58	111

* not including Dodgers

When you break those figures down even further, the burden borne by the Dodgers' Big Three is even more apparent. Because at the same time that the Dodgers were blessed with a better than average Big Three, they were also cursed with a sub par Little Two. That Little Two (the fourth and fifth spots in the rotation) was really a Little Eight, since Lasorda used eight other starting pitchers last season: Rick Honeycutt (20 starts), Tim Leary (12), Shawn Hillegas (10), Alejandro Pena (7), Tim Belcher (5), Ken Howell (2), Brad Havens (1), and Brian Holton (1). But if Tommy was free to talk to Sinatra when his aces threw, he had to keep those lines to the bullpen clear the rest of the time. The drop-off in quality is evident in these figures:

	Starts	Innings	Innings Per Start	Personal W–L	Team W–L
Big Three	104	765	7.36	45–38	55–49
Little Two	58	310.2	5.36	12–30	18–40

The Dodgers were a .529 team last season in games started by Valenzuela, Hershiser, or Welch; they were a .310 team when other guys started. The Big Three pitched at least five innings in 102 of their 104 starts, including the last 80-of-80 after May 16. The Little Two failed to complete five innings in 16 of their 58 starts.

Now it stands to reason that a team's top three pitchers would go deeper into their starts than would a team's fourth or fifth starters, but look at the extremes to which the Dodgers' top starters reflected that pattern. These figures compare the number of innings pitched by Dodgers starters with the averages of the 11 other teams in the league. The top three starters on each team are defined as those with the most starts:

	Innings by Top 3 Starters	Innings by Other Starters
Dodgers	765	310.2
*N.L. Average	557	408
Difference	+208	−97.1

* not including Dodgers

What a remarkable difference! The Dodgers' Top Three threw more than 200 more innings than the top three pitchers on the average staff of other National League teams, but they got nearly 100 fewer innings out of their fourth and fifth starters.

That kind of distribution of the work load certainly made for some interesting individual statistics. If they played municipal anthems for statistical categories, Randy Newman's "I Love L.A." would surely have gotten a workout. Hershiser, Welch, and Valenzuela finished one-two-three in the league in innings pitched last season, with Hershiser even pitching two and one-third innings in relief. The Dodgers also took the gold, silver, and bronze in the category of average innings per start among National League pitchers who made at least 20 starts last season. In fact, only two other pitchers in the league averaged seven innings per start:

	GS	IP	Avg.
Hershiser, L.A.	35	262.1	7.50
Valenzuela, L.A.	34	251	7.38
Welch, L.A.	35	251.2	7.190
Gooden, N.Y.	25	179.2	7.187
Dunne, Pitt.	23	163.1	7.10

Neither Gooden nor Dunne pitched a full major-league season last year. Gooden wasn't cleared to play until June 5, when he coincidentally opposed Dunne, who was making his major-league debut that night. Among National League pitchers who were regular starters for the entire season, only three averaged seven innings per start, and all three were Dodgers.

Lasorda's strategy of "going farther with his starters" also paid off in the win column. In 1986, the Dodgers led the National League with 13 losses in games in which they led going into the eighth inning, and they led the majors with seven losses in games in which they led going into the ninth. Last season, they cut those figures by more than 50 percent each, losing only six games in which they led after seven, and only three in which they led through eight.

Nevertheless, heading into the off-season, the Dodgers faced a couple of problems: first, to produce decent fourth and fifth starters; second, to develop a bullpen in which the manager could have confidence on a daily basis.

Even while building that bullpen in a single bold stroke,

the Welch trade opened up another spot in the rotation. But considering the Dodgers' position in the standings for the past two years, it might be wise to note that you can't be hurt too badly falling out of a ground-floor window. And whatever downside risk the gamble entailed was softened by the addition of Don Sutton and the development of two rookies who pitched for the Dodgers late last season and appeared ready to join the rotation in 1988.

Twenty-six-year-old Tim Belcher, the former number-one amateur draft choice (he chose not to sign when the Twins selected him in 1983) is one of them. He pitched only 37 innings in Double-A ball in an injury-plagued 1986 season, but bounced back to strike out 136 batters in 163 innings at Tacoma in 1987. Sent to the Dodgers on September 3 as payment in the Honeycutt deal, Belcher went 4–2 with a 2.38 ERA in six games. Shawn Hillegas might also become a regular starter. He was 4–3 with a 3.57 ERA in 12 late-season appearances with the Dodgers.

But the trade looks great on paper because of what it did for the Dodgers' bullpen. Neither Orosco nor Howell had a good year in 1987, but chances are that one of them—or Pena, who was the best reliever in the league at the close of the '87 season—can succeed as a true stopper where so many have failed: Steve Howe, Tom Niedenfuer, Carlos Diaz, Ken Howell, Ed Vande Berg, and Matt Young. Remember that Pena saved nine games over the last four weeks of the season, and allowed only one earned run in his last 23 2/3 innings. But his past medical history made him a risky basket in which to put all of the Dodgers' bullpen eggs. Thus, the trade leaves Lasorda with a choice on whether to leave Pena in the pen, as the supporter or supportee of Orosco and Howell, or to return him to the rotation.

Whatever his decision, the fact remains that very few pitchers in current-day baseball in either league are asked to pitch the number of innings that the Dodgers' ace starters are. When Billy Martin made similar demands on his Oakland A's staff in 1980, there were cries from every bully pulpit on the continent that he was ruining the arms of his pitchers. And indeed, the names of Rick Langford, Mike Norris, Matt Keough, Steve McCatty, and Brian Kingman are no longer found in major league box scores. Only time will tell if there will be an adverse long-term effect on the Dodgers' pitchers.

Meanwhile, an aside to Sinatra, Rickles, and the rest of Lasorda's Hollywood pals: Check the daily pitching form before putting in a call to your buddy at Chavez Ravine. If the probable pitcher is listed as Fernando or Hershiser, go ahead and dial. But if you see some other name listed, save yourself the trouble—the line is probably busy.

Just to Complete the Thought...

To paraphrase a famous baseball fan who used to spend a lot of time in California, you don't have Pedro Guerrero to kick around anymore. Dodgers fans can no longer blame the team's dismal performance in 1986 on the preseason injury to their star outfielder. You'll recall that Guerrero missed nearly the entire season that year after tearing up his knee in spring training, and the temptation was strong to place the blame for the Dodgers' fall from a 1985 division title to a fifth-place finish, 16 games below the .500 mark, on Guerrero's wobbly knees. But last season, Guerrero not only returned, he posted numbers that in another season might have spelled MVP: a .338 batting average, with 27 home runs and 89 RBI. But once again, the Dodgers finished 16 games below .500, with the same 73–89 mark they posted a year earlier without him.

We're proud to say that we told readers of the 1987 *Analyst* that the loss of Guerrero was only a small part of what ailed the Dodgers in 1986. (By way of coming clean, we're not so proud that we also wrote that the Dodgers would rebound in 1987.) We based our assessment of the Guerrero situation on two points: First, that pitching was more responsible for the team's demise in 1986 than offense. (The Dodgers allowed 100 more runs in 1986 than in 1985; they scored only 44 fewer.) And second, that the value of a star player of Guerrero's stature is much less than most people think—about five wins per season.

Not that we think that five wins over the course of a season is a meager amount. Just ask the Mets, Expos, Royals, Athletics, or Blue Jays: each team lost its division title last season by less than that margin. In fact, 51 percent of all of baseball's division titles since 1969 have been decided by five games or less.

Nevertheless, our five-game estimate didn't sit well with Vin Scully, the Hall-of-Fame broadcaster for the Dodgers and for the NBC Game of the Week. Now judging from some of the material that he uses on his broadcasts, Vin may be one of the *Analyst*'s biggest fans. Just follow along some time and see for yourself. But on a national telecast last spring, Scully opined that our estimate of five wins was far below Guerrero's true worth to the '86 Dodgers. Although he didn't pin an exact number on it, Vin apparently felt that a player of Guerrero's ability would account for, as he might put it, oh, anywhere between a half-a-dozen and a dozen victories over the course of a season. In looking at the Dodgers' fall from 95 wins in 1985 to 73 in '86, perhaps Vin believed that Guerrero was responsible for, oh, up to a score of wins.

We're reasonable guys, and two of us, like Vin, are Fordham graduates, so we reexamined the question based on data from the 1987 season, and found no evidence that we'd understated a superstar's impact with our five-win estimate. The following table contains a summary of the data from last year's edition, followed by last season's information. The column headings "Yes" and "No" indicate the winning percentage or record of each player's team according to whether or not he was in the starting lineup. After all, if you're trying to measure a player's worth, what better way than to compare his team's record in the games he's started to their mark in games he's missed. In the long run, over the course of

hundreds of games by dozens of players, the truth will out. The statistics:

Player	1982 through 1986			1987 Season		
	Yes	No	Diff.	Yes	No	Diff.
Jesse Barfield	.554	.523	+ .031	84–62	12–4	− .175
Wade Boggs	.530	.532	− .002	70–76	8–8	− .021
George Brett	.533	.465	+ .068	57–58	26–21	− .058
Gary Carter	.561	.542	+ .018	76–57	16–13	+ .020
Jack Clark	.512	.504	+ .009	76–50	19–17	+ .075
Andre Dawson	.512	.466	+ .046	70–81	6–4	− .136
Kirk Gibson	.565	.558	+ .008	80–43	18–21	+ .189
Pedro Guerrero	.539	.491	+ .048	66–81	7–8	− .018
Rickey Henderson	.501	.505	− .003	50–43	39–30	− .028
Keith Hernandez	.575	.559	+ .016	87–64	5–6	+ .122
Kent Hrbek	.447	.413	+ .034	69–66	16–11	− .081
Eddie Murray	.537	.517	+ .020	66–94	1–1	− .088
Tim Raines	.507	.490	+ .016	82–57	9–14	+ .199
Jim Rice	.537	.439	+ .099	52–54	26–30	+ .026
Ryne Sandberg	.483	.421	+ .062	62–68	14–17	+ .025
Mike Schmidt	.521	.508	+ .013	68–73	12–9	− .089
Ozzie Smith	.541	.511	+ .030	90–63	5–4	+ .033
Darryl Strawberry	.589	.474	+ .115	84–65	8–5	− .052
Dave Winfield	.554	.500	+ .054	82–68	7–5	− .037
Robin Yount	.490	.505	− .015	89–68	2–3	+ .167

Based on the five-year sample, we concluded that a superstar such as those listed above is worth 5.41 wins for every 162 games. (That figure represents the average difference, .033, multiplied by 162.) But that number has to be reduced, since it's rare for anyone to play all 162 games. After accounting for the games missed by each player, our estimate of the worth of the typical superstar fell to 4.66 wins per season.

The 1987 data makes us wonder if that estimate wasn't a little high. The teams of 11 of the 20 players compiled better records *without them* in the starting lineup than with them. Of course, that's a reflection of the inadequacy of a single season's worth of statistics (which is why we used a five-year study in the first place). But even if we study only the players who failed to start at least 20 games last season—reducing the margin of error on an individual basis—we still find that only six of 10 players had a positive impact when judged according to their teams' won-lost records. On average, those 10 players increased their teams' winning percentages by .028, or 4.51 wins per 162 games played. That's satisfyingly close to the figure we computed last season, and lends further credence to our contention that even the best everyday players are rarely worth five wins a season.

So, Vin, we promise that we won't offer you any tips on play-by-play, but please don't offer us any on analyzing statistics. For as Dryden wrote, "Errors, like straws, upon the surface flow; He who would search for pearls must dive below."

WON-LOST RECORD BY STARTING POSITION

LOS ANGELES 73-89	C	1B	2B	3B	SS	LF	CF	RF	P	Leadoff	Relief	Starts
Dave Anderson	-	-	1-0	5-6	22-33	-	-	-	-	18-24	-	28-39
Tim Belcher	-	-	-	-	-	-	-	-	3-2	-	1-0	3-2
Ralph Bryant	-	-	-	-	-	5-2	3-3	-	-	-	-	8-5
Tim Crews	-	-	-	-	-	-	-	-	-	-	10-10	-
Ron Davis	-	-	-	-	-	-	-	-	-	-	0-4	-
Mike Devereaux	-	-	-	-	-	4-4	0-1	0-2	-	-	-	4-7
Mariano Duncan	-	-	1-3	-	30-32	-	-	0-1	-	16-13	-	31-36
Phil Garner	-	-	1-2	11-18	0-1	-	-	-	-	-	-	12-21
Jose Gonzalez	-	-	-	-	-	1-1	1-1	-	-	1-1	-	2-2
Pedro Guerrero	-	17-22	-	-	-	49-59	-	-	-	-	-	66-81
Chris Gwynn	-	-	-	-	-	4-4	-	-	-	-	-	4-4
Jeff Hamilton	-	-	-	11-12	-	-	-	-	-	-	-	11-12
Mickey Hatcher	-	13-16	-	20-22	-	-	-	2-4	-	-	-	35-42
Brad Havens	-	-	-	-	-	-	-	-	0-1	-	4-26	0-1
Danny Heep	-	2-1	-	-	-	3-6	-	2-2	-	-	-	7-9
Orel Hershiser	-	-	-	-	-	-	-	-	17-18	-	1-1	17-18
Shawn Hillegas	-	-	-	-	-	-	-	-	5-5	-	0-2	5-5
Glenn Hoffman	-	-	-	19-21	-	-	-	-	-	0-1	-	19-21
Brian Holton	-	-	-	-	-	-	-	-	1-0	-	12-40	1-0
Rick Honeycutt	-	-	-	-	-	-	-	-	3-17	-	2-5	3-17
Ken Howell	-	-	-	-	-	-	-	-	1-1	-	9-29	1-1
Bill Krueger	-	-	-	-	-	-	-	-	-	-	0-2	-
Ken Landreaux	-	-	-	-	-	1-3	1-2	12-15	-	-	-	14-20
Tito Landrum	-	-	-	-	-	1-4	-	2-3	-	-	-	3-7
Tim Leary	-	-	-	-	-	-	-	-	4-8	-	5-22	4-8
Bill Madlock	-	-	-	6-10	-	-	-	-	-	-	-	6-10
Mike Marshall	-	-	-	-	-	-	49-53	-	-	-	-	49-53
Len Matuszek	-	0-1	-	-	-	-	-	-	-	-	-	0-1
Orlando Mercado	1-0	-	-	-	-	-	-	-	-	-	-	1-0
Tom Niedenfuer	-	-	-	-	-	-	-	-	-	-	5-10	-
Alejandro Pena	-	-	-	-	-	-	-	1-6	-	-	16-14	1-6
Mike Ramsey	-	-	-	-	-	17-17	-	-	-	-	-	17-17
Jerry Reuss	-	-	-	-	-	-	-	-	-	-	0-1	-
Gilberto Reyes	-	-	-	-	-	-	-	-	-	-	-	-
Jack Savage	-	-	-	-	-	-	-	-	-	-	1-2	-
Steve Sax	-	-	68-83	-	-	-	-	-	-	37-50	-	68-83
Mike Scioscia	61-67	-	-	-	-	-	-	-	-	-	-	61-67
Mike Sharperson	-	-	2-1	5-2	-	-	-	-	-	1-0	-	7-3
John Shelby	-	-	-	-	-	-	52-65	-	-	-	-	52-65
Craig Shipley	-	-	-	0-1	2-2	-	-	-	-	-	-	2-3
Franklin Stubbs	-	40-46	-	-	-	4-6	-	1-5	-	-	-	45-57
Alex Trevino	11-22	-	-	-	-	1-0	-	-	-	-	-	12-22
Fernando Valenzuela	-	-	-	-	-	-	-	-	16-18	-	-	16-18
Bob Welch	-	-	-	-	-	-	-	-	22-13	-	-	22-13
Brad Wellman	-	-	-	-	-	-	-	-	-	-	-	-
Reggie Williams	-	-	-	-	-	2-3	2-1	-	-	-	-	4-4
Tracy Woodson	-	1-3	-	15-18	-	-	-	-	-	-	-	16-21
Matt Young	-	-	-	-	-	-	-	-	-	-	22-25	-

Batting vs. Left and Right Handed Pitchers

		BA	Rank	SA	Rank	OBA	Rank	HR %	Rank	BB %	Rank	SO %	Rank
Dave Anderson	vs. Lefties	.250	95	.333	109	.316	91	0.00	113	8.43	72	9.64	40
	vs. Righties	.228	119	.306	125	.292	108	0.52	122	7.94	87	16.36	92
Mariano Duncan	vs. Lefties	.275	66	.451	56	.305	106	4.40	33	4.12	119	19.59	118
	vs. Righties	.182	134	.253	135	.247	134	1.18	102	6.84	100	22.63	127
Phil Garner	vs. Lefties	.231	110	.357	103	.311	97	2.80	71	10.91	37	13.94	75
	vs. Righties	.168	--	.232	--	.245	--	1.05	--	9.09	--	19.09	--
Pedro Guerrero	vs. Lefties	.365	4	.575	9	.451	6	4.79	29	13.85	19	10.77	47
	vs. Righties	.325	9	.524	20	.400	15	5.03	21	10.80	41	14.71	75
Mickey Hatcher	vs. Lefties	.328	21	.528	27	.384	29	3.20	59	8.63	69	4.32	4
	vs. Righties	.247	99	.352	103	.283	114	1.85	84	4.57	121	7.43	11
Glenn Hoffman	vs. Lefties	.224	119	.286	125	.269	127	0.00	113	3.70	129	18.52	110
	vs. Righties	.217	--	.241	--	.270	--	0.00	--	5.43	--	14.13	--
Ken Landreaux	vs. Lefties	.200	--	.250	--	.238	--	0.00	--	4.35	--	17.39	--
	vs. Righties	.204	128	.333	110	.272	126	3.70	42	8.29	78	13.26	60
Tito Landrum	vs. Lefties	.230	112	.276	128	.287	117	0.00	113	6.32	95	24.21	131
	vs. Righties	.200	--	.300	--	.294	--	3.33	--	11.76	--	20.59	--
Mike Marshall	vs. Lefties	.280	58	.464	47	.313	95	4.00	45	3.73	128	14.93	80
	vs. Righties	.300	23	.458	48	.333	69	3.97	34	4.42	124	20.07	115
Steve Sax	vs. Lefties	.278	60	.376	94	.330	75	0.98	106	6.76	90	6.31	8
	vs. Righties	.281	51	.365	97	.332	73	0.99	107	6.58	102	10.66	31
Mike Scioscia	vs. Lefties	.273	68	.348	105	.356	48	0.00	113	10.60	38	7.28	17
	vs. Righties	.261	80	.371	92	.338	65	1.82	85	10.48	46	3.23	1
John Shelby	vs. Lefties	.335	16	.595	7	.366	39	6.33	16	5.81	102	17.44	100
	vs. Righties	.248	97	.399	73	.293	107	3.46	47	6.07	108	19.36	111
Franklin Stubbs	vs. Lefties	.186	133	.186	135	.205	135	0.00	113	1.10	135	24.18	130
	vs. Righties	.247	100	.480	33	.313	95	5.33	19	9.04	66	18.98	107
Alex Trevino	vs. Lefties	.222	120	.370	97	.297	112	2.47	74	6.59	91	18.68	113
	vs. Righties	.222	--	.317	--	.234	--	1.59	--	0.00	--	16.92	--
Team Average	vs. Lefties	.265	5	.389	10	.322	9	2.10	11	7.27	11	13.79	2
	vs. Righties	.245	12	.362	12	.303	12	2.35	7	7.28	12	15.74	7
League Average	vs. Lefties	.263		.409		.332		2.81		9.08		15.22	
	vs. Righties	.260		.401		.327		2.73		8.70		15.85	

Batting with Runners on Base and Bases Empty

		BA	Rank	SA	Rank	OBA	Rank	HR %	Rank	BB %	Rank	SO %	Rank
Dave Anderson	Runners On	.293	51	.380	93	.327	98	0.00	122	3.85	129	16.35	96
	Bases Empty	.202	130	.277	129	.285	112	0.58	119	10.36	36	13.47	59
Mariano Duncan	Runners On	.208	127	.292	127	.238	131	1.04	108	3.74	130	18.69	117
	Bases Empty	.218	121	.339	111	.283	115	3.03	61	7.22	75	23.33	130
Phil Garner	Runners On	.211	124	.305	120	.325	101	2.11	80	14.75	19	12.30	55
	Bases Empty	.203	129	.308	119	.255	129	2.10	83	6.54	88	18.95	107
Pedro Guerrero	Runners On	.337	11	.514	18	.421	12	4.53	26	13.10	31	13.45	65
	Bases Empty	.338	4	.560	13	.412	6	5.30	25	10.59	29	13.53	61
Mickey Hatcher	Runners On	.294	50	.445	58	.365	51	2.52	65	10.00	69	5.71	9
	Bases Empty	.274	61	.417	63	.299	98	2.38	74	3.45	131	6.32	6
Ken Landreaux	Runners On	.263	66	.438	66	.299	112	5.00	19	5.56	116	16.67	99
	Bases Empty	.157	137	.235	136	.246	134	1.96	85	9.65	44	11.40	38
Mike Marshall	Runners On	.329	13	.538	12	.358	58	4.76	22	4.42	125	14.60	86
	Bases Empty	.255	81	.375	95	.292	106	3.13	58	3.96	127	22.77	127
Steve Sax	Runners On	.263	88	.335	113	.326	99	0.48	119	8.51	87	10.21	32
	Bases Empty	.289	38	.387	84	.334	61	1.25	102	5.61	108	8.64	14
Mike Scioscia	Runners On	.257	97	.294	126	.335	85	0.00	122	10.65	57	3.70	2
	Bases Empty	.270	65	.412	66	.349	45	2.19	79	10.42	35	4.89	2
John Shelby	Runners On	.278	75	.450	55	.301	111	3.83	39	4.78	121	22.61	132
	Bases Empty	.277	58	.476	36	.330	67	4.87	30	6.94	78	15.63	85
Franklin Stubbs	Runners On	.289	54	.503	25	.350	71	5.03	18	8.89	81	16.67	99
	Bases Empty	.194	132	.352	104	.247	133	3.52	53	6.17	101	22.63	126
Team Average	Runners On	.262	8	.380	11	.322	12	2.19	9	7.91	12	15.06	7
	Bases Empty	.244	12	.365	10	.300	12	2.32	8	6.80	11	15.13	4
League Average	Runners On	.267		.410		.341		2.66		9.88		14.92	
	Bases Empty	.256		.399		.319		2.82		7.98		16.22	

Overall Batting Compared to Late Inning Pressure Situations

		BA	Rank	SA	Rank	OBA	Rank	HR %	Rank	BB %	Rank	SO %	Rank	RDI %	Rank
Dave Anderson	Overall	.234	118	.313	124	.299	116	0.38	127	8.08	82	14.48	75	.129	135
	Pressure	.317	26	.488	29	.356	58	0.00	105	6.12	106	18.37	93	.250	71
Mariano Duncan	Overall	.215	126	.322	123	.267	131	2.30	79	5.92	119	21.60	130	.175	130
	Pressure	.324	22	.471	31	.439	6	0.00	105	13.95	22	20.93	108	.333	--
Phil Garner	Overall	.206	132	.307	128	.285	124	2.10	83	10.18	49	16.00	90	.230	113
	Pressure	.279	56	.395	66	.340	70	2.33	70	7.84	87	21.57	115	.400	15
Pedro Guerrero	Overall	.338	2	.539	11	.416	8	4.95	16	11.75	25	13.49	62	.354	10
	Pressure	.256	78	.359	86	.376	43	1.28	96	16.13	13	12.90	42	.471	7
Mickey Hatcher	Overall	.282	56	.429	60	.328	79	2.44	74	6.37	111	6.05	7	.349	14
	Pressure	.188	127	.250	130	.250	126	2.08	72	7.55	91	15.09	63	.200	96
Danny Heep	Overall	.163	--	.204	--	.226	--	0.00	--	7.48	--	9.35	--	.167	--
	Pressure	.069	--	.103	--	.156	--	0.00	--	9.09	--	15.15	--	.067	137
Ken Landreaux	Overall	.203	134	.324	122	.269	128	3.30	53	7.84	84	13.73	65	.211	119
	Pressure	.178	129	.200	134	.275	117	0.00	105	11.32	43	11.32	30	.188	101
Tito Landrum	Overall	.222	--	.282	--	.289	--	0.85	--	7.75	--	23.26	--	.233	--
	Pressure	.103	--	.103	--	.103	--	0.00	--	0.00	--	34.48	--	.077	136
Mike Marshall	Overall	.294	29	.460	40	.327	83	3.98	38	4.21	129	18.46	108	.343	18
	Pressure	.196	124	.339	103	.220	134	3.57	39	1.69	135	32.20	138	.333	36
Steve Sax	Overall	.280	58	.369	98	.331	72	0.98	116	6.64	108	9.20	17	.252	93
	Pressure	.351	13	.468	36	.408	23	1.06	102	8.74	73	10.68	27	.256	70
Mike Scioscia	Overall	.265	82	.364	102	.343	62	1.30	105	10.52	40	4.40	1	.270	82
	Pressure	.247	85	.397	65	.329	79	2.74	54	10.71	50	5.95	6	.429	10
John Shelby	Overall	.277	62	.464	38	.317	94	4.41	31	5.98	118	18.73	111	.272	80
	Pressure	.169	131	.268	127	.234	131	2.82	51	7.79	89	25.97	131	.154	118
Franklin Stubbs	Overall	.233	119	.415	73	.290	120	4.15	36	7.33	94	20.09	125	.261	88
	Pressure	.169	130	.356	90	.279	110	5.08	19	13.04	30	24.64	124	.188	101
Alex Trevino	Overall	.222	--	.347	--	.271	--	2.08	--	3.85	--	17.95	--	.213	118
	Pressure	.194	125	.278	120	.216	135	0.00	105	2.63	127	13.16	44	.348	33
Team Average	Overall	.252	12	.371	12	.309	12	2.27	8	7.28	12	15.10	6	.263	8
	Pressure	.222	12	.321	12	.300	12	1.40	11	9.62	6	17.71	9	.240	10
League Average	Overall	.261		.404		.328		2.75		8.83		15.64		.272	
	Pressure	.258		.385		.331		2.46		9.54		16.95		.261	

Additional Miscellaneous Batting Comparisons

	Grass Surface		Artificial Surface		Home Games		Road Games		Runners in Scoring Position		Runners in Scoring Pos and Two Outs		Leading Off Inning		Runners on 3B with less than 2 Outs	
	BA	Rank	BA	Rank	BA	Rank	BA	Rank	BA	Rank	BA	Rank	OBA	Rank	RDI %	Rank
Dave Anderson	.225	116	.256	87	.250	102	.216	125	.200	121	.136	--	.269	122	.308	136
Mariano Duncan	.221	121	.197	129	.227	118	.205	129	.170	129	.154	125	.250	130	.364	130
Phil Garner	.221	119	.192	131	.198	130	.213	127	.231	109	.115	130	.304	100	.750	11
Pedro Guerrero	.333	9	.354	5	.324	16	.352	3	.344	7	.319	22	.391	17	.641	38
Mickey Hatcher	.249	93	.372	2	.255	95	.307	21	.296	43	.243	74	.313	92	.727	15
Glenn Hoffman	.235	106	.167	--	.262	--	.183	--	.143	--	.133	--	.229	--	.545	79
Ken Landreaux	.230	110	.143	--	.297	39	.110	136	.213	--	.190	--	.233	132	.500	91
Mike Marshall	.286	42	.317	19	.284	58	.301	26	.328	13	.323	17	.333	62	.429	118
Mike Ramsey	.236	105	.222	--	.236	--	.229	--	.219	--	.235	--	.240	--	.545	79
Steve Sax	.280	51	.281	56	.260	89	.299	28	.269	71	.271	53	.326	77	.483	101
Mike Scioscia	.280	52	.224	119	.260	87	.269	69	.267	74	.196	113	.318	86	.650	34
John Shelby	.269	69	.299	30	.243	108	.312	17	.259	82	.279	48	.313	92	.480	104
Franklin Stubbs	.205	130	.326	15	.167	135	.311	19	.277	64	.271	54	.261	128	.389	127
Alex Trevino	.204	131	.268	--	.187	--	.261	--	.178	--	.136	--	.265	--	.583	67
Tracy Woodson	.215	125	.256	--	.185	--	.256	--	.154	--	.000	--	.200	--	.556	--
Team Average	.249	10	.259	7	.240	12	.262	4	.251	9	.233	9	.298	12	.505	11
League Average	.260		.261		.265		.256		.258		.241		.324		.554	

Pitching vs. Left and Right Handed Batters

		BA	Rank	SA	Rank	OBA	Rank	HR %	Rank	BB %	Rank	SO %	Rank
Orel Hershiser	vs. Lefties	.272	67	.385	51	.330	47	1.70	37	7.60	24	14.11	50
	vs. Righties	.212	16	.304	10	.266	14	1.70	17	5.58	19	22.10	20
Shawn Hillegas	vs. Lefties	.275	74	.404	62	.398	104	2.75	81	17.16	111	20.15	17
	vs. Righties	.206	--	.280	--	.261	--	1.87	--	6.78	--	20.34	--
Brian Holton	vs. Lefties	.272	68	.392	54	.361	81	2.53	69	12.15	89	8.84	98
	vs. Righties	.267	73	.461	94	.303	39	4.24	97	5.59	20	23.46	10
Rick Honeycutt	vs. Lefties	.218	9	.333	23	.253	3	2.30	57	4.40	5	18.68	26
	vs. Righties	.292	100	.435	83	.362	100	2.05	24	9.45	86	17.28	49
Ken Howell	vs. Lefties	.271	65	.375	43	.381	98	1.04	13	14.91	107	21.93	11
	vs. Righties	.259	--	.509	--	.333	--	5.56	--	9.60	--	28.00	--
Tim Leary	vs. Lefties	.289	86	.451	87	.344	64	2.45	64	7.21	20	8.11	100
	vs. Righties	.282	92	.473	98	.343	89	4.55	99	8.10	62	17.41	48
Alejandro Pena	vs. Lefties	.237	28	.305	12	.320	40	1.13	17	11.06	71	18.75	23
	vs. Righties	.267	73	.473	99	.331	73	4.67	102	8.28	75	21.89	22
Fernando Valenzuela	vs. Lefties	.228	18	.377	46	.283	10	2.40	63	7.07	19	23.37	9
	vs. Righties	.270	78	.406	58	.361	99	2.62	47	11.91	101	15.77	67
Bob Welch	vs. Lefties	.236	27	.345	32	.301	24	1.88	43	8.42	31	16.84	38
	vs. Righties	.201	12	.338	21	.273	19	2.84	51	8.31	76	22.17	19
Matt Young	vs. Lefties	.234	--	.313	--	.279	--	1.56	--	5.88	--	16.18	--
	vs. Righties	.311	107	.411	65	.364	101	1.32	11	7.83	56	18.67	38
Team Average	vs. Lefties	.257	3	.370	1	.326	3	1.92	2	9.15	4	15.47	3
	vs. Righties	.253	7	.391	3	.324	9	2.66	1	8.99	10	19.19	2
League Average	vs. Lefties	.268		.404		.341		2.34		9.74		14.31	
	vs. Righties	.255		.403		.319		3.05		8.16		16.61	

Pitching with Runners on Base and Bases Empty

		BA	Rank	SA	Rank	OBA	Rank	HR %	Rank	BB %	Rank	SO %	Rank
Orel Hershiser	Runners On	.254	46	.353	25	.317	23	1.51	23	7.43	15	17.12	38
	Bases Empty	.242	39	.352	24	.296	27	1.82	23	6.32	28	17.57	40
Shawn Hillegas	Runners On	.271	--	.333	--	.336	--	2.08	--	9.01	--	19.82	--
	Bases Empty	.217	14	.350	22	.333	78	2.50	49	14.89	112	20.57	20
Brian Holton	Runners On	.239	26	.374	37	.320	31	2.58	61	11.11	80	18.33	25
	Bases Empty	.298	101	.476	100	.344	93	4.17	96	6.67	34	13.89	79
Rick Honeycutt	Runners On	.291	95	.447	86	.379	102	2.43	52	11.49	84	17.02	41
	Bases Empty	.268	76	.393	63	.314	54	1.84	26	6.21	24	17.93	37
Tim Leary	Runners On	.313	108	.506	108	.381	104	3.98	99	9.36	49	10.84	94
	Bases Empty	.266	72	.431	86	.316	57	3.23	80	6.39	30	14.66	66
Alejandro Pena	Runners On	.248	36	.383	42	.333	52	2.84	68	10.98	79	20.81	14
	Bases Empty	.253	57	.382	55	.319	61	2.69	60	8.82	79	19.61	27
Fernando Valenzuela	Runners On	.257	50	.388	47	.330	44	2.30	48	9.24	44	15.94	50
	Bases Empty	.268	75	.413	76	.365	104	2.86	67	12.94	110	18.09	34
Bob Welch	Runners On	.249	37	.404	61	.332	47	3.47	88	10.93	78	17.60	30
	Bases Empty	.207	7	.310	11	.265	5	1.66	19	6.90	41	19.94	24
Matt Young	Runners On	.312	107	.416	67	.370	97	1.60	27	8.63	27	17.27	36
	Bases Empty	.256	--	.333	--	.295	--	1.11	--	5.26	--	18.95	--
Team Average	Runners On	.266	7	.399	5	.344	9	2.52	5	10.14	8	16.70	2
	Bases Empty	.247	4	.370	1	.311	3	2.21	1	8.19	7	18.29	2
League Average	Runners On	.267		.410		.341		2.66		9.88		14.92	
	Bases Empty	.256		.399		.319		2.82		7.98		16.22	

Overall Pitching Compared to Late Inning Pressure Situations

		BA	Rank	SA	Rank	OBA	Rank	HR %	Rank	BB %	Rank	SO %	Rank
Tim Crews	Overall	.268	--	.384	--	.325	--	1.79	--	6.45	--	16.13	--
	Pressure	.250	46	.357	43	.304	31	1.19	28	7.53	32	18.28	43
Orel Hershiser	Overall	.247	41	.352	24	.304	22	1.70	17	6.77	17	17.38	31
	Pressure	.315	98	.469	92	.395	98	2.10	50	10.98	77	12.80	74
Shawn Hillegas	Overall	.241	23	.343	18	.335	79	2.31	43	12.30	107	20.24	18
	Pressure	.158	--	.158	--	.273	--	0.00	--	13.64	--	27.27	--
Brian Holton	Overall	.269	77	.427	79	.332	73	3.41	87	8.89	63	16.11	47
	Pressure	.247	43	.416	77	.324	45	3.37	83	10.78	73	15.69	59
Rick Honeycutt	Overall	.278	91	.416	72	.343	89	2.09	32	8.57	50	17.52	30
	Pressure	.500	--	.625	--	.600	--	0.00	--	20.00	--	10.00	--
Ken Howell	Overall	.265	--	.446	--	.356	--	3.43	--	12.13	--	25.10	--
	Pressure	.278	78	.380	59	.367	84	1.27	31	11.96	87	23.91	16
Tim Leary	Overall	.285	100	.462	103	.343	90	3.54	95	7.68	27	13.01	83
	Pressure	.257	57	.329	24	.307	33	1.43	37	6.67	23	14.67	64
Alejandro Pena	Overall	.251	47	.382	48	.325	55	2.75	66	9.81	78	20.16	20
	Pressure	.211	17	.289	11	.301	27	1.11	27	11.32	83	26.42	8
Fernando Valenzuela	Overall	.262	66	.401	59	.348	94	2.58	60	11.11	102	17.03	38
	Pressure	.229	28	.300	15	.312	37	0.71	23	10.56	69	17.39	47
Bob Welch	Overall	.221	9	.342	16	.289	7	2.28	40	8.37	45	19.08	24
	Pressure	.248	44	.347	33	.315	41	1.98	48	8.85	47	8.85	101
Matt Young	Overall	.288	--	.381	--	.339	--	1.40	--	7.26	--	17.95	--
	Pressure	.316	99	.406	71	.367	85	1.29	34	7.65	33	18.82	40
Team Average	Overall	.255	4	.382	1	.325	6	2.34	2	9.06	7	17.59	2
	Pressure	.264	9	.363	3	.340	7	1.44	2	10.12	7	16.61	9
League Average	Overall	.261		.404		.328		2.75		8.83		15.64	
	Pressure	.260		.391		.337		2.47		10.04		17.14	

Additional Miscellaneous Pitching Comparisons

	Grass Surface BA	Rank	Artificial Surface BA	Rank	Home Games BA	Rank	Road Games BA	Rank	Runners in Scoring Position BA	Rank	Runners in Scoring Pos and Two Outs BA	Rank	Leading Off Inning OBA	Rank
Tim Belcher	.217	11	.368	--	.217	--	.368	--	.250	--	.091	--	.353	--
Ron Davis	.364	111	.268	--	.423	--	.260	--	.417	--	.500	--	.297	--
Brad Havens	.255	54	.147	--	.259	--	.203	--	.353	--	.429	112	.242	--
Orel Hershiser	.247	39	.247	37	.236	28	.259	49	.225	29	.196	29	.296	24
Shawn Hillegas	.254	50	.179	--	.297	--	.181	3	.286	--	.136	--	.377	99
Brian Holton	.262	61	.284	85	.255	56	.282	78	.256	61	.224	51	.316	48
Rick Honeycutt	.280	83	.273	71	.281	90	.275	66	.272	77	.236	64	.298	28
Ken Howell	.247	38	.310	--	.213	--	.295	95	.300	--	.333	--	.474	112
Tim Leary	.278	78	.302	97	.280	89	.290	86	.300	94	.315	100	.321	57
Alejandro Pena	.239	29	.281	--	.235	27	.276	70	.189	6	.143	8	.306	41
Fernando Valenzuela	.251	43	.307	98	.251	48	.273	62	.216	20	.228	56	.339	77
Bob Welch	.217	10	.243	30	.225	23	.217	14	.241	43	.198	32	.232	4
Matt Young	.254	48	.356	--	.243	--	.337	--	.267	74	.194	28	.364	--
Team Average	.249	3	.271	9	.249	5	.261	4	.249	4	.224	5	.308	3
League Average	.260		.261		.256		.265		.258		.241		.324	

MONTREAL EXPOS

There aren't many guarantees in baseball. This is as close as you'll come: The Montreal Expos won't match last season's 91–71 record.

How can we be so sure? Simple. Montreal had an record of 28–14 (.667) in one-run games last season, the best in either league. Such a good record in one-run games is one of the most reliable leading indicators of a team that will fail to equal its overall record the next season. (On the other hand, a poor record in one-run games signals likely improvement a year later.)

The following table shows the number of teams since 1969 that improved their overall won-lost records according to their records in games decided by one run the previous season. It's clear that the better a team's record in one-run games, the greater the chance that its overall mark will decline a year later:

| | Overall Mark Next Season | | |
Pct. in One-run Games	Better	Worse	Pct. Better
Less than .450	75	31	.708
Between .450 and .500	51	44	.537
Between .501 and .550	39	46	.459
Better than .550	29	72	.287

If we examine teams with records similar to Montreal's last season, both in one-run games and overall, the picture becomes even more dismal for the Expos. Since 1969, 32 teams won 60 percent or more of their one-run games with at least as many overall wins as the 1987 Expos. Only one improved its overall record a year later: the Baltimore Orioles, by a paper-thin .004 margin (from 91–71 in 1974 to 90–69 in 1975). On the down side, 10 of those 32 teams fell more than 100 percentage points short (equal to 16 wins over a 162-game schedule) of their overall records the next season:

| | | 1-Run Games | | | Overall | | | Next Season | | |
Year	Team	W	L	Pct.	W	L	Pct.	W	L	Pct.
1963	Dodgers	33	18	.647	99	63	.611	80	82	.494
1966	Dodgers	34	19	.642	95	67	.586	73	89	.451
1969	Braves	28	17	.622	93	69	.574	76	86	.469
1969	Mets	41	23	.641	100	62	.617	83	79	.512
1970	Reds	27	15	.643	102	60	.630	79	83	.488
1980	Royals	29	12	.707	97	65	.599	50	53	.485
1983	White Sox	28	17	.622	99	63	.611	74	88	.457
1984	Tigers	25	11	.694	104	58	.642	84	77	.522
1986	Red Sox	24	10	.706	95	66	.590	78	84	.481
1986	Angels	28	16	.636	92	70	.568	75	87	.463

Why should a good record in one-run games portend an overall decline in a team's performance? After all, according to conventional thinking, teams that win more than their share of one-run contests are considered to be gritty teams with first-class bullpens.

Actually, the relationship is quite a logical one. Games decided by large margins are usually won by the better team. The smaller the margin of victory, the greater the element of chance in determining the outcome, and the greater the likelihood that the inferior team might win the game. The following table illustrates that rule, showing the results of all National League games over the past 10 seasons:

Margin	Won by Better Team	Won by Worse Team	Won by Better Team
1 run	1733	1368	.559
2–3 runs	1820	1376	.569
4–5 runs	1013	706	.589
6+ runs	763	508	.600

Because games decided by one run are less likely than others to indicate which of the teams is better, an extremely good or bad record in one-run contests distorts our picture of that team's quality. Montreal's record of 91–71 last season is one of those distortions. Consider, for example, that the Expos outscored their opponents by only 21 runs last season, a margin that is more typical of a team with a humbler record. There have been 27 teams during the divisional era that outscored their opponents by a margin of between 15 and 25 runs. They had a combined record of 2,147 wins and 2,003 losses. A 162-game slice of that humble pie tastes like 84–78 to us.

Exposing the Expos' Chances

All this must come as pretty bad news to those who thought the Expos were one step from bringing the provinces their first World Series, eh? Actually, there are several reasons not to despair totally. First, five of the 18 National League East titles (not including the Expos' pennant in the post-season circus following the 1981 players' strike) have been won by teams with records worse than Montreal's 1987 mark. Second, Montreal didn't add Pascual Perez to its roster until the end of August last season, three weeks before Floyd Youmans's season came to an abrupt end. If Pascual and Floyd behave themselves this season, the Expos' starting rotation will be vastly improved.

The third reason is another of those quirky statistical patterns that we often use to point us in the right direction. Montreal had an 86–76 record in 1982, and has alternated losing seasons with winning ones since then. The Expos are only the ninth team in modern major-league history to manufacture such a plus-minus-plus-minus-plus pattern. And although you might expect those teams to have continued their streaks by dropping below the .500 mark once again in the sixth season, only one of them failed to win a majority of its games in Year 6. But even more noteworthy, five of the eight snapped their streaks by compiling sixth-season records good enough for league or division titles (marked with asterisks in the following table):

Years	Team	Year 1	Year 2	Year 3	Year 4	Year 5	Year 6
1911–16	Phillies	79–73	73–79	88–63	74–80	90–62	91–62
1943–48	Cleve.	82–71	72–82	73–72	68–86	80–74	97–58*
1951–56	Red Sox	87–67	76–78	84–69	69–85	84–70	84–70
1971–76	K.C.	85–76	76–78	88–74	77–85	91–71	90–72*
1975–80	St. Lou.	82–80	72–90	83–79	69–93	86–76	74–88
1977–82	St. Lou.	83–79	69–93	86–76	74–88	59–43	92–70*
1980–85	K.C.	97–65	50–53	90–72	79–83	84–78	91–71*
1981–86	Houst.	61–49	77–85	85–77	80–82	83–79	96–66*
1983–87	Mont.	82–80	78–83	84–77	78–83	91–71	—

So what we have here is a case of dueling indicators, one pointing the Expos south, the other suggesting that they might be on the verge of at least a division title. We think that the one-run games indicator is far more powerful than the pattern of alternating winning and losing seasons, so we stand by our guarantee. But Buck Rodgers and Co. have surprised us before; maybe this will be a season in which an 89–73 mark will capture the division title, and both indicators will prove to be right.

Look Out, Lefties!

Once again last season, Montreal compiled a much higher batting average against left-handed pitchers than against right-handers. In fact, the difference of 28 batting-average points was the highest in either league since 1984, when the Expos hit 33 points higher against lefties. But once again, that difference failed to make the Expos a better team against southpaws than right-handers. Over the past four seasons, the Expos hit 23 points better against left-handers, but had a better record against right-handers in all but one of those years:

	Vs. Left-Handed Pitchers				Vs. Right-Handed Pitchers			
Year	BA	SA	W–L	Pct.	BA	SA	W–L	Pct.
1984	.275	.398	21–23	.477	.242	.348	57–60	.487
1985	.254	.392	26–22	.542	.244	.367	58–55	.513
1986	.269	.414	22–32	.409	.248	.364	56–51	.523
1987	.285	.430	28–22	.560	.257	.388	63–49	.563
Totals	.271	.409	97–99	.495	.248	.367	234–215	.521

We're not sure why Montreal hasn't been able to translate that difference in batting and slugging averages into more

wins against left-handed pitchers. But we did notice that the gap between those averages has given the Expos an unexpected advantage at crunch time.

You might think that teams that hit far better against one type of pitching than against another can be played like a fiddle by opposing managers in the late innings; that those managers can alternate left- and right-handed relievers to exploit a lineup with strength against only one type of pitching. But actually, just the opposite is true: Teams that hit much better one way or another—it doesn't matter whether the advantage is against left- or right-handers—are more likely to thrive on Late-Inning Pressure Situations than are teams who have balanced hitting against pitchers from both sides.

We divided every team of the past 10 seasons into one of three categories: those with balanced hitting against left- and right-handed pitchers (no more than four points difference in batting average), those with a moderate imbalance (between four and 20 points difference), and those with a pronounced imbalance (more than 20 points). Notice in the following table that it's that last group, in which the 1987 Expos are included, that is most likely to hit better in Late-Inning Pressure Situations than overall:

	Better in LIP	Worse in LIP	Better in LIP
Balanced hitting	25	41	.379
Moderate imbalance	71	95	.428
Pronounced imbalance	26	20	.565

Many teams strive to attain a balance that will allow them to "play the percentages" with pinch-hitters in the late innings of close games. But it appears that those are the very teams that are *least* likely to match the batter to the appropriate late-game situation. Apparently, a lineup stacked against one side is more likely to freeze an opposing manager into strategic paralysis. After all, with Brooks, Wallach, Galarraga, and Raines drooling at the chance to swing against southpaws, it's tough to slip a left-handed reliever into and out of a game fast enough to survive the assault.

Going for Four in a Row

Do you think the Expos would be more likely to win tonight's game if they were on a winning streak than if they were on a losing streak? That assumption seems to be the basis for much of the "advice" provided by newspaper betting touts. You've all seen that trash: "Phillies on a roll. Major wager at home." "Padres shaky for past week. Take streaking Cardinals instead."

Expos fans would've gone broke betting on that angle last season. That is, if they had any money left after betting on the same scam during the past few seasons, because in each of past five years, Montreal has had a better record when it's lost the past three games than coming off three consecutive wins. Last season, Montreal took the field 26 times with winning streaks of three (or more) games. They split those 26, hardly a good enough record to save those bettors who'd wagered *against* Les Expos on each of the 13 occasions they took the field with a three-game losing streak: Montreal *won* 11 of those 13 games. The five-year figures:

Results of last 3 games	1983	1984	1985	1986	1987	Total
Following three wins	8–11	7–9	7–12	8–8	13–13	43–53
Following three losses	7–9	13–6	8–8	10–7	11–2	49–32

For the three-year period, Montreal had a .605 winning percentage coming off three losses, compared to .448 coming off three wins. And the Expos aren't an exception; they prove the rule. Last season, 17 of the 26 major-league teams had better records off three losses than off three wins, a pattern typical of the past few seasons. The year by year breakdown during the 1980s:

	1980	1981	1982	1983	1984	1985	1986	1987
Better off 3 wins	14	9	13	7	10	11	8	9
Better off 3 losses	12	14	13	19	16	15	18	17

Don't bother to grab your calculator; we'll add those totals for you. During the 1980s, 81 teams compiled better records off three game winning streaks and 124 had better records off three-game losing streaks. That three-to-two margin is greater than at any other time in major-league history. But it's a fact that for the past seven decades, teams have invariably played better off losing streaks than winning streaks. All together since 1920, 693 teams had better records following three consecutive losses, 580 had better records coming off three straight wins:

	1920s	1930s	1940s	1950s	1960s	1970s	1980s
Better off 3 wins	74	75	72	67	96	115	81
Better off 3 losses	82	83	85	89	102	128	124

Now maybe you're thinking that three games isn't enough to indicate whether a team is truly hot or cold. Well, if you extend the length of the streak to five games, the differences become even greater—597 teams were better coming off five losses, 317 were better off five wins:

	1980s	1970s	1960s	1950s	1940s	1930s	1920s
Better off 5 wins	56	59	51	38	36	32	45
Better off 5 losses	97	121	89	79	77	69	65

What does all this prove? Simply that you can't use a baseball team's past performances like those of a five-thousand-dollar claimer at Blue Bonnet. A short losing streak doesn't mean that a team is likely to continue losing; in fact, just the opposite is true. Obedient to the law of averages, teams tend to play better following losses than following wins.

There's no question that over the course of a 162-game season, every team goes through streaks during which it wins a series of games, or loses a series, usually both. But do teams really get hot and cold? Or are those streaks merely the result of random chance, the same as a long streak of heads or tails when tossing an honest coin? The evidence proves that the latter is true. That would be more surprising to us had we not found the same result last year when we studied the question with regard not to teams but to individual players. (That study is updated in the Atlanta Braves essay on page 112.) But whether dealing with players or teams, the fact remains that they fare no better coming off a streak of recent success than off one of failure.

WON-LOST RECORD BY STARTING POSITION

MONTREAL 91-71	C	1B	2B	3B	SS	LF	CF	RF	P	Leadoff	Relief	Starts
Hubie Brooks	·	·	·	·	61-48	·	·	·	·	·	·	61-48
Curt Brown	·	·	·	·	·	·	·	·	·	·	1-4	·
Tim Burke	·	·	·	·	·	·	·	·	·	·	43-12	·
Bill Campbell	·	·	·	·	·	·	·	·	·	·	1-6	·
Casey Candaele	·	·	11-18	·	11-4	1-5	24-14	11-3	·	48-34	·	58-44
Jack Daugherty	·	·	·	·	·	·	·	·	·	·	·	·
Dave Engle	·	·	·	·	·	3-5	·	0-1	·	·	·	3-6
Jeff Fischer	·	·	·	·	·	·	·	·	1-1	·	0-2	1-1
Mike Fitzgerald	47-40	·	·	·	·	·	·	·	·	·	·	47-40
Tom Foley	·	·	22-14	0-1	16-14	·	·	·	·	1-1	·	38-29
Andres Galarraga	·	80-63	·	·	·	·	·	·	·	·	·	80-63
Neal Heaton	·	·	·	·	·	·	·	·	19-13	·	·	19-13
Ubaldo Heredia	·	·	·	·	·	·	·	·	1-1	·	·	1-1
Joe Hesketh	·	·	·	·	·	·	·	·	·	·	8-10	·
Wallace Johnson	·	5-2	·	·	·	·	·	·	·	0-1	·	5-2
Vance Law	·	5-5	58-39	4-7	·	·	·	·	·	·	0-3	67-51
Charlie Lea	·	·	·	·	·	·	·	·	0-1	·	·	0-1
Dennis Martinez	·	·	·	·	·	·	·	·	18-4	·	·	18-4
Bob McClure	·	·	·	·	·	·	·	·	·	·	27-25	·
Andy McGaffigan	·	·	·	·	·	·	·	·	·	·	35-34	·
Reid Nichols	·	·	·	·	·	·	24-18	·	·	7-3	·	24-18
Nelson Norman	·	·	·	·	0-1	·	·	·	·	·	·	0-1
Jeff Parrett	·	·	·	·	·	·	·	·	·	·	19-26	·
Pascual Perez	·	·	·	·	·	·	·	·	9-1	·	·	9-1
Alonzo Powell	·	·	·	·	·	5-4	·	·	·	1-4	·	5-4
Tim Raines	·	·	·	·	·	82-57	·	·	·	33-25	·	82-57
Jeff Reed	37-24	·	·	·	·	·	·	·	·	·	·	37-24
Luis Rivera	·	·	·	·	3-4	·	·	·	·	·	·	3-4
Tom Romano	·	·	·	·	·	·	·	·	·	·	·	·
Nelson Santovenia	·	·	·	·	·	·	·	·	·	·	·	·
Bob Sebra	·	·	·	·	·	·	·	·	10-17	·	1-8	10-17
Ray Shines	·	1-1	·	·	·	·	·	·	·	·	·	1-1
Bryn Smith	·	·	·	·	·	·	·	·	13-13	·	·	13-13
Lary Sorensen	·	·	·	·	·	·	·	·	2-3	·	7-11	2-3
Randy St. Claire	·	·	·	·	·	·	·	·	·	·	16-28	·
John Stefero	7-7	·	·	·	·	·	·	·	·	·	·	7-7
Jay Tibbs	·	·	·	·	·	·	·	·	5-7	·	0-7	5-7
Tim Wallach	·	·	·	87-63	·	·	·	·	·	·	0-1	87-63
Mitch Webster	·	·	·	·	·	·	·	80-67	·	·	·	80-67
Herm Winningham	·	·	·	·	·	·	·	43-39	·	1-3	·	43-39
Floyd Youmans	·	·	·	·	·	·	·	·	13-10	·	·	13-10

Batting vs. Left and Right Handed Pitchers

		BA	Rank	SA	Rank	OBA	Rank	HR %	Rank	BB %	Rank	SO %	Rank
Hubie Brooks	vs. Lefties	.331	20	.554	16	.354	49	4.13	42	3.94	122	14.17	76
	vs. Righties	.236	111	.375	89	.280	118	2.91	59	5.72	110	16.27	89
Casey Candaele	vs. Lefties	.310	31	.407	81	.352	52	0.00	113	6.56	92	1.64	1
	vs. Righties	.259	84	.327	114	.322	85	0.30	125	8.04	85	6.97	9
Mike Fitzgerald	vs. Lefties	.214	123	.294	120	.327	82	1.59	92	13.51	20	20.27	119
	vs. Righties	.261	81	.323	116	.348	56	0.62	120	11.83	24	12.90	53
Tom Foley	vs. Lefties	.190	--	.238	--	.190	--	0.00	--	0.00	--	23.81	--
	vs. Righties	.301	21	.448	44	.332	72	1.93	83	4.04	126	12.87	52
Andres Galarraga	vs. Lefties	.323	22	.543	21	.385	27	4.27	37	9.34	57	18.13	107
	vs. Righties	.297	27	.424	56	.351	92	1.55	92	5.66	112	22.17	123
Vance Law	vs. Lefties	.288	51	.412	79	.384	28	1.96	84	13.48	21	11.80	54
	vs. Righties	.265	78	.428	54	.326	79	3.18	53	8.60	74	13.06	58
Reid Nichols	vs. Lefties	.278	59	.451	54	.342	66	3.01	65	8.72	68	6.04	7
	vs. Righties	.143	--	.214	--	.200	--	0.00	--	6.67	--	26.67	--
Tim Raines	vs. Lefties	.396	2	.616	6	.471	5	3.05	63	11.23	35	9.63	39
	vs. Righties	.301	22	.486	29	.411	9	3.55	46	15.68	6	7.73	12
Jeff Reed	vs. Lefties	.258	--	.387	--	.294	--	0.00	--	5.71	--	11.43	--
	vs. Righties	.205	127	.261	133	.247	133	0.57	121	5.18	116	8.29	15
Tim Wallach	vs. Lefties	.306	35	.444	61	.353	51	0.63	112	6.36	94	16.18	94
	vs. Righties	.296	29	.540	11	.340	64	5.77	14	5.52	113	14.86	77
Mitch Webster	vs. Lefties	.285	53	.455	52	.344	63	3.50	54	7.73	79	13.18	67
	vs. Righties	.278	59	.425	55	.369	30	2.06	80	11.62	26	14.47	74
Herm Winningham	vs. Lefties	.345	--	.448	--	.394	--	0.00	--	9.09	--	27.27	--
	vs. Righties	.230	116	.340	106	.295	104	1.26	99	8.78	71	16.71	94
Team Average	vs. Lefties	.285	1	.430	3	.346	2	2.16	10	8.32	9	14.59	5
	vs. Righties	.257	8	.388	8	.321	11	2.18	10	8.05	9	15.03	4
League Average	vs. Lefties	.263		.409		.332		2.81		9.08		15.22	
	vs. Righties	.260		.401		.327		2.73		8.70		15.85	

Batting with Runners on Base and Bases Empty

		BA	Rank	SA	Rank	OBA	Rank	HR %	Rank	BB %	Rank	SO %	Rank
Hubie Brooks	Runners On	.299	43	.450	54	.324	102	1.90	85	4.00	127	13.78	76
	Bases Empty	.228	117	.402	74	.278	120	4.57	33	6.41	92	17.52	99
Casey Candaele	Runners On	.263	90	.299	125	.322	103	0.00	122	7.69	100	3.85	3
	Bases Empty	.276	59	.369	100	.333	62	0.32	127	7.67	63	6.49	7
Mike Fitzgerald	Runners On	.237	112	.302	123	.355	61	0.72	116	14.79	18	17.16	106
	Bases Empty	.243	101	.318	116	.321	78	1.35	101	10.30	37	15.15	81
Tom Foley	Runners On	.256	98	.385	92	.256	129	1.71	89	0.00	136	17.80	112
	Bases Empty	.319	15	.466	44	.366	29	1.84	89	6.29	97	10.86	35
Andres Galarraga	Runners On	.344	7	.515	17	.415	17	2.29	77	9.30	76	22.59	131
	Bases Empty	.270	66	.408	70	.308	91	2.42	72	4.26	123	19.34	111
Vance Law	Runners On	.266	82	.375	94	.366	50	1.56	90	13.97	25	11.35	43
	Bases Empty	.279	54	.459	46	.331	65	3.69	49	7.22	74	13.69	63
Tim Raines	Runners On	.325	15	.505	24	.460	2	3.61	41	20.56	3	10.08	31
	Bases Empty	.333	5	.539	19	.409	9	3.27	56	10.29	38	7.12	10
Jeff Reed	Runners On	.226	119	.321	117	.281	122	1.19	100	7.00	111	7.00	15
	Bases Empty	.203	128	.252	133	.234	135	0.00	128	3.91	128	10.16	27
Tim Wallach	Runners On	.288	57	.485	32	.351	68	3.34	44	8.26	91	12.98	60
	Bases Empty	.310	19	.544	15	.334	60	5.44	21	2.95	133	17.70	101
Mitch Webster	Runners On	.285	61	.438	65	.372	41	2.41	72	12.08	35	12.75	58
	Bases Empty	.277	57	.434	60	.352	41	2.65	67	8.99	46	15.08	80
Herm Winningham	Runners On	.283	66	.449	56	.360	53	2.90	50	11.73	41	16.67	99
	Bases Empty	.211	124	.282	128	.263	128	0.00	128	6.70	83	18.30	104
Team Average	Runners On	.276	4	.411	6	.350	4	2.04	12	9.87	6	14.73	5
	Bases Empty	.258	4	.394	8	.311	10	2.26	9	6.74	12	15.03	3
League Average	Runners On	.267		.410		.341		2.66		9.88		14.92	
	Bases Empty	.256		.399		.319		2.82		7.98		16.22	

Overall Batting Compared to Late Inning Pressure Situations

		BA	Rank	SA	Rank	OBA	Rank	HR %	Rank	BB %	Rank	SO %	Rank	RDI %	Rank
Hubie Brooks	Overall	.263	86	.426	61	.301	113	3.26	57	5.23	125	15.69	88	.311	40
	Pressure	.219	112	.406	58	.239	130	4.69	24	2.99	124	19.40	100	.250	71
Casey Candaele	Overall	.272	74	.347	112	.330	75	0.22	132	7.68	85	5.66	6	.204	123
	Pressure	.328	20	.469	34	.362	51	1.56	88	5.63	111	5.63	5	.167	111
Dave Engle	Overall	.226	--	.310	--	.278	--	1.19	--	6.67	--	12.22	--	.452	--
	Pressure	.321	--	.464	--	.321	--	3.57	--	0.00	--	17.86	--	.556	3
Mike Fitzgerald	Overall	.240	111	.310	126	.338	65	1.05	113	12.57	18	16.17	94	.248	99
	Pressure	.250	83	.273	126	.313	89	0.00	105	8.16	81	16.33	79	.211	91
Tom Foley	Overall	.293	33	.432	57	.322	90	1.79	90	3.75	132	13.65	64	.247	101
	Pressure	.395	2	.581	9	.435	9	2.33	70	6.38	104	8.51	15	.286	--
Andres Galarraga	Overall	.305	16	.459	41	.361	38	2.36	76	6.77	104	20.96	128	.346	16
	Pressure	.282	52	.462	37	.321	85	2.56	62	3.57	122	21.43	114	.391	19
Vance Law	Overall	.273	71	.422	65	.347	54	2.75	66	10.37	43	12.60	52	.284	67
	Pressure	.259	74	.362	83	.338	71	1.72	81	10.77	49	9.23	19	.444	9
Tim Raines	Overall	.330	5	.526	14	.429	3	3.40	51	14.35	10	8.29	12	.290	60
	Pressure	.394	3	.690	2	.482	3	4.23	27	15.29	18	7.06	9	.389	20
Jeff Reed	Overall	.213	128	.280	134	.254	133	0.48	122	5.26	124	8.77	14	.277	71
	Pressure	.211	--	.263	--	.286	--	0.00	--	9.09	--	4.55	--	.333	--
Tim Wallach	Overall	.298	23	.514	17	.343	61	4.38	32	5.75	121	15.22	84	.351	12
	Pressure	.301	38	.589	8	.320	88	8.22	5	2.67	126	24.00	120	.308	55
Mitch Webster	Overall	.281	57	.435	54	.361	39	2.55	70	10.36	45	14.05	71	.265	86
	Pressure	.282	55	.394	67	.341	69	2.82	51	8.43	77	18.07	88	.188	101
Herm Winningham	Overall	.239	113	.349	110	.304	109	1.15	107	8.81	65	17.62	105	.333	22
	Pressure	.160	134	.240	131	.288	105	2.00	75	15.25	19	30.51	137	.333	36
Team Average	Overall	.265	3	.401	8	.328	7	2.17	10	8.13	11	14.90	4	.290	2
	Pressure	.282	2	.440	1	.335	7	3.00	4	7.39	12	15.52	3	.304	2
League Average	Overall	.261		.404		.328		2.75		8.83		15.64		.272	
	Pressure	.258		.385		.331		2.46		9.54		16.95		.261	

Additional Miscellaneous Batting Comparisons

	Grass Surface BA	Rank	Artificial Surface BA	Rank	Home Games BA	Rank	Road Games BA	Rank	Runners in Scoring Position BA	Rank	Runners in Scoring Pos and Two Outs BA	Rank	Leading Off Inning OBA	Rank	Runners on 3B with less than 2 Outs RDI %	Rank
Hubie Brooks	.241	102	.268	74	.289	50	.233	113	.300	35	.321	20	.231	133	.517	89
Casey Candaele	.286	42	.267	75	.270	75	.273	62	.205	118	.217	91	.311	94	.533	86
Mike Fitzgerald	.273	--	.229	114	.253	96	.226	116	.264	77	.214	95	.333	62	.632	44
Tom Foley	.295	30	.291	40	.314	21	.277	55	.254	86	.207	103	.389	20	.417	122
Andres Galarraga	.288	40	.311	23	.314	20	.296	30	.331	11	.357	9	.367	37	.571	72
Vance Law	.263	78	.277	62	.268	76	.278	50	.277	63	.274	50	.287	112	.607	53
Reid Nichols	.310	--	.254	91	.293	--	.236	--	.387	--	.353	--	.260	129	.625	--
Tim Raines	.340	3	.326	14	.337	10	.323	9	.336	9	.286	42	.431	7	.565	76
Jeff Reed	.211	--	.213	125	.163	136	.248	96	.235	106	.185	120	.275	118	.583	67
Tim Wallach	.305	23	.296	34	.300	33	.297	29	.280	58	.279	47	.361	43	.600	57
Mitch Webster	.297	29	.274	66	.267	79	.294	32	.287	50	.264	60	.340	59	.462	111
Herm Winningham	.250	92	.236	109	.272	73	.204	131	.318	23	.343	14	.186	136	.833	2
Team Average	.267	3	.265	3	.272	4	.259	6	.277	2	.267	1	.310	10	.558	7
League Average	.260		.261		.265		.256		.258		.241		.324		.554	

Pitching vs. Left and Right Handed Batters

		BA	Rank	SA	Rank	OBA	Rank	HR %	Rank	BB %	Rank	SO %	Rank
Tim Burke	vs. Lefties	.218	8	.288	6	.264	5	1.18	19	5.82	11	11.64	72
	vs. Righties	.172	1	.217	2	.201	1	0.64	4	3.64	1	21.82	23
Neal Heaton	vs. Lefties	.244	36	.415	69	.266	7	3.25	95	3.08	2	18.46	28
	vs. Righties	.280	91	.428	78	.316	55	3.32	73	4.87	9	11.96	99
Dennis Martinez	vs. Lefties	.238	30	.343	29	.294	18	1.45	27	7.47	22	14.40	48
	vs. Righties	.252	53	.376	37	.312	47	1.98	21	5.36	16	13.39	85
Andy McGaffigan	vs. Lefties	.271	65	.392	53	.343	62	1.67	35	9.56	53	18.75	23
	vs. Righties	.193	7	.237	3	.254	7	0.48	3	7.02	42	21.49	25
Jeff Parrett	vs. Lefties	.250	41	.407	64	.333	50	3.57	100	11.11	73	17.90	32
	vs. Righties	.198	--	.352	--	.291	--	3.30	--	11.43	--	25.71	--
Pascual Perez	vs. Lefties	.223	13	.291	8	.286	12	1.35	24	7.41	21	20.37	16
	vs. Righties	.183	--	.308	--	.211	--	2.88	--	3.60	--	22.52	--
Bob Sebra	vs. Lefties	.259	50	.398	59	.329	46	2.14	54	9.22	47	18.68	27
	vs. Righties	.288	99	.424	74	.347	93	2.32	36	8.19	66	22.51	15
Bryn Smith	vs. Lefties	.259	51	.372	41	.293	16	2.31	58	4.84	8	13.17	57
	vs. Righties	.295	101	.462	95	.333	76	3.19	70	4.80	8	16.61	57
Lary Sorensen	vs. Lefties	.311	108	.511	108	.373	94	4.44	107	8.65	37	7.69	105
	vs. Righties	.264	--	.415	--	.297	--	2.83	--	2.70	--	11.71	--
Randy St. Claire	vs. Lefties	.278	76	.373	42	.314	32	1.59	32	5.80	10	14.49	47
	vs. Righties	.223	--	.415	--	.294	--	5.38	--	8.33	--	15.97	--
Jay Tibbs	vs. Lefties	.294	92	.479	100	.370	90	2.45	65	10.87	66	11.96	70
	vs. Righties	.283	95	.422	72	.339	83	3.61	81	7.69	52	17.58	44
Floyd Youmans	vs. Lefties	.282	79	.444	82	.361	82	2.32	60	11.07	72	12.75	63
	vs. Righties	.209	14	.374	36	.261	12	3.74	83	6.76	36	27.05	6
Team Average	vs. Lefties	.259	5	.393	5	.320	1	2.26	5	8.06	1	15.31	4
	vs. Righties	.254	8	.394	5	.305	1	2.95	7	6.45	1	17.59	4
League Average	vs. Lefties	.268		.404		.341		2.34		9.74		14.31	
	vs. Righties	.255		.403		.319		3.05		8.16		16.61	

Pitching with Runners on Base and Bases Empty

		BA	Rank	SA	Rank	OBA	Rank	HR %	Rank	BB %	Rank	SO %	Rank
Tim Burke	Runners On	.180	1	.223	1	.232	1	0.72	10	6.29	7	16.35	45
	Bases Empty	.207	8	.277	4	.236	2	1.06	4	3.59	2	16.41	50
Neal Heaton	Runners On	.306	106	.515	110	.348	77	5.22	110	6.38	8	12.42	77
	Bases Empty	.256	65	.377	50	.285	17	2.25	38	3.54	1	13.36	88
Dennis Martinez	Runners On	.253	44	.359	32	.318	27	1.84	35	7.32	13	17.07	39
	Bases Empty	.237	34	.353	25	.289	21	1.52	15	6.23	26	11.90	95
Andy McGaffigan	Runners On	.202	5	.261	3	.283	4	0.49	5	9.36	50	20.85	13
	Bases Empty	.262	69	.369	36	.321	65	1.64	17	7.55	54	19.25	28
Jeff Parrett	Runners On	.245	31	.408	63	.353	87	3.06	76	14.05	108	18.18	26
	Bases Empty	.218	15	.368	33	.288	19	3.76	90	8.90	81	23.29	11
Pascual Perez	Runners On	.244	--	.378	--	.300	--	3.66	--	6.45	--	16.13	--
	Bases Empty	.188	2	.259	1	.233	1	1.18	6	5.56	14	23.89	8
Bob Sebra	Runners On	.302	103	.456	89	.366	96	2.11	43	9.79	59	18.40	23
	Bases Empty	.251	52	.376	48	.315	56	2.30	40	7.94	59	21.96	14
Bryn Smith	Runners On	.293	97	.475	98	.328	40	3.31	83	5.58	5	15.61	54
	Bases Empty	.261	68	.365	31	.297	28	2.25	36	4.28	5	13.90	78
Randy St. Claire	Runners On	.255	47	.427	78	.320	29	4.55	107	8.66	30	14.17	63
	Bases Empty	.247	46	.370	39	.290	23	2.74	62	5.81	16	16.13	53
Jay Tibbs	Runners On	.317	109	.489	103	.381	103	3.60	93	9.55	55	14.01	68
	Bases Empty	.268	77	.421	80	.335	79	2.63	57	9.09	82	15.31	58
Floyd Youmans	Runners On	.284	89	.472	97	.348	78	2.27	47	9.18	41	19.32	16
	Bases Empty	.230	21	.378	51	.302	33	3.33	83	9.40	86	18.12	33
Team Average	Runners On	.272	9	.426	8	.335	4	2.92	9	8.42	1	16.13	5
	Bases Empty	.245	3	.370	2	.296	1	2.39	2	6.37	1	16.70	6
League Average	Runners On	.267		.410		.341		2.66		9.88		14.92	
	Bases Empty	.256		.399		.319		2.82		7.98		16.22	

Overall Pitching Compared to Late Inning Pressure Situations

		BA	Rank	SA	Rank	OBA	Rank	HR %	Rank	BB %	Rank	SO %	Rank
Tim Burke	Overall	.196	2	.254	1	.234	1	0.92	3	4.80	3	16.38	43
	Pressure	.189	6	.239	6	.218	2	0.56	21	3.59	8	20.00	31
Neal Heaton	Overall	.274	86	.426	77	.308	27	3.31	82	4.58	2	13.01	82
	Pressure	.347	104	.429	80	.396	99	0.00	1	5.56	20	11.11	86
Dennis Martinez	Overall	.244	28	.355	26	.301	17	1.65	14	6.68	13	14.02	71
	Pressure	.206	13	.265	7	.250	7	0.00	1	5.56	20	16.67	51
Bob McClure	Overall	.241	--	.431	--	.309	--	4.10	--	9.01	--	14.86	--
	Pressure	.221	23	.364	47	.259	8	2.60	64	4.76	15	17.86	45
Andy McGaffigan	Overall	.235	16	.320	6	.303	18	1.12	5	8.40	46	20.00	22
	Pressure	.228	26	.323	21	.303	28	1.27	31	9.71	59	21.14	24
Jeff Parrett	Overall	.229	13	.385	51	.317	36	3.46	89	11.24	103	20.97	14
	Pressure	.271	68	.439	84	.358	76	3.74	89	11.81	85	18.90	39
Pascual Perez	Overall	.206	5	.298	3	.256	2	1.98	26	5.86	8	21.25	13
	Pressure	.219	21	.344	31	.219	3	3.13	79	0.00	1	12.12	77
Bob Sebra	Overall	.272	83	.410	66	.337	86	2.22	37	8.76	58	20.39	16
	Pressure	.189	8	.270	8	.211	1	2.70	67	2.56	4	20.51	29
Bryn Smith	Overall	.274	88	.410	65	.310	30	2.68	62	4.82	4	14.62	68
	Pressure	.500	--	.625	--	.500	--	0.00	--	0.00	--	10.00	--
Randy St. Claire	Overall	.250	45	.395	58	.304	20	3.52	94	7.09	19	15.25	57
	Pressure	.267	88	.367	51	.333	53	2.22	54	9.00	51	13.00	73
Jay Tibbs	Overall	.289	103	.450	96	.354	100	3.04	75	9.29	67	14.75	66
	Pressure	.222	--	.611	--	.333	--	11.11	--	14.29	--	9.52	--
Floyd Youmans	Overall	.251	48	.415	71	.321	44	2.91	72	9.31	68	18.61	27
	Pressure	.148	1	.185	1	.303	29	0.00	1	17.65	107	20.59	28
Team Average	Overall	.257	7	.393	5	.313	1	2.61	5	7.25	1	16.45	5
	Pressure	.233	1	.336	1	.295	1	1.85	3	7.86	1	17.68	4
League Average	Overall	.261		.404		.328		2.75		8.83		15.64	
	Pressure	.260		.391		.337		2.47		10.04		17.14	

Additional Miscellaneous Pitching Comparisons

	Grass Surface BA	Rank	Artificial Surface BA	Rank	Home Games BA	Rank	Road Games BA	Rank	Runners in Scoring Position BA	Rank	Runners in Scoring Pos and Two Outs BA	Rank	Leading Off Inning OBA	Rank
Tim Burke	.167	--	.208	9	.201	10	.190	5	.195	8	.162	18	.250	10
Neal Heaton	.296	99	.268	62	.262	66	.290	85	.305	100	.169	20	.248	8
Dennis Martinez	.246	35	.243	31	.217	17	.275	67	.258	66	.300	96	.325	62
Bob McClure	.205	--	.252	43	.248	41	.231	--	.203	--	.241	--	.188	--
Andy McGaffigan	.186	3	.251	42	.266	74	.205	8	.236	36	.210	40	.292	22
Jeff Parrett	.333	--	.208	11	.195	6	.276	--	.219	23	.135	6	.271	12
Pascual Perez	.167	--	.226	16	.258	61	.156	1	.261	--	.250	--	.292	20
Bob Sebra	.290	97	.266	60	.253	53	.291	87	.255	60	.255	73	.335	73
Bryn Smith	.287	91	.269	63	.272	84	.277	73	.301	95	.242	66	.226	2
Lary Sorensen	.194	--	.328	107	.387	--	.194	--	.291	--	.273	--	.356	--
Randy St. Claire	.203	--	.269	64	.252	52	.248	38	.262	70	.273	81	.186	1
Jay Tibbs	.328	--	.280	79	.272	83	.301	98	.314	106	.238	65	.329	69
Floyd Youmans	.274	76	.241	27	.270	79	.236	25	.236	37	.149	12	.320	55
Team Average	.253	5	.258	5	.257	7	.257	2	.259	8	.224	4	.290	2
League Average	.260		.261		.256		.265		.258		.241		.324	

NEW YORK METS

Everyone already knows why the Mets didn't repeat as division, league, and world champions last year. The analysis began last spring, and continued right through the season: Doc did drugs, McDowell had a hernia, Ojeda hurt his elbow, Sid ate too much, Darling thought too much, and Davey preened too much. Apart from the injuries to the pitchers and the alleged managerial blunders, everything at Shea was just as fine as could be.

After all, didn't Strawberry and Johnson become the first teammates in planetary history to join the 30/30 Club in the same season? And didn't Hernandez hit .292, McReynolds drive in 95 runs, and Carter, even in an off-year, knock out 20 dingers? Not to mention Teufel's 43 extra-base hits, Dykstra and Wilson hitting a combined (albeit unhappy) .290, and Magadan and Mazzilli having daily discussions on what it's like to hit .300 and not be able to crack the starting lineup.

Well gather 'round, boys and girls, all three million of you who danced into Shea last summer, and hear the real reason that the Mets didn't beat out the Cardinals:

They didn't hit well enough in the clutch.

Now, hold on a minute, Mets fans. Before you storm the Elias Sports Bureau Building, let's discuss this like calm, reasonable adults. Yes, we know that the Mets led the National League in runs scored (823). Yes, we know that no other team in the league averaged five runs per game. And we know that they outscored their opponents by the widest margin in the league (125 runs).

But consider the run-scoring components that the Mets' offense produced last season, and you'll see what we mean. The Mets led the league in hits, extra-base hits, and total bases, and despite all of those base runners, they grounded into the fewest double plays. They hit 192 home runs. Their total of 592 walks was third highest in the league, and they didn't run the bases recklessly, either (76.4 stolen-base percentage, compared to the overall National League average of 69.2).

When you compare the effort that went into the Mets' offense with the resulting output, you get that old Peggy Lee feeling, "Is that all there is?" They sure didn't get as much as they could from what they had. That feeling is fortified when you compare the Mets' "input and output" lines with those of their divisional rivals, the Cardinals and the Expos:

			Input					Output
	H	2B	3B	HR	BB	SB	GDP	Runs
Mets	1499	287	34	192	592	159	94	823
Cardinals	1449	252	49	94	644	248	126	798
Expos	1467	310	39	120	501	166	100	741

Sure, the Mets scored more runs than their rivals, but unlike the Cardinals and the Expos, the Mets didn't score as many as they should have. The linear weights formula that we mentioned in the Kansas City essay indicates that on the basis of their component parts, the 1987 Cardinals scored 58 more runs than they were expected to and the Expos scored 26 more runs than they should have. But the Mets came up short, scoring 11 fewer runs than they should have, given their component numbers.

So where did the Mets go wrong? Certainly their 1987 lineup was the most powerful that they have assembled in the team's 26-year history. But they lacked the key hit at the key time, especially early in the season, when the Cardinals built what turned out to be an insurmountable lead.

Let's look at the clutch hitting statistics. To start, let's compare each National League team's overall batting average to its average with runners in scoring position. The teams are ranked here according to the difference (in terms of batting average points) between the two figures:

Team	Overall	Scor. Pos.	Difference	W–L
Montreal	.265	.277	+ 12	92–70
Cincinnati	.266	.277	+ 11	84–78
San Francisco	.260	.271	+ 11	90–72
St. Louis	.263	.268	+ 5	95–67
Atlanta	.258	.260	+ 2	69–92
Los Angeles	.252	.251	− 1	73–89
Pittsburgh	.264	.261	− 3	80–82
Houston	.253	.247	− 6	76–86
San Diego	.260	.252	− 8	65–97
New York	.268	.254	− 14	92–70
Philadelphia	.254	.235	− 19	80–82
Chicago	.264	.239	− 25	76–85

Of the five National League teams that finished with winning records last season, four of them were helped by their scoring-position performances: they finished one-two-three-four in that category. The other winning team, the Mets, stand 10th on the list, keeping company with the Cubs, Phillies, and Padres. During the month of May, when the Mets lost four and one half games in the standings to the Cardinals, they batted .296 when there were no runners in scoring position, .194 when there were.

Now let's turn the pressure up a notch and look at each

team's overall batting average compared to its average with runners in scoring position *in Late-Inning Pressure Situations*. (Remember that, by definition, this last group includes all late-game, close-game situations in which the team at bat needs to score in order to win. Considering only those situations, with the additional pressure of having runners in scoring position, heightens the cruciality of the particular at bat.) Again, the teams appear in order of the difference between the two figures:

Team	Overall	LIP Scor. Pos.	Difference
Montreal	.265	.335	+70
Houston	.253	.277	+24
San Francisco	.260	.272	+12
Atlanta	.258	.262	+4
Philadelphia	.254	.255	+1
Cincinnati	.266	.262	−4
Chicago	.264	.259	−5
St. Louis	.263	.245	−18
San Diego	.260	.227	−33
Los Angeles	.252	.217	−35
Pittsburgh	.264	.227	−37
New York	.268	.224	−44

Not that the 44-point difference in respective batting averages isn't bad enough, but the Mets' .224 late-inning scoring-position average was more than 100 points lower than their corresponding average from *That Championship Season*. Note the difference:

	Overall	LIP Scor. Pos.	Difference
1986 Mets	.263	.326	+63 (best in majors)
1987 Mets	.268	.224	−44 (worst in majors)

The 1986 Mets finished with the *best* differential in either league and the '87 Mets finished with the *worst* differential in either league (the White Sox, at minus 43, finished last in the American League). What makes this an especially bitter pill to swallow is that the meat of the batting order—the guys who batted third, fourth, fifth, and sixth practically all season —were the very guys who failed to produce at these key times. Contrast the performance of the Big Four—Hernandez, Strawberry, McReynolds and Carter—with that of the guys who usually batted first, second, seventh, and eighth (six players are included because of platoon situations at second base and center field)—Wilson, Dykstra, Teufel, Backman, Johnson, and Santana. Their numbers in Late-Inning Pressure Situations with runners in scoring position:

	AB	H	2B	3B	HR	BA	Driving In Runs From Scor. Pos.	
3-4-5-6 Hitters	82	13	2	0	1	.159	16/97	16%
1-2-7-8 Hitters	82	25	5	2	3	.305	35/105	33%

In the same number of at bats, the Little Guys outhit the Big Guys by 146 points. They drove in more than twice as many runners from scoring position as the supposed RBI guys did in only a few more chances. And none of that had anything to do with drugs, hernias, or elbows. Even though the total number of at bats involved in these situations may seem small at first glance, go back and reread our definition of Late-Inning Pressure Situations. The Mets' 205 at bats in Late-Inning Pressure Situations with runners in scoring position may have been their most important 205 at bats of the season. And, we submit, it was probably those 205 at bats that kept the Mets from repeating.

Strawberry in Right Field Forever?

Having said all of that, let's focus now on the career of Darryl Strawberry. The Mets were still basking in the warmth of the Florida sun last March when the opening bell sounded and the debate began: Should Darryl be traded?

Like the winds of Shea fans have blown warm and cold on the issue, as they have on the player himself. Recognized as a budding superstar in 1983, Strawberry has been the centerpiece around which the rest of the Mets' superstar cast has been assembled. In terms of continuous service with the team, he outranks Hernandez, Carter, Gooden, Darling, and Davey Johnson; in fact, among the players on last year's team, only Mookie Wilson and Jesse Orosco had more consecutive years of Met's seniority.

But Strawberry's years with the Mets have not been without sin. His blowup after Game Six of the '86 Series, when he sulked after being removed on a double-switch, rather than celebrate the Mets' improbable win, was the tip of an oxymoron: A smoking iceberg. He was fined for being late to work one day last spring, and was fined and benched after reporting late to Wrigley Field for a game in June. He has heard the boos at Shea on more than one occasion.

On the field, the critics have found fault at various times with Darryl's defense, attitude, and hustle. But how about a little thing called performance? Let's go to the books to see how he stacks up.

First, some general statistics:

- Over the past five years, Strawberry has hit 147 home runs and has stolen 136 bases. No other player in the majors has averaged 25 homers and 25 steals over the last five years.
- That total of 147 home runs since 1983 ranks fourth in the majors behind Dale Murphy (182), Mike Schmidt (181) and Darrell Evans (149).
- Strawberry achieved career-bests in 1987 with 39 home runs, 104 RBI's, 97 walks, 36 stolen bases, a .284 batting average, a .583 slugging average, and a strikeout rate of one for every 5.2 plate appearances.

Some will contend, however, that Straw is not as good as his "traditional" numbers would indicate. But we say that those numbers actually understate his value. Consider his performance in some of the categories that we track in the

Analyst.

We noted earlier that the Mets' big guns were silent during the key late-game moments in 1987, and Strawberry's name is included in that indictment. Nevertheless, if there is any pattern to Darryl's *career* batting statistics, it is that he has hit much better with runners on base than with the bases empty. In fact, he has done that by significant margins each year in his major league career:

	1983	1984	1985	1986	1987	Total
Runners on Base	.269	.285	.303	.292	.314	.293
Bases Empty	.249	.220	.256	.226	.260	.242
Difference (Points)	+20	+65	+47	+66	+54	+51

How big is a 51-point difference between those averages? Sort of like the difference between having Steve Garvey or Brian Bosworth date your daughter. Of the 79 players in the major leagues since 1983 who had at least 1000 at bats in each situation, only one player's eyes grew wider than Strawberry's with runners on base. Here are the top five:

	Runners On Base	Bases Empty	Diff.
Dave Parker	.312	.252	+60
Darryl Strawberry	.293	.242	+51
Eddie Murray	.323	.275	+48
Harold Baines	.322	.275	+47
Pat Tabler	.323	.277	+46

One more thing. Let's look at Darryl's numbers compared with those fashioned by the New York superstars of 30 years ago. Here are the figures for Darryl compared with those of Willie, Mickey, and The Duke, each through his first career 2342 at bats (Strawberry's total through the end of the 1987 season):

	AB	H	2B	3B	HR	RBI	BB	SO	SB	BA
Strawberry	2342	622	116	25	147	447	364	618	136	.266
Mays	2342	717	103	43	155	422	286	260	84	.306
Mantle	2342	698	111	36	117	432	402	469	33	.298
Snider	2342	682	108	35	100	383	232	370	52	.291

There's no argument that from the starts of their careers, the Blessed Trinity of a generation ago hit for a far better average than Strawberry has. But would Darryl's detractors have dreamed that he has driven in more runs in a corresponding number of at bats than these demigods of New York baseball history? And what of the home run totals, which show Strawberry significantly ahead of Snider (career total: 407) and Mantle (career total: 536), and only slightly behind Mays (career total: 660). True, he has struck out more, as have most current sluggers when compared to those of earlier eras. But he has drawn more walks than Mays or Snider, and has stolen more bases (again, another generation-

al bias) than any of the hallowed three.

So be gentle, boo birds. Whatever sins Strawberry hath committed are venial. The mortal sin would be hounding him into an escape from New York through free agency when his contract permits.

"Once You Leave, It's Tough To Go Back"

Will the Mets rebound? Were their problems of last year temporary and nontransferable to this season? Will they come out for 1988 hungrier (except for Sid) than ever?

Let's look at baseball history to see which teams most closely fit the Mets' recent profile. First, recent history. In the divisional era, there have been nine teams that won a division title in Year One, but finished second in Year Two:

	Yr. 1	Next Title	Yr. 1 Pct.	Yr. 2 Pct.	Yr. 3 Pct.
Cincinnati	1973	**1975	.611	.605	.667
Baltimore	1974	*1979	.562	.566	.543
Los Angeles	*1974	*1977	.630	.543	.568
Oakland	1975	1981	.605	.540	.591
Pittsburgh	1975	**1979	.571	.568	.593
Cincinnati	**1976	1979	.630	.543	.571
Kansas City	1978	*1980	.568	.525	.599
Baltimore	*1979	**1983	.642	.617	.562
Atlanta	1982	None	.549	.543	.494

* league champion
** world champion

Eight of the nine teams played over .500 ball in the season two years after their division title ("Yr. 3 Pct."), although only two of them (Reds in 1975 and Royals in 1980) won so much as a division title while doing so. But since only one of these nine division winners (1976 Reds) was also a *World Series* winner, the parallel to the Mets' situation is not a strong one.

So let's enlarge the scope of our research and look at all teams since 1905 (when the World Series became an annual event) that have won the World Series, but failed to reach the Series the following year. There have been 50 such teams in this century, and only five of them have come back to win the Series again after a year's absence:

Champ. Yrs.	Team	Non-Title Season
1911–13	Athletics	1912: 90–62, 3rd place, 15 GB
1916–18	Red Sox	1917: 90–62, 2nd place, 9 GB
1944–46	Cardinals	1945: 95–59, 2nd place, 3 GB
1947–49	Yankees	1948: 94–60, 3rd place, 2.5 GB
1963–65	Dodgers	1964: 80–82, 6th place tie, 13 GB

Five times out of 50, and only once since the Korean War, is a pretty strong trend to buck. But lame duck manager Davey Johnson may have more to look forward to than some other prominent lame ducks. At least he doesn't have to make any Supreme Court nominations.

WON-LOST RECORD BY STARTING POSITION

NEW YORK 92-70	C	1B	2B	3B	SS	LF	CF	RF	P	Leadoff	Relief	Starts
Rick Aguilera	-	-	-	-	-	-	-	-	11-6	-	1-0	11-6
Bill Almon	-	-	0-1	-	1-3	-	-	-	-	-	-	1-4
Wally Backman	-	-	45-32	-	-	-	-	-	-	-	-	45-32
John Candelaria	-	-	-	-	-	-	-	-	2-1	-	-	2-1
Mark Carreon	-	-	-	-	-	1-1	-	-	-	-	-	1-1
Gary Carter	75-57	-	-	-	-	-	1-0	-	-	-	-	76-57
David Cone	-	-	-	-	-	-	-	-	6-7	-	5-3	6-7
Ron Darling	-	-	-	-	-	-	-	-	17-15	-	-	17-15
Len Dykstra	-	-	-	-	-	56-44	-	-	-	55-44	-	56-44
Tom Edens	-	-	-	-	-	-	-	-	0-2	-	-	0-2
Kevin Elster	-	-	-	-	1-1	-	-	-	-	-	-	1-1
Sid Fernandez	-	-	-	-	-	-	-	-	16-11	-	0-1	16-11
Bob Gibson	-	-	-	-	-	-	-	-	-	-	0-1	-
Dwight Gooden	-	-	-	-	-	-	-	-	15-10	-	-	15-10
Keith Hernandez	-	87-64	-	-	-	-	-	-	-	-	-	87-64
Clint Hurdle	-	-	-	-	-	-	-	-	-	-	-	-
Jeff Innis	-	-	-	-	-	-	-	-	1-0	-	3-13	1-0
Gregg Jefferies	-	-	-	-	-	-	-	-	-	-	-	-
Howard Johnson	-	-	-	76-51	11-15	-	-	-	-	-	-	87-66
Terry Leach	-	-	-	-	-	-	-	-	10-2	-	12-20	10-2
Barry Lyons	17-13	-	-	-	-	-	-	-	-	-	-	17-13
Dave Magadan	-	3-4	-	16-19	-	-	-	-	-	-	-	19-23
Lee Mazzilli	-	2-2	-	-	-	4-2	3-2	-	-	-	-	9-6
Roger McDowell	-	-	-	-	-	-	-	-	-	-	42-14	-
Kevin McReynolds	-	-	-	-	-	82-65	-	-	-	-	-	82-65
Keith Miller	-	-	9-4	-	-	-	-	-	-	-	-	9-4
Randy Milligan	-	-	-	-	-	-	-	-	-	-	-	-
John Mitchell	-	-	-	-	-	-	-	-	9-10	-	0-1	9-10
Randy Myers	-	-	-	-	-	-	-	-	-	-	20-34	-
Bob Ojeda	-	-	-	-	-	-	-	-	3-4	-	1-2	3-4
Jesse Orosco	-	-	-	-	-	-	-	-	-	-	32-26	-
Al Pedrique	-	-	-	-	0-1	-	-	-	-	-	-	0-1
Rafael Santana	-	-	-	-	79-50	-	-	-	-	-	-	79-50
Don Schulze	-	-	-	-	-	-	2-2	-	-	-	0-1	2-2
Doug Sisk	-	-	-	-	-	-	-	-	-	-	20-35	-
Darryl Strawberry	-	-	-	-	-	-	-	84-65	-	-	-	84-65
Tim Teufel	-	-	38-33	-	-	-	-	-	-	-	-	38-33
Gene Walter	-	-	-	-	-	-	-	-	-	-	4-17	-
Mookie Wilson	-	-	-	-	-	5-2	36-26	4-3	-	37-26	-	45-31

Batting vs. Left and Right Handed Pitchers

		BA	Rank	SA	Rank	OBA	Rank	HR %	Rank	BB %	Rank	SO %	Rank
Wally Backman	vs. Lefties	.086	--	.086	--	.158	--	0.00	--	7.89	--	13.16	--
	vs. Righties	.272	68	.313	123	.326	78	0.38	124	7.41	92	12.79	51
Gary Carter	vs. Lefties	.240	103	.404	85	.322	87	3.83	51	11.32	33	7.08	12
	vs. Righties	.232	113	.385	81	.271	127	3.82	39	4.99	119	16.07	88
Len Dykstra	vs. Lefties	.203	128	.324	112	.289	116	1.35	94	9.41	54	15.29	88
	vs. Righties	.303	19	.482	32	.365	34	2.52	66	8.12	83	13.71	66
Keith Hernandez	vs. Lefties	.254	91	.373	96	.343	64	2.38	76	11.07	36	17.65	102
	vs. Righties	.316	12	.484	31	.403	13	3.58	45	12.66	16	13.70	65
Howard Johnson	vs. Lefties	.289	48	.552	18	.376	32	7.73	6	11.76	32	17.65	102
	vs. Righties	.253	93	.478	35	.358	42	5.83	13	13.44	12	17.45	102
Dave Magadan	vs. Lefties	.438	1	.625	5	.481	2	4.17	40	9.26	58	7.41	18
	vs. Righties	.278	61	.382	86	.354	47	0.69	119	10.49	45	11.11	36
Kevin McReynolds	vs. Lefties	.290	46	.534	25	.325	84	5.43	18	4.70	115	10.68	46
	vs. Righties	.268	76	.472	37	.314	94	4.61	26	6.91	99	11.11	36
Rafael Santana	vs. Lefties	.262	80	.363	99	.322	86	1.79	87	7.65	82	8.74	31
	vs. Righties	.251	94	.336	109	.289	110	0.74	118	5.23	115	14.29	73
Darryl Strawberry	vs. Lefties	.248	98	.517	30	.330	76	6.96	10	9.58	47	22.22	123
	vs. Righties	.311	14	.632	2	.446	4	7.62	5	19.00	3	16.89	96
Tim Teufel	vs. Lefties	.321	24	.563	13	.412	14	4.21	39	13.45	22	12.11	57
	vs. Righties	.284	47	.514	21	.373	26	5.50	36	10.94	36	20.31	117
Mookie Wilson	vs. Lefties	.271	71	.404	84	.329	77	1.33	95	7.69	80	18.62	111
	vs. Righties	.338	5	.525	19	.401	14	3.75	41	8.99	67	21.91	122
Team Average	vs. Lefties	.264	6	.433	2	.335	6	3.62	2	9.19	5	15.48	7
	vs. Righties	.270	1	.434	2	.341	1	3.32	4	9.43	3	16.27	8
League Average	vs. Lefties	.263		.409		.332		2.81		9.08		15.22	
	vs. Righties	.260		.401		.327		2.73		8.70		15.85	

Batting with Runners on Base and Bases Empty

		BA	Rank	SA	Rank	OBA	Rank	HR %	Rank	BB %	Rank	SO %	Rank
Wally Backman	Runners On	.328	14	.345	108	.388	32	0.00	122	8.70	84	10.87	40
	Bases Empty	.201	131	.250	134	.254	130	0.54	121	6.60	86	14.21	71
Gary Carter	Runners On	.241	111	.402	78	.297	115	3.83	38	7.90	96	13.75	75
	Bases Empty	.229	116	.382	89	.284	114	3.82	48	6.74	82	11.70	43
Len Dykstra	Runners On	.303	37	.485	33	.387	33	3.03	48	9.74	71	10.39	34
	Bases Empty	.278	56	.441	54	.335	57	2.01	84	7.69	62	15.69	86
Keith Hernandez	Runners On	.299	41	.430	68	.399	27	2.46	69	14.20	22	13.31	62
	Bases Empty	.281	49	.442	51	.355	39	3.63	50	9.76	42	17.46	98
Howard Johnson	Runners On	.306	34	.548	10	.405	23	6.05	9	13.95	26	17.01	105
	Bases Empty	.232	111	.467	42	.330	66	6.86	12	11.97	15	17.95	103
Dave Magadan	Runners On	.311	25	.400	79	.388	31	0.00	122	11.54	44	10.58	36
	Bases Empty	.324	12	.480	34	.384	20	2.94	62	8.93	48	9.82	25
Kevin McReynolds	Runners On	.222	120	.409	75	.274	125	3.94	34	7.40	107	13.83	77
	Bases Empty	.325	11	.572	8	.360	33	5.79	19	4.88	114	8.23	12
Rafael Santana	Runners On	.282	68	.388	89	.346	77	1.06	106	9.13	78	10.58	36
	Bases Empty	.235	105	.315	117	.267	127	1.20	104	3.82	129	13.36	56
Darryl Strawberry	Runners On	.314	22	.695	1	.447	5	9.75	1	19.33	4	17.00	104
	Bases Empty	.260	76	.493	30	.356	38	5.41	22	11.47	18	20.88	121
Tim Teufel	Runners On	.289	55	.563	7	.380	39	5.63	11	12.94	33	15.29	93
	Bases Empty	.325	10	.529	23	.414	4	3.82	47	12.15	14	14.92	78
Mookie Wilson	Runners On	.265	86	.397	83	.348	75	1.47	92	11.46	45	18.47	115
	Bases Empty	.317	16	.486	32	.366	30	2.81	64	6.34	96	20.90	122
Team Average	Runners On	.270	6	.440	2	.351	2	3.46	2	10.95	2	15.23	9
	Bases Empty	.266	2	.429	2	.329	2	3.40	3	8.00	5	16.60	8
League Average	Runners On	.267		.410		.341		2.66		9.88		14.92	
	Bases Empty	.256		.399		.319		2.82		7.98		16.22	

Overall Batting Compared to Late Inning Pressure Situations

		BA	Rank	SA	Rank	OBA	Rank	HR %	Rank	BB %	Rank	SO %	Rank	RDI %	Rank
Bill Almon	Overall	.230	--	.284	--	.313	--	0.00	--	10.84	--	25.30	--	.263	--
	Pressure	.300	--	.350	--	.391	--	0.00	--	13.04	--	30.43	--	.111	123
Wally Backman	Overall	.250	99	.287	132	.307	107	0.33	130	7.46	89	12.84	56	.312	38
	Pressure	.208	--	.208	--	.387	--	0.00	--	21.88	--	12.50	--	.167	--
Gary Carter	Overall	.235	116	.392	87	.290	121	3.82	40	7.33	93	12.74	54	.277	71
	Pressure	.230	98	.378	75	.288	106	4.05	32	6.17	105	19.75	102	.091	131
Len Dykstra	Overall	.285	48	.455	44	.352	46	2.32	78	8.35	74	13.99	69	.301	52
	Pressure	.220	110	.400	63	.304	96	4.00	34	10.53	53	12.28	37	.111	123
Keith Hernandez	Overall	.290	39	.436	53	.377	26	3.07	60	11.98	23	15.38	85	.311	41
	Pressure	.269	63	.359	86	.352	61	2.56	62	10.23	59	21.59	116	.174	110
Howard Johnson	Overall	.265	81	.504	22	.364	36	6.50	10	12.87	16	17.52	103	.284	66
	Pressure	.316	27	.595	7	.398	27	7.59	6	12.90	31	18.28	91	.370	24
Barry Lyons	Overall	.254	--	.392	--	.301	--	3.08	--	5.59	--	16.78	--	.321	31
	Pressure	.273	--	.318	--	.273	--	0.00	--	0.00	--	18.18	--	.333	36
Dave Magadan	Overall	.318	9	.443	48	.386	20	1.56	96	10.19	48	10.19	22	.258	91
	Pressure	.282	52	.513	22	.333	73	5.13	18	6.98	99	13.95	57	.063	138
Lee Mazzilli	Overall	.306	--	.460	--	.399	--	2.42	--	14.19	--	9.46	--	.423	--
	Pressure	.327	21	.469	33	.404	25	2.04	73	12.28	35	15.79	69	.421	13
Kevin McReynolds	Overall	.276	65	.495	25	.318	92	4.92	17	6.10	116	10.95	37	.247	102
	Pressure	.218	114	.276	122	.278	112	1.15	101	8.16	81	6.12	7	.270	64
Rafael Santana	Overall	.255	92	.346	113	.302	112	1.14	108	6.17	115	12.13	48	.261	90
	Pressure	.229	100	.333	104	.245	128	0.00	105	2.04	134	14.29	58	.333	36
Darryl Strawberry	Overall	.284	51	.583	4	.398	14	7.33	5	15.16	7	19.06	115	.295	56
	Pressure	.213	116	.333	104	.344	67	2.67	59	15.56	16	21.11	113	.000	140
Tim Teufel	Overall	.308	15	.545	9	.398	15	4.68	23	12.54	19	15.10	81	.374	3
	Pressure	.341	15	.561	11	.460	5	4.88	21	17.65	10	9.80	22	.588	1
Mookie Wilson	Overall	.299	22	.455	45	.359	41	2.34	77	8.24	78	20.00	123	.229	115
	Pressure	.279	57	.393	68	.333	73	1.64	82	5.97	107	25.37	126	.316	47
Team Average	Overall	.268	1	.434	1	.339	2	3.43	4	9.34	4	15.97	8	.276	5
	Pressure	.261	6	.396	6	.341	4	2.91	5	10.45	2	16.72	5	.252	8
League Average	Overall	.261		.404		.328		2.75		8.83		15.64		.272	
	Pressure	.258		.385		.331		2.46		9.54		16.95		.261	

Additional Miscellaneous Batting Comparisons

	Grass Surface		Artificial Surface		Home Games		Road Games		Runners in Scoring Position		Runners in Scoring Pos and Two Outs		Leading Off Inning		Runners on 3B with less than 2 Outs	
	BA	Rank	BA	Rank	BA	Rank	BA	Rank	BA	Rank	BA	Rank	OBA	Rank	RDI %	Rank
Wally Backman	.272	66	.158	--	.284	59	.206	128	.279	59	.355	11	.328	74	.583	67
Gary Carter	.243	101	.217	124	.231	117	.239	105	.245	94	.289	39	.233	131	.526	88
Len Dykstra	.301	27	.248	101	.292	45	.279	46	.268	73	.297	33	.346	53	.750	11
Keith Hernandez	.290	36	.289	44	.288	53	.291	34	.257	84	.188	119	.333	62	.667	25
Howard Johnson	.282	49	.230	112	.262	86	.269	70	.277	62	.212	97	.291	108	.471	107
Barry Lyons	.259	83	.244	--	.259	--	.250	--	.250	--	.188	--	.167	--	.636	40
Dave Magadan	.338	5	.274	--	.382	2	.262	77	.259	80	.207	103	.381	28	.500	--
Lee Mazzilli	.356	2	.189	--	.429	--	.206	--	.308	--	.250	--	.444	--	.857	1
Kevin McReynolds	.272	64	.287	49	.275	70	.277	51	.213	115	.265	59	.432	5	.543	82
Rafael Santana	.255	89	.256	88	.244	107	.266	73	.254	85	.250	69	.262	126	.500	91
Darryl Strawberry	.299	28	.248	99	.322	17	.246	98	.267	74	.254	68	.328	73	.556	77
Tim Teufel	.285	44	.354	6	.326	15	.293	33	.368	4	.325	15	.429	8	.588	63
Mookie Wilson	.304	25	.288	46	.267	78	.325	8	.241	99	.200	108	.386	23	.571	72
Team Average	.274	1	.252	11	.278	1	.258	7	.254	7	.239	6	.328	5	.563	5
League Average	.260		.261		.265		.256		.258		.241		.324		.554	

Pitching vs. Left and Right Handed Batters

		BA	Rank	SA	Rank	OBA	Rank	HR %	Rank	BB %	Rank	SO %	Rank
Rick Aguilera	vs. Lefties	.301	94	.447	84	.361	80	2.74	79	7.88	26	12.86	61
	vs. Righties	.252	52	.396	49	.297	32	2.61	45	5.53	18	18.18	42
David Cone	vs. Lefties	.233	21	.376	44	.338	55	2.65	75	12.44	96	11.56	73
	vs. Righties	.246	39	.400	51	.314	53	3.43	75	8.21	67	21.54	24
Ron Darling	vs. Lefties	.223	13	.356	34	.299	20	2.25	56	9.64	55	18.27	29
	vs. Righties	.247	45	.412	67	.343	88	4.12	94	12.21	105	19.34	33
Sid Fernandez	vs. Lefties	.225	--	.408	--	.291	--	2.82	--	8.86	--	17.72	--
	vs. Righties	.224	24	.357	28	.312	46	2.75	50	10.24	93	20.48	29
Dwight Gooden	vs. Lefties	.239	31	.318	17	.304	26	1.36	25	8.52	34	18.73	25
	vs. Righties	.249	49	.377	39	.293	31	2.02	22	5.64	21	22.26	18
Terry Leach	vs. Lefties	.275	72	.429	74	.323	42	2.50	68	6.56	15	7.34	108
	vs. Righties	.251	51	.380	42	.285	24	3.04	63	4.24	3	14.84	73
Roger McDowell	vs. Lefties	.243	35	.320	18	.314	33	1.78	39	8.81	42	9.84	90
	vs. Righties	.309	106	.411	66	.346	90	2.29	33	5.76	22	6.81	112
John Mitchell	vs. Lefties	.296	93	.363	35	.358	77	0.83	6	8.92	44	8.92	97
	vs. Righties	.260	65	.368	33	.301	35	1.96	20	5.36	16	14.73	75
Randy Myers	vs. Lefties	.175	3	.300	10	.244	2	1.25	22	8.79	41	39.56	1
	vs. Righties	.246	40	.361	31	.318	58	2.62	46	9.87	88	25.11	8
Jesse Orosco	vs. Lefties	.230	--	.243	--	.275	--	0.00	--	6.25	--	26.25	--
	vs. Righties	.279	89	.397	50	.356	96	2.28	32	10.20	92	22.35	17
Doug Sisk	vs. Lefties	.268	61	.341	28	.325	43	0.00	1	7.89	27	8.55	99
	vs. Righties	.272	82	.408	60	.322	63	2.96	58	5.35	15	12.83	90
Team Average	vs. Lefties	.256	2	.379	4	.323	2	2.03	3	8.76	2	14.55	5
	vs. Righties	.253	5	.386	2	.315	4	2.75	2	7.84	4	18.30	3
League Average	vs. Lefties	.268		.404		.341		2.34		9.74		14.31	
	vs. Righties	.255		.403		.319		3.05		8.16		16.61	

Pitching with Runners on Base and Bases Empty

		BA	Rank	SA	Rank	OBA	Rank	HR %	Rank	BB %	Rank	SO %	Rank
Rick Aguilera	Runners On	.227	18	.379	40	.286	8	3.03	73	7.14	12	17.86	28
	Bases Empty	.315	108	.454	90	.363	101	2.39	47	6.30	27	13.70	82
David Cone	Runners On	.227	17	.393	56	.328	38	3.33	85	13.26	103	16.02	49
	Bases Empty	.248	48	.383	57	.326	73	2.80	65	8.37	69	16.32	51
Ron Darling	Runners On	.234	22	.392	52	.324	34	3.04	74	11.52	85	15.71	52
	Bases Empty	.233	25	.371	41	.314	55	3.08	75	10.22	96	21.02	18
Sid Fernandez	Runners On	.235	25	.376	38	.320	28	2.56	59	10.55	73	19.64	15
	Bases Empty	.216	12	.354	27	.303	34	2.88	69	9.74	90	20.51	21
Dwight Gooden	Runners On	.231	20	.311	11	.283	5	1.10	18	6.89	11	18.69	21
	Bases Empty	.253	56	.367	32	.311	46	2.04	31	7.53	53	21.41	15
Terry Leach	Runners On	.225	15	.289	6	.284	7	0.49	4	7.39	14	11.74	88
	Bases Empty	.288	94	.482	101	.317	59	4.35	104	3.85	3	10.90	102
Roger McDowell	Runners On	.283	87	.342	22	.332	49	1.09	17	6.67	10	10.48	95
	Bases Empty	.269	79	.394	64	.328	75	3.13	77	8.05	61	5.75	112
John Mitchell	Runners On	.281	85	.402	58	.339	66	2.01	39	8.70	31	11.30	92
	Bases Empty	.278	87	.335	16	.327	74	0.82	3	6.08	21	11.79	97
Randy Myers	Runners On	.210	8	.306	9	.262	2	2.42	51	7.43	15	31.76	1
	Bases Empty	.238	35	.374	47	.325	71	2.04	31	11.45	104	27.11	3
Jesse Orosco	Runners On	.256	49	.350	24	.335	59	1.88	36	10.53	71	23.16	9
	Bases Empty	.278	88	.368	33	.338	83	1.50	14	7.59	55	23.45	10
Doug Sisk	Runners On	.319	112	.489	104	.376	100	3.55	92	8.02	22	8.02	110
	Bases Empty	.229	20	.283	5	.277	10	0.00	1	5.08	11	13.56	84
Team Average	Runners On	.248	1	.369	1	.315	1	2.23	2	8.83	2	16.42	4
	Bases Empty	.259	7	.394	6	.321	7	2.60	5	7.75	5	16.88	5
League Average	Runners On	.267		.410		.341		2.66		9.88		14.92	
	Bases Empty	.256		.399		.319		2.82		7.98		16.22	

Overall Pitching Compared to Late Inning Pressure Situations

		BA	Rank	SA	Rank	OBA	Rank	HR %	Rank	BB %	Rank	SO %	Rank
Rick Aguilera	Overall	.276	90	.421	74	.329	64	2.67	61	6.68	14	15.59	54
	Pressure	.314	97	.343	30	.368	87	0.00	1	7.32	29	19.51	35
David Cone	Overall	.239	19	.387	54	.327	60	3.02	74	10.48	93	16.19	45
	Pressure	.333	--	.444	--	.419	--	0.00	--	12.50	--	25.00	--
Ron Darling	Overall	.233	14	.380	47	.318	39	3.06	76	10.77	97	18.74	26
	Pressure	.343	103	.586	105	.397	100	7.14	106	8.97	50	16.67	51
Sid Fernandez	Overall	.224	10	.363	31	.310	29	2.75	67	10.08	84	20.15	21
	Pressure	.182	4	.205	3	.265	10	0.00	1	8.16	34	24.49	12
Dwight Gooden	Overall	.244	29	.344	20	.299	15	1.65	15	7.26	20	20.27	17
	Pressure	.273	71	.398	68	.337	57	2.27	55	8.16	34	19.39	37
Terry Leach	Overall	.262	68	.404	62	.303	19	2.78	69	5.35	5	11.25	98
	Pressure	.308	92	.446	85	.338	58	3.08	78	4.35	12	21.74	20
Roger McDowell	Overall	.276	89	.366	36	.330	66	2.03	30	7.29	21	8.33	110
	Pressure	.277	77	.391	65	.339	59	2.97	77	8.30	36	6.55	105
John Mitchell	Overall	.279	93	.365	32	.333	74	1.35	10	7.30	22	11.56	97
	Pressure	.385	--	.538	--	.429	--	3.85	--	6.90	--	3.45	--
Randy Myers	Overall	.225	11	.343	19	.296	10	2.21	36	9.55	74	29.30	3
	Pressure	.198	11	.326	22	.307	34	3.49	85	13.21	92	27.36	5
Jesse Orosco	Overall	.266	72	.358	28	.336	84	1.71	18	9.25	66	23.28	10
	Pressure	.258	58	.352	39	.344	64	2.20	53	11.21	81	23.36	18
Doug Sisk	Overall	.270	80	.378	43	.323	51	1.63	13	6.49	11	10.91	100
	Pressure	.288	85	.368	52	.346	66	1.60	43	7.19	28	10.07	94
Gene Walter	Overall	.243	--	.351	--	.360	--	1.35	--	14.61	--	12.36	--
	Pressure	.276	75	.345	32	.382	94	0.00	1	14.71	104	2.94	112
Team Average	Overall	.254	3	.383	2	.319	3	2.44	3	8.24	3	16.67	4
	Pressure	.274	11	.390	7	.344	8	2.65	8	9.21	4	16.87	7
League Average	Overall	.261		.404		.328		2.75		8.83		15.64	
	Pressure	.260		.391		.337		2.47		10.04		17.14	

Additional Miscellaneous Pitching Comparisons

	Grass Surface BA	Rank	Artificial Surface BA	Rank	Home Games BA	Rank	Road Games BA	Rank	Runners in Scoring Position BA	Rank	Runners in Scoring Pos and Two Outs BA	Rank	Leading Off Inning OBA	Rank
Rick Aguilera	.262	60	.315	104	.272	82	.282	77	.204	12	.192	27	.364	92
David Cone	.246	36	.220	--	.264	70	.216	13	.205	15	.214	42	.356	89
Ron Darling	.231	22	.238	23	.237	29	.231	20	.245	48	.258	75	.323	59
Sid Fernandez	.202	5	.274	75	.198	8	.259	50	.219	22	.215	45	.292	21
Dwight Gooden	.246	37	.235	19	.246	38	.241	32	.220	24	.203	35	.322	58
Terry Leach	.292	98	.208	10	.308	106	.240	28	.223	27	.158	17	.336	75
Roger McDowell	.286	89	.240	--	.255	57	.304	101	.306	101	.345	105	.368	95
John Mitchell	.278	79	.282	82	.269	77	.294	94	.293	90	.322	102	.304	39
Randy Myers	.225	18	.225	--	.233	24	.218	15	.203	11	.171	22	.319	52
Bob Ojeda	.271	72	.225	--	.262	--	.240	--	.239	--	.316	--	.277	--
Jesse Orosco	.265	65	.270	--	.248	44	.287	81	.212	18	.229	58	.379	100
Doug Sisk	.263	64	.287	--	.301	103	.244	34	.303	97	.357	109	.303	31
Team Average	.255	6	.253	2	.254	6	.255	1	.243	3	.249	7	.330	7
League Average	.260		.261		.256		.265		.258		.241		.324	

PHILADELPHIA PHILLIES

Every school child in America knows that in the story of the tortoise and the hare, it's slow and steady that wins the race, and that jackrabbit starts lead to overconfidence later on. But in the town where they once booed Santa Claus, that late-starting tortoise may not be too popular, either. Seems that he bears an unusual resemblance to the local baseball team, but with one significant difference. The baseball team has modified the tortoise's it's-not-how-you-start-it's-how-you-finish approach, making it read: If you start slowly enough, no one will care how well you finish.

The Phillies' remarkably slow starts over the last three years have depressed the most ardent of optimists before the Mother's Day cards are even in the stores. The results are painfully clear regardless of which early-season milepost you look at:

	First 10 Games	First 20 Games	First 30 Games	First 40 Games
1985	2–8	8–12	11–19	15–25
1986	3–7	9–11	13–17	16–24
1987	2–8	7–13	11–19	17–23
Totals	7–23	24–36	35–55	48–72
	(.233)	(.400)	(.389)	(.400)

No matter how you slice the pie, the Phillies come out with just a few crumbs. Here are the worst records in the majors over the past three seasons, based on the three-year cumulative record of the teams to that point in the season:

Worst First 10 Games 1985–87		Worst First 20 Games 1985–87	
Philadelphia	7–23	Philadelphia	24–36
Cleveland	9–21	Chi. White Sox	25–35
Seattle	10–20	Cleveland	25–35
Chi. White Sox	10–20	Seattle	25–35
Four teams	13–17	Texas	25–35

Worst First 30 Games 1985–87		Worst First 40 Games 1985–87	
Philadelphia	35–55	Philadelphia	48–72
Pittsburgh	36–54	Cleveland	50–70
Chi. White Sox	37–53	Texas	50–70
San Diego	39–51	Pittsburgh	51–69
Seattle	39–51	Seattle	53–67
Texas	39–51		

For clarity, let's focus on the first 10 games of each season, the period that has been most troublesome for the Phillies. Only three major-league teams in this century have had a worse cumulative first-10-games record over a three-season span:

Team	Seasons	Yr. 1	Yr. 2	Yr. 3	3-Year Totals
Brooklyn	1905–06–07	3–7	1–9	1–9	5–25
N.Y. Mets	1962–63–64	1–9	2–8	2–8	5–25
Chi. Cubs	1981–82–83	1–9	3–7	2–8	6–24

There have also been three other teams that, like the Phillies, had 7–23 records: the Tigers (in any of three three-year sequences from 1918 through 1922); the Athletics (1950–52, as Connie Mack turned the managerial reins over to Jimmie Dykes); and the Astros (1981–83, concurrent with the Cubs). Brooklyn also had a 7–23 mark in 1906–08, a period that overlaps the one listed in the table.

Ask any major-league manager in spring training about the importance of a good start and you'll get a unanimous opinion: It's as important as your next paycheck. It's easy to overstate the significance of getting off to a fast start, but a look at baseball history shows that the managers know what they're talking about: A poor first 10 games more often than not translates into a sub-.500 season.

We looked at the first 10 games of every major-league team in this century. Listed below is a summary of the data, showing how many teams started a season with a particular record over the first 10 games, and the distribution of the season winning percentages for those teams. (For example, of the 184 teams that started a season with a 3–7 mark, 5 percent had final winning percentages in the .200s, 23 percent finished in the .300s, etc.) The category marked "Winner" shows the percentage of teams that went on to win either a (pre-1969) league or ('69 and later) division title; for the 1981 strike season, the best overall record in the division is considered the division winner:

First 10 Games	Teams	.200s	.300s	.400s	.500s	.600s	.700s	Winner
0–10	3	33%	33%	33%	0	0	0	0
1–9	26	4%	35%	38%	23%	0	0	0
2–8	97	3%	31%	40%	22%	4%	0	5%
3–7	184	5%	23%	41%	28%	3%	0	4%

4–6	314	1%	18%	43%	31%	6%	.3%	5%
5–5	350	0	12%	35%	44%	8%	1%	9%
6–4	314	.3%	6%	27%	49%	18%	.3%	18%
7–3	211	0	1%	22%	51%	24%	1%	27%
8–2	81	0	1%	14%	44%	38%	2%	40%
9–1	18	0	0	6%	61%	33%	0	44%
10–0	6	0	0	0	83%	17%	0	50%

In other words, the pattern of a poor start begetting a poor season is striking. Only 22 of the 97 teams that started a season with a 2–8 record went on to play over .500 ball, and only 54 of 184 teams that had 3–7 starts did the same. The figures come into even sharper focus if, rather than sorting the records into 11 groups, we sort them into three: poor starts (3–7 or worse), average starts (4–6 to 6–4) and good starts (7–3 or better):

First 10 Games	Teams	.200s	.300s	.400s	.500s	.600s	.700s	Winner
Poor	310	5%	27%	41%	25%	3%	0	4%
Average	978	1%	12%	35%	41%	11%	.4%	10%
Good	316	0	1%	19%	51%	28%	1%	31%

Throughout modern major-league history, only one of every four teams that have had as bad a first-10-games record as the 1985–87 Phillies has finished above the .500 mark. And only 12 of the 310 teams that have started that badly have gone on to finish first in their league or division:

Finished First After 2–8 Start	Finished First After 3–7 Start
1914 Braves	1908 Tigers
1935 Tigers	1925 Pirates
1951 Giants	1934 Cardinals
1974 Pirates	1969 Mets
1977 Yankees	1973 A's
	1977 Phillies
	1979 Orioles

Given these annual April thuds, it's not surprising that the Phillies haven't played a crucial late-season game since Game Five of the 1983 World Series. But even though they've been saddled with three consecutive poor starts, the team deserves some credit for rebounding to respectability in each of those seasons. Over those three seasons, after playing .400 ball over their first 40 games, the Phillies have been a .529 team in Games 41 through 162 (see chart below). Not that .529 is a pennant-winning pace, but only three National League teams (the Mets, Cardinals, and Reds) have a better record over the corresponding period of games:

	First 10 Games		Next 30 Games		Rest Of Season		Totals	
1985	2–8	.200	13–17	.433	60–62	.492	75–87	.463
1986	3–7	.300	13–17	.433	70–51	.579	86–75	.534
1987	2–8	.200	15–15	.500	63–59	.516	80–82	.494
Totals	7–23	.233	41–49	.456	193–172	.529	241–244	.497

And say this for the Philadelphia front office: It has never been lulled into inaction by the team's prolonged salary drives. In each of the past three off-seasons, the Phillies have done some significant trading. They hit a home run with the Virgil-for-Bedrosian deal following 1985, but struck out with the Easler-for-Hudson deal a year later. They signed Lance Parrish as a free agent before last season, and then in December, they acquired Phil Bradley from the Mariners for Glenn Wilson and Mike Jackson.

Nevertheless, the annual let's-shoot-ourselves-in-the-foot ritual will continue to cripple the Phillies unless they convince the National League to ignore spring results in the summer game's standings. Or maybe a little positive thinking can set things right: Instead of pushing the clocks ahead an hour in the first week of April, maybe the Phillies should push them ahead two months. Then have the Phillie Phanatic model summer swimwear on a frigid April night; or distribute special Calendar Night merchandise with April and May torn out. Whatever the solution, it sure would be interesting to see how the Phillies' players perform without the burden of a poor start.

Clones On The Surface, But...

Rarely in the history of baseball have the earned run averages of four regular starting pitchers on the same team been as closely similar as those of the 1987 Phillies: Don Carman finished at 4.22, Kevin Gross and Bruce Ruffin at 4.35, and Shane Rawley at 4.39. But despite the proximity of their earned run averages, the won-lost records of the four were widely divergent: Rawley was 17–11 and a Cy Young candidate; Carman was 13–11 and steady; Ruffin was 11–14 and disappointing; and Gross was 9–16 and suspended. How can pitchers on the same team with nearly identical earned run averages have such disparate won-lost records? What did Rawley have that the others didn't? (OK, besides the talent to write screenplays for "Miami Vice.") If you restrict yourself to looking at just those two categories—ERA and winning percentage—you'll dance around from now till Granny Hamner's election to the Hall of Fame without solving this conundrum.

The answer lies in a category that some baseball fans don't think about at all, and that others regard merely as an unimportant extra, a piece of statistical flotsam. And the illustration provided by the Phillies' pitchers in 1987 is an almost too good example of why it is that some pitchers win and some pitchers lose, even though their other performance statistics are similar. The category is *run support*; that is, the average number of runs that a pitcher's own team scores in the games in which he starts.

Let's take another look at the statistics of those four pitchers, this time with each pitcher's run support listed alongside his other statistics:

	ERA	W–L	Pct.	Run Support		
				Avg.	Starts	Runs
Rawley	4.39	17–11	.607	4.92	36	177
Carman	4.22	13–11	.542	4.54	35	159

Ruffin	4.35	11–14	.440	3.89	35	136
*Gross	4.35	9–16	.360	3.58	33	118

* ERA and W–L include one relief appearance (a win).

The distribution of the pitchers' won-lost percentages and the average run support per start mirror each other almost exactly. The Phillies were an 80–82 team that averaged 4.33 runs per game, but they scored nearly five runs per start for Rawley, and he finished at .607. (Actually, the 4.92 runs that the team averaged for Shane were a decline from his 1986 support of 5.65 runs per start, best in the league.) Carman was afforded better-than-average support, and he produced a better-than-average record. Ruffin, given poor support, produced a poor record. And Gross, given the fewest runs to work with, had the worst record among the four.

Certainly, a pitcher whose earned run average is low and whose run support is high is guaranteed a good record; check out Roger Clemens in 1986, when he led the American League in both ERA (2.48) and run support (6.09 runs per start) and finished with a 24–4 record, the Cy Young Award, and the MVP. The broader question is, are the starting pitchers with the best won-lost records those who have the best earned run averages, or are they those who benefit from the most robust batting support?

Listed below are the top 12 National League pitchers for 1987 listed according to three categories: won-lost percentage, earned run average, and run support. Only those statistics compiled as a starting pitcher were considered, and a minimum of 20 starts was necessary for inclusion in any of the lists:

Winning Pct.		Earned Run Average		Run Support	
Dennis Martinez	.733	Nolan Ryan	2.76	Mike Krukow	5.64
Mike Dunne	.684	Rick Reuschel	2.92	Bob Forsch	5.63
Dwight Gooden	.682	Orel Hershiser	3.02	Rick Sutcliffe	5.38
Jim Deshaies	.647	Mike Dunne	3.03	Dennis Martinez	5.27
Rick Sutcliffe	.643	Dwight Gooden	3.21	Sid Fernandez	5.22
Bob Welch	.625	Bob Welch	3.22	Zane Smith	5.22
Rick Reuschel	.619	Mike Scott	3.23	Bryn Smith	5.19
Bob Forsch	.611	Dennis Martinez	3.30	Dwight Gooden	5.04
Shane Rawley	.607	Dave Dravecky	3.35	Ron Darling	5.03
Ron Darling	.600	Joe Magrane	3.39	Jimmy Jones	5.00
Sid Fernandez	.600	Danny Darwin	3.56	David Palmer	4.96
Zane Smith	.600	Mike LaCoss	3.60	Guy Hoffman	4.95

Martinez and Gooden are the only pitchers among the top 12 in both earned run average and run support. Predictably, they ranked first and third in the league in winning percentage. But of the other 10 pitchers with 20 or more starts and a won-lost percentage of .600 or higher, only three (Reuschel, Dunne, and Welch) were found among the ERA leaders, while five (Forsch, Sutcliffe, Fernandez, Zane Smith, and Darling) were among the pitchers best supported by their teammates.

Because these pitchers all played for different teams, and in different home stadiums, it might be argued that "all runs are not created equal," and that the 5.22 runs per start with which the Mets, playing in a pitchers' park, supported Fernandez are not the same as the 5.22 runs with which the Braves, playing in the Launching Pad, supported Zane Smith. But come back to the Phillies: What makes this case such a spectacular example is that we have a self-contained test case in which not only was the qualitative pitching of four individuals virtually identical, but the biases are eliminated because they all pitched for the same team. The results could not be more revealing, in terms of the almost parabolic distribution of the data.

Just to check the matter out a little further, we ran the same tests on the National League starting pitchers in both 1986 and 1985. The results from each of those years were identical: seven starters who were among the top 12 in ERA were also among the top 12 in winning percentage, while five names from the list of run-support leaders were repeated among the top winning percentages. So over the last three years, we have 19 matches between ERA and winning percentage; 17 matches between run support and winning percentage.

The point is that there are two components that go into a won-lost record: a defensive component, measured by ERA, and an offensive component, measured by run support. Any consideration of a pitcher's won-lost record—such as Cy Young voting, All-Star selection, or arbitration hearing—should take both of those elements into account.

WON-LOST RECORD BY STARTING POSITION

PHILADELPHIA 80-82	C	1B	2B	3B	SS	LF	CF	RF	P	Leadoff	Relief	Starts
Luis Aguayo	-	-	1-2	-	27-22	-	-	-	-	1-0	-	28-24
Doug Bair	-	-	-	-	-	-	-	-	-	-	5-6	-
Steve Bedrosian	-	-	-	-	-	-	-	-	-	-	50-15	-
Jeff Calhoun	-	-	-	-	-	-	-	-	-	-	17-25	-
Don Carman	-	-	-	-	-	-	-	-	18-17	-	-	18-17
Joe Cowley	-	-	-	-	-	-	-	-	0-4	-	0-1	0-4
Darren Daulton	16-17	0-1	-	-	-	-	-	-	-	-	-	16-18
Ken Dowell	-	-	-	9-4	-	-	-	-	-	-	-	9-4
Mike Easler	-	-	-	-	-	14-16	-	-	-	-	-	14-16
Todd Frohwirth	-	-	-	-	-	-	-	-	-	-	4-6	-
Greg Gross	-	1-0	-	-	-	7-8	-	1-0	-	-	-	9-8
Kevin Gross	-	-	-	-	-	-	-	-	14-19	-	1-0	14-19
Von Hayes	-	66-64	-	-	-	0-2	13-8	0-1	-	-	-	79-75
Keith Hughes	-	-	-	-	-	2-7	-	2-4	-	-	-	4-11
Tom Hume	-	-	-	-	-	-	-	-	2-4	-	4-28	2-4
Ken Jackson	-	-	-	1-4	-	-	-	-	-	-	-	1-4
Mike Jackson	-	-	-	-	-	-	-	-	3-4	-	14-34	3-4
Chris James	-	-	-	-	-	41-36	1-9	2-1	-	1-7	-	44-46
Greg Jelks	-	0-1	-	0-1	-	1-0	-	-	-	-	-	1-2
Steve Jeltz	-	-	-	-	43-52	-	-	-	-	-	-	43-52
Greg Legg	-	-	-	-	-	-	-	-	-	-	-	-
Mike Maddux	-	-	-	-	-	-	-	-	2-0	-	1-4	2-0
Tom Newell	-	-	-	-	-	-	-	-	-	-	0-2	-
Lance Parrish	62-62	-	-	-	-	-	-	-	-	-	-	62-62
Shane Rawley	-	-	-	-	-	-	-	-	23-13	-	-	23-13
Wally Ritchie	-	-	-	-	-	-	-	-	-	-	14-35	-
Ron Roenicke	-	-	-	-	-	-	2-3	1-1	-	-	-	3-4
Bruce Ruffin	-	-	-	-	-	-	-	-	15-20	-	-	15-20
John Russell	2-3	-	-	-	-	1-9	-	-	-	-	-	3-12
Juan Samuel	-	-	79-80	-	-	-	-	-	-	49-44	-	79-80
Dan Schatzeder	-	-	-	-	-	-	-	-	-	-	6-20	-
Mike Schmidt	-	2-6	-	66-67	-	-	-	-	-	-	-	68-73
Rick Schu	-	11-10	-	14-14	-	-	-	-	-	-	-	25-24
Jeff Stone	-	-	-	-	-	14-4	1-2	-	-	0-1	-	15-6
Kent Tekulve	-	-	-	-	-	-	-	-	-	-	42-48	-
Milt Thompson	-	-	-	-	-	-	63-60	1-0	-	29-30	-	64-60
Fred Toliver	-	-	-	-	-	-	-	-	3-1	-	0-6	3-1
Glenn Wilson	-	-	-	-	-	-	-	73-75	-	-	0-1	73-75

Batting vs. Left and Right Handed Pitchers

		BA	Rank	SA	Rank	OBA	Rank	HR %	Rank	BB %	Rank	SO %	Rank
Luis Aguayo	vs. Lefties	.276	63	.645	4	.304	108	9.21	3	2.53	134	22.78	128
	vs. Righties	.165	136	.308	124	.257	132	3.76	40	8.39	76	24.52	130
Darren Daulton	vs. Lefties	.125	--	.250	--	.222	--	0.00	--	10.00	--	30.00	--
	vs. Righties	.198	131	.314	122	.285	113	2.48	68	10.71	42	24.29	129
Greg Gross	vs. Lefties	.300	--	.300	--	.364	--	0.00	--	9.09	--	9.09	--
	vs. Righties	.285	46	.358	102	.397	17	0.81	115	15.79	5	7.24	10
Von Hayes	vs. Lefties	.232	108	.345	106	.361	46	1.79	87	17.07	7	15.12	84
	vs. Righties	.296	28	.528	17	.422	7	4.64	25	18.07	4	9.66	21
Chris James	vs. Lefties	.282	56	.570	10	.327	81	6.04	17	6.79	89	16.05	92
	vs. Righties	.301	26	.493	26	.355	46	3.83	38	6.99	98	17.90	106
Steve Jeltz	vs. Lefties	.175	134	.263	131	.258	130	0.00	113	10.00	44	17.78	105
	vs. Righties	.254	92	.319	117	.348	53	0.00	126	12.15	21	15.38	81
Lance Parrish	vs. Lefties	.304	35	.464	48	.391	35	4.35	35	13.04	23	18.63	112
	vs. Righties	.220	123	.372	91	.278	121	3.35	51	7.28	95	20.73	118
Juan Samuel	vs. Lefties	.249	97	.492	36	.344	62	4.97	24	11.96	30	22.49	125
	vs. Righties	.281	53	.506	25	.331	76	4.01	33	6.77	101	22.24	125
Mike Schmidt	vs. Lefties	.331	18	.556	14	.442	8	5.26	19	16.97	8	6.67	11
	vs. Righties	.280	55	.545	9	.368	31	7.20	7	12.28	20	15.40	82
Rick Schu	vs. Lefties	.265	77	.471	43	.330	74	4.90	27	8.93	65	12.50	59
	vs. Righties	.202	--	.330	--	.290	--	2.13	--	9.35	--	20.56	--
Jeff Stone	vs. Lefties	.100	--	.200	--	.308	--	0.00	--	7.69	--	46.15	--
	vs. Righties	.270	71	.365	98	.317	92	0.87	112	5.69	111	26.02	134
Milt Thompson	vs. Lefties	.214	123	.250	132	.283	123	0.00	113	8.60	71	15.05	83
	vs. Righties	.318	11	.458	42	.365	35	1.58	91	7.05	97	15.15	80
Glenn Wilson	vs. Lefties	.271	72	.355	104	.307	102	1.29	98	5.42	109	9.04	34
	vs. Righties	.261	81	.391	78	.308	100	2.90	60	6.47	103	14.96	79
Team Average	vs. Lefties	.250	11	.417	6	.328	8	3.40	3	10.19	3	16.99	10
	vs. Righties	.255	10	.408	5	.326	6	2.97	5	9.21	4	18.27	12
League Average	vs. Lefties	.263		.409		.332		2.81		9.08		15.22	
	vs. Righties	.260		.401		.327		2.73		8.70		15.85	

Batting with Runners on Base and Bases Empty

		BA	Rank	SA	Rank	OBA	Rank	HR %	Rank	BB %	Rank	SO %	Rank
Luis Aguayo	Runners On	.163	135	.233	136	.204	136	1.16	101	4.17	126	19.79	120
	Bases Empty	.236	104	.569	10	.319	82	8.94	2	7.97	60	26.81	135
Von Hayes	Runners On	.298	44	.512	19	.426	9	3.23	46	18.71	5	8.71	23
	Bases Empty	.260	77	.442	53	.385	18	4.22	37	16.98	5	13.48	60
Chris James	Runners On	.247	106	.462	45	.299	112	4.43	27	7.43	105	20.00	121
	Bases Empty	.330	6	.575	7	.380	22	5.00	29	6.48	89	14.81	75
Steve Jeltz	Runners On	.172	133	.250	134	.274	126	0.00	122	11.33	48	17.33	107
	Bases Empty	.279	53	.345	107	.364	31	0.00	128	11.76	17	14.97	79
Lance Parrish	Runners On	.258	95	.458	49	.310	107	4.66	24	7.34	108	20.85	126
	Bases Empty	.230	113	.339	112	.317	84	2.61	69	10.81	26	19.31	110
Juan Samuel	Runners On	.311	26	.558	8	.358	57	4.38	30	7.53	104	20.07	123
	Bases Empty	.248	95	.468	41	.320	81	4.21	40	8.72	52	23.71	131
Mike Schmidt	Runners On	.300	38	.552	9	.393	30	6.30	8	13.40	29	12.46	57
	Bases Empty	.286	41	.544	17	.384	21	7.14	10	13.70	8	13.70	64
Rick Schu	Runners On	.221	121	.390	88	.337	82	3.90	36	14.13	24	19.57	119
	Bases Empty	.244	100	.412	67	.291	107	3.36	54	5.51	109	14.17	70
Milt Thompson	Runners On	.313	23	.443	59	.371	44	1.14	102	9.00	79	14.50	85
	Bases Empty	.296	31	.416	64	.341	51	1.42	99	6.40	94	15.47	83
Glenn Wilson	Runners On	.244	108	.316	118	.284	121	1.13	104	5.88	114	13.49	66
	Bases Empty	.281	49	.439	56	.329	68	3.63	50	6.46	90	13.23	55
Team Average	Runners On	.252	11	.405	7	.326	9	2.78	5	9.72	7	17.45	12
	Bases Empty	.255	7	.414	5	.328	3	3.32	4	9.29	2	18.29	11
League Average	Runners On	.267		.410		.341		2.66		9.88		14.92	
	Bases Empty	.256		.399		.319		2.82		7.98		16.22	

Overall Batting Compared to Late Inning Pressure Situations

		BA	Rank	SA	Rank	OBA	Rank	HR %	Rank	BB %	Rank	SO %	Rank	RDI %	Rank
Luis Aguayo	Overall	.206	133	.431	58	.273	127	5.74	15	6.41	110	23.93	133	.143	134
	Pressure	.268	66	.537	16	.302	98	7.32	8	2.17	133	26.09	132	.143	120
Greg Gross	Overall	.286	--	.353	--	.395	--	0.75	--	15.34	--	7.36	--	.250	--
	Pressure	.267	68	.289	118	.433	10	0.00	105	22.95	2	6.56	8	.214	87
Von Hayes	Overall	.277	63	.473	31	.404	11	3.78	42	17.77	3	11.31	41	.289	61
	Pressure	.293	43	.451	42	.410	20	2.44	66	17.00	11	9.00	17	.400	15
Chris James	Overall	.293	30	.525	15	.344	59	4.75	21	6.91	101	17.14	101	.267	84
	Pressure	.306	35	.449	44	.370	47	4.08	30	9.26	66	16.67	80	.059	139
Steve Jeltz	Overall	.232	120	.304	129	.324	86	0.00	133	11.57	26	16.02	91	.122	136
	Pressure	.290	45	.452	41	.389	35	0.00	105	10.53	53	13.16	44	.000	--
Lance Parrish	Overall	.245	107	.399	84	.313	98	3.65	45	9.07	59	20.08	124	.236	108
	Pressure	.211	118	.382	73	.302	98	5.26	16	11.49	41	20.69	106	.219	86
Ron Roenicke	Overall	.167	--	.269	--	.293	--	1.28	--	15.22	--	16.30	--	.033	--
	Pressure	.219	112	.344	97	.342	68	3.13	44	15.79	14	21.05	110	.000	140
Juan Samuel	Overall	.272	73	.502	23	.335	69	4.27	33	8.26	77	22.31	131	.361	6
	Pressure	.322	23	.529	19	.412	17	3.45	40	13.73	24	24.51	122	.333	36
Mike Schmidt	Overall	.293	32	.548	8	.388	19	6.70	7	13.54	13	13.05	58	.337	21
	Pressure	.264	72	.448	45	.379	41	4.60	25	15.53	17	13.59	52	.267	65
Rick Schu	Overall	.235	117	.403	81	.311	101	3.57	47	9.13	58	16.44	96	.210	121
	Pressure	.167	--	.267	--	.194	--	0.00	--	3.23	--	22.58	--	.273	61
Jeff Stone	Overall	.256	--	.352	--	.316	--	0.80	--	5.88	--	27.94	--	.310	--
	Pressure	.192	--	.269	--	.323	--	0.00	--	12.90	--	32.26	--	.091	131
Milt Thompson	Overall	.302	18	.425	63	.351	48	1.33	102	7.30	95	15.13	82	.248	98
	Pressure	.297	40	.405	59	.325	83	2.70	56	3.80	121	25.32	125	.231	81
Glenn Wilson	Overall	.264	85	.381	93	.308	105	2.46	73	6.19	114	13.36	60	.231	112
	Pressure	.232	96	.274	125	.291	103	1.05	103	7.77	90	15.53	66	.207	94
Team Average	Overall	.254	10	.410	5	.327	8	3.09	5	9.48	3	17.92	12	.251	12
	Pressure	.260	7	.400	5	.351	1	3.00	3	11.87	1	18.27	10	.223	11
League Average	Overall	.261		.404		.328		2.75		8.83		15.64		.272	
	Pressure	.258		.385		.331		2.46		9.54		16.95		.261	

Additional Miscellaneous Batting Comparisons

	Grass Surface		Artificial Surface		Home Games		Road Games		Runners in Scoring Position		Runners in Scoring Pos and Two Outs		Leading Off Inning		Runners on 3B with less than 2 Outs	
	BA	Rank	BA	Rank	BA	Rank	BA	Rank	BA	Rank	BA	Rank	OBA	Rank	RDI %	Rank
Luis Aguayo	.218	--	.201	127	.207	128	.205	130	.118	136	.120	129	.348	51	.429	--
Darren Daulton	.205	--	.189	132	.259	--	.147	--	.171	--	.190	116	.343	--	.400	--
Mike Easler	.320	--	.271	72	.261	--	.317	--	.250	--	.077	--	.382	--	.500	--
Greg Gross	.292	--	.282	53	.316	--	.263	--	.222	--	.250	--	.431	6	.500	--
Von Hayes	.275	59	.278	59	.252	100	.302	25	.259	79	.291	36	.435	4	.618	49
Chris James	.235	106	.311	21	.302	31	.285	38	.233	108	.208	100	.385	24	.611	51
Steve Jeltz	.263	79	.221	121	.209	126	.262	78	.101	137	.059	136	.415	11	.364	130
Lance Parrish	.246	97	.244	104	.252	99	.237	108	.241	101	.197	111	.262	127	.650	34
Juan Samuel	.244	100	.282	54	.288	54	.257	83	.321	19	.270	55	.342	56	.771	7
Mike Schmidt	.258	85	.305	27	.342	7	.244	102	.311	28	.350	12	.388	21	.588	63
Rick Schu	.143	--	.271	70	.250	102	.219	123	.135	134	.091	135	.333	62	.600	--
Jeff Stone	.258	--	.255	89	.246	--	.266	--	.278	--	.333	--	.391	--	.333	--
Milt Thompson	.252	90	.318	18	.330	14	.272	64	.270	70	.231	82	.344	55	.750	11
Glenn Wilson	.291	34	.253	92	.252	100	.275	60	.241	99	.208	101	.350	50	.625	47
Team Average	.241	12	.258	8	.263	9	.245	10	.235	12	.220	11	.347	2	.566	4
League Average	.260		.261		.265		.256		.258		.241		.324		.554	

Pitching vs. Left and Right Handed Batters

		BA	Rank	SA	Rank	OBA	Rank	HR %	Rank	BB %	Rank	SO %	Rank
Steve Bedrosian	vs. Lefties	.249	40	.394	56	.315	34	4.15	104	8.84	43	20.93	13
	vs. Righties	.220	20	.319	14	.272	18	2.13	25	5.96	26	19.21	36
Don Carman	vs. Lefties	.312	102	.468	95	.364	84	2.75	81	4.92	9	11.48	75
	vs. Righties	.233	30	.425	75	.297	33	4.51	98	8.25	73	14.53	77
Kevin Gross	vs. Lefties	.278	77	.432	76	.369	89	2.83	83	11.69	85	10.48	81
	vs. Righties	.254	54	.426	76	.318	59	4.08	93	7.59	51	15.18	71
Mike Jackson	vs. Lefties	.265	56	.407	65	.397	103	3.17	94	17.17	112	13.30	56
	vs. Righties	.178	2	.352	25	.236	3	4.69	103	6.81	38	26.38	7
Shane Rawley	vs. Lefties	.294	91	.471	97	.357	75	2.94	87	8.47	33	9.32	94
	vs. Righties	.277	86	.422	73	.341	85	2.52	42	8.57	78	12.63	94
Wally Ritchie	vs. Lefties	.323	--	.523	--	.371	--	3.08	--	6.94	--	18.06	--
	vs. Righties	.228	27	.392	46	.323	65	3.51	78	11.94	102	15.92	65
Bruce Ruffin	vs. Lefties	.269	62	.351	33	.333	50	1.49	28	8.72	39	14.09	51
	vs. Righties	.305	103	.441	87	.360	98	2.29	34	8.16	64	9.80	105
Kent Tekulve	vs. Lefties	.309	99	.467	94	.377	96	3.03	90	9.73	57	8.11	100
	vs. Righties	.196	9	.265	6	.230	2	1.30	10	4.45	4	18.22	41
Team Average	vs. Lefties	.285	10	.431	10	.371	11	2.72	10	11.62	12	12.55	11
	vs. Righties	.253	6	.406	7	.317	6	3.16	9	8.27	7	14.71	10
League Average	vs. Lefties	.268		.404		.341		2.34		9.74		14.31	
	vs. Righties	.255		.403		.319		3.05		8.16		16.61	

Pitching with Runners on Base and Bases Empty

		BA	Rank	SA	Rank	OBA	Rank	HR %	Rank	BB %	Rank	SO %	Rank
Steve Bedrosian	Runners On	.220	11	.313	13	.293	11	2.00	38	9.47	53	18.93	19
	Bases Empty	.250	50	.402	69	.299	30	4.35	104	6.09	22	21.32	16
Don Carman	Runners On	.280	83	.457	91	.353	86	4.15	101	9.12	39	12.35	78
	Bases Empty	.223	18	.416	78	.278	11	4.34	103	6.96	43	15.20	60
Kevin Gross	Runners On	.246	32	.345	23	.312	21	0.85	14	8.64	29	12.35	79
	Bases Empty	.286	92	.501	105	.376	108	5.57	112	10.99	99	12.68	93
Mike Jackson	Runners On	.226	16	.429	81	.312	20	5.65	111	11.54	86	19.23	17
	Bases Empty	.213	11	.338	17	.319	64	2.67	58	12.31	107	20.38	22
Shane Rawley	Runners On	.270	69	.427	76	.336	60	2.83	67	9.31	47	11.97	83
	Bases Empty	.287	93	.429	85	.348	97	2.37	44	7.94	58	12.45	94
Wally Ritchie	Runners On	.223	14	.388	48	.349	81	3.88	97	15.27	112	14.50	60
	Bases Empty	.278	88	.459	93	.324	70	3.01	72	6.34	29	18.31	31
Bruce Ruffin	Runners On	.280	81	.393	54	.344	72	2.08	41	9.44	51	11.73	89
	Bases Empty	.313	107	.449	89	.365	103	2.20	35	7.32	50	9.55	108
Kent Tekulve	Runners On	.212	9	.302	8	.284	6	1.68	29	9.22	42	13.59	70
	Bases Empty	.269	78	.389	60	.301	32	2.31	42	4.42	7	14.16	75
Team Average	Runners On	.254	2	.391	2	.336	5	2.61	6	10.73	10	13.25	11
	Bases Empty	.270	11	.432	12	.334	11	3.35	10	8.23	8	14.63	9
League Average	Runners On	.267		.410		.341		2.66		9.88		14.92	
	Bases Empty	.256		.399		.319		2.82		7.98		16.22	

Overall Pitching Compared to Late Inning Pressure Situations

		BA	Rank	SA	Rank	OBA	Rank	HR %	Rank	BB %	Rank	SO %	Rank
Steve Bedrosian	Overall	.237	17	.362	30	.297	11	3.29	80	7.65	26	20.22	19
	Pressure	.249	45	.357	44	.300	25	2.81	71	6.69	24	20.45	30
Jeff Calhoun	Overall	.168	--	.255	--	.292	--	0.67	--	14.21	--	16.94	--
	Pressure	.156	2	.229	4	.281	18	0.00	1	14.66	103	19.83	33
Don Carman	Overall	.244	30	.431	86	.306	24	4.27	107	7.79	31	14.11	70
	Pressure	.239	37	.348	35	.327	48	2.17	52	11.32	83	11.32	83
Kevin Gross	Overall	.267	75	.429	84	.347	93	3.39	85	9.91	79	12.53	88
	Pressure	.271	69	.525	99	.358	77	6.78	105	11.94	86	13.43	71
Mike Jackson	Overall	.219	8	.378	45	.316	35	3.98	104	11.97	105	19.87	23
	Pressure	.250	46	.354	41	.345	65	2.08	49	10.81	74	15.32	61
Shane Rawley	Overall	.279	94	.428	81	.343	88	2.57	58	8.56	49	12.24	91
	Pressure	.280	79	.451	86	.344	63	4.88	95	8.79	46	12.09	79
Wally Ritchie	Overall	.254	53	.428	82	.336	80	3.39	85	10.62	96	16.48	42
	Pressure	.409	111	.727	111	.500	110	9.09	109	12.96	91	7.41	104
Bruce Ruffin	Overall	.299	108	.425	76	.355	101	2.15	33	8.26	42	10.52	103
	Pressure	.308	92	.513	98	.341	60	5.13	98	4.76	15	9.52	97
Kent Tekulve	Overall	.243	27	.349	22	.293	8	2.03	29	6.71	15	13.89	73
	Pressure	.218	20	.340	28	.266	11	2.91	72	6.19	22	14.16	67
Team Average	Overall	.263	8	.414	9	.335	10	3.02	10	9.37	10	14.00	10
	Pressure	.252	4	.387	6	.323	3	3.17	10	8.98	3	14.96	11
League Average	Overall	.261		.404		.328		2.75		8.83		15.64	
	Pressure	.260		.391		.337		2.47		10.04		17.14	

Additional Miscellaneous Pitching Comparisons

	Grass Surface		Artificial Surface		Home Games		Road Games		Runners in Scoring Position		Runners in Scoring Pos and Two Outs		Leading Off Inning	
	BA	Rank	BA	Rank	BA	Rank	BA	Rank	BA	Rank	BA	Rank	OBA	Rank
Steve Bedrosian	.230	--	.239	24	.251	51	.222	16	.156	1	.149	12	.286	17
Jeff Calhoun	.306	--	.124	1	.102	--	.262	--	.190	--	.111	--	.333	--
Don Carman	.247	40	.243	29	.243	34	.245	36	.275	78	.313	99	.311	43
Kevin Gross	.324	109	.250	39	.251	49	.289	84	.261	69	.225	53	.393	106
Mike Jackson	.297	100	.189	4	.151	1	.276	71	.200	10	.170	21	.312	44
Shane Rawley	.269	70	.283	84	.284	94	.275	64	.229	31	.217	47	.360	91
Wally Ritchie	.196	--	.272	69	.284	93	.216	--	.176	4	.167	19	.339	78
Bruce Ruffin	.303	102	.297	93	.305	104	.294	92	.309	103	.293	92	.389	105
Dan Schatzeder	.303	--	.270	66	.225	--	.344	--	.289	--	.211	--	.250	--
Kent Tekulve	.256	55	.237	22	.251	50	.233	22	.180	5	.151	14	.326	64
Team Average	.284	12	.256	4	.257	8	.270	10	.238	2	.217	3	.351	12
League Average	.260		.261		.256		.265		.258		.241		.324	

PITTSBURGH PIRATES

Anyone who has seen *Angels in the Outfield*, a 1950s movie shot on location at Forbes Field, has to wonder whether those heavenly aides have returned to the City of Steel and taken up temporary residence at Three Rivers Stadium to bail the Pirates out of another sticky situation. Because what's happened in Pittsburgh over the past two seasons is almost miraculous.

Three seasons ago, the Pittsburgh Pirates compiled a record of 57–104, the worst in the National League since 1976, and the worst by a Pirates team since 1954, when Pittsburgh suffered the last of three consecutive 100-loss seasons. But the Pirates are one of only four teams in either league to improve its record in both seasons since then, the others being San Francisco, Detroit, and Milwaukee. And last season, Pittsburgh fell only one win short of the .500 mark.

General Manager Syd Thrift and field manager Jim Leyland, both hired shortly after the end of the 1985 season, have been active directors of the team's turnaround. Although Thrift didn't move a single player for nearly five months after taking charge, he has engineered a nearly total overhaul of the team since then. Of the 25 players on the Pirates roster as of August 31, 1985, only two remained with the team at the close of the 1987 season: Junior Ortiz and Bob Walk.

The turnover in personnel has dramatically reduced the team's age. At the close of the 1985 season, Pittsburgh's everyday players were, on average, 28.8 years old; its pitchers averaged 29.1 years of age. By the final month of the 1987, when the Pirates gave their fans a glimpse of the future with rookies like Jose Lind and Vicente Palacios making their major-league debuts, those figures fell to 26.8 years for the batters, and 25.8 for the pitchers, the second-lowest and lowest marks in the majors respectively.

But the *piece de resistance* of Thrift's dealing was last April's trade in which he acquired Andy Van Slyke, Mike LaValliere, and Mike Dunne from St. Louis for Tony Pena. LaValliere batted nearly 100 points higher than Pena, and the addition of Van Slyke solidified the Pirates' lineup. Dunne, an ex-Olympian largely ignored at the time of the trade, joined the team in early June, and compiled the league's second-best ERA. The only pitcher who won more games over the second half of the season was teammate Doug Drabek, the key man in a six-player deal in which Pittsburgh sent Rick Rhoden to the Yankees following the 1986 season.

The Pirates still have several holes, with the shortstop and right field positions unsettled as the 1988 season begins. But if their young pitchers fulfill their potential, Pittsburgh may be contenders for a division title before the end of the decade.

For Openers, Beware of Rookies

Although the Pirates have introduced two of the best rookies in the National League over the past two years, Pittsburgh hasn't started a rookie on opening day since long-forgotten Doug Frobel started in right field in 1984. Barry Bonds and Mike Dunne, Pittsburgh's best rookies of the 1986 and 1987 seasons, respectively, spent the first few weeks of those seasons in the minors before late-spring recalls.

We mention this because one of the biggest mistakes that fantasy-league owners make each season is to overbid for rookies who make their teams' opening-day lineups. Occasionally, rookies who earn a starting spot with an outstanding training camp prove to be exceptional players. Certainly no one who drafted Jose Canseco, Wally Joyner, or Pete Incaviglia—all starters on opening day in 1986—felt cheated. But what about those who plunked down big bucks last season for Jim Lindeman, the rookie sensation of spring training in 1987? Unfortunately, many fantasy-league owners have learned the hard way that disappointments like Lindeman are the rule, not the exception, and that few rookies justify the premium prices usually required to land them.

Need convincing? Here are the statistics of National League rookies who started on opening day last season. Of course, Santiago had an outstanding season, but the others all proved to be disappointments:

Player, Team	Pos.	AB	H	2B	3B	HR	RBI	SB	BA	SA	OBA
Mike Ramsey, L.A.	CF	125	29	4	2	0	12	2	.232	.296	.287
Alonzo Powell, Mtl.	LF	41	8	3	0	0	4	0	.195	.268	.283
Jim Lindeman, St.L.	RF	207	43	13	0	8	28	3	.208	.386	.253
Benito Santiago, S.D.	C	546	164	33	2	18	79	21	.300	.467	.324
Joey Cora, S.D.	2B	241	57	7	2	0	13	15	.237	.282	.317

American League rookies who started on opening day last season were slightly better. Bo Jackson, Fred McGriff, Kevin Seitzer, and Devon White were worth a substantial investment. But how about the owner who drafted the only A.L. rookie catcher to start on opening day—not Matt Nokes, but Chicago's Ron Karkovice, who managed only six hits in 85 at bats? Other A.L. rookies who started on opening day last season included Ken Gerhart, Mark McLemore, Mark Davidson, Rob Nelson (who started over another rookie, Mark McGwire, at first base for the A's), Donell Nixon, Jerry Browne, and Mike Sharperson. Anyone who paid more than the minimum for any of those players overspent.

We've compiled lists of all the opening-day rookie starters for the previous five seasons as well. There's no doubt that some of the players listed have been worth every penny paid, but the message of the majority of the names below is *caveat emptor*.

1986—Wally Joyner, John Cangelosi, Andy Allanson, Billy Jo Robidoux, Mike Felder, Steve Lombardozzi, Jose Canseco, Danny Tartabull, Pete Incaviglia, and Cecil Fielder in the American League; Tracy Jones, Eric Bullock, Tony Walker, Bip Roberts, Rob Thompson, and Will Clark in the National League.

1985—Larry Sheets, Ozzie Guillen, Daryl Boston, Chris Pittaro, and Doug Loman; Shawon Dunston, Sid Bream, Herm Winningham, Steve Jeltz, John Russell, Gerry Davis, and Chris Brown.

1984—Dick Schofield, Gary Pettis, Brook Jacoby, Otis Nixon, Butch Davis, Randy Ready, Tim Teufel, and Curtis Wilkerson; German Rivera, Angel Salazar, Juan Samuel, Doug Frobel, and Carmelo Martinez.

1983—Leo Hernandez, John Shelby, Daryl Sconiers, Scott Fletcher, Greg Walker, Julio Franco, Bob Kearney, Kelvin Moore, and Pete O'Brien; Mel Hall, Jeff Jones, Gary Redus, Bill Doran, Greg Brock, Bryan Little, and Mike Howard.

1982—Cal Ripken, Jack Perconte, Gary Gaetti, Kent Hrbek, Jim Eisenreich, Bob Kearney, Manny Castillo, Jim Maler, Mike Richardt, George Wright, and Jesse Barfield; Brett Butler, Ryne Sandberg, Paul Householder, Steve Sax, Wallace Johnson, Ron Gardenhire, Johnny Ray, and Chili Davis.

Win One for the Kipper

In the 1987 *Analyst*, we challenged the assumption that a player's past few games provide an indication as to how well he might hit in an upcoming contest. That study, which is updated in the Atlanta Braves essay of this book, proved that players are just as likely to hit well when they've been mired in slumps as when they've come off hot streaks.

This season, we examined the same question on a team basis—that is, whether a team is more likely to win its next game having won its last few games than it is having lost a few in a row. The evidence, which you can find in the Montreal Expos essay, demonstrates that teams are no more likely to win if they've lost the last few games than if they've won them.

There remains one unanswered question: Do pitchers follow the same rule as well? If the recent past performances of teams and batters provide no indication of how they are likely to play in their next game, can we also ignore a pitcher's last few outings as a guide to his performance in his next start?

The answer is yes. Pitchers are no more likely to win a start following a win in their last outing than they are following a loss their last time out. Over the course of each season, some pitchers are nearly unbeatable coming off wins—the late-season success of Doyle Alexander in 1987 comes to mind. But just as many pitchers do their best work following losses.

No pitcher has illustrated that rule better over the past few years than Bob Kipper has. The following table classifies each start of Kipper's career—excluding his initial appearance of each season—according to the result of his previous appearance:

Last Appearance	GS	W	L	IP	H	ER	BB	SO	ERA
Started and won	11	0	8	47.2	71	48	20	38	9.06
No-decision starts	12	3	5	73.0	65	33	24	49	4.07
Started and lost	19	9	3	112.2	101	39	39	75	3.12
Relief appearances	5	0	2	9.2	18	13	7	8	12.10

Kipper has been extremely effective in starts that followed losses. But in three seasons in the majors, he is winless in 11 starts coming off winning starts, and he's allowed more than one earned run per inning in those games.

But let's not get sidetracked by individual cases. The fact is that if you examine all the starting pitchers in the majors over a period of time, their composite record will be better following losing starts than following no decisions; and better after no-decisions than after winning starts. The following table shows the major-league winning percentages for starters in each of those situations. The records include statistics for all starting pitchers in a given season with at least one start following a winning start, one following a losing start, and one following a start without a decision:

Year	No. of Pitchers	After Wins	After ND's	After Losses
1982	144	.443	.492	.521
1983	155	.461	.595	.523
1984	151	.469	.477	.543
1985	151	.480	.486	.506
1986	156	.437	.471	.547
1987	157	.442	.506	.504
Totals	914	.455	.489	.524

Let's examine the question in another way. There were 96 pitchers who made at least 100 starts following other starts over the past six seasons. If pitchers were truly more effective coming off other good outings, then a solid majority of those 96 should have compiled better records following winning starts than they did following losses. But only a weak majority of 51 actually did, compared to 45 who had better records after losses than after wins.

Some individual pitchers were much more effective following wins. The following table shows the statistics after wins and after losses for those with the widest margins:

Pitcher	Following Wins			Following Losses			
	W	L	Pct.	W	L	Pct.	Diff.
Doyle Alexander	29	13	.690	15	21	.417	.274
Richard Dotson	37	19	.661	22	34	.393	.268
Bill Laskey	19	14	.576	12	24	.333	.242
Dave Stewart	20	10	.667	12	16	.429	.238
Lamarr Hoyt	44	21	.677	22	27	.449	.228
Mike Boddicker	40	23	.635	19	26	.422	.213
Jose DeLeon	11	9	.550	12	23	.343	.207

Pitcher							
Charles Hudson	13	10	.565	11	19	.367	.199
Pascual Perez	19	11	.633	8	10	.444	.189
Nolan Ryan	28	22	.560	17	28	.378	.182

But, as we pointed out earlier, individual cases can be misleading. There were nearly as many wide swings in the opposite direction as well, indicative of pitchers who were much better following losses than wins. Those with the 10 widest such margins:

Pitcher	Following Wins			Following Losses			
	W	L	Pct.	W	L	Pct.	Diff.
Danny Cox	14	23	.378	21	11	.656	.278
John Butcher	6	13	.316	13	9	.591	.275
Len Barker	7	18	.280	15	13	.536	.256
Rick Reuschel	11	15	.423	14	7	.667	.244
Bert Blyleven	28	30	.483	33	16	.673	.191
Bob Forsch	17	18	.486	20	10	.667	.181
Jimmy Key	16	12	.571	12	4	.750	.179
Moose Haas	19	15	.559	14	5	.737	.178
Oil Can Boyd	20	23	.465	19	11	.633	.168
Mike Scott	29	28	.509	22	12	.647	.138

Incidentally, don't go betting the rent money on Kipper or any of the pitchers in the preceding table the next time they take the mound coming off a defeat. The statistics for the past six seasons also suggest that pitching well off wins (or losses) isn't a trait that is reproduced from one season to the next.

We found 57 pitchers who made at least 100 starts following other starts from 1982 through 1986, and who also made starts following both wins and losses last season. Among those 57 pitchers, 28 were better following wins during the five-year period prior to the 1987 season; the other 29 were better following losses. But last season, the first group was only slightly better following wins than the second:

Tendency during 1982–1987	Better After Wins in 1987	Better After Losses in 1987
Better following wins	15	13
Better following losses	13	16

We found last year that it wasn't easy to convince anyone that a player's last few games have no bearing on his performance in his next game. Fans, players, and the media have always assumed that when you're hot, you're hot, and when you're not, you're benched. But the evidence is as clear as it is unanimous: Whether you're talking about batters, pitchers, or teams, past performance has about as much to do with the outcome of an upcoming game as does the weather, the day of the week, or the price of popcorn in the bleachers.

WON-LOST RECORD BY STARTING POSITION

PITTSBURGH 80-82	C	1B	2B	3B	SS	LF	CF	RF	P	Leadoff	Relief	Starts
Bill Almon	-	-	-	-	1-2	-	-	-	-	-	-	1-2
Rafael Belliard	-	-	2-2	-	29-34	-	-	-	-	-	-	31-36
Mike Bielecki	-	-	-	-	-	-	-	-	4-4	-	-	4-4
Barry Bonds	-	-	-	-	-	41-42	19-24	-	-	57-58	-	60-66
Bobby Bonilla	-	1-1	-	39-36	-	3-5	-	11-14	-	2-2	-	54-56
Sid Bream	-	67-64	-	-	-	-	-	-	-	-	-	67-64
John Cangelosi	-	-	-	-	-	8-12	9-5	1-3	-	18-20	-	18-20
Darnell Coles	-	-	-	5-5	-	-	-	16-7	-	1-1	-	21-12
Onix Concepcion	-	-	-	-	-	-	-	-	-	-	-	-
Butch Davis	-	-	-	-	-	0-1	-	-	-	-	-	0-1
Mike Diaz	0-2	12-16	-	-	-	13-9	-	4-6	-	-	-	29-33
Doug Drabek	-	-	-	-	-	-	-	-	12-16	-	1-0	12-16
Tim Drummond	-	-	-	-	-	-	-	-	-	-	2-4	-
Mike Dunne	-	-	-	-	-	-	-	-	13-10	-	-	13-10
Logan Easley	-	-	-	-	-	-	-	-	-	-	6-11	-
Felix Fermin	-	-	-	-	12-7	-	-	-	-	1-1	-	12-7
Brian Fisher	-	-	-	-	-	-	-	-	14-12	-	2-9	14-12
Miguel Garcia	-	-	-	-	-	-	-	-	-	-	0-1	-
Brett Gideon	-	-	-	-	-	-	-	-	-	-	6-23	-
Denny Gonzalez	-	-	-	0-1	-	-	-	-	-	-	-	0-1
Jim Gott	-	-	-	-	-	-	-	-	-	17-8	-	-
Tommy Gregg	-	-	-	-	-	-	-	-	-	-	-	-
Terry Harper	-	-	-	-	-	6-3	1-8	-	-	-	-	7-11
Houston Jimenez	-	-	-	-	0-1	-	-	-	-	-	-	0-1
Dave Johnson	-	-	-	-	-	-	-	-	-	-	0-5	-
Barry Jones	-	-	-	-	-	-	-	-	-	12-20	-	-
Sammy Khalifa	-	-	-	-	2-3	-	-	-	-	-	-	2-3
Bob Kipper	-	-	-	-	-	-	-	-	10-10	-	1-3	10-10
Mike LaValliere	53-46	-	-	-	-	-	-	-	-	-	-	53-46
Jose Lind	-	-	23-11	-	-	-	-	-	-	-	-	23-11
Jim Morrison	-	-	2-7	36-41	0-1	-	-	-	-	-	-	38-49
Junior Ortiz	23-32	-	-	-	-	-	-	-	-	-	-	23-32
Vicente Palacios	-	-	-	-	-	-	-	-	2-2	-	0-2	2-2
Bob Patterson	-	-	-	-	-	-	-	-	1-6	-	3-5	1-6
Al Pedrique	-	-	-	-	35-33	-	-	-	-	1-0	-	35-33
Hipolito Pena	-	-	-	-	-	-	-	-	0-1	-	4-11	0-1
Tom Prince	1-2	-	-	-	-	-	-	-	-	-	-	1-2
Johnny Ray	-	-	53-62	-	-	-	-	-	-	-	-	53-62
Rick Reuschel	-	-	-	-	-	-	-	-	12-13	-	-	12-13
R.J. Reynolds	-	-	-	-	-	9-10	-	35-25	-	-	-	44-35
Don Robinson	-	-	-	-	-	-	-	-	-	23-19	-	-
Jeff D. Robinson	-	-	-	-	-	-	-	-	-	11-7	-	-
Mark Ross	-	-	-	-	-	-	-	-	-	-	0-1	-
Mackey Sasser	3-0	-	-	-	-	-	-	-	-	-	-	3-0
John Smiley	-	-	-	-	-	-	-	-	-	23-40	-	-
Dorn Taylor	-	-	-	-	-	-	-	-	4-4	-	2-4	4-4
Andy Van Slyke	-	0-1	-	-	-	52-53	12-19	-	-	-	-	64-73
Bob Walk	-	-	-	-	-	-	-	-	8-4	-	4-23	8-4
U.L. Washington	-	-	-	-	1-0	-	-	-	-	-	-	1-0

Batting vs. Left and Right Handed Pitchers

		BA	Rank	SA	Rank	OBA	Rank	HR %	Rank	BB %	Rank	SO %	Rank
Rafael Belliard	vs. Lefties	.213	125	.293	121	.306	104	0.00	113	9.41	54	11.76	52
	vs. Righties	.203	129	.258	134	.275	124	0.78	117	8.33	77	10.42	29
Barry Bonds	vs. Lefties	.228	115	.456	50	.303	109	3.88	49	8.77	67	18.42	109
	vs. Righties	.281	52	.513	22	.345	60	4.93	22	8.88	69	12.01	44
Bobby Bonilla	vs. Lefties	.308	32	.474	41	.345	61	2.99	66	5.56	107	8.33	29
	vs. Righties	.293	34	.487	28	.357	44	3.45	48	9.51	60	16.35	90
Sid Bream	vs. Lefties	.275	67	.456	51	.314	94	4.15	41	5.71	104	13.81	71
	vs. Righties	.276	64	.384	84	.348	54	1.55	93	10.22	53	11.05	35
John Cangelosi	vs. Lefties	.282	57	.485	37	.400	18	3.88	49	15.08	14	11.90	55
	vs. Righties	.266	--	.329	--	.458	--	0.00	--	25.23	--	16.82	--
Darnell Coles	vs. Lefties	.247	99	.545	19	.362	43	7.79	5	14.89	15	10.64	45
	vs. Righties	.190	--	.262	--	.277	--	0.00	--	10.00	--	20.00	--
Mike Diaz	vs. Lefties	.256	88	.565	12	.350	54	8.33	4	12.12	27	13.13	66
	vs. Righties	.205	--	.315	--	.271	--	2.74	--	8.24	--	18.82	--
Terry Harper	vs. Lefties	.298	39	.386	88	.365	40	1.75	90	9.52	48	12.70	61
	vs. Righties	.222	--	.333	--	.300	--	0.00	--	10.00	--	30.00	--
Mike LaValliere	vs. Lefties	.221	121	.273	129	.302	110	0.00	113	10.34	41	14.94	81
	vs. Righties	.323	10	.392	77	.399	16	0.38	123	11.22	34	6.27	7
Jose Lind	vs. Lefties	.342	9	.507	32	.368	37	0.00	113	3.75	127	5.00	6
	vs. Righties	.300	--	.357	--	.347	--	0.00	--	6.49	--	10.39	--
Jim Morrison	vs. Lefties	.289	47	.472	42	.370	36	3.52	53	12.12	27	11.52	50
	vs. Righties	.248	98	.369	95	.273	125	1.94	81	3.23	132	17.51	103
Junior Ortiz	vs. Lefties	.275	64	.325	111	.316	92	0.00	113	5.71	104	9.71	41
	vs. Righties	.250	--	.406	--	.351	--	3.13	--	13.16	--	15.79	--
Al Pedrique	vs. Lefties	.296	42	.326	110	.351	53	0.00	113	7.19	85	7.84	22
	vs. Righties	.291	39	.385	82	.346	57	0.85	113	6.25	107	13.28	61
Johnny Ray	vs. Lefties	.257	86	.319	115	.322	87	1.05	103	9.00	63	8.06	24
	vs. Righties	.285	45	.384	83	.332	71	1.07	106	7.17	96	6.19	5
R.J. Reynolds	vs. Lefties	.351	7	.386	88	.391	24	0.00	113	7.81	78	3.13	2
	vs. Righties	.241	105	.403	68	.309	99	2.52	67	9.32	62	25.08	132

Batting vs. Left and Right Handed Pitchers

		BA	Rank	SA	Rank	OBA	Rank	HR %	Rank	BB %	Rank	SO %	Rank
Andy Van Slyke	vs. Lefties	.231	109	.358	102	.292	113	1.31	97	7.14	86	22.22	123
	vs. Righties	.334	6	.609	4	.403	12	5.37	18	10.00	55	17.37	100
Team Average	vs. Lefties	.257	9	.396	9	.322	10	2.48	7	8.31	10	13.93	3
	vs. Righties	.270	2	.408	6	.336	3	2.28	8	8.82	6	15.26	6
League Average	vs. Lefties	.263		.409		.332		2.81		9.08		15.22	
	vs. Righties	.260		.401		.327		2.73		8.70		15.85	

Batting with Runners on Base and Bases Empty

		BA	Rank	SA	Rank	OBA	Rank	HR %	Rank	BB %	Rank	SO %	Rank
Rafael Belliard	Runners On	.207	129	.304	122	.302	110	1.09	105	10.19	64	12.04	49
	Bases Empty	.207	127	.243	135	.273	123	0.00	128	7.44	66	9.92	26
Barry Bonds	Runners On	.256	98	.487	31	.339	81	5.13	17	11.61	43	17.41	108
	Bases Empty	.264	70	.494	29	.323	76	4.21	38	7.24	73	12.66	51
Bobby Bonilla	Runners On	.299	42	.477	37	.352	67	2.49	66	8.42	88	14.29	83
	Bases Empty	.302	22	.484	33	.351	43	4.00	45	6.61	85	10.33	31
Sid Bream	Runners On	.265	85	.392	87	.345	78	2.45	70	11.27	50	11.27	42
	Bases Empty	.284	45	.428	61	.326	72	2.58	70	5.90	103	12.85	53
John Cangelosi	Runners On	.311	--	.511	--	.467	--	2.22	--	18.03	--	16.39	--
	Bases Empty	.263	72	.387	83	.413	5	2.19	79	20.35	2	13.37	57
Mike Diaz	Runners On	.231	116	.375	94	.351	69	2.88	51	14.93	17	14.18	82
	Bases Empty	.248	92	.577	6	.304	94	9.49	1	7.38	68	15.44	82
Mike LaValliere	Runners On	.289	55	.338	111	.416	15	0.00	122	18.23	7	6.63	12
	Bases Empty	.308	21	.384	85	.344	48	0.51	123	4.78	118	9.57	18
Jim Morrison	Runners On	.278	73	.411	73	.331	88	2.53	63	7.82	99	15.08	88
	Bases Empty	.253	86	.411	68	.300	96	2.63	68	6.40	93	14.78	74
Junior Ortiz	Runners On	.324	--	.380	--	.372	--	0.00	--	7.23	--	7.23	--
	Bases Empty	.240	103	.314	118	.292	105	0.83	112	6.92	79	13.08	54
Al Pedrique	Runners On	.374	2	.477	38	.419	13	0.93	112	6.50	113	5.69	8
	Bases Empty	.234	106	.262	131	.297	99	0.00	128	6.96	77	13.92	66
Johnny Ray	Runners On	.266	81	.369	100	.331	91	1.35	94	9.56	75	7.97	18
	Bases Empty	.280	51	.348	106	.326	73	0.80	113	6.37	95	5.99	5
R.J. Reynolds	Runners On	.265	83	.420	71	.335	84	2.47	67	10.64	58	22.34	130
	Bases Empty	.254	84	.382	90	.310	90	1.73	94	7.49	65	20.32	116
Andy Van Slyke	Runners On	.288	58	.498	28	.360	54	4.29	32	9.70	73	18.66	116
	Bases Empty	.296	32	.514	26	.358	36	3.32	55	8.24	58	19.78	113
Team Average	Runners On	.274	5	.412	4	.348	5	2.34	7	10.15	4	14.33	4
	Bases Empty	.257	5	.395	7	.315	7	2.39	7	7.31	10	14.97	2
League Average	Runners On	.267		.410		.341		2.66		9.88		14.92	
	Bases Empty	.256		.399		.319		2.82		7.98		16.22	

Overall Batting Compared to Late Inning Pressure Situations

		BA	Rank	SA	Rank	OBA	Rank	HR %	Rank	BB %	Rank	SO %	Rank	RDI %	Rank
Rafael Belliard	Overall	.207	131	.271	135	.286	123	0.49	121	8.73	66	10.92	36	.186	127
	Pressure	.211	--	.211	--	.348	--	0.00	--	12.50	--	4.17	--	.000	--
Barry Bonds	Overall	.261	89	.492	26	.329	76	4.54	25	8.84	64	14.40	73	.152	133
	Pressure	.239	91	.507	24	.321	86	5.63	14	11.11	46	16.05	77	.091	131
Bobby Bonilla	Overall	.300	19	.481	29	.351	47	3.22	58	7.57	87	12.43	50	.302	51
	Pressure	.278	58	.443	46	.352	61	1.27	97	10.23	59	15.91	74	.259	69
Sid Bream	Overall	.275	67	.411	78	.336	68	2.52	72	8.57	69	12.06	47	.247	100
	Pressure	.254	81	.492	26	.353	60	5.08	19	12.86	32	8.57	16	.083	135
John Cangelosi	Overall	.275	68	.418	71	.427	5	2.20	82	19.74	2	14.16	72	.263	--
	Pressure	.238	92	.310	112	.418	13	2.38	67	23.21	1	19.64	101	.000	--
Mike Diaz	Overall	.241	110	.490	27	.326	84	6.64	8	10.95	34	14.84	79	.354	11
	Pressure	.208	121	.358	88	.274	118	3.77	37	7.94	84	19.05	97	.333	36
Mike LaValliere	Overall	.300	21	.365	101	.377	25	0.29	131	11.03	32	8.21	11	.292	59
	Pressure	.333	17	.405	60	.391	32	0.00	105	8.33	78	10.42	24	.200	96
Jim Morrison	Overall	.264	83	.411	76	.315	91	2.59	68	7.07	97	14.92	80	.286	64
	Pressure	.231	97	.365	82	.310	91	1.92	78	10.34	57	18.97	96	.118	121
Junior Ortiz	Overall	.271	76	.339	117	.322	89	0.52	120	7.04	99	10.80	35	.317	33
	Pressure	.208	--	.208	--	.240	--	0.00	--	3.70	--	7.41	--	.182	105
Al Pedrique	Overall	.294	28	.353	108	.349	51	0.40	125	6.76	105	10.32	25	.329	27
	Pressure	.225	107	.275	123	.262	122	0.00	105	2.27	132	13.64	53	.167	111
Johnny Ray	Overall	.273	70	.358	106	.328	78	1.06	112	7.92	83	6.95	9	.272	79
	Pressure	.303	37	.470	32	.361	53	3.03	45	8.33	78	5.56	4	.190	100
R.J. Reynolds	Overall	.260	90	.400	82	.323	88	2.09	84	9.07	60	21.33	129	.314	35
	Pressure	.265	71	.367	80	.356	57	2.04	73	13.56	25	25.42	127	.310	52
Andy Van Slyke	Overall	.293	34	.507	21	.359	42	3.72	44	8.86	63	19.30	117	.293	58
	Pressure	.267	68	.533	17	.278	111	6.67	10	2.47	130	25.93	130	.303	58
Team Average	Overall	.264	4	.403	7	.330	5	2.37	7	8.59	6	14.68	2	.271	7
	Pressure	.253	8	.403	4	.331	8	2.91	6	10.06	3	16.00	4	.216	12
League Average	Overall	.261		.404		.328		2.75		8.83		15.64		.272	
	Pressure	.258		.385		.331		2.46		9.54		16.95		.261	

Additional Miscellaneous Batting Comparisons

	Grass Surface		Artificial Surface		Home Games		Road Games		Runners in Scoring Position		Runners in Scoring Pos and Two Outs		Leading Off Inning		Runners on 3B with less than 2 Outs	
	BA	Rank	BA	Rank	BA	Rank	BA	Rank	BA	Rank	BA	Rank	OBA	Rank	RDI %	Rank
Rafael Belliard	.261	--	.179	134	.187	132	.223	120	.200	121	.211	99	.353	47	.571	72
Barry Bonds	.260	82	.262	80	.265	83	.258	81	.159	132	.149	127	.350	49	.300	137
Bobby Bonilla	.336	6	.289	45	.265	84	.333	6	.281	55	.279	48	.330	70	.714	16
Sid Bream	.289	37	.270	73	.282	61	.268	71	.204	120	.216	93	.317	87	.469	108
John Cangelosi	.205	--	.297	33	.294	42	.250	91	.375	--	.333	--	.422	10	.667	--
Darnell Coles	.095	--	.255	90	.286	--	.161	--	.231	--	.182	--	.333	--	.417	122
Mike Diaz	.309	--	.220	122	.231	116	.250	91	.297	41	.296	34	.292	107	.667	25
Mike LaValliere	.274	60	.309	24	.305	28	.295	31	.290	48	.261	63	.325	79	.750	11
Jose Lind	.320	--	.322	16	.313	--	.333	--	.310	--	.467	--	.367	--	.000	--
Jim Morrison	.270	68	.262	79	.303	29	.225	117	.281	54	.302	30	.309	95	.583	67
Junior Ortiz	.296	--	.261	82	.271	74	.271	--	.292	46	.320	21	.273	120	.667	25
Al Pedrique	.265	--	.300	29	.308	24	.277	53	.458	1	.500	1	.364	40	.636	40
Johnny Ray	.246	96	.284	51	.303	30	.246	101	.250	88	.240	75	.282	116	.475	105
R.J. Reynolds	.229	112	.272	68	.267	77	.252	90	.237	105	.196	112	.329	71	.762	9
Andy Van Slyke	.289	38	.294	37	.273	71	.311	18	.306	30	.293	35	.376	30	.382	129
Team Average	.258	8	.267	2	.271	5	.258	8	.261	5	.254	3	.326	6	.555	8
League Average	.260		.261		.265		.256		.258		.241		.324		.554	

Pitching vs. Left and Right Handed Batters

		BA	Rank	SA	Rank	OBA	Rank	HR %	Rank	BB %	Rank	SO %	Rank
Mike Bielecki	vs. Lefties	.253	42	.442	80	.305	27	3.16	93	6.36	14	9.09	96
	vs. Righties	.250	--	.461	--	.296	--	3.95	--	6.10	--	18.29	--
Doug Drabek	vs. Lefties	.275	73	.479	99	.332	49	4.30	105	7.87	25	14.17	49
	vs. Righties	.216	19	.345	24	.251	5	2.19	27	4.71	6	19.41	32
Mike Dunne	vs. Lefties	.275	71	.407	65	.366	88	2.47	66	12.20	92	6.10	110
	vs. Righties	.199	11	.254	4	.256	8	0.74	6	7.26	47	16.17	63
Brian Fisher	vs. Lefties	.265	57	.438	78	.350	70	2.39	62	11.55	82	12.93	60
	vs. Righties	.259	64	.482	102	.311	43	5.49	109	6.13	99	16.99	52
Jim Gott	vs. Lefties	.292	88	.422	73	.401	105	2.48	67	15.03	108	24.35	7
	vs. Righties	.193	6	.216	1	.245	4	0.00	1	5.82	23	22.75	14
Barry Jones	vs. Lefties	.286	83	.393	55	.365	85	1.19	21	11.34	79	10.31	84
	vs. Righties	.341	--	.593	--	.413	--	5.49	--	11.32	--	16.98	--
Bob Kipper	vs. Lefties	.203	--	.241	--	.241	--	0.00	--	3.57	--	19.05	--
	vs. Righties	.286	97	.578	111	.372	103	7.08	112	11.98	103	16.38	59
Bob Patterson	vs. Lefties	.220	--	.366	--	.319	--	2.44	--	11.76	--	17.65	--
	vs. Righties	.315	108	.512	107	.388	108	3.15	69	10.67	98	12.00	98
Jeff D. Robinson	vs. Lefties	.232	20	.367	39	.319	39	2.53	69	10.99	69	20.15	18
	vs. Righties	.180	3	.296	8	.270	16	2.65	48	10.81	99	20.72	28
John Smiley	vs. Lefties	.195	5	.299	9	.287	14	1.15	18	11.88	87	20.79	14
	vs. Righties	.265	71	.429	79	.383	106	3.06	64	16.17	112	15.74	68
Dorn Taylor	vs. Lefties	.273	69	.515	109	.365	86	5.05	110	13.04	98	12.17	69
	vs. Righties	.221	--	.400	--	.318	--	5.26	--	11.71	--	20.72	--
Bob Walk	vs. Lefties	.253	43	.380	49	.331	48	1.75	38	10.00	61	12.31	67
	vs. Righties	.238	36	.374	35	.325	70	3.40	74	10.50	96	19.33	34
Team Average	vs. Lefties	.258	4	.402	7	.328	5	2.39	7	9.33	5	12.47	12
	vs. Righties	.249	4	.412	9	.319	8	3.59	11	9.02	11	17.13	6
League Average	vs. Lefties	.268		.404		.341		2.34		9.74		14.31	
	vs. Righties	.255		.403		.319		3.05		8.16		16.61	

Pitching with Runners on Base and Bases Empty

		BA	Rank	SA	Rank	OBA	Rank	HR %	Rank	BB %	Rank	SO %	Rank
Doug Drabek	Runners On	.270	71	.488	102	.291	10	4.44	104	3.41	1	17.80	29
	Bases Empty	.233	26	.371	41	.295	26	2.62	56	8.10	63	15.97	54
Mike Dunne	Runners On	.221	12	.283	5	.315	22	0.83	12	12.07	93	9.66	102
	Bases Empty	.253	58	.374	45	.318	60	2.25	36	8.46	70	11.28	101
Brian Fisher	Runners On	.252	41	.455	88	.317	25	3.10	78	9.06	83	14.80	59
	Bases Empty	.270	82	.460	94	.343	92	4.34	102	9.11	83	14.75	65
Jim Gott	Runners On	.259	55	.328	19	.326	36	0.57	6	9.23	43	23.59	7
	Bases Empty	.221	17	.301	8	.321	66	1.84	27	11.76	105	23.53	9
Bob Kipper	Runners On	.288	94	.582	113	.355	88	6.21	113	9.80	60	15.20	57
	Bases Empty	.259	67	.471	98	.346	96	5.49	110	11.07	100	17.99	36
Jeff D. Robinson	Runners On	.209	7	.316	15	.321	32	2.26	46	13.51	106	18.47	22
	Bases Empty	.209	9	.349	21	.278	11	2.81	66	8.79	77	21.98	13
John Smiley	Runners On	.278	80	.421	71	.397	111	2.38	50	17.31	113	14.10	65
	Bases Empty	.217	13	.363	29	.317	58	2.55	52	12.78	109	20.00	23
Dorn Taylor	Runners On	.325	--	.623	--	.400	--	6.49	--	10.99	--	9.89	--
	Bases Empty	.197	6	.350	23	.304	36	4.27	98	13.33	111	20.74	19
Bob Walk	Runners On	.262	56	.385	44	.330	45	2.56	59	8.89	35	17.33	34
	Bases Empty	.233	26	.371	40	.326	72	2.50	49	11.36	103	14.29	72
Team Average	Runners On	.264	5	.430	10	.333	2	3.13	12	9.45	4	13.94	8
	Bases Empty	.245	2	.391	5	.316	6	2.93	9	8.95	11	15.65	8
League Average	Runners On	.267		.410		.341		2.66		9.88		14.92	
	Bases Empty	.256		.399		.319		2.82		7.98		16.22	

Overall Pitching Compared to Late Inning Pressure Situations

		BA	Rank	SA	Rank	OBA	Rank	HR %	Rank	BB %	Rank	SO %	Rank
Doug Drabek	Overall	.247	42	.415	70	.294	9	3.29	80	6.38	10	16.64	41
	Pressure	.440	--	.600	--	.462	--	4.00	--	3.57	--	3.57	--
Mike Dunne	Overall	.240	21	.337	11	.317	37	1.68	16	10.00	82	10.59	102
	Pressure	.250	46	.375	54	.289	20	2.78	69	5.26	19	9.21	99
Brian Fisher	Overall	.262	67	.458	102	.332	70	3.83	102	9.09	65	14.77	65
	Pressure	.241	39	.426	79	.317	42	3.70	88	8.33	38	16.67	51
Brett Gideon	Overall	.243	--	.393	--	.298	--	4.29	--	6.54	--	20.26	--
	Pressure	.270	67	.459	88	.308	35	5.41	99	3.75	10	20.00	31
Jim Gott	Overall	.240	22	.315	5	.324	52	1.19	6	10.47	91	23.56	7
	Pressure	.215	19	.271	9	.300	26	0.93	24	10.74	71	21.49	21
Barry Jones	Overall	.314	--	.497	--	.390	--	3.43	--	11.33	--	13.79	--
	Pressure	.284	84	.388	64	.347	67	1.49	40	9.09	53	11.69	81
Bob Kipper	Overall	.271	82	.516	112	.350	95	5.79	112	10.55	94	16.84	39
	Pressure	.143	--	.143	--	.333	--	0.00	--	22.22	--	33.33	--
Jeff D. Robinson	Overall	.209	6	.336	10	.297	12	2.58	59	10.91	99	20.40	15
	Pressure	.210	15	.347	34	.297	24	2.95	75	10.86	75	21.41	22
John Smiley	Overall	.244	31	.389	55	.354	99	2.47	53	14.88	112	17.26	33
	Pressure	.244	42	.378	58	.381	92	1.48	39	18.45	108	16.67	51
Bob Walk	Overall	.246	36	.377	41	.328	63	2.53	56	10.24	87	15.66	53
	Pressure	.333	--	.583	--	.407	--	4.17	--	10.71	--	21.43	--
Team Average	Overall	.253	2	.407	7	.324	5	3.02	9	9.17	8	14.91	7
	Pressure	.252	5	.384	5	.331	5	2.50	6	10.16	8	17.09	6
League Average	Overall	.261		.404		.328		2.75		8.83		15.64	
	Pressure	.260		.391		.337		2.47		10.04		17.14	

Additional Miscellaneous Pitching Comparisons

	Grass Surface BA	Rank	Artificial Surface BA	Rank	Home Games BA	Rank	Road Games BA	Rank	Runners in Scoring Position BA	Rank	Runners in Scoring Pos and Two Outs BA	Rank	Leading Off Inning OBA	Rank
Mike Bielecki	.327	--	.218	14	.220	--	.296	--	.262	--	.250	--	.313	--
Doug Drabek	.227	20	.252	47	.256	58	.240	29	.271	76	.250	72	.341	80
Mike Dunne	.252	45	.237	21	.221	20	.254	43	.204	14	.211	41	.304	35
Brian Fisher	.207	6	.280	79	.324	111	.207	9	.223	28	.125	4	.359	90
Brett Gideon	.171	--	.267	61	.228	--	.262	--	.294	--	.091	--	.273	--
Jim Gott	.227	19	.255	48	.224	22	.254	45	.215	19	.143	8	.296	25
Barry Jones	.224	--	.349	110	.306	--	.325	--	.303	96	.231	--	.425	--
Bob Kipper	.271	71	.271	68	.269	78	.273	61	.286	84	.214	42	.345	84
Bob Patterson	.350	--	.259	53	.262	66	.344	--	.283	--	.292	--	.455	--
Jeff D. Robinson	.222	16	.188	3	.209	13	.209	11	.161	3	.083	1	.333	71
John Smiley	.387	--	.204	8	.162	2	.362	111	.310	104	.129	5	.303	31
Dorn Taylor	.217	--	.257	51	.255	--	.239	--	.289	--	.222	--	.304	35
Bob Walk	.262	--	.243	32	.234	25	.265	56	.241	43	.217	46	.330	70
Team Average	.249	2	.255	3	.249	4	.258	3	.253	5	.201	1	.336	9
League Average	.260		.261		.256		.265		.258		.241		.324	

ST. LOUIS CARDINALS

The Yankees had barely announced that they'd arranged the safe passage of Jack Clark from St. Louis to the city that Cardinals fans love to hate when St. Louis manager Whitey Herzog made an announcement of his own. The manager who New York fans love to hate announced that the Cardinals were no longer contenders in the National League East, that they were now nothing more than a .500 team. Given Clark's enormous impact on the 1987 Cardinals, we'd have to agree.

For the first half of the 1987 season, the most valuable player in the National League was Jack Clark. Not even the electorate from the Baseball Writers Association, or talk-show hosts, or talk-show callers could dispute the fact that over the first three months of the season, Clark *was* the offense for the division-leading St. Louis Cardinals. As late as July 3, he had hit as many home runs as the rest of his teammates combined (24), something no player had done over an entire season since 1946, when since Sam Chapman matched the 20 home runs that his Philadelphia A's teammates hit. Even more, Clark maintained a rate of one RBI per game until the All-Star break, despite a major-league-leading total of 82 walks.

But shortly after the break, Clark's season turned sour. During the first half of the season, pitchers were hesitant to give Clark anything good to hit; by July, they flat out refused. Clark was walked at least once in 16 consecutive games from July 18 through August 10, the longest streak in National League history. And when the pace really picked up—from July 21 through August 9, Clark batted 27 times with runners on base and drew 17 walks—he fell apart. Clark batted only .185 with five RBIs during that 13-game period, and never regained his earlier form.

As Clark stumbled, so did the Cardinals. St. Louis led the division by nine games at the All-Star break last season, a lead nearly as large as that of the New York Mets a year earlier as of the same date. But by September 9, St. Louis' lead had dwindled to two and one-half games over the Mets and three over the Montreal Expos. It was at that point that Clark assumed his customary position on the disabled list, not to be seen again except for two futile pinch-hit appearances during the final weekend of the season.

The disintegration of the Cardinals—first with a slumping Clark, then entirely without him—was so total that three teams in their division had a better second-half record than the Cardinals had. The major-league standings *after* the All-Star break:

N.L. East	W	L	Pct.		A.L. East	W	L	Pct.
New York	45	30	.600		Detroit	50	27	.649
Montreal	44	32	.579		Milwaukee	49	28	.636
Pittsburgh	41	34	.547		Toronto	45	30	.600
St. Louis	39	37	.513		Boston	37	37	.500
Philadelphia	38	38	.500		New York	34	39	.466
Chicago	29	44	.397		Baltimore	32	42	.432
					Cleveland	30	45	.400

N.L. West	W	L	Pct.		A.L. West	W	L	Pct.
San Francisco	46	28	.622		Chicago	43	34	.558
Cincinnati	37	37	.500		Kansas City	37	38	.493
San Diego	35	39	.473		Minnesota	36	37	.493
Los Angeles	34	40	.459		Oakland	35	40	.467
Houston	32	43	.427		Texas	34	42	.447
Atlanta	28	46	.378		Seattle	33	41	.446
					California	29	44	.397

Before you think that such a dramatic turnaround must be at least partially attributable to pitching, understand this: The collapse of St. Louis's offense was wholly responsible for its second-half decline. Prior to the All-Star break, the Cardinals led the National League with an average 5.65 runs scored per game; after the break, they ranked ninth with an average of 4.11 runs. St. Louis's pitchers actually allowed fewer runs per game during the second half of the season (4.17) than the first (4.37), ranking third in the league both before and after the break.

We could recite a litany of Clark's personal statistics to further demonstrate his value to the Cardinals' offense. But look at the following table, which compares the batting statistics of Clark's teammates when he was in the starting lineup to those compiled when he wasn't. The team totals with Clark in the starting lineup do not include Clark's own statistics:

Player	With Clark in Lineup				Without Clark in Lineup			
	G	HR	RBI	BA	G	HR	RBI	BA
Coleman	118	1	32	.294	33	2	11	.270
Ford	31	3	21	.309	18	0	5	.175
Herr	107	2	64	.272	34	0	19	.233
Lindeman	55	6	23	.219	20	2	5	.179
McGee	121	10	93	.287	32	1	12	.278
Morris	74	3	14	.296	27	0	9	.203
Oquendo	92	1	22	.307	24	0	2	.152
Pena	84	4	34	.222	32	1	10	.187
Pendleton	124	9	81	.303	35	3	15	.220

| Smith | 124 | 0 | 66 | .292 | 34 | 0 | 9 | .343 |
| Team Totals | 126 | 46 | 519 | .271 | 36 | 13 | 121 | .229 |

Only Ozzie Smith had a higher batting average when Clark didn't start. But notice the precipitous decline even in Ozzie's productivity: On a prorated basis, his RBI rate was halved from 86 to 43 per 162 games. Clark's presence was especially beneficial to the Cardinals' part-time starters. Curt Ford, Jim Lindeman, John Morris, and Jose Oquendo had a collective .285 batting average when Clark started; when Clark sat, they batted .181.

Clark's contribution to the Cardinals' attack was formidable. But the decline in the productivity of the rest of the team without him in the lineup suggests that his greatest contribution to the Cardinals' attack last season wasn't what he did on his own, but what he did for his teammates. And it illustrates that the 1988 Cardinals will have a lot more to compensate for than simply Clark's own 35 home runs and 106 RBIs.

A Guarantee for Success

One of the most noteworthy but least noted streaks of the 1987 season was the Cardinals' string of 16 consecutive games scoring at least four runs, from May 10 through May 29. It may not sound like much—we suppose that's why so little attention was paid to it—but consider this: St. Louis's streak was the longest of its type in the National League since 1950.

It's funny how baseball writers and publicists note the daily progress of streaks like Jack Clark's 16 consecutive games with walks, but often ignore streaks that represent true accomplishment. To be sure, Clark's streak measures the respect that other teams have for him; but it represents a *passive* achievement, derived as much from the defensive strategy of opposing teams as from Clark's own batting skill. But scoring four or more runs in a game, day in and day out over an extended period, is a guarantee of a team's success. Last season, for example, National League teams that scored at least four runs won 813 of 1,129 games, a .720 winning percentage. St. Louis had a 78–27 mark in games in which they scored four or more runs (.742), 12–4 during its streak.

The following table lists the longest streaks of four-run games in modern major-league history.

National League		American League	
Pittsburgh, 1922	29	Detroit, 1927	28
St. Louis, 1921	21	Philadelphia, 1930	27
New York, 1922	19	Boston, 1936	23
New York, 1930	19	New York, 1937	23
Chicago, 1935	19	Chicago, 1901	22
Pittsburgh, 1925	18	Cleveland, 1938	22
New York, 1930	18	St. Louis, 1921	21
Philadelphia, 1934	17	New York, 1938	21
Chicago, 1912	16	Boston, 1977–78	21
New York, 1944	16	Kansas City, 1985	20
Philadelphia, 1950	16	six teams	19
St. Louis, 1987	16		

Making Crime Pay on the Bases

Two seasons ago, with St. Louis trailing the Mets by more than 20 games in early July, Whitey Herzog gave Vince Coleman a green light to steal as many bases as he could, without regard to game situations, in an effort to break Rickey Henderson's modern major-league record of 130. "As far as I'm concerned," said Herzog, "nothing else is happening. Not that I'm a showman, but [baseball fans] like to see him run. With a team out of the race, he could get [an extra] 20 steals."

Herzog's lenient approach to aggrandizing an individual achievement at the risk of team goals failed to produce the intended result: Vincent Van Go stole 50 bases in 70 games prior to Whitey's proclamation, 49 in the next 70. But the episode did tarnish Coleman's reputation, perhaps unfairly according to a study of 1987 stolen base data.

It's not unusual for superstars, in their quests for statistical titles or records, to be subjected to baseless accusations. Rod Carew was often called a poor clutch hitter, a claim that went unchallenged before we published data demonstrating his ability at the plate with runners in scoring position. Last season, George Steinbrenner even criticized Don Mattingly for swinging for home runs during his eight-game homer streak. Maybe he'd have preferred an eight-game singles streak. Herzog's go-for-the-record exhortation prompted similar criticism of Coleman by the media and fans.

But last season, with St. Louis involved in a pennant race, Coleman disdained the so-called cheap steal. Only 12 of his stolen base attempts came with the Cardinals leading by more than three runs or trailing by that margin. That represented only 9 percent of his season's total of 131 attempts, far below the N.L. average of 14 percent.

For the most part, Coleman chose key situations for his steals. He made 82 stolen-base attempts in lead-changing situations (with the score tied or the Cardinals trailing by a single run). And Coleman's total of 67 steals in those situations was *more than three times as many* as all but three other players in the National League. The major-league leaders in potential lead-changing stolen bases:

National League		American League	
Coleman, St.L.	67	Wilson, K.C.	37
Gwynn, S.D.	30	Redus, Chi.	31
Hatcher, Hou.	26	Henderson, N.Y.	25
Thompson, Phil.	24	Reynolds, Sea.	23
Jefferson, S.D.	22	Molitor, Mil.	20

Coleman also led the majors with 17 steals in Late-Inning Pressure Situations. No other player in either league had more than 10.

So it appears that whatever criticism was directed at Coleman *last* season was unfairly aimed. If Herzog is serious when he says that the Clark-less Cardinals have no shot at the division title this season, maybe he will once again encourage Coleman to sacrifice the good of the team for the sake of Vince's own personal goals. But to conclude that Coleman is, therefore, a player incapable of compromising personal achievement for team goals is absolutely wrong. Coleman is a man for all seasons.

Whitey's Magic Carpet

For many years, Whitey Herzog has received well-deserved credit for tailoring his lineup to his home fields, Busch Stadium in St. Louis and its Kansas City clone, Royals Stadium. In the past, we've questioned whether the value of custom-crafted personnel is as great as many consider it to be (see the Houston Astros essay in the 1986 *Analyst*). But there's no doubt that, whatever the value of customizing a team's roster to the demands of a particular stadium, Whitey does it as well as anyone.

But with all the attention paid to the defensive speed of Herzog's outfielders and the base-running speed of the rest of his team as well, the profile of his pitching staff has been ignored. No one to our knowledge has noted that of the six National League teams that play their home games on artificial turf, only St. Louis has a pitching staff suited to the demands of plastic grass.

Maybe that's because of an erroneous assumption—namely, that ground-ball pitchers thrive on grass surfaces and have trouble on the man-made stuff. Actually, ground-ball pitchers pitch about as well on artificial turf as on grass.

We found 48 pitchers who made at least 100 starts over the past six seasons and compiled ground outs-to-air outs ratios above the major-league average during that time. The following table shows that those ground-ball pitchers had nearly identical winning percentages on grass and turf:

Surface	W	L	Pct.
Grass surfaces	1497	1420	.513
Artificial turf	1195	1138	.512

Of course, not even Herzog could exploit such a narrow margin to a strategic advantage. But a subgroup of ground-ball pitchers—those with good control as well—has a significant advantage on artificial turf. We classified those 48 ground-ball pitchers as having good or poor control according to whether they fell above or below the major-league average for walks per 100 batters faced over the past six seasons. The pitchers with good control had a decided edge on synthetic surfaces:

	Grass Surfaces			Artificial Turf			
	W	L	Pct.	W	L	Pct.	Diff.
Good control	895	844	.515	768	683	.529	+.015
Poor control	602	576	.511	427	455	.484	−.027

During the past six seasons, only Whitey Herzog's Cardinals have taken advantage of that edge. The following table lists the ground outs-to-air outs ratios and walks per 100 opposing batters faced since 1982 for the six National League teams that play their home games on artificial turf. Of those six, only St. Louis has both a higher G/A ratio and a lower walk percentage than the league averages:

Team	G/A Ratio	BB Per 100 BFP
Cincinnati	1.05	8.92
Houston	1.21	8.60
Montreal	1.13	7.97
Philadelphia	1.19	8.39
Pittsburgh	1.26	8.91
St. Louis	1.26	8.13
N.L. Averages	1.22	8.57

Two Cardinals starters match the profile of those who benefit most from artificial turf: Danny Cox and Bob Forsch. Over the past six years, Cox walked 7.2 batters for every 100 he faced, and compiled a ratio of 1.39 ground outs per air out (compared to major-league averages of 8.6 and 1.15, respectively). Forsch's figures were 6.8 walks per 100 batters faced, with a 1.20 G/A ratio. Both had enormous advantages on artificial turf:

	Danny Cox			Bob Forsch		
Surface	W	L	Pct.	W	L	Pct.
Home games (turf)	30	20	.600	34	21	.618
Road turf surfaces	13	12	.520	13	12	.520
Grass surfaces	10	16	.385	14	16	.467

So the next time you hear about how well Herzog has crafted his roster to suit the needs of Busch Stadium, point out that his tailoring includes the pitching staff as well. It appears that no one understands the unique demands of playing on artificial turf as well as Whitey.

WON-LOST RECORD BY STARTING POSITION

ST. LOUIS 95-67	C	1B	2B	3B	SS	LF	CF	RF	P	Leadoff	Relief	Starts
Skeeter Barnes	·	·	·	·	·	·	·	·	·	·	·	·
Rod Booker	·	·	3-2	·	·	·	·	·	·	·	·	3-2
Jack Clark	·	76-49	·	·	·	·	·	0-1	·	·	·	76-50
Vince Coleman	·	·	·	·	·	88-62	·	·	·	88-62	·	88-62
Tim Conroy	·	·	·	·	·	·	·	·	6-3	·	0-1	6-3
Danny Cox	·	·	·	·	·	·	·	·	19-12	·	·	19-12
Bill Dawley	·	·	·	·	·	·	·	·	·	·	28-32	·
Ken Dayley	·	·	·	·	·	·	·	·	·	·	30-23	·
Doug DeCinces	·	·	·	1-0	·	·	·	·	·	·	·	1-0
Dan Driessen	·	9-7	·	·	·	·	·	·	·	·	·	9-7
Curt Ford	·	·	·	·	·	3-2	1-0	30-20	·	·	·	34-22
Bob Forsch	·	·	·	·	·	·	·	·	16-14	·	2-1	16-14
David Green	·	·	·	·	·	0-1	·	2-4	·	·	·	2-5
Tom Herr	·	·	81-56	·	·	·	·	·	·	·	·	81-56
Ricky Horton	·	·	·	·	·	·	·	·	4-2	·	35-26	4-2
Lance Johnson	·	·	·	·	·	·	1-1	7-4	·	1-1	·	8-5
Mike Laga	·	3-4	·	·	·	·	·	·	·	·	·	3-4
Steve Lake	32-18	·	·	·	·	·	·	·	·	·	·	32-18
Tito Landrum	·	·	·	·	·	0-2	2-3	4-1	·	·	·	6-6
Dave LaPoint	·	·	·	·	·	·	·	·	1-1	·	1-3	1-1
Tom Lawless	·	·	1-1	·	·	·	0-1	·	·	·	·	1-2
Jim Lindeman	·	7-5	·	·	·	·	·	27-18	·	·	·	34-23
Joe Magrane	·	·	·	·	·	·	·	·	14-12	·	0-1	14-12
Greg Mathews	·	·	·	·	·	·	·	·	14-18	·	·	14-18
Willie McGee	·	·	·	·	·	·	89-60	·	·	·	·	89-60
John Morris	·	·	·	·	·	2-0	15-9	·	·	·	·	17-9
Randy O'Neal	·	·	·	·	·	·	·	·	0-1	·	·	0-1
Jose Oquendo	·	0-1	10-8	1-2	5-4	4-0	0-3	9-8	·	·	0-1	29-26
Tom Pagnozzi	7-2	0-1	·	·	·	·	·	·	·	·	·	7-3
Tony Pena	56-47	·	·	·	·	·	·	1-1	·	·	·	57-48
Terry Pendleton	·	·	·	93-65	·	·	·	·	·	·	·	93-65
Pat Perry	·	·	·	·	·	·	·	·	·	·	20-25	·
Steve Peters	·	·	·	·	·	·	·	·	·	·	4-8	·
Ozzie Smith	·	·	·	·	90-63	·	·	·	·	6-4	·	90-63
Ray Soff	·	·	·	·	·	·	·	·	·	·	4-8	·
Scott Terry	·	·	·	·	·	·	·	·	·	·	6-5	·
John Tudor	·	·	·	·	·	·	·	·	14-2	·	·	14-2
Lee Tunnell	·	·	·	·	·	·	·	·	7-2	·	8-15	7-2
Todd Worrell	·	·	·	·	·	·	·	·	·	·	53-22	·

Batting vs. Left and Right Handed Pitchers

		BA	Rank	SA	Rank	OBA	Rank	HR %	Rank	BB %	Rank	SO %	Rank
Jack Clark	vs. Lefties	.261	81	.543	20	.480	3	7.25	8	29.65	1	22.61	126
	vs. Righties	.299	25	.623	3	.447	3	8.90	1	21.39	1	26.11	135
Vince Coleman	vs. Lefties	.268	74	.416	76	.361	45	1.44	93	11.93	31	18.93	116
	vs. Righties	.300	24	.329	113	.364	36	0.00	126	8.93	68	17.43	101
Curt Ford	vs. Lefties	.286	--	.333	--	.348	--	0.00	--	8.33	--	20.83	--
	vs. Righties	.285	43	.415	63	.323	84	1.45	95	5.38	114	12.11	45
Tom Herr	vs. Lefties	.298	38	.398	87	.386	26	1.05	103	12.89	24	7.11	13
	vs. Righties	.241	104	.292	128	.322	86	0.00	126	10.46	47	12.33	47
Steve Lake	vs. Lefties	.308	32	.423	72	.337	70	2.56	73	4.76	114	8.33	29
	vs. Righties	.208	--	.287	--	.252	--	0.00	--	5.41	--	9.91	--
Jim Lindeman	vs. Lefties	.208	126	.366	98	.252	131	3.96	47	6.31	97	24.32	132
	vs. Righties	.208	--	.406	--	.254	--	3.77	--	3.45	--	25.00	--
Willie McGee	vs. Lefties	.288	49	.500	35	.309	100	2.88	70	3.64	130	15.91	91
	vs. Righties	.284	48	.400	71	.313	96	1.21	100	3.70	130	12.73	50
John Morris	vs. Lefties	.200	--	.250	--	.200	--	0.00	--	0.00	--	20.00	--
	vs. Righties	.270	70	.431	53	.329	77	2.19	78	7.33	93	12.00	43
Jose Oquendo	vs. Lefties	.277	62	.339	108	.375	33	0.89	108	14.71	17	8.09	25
	vs. Righties	.294	32	.331	112	.435	6	0.00	126	19.32	2	10.23	25
Tony Pena	vs. Lefties	.226	118	.321	113	.280	124	2.19	79	7.33	84	10.00	42
	vs. Righties	.206	126	.300	126	.282	116	0.81	116	9.09	64	14.18	72
Terry Pendleton	vs. Lefties	.337	15	.447	59	.386	25	1.92	85	7.86	77	8.30	28
	vs. Righties	.259	85	.392	76	.346	58	2.13	79	11.87	23	12.56	48
Ozzie Smith	vs. Lefties	.250	95	.318	116	.346	60	0.00	113	12.69	25	4.62	5
	vs. Righties	.334	7	.421	59	.419	8	0.00	126	12.56	17	5.38	4
Team Average	vs. Lefties	.263	7	.389	11	.342	4	2.00	12	10.85	2	14.36	4
	vs. Righties	.264	4	.373	10	.339	2	1.55	12	9.89	1	15.05	5
League Average	vs. Lefties	.263		.409		.332		2.81		9.08		15.22	
	vs. Righties	.260		.401		.327		2.73		8.70		15.85	

Batting with Runners on Base and Bases Empty

		BA	Rank	SA	Rank	OBA	Rank	HR %	Rank	BB %	Rank	SO %	Rank
Jack Clark	Runners On	.330	12	.665	2	.500	1	8.81	2	25.81	1	21.29	127
	Bases Empty	.234	108	.516	25	.407	11	7.81	8	22.49	1	29.32	137
Vince Coleman	Runners On	.318	18	.387	90	.371	43	0.46	121	7.85	98	16.12	95
	Bases Empty	.273	63	.342	110	.359	35	0.49	124	11.09	24	18.91	106
Curt Ford	Runners On	.300	38	.440	64	.330	93	1.00	110	5.45	118	11.82	46
	Bases Empty	.273	62	.383	87	.321	79	1.56	97	5.84	105	13.87	65
Tom Herr	Runners On	.274	77	.361	103	.357	59	0.75	115	12.04	36	10.49	35
	Bases Empty	.250	89	.299	121	.332	64	0.00	128	10.58	30	10.22	28
Steve Lake	Runners On	.354	4	.456	50	.402	26	1.27	96	7.61	102	7.61	17
	Bases Empty	.170	136	.260	132	.194	137	1.00	108	2.91	134	10.68	34
Jim Lindeman	Runners On	.181	132	.277	129	.221	135	2.13	79	5.66	115	25.47	135
	Bases Empty	.230	114	.478	35	.281	117	5.31	24	4.13	125	23.97	133
Willie McGee	Runners On	.295	49	.463	44	.328	96	2.80	54	4.62	123	13.58	71
	Bases Empty	.275	60	.403	73	.294	102	0.67	117	2.61	136	14.05	67
Jose Oquendo	Runners On	.298	45	.375	94	.417	14	0.96	111	17.39	10	8.70	22
	Bases Empty	.278	55	.306	120	.402	12	0.00	128	17.24	3	9.77	24
Tony Pena	Runners On	.210	125	.333	114	.290	118	2.47	67	10.27	62	8.65	21
	Bases Empty	.216	122	.288	127	.275	121	0.45	125	7.08	76	15.83	87
Terry Pendleton	Runners On	.320	16	.476	39	.393	29	2.55	62	11.35	46	10.74	38
	Bases Empty	.256	78	.354	103	.328	69	1.62	95	9.68	43	11.44	39
Ozzie Smith	Runners On	.308	31	.400	79	.385	36	0.00	122	10.93	55	5.14	5
	Bases Empty	.300	25	.371	99	.397	14	0.00	128	13.92	7	5.06	3
Team Average	Runners On	.283	1	.412	5	.359	1	2.09	11	10.81	3	13.45	2
	Bases Empty	.248	10	.350	12	.323	6	1.40	12	9.71	1	16.01	7
League Average	Runners On	.267		.410		.341		2.66		9.88		14.92	
	Bases Empty	.256		.399		.319		2.82		7.98		16.22	

Overall Batting Compared to Late Inning Pressure Situations

		BA	Rank	SA	Rank	OBA	Rank	HR %	Rank	BB %	Rank	SO %	Rank	RDI %	Rank
Rod Booker	Overall	.277	--	.340	--	.370	--	0.00	--	12.50	--	12.50	--	.333	--
	Pressure	.059	--	.059	--	.200	--	0.00	--	13.64	--	22.73	--	.214	87
Jack Clark	Overall	.286	44	.597	2	.459	1	8.35	1	24.33	1	24.87	135	.337	20
	Pressure	.269	64	.731	1	.412	17	13.43	1	20.00	5	28.24	135	.304	57
Vince Coleman	Overall	.289	40	.358	107	.363	37	0.48	123	9.97	54	17.95	107	.227	116
	Pressure	.389	4	.433	50	.439	7	0.00	105	7.92	86	16.83	81	.188	101
Curt Ford	Overall	.285	49	.408	79	.325	85	1.32	103	5.67	122	12.96	57	.296	55
	Pressure	.288	48	.346	96	.333	73	0.00	105	7.02	98	12.28	37	.471	7
Tom Herr	Overall	.263	87	.331	120	.346	55	0.39	126	11.37	29	10.37	26	.357	8
	Pressure	.289	46	.368	79	.349	64	1.32	95	9.09	70	17.05	83	.475	6
Jim Lindeman	Overall	.208	130	.386	89	.253	134	3.86	39	4.85	126	24.67	134	.234	110
	Pressure	.176	--	.206	--	.200	--	0.00	--	2.86	--	28.57	--	.000	--
Willie McGee	Overall	.285	47	.434	55	.312	99	1.77	91	3.68	133	13.80	67	.300	54
	Pressure	.240	90	.344	97	.277	114	0.00	105	3.96	120	17.82	87	.313	48
John Morris	Overall	.261	--	.408	--	.314	--	1.91	--	6.47	--	12.94	--	.367	5
	Pressure	.256	78	.333	104	.356	58	2.56	62	13.33	28	13.33	48	.429	--
Jose Oquendo	Overall	.286	45	.335	119	.408	9	0.40	124	17.31	4	9.29	19	.317	34
	Pressure	.226	105	.323	111	.377	42	1.61	86	13.29	9	12.20	33	.313	48
Tony Pena	Overall	.214	127	.307	127	.281	125	1.30	104	8.47	71	12.71	53	.312	37
	Pressure	.219	111	.329	109	.288	106	1.37	94	7.50	92	13.75	56	.118	121
Terry Pendleton	Overall	.286	43	.412	74	.360	40	2.06	85	10.49	42	11.09	39	.368	4
	Pressure	.315	29	.539	15	.384	38	3.37	42	8.91	71	18.81	94	.385	21
Ozzie Smith	Overall	.303	17	.383	91	.392	18	0.00	133	12.61	17	5.10	2	.330	24
	Pressure	.297	42	.341	102	.396	29	0.00	105	13.51	26	1.80	1	.326	45
Team Average	Overall	.263	6	.378	9	.340	1	1.71	12	10.22	2	14.81	3	.307	1
	Pressure	.264	5	.379	8	.341	5	1.91	9	9.98	4	17.03	6	.307	1
League Average	Overall	.261		.404		.328		2.75		8.83		15.64		.272	
	Pressure	.258		.385		.331		2.46		9.54		16.95		.261	

Additional Miscellaneous Batting Comparisons

	Grass Surface BA	Rank	Artificial Surface BA	Rank	Home Games BA	Rank	Road Games BA	Rank	Runners in Scoring Position BA	Rank	Runners in Scoring Pos and Two Outs BA	Rank	Leading Off Inning OBA	Rank	Runners on 3B with less than 2 Outs RDI %	Rank
Jack Clark	.276	56	.291	42	.292	46	.281	41	.304	31	.288	41	.398	15	.553	78
Vince Coleman	.335	7	.271	71	.275	69	.301	27	.299	36	.263	61	.390	19	.483	101
Curt Ford	.276	57	.291	41	.279	68	.290	35	.308	29	.207	103	.353	47	.600	57
Tom Herr	.223	117	.275	64	.280	65	.246	99	.269	72	.283	45	.322	81	.755	10
Steve Lake	.216	--	.266	76	.253	--	.250	--	.311	26	.273	51	.162	--	.429	--
Jim Lindeman	.200	--	.209	126	.196	131	.221	121	.190	126	.207	103	.362	41	.333	133
Willie McGee	.268	73	.292	39	.297	40	.275	59	.246	91	.219	90	.285	114	.679	24
John Morris	.255	--	.264	78	.232	--	.284	--	.286	51	.227	87	.316	--	.786	6
Jose Oquendo	.310	18	.277	60	.297	38	.277	52	.279	60	.226	88	.400	14	.833	2
Tony Pena	.167	135	.228	116	.225	122	.203	132	.209	117	.156	124	.263	125	.606	56
Terry Pendleton	.316	15	.275	63	.266	82	.307	20	.323	17	.384	6	.365	39	.638	39
Ozzie Smith	.317	14	.298	32	.287	55	.318	13	.299	37	.260	64	.469	1	.658	31
Team Average	.267	2	.262	4	.264	7	.263	3	.268	4	.252	4	.350	1	.615	1
League Average	.260		.261		.265		.256		.258		.241		.324		.554	

Pitching vs. Left and Right Handed Batters

		BA	Rank	SA	Rank	OBA	Rank	HR %	Rank	BB %	Rank	SO %	Rank
Tim Conroy	vs. Lefties	.313	--	.375	--	.389	--	0.00	--	10.81	--	16.22	--
	vs. Righties	.304	102	.400	51	.403	112	0.00	1	13.91	109	10.60	104
Danny Cox	vs. Lefties	.316	106	.450	86	.382	100	1.84	42	9.63	54	8.03	102
	vs. Righties	.265	71	.393	47	.319	60	2.55	44	6.78	37	15.42	69
Bill Dawley	vs. Lefties	.254	45	.377	45	.353	74	2.31	59	13.16	100	9.21	95
	vs. Righties	.262	68	.502	104	.316	54	5.24	108	7.09	43	20.08	31
Ken Dayley	vs. Lefties	.247	--	.301	--	.337	--	0.00	--	10.71	--	30.95	--
	vs. Righties	.228	28	.356	26	.337	81	1.34	12	13.64	108	21.02	26
Bob Forsch	vs. Lefties	.264	55	.363	36	.313	31	1.07	14	6.80	16	10.92	79
	vs. Righties	.283	94	.465	97	.324	69	3.46	77	4.96	12	12.83	92
Ricky Horton	vs. Lefties	.225	15	.333	23	.288	15	0.83	6	8.15	43	15.56	43
	vs. Righties	.277	85	.479	100	.332	75	3.88	86	7.79	54	8.54	110
Joe Magrane	vs. Lefties	.226	16	.312	14	.301	23	1.08	15	8.57	35	20.00	19
	vs. Righties	.249	46	.342	23	.321	45	1.46	14	8.27	74	12.97	87
Greg Mathews	vs. Lefties	.240	33	.336	26	.321	41	1.60	34	10.71	65	10.00	88
	vs. Righties	.250	50	.395	48	.312	45	2.44	39	8.21	68	13.78	81
Randy O'Neal	vs. Lefties	.341	112	.489	105	.419	109	2.22	55	12.18	90	11.54	74
	vs. Righties	.263	--	.504	--	.308	--	6.77	--	4.86	--	13.19	--
John Tudor	vs. Lefties	.246	--	.446	--	.310	--	3.08	--	8.22	--	24.66	--
	vs. Righties	.278	87	.457	93	.335	78	2.98	60	7.83	56	10.84	103
Lee Tunnell	vs. Lefties	.254	44	.328	20	.348	69	0.00	1	12.82	97	16.67	39
	vs. Righties	.352	112	.516	108	.401	111	3.14	68	7.82	55	12.85	89
Todd Worrell	vs. Lefties	.233	23	.315	16	.333	50	2.05	51	13.29	102	24.86	6
	vs. Righties	.249	47	.402	55	.286	26	2.39	38	4.95	11	22.07	21
Team Average	vs. Lefties	.267	7	.376	3	.338	6	1.36	1	9.62	6	14.09	7
	vs. Righties	.265	11	.418	11	.327	10	2.77	3	7.98	5	13.90	11
League Average	vs. Lefties	.268		.404		.341		2.34		9.74		14.31	
	vs. Righties	.255		.403		.319		3.05		8.16		16.61	

Pitching with Runners on Base and Bases Empty

		BA	Rank	SA	Rank	OBA	Rank	HR %	Rank	BB %	Rank	SO %	Rank
Danny Cox	Runners On	.275	75	.365	35	.332	48	1.46	22	7.67	19	12.79	74
	Bases Empty	.302	103	.465	95	.366	105	2.79	63	8.67	74	10.78	103
Bill Dawley	Runners On	.280	82	.440	83	.385	108	2.67	66	14.59	109	16.22	47
	Bases Empty	.244	43	.469	97	.285	16	5.26	108	4.98	9	15.84	56
Ken Dayley	Runners On	.222	13	.316	14	.343	70	0.85	15	14.79	110	21.13	12
	Bases Empty	.248	--	.362	--	.331	--	0.95	--	10.17	--	27.97	--
Bob Forsch	Runners On	.303	104	.457	92	.349	80	3.00	72	6.62	9	9.27	105
	Bases Empty	.254	61	.380	54	.298	29	1.64	18	5.52	13	13.47	87
Ricky Horton	Runners On	.257	52	.427	77	.325	35	1.94	37	9.28	46	12.24	81
	Bases Empty	.269	80	.455	91	.319	62	4.00	92	6.76	36	8.78	109
Joe Magrane	Runners On	.282	86	.388	46	.361	94	1.57	25	10.33	67	13.67	69
	Bases Empty	.221	16	.304	9	.289	22	1.30	8	6.87	39	14.22	74
Greg Mathews	Runners On	.245	30	.390	49	.322	33	2.48	55	10.12	65	11.35	91
	Bases Empty	.251	53	.382	56	.308	44	2.18	34	7.66	56	14.31	71
Randy O'Neal	Runners On	.258	53	.427	79	.333	52	3.23	81	10.49	70	9.79	101
	Bases Empty	.340	111	.556	112	.395	112	5.56	111	7.01	44	14.65	67
John Tudor	Runners On	.234	22	.383	42	.317	24	2.84	68	10.37	68	12.80	73
	Bases Empty	.296	100	.500	104	.340	86	3.10	76	6.22	25	13.69	83
Lee Tunnell	Runners On	.306	105	.403	59	.385	107	0.69	8	12.21	95	13.37	71
	Bases Empty	.309	106	.456	92	.368	106	2.68	59	7.98	60	15.95	55
Todd Worrell	Runners On	.200	3	.274	4	.277	3	1.58	26	9.68	56	23.50	8
	Bases Empty	.291	98	.473	99	.343	91	3.03	73	7.30	49	23.03	12
Team Average	Runners On	.265	6	.392	3	.339	6	2.01	1	9.89	7	13.74	10
	Bases Empty	.266	9	.414	9	.324	9	2.53	3	7.43	3	14.14	11
League Average	Runners On	.267		.410		.341		2.66		9.88		14.92	
	Bases Empty	.256		.399		.319		2.82		7.98		16.22	

Overall Pitching Compared to Late Inning Pressure Situations

		BA	Rank	SA	Rank	OBA	Rank	HR %	Rank	BB %	Rank	SO %	Rank
Danny Cox	Overall	.290	104	.421	75	.351	96	2.20	35	8.22	41	11.69	94
	Pressure	.300	91	.467	90	.348	70	3.33	82	7.46	31	10.45	91
Bill Dawley	Overall	.259	61	.457	101	.330	67	4.18	106	9.36	71	16.01	51
	Pressure	.312	95	.493	95	.391	97	3.62	87	11.18	80	14.91	63
Ken Dayley	Overall	.234	15	.338	14	.337	85	0.90	2	12.69	110	24.23	5
	Pressure	.242	40	.348	37	.349	71	0.56	22	13.27	94	27.01	7
Bob Forsch	Overall	.273	85	.410	67	.318	38	2.16	34	5.96	9	11.79	93
	Pressure	.242	41	.303	16	.324	46	0.00	1	10.53	68	21.05	26
Ricky Horton	Overall	.264	69	.443	93	.321	46	3.12	77	7.88	34	10.32	106
	Pressure	.255	56	.414	74	.319	43	3.45	84	8.48	42	14.55	65
Joe Magrane	Overall	.245	34	.338	13	.318	46	1.41	11	8.31	44	13.99	72
	Pressure	.270	66	.333	26	.378	91	0.00	1	13.33	96	10.67	88
Greg Mathews	Overall	.249	44	.385	50	.314	34	2.30	42	8.64	52	13.14	81
	Pressure	.228	27	.368	53	.313	38	1.75	44	10.77	72	12.31	76
Randy O'Neal	Overall	.302	109	.496	110	.366	105	4.48	108	8.67	54	12.33	90
	Pressure	.286	--	.857	--	.375	--	14.29	--	12.50	--	12.50	--
John Tudor	Overall	.272	84	.455	100	.331	68	3.00	73	7.90	35	13.33	78
	Pressure	.375	--	.563	--	.444	--	0.00	--	11.11	--	0.00	--
Lee Tunnell	Overall	.307	110	.430	85	.377	111	1.71	18	10.15	86	14.63	67
	Pressure	.283	82	.348	35	.441	107	0.00	1	19.67	110	8.20	102
Todd Worrell	Overall	.242	25	.366	34	.307	25	2.25	38	8.61	51	23.29	9
	Pressure	.254	53	.409	72	.329	50	2.78	69	10.10	63	24.74	10
Team Average	Overall	.266	9	.404	6	.331	8	2.31	1	8.52	4	13.96	11
	Pressure	.261	7	.400	8	.350	10	2.12	5	11.52	11	17.58	5
League Average	Overall	.261		.404		.328		2.75		8.83		15.64	
	Pressure	.260		.391		.337		2.47		10.04		17.14	

Additional Miscellaneous Pitching Comparisons

	Grass Surface		Artificial Surface		Home Games		Road Games		Runners in Scoring Position		Runners in Scoring Pos and Two Outs		Leading Off Inning	
	BA	Rank	BA	Rank	BA	Rank	BA	Rank	BA	Rank	BA	Rank	OBA	Rank
Tim Conroy	.292	--	.308	99	.315	--	.298	--	.262	--	.222	--	.435	--
Danny Cox	.279	81	.293	89	.287	98	.295	97	.243	46	.247	71	.364	92
Bill Dawley	.242	--	.265	58	.273	85	.240	30	.257	64	.296	93	.370	97
Ken Dayley	.140	--	.262	56	.317	--	.161	2	.279	82	.286	88	.250	--
Bob Forsch	.271	74	.274	72	.270	80	.275	65	.281	83	.243	67	.304	37
Ricky Horton	.269	69	.263	57	.255	54	.272	60	.233	32	.172	23	.314	47
Joe Magrane	.233	23	.249	38	.249	46	.241	33	.277	79	.286	88	.305	40
Greg Mathews	.221	14	.261	55	.256	60	.240	31	.247	51	.215	44	.319	53
Randy O'Neal	.309	105	.284	--	.266	75	.351	109	.221	25	.243	67	.406	110
John Tudor	.306	--	.266	59	.258	61	.287	83	.263	71	.289	90	.323	61
Lee Tunnell	.378	--	.294	91	.263	69	.369	112	.315	107	.263	78	.395	109
Todd Worrell	.263	62	.234	18	.235	26	.249	39	.207	16	.206	38	.342	81
Team Average	.260	7	.267	7	.265	9	.266	6	.258	7	.240	6	.330	6
League Average	.260		.261		.256		.265		.258		.241		.324	

SAN DIEGO PADRES

The best team in the National League West for most of the 1987 season was the team that spent every single day of the season in last place: The San Diego Padres.

In fact, about the only national attention the Padres drew last season was for their horrendous start. On the morning of June 12, baseball fans all over San Diego could have spit up their Eggs McMuffin when they looked at the standings and found the Padres 19 games out of first place with the season only two months old. At the time, the Padres had just become the fifth team in modern National League history, and the first in 42 years, to lose 46 of its first 61 games:

Year	Team	First 61 Games	Record Thereafter	Final W–L	Pct.	GB
1904	Philadelphia	15–46	37–54	52–100	.342	53.5
1907	St. Louis	15–46	37–55	52–101	.340	55.5
1911	Boston	14–47	30–60	44–107	.291	54
1945	Philadelphia	15–46	31–62	46–108	.299	52
1987	San Diego	15–46	50–51	65–97	.401	25

Even San Diego's rookie manager, Larry Bowa, would have forgiven Padres fans for surrendering by that point, because that's exactly what he himself had done *a month earlier*. On May 4, after San Diego had lost 20 of its first 26 games, Bowa matter-of-factly said, "It's obvious we're not going to win the division." But don't think for a minute that Bowa was giving up entirely; he was simply giving up the race for the pennant.

Over the next two months, Bowa overhauled the lineup. Only Tony Gwynn, Garry Templeton, and Benito Santiago were unaffected. Bowa's first and perhaps his most controversial move was to replace Steve Garvey at first base with a platoon of John Kruk against right-handers and Carmelo Martinez against southpaws. Martinez retained his spot in left field when Kruk played first base, but against left-handed pitchers, the left-field spot opened up for Stan Jefferson, who also shared the center field post with Shane Mack. Tim Flannery and Randy Ready replaced Joey Cora at second base; Ready and eventually Chris Brown succeeded Kevin Mitchell at third. Jefferson also inherited the leadoff position in the Padres' batting order from Cora.

Storm Davis and Andy Hawkins lost their spots in the starting rotation; they were replaced, in time, by Jimmy Jones and Eric Nolte. And Goose Gossage regained his role as the bullpen stopper from Lance McCullers.

The Padres survived another five weeks of almost daily

failure before finding their stride. But on June 12, San Diego started a miraculous turnaround, compiling the best record in its division over the next 100 days (through September 19):

Team	W	L	Pct.
San Diego	48	39	.552
San Francisco	49	40	.551
Houston	41	49	.456
Cincinnati	40	49	.449
Los Angeles	35	54	.393
Atlanta	34	54	.386

Only a nine-game losing streak during the final two weeks of the season kept the Padres from a winning record following those disastrous first 61 games. That's an enormous achievement considering that the other teams listed in the table of poor starts (above) had a combined record of 135 wins and 231 losses (.369) over the remainder of those seasons. And for those few diehards who thought that Bowa might have surrendered prematurely after only 26 games, consider this: No team in modern major-league history has ever won a pennant after losing 20 of its first 26 games. In fact, none of the other 29 teams that won six or fewer of their first 26 games even finished with a winning record. (For the record, we'll note that the 1973 St. Louis Cardinals came close on both counts, compiling an 81-81 mark, good for second place, one and one-half games behind the New York Mets.)

By signing the death certificate for San Diego's pennant hopes before the season was a month old, Bowa gave himself and his players an opportunity to explore the future, and in so doing, he advanced San Diego's rebuilding schedule by a full season. He must have liked what he saw, even if no one else noticed.

Coming Home

One of the most unusual aspects of the Padres' season was the team's 8–2 record in the opening games of its 10 home stands. Remember that these are the same Padres who had a record of 29–42 in their other home games. But upon returning home, not just last season but for the past five years, they've been nearly unbeatable. San Diego's record as its home stands progressed over the past five seasons:

Game	W	L	Pct.
First game	33	13	.717

Second game	29	18	.617
Third & after	157	155	.503
Totals	219	186	.541

Of course, if that pattern were typical of every major-league team, we'd be booked on the first flight to Las Vegas, and not to see Wayne Newton. And for half a century, teams did enjoy a greater than average home-field advantage in the opening game of each home stand than in later games. But the following table reveals that extra edge has all but disappeared over the past 20 years:

	First Game			Second Game			Third & After		
Years	W	L	Pct.	W	L	Pct.	W	L	Pct.
1900–19	1316	1123	.540	1207	983	.551	10051	8352	.546
1920–69	4203	3249	.564	3806	3260	.539	27326	23146	.541
1970–79	1447	1253	.535	1430	1249	.534	7646	6559	.538
1980–87	1238	1035	.545	1203	1067	.530	6269	5302	.542
Totals	8204	6660	.552	7646	6559	.538	51292	43359	.542

It's odd that as the increased home-field advantage in the opening games of home stands has evaporated, the corresponding disadvantage of the first game of a road trip has grown to an almost unprecedented level. Throughout most of modern major-league history, the road-field disadvantage was greatest in the first game of a road trip. (The 1970s was a notable exception.) But during the 1980s, the first-game disadvantage has increased sharply, while the disadvantage associated with the latter parts of long road trips (that is, after the seventh game) has disappeared:

	First Game			Games 2 through 7			Eighth & After		
Years	W	L	Pct.	W	L	Pct.	W	L	Pct.
1900–19	1120	1329	.457	4633	5424	.461	4705	5821	.447
1920–69	3334	4112	.448	15265	17803	.462	11056	13420	.452
1970–79	1252	1448	.464	6088	7079	.462	1812	2116	.461
1980–87	1002	1271	.441	5086	5932	.462	1316	1507	.466
Totals	6708	8160	.451	31072	36238	.462	18889	22864	.452

It's important to understand that the trends associated with how teams play over the course of home stands and road trips probably don't happen merely by accident. The difference between records in the first games of road trips and all road games thereafter is small (.007), but the odds that such a margin would occur merely by chance *over so many thousands of games* are roughly eight to one. But it's also true that the differences are trivial; the patterns are thus useless in predicting how any particular team will play or in analyzing why that team won or lost. Why, then, has San Diego been so successful when it returns home following road trips? Some things have no explanation—they just *happen*.

Ignoring the Ground Rules

Certain ballparks have such unique characteristics that teams try to tailor their personnel to exploit those traits. For example, the Red Sox spent most of the twentieth century gathering right-handed power hitters for an assault on Fenway Park's Green Monster. But what happens when those ballpark characteristics aren't so obvious or well-publicized? Let's consider the case of the San Diego Padres.

No stadium in the National League increases strikeouts to even half the extent that San Diego-Jack Murphy Stadium does (see page 435). But the Padres have failed to exploit that characteristic, building exactly the wrong type of pitching staff for its stadium.

Power pitchers thrive in ballparks that increase strikeouts; finesse pitchers flounder in that environment. But over the past five seasons, only one National League team has struck out fewer opposing batters than the Padres; and if you consider only road games (to eliminate the home-field bias), San Diego ranks dead last. Road-game strikeouts over the past five seasons:

Los Angeles	2,539	Montreal	2,250
Houston	2,410	Philadelphia	2,174
Pittsburgh	2,298	Atlanta	2,121
New York	2,279	Chicago	2,094
San Francisco	2,277	St. Louis	2,024
Cincinnati	2,259	San Diego	1,944

We examined the home and road records of all San Diego pitchers with at least 20 starts in any of the past five seasons. They are listed below, ranked according to their strikeout rates (per nine innings). The plus and minus designations refer to whether they had better records at home (+) or on the road (-). Notice that only one of the seven pitchers with rates of less than four strikeouts per nine innings had a better record at San Diego Stadium; eight of the 15 others, with rates higher than 4.00, were better at home:

Year	Pitcher	SO/9	Home	Road	+/–
1983	Lollar	6.92	4–5	3–7	+
1986	Show	6.21	5–3	4–2	–
1984	Lollar	6.03	5–6	6–7	–
1987	Whitson	5.91	5–7	5–6	–
1985	Show	5.45	6–5	6–6	+
1983	Show	5.38	10–3	5–9	+
1987	Show	5.10	5–6	3–10	+
1983	Whitson	5.05	1–3	4–4	–
1986	Hawkins	5.03	6–2	4–6	+
1984	Whitson	4.90	9–4	5–4	+
1986	Dravecky	4.85	3–6	6–5	–
1986	Hoyt	4.81	5–3	3–8	+
1984	Hawkins	4.75	5–5	3–4	–
1984	Show	4.53	6–5	9–4	–
1985	Dravecky	4.40	6–3	7–8	+
1987	Hawkins	3.90	1–5	2–5	–
1985	Thurmond	3.71	3–5	4–6	–
1983	Dravecky	3.63	8–5	6–5	+
1985	Hoyt	3.55	9–5	7–3	–
1987	Jones	3.15	4–5	4–2	–
1984	Thurmond	2.87	5–6	9–2	–
1985	Hawkins	2.72	10–6	8–2	–

The statistics strongly suggest that a pitcher's advantage at San Diego Stadium grows in proportion to his strikeout rate. Power pitchers exploit the stadium's strikeout potential; finesse pitchers are victimized by their inability to capitalize on it. But 22 pitchers' worth of evidence can't be considered conclusive, so we checked the stadiums that rank second and third in promoting strikeouts, specifically the Metrodome and Shea Stadium, and found similar results. We've summarized those results in the table below by grouping pitchers of similar strikeout rates:

SO Rate	San Diego Stadium			Metrodome			Shea Stadium		
	Home	Road	Diff.	Home	Road	Diff.	Home	Road	Diff.
0.00–3.99	40–37	40–25	–.096	29–28	26–30	+.044	18–21	20–22	–.015
4.00–5.99	67–52	60–74	+.115	62–55	53–68	+.092	16–16	16–19	+.043
6.00–up	14–14	13–16	+.052	32–16	24–24	+.167	101–39	54–29	+.071

At all three stadiums, the low-strikeout group had a lesser home-field advantage than the middle group; and in two of three cases, the high-strikeout group had a greater advantage than the middle group. San Diego Stadium is the exception, and that's explained by the fact that the Padres had only three qualifiers for the highest strikeout level—not enough to provide a reliable reading. But by combining the statistics of all three teams over the past five seasons, the trend is obvious:

SO Rate	Home Games		Road Games		
	W–L	Pct.	W–L	Pct.	Diff.
0.00–3.99	87–86	.503	86–77	.528	–.025
4.00–5.99	145–123	.541	129–161	.445	+.096
6.00–up	147–69	.681	91–69	.569	+.112

The Twins and the Mets both won world championships after discarding moderately successful pitchers who nevertheless had low strikeout rates and therefore didn't maximize their potential at the Metrodome (Ken Schrom and John Butcher) and Shea Stadium (Ed Lynch and Walt Terrell). Of course, San Diego doesn't have Frank Viola, Bert Blyleven, Dwight Gooden, or Ron Darling to fall back on, so until the Padres do develop a cadre of power pitchers for their starting rotation, they'll be working against rather than with an undeniable stadium bias.

Setting the Records Straight

Benito Santiago's 34-game hitting streak enlivened the last few weeks of the 1987 season. The streak was noteworthy in several respects: It was the longest ever by a rookie, the longest ever by a catcher, and the longest by a National Leaguer since Pete Rose's 44-gamer in 1978. Unlike Paul Molitor, who batted leadoff throughout his 39-game streak earlier in the summer, Santiago fashioned his streak from either the five or four spots in the order (until Game 31, when Bowa moved him up to the second spot). Not that Benito hadn't been getting his swings in from the middle of the order. He walked exactly twice during the 34 games: once in Game 1, before anyone knew that there *was* a streak, and an intentional walk in Game 7.

A side issue to the streak that turned out to be a moot point was the matter of whether Santiago would be "allowed" to carry over a hitting streak from one season to the next, in order to challenge Joe DiMaggio's record of 56 games. Newspaper stories, purporting to quote the Elias Bureau as baseball's official statistician, reported that Santiago wouldn't have a streak intact to start the 1988 season even if he hit in all remaining games in 1987. In fact, what we said was exactly the opposite. So even though the matter faded from public attention after Santiago was stopped by Orel Hershiser on the next-to-last day of the season, the question still deserves an answer.

Even a casual glance through baseball's record books reveals that streak records come in many varieties: streaks within an inning, streaks within a game, streaks within a season, and streaks without limits (career streaks). For example, the major-league record for consecutive games won by a pitcher in a season is 19, by Tim Keefe and Rube Marquard; but the overall record for consecutive games won in a career is 24, by Carl Hubbell. The major-league record for consecutive chances at shortstop without an error in a season is 331, by Ed Brinkman; the same record, without the one-season limitation, is 383, by Buddy Kerr. One set of records recognizes achievements within the confines of a particular season; another recognizes those with no such restriction. In a sport whose followers are as statistically wired as baseball's are, it's not a difficult distinction to grasp.

But some people have a hard time understanding or accepting this distinction when it comes to *batting* streaks. Perhaps some of the same public resentment that Roger Maris faced when he challenged Babe Ruth's record of 60 home runs in a season a generation ago will be brought to bear unfairly against any modern player who has the temerity to challenge DiMaggio's legendary record. But the fact is that any player who hits safely in 57 consecutive games—even over two (or more) seasons—would hold the all-time major-league record for the longest hitting streak, while Mr. Coffee would continue to hold the record for the longest *single-season* streak.

Actually, record keepers faced a similar situation 10 years ago. When Rose hit safely in his 44 straight games in 1978, it was widely reported that his streak tied the National League record set by Willie Keeler in 1897. That wasn't quite correct; Rose had only tied the N.L. *single-season* mark. The overall National League record for hitting safely in consecutive games was, and still is, 45, by Keeler, who hit safely in his final game in 1896 and in his first 44 the next year.

That's nothing new: ask Kerr and Brinkman, ask Hubbell, and the Keefe and Marquard heirs. The fact that some record books don't list Keeler's 45 is a matter of editorial judgment, not a definitive statement on what constitutes a record. Hundreds of achievement records are listed in those books: Most Home Runs, Season; Most Putouts, First Baseman, Game; Most Innings Pitched, Lifetime. But there are also thousands and thousands (sorry, Carl Sagan wasn't available) of records that are *not* routinely listed.

The term *record*, used in this sense, means the best achievement by a particular player or team in a specific category, and sometimes within a specific time frame. And with the price of paper being what it is, no book could possibly list all of the records that exist, whether or not the record-holder is known: Most Games Won Against Right-Handed Pitchers, Season; Most Consecutive Second Games of Doubleheaders Won; Most Foul Balls Hit, Lifetime; Fewest Pitches Thrown, Two Consecutive Complete Games, Rookie.

Some of these records are researchable, others are not, but theoretically all of them exist. Records are like numbers themselves: There's an infinite number of unprinted, unresearched records scattered between and among those that are printed in the books. Just because a particular record book doesn't print a record does not mean it doesn't exist.

And since Santiago had a hit in his final game of the '87 season, he starts the 1988 season only 44 games shy of the National League record for the longest hitting streak: 45 games, by Willie Keeler, in 1896 and 1897.

WON-LOST RECORD BY STARTING POSITION

SAN DIEGO 65-97	C	1B	2B	3B	SS	LF	CF	RF	P	Leadoff	Relief	Starts
Shawn Abner	-	-	-	-	-	3-3	0-1	0-3	-	-	-	3-7
Bruce Bochy	11-7	-	-	-	-	-	-	-	-	-	-	11-7
Greg Booker	-	-	-	-	-	-	-	-	-	-	3-41	-
Chris Brown	-	-	-	21-21	-	-	-	-	-	-	-	21-21
Randell Byers	-	-	-	-	1-2	-	-	-	-	-	-	1-2
Keith Comstock	-	-	-	-	-	-	-	-	-	-	6-20	-
Joey Cora	-	-	14-44	-	0-4	-	-	-	-	7-21	-	14-48
Mark Davis	-	-	-	-	-	-	-	-	-	-	18-25	-
Storm Davis	-	-	-	-	-	-	-	-	3-7	-	0-11	3-7
Dave Dravecky	-	-	-	-	-	-	-	-	3-7	-	3-17	3-7
Tim Flannery	-	-	30-35	2-5	-	-	-	-	-	1-2	-	32-40
Steve Garvey	-	5-14	-	-	-	-	-	-	-	-	-	5-14
Tom Gorman	-	-	-	-	-	-	-	-	-	-	0-6	-
Rich Gossage	-	-	-	-	-	-	-	-	-	-	23-17	-
Mark Grant	-	-	-	-	-	-	-	-	8-9	-	-	8-9
Tony Gwynn	-	-	-	-	-	-	-	63-91	-	11-14	-	63-91
Andy Hawkins	-	-	-	-	-	-	-	-	7-13	-	0-4	7-13
Ray Hayward	-	-	-	-	-	-	-	-	-	-	1-3	-
Stan Jefferson	-	-	-	-	-	13-7	31-46	-	-	37-44	-	44-53
Jimmy Jones	-	-	-	-	-	-	-	-	10-12	-	3-5	10-12
John Kruk	-	42-51	-	-	-	5-24	-	-	-	-	-	47-75
Craig Lefferts	-	-	-	-	-	-	-	-	-	-	9-24	-
Dave Leiper	-	-	-	-	-	-	-	-	-	-	2-10	-
Shane Mack	-	-	-	-	-	-	25-26	0-2	-	3-5	-	25-28
Carmelo Martinez	-	18-32	-	-	-	32-44	-	-	-	-	-	50-76
Lance McCullers	-	-	-	-	-	-	-	-	-	-	35-43	-
Kevin Mitchell	-	-	-	20-30	2-1	-	-	-	-	-	-	22-31
Rob Nelson	-	-	-	-	-	-	-	-	-	-	-	-
Eric Nolte	-	-	-	-	-	-	-	-	4-8	-	-	4-8
Mark Parent	1-3	-	-	-	-	-	-	-	-	-	-	1-3
Randy Ready	-	-	21-18	14-26	-	3-7	-	-	-	3-3	-	38-51
Luis Salazar	-	-	-	8-15	7-10	-	0-3	2-0	-	-	0-2	17-28
Benito Santiago	53-87	-	-	-	-	-	-	-	-	-	-	53-87
Eric Show	-	-	-	-	-	-	-	-	13-21	-	-	13-21
James Steels	-	-	-	-	-	1-1	2-2	-	-	-	-	3-3
Garry Templeton	-	-	-	-	58-83	-	-	-	-	-	-	58-83
Ed Whitson	-	-	-	-	-	-	-	-	17-17	-	0-2	17-17
Ed Wojna	-	-	-	-	-	-	-	-	0-3	-	0-2	0-3
Marvell Wynne	-	-	-	-	-	5-8	7-19	0-1	-	3-8	-	12-28

Batting vs. Left and Right Handed Pitchers

		BA	Rank	SA	Rank	OBA	Rank	HR %	Rank	BB %	Rank	SO %	Rank
Chris Brown	vs. Lefties	.265	75	.449	58	.339	69	5.10	22	9.09	61	12.73	63
	vs. Righties	.222	122	.365	99	.278	122	3.70	42	4.83	120	15.46	83
Joey Cora	vs. Lefties	.245	100	.286	125	.308	101	0.00	113	8.11	75	9.01	33
	vs. Righties	.231	114	.280	131	.323	83	0.00	126	11.52	28	9.70	22
Tim Flannery	vs. Lefties	.244	--	.268	--	.311	--	0.00	--	8.70	--	8.70	--
	vs. Righties	.226	120	.251	136	.336	66	0.00	126	13.57	11	9.29	19
Tony Gwynn	vs. Lefties	.361	5	.470	44	.433	10	1.20	100	10.53	40	3.51	3
	vs. Righties	.376	1	.541	10	.457	2	1.18	102	13.16	14	6.33	8
Stan Jefferson	vs. Lefties	.240	104	.273	129	.310	99	0.65	111	8.62	70	17.24	99
	vs. Righties	.224	121	.377	88	.288	111	2.61	64	8.14	81	21.02	120
John Kruk	vs. Lefties	.255	89	.380	91	.329	78	2.92	68	10.26	43	24.36	133
	vs. Righties	.339	3	.535	15	.439	5	5.16	20	15.36	7	14.82	76
Shane Mack	vs. Lefties	.265	76	.417	75	.313	96	3.03	64	4.79	113	16.44	96
	vs. Righties	.208	125	.292	127	.282	116	0.00	126	9.09	64	19.01	108
Carmelo Martinez	vs. Lefties	.272	69	.478	39	.395	20	4.89	28	16.59	9	13.45	69
	vs. Righties	.274	66	.395	75	.355	45	2.28	73	10.93	37	17.22	98
Randy Ready	vs. Lefties	.331	17	.566	11	.473	4	3.43	56	20.72	3	8.11	26
	vs. Righties	.286	42	.474	36	.367	32	3.43	49	10.45	48	12.94	55
Luis Salazar	vs. Lefties	.258	84	.361	100	.287	118	2.06	81	3.92	123	17.65	102
	vs. Righties	.250	--	.293	--	.317	--	1.09	--	9.62	--	11.54	--
Benito Santiago	vs. Lefties	.341	10	.577	8	.363	41	4.40	33	3.16	131	16.84	97
	vs. Righties	.280	54	.412	66	.304	101	2.75	61	2.62	135	20.94	119
Garry Templeton	vs. Lefties	.233	107	.307	118	.284	122	1.06	102	6.86	87	16.18	93
	vs. Righties	.215	124	.290	129	.278	120	0.93	109	7.84	89	16.53	93
Marvell Wynne	vs. Lefties	.231	--	.256	--	.318	--	0.00	--	11.36	--	34.09	--
	vs. Righties	.255	90	.369	94	.321	88	1.34	97	8.88	70	13.02	56
Team Average	vs. Lefties	.271	2	.402	8	.343	3	2.45	8	9.58	4	15.21	6
	vs. Righties	.254	11	.364	11	.325	8	1.84	11	9.20	5	16.57	9
League Average	vs. Lefties	.263		.409		.332		2.81		9.08		15.22	
	vs. Righties	.260		.401		.327		2.73		8.70		15.85	

Batting with Runners on Base and Bases Empty

		BA	Rank	SA	Rank	OBA	Rank	HR %	Rank	BB %	Rank	SO %	Rank
Chris Brown	Runners On	.258	96	.477	36	.331	89	5.30	15	7.28	109	16.56	97
	Bases Empty	.219	120	.323	113	.271	125	3.23	57	5.42	111	12.65	50
Joey Cora	Runners On	.218	122	.269	131	.279	123	0.00	122	7.69	100	8.79	24
	Bases Empty	.245	98	.288	126	.335	58	0.00	128	11.35	20	9.73	21
Tim Flannery	Runners On	.311	24	.349	106	.385	34	0.00	122	11.11	52	7.14	16
	Bases Empty	.176	134	.194	137	.300	97	0.00	128	14.00	6	10.50	33
Tony Gwynn	Runners On	.339	9	.474	41	.447	4	0.00	122	16.55	12	2.46	1
	Bases Empty	.390	1	.535	20	.447	1	1.95	86	8.84	51	7.07	9
Stan Jefferson	Runners On	.168	134	.252	133	.238	132	1.40	93	8.59	86	13.50	67
	Bases Empty	.262	73	.384	86	.327	70	2.15	81	8.17	59	22.88	128
John Kruk	Runners On	.304	28	.512	20	.406	22	4.83	20	15.08	16	20.63	125
	Bases Empty	.321	14	.467	43	.407	10	4.17	41	12.73	10	14.91	76
Shane Mack	Runners On	.297	46	.441	62	.328	95	0.90	114	3.20	134	19.20	118
	Bases Empty	.189	133	.291	125	.275	122	2.36	75	9.86	40	16.20	89
Carmelo Martinez	Runners On	.310	27	.441	63	.415	18	1.75	88	15.11	15	14.03	81
	Bases Empty	.234	109	.417	62	.324	74	5.05	28	11.34	21	17.41	97
Randy Ready	Runners On	.342	8	.519	16	.439	6	2.53	63	14.29	21	8.99	26
	Bases Empty	.281	47	.521	24	.410	8	4.17	41	17.09	4	11.54	41
Luis Salazar	Runners On	.264	87	.368	101	.313	106	2.30	76	7.22	110	13.40	64
	Bases Empty	.245	99	.294	123	.294	103	0.98	109	6.42	91	15.60	84
Benito Santiago	Runners On	.310	28	.502	26	.333	87	4.31	31	3.69	131	14.76	87
	Bases Empty	.292	34	.436	59	.316	85	2.41	73	1.99	137	23.92	132
Garry Templeton	Runners On	.207	128	.302	124	.275	124	1.35	94	8.33	90	16.67	99
	Bases Empty	.233	110	.292	124	.285	113	0.69	115	6.80	81	16.18	88
Marvell Wynne	Runners On	.284	64	.407	76	.359	56	1.23	98	10.42	59	13.54	69
	Bases Empty	.224	119	.299	122	.291	109	0.93	111	8.55	54	20.51	119
Team Average	Runners On	.268	7	.399	8	.343	8	2.13	10	9.99	5	14.78	6
	Bases Empty	.254	8	.362	11	.323	5	2.03	11	8.82	4	17.09	9
League Average	Runners On	.267		.410		.341		2.66		9.88		14.92	
	Bases Empty	.256		.399		.319		2.82		7.98		16.22	

Overall Batting Compared to Late Inning Pressure Situations

		BA	Rank	SA	Rank	OBA	Rank	HR %	Rank	BB %	Rank	SO %	Rank	RDI %	Rank
Chris Brown	Overall	.237	114	.394	86	.299	115	4.18	35	6.31	113	14.51	76	.234	109
	Pressure	.229	100	.292	117	.327	81	0.00	105	8.62	75	10.34	23	.176	109
Joey Cora	Overall	.237	115	.282	133	.317	93	0.00	133	10.14	50	9.42	20	.176	129
	Pressure	.146	135	.146	137	.239	129	0.00	105	10.42	56	14.58	59	.000	140
Tim Flannery	Overall	.228	123	.254	136	.332	71	0.00	133	12.88	15	9.20	18	.269	83
	Pressure	.132	137	.151	136	.233	132	0.00	105	11.48	42	14.75	61	.158	116
Tony Gwynn	Overall	.370	1	.511	19	.447	2	1.19	106	12.06	22	5.15	4	.280	69
	Pressure	.337	16	.449	43	.417	14	0.00	105	12.50	33	9.62	21	.167	111
Stan Jefferson	Overall	.230	122	.339	115	.296	118	1.90	88	8.32	76	19.62	121	.188	126
	Pressure	.119	138	.179	138	.178	138	1.49	90	6.67	101	29.33	136	.107	129
John Kruk	Overall	.313	11	.488	28	.406	10	4.47	27	13.85	12	17.65	106	.355	9
	Pressure	.322	23	.437	48	.422	12	3.45	40	14.42	21	17.31	86	.290	60
Shane Mack	Overall	.239	112	.361	104	.299	117	1.68	93	6.74	106	17.60	104	.250	95
	Pressure	.190	126	.238	132	.261	123	0.00	105	7.84	87	13.73	55	.111	123
Carmelo Martinez	Overall	.273	72	.430	59	.372	27	3.36	52	13.33	14	15.62	87	.287	63
	Pressure	.208	120	.306	114	.288	106	1.39	93	9.88	62	20.99	109	.421	13
Randy Ready	Overall	.309	13	.520	16	.423	6	3.43	50	15.84	6	10.40	27	.308	45
	Pressure	.259	73	.370	78	.437	8	1.85	79	21.92	4	13.70	54	.211	91
Luis Salazar	Overall	.254	94	.328	121	.302	111	1.59	95	6.80	103	14.56	77	.190	125
	Pressure	.162	133	.216	133	.179	137	0.00	105	2.56	129	25.64	128	.385	21
Benito Santiago	Overall	.300	20	.467	35	.324	87	3.30	53	2.80	135	19.58	120	.295	57
	Pressure	.379	7	.544	14	.385	36	2.91	47	0.95	138	25.71	129	.371	23
Garry Templeton	Overall	.222	125	.296	130	.281	126	0.98	117	7.49	88	16.40	95	.253	92
	Pressure	.217	115	.348	94	.294	101	3.26	43	9.62	63	18.27	90	.091	131
Marvell Wynne	Overall	.250	99	.346	114	.321	91	1.06	111	9.39	56	17.37	102	.400	--
	Pressure	.292	44	.354	91	.352	63	0.00	105	8.77	72	15.79	69	.588	1
Team Average	Overall	.260	7	.378	10	.332	4	2.07	11	9.34	5	16.06	9	.262	9
	Pressure	.240	10	.326	11	.315	11	1.31	12	9.61	7	19.03	12	.251	9
League Average	Overall	.261		.404		.328		2.75		8.83		15.64		.272	
	Pressure	.258		.385		.331		2.46		9.54		16.95		.261	

Additional Miscellaneous Batting Comparisons

	Grass Surface BA	Rank	Artificial Surface BA	Rank	Home Games BA	Rank	Road Games BA	Rank	Runners in Scoring Position BA	Rank	Runners in Scoring Pos and Two Outs BA	Rank	Leading Off Inning OBA	Rank	Runners on 3B with less than 2 Outs RDI %	Rank
Chris Brown	.245	98	.184	--	.219	124	.253	85	.259	80	.231	82	.214	134	.467	109
Joey Cora	.230	109	.250	96	.207	127	.262	78	.164	130	.269	56	.267	124	.400	125
Tim Flannery	.241	103	.195	130	.246	106	.214	126	.313	25	.306	28	.306	97	.455	113
Tony Gwynn	.374	1	.360	4	.390	1	.352	4	.302	33	.268	58	.397	16	.815	4
Stan Jefferson	.220	122	.257	85	.211	125	.249	94	.149	133	.151	126	.316	89	.692	20
John Kruk	.302	26	.345	7	.298	37	.328	7	.331	12	.349	13	.366	38	.541	83
Shane Mack	.263	77	.179	134	.225	121	.252	89	.213	115	.281	46	.305	98	.600	57
Carmelo Martinez	.285	45	.242	106	.282	60	.264	76	.295	44	.190	116	.324	80	.667	25
Randy Ready	.335	8	.240	107	.339	9	.279	44	.326	15	.385	5	.383	26	.588	63
Luis Salazar	.277	54	.203	--	.284	57	.223	119	.226	111	.231	82	.204	135	.357	132
Benito Santiago	.284	46	.342	8	.281	64	.320	12	.292	45	.324	16	.304	101	.607	53
Garry Templeton	.210	126	.252	95	.204	129	.238	106	.187	128	.169	122	.317	88	.654	32
Marvell Wynne	.225	115	.320	--	.163	--	.315	16	.349	6	.450	3	.269	122	.500	91
Team Average	.260	7	.261	5	.255	11	.265	1	.252	8	.257	2	.306	11	.560	6
League Average	.260		.261		.265		.256		.258		.241		.324		.554	

Pitching vs. Left and Right Handed Batters

		BA	Rank	SA	Rank	OBA	Rank	HR %	Rank	BB %	Rank	SO %	Rank
Greg Booker	vs. Lefties	.309	99	.409	67	.424	111	2.73	78	15.67	110	2.24	112
	vs. Righties	.197	10	.261	5	.253	6	1.41	13	5.84	24	9.09	108
Keith Comstock	vs. Lefties	.290	--	.377	--	.351	--	1.45	--	8.97	--	17.95	--
	vs. Righties	.234	31	.358	29	.341	86	2.92	54	14.46	111	27.11	5
Mark Davis	vs. Lefties	.221	10	.345	31	.302	25	2.65	76	8.46	32	15.38	44
	vs. Righties	.259	62	.404	56	.346	92	2.90	53	11.01	100	17.89	43
Storm Davis	vs. Lefties	.315	105	.465	92	.420	110	1.57	31	15.33	109	10.67	80
	vs. Righties	.244	--	.398	--	.321	--	2.44	--	9.15	--	14.79	--
Rich Gossage	vs. Lefties	.248	38	.396	57	.342	60	1.98	46	13.22	101	17.36	34
	vs. Righties	.239	--	.370	--	.263	--	2.17	--	3.13	--	23.96	--
Mark Grant	vs. Lefties	.259	49	.379	47	.344	63	1.91	44	11.37	80	11.14	78
	vs. Righties	.285	96	.510	105	.349	94	5.70	110	8.39	77	14.43	78
Andy Hawkins	vs. Lefties	.336	110	.515	110	.415	108	3.06	92	12.31	93	6.34	109
	vs. Righties	.237	34	.421	70	.293	30	3.95	90	6.45	31	13.71	83
Jimmy Jones	vs. Lefties	.268	59	.366	37	.338	56	1.96	45	9.28	49	7.83	103
	vs. Righties	.273	83	.409	62	.333	76	3.03	62	7.48	50	8.16	111
Lance McCullers	vs. Lefties	.226	17	.301	11	.340	58	0.84	9	14.89	106	23.40	8
	vs. Righties	.263	69	.453	92	.317	56	3.88	87	6.59	34	23.26	11
Eric Nolte	vs. Lefties	.250	--	.444	--	.341	--	5.56	--	7.32	--	9.76	--
	vs. Righties	.222	21	.319	15	.324	67	1.85	19	13.10	106	15.87	66
Eric Show	vs. Lefties	.248	39	.401	61	.329	45	2.83	83	10.95	68	13.84	52
	vs. Righties	.234	32	.407	59	.312	48	3.95	91	7.94	60	12.41	96
Ed Whitson	vs. Lefties	.286	83	.443	81	.351	73	3.28	96	8.70	38	13.59	55
	vs. Righties	.210	15	.443	88	.258	11	6.16	111	5.94	25	18.35	40
Team Average	vs. Lefties	.267	8	.406	8	.350	9	2.53	8	11.13	11	12.96	9
	vs. Righties	.247	1	.412	8	.316	5	3.77	12	8.45	8	15.76	9
League Average	vs. Lefties	.268		.404		.341		2.34		9.74		14.31	
	vs. Righties	.255		.403		.319		3.05		8.16		16.61	

Pitching with Runners on Base and Bases Empty

		BA	Rank	SA	Rank	OBA	Rank	HR %	Rank	BB %	Rank	SO %	Rank
Greg Booker	Runners On	.254	45	.320	16	.328	42	1.64	28	8.63	27	4.32	113
	Bases Empty	.238	36	.331	14	.336	80	2.31	41	12.08	106	7.38	111
Keith Comstock	Runners On	.281	84	.385	45	.360	92	2.08	41	11.97	91	18.80	20
	Bases Empty	.227	--	.345	--	.331	--	2.73	--	13.39	--	29.13	--
Mark Davis	Runners On	.247	33	.414	65	.335	56	3.52	91	10.49	69	16.85	43
	Bases Empty	.253	59	.370	38	.338	82	2.26	39	10.37	97	17.73	39
Storm Davis	Runners On	.292	96	.478	99	.406	113	2.65	65	15.00	111	10.00	100
	Bases Empty	.270	83	.394	65	.342	89	1.46	10	9.87	92	15.13	61
Mark Grant	Runners On	.265	62	.463	95	.355	89	4.85	109	11.80	88	11.80	86
	Bases Empty	.273	85	.412	74	.339	85	2.49	48	8.79	78	13.07	91
Andy Hawkins	Runners On	.248	28	.391	50	.320	30	2.48	54	9.44	52	9.44	103
	Bases Empty	.318	109	.529	110	.385	109	4.31	100	9.54	87	10.25	107
Jimmy Jones	Runners On	.317	111	.465	96	.376	101	3.29	82	8.60	26	8.60	109
	Bases Empty	.235	32	.327	13	.306	39	1.83	24	8.33	68	7.50	110
Lance McCullers	Runners On	.242	28	.356	31	.347	74	2.12	44	13.07	101	26.50	5
	Bases Empty	.247	47	.396	67	.311	49	2.55	54	8.56	71	19.84	25
Eric Nolte	Runners On	.195	2	.292	7	.303	14	1.77	31	13.43	105	15.67	53
	Bases Empty	.252	54	.374	46	.346	95	2.88	68	11.32	102	14.47	68
Eric Show	Runners On	.230	19	.355	30	.343	71	1.74	30	13.60	107	12.18	82
	Bases Empty	.248	49	.432	87	.308	42	4.28	99	6.93	42	13.86	80
Ed Whitson	Runners On	.276	78	.505	107	.310	19	4.78	108	4.44	2	16.83	44
	Bases Empty	.236	33	.405	70	.309	45	4.48	106	9.21	84	15.10	62
Team Average	Runners On	.259	3	.410	7	.343	8	2.98	10	10.85	11	14.40	6
	Bases Empty	.254	6	.408	7	.324	8	3.36	11	8.78	10	14.49	10
League Average	Runners On	.267		.410		.341		2.66		9.88		14.92	
	Bases Empty	.256		.399		.319		2.82		7.98		16.22	

Overall Pitching Compared to Late Inning Pressure Situations

		BA	Rank	SA	Rank	OBA	Rank	HR %	Rank	BB %	Rank	SO %	Rank
Greg Booker	Overall	.246	38	.325	7	.332	71	1.98	26	10.42	89	5.90	112
	Pressure	.261	--	.348	--	.452	--	0.00	--	22.58	--	3.23	--
Keith Comstock	Overall	.252	--	.364	--	.344	--	2.43	--	12.70	--	24.18	--
	Pressure	.268	64	.375	54	.368	86	1.79	45	14.49	102	17.39	47
Mark Davis	Overall	.250	45	.390	56	.336	83	2.85	71	10.42	90	17.31	32
	Pressure	.215	18	.363	46	.333	53	2.96	76	13.58	97	19.14	38
Storm Davis	Overall	.280	95	.432	87	.372	109	2.00	28	12.33	109	12.67	86
	Pressure	.308	--	.846	--	.471	--	15.38	--	23.53	--	23.53	--
Rich Gossage	Overall	.244	--	.383	--	.307	--	2.07	--	8.76	--	20.28	--
	Pressure	.232	30	.384	62	.313	38	2.40	59	10.96	76	18.49	41
Mark Grant	Overall	.270	78	.433	88	.346	91	3.49	91	10.14	85	12.50	89
	Pressure	.400	110	.625	106	.467	109	5.00	97	10.00	61	6.00	107
Andy Hawkins	Overall	.287	101	.468	105	.356	103	3.50	92	9.50	73	9.88	107
	Pressure	.269	--	.462	--	.367	--	3.85	--	13.33	--	16.67	--
Jimmy Jones	Overall	.270	79	.386	53	.336	81	2.46	51	8.45	48	7.98	111
	Pressure	.250	46	.375	54	.273	15	3.13	79	3.03	7	12.12	77
Lance McCullers	Overall	.244	32	.376	40	.330	65	2.34	44	10.93	100	23.33	8
	Pressure	.261	62	.400	69	.362	81	2.14	51	13.29	95	21.15	23
Eric Nolte	Overall	.226	12	.337	12	.326	58	2.38	47	12.29	106	15.02	60
	Pressure	.067	--	.067	--	.176	--	0.00	--	11.76	--	29.41	--
Eric Show	Overall	.242	24	.404	63	.322	47	3.34	84	9.58	76	13.19	80
	Pressure	.188	5	.375	54	.235	5	6.25	102	3.92	11	23.53	17
Ed Whitson	Overall	.251	49	.443	92	.309	28	4.59	109	7.46	24	15.73	52
	Pressure	.333	102	.650	107	.365	83	10.00	110	4.76	15	20.63	27
Team Average	Overall	.256	6	.409	8	.332	9	3.20	12	9.70	11	14.45	9
	Pressure	.261	8	.436	11	.348	9	3.70	12	11.31	10	18.98	3
League Average	Overall	.261		.404		.328		2.75		8.83		15.64	
	Pressure	.260		.391		.337		2.47		10.04		17.14	

Additional Miscellaneous Pitching Comparisons

	Grass Surface		Artificial Surface		Home Games		Road Games		Runners in Scoring Position		Runners in Scoring Pos and Two Outs		Leading Off Inning	
	BA	Rank	BA	Rank	BA	Rank	BA	Rank	BA	Rank	BA	Rank	OBA	Rank
Greg Booker	.257	56	.167	--	.271	81	.206	--	.250	57	.200	33	.290	19
Keith Comstock	.277	77	.176	--	.231	--	.276	69	.327	--	.259	--	.382	--
Mark Davis	.238	26	.288	87	.220	19	.275	68	.260	68	.246	70	.344	82
Storm Davis	.250	41	.330	109	.248	41	.308	105	.295	92	.353	108	.394	108
Rich Gossage	.231	21	.270	--	.226	--	.260	--	.193	--	.257	74	.239	--
Mark Grant	.250	41	.329	108	.244	36	.304	100	.247	52	.233	61	.335	74
Andy Hawkins	.303	104	.252	44	.308	106	.265	54	.239	39	.273	81	.385	104
Jimmy Jones	.255	53	.312	102	.261	65	.281	75	.324	108	.333	103	.327	66
Lance McCullers	.243	31	.246	36	.224	21	.265	55	.221	26	.200	33	.276	14
Eric Nolte	.239	27	.204	--	.205	--	.237	26	.157	2	.097	2	.352	87
Eric Show	.208	7	.376	112	.201	11	.287	82	.244	47	.205	37	.312	44
Ed Whitson	.253	47	.241	26	.249	45	.254	44	.293	89	.365	111	.316	50
Team Average	.246	1	.283	12	.242	3	.271	11	.257	6	.261	10	.328	5
League Average	.260		.261		.256		.265		.258		.241		.324	

SAN FRANCISCO GIANTS

Imagine Carl Lewis trying to set a new world record in the 100-meter dash running on a sand track. Or Secretariat trying to win the Belmont Stakes with Willie McCovey on his back. Or Tom Dempsey trying to kick his NFL-record 62-yard field goal into the wind at Candlestick Park.

It's a rare and noteworthy achievement when a player or team overcomes uncooperative circumstances to set a record or win a title. Conversely, players and teams that lead leagues in various statistical categories usually do so with a strong assist from their home fields. The Chicago Cubs, for example, have led the National League in home runs in each of the past three seasons. Sure, Andre Dawson, Ryne Sandberg, and Leon Durham had a lot to do with that, but not nearly as much as Wrigley Field did. Put those same players in the Astrodome and Houston would be lucky to finish in the top half of the league in homers. The story's the same in the American League: Only Detroit and Baltimore have led the league in home runs for the past five years. Both play in stadiums that are generous to home run hitters.

There are similar reasons why the Dodgers have led the National League in ERA 14 times in the past 28 years; why Houston's led the league in shutouts six times in the past 10 years; and why either Kansas City or Toronto has led the A.L. in triples 11 times in the past 13 years. The reasons, quite simply, are Dodger Stadium, the Astrodome, Royals Stadium, and Exhibition Stadium.

Occasionally, teams win a statistical title despite a negative stadium bias, a tip-off that the team stands head and shoulders above the rest of the league. The New York Mets, for example, have led the National League in runs scored for the past two seasons despite playing their home games in Shea Stadium, a poor hitters' park. And on a rare occasion, a team will overcome an extremely strong negative bias, the sign of a team with extraordinary talent. The 1973 Oakland A's were a classic example: They led the American League in scoring despite playing in the Oakland Coliseum, the A.L.'s worst park for hitters.

Last season, the San Francisco Giants performed a similar feat— albeit one of a lesser note—when they led the National League in handling double plays for the first time since the franchise left New York's Polo Grounds in 1957. Throughout its history, Candlestick Park has offered one of the most diabolical infield surfaces in the majors. As a result, during their first 29 years in San Francisco, the Giants had the lowest average of double plays per season in the National League. The figures from 1958 through 1986 (Atlanta'a aver-

age includes eight seasons in Milwaukee. New York and Houston entered the league in 1962, Montreal and San Diego in 1969):

Team	DP
Pittsburgh	161.48
St. Louis	157.45
Chicago	148.31
Philadelphia	147.69
Atlanta	147.62
Montreal	146.72
San Diego	146.28
Cincinnati	144.55
New York	143.88
Los Angeles	139.72
Houston	137.84
San Francisco	134.72

But last season, the Giants' total of 183 twin killings was not only the highest in the National League, it led the entire majors. And it wasn't only their highest total since moving west, *it was the highest in the entire history of the franchise.* And they turned those 183 double plays despite one of baseball's most uncooperative home fields.

The following table, similar to those in the back of the Ballparks section, ranks the 26 major-league stadiums according to their effect on ground-ball double plays over the past five seasons. Stadiums with artificial turf are marked with asterisks:

Stadium	Home Games	Road Games	Pct. Diff.
Atlanta Stadium	773	631	+19.5
Wrigley Field	634	532	+17.2
Anaheim Stadium	722	672	+10.0
Memorial Stadium	726	678	+8.2
Arlington Stadium	649	600	+7.4
Fenway Park	713	668	+5.8
*Astrodome	566	536	+5.2
San Diego Stadium	612	589	+4.9
Oakland Coliseum	585	565	+4.7
Cleveland Stadium	654	627	+3.6
*Olympic Stadium	551	543	+2.9
*Three Rivers Stadium	605	594	+1.6
Yankee Stadium	675	695	-0.6
Comiskey Park	604	619	-1.6
*Kingdome	644	639	-2.1
*Royals Stadium	630	633	-2.1
County Stadium	636	659	-2.7
*Veterans Stadium	562	592	-5.1
*Riverfront Stadium	560	590	-6.4

* Busch Stadium	605	656	− 6.8		
Shea Stadium	566	624	− 7.8		
Tiger Stadium	543	602	− 8.6		
Candlestick Park	538	609	− 10.5		
* Exhibition Stadium	563	639	− 10.7		
* Metrodome	597	645	− 11.3		
Dodger Stadium	513	589	− 12.9		

1957	New York	183	3.00	98	56	.636	1st
1955	New York	180	3.23	96	58	.623	1st
1952	New York	199	3.14	95	59	.617	1st
1942	New York	190	2.91	103	51	.669	1st
1925	Washington	166	3.67	96	55	.636	1st

Last season, as half the baseball world waited for the Giants to crumble, and the other half searched for obscure reasons to explain their unexpected success, few of us understood the significance of San Francisco's unprecedented rate of double plays. Some even questioned whether it was advantageous to lead the league in double plays in the first place. After all, the teams that turn the most DPs are usually those with the most opportunities, and those with the most opportunities are the ones that allow the most batters to reach base, and the ones that allow the most batters to reach base ... well, you get the picture. And to a degree, that's correct. Over the past five years, teams that made at least 160 double plays over the course of a season have lost more games than they've won:

	W	L	Pct.
More than 160 DP's	3133	3179	.496
140–160 double plays	4782	4600	.510
Less than 140 DP's	2603	2739	.488

Not a major difference, but a significant one. Too many double plays indicate that you're allowing too many base runners; too few indicate that your defense isn't up to par. On average, teams with moderate double-play totals fare best. *On average.*

But San Francisco wasn't your average double-play leader. The missing piece to the puzzle was that the Giants also led the National League in ERA last season. They turned the most double plays not only despite Candlestick Park, but also despite a pitching staff that "refused to cooperate" by putting runners on base. San Francisco became only the second team in the past 40 seasons to lead the National League in both categories, and the seventh since guys like us starting counting up double plays in 1919. Another seven teams led the A.L. in ERA and double plays during that period. As you would imagine, the DP/ERA parley produces sensational results. The 14 teams had a composite winning percentage of .609; nine won either a division or league title, and none had a losing record.

Year	Team	DP	ERA	W	L	Pct.	Finish
1987	San Francisco	183	3.68	90	72	.556	1st
1962	Pittsburgh	177	3.38	93	68	.578	4th
1947	St. Louis	169	3.53	89	65	.578	2d
1944	St. Louis	162	2.67	105	49	.682	1st
1935	Chicago	163	3.26	100	54	.649	1st
1934	New York	141	3.19	93	60	.608	2d
1926	Chicago	174	3.26	82	72	.532	4th
1975	Baltimore	175	3.17	90	69	.566	2d
1958	New York	182	3.22	92	62	.597	1st

A final thought: If, on average, the teams that make a lot of double plays have no advantage, what are we to make of these figures for the 1987 season, which indicate that the more DPs you make *in a game*, the better your chances of winning that game:

DP	W	L	Pct.
0	769	877	.467
1	806	764	.513
2	383	358	.517
3	115	83	.581
4 +	32	23	.582

Mom and Dad always told us to go into medicine. But, no—we had to be *statisticians.*

One Last Look

Just when you thought it was safe to go back in the batter's box ... *Arrrrrgh! Another essay on the lively-ball controversy!*

Frankly, this is a topic that we, too, hoped would go away. But for all that was said and written about the enormous increase in home runs last season, it's amazing how much pertinent information was either missed or misrepresented. For the record, we'd like to present our revisionist theory on last season's 16-percent increase in home runs. First, let's look at the numbers: A 14.4 percent rise in the American League, 18.8 percent in the National League:

	American League			National League		
	AB	HR	AB/HR	AB	HR	AB/HR
1986	77,376	2,290	33.8	65,730	1,523	43.2
1987	77,819	2,634	29.5	66,276	1,824	36.3

Only once before in the history of baseball had more than one team hit 200 home runs in the same season. That was in 1962 when Detroit hit 209 and San Francisco hit 204. Last season, five different teams topped the 200 mark: Detroit (225), Toronto (215), and Baltimore (211) in the A.L., Chicago (209) and San Francisco (205) in the N.L. And some of the gains were enormous. In fact, the Giants hit only 114 home runs in 1986; last season's leap to 205 represented the fourth-largest single-season increase in the history of major-league baseball:

Years	Team	Year 1	Year 2	Diff.
1946–1947	New York Giants	121	221	+ 100
1976–1977	Los Angeles Dodgers	91	191	+ 100
1946–1947	Pittsburgh Pirates	60	156	+ 96
1986–1987	San Francisco Giants	114	205	+ 91

For some reason, many fans agreed that a juiced-up baseball was solely responsible for the increase. Sure, a livelier ball provided a logical explanation for the phenomenon. But there were several scientific tests by credible organizations that concluded that the balls used last season were essentially the same as those used a year earlier. And, of course, there were other possible explanations for the record number of home runs that were every bit as plausible as a souped-up baseball. We'll examine two of them.

First, we'll study the contention that the increase in home runs resulted from a major-league-wide deterioration in pitching skill. Throughout the summer, we heard with increasing regularity the lament that "they just don't make pitchers like they used to." That sounded to us like a rehash of the claim that the players of old would've kicked the assets of today's millionaires, especially since we didn't hear that plaint from anyone under the age of thirty. But we're always willing to take a fresh look at an old question.

If the new pitchers were responsible for the home run increase, then you'd expect that the rise would be negligible among a group of established pitchers, or at least much smaller than among the rest of the major leagues' pitchers. So we divided each league into two groups: the first was composed of all pitchers who worked at least 162 innings in each of the past two seasons, the other included everyone else.

In the American League, the group of 17 established pitchers (see names below) allowed 13.6 percent more home runs last season, compared to a 14.7-percent increase among the others. Hardly the type of difference it would take to support the contention that the new guys on the block can't pitch. But in the National League, the home-run leap was nearly *twice as great* among the veteran subgroup as it was among all other pitchers. The following table shows the number of home runs per 100 at bats allowed by each group over the past two seasons:

Year	American League		National League	
	Vets	Others	Vets	Others
1987	3.23	3.42	2.70	2.76
1986	2.85	2.98	2.05	2.37
	+13.6%	+14.7%	+32.0%	+16.5%

(The pitchers included in the group of established A.L. pitchers are: Floyd Bannister, Bert Blyleven, Tom Candiotti, Jim Clancy, Roger Clemens, Mark Gubicza, Ted Higuera, Charlie Hough, Bruce Hurst, Danny Jackson, Jimmy Key, Charlie Leibrandt, Jack Morris, Don Sutton, Frank Tanana, Mike Witt, and Curt Young. The established N.L. pitchers: Danny Cox, Ron Darling, Bob Forsch, Dwight Gooden, Bill Gullickson, Bob Knepper, Mike Krukow, Mike LaCoss, Nolan Ryan, Mike Scott, Fernando Valenzuela, and Bob Welch.)

Bat Day: August 6th

So much for the notion that poor pitchers were responsible for the home run increase. But while everyone else pointed a finger at the baseball, we couldn't help but wonder about the bats. So we thought we'd examine the other side of the contact equation.

For those who study financial charts, the date of the crash of '87 was October 19; for those who study home run charts, the date was Aug. 6, the day that National League umpire John Kibler impounded the bat of Howard Johnson on the suspicion of corkedness. *From that day on, home-run rates retreated from their earlier record levels more than halfway back to the levels of the 1986 season*:

	American League			National League		
	AB	HR	AB/HR	AB	HR	AB/HR
Entire 1986 season	77,376	2,290	33.8	65,730	1,523	43.2
1987 through August 6	51,540	1,810	28.5	44,113	1,262	35.0
1987 after August 6	26,279	824	31.9	22,163	562	39.4

Some fluctuations are to be expected over the course of any season; that's normal. But the degree of change that occurred following the first bat confiscation last August—with the threat of further checks to come when opposing managers challenged bats they suspected—would occur merely by chance only once in 3,309 trials. To us, that's conclusive evidence.

The degree to which home runs declined—a drop that began *at exactly the time when major-league baseball announced that it would check for tampering*—is demonstrated vividly in the following table, which shows the major-league home run percentage (home runs per 100 at bats) week by week throughout the 1987 season:

Week of	HR%	Week of	HR%	Week of	HR%	Week of	HR%
Apr. 6	2.90	May 25	3.46	July 13	2.90	Aug. 24	2.75
Apr. 13	2.78	June 1	3.38	July 20	2.99	Aug. 31	2.45
Apr. 20	3.06	June 8	3.19	July 27	3.10	Sept. 7	2.86
Apr. 27	3.62	June 15	3.78	Aug. 3	3.44	Sept. 14	3.15
May 4	3.20	June 22	3.12	Aug. 10	3.16	Sept. 21	2.76
May 11	3.28	June 29	2.48	Aug. 17	2.96	Sept. 28	2.43
May 18	3.28	July 6	3.77				

Six of the 10 lowest weekly home run rates occurred in the eight weeks following the first bat confiscation. That incident prompted the only streak of four consecutive weekly declines during the entire season. (In the interest of fairness, we're obliged to mention that none of the bats that were challenged and checked were found to have been altered.)

We don't doubt that there might have been a livelier baseball used during the 1987 season. But we're certain that last year's drastic increase in home runs was in large measure due to the bats as well. Or, as Keith Jackson might say, "Perhaps it was the spheroid. But we suspect the bludgeon."

WON-LOST RECORD BY STARTING POSITION

SAN FRANCISCO 90-72	C	1B	2B	3B	SS	LF	CF	RF	P	Leadoff	Relief	Starts
Mike Aldrete	-	14-5	-	-	-	18-17	6-4	14-12	-	11-11	-	52-38
Randy Bockus	-	-	-	-	-	-	-	-	-	-	4-8	-
Bob Brenly	54-46	2-3	-	-	-	-	-	-	-	-	-	56-49
Chris Brown	-	-	-	21-15	-	-	-	-	-	-	-	21-15
John Burkett	-	-	-	-	-	-	-	-	-	-	1-2	-
Will Clark	-	72-61	-	-	-	-	-	-	-	11-8	-	72-61
Keith Comstock	-	-	-	-	-	-	-	-	-	-	3-12	-
Chili Davis	-	-	-	-	-	3-2	57-48	8-7	-	-	2-7	68-57
Mark Davis	-	-	-	-	-	-	-	-	6-5	-	2-7	6-5
Ivan DeJesus	-	-	-	-	1-1	-	-	-	-	-	-	1-1
Kelly Downs	-	-	-	-	-	-	-	-	14-14	-	8-5	14-14
Dave Dravecky	-	-	-	-	-	-	-	-	11-7	-	-	11-7
Scott Garrelts	-	-	-	-	-	-	-	-	-	-	38-26	-
Jim Gott	-	-	-	-	-	-	-	-	1-2	-	6-21	1-2
Mark Grant	-	-	-	-	-	-	-	-	4-4	-	3-5	4-4
Atlee Hammaker	-	-	-	-	-	-	-	-	14-13	-	3-1	14-13
Dave Henderson	-	-	-	-	-	-	3-2	-	-	-	-	3-2
Mike Krukow	-	-	-	-	-	-	-	-	18-10	-	1-1	18-10
Randy Kutcher	-	-	0-1	0-1	-	1-0	-	-	-	0-1	-	1-2
Mike LaCoss	-	-	-	-	-	-	-	-	12-14	-	3-10	12-14
Craig Lefferts	-	-	-	-	-	-	-	-	-	-	20-24	-
Jeffrey Leonard	-	-	-	-	-	63-50	0-1	-	-	1-0	-	63-51
Candy Maldonado	-	-	-	-	-	1-0	-	64-49	-	1-0	-	65-49
Kirt Manwaring	1-0	-	-	-	-	-	-	-	-	-	-	1-0
Roger Mason	-	-	-	-	-	-	-	-	4-1	-	-	4-1
Francisco Melendez	-	1-0	-	-	-	-	-	-	-	-	-	1-0
Bob Melvin	35-25	0-1	-	-	-	-	-	-	-	-	-	35-26
Eddie Milner	-	-	-	-	-	-	23-17	-	-	23-17	-	23-17
Greg Minton	-	-	-	-	-	-	-	-	-	-	5-10	-
Kevin Mitchell	-	-	-	38-27	-	1-0	-	-	-	-	-	39-27
Jon Perlman	-	-	-	-	-	-	-	-	-	-	1-9	-
Joe Price	-	-	-	-	-	-	-	-	-	-	7-13	-
Jessie Reid	-	-	-	-	-	-	1-0	-	-	-	-	1-0
Rick Reuschel	-	-	-	-	-	-	-	-	6-2	-	0-1	6-2
Don Robinson	-	-	-	-	-	-	-	-	-	-	17-8	-
Jeff D. Robinson	-	-	-	-	-	-	-	-	-	-	27-36	0-1
Mackey Sasser	0-1	-	-	-	-	-	-	-	-	-	-	0-1
Chris Speier	-	-	16-17	20-15	2-5	-	-	-	-	6-12	-	38-37
Harry Spilman	-	1-2	2-1	-	-	-	-	-	-	-	-	3-3
Rob Thompson	-	-	67-51	-	-	-	-	-	-	24-11	-	67-51
Jose Uribe	-	-	-	-	56-34	-	-	-	-	4-4	-	56-34
Mark Wasinger	-	-	3-2	5-6	-	-	-	-	-	6-7	-	8-8
Rob Wilfong	-	-	2-0	-	-	-	-	-	-	2-0	-	2-0
Matt Williams	-	-	-	4-6	31-32	-	-	-	-	-	-	35-38
Mike Woodard	-	-	2-1	?	-	-	-	-	-	-	1-1	2-1
Joel Youngblood	-	-	-	0-1	-	4-3	-	3-4	-	-	-	7-8

Batting vs. Left and Right Handed Pitchers

		BA	Rank	SA	Rank	OBA	Rank	HR %	Rank	BB %	Rank	SO %	Rank
Mike Aldrete	vs. Lefties	.314	27	.443	62	.342	65	0.00	113	3.95	121	9.21	36
	vs. Righties	.328	8	.467	40	.407	10	3.14	55	12.12	22	13.03	57
Bob Brenly	vs. Lefties	.238	106	.535	24	.304	107	6.93	11	9.40	56	18.80	114
	vs. Righties	.277	62	.442	48	.364	37	4.01	32	11.29	31	19.75	113
Will Clark	vs. Lefties	.318	26	.555	15	.341	67	4.05	43	2.73	133	18.03	106
	vs. Righties	.303	18	.593	5	.385	20	7.87	4	10.86	40	16.05	87
Chili Davis	vs. Lefties	.262	79	.536	23	.337	72	7.65	7	9.76	45	23.41	129
	vs. Righties	.243	103	.388	80	.349	52	3.15	54	13.94	10	16.35	91
Jeffrey Leonard	vs. Lefties	.283	54	.462	49	.306	105	3.45	55	3.82	126	10.83	48
	vs. Righties	.279	56	.469	39	.310	97	3.91	35	4.01	128	13.64	62
Candy Maldonado	vs. Lefties	.295	43	.515	31	.371	34	4.55	31	11.26	34	13.91	74
	vs. Righties	.290	40	.506	24	.334	68	4.52	52	5.03	118	16.86	95
Bob Melvin	vs. Lefties	.242	102	.414	78	.272	125	5.05	23	3.88	125	7.77	21
	vs. Righties	.170	135	.333	110	.235	136	4.08	31	8.02	86	22.22	124
Eddie Milner	vs. Lefties	.156	--	.156	--	.229	--	0.00	--	8.57	--	34.29	--
	vs. Righties	.269	72	.412	66	.345	59	2.20	77	10.29	51	10.29	27
Kevin Mitchell	vs. Lefties	.338	14	.647	3	.418	13	7.19	9	12.03	29	12.66	60
	vs. Righties	.255	89	.400	72	.319	90	3.69	44	8.12	82	19.05	109
Chris Speier	vs. Lefties	.272	69	.424	71	.337	71	4.35	35	8.91	66	14.85	79
	vs. Righties	.240	107	.382	85	.344	61	3.11	56	12.55	18	13.69	64
Rob Thompson	vs. Lefties	.310	28	.465	46	.382	31	2.33	77	6.80	88	12.24	58
	vs. Righties	.241	106	.399	74	.318	91	2.41	70	9.17	63	22.32	126
Jose Uribe	vs. Lefties	.260	83	.406	82	.311	98	3.13	61	5.77	103	9.62	38
	vs. Righties	.305	17	.432	51	.358	43	0.94	108	7.63	90	10.59	30
Matt Williams	vs. Lefties	.192	132	.385	90	.241	132	5.13	21	5.95	100	22.62	127
	vs. Righties	.186	133	.317	119	.239	135	2.40	71	6.04	109	26.92	136
Joel Youngblood	vs. Lefties	.169	135	.288	124	.231	134	3.39	57	6.15	98	13.85	73
	vs. Righties	.406	--	.563	--	.424	--	3.13	--	3.03	--	12.12	--
Team Average	vs. Lefties	.263	8	.446	1	.319	11	4.01	1	7.18	12	17.06	12
	vs. Righties	.259	6	.423	4	.326	5	3.51	2	8.59	7	17.69	11
League Average	vs. Lefties	.263		.409		.332		2.81		9.08		15.22	
	vs. Righties	.260		.401		.327		2.73		8.70		15.85	

Batting with Runners on Base and Bases Empty

Player	Situation	BA	Rank	SA	Rank	OBA	Rank	HR %	Rank	BB %	Rank	SO %	Rank
Mike Aldrete	Runners On	.406	1	.545	11	.460	3	2.80	53	9.70	74	13.94	80
	Bases Empty	.271	64	.407	71	.353	40	2.34	77	11.20	23	11.20	37
Bob Brenly	Runners On	.269	79	.407	77	.349	74	2.76	56	11.30	49	18.08	114
	Bases Empty	.265	69	.504	28	.347	46	6.09	17	10.42	34	20.46	118
Will Clark	Runners On	.338	10	.641	3	.412	19	7.58	4	10.04	68	15.28	91
	Bases Empty	.290	36	.544	16	.345	47	6.04	18	7.24	72	17.55	100
Chili Davis	Runners On	.279	72	.500	27	.403	25	5.77	10	17.44	9	17.44	109
	Bases Empty	.229	115	.401	75	.297	100	4.11	44	8.44	55	20.00	114
Jeffrey Leonard	Runners On	.259	94	.386	91	.297	114	2.73	59	5.02	119	13.39	63
	Bases Empty	.297	30	.530	22	.318	83	4.59	32	3.08	132	12.33	48
Candy Maldonado	Runners On	.284	63	.463	43	.335	86	2.75	57	6.53	112	15.10	90
	Bases Empty	.299	27	.554	14	.357	37	6.25	15	7.38	69	16.80	93
Bob Melvin	Runners On	.234	114	.333	114	.293	116	1.80	87	8.13	92	12.20	53
	Bases Empty	.170	135	.393	79	.211	86	6.67	13	4.93	113	20.42	117
Eddie Milner	Runners On	.290	--	.377	--	.355	--	0.00	--	9.09	--	14.29	--
	Bases Empty	.234	106	.372	97	.315	86	2.76	65	10.49	32	13.58	62
Kevin Mitchell	Runners On	.319	17	.512	21	.384	37	5.16	16	9.70	72	16.88	103
	Bases Empty	.247	96	.442	52	.320	80	4.38	35	8.99	47	17.27	95
Chris Speier	Runners On	.244	109	.370	99	.331	90	2.36	73	11.64	42	13.01	61
	Bases Empty	.253	86	.411	68	.349	44	4.21	39	11.47	19	14.68	73
Rob Thompson	Runners On	.287	59	.426	70	.366	49	2.94	49	7.55	103	15.09	89
	Bases Empty	.250	89	.415	65	.324	75	2.11	82	8.89	49	21.27	123
Jose Uribe	Runners On	.306	34	.476	40	.383	38	2.42	71	10.27	61	8.22	19
	Bases Empty	.281	48	.389	82	.314	87	1.08	106	4.64	120	11.86	46
Matt Williams	Runners On	.158	136	.257	132	.225	134	1.98	82	7.89	97	23.68	134
	Bases Empty	.208	126	.396	76	.250	131	4.17	41	4.61	121	26.97	136
Team Average	Runners On	.278	3	.436	3	.346	7	3.30	3	8.94	11	15.76	10
	Bases Empty	.247	11	.425	3	.309	11	3.90	2	7.62	7	18.79	12
League Average	Runners On	.267		.410		.341		2.66		9.88		14.92	
	Bases Empty	.256		.399		.319		2.82		7.98		16.22	

Overall Batting Compared to Late Inning Pressure Situations

Player	Situation	BA	Rank	SA	Rank	OBA	Rank	HR %	Rank	BB %	Rank	SO %	Rank	RDI %	Rank
Mike Aldrete	Overall	.325	6	.462	39	.396	17	2.52	71	10.59	38	12.32	49	.384	1
	Pressure	.222	109	.389	70	.311	90	3.70	38	11.29	44	11.29	29	.313	48
Bob Brenly	Overall	.267	79	.467	36	.348	52	4.80	18	10.78	36	19.50	118	.237	107
	Pressure	.314	30	.643	3	.400	26	8.57	3	10.98	48	15.85	72	.267	65
Will Clark	Overall	.308	14	.580	5	.371	29	6.62	9	8.33	75	16.67	98	.310	43
	Pressure	.266	70	.468	35	.348	65	3.80	36	10.11	61	19.10	98	.211	91
Chili Davis	Overall	.250	99	.442	49	.344	57	4.80	18	12.46	20	18.86	113	.305	48
	Pressure	.211	118	.408	57	.358	56	5.26	16	18.95	8	18.95	95	.238	77
Jeffrey Leonard	Overall	.280	59	.467	34	.309	104	3.78	41	3.95	131	12.81	55	.244	104
	Pressure	.257	77	.432	52	.305	95	2.70	56	7.32	94	12.20	33	.214	87
Candy Maldonado	Overall	.292	36	.509	20	.346	56	4.52	26	6.95	100	15.95	89	.350	13
	Pressure	.380	6	.620	5	.405	24	4.23	27	2.70	125	13.51	49	.393	18
Bob Melvin	Overall	.199	135	.366	100	.249	135	4.47	28	6.42	109	16.60	97	.205	122
	Pressure	.286	49	.452	40	.333	73	4.76	23	6.67	101	22.22	117	.231	81
Eddie Milner	Overall	.252	97	.374	96	.328	81	1.87	89	10.04	53	13.81	68	.302	--
	Pressure	.270	62	.459	38	.372	46	2.70	56	13.95	22	16.28	78	.111	123
Kevin Mitchell	Overall	.280	60	.474	30	.350	50	4.74	22	9.32	57	17.09	100	.284	67
	Pressure	.225	106	.282	119	.276	115	1.41	91	6.58	103	21.05	110	.310	52
Chris Speier	Overall	.249	102	.394	85	.342	64	3.47	49	11.54	27	14.01	70	.301	52
	Pressure	.228	103	.342	100	.274	119	2.53	65	5.88	109	15.29	65	.310	52
Harry Spilman	Overall	.267	--	.356	--	.327	--	1.11	--	8.91	--	19.80	--	.261	--
	Pressure	.298	39	.383	72	.358	55	0.00	105	9.43	65	24.53	123	.261	68
Rob Thompson	Overall	.262	88	.419	67	.338	66	2.38	75	8.44	72	19.20	116	.303	50
	Pressure	.230	99	.361	85	.329	80	1.64	82	10.67	51	20.00	103	.538	4
Jose Uribe	Overall	.291	37	.424	64	.343	60	1.62	94	7.06	98	10.29	24	.224	117
	Pressure	.333	17	.429	53	.417	15	2.38	67	12.00	39	8.00	13	.182	105
Matt Williams	Overall	.188	136	.339	116	.240	136	3.27	55	6.02	117	25.56	136	.165	131
	Pressure	.136	--	.364	--	.200	--	4.55	--	7.14	--	28.57	--	.250	71
Joel Youngblood	Overall	.253	--	.385	--	.296	--	3.30	--	5.10	--	13.27	--	.241	--
	Pressure	.267	--	.433	--	.267	--	3.33	--	0.00	--	13.33	--	.333	36
Team Average	Overall	.260	8	.430	3	.324	10	3.66	2	8.18	9	17.50	11	.272	6
	Pressure	.267	4	.440	2	.338	6	3.49	2	9.21	8	17.23	7	.273	4
League Average	Overall	.261		.404		.328		2.75		8.83		15.64		.272	
	Pressure	.258		.385		.331		2.46		9.54		16.95		.261	

Additional Miscellaneous Batting Comparisons

	Grass Surface BA	Rank	Artificial Surface BA	Rank	Home Games BA	Rank	Road Games BA	Rank	Runners in Scoring Position BA	Rank	Runners in Scoring Pos and Two Outs BA	Rank	Leading Off Inning OBA	Rank	Runners on 3B with less than 2 Outs RDI %	Rank
Mike Aldrete	.306	22	.365	3	.335	11	.315	15	.419	3	.378	7	.315	90	.714	16
Bob Brenly	.269	70	.261	82	.301	32	.238	107	.223	112	.200	108	.371	35	.407	124
Will Clark	.311	17	.298	31	.339	8	.275	61	.311	27	.254	67	.336	61	.615	50
Chili Davis	.260	81	.222	120	.242	109	.256	84	.273	66	.232	81	.330	69	.600	57
Jeffrey Leonard	.277	55	.290	43	.280	67	.281	42	.246	92	.231	82	.333	62	.514	90
Candy Maldonado	.278	53	.336	12	.241	110	.346	5	.296	42	.286	42	.375	31	.583	67
Bob Melvin	.210	127	.171	136	.175	134	.220	122	.214	114	.233	80	.176	137	.429	118
Eddie Milner	.248	94	.264	--	.236	112	.269	67	.282	--	.167	--	.309	96	.500	--
Kevin Mitchell	.293	32	.248	100	.291	48	.270	66	.301	34	.373	8	.344	54	.421	120
Chris Speier	.218	123	.311	22	.226	120	.272	65	.240	102	.235	77	.341	58	.692	20
Rob Thompson	.266	75	.250	96	.263	85	.260	80	.333	10	.452	2	.305	99	.333	133
Jose Uribe	.324	11	.229	114	.316	18	.266	72	.239	103	.147	128	.358	44	.500	91
Matt Williams	.198	132	.151	--	.179	133	.195	134	.159	131	.114	132	.273	120	.313	135
Team Average	.262	6	.256	10	.259	10	.261	5	.271	3	.248	5	.313	9	.497	12
League Average	.260		.261		.265		.256		.258		.241		.324		.554	

Pitching vs. Left and Right Handed Batters

		BA	Rank	SA	Rank	OBA	Rank	HR %	Rank	BB %	Rank	SO %	Rank
Kelly Downs	vs. Lefties	.278	75	.367	38	.339	57	1.18	19	8.14	28	16.06	40
	vs. Righties	.229	29	.362	32	.302	38	3.07	65	8.79	82	18.79	37
Dave Dravecky	vs. Lefties	.142	1	.245	3	.222	1	2.83	83	9.32	50	28.81	4
	vs. Righties	.279	90	.401	54	.338	82	2.45	40	7.76	53	15.23	70
Scott Garrelts	vs. Lefties	.180	4	.284	5	.283	9	2.06	52	12.39	95	29.65	2
	vs. Righties	.206	13	.341	22	.313	50	3.53	79	13.37	107	29.70	4
Atlee Hammaker	vs. Lefties	.168	2	.215	1	.258	4	0.93	11	9.17	46	20.00	19
	vs. Righties	.265	70	.420	69	.322	64	3.94	89	7.85	58	14.16	80
Mike Krukow	vs. Lefties	.313	103	.486	103	.371	93	3.74	103	8.74	40	12.85	62
	vs. Righties	.256	57	.435	84	.286	25	3.86	85	3.87	2	17.42	47
Mike LaCoss	vs. Lefties	.302	95	.466	93	.371	91	3.00	89	9.90	59	9.90	89
	vs. Righties	.257	60	.359	30	.314	51	1.76	18	7.01	41	12.10	97
Craig Lefferts	vs. Lefties	.228	19	.412	68	.264	6	4.39	106	4.10	4	20.49	15
	vs. Righties	.255	56	.409	64	.329	72	3.09	66	9.52	87	10.88	102
Rick Reuschel	vs. Lefties	.257	46	.390	52	.293	17	1.44	26	4.43	6	7.71	104
	vs. Righties	.223	23	.297	9	.267	15	1.63	16	4.74	7	16.71	55
Don Robinson	vs. Lefties	.242	34	.332	22	.317	37	0.90	10	9.96	60	17.93	31
	vs. Righties	.273	83	.433	82	.324	66	2.67	49	7.18	45	16.27	62
Team Average	vs. Lefties	.265	6	.394	6	.338	7	2.36	6	9.74	7	16.24	2
	vs. Righties	.247	2	.381	1	.311	3	2.86	4	8.10	6	17.12	7
League Average	vs. Lefties	.268		.404		.341		2.34		9.74		14.31	
	vs. Righties	.255		.403		.319		3.05		8.16		16.61	

Pitching with Runners on Base and Bases Empty

		BA	Rank	SA	Rank	OBA	Rank	HR %	Rank	BB %	Rank	SO %	Rank
Kelly Downs	Runners On	.277	79	.416	68	.348	76	2.58	61	8.81	34	17.90	27
	Bases Empty	.243	41	.326	12	.306	40	1.47	11	8.09	62	16.63	46
Dave Dravecky	Runners On	.267	66	.378	39	.332	50	2.43	53	8.73	32	18.37	24
	Bases Empty	.253	60	.378	52	.313	52	2.55	53	7.46	52	16.42	49
Scott Garrelts	Runners On	.201	4	.354	28	.307	18	4.27	102	13.07	100	26.63	4
	Bases Empty	.185	1	.275	3	.288	20	1.50	13	12.66	108	32.31	2
Atlee Hammaker	Runners On	.270	68	.397	57	.342	68	3.17	80	9.06	37	17.07	39
	Bases Empty	.235	29	.379	53	.291	24	3.61	87	7.40	51	13.84	81
Mike Krukow	Runners On	.301	101	.457	94	.351	83	3.13	79	7.72	20	14.43	61
	Bases Empty	.279	90	.467	96	.322	67	4.24	97	5.74	15	15.21	59
Mike LaCoss	Runners On	.270	70	.409	64	.351	84	2.55	58	10.87	75	10.25	99
	Bases Empty	.292	99	.427	84	.342	90	2.39	46	6.90	40	11.33	100
Craig Lefferts	Runners On	.243	29	.393	55	.335	58	2.89	70	11.65	87	14.08	66
	Bases Empty	.250	50	.425	83	.286	18	4.00	92	4.29	6	13.33	89
Rick Reuschel	Runners On	.255	48	.365	34	.290	9	1.78	32	5.09	3	8.85	107
	Bases Empty	.234	28	.340	18	.276	8	1.35	9	4.20	4	13.53	86
Don Robinson	Runners On	.273	74	.404	62	.335	57	1.52	24	8.77	33	17.54	32
	Bases Empty	.241	37	.354	26	.306	41	1.89	28	8.62	73	16.81	43
Team Average	Runners On	.261	4	.395	4	.334	3	2.71	7	9.68	5	16.55	3
	Bases Empty	.251	5	.381	4	.315	5	2.60	4	8.14	6	16.88	4
League Average	Runners On	.267		.410		.341		2.66		9.88		14.92	
	Bases Empty	.256		.399		.319		2.82		7.98		16.22	

Overall Pitching Compared to Late Inning Pressure Situations

		BA	Rank	SA	Rank	OBA	Rank	HR %	Rank	BB %	Rank	SO %	Rank
Kelly Downs	Overall	.258	59	.365	33	.324	53	1.95	25	8.41	47	17.19	36
	Pressure	.239	38	.310	18	.353	72	1.41	36	15.12	106	13.95	70
Dave Dravecky	Overall	.259	60	.378	46	.321	45	2.50	55	7.99	38	17.23	34
	Pressure	.268	65	.488	94	.375	89	7.32	108	14.00	99	24.00	14
Scott Garrelts	Overall	.192	1	.310	4	.297	13	2.75	65	12.85	111	29.67	2
	Pressure	.195	10	.307	17	.294	22	2.39	58	12.16	88	32.09	2
Atlee Hammaker	Overall	.248	43	.386	52	.312	32	3.44	88	8.07	40	15.16	59
	Pressure	.317	100	.415	75	.370	88	2.44	60	8.70	45	17.39	47
Mike Krukow	Overall	.288	102	.463	104	.334	78	3.79	99	6.58	12	14.88	63
	Pressure	.388	109	.653	108	.404	101	6.12	101	3.64	9	12.73	75
Mike LaCoss	Overall	.283	97	.419	73	.346	92	2.46	52	8.65	53	10.85	101
	Pressure	.277	76	.508	97	.415	102	4.62	92	19.05	109	9.52	97
Craig Lefferts	Overall	.247	39	.410	68	.310	31	3.49	90	7.93	37	13.70	75
	Pressure	.275	74	.487	93	.330	51	4.76	93	7.11	27	11.85	80
Joe Price	Overall	.154	--	.301	--	.241	--	4.07	--	9.49	--	30.66	--
	Pressure	.281	80	.688	110	.343	62	12.50	112	8.57	43	28.57	4
Rick Reuschel	Overall	.242	26	.350	23	.282	5	1.52	12	4.57	1	11.63	95
	Pressure	.224	24	.342	29	.294	22	2.63	65	6.98	25	16.28	56
Don Robinson	Overall	.256	56	.378	44	.320	43	1.71	20	8.70	55	17.17	37
	Pressure	.272	70	.416	76	.342	61	2.47	61	9.49	58	17.88	44
Team Average	Overall	.255	5	.387	4	.323	4	2.65	6	8.82	6	16.74	3
	Pressure	.246	2	.403	10	.336	6	3.45	11	11.65	12	19.72	2
League Average	Overall	.261		.404		.328		2.75		8.83		15.64	
	Pressure	.260		.391		.337		2.47		10.04		17.14	

Additional Miscellaneous Pitching Comparisons

	Grass Surface BA	Rank	Artificial Surface BA	Rank	Home Games BA	Rank	Road Games BA	Rank	Runners in Scoring Position BA	Rank	Runners in Scoring Pos and Two Outs BA	Rank	Leading Off Inning OBA	Rank
Kelly Downs	.245	34	.294	90	.238	31	.274	63	.241	41	.225	53	.326	65
Dave Dravecky	.239	28	.300	95	.240	33	.279	74	.256	62	.275	83	.316	49
Scott Garrelts	.179	2	.220	15	.200	9	.187	4	.204	13	.190	26	.347	86
Atlee Hammaker	.253	46	.236	20	.217	16	.292	89	.217	21	.229	57	.303	33
Mike Krukow	.282	84	.308	99	.275	87	.301	99	.257	63	.230	59	.384	102
Mike LaCoss	.284	88	.279	78	.266	73	.305	103	.246	50	.236	63	.385	103
Craig Lefferts	.221	15	.300	95	.204	12	.282	76	.225	30	.152	15	.333	71
Roger Mason	.303	103	.000	--	.212	--	.404	--	.276	--	.400	--	.500	--
Joe Price	.140	1	.217	--	.190	--	.136	--	.067	--	.125	--	.273	--
Rick Reuschel	.217	12	.258	52	.238	32	.247	37	.247	53	.197	31	.303	34
Don Robinson	.263	63	.251	41	.258	61	.254	46	.260	67	.203	36	.317	51
Team Average	.252	4	.263	6	.241	2	.269	9	.235	1	.212	2	.342	11
League Average	.260		.261		.256		.265		.258		.241		.324	
League Average	.260		.261		.256		.265		.258		.241		.324	

III
Batter Section

Batter Section

The Batter Section is an alphabetical listing of every player who had at least 200 plate appearances in either the American or the National League last season. Also included are key players who did not meet the 200-plate-appearance requirement. Players are listed alphabetically within each league, followed by the totals for each team and the league as a whole.

Column Headings Information

Tony Armas   Bats Right

Boston Red Sox	AB	H	2B	3B	HR	RRF	BB	SO	BA	SA	OBA

AB	At Bats
H	Hits
2B	Doubles
3B	Triples
HR	Home Runs
RRF	Runs Responsible For (See below)
BB	Bases on Balls
SO	Strikeouts
BA	Batting Average
SA	Slugging Average
OBA	On-Base Average

For each player, information is provided in eleven offensive categories. The only one that may be unfamiliar is RRF, *Runs Responsible For*. RRF includes official runs batted in, but also includes all other plays on which runners score following a batter's action, even if no RBI is officially given. (Examples include a runner scoring from third on a ground-ball double play, a runner scoring as a result of a fielder's error on a batted ball, or a batter hitting a triple and scoring on an error on the same play. Runs scored on such plays as a wild pitch or an error resulting from a pickoff attempt are not credited to the batter.)

Season Summary Information

Season	493	129	29	1	27	91	38	68	.262	.489	.341
vs. Left-Handed Pitchers	188	53	9	0	9	38	18	27	.282	.473	.366
vs. Right-Handed Pitchers	305	76	20	1	18	53	20	41	.249	.498	.326
Home	223	55	11	0	10	43	18	38	.247	.430	.325
Road	270	74	18	1	17	48	20	30	.274	.537	.354
Grass	409	106	26	0	21	79	33	57	.259	.477	.336
Artificial Turf	84	23	3	1	6	12	5	11	.274	.548	.365
April	74	16	6	0	3	7	0	9	.216	.419	.244
May	75	21	4	0	6	12	10	12	.280	.573	.386
June	87	23	3	0	7	24	11	9	.264	.540	.360
July	88	22	6	0	3	11	6	10	.250	.420	.316
August	98	25	4	1	5	21	7	14	.255	.469	.333
Sept./Oct.	71	22	6	0	3	16	4	14	.310	.521	.402

Each player's seasonal performance is broken down into a variety of special categories. The first line for each player gives his totals for the whole season. This is followed by breakdowns of his performance against left- and right-handed pitchers, in home and road games, on grass fields and on artificial turf, and in each month. (For players who played for more than one team within a league, all totals are combined. The "home" totals for Kevin Mitchell, for example, include all games he played in San Diego while with the Padres, and all games played in San Francisco while with the Giants.)

Leading Off Inn.	107	25	5	0	6	6	8	16	.234	.449	.311
Runners On	272	72	18	0	13	77	20	39	.265	.474	.343
Runners/Scor. Pos.	140	35	9	0	3	51	13	15	.250	.379	.337
Runners On/2 Out	133	29	6	0	5	26	11	19	.218	.376	.325
Scor. Pos./2 Out	60	11	2	0	0	12	7	7	.183	.217	.319

Following these breakdowns, each batter's performance is divided into specific game situations. Totals are given for each batter when he led off an inning and when he batted with runners on base. These are followed by his performance with runners in scoring position (on second or third base, or both), with runners on base and two out, and with runners in scoring position and two out.

Late Inning Pressure	90	23	6	1	3	13	5	13	.256	.444	.299
Bases Empty	42	12	5	1	2	2	1	7	.286	.595	.318
Runners On	48	11	1	0	1	11	4	6	.229	.313	.283
Runners/Scor. Pos.	26	7	1	0	1	11	3	2	.269	.423	.333

The next group shows the batter's performance in late-inning pressure situations: any plate appearances occurring in the seventh inning or later with the score tied or with the batter's team trailing by one, two, or three runs (or four runs if the bases are loaded).

Each player's totals are listed for all late-inning pressure situations, then broken out for his performance when leading off an inning, with runners on base, and with runners in scoring position.

DRIVING IN RUNS	From 1B	From 2B	From 3B	Scoring Position
Total	6/138	14/80	21/57	35/137
Percentage	4%	18%	37%	26%
Driving In Runners from 3B with Less than Two Out:			15/30	50%

The next section, labeled "Driving In Runs," is a measure of the player's ability to drive in runners from each base. For every base, two numbers are listed: the first is the number of RRFs credited to the batter for bringing home runners from that base; the second is the total number of opportunities the batter faced for that situation. (For example, the notation "14/31" under runners on second would mean that the player batted 31 times with runners on second and drove home 14 of the runners.) Plate appearances that result in a base on balls, hit batsman, sacrifice bunt, or an award of first base through catcher's interference are not treated as "opportunities" if they do not result in a run.

If there is more than one runner on base, the batter is charged with an "opportunity" to drive in each base runner. A single with the bases loaded that scores only the runner from third is an opportunity and an RRF for the "From 3B" line, but an unsuccessful opportunity for the "From 2B" and "From 1B" lines. (The exception to this is when a base on balls, hit batsman, sacrifice bunt, or award through interference results in a run. A walk with the bases loaded would result in an RRF and an opportunity for the "From 3B" line, but would not be charged as an unsuccessful opportunity for the other two.)

Also given is the percentage of successful opportunities; runners driven in from scoring position (combining the "From 3B" and "From 2B" totals); and a line summarizing the batter's performance driving in runners from third with less than two out.

Following the "Driving In Runs" information are comments for each player. Included are the pitchers each batter loves to face and hates to face. The statistics listed for each individual match-up are from regular season games since 1975.

American League

Harold Baines

Chicago White Sox   Bats Left

	AB	H	2B	3B	HR	RRF	BB	SO	BA	SA	OBA
Season	505	148	26	4	20	97	46	82	.293	.479	.352
vs. Left-Handers	181	46	8	1	6	25	13	45	.254	.409	.308
vs. Right-Handers	324	102	18	3	14	72	33	37	.315	.519	.376
Home	253	79	15	3	12	54	16	37	.312	.538	.353
Road	252	69	11	1	8	43	30	45	.274	.421	.351
Grass	438	130	22	3	18	86	37	72	.297	.484	.351
Artificial Turf	67	18	4	1	2	11	9	10	.269	.448	.355
April	4	2	1	0	0	2	1	0	.500	.750	.600
May	84	25	3	0	3	17	9	21	.298	.440	.366
June	99	26	2	2	7	19	13	11	.263	.535	.354
July	105	36	6	0	6	22	10	16	.343	.571	.400
August	97	19	5	1	1	16	8	18	.196	.299	.255
Sept./Oct.	116	40	9	1	3	21	5	16	.345	.517	.369
Leading Off Inn.	99	24	2	0	0	0	8	14	.242	.263	.299
Runners On	216	73	17	2	13	90	21	35	.338	.616	.396
Runners/Scor. Pos.	133	46	9	2	7	73	17	21	.346	.602	.414
Runners On/2 Out	71	23	7	0	3	29	11	15	.324	.549	.415
Scor. Pos./2 Out	45	15	4	0	2	24	10	8	.333	.556	.455
Late Inning Pressure	71	22	4	1	2	7	8	9	.310	.479	.380
Leading Off	17	5	0	0	0	0	2	2	.294	.294	.368
Runners On	25	8	2	1	1	6	4	4	.320	.600	.414
Runners/Scor. Pos.	10	3	0	1	1	5	3	1	.300	.800	.462

DRIVING IN RUNS	From 1B	From 2B	From 3B	Scoring Position
Totals	14/127	31/99	32/54	63/153
Percentage	11%	31%	59%	41%
Driving In Runners from 3B with Less than Two Out:		25/35		71%

Loves to face: Eric Plunk (.833, 5-for-6)
Hates to face: Mark Langston (.125, 3-for-24)
Only player in the majors with 20+ HR and a batting average of .280+ in each of last five seasons.... Those 20 home runs boosted his career total to 160, breaking old Chisox mark of 154 by Bill Melton; only three franchises, all from expansion era, have lower records: Mets (156), Blue Jays (156), Mariners (89).... Needs 13 home runs to break Bill Melton's record of 90 at Comiskey Park. Baines has averaged 12 HR a year at Comiskey since 1982.... Only player to hit at least .320 with runners on base in each of the last four seasons (minimum: 100 AB in each). Year by year since 1984: .322, .337, .322, .338.... Drove in 41.2 percent of runners from scoring position, highest rate of his career (career average: 33.2%).

Chris Bando

Cleveland Indians   Bats Left and Right

	AB	H	2B	3B	HR	RRF	BB	SO	BA	SA	OBA
Season	211	46	9	0	5	17	12	28	.218	.332	.260
vs. Left-Handers	51	9	0	0	0	0	2	6	.176	.176	.208
vs. Right-Handers	160	37	9	0	5	17	10	22	.231	.381	.276
Home	103	24	3	0	2	8	6	12	.233	.320	.275
Road	108	22	6	0	3	9	6	16	.204	.343	.246
Grass	170	34	7	0	3	13	10	21	.200	.294	.244
Artificial Turf	41	12	2	0	2	4	2	7	.293	.488	.326
April	29	6	2	0	0	1	3	6	.207	.276	.281
May	27	5	0	0	1	1	2	5	.185	.296	.241
June	51	12	0	0	2	8	2	5	.235	.353	.264
July	39	7	2	0	0	3	1	6	.179	.231	.200
August	29	9	3	0	1	3	1	2	.310	.517	.333
Sept./Oct.	36	7	2	0	1	1	3	4	.194	.333	.256
Leading Off Inn.	59	14	5	0	2	2	2	11	.237	.424	.262
Runners On	80	18	2	0	2	14	4	11	.225	.325	.262
Runners/Scor. Pos.	43	6	1	0	0	10	3	9	.140	.163	.196
Runners On/2 Out	31	9	0	0	2	8	3	3	.290	.484	.353
Scor. Pos./2 Out	16	4	0	0	0	4	2	3	.250	.250	.333
Late Inning Pressure	22	4	1	0	1	1	3	2	.182	.364	.280
Leading Off	7	2	1	0	0	0	0	2	.286	.429	.286
Runners On	9	1	0	0	0	0	2	0	.111	.111	.273
Runners/Scor. Pos.	5	0	0	0	0	0	2	0	.000	.000	.286

DRIVING IN RUNS	From 1B	From 2B	From 3B	Scoring Position
Totals	2/64	7/39	3/10	10/49
Percentage	3%	18%	30%	20%
Driving In Runners from 3B with Less than Two Out:		3/7		43%

Loves to face: Les Straker (.800, 4-for-5, 1 HR)
Hates to face: Roger Clemens (0-for-11, 6 SO)
Opponents were successful on 67 percent of stolen-base attempts in 1987 (A.L. average was 69 percent); but he was the best in A.L. at throwing out the league's *best* runners: the 13 players who stole 30+ bases last season, a group that had an overall success rate of 79 percent, was only 11-for-17 (65 percent) against Bando—a worse rate than less notable runners had.... Home run off Frank Viola in September 1986 is only one against a lefty in last three seasons; didn't have any extra-base hits in 51 at bats vs. left-handers in 1987. ... Has hit for higher average in home games than in road games in each of seven seasons in majors.... Career batting average of .340 outside the United States; OK, that means Toronto.

Steve Balboni

Kansas City Royals   Bats Right

	AB	H	2B	3B	HR	RRF	BB	SO	BA	SA	OBA
Season	386	80	11	1	24	61	34	97	.207	.427	.273
vs. Left-Handers	103	20	1	0	6	11	10	27	.194	.379	.265
vs. Right-Handers	283	60	10	1	18	50	24	70	.212	.445	.276
Home	190	36	6	0	8	23	16	49	.189	.347	.255
Road	196	44	5	1	16	38	18	48	.224	.505	.290
Grass	146	33	3	1	13	29	11	34	.226	.527	.277
Artificial Turf	240	47	8	0	11	32	23	63	.196	.367	.271
April	58	9	1	0	2	6	5	10	.155	.276	.222
May	91	19	3	0	5	12	8	23	.209	.407	.273
June	71	18	3	0	4	11	6	12	.254	.465	.329
July	23	4	0	0	1	4	2	6	.174	.304	.231
August	74	20	3	0	6	13	8	19	.270	.554	.341
Sept./Oct.	69	10	1	1	6	15	5	27	.145	.449	.197
Leading Off Inn.	68	10	1	0	2	2	6	20	.147	.250	.216
Runners On	190	41	8	1	11	48	13	43	.216	.442	.262
Runners/Scor. Pos.	108	20	4	0	6	35	8	28	.185	.389	.235
Runners On/2 Out	91	23	5	1	8	29	7	18	.253	.593	.306
Scor. Pos./2 Out	58	10	3	0	4	19	4	15	.172	.431	.226
Late Inning Pressure	61	12	0	0	6	12	2	17	.197	.492	.219
Leading Off	14	1	0	0	1	1	0	4	.071	.286	.071
Runners On	27	6	0	0	3	9	1	8	.222	.556	.241
Runners/Scor. Pos.	16	2	0	0	2	7	1	5	.125	.500	.167

DRIVING IN RUNS	From 1B	From 2B	From 3B	Scoring Position
Totals	13/137	10/86	14/48	24/134
Percentage	9%	12%	29%	18%
Driving In Runners from 3B with Less than Two Out:		8/25		32%

Loves to face: Walt Terrell (.500, 12-for-24, 4 HR)
Hates to face: Willie Fraser (0-for-9, 4 SO)
Batting average vs. right-handed pitchers was .212 in both 1986 and 1987, but his average against southpaws dropped from .276 to .194. ... Hitless in 31 consecutive at bats from April 19 to May 2.... Hit his first home run for Yankees in 1983, and in every season since then has hit more home runs on the road than he has in his home ballpark.... Hitless in 10 consecutive pinch-hit at bats between pinch-hit HR on July 8 and Sept. 10.... Drove in 32 percent of runners from third base with less than two out, 2d-lowest rate in A.L. last season (minimum: 15 opportunities).... Pinch ran for Bill Pecota on April 24. Did you know that Harmon Killebrew made his major-league debut as a pinch-runner?

Jesse Barfield

Toronto Blue Jays   Bats Right

	AB	H	2B	3B	HR	RRF	BB	SO	BA	SA	OBA
Season	590	155	25	3	28	86	58	141	.263	.458	.331
vs. Left-Handers	177	53	9	2	9	22	23	43	.299	.525	.380
vs. Right-Handers	413	102	16	1	19	64	35	98	.247	.429	.309
Home	302	92	18	2	11	41	31	59	.305	.487	.371
Road	288	63	7	1	17	45	27	82	.219	.427	.288
Grass	222	51	5	0	17	42	23	63	.230	.482	.302
Artificial Turf	368	104	20	3	11	44	35	78	.283	.443	.348
April	71	20	6	0	5	11	6	4	.282	.577	.407
May	97	26	2	0	7	14	11	23	.268	.505	.349
June	112	34	3	1	7	25	5	25	.304	.536	.328
July	100	23	3	0	2	10	11	25	.230	.320	.313
August	98	17	2	1	6	13	7	31	.173	.398	.229
Sept./Oct.	112	35	9	1	1	13	10	21	.313	.438	.369
Leading Off Inn.	115	30	5	1	6	6	4	29	.261	.478	.286
Runners On	261	67	12	2	8	66	34	55	.257	.410	.342
Runners/Scor. Pos.	153	36	5	1	5	56	27	33	.235	.379	.346
Runners On/2 Out	104	25	6	0	3	26	20	25	.240	.385	.363
Scor. Pos./2 Out	63	14	2	0	3	24	16	16	.222	.397	.380
Late Inning Pressure	96	27	5	0	3	14	9	22	.281	.427	.349
Leading Off	23	7	2	0	1	1	1	5	.304	.522	.333
Runners On	35	9	2	0	1	12	6	6	.257	.400	.381
Runners/Scor. Pos.	22	7	1	0	1	11	6	5	.318	.500	.464

DRIVING IN RUNS	From 1B	From 2B	From 3B	Scoring Position
Totals	11/182	23/113	24/63	47/176
Percentage	6%	20%	38%	27%
Driving In Runners from 3B with Less than Two Out:		16/36		44%

Loves to face: Dave Schmidt (.538, 7-for-13, 1 HR)
Hates to face: Bob Stoddard (0-for-9, 6 SO)
It was reported last July that Don Mattingly set an A.L. record with extra-base hits in 10 games in a row. We don't know what the record is, but we know Mattingly didn't set it because Barfield had extra-base hits in 11 straight games in 1985.... One of five players with six consecutive hits with two outs and runners on in 1987. Odd that he hit only .240 for season in those situations.... Only 27 HR at home, 41 on road over last two years; from 1982 to 1985, he hit 59 at home, 29 on road.... California dreamin'? Career averages of .191 at Anaheim and .195 at Oakland, only parks in which he's below .200.... Led outfielders with 59 assists from April 1985 to October 1987. Manute Bol had 34 assists during that period.

Marty Barrett
Boston Red Sox — Bats Right

	AB	H	2B	3B	HR	RRF	BB	SO	BA	SA	OBA
Season	559	164	23	0	3	46	51	38	.293	.351	.351
vs. Left-Handers	150	52	5	0	2	18	18	4	.347	.420	.412
vs. Right-Handers	409	112	18	0	1	28	33	34	.274	.325	.327
Home	274	80	15	0	2	19	24	18	.292	.369	.350
Road	285	84	8	0	1	27	27	20	.295	.333	.351
Grass	487	142	20	0	3	37	42	37	.292	.351	.348
Artificial Turf	72	22	3	0	0	9	9	1	.306	.347	.369
April	32	6	0	0	0	5	1	3	.188	.188	.235
May	92	18	2	0	1	6	11	10	.196	.250	.282
June	112	34	4	0	1	9	13	7	.304	.384	.373
July	93	30	3	0	0	8	10	6	.323	.355	.381
August	106	29	5	0	0	7	10	5	.274	.321	.336
Sept./Oct.	124	47	7	0	1	11	6	7	.379	.460	.402
Leading Off Inn.	102	26	6	0	0	0	6	9	.255	.314	.296
Runners On	206	71	9	0	2	45	32	11	.345	.417	.426
Runners/Scor. Pos.	110	33	2	0	2	44	28	9	.300	.373	.431
Runners On/2 Out	83	24	3	0	1	16	16	6	.289	.361	.422
Scor. Pos./2 Out	54	13	1	0	1	15	15	6	.241	.315	.414
Late Inning Pressure	66	18	2	0	0	6	12	4	.273	.303	.385
Leading Off	14	3	0	0	0	0	2	2	.214	.214	.313
Runners On	26	11	2	0	0	6	7	1	.423	.500	.545
Runners/Scor. Pos.	17	5	0	0	0	6	6	0	.294	.294	.478

DRIVING IN RUNS	From 1B	From 2B	From 3B	Scoring Position
Totals	4/148	15/103	24/39	39/142
Percentage	3%	15%	62%	27%
Driving In Runners from 3B with Less than Two Out:			19/26	73%

Loves to face: Dave Stewart (.556, 10-for-18, 1 HR)
Hates to face: Jack Morris (.069, 2-for-29)
Led majors with 22 sacrifice bunts last season; he also won the inter-sport competition in sacs, by one, over Eagles' Reggie White. . . . Averaged one strikeout every 16.8 plate appearances last season, 3d-best in A.L. . . . Stole 15 of 17 bases in 1987, 5th-best rate (.882) in A.L. (minimum: 10 SB). . . . Batting average after Sept. 1 was 3d-highest in A.L. . . . Averaged 3.31 assists per nine innings, highest rate among A.L. second basemen (minimum: 500 innings). . . . Career ratio of 3.12 walks per strikeout vs. left-handers is best in majors since we've been keeping track (minimum: 500 PA since 1975). . . . Batted .529 vs. Orioles last season, only player in A.L. to hit .500+ against any one team.

Don Baylor
Red Sox/Twins — Bats Right

	AB	H	2B	3B	HR	RRF	BB	SO	BA	SA	OBA
Season	388	95	9	0	16	63	45	59	.245	.392	.360
vs. Left-Handers	135	36	1	0	6	23	12	15	.267	.407	.353
vs. Right-Handers	253	59	8	0	10	40	33	44	.233	.383	.363
Home	183	49	3	0	10	39	17	31	.268	.448	.376
Road	205	46	6	0	6	24	28	28	.224	.341	.346
Grass	288	70	3	0	14	54	40	41	.243	.399	.374
Artificial Turf	100	25	6	0	2	9	5	18	.250	.370	.312
April	77	19	4	0	4	13	13	15	.247	.455	.376
May	90	18	2	0	5	12	12	11	.200	.389	.327
June	90	27	1	0	5	17	9	10	.300	.478	.407
July	46	7	1	0	1	6	4	4	.152	.239	.222
August	36	10	0	0	1	9	2	7	.278	.361	.409
Sept./Oct.	49	14	1	0	0	6	5	12	.286	.306	.397
Leading Off Inn.	91	21	1	0	7	7	8	7	.231	.473	.340
Runners On	182	50	6	0	8	55	24	31	.275	.440	.392
Runners/Scor. Pos.	113	35	3	0	7	53	17	15	.310	.522	.436
Runners On/2 Out	73	18	1	0	3	22	10	9	.247	.384	.396
Scor. Pos./2 Out	52	16	0	0	3	22	7	4	.308	.481	.446
Late Inning Pressure	61	15	3	0	1	4	8	9	.246	.344	.351
Leading Off	15	5	1	0	1	1	4	1	.333	.600	.500
Runners On	28	6	1	0	0	3	4	3	.214	.250	.333
Runners/Scor. Pos.	11	1	0	0	0	3	3	0	.091	.091	.333

DRIVING IN RUNS	From 1B	From 2B	From 3B	Scoring Position
Totals	6/139	19/94	22/49	41/143
Percentage	4%	20%	45%	29%
Driving In Runners from 3B with Less than Two Out:			16/29	55%

Loves to face: Mike Flanagan (.392, 20-for-51, 6 HR)
Hates to face: Ken Dixon (.105, 2-for-19)
Leaning into more pitches than ever before, here are his career hit-by-pitch totals, broken into four-year segments: 1972–75: 45; 1976–79: 61; 1980–83: 38; 1984–87: 110 (he also had one in his only game in 1971). . . . One of two players on Twins World Series roster who are older than Tom Kelly; Joe Niekro is the other, and that doesn't even count Steve Carlton, ineligible for the Series. . . . Has now played in six A.L. Championship Series with four different clubs (Baltimore, California, Boston, and Minnesota). . . . Had five steals last season, leaving him 15 shy of 300 mark for his career; if he gets the 15, he would join Bobby Bonds and Willie Mays as the only members of the 300/300 Club for career HR and SB.

George Bell
Toronto Blue Jays — Bats Right

	AB	H	2B	3B	HR	RRF	BB	SO	BA	SA	OBA
Season	610	188	32	4	47	137	39	75	.308	.605	.352
vs. Left-Handers	175	60	8	2	16	47	12	25	.343	.686	.385
vs. Right-Handers	435	128	24	2	31	90	27	50	.294	.572	.339
Home	302	88	13	3	19	57	23	41	.291	.543	.346
Road	308	100	19	1	28	80	16	34	.325	.666	.357
Grass	244	76	14	0	22	64	15	28	.311	.639	.351
Artificial Turf	366	112	18	4	25	73	24	47	.306	.582	.353
April	79	20	5	1	5	13	4	10	.253	.532	.306
May	105	37	4	2	11	31	1	14	.352	.743	.352
June	110	30	3	0	11	27	9	19	.273	.600	.322
July	93	31	4	0	5	16	5	11	.333	.538	.363
August	106	34	10	0	9	28	9	8	.321	.670	.376
Sept./Oct.	117	36	6	1	6	22	11	13	.308	.530	.379
Leading Off Inn.	164	56	13	3	13	13	9	20	.341	.695	.386
Runners On	300	91	13	1	21	111	26	36	.303	.563	.355
Runners/Scor. Pos.	176	56	10	1	10	89	19	18	.318	.557	.368
Runners On/2 Out	148	42	7	0	10	45	17	21	.284	.534	.365
Scor. Pos./2 Out	84	21	5	0	5	35	12	12	.250	.488	.344
Late Inning Pressure	95	30	5	1	5	16	5	8	.316	.547	.353
Leading Off	30	10	3	1	0	0	1	1	.333	.500	.355
Runners On	44	12	2	0	4	15	4	5	.273	.591	.327
Runners/Scor. Pos.	24	8	2	0	2	11	4	2	.333	.667	.414

DRIVING IN RUNS	From 1B	From 2B	From 3B	Scoring Position
Totals	21/211	35/125	34/81	69/206
Percentage	10%	28%	42%	33%
Driving In Runners from 3B with Less than Two Out:			25/39	64%

Loves to face: Scott Bankhead (.533, 8-for-15, 4 HR)
Hates to face: Mark Clear (.071, 1-for-14)
In last year's *Analyst* we told you that he had no home runs in 99 career at bats at Yankee Stadium. So in '87, Bell hits four home runs there, more than any visiting player; also led Kingdome visitors with five HR. . . . Has batted .458 (11-for-24) with the bases loaded since 1985, including five grand slams; has never drawn a walk in 42 career plate appearances with the bags full. . . . Career batting average of .304 in Late-Inning Pressure Situations, and .343 in LIPS with runners in scoring position. . . . Led A.L. left fielders with 14 assists, but averaged only 1.76 putouts per nine innings, 3d-lowest among A.L. left fielders (minimum: 500 innings). . . . First league MVP from a Canadian club.

Juan Beniquez
Royals/Blue Jays — Bats Right

	AB	H	2B	3B	HR	RRF	BB	SO	BA	SA	OBA
Season	255	64	12	1	8	47	16	39	.251	.400	.297
vs. Left-Handers	116	31	8	0	6	26	6	16	.267	.491	.306
vs. Right-Handers	139	33	4	1	2	21	10	23	.237	.324	.289
Home	112	26	6	1	2	21	7	16	.232	.357	.279
Road	143	38	6	0	6	26	9	23	.266	.434	.312
Grass	120	33	5	0	6	25	7	18	.275	.467	.318
Artificial Turf	135	31	7	1	2	22	9	21	.230	.341	.279
April	28	7	1	0	0	5	4	6	.250	.286	.344
May	82	22	5	0	2	14	4	9	.268	.402	.303
June	40	6	1	0	1	4	2	6	.150	.250	.190
July	39	10	1	0	1	7	2	8	.256	.359	.310
August	25	10	2	0	2	6	1	4	.400	.720	.423
Sept./Oct.	41	9	2	1	2	11	3	6	.220	.463	.267
Leading Off Inn.	50	11	1	0	2	2	6	10	.220	.304	.304
Runners On	122	35	8	1	4	43	6	19	.287	.467	.323
Runners/Scor. Pos.	66	21	6	1	3	40	3	12	.318	.576	.342
Runners On/2 Out	41	12	1	0	2	14	3	4	.293	.463	.341
Scor. Pos./2 Out	25	7	0	0	2	13	1	4	.280	.520	.308
Late Inning Pressure	45	11	0	1	1	10	2	9	.244	.356	.292
Leading Off	10	0	0	0	0	0	0	3	.000	.000	.000
Runners On	23	8	0	1	1	10	2	3	.348	.565	.423
Runners/Scor. Pos.	13	5	0	1	1	10	1	2	.385	.769	.429

DRIVING IN RUNS	From 1B	From 2B	From 3B	Scoring Position
Totals	5/98	16/50	18/32	34/82
Percentage	5%	32%	56%	41%
Driving In Runners from 3B with Less than Two Out:			15/18	83%

Loves to face: Curt Young (.471, 8-for-17, 1 HR)
Hates to face: Charlie Hough (.071, 1-for-14, 1 HR)
One of two A.L. players to start at six different positions. The other was Jim Morrison, who started at six positions in less than two months for Sparky. . . . Percentage of runners driven in from third base with less than two out was highest in A.L. last season (minimum: 10 RRF). . . . First player in history to play for eight different A.L. clubs. . . . Over the past ten years he hit 65 points higher on grass fields than on artificial turf, largest difference in the majors (minimum: 500 career AB on both). . . . The only A.L. player to hit at least 25 points higher vs. left-handers than vs. right-handers in each of the past six seasons. Floyd Rayford and Bob Forsch have streaks of seven seasons, including time in N.L.

Todd Benzinger

Boston Red Sox — Bats Left and Right

	AB	H	2B	3B	HR	RRF	BB	SO	BA	SA	OBA
Season	223	62	11	1	8	44	22	41	.278	.444	.344
vs. Left-Handers	80	26	4	0	2	18	7	12	.325	.450	.371
vs. Right-Handers	143	36	7	1	6	26	15	29	.252	.441	.329
Home	106	33	6	1	5	22	14	18	.311	.528	.390
Road	117	29	5	0	3	22	8	23	.248	.368	.299
Grass	199	56	9	1	8	43	21	35	.281	.457	.351
Artificial Turf	24	6	2	0	0	1	1	6	.250	.333	.280
April	0	0	0	0	0	0	0	0	—	—	—
May	0	0	0	0	0	0	0	0	—	—	—
June	29	9	1	0	0	7	7	3	.310	.345	.459
July	30	8	2	0	1	4	2	10	.267	.433	.313
August	48	8	1	0	0	6	5	10	.167	.188	.241
Sept./Oct.	116	37	7	1	7	27	8	18	.319	.578	.362
Leading Off Inn.	55	13	3	0	1	1	1	14	.236	.345	.250
Runners On	104	26	4	1	6	42	15	17	.250	.481	.341
Runners/Scor. Pos.	69	17	2	0	3	34	12	13	.246	.406	.353
Runners On/2 Out	35	10	0	0	3	17	5	5	.286	.543	.390
Scor. Pos./2 Out	26	9	0	0	3	17	4	3	.346	.692	.452
Late Inning Pressure	32	7	0	0	1	5	3	9	.219	.313	.286
Leading Off	9	1	0	0	0	0	1	4	.111	.111	.200
Runners On	17	3	0	0	1	5	0	3	.176	.353	.176
Runners/Scor. Pos.	11	1	0	0	0	3	0	2	.091	.091	.091

DRIVING IN RUNS	From 1B	From 2B	From 3B	Scoring Position
Totals	7/81	11/55	18/40	29/95
Percentage	9%	20%	45%	31%
Driving In Runners from 3B with Less than Two Out:		13/26		50%

Loves to face: Jerry Reuss (3-for-3)
Hates to face: Bert Blyleven (0-for-4, 4 SO)
Started 30 of 33 games for the Red Sox after Sept. 1 and drove in 26 runs during that period, 2d-most in A.L. to Don Mattingly's 28. . . . Started 45 games in right field, five in center, five in left, and one game at first base. . . . Didn't have a streak of more than 11 at bats without a hit. . . . Batted .313 (5-for-16, one HR) with the bases loaded. . . . Drew only one walk in the 56 innings that he led off. That qualifies as patient if you're Garth Iorg, who was 0-for-70. At other times, Benzinger's rate was one BB for every 9.4 plate appearances. . . . Oldest of the Red Sox' crew of 1987 rookies, celebrated his 25th birthday this past winter. One day younger than Mets' Lenny Dykstra, three days older than John Marzano.

Dave Bergman

Detroit Tigers — Bats Left

	AB	H	2B	3B	HR	RRF	BB	SO	BA	SA	OBA
Season	172	47	7	3	6	23	30	23	.273	.453	.379
vs. Left-Handers	19	5	0	0	0	2	0	4	.263	.263	.263
vs. Right-Handers	153	42	7	3	6	21	30	19	.275	.477	.390
Home	85	26	3	0	4	10	13	15	.306	.482	.394
Road	87	21	4	3	2	13	17	8	.241	.425	.364
Grass	151	42	7	2	6	20	28	20	.278	.470	.387
Artificial Turf	21	5	0	1	0	3	2	3	.238	.333	.320
April	27	10	0	0	3	6	7	2	.370	.704	.486
May	28	7	1	0	1	3	4	3	.250	.393	.364
June	13	4	1	1	0	0	6	2	.308	.538	.526
July	24	7	1	0	1	1	5	7	.292	.458	.414
August	48	15	4	2	1	8	7	4	.313	.542	.393
Sept./Oct.	32	4	0	0	0	5	1	5	.125	.125	.147
Leading Off Inn.	43	7	3	0	0	0	9	6	.163	.233	.308
Runners On	72	19	3	0	2	19	14	9	.264	.389	.378
Runners/Scor. Pos.	43	9	2	0	1	17	9	6	.209	.326	.339
Runners On/2 Out	41	8	1	0	1	9	7	6	.195	.293	.327
Scor. Pos./2 Out	30	6	1	0	0	7	6	4	.200	.233	.351
Late Inning Pressure	27	7	0	0	2	4	3	6	.259	.481	.323
Leading Off	3	0	0	0	0	0	2	1	.000	.000	.400
Runners On	14	2	0	0	0	2	1	3	.143	.143	.188
Runners/Scor. Pos.	9	1	0	0	0	2	0	2	.111	.111	.100

DRIVING IN RUNS	From 1B	From 2B	From 3B	Scoring Position
Totals	3/58	7/36	7/18	14/54
Percentage	5%	19%	39%	26%
Driving In Runners from 3B with Less than Two Out:		6/9		67%

Loves to face: Ken Schrom (.571, 4-for-7, 1 HR)
Hates to face: Oil Can Boyd (0-for-10)
Batted .329 in day games, .232 at night. . . . Started 41 games last season, all against right-handers. Has never batted more than 28 times in one season vs. southpaws. In four years under Sparky he has faced left-handers only 63 times. Two career HR vs. lefties were both hit off of Gary Lucas (1982 and 1983). . . . Batting average of .153 with runners in scoring position since 1985. . . . Career batting average of .423 (11-for-26) with the bases loaded. Most plate appearances among active players who have never struck out with the bags full (40). . . . Made his major-league debut for Billy Martin's 1975 Yankees. Hitless in 17 at bats for that club. . . . Career average of .415 (17-for-41, 1 HR) at Cleveland Stadium.

Tony Bernazard

Indians/As — Bats Left and Right

	AB	H	2B	3B	HR	RRF	BB	SO	BA	SA	OBA
Season	507	127	26	2	14	49	55	79	.250	.393	.323
vs. Left-Handers	139	32	7	1	4	16	19	22	.230	.381	.323
vs. Right-Handers	368	95	19	1	10	33	36	57	.258	.397	.324
Home	227	54	12	1	3	16	24	31	.238	.339	.313
Road	280	73	14	1	11	33	31	48	.261	.436	.331
Grass	410	102	23	1	7	37	50	66	.249	.361	.330
Artificial Turf	97	25	3	1	7	12	5	13	.258	.526	.291
April	73	16	5	0	2	8	2	8	.219	.370	.240
May	91	17	1	0	4	5	6	22	.187	.330	.245
June	85	24	3	1	5	14	11	15	.282	.518	.361
July	91	31	8	0	1	6	10	13	.341	.462	.402
August	99	27	7	0	1	15	17	12	.273	.404	.376
Sept./Oct.	68	12	2	1	0	1	9	9	.176	.235	.273
Leading Off Inn.	146	26	4	1	3	3	10	27	.178	.281	.231
Runners On	192	47	9	0	3	38	31	34	.245	.339	.345
Runners/Scor. Pos.	106	23	6	0	2	34	22	20	.217	.330	.344
Runners On/2 Out	85	19	5	0	2	21	12	18	.224	.353	.320
Scor. Pos./2 Out	60	11	3	0	1	18	9	13	.183	.283	.290
Late Inning Pressure	56	17	6	0	2	5	10	13	.304	.518	.409
Leading Off	16	4	2	0	0	0	2	2	.250	.375	.333
Runners On	18	3	0	0	0	3	5	6	.167	.167	.348
Runners/Scor. Pos.	9	3	0	0	0	3	4	3	.333	.333	.538

DRIVING IN RUNS	From 1B	From 2B	From 3B	Scoring Position
Totals	5/138	16/83	14/45	30/128
Percentage	4%	19%	31%	23%
Driving In Runners from 3B with Less than Two Out:		8/16		50%

Loves to face: Bob Stanley (.524, 11-for-21)
Hates to face: Dan Petry (.122, 5-for-41, 1 HR)
Lowest fielding percentage (.971) of any second baseman in majors last season (minimum: 100 games); 3d-lowest average of assists per nine innings (2.66). . . . One home run in 173 at bats in day games, 13 home runs (one per 25.7 AB) at night. . . . Failed to reach base safely in 32 consecutive innings that he led off (April 15 to May 24), longest streak in the majors last season. . . . Career batting average of .207 with runners in scoring position in Late-Inning Pressure Situations. . . . Has homered at every A.L. ballpark except Arlington Stadium (135 career AB). . . . The least likely of 17 players who have stolen more than 10 bases and hit more than 10 home runs in each of the past three seasons.

Wade Boggs

Boston Red Sox — Bats Left

	AB	H	2B	3B	HR	RRF	BB	SO	BA	SA	OBA
Season	551	200	40	6	24	92	105	48	.363	.588	.461
vs. Left-Handers	169	56	11	2	7	38	20	14	.331	.544	.403
vs. Right-Handers	382	144	29	4	17	54	85	34	.377	.607	.484
Home	282	116	28	3	10	51	53	24	.411	.638	.500
Road	269	84	12	3	14	41	52	24	.312	.535	.421
Grass	452	167	33	5	17	73	91	41	.369	.577	.471
Artificial Turf	99	33	7	1	7	19	14	7	.333	.636	.412
April	80	22	2	0	5	16	7	5	.275	.375	.392
May	98	38	8	0	7	22	16	14	.388	.684	.466
June	101	49	8	4	4	19	22	5	.485	.762	.581
July	111	36	11	2	5	20	12	9	.324	.595	.392
August	93	32	4	0	3	12	22	8	.344	.484	.462
Sept./Oct.	68	23	7	0	3	14	17	5	.338	.574	.460
Leading Off Inn.	130	48	8	0	8		21	14	.369	.615	.457
Runners On	229	82	14	3	11	79	60	16	.358	.590	.480
Runners/Scor. Pos.	129	43	12	1	4	63	50	11	.333	.535	.500
Runners On/2 Out	83	23	5	1	2	21	21	8	.277	.434	.429
Scor. Pos./2 Out	55	16	5	0	1	18	19	6	.291	.436	.480
Late Inning Pressure	76	19	3	1	1	10	14	8	.250	.355	.363
Leading Off	19	4	0	0	0	3	3	1	.211	.211	.318
Runners On	34	10	2	0	0	9	7	2	.294	.353	.405
Runners/Scor. Pos.	23	6	1	0	0	9	6	1	.261	.304	.400

DRIVING IN RUNS	From 1B	From 2B	From 3B	Scoring Position
Totals	14/168	21/100	33/57	54/157
Percentage	8%	21%	58%	34%
Driving In Runners from 3B with Less than Two Out:		27/36		75%

Loves to face: Bret Saberhagen (.500, 11-for-22, 1 HR)
Hates to face: Matt Young (.053, 1-for-19)
Here's a man who knows when to quit. He rested for the final regular-season series in 1986, and in the process held on to the A.L. batting crown. In 1987, he missed Boston's final 10 games with a knee injury, but played through the injury long enough to reach the 200-hit mark for the fifth consecutive season. . . . Percentage of runners driven in from scoring position has decreased in each season since 1985: .372, .368, .338. . . . Batted .424 vs. right-handed pitchers at Fenway Park, raising his career mark to .402. . . . Has scored 100+ runs in each of last five seasons; no other player has done it for more than the last two. . . . Career batting average of .388 at Anaheim (highest at any ballpark), .252 at Oakland (lowest).

Bob Boone

California Angels — Bats Right

	AB	H	2B	3B	HR	RRF	BB	SO	BA	SA	OBA
Season	389	94	18	0	3	37	35	36	.242	.311	.304
vs. Left-Handers	134	38	5	0	0	14	11	8	.284	.321	.333
vs. Right-Handers	255	56	13	0	3	23	24	28	.220	.306	.288
Home	186	45	7	0	1	14	20	19	.242	.296	.316
Road	203	49	11	0	2	23	15	17	.241	.325	.292
Grass	329	82	16	0	2	30	29	29	.249	.316	.310
Artificial Turf	60	12	2	0	1	7	6	7	.200	.283	.269
April	0	0	0	0	0	0	0	0	—	—	—
May	64	18	3	0	0	6	6	6	.281	.328	.343
June	80	20	3	0	1	7	12	8	.250	.325	.348
July	81	20	6	0	1	12	3	8	.247	.358	.267
August	89	21	5	0	0	6	9	8	.236	.292	.313
Sept./Oct.	75	15	1	0	1	6	5	6	.200	.253	.247
Leading Off Inn.	92	16	1	0	1	1	9	9	.174	.217	.248
Runners On	163	43	13	0	0	34	11	13	.264	.344	.309
Runners/Scor. Pos.	96	26	9	0	0	33	10	9	.271	.365	.330
Runners On/2 Out	88	20	7	0	0	16	6	8	.227	.307	.277
Scor. Pos./2 Out	60	15	5	0	0	15	6	5	.250	.333	.318
Late Inning Pressure	55	10	0	0	1		6	7	.182	.236	.274
Leading Off	16	4	0	0	1	1	3	2	.250	.438	.368
Runners On	18	1	0	0	0	0	0	3	.056	.056	.105
Runners/Scor. Pos.	9	0	0	0	0	0	0	1	.000	.000	.000

DRIVING IN RUNS	From 1B	From 2B	From 3B	Scoring Position
Totals	2/117	10/69	22/47	32/116
Percentage	2%	14%	47%	28%
Driving In Runners from 3B with Less than Two Out:		13/17		76%

Loves to face: Frank Tanana (.476, 10-for-21)
Hates to face: Charlie Leibrandt (.083, 2-for-24)
Needs one home run to reach 100 in his career. Bob and Ray (the Boones, not the comedy team) would then join Buddy and Gus Bell as the only father-son combinations in baseball history with 100 home runs apiece.... One of two players to hit below .250 with at least 300 at bats in each of last four seasons. The other: Steve Balboni. (Special mention goes to perennial cup-of-coffee outfielder Tim Tolman, who has never had even 60 major-league at bats in a season, but whose annual averages since 1981 are .125, .192, .196, .176, .140, .176, and .083.).... Won the Rawlings Gold Glove Award for A.L. catchers last season despite having the *lowest* fielding percentage of the 12 qualifying catchers in the A.L.

Daryl Boston

Chicago White Sox — Bats Left

	AB	H	2B	3B	HR	RRF	BB	SO	BA	SA	OBA
Season	337	87	21	2	10	31	25	68	.258	.421	.307
vs. Left-Handers	59	18	4	0	0	5	1	17	.305	.373	.311
vs. Right-Handers	278	69	17	2	10	26	24	51	.248	.432	.306
Home	168	54	9	2	5	18	12	37	.321	.488	.365
Road	169	33	12	0	5	13	13	31	.195	.355	.250
Grass	296	82	20	2	8	24	24	61	.277	.439	.330
Artificial Turf	41	5	1	0	2	7	1	7	.122	.293	.136
April	46	10	2	0	1	6	3	10	.217	.326	.260
May	95	28	6	0	4	4	11	20	.295	.484	.368
June	80	14	5	0	3	10	7	15	.175	.350	.236
July	49	12	3	1	0		1	9	.245	.347	.260
August	6	0	0	0	0	0	1	1	.000	.000	.143
Sept./Oct.	61	23	5	1	2	9	2	13	.377	.590	.397
Leading Off Inn.	108	37	10	0	6	6	6	22	.343	.602	.377
Runners On	127	27	5	1	2	23	13	26	.213	.315	.280
Runners/Scor. Pos.	65	12	3	0	2	20	8	16	.185	.323	.263
Runners On/2 Out	48	7	2	0	2	11	9	11	.146	.313	.281
Scor. Pos./2 Out	32	5	2	0	1	10	4	8	.156	.406	.250
Late Inning Pressure	51	10	3	1	0	2	4	14	.196	.294	.255
Leading Off	18	3	1	0	0		1	6	.167	.222	.211
Runners On	14	4	1	0	0	2	3	5	.286	.357	.412
Runners/Scor. Pos.	8	1	1	0	0		2	1	.125	.250	.222

DRIVING IN RUNS	From 1B	From 2B	From 3B	Scoring Position
Totals	7/96	7/56	7/24	14/80
Percentage	7%	13%	29%	18%
Driving In Runners from 3B with Less than Two Out:		5/12		42%

Loves to face: Charlie Hough (.400, 10-for-25, 1 HR)
Hates to face: Tom Candiotti (0-for-6)
Batted 126 points higher in home games than road games, 2d-largest difference among A.L. players (minimum: 100 AB each way).... Made 32 plate appearances in a row from May 3 to May 12 without a runner in scoring position, tying Willie Upshaw for longest streak in A.L. last season.... Yearly averages at Comiskey Park: .163, .175, .309, .321.... Career average of .161 in Late-Inning Pressure Situations, .256 in other situations. Has driven in only two of 21 runners from scoring position in LIP Situations.... Leads active A.L. players with career total of 928 plate appearances without being hit by a pitch. He's just 35 behind Herm Winningham, who is the overall major-league leader in that painless category.

Phil Bradley

Seattle Mariners — Bats Right

	AB	H	2B	3B	HR	RRF	BB	SO	BA	SA	OBA
Season	603	179	38	10	14	70	84	119	.297	.463	.387
vs. Left-Handers	176	61	15	2	11	29	25	30	.347	.642	.426
vs. Right-Handers	427	118	23	8	3	41	59	89	.276	.389	.371
Home	304	94	18	5	12	44	43	64	.309	.520	.398
Road	299	85	20	5	2	26	41	55	.284	.405	.376
Grass	231	62	15	4	2	20	30	46	.268	.394	.358
Artificial Turf	372	117	23	6	12	50	54	73	.315	.505	.405
April	76	14	1	1	1	9	21	18	.184	.263	.374
May	103	26	8	5	1	12	11	25	.252	.456	.322
June	100	34	8	2	3	10	16	17	.340	.550	.436
July	87	30	6	2	5	14	8	14	.345	.632	.402
August	113	36	8	0	4	12	12	22	.319	.496	.391
Sept./Oct.	124	39	7	0	0	13	16	23	.315	.371	.397
Leading Off Inn.	104	39	10	3	1		17	14	.375	.558	.463
Runners On	247	60	11	3	3	59	44	54	.243	.348	.358
Runners/Scor. Pos.	165	37	9	0	1	52	37	44	.224	.297	.364
Runners On/2 Out	74	19	4	2	1	18	21	20	.257	.405	.421
Scor. Pos./2 Out	58	14	3	0	1	16	19	19	.241	.345	.429
Late Inning Pressure	65	20	3	1	1	6	6	18	.308	.431	.366
Leading Off	15	5	2	1	0		0	3	.333	.600	.333
Runners On	29	9	0	0	1	6	5	7	.310	.414	.412
Runners/Scor. Pos.	19	4	0	0	0	4	3	5	.211	.211	.318

DRIVING IN RUNS	From 1B	From 2B	From 3B	Scoring Position
Totals	7/139	20/139	29/59	49/198
Percentage	5%	14%	49%	25%
Driving In Runners from 3B with Less than Two Out:		22/37		59%

Loves to face: Al Nipper (.387, 12-for-31)
Hates to face: Bob Ojeda (0-for-7)
Only major leaguer to play more than 150 games in left field last season (played 158).... Twelve HR at Kingdome ranked third on the club, but two HR in road games ranked eighth.... Batted 91 points lower with men on base than he did with the bases empty, 2d-largest difference in A.L. last season (minimum: 75 AB each way).... Ranked 7th in A.L. with 55 multiple-hit games.... Batting average vs. left-handers has steadily improved (since 1984: .205, .267, .325, .347), while his average vs. right-handers has declined (.352, .312, .305, .276).... Has batted above .300 at the Kingdome and below .300 on the road in each of the last four seasons.... Homered in every A.L. ballpark except Fenway (70 career AB).

Scott Bradley

Seattle Mariners — Bats Left

	AB	H	2B	3B	HR	RRF	BB	SO	BA	SA	OBA
Season	342	95	15	1	5	45	15	18	.278	.371	.310
vs. Left-Handers	54	14	2	0	1	9	1	3	.259	.352	.273
vs. Right-Handers	288	81	13	1	4	36	14	15	.281	.375	.317
Home	145	42	6	1	5	24	9	4	.290	.448	.329
Road	197	53	9	0	0	21	6	14	.269	.315	.297
Grass	155	46	9	0	0	19	2	13	.297	.355	.309
Artificial Turf	187	49	6	1	5	26	13	5	.262	.385	.312
April	49	18	1	0	2	7	3	1	.367	.510	.404
May	67	22	4	0	0	9	0	4	.328	.388	.324
June	69	15	3	0	0	8	3	3	.217	.261	.260
July	62	13	1	1	0	5	2	4	.210	.258	.234
August	44	12	4	0	3	11	4	2	.273	.568	.340
Sept./Oct.	51	15	2	0	0	5	3	4	.294	.333	.333
Leading Off Inn.	64	18	6	0	1	1	1	2	.281	.422	.292
Runners On	170	41	5	1	3	43	10	9	.241	.335	.289
Runners/Scor. Pos.	101	23	3	1	1	38	6	7	.228	.307	.274
Runners On/2 Out	60	14	2	0	1	13	3	4	.233	.317	.270
Scor. Pos./2 Out	42	9	2	0	0	11	0	4	.214	.262	.214
Late Inning Pressure	39	13	1	1	1	12	2	4	.333	.487	.366
Leading Off	5	2	1	0	0	0	0	0	.400	.600	.400
Runners On	24	7	0	1	1	12	1	2	.292	.500	.320
Runners/Scor. Pos.	22	7	0	1	1	12	1	2	.318	.545	.348

DRIVING IN RUNS	From 1B	From 2B	From 3B	Scoring Position
Totals	4/112	14/75	22/39	36/114
Percentage	4%	19%	56%	32%
Driving In Runners from 3B with Less than Two Out:		17/24		71%

Loves to face: Dave Stewart (.714, 5-for-7, 2 HR)
Hates to face: Dave Stieb (.071, 1-for-14)
Career batting average of .248 with runners on base, .302 with the bases empty. 54 points is 2d-largest difference of any active player over the last 10 seasons (minimum: 200 AB each way).... Started 80 games against right-handed pitchers, but only four games against southpaws.... Career average of .225 (one HR) vs. left-handers, .284 (nine HR) vs. right-handers.... Nine of his 10 career HR were at the Kingdome.... Career average of under .200 at four different A.L. ballparks: Exhibition (.162), Metrodome (.148), Anaheim (.143), Fenway (.143).... Career average of one strikeout for every 20.4 plate appearances ranks 2d to Bill Buckner (21.1) among active players who've batted at least as often as Bradley.

Glenn Braggs
Milwaukee Brewers — Bats Right

	AB	H	2B	3B	HR	RRF	BB	SO	BA	SA	OBA
Season	505	136	28	7	13	78	47	96	.269	.430	.332
vs. Left-Handers	168	46	10	2	2	23	18	29	.274	.393	.349
vs. Right-Handers	337	90	18	5	11	55	29	67	.267	.448	.324
Home	253	66	11	4	4	43	25	51	.261	.383	.323
Road	252	70	17	3	9	35	22	45	.278	.476	.342
Grass	421	117	25	7	10	69	40	78	.278	.442	.341
Artificial Turf	84	19	3	0	3	9	7	18	.226	.369	.286
April	88	26	5	1	4	14	10	18	.295	.511	.364
May	75	15	3	1	2	8	11	20	.200	.347	.310
June	58	12	2	0	1	6	7	13	.207	.293	.313
July	96	29	8	3	3	20	9	13	.302	.542	.355
August	90	23	5	1	1	14	5	17	.256	.367	.296
Sept./Oct.	98	31	5	1	2	16	5	15	.316	.449	.343
Leading Off Inn.	90	25	4	1	4	4	11	16	.278	.478	.363
Runners On	232	62	16	2	3	68	23	44	.267	.392	.332
Runners/Scor. Pos.	148	42	9	1	2	62	20	29	.284	.399	.358
Runners On/2 Out	99	25	7	2	2	30	8	23	.253	.424	.327
Scor. Pos./2 Out	78	20	5	1	2	28	8	19	.256	.423	.333
Late Inning Pressure	67	19	5	1	0	9	9	18	.284	.388	.359
Leading Off	17	5	2	0	0		3	2	.294	.412	.400
Runners On	28	8	3	1	0	9	5	7	.286	.464	.371
Runners/Scor. Pos.	19	6	2	1	0	9	4	5	.316	.526	.400

DRIVING IN RUNS	From 1B	From 2B	From 3B	Scoring Position
Totals	7/161	28/119	30/69	58/188
Percentage	4%	24%	43%	31%
Driving In Runners from 3B with Less than Two Out:		22/33		67%

Loves to face: Greg Swindell (.714, 5-for-7)
Hates to face: Jim Clancy (0-for-9)
Averaged 2.61 putouts per nine innings last season, highest of any major-league right fielder (minimum: 500 innings).... Grounded into 14 double plays in 75 double-play situations, 7th-highest rate (.180) in A.L. (minimum: 40 opportunities).... Has had an extra-base hit at every A.L. ballpark except Cleveland Stadium (.229, 8-for-35).... Career batting average of .325 (13-for-40, 3 HR) at Arlington Stadium.... No home runs in 97 career at bats in Late-Inning Pressure Situations.... *Baseball America* rated him best prospect in the Pacific Coast League after the 1986 season, but he's been eclipsed by many of those below him in the top ten. They include Devon White, Benito Santiago, and Mark McGwire.

Mickey Brantley
Seattle Mariners — Bats Right

	AB	H	2B	3B	HR	RRF	BB	SO	BA	SA	OBA
Season	351	106	23	2	14	56	24	44	.302	.499	.344
vs. Left-Handers	127	36	8	1	7	27	8	14	.283	.528	.324
vs. Right-Handers	224	70	15	1	7	29	16	30	.313	.482	.355
Home	159	51	8	2	11	31	8	17	.321	.604	.347
Road	192	55	15	0	3	25	16	27	.286	.411	.341
Grass	146	48	13	0	3	22	10	19	.329	.479	.372
Artificial Turf	205	58	10	2	11	34	14	25	.283	.512	.324
April	23	5	1	0	0	2	2	4	.217	.261	.280
May	0	0	0	0	0	0	0	0	—	—	—
June	86	23	5	1	3	17	4	9	.267	.453	.293
July	57	19	2	0	1	3	4	6	.333	.421	.377
August	79	20	6	0	3	10	4	11	.253	.443	.289
Sept./Oct.	106	39	9	1	7	24	10	14	.368	.670	.419
Leading Off Inn.	106	28	6	1	4		9	9	.264	.453	.322
Runners On	130	42	11	0	7	49	9	16	.323	.569	.359
Runners/Scor. Pos.	85	32	8	0	4	43	4	8	.376	.612	.391
Runners On/2 Out	42	11	2	0	1	10	4	3	.262	.381	.326
Scor. Pos./2 Out	30	9	2	0	1	10	2	1	.300	.467	.344
Late Inning Pressure	45	13	2	0	1	3	3	7	.289	.400	.333
Leading Off	13	2	0	0	0		0	1	.154	.154	.154
Runners On	15	4	1	0	0		2	3	.267	.333	.353
Runners/Scor. Pos.	9	3	0	0	0	2	0	1	.333	.333	.333

DRIVING IN RUNS	From 1B	From 2B	From 3B	Scoring Position
Totals	5/70	21/65	16/35	37/100
Percentage	7%	32%	46%	37%
Driving In Runners from 3B with Less than Two Out:		15/25		60%

Loves to face: Greg Harris (.545, 6-for-11, 1 HR)
Hates to face: Mark Gubicza (0-for-7)
One of four A.L. rookies (minimum: 200 PA) to bat over .300.... Mariners had a record of 10–2 in games in which he homered.... Hit six home runs in 68 at bats vs. left-handed pitchers at the Kingdome.... Batting average after September 1 was 5th highest in A.L.... One of eight A.L. players to collect five hits in a game (Sept. 14 vs. Cleveland).... A Wade Boggs disciple? Brantley raised his average above .300 with two hits in four at bats on the final Friday of the season, then sat out the final two games, preserving his .300 status. Just like the master.... Career average of .333 with runners in scoring position.... One hit in 25 career at bats at Royals Stadium.

George Brett
Kansas City Royals — Bats Left

	AB	H	2B	3B	HR	RRF	BB	SO	BA	SA	OBA
Season	427	124	18	2	22	79	72	47	.290	.496	.388
vs. Left-Handers	149	40	3	0	7	25	12	22	.268	.430	.317
vs. Right-Handers	278	84	15	2	15	54	60	25	.302	.532	.422
Home	231	62	6	2	14	48	36	26	.268	.494	.364
Road	196	62	12	0	8	31	36	21	.316	.500	.415
Grass	160	52	9	0	6	26	29	17	.325	.494	.422
Artificial Turf	267	72	9	2	16	53	43	30	.270	.498	.367
April	22	7	1	0	1	3	9	2	.318	.500	.500
May	13	5	1	0	0	2	2	3	.385	.462	.467
June	66	20	6	0	4	12	7	7	.303	.576	.378
July	107	29	4	0	2	17	15	12	.271	.364	.355
August	110	34	1	1	10	24	22	14	.309	.609	.418
Sept./Oct.	109	29	5	1	5	21	17	9	.266	.468	.357
Leading Off Inn.	69	19	1	0	8	8	5	7	.275	.638	.333
Runners On	231	66	9	1	8	65	43	25	.286	.437	.387
Runners/Scor. Pos.	119	38	3	1	4	53	31	15	.319	.462	.437
Runners On/2 Out	81	13	0	1	2	13	21	11	.160	.259	.333
Scor. Pos./2 Out	50	11	0	1	1	11	15	8	.220	.320	.400
Late Inning Pressure	53	16	3	0	2	11	9	6	.302	.472	.397
Leading Off	9	2	0	0	1	1	0	0	.222	.556	.222
Runners On	27	8	2	0	0	9	7	3	.296	.370	.429
Runners/Scor. Pos.	15	5	0	0	0	8	6	1	.333	.333	.500

DRIVING IN RUNS	From 1B	From 2B	From 3B	Scoring Position
Totals	9/173	19/93	29/49	48/142
Percentage	5%	20%	59%	34%
Driving In Runners from 3B with Less than Two Out:		26/33		79%

Loves to face: Mike Smithson (.607, 17-for-28, 2 HR)
Hates to face: Steve Ontiveros (0-for-14)
At which ballpark does Brett have his highest career batting average? We'll give you 14 guesses. You're wrong unless you said Shea Stadium (.387, 12-for-31). The Yankees played their home games there in 1974 and 1975.... Batting average at Royals Stadium last season was his lowest since going 0-for-15 there in 1973.... Had hit .300 or better on artificial surfaces 11 times in 12 seasons prior to 1987.... Has never struck out more than 51 times in a season. Teammate Bo Jackson surpassed that figure on May 22 last season.... How difficult will it be for anyone to break Pete Rose's record of 4,256 hits in a career? Consider this: Brett, a 15-year veteran and nine-time .300-hitter, reached *the halfway point* last July.

Greg Brock
Milwaukee Brewers — Bats Left

	AB	H	2B	3B	HR	RRF	BB	SO	BA	SA	OBA
Season	532	159	29	3	13	85	57	63	.299	.438	.371
vs. Left-Handers	157	45	6	1	3	27	14	22	.287	.395	.351
vs. Right-Handers	375	114	23	2	10	58	43	41	.304	.456	.380
Home	270	81	15	2	5	45	26	28	.300	.426	.370
Road	262	78	14	1	8	40	31	35	.298	.450	.372
Grass	456	138	24	2	13	78	45	55	.303	.450	.371
Artificial Turf	76	21	5	1	0	7	12	8	.276	.368	.375
April	71	23	2	0	4	18	7	9	.324	.521	.407
May	79	16	5	0	3	12	4	7	.203	.380	.250
June	50	15	2	0	1	5	9	4	.300	.400	.407
July	101	32	3	1	2	16	9	14	.317	.426	.377
August	110	35	7	1	2	16	9	12	.318	.455	.370
Sept./Oct.	121	38	10	1	1	18	19	17	.314	.438	.404
Leading Off Inn.	136	33	5	1	3	3	12	16	.243	.360	.313
Runners On	262	91	15	2	7	79	30	33	.347	.500	.416
Runners/Scor. Pos.	166	54	10	1	4	72	24	25	.325	.470	.413
Runners On/2 Out	139	42	8	1	4	39	14	23	.302	.460	.370
Scor. Pos./2 Out	91	29	7	0	3	36	13	17	.319	.495	.410
Late Inning Pressure	69	20	4	0	0	5	9	6	.290	.348	.372
Leading Off	19	4	0	0	0	0	1	2	.211	.211	.250
Runners On	32	11	2	0	0	5	6	2	.344	.406	.447
Runners/Scor. Pos.	16	4	1	0	0	5	5	2	.250	.313	.429

DRIVING IN RUNS	From 1B	From 2B	From 3B	Scoring Position
Totals	9/176	36/127	27/58	63/185
Percentage	5%	28%	47%	34%
Driving In Runners from 3B with Less than Two Out:		18/30		60%

Loves to face: Frank Viola (.800, 4-for-5)
Hates to face: Jeff Reardon (.067, 1-for-15)
Brewers had a record of 63–38 with him in the cleanup spot, 28–33 with others there.... One of six A.L. players to collect four or more hits in four different games. The others: Barfield, Barrett, Boggs, McGwire, and Puckett (6 games).... One of five players to take one for the team with the bases loaded last season. The others: Joe Carter, Tom Brunansky, Don Baylor, and Willie McGee. The last two did it twice.... Career average of .191 (one home run per 76.0 AB) in Late-Inning Pressure Situations, .261 (one HR per 21.7 AB) in other situations.... Percentage of runners driven in from scoring position was a career-high (previous high was 27 percent in 1983).... Career breakdown: .217 vs. left-handers, .260 vs. right-handers.

Tom Brookens

Detroit Tigers   Bats Right

	AB	H	2B	3B	HR	RRF	BB	SO	BA	SA	OBA
Season	444	107	15	3	13	62	33	63	.241	.376	.295
vs. Left-Handers	154	37	7	0	7	27	16	24	.240	.422	.310
vs. Right-Handers	290	70	8	3	6	35	17	39	.241	.352	.287
Home	212	48	3	0	6	27	18	32	.226	.325	.291
Road	232	59	12	3	7	35	15	31	.254	.422	.300
Grass	378	96	11	1	13	57	30	55	.254	.392	.311
Artificial Turf	66	11	4	2	0	5	3	8	.167	.288	.203
April	58	15	4	2	1	11	5	4	.259	.448	.317
May	64	17	1	0	3	9	8	12	.266	.422	.347
June	89	20	5	1	3	13	7	12	.225	.404	.281
July	87	20	1	0	1	8	4	9	.230	.276	.261
August	49	11	0	0	1	7	4	8	.224	.286	.291
Sept./Oct.	97	24	4	0	4	14	5	18	.247	.412	.291
Leading Off Inn.	91	21	2	1	1	1	9	13	.231	.308	.307
Runners On	215	52	7	1	7	56	17	38	.242	.381	.298
Runners/Scor. Pos.	128	30	3	1	4	50	10	25	.234	.367	.286
Runners On/2 Out	103	28	2	1	5	33	8	21	.272	.456	.324
Scor. Pos./2 Out	74	19	2	1	3	29	5	17	.257	.432	.304
Late Inning Pressure	40	11	2	0	1	3	2	6	.275	.400	.310
Leading Off	10	5	1	0	0	0	0	2	.500	.600	.500
Runners On	20	4	0	0	1	3	1	3	.200	.350	.238
Runners/Scor. Pos.	13	3	0	0	1	3	1	2	.231	.462	.286

DRIVING IN RUNS	From 1B	From 2B	From 3B	Scoring Position
Totals	8/152	23/110	18/53	41/163
Percentage	5%	21%	34%	25%
Driving In Runners from 3B with Less than Two Out:		10/21		48%

Loves to face: Mark Langston (.458, 11-for-24)
Hates to face: Ken Schrom (.063, 1-for-16)
Played 122 games at third base, 16 games at shortstop, and 11 games at second base. . . . Career fielding percentage at third base is .943, 3d-lowest among active players with 500+ games there. The two third basemen with worse percentages (Hubie Brooks and Larry Parrish) no longer play that position. . . . Batting average in Late-Inning Pressure Situations has been higher than his overall average in each of the last five seasons. . . . Only player to hit below .200 with at least 300 at bats over the past five Julys. His average: .198. . . . Career breakdowns: .277 vs. left-handers, .223 vs. right-handers; .251 on grass fields, .215 on artificial surfaces. . . . Hitless in 18 post-season at bats for his career.

Bob Brower

Texas Rangers   Bats Right

	AB	H	2B	3B	HR	RRF	BB	SO	BA	SA	OBA
Season	303	79	10	3	14	46	36	66	.261	.452	.338
vs. Left-Handers	176	48	8	1	8	21	23	39	.273	.466	.355
vs. Right-Handers	127	31	2	2	6	25	13	27	.244	.433	.314
Home	155	46	7	2	7	20	16	40	.297	.503	.363
Road	148	33	3	1	7	26	20	26	.223	.399	.314
Grass	269	76	10	3	14	44	29	60	.283	.498	.351
Artificial Turf	34	3	0	0	0	2	7	6	.088	.088	.244
April	39	11	3	0	1	5	8	9	.282	.436	.404
May	44	9	1	0	2	2	8	13	.205	.364	.327
June	18	4	1	0	2	7	4	5	.222	.611	.364
July	59	20	0	2	4	13	5	12	.339	.610	.391
August	53	8	0	1	2	7	5	10	.151	.302	.220
Sept./Oct.	90	27	5	0	3	12	6	17	.300	.456	.344
Leading Off Inn.	88	19	4	1	4	4	11	21	.216	.420	.303
Runners On	119	40	4	1	6	38	19	23	.336	.538	.424
Runners/Scor. Pos.	63	19	1	1	2	30	10	13	.302	.444	.392
Runners On/2 Out	52	20	1	0	3	19	7	11	.385	.577	.458
Scor. Pos./2 Out	34	12	0	0	2	17	3	8	.353	.529	.405
Late Inning Pressure	37	6	1	0	0	3	8	10	.162	.189	.304
Leading Off	10	3	1	0	0	0	0	2	.300	.400	.300
Runners On	16	2	0	0	0	3	7	5	.125	.125	.375
Runners/Scor. Pos.	11	2	0	0	0	3	5	2	.182	.182	.412

DRIVING IN RUNS	From 1B	From 2B	From 3B	Scoring Position
Totals	5/87	10/41	17/34	27/75
Percentage	6%	24%	50%	36%
Driving In Runners from 3B with Less than Two Out:		10/17		59%

Loves to face: Rich Bordi (3-for-3, 2 HR)
Hates to face: Charlie Leibrandt (0-for-8)
Grounded into 2 double plays in 64 DP situations, 3d-lowest rate in A.L. (minimum: 40 opportunities). . . . Batted 124 points higher with men on base than with the bases empty, 2d-largest difference among A.L. batters last season (minimum: 75 AB each way). . . . Hit an inside-the-park grand-slam home run at Oakland on June 21. . . . Started 52 of 62 games (84 percent) in which the Rangers faced a left-handed starter, but only 29 of 100 games against right-handers. . . . One hit, six strikeouts in 11 appearances as a pinch-hitter. . . . Attended Duke on football scholarship, and was named ACC Offensive Back of the Week for a 130-yard performance vs. North Carolina in 1979. Where was L.T. that day?

Jerry Browne

Texas Rangers   Bats Left and Right

	AB	H	2B	3B	HR	RRF	BB	SO	BA	SA	OBA
Season	454	123	16	6	1	40	61	50	.271	.339	.358
vs. Left-Handers	119	37	4	3	1	17	18	8	.311	.420	.403
vs. Right-Handers	335	86	12	3	0	23	43	42	.257	.310	.342
Home	245	75	9	3	1	23	33	29	.306	.380	.390
Road	209	48	7	3	0	17	28	21	.230	.292	.321
Grass	393	108	13	6	1	36	52	41	.275	.346	.361
Artificial Turf	61	15	3	0	0	4	9	9	.246	.295	.343
April	54	14	2	3	0	3	10	3	.259	.407	.375
May	63	15	4	0	0	9	12	5	.238	.302	.364
June	101	24	1	2	0	8	13	17	.238	.287	.322
July	74	24	3	1	0	5	11	8	.324	.392	.412
August	84	24	3	0	1	8	4	7	.286	.357	.318
Sept./Oct.	78	22	3	0	0	7	11	10	.282	.321	.378
Leading Off Inn.	187	49	5	2	1	1	18	29	.262	.326	.330
Runners On	138	35	5	3	0	39	25	9	.254	.333	.364
Runners/Scor. Pos.	90	26	4	2	0	38	17	6	.289	.378	.394
Runners On/2 Out	53	14	1	3	0	18	15	5	.264	.396	.426
Scor. Pos./2 Out	40	12	1	2	0	17	11	4	.300	.425	.451
Late Inning Pressure	57	19	2	1	0	7	16	3	.333	.404	.479
Leading Off	15	9	0	0	0	0	3	1	.600	.600	.667
Runners On	23	5	1	0	0	7	11	2	.217	.261	.471
Runners/Scor. Pos.	17	4	0	0	0	7	7	1	.235	.235	.458

DRIVING IN RUNS	From 1B	From 2B	From 3B	Scoring Position
Totals	2/92	12/64	25/45	37/109
Percentage	2%	19%	56%	34%
Driving In Runners from 3B with Less than Two Out:		15/23		65%

Loves to face: Bill Wegman (.500, 5-for-10)
Hates to face: Moose Haas (0-for-7)
Youngest position player on a major-league opening-day roster last season. . . . Hit safely in 15 consecutive games (Aug. 11 to Sept. 10), tying Scott Fletcher and Pete O'Brien for club lead. . . . Caught stealing 17 times (in 44 attempts) last season, 2d-most in A.L, including four times in four attempts vs. Seattle. . . . One of three A.L. players to walk four times with the bases loaded last season. Mike Greenwell and Eddie Murray were the others. . . . Career average of .315 at Arlington Stadium, .232 on the road. . . . Had hits in five consecutive at bats in Late-Inning Pressure Situations (June 22–July 4). Career averages: .344 in LIP Situations, .269 in unpressured at bats.

Tom Brunansky

Minnesota Twins   Bats Right

	AB	H	2B	3B	HR	RRF	BB	SO	BA	SA	OBA
Season	532	138	22	2	32	91	74	104	.259	.489	.352
vs. Left-Handers	158	36	8	1	10	29	23	20	.228	.481	.321
vs. Right-Handers	374	102	14	1	22	62	51	84	.273	.492	.365
Home	277	83	15	2	19	56	37	57	.300	.574	.384
Road	255	55	7	0	13	35	37	47	.216	.396	.318
Grass	197	43	5	0	12	32	29	38	.218	.426	.323
Artificial Turf	335	95	17	2	20	59	45	66	.284	.525	.369
April	67	16	0	0	2	7	7	18	.239	.328	.320
May	95	28	4	1	8	24	14	21	.295	.611	.391
June	86	22	4	0	6	14	16	15	.256	.512	.365
July	86	22	4	0	5	12	14	8	.256	.477	.356
August	105	27	6	0	6	21	9	22	.257	.486	.316
Sept./Oct.	93	23	4	1	5	13	14	20	.247	.473	.355
Leading Off Inn.	126	30	5	0	10	10	14	22	.238	.516	.314
Runners On	223	60	14	1	12	71	39	39	.269	.502	.379
Runners/Scor. Pos.	122	36	10	0	8	59	22	25	.295	.574	.404
Runners On/2 Out	100	18	3	0	6	25	17	25	.180	.311	.311
Scor. Pos./2 Out	58	12	2	0	4	20	11	12	.207	.448	.352
Late Inning Pressure	66	18	3	0	5	8	11	17	.273	.545	.377
Leading Off	23	7	1	0	3	3	3	5	.304	.739	.385
Runners On	27	7	2	0	0	3	4	8	.259	.333	.355
Runners/Scor. Pos.	12	2	1	0	0	2	3	3	.167	.250	.333

DRIVING IN RUNS	From 1B	From 2B	From 3B	Scoring Position
Totals	11/164	21/89	27/58	48/147
Percentage	7%	24%	47%	33%
Driving In Runners from 3B with Less than Two Out:		20/30		67%

Loves to face: Bruce Hurst (.577, 15-for-26, 1 HR)
Hates to face: Bobby Witt (0-for-13, 9 SO)
One of seven players with at least 20 home runs in every season since 1982. He's also one of six to play 150 or more games in each of those seasons. . . . Topped the 100 strikeout mark for the first time since 1982 when he fanned 101 times in only 463 at bats. . . . Batting average with runners in scoring position and percentage of runners driven in from scoring position were both career highs. . . . His only hit in 11 at bats with the bases loaded was a grand slam off Tom Candiotti. . . . Career averages are .302 at Fenway Park (his highest at any ballpark), .194 at Oakland Coliseum (his lowest). . . . Has hit between .240 and .260 in each of the past four seasons, with between 75 and 90 RBI in each.

Bill Buckner
Red Sox/Angels   Bats Left

	AB	H	2B	3B	HR	RRF	BB	SO	BA	SA	OBA
Season	469	134	18	2	5	79	22	26	.286	.365	.314
vs. Left-Handers	119	31	1	1	0	17	3	11	.261	.286	.272
vs. Right-Handers	350	103	17	1	5	62	19	15	.294	.391	.328
Home	238	72	8	2	2	45	13	14	.303	.378	.333
Road	231	62	10	0	3	34	9	12	.268	.351	.293
Grass	378	104	12	2	4	66	18	21	.275	.349	.303
Artificial Turf	91	30	6	0	1	13	4	5	.330	.429	.358
April	84	22	2	1	0	12	1	3	.262	.310	.267
May	95	22	1	0	2	14	5	9	.232	.305	.262
June	47	17	1	0	0	14	2	3	.362	.383	.380
July	72	20	3	0	0	5	6	5	.278	.319	.333
August	86	26	4	0	2	15	3	2	.302	.419	.326
Sept./Oct.	85	27	7	1	1	19	5	4	.318	.459	.352
Leading Off Inn.	90	29	4	0	1	1	3	5	.322	.400	.344
Runners On	209	66	9	2	3	77	12	11	.316	.421	.344
Runners/Scor. Pos.	129	39	4	1	3	72	9	9	.302	.419	.333
Runners On/2 Out	87	25	4	1	2	26	4	8	.287	.425	.319
Scor. Pos./2 Out	57	16	0	1	2	23	4	7	.281	.421	.328
Late Inning Pressure	74	20	2	1	0	8	5	4	.270	.324	.316
Leading Off	22	5	1	0	0		1	2	.227	.273	.261
Runners On	28	9	0	1	0	8	3	1	.321	.393	.387
Runners/Scor. Pos.	19	5	0	1	0	8	2	1	.263	.368	.333

DRIVING IN RUNS	From 1B	From 2B	From 3B	Scoring Position
Totals	8/163	23/103	43/74	66/177
Percentage	5%	22%	58%	37%
Driving In Runners from 3B with Less than Two Out:			33/43	77%

Loves to face: Bob Welch (.367, 18-for-49, 2 HR)
Hates to face: Curt Young (.067, 1-for-15)
Homered vs. every A.L. club except the Angels last season.... Played 18 games against the A's, a scheduling impossibility were it not for his mid-season trade from Boston to California.... Batted .533 (8-for-15) as a pinch-hitter.... Something to remember me by: Committed an error in his final game with the Red Sox.... Played only one game in the field for the Angels after August 13.... Was struck out on July 5 by Gene Nelson with two outs and runners in scoring position in a Late-Inning Pressure Situation, his first whiff in 93 times up under those conditions since 1978.... Has never struck out three times in one game.... Career average of .394 (39-for-99, 5 HR) at Memorial Stadium.

Steve Buechele
Texas Rangers   Bats Right

	AB	H	2B	3B	HR	RRF	BB	SO	BA	SA	OBA
Season	363	86	20	0	13	54	28	66	.237	.399	.290
vs. Left-Handers	177	51	13	0	8	31	12	28	.288	.497	.333
vs. Right-Handers	186	35	7	0	5	23	16	38	.188	.306	.250
Home	188	47	11	0	6	31	18	32	.250	.404	.316
Road	175	39	9	0	7	23	10	34	.223	.394	.262
Grass	305	71	16	0	10	47	24	56	.233	.384	.287
Artificial Turf	58	15	4	0	3	7	4	10	.259	.483	.306
April	61	13	3	0	2	5	6	17	.213	.361	.294
May	67	14	3	0	2	6	4	14	.209	.343	.250
June	75	16	8	0	3	15	4	10	.213	.440	.247
July	70	21	2	0	3	17	8	5	.300	.457	.367
August	40	9	2	0	1	1	2	9	.225	.275	.262
Sept./Oct.	50	13	2	0	3	10	4	11	.260	.480	.315
Leading Off Inn.	86	19	2	0	7	7	5	17	.221	.488	.264
Runners On	167	38	11	0	3	44	14	30	.228	.347	.281
Runners/Scor. Pos.	85	21	5	0	1	38	10	16	.247	.341	.313
Runners On/2 Out	89	20	5	0	0	21	3	14	.225	.281	.250
Scor. Pos./2 Out	51	15	4	0	0	20	2	8	.294	.373	.321
Late Inning Pressure	45	12	4	0	1	4	7	8	.267	.422	.377
Leading Off	10	2	0	0	1	1	3	3	.200	.500	.385
Runners On	19	5	1	0	0	3	4	4	.263	.316	.391
Runners/Scor. Pos.	9	4	0	0	0	3	4	1	.444	.444	.615

DRIVING IN RUNS	From 1B	From 2B	From 3B	Scoring Position
Totals	6/127	16/63	19/45	35/108
Percentage	5%	25%	42%	32%
Driving In Runners from 3B with Less than Two Out:			14/21	67%

Loves to face: Juan Nieves (.556, 5-for-9, 2 HR)
Hates to face: Oil Can Boyd (0-for-12)
Played 123 games at third base, 18 games at second base, and two games in left field.... Started 61 of 62 games in which the Rangers faced a left-handed starter, 49 of 100 games against right-handers.... Taken out for a pinch-hitter 38 times last season, tied with Jays' Cecil Fielder and Reds' pitcher Rob Murphy for most in majors.... One hit in 13 career at bats with the bases loaded.... Career batting average of .279 vs. left-handers, .210 vs. right-handers.... Career batting average is under .200 at three different ballparks: Metrodome (.198), Oakland (.128), Exhibition (.125).... Born Sept. 26, 1961, the day that Roger Maris blasted his 60th home run of the season, tying Babe Ruth's record.

Ellis Burks
Boston Red Sox   Bats Right

	AB	H	2B	3B	HR	RRF	BB	SO	BA	SA	OBA
Season	558	152	30	2	20	60	41	98	.272	.441	.324
vs. Left-Handers	151	49	12	0	4	19	14	30	.325	.483	.380
vs. Right-Handers	407	103	18	2	16	41	27	68	.253	.425	.303
Home	256	74	14	1	11	30	30	43	.289	.480	.365
Road	302	78	16	1	9	30	11	55	.258	.407	.287
Grass	466	130	24	2	17	56	39	78	.279	.448	.335
Artificial Turf	92	22	6	0	3	4	2	20	.239	.402	.263
April	3	0	0	0	0	0	0	1	.000	.000	.000
May	113	27	8	0	5	14	6	22	.239	.442	.277
June	81	21	4	0	7	19	8	16	.259	.568	.326
July	113	36	8	1	4	10	6	22	.319	.513	.358
August	111	30	4	1	3	12	15	20	.270	.405	.359
Sept./Oct.	137	38	6	0	1	5	6	17	.277	.343	.308
Leading Off Inn.	228	72	11	0	7	7	12	35	.316	.456	.350
Runners On	178	44	10	2	8	48	21	36	.247	.461	.332
Runners/Scor. Pos.	117	26	4	2	6	43	14	28	.222	.444	.308
Runners On/2 Out	83	15	5	1	2	17	10	17	.181	.337	.269
Scor. Pos./2 Out	62	8	2	1	2	16	6	16	.129	.290	.206
Late Inning Pressure	68	12	0	1	1	8	6	14	.176	.250	.243
Leading Off	20	5	0	0	0	0	0	5	.250	.250	.250
Runners On	28	6	0	1	1	8	4	5	.214	.393	.313
Runners/Scor. Pos.	19	4	0	1	0	6	2	4	.211	.316	.286

DRIVING IN RUNS	From 1B	From 2B	From 3B	Scoring Position
Totals	6/113	18/104	16/41	34/145
Percentage	4%	17%	39%	23%
Driving In Runners from 3B with Less than Two Out:			10/17	59%

Loves to face: Bill Wegman (4-for-4, 1 HR)
Hates to face: Tom Candiotti (0-for-9)
Grounded into only one double play in 72 double-play situations, lowest rate in the major leagues (minimum: 40 opportunities).... Batted ninth in his first four games, in the leadoff spot in each of 124 starts thereafter.... Averaged one home run per 20.6 at bats through games of August 21, but hit only one in 167 at bats after that.... One of three major leaguers who hit 20+ home runs without being walked intentionally, and the only one without either a 927-consecutive-game playing streak or a 91-yard TD run.... Tied a major-league record by hitting two grand slams in his rookie season, joining an eclectic group that includes Marv Throneberry's brother Faye and Dale Berra's dad, Lawrence.

Rick Burleson
Baltimore Orioles   Bats Right

	AB	H	2B	3B	HR	RRF	BB	SO	BA	SA	OBA
Season	206	43	14	1	2	16	17	30	.209	.316	.279
vs. Left-Handers	77	15	6	1	0	5	8	13	.195	.299	.279
vs. Right-Handers	129	28	8	0	2	11	9	17	.217	.326	.279
Home	110	24	9	1	2	9	8	16	.218	.373	.283
Road	96	19	5	0	0	7	9	14	.198	.250	.274
Grass	171	37	11	1	2	14	17	26	.216	.327	.298
Artificial Turf	35	6	3	0	0	2	0	4	.171	.257	.171
April	67	11	3	0	0	4	9	14	.164	.209	.282
May	68	16	2	1	2	8	5	9	.235	.382	.288
June	57	15	8	0	0	4	3	6	.263	.404	.311
July	14	1	1	0	0	0	0	1	.071	.143	.071
August	0	0	0	0	0	0	0	0	—	—	—
Sept./Oct.	0	0	0	0	0	0	0	0	—	—	—
Leading Off Inn.	40	10	5	0	1	1	2	7	.250	.450	.286
Runners On	80	15	4	1	0	14	9	8	.188	.263	.286
Runners/Scor. Pos.	42	8	4	0	0	13	6	4	.190	.286	.277
Runners On/2 Out	29	3	1	0	0	4	4	4	.103	.138	.212
Scor. Pos./2 Out	19	3	1	0	0	4	4	1	.158	.211	.304
Late Inning Pressure	31	5	2	0	0	3	1	4	.161	.226	.188
Leading Off	3	0	0	0	0	0	0	1	.000	.000	.000
Runners On	14	4	1	0	0	3	1	1	.286	.357	.333
Runners/Scor. Pos.	7	2	1	0	0	3	0	1	.286	.429	.286

DRIVING IN RUNS	From 1B	From 2B	From 3B	Scoring Position
Totals	2/55	7/33	5/17	12/50
Percentage	4%	21%	29%	24%
Driving In Runners from 3B with Less than Two Out:			4/8	50%

Loves to face: Doyle Alexander (.354, 17-for-48, 4 HR)
Hates to face: Dan Quisenberry (.067, 1-for-15, 14 ground outs)
His only home runs were hit in back-to-back games against the Angels.... Last 11 home runs were hit with the bases empty. Hasn't hit a home run with a runner on base since he connected off Pete Redfern on April 25, 1981.... Orioles lost 17 of his last 19 starts.... Caught stealing on both attempts last season, running his total over past five seasons to one steal in eight tries. Career totals: 72-for-138 (52 percent).... Batted .215 in Late-Inning Pressure Situations over the last nine years.... Career batting average of .309 at the Kingdome.... Made three errors in his major-league debut in 1974, tying an A.L. record.... Anyone remember the Boston shortstop who lost his spot to Burleson in 1974? Mario Guerrero.

Randy Bush
Minnesota Twins   Bats Left

	AB	H	2B	3B	HR	RRF	BB	SO	BA	SA	OBA
Season	293	74	10	2	11	48	43	49	.253	.413	.349
vs. Left-Handers	9	2	0	0	0	2	3	2	.222	.222	.417
vs. Right-Handers	284	72	10	2	11	46	40	47	.254	.419	.346
Home	128	33	3	1	3	20	25	21	.258	.367	.380
Road	165	41	7	1	8	28	18	28	.248	.448	.323
Grass	125	33	6	1	6	20	16	20	.264	.472	.347
Artificial Turf	168	41	4	1	5	28	27	29	.244	.369	.350
April	54	12	2	1	2	6	7	6	.222	.407	.306
May	38	8	2	0	0	6	10	3	.211	.263	.375
June	37	12	1	0	3	8	2	5	.324	.595	.359
July	33	6	1	0	1	6	2	8	.182	.303	.229
August	62	16	2	1	1	4	8	15	.258	.371	.343
Sept./Oct.	69	20	2	0	4	18	14	12	.290	.493	.411
Leading Off Inn.	64	17	1	1	3	3	7	14	.266	.453	.347
Runners On	128	37	7	1	4	41	23	17	.289	.453	.385
Runners/Scor. Pos.	70	20	4	0	2	34	16	10	.286	.429	.396
Runners On/2 Out	53	13	2	0	2	16	11	5	.245	.396	.375
Scor. Pos./2 Out	33	8	1	0	1	13	7	4	.242	.364	.375
Late Inning Pressure	37	9	2	1	0	6	6	10	.243	.351	.364
Leading Off	5	1	0	0	0	0	1	2	.200	.200	.429
Runners On	22	7	2	1	0	6	5	4	.318	.500	.444
Runners/Scor. Pos.	16	6	2	0	0	5	5	3	.375	.500	.524

DRIVING IN RUNS	From 1B	From 2B	From 3B	Scoring Position
Totals	8/86	16/63	13/31	29/94
Percentage	9%	25%	42%	31%
Driving In Runners from 3B with Less than Two Out:		9/15		60%

Loves to face: Bob James (.800, 4-for-5, 1 HR)
Hates to face: Dave Schmidt (0-for-8)

Started 73 games last season, all against right-handed pitchers.... Twins' most often used pinch hitter last season, sent up to the plate 40 times by Tom Kelly. Batted .233 and led A.L. with nine pinch-hit walks.... Has only 67 career plate appearances vs. left-handed pitchers (.130, 7-for-54, 0 HR); 1,851 appearances vs. right-handers (.251 average).... Career batting average of .227 leading off innings.... Has hit for a higher average at the Metrodome than he has in road games in each of the last five seasons.... Has hit at least 40 points higher with runners on than with the bases empty in four of the last five seasons.... Part of Minnesota's great rookie crop of '82 that included Hrbek, Gaetti, and Brunansky.

Brett Butler
Cleveland Indians   Bats Left

	AB	H	2B	3B	HR	RRF	BB	SO	BA	SA	OBA
Season	522	154	25	8	9	42	91	55	.295	.425	.399
vs. Left-Handers	146	39	5	0	2	16	32	25	.267	.342	.397
vs. Right-Handers	376	115	20	8	7	26	59	30	.306	.457	.400
Home	246	83	12	7	4	16	47	29	.337	.492	.443
Road	276	71	13	1	5	26	44	26	.257	.366	.359
Grass	425	136	21	8	7	35	80	41	.320	.456	.427
Artificial Turf	97	18	4	0	2	7	11	14	.186	.289	.269
April	13	2	2	0	0	1	2	1	.154	.308	.267
May	103	31	6	2	1	9	21	12	.301	.427	.424
June	92	27	4	3	0	6	19	7	.293	.402	.414
July	93	25	4	1	1	6	11	6	.269	.366	.346
August	112	36	4	0	3	9	16	14	.321	.438	.406
Sept./Oct.	109	33	5	2	4	11	22	15	.303	.495	.414
Leading Off Inn.	202	64	6	4	4	4	31	20	.317	.446	.408
Runners On	165	50	8	2	2	35	38	17	.303	.412	.432
Runners/Scor. Pos.	90	29	4	2	2	34	29	9	.322	.478	.479
Runners On/2 Out	67	18	3	1	0	16	14	6	.269	.343	.395
Scor. Pos./2 Out	42	10	1	1	0	9	11	4	.238	.310	.396
Late Inning Pressure	62	19	3	0	3	10	8	9	.306	.500	.380
Leading Off	16	5	0	0	1	1	3	2	.313	.500	.421
Runners On	18	6	1	0	2	9	1	3	.333	.722	.350
Runners/Scor. Pos.	10	5	1	0	2	9	1	1	.500	1.200	.500

DRIVING IN RUNS	From 1B	From 2B	From 3B	Scoring Position
Totals	2/112	16/73	15/34	31/107
Percentage	2%	22%	44%	29%
Driving In Runners from 3B with Less than Two Out:		11/20		55%

Loves to face: Neal Heaton (.800, 4-for-5)
Hates to face: Mario Soto (.138, 4-for-29, 1 HR)

Led major-league center fielders with 401 fielding chances last season.... One of three center fielders to average better than 3.00 putouts per nine innings last season. (Pettis 3.15, E.Davis 3.12, Butler 3.02).... Caught stealing 16 times (in 49 attempts), 3d most in A.L.... Yearly batting averages with runners in scoring position since 1984: .346, .351, .273, .322.... Here's a left-handed batter with a career average 23 points higher vs. southpaws (.297) than vs. right-handers (.274).... Leaving Cleveland Stadium for Candlestick ought to cost him roughly 15 points on his batting average, judging by our Ballpark Effects data (page 433). Career mark at the 'Stick is .283 (13-for-46).

Ivan Calderon
Chicago White Sox   Bats Right

	AB	H	2B	3B	HR	RRF	BB	SO	BA	SA	OBA
Season	542	159	38	2	28	84	60	109	.293	.526	.362
vs. Left-Handers	190	53	11	0	13	25	24	40	.279	.542	.360
vs. Right-Handers	352	106	27	2	15	59	36	69	.301	.517	.364
Home	260	82	20	1	15	49	39	47	.315	.573	.402
Road	282	77	18	1	13	35	21	62	.273	.482	.324
Grass	450	136	30	1	26	78	59	91	.302	.547	.382
Artificial Turf	92	23	8	1	2	6	1	18	.250	.424	.255
April	66	17	5	0	1	2	6	10	.258	.379	.319
May	50	19	6	0	5	12	10	11	.380	.800	.492
June	111	32	9	1	4	21	6	23	.288	.495	.325
July	105	29	4	0	5	17	11	22	.276	.457	.342
August	102	31	3	0	7	16	13	24	.304	.539	.379
Sept./Oct.	108	31	11	1	6	16	14	19	.287	.574	.363
Leading Off Inn.	129	40	12	1	7	7	10	25	.310	.581	.364
Runners On	255	67	14	0	9	65	28	57	.263	.424	.331
Runners/Scor. Pos.	136	37	7	0	4	53	18	33	.272	.412	.348
Runners On/2 Out	103	18	3	0	2	18	17	25	.175	.262	.292
Scor. Pos./2 Out	56	11	1	0	1	15	11	13	.196	.268	.328
Late Inning Pressure	79	27	4	0	2	10	13	17	.342	.468	.426
Leading Off	18	8	2	0	0	0	1	2	.444	.556	.474
Runners On	36	12	2	0	1	9	6	9	.333	.472	.409
Runners/Scor. Pos.	17	4	2	0	0	7	3	6	.235	.353	.318

DRIVING IN RUNS	From 1B	From 2B	From 3B	Scoring Position
Totals	12/183	22/106	22/55	44/161
Percentage	7%	21%	40%	27%
Driving In Runners from 3B with Less than Two Out:		15/28		54%

Loves to face: Mike Moore (.700, 7-for-10)
Hates to face: Mike Smithson (.048, 1-for-21)

Ranked fifth in A.L. with 17 home runs after the All-Star break.... Had never hit more than 24 home runs at any level of professional baseball prior to 1987.... White Sox had a record of 49-37 with him in the cleanup spot, 28-48 without him there.... Batted .465 (20-for-43) in 10 games against the Brewers last season. Career batting average of .400 (14-for-35) at County Stadium is his highest at any ballpark.... Career average of .267 with runners in scoring position is broken down like this: .326 with less than two out, .170 with two out.... Career average of .259 (1 HR per 35.4 AB) with runners on base, .301 (1 HR per 19.1 AB) with the bases empty.... Career average of .326 in LIP Situations, .274 otherwise.

Jose Canseco
Oakland As   Bats Right

	AB	H	2B	3B	HR	RRF	BB	SO	BA	SA	OBA
Season	630	162	35	3	31	117	50	157	.257	.470	.310
vs. Left-Handers	204	63	12	3	15	48	16	46	.309	.618	.356
vs. Right-Handers	426	99	23	0	16	69	34	111	.232	.399	.288
Home	298	82	17	2	16	60	28	66	.275	.507	.332
Road	332	80	18	1	15	57	22	91	.241	.437	.289
Grass	530	141	29	3	29	104	38	130	.266	.496	.311
Artificial Turf	100	21	6	0	2	13	12	27	.210	.330	.301
April	80	23	5	0	1	11	0	27	.288	.388	.284
May	104	24	3	0	5	14	7	22	.231	.404	.274
June	105	30	4	1	8	24	13	20	.286	.571	.361
July	113	36	8	0	8	29	6	27	.319	.602	.355
August	118	29	8	2	5	21	9	29	.246	.475	.302
Sept./Oct.	110	20	7	0	4	18	15	32	.182	.355	.273
Leading Off Inn.	122	32	8	0	7	7	7	27	.262	.500	.308
Runners On	289	78	15	2	12	98	26	62	.270	.460	.327
Runners/Scor. Pos.	187	49	6	2	8	83	21	41	.262	.444	.323
Runners On/2 Out	131	36	7	2	5	45	8	35	.275	.473	.317
Scor. Pos./2 Out	88	24	1	2	4	37	8	23	.273	.466	.333
Late Inning Pressure	84	22	6	0	3	20	6	22	.262	.440	.315
Leading Off	18	7	4	0	1	1	2	2	.389	.778	.450
Runners On	42	14	1	0	2	19	3	10	.333	.500	.383
Runners/Scor. Pos.	27	12	1	0	2	19	3	5	.444	.704	.484

DRIVING IN RUNS	From 1B	From 2B	From 3B	Scoring Position
Totals	18/193	34/146	34/81	68/227
Percentage	9%	23%	42%	30%
Driving In Runners from 3B with Less than Two Out:		22/47		47%

Loves to face: Oil Can Boyd (.500, 5-for-10, 4 HR)
Hates to face: Greg Harris (0-for-10, 7 SO)

A's led A.L. with 28 steals of third. Who led A's? Canseco, who was six for six.... Batted .300 in day games (1 HR per 15.7 AB), .234 at night (1 HR per 24.1 AB).... Had 10 extra-base hits without a single (Aug. 5-Aug. 15), tying Kent Hrbek for longest streak in A.L. last season.... A's had a 22-5 record in games in which he homered, but only a 23-18 record when McGwire connected.... Career batting average of .304 with runners in scoring position, .234 in all other at bats combined. Difference of 70 points is largest by any player for the last 10 years (minimum: 300 AB with RISP).... Career average of .357 at Cleveland Stadium. Has hit more HR there (6) as a visiting player than in any other ballpark.

Joe Carter
Bats Right

Cleveland Indians	AB	H	2B	3B	HR	RRF	BB	SO	BA	SA	OBA
Season	588	155	27	2	32	109	27	105	.264	.480	.304
vs. Left-Handers	153	38	5	1	7	26	7	28	.248	.431	.287
vs. Right-Handers	435	117	22	1	25	83	20	77	.269	.497	.310
Home	279	70	15	1	9	46	17	43	.251	.409	.298
Road	309	85	12	1	23	63	10	62	.275	.544	.310
Grass	509	135	23	2	30	97	24	90	.265	.495	.304
Artificial Turf	79	20	4	0	2	12	3	15	.253	.380	.302
April	91	23	5	0	6	14	5	19	.253	.505	.299
May	110	26	3	2	6	18	5	21	.236	.464	.274
June	79	19	4	0	4	17	2	16	.241	.443	.302
July	111	30	5	0	8	27	6	15	.270	.532	.305
August	91	25	1	0	4	11	3	15	.275	.418	.302
Sept./Oct.	106	32	9	0	4	22	6	19	.302	.500	.342
Leading Off Inn.	134	36	7	0	12	12	4	22	.269	.590	.300
Runners On	303	73	12	1	11	88	13	57	.241	.396	.278
Runners/Scor. Pos.	198	49	6	1	6	77	12	39	.247	.379	.298
Runners On/2 Out	141	29	6	1	3	30	2	29	.206	.326	.233
Scor. Pos./2 Out	94	21	3	1	1	26	2	20	.223	.309	.263
Late Inning Pressure	79	19	2	0	4	16	7	16	.241	.418	.318
Leading Off	16	6	1	0	1	1	0	2	.375	.625	.375
Runners On	43	12	0	0	3	15	7	8	.279	.488	.392
Runners/Scor. Pos.	26	8	0	0	2	13	7	4	.308	.538	.471

DRIVING IN RUNS	From 1B	From 2B	From 3B	Scoring Position
Totals	12/197	26/135	39/97	65/232
Percentage	6%	19%	40%	28%
Driving In Runners from 3B with Less than Two Out:	26/49			53%

Loves to face: Jose Nunez (2-for-2, 2 HR)
Hates to face: Tommy John (0-for-9)

Averaged one walk per 23.3 plate appearances, 3d-lowest rate in A.L.... Although he started the majority of his games at first base (80), he was one of three A.L. players to start at least 10 games at each of the three outfield positions. Gary Redus and Mark Davidson were the others.... Most HR of any visiting player at Memorial Stadium (4) and Fenway Park (7). Seven home runs at Fenway were the most by a visiting player at any stadium since Mike Schmidt hit eight at Wrigley Field in 1980. The last visiting player to hit seven at Fenway was Vic Wertz in 1957.... Career totals: 34 HR with runners on base, 55 with the bases empty.... Career batting average of .235 during month of April, .308 from Sept. 1 on.

Carmen Castillo
Bats Right

Cleveland Indians	AB	H	2B	3B	HR	RRF	BB	SO	BA	SA	OBA
Season	220	55	17	0	11	31	16	52	.250	.477	.296
vs. Left-Handers	124	33	10	0	7	21	14	29	.266	.516	.336
vs. Right-Handers	96	22	7	0	4	10	2	23	.229	.427	.240
Home	118	37	12	0	8	21	12	28	.314	.619	.368
Road	102	18	5	0	3	10	4	24	.176	.314	.206
Grass	192	48	14	0	11	28	14	44	.250	.495	.295
Artificial Turf	28	7	3	0	0	3	2	8	.250	.357	.300
April	16	3	0	0	1	2	0	7	.188	.375	.188
May	26	9	2	0	3	4	3	4	.346	.769	.414
June	35	11	2	0	2	5	0	10	.314	.543	.306
July	49	10	3	0	2	4	6	9	.204	.388	.286
August	67	15	8	0	1	11	7	14	.224	.388	.293
Sept./Oct.	27	7	2	0	2	5	0	8	.259	.556	.250
Leading Off Inn.	47	13	4	0	2	2	3	10	.277	.489	.320
Runners On	89	19	7	0	2	22	8	20	.213	.360	.267
Runners/Scor. Pos.	60	14	6	0	1	20	3	11	.233	.383	.254
Runners On/2 Out	40	8	3	0	1	11	3	6	.200	.350	.256
Scor. Pos./2 Out	31	8	3	0	1	11	1	3	.258	.452	.281
Late Inning Pressure	41	6	1	0	1	3	0	7	.146	.244	.143
Leading Off	5	0	0	0	0	0	0	0	.000	.000	.000
Runners On	18	3	1	0	0	2	0	2	.167	.222	.158
Runners/Scor. Pos.	14	1	1	0	0	2	0	2	.071	.143	.067

DRIVING IN RUNS	From 1B	From 2B	From 3B	Scoring Position
Totals	3/58	5/45	12/30	17/75
Percentage	5%	11%	40%	23%
Driving In Runners from 3B with Less than Two Out:	6/13			46%

Loves to face: Tommy John (.556, 5-for-9, 1 HR)
Hates to face: Ron Guidry (.080, 2-for-25)

Batted .141 in day games, .302 at night. That 161-point difference was the largest of the 1987 season (minimum: 50 AB each way). His career numbers (.194 daytime, .276 night) also represent the largest difference over the last 10 years. Now look at Juan Castillo.... Batting average 137 points higher at home than on the road was the largest difference of *that* type in A.L. last season (minimum: 100 AB each way), marking the sixth year in a row that he's hit better at Cleveland Stadium than he has on the road.... Combined strengths: .403 in night games at home last season; combined weaknesses: .133 in day games on the road.... Started 41 of 48 games vs. opposing southpaw starters, 16 of 114 vs. right-handers.

Juan Castillo
Bats Left and Right

Milwaukee Brewers	AB	H	2B	3B	HR	RRF	BB	SO	BA	SA	OBA
Season	321	72	11	4	3	31	33	76	.224	.312	.302
vs. Left-Handers	138	30	4	2	1	10	2	28	.217	.297	.229
vs. Right-Handers	183	42	7	2	2	21	31	48	.230	.322	.349
Home	164	43	6	2	3	18	16	35	.262	.378	.330
Road	157	29	5	2	0	13	17	41	.185	.242	.273
Grass	262	60	9	4	3	27	24	65	.229	.328	.300
Artificial Turf	59	12	2	0	0	4	9	11	.203	.237	.309
April	13	4	0	0	1	2	2	1	.308	.538	.400
May	75	20	3	0	2	7	12	16	.267	.387	.368
June	49	14	2	3	0	7	4	12	.286	.449	.340
July	30	3	1	0	0	0	3	12	.100	.133	.182
August	98	18	4	1	0	12	5	20	.184	.245	.236
Sept./Oct.	56	13	1	0	0	3	7	15	.232	.250	.328
Leading Off Inn.	99	26	3	1	2	2	8	20	.263	.374	.318
Runners On	128	27	7	1	1	29	13	36	.211	.305	.287
Runners/Scor. Pos.	74	14	5	0	0	25	8	26	.189	.257	.265
Runners On/2 Out	64	12	4	1	0	13	6	22	.188	.281	.257
Scor. Pos./2 Out	36	6	2	0	0	11	5	16	.167	.222	.268
Late Inning Pressure	34	9	2	0	0	4	4	6	.265	.324	.342
Leading Off	10	2	1	0	0	0	1	2	.200	.300	.273
Runners On	12	3	1	0	0	4	2	2	.250	.333	.357
Runners/Scor. Pos.	9	3	1	0	0	4	2	1	.333	.444	.455

DRIVING IN RUNS	From 1B	From 2B	From 3B	Scoring Position
Totals	6/80	10/61	12/31	22/92
Percentage	8%	16%	39%	24%
Driving In Runners from 3B with Less than Two Out:	8/12			67%

Loves to face: Ken Schrom (.600, 3-for-5, 1 HR)
Hates to face: Roger Clemens (0-for-3, 3 SO)

What's with these Castillos? This one batted .313 in day games, .177 at night. 135 points is largest difference among A.L. players last season (minimum: 50 AB each way). Night-game average was 2d-lowest among 299 major-league qualifiers.... Batted .214 in day games in 1986, .115 at night.... Played 97 games at second base, 13 games at shortstop, and 7 games at third base.... Averaged 2.62 assists per nine innings, 2d-lowest among major-league second basemen (minimum: 500 innings).... Tied for third in A.L. with 14 sacrifice bunts.... Failed to drive in a run in his final 18 games last season.... Career breakdown: .232 with bases empty, .194 with runners on base, .174 with runners in scoring position.

Rick Cerone
Bats Right

New York Yankees	AB	H	2B	3B	HR	RRF	BB	SO	BA	SA	OBA
Season	284	69	12	1	4	24	30	46	.243	.335	.320
vs. Left-Handers	132	36	6	0	1	11	10	20	.273	.341	.329
vs. Right-Handers	152	33	6	1	3	13	20	26	.217	.329	.313
Home	148	28	4	1	1	13	18	26	.189	.250	.282
Road	136	41	8	0	3	11	12	20	.301	.426	.362
Grass	242	56	9	1	4	24	23	38	.231	.326	.304
Artificial Turf	42	13	3	0	0	0	7	8	.310	.381	.408
April	19	2	0	0	0	1	2	3	.105	.105	.250
May	38	11	3	0	0	2	3	5	.289	.368	.341
June	55	11	1	0	1	9	8	7	.200	.273	.297
July	46	13	3	0	1	6	5	7	.283	.413	.365
August	67	17	3	0	1	3	9	9	.254	.343	.292
Sept./Oct.	59	15	2	1	1	3	9	15	.254	.373	.348
Leading Off Inn.	68	22	3	0	2	2	9	9	.324	.456	.403
Runners On	111	22	4	0	1	21	14	19	.198	.261	.295
Runners/Scor. Pos.	59	12	1	0	1	20	14	10	.203	.271	.354
Runners On/2 Out	48	11	1	0	0	9	11	9	.229	.250	.403
Scor. Pos./2 Out	32	7	1	0	0	9	11	5	.219	.250	.444
Late Inning Pressure	30	6	1	0	0	2	5	4	.200	.233	.314
Leading Off	6	1	0	0	0	0	3	0	.167	.167	.444
Runners On	14	1	0	0	0	2	1	2	.071	.071	.133
Runners/Scor. Pos.	9	1	0	0	0	2	1	1	.111	.111	.200

DRIVING IN RUNS	From 1B	From 2B	From 3B	Scoring Position
Totals	1/85	7/51	12/24	19/75
Percentage	1%	14%	50%	25%
Driving In Runners from 3B with Less than Two Out:	8/12			67%

Loves to face: Mike Smithson (.375, 3-for-8, 2 HR)
Hates to face: Frank Viola (.083, 2-for-24)

Batted 112 points higher in road games than he did in home games, largest difference in A.L. last season (minimum: 100 AB each way). ... Batting average with runners on base was the lowest of his career.... Career batting average of .197 (13-for-66) with the bases loaded.... First player to pitch and catch in the same game since Jeff Newman in 1977. First "nonpitcher" to pitch for the Yankees since Gene Michael mopped up a doubleheader in a 10–2 loss to the Angels on August 26, 1968. On previous day, Rocky Colavito was the winner in a 6–5 victory vs. the Tigers.... Hit 14 home runs with 85 RBI for the 1980 Yankees, and hasn't produced even half those totals in any season since.

Cecil Cooper

Bats Left

Milwaukee Brewers

	AB	H	2B	3B	HR	RRF	BB	SO	BA	SA	OBA
Season	250	62	13	0	6	37	17	51	.248	.372	.293
vs. Left-Handers	81	21	5	0	1	13	7	19	.259	.358	.308
vs. Right-Handers	169	41	8	0	5	24	10	32	.243	.379	.285
Home	108	32	6	0	4	22	8	18	.296	.463	.342
Road	142	30	7	0	2	15	9	33	.211	.303	.255
Grass	208	55	11	0	6	34	16	37	.264	.404	.313
Artificial Turf	42	7	2	0	0	3	1	14	.167	.214	.186
April	57	10	2	0	0	8	1	10	.175	.211	.183
May	60	16	5	0	3	7	0	14	.267	.500	.267
June	105	30	5	0	3	21	13	21	.286	.419	.361
July	28	6	1	0	0	1	3	6	.214	.250	.290
August	0	0	0	0	0	0	0	0	—	—	—
Sept./Oct.	0	0	0	0	0	0	0	0	—	—	—
Leading Off Inn.	40	12	4	0	0	0	2	10	.300	.400	.333
Runners On	108	30	5	0	3	34	12	20	.278	.407	.341
Runners/Scor. Pos.	60	19	3	0	1	28	9	11	.317	.417	.389
Runners On/2 Out	42	12	2	0	2	14	4	8	.286	.476	.348
Scor. Pos./2 Out	24	7	1	0	1	11	4	5	.292	.458	.393
Late Inning Pressure	31	14	2	0	1	7	1	5	.452	.613	.455
Leading Off	9	6	2	0	0	0	0	0	.667	.889	.667
Runners On	14	6	0	0	1	7	1	3	.429	.643	.438
Runners/Scor. Pos.	9	4	0	0	1	7	1	2	.444	.778	.455

DRIVING IN RUNS	From 1B	From 2B	From 3B	Scoring Position
Totals	6/88	10/44	15/26	25/70
Percentage	7%	23%	58%	36%
Driving In Runners from 3B with Less than Two Out:			12/15	80%

Loves to face: Dan Quisenberry (.500, 10-for-20, 2 HR)
Hates to face: Storm Davis (.138, 4-for-29)

Did not play the field in 1987. Appeared in 62 games as a designated hitter and one game as a pinch-hitter. Didn't play at all after July 12. It's a crazy world. . . . Through June 6, Cooper had one walk and 25 strikeouts. . . . Batting average with runners in scoring position was over .290 in seven of the previous eight seasons. . . . Batting average in Late-Inning Pressure Situations was the highest among 302 major-league qualifiers. Has batted .340 in LIP Situations from 1985 to 1987. . . . Only left-handed hitter with a higher batting average vs. southpaws than vs. right-handers in each of the last four seasons. . . . Names from box-score of his major-league debut (Sept. 8, 1971): Ron Swoboda, Jake Gibbs, Bob Bolin, Felipe Alou.

Alvin Davis

Bats Left

Seattle Mariners

	AB	H	2B	3B	HR	RRF	BB	SO	BA	SA	OBA
Season	580	171	37	2	29	101	72	84	.295	.516	.370
vs. Left-Handers	208	50	14	0	5	26	19	38	.240	.380	.301
vs. Right-Handers	372	121	23	2	24	75	53	46	.325	.591	.406
Home	277	85	17	1	18	56	44	39	.307	.570	.402
Road	303	86	20	1	11	45	28	45	.284	.465	.339
Grass	233	71	18	0	9	38	22	31	.305	.498	.359
Artificial Turf	347	100	19	2	20	63	50	53	.288	.527	.377
April	76	19	7	0	1	9	11	15	.250	.382	.337
May	96	33	6	0	2	13	12	17	.344	.469	.405
June	92	28	5	1	3	14	14	12	.304	.478	.393
July	98	33	7	1	8	18	9	9	.337	.673	.394
August	108	32	7	0	8	26	20	12	.296	.583	.406
Sept./Oct.	110	26	5	0	7	21	6	19	.236	.473	.280
Leading Off Inn.	132	44	15	0	8	8	8	17	.333	.629	.371
Runners On	269	79	16	1	17	89	42	36	.294	.550	.381
Runners/Scor. Pos.	160	41	10	1	9	70	27	19	.256	.500	.352
Runners On/2 Out	116	39	8	1	8	39	23	15	.336	.629	.446
Scor. Pos./2 Out	78	21	4	1	5	31	17	10	.269	.538	.400
Late Inning Pressure	67	21	5	0	4	11	11	6	.313	.567	.405
Leading Off	18	6	2	0	1	1	2	3	.333	.611	.400
Runners On	29	10	3	0	3	10	7	1	.345	.759	.459
Runners/Scor. Pos.	14	4	2	0	1	6	5	0	.286	.643	.450

DRIVING IN RUNS	From 1B	From 2B	From 3B	Scoring Position
Totals	18/186	25/131	29/62	54/193
Percentage	10%	19%	47%	28%
Driving In Runners from 3B with Less than Two Out:			22/33	67%

Loves to face: Roger Clemens (.526, 10-for-19, 2 HR)
Hates to face: Bert Blyleven (.100, 4-for-40)

Ranked second in A.L. with 19 HR after the All-Star break, one fewer than Danny Tartabull. . . . Drove in at least one run in each of his last three games, including one in his final at bat, to reach the 100-RBI plateau. . . . More strikeouts than walks for the first time in his career. . . . One home run and 30 stolen bases shy of the 30/30 Club. . . . Streak of 54 consecutive errorless games at first base (May 25 to July 25). . . . On-going race for the Mariners all-time HR leadership: Davis (92), Phelps (91), Presley (89). . . . Career average of .254 (1 HR per 50.9 AB) vs. left-handed pitchers, .300 (one HR per 19.1 AB) vs. right-handers. . . . Has homered in every A.L. ballpark except Exhibition Stadium (80 career AB).

Mike Davis

Bats Left

Oakland As

	AB	H	2B	3B	HR	RRF	BB	SO	BA	SA	OBA
Season	494	131	32	1	22	74	42	94	.265	.468	.320
vs. Left-Handers	126	35	8	1	6	29	10	31	.278	.500	.326
vs. Right-Handers	368	96	24	0	16	45	32	63	.261	.457	.319
Home	234	61	17	0	9	32	21	45	.261	.449	.318
Road	260	70	15	1	13	42	21	49	.269	.485	.323
Grass	403	111	26	1	17	57	37	70	.275	.471	.334
Artificial Turf	91	20	6	0	5	17	5	24	.220	.451	.258
April	71	18	7	0	5	13	4	12	.254	.563	.289
May	84	27	7	1	7	19	9	11	.321	.679	.385
June	98	29	3	0	5	16	13	20	.296	.480	.378
July	73	16	6	0	3	10	6	19	.219	.425	.272
August	78	16	5	0	0	8	7	14	.205	.269	.267
Sept./Oct.	90	25	4	0	2	8	3	18	.278	.389	.301
Leading Off Inn.	104	32	9	0	6	6	5	21	.308	.567	.339
Runners On	212	57	13	1	8	60	23	41	.269	.453	.332
Runners/Scor. Pos.	123	32	10	1	5	52	15	26	.260	.480	.326
Runners On/2 Out	80	26	7	1	3	27	9	13	.325	.550	.393
Scor. Pos./2 Out	53	18	6	1	2	24	6	9	.340	.604	.407
Late Inning Pressure	64	20	5	0	4	13	10	19	.313	.578	.400
Leading Off	21	8	3	0	2	2	2	5	.381	.810	.435
Runners On	25	9	1	0	2	11	5	6	.360	.640	.452
Runners/Scor. Pos.	17	7	1	0	2	11	2	5	.412	.824	.450

DRIVING IN RUNS	From 1B	From 2B	From 3B	Scoring Position
Totals	8/150	24/98	20/47	44/145
Percentage	5%	24%	43%	30%
Driving In Runners from 3B with Less than Two Out:			14/23	61%

Loves to face: Danny Darwin (.310, 9-for-29, 1 HR)
Hates to face: Chuck Cary (0-for-4)

Hit 20 home runs before the All-Star break, but only two after that, the fewest 2d-half HR by a 1st-half 20-HR man since—well—since 1986 when Wally Joyner posted that same 20–2 split. . . . How will A's replace his 13 errors in right field, last season's major-league high? They've brought in Dave Parker, who led N.L. right fielders with 10. . . . But seriously folks, over the past four seasons, Oakland has allowed 4.72 runs per nine innings with Davis in RF, 5.24 with other RFs. . . . Only four players have equalled or surpassed Davis in HR (65), SB (70), and BA (.274) over past three seasons: Joe Carter, namesake Eric, Rickey Henderson, and new teammate Kirk Gibson.

Doug DeCinces

Bats Right

California Angels

	AB	H	2B	3B	HR	RRF	BB	SO	BA	SA	OBA
Season	453	106	23	0	16	67	70	87	.234	.391	.337
vs. Left-Handers	159	45	7	0	7	28	36	27	.283	.459	.413
vs. Right-Handers	294	61	16	0	9	39	34	60	.207	.354	.292
Home	226	62	10	0	10	34	40	35	.274	.451	.385
Road	227	44	13	0	6	33	30	52	.194	.330	.287
Grass	374	92	19	0	13	54	64	67	.246	.401	.357
Artificial Turf	79	14	4	0	3	13	6	20	.177	.342	.235
April	58	17	4	0	2	12	15	12	.293	.466	.440
May	90	17	4	0	3	12	11	17	.189	.333	.277
June	86	18	3	0	4	11	13	19	.209	.384	.320
July	85	24	4	0	2	12	18	15	.282	.400	.400
August	91	24	5	0	5	13	9	15	.264	.484	.330
Sept./Oct.	43	6	3	0	0	7	4	9	.140	.209	.213
Leading Off Inn.	108	32	8	0	6	6	17	20	.296	.537	.392
Runners On	197	45	9	0	6	57	37	45	.228	.365	.351
Runners/Scor. Pos.	129	27	7	0	5	54	28	32	.209	.380	.348
Runners On/2 Out	86	21	4	0	4	26	19	23	.244	.430	.387
Scor. Pos./2 Out	53	12	3	0	3	23	13	17	.226	.453	.379
Late Inning Pressure	61	13	2	0	2	7	13	11	.213	.344	.351
Leading Off	13	5	1	0	0	0	2	2	.385	.462	.467
Runners On	24	3	1	0	1	6	7	6	.125	.292	.323
Runners/Scor. Pos.	17	2	1	0	0	4	7	4	.118	.176	.375

DRIVING IN RUNS	From 1B	From 2B	From 3B	Scoring Position
Totals	9/137	17/102	24/48	41/150
Percentage	7%	17%	50%	27%
Driving In Runners from 3B with Less than Two Out:			16/36	44%

Loves to face: Luis Sanchez (1-for-1)
Hates to face: Matt Keough (.235, 4-for-17, 1 HR)

Has never faced Brad Lesley, the other former major-leaguer who pitched in Japan last season; nor has he faced Bill Gullickson, who's headed there this season. . . . Played 131 games at third base, four at first base, and one at shortstop for Angels, who allowed 4.81 runs per nine innings with DeCinces at third base, 5.35 with other third basemen. . . . Hit well at Anaheim Stadium and vs. left-handed pitchers, but combine his weaknesses and what do you get? A .167 batting average (24-for-144 with two HR) vs. right-handers in road games. . . . Results Guaranteed in 7 Days, Or Your Money Back: Cardinals clinched the N.L. East title in DeCinces's first game with them.

Rob Deer
Milwaukee Brewers — Bats Right

	AB	H	2B	3B	HR	RRF	BB	SO	BA	SA	OBA
Season	474	113	15	2	28	84	86	186	.238	.456	.360
vs. Left-Handers	152	39	6	1	8	31	35	48	.257	.467	.394
vs. Right-Handers	322	74	9	1	20	53	51	138	.230	.450	.344
Home	232	53	7	1	11	37	33	94	.228	.409	.332
Road	242	60	8	1	17	47	53	92	.248	.500	.386
Grass	403	95	11	2	21	67	72	163	.236	.429	.356
Artificial Turf	71	18	4	0	7	17	14	23	.254	.606	.384
April	74	25	1	2	9	22	14	25	.338	.770	.444
May	62	18	6	0	2	5	11	16	.290	.484	.397
June	94	19	3	0	5	17	10	39	.202	.394	.279
July	80	20	1	0	6	10	17	32	.250	.488	.394
August	81	14	1	0	4	16	21	37	.173	.333	.350
Sept./Oct.	83	17	3	0	2	14	13	37	.205	.313	.320
Leading Off Inn.	122	30	5	1	9	9	19	49	.246	.525	.361
Runners On	235	55	7	0	14	70	41	102	.234	.443	.351
Runners/Scor. Pos.	131	34	6	0	8	58	34	54	.260	.489	.410
Runners On/2 Out	95	24	5	0	4	30	27	41	.253	.432	.423
Scor. Pos./2 Out	55	16	5	0	1	24	23	18	.291	.436	.500
Late Inning Pressure	52	16	3	0	3	10	10	18	.308	.538	.438
Leading Off	16	3	1	0	1	1	1	7	.188	.438	.278
Runners On	24	12	2	0	2	9	4	6	.500	.833	.586
Runners/Scor. Pos.	16	8	2	0	2	9	3	4	.500	1.000	.579

DRIVING IN RUNS

	From 1B	From 2B	From 3B	Scoring Position
Totals	14/180	18/95	23/59	41/154
Percentage	8%	19%	39%	27%
Driving In Runners from 3B with Less than Two Out:		14/35		40%

Loves to face: Mike Moore (.583, 7-for-12, 2 HR)
Hates to face: Mark Eichhorn (0-for-7, 6 SO)

Became the first player to hit grand slams in consecutive games since Greg Luzinski in 1984.... Only player in majors with at least 80 RBI in each of last two seasons, but with sub-.250 batting average in each.... Batting average vs. right-handers has increased in each of his seasons in the majors: .143, .168, .214, .230.... Career ratio of 0.58 ground outs-to-air outs is lowest of any player over the last 13 years (minimum: 1,000 PA).... Has homered in every A.L. ballpark except Yankee Stadium (34 AB) and Fenway Park (40 AB).... Was born on Sept. 29, 1960, the day that Ted Williams announced his retirement, and a day after the Splinter hit a 420-foot homer in his final at bat.

Brian Downing
California Angels — Bats Right

	AB	H	2B	3B	HR	RRF	BB	SO	BA	SA	OBA
Season	567	154	29	3	29	78	106	85	.272	.487	.400
vs. Left-Handers	177	53	10	1	11	24	41	35	.299	.554	.432
vs. Right-Handers	390	101	19	2	18	54	65	50	.259	.456	.384
Home	280	78	18	2	11	36	56	43	.279	.475	.412
Road	287	76	11	1	18	42	50	42	.265	.498	.388
Grass	482	131	24	3	21	63	85	69	.272	.465	.398
Artificial Turf	85	23	5	0	8	15	21	16	.271	.612	.411
April	88	31	7	1	9	22	18	12	.352	.761	.472
May	91	21	3	0	5	13	17	14	.231	.429	.358
June	100	26	6	1	3	8	17	15	.260	.430	.388
July	99	26	4	1	2	13	14	13	.263	.384	.370
August	93	23	5	0	4	9	14	18	.247	.430	.355
Sept./Oct.	96	27	4	0	6	13	26	13	.281	.510	.452
Leading Off Inn.	201	62	13	2	17	17	37	28	.308	.647	.433
Runners On	216	58	9	0	7	56	37	32	.269	.407	.388
Runners/Scor. Pos.	130	28	3	0	3	44	29	20	.215	.308	.367
Runners On/2 Out	87	19	2	0	3	16	15	14	.218	.345	.340
Scor. Pos./2 Out	58	11	1	0	2	13	12	7	.190	.310	.338
Late Inning Pressure	82	20	3	0	2	12	15	12	.244	.354	.364
Leading Off	18	5	2	0	0	0	2	3	.278	.389	.350
Runners On	45	12	0	0	2	12	5	6	.267	.400	.346
Runners/Scor. Pos.	26	5	0	0	0	8	2	3	.192	.192	.241

DRIVING IN RUNS

	From 1B	From 2B	From 3B	Scoring Position
Totals	9/141	22/104	17/54	39/158
Percentage	6%	21%	31%	25%
Driving In Runners from 3B with Less than Two Out:		17/27		63%

Loves to face: Charlie Leibrandt (.609, 14-for-23, 2 HR)
Hates to face: Jim Clancy (.059, 2-for-34, 1 HR)

Only A.L. player to start at least 10 games in both the leadoff and cleanup spots in the batting order.... Hitless in 28 consecutive at bats with runners in scoring position from May 25 to July 2, 2d-longest streak in majors last season.... 41 walks off left-handed pitchers were the most in A.L.... Of his 29 HR, 22 were solo shots and the other seven were hit with one man on base.... Led designated hitters in plate appearances (544), extra-base hits (49), and walks (84).... If the season were only a month long, Downing would be a sure-shot Hall of Famer. Last season, he hit nine HR in April, raising his total over the past six seasons to 30. Only Dale Murphy has hit more (35).

Jim Dwyer
Baltimore Orioles — Bats Left

	AB	H	2B	3B	HR	RRF	BB	SO	BA	SA	OBA
Season	241	66	7	1	15	35	37	57	.274	.498	.371
vs. Left-Handers	13	4	0	0	1	2	0	4	.308	.538	.308
vs. Right-Handers	228	62	7	1	14	33	37	53	.272	.496	.375
Home	84	20	3	0	3	11	19	20	.238	.381	.375
Road	157	46	4	1	12	24	18	37	.293	.561	.369
Grass	201	51	6	1	11	26	35	48	.254	.458	.366
Artificial Turf	40	15	1	0	4	9	2	9	.375	.700	.405
April	12	3	1	0	0	0	2	1	.250	.333	.400
May	73	23	1	0	8	16	8	11	.315	.658	.383
June	47	10	1	1	1	6	10	16	.213	.340	.345
July	25	7	0	0	1	2	4	7	.280	.400	.379
August	51	15	2	0	3	5	7	14	.294	.510	.379
Sept./Oct.	33	8	2	0	2	6	6	8	.242	.485	.359
Leading Off Inn.	54	21	4	0	3	3	8	12	.389	.630	.468
Runners On	98	19	0	1	7	27	21	30	.194	.429	.339
Runners/Scor. Pos.	54	9	0	1	2	17	10	17	.167	.315	.303
Runners On/2 Out	35	3	0	1	0	3	9	12	.086	.143	.273
Scor. Pos./2 Out	23	2	0	1	0	3	6	8	.087	.174	.276
Late Inning Pressure	33	8	1	0	2	4	7	8	.242	.455	.375
Leading Off	9	2	1	0	0	0	0	2	.222	.333	.222
Runners On	14	2	0	0	1	3	6	3	.143	.357	.400
Runners/Scor. Pos.	6	0	0	0	0	4	0		.000	.000	.400

DRIVING IN RUNS

	From 1B	From 2B	From 3B	Scoring Position
Totals	7/76	6/39	7/25	13/64
Percentage	9%	15%	28%	20%
Driving In Runners from 3B with Less than Two Out:		5/10		50%

Loves to face: Joe Johnson (3-for-3, 2 2B, 1 HR)
Hates to face: Gene Garber (0-for-11)

Came within 19 at bats of the highest total of his 15-year career (260 in 1980). Excluding pitchers, only one other player with at least 15 seasons never had more than 260 at bats in any of them: Terry Crowley, whose 15-year career high was 247 AB.... Had never before reached double figures in home runs.... Pinch HR on June 14 was his eighth in an Orioles uniform, breaking the club record he had shared with Benny Ayala.... Batting average with runners on base was 135 points lower than with bases empty, largest difference in majors (minimum: 75 AB each way).... On-base average leading off innings was highest among 162 A.L. qualifiers.

Darrell Evans
Detroit Tigers — Bats Left

	AB	H	2B	3B	HR	RRF	BB	SO	BA	SA	OBA
Season	499	128	20	0	34	103	100	84	.257	.501	.379
vs. Left-Handers	148	31	4	0	5	21	22	31	.209	.338	.312
vs. Right-Handers	351	97	16	0	29	82	78	53	.276	.570	.406
Home	246	61	8	0	19	52	45	43	.248	.512	.359
Road	253	67	12	0	15	51	55	41	.265	.490	.397
Grass	435	111	18	0	29	92	82	72	.255	.497	.370
Artificial Turf	64	17	2	0	5	11	18	12	.266	.531	.434
April	67	16	5	0	2	7	13	6	.239	.403	.366
May	76	17	1	0	5	15	18	9	.224	.434	.368
June	75	22	7	0	7	21	16	14	.293	.667	.413
July	76	20	1	0	7	15	11	15	.263	.553	.356
August	90	22	4	0	4	17	19	21	.244	.422	.369
Sept./Oct.	115	31	2	0	9	28	23	19	.270	.522	.393
Leading Off Inn.	112	26	2	0	10	10	16	19	.232	.518	.328
Runners On	234	68	14	0	16	85	47	40	.291	.556	.401
Runners/Scor. Pos.	126	36	10	0	8	67	32	23	.286	.556	.415
Runners On/2 Out	90	31	9	0	5	38	20	13	.344	.611	.464
Scor. Pos./2 Out	57	21	7	0	3	32	15	9	.368	.649	.500
Late Inning Pressure	63	17	2	0	2	6	9	6	.270	.397	.370
Leading Off	18	3	0	0	1	1	2	1	.167	.333	.250
Runners On	27	8	2	0	1	5	5	4	.296	.481	.406
Runners/Scor. Pos.	11	3	1	0	0	2	4	1	.273	.364	.467

DRIVING IN RUNS

	From 1B	From 2B	From 3B	Scoring Position
Totals	21/179	24/102	24/49	48/151
Percentage	12%	24%	49%	32%
Driving In Runners from 3B with Less than Two Out:		17/32		53%

Loves to face: Mike Boddicker (.471, 8-for-17, 2 HR)
Hates to face: Jimmy Key (.059, 1-for-17)

Reached 99-RBI mark with four games to play, but failed to become first 40-year-old ever to attain the 100 level.... Grounded into two double plays in 132 double-play situations, 2d-lowest rate in the majors (minimum: 40 opportunities).... Homered vs. every A.L. club except the Angels.... Started all 110 games in which Tigers faced a right-handed pitcher, half of their 52 games vs. southpaws.... They all laughed when Darnell Coles made 15 errors in his first 29 games at third base last season. But the Tigers allowed 23 runs in the 20.1 innings that Evans played at third, compared to 4.10 per nine innings with Coles there, and 4.55 with anyone else. We promise not to mention the A.L.C.S.

Dwight Evans

Bats Right

Boston Red Sox	AB	H	2B	3B	HR	RRF	BB	SO	BA	SA	OBA
Season	541	165	37	2	34	126	106	98	.305	.569	.417
vs. Left-Handers	144	53	10	0	12	38	27	17	.368	.688	.465
vs. Right-Handers	397	112	27	2	22	88	79	81	.282	.526	.400
Home	263	80	23	2	14	66	43	44	.304	.567	.399
Road	278	85	14	0	20	60	63	54	.306	.572	.433
Grass	458	139	34	2	27	106	88	80	.303	.563	.414
Artificial Turf	83	26	3	0	7	20	18	18	.313	.602	.436
April	71	21	7	1	4	17	19	7	.296	.592	.444
May	74	22	4	0	4	18	9	15	.297	.514	.373
June	101	32	8	0	5	24	15	23	.317	.545	.403
July	95	33	5	0	7	21	18	16	.347	.621	.451
August	104	38	9	1	13	31	11	19	.365	.846	.429
Sept./Oct.	96	19	4	0	1	15	34	18	.198	.271	.398
Leading Off Inn.	117	32	6	0	6	6	13	22	.274	.479	.450
Runners On	256	83	18	0	16	108	62	45	.324	.582	.450
Runners/Scor. Pos.	149	51	8	0	10	95	43	29	.342	.597	.475
Runners On/2 Out	113	32	5	0	5	40	30	23	.283	.460	.438
Scor. Pos./2 Out	67	21	3	0	4	37	24	14	.313	.537	.500
Late Inning Pressure	81	24	5	0	3	12	11	15	.296	.469	.376
Leading Off	18	5	0	0	0	0	1	2	.278	.278	.316
Runners On	42	12	4	0	3	12	8	9	.286	.595	.392
Runners/Scor. Pos.	20	4	1	0	1	8	6	4	.200	.400	.370

DRIVING IN RUNS	From 1B	From 2B	From 3B	Scoring Position
Totals	19/203	32/123	41/81	73/204
Percentage	9%	26%	51%	36%
Driving In Runners from 3B with Less than Two Out:		28/51		55%

Loves to face: Bryan Clark (.600, 12-for-20)
Hates to face: Mike Witt (.105, 4-for-38)

Played 79 games at first base, a position he hadn't tried since 1971, when he played four games there for Winston-Salem. . . . Batted .300+ for first time in 16-year career. . . . Percentage of runners driven in from scoring position was his highest in past 13 years. Ditto his batting average with runners in scoring position. . . . Led A.L. with 65 RBI in home games. . . . Reached base safely in eight consecutive innings that he led off (Aug. 11–21), longest A.L. streak last season. . . . Leads A.L. with 197 home runs over past seven seasons. . . . Three teammates with 300 or more HR: Banks, Santo, Williams (1971 Cubs); Cash, Howard, Kaline (1972–73 Tigers); Baylor, Rice, Evans (1987 Red Sox).

Mike Felder

Bats Left and Right

Milwaukee Brewers	AB	H	2B	3B	HR	RRF	BB	SO	BA	SA	OBA
Season	289	77	5	7	2	32	28	23	.266	.353	.330
vs. Left-Handers	94	29	2	2	0	10	12	6	.309	.372	.383
vs. Right-Handers	195	48	3	5	2	22	16	17	.246	.344	.303
Home	126	38	2	5	1	19	21	9	.302	.421	.401
Road	163	39	3	2	1	13	7	14	.239	.301	.269
Grass	253	67	4	7	2	31	27	21	.265	.360	.335
Artificial Turf	36	10	1	0	0	1	1	2	.278	.306	.297
April	0	0	0	0	0	0	0	0	—	—	—
May	18	3	0	0	0	1	0	1	.167	.167	.167
June	66	19	1	3	0	7	5	4	.288	.394	.333
July	67	17	0	1	1	8	4	6	.254	.328	.296
August	54	12	0	1	0	5	15	3	.222	.259	.391
Sept./Oct.	84	26	4	2	1	11	4	9	.310	.440	.341
Leading Off Inn.	81	21	3	1	0	0	3	4	.259	.321	.286
Runners On	116	34	1	5	1	31	14	8	.293	.414	.366
Runners/Scor. Pos.	68	19	1	3	1	29	10	5	.279	.426	.367
Runners On/2 Out	51	15	0	3	1	14	9	3	.294	.471	.400
Scor. Pos./2 Out	36	10	0	2	1	13	8	3	.278	.472	.409
Late Inning Pressure	47	16	1	0	0	3	4	4	.340	.362	.392
Leading Off	14	5	1	0	0	0	0	2	.357	.429	.357
Runners On	20	8	0	0	0	3	3	2	.400	.400	.478
Runners/Scor. Pos.	8	4	0	0	0	3	2	1	.500	.500	.600

DRIVING IN RUNS	From 1B	From 2B	From 3B	Scoring Position
Totals	5/76	3/47	22/35	25/82
Percentage	7%	6%	63%	30%
Driving In Runners from 3B with Less than Two Out:		13/18		72%

Loves to face: Jeff Musselman (3-for-3)
Hates to face: Ken Dixon (0-for-8)

Averaged 2.51 putouts per nine innings last season, highest rate among A.L. left fielders (minimum: 500 innings). . . . Only major leaguer with 150+ AB and more triples than doubles last season. . . . One of eight A.L. players with five hits in a game last season (June 11 at Detroit). . . . One of two A.L. players to increase his batting average by at least 25 points in each of the last two seasons (minimum: 50 AB in 1985, 1986, and 1987). . . . Career average of .306 vs. left-handers, .224 (and all three HR) vs. right-handers. . . . Has never driven in a runner from either first or second base in Late-Inning Pressure Situations. . . . Career average of .254 (1 XBH per 21.0 AB) on grass, .220 (1 XBH in 59 AB) on artificial turf.

Tony Fernandez

Bats Left and Right

Toronto Blue Jays	AB	H	2B	3B	HR	RRF	BB	SO	BA	SA	OBA
Season	578	186	29	8	5	71	51	48	.322	.426	.379
vs. Left-Handers	192	57	8	1	2	17	21	18	.297	.380	.367
vs. Right-Handers	386	129	21	7	3	54	30	30	.334	.448	.385
Home	299	90	15	5	1	45	27	16	.301	.395	.363
Road	279	96	14	3	4	26	24	32	.344	.459	.397
Grass	207	68	9	3	3	19	16	24	.329	.444	.379
Artificial Turf	371	118	20	5	2	52	35	24	.318	.415	.380
April	82	19	0	2	1	6	7	6	.232	.317	.293
May	102	36	7	1	1	14	16	11	.353	.471	.441
June	108	37	11	2	2	17	14	9	.343	.537	.419
July	116	36	5	1	0	12	6	15	.310	.371	.344
August	88	33	3	2	1	9	5	3	.375	.489	.427
Sept./Oct.	82	25	3	0	0	13	3	4	.305	.341	.326
Leading Off Inn.	208	56	8	2	1	1	23	25	.269	.341	.345
Runners On	210	68	16	2	0	66	21	13	.324	.419	.387
Runners/Scor. Pos.	130	49	11	2	0	63	13	11	.377	.492	.433
Runners On/2 Out	84	25	7	2	0	28	9	6	.298	.429	.379
Scor. Pos./2 Out	56	21	4	2	0	26	7	6	.375	.518	.462
Late Inning Pressure	80	29	6	1	1	17	9	7	.363	.500	.418
Leading Off	17	8	2	0	0	0	3	0	.471	.588	.550
Runners On	41	12	4	0	0	16	3	4	.293	.390	.326
Runners/Scor. Pos.	29	8	3	0	0	15	2	4	.276	.379	.303

DRIVING IN RUNS	From 1B	From 2B	From 3B	Scoring Position
Totals	6/143	30/102	30/54	60/156
Percentage	4%	29%	56%	38%
Driving In Runners from 3B with Less than Two Out:		19/31		61%

Loves to face: Mike Morgan (.538, 7-for-13)
Hates to face: Jack Morris (.111, 3-for-27)

Batting average has increased in each of his major-league seasons (.265, .270, .289, .310, .322), as have his stolen base totals (0, 5, 13, 25, 32). . . . Stole 32 bases last season, but none in 33 games after August 14. . . . Was switched from the leadoff position to the third slot in the order on August 25. He proceeded to reach base safely in each of his next 21 games. Blue Jays had a record of 20–6 in games in which he batted third. . . . The Rice Krispies collision: Madlock upends Fernandez on Sept. 24. Snap goes Tony's streak of 12 games in a row with a double play. Crackle goes his elbow, which required surgery. Pop go Toronto's pennant hopes. . . . Only career .300-hitter in Blue Jays history (minimum: 300 games).

Cecil Fielder

Bats Right

Toronto Blue Jays	AB	H	2B	3B	HR	RRF	BB	SO	BA	SA	OBA
Season	175	47	7	1	14	32	20	48	.269	.560	.345
vs. Left-Handers	153	41	7	1	13	30	17	40	.268	.582	.343
vs. Right-Handers	22	6	0	0	1	2	3	8	.273	.409	.360
Home	90	31	5	1	10	21	11	24	.344	.756	.422
Road	85	16	2	0	4	11	9	24	.188	.353	.263
Grass	61	9	1	0	1	6	6	18	.148	.213	.221
Artificial Turf	114	38	6	1	13	26	14	30	.333	.746	.411
April	16	4	2	0	1	5	2	3	.250	.563	.316
May	24	8	1	0	2	7	8	6	.333	.625	.500
June	46	13	3	1	4	8	4	12	.283	.652	.340
July	32	7	0	0	3	3	2	7	.219	.500	.286
August	27	7	0	0	1	2	4	6	.259	.370	.355
Sept./Oct.	30	8	1	0	3	7	0	14	.267	.600	.267
Leading Off Inn.	44	11	1	1	5	5	3	12	.250	.659	.298
Runners On	88	23	5	0	3	29	25	25	.261	.420	.333
Runners/Scor. Pos.	48	10	5	0	1	17	9	13	.208	.375	.339
Runners On/2 Out	38	8	1	0	2	6	3	9	.211	.395	.286
Scor. Pos./2 Out	22	2	1	0	1	4	3	5	.091	.273	.231
Late Inning Pressure	27	7	1	1	2	2	5	11	.259	.593	.375
Leading Off	11	4	0	1	1	1	0	5	.364	.818	.364
Runners On	9	1	0	0	0	0	3	2	.111	.111	.333
Runners/Scor. Pos.	3	0	0	0	0	0	3	2	.000	.000	.500

DRIVING IN RUNS	From 1B	From 2B	From 3B	Scoring Position
Totals	3/65	5/37	10/22	15/59
Percentage	5%	14%	45%	25%
Driving In Runners from 3B with Less than Two Out:		9/12		75%

Loves to face: Charlie Leibrandt (.400, 6-for-15, 3 HR)
Hates to face: Scott McGregor (0-for-7, 5 SO)

Fourth-best home run rate (one per 12.5 AB) in A.L. last season (minimum: 10 HR). . . . Batted .193 in day games, .305 at night, for 2d-largest difference among A.L. players last season (minimum: 50 AB each way). . . . Increase of 186 points from grass to artificial turf was largest gain in the majors last season. . . . Started 49 of 50 games against left-handed starters, but didn't start a game against a right-hander. . . . Fielder's fielding? Played 16 errorless games at first base, two games without a fielding chance at third. Now, about Earl Battey. . . . Led A.L. in one category last year: "Most Times as an Announced Pinch-Hitter." Six times Fielder was removed for *another* pinch-hitter before he even got a chance to hit!

Carlton Fisk
Chicago White Sox — Bats Right

	AB	H	2B	3B	HR	RRF	BB	SO	BA	SA	OBA
Season	454	116	22	1	23	72	39	72	.256	.460	.321
vs. Left-Handers	182	43	10	1	9	27	17	26	.236	.451	.305
vs. Right-Handers	272	73	12	0	14	45	22	46	.268	.467	.332
Home	218	58	13	0	5	25	19	36	.266	.394	.328
Road	236	58	9	1	18	47	20	36	.246	.521	.316
Grass	393	110	21	1	22	66	32	63	.280	.506	.338
Artificial Turf	61	6	1	0	1	6	7	9	.098	.164	.222
April	56	15	1	1	1	8	7	7	.268	.375	.369
May	67	10	3	0	2	8	7	18	.149	.284	.256
June	87	18	3	0	4	11	3	16	.207	.379	.245
July	94	29	3	0	6	17	5	12	.309	.532	.343
August	59	20	4	0	5	11	5	11	.339	.661	.385
Sept./Oct.	91	24	8	0	5	17	11	8	.264	.516	.349
Leading Off Inn.	113	28	8	0	4	4	8	15	.248	.425	.309
Runners On	195	45	6	1	10	59	17	44	.231	.426	.300
Runners/Scor. Pos.	107	26	3	0	3	42	13	28	.243	.355	.326
Runners On/2 Out	89	17	2	1	3	23	6	24	.191	.337	.258
Scor. Pos./2 Out	54	11	1	0	1	16	5	15	.204	.278	.295
Late Inning Pressure	73	17	1	0	2	10	9	22	.233	.329	.325
Leading Off	23	4	0	0	1	1	0	4	.174	.304	.174
Runners On	41	9	1	0	0	8	4	17	.220	.244	.304
Runners/Scor. Pos.	28	8	1	0	0	8	3	11	.286	.321	.355

DRIVING IN RUNS	From 1B	From 2B	From 3B	Scoring Position
Totals	11/141	12/85	26/53	38/138
Percentage	8%	14%	49%	28%
Driving In Runners from 3B with Less than Two Out:			17/27	63%

Loves to face: Dan Quisenberry (.458, 11-for-24, 1 HR)
Hates to face: Curt Young (.063, 1-for-16)
Active career leaders, games behind the plate: Boone 1,935, Sundberg 1,798, Simmons 1,762, Fisk 1,761, Carter 1,657.... Played 122 games as catcher, nine games at first base, and two games in left field last season.... Batted 181 points higher on artificial turf than on grass, largest increase in the majors (minimum: 50 AB each way).... Batting average on artificial turf was lowest among 298 major-league qualifiers.... Struck out 17 times with runners on base in Late-Inning Pressure Situations, highest A.L. total since Jeff Burroughs had 17 in 1977.... He ain't done yet: Batted .301 with 16 HR and 44 RBI in 71 games after July 2.... Only player ever to hit home runs in three straight at bats vs. Roger Clemens.

Scott Fletcher
Texas Rangers — Bats Right

	AB	H	2B	3B	HR	RRF	BB	SO	BA	SA	OBA
Season	588	169	28	4	5	69	61	66	.287	.374	.358
vs. Left-Handers	220	70	9	1	3	24	24	18	.318	.409	.388
vs. Right-Handers	368	99	19	3	2	45	37	48	.269	.353	.341
Home	287	98	17	3	4	41	31	25	.341	.463	.413
Road	301	71	11	1	1	28	30	41	.236	.289	.305
Grass	489	154	25	4	5	64	50	50	.315	.413	.383
Artificial Turf	99	15	3	0	0	5	11	16	.152	.182	.234
April	75	27	3	1	1	13	5	9	.360	.467	.407
May	103	30	3	1	1	12	9	11	.291	.369	.330
June	110	33	8	2	2	13	13	15	.300	.464	.376
July	103	32	6	0	0	12	13	10	.311	.369	.388
August	97	24	4	0	0	8	9	13	.247	.289	.321
Sept./Oct.	100	23	4	0	1	11	15	8	.230	.300	.336
Leading Off Inn.	109	25	2	0	3	3	17	10	.229	.339	.309
Runners On	236	76	12	2	1	65	20	23	.322	.403	.377
Runners/Scor. Pos.	133	45	7	0	0	57	15	17	.338	.391	.400
Runners On/2 Out	96	29	5	0	0	28	9	9	.302	.354	.368
Scor. Pos./2 Out	66	23	5	0	0	28	7	8	.348	.424	.411
Late Inning Pressure	83	20	4	0	0	11	12	11	.241	.289	.333
Leading Off	20	2	0	0	0	0	6	2	.100	.100	.308
Runners On	44	12	3	0	0	11	3	6	.273	.341	.313
Runners/Scor. Pos.	30	9	3	0	0	11	2	4	.300	.400	.333

DRIVING IN RUNS	From 1B	From 2B	From 3B	Scoring Position
Totals	7/159	26/104	30/66	56/170
Percentage	4%	25%	45%	33%
Driving In Runners from 3B with Less than Two Out:			17/27	63%

Loves to face: Frank Tanana (.500, 9-for-18, 2 HR)
Hates to face: Richard Dotson (.067, 1-for-15)
Batted 106 points higher in home games than he did in road games, 3d-largest difference in A.L. last season (minimum: 100 AB each way).... Started all 62 games in which the Rangers faced a southpaw starter, 85 of 100 games against right-handers.... Committed 23 errors last season, 4th-most in A.L.... Career batting averages of .347 at County Stadium (his highest at any A.L. ballpark), .226 at Yankee Stadium (his lowest). ..Career average of .313 with runners in scoring position.... One of six major leaguers to have driven in more than 30 percent of runners from scoring position in each of the last five seasons (minimum: 75 opportunities). The others: Brett, Hrbek, Murray, Tabler, and Winfield.

Julio Franco
Cleveland Indians — Bats Right

	AB	H	2B	3B	HR	RRF	BB	SO	BA	SA	OBA
Season	495	158	24	3	8	58	57	56	.319	.428	.389
vs. Left-Handers	130	40	10	1	4	13	18	21	.308	.492	.389
vs. Right-Handers	365	118	14	2	4	45	39	35	.323	.405	.389
Home	242	75	12	0	5	28	28	24	.310	.421	.383
Road	253	83	12	3	3	30	29	32	.328	.435	.395
Grass	431	131	21	1	5	48	49	49	.304	.392	.376
Artificial Turf	64	27	3	2	3	10	8	7	.422	.672	.479
April	89	29	7	0	2	13	11	10	.326	.472	.400
May	99	33	5	1	1	11	17	13	.333	.434	.429
June	103	29	2	2	1	12	6	9	.282	.369	.318
July	45	15	2	0	2	6	9	4	.333	.511	.444
August	81	28	5	0	1	6	8	14	.346	.444	.418
Sept./Oct.	78	24	3	0	1	10	6	6	.308	.385	.349
Leading Off Inn.	102	39	8	0	0	0	4	8	.382	.461	.406
Runners On	212	59	10	0	4	54	29	25	.278	.382	.365
Runners/Scor. Pos.	128	32	4	0	4	50	17	18	.250	.375	.336
Runners On/2 Out	73	26	4	0	3	22	7	10	.356	.534	.420
Scor. Pos./2 Out	51	15	3	0	3	21	7	8	.294	.529	.390
Late Inning Pressure	66	25	6	0	1	7	9	9	.379	.515	.447
Leading Off	20	8	3	0	0	0	0	3	.400	.550	.400
Runners On	25	10	2	0	0	6	5	3	.400	.480	.484
Runners/Scor. Pos.	13	2	0	0	0	5	3	2	.154	.154	.294

DRIVING IN RUNS	From 1B	From 2B	From 3B	Scoring Position
Totals	6/138	18/105	26/47	44/152
Percentage	4%	17%	55%	29%
Driving In Runners from 3B with Less than Two Out:			20/33	61%

Loves to face: Richard Dotson (.483, 14-for-29)
Hates to face: Dan Quisenberry (0-for-16)
Like the Browns' Bernie Kosar, he'll be only 36 at the turn of the century, but has already compiled some formidable career stats. No active player as young as Franco is within 200 hits of Franco's career total of 873. And only one, Darryl Strawberry, has more RBI than Franco (447 to 378).... Has grounded into 20 or more DP in each of the last five seasons. No other player has done it for more than the last two years.... Ratio of ground outs to air outs, year by year since 1983: 1.49, 1.42, 1.41, 1.54, 2.72.... Has hit better than .300 at Cleveland Stadium in four of the last five seasons.... Career average of .315 (1 XBH per 10.6 AB) vs. left-handers, .284 (1 XBH per 18.8 AB) vs. right-handers.

Gary Gaetti
Minnesota Twins — Bats Right

	AB	H	2B	3B	HR	RRF	BB	SO	BA	SA	OBA
Season	584	150	36	2	31	112	37	92	.257	.485	.303
vs. Left-Handers	166	39	6	2	7	29	12	29	.235	.422	.287
vs. Right-Handers	418	111	30	0	24	83	25	63	.266	.510	.309
Home	301	92	23	2	18	59	20	47	.306	.575	.352
Road	283	58	13	0	13	53	17	45	.205	.389	.250
Grass	219	48	11	0	9	43	15	35	.219	.393	.269
Artificial Turf	365	102	25	2	22	69	22	57	.279	.540	.323
April	81	17	3	1	6	17	6	15	.210	.494	.264
May	108	34	6	0	6	17	7	21	.315	.537	.353
June	79	20	4	0	3	15	9	11	.253	.418	.326
July	101	22	7	0	6	19	5	15	.218	.465	.255
August	108	31	9	1	7	31	4	17	.287	.583	.325
Sept./Oct.	107	26	7	0	3	13	6	13	.243	.393	.287
Leading Off Inn.	128	28	9	0	9	9	9	16	.219	.500	.281
Runners On	283	78	20	1	12	93	21	42	.276	.481	.325
Runners/Scor. Pos.	170	51	15	1	8	84	15	26	.300	.541	.354
Runners On/2 Out	121	40	8	0	8	49	10	19	.331	.595	.382
Scor. Pos./2 Out	86	28	7	0	5	43	7	13	.326	.581	.376
Late Inning Pressure	63	16	3	0	4	8	6	14	.254	.492	.329
Leading Off	14	3	1	0	2	2	0	4	.214	.714	.267
Runners On	25	5	1	0	1	5	6	5	.200	.360	.355
Runners/Scor. Pos.	6	2	0	0	1	5	5	0	.333	.833	.636

DRIVING IN RUNS	From 1B	From 2B	From 3B	Scoring Position
Totals	15/202	30/126	36/76	66/202
Percentage	7%	24%	47%	33%
Driving In Runners from 3B with Less than Two Out:			21/39	54%

Loves to face: Floyd Bannister (.471, 16-for-34, 7 HR)
Hates to face: Charlie Leibrandt (.111, 3-for-27, 1 HR)
One of five major leaguers with 30+ home runs and 100+ RBI in both 1986 and 1987. The others: Bell, Canseco, Mattingly, and Schmidt.... Led majors by grounding into 25 double plays.... Has played 790 games over past five seasons. Only one A.L. player has played more, consecutive or otherwise: Cal's son Cal.... Career batting average of .155 with runners in scoring position in Late-Inning Pressure Situations.... Career average of .168 at Royals Stadium, with only one HR in 137 AB.... First player to hit home runs on each of his first two post-season at bats; also homered on first major-league at bat in 1981.... Born August 19, 1958, the same day as Michael Jackson. The Pepsi salesman, not the pitcher.

Greg Gagne

Minnesota Twins — Bats Right

	AB	H	2B	3B	HR	RRF	BB	SO	BA	SA	OBA
Season	437	116	28	7	10	43	25	84	.265	.430	.310
vs. Left-Handers	128	34	7	3	0	12	6	28	.266	.367	.294
vs. Right-Handers	309	82	21	4	10	31	19	56	.265	.456	.316
Home	212	51	10	5	7	25	18	45	.241	.434	.303
Road	225	65	18	2	3	18	7	39	.289	.427	.316
Grass	171	46	13	2	3	12	5	30	.269	.421	.298
Artificial Turf	266	70	15	5	7	31	20	54	.263	.436	.317
April	50	14	3	0	3	7	2	12	.280	.520	.315
May	51	8	2	1	0	4	5	8	.157	.235	.232
June	80	23	9	1	2	11	6	18	.288	.500	.337
July	77	24	6	1	0	5	3	14	.312	.416	.338
August	88	25	3	4	1	9	1	18	.284	.443	.289
Sept./Oct.	91	22	5	0	4	7	8	14	.242	.429	.324
Leading Off Inn.	88	26	6	1	2	2	6	15	.295	.455	.347
Runners On	172	43	9	4	2	35	11	36	.250	.384	.292
Runners/Scor. Pos.	84	20	6	2	1	29	7	15	.238	.393	.290
Runners On/2 Out	67	15	4	2	1	15	5	14	.224	.388	.278
Scor. Pos./2 Out	38	8	3	1	1	14	4	6	.211	.421	.286
Late Inning Pressure	40	6	1	0	1	2	4	7	.150	.250	.227
Leading Off	13	3	0	0	0	0	2	3	.231	.231	.333
Runners On	9	0	0	0	0	1	1	2	.000	.000	.100
Runners/Scor. Pos.	3	0	0	0	0	1	1	0	.000	.000	.250

DRIVING IN RUNS	From 1B	From 2B	From 3B	Scoring Position
Totals	7/125	12/73	13/32	25/105
Percentage	6%	16%	41%	24%
Driving In Runners from 3B with Less than Two Out:			9/18	50%

Loves to face: Frank Tanana (.462, 6-for-13, 2 HR)
Hates to face: Walt Terrell (.095, 2-for-21)
Removed for pinch-hitter 26 times last season, most on the team. . . . Batted .057 vs. left-handers in April and May, .344 the rest of the way. No home runs vs. southpaws during the regular season, but connected off Tanana and Mathews in October. . . . One of two players with 10+ sacrifice bunts and 10+ home runs last season. The other: Devon White. . . . Averaged 3.26 assists per nine innings, 3d-highest among A.L. shortstops. . . . Grounded into three double plays in 90 DP situations, 5th-lowest rate in A.L. (minimum: 40 opp's). . . . Though his overall average has increased in each of the last three seasons (.225, .250, .265), his average in Late-Inning Pressure Situations has decreased (.292, .250, .150).

Jim Gantner

Milwaukee Brewers — Bats Left

	AB	H	2B	3B	HR	RRF	BB	SO	BA	SA	OBA
Season	265	72	14	0	4	30	19	22	.272	.370	.331
vs. Left-Handers	86	20	4	0	0	9	4	9	.233	.279	.280
vs. Right-Handers	179	52	10	0	4	21	15	13	.291	.413	.355
Home	121	36	6	0	0	11	11	12	.298	.347	.370
Road	144	36	8	0	4	19	8	10	.250	.389	.297
Grass	216	58	12	0	2	20	18	18	.269	.352	.339
Artificial Turf	49	14	2	0	2	10	1	4	.286	.449	.294
April	66	19	5	0	1	7	6	8	.288	.409	.365
May	80	22	5	0	2	8	7	5	.275	.413	.333
June	86	23	2	0	1	12	6	5	.267	.326	.326
July	32	8	2	0	0	3	0	3	.250	.313	.273
August	0	0	0	0	0	0	0	0	—	—	—
Sept./Oct.	1	0	0	0	0	0	0	1	.000	.000	.000
Leading Off Inn.	57	21	3	0	1	1	4	2	.368	.474	.419
Runners On	124	28	4	0	3	29	9	13	.226	.331	.287
Runners/Scor. Pos.	68	17	1	0	2	24	9	11	.250	.353	.350
Runners On/2 Out	59	11	2	0	1	12	6	4	.186	.271	.273
Scor. Pos./2 Out	41	8	0	0	1	10	6	3	.195	.268	.313
Late Inning Pressure	37	11	1	0	0	2	3	4	.297	.324	.341
Leading Off	9	4	0	0	0	0	0	1	.444	.444	.444
Runners On	14	3	0	0	0	2	1	1	.214	.214	.294
Runners/Scor. Pos.	6	0	0	0	0	2	1	1	.000	.000	.222

DRIVING IN RUNS	From 1B	From 2B	From 3B	Scoring Position
Totals	4/78	13/57	9/22	22/79
Percentage	5%	23%	41%	28%
Driving In Runners from 3B with Less than Two Out:			6/9	67%

Loves to face: Don Schulze (.833, 5-for-6, 2 HR)
Hates to face: Roger Clemens (0-for-16)
Struck out as a pinch-hitter on Sept. 20 in his only appearance after tearing a hamstring on July 27. . . . Has hit for a higher average on artificial surfaces than he has on grass fields in each of the last five seasons. . . . Has homered at every A.L. ballpark except Royals Stadium (171 career AB). . . . A potential couch potato? Career batting average of .368 in Metrodome, .310 in Kingdome, .272 outdoors. . . . Only player who's batted 100 points higher at Oakland Coliseum (.355) than at Fenway Park (.255) over the past five seasons (minimum: 100 AB at each). . . . Only two of his 44 career home runs have been hit against left-handed pitchers, both in 1983, off Ed Vande Berg and Frank Viola.

Ken Gerhart

Baltimore Orioles — Bats Right

	AB	H	2B	3B	HR	RRF	BB	SO	BA	SA	OBA
Season	284	69	10	2	14	35	17	53	.243	.440	.286
vs. Left-Handers	129	31	4	0	4	10	6	24	.240	.364	.272
vs. Right-Handers	155	38	6	2	10	25	11	29	.245	.503	.298
Home	134	29	6	0	5	13	8	24	.216	.373	.264
Road	150	40	4	2	9	22	9	29	.267	.500	.306
Grass	233	59	9	1	13	29	15	43	.253	.468	.299
Artificial Turf	51	10	1	1	1	6	2	10	.196	.314	.226
April	74	22	3	1	3	8	3	20	.297	.486	.325
May	45	10	2	1	1	4	1	6	.222	.378	.234
June	49	11	2	0	3	4	3	11	.224	.449	.269
July	78	18	2	0	5	14	3	9	.231	.449	.256
August	38	8	1	0	2	5	7	7	.211	.395	.348
Sept./Oct.	0	0	0	0	0	0	0	0	—	—	—
Leading Off Inn.	80	23	5	1	5	5	6	12	.288	.563	.337
Runners On	122	25	4	1	4	25	4	20	.205	.352	.227
Runners/Scor. Pos.	58	13	2	1	2	20	2	12	.224	.397	.242
Runners On/2 Out	49	10	3	1	1	9	3	11	.204	.367	.250
Scor. Pos./2 Out	25	6	1	1	0	6	2	7	.240	.360	.296
Late Inning Pressure	43	6	1	0	0	3	3	10	.140	.163	.208
Leading Off	12	2	1	0	0	0	1	3	.167	.250	.231
Runners On	15	1	0	0	0	3	0	4	.067	.067	.063
Runners/Scor. Pos.	7	1	0	0	0	3	0	3	.143	.143	.125

DRIVING IN RUNS	From 1B	From 2B	From 3B	Scoring Position
Totals	5/100	7/49	9/21	16/70
Percentage	5%	14%	43%	23%
Driving In Runners from 3B with Less than Two Out:			6/12	50%

Loves to face: Walt Terrell (.400, 4-for-10, 2 HR)
Hates to face: Frank Tanana (0-for-7)
Had hit .310 with seven home runs and 12 RBI over previous 12 games when Doug Jones broke his wrist with a pitched ball, ending his season on Aug. 12. . . . Second Orioles rookie to start on opening day since Ripken in 1982. The other: Larry Sheets (1985). . . . Batting average in Late-Inning Pressure Situations was 2d-lowest among 164 A.L. qualifiers last season. One hit in 18 career at bats (.056) with runners on base in LIP Situations. . . . We think Harry's a swell name. So what gives with Harold Kenneth Gerhart, Harold ("Butch") Wynegar, and Harry ("Bud") Black, not to mention Harry Rasmussen, who changed his name to Eric by law? We'll check this out with our colleague Harry ("Jay") Chesler.

Kirk Gibson

Detroit Tigers — Bats Left

	AB	H	2B	3B	HR	RRF	BB	SO	BA	SA	OBA
Season	487	135	25	3	24	83	71	117	.277	.489	.372
vs. Left-Handers	179	48	9	0	4	23	28	50	.268	.385	.374
vs. Right-Handers	308	87	16	3	20	60	43	67	.282	.549	.371
Home	240	58	9	2	14	45	37	57	.242	.471	.350
Road	247	77	16	1	10	38	34	60	.312	.506	.394
Grass	404	113	21	3	22	72	62	90	.280	.510	.378
Artificial Turf	83	22	4	0	2	11	9	27	.265	.386	.340
April	0	0	0	0	0	0	0	0	—	—	—
May	89	25	4	1	5	15	13	20	.281	.517	.385
June	109	34	9	1	4	21	14	24	.312	.523	.392
July	86	18	3	0	5	15	7	23	.209	.419	.274
August	98	29	5	0	4	19	19	29	.296	.469	.412
Sept./Oct.	105	29	4	1	6	13	18	21	.276	.505	.379
Leading Off Inn.	94	26	5	1	6	6	8	27	.277	.543	.333
Runners On	221	64	6	1	10	68	38	44	.290	.462	.392
Runners/Scor. Pos.	129	36	4	1	6	59	23	18	.279	.465	.378
Runners On/2 Out	67	16	3	0	3	20	13	14	.239	.418	.363
Scor. Pos./2 Out	47	12	3	0	3	20	8	6	.255	.511	.364
Late Inning Pressure	45	14	0	0	3	9	12	13	.311	.578	.466
Leading Off	8	4	0	0	2	2	1	1	.500	1.250	.556
Runners On	25	6	1	0	1	7	9	9	.240	.400	.441
Runners/Scor. Pos.	15	3	1	0	0	5	7	6	.200	.267	.455

DRIVING IN RUNS	From 1B	From 2B	From 3B	Scoring Position
Totals	10/156	22/97	26/53	48/150
Percentage	6%	23%	49%	32%
Driving In Runners from 3B with Less than Two Out:			19/29	66%

Loves to face: Doug Drabek (0-for-4)
Hates to face: Jose Rijo (0-for-11)
One of baseball's highest percentage base stealers, with 107 steals in his last 125 attempts (86 percent). Stole third base six times in six attempts last season. . . . Career average of one home run per 21.4 at bats, but has never homered in 64 career AB with the bases loaded (19-for-64, .297). . . . California, here I come: .336 career batting average with seven home runs in 122 AB at Anaheim Stadium; .255 (7 HR in 137 AB) at Oakland Coliseum. . . . One of two A.L. players to strike out 100+ times in each of the past four seasons. The other: Gibson's almost-teammate Gary Pettis. Juan Samuel has four straight 100-SO seasons in N.L.; Dale Murphy has six in a row. . . . Gibson's middle name is Harold.

Dan Gladden

Minnesota Twins — Bats Right

	AB	H	2B	3B	HR	RRF	BB	SO	BA	SA	OBA
Season	438	109	21	2	8	38	38	72	.249	.361	.312
vs. Left-Handers	163	42	11	0	2	13	11	19	.258	.362	.307
vs. Right-Handers	275	67	10	2	6	25	27	53	.244	.360	.315
Home	203	55	11	2	4	15	21	23	.271	.404	.342
Road	235	54	10	0	4	23	17	49	.230	.323	.285
Grass	176	42	7	0	4	18	14	37	.239	.347	.301
Artificial Turf	262	67	14	2	4	20	24	35	.256	.370	.319
April	40	12	3	0	0	6	1	10	.300	.375	.310
May	79	19	3	0	1	7	8	13	.241	.316	.315
June	100	27	5	0	3	10	11	11	.270	.410	.348
July	108	28	5	1	1	5	9	13	.259	.352	.316
August	47	9	1	0	0	2	3	13	.191	.213	.240
Sept./Oct.	64	14	4	1	3	8	6	12	.219	.453	.296
Leading Off Inn.	161	44	9	1	2	2	14	28	.273	.379	.339
Runners On	161	35	7	1	2	32	15	20	.217	.311	.285
Runners/Scor. Pos.	92	19	4	0	1	26	10	14	.207	.283	.286
Runners On/2 Out	66	12	3	0	1	10	7	12	.182	.273	.260
Scor. Pos./2 Out	44	9	3	0	1	10	4	9	.205	.341	.271
Late Inning Pressure	53	9	0	1	2	9	5	14	.170	.321	.237
Leading Off	17	3	0	0	0	0	0	5	.176	.176	.176
Runners On	21	4	0	0	1	8	2	4	.190	.429	.250
Runners/Scor. Pos.	15	2	0	0	1	7	0	3	.133	.333	.125

DRIVING IN RUNS	From 1B	From 2B	From 3B	Scoring Position
Totals	5/103	6/62	19/44	25/106
Percentage	5%	10%	43%	24%
Driving In Runners from 3B with Less than Two Out:		13/22		59%

Loves to face: Tommy John (.500, 6-for-12)
Hates to face: Charlie Hough (0-for-8)

Led Twins with 25 stolen bases, most by a Minnesota player since 1978 when Rod Carew stole 27 and Willie Norwood stole 25. . . . Averaged 2.30 putouts per nine innings, 3d-highest rate among A.L. left fielders (minimum: 500 innings). . . . Batted .283 before the All-Star break, but only .195 thereafter. . . . Ended the regular season with 17 consecutive hitless at bats. . . . Batting average in Late-Inning Pressure Situations has been lower than his overall average in each of his five seasons in the majors. Career averages: .211 in LIP Situations, .285 in other situations. . . . Percentage of runners driven in from scoring position has decreased in each of his seasons in the majors: .333, .301, .297, .286, .236.

Mike Greenwell

Boston Red Sox — Bats Left

	AB	H	2B	3B	HR	RRF	BB	SO	BA	SA	OBA
Season	412	135	31	6	19	93	35	40	.328	.570	.386
vs. Left-Handers	74	28	5	1	1	14	4	6	.378	.514	.420
vs. Right-Handers	338	107	26	5	18	79	31	34	.317	.583	.379
Home	217	71	19	5	8	46	19	16	.327	.571	.387
Road	195	64	12	1	11	47	16	24	.328	.569	.385
Grass	354	108	26	5	13	74	32	35	.305	.517	.368
Artificial Turf	58	27	5	1	6	19	3	5	.466	.897	.500
April	19	6	2	0	2	5	0	2	.316	.737	.350
May	57	14	5	0	2	19	4	5	.246	.439	.306
June	60	21	5	0	5	17	3	8	.350	.683	.394
July	80	27	8	0	3	10	7	7	.338	.550	.398
August	78	28	3	4	3	17	15	7	.359	.615	.468
Sept./Oct.	118	39	8	2	4	25	6	11	.331	.534	.357
Leading Off Inn.	70	22	7	0	5	5	9	9	.314	.629	.392
Runners On	234	84	18	3	10	84	17	23	.359	.590	.405
Runners/Scor. Pos.	145	46	10	2	6	73	15	20	.317	.538	.378
Runners On/2 Out	105	34	11	1	4	39	7	15	.324	.562	.372
Scor. Pos./2 Out	73	22	6	1	3	36	7	13	.301	.534	.370
Late Inning Pressure	67	22	7	1	5	19	6	8	.328	.687	.392
Leading Off	9	4	2	0	0		2	1	.444	.667	.545
Runners On	38	14	5	1	3	17	2	5	.368	.789	.415
Runners/Scor. Pos.	25	8	2	1	2	15	2	4	.320	.720	.393

DRIVING IN RUNS	From 1B	From 2B	From 3B	Scoring Position
Totals	15/181	35/125	24/57	59/182
Percentage	8%	28%	42%	32%
Driving In Runners from 3B with Less than Two Out:		15/26		58%

Loves to face: Jeff Reardon (3-for-3, 1 2B, 1 HR)
Hates to face: Jose Guzman (0-for-7)

Forget the platoon, Mac. Greenwell started 92 of Boston's 114 games vs. right-handers, 11 of 48 vs. left-handers. But he's had a higher batting average vs. southpaws than vs. right-handers in each of his three seasons in majors, and has compiled a career .398 mark vs. his fellow lefties. . . . Need more convincing? He's the only lefty hitter in the A.L. with a lower strikeout rate vs. left-handers than vs. right-handers in each of those seasons. . . . Highest batting average among major-league rookies last season (minimum: 200 PA). Ranked second with 89 RBI. . . . Led majors with 13 extra-base hits in LIP Situations. . . . Has 101 career RBI in only 530 plate appearances, the highest rate among active players (minimum: 500 PA).

Alfredo Griffin

Oakland As — Bats Left and Right

	AB	H	2B	3B	HR	RRF	BB	SO	BA	SA	OBA
Season	494	130	23	5	3	66	28	41	.263	.348	.306
vs. Left-Handers	188	46	7	1	1	21	11	13	.245	.309	.292
vs. Right-Handers	306	84	16	4	2	45	17	28	.275	.373	.315
Home	233	55	9	2	2	32	12	22	.236	.318	.278
Road	261	75	14	3	1	34	16	19	.287	.375	.331
Grass	411	106	19	3	2	55	24	38	.258	.333	.303
Artificial Turf	83	24	4	2	1	11	4	3	.289	.422	.322
April	86	22	4	1	1	10	1	7	.256	.360	.264
May	82	24	5	1	0	12	8	5	.293	.378	.363
June	77	19	3	0	0	6	6	6	.247	.286	.310
July	97	27	4	0	0	9	6	10	.278	.320	.327
August	107	28	6	3	2	20	6	8	.262	.430	.301
Sept./Oct.	45	10	1	0	0	9	1	5	.222	.244	.234
Leading Off Inn.	99	17	3	1	0	0	12	9	.172	.222	.268
Runners On	215	69	10	1	3	66	8	16	.321	.419	.346
Runners/Scor. Pos.	133	38	7	1	1	60	8	10	.286	.376	.324
Runners On/2 Out	91	31	5	1	1	30	6	8	.341	.451	.388
Scor. Pos./2 Out	62	19	3	1	0	27	6	6	.306	.387	.377
Late Inning Pressure	69	22	2	0	0	15	4	6	.319	.348	.351
Leading Off	12	2	1	0	0	0	3	1	.167	.250	.333
Runners On	34	14	0	0	0	15	0	3	.412	.412	.400
Runners/Scor. Pos.	21	10	0	0	0	15	0	2	.476	.476	.455

DRIVING IN RUNS	From 1B	From 2B	From 3B	Scoring Position
Totals	6/165	25/104	31/61	56/165
Percentage	4%	24%	51%	34%
Driving In Runners from 3B with Less than Two Out:		20/36		56%

Loves to face: John Tudor (.476, 10-for-21)
Hates to face: Dennis Martinez (.167, 6-for-36)

Committed 24 errors last season, 2d-most in A.L., but ended the season with 14 consecutive errorless games at shortstop. . . . Percentage of runners driven in from scoring position was the highest of his career. . . . Handwriting may have been on the wall for Alfredo in September. He didn't bat or play the field after Sept. 16, appearing in just five of Oakland's last 16 games, all as a pinch-runner. . . . Has played 1,188 games in the 1980's, second only to Dale Murphy's total of 1,227. . . . But he's made only one appearance in the majors as a pinch-hitter, and that was in 1981. . . . With addition of Davis, Gibson, and Griffin, Dodgers have added an average of 81 stolen bases per season, based on past three years.

Kelly Gruber

Toronto Blue Jays — Bats Right

	AB	H	2B	3B	HR	RRF	BB	SO	BA	SA	OBA
Season	341	80	14	3	12	38	17	70	.235	.399	.283
vs. Left-Handers	152	35	7	3	4	17	12	35	.230	.395	.289
vs. Right-Handers	189	45	7	0	8	21	5	35	.238	.402	.279
Home	144	32	6	2	5	21	10	29	.222	.396	.283
Road	197	48	8	1	7	17	7	41	.244	.401	.284
Grass	139	33	6	0	4	12	6	31	.237	.367	.279
Artificial Turf	202	47	8	3	8	26	11	39	.233	.421	.286
April	25	4	0	0	0	2	1	2	.160	.160	.222
May	80	26	6	0	3	6	4	13	.325	.513	.365
June	76	21	5	0	3	11	4	22	.276	.461	.321
July	64	12	0	2	2	6	0	13	.188	.344	.206
August	68	14	3	0	3	11	2	11	.206	.382	.239
Sept./Oct.	28	3	0	1	1	2	6	9	.107	.286	.286
Leading Off Inn.	80	18	4	1	4	4	3	19	.225	.450	.262
Runners On	136	34	8	1	2	28	11	26	.250	.368	.311
Runners/Scor. Pos.	76	20	6	0	0	22	10	19	.263	.342	.348
Runners On/2 Out	59	10	3	0	0	7	5	17	.169	.220	.246
Scor. Pos./2 Out	38	8	3	0	0	4	4	11	.211	.289	.286
Late Inning Pressure	50	12	1	0	3	8	6	12	.240	.440	.328
Leading Off	12	3	0	0	2	2	1	5	.250	.750	.308
Runners On	21	5	0	0	0	5	4	4	.238	.238	.370
Runners/Scor. Pos.	12	4	0	0	0	5	4	2	.333	.333	.500

DRIVING IN RUNS	From 1B	From 2B	From 3B	Scoring Position
Totals	4/90	10/59	12/33	22/92
Percentage	4%	17%	36%	24%
Driving In Runners from 3B with Less than Two Out:		10/21		48%

Loves to face: Scott Bankhead (.600, 3-for-5, 1 HR)
Hates to face: Mike Morgan (0-for-7)

Played 119 games at third base, 21 games at shortstop, seven games at second base, and two games in center field. . . . Walked only once in 138 plate appearances from June 29 to August 29. . . . Grounded into 11 double plays in 57 double-play situations, 5th-highest rate in A.L. (minimum: 40 opportunities). . . . Struck out in six straight appearances with runners in scoring position (July 21–Aug. 1), longest streak in the A.L. last season. Dave Dravecky (as a batter) duplicated that streak in N.L. . . . Only player in either league with doubles in five consecutive games last season. . . . Career batting average below .100 at three ballparks: .056 (1-for-18) at Royals Stadium and Yankee Stadium, .048 (1-for-21) at Oakland Coliseum.

Ozzie Guillen
Chicago White Sox — Bats Left

	AB	H	2B	3B	HR	RRF	BB	SO	BA	SA	OBA
Season	560	156	22	7	2	52	22	52	.279	.354	.303
vs. Left-Handers	164	33	4	1	0	10	6	18	.201	.238	.227
vs. Right-Handers	396	123	18	6	2	42	16	34	.311	.402	.334
Home	269	85	11	4	2	32	17	20	.316	.409	.352
Road	291	71	11	3	0	20	5	32	.244	.302	.256
Grass	489	141	20	5	2	48	19	46	.288	.362	.312
Artificial Turf	71	15	2	2	0	4	3	6	.211	.296	.240
April	63	20	4	1	0	2	7	6	.317	.413	.386
May	87	26	1	2	1	7	5	11	.299	.391	.344
June	100	25	4	1	0	8	2	5	.250	.310	.262
July	107	31	4	0	0	12	2	10	.290	.327	.292
August	113	34	5	2	0	8	3	11	.301	.381	.316
Sept./Oct.	90	20	4	1	1	15	3	9	.222	.322	.242
Leading Off Inn.	165	55	8	2	0	0	8	19	.333	.406	.364
Runners On	209	53	7	0	2	52	10	15	.254	.316	.278
Runners/Scor. Pos.	121	34	3	0	1	50	10	9	.281	.331	.317
Runners On/2 Out	94	23	1	0	1	15	6	11	.245	.287	.290
Scor. Pos./2 Out	60	17	1	0	1	15	6	8	.283	.350	.348
Late Inning Pressure	89	23	2	1	1	7	2	7	.258	.337	.280
Leading Off	18	10	1	1	0	0	0	1	.556	.722	.556
Runners On	35	5	0	0	1	7	2	3	.143	.229	.184
Runners/Scor. Pos.	22	3	0	0	0	5	2	2	.136	.136	.200

DRIVING IN RUNS	From 1B	From 2B	From 3B	Scoring Position
Totals	1/148	16/91	33/59	49/150
Percentage	1%	18%	56%	33%
Driving In Runners from 3B with Less than Two Out:			27/38	71%

Loves to face: Mike Moore (.500, 10-for-20, 1 HR)
Hates to face: Bud Black (0-for-12)

Averaged one walk per 27.5 plate appearances, lowest rate in the A.L. ... Averaged 3.31 assists per nine innings last season, 2d-highest rate among A.L. shortstops (minimum: 500 innings). Ended the season with 20 consecutive errorless games at shortstop, his longest streak of the year.... Hitless in 22 consecutive at bats with runners in scoring position from Aug. 3 to Aug. 28.... As that streak ended he started another one: 28 consecutive at bats without a hit vs. southpaws from Aug. 28 to Oct. 3.... Batted 109 points higher against right-handed pitchers than he did against lefties, 3d-largest difference in A.L. last season (minimum: 50 AB each way).... No extra-base hits in 60 career at bats at the Metrodome.

Mel Hall
Cleveland Indians — Bats Left

	AB	H	2B	3B	HR	RRF	BB	SO	BA	SA	OBA
Season	485	136	21	1	18	79	20	68	.280	.439	.309
vs. Left-Handers	33	12	2	0	1	7	3	8	.364	.515	.417
vs. Right-Handers	452	124	19	1	17	72	17	60	.274	.434	.301
Home	222	64	10	0	8	41	10	25	.288	.441	.319
Road	263	72	11	1	10	38	10	43	.274	.437	.301
Grass	416	116	18	0	16	68	13	54	.279	.438	.300
Artificial Turf	69	20	3	1	2	11	7	14	.290	.449	.359
April	58	13	0	0	3	9	4	12	.224	.379	.274
May	88	23	1	0	4	9	1	17	.261	.409	.270
June	80	18	4	1	1	10	4	12	.225	.338	.262
July	79	24	4	0	2	7	2	3	.304	.430	.321
August	75	25	6	0	1	14	3	13	.333	.453	.359
Sept./Oct.	105	33	6	0	7	30	6	11	.314	.571	.351
Leading Off Inn.	130	35	4	0	9	9	4	19	.269	.508	.291
Runners On	210	57	8	1	5	66	12	30	.271	.390	.308
Runners/Scor. Pos.	123	36	5	1	2	58	11	15	.293	.398	.346
Runners On/2 Out	89	21	3	0	2	23	9	13	.236	.337	.306
Scor. Pos./2 Out	56	13	2	0	1	20	8	6	.232	.321	.328
Late Inning Pressure	72	21	3	0	3	7	2	6	.292	.458	.311
Leading Off	27	6	0	0	2	0	3	2	.222	.444	.222
Runners On	23	7	2	0	1	5	2	1	.304	.522	.360
Runners/Scor. Pos.	10	3	1	0	1	4	2	1	.300	.700	.417

DRIVING IN RUNS	From 1B	From 2B	From 3B	Scoring Position
Totals	10/137	26/97	25/57	51/154
Percentage	7%	27%	44%	33%
Driving In Runners from 3B with Less than Two Out:			19/30	63%

Loves to face: Bob Stanley (.500, 7-for-14, 1 HR)
Hates to face: Tom Henke (0-for-7)

Batted .238 before the All-Star break, but after the break he batted .330 with 10 HR and 44 RBI in 64 games.... Averaged one walk per 25.4 plate appearances, 2d-lowest rate in A.L. ... Ranked second among A.L. left fielders with 2.46 putouts per nine innings (minimum: 500 innings). ... Started all 114 games in which the Tribe faced a right-handed starting pitcher, but only one of 48 games in which they faced a southpaw.... Career batting averages: .165 vs. left-handers, .293 vs. right-handers. Home run off Gary Lucas on Sept. 25 is the only one he's hit in 182 career at bats against lefties.... Career average of .356 with one home run with the bases loaded, but he hasn't walked once in those 49 plate appearances.

Mike Heath
Detroit Tigers — Bats Right

	AB	H	2B	3B	HR	RRF	BB	SO	BA	SA	OBA
Season	270	76	16	0	8	34	21	42	.281	.430	.339
vs. Left-Handers	159	48	11	0	5	19	12	15	.302	.465	.356
vs. Right-Handers	111	28	5	0	3	15	9	27	.252	.378	.314
Home	145	43	10	0	8	22	12	23	.297	.531	.352
Road	125	33	6	0	0	12	9	19	.264	.312	.324
Grass	227	66	14	0	8	31	18	38	.291	.458	.349
Artificial Turf	43	10	2	0	0	3	3	4	.233	.279	.283
April	20	7	3	0	1	3	5	0	.350	.650	.480
May	85	28	7	0	4	10	8	14	.329	.553	.394
June	37	8	0	0	0	5	1	7	.216	.216	.231
July	46	12	3	0	2	10	1	8	.261	.457	.277
August	43	10	0	0	1	4	6	9	.233	.302	.340
Sept./Oct.	39	11	3	0	0	2	0	4	.282	.359	.300
Leading Off Inn.	52	15	5	0	3	3	3	9	.288	.558	.362
Runners On	113	34	5	0	4	30	12	17	.301	.451	.365
Runners/Scor. Pos.	69	19	4	0	1	24	9	14	.275	.377	.354
Runners On/2 Out	48	11	1	0	1	9	9	9	.229	.313	.351
Scor. Pos./2 Out	34	7	1	0	0	7	6	7	.206	.235	.325
Late Inning Pressure	40	6	3	0	0	5	4	8	.150	.225	.222
Leading Off	12	2	1	0	0	0	1	3	.167	.250	.231
Runners On	16	4	2	0	0	5	2	1	.250	.375	.316
Runners/Scor. Pos.	12	3	1	0	0	5	2	1	.250	.333	.333

DRIVING IN RUNS	From 1B	From 2B	From 3B	Scoring Position
Totals	4/78	13/60	9/25	22/85
Percentage	5%	22%	36%	26%
Driving In Runners from 3B with Less than Two Out:			7/14	50%

Loves to face: Curt Young (.600, 6-for-10, 2 HR)
Hates to face: Juan Berenguer (0-for-14)

Started 51 of 52 games in which the Tigers faced left-handed starters, 16 of 110 games vs. right-handers.... Played eight positions last season: catcher (67 games), right field (20), first base (4), third base (4), left field (4), shortstop (2), second base (1), and center field (1). ... Opponents stole only 34 bases in 56 attempts, a rate of 61 percent. Against other Detroit catchers (primarily Nokes), the rate was 81 percent.... Lowest career fielding percentage (.979) of the 27 catchers active in 1987 who have played 500+ games... Has hit for a higher average on grass fields than he has on artificial surfaces in each of the last five seasons; lower in Late-Inning Pressure Situations than overall in each of the last six.

Dave Henderson
Boston Red Sox — Bats Right

	AB	H	2B	3B	HR	RRF	BB	SO	BA	SA	OBA
Season	184	43	10	0	8	28	22	48	.234	.418	.313
vs. Left-Handers	66	17	5	0	4	10	6	17	.258	.515	.319
vs. Right-Handers	118	26	5	0	4	18	16	31	.220	.364	.309
Home	107	25	7	0	4	16	14	26	.234	.411	.320
Road	77	18	3	0	4	12	8	22	.234	.429	.302
Grass	155	35	10	0	6	23	20	40	.226	.406	.311
Artificial Turf	29	8	0	0	2	5	2	8	.276	.483	.323
April	71	17	3	0	3	8	8	18	.239	.408	.316
May	25	6	2	0	0	3	2	6	.240	.320	.296
June	40	5	3	0	0	3	8	12	.125	.200	.265
July	6	3	0	0	1	3	0	3	.500	1.000	.500
August	42	12	2	0	1	7	4	9	.286	.405	.340
Sept./Oct.	0	0	0	0	0	0	0	0	—	—	—
Leading Off Inn.	41	11	4	0	2	2	7	10	.268	.512	.375
Runners On	86	15	3	0	4	24	9	23	.174	.349	.247
Runners/Scor. Pos.	52	8	2	0	2	19	5	15	.154	.308	.220
Runners On/2 Out	34	3	3	0	0	5	6	11	.088	.176	.225
Scor. Pos./2 Out	25	2	2	0	0	4	3	8	.080	.160	.179
Late Inning Pressure	28	6	0	0	1	3	3	9	.214	.321	.290
Leading Off	5	0	0	0	0	0	0	1	.000	.000	.000
Runners On	10	1	0	0	1	3	2	6	.100	.400	.250
Runners/Scor. Pos.	5	0	0	0	0	1	1	2	.000	.000	.167

DRIVING IN RUNS	From 1B	From 2B	From 3B	Scoring Position
Totals	4/65	6/36	10/33	16/69
Percentage	6%	17%	30%	23%
Driving In Runners from 3B with Less than Two Out:			8/18	44%

Loves to face: Ray Searage (5-for-5, 2 2B, 1 HR)
Hates to face: Bert Blyleven (.056, 1-for-18)

Batting average with runners on base was the lowest among 162 A.L. qualifiers last season.... Stole 11 bases vs. the Twins, the most by one player against a single A.L. club.... Career batting average of .131 with two outs and runners on base in Late-Inning Pressure Situations. Of course, that's only in the regular season.... Career batting average of .226 on grass fields, .275 on artificial turf. Difference of 49 points is 2d largest among players with at least 1,000 at bats on each surface over the last 10 years.... Has batted .225 during the past five Aprils, 2d-lowest mark in majors to Bill Doran's .217 (minimum: 300 AB).... Has homered in every A.L. ballpark except Tiger Stadium (74 career AB).

Rickey Henderson
New York Yankees — Bats Right

	AB	H	2B	3B	HR	RRF	BB	SO	BA	SA	OBA
Season	358	104	17	3	17	38	80	52	.291	.497	.423
vs. Left-Handers	118	37	7	2	7	13	28	14	.314	.585	.445
vs. Right-Handers	240	67	10	1	10	25	52	38	.279	.454	.412
Home	161	51	8	3	10	20	39	25	.317	.590	.453
Road	197	53	9	0	7	18	41	27	.269	.421	.397
Grass	289	84	13	3	16	35	68	42	.291	.522	.429
Artificial Turf	69	20	4	0	1	3	12	10	.290	.391	.395
April	68	26	3	2	6	13	18	7	.382	.750	.512
May	100	29	7	0	4	6	17	14	.290	.480	.398
June	11	2	0	0	0	0	3	3	.182	.182	.357
July	79	20	2	0	1	7	17	10	.253	.316	.392
August	0	0	0	0	0	0	0	0	—	—	—
Sept./Oct.	100	27	5	1	6	12	25	18	.270	.520	.416
Leading Off Inn.	136	43	6	3	10	10	20	14	.316	.625	.408
Runners On	119	29	4	0	4	25	37	19	.244	.378	.423
Runners/Scor. Pos.	64	13	2	0	0	16	24	14	.203	.234	.420
Runners On/2 Out	41	9	2	0	2	8	18	9	.220	.415	.458
Scor. Pos./2 Out	22	3	1	0	0	4	13	7	.136	.182	.457
Late Inning Pressure	51	22	3	0	3	10	10	11	.431	.725	.525
Leading Off	7	4	2	0	1	1	0	0	.571	1.286	.571
Runners On	24	10	2	0	2	9	6	5	.417	.750	.533
Runners/Scor. Pos.	11	5	1	0	0	4	4	1	.455	.545	.600

DRIVING IN RUNS	From 1B	From 2B	From 3B	Scoring Position
Totals	5/96	6/45	9/30	15/75
Percentage	5%	13%	30%	20%
Driving In Runners from 3B with Less than Two Out:		7/18		39%

Loves to face: Storm Davis (.423, 11-for-26)
Hates to face: Dennis Eckersley (.135, 5-for-37)
Stole third base nine times (2d in A.L. to Molitor's 10), without being caught.... Averaged one walk per 5.5 plate appearances, 3d best in A.L. (minimum: 50 BB).... Batted .367 (and stole 15 bases in 15 attempts) in day games, .252 at night, a difference of 115 points, the 2d largest among A.L. players last season (minimum: 50 AB each way).... Has homered in every A.L. ballpark except Fenway Park (165 career AB).... Yearly batting averages with runners in scoring position since 1983: .327, .275, .288, .211, .203. ... Career average of .302 under Billy Martin, .280 for other managers. Has stolen 117 bases per 162 games with a 78-percent success rate under Billy; 81 SB per 162 games, 82-percent for others.

Larry Herndon
Detroit Tigers — Bats Right

	AB	H	2B	3B	HR	RRF	BB	SO	BA	SA	OBA
Season	225	73	13	2	9	48	23	35	.324	.520	.378
vs. Left-Handers	177	66	11	2	8	41	20	24	.373	.593	.426
vs. Right-Handers	48	7	2	0	1	7	3	11	.146	.250	.192
Home	115	36	6	2	7	28	12	15	.313	.583	.372
Road	110	37	7	0	2	20	11	20	.336	.455	.384
Grass	185	57	10	2	8	41	19	27	.308	.514	.364
Artificial Turf	40	16	3	0	1	7	4	8	.400	.550	.444
April	39	13	1	1	2	7	5	8	.333	.564	.400
May	36	10	3	0	0	8	7	6	.278	.361	.370
June	35	13	2	0	2	8	1	4	.371	.600	.378
July	33	9	1	0	2	7	1	6	.273	.485	.294
August	44	17	4	1	2	12	4	4	.386	.659	.438
Sept./Oct.	38	11	2	0	1	6	5	7	.289	.421	.364
Leading Off Inn.	38	15	4	1	2	2	5	7	.395	.711	.465
Runners On	106	32	3	0	6	45	14	19	.302	.500	.365
Runners/Scor. Pos.	67	19	2	0	2	37	9	12	.284	.403	.341
Runners On/2 Out	44	13	2	0	1	16	3	8	.295	.409	.340
Scor. Pos./2 Out	31	8	2	0	0	14	1	6	.258	.323	.281
Late Inning Pressure	33	13	3	0	0	1	3	6	.394	.485	.444
Leading Off	6	3	1	0	0	0	1	1	.500	.667	.571
Runners On	16	3	0	0	0	1	1	4	.188	.188	.235
Runners/Scor. Pos.	7	1	0	0	0	1	1	2	.143	.143	.250

DRIVING IN RUNS	From 1B	From 2B	From 3B	Scoring Position
Totals	7/77	15/59	17/33	32/92
Percentage	9%	25%	52%	35%
Driving In Runners from 3B with Less than Two Out:		13/20		65%

Loves to face: Scott McGregor (.469, 15-for-32, 4 HR)
Hates to face: Jim Clancy (0-for-18)
Batted 77 points higher in 1987 than in 1986, 2d-largest increase in majors (minimum: 200 AB in both years).... Batted .381 (8-for-21) as a pinch-hitter, highest average in A.L. (minimum: 20 AB). ... Grounded into 12 double plays in 55 DP situations, highest rate in A.L. (minimum: 40 opportunities). ... Started all 52 games in which the Tigers faced southpaws, but only five of 110 vs. right-handers.... Career average of .301 vs. left-handers, .258 vs. right-handers.... Career average of .402 (47-for-117, 3 HR) at Yankee Stadium, his highest at any major-league ballpark.... Never had more than nine consecutive at bats without a hit last season.

Donnie Hill
Chicago White Sox — Bats Left and Right

	AB	H	2B	3B	HR	RRF	BB	SO	BA	SA	OBA
Season	410	98	14	6	9	46	30	35	.239	.368	.290
vs. Left-Handers	130	34	3	0	5	14	12	13	.262	.400	.319
vs. Right-Handers	280	64	11	6	4	32	18	22	.229	.354	.276
Home	201	51	11	4	1	19	14	11	.254	.363	.303
Road	209	47	3	2	8	27	16	24	.225	.373	.278
Grass	326	81	13	5	6	36	24	23	.248	.374	.299
Artificial Turf	84	17	1	1	3	10	6	12	.202	.345	.253
April	58	11	3	1	2	7	7	8	.190	.379	.277
May	33	3	0	0	0	3	4	4	.091	.091	.184
June	50	13	4	1	0	3	3	1	.260	.380	.302
July	88	18	1	2	2	8	4	6	.205	.330	.234
August	57	21	4	0	3	14	4	6	.368	.596	.419
Sept./Oct.	124	32	2	2	2	11	8	10	.258	.355	.301
Leading Off Inn.	94	25	4	0	1	1	4	7	.266	.340	.296
Runners On	174	43	7	3	3	40	15	15	.247	.374	.301
Runners/Scor. Pos.	112	27	3	3	2	36	13	10	.241	.375	.310
Runners On/2 Out	69	19	3	2	2	18	7	7	.275	.464	.342
Scor. Pos./2 Out	50	13	1	2	1	15	7	5	.260	.420	.351
Late Inning Pressure	51	15	2	0	2	7	6	4	.294	.451	.368
Leading Off	18	5	1	0	0	0	2	1	.278	.333	.350
Runners On	21	7	1	0	2	7	0	2	.333	.667	.333
Runners/Scor. Pos.	12	5	0	0	1	5	0	2	.417	.667	.417

DRIVING IN RUNS	From 1B	From 2B	From 3B	Scoring Position
Totals	4/101	18/96	15/34	33/130
Percentage	4%	19%	44%	25%
Driving In Runners from 3B with Less than Two Out:		11/18		61%

Loves to face: Rick Honeycutt (.571, 4-for-7, 1 HR)
Hates to face: Richard Dotson (0-for-10)
Now he's a member: Was hit by a pitch for first time in career on August 29, after 1,460 plate appearances. Mark Gubicza presided over the initiation rites.... White Sox allowed 4.26 runs per nine innings with Hill at second base, 4.97 with other second basemen. ... Committed nine errors in 14 games at third base on grass fields. ... Career batting averages of .358 at the Metrodome (his highest at any A.L. ballpark), .169 at Tiger Stadium (lowest).... Career breakdown: .251 with bases empty, .279 with runners on base, .286 with runners in scoring position, .301 with two out and runners in scoring position.... Ranks 10th in majors with a .332 average during past three Augusts (minimum: 200 AB).

Tommy Hinzo
Cleveland Indians — Bats Left and Right

	AB	H	2B	3B	HR	RRF	BB	SO	BA	SA	OBA
Season	257	68	9	3	3	21	10	47	.265	.358	.296
vs. Left-Handers	64	25	4	0	2	8	5	5	.391	.547	.443
vs. Right-Handers	193	43	5	3	1	13	5	42	.223	.295	.245
Home	116	27	5	1	3	7	6	25	.233	.371	.276
Road	141	41	4	2	0	14	4	22	.291	.348	.313
Grass	213	55	8	2	3	18	9	38	.258	.357	.293
Artificial Turf	44	13	1	1	0	3	1	9	.295	.364	.311
April	0	0	0	0	0	0	0	0	—	—	—
May	0	0	0	0	0	0	0	0	—	—	—
June	0	0	0	0	0	0	0	0	—	—	—
July	55	12	2	0	0	4	3	6	.218	.255	.254
August	110	29	5	0	2	10	5	25	.264	.364	.302
Sept./Oct.	92	27	2	3	1	7	2	16	.293	.413	.316
Leading Off Inn.	41	9	2	0	2	2	0	9	.220	.415	.220
Runners On	113	25	3	1	0	18	4	22	.221	.265	.252
Runners/Scor. Pos.	56	9	1	1	0	17	2	14	.161	.214	.200
Runners On/2 Out	42	8	2	0	0	4	1	6	.190	.238	.227
Scor. Pos./2 Out	26	2	1	0	0	3	1	8	.077	.115	.111
Late Inning Pressure	33	7	1	0	1	1	2	5	.212	.333	.257
Leading Off	6	1	0	0	1	1	0	2	.167	.667	.167
Runners On	10	0	0	0	0	0	1	3	.000	.000	.091
Runners/Scor. Pos.	6	0	0	0	0	0	0	2	.000	.000	.000

DRIVING IN RUNS	From 1B	From 2B	From 3B	Scoring Position
Totals	2/81	6/41	10/28	16/69
Percentage	2%	15%	36%	23%
Driving In Runners from 3B with Less than Two Out:		8/13		62%

Loves to face: Gary Lavelle (3-for-3)
Hates to face: Ken Dixon (0-for-2, 2 SO)
Joined the Indians at the All-Star break and started 63 of 77 games in the second half of the season.... Averaged 3.29 assists per nine innings last season, 2d-highest among A.L. second basemen (minimum: 500 innings).... Indians allowed an average of 5.52 runs per nine innings with Hinzo at second, 6.23 with Bernazard there, and 7.48 with Noboa there.... Looks like another bogus switch hitter. Batted 168 points higher against left-handers than he did against right-handers, largest difference in A.L. last season (minimum: 50 AB each way). Batting average against lefties was the highest among 163 A.L. qualifiers.... One of eight A.L. players to collect five hits in a single game last season.

Sam Horn

Boston Red Sox — Bats Left

	AB	H	2B	3B	HR	RRF	BB	SO	BA	SA	OBA
Season	158	44	7	0	14	35	17	55	.278	.589	.356
vs. Left-Handers	29	8	2	0	3	9	4	15	.276	.655	.382
vs. Right-Handers	129	36	5	0	11	26	13	40	.279	.574	.350
Home	72	22	3	0	6	18	8	22	.306	.597	.383
Road	86	22	4	0	8	17	9	33	.256	.581	.333
Grass	141	39	6	0	12	31	15	48	.277	.574	.354
Artificial Turf	17	5	1	0	2	4	2	7	.294	.706	.368
April	0	0	0	0	0	0	0	0	——	——	——
May	0	0	0	0	0	0	0	0	——	——	——
June	0	0	0	0	0	0	0	0	——	——	——
July	22	9	1	0	4	9	2	7	.409	1.000	.458
August	69	19	4	0	5	12	8	20	.275	.551	.359
Sept./Oct.	67	16	2	0	5	14	7	28	.239	.493	.320
Leading Off Inn.	36	11	2	0	4	4	3	12	.306	.694	.359
Runners On	73	21	3	0	5	26	8	25	.288	.534	.373
Runners/Scor. Pos.	44	10	1	0	2	20	4	16	.227	.386	.306
Runners On/2 Out	29	9	1	0	3	13	2	12	.310	.655	.355
Scor. Pos./2 Out	19	6	1	0	2	11	0	8	.316	.684	.316
Late Inning Pressure	19	2	1	0	1	4	0	7	.105	.263	.150
Leading Off	5	2	0	0	1	1	0	0	.400	1.000	.400
Runners On	9	0	0	0	0	3	0	3	.000	.000	.100
Runners/Scor. Pos.	6	0	0	0	0	3	0	3	.000	.000	.143

DRIVING IN RUNS	From 1B	From 2B	From 3B	Scoring Position
Totals	5/54	6/33	10/21	16/54
Percentage	9%	18%	48%	30%
Driving In Runners from 3B with Less than Two Out:			6/10	60%

Loves to face: Jose Nunez (.750, 3-for-4, 2 HR)
Hates to face: Ted Higuera (0-for-6, 5 SO)
Best home run rate (one per 11.3 AB) in the major leagues last season (minimum: 10 HR). . . . Strikeout rate was also near the top (or is it the bottom?): one strikeout per 3.2 plate appearances was 3d-worst in A.L. (minimum: 50 SO). . . . Batted .222 in day games, .308 at night. . . . He's listed as a first baseman in the Red Sox' media guide, but has yet to play the field in a major-league game. Played 46 games after his debut on July 25, 40 games as the designated hitter and six games as a pinch-hitter. . . . Made 29 errors at first base for Winston-Salem in 1984. Sounded pretty gruesome until we found that Wesley Kent, a first baseman for San Jose, made 31 that year and hit only .200 to boot!

Jack Howell

California Angels — Bats Left

	AB	H	2B	3B	HR	RRF	BB	SO	BA	SA	OBA
Season	449	110	18	5	23	68	57	118	.245	.461	.331
vs. Left-Handers	73	9	3	2	1	13	7	25	.123	.260	.200
vs. Right-Handers	376	101	15	3	22	55	50	93	.269	.500	.356
Home	230	62	8	3	15	43	26	56	.270	.526	.344
Road	219	48	10	2	8	25	31	62	.219	.393	.319
Grass	368	91	13	3	23	65	50	90	.247	.486	.338
Artificial Turf	81	19	5	2	0	3	7	28	.235	.346	.300
April	66	20	4	0	4	10	10	17	.303	.545	.385
May	73	17	3	1	6	10	6	21	.233	.548	.291
June	82	20	5	1	2	14	15	17	.244	.402	.361
July	76	17	1	1	3	13	13	16	.224	.382	.337
August	69	17	4	1	3	5	5	23	.246	.377	.307
Sept./Oct.	83	19	1	1	7	18	8	24	.229	.518	.304
Leading Off Inn.	102	25	5	0	4	4	17	19	.245	.412	.353
Runners On	196	48	5	3	10	55	27	51	.245	.454	.339
Runners/Scor. Pos.	114	20	2	1	5	42	15	31	.175	.342	.278
Runners On/2 Out	75	18	1	1	4	19	9	17	.240	.440	.321
Scor. Pos./2 Out	46	9	1	0	3	16	5	11	.196	.413	.275
Late Inning Pressure	75	19	1	5	5	9	11	23	.253	.533	.349
Leading Off	15	5	1	0	0	0	3	5	.333	.400	.444
Runners On	30	5	2	0	1	5	7	9	.167	.333	.324
Runners/Scor. Pos.	16	1	0	0	1	4	6	3	.063	.250	.318

DRIVING IN RUNS	From 1B	From 2B	From 3B	Scoring Position
Totals	14/147	10/79	20/57	30/136
Percentage	10%	13%	35%	22%
Driving In Runners from 3B with Less than Two Out:			13/29	45%

Loves to face: Steve Ontiveros (.600, 3-for-5, 1 HR)
Hates to face: Dave Righetti (0-for-7, 6 SO)
Angels had a record of 15–12 with Howell batting cleanup, 60–75 with others there. . . . Started 104 of 111 games in which the Angels faced a right-handed starter, seven of 51 games vs. lefties. . . . Batted 145 points higher vs. right-handers than vs. southpaws, 2d-largest difference in A.L. last season (minimum: 50 AB each way). Career averages: .153 (two HR) vs. southpaws, .262 (30 HR) vs. right-handers. . . . Only homer run vs. a left-hander: April 27 off Juan Nieves. . . . Had seven consecutive extra-base hits without a single from May 3 to May 20. Hit home runs in three consecutive games from May 3 to May 6, and in four in a row from Sept. 30 to Oct. 3. . . . Career average of .213 with runners in scoring position.

Kent Hrbek

Minnesota Twins — Bats Left

	AB	H	2B	3B	HR	RRF	BB	SO	BA	SA	OBA
Season	477	136	20	1	34	92	84	60	.285	.545	.389
vs. Left-Handers	138	31	2	0	6	22	14	23	.225	.370	.290
vs. Right-Handers	339	105	18	1	28	70	70	37	.310	.617	.426
Home	234	69	8	1	20	51	48	30	.295	.594	.413
Road	243	67	12	0	14	41	36	30	.276	.498	.364
Grass	197	59	10	0	13	36	30	26	.299	.548	.387
Artificial Turf	280	77	10	1	21	56	54	34	.275	.543	.390
April	74	19	2	0	2	14	12	11	.257	.365	.360
May	88	24	1	0	8	16	14	12	.273	.557	.369
June	84	24	2	0	10	20	9	11	.286	.667	.355
July	79	21	3	0	4	11	17	11	.266	.456	.396
August	92	30	8	1	8	22	19	8	.326	.696	.438
Sept./Oct.	60	18	4	0	2	9	13	7	.300	.467	.408
Leading Off Inn.	112	30	3	0	6	6	15	13	.268	.473	.354
Runners On	225	68	9	0	16	74	48	29	.302	.556	.417
Runners/Scor. Pos.	115	27	3	0	6	52	32	18	.235	.417	.388
Runners On/2 Out	106	31	5	0	5	22	26	17	.292	.481	.432
Scor. Pos./2 Out	62	11	1	0	1	13	17	11	.177	.242	.354
Late Inning Pressure	67	24	4	0	4	14	4	5	.358	.597	.384
Leading Off	16	7	0	0	1	1	0	0	.438	.625	.471
Runners On	29	8	0	0	2	12	2	4	.276	.483	.303
Runners/Scor. Pos.	16	4	0	0	0	8	1	1	.250	.250	.263

DRIVING IN RUNS	From 1B	From 2B	From 3B	Scoring Position
Totals	15/162	18/89	25/49	43/138
Percentage	9%	20%	51%	31%
Driving In Runners from 3B with Less than Two Out:			21/30	70%

Loves to face: Jose Guzman (.727, 8-for-11, 2 HR)
Hates to face: Gene Nelson (.100, 2-for-20, 1 HR, 9 SO)
One of three players with 20+ home runs and 90+ RBI in each of last four years. Others: Mattingly and Schmidt. . . . Belted his 34 home runs in 34 separate games, just one shy of the A.L. record for that sort of thing: Ron Kittle hit 35 HR in 35 different games in 1983; Willie Mays set the major-league mark of 37 HR without a multiple-HR game in 1966. . . . Batted career-low .225 vs. left-handers, but made up for it with one Series swing against Ken Dayley. . . . Walks have increased every full year in majors: 54, 57, 65, 67, 71, 84. . . . Has hit for a higher average at the Metrodome than in road games in each of the last six seasons. . . . Only one home run in 143 career at bats at the Oakland Coliseum.

Tim Hulett

Chicago White Sox — Bats Right

	AB	H	2B	3B	HR	RRF	BB	SO	BA	SA	OBA
Season	240	52	10	0	7	28	10	41	.217	.346	.246
vs. Left-Handers	81	20	3	0	4	11	2	13	.247	.432	.265
vs. Right-Handers	159	32	7	0	3	17	8	28	.201	.302	.237
Home	112	18	3	0	3	10	4	21	.161	.268	.188
Road	128	34	7	0	4	18	6	20	.266	.414	.296
Grass	204	39	7	0	6	19	9	38	.191	.314	.224
Artificial Turf	36	13	3	0	1	9	1	3	.361	.528	.368
April	70	19	2	0	3	14	1	13	.271	.429	.282
May	98	19	4	0	4	11	5	17	.194	.357	.231
June	56	11	4	0	0	3	4	8	.196	.268	.246
July	5	1	0	0	0	0	0	2	.200	.200	.200
August	11	2	0	0	0	0	0	1	.182	.182	.182
Sept./Oct.	0	0	0	0	0	0	0	0	——	——	——
Leading Off Inn.	58	10	1	0	2	2	3	10	.172	.293	.213
Runners On	92	23	6	0	1	22	6	17	.250	.348	.290
Runners/Scor. Pos.	59	15	5	0	0	20	5	12	.254	.339	.303
Runners On/2 Out	45	12	4	0	1	11	2	7	.267	.422	.298
Scor. Pos./2 Out	31	8	4	0	0	9	2	6	.258	.387	.303
Late Inning Pressure	35	5	2	0	0	4	3	6	.143	.200	.200
Leading Off	13	1	0	0	0	0	0	3	.077	.077	.077
Runners On	12	2	1	0	0	4	3	2	.167	.250	.294
Runners/Scor. Pos.	7	2	1	0	0	4	2	1	.286	.429	.364

DRIVING IN RUNS	From 1B	From 2B	From 3B	Scoring Position
Totals	1/59	14/48	6/22	20/70
Percentage	2%	29%	27%	29%
Driving In Runners from 3B with Less than Two Out:			5/10	50%

Loves to face: Bud Black (.500, 7-for-14, 1 HR)
Hates to face: Joe Niekro (0-for-15)
Hit seven HR in his first 40 games, none in his last 28. . . . Batted .282 in day games last season, .189 at night. Career averages are 85 points apart (.301 in day, .216 at night), largest difference of any player over the last ten years (minimum: 200 AB each way). . . . Batted 105 points higher in road games than in home games, 2d-largest difference in the A.L. last season (minimum: 100 AB each way). . . . Yearly batting average vs. right-handed pitchers since 1985: .250, .218, .201. . . . Career breakdown: .245 with bases empty, .231 with runners on base, .217 with runners in scoring position. . . . Career batting average of .356 (16-for-45, 2 HR) at Memorial Stadium.

Pete Incaviglia
Texas Rangers   Bats Right

	AB	H	2B	3B	HR	RRF	BB	SO	BA	SA	OBA
Season	509	138	26	4	27	84	48	168	.271	.497	.332
vs. Left-Handers	182	62	12	1	13	39	21	54	.341	.632	.407
vs. Right-Handers	327	76	14	3	14	45	27	114	.232	.422	.290
Home	255	66	12	2	11	43	30	85	.259	.451	.336
Road	254	72	14	2	16	41	18	83	.283	.543	.328
Grass	423	114	22	2	22	72	43	136	.270	.487	.335
Artificial Turf	86	24	4	2	5	12	5	32	.279	.547	.319
April	74	24	1	0	8	19	8	23	.324	.662	.390
May	97	28	7	1	3	12	12	31	.289	.474	.360
June	102	22	5	2	5	15	5	39	.216	.451	.259
July	93	25	8	0	4	15	17	28	.269	.484	.378
August	100	28	2	1	6	18	4	30	.280	.500	.305
Sept./Oct.	43	11	3	0	1	5	2	17	.256	.395	.283
Leading Off Inn.	137	41	7	0	4	4	14	40	.299	.438	.368
Runners On	231	60	8	2	11	68	19	75	.260	.455	.310
Runners/Scor. Pos.	119	30	3	1	6	54	15	45	.252	.445	.324
Runners On/2 Out	104	27	2	2	5	26	9	35	.260	.462	.319
Scor. Pos./2 Out	61	14	1	.1	3	21	7	23	.230	.492	.309
Late Inning Pressure	70	17	6	0	4	11	9	27	.243	.500	.321
Leading Off	21	4	1	0	0	0	4	9	.190	.238	.320
Runners On	27	8	3	0	2	9	3	9	.296	.630	.344
Runners/Scor. Pos.	11	1	0	0	0	3	2	5	.091	.091	.200

DRIVING IN RUNS	From 1B	From 2B	From 3B	Scoring Position
Totals	12/160	18/98	27/57	45/155
Percentage	8%	18%	47%	29%
Driving In Runners from 3B with Less than Two Out:	20/33	61%		

Loves to face: Lee Guetterman (.667, 6-for-9)
Hates to face: Oil Can Boyd (0-for-11, 8 SO)
Batted 108 points higher against left-handers than he did against right-handers last season, largest difference among everyday players in the A.L. last season.... Career slugging average vs. left-handed pitchers (.617) is the highest in the majors over the 13 years that we've been keeping track of such things (minimum: 200 TB).... Batted .323 (1 HR per 9.6 AB) in day games, .259 (one HR per 24.3 AB) in night games.... Rangers had a record of 28–48 with him in the cleanup spot, 47–39 record with others there.... Hitless in nine at bats with the bases loaded last season, largest 0-for in the A.L. Career average of .130 (3-for-23, 2 HR).... Has homered at every A.L. ballpark except Yankee Stadium (36 career AB).

Garth Iorg
Toronto Blue Jays   Bats Right

	AB	H	2B	3B	HR	RRF	BB	SO	BA	SA	OBA
Season	310	65	11	0	4	32	21	52	.210	.284	.262
vs. Left-Handers	138	25	3	0	1	14	11	18	.181	.225	.238
vs. Right-Handers	172	40	8	0	3	18	10	34	.233	.331	.281
Home	148	31	5	0	1	17	10	26	.209	.264	.267
Road	162	34	6	0	3	15	11	26	.210	.302	.257
Grass	128	28	6	0	3	11	9	22	.219	.336	.266
Artificial Turf	182	37	5	0	1	21	12	30	.203	.247	.259
April	23	2	0	0	0	1	3	2	.087	.087	.214
May	48	8	0	0	0	5	3	8	.167	.167	.216
June	65	19	1	0	0	6	3	5	.292	.308	.314
July	79	23	5	0	3	15	6	15	.291	.468	.349
August	78	12	4	0	1	5	6	14	.154	.244	.214
Sept./Oct.	17	1	1	0	0	0	0	8	.059	.118	.059
Leading Off Inn.	68	12	3	0	1	1	0	17	.176	.265	.200
Runners On	135	29	4	0	1	29	14	17	.215	.267	.283
Runners/Scor. Pos.	80	21	2	0	1	29	10	9	.263	.325	.333
Runners On/2 Out	55	14	1	0	0	14	4	9	.255	.273	.305
Scor. Pos./2 Out	39	12	1	0	0	14	4	6	.308	.333	.372
Late Inning Pressure	54	13	2	0	0	8	5	7	.241	.278	.295
Leading Off	11	2	1	0	0	0	0	2	.182	.273	.182
Runners On	22	7	1	0	0	8	2	2	.318	.364	.346
Runners/Scor. Pos.	11	4	0	0	0	8	2	0	.364	.364	.400

DRIVING IN RUNS	From 1B	From 2B	From 3B	Scoring Position
Totals	1/96	11/61	16/35	27/96
Percentage	1%	18%	46%	28%
Driving In Runners from 3B with Less than Two Out:	11/19	58%		

Loves to face: Charlie Hough (.481, 13-for-27, 2 HR)
Hates to face: Kirk McCaskill (0-for-8, 4 SO)
Has lost 50+ points on his batting average in each of the last two seasons. Year by year since 1985: .313, .260, .210. Only comparable player: the incomparable Wayne Tolleson (.313, .265, .221).... Batting average in LIPS has been higher than his overall average in each of the last nine seasons, the longest streak in the 13 years we've compiled that stat. Career averages: .304 in LIPS, .250 at other times.... Percentage of runners driven in from scoring position in Late-Inning Pressure Situations (8-for-17, 47%) was a career-high (career average: 34.6 percent).... Batting average with runners in scoring position has been higher than overall batting average in each of the last five seasons.

Bo Jackson
Kansas City Royals   Bats Right

	AB	H	2B	3B	HR	RRF	BB	SO	BA	SA	OBA
Season	396	93	17	2	22	53	30	158	.235	.455	.296
vs. Left-Handers	113	28	5	1	7	13	10	46	.248	.496	.315
vs. Right-Handers	283	65	12	1	15	40	20	112	.230	.438	.288
Home	197	56	14	1	14	39	18	59	.284	.579	.344
Road	199	37	3	1	8	14	12	99	.186	.332	.247
Grass	157	28	3	1	5	10	11	79	.178	.306	.246
Artificial Turf	239	65	14	1	17	43	19	79	.272	.552	.328
April	68	22	5	0	4	15	6	25	.324	.574	.378
May	88	19	2	1	5	14	8	34	.216	.432	.289
June	81	23	3	0	7	12	5	33	.284	.580	.341
July	90	20	4	1	4	7	8	39	.222	.422	.287
August	47	7	2	0	1	2	2	22	.149	.255	.200
Sept./Oct.	22	2	1	0	1	3	1	5	.091	.273	.130
Leading Off Inn.	88	22	2	0	8	10	10	32	.250	.545	.333
Runners On	179	37	8	1	6	37	12	75	.207	.363	.258
Runners/Scor. Pos.	103	20	4	1	3	30	8	42	.194	.340	.254
Runners On/2 Out	72	19	3	1	6	27	6	24	.264	.483	.329
Scor. Pos./2 Out	48	12	3	1	3	21	5	16	.250	.542	.333
Late Inning Pressure	47	11	1	0	1	3	7	19	.234	.319	.339
Leading Off	11	1	0	0	0	0	3	3	.091	.091	.286
Runners On	15	3	1	0	0	2	2	9	.200	.267	.278
Runners/Scor. Pos.	11	1	0	0	0	1	1	8	.091	.091	.154

DRIVING IN RUNS	From 1B	From 2B	From 3B	Scoring Position
Totals	7/132	8/84	16/40	24/124
Percentage	5%	10%	40%	19%
Driving In Runners from 3B with Less than Two Out:	7/20	35%		

Loves to face: Dan Petry (.714, 5-for-7, 1 HR)
Hates to face: Tom Candiotti (0-for-7)
Averaged one strikeout every 2.7 plate appearances, highest rate in major-league history among players with 400+ plate appearances. ... Struck out in his first plate appearance in 54 of the 122 games in which he batted. That rate (44%) is 33 percent higher than even his own whopping rate at other times. Composite totals for his first time up in each game: .162 (18-for-111) with 2 HR and 11 BB.... Struck out 10 consecutive times with runners on base from June 6 to June 18.... Averaged 1.74 putouts per nine innings, 2d-lowest rate among A.L. left fielders (minimum: 500 innings).... Percentage of runners driven in from scoring position with less than two out was the lowest in the majors (minimum: 40 opportunities).

Reggie Jackson
Oakland As   Bats Left

	AB	H	2B	3B	HR	RRF	BB	SO	BA	SA	OBA
Season	336	74	14	1	15	45	33	97	.220	.402	.297
vs. Left-Handers	48	14	5	0	2	8	2	15	.292	.521	.333
vs. Right-Handers	288	60	9	1	13	37	31	82	.208	.382	.291
Home	165	36	8	0	7	25	17	57	.218	.394	.303
Road	171	38	6	1	8	20	16	40	.222	.409	.291
Grass	287	63	12	0	14	39	30	84	.220	.408	.301
Artificial Turf	49	11	2	1	1	6	3	13	.224	.367	.269
April	74	17	3	1	4	12	9	20	.230	.459	.321
May	61	9	2	0	0	1	7	14	.148	.180	.235
June	72	17	4	0	6	18	7	17	.236	.514	.309
July	76	14	4	0	4	6	3	30	.184	.395	.215
August	37	10	2	0	1	4	4	12	.270	.405	.372
Sept./Oct.	16	7	1	0	0	4	3	4	.438	.500	.526
Leading Off Inn.	82	25	5	0	2	2	8	20	.305	.439	.374
Runners On	143	31	4	0	10	40	13	37	.217	.455	.289
Runners/Scor. Pos.	83	14	1	0	3	24	6	22	.169	.289	.239
Runners On/2 Out	72	13	2	0	3	13	8	17	.181	.333	.272
Scor. Pos./2 Out	45	6	1	0	1	9	4	12	.133	.222	.220
Late Inning Pressure	66	14	1	0	3	6	4	18	.212	.394	.257
Leading Off	24	7	2	0	1	1	1	7	.292	.500	.320
Runners On	20	3	0	0	1	4	2	4	.150	.300	.227
Runners/Scor. Pos.	11	1	0	0	0	2	0	1	.091	.091	.091

DRIVING IN RUNS	From 1B	From 2B	From 3B	Scoring Position
Totals	9/106	8/60	13/44	21/104
Percentage	8%	13%	30%	20%
Driving In Runners from 3B with Less than Two Out:	7/19	37%		

Loves to face: Floyd Bannister (.423, 11-for-26, 2 HR)
Hates to face: Bret Saberhagen (.065, 2-for-31, 1 HR)
Struck out on nine consecutive plate appearances (July 6–11), tying a major-league record for nonpitchers. Eric Davis received considerably more press for tying same record in April. They join Adolfo Phillips (1966) and Steve Balboni (1984).... Started 78 games vs. right-handers, but only five against southpaws.... Season finale was his first appearance in the starting lineup since August 30, and his first time in the cleanup spot since May 6.... Played 20 games in right field without committing an error last season.... If it is all over for Reggie, Mike Witt will have the distinction of having allowed his last home run, one month short of 20 years to the day that Jackson hit his first (off Floyd Weaver on Sept. 17, 1967).

Brook Jacoby

Cleveland Indians — Bats Right

	AB	H	2B	3B	HR	RRF	BB	SO	BA	SA	OBA
Season	540	162	26	4	32	73	75	73	.300	.541	.387
vs. Left-Handers	142	37	9	1	5	11	28	20	.261	.444	.382
vs. Right-Handers	398	125	17	3	27	62	47	53	.314	.575	.389
Home	280	78	13	2	21	42	38	40	.279	.564	.366
Road	260	84	13	2	11	31	37	33	.323	.515	.410
Grass	449	132	20	4	28	58	65	62	.294	.543	.384
Artificial Turf	91	30	6	0	4	15	10	11	.330	.527	.402
April	76	18	4	0	3	9	11	9	.237	.408	.341
May	99	23	2	1	2	8	13	21	.232	.333	.321
June	87	24	5	1	8	16	9	10	.276	.632	.357
July	97	35	5	1	8	12	9	13	.361	.680	.415
August	95	30	9	0	3	10	22	12	.316	.505	.441
Sept./Oct.	86	32	1	1	8	18	11	8	.372	.686	.439
Leading Off Inn.	126	41	11	1	10	10	13	16	.325	.667	.388
Runners On	219	60	9	1	5	46	38	31	.274	.393	.383
Runners/Scor. Pos.	122	27	3	0	2	36	27	19	.221	.295	.362
Runners On/2 Out	84	17	3	0	2	15	18	14	.202	.310	.350
Scor. Pos./2 Out	57	9	0	0	1	12	14	10	.158	.211	.333
Late Inning Pressure	86	23	0	2	6	10	6	11	.267	.523	.323
Leading Off	18	6	0	0	2	2	2	1	.333	.667	.400
Runners On	37	10	0	1	1	5	3	6	.270	.405	.341
Runners/Scor. Pos.	20	2	0	0	0	2	1	5	.100	.100	.143

DRIVING IN RUNS	From 1B	From 2B	From 3B	Scoring Position
Totals	7/145	20/93	14/49	34/142
Percentage	5%	22%	29%	24%
Driving In Runners from 3B with Less than Two Out:			7/21	33%

Loves to face: Doyle Alexander (.556, 10-for-18, 1 HR)
Hates to face: Willie Hernandez (.071, 1-for-14)
Hit 27 of 32 home runs with the bases empty, the other five with only one runner on base. . . . Hit 21 HR in home games, tying McGwire and Sheets for most in A.L. . . . Ranked second in A.L. in batting average (.366) after the All-Star break. . . . Fielding percentage of .940 on grass fields, .974 on artificial surfaces. . . . Lost 102 points on his batting average when runners were in scoring position, 2d-largest decrease in the majors last season (minimum: 100 AB each way). . . . Career totals of 334 strikeouts and 136 walks through 1986. Last season's turnaround (75 BB, 73 SO) pretty impressive by itself, but even more so when you consider his yearly home run totals for the last four seasons: 7, 20, 17, 32.

Ruppert Jones

California Angels — Bats Left

	AB	H	2B	3B	HR	RRF	BB	SO	BA	SA	OBA
Season	192	47	8	2	8	29	20	38	.245	.432	.316
vs. Left-Handers	14	5	1	0	1	5	1	1	.357	.643	.400
vs. Right-Handers	178	42	7	2	7	24	19	37	.236	.416	.310
Home	85	22	1	1	3	8	8	16	.259	.400	.323
Road	107	25	7	1	5	21	12	22	.234	.458	.311
Grass	158	36	4	2	5	22	18	32	.228	.373	.307
Artificial Turf	34	11	4	0	3	7	2	6	.324	.706	.361
April	20	4	1	0	1	4	2	3	.200	.400	.273
May	19	4	0	0	2	3	7	5	.211	.526	.423
June	29	7	0	1	3	6	2	6	.241	.621	.290
July	43	9	3	1	0	10	4	8	.209	.326	.277
August	47	12	0	0	2	4	1	9	.255	.383	.271
Sept./Oct.	34	11	4	0	0	2	4	7	.324	.441	.395
Leading Off Inn.	56	14	2	0	3	3	3	7	.250	.446	.288
Runners On	72	21	4	2	3	24	11	16	.292	.528	.386
Runners/Scor. Pos.	38	8	3	1	0	16	8	12	.211	.342	.348
Runners On/2 Out	22	4	1	0	0	5	5	5	.182	.227	.333
Scor. Pos./2 Out	17	3	1	0	0	5	4	4	.176	.235	.333
Late Inning Pressure	41	10	2	0	1	9	10	9	.244	.366	.392
Leading Off	15	2	0	0	1	1	2	3	.133	.333	.188
Runners On	12	5	1	0	0	8	7	2	.417	.500	.632
Runners/Scor. Pos.	8	4	1	0	0	6	6	1	.500	.625	.714

DRIVING IN RUNS	From 1B	From 2B	From 3B	Scoring Position
Totals	8/49	8/32	5/13	13/45
Percentage	16%	25%	38%	29%
Driving In Runners from 3B with Less than Two Out:			4/6	67%

Loves to face: Mark Eichhorn (.714, 5-for-7, 1 HR)
Hates to face: Steve Trout (.138, 4-for-29)
Started 40 games, all against right-handed pitchers. . . . Don't be misled by last season's performance against lefties. The reason he batted only 15 times vs. left-handers is his .212 career average against them. . . . Only 1987 home run vs. a left-hander: August 12 off Dan Schatzeder. . . . Used as a pinch-hitter 37 times last season with a .222 average (6-for-27, 2 HR). . . . Percentage of runners driven in from scoring position in Late-Inning Pressure Situations (7-for-11, 64%) was the highest among 298 major-league qualifiers. . . . Career average of .192 (24 of 125, 1 HR) at Memorial Stadium.

Wally Joyner

California Angels — Bats Left

	AB	H	2B	3B	HR	RRF	BB	SO	BA	SA	OBA
Season	564	161	33	1	34	120	72	64	.285	.528	.366
vs. Left-Handers	201	57	15	0	8	41	20	25	.284	.478	.347
vs. Right-Handers	363	104	18	1	26	79	52	39	.287	.556	.376
Home	307	80	16	1	19	60	37	38	.261	.505	.336
Road	257	81	17	0	15	60	35	26	.315	.556	.399
Grass	471	127	24	1	30	99	61	54	.270	.516	.352
Artificial Turf	93	34	9	0	4	21	11	10	.366	.591	.431
April	91	27	4	0	5	20	9	6	.297	.505	.350
May	83	22	4	0	6	17	9	10	.265	.530	.344
June	99	29	7	0	7	29	22	15	.293	.576	.408
July	75	22	5	1	4	17	8	4	.293	.547	.365
August	97	28	7	0	5	16	13	11	.289	.515	.369
Sept./Oct.	119	33	6	0	7	21	11	18	.277	.504	.351
Leading Off Inn.	114	30	6	0	8	8	10	11	.263	.526	.328
Runners On	266	82	22	1	13	99	45	32	.308	.545	.399
Runners/Scor. Pos.	158	52	15	1	8	86	32	18	.329	.589	.426
Runners On/2 Out	92	22	8	1	3	22	17	11	.239	.446	.369
Scor. Pos./2 Out	49	11	3	1	2	17	15	7	.224	.449	.424
Late Inning Pressure	92	17	7	0	2	15	11	9	.185	.326	.283
Leading Off	27	3	2	0	1	1	3	3	.111	.296	.226
Runners On	45	10	4	0	0	13	7	3	.222	.311	.333
Runners/Scor. Pos.	30	7	3	0	0	12	7	2	.233	.333	.385

DRIVING IN RUNS	From 1B	From 2B	From 3B	Scoring Position
Totals	14/189	32/122	40/71	72/193
Percentage	7%	26%	56%	37%
Driving In Runners from 3B with Less than Two Out:			37/49	76%

Loves to face: Ken Schrom (.571, 8-for-14, 2 HR)
Hates to face: Bill Wegman (.105, 2-for-19)
Successor to Charlie Maxwell as the Sunday Bomber: Joyner led majors with 12 Sunday HR in 1987. . . . Finished season with 52 consecutive errorless games at first base. If he keeps that up, he'll break Mike Hegan's A.L. record some time in August. . . . Started 17 double plays in the field last season, most among major-league first basemen. . . . Career average of .314 with runners on base, .265 with the bases empty. . . . Has homered at every A.L. ballpark except Royals Stadium (36 career AB) and Oakland Coliseum (43 career AB). . . . Has hit .300+ in road games in each of his two seasons in the majors, below .300 at Anaheim Stadium in both seasons. His HR rate is similar in Anaheim and on the road.

Terry Kennedy

Baltimore Orioles — Bats Left

	AB	H	2B	3B	HR	RRF	BB	SO	BA	SA	OBA
Season	512	128	13	1	18	64	35	112	.250	.385	.299
vs. Left-Handers	183	40	4	0	6	23	8	51	.219	.339	.255
vs. Right-Handers	329	88	9	1	12	41	27	61	.267	.410	.323
Home	240	51	6	1	11	28	22	59	.213	.383	.279
Road	272	77	7	0	7	36	13	53	.283	.386	.318
Grass	436	105	10	1	17	56	31	100	.241	.385	.291
Artificial Turf	76	23	3	0	1	8	4	12	.303	.382	.346
April	74	21	3	0	2	10	6	15	.284	.405	.338
May	102	27	3	0	4	11	5	20	.265	.412	.306
June	97	25	3	0	7	17	6	21	.258	.505	.301
July	73	19	1	1	0	6	9	13	.260	.301	.341
August	88	20	2	0	3	12	8	21	.227	.352	.292
Sept./Oct.	78	16	1	0	2	8	1	22	.205	.295	.215
Leading Off Inn.	118	36	1	0	7	7	7	22	.305	.492	.344
Runners On	218	52	7	1	6	52	22	44	.239	.362	.308
Runners/Scor. Pos.	127	31	3	1	3	46	16	31	.244	.354	.329
Runners On/2 Out	92	22	2	0	1	24	7	24	.239	.293	.293
Scor. Pos./2 Out	63	16	2	0	0	22	6	20	.254	.286	.319
Late Inning Pressure	73	17	0	1	5	11	8	18	.233	.466	.309
Leading Off	19	5	0	0	3	3	0	3	.263	.737	.263
Runners On	33	7	0	1	1	7	7	9	.212	.364	.350
Runners/Scor. Pos.	21	5	0	1	1	7	5	7	.238	.476	.385

DRIVING IN RUNS	From 1B	From 2B	From 3B	Scoring Position
Totals	6/162	18/103	22/56	40/159
Percentage	4%	17%	39%	25%
Driving In Runners from 3B with Less than Two Out:			9/20	45%

Loves to face: Steve Trout (.421, 8-for-19, 1 HR)
Hates to face: Jeff Reardon (.087, 2-for-23)
Homered against every A.L. club except Minnesota. . . . Career strikeout-to-walk ratio of 5.66 vs. left-handers is 2d worst in baseball over the past 13 years (minimum: 500 AB vs. LHP). . . . Hitless in five at bats as a pinch-hitter last season after leading the N.L. with a .478 mark (11-for-23) in the previous year. . . . One of four catchers with 120+ games caught in each of last six years. Others: Boone, Carter, Jody Davis. . . . One of 11 players active in 1987 who have caught at least 1,000 games. Another five players (Cerone, Whitt, Pena, Moore, Davis) can join the club in 1988. . . . Will all this result in a revision of the estimate of the genetic limit of games a human body can withstand behind the plate?

Mike Kingery

Seattle Mariners — Bats Left

	AB	H	2B	3B	HR	RRF	BB	SO	BA	SA	OBA
Season	354	99	25	4	9	53	27	43	.280	.449	.329
vs. Left-Handers	39	7	1	0	1	1	1	8	.179	.282	.200
vs. Right-Handers	315	92	24	4	8	52	26	35	.292	.470	.344
Home	174	53	17	3	5	26	12	22	.305	.523	.349
Road	180	46	8	1	4	27	15	21	.256	.378	.310
Grass	140	35	6	0	4	26	12	18	.250	.379	.308
Artificial Turf	214	64	19	4	5	27	15	25	.299	.495	.343
April	59	15	1	1	1	7	3	7	.254	.356	.290
May	57	18	4	2	2	16	1	5	.316	.561	.311
June	42	7	0	1	1	4	6	10	.167	.286	.294
July	56	16	5	0	2	9	6	11	.286	.482	.355
August	78	25	9	0	3	12	5	5	.321	.551	.357
Sept./Oct.	62	18	6	0	0	5	6	5	.290	.387	.348
Leading Off Inn.	85	29	9	0	3	3	5	10	.341	.553	.385
Runners On	151	45	9	3	4	48	13	16	.298	.477	.341
Runners/Scor. Pos.	91	29	4	2	3	43	11	8	.319	.505	.370
Runners On/2 Out	71	23	5	2	4	27	7	8	.324	.620	.385
Scor. Pos./2 Out	43	14	3	1	3	22	6	6	.326	.651	.408
Late Inning Pressure	43	11	3	1	1	6	5	5	.256	.442	.333
Leading Off	12	3	0	0	1	0	0	3	.250	.500	.250
Runners On	19	5	2	1	0	5	4	1	.263	.474	.391
Runners/Scor. Pos.	14	4	1	1	0	5	4	1	.286	.500	.444

DRIVING IN RUNS	From 1B	From 2B	From 3B	Scoring Position
Totals	8/101	17/75	19/40	36/115
Percentage	8%	23%	48%	31%
Driving In Runners from 3B with Less than Two Out:		14/21		67%

Loves to face: Chris Bosio (4-for-4, 1 HR)
Hates to face: The Niekros (0-for-7 vs. Joe; 1-for-7 vs. Phil)
Averaged 2.40 putouts per nine innings, 2d-highest rate among major-league right fielders (minimum: 500 innings). . . . Reached base on catchers' interference five times last season, most in A.L. . . . Batted .220 in day games, .309 at night. . . . Improved his average with runners in scoring position from .146 in 1986. . . . Started 97 games last season, all against right-handed pitchers. . . . Career average of .130 (9-for-69, 1 HR) vs. left-handers, .291 (11 HR) vs. right-handers. Only home run against a southpaw was off Orioles' Jack O'Connor on Aug. 22. . . . Career batting averages of .433 at the Metrodome (his highest at any A.L. ballpark), .087 at Exhibition Stadium (his lowest).

Ray Knight

Baltimore Orioles — Bats Right

	AB	H	2B	3B	HR	RRF	BB	SO	BA	SA	OBA
Season	563	144	24	0	14	66	39	90	.256	.373	.310
vs. Left-Handers	206	45	4	0	8	24	21	34	.218	.354	.293
vs. Right-Handers	357	99	20	0	6	42	18	56	.277	.384	.321
Home	270	74	13	0	8	33	16	42	.274	.411	.319
Road	293	70	11	0	6	33	23	48	.239	.338	.302
Grass	481	124	18	0	14	58	32	72	.258	.383	.312
Artificial Turf	82	20	6	0	0	8	7	18	.244	.317	.303
April	71	24	5	0	2	14	9	8	.338	.493	.427
May	98	23	5	0	3	13	7	14	.235	.378	.292
June	108	29	4	0	3	8	5	18	.269	.389	.298
July	89	22	2	0	1	9	6	12	.247	.303	.295
August	100	23	6	0	2	11	6	17	.230	.350	.280
Sept./Oct.	97	23	2	0	3	11	6	21	.237	.351	.295
Leading Off Inn.	106	23	1	0	3	3	3	21	.217	.311	.252
Runners On	262	75	14	0	8	60	19	42	.286	.431	.336
Runners/Scor. Pos.	145	39	8	0	4	48	14	24	.269	.386	.335
Runners On/2 Out	109	30	5	0	4	32	7	16	.275	.431	.325
Scor. Pos./2 Out	70	19	4	0	1	25	7	10	.271	.371	.346
Late Inning Pressure	80	26	2	0	2	13	6	11	.325	.425	.368
Leading Off	15	3	0	0	0	1	1	2	.200	.200	.250
Runners On	42	15	2	0	2	13	4	7	.357	.548	.404
Runners/Scor. Pos.	21	7	1	0	2	13	3	4	.333	.667	.400

DRIVING IN RUNS	From 1B	From 2B	From 3B	Scoring Position
Totals	8/199	26/118	18/62	44/180
Percentage	4%	22%	29%	24%
Driving In Runners from 3B with Less than Two Out:		9/33		27%

Loves to face: Gary Lavelle (.379, 11-for-29)
Hates to face: Greg Minton (.107, 3-for-28)
Led A.L. third basemen with 2.26 assists per nine innings (minimum: 500 innings). . . . Tied his personal high with 14 home runs. . . . Has hit for a higher average with men on base than he has with the bases empty in each of the last four seasons. . . . But the percentage of runners he drove in from third base with less than two out was the lowest in the majors last season (minimum: 15 opportunities). RDI% with runners in scoring position dropped from .403 (best in N.L.) in 1986 to .244 in '87. . . . Yearly batting averages since 1983 show no pattern: .304, .237, .218, .298, .256. . . . Batting average of .338 in Late-Inning Pressure Situations over the last two seasons. And that doesn't even include heroics in '86 Series.

Lee Lacy

Baltimore Orioles — Bats Right

	AB	H	2B	3B	HR	RRF	BB	SO	BA	SA	OBA
Season	258	63	13	3	7	27	32	49	.244	.399	.326
vs. Left-Handers	156	37	10	2	4	19	16	24	.237	.404	.306
vs. Right-Handers	102	26	3	1	3	8	16	25	.255	.392	.356
Home	130	30	7	1	2	7	17	32	.231	.346	.318
Road	128	33	6	2	5	20	15	17	.258	.453	.336
Grass	217	50	11	2	6	23	28	42	.230	.382	.317
Artificial Turf	41	13	2	1	1	4	4	7	.317	.488	.378
April	16	3	0	0	1	3	3	1	.188	.375	.316
May	63	13	4	0	1	5	11	14	.206	.317	.324
June	59	16	3	1	2	10	7	10	.271	.458	.348
July	29	10	1	1	0	3	4	4	.345	.552	.424
August	47	8	1	1	1	4	2	9	.170	.298	.204
Sept./Oct.	44	13	4	0	1	2	5	11	.295	.455	.360
Leading Off Inn.	66	21	4	1	4	4	7	15	.318	.591	.384
Runners On	90	18	5	2	1	21	10	19	.200	.333	.277
Runners/Scor. Pos.	45	13	4	1	0	18	5	8	.289	.422	.353
Runners On/2 Out	39	8	2	1	0	10	6	9	.205	.308	.311
Scor. Pos./2 Out	22	8	2	1	0	10	3	3	.364	.545	.440
Late Inning Pressure	33	11	2	0	1	5	6	5	.333	.485	.436
Leading Off	9	2	0	0	1	1	1	2	.222	.556	.300
Runners On	10	2	1	0	0	4	3	3	.200	.300	.385
Runners/Scor. Pos.	7	2	1	0	0	4	1	2	.286	.429	.375

DRIVING IN RUNS	From 1B	From 2B	From 3B	Scoring Position
Totals	3/68	6/33	11/22	17/55
Percentage	4%	18%	50%	31%
Driving In Runners from 3B with Less than Two Out:		7/11		64%

Loves to face: Willie Hernandez (.455, 10-for-22)
Hates to face: Walt Terrell (0-for-12, 6 SO)
Batting average was his lowest since .207 in 135 AB for Dodgers in 1973. . . . Appeared in eight of nine batting-order positions, missing only the cleanup spot. . . . Plate appearances vs. right-handers, year by year since 1984: 336, 355, 366, 119. . . . Career batting average of .391 (18-for-46) at Exhibition Stadium is his highest at any ballpark. . . . Has been on N.L.C.S. roster four times (L.A. in '74, '77, and '78, Pittsburgh in '79), and in each case his team has reached the World Series. . . . Of the 11 nonpitchers active in 1987 older than Lacy, how many will be around at the end of 1988: Nettles, McRae, Lopes, Reggie, Paciorek, Darrell Evans, Cruz, Boone, Fisk, Concepcion, Grubb, and Garvey?

Carney Lansford

Oakland As — Bats Right

	AB	H	2B	3B	HR	RRF	BB	SO	BA	SA	OBA
Season	554	160	27	4	19	78	60	44	.289	.455	.366
vs. Left-Handers	175	49	4	0	8	23	17	16	.280	.440	.352
vs. Right-Handers	379	111	23	4	11	55	43	28	.293	.462	.372
Home	271	78	16	3	9	32	31	25	.288	.469	.371
Road	283	82	11	1	10	46	29	19	.290	.441	.361
Grass	458	131	24	4	14	59	49	35	.286	.448	.363
Artificial Turf	96	29	3	0	5	19	11	9	.302	.490	.380
April	81	24	3	1	2	12	12	12	.296	.432	.396
May	74	14	3	0	1	4	10	7	.189	.270	.286
June	92	30	9	0	4	16	13	8	.326	.554	.426
July	99	32	2	2	3	11	8	6	.323	.475	.376
August	106	36	5	0	7	22	8	6	.340	.585	.388
Sept./Oct.	102	24	5	1	2	13	9	5	.235	.363	.310
Leading Off Inn.	119	37	7	0	8	8	6	6	.311	.571	.349
Runners On	230	68	9	3	8	67	32	27	.296	.465	.380
Runners/Scor. Pos.	123	41	6	3	6	62	25	13	.333	.577	.437
Runners On/2 Out	92	27	3	1	4	27	10	12	.293	.478	.363
Scor. Pos./2 Out	56	18	3	1	3	25	7	8	.321	.571	.397
Late Inning Pressure	81	19	3	0	3	12	11	8	.235	.333	.333
Leading Off	18	7	1	0	2	2	2	0	.389	.778	.450
Runners On	34	8	2	0	0	9	6	4	.235	.294	.350
Runners/Scor. Pos.	22	5	1	0	0	9	6	2	.227	.273	.393

DRIVING IN RUNS	From 1B	From 2B	From 3B	Scoring Position
Totals	12/170	26/94	21/46	47/140
Percentage	7%	28%	46%	34%
Driving In Runners from 3B with Less than Two Out:		12/23		52%

Loves to face: Mike Boddicker (.424, 14-for-33, 4 HR)
Hates to face: Tim Stoddard (0-for-15)
Averaged one strikeout per 14.3 plate appearances last season, 5th-best in A.L. . . . Walks exceeded strikeouts for only the second time in his 10-year career. . . . Career high of 27 stolen bases in his 10th big–league season. Had stolen only 30 bases the previous four seasons combined. . . . Third time he's hit 19 home runs, but he's never hit 20. . . . Eight doubles vs. Texas were the most by an A.L. player against any club last season. . . . Highest career fielding percentage (.965) of any active third baseman (minimum: 1,000 games). . . . Batting average in Late-Inning Pressure Situations has fallen at least 50 points short of his unpressured average for three straight seasons. Only one other A.L. player has done that: Dick Schofield.

Gene Larkin

Minnesota Twins — Bats Left and Right

Minnesota Twins	AB	H	2B	3B	HR	RRF	BB	SO	BA	SA	OBA
Season	233	62	11	2	4	28	25	31	.266	.382	.340
vs. Left-Handers	77	22	2	1	1	9	11	11	.286	.377	.375
vs. Right-Handers	156	40	9	1	3	19	14	20	.256	.385	.322
Home	112	33	6	2	0	13	13	13	.295	.384	.367
Road	121	29	5	0	4	15	12	18	.240	.380	.313
Grass	95	25	4	0	3	12	11	15	.263	.400	.346
Artificial Turf	138	37	7	2	1	16	14	16	.268	.370	.335
April	0	0	0	0	0	0	0	0	—	—	—
May	26	8	1	0	1	5	0	2	.308	.462	.296
June	58	17	2	1	1	9	9	12	.293	.414	.388
July	32	7	1	1	1	3	2	2	.219	.406	.265
August	66	18	4	0	1	7	11	8	.273	.379	.380
Sept./Oct.	51	12	3	0	0	4	3	7	.235	.294	.291
Leading Off Inn.	46	14	2	0	2	2	2	4	.304	.478	.333
Runners On	108	28	5	1	0	24	14	16	.259	.324	.344
Runners/Scor. Pos.	70	16	3	1	0	23	11	9	.229	.300	.333
Runners On/2 Out	47	11	2	0	0	8	6	5	.234	.277	.333
Scor. Pos./2 Out	35	8	1	0	0	7	4	4	.229	.257	.325
Late Inning Pressure	39	14	1	2	0	8	4	7	.359	.487	.419
Leading Off	8	3	0	0	0		0	1	.375	.375	.444
Runners On	19	7	0	1	0	8	1	4	.368	.474	.400
Runners/Scor. Pos.	14	6	0	1	0	8	1	1	.429	.571	.467

DRIVING IN RUNS	From 1B	From 2B	From 3B	Scoring Position
Totals	3/69	10/51	11/35	21/86
Percentage	4%	20%	31%	24%
Driving In Runners from 3B with Less than Two Out:		9/17		53%

Loves to face: Curt Young (.600, 3-for-5, 1 HR)
Hates to face: Chris Bosio (0-for-4, 3 SO)
Was also a perfect 2-for-2 against a pair of Cleveland relievers: right-hander Doug Jones and southpaw Ed Vande Berg.... Started 57 games, 31 as DH and 26 at first base.... Batted .294 (5-for-17) as a pinch-hitter.... Started a streak of hits in six consecutive at bats on June 3, less than two weeks after his major-league debut.... Of the 28 runs he drove in, five were game winners and another five gave the Twins leads that they eventually surrendered.... Batted over .300 at each of his four stops in the minors before joining the Twins in May 1987.... Not too young for a rookie. Larkin was born the same month as Danny Tartabull and Sid Fernandez. Still, he's nearly three years younger than DeWayne Buice.

Tim Laudner

Minnesota Twins — Bats Right

Minnesota Twins	AB	H	2B	3B	HR	RRF	BB	SO	BA	SA	OBA
Season	288	55	7	1	16	44	23	80	.191	.389	.252
vs. Left-Handers	98	19	2	1	7	19	12	22	.194	.449	.279
vs. Right-Handers	190	36	5	0	9	25	11	58	.189	.358	.236
Home	151	26	3	1	7	17	14	42	.172	.344	.247
Road	137	29	4	0	9	27	9	38	.212	.438	.257
Grass	109	24	4	0	7	23	7	30	.220	.450	.263
Artificial Turf	179	31	3	1	9	21	16	50	.173	.352	.245
April	11	1	0	0	1	2	1	5	.091	.364	.167
May	61	11	1	0	3	13	3	15	.180	.344	.219
June	47	9	1	0	4	10	5	13	.191	.468	.264
July	60	14	1	1	4	8	7	16	.233	.483	.313
August	62	11	3	0	3	8	6	21	.177	.371	.257
Sept./Oct.	47	9	1	0	1	3	1	10	.191	.277	.208
Leading Off Inn.	74	14	1	0	4	4	5	14	.189	.432	.250
Runners On	113	25	3	0	9	37	14	30	.221	.487	.302
Runners/Scor. Pos.	66	15	1	0	6	31	11	18	.227	.515	.329
Runners On/2 Out	36	6	2	0	3	8	10	7	.167	.472	.348
Scor. Pos./2 Out	23	3	0	0	2	6	8	6	.130	.391	.355
Late Inning Pressure	36	7	1	0	2	5	4	13	.194	.389	.275
Leading Off	10	4	1	0	2	2	0	0	.400	1.100	.400
Runners On	14	1	0	0	0	3	3	6	.071	.071	.235
Runners/Scor. Pos.	9	1	0	0	0	3	3	3	.111	.111	.333

DRIVING IN RUNS	From 1B	From 2B	From 3B	Scoring Position
Totals	5/78	13/56	10/28	23/84
Percentage	6%	23%	36%	27%
Driving In Runners from 3B with Less than Two Out:		9/17		53%

Loves to face: Tommy John (.409, 9-for-22, 2 HR)
Hates to face: Jack Morris (.053, 1-for-19)
This wasn't the first time he failed to hit his weight. He batted .206 in 1984, and .185 the year before that. Not to mention—never mind. ... Batted .137 in day games, lowest average among 162 A.L. qualifiers.... Career average of .197 vs. right-handers. Has hit below .200 against them in five of seven seasons. More bad news for Laudner: his average vs. lefties has slipped every year since 1984: .274, .270, .261, .194.... Has driven in only 19 percent (10-for-53) of runners from scoring position in Late-Inning Pressure Situations. ... Career batting average of .086 (3-for-35, one HR) at Memorial Stadium.... One stolen base in 517 career games.... But he's got one more Series ring than Ernie Banks, so there!

Rick Leach

Toronto Blue Jays — Bats Left

Toronto Blue Jays	AB	H	2B	3B	HR	RRF	BB	SO	BA	SA	OBA
Season	195	55	13	1	3	25	25	25	.282	.405	.371
vs. Left-Handers	16	6	3	0	0	3	4	6	.375	.563	.500
vs. Right-Handers	179	49	10	1	3	22	21	19	.274	.391	.358
Home	110	29	8	1	3	13	14	13	.264	.436	.357
Road	85	26	5	0	0	12	11	12	.306	.365	.388
Grass	66	17	2	0	0	6	9	10	.258	.288	.351
Artificial Turf	129	38	11	1	3	19	16	15	.295	.465	.381
April	7	4	0	0	0	1	5	1	.571	.571	.750
May	26	8	1	0	1	7	2	5	.308	.462	.367
June	28	5	3	0	0	1	3	4	.179	.286	.281
July	40	12	3	0	1	6	8	3	.300	.450	.417
August	50	15	4	0	0	6	5	7	.300	.380	.364
Sept./Oct.	44	11	2	1	1	4	2	5	.250	.409	.298
Leading Off Inn.	53	14	4	0	0		3	6	.264	.340	.304
Runners On	72	26	4	0	2	24	13	10	.361	.500	.466
Runners/Scor. Pos.	39	17	3	0	2	24	8	4	.436	.667	.540
Runners On/2 Out	27	9	1	0	1	8	5	4	.333	.481	.438
Scor. Pos./2 Out	14	6	1	0	1	8	3	1	.429	.714	.529
Late Inning Pressure	49	14	3	0	2	9	6	8	.286	.469	.375
Leading Off	13	5	1	0	0		2	3	.385	.462	.467
Runners On	24	6	1	0	1	8	4	3	.250	.417	.379
Runners/Scor. Pos.	16	5	0	0	1	8	3	1	.313	.500	.450

DRIVING IN RUNS	From 1B	From 2B	From 3B	Scoring Position
Totals	2/57	10/32	10/14	20/46
Percentage	4%	31%	71%	43%
Driving In Runners from 3B with Less than Two Out:		6/8		75%

Loves to face: Eric Plunk (.571, 4-for-7)
Hates to face: Kirk McCaskill (0-for-8)
Started 47 games last season, all but one against right-handed pitchers.... Over 1,000 career at bats vs. right-handers, but only 70 against southpaws. Career: .214 (no home runs) vs. lefties, .264 vs. right-handers.... Batting average with runners in scoring position was 2d-highest among 163 A.L. qualifiers. In 1986, Leach batted .343 (24-for-70) with runners on second and/or third base.... Hits well indoors. He's the only player active in 1987 with .350+ career batting averages at both the Kingdome (.395, 15-for-38) and the Metrodome (.400, 18-for-45) among those with at least 25 AB at each.... Career breakdown: .244 with bases empty, .285 with runners on base, .308 with runners in scoring position.

Chet Lemon

Detroit Tigers — Bats Right

Detroit Tigers	AB	H	2B	3B	HR	RRF	BB	SO	BA	SA	OBA
Season	470	130	30	3	20	76	70	82	.277	.481	.376
vs. Left-Handers	180	49	14	1	8	25	32	26	.272	.494	.382
vs. Right-Handers	290	81	16	2	12	51	38	56	.279	.472	.372
Home	223	58	17	0	10	35	40	44	.260	.471	.379
Road	247	72	13	3	10	41	30	38	.291	.490	.373
Grass	399	110	25	3	17	62	65	70	.276	.481	.382
Artificial Turf	71	20	5	0	3	14	5	12	.282	.479	.338
April	61	11	3	1	2	6	15	9	.180	.361	.354
May	43	12	3	0	2	8	9	9	.279	.488	.415
June	87	25	7	0	5	21	10	14	.287	.540	.360
July	74	22	2	0	4	13	10	14	.297	.486	.388
August	92	35	11	0	4	15	6	18	.380	.630	.426
Sept./Oct.	113	25	4	2	3	13	20	18	.221	.372	.341
Leading Off Inn.	109	28	6	0	4	4	9	19	.257	.422	.325
Runners On	217	64	18	1	8	64	32	31	.295	.498	.390
Runners/Scor. Pos.	122	39	11	0	6	58	23	19	.320	.557	.421
Runners On/2 Out	80	20	4	1	3	21	25	10	.250	.438	.434
Scor. Pos./2 Out	46	11	3	0	2	17	18	6	.239	.435	.453
Late Inning Pressure	54	7	3	0	0	4	6	13	.130	.185	.217
Leading Off	16	1	0	0	0		1	1	.063	.063	.118
Runners On	19	6	3	0	0	4	3	3	.316	.474	.409
Runners/Scor. Pos.	8	4	2	0	0	4	2	1	.500	.750	.600

DRIVING IN RUNS	From 1B	From 2B	From 3B	Scoring Position
Totals	8/176	24/88	24/61	48/149
Percentage	5%	27%	39%	32%
Driving In Runners from 3B with Less than Two Out:		18/39		46%

Loves to face: Matt Young (.529, 9-for-17, 4 HR)
Hates to face: Juan Nieves (.059, 1-for-17)
Batting average in August was 3d-highest in A.L. ... Collected seven consecutive hits off left-handed pitchers (Aug. 9–21), longest streak by an A.L. batter last season. A.L.C.S. teammate Jim Morrison had a streak of equal length while playing for the Pirates in April.... Led the league with a .455 mark in regular-season games vs. the Twins. Batted .278 (5-for-18) against them in the A.L.C.S. ... Career batting average at the Metrodome (.388, 50-for-129, 3 HR) is his highest at any ballpark.... Ranks second among active outfielders with 4,299 career putouts. (Jose Cruz leads with 4,383.) Lemon is seven or eight years away from Tris Speaker's A.L. record of 6,794 putouts. ... Yeah, right.

Steve Lombardozzi

Bats Right

Minnesota Twins	AB	H	2B	3B	HR	RRF	BB	SO	BA	SA	OBA
Season	432	103	19	3	8	39	33	66	.238	.352	.298
vs. Left-Handers	139	40	10	1	2	10	9	17	.288	.417	.333
vs. Right-Handers	293	63	9	2	6	29	24	49	.215	.321	.281
Home	213	45	9	2	3	16	18	29	.211	.315	.272
Road	219	58	10	1	5	23	15	37	.265	.388	.324
Grass	165	44	5	1	4	18	11	29	.267	.382	.328
Artificial Turf	267	59	14	2	4	21	22	37	.221	.333	.279
April	49	12	2	0	1	3	9	11	.245	.347	.362
May	89	27	3	0	2	6	6	5	.303	.404	.347
June	69	10	2	0	0	1	2	8	.145	.174	.192
July	80	20	5	3	1	10	3	9	.250	.425	.286
August	79	19	5	0	2	13	9	18	.241	.380	.322
Sept./Oct.	66	15	2	0	2	6	4	15	.227	.348	.271
Leading Off Inn.	113	32	6	0	3	3	7	23	.283	.416	.325
Runners On	160	39	5	3	3	34	13	26	.244	.369	.303
Runners/Scor. Pos.	95	25	5	3	3	32	9	15	.263	.474	.330
Runners On/2 Out	70	17	2	2	2	19	6	14	.243	.414	.312
Scor. Pos./2 Out	45	12	2	2	2	18	5	7	.267	.533	.353
Late Inning Pressure	43	13	1	0	2	8	9	9	.302	.465	.423
Leading Off	14	3	0	0	0	0	3	5	.214	.214	.353
Runners On	14	6	0	0	1	7	4	3	.429	.643	.556
Runners/Scor. Pos.	8	5	0	0	1	6	3	2	.625	1.000	.727

DRIVING IN RUNS	From 1B	From 2B	From 3B	Scoring Position
Totals	5/112	15/84	11/29	26/113
Percentage	4%	18%	38%	23%
Driving In Runners from 3B with Less than Two Out:			7/15	47%

Loves to face: Tommy John (.500, 6-for-12, 1 HR)
Hates to face: Roger Clemens (0-for-19, 8 SO)
Batted .344 in 1987 post-season, including seven hits in 17 at bats (.412) in the World Series. Homered in Game One of the Series.... Committed four errors in his first seven games at second base last season after leading A.L. second basemen with a .991 fielding percentage in 1986.... Fielding percentage of .965 on grass fields, .984 on artificial surfaces. Committed 11 of his 14 errors in road games. ... Two hits in 42 career AB (.048) at Fenway Park.... Over the past 13 years, 707 players have had more than 30 opportunities to drive in runners from third base with less than two outs. Only one has driven in those runners at a lower rate than Lombardozzi, who has delivered only seven of 32 (22%). Take a bow, Joaquin.

Fred Lynn

Bats Left

Baltimore Orioles	AB	H	2B	3B	HR	RRF	BB	SO	BA	SA	OBA
Season	396	100	24	0	23	62	39	72	.253	.487	.320
vs. Left-Handers	125	28	7	0	5	13	13	28	.224	.400	.297
vs. Right-Handers	271	72	17	0	18	49	26	44	.266	.528	.330
Home	191	46	9	0	11	28	14	30	.241	.461	.290
Road	205	54	15	0	12	34	25	42	.263	.512	.346
Grass	351	88	19	0	23	60	36	64	.251	.501	.321
Artificial Turf	45	12	5	0	0	2	3	8	.267	.378	.313
April	77	16	5	0	1	7	11	14	.208	.312	.311
May	79	25	3	0	7	17	11	14	.316	.620	.396
June	79	18	2	0	4	13	8	13	.228	.405	.299
July	38	10	6	0	2	7	1	5	.263	.579	.282
August	68	20	3	0	7	13	4	20	.294	.647	.333
Sept./Oct.	55	11	5	0	2	5	4	6	.200	.400	.254
Leading Off Inn.	100	23	5	0	5	5	5	13	.230	.430	.267
Runners On	156	40	8	0	10	49	24	34	.256	.500	.352
Runners/Scor. Pos.	83	21	3	0	8	44	19	23	.253	.578	.385
Runners On/2 Out	61	10	1	0	4	17	10	15	.164	.377	.282
Scor. Pos./2 Out	35	6	1	0	4	17	8	11	.171	.543	.326
Late Inning Pressure	70	17	2	0	3	7	5	17	.243	.400	.303
Leading Off	16	2	0	0	0	0	0	4	.125	.125	.125
Runners On	31	8	2	0	2	6	5	8	.258	.516	.361
Runners/Scor. Pos.	13	1	0	0	1	4	3	6	.077	.308	.250

DRIVING IN RUNS	From 1B	From 2B	From 3B	Scoring Position
Totals	11/130	13/63	15/38	28/101
Percentage	8%	21%	39%	28%
Driving In Runners from 3B with Less than Two Out:			12/23	52%

Loves to face: Bert Blyleven (.391, 18-for-46, 4 HR)
Hates to face: Frank Tanana (.122, 5-for-41)
Hit five home runs in 35 at bats vs. California last season.... Active career leaders in fielding percentage for outfielders: Terry Puhl .993, Lynn .9878, Willie Wilson .9876, Dwight Evans .9875.... Hit more HR in road games than in home games last season, something he hadn't done since he played for Boston in 1976.... Yearly home run totals since 1982: 21, 22, 23, 23, 23, 23.... Batting average in Late-Inning Pressure Situations has been lower than his overall average in each of the last five seasons.... Career average of .448 (13-for-29, 2 HR) at Shea Stadium is his highest at any major-league ballpark.... Has played 150+ games in a season only once. Has averaged 128 games played in his 13 full major-league seasons.

Steve Lyons

Bats Left

Chicago White Sox	AB	H	2B	3B	HR	RRF	BB	SO	BA	SA	OBA
Season	193	54	11	1	1	20	12	37	.280	.363	.320
vs. Left-Handers	25	8	1	0	0	2	0	6	.320	.360	.320
vs. Right-Handers	168	46	10	1	1	18	12	31	.274	.363	.320
Home	107	30	6	0	0	13	6	23	.280	.336	.316
Road	86	24	5	1	1	7	6	14	.279	.395	.326
Grass	169	48	10	1	1	18	12	33	.284	.373	.330
Artificial Turf	24	6	1	0	0	2	0	4	.250	.292	.250
April	9	0	0	0	0	0	0	3	.000	.000	.000
May	1	0	0	0	0	0	0	0	.000	.000	.000
June	12	4	0	0	0	1	1	4	.333	.333	.385
July	49	15	2	1	0	3	5	8	.306	.388	.370
August	56	16	4	0	1	7	6	7	.286	.411	.355
Sept./Oct.	66	19	5	0	0	9	0	15	.288	.364	.284
Leading Off Inn.	48	11	2	0	0	2	10	12	.229	.271	.260
Runners On	87	27	6	0	1	20	6	12	.310	.414	.351
Runners/Scor. Pos.	57	19	4	0	1	19	4	9	.333	.456	.371
Runners On/2 Out	34	9	3	0	0	6	2	6	.265	.353	.306
Scor. Pos./2 Out	20	5	1	0	0	5	1	4	.250	.300	.286
Late Inning Pressure	19	4	0	0	0	1	1	6	.211	.211	.250
Leading Off	8	1	0	0	0	0	0	3	.125	.125	.125
Runners On	6	2	0	0	0	1	0	0	.333	.333	.333
Runners/Scor. Pos.	4	2	0	0	0	1	0	0	.500	.500	.500

DRIVING IN RUNS	From 1B	From 2B	From 3B	Scoring Position
Totals	1/61	8/45	10/21	18/66
Percentage	2%	18%	48%	27%
Driving In Runners from 3B with Less than Two Out:			8/14	57%

Loves to face: Walt Terrell (.462, 6-for-13)
Hates to face: Chris Codiroli (0-for-9)
Played majority of his games (51) at third base, but also appeared at second base and all three outfield positions.... Batted .288 in 54 games in the starting lineup.... Batted .563 (9-for-16) in 11 games vs. Cleveland.... Career breakdown: .253 with bases empty, .261 with runners on base, .288 with runners in scoring position.... This left-hander had a higher batting average vs. southpaws than vs. right-handers in each of his three seasons in the majors. But he's hit six of his seven career home runs against right-handed pitchers. Only homer vs. a lefty was hit off of Mike Jones in 1985.... Expos' Jack Daugherty joins Steve and Barry Lyons as the only active players born on June 3, 1960. None of them are brothers.

Bill Madlock

Bats Right

Detroit Tigers	AB	H	2B	3B	HR	RRF	BB	SO	BA	SA	OBA
Season	326	91	17	0	14	50	28	45	.279	.460	.351
vs. Left-Handers	151	42	9	0	7	26	10	26	.278	.477	.323
vs. Right-Handers	175	49	8	0	7	24	18	19	.280	.446	.373
Home	152	41	6	0	7	25	10	21	.270	.447	.323
Road	174	50	11	0	7	25	18	24	.287	.471	.373
Grass	277	77	14	0	12	46	16	36	.278	.458	.325
Artificial Turf	49	14	3	0	2	4	12	9	.286	.469	.470
April	0	0	0	0	0	0	0	0	—	—	—
May	0	0	0	0	0	0	0	0	—	—	—
June	83	25	2	0	6	13	3	7	.301	.542	.344
July	64	19	1	0	4	10	10	12	.297	.500	.416
August	76	27	9	0	2	13	10	7	.355	.553	.451
Sept./Oct.	103	20	5	0	2	14	5	19	.194	.301	.227
Leading Off Inn.	54	20	5	0	3	3	4	7	.370	.630	.414
Runners On	144	44	6	0	6	42	13	18	.306	.472	.388
Runners/Scor. Pos.	75	20	2	0	1	30	10	11	.267	.333	.372
Runners On/2 Out	52	16	4	0	2	17	4	7	.308	.500	.400
Scor. Pos./2 Out	35	11	2	0	0	12	3	4	.314	.371	.400
Late Inning Pressure	29	13	2	0	1	3	3	2	.448	.621	.500
Leading Off	9	4	1	0	0	0	0	0	.444	.556	.444
Runners On	11	4	0	0	0	2	2	1	.364	.364	.462
Runners/Scor. Pos.	4	2	0	0	0	2	1	0	.500	.500	.600

DRIVING IN RUNS	From 1B	From 2B	From 3B	Scoring Position
Totals	7/100	10/51	19/38	29/89
Percentage	7%	20%	50%	33%
Driving In Runners from 3B with Less than Two Out:			14/23	61%

Loves to face: Bob Welch (.381, 16-for-42, 4 HR, 0 SO)
Hates to face: Chris Bosio (0-for-6)
Has been traded in mid-season three times in his career, and in each case his new team has gone on to win a division title: Pittsburgh in 1979, Los Angeles in 1985, and Detroit in 1987.... Think Mad Dog hasn't had something to do with that? Consider that Detroit was 25–24, in fifth place when he first took the field for the Tigers.... Started 85 games for Detroit, batting in the second slot for all but one of them.... Homered in his first game with the Tigers, returning to the A.L. after 13 seasons in the National League. Only previous A.L. HR was hit off Jim Kaat on Sept. 17, 1973.... Batting average of .319 leading off innings over the last 13 years.

Fred Manrique

Chicago White Sox — Bats Right

	AB	H	2B	3B	HR	RRF	BB	SO	BA	SA	OBA
Season	298	77	13	3	4	29	19	69	.258	.362	.302
vs. Left-Handers	144	43	10	3	2	9	13	34	.299	.451	.361
vs. Right-Handers	154	34	3	0	2	20	6	35	.221	.279	.245
Home	141	43	7	3	2	19	13	29	.305	.440	.359
Road	157	34	6	0	2	10	6	40	.217	.293	.248
Grass	250	69	12	3	2	24	18	57	.276	.372	.324
Artificial Turf	48	8	1	0	2	5	1	12	.167	.313	.184
April	13	6	1	0	0	1	2	2	.462	.538	.533
May	57	10	3	0	0	4	0	15	.175	.228	.172
June	31	6	0	0	1	2	1	7	.194	.290	.219
July	27	11	3	0	0	3	4	6	.407	.519	.484
August	100	30	5	2	3	15	8	26	.300	.480	.345
Sept./Oct.	70	14	1	1	0	4	4	13	.200	.243	.253
Leading Off Inn.	64	12	1	1	2	2	1	22	.188	.328	.200
Runners On	118	31	6	0	2	27	14	25	.263	.364	.333
Runners/Scor. Pos.	66	19	4	0	2	27	11	14	.288	.439	.375
Runners On/2 Out	55	15	3	0	1	13	9	16	.273	.382	.375
Scor. Pos./2 Out	34	11	3	0	1	13	6	10	.324	.500	.425
Late Inning Pressure	40	8	0	0	0	1	0	12	.200	.200	.200
Leading Off	13	1	0	0	0	0	0	5	.077	.077	.077
Runners On	15	3	0	0	0	1	0	6	.200	.200	.200
Runners/Scor. Pos.	7	2	0	0	0	1	0	3	.286	.286	.286

DRIVING IN RUNS	From 1B	From 2B	From 3B	Scoring Position
Totals	1/75	9/55	15/29	24/84
Percentage	1%	16%	52%	29%
Driving In Runners from 3B with Less than Two Out:		10/14		71%

Loves to face: Jeff M. Robinson (.600, 3-for-5, 1 HR)
Hates to face: Curt Young (0-for-9)
Started 52 of 60 games in which the Sox faced left-handed starters, 38 of 102 vs. right-handers.... Walked three times in his first 113 plate appearances, three more in his next eight times up.... Made nine assists in first six innings vs. Detroit on July 27. Modern record for second basemen in a nine-inning game is 12, but Manrique didn't handle another chance in that game.... Batted .375 (27-for-72) vs. southpaws at Comiskey Park.... Career average of .277 vs. left-handers, .218 vs. right-handers.... Career average of .299 with runners in scoring position.... Before 1987, had played parts of four seasons with the Blue Jays, Expos, and Cardinals. Previous career high in plate appearances was 29 in 1981.

Don Mattingly

New York Yankees — Bats Left

	AB	H	2B	3B	HR	RRF	BB	SO	BA	SA	OBA
Season	569	186	38	2	30	118	51	38	.327	.559	.378
vs. Left-Handers	199	60	9	1	11	52	16	15	.302	.523	.355
vs. Right-Handers	370	126	29	1	19	66	35	23	.341	.578	.391
Home	283	95	14	1	17	58	24	25	.336	.572	.384
Road	286	91	24	1	13	60	27	13	.318	.545	.373
Grass	474	153	30	2	25	92	41	32	.323	.553	.374
Artificial Turf	95	33	8	0	5	26	10	6	.347	.589	.402
April	83	22	9	2	2	20	10	9	.265	.494	.337
May	109	35	5	0	4	16	17	4	.321	.477	.409
June	39	16	1	0	2	11	4	3	.410	.590	.465
July	99	37	8	0	10	24	7	6	.374	.758	.415
August	111	34	8	0	6	17	7	3	.306	.541	.354
Sept./Oct.	128	42	7	0	6	30	6	13	.328	.523	.353
Leading Off Inn.	86	26	1	0	4	4	8	5	.302	.453	.362
Runners On	279	94	18	1	17	105	31	22	.337	.591	.395
Runners/Scor. Pos.	150	48	11	0	13	94	22	14	.320	.653	.392
Runners On/2 Out	97	26	5	0	5	31	18	9	.268	.474	.388
Scor. Pos./2 Out	66	16	4	0	3	26	14	7	.242	.439	.383
Late Inning Pressure	65	13	2	1	1	7	10	6	.200	.308	.303
Leading Off	20	5	0	0	0	0	3	3	.250	.250	.348
Runners On	33	7	1	1	1	7	5	3	.212	.394	.308
Runners/Scor. Pos.	15	2	0	1	0	5	6	5	.133	.333	.333

DRIVING IN RUNS	From 1B	From 2B	From 3B	Scoring Position
Totals	18/212	30/108	40/78	70/186
Percentage	9%	28%	51%	38%
Driving In Runners from 3B with Less than Two Out:		32/46		70%

Loves to face: Scott McGregor (.500, 16-for-32, 3 HR)
Hates to face: Storm Davis (.105, 2-for-19)
Has led Yankees in batting average for four straight years, tying club record shared by Gehrig (1932–35), DiMaggio (1938–41), and Mantle (1955–58).... Four straight seasons of .300+ batting average and 20+ HR.... No other player has current streak of more than two seasons; only two have two-year streaks: George Bell and Kirby Puckett.... Yearly batting averages vs. right-handers since 1984: .351, .348, .348, .341.... Career percentage of runners driven in from scoring position (.375) is the highest over the past 13 seasons. ... Career batting average of over .400 at three different ballparks: Fenway (.409), Kingdome (.411), and Exhibition (.413). Has homered at every A.L. park except County Stadium (118 AB).

Oddibe McDowell

Texas Rangers — Bats Left

	AB	H	2B	3B	HR	RRF	BB	SO	BA	SA	OBA
Season	407	98	26	4	14	54	51	99	.241	.428	.324
vs. Left-Handers	71	16	3	0	2	13	17	16	.225	.352	.371
vs. Right-Handers	336	82	23	4	12	41	34	83	.244	.443	.313
Home	196	49	11	3	5	25	19	46	.250	.413	.315
Road	211	49	15	1	9	29	32	53	.232	.441	.332
Grass	335	75	21	3	7	39	34	82	.224	.367	.294
Artificial Turf	72	23	5	1	7	15	17	17	.319	.708	.449
April	38	7	2	0	1	4	6	8	.184	.316	.295
May	62	11	4	0	1	6	13	17	.177	.290	.316
June	95	34	9	1	6	21	15	27	.358	.663	.445
July	54	15	5	2	2	9	1	8	.278	.556	.286
August	79	12	5	0	1	5	6	20	.152	.253	.212
Sept./Oct.	79	19	1	1	3	9	10	19	.241	.392	.326
Leading Off Inn.	102	26	10	0	4	13	20		.255	.471	.339
Runners On	167	38	11	2	4	44	25	45	.228	.389	.325
Runners/Scor. Pos.	91	25	9	1	2	38	19	24	.275	.462	.393
Runners On/2 Out	69	16	5	1	1	18	13	21	.232	.377	.354
Scor. Pos./2 Out	45	12	5	1	0	16	10	13	.267	.422	.400
Late Inning Pressure	57	18	2	1	1	9	13	8	.316	.439	.443
Leading Off	19	5	1	0	0	0	3	3	.263	.316	.364
Runners On	20	6	1	0	1	9	8	3	.300	.500	.500
Runners/Scor. Pos.	12	5	1	0	1	9	4	2	.417	.750	.563

DRIVING IN RUNS	From 1B	From 2B	From 3B	Scoring Position
Totals	9/126	17/75	14/37	31/112
Percentage	7%	23%	38%	28%
Driving In Runners from 3B with Less than Two Out:		11/21		52%

Loves to face: Bert Blyleven (.417, 10-for-24, 5 HR)
Hates to face: Walt Terrell (.050, 1-for-20)
Stole 24 bases in 26 attempts last season (.923), best percentage in A.L. (minimum: 10 SB).... Started 91 of 100 games in which the Rangers faced a right-handed starter, but only 15 of 62 games against southpaws.... Has hit 42 of his 50 career home runs against right-handed pitchers.... Batted .132 in 27 games in the leadoff position. Rangers' record in those games was 10–17.... Led visiting players in home runs (5) and batting average (.526) at the Metrodome last season.... Has homered at every A.L. ballpark except Tiger Stadium, where he has his lowest average (.064, 3-for-47, 0 XBH) of any stadium.... Batting average on artificial turf has been higher than on grass in each of his three seasons in the majors.

Fred McGriff

Toronto Blue Jays — Bats Left

	AB	H	2B	3B	HR	RRF	BB	SO	BA	SA	OBA
Season	295	73	16	0	20	45	60	104	.247	.505	.376
vs. Left-Handers	26	4	2	0	1	1	3	14	.154	.346	.241
vs. Right-Handers	269	69	14	0	19	44	57	90	.257	.520	.388
Home	139	31	11	0	7	20	31	52	.223	.453	.368
Road	156	42	5	0	13	25	29	52	.269	.551	.384
Grass	124	34	4	0	9	17	24	39	.274	.524	.392
Artificial Turf	171	39	12	0	11	28	36	65	.228	.491	.365
April	45	12	4	0	1	5	9	12	.267	.422	.389
May	46	9	1	0	2	5	9	14	.196	.348	.327
June	36	11	1	0	4	7	8	14	.306	.667	.444
July	57	16	2	0	6	15	11	20	.281	.632	.397
August	76	20	7	0	5	11	14	30	.263	.553	.378
Sept./Oct.	35	5	1	0	2	2	9	14	.143	.343	.318
Leading Off Inn.	72	18	6	0	5	5	12	24	.250	.542	.357
Runners On	128	29	6	0	6	31	22	52	.227	.414	.365
Runners/Scor. Pos.	68	13	3	0	2	22	18	34	.191	.324	.368
Runners On/2 Out	47	11	3	0	2	10	10	23	.234	.426	.379
Scor. Pos./2 Out	28	5	1	0	1	7	7	16	.179	.321	.361
Late Inning Pressure	35	7	1	0	2	5	10	11	.200	.400	.378
Leading Off	10	0	0	0	0	0	1	3	.000	.000	.091
Runners On	13	3	0	0	0	3	6	7	.231	.308	.474
Runners/Scor. Pos.	9	2	1	0	0	3	4	5	.222	.333	.462

DRIVING IN RUNS	From 1B	From 2B	From 3B	Scoring Position
Totals	7/95	7/49	11/36	18/85
Percentage	7%	14%	31%	21%
Driving In Runners from 3B with Less than Two Out:		9/20		45%

Loves to face: Wes Gardner (.667, 4-for-6, 3 2B, 1 HR)
Hates to face: Scott Bankhead (0-for-5, 4 SO)
Played 90 games as designated hitter, 14 games at first base.... Batted .071 (1-for-14) as a pinch-hitter. His only hit was a home run off Brewers' Jay Aldrich.... Started 87 games vs. right-handed pitchers, but only one against a southpaw.... Only home run vs. a left-hander in his career: August 27 off Greg Cadaret.... Ranked third on Blue Jays with 13 home runs in road games, but ranked only 6th on the club with seven HR at Exhibition Stadium.... Averaged one walk per 5.9 plate appearances last season, 4th-best in A.L. (minimum: 50 BB).... A power-hitting Blue Jays first baseman who can't hit left-handers, and had no triples or sac bunts? Wait a minute—is this guy really Willie Aikens?

Mark McGwire — Oakland As — Bats Right

	AB	H	2B	3B	HR	RRF	BB	SO	BA	SA	OBA
Season	557	161	28	4	49	119	71	131	.289	.618	.370
vs. Left-Handers	171	49	10	0	16	38	35	40	.287	.626	.400
vs. Right-Handers	386	112	18	4	33	81	36	91	.290	.614	.355
Home	278	77	15	2	21	49	38	67	.277	.572	.366
Road	279	84	13	2	28	70	33	64	.301	.663	.373
Grass	486	140	25	2	44	106	59	115	.288	.619	.366
Artificial Turf	71	21	3	2	5	13	12	16	.296	.606	.395
April	52	13	2	0	4	12	9	16	.250	.519	.361
May	91	25	0	2	15	24	18	20	.275	.813	.391
June	102	31	6	1	9	21	10	19	.304	.647	.363
July	102	32	4	0	9	27	4	23	.314	.618	.360
August	99	21	5	1	3	12	15	28	.212	.374	.316
Sept./Oct.	111	39	11	0	9	23	15	23	.351	.694	.419
Leading Off Inn.	142	43	7	0	20	20	14	37	.303	.775	.365
Runners On	242	73	14	3	17	87	34	56	.302	.595	.383
Runners/Scor. Pos.	141	41	5	2	8	64	27	37	.291	.525	.393
Runners On/2 Out	113	33	9	1	5	33	21	27	.292	.522	.407
Scor. Pos./2 Out	70	19	4	1	3	27	17	21	.271	.486	.420
Late Inning Pressure	80	23	2	1	7	11	6	22	.288	.600	.345
Leading Off	29	10	0	0	5	5	2	8	.345	.862	.387
Runners On	28	5	1	0	1	5	2	6	.179	.321	.258
Runners/Scor. Pos.	17	3	0	0	0	2	2	5	.176	.176	.300

DRIVING IN RUNS	From 1B	From 2B	From 3B	Scoring Position
Totals	22/178	18/99	30/71	48/170
Percentage	12%	18%	42%	28%
Driving In Runners from 3B with Less than Two Out:		19/34		56%

Loves to face: Jack Morris (2-for-2, 2 HR)
Hates to face: Ron Guidry (.077, 1-for-13, 8 SO)
Name the rookie who started at first base for Oakland on opening day last season. Answer below. . . . Previous record for home runs by a rookie had stood for 57 years. Wally Berger hit 38 in 1930; his mark was equalled by Frank Robinson in 1956. . . . Hit 21 home runs at the Oakland Coliseum, five short of the stadium record set by Reggie Jackson in 1970. . . . Had as many home runs as singles through June 10 (19). Then kicked into high gear, hitting .305 the rest of the way. . . . Batting average didn't suffer during quest for 50 home runs. Batted .374 after Sept. 1, 3d-highest mark in A.L. . . . Struck out nine times (in 14 appearances) with the bags full, highest total in the majors. . . . Answer: Rob Nelson.

Mark McLemore — California Angels — Bats Left and Right

	AB	H	2B	3B	HR	RRF	BB	SO	BA	SA	OBA
Season	433	102	13	3	3	45	48	72	.236	.300	.310
vs. Left-Handers	126	28	4	1	1	10	13	12	.222	.294	.293
vs. Right-Handers	307	74	9	2	2	35	35	60	.241	.303	.317
Home	213	50	7	1	3	28	26	32	.235	.319	.315
Road	220	52	6	2	0	17	22	40	.236	.282	.305
Grass	363	85	11	2	3	40	39	59	.234	.300	.306
Artificial Turf	70	17	2	1	0	5	9	13	.243	.300	.329
April	76	20	3	0	0	8	12	13	.263	.303	.364
May	91	19	4	1	0	5	9	14	.209	.275	.280
June	85	18	2	1	0	6	9	20	.212	.259	.287
July	86	17	2	0	1	10	6	12	.198	.256	.242
August	79	22	1	1	2	8	10	12	.278	.392	.360
Sept./Oct.	16	6	1	0	0	8	2	1	.375	.438	.444
Leading Off Inn.	100	24	1	0	1	1	11	14	.240	.280	.315
Runners On	193	46	8	2	1	43	29	35	.238	.316	.333
Runners/Scor. Pos.	118	27	5	1	0	39	16	26	.229	.288	.314
Runners On/2 Out	96	18	3	0	1	19	10	20	.188	.250	.264
Scor. Pos./2 Out	70	13	2	0	0	16	7	16	.186	.214	.260
Late Inning Pressure	71	27	0	1	1	10	8	8	.380	.451	.443
Leading Off	17	8	0	0	0		3	0	.471	.471	.550
Runners On	28	11	0	1	1	10	4	3	.393	.571	.469
Runners/Scor. Pos.	15	6	1	0	0	8	3	3	.400	.533	.500

DRIVING IN RUNS	From 1B	From 2B	From 3B	Scoring Position
Totals	4/131	14/94	24/53	38/147
Percentage	3%	15%	45%	26%
Driving In Runners from 3B with Less than Two Out:		15/20		75%

Loves to face: Charles Hudson (3-for-3)
Hates to face: Mark Gubicza (0-for-9, 8 ground outs)
One of six Angels rookies to start on opening day over past five seasons. The others: Devon White (1987), Wally Joyner (1986), Dick Schofield and Gary Pettis (1984), and Daryl Sconiers (1983). . . . Started only three games after Johnny Ray joined the team on August 30. Played 11 games after September 1, eight as a pinch-runner. . . . Hitless in 23 consecutive at bats vs. southpaws (April 22–May 16), longest streak by a right-handed batter last season. . . . Ranked second in the major leagues with 15 sacrifice bunts. Marty Barrett led with 22. . . . Born October 4, 1964, the day that Gene Mauch's Phillies were eliminated on the final day of N.L. season after blowing a 6.5–game lead over the last 12 days.

Bobby Meacham — New York Yankees — Bats Right

	AB	H	2B	3B	HR	RRF	BB	SO	BA	SA	OBA
Season	203	55	11	1	5	22	19	33	.271	.409	.349
vs. Left-Handers	85	26	4	0	3	14	10	16	.306	.459	.379
vs. Right-Handers	118	29	7	1	2	8	9	17	.246	.373	.328
Home	93	26	6	0	2	10	7	14	.280	.409	.352
Road	110	29	5	1	3	12	12	19	.264	.409	.347
Grass	164	45	8	1	3	17	13	24	.274	.390	.348
Artificial Turf	39	10	3	0	2	5	6	9	.256	.487	.356
April	0	0	0	0	0	0	0	0	—	—	—
May	5	1	1	0	0	1	1	0	.200	.400	.333
June	15	4	0	0	0	0	0	6	.267	.267	.313
July	19	4	0	0	0	1	3	2	.211	.211	.318
August	79	20	3	1	4	8	7	13	.253	.468	.337
Sept./Oct.	85	26	7	0	1	12	8	12	.306	.424	.375
Leading Off Inn.	44	9	5	0	2	2	3	7	.205	.455	.286
Runners On	85	27	2	0	2	19	11	12	.318	.412	.398
Runners/Scor. Pos.	49	14	1	0	0	15	6	7	.286	.306	.357
Runners On/2 Out	38	11	1	0	2	14	4	7	.289	.474	.357
Scor. Pos./2 Out	26	8	1	0	0	10	3	5	.308	.346	.379
Late Inning Pressure	24	8	2	0	0	2	4	6	.333	.417	.429
Leading Off	6	1	0	0	0	0	0	3	.167	.167	.167
Runners On	9	5	1	0	0	2	4	1	.556	.667	.692
Runners/Scor. Pos.	1	1	1	0	0	2	2	0	1.000	2.000	1.000

DRIVING IN RUNS	From 1B	From 2B	From 3B	Scoring Position
Totals	3/64	4/36	10/22	14/58
Percentage	5%	11%	45%	24%
Driving In Runners from 3B with Less than Two Out:		4/6		67%

Loves to face: David Wells (.750, 3-for-4)
Hates to face: Dan Petry (.100, 2-for-20)
Only two games at second base prior to 1987, but started 17 there last season while Willie Randolph was injured. . . . Started at shortstop in each of Yankees' final 22 games, batting .338 (23-for-68) in the process. . . . Career fielding percentage of .957 at shortstop ranks 27th among 31 active players with at least 350 games played there. . . . Career batting average of .209 in Late-Inning Pressure Situations not as bad as it appears. Career LIPS breakdown: .154 with bases empty, .341 with runners on base, .353 with runners in scoring position. . . . Has spent only one full season in the majors (1985). . . . Made the first and only appearance of his career as a pinch hitter on June 5. Answer to trivia question: He hit for Randolph.

Paul Molitor — Milwaukee Brewers — Bats Right

	AB	H	2B	3B	HR	RRF	BB	SO	BA	SA	OBA
Season	465	164	41	5	16	76	69	67	.353	.566	.438
vs. Left-Handers	145	48	12	0	3	14	23	15	.331	.476	.426
vs. Right-Handers	320	116	29	5	13	62	46	52	.363	.606	.443
Home	231	91	21	4	7	38	33	35	.394	.610	.470
Road	234	73	20	1	9	38	36	32	.312	.521	.406
Grass	404	152	35	5	15	72	57	57	.376	.599	.455
Artificial Turf	61	12	6	0	1	4	12	10	.197	.344	.329
April	81	32	9	1	3	16	10	7	.395	.642	.462
May	23	5	0	0	0	3	3	5	.217	.217	.308
June	51	13	5	0	1	6	6	9	.255	.412	.333
July	65	27	6	2	3	17	7	9	.415	.708	.472
August	118	45	12	1	4	16	21	16	.381	.602	.479
Sept./Oct.	127	42	9	1	5	18	22	21	.331	.535	.430
Leading Off Inn.	160	54	11	2	6	6	23	21	.338	.544	.421
Runners On	166	70	17	1	8	68	23	25	.422	.681	.495
Runners/Scor. Pos.	107	48	13	0	5	59	15	18	.449	.710	.520
Runners On/2 Out	73	28	9	1	2	24	14	14	.384	.616	.489
Scor. Pos./2 Out	45	18	8	0	1	21	12	8	.400	.644	.534
Late Inning Pressure	54	23	1	1	4	13	6	11	.426	.704	.483
Leading Off	9	4	0	0	1	1	0	0	.444	.778	.444
Runners On	24	12	1	0	1	10	2	5	.500	.667	.538
Runners/Scor. Pos.	18	9	1	0	1	10	1	4	.500	.722	.526

DRIVING IN RUNS	From 1B	From 2B	From 3B	Scoring Position
Totals	13/99	25/77	22/44	47/121
Percentage	13%	32%	50%	39%
Driving In Runners from 3B with Less than Two Out:		15/25		60%

Loves to face: Frank Tanana (.460, 23-for-50, 1 HR)
Hates to face: Tim Stoddard (.045, 1-for-22)
Led A.L. in runs scored despite playing only 118 games, the fewest by a "runs leader" in either league since 1900. Should give Rickey Henderson and his hammies something to shoot for. . . . Other streaks: Scored a run in 16 consecutive games, and scored or drove in a run in 23 in a row (Sept. 9–Oct. 3). We don't know the records; we do know Molitor's streaks were the longest of the past six seasons. . . . Stole 3d base 10 times (most in A.L.), and wasn't thrown out. . . . First A.L. player to steal three bases in an inning (July 26 vs. Minn.) since Dave Nelson in 1974. . . . Batting average on grass fields was highest among 298 major-league qualifiers. But he's hit below .200 on artificial turf in three of the last four seasons.

Lloyd Moseby

Toronto Blue Jays — Bats Left

	AB	H	2B	3B	HR	RBI	BB	SO	BA	SA	OBA
Season	592	167	27	4	26	102	70	124	.282	.473	.358
vs. Left-Handers	198	55	9	2	5	28	25	45	.278	.419	.362
vs. Right-Handers	394	112	18	2	21	74	45	79	.284	.500	.357
Home	298	87	12	3	15	50	37	66	.292	.503	.371
Road	294	80	15	1	11	52	33	58	.272	.442	.345
Grass	229	64	12	1	7	40	25	43	.279	.432	.350
Artificial Turf	363	103	15	3	19	62	45	81	.284	.499	.363
April	84	20	4	0	2	10	5	22	.238	.357	.281
May	96	26	5	0	5	19	4	25	.271	.479	.307
June	102	29	2	2	6	23	19	20	.284	.520	.397
July	91	20	4	1	4	14	25	22	.220	.418	.388
August	98	30	2	0	5	16	5	15	.306	.480	.333
Sept./Oct.	121	42	10	1	4	20	12	20	.347	.545	.407
Leading Off Inn.	106	28	8	0	2		10	19	.264	.396	.328
Runners On	266	73	9	2	15	91	28	48	.274	.492	.340
Runners/Scor. Pos.	162	51	8	2	9	78	22	30	.315	.556	.390
Runners On/2 Out	98	25	3	2	5	30	15	21	.255	.480	.354
Scor. Pos./2 Out	64	15	3	2	2	23	13	15	.234	.438	.364
Late Inning Pressure	82	18	3	0	4	13	12	23	.220	.402	.319
Leading Off	20	7	1	0	2	2	5	3	.350	.700	.480
Runners On	38	6	2	0	2	11	2	12	.158	.368	.200
Runners/Scor. Pos.	25	3	2	0	0	7	1	7	.120	.200	.154

DRIVING IN RUNS	From 1B	From 2B	From 3B	Scoring Position
Totals	14/164	32/134	30/65	62/199
Percentage	9%	24%	46%	31%
Driving In Runners from 3B with Less than Two Out:		23/36		64%

Loves to face: Frank Viola (.378, 14-for-37, 3 HR)
Hates to face: Steve Ontiveros (0-for-10)
One of three major leaguers with 100+ HR and 100+ SB over past five years. The two others (Strawberry and Gibson) get a lot more pub. ... Drove in or scored a run in 15 consecutive games (Sept. 8–24), 2d-longest streak in majors to Molitor's 23-gamer. ... Won triple crown in games against the Brewers, leading their opponents in batting average (.490), HR (5), and RBI (19). ... Batting average of .195 during the past three Julys is lowest in majors (minimum: 200 AB). ... One of eight players in baseball history to have maintained or increased their home run totals in seven consecutive years. (We don't count players who never hit one.) No player has ever done it for eight straight years.

John Moses

Seattle Mariners — Bats Left and Right

	AB	H	2B	3B	HR	RBI	BB	SO	BA	SA	OBA
Season	390	96	16	4	3	41	29	49	.246	.331	.301
vs. Left-Handers	129	27	3	0	1	8	11	11	.209	.256	.277
vs. Right-Handers	261	69	13	4	2	33	18	38	.264	.368	.313
Home	214	47	8	1	2	17	17	26	.220	.294	.286
Road	176	49	8	3	1	24	12	23	.278	.375	.319
Grass	130	37	4	3	1	19	12	17	.285	.385	.340
Artificial Turf	260	59	12	1	2	22	17	32	.227	.304	.281
April	75	24	3	1	1	9	4	11	.320	.427	.354
May	110	28	2	2	0	7	12	18	.255	.309	.333
June	66	14	4	1	0	7	2	6	.212	.303	.246
July	60	12	3	0	1	6	1	7	.200	.300	.206
August	56	10	3	0	1	9	7	4	.179	.286	.281
Sept./Oct.	23	8	1	0	0	3	3	3	.348	.391	.407
Leading Off Inn.	141	28	4	1	1	1	12	19	.199	.262	.266
Runners On	141	38	6	1	2	40	12	17	.270	.369	.325
Runners/Scor. Pos.	95	23	3	1	0	33	9	15	.242	.295	.306
Runners On/2 Out	64	13	2	0	1	18	4	8	.203	.281	.250
Scor. Pos./2 Out	51	12	2	0	0	16	3	8	.235	.275	.278
Late Inning Pressure	45	10	1	0	1	4	2	6	.222	.289	.255
Leading Off	10	3	0	0	0	0	1	1	.300	.300	.364
Runners On	20	5	1	0	0	4	1	1	.250	.300	.286
Runners/Scor. Pos.	12	3	1	0	0	4	0	0	.250	.333	.250

DRIVING IN RUNS	From 1B	From 2B	From 3B	Scoring Position
Totals	6/76	12/78	20/42	32/120
Percentage	8%	15%	48%	27%
Driving In Runners from 3B with Less than Two Out:		14/20		70%

Loves to face: John Habyan (.800, 4-for-5)
Hates to face: Dan Petry (0-for-10)
1987 was his first full major-league season after spending parts of the previous five years with the Mariners. ... Started only five games after September 1. ... Failed to reach base safely in 32 consecutive innings that he led off (June 22–July 8), 2d-longest streak in A.L. last season. ... Batted 32 consecutive times from May 13 to May 20 without a runner in scoring position, one short of the longest streak in the A.L. last season. ... Caught stealing 15 times (in 38 attempts) last season, 4th-most in A.L. ... Career average of .400 (14-for-35) at County Stadium. ... Five hits (all singles) in 11 career at bats with the bases loaded. ... Career average of .276 with runners on base, .233 with the bases empty.

Rance Mulliniks

Toronto Blue Jays — Bats Left

	AB	H	2B	3B	HR	RBI	BB	SO	BA	SA	OBA
Season	332	103	28	1	11	47	34	55	.310	.500	.371
vs. Left-Handers	18	7	2	0	1	2	2	4	.389	.667	.450
vs. Right-Handers	314	96	26	1	10	45	32	51	.306	.490	.367
Home	162	51	15	1	6	23	13	32	.315	.531	.364
Road	170	52	13	0	5	24	21	23	.306	.471	.378
Grass	141	42	11	0	3	16	19	21	.298	.440	.377
Artificial Turf	191	61	17	1	8	31	15	34	.319	.545	.367
April	43	15	4	0	1	4	6	6	.349	.512	.420
May	53	11	3	0	0	4	4	10	.208	.264	.263
June	40	11	2	0	2	3	4	6	.275	.475	.341
July	51	15	5	0	3	10	2	9	.294	.569	.321
August	80	29	8	1	1	15	8	16	.363	.525	.416
Sept./Oct.	65	22	6	0	4	11	10	8	.338	.615	.421
Leading Off Inn.	67	20	3	0	2	2	8	11	.299	.433	.373
Runners On	129	39	11	1	5	41	17	19	.302	.519	.376
Runners/Scor. Pos.	81	23	9	1	3	36	13	11	.284	.531	.371
Runners On/2 Out	56	17	2	1	3	19	5	5	.304	.536	.361
Scor. Pos./2 Out	38	10	1	1	2	16	4	4	.263	.500	.333
Late Inning Pressure	48	15	3	0	1	7	11	12	.313	.438	.441
Leading Off	10	3	0	0	0	0	2	3	.300	.300	.417
Runners On	20	5	1	0	1	7	6	4	.250	.450	.423
Runners/Scor. Pos.	12	3	1	0	0	5	5	1	.250	.333	.471

DRIVING IN RUNS	From 1B	From 2B	From 3B	Scoring Position
Totals	7/92	16/66	13/34	29/100
Percentage	8%	24%	38%	29%
Driving In Runners from 3B with Less than Two Out:		10/19		53%

Loves to face: Mike Moore (.354, 17-for-48)
Hates to face: Dave Stewart (.059, 1-for-17)
Batting average in August was 6th-highest in A.L. ... Batted .324 in 79 games started at third base, .241 in 13 starts as the Jays' designated hitter. ... Started 92 games, all but two of them vs. right-handers. ... Has averaged less than 20 at bats per season vs. left-handed pitchers over his 11-year career. Has hit only three home runs vs. southpaws, but at regular intervals (1979, 1983, and 1987). ... Has hit for a higher average on artificial surfaces than he has on grass fields in each of the last six seasons. ... Career average of .254 on grass fields, .292 on artificial turf. ... Yearly batting averages with runners in scoring position since 1984: .372, .381, .310, .284.

Dwayne Murphy

Oakland As — Bats Left

	AB	H	2B	3B	HR	RBI	BB	SO	BA	SA	OBA
Season	219	51	7	0	8	35	58	61	.233	.374	.388
vs. Left-Handers	66	12	1	0	2	6	12	22	.182	.288	.304
vs. Right-Handers	153	39	6	0	6	29	46	39	.255	.412	.421
Home	101	18	6	0	2	12	25	27	.178	.297	.339
Road	118	33	1	0	6	23	33	34	.280	.441	.429
Grass	178	40	6	0	6	28	38	51	.225	.360	.358
Artificial Turf	41	11	1	0	2	7	20	10	.268	.439	.492
April	45	12	2	0	2	8	10	12	.267	.444	.400
May	0	0	0	0	0	0	0	0	—	—	—
June	6	0	0	0	0	0	2	2	.000	.000	.250
July	20	5	1	0	0	2	2	3	.250	.300	.304
August	64	15	2	0	0	11	26	19	.234	.266	.451
Sept./Oct.	84	19	2	0	6	14	18	25	.226	.464	.356
Leading Off Inn.	50	9	0	0	0		15	13	.180	.180	.369
Runners On	88	29	6	0	3	30	25	22	.330	.500	.462
Runners/Scor. Pos.	57	19	4	0	2	26	16	15	.333	.509	.455
Runners On/2 Out	41	11	3	0	1	13	10	11	.268	.415	.412
Scor. Pos./2 Out	32	9	2	0	0	10	8	8	.281	.344	.425
Late Inning Pressure	39	7	1	0	1	3	7	12	.179	.282	.304
Leading Off	9	1	0	0	0	0	2	3	.111	.111	.273
Runners On	15	6	1	0	0	3	2	2	.400	.667	.471
Runners/Scor. Pos.	10	4	1	0	1	3	1	1	.400	.800	.455

DRIVING IN RUNS	From 1B	From 2B	From 3B	Scoring Position
Totals	3/60	10/41	14/28	24/69
Percentage	5%	24%	50%	35%
Driving In Runners from 3B with Less than Two Out:		10/14		71%

Loves to face: Bob Stoddard (.615, 8-for-13, 3 HR)
Hates to face: Tom Henke (0-for-8, 7 SO)
Averaged one walk per 4.9 plate appearances, highest rate in the A.L. (minimum: 50 BB). ... Batted 162 points higher with men on base than with the bases empty, largest difference among A.L. players (minimum: 75 AB each way). ... Batted 101 points higher at home than on the road, 3d-largest difference in the league (minimum: 100 AB each way). ... Three hits in three at bats with bases loaded last season. Nobody did it better, except maybe Mike Stanley, who was 3-for-3 with two HR. ... Batting average in Late-Inning Pressure Situations has been lower than his overall average in each of the last six seasons. ... Career averages: .219 vs. left-handers, .262 vs. right-handers.

Eddie Murray

Bats Left and Right

Baltimore Orioles	AB	H	2B	3B	HR	RRF	BB	SO	BA	SA	OBA
Season	618	171	28	3	30	94	73	80	.277	.477	.352
vs. Left-Handers	221	60	10	1	11	35	22	33	.271	.475	.336
vs. Right-Handers	397	111	18	2	19	59	51	47	.280	.479	.360
Home	300	79	9	0	14	38	39	45	.263	.433	.347
Road	318	92	19	3	16	56	34	35	.289	.519	.356
Grass	524	140	22	0	26	79	64	71	.267	.458	.345
Artificial Turf	94	31	6	3	4	15	9	9	.330	.585	.388
April	83	15	5	1	1	14	9	12	.181	.301	.255
May	108	37	5	1	11	29	13	8	.343	.713	.410
June	109	28	7	0	2	4	8	18	.257	.376	.308
July	98	27	3	1	11	28	16	10	.276	.663	.377
August	106	34	2	0	3	11	12	17	.321	.425	.390
Sept./Oct.	114	30	6	0	2	8	15	15	.263	.368	.349
Leading Off Inn.	155	42	8	2	7	7	14	11	.271	.484	.331
Runners On	288	79	14	1	15	79	44	41	.274	.486	.367
Runners/Scor. Pos.	136	39	5	1	7	61	30	28	.287	.493	.408
Runners On/2 Out	142	35	5	0	12	38	28	19	.246	.535	.371
Scor. Pos./2 Out	64	13	1	0	4	20	19	15	.203	.406	.386
Late Inning Pressure	91	27	5	0	4	15	11	15	.297	.484	.373
Leading Off	22	6	2	0	0	0	3	2	.273	.364	.360
Runners On	35	12	3	0	1	12	3	5	.343	.514	.395
Runners/Scor. Pos.	19	8	2	0	0	10	2	3	.421	.526	.476

DRIVING IN RUNS	From 1B	From 2B	From 3B	Scoring Position
Totals	14/221	27/113	23/51	50/164
Percentage	6%	24%	45%	30%
Driving In Runners from 3B with Less than Two Out:			17/25	68%

Loves to face: Mark Langston (.429, 12-for-28, 1 HR)
Hates to face: Eric King (0-for-17)
Hit eight home runs vs. White Sox, twice as many as anyone else. ... Passed Boog Powell as Orioles' all-time HR leader. ... Batting average with runners in scoring position was higher than overall average in each of last six seasons. ... All things must pass: One hit in nine at bats with bases loaded represented his first season below the .400 mark since 1979, and his first ever below .300. His streak of six consecutive seasons with a grand slam was broken as well, one short of Vern Stephens's A.L. record. ... The more things change, the more they stay the same. The best clutch hitter of the 1980s *raised* his career average with runners in scoring position in Late-Inning Pressure Situations from .383 to .387 by going 8-for-19.

Al Newman

Bats Left and Right

Minnesota Twins	AB	H	2B	3B	HR	RRF	BB	SO	BA	SA	OBA
Season	307	68	15	5	0	30	34	27	.221	.303	.298
vs. Left-Handers	94	30	10	3	0	11	14	12	.319	.489	.407
vs. Right-Handers	213	38	5	2	0	19	20	15	.178	.221	.248
Home	153	36	8	3	0	21	24	15	.235	.327	.339
Road	154	32	7	2	0	9	10	12	.208	.279	.255
Grass	128	24	6	2	0	8	10	10	.188	.266	.245
Artificial Turf	179	44	9	3	0	22	24	17	.246	.330	.335
April	54	14	2	1	0	9	4	3	.259	.333	.310
May	64	9	3	2	0	4	8	9	.141	.250	.233
June	66	14	4	1	0	9	8	7	.212	.303	.297
July	35	9	3	1	0	3	1	2	.257	.400	.278
August	47	14	2	0	0	2	8	1	.298	.340	.400
Sept./Oct.	41	8	1	0	0	3	5	5	.195	.220	.283
Leading Off Inn.	95	21	4	1	0	0	17	12	.221	.284	.339
Runners On	133	32	8	3	0	30	7	7	.241	.346	.277
Runners/Scor. Pos.	79	19	6	2	0	28	6	6	.241	.367	.291
Runners On/2 Out	57	14	3	3	0	13	4	4	.246	.404	.283
Scor. Pos./2 Out	35	9	2	2	0	12	3	4	.257	.429	.316
Late Inning Pressure	31	6	1	0	0	2	4	4	.194	.226	.286
Leading Off	9	0	0	0	0	0	3	3	.000	.000	.250
Runners On	13	4	1	0	0	2	1	0	.308	.385	.357
Runners/Scor. Pos.	5	2	1	0	0	2	1	0	.400	.600	.500

DRIVING IN RUNS	From 1B	From 2B	From 3B	Scoring Position
Totals	4/88	12/68	14/27	26/95
Percentage	5%	18%	52%	27%
Driving In Runners from 3B with Less than Two Out:			9/13	69%

Loves to face: Curt Young (2-for-2)
Hates to face: Charles Hudson (.063, 1-for-16)
Played 55 games at shortstop, 47 games at second base, 12 games at third base, and two games in left field. ... Fielding percentage at his three infield positions of .962 on grass fields (four errors in 106 chances), .996 on artificial surfaces (one error in 228 chances). ... Batted 141 points higher against southpaws than he did against right-handers last season, 2d-largest difference in A.L. (minimum: 50 AB each way). ... Still hitless at three different A.L. cities: Cleveland (14 AB), Chicago (11 AB), and Detroit (11 AB). ... Career average of .241 with runners on base, .192 with the bases empty. ... His only career home run was hit against Zane Smith in 1986.

Matt Nokes

Bats Left

Detroit Tigers	AB	H	2B	3B	HR	RRF	BB	SO	BA	SA	OBA
Season	461	133	14	2	32	90	35	70	.289	.536	.345
vs. Left-Handers	87	18	1	0	4	13	8	23	.207	.356	.278
vs. Right-Handers	374	115	13	2	28	77	27	47	.307	.578	.360
Home	214	66	4	2	14	37	19	39	.308	.542	.374
Road	247	67	10	0	18	53	16	31	.271	.530	.318
Grass	398	123	12	2	29	74	31	60	.309	.568	.365
Artificial Turf	63	10	2	0	3	16	4	10	.159	.333	.209
April	58	18	2	0	4	14	5	10	.310	.552	.359
May	80	24	2	0	5	17	8	12	.300	.513	.360
June	82	28	3	1	7	15	6	13	.341	.659	.393
July	68	18	3	0	6	12	2	11	.265	.574	.315
August	82	17	3	0	3	16	5	9	.207	.354	.258
Sept./Oct.	91	28	1	1	7	16	9	15	.308	.571	.376
Leading Off Inn.	91	31	6	0	9	9	5	9	.341	.703	.394
Runners On	245	71	7	0	12	70	13	46	.290	.465	.324
Runners/Scor. Pos.	145	34	5	0	5	54	10	26	.234	.372	.283
Runners On/2 Out	104	24	3	0	4	30	6	20	.231	.375	.273
Scor. Pos./2 Out	68	18	3	0	3	28	5	12	.265	.441	.315
Late Inning Pressure	54	13	0	0	3	10	2	9	.241	.407	.268
Leading Off	13	3	0	0	2	2	0	1	.231	.692	.231
Runners On	24	7	0	0	0	7	1	6	.292	.292	.320
Runners/Scor. Pos.	11	4	0	0	0	7	1	1	.364	.364	.417

DRIVING IN RUNS	From 1B	From 2B	From 3B	Scoring Position
Totals	15/177	19/117	24/62	43/179
Percentage	8%	16%	39%	24%
Driving In Runners from 3B with Less than Two Out:			15/30	50%

Loves to face: Mike Witt (.833, 5-for-6, 2 HR)
Hates to face: Tom Bolton (0-for-3, 3 SO)
12th-highest HR total by a rookie in baseball history was overshadowed by Canseco's 33 and McGwire's 49 in back-to-back seasons. ... Opponents were successful on 81 percent of stolen-base attempts, including 11-for-11 stealing third. ... Batted 101 points higher vs. right-handers than vs. left-handers, 5th-largest difference in A.L. last season (minimum: 50 AB each way). Career averages: .198 vs. LHP, .300 vs. RHP. ... Started 109 of 110 games in which the Tigers faced a right-hander, but only four of 52 games against southpaws. ... Career batting average of .500 with five HR in 18 AB at Anaheim Stadium. ... The only rookie catcher in A.L. to start a 1987 season opener? Ron Karkovice.

Pete O'Brien

Bats Left

Texas Rangers	AB	H	2B	3B	HR	RRF	BB	SO	BA	SA	OBA
Season	569	163	26	1	23	93	59	61	.286	.457	.348
vs. Left-Handers	186	46	8	0	3	23	13	30	.247	.339	.294
vs. Right-Handers	383	117	18	1	20	70	46	31	.305	.514	.373
Home	265	72	14	0	9	44	32	28	.272	.426	.341
Road	304	91	12	1	14	49	27	33	.299	.484	.354
Grass	469	133	22	1	17	72	51	45	.284	.443	.347
Artificial Turf	100	30	4	0	6	21	8	16	.300	.520	.352
April	67	13	4	0	2	8	8	8	.194	.343	.273
May	99	27	1	0	9	23	9	10	.273	.556	.333
June	103	36	5	0	6	23	10	9	.350	.573	.400
July	92	27	6	0	3	11	9	8	.293	.457	.350
August	104	34	5	1	0	16	11	9	.327	.394	.388
Sept./Oct.	104	26	5	0	3	12	12	17	.250	.385	.319
Leading Off Inn.	132	37	6	0	6	6	10	11	.280	.462	.331
Runners On	248	77	13	1	8	78	31	29	.310	.468	.374
Runners/Scor. Pos.	148	40	4	1	6	65	19	17	.270	.432	.333
Runners On/2 Out	110	32	3	1	5	32	18	13	.291	.473	.391
Scor. Pos./2 Out	80	21	1	1	5	29	12	11	.263	.488	.359
Late Inning Pressure	91	27	3	0	8	16	10	8	.297	.593	.363
Leading Off	31	9	0	0	3	3	0	2	.290	.581	.290
Runners On	32	10	3	0	2	10	5	4	.313	.594	.395
Runners/Scor. Pos.	19	3	0	0	1	6	3	4	.158	.316	.261

DRIVING IN RUNS	From 1B	From 2B	From 3B	Scoring Position
Totals	13/165	27/115	28/61	55/176
Percentage	8%	23%	46%	31%
Driving In Runners from 3B with Less than Two Out:			18/28	64%

Loves to face: Roger Clemens (.471, 8-for-17, 5 BB)
Hates to face: Willie Hernandez (0-for-17)
Hit two extra-inning home runs last season, and led the league with eight HR in Late-Inning Pressure Situations. ... Averaged 1.01 assists per nine innings last season, one of three A.L. first basemen to average above 1.00 (minimum: 500 innings). Started 16 double plays, one fewer than the major-league leader at first base, Wally Joyner. ... Has homered at every A.L. ballpark except Yankee Stadium (101 career AB). ... Although he's never batted .300+ in any of his six seasons in the majors, he has batted .300 or better with runners on base in three of the last four. ... Career RDI% of only 21 percent from scoring position in Late-Inning Pressure Situations, 34 percent at other times.

Spike Owen
Boston Red Sox — Bats Left and Right

	AB	H	2B	3B	HR	RRF	BB	SO	BA	SA	OBA
Season	437	113	17	7	2	52	53	43	.259	.343	.337
vs. Left-Handers	134	43	8	2	2	19	16	14	.321	.455	.393
vs. Right-Handers	303	70	9	5	0	33	37	29	.231	.294	.313
Home	224	59	8	5	2	29	28	21	.263	.371	.341
Road	213	54	9	2	0	23	25	22	.254	.315	.333
Grass	381	98	13	7	2	46	46	35	.257	.344	.335
Artificial Turf	56	15	4	0	0	6	7	8	.268	.339	.354
April	36	5	2	0	0	2	4	5	.139	.194	.225
May	35	9	2	1	0	3	5	4	.257	.371	.350
June	99	27	7	3	0	13	12	7	.273	.404	.348
July	79	23	1	2	0	11	7	3	.291	.354	.341
August	94	22	2	0	1	14	13	13	.234	.287	.324
Sept./Oct.	94	27	3	1	1	9	12	11	.287	.372	.374
Leading Off Inn.	101	25	5	0	0	8	9	8	.248	.297	.309
Runners On	186	52	9	6	1	51	23	15	.280	.409	.352
Runners/Scor. Pos.	103	33	6	3	0	43	14	8	.320	.437	.388
Runners On/2 Out	72	19	2	2	0	14	10	8	.264	.347	.354
Scor. Pos./2 Out	39	11	2	0	0	12	7	3	.282	.333	.391
Late Inning Pressure	59	14	0	1	1	4	8	3	.237	.322	.328
Leading Off	16	3	0	0	0		2	1	.188	.188	.278
Runners On	20	5	0	1	0	3	4	1	.250	.350	.375
Runners/Scor. Pos.	9	3	0	0	0	2	2	1	.333	.333	.455

DRIVING IN RUNS	From 1B	From 2B	From 3B	Scoring Position
Totals	9/144	16/81	24/48	40/129
Percentage	6%	20%	50%	31%
Driving In Runners from 3B with Less than Two Out:		18/27		67%

Loves to face: Dave Schmidt (.563, 9-for-16, 1 HR)
Hates to face: Tom Candiotti (.040, 1-for-25)
Batted .216 in day games, .282 at night. . . . Drove in 31 percent of runners from scoring position. Jim Rice drove in 29 percent. . . . Fielding percentages at shortstop, year by year since 1984: .977, .975, .973, .975. The only other shortstop to top the .970 mark in at least 100 games in each of the last four seasons is Ozzie Smith. . . . Batting average in Late-Inning Pressure Situations has been lower than his overall average in each of his five seasons in the majors. Career marks: .179 in LIPS, .249 otherwise. . . . Hasn't hit a home run against a right-hander since he connected against Gene Nelson in October 1985. . . . Scored six runs in one game in 1986, but didn't score his sixth run until his 21st game last season.

Mike Pagliarulo
New York Yankees — Bats Left

	AB	H	2B	3B	HR	RRF	BB	SO	BA	SA	OBA
Season	522	122	26	3	32	89	53	111	.234	.479	.305
vs. Left-Handers	152	35	7	0	4	21	11	43	.230	.355	.283
vs. Right-Handers	370	87	19	3	28	68	42	68	.235	.530	.314
Home	243	52	10	1	17	48	32	56	.214	.473	.308
Road	279	70	16	2	15	41	21	55	.251	.484	.302
Grass	435	101	20	3	27	75	45	87	.232	.478	.305
Artificial Turf	87	21	6	0	5	14	8	24	.241	.483	.305
April	68	11	2	0	1	7	8	13	.162	.235	.260
May	90	21	4	2	5	14	10	17	.233	.489	.317
June	92	26	5	0	6	19	11	25	.283	.533	.352
July	77	21	4	0	8	17	14	15	.273	.636	.380
August	105	24	6	0	9	16	3	23	.229	.543	.250
Sept./Oct.	90	19	5	1	3	16	7	18	.211	.389	.268
Leading Off Inn.	124	27	5	2	6	6	13	18	.218	.435	.297
Runners On	215	54	14	0	14	71	27	52	.251	.512	.333
Runners/Scor. Pos.	121	28	5	0	6	53	19	31	.231	.421	.333
Runners On/2 Out	98	19	7	0	2	18	13	30	.194	.327	.288
Scor. Pos./2 Out	60	9	3	0	2	17	8	18	.150	.300	.250
Late Inning Pressure	69	13	1	0	7	16	9	10	.188	.507	.278
Leading Off	19	5	0	0	3	3	5	0	.263	.737	.417
Runners On	25	2	1	0	1	10	3	5	.080	.240	.172
Runners/Scor. Pos.	14	2	1	0	1	10	3	2	.143	.429	.278

DRIVING IN RUNS	From 1B	From 2B	From 3B	Scoring Position
Totals	14/164	17/103	26/51	43/154
Percentage	9%	17%	51%	28%
Driving In Runners from 3B with Less than Two Out:		21/30		70%

Loves to face: Bret Saberhagen (.368, 7-for-19, 4 HR)
Hates to face: Bert Blyleven (.038, 1-for-26)
Only player in majors with 100+ at bats in each of last four years who hasn't hit .240 in any of the four years. . . . Ranks second in A.L. with 71 home runs vs. right-handers over past three seasons. Darrell Evans leads the majors with 80. . . . Started all 105 games in which Yankees faced a right-hander, 33 of 57 vs. southpaws. . . . Career average of .209 (one HR per 49.5 AB) vs. left-handers, .247 (one HR per 15.5 AB) vs. right-handers. . . . No HR in his final 68 AB last season; none in last 99 AB of 1986. Career batting average from Sept. 1 on: .195. . . . Has hit 86 career HR: 43 at Yankee Stadium, 43 on the road. . . . Career average of .195 at Memorial Stadium, the only A.L. ballpark in which he has not homered.

Larry Parrish
Texas Rangers — Bats Right

	AB	H	2B	3B	HR	RRF	BB	SO	BA	SA	OBA
Season	557	149	22	1	32	101	49	154	.268	.483	.328
vs. Left-Handers	190	51	5	0	14	35	22	60	.268	.516	.346
vs. Right-Handers	367	98	17	1	18	66	27	94	.267	.466	.318
Home	277	73	11	0	16	47	29	69	.264	.477	.335
Road	280	76	11	1	16	54	20	85	.271	.489	.320
Grass	484	130	22	1	29	89	41	133	.269	.498	.326
Artificial Turf	73	19	0	0	3	12	8	21	.260	.384	.341
April	71	16	1	0	4	5	3	22	.225	.408	.267
May	89	35	7	0	7	35	10	16	.393	.708	.450
June	102	25	6	0	7	16	9	32	.245	.510	.304
July	89	20	3	0	5	16	10	20	.225	.427	.300
August	94	23	4	0	4	11	10	30	.245	.415	.317
Sept./Oct.	112	30	1	1	5	18	7	34	.268	.429	.320
Leading Off Inn.	117	26	3	1	5	5	8	30	.222	.393	.278
Runners On	258	84	11	0	19	88	27	64	.326	.589	.388
Runners/Scor. Pos.	135	48	6	0	14	74	17	30	.356	.711	.424
Runners On/2 Out	107	30	2	0	7	35	15	26	.280	.495	.379
Scor. Pos./2 Out	68	24	2	0	6	33	11	12	.353	.647	.457
Late Inning Pressure	76	18	0	0	3	11	7	23	.237	.355	.310
Leading Off	15	2	0	0	0	0	0	4	.133	.133	.133
Runners On	38	13	0	0	1	10	6	7	.342	.500	.444
Runners/Scor. Pos.	16	5	0	0	2	10	4	3	.313	.688	.476

DRIVING IN RUNS	From 1B	From 2B	From 3B	Scoring Position
Totals	16/188	25/96	28/58	53/154
Percentage	9%	26%	48%	34%
Driving In Runners from 3B with Less than Two Out:		17/27		63%

Loves to face: Dave Stieb (.485, 16-for-33, 3 HR)
Hates to face: Gene Nelson (.111, 2-for-18)
Led designated hitters in games (122) and home runs (26, tied with Phelps) last season. . . . Batting average in May was highest in A.L. . . . Homered against every opposing team except Boston. . . . Hit safely in seven consecutive at bats with runners in scoring position (May 25–June 1), longest streak in A.L. last season. Batting average was 116 points higher with runners in scoring position than otherwise, 2d-largest gain in the majors (minimum: 100 AB each way). . . . Has hit an equal number of HR at home and on the road in three of the last four seasons. The only exception: 1985 (9 on the road, 8 at home). . . . Needs 51 RBI to overtake Toby Harrah as Rangers' all-time leader. He's currently tied for second with Buddy Bell.

Dan Pasqua
New York Yankees — Bats Left

	AB	H	2B	3B	HR	RRF	BB	SO	BA	SA	OBA
Season	318	74	7	1	17	42	40	99	.233	.421	.319
vs. Left-Handers	55	9	2	0	0	3	6	19	.164	.200	.246
vs. Right-Handers	263	65	5	1	17	39	34	80	.247	.468	.334
Home	141	39	1	0	6	13	21	43	.277	.411	.372
Road	177	35	6	1	11	29	19	56	.198	.429	.276
Grass	273	64	5	0	13	34	36	84	.234	.396	.325
Artificial Turf	45	10	2	1	4	8	4	15	.222	.578	.286
April	46	6	1	0	1	4	7	18	.130	.217	.241
May	70	17	0	0	5	11	16	20	.243	.457	.391
June	53	11	2	0	2	8	9	23	.208	.358	.323
July	25	4	2	1	1	3	0	6	.160	.440	.160
August	67	19	1	0	4	10	3	18	.284	.478	.314
Sept./Oct.	57	17	1	0	4	6	5	14	.298	.526	.355
Leading Off Inn.	73	19	2	0	5	5	4	19	.260	.493	.299
Runners On	138	29	2	0	8	33	25	44	.210	.399	.333
Runners/Scor. Pos.	76	15	1	0	5	27	16	28	.197	.408	.333
Runners On/2 Out	53	7	0	0	2	6	9	17	.132	.245	.270
Scor. Pos./2 Out	29	2	0	0	1	4	5	12	.069	.172	.206
Late Inning Pressure	44	12	1	0	4	9	7	12	.273	.568	.365
Leading Off	14	4	0	0	2		1	5	.286	.714	.333
Runners On	14	4	0	0	2	7	4	3	.286	.714	.421
Runners/Scor. Pos.	9	3	0	0	2	7	4	1	.333	1.000	.500

DRIVING IN RUNS	From 1B	From 2B	From 3B	Scoring Position
Totals	4/104	10/57	11/30	21/87
Percentage	4%	18%	37%	24%
Driving In Runners from 3B with Less than Two Out:		10/17		59%

Loves to face: Mike Moore (.579, 11-for-19, 2 HR)
Hates to face: Dave Stieb (.100, 2-for-20)
Played 74 games in the outfield, 12 at first base, and 20 as a designated hitter last season. . . . His three hits in 22 at bats as a pinch-hitter last season were all home runs. . . . Started 76 of 105 games in which the Yankees faced a right-handed starter, six of 57 games against southpaws. Career breakdown: .182 (one HR per 40.4 AB) vs. lefties, .264 (one HR every 16.0 AB) vs. right-handers. . . . Career at Comiskey: .292 (7-for-24), two home runs. . . . Has a career average of under .200 at five different A.L. ballparks (Memorial Stadium, Cleveland Stadium, Tiger Stadium, Oakland Coliseum, and Exhibition Stadium). . . . Career average of .227 with runners in scoring position.

Geno Petralli

Texas Rangers — Bats Left and Right

	AB	H	2B	3B	HR	RRF	BB	SO	BA	SA	OBA
Season	202	61	11	2	7	31	27	29	.302	.480	.388
vs. Left-Handers	15	4	0	0	0	0	2	3	.267	.267	.353
vs. Right-Handers	187	57	11	2	7	31	25	26	.305	.497	.391
Home	94	30	6	1	4	15	16	12	.319	.532	.423
Road	108	31	5	1	3	16	11	17	.287	.435	.355
Grass	163	51	8	2	6	26	25	21	.313	.497	.411
Artificial Turf	39	10	3	0	1	5	2	8	.256	.410	.286
April	11	5	0	0	0	3	4	2	.455	.455	.600
May	41	8	4	0	1	7	9	5	.195	.366	.340
June	27	12	3	0	1	5	3	4	.444	.667	.500
July	29	7	1	1	0	1	2	4	.241	.345	.281
August	43	12	2	0	2	8	5	10	.279	.465	.367
Sept./Oct.	51	17	1	1	3	7	4	4	.333	.569	.393
Leading Off Inn.	52	20	5	1	3	3	5	5	.385	.692	.448
Runners On	97	25	3	1	1	25	18	16	.258	.340	.376
Runners/Scor. Pos.	58	17	2	1	1	24	14	8	.293	.414	.432
Runners On/2 Out	36	9	1	0	0	8	11	5	.250	.278	.426
Scor. Pos./2 Out	20	6	1	0	0	8	9	2	.300	.350	.517
Late Inning Pressure	42	11	2	0	1	6	5	4	.262	.381	.347
Leading Off	11	5	2	0	1	0	0	0	.455	.909	.500
Runners On	22	4	0	0	0	5	5	4	.182	.182	.321
Runners/Scor. Pos.	14	3	0	0	0	5	4	3	.214	.214	.368

DRIVING IN RUNS	From 1B	From 2B	From 3B	Scoring Position
Totals	3/69	11/47	10/19	21/66
Percentage	4%	23%	53%	32%
Driving In Runners from 3B with Less than Two Out:	7/13			54%

Loves to face: Bill Long (.667, 4-for-6)
Hates to face: Mark Gubicza (0-for-10)
Played six different positions last season (C-3B-1B-2B-RF-LF), plus two games as designated hitter. ... Started 53 games vs. right-handed pitchers, but only three against southpaws. ... Nine hits (1 XBH, a double) in 45 career at bats vs. left-handed pitchers. .292 career average vs. right-handers. ... Career breakdown: .277 with bases empty, .292 with runners on base, .317 with runners in scoring position, .327 with two out and runners in scoring position. ... No home runs in first 228 at bats of his career, nine in 262 AB since then. Seven of his nine HR have been hit with the bases empty. ... Career average of .414 (12-for-29, 1 HR) at the Metrodome.

Gary Pettis

California Angels — Bats Left and Right

	AB	H	2B	3B	HR	RRF	BB	SO	BA	SA	OBA
Season	394	82	13	2	1	19	52	124	.208	.259	.302
vs. Left-Handers	128	22	5	1	1	6	13	28	.172	.250	.248
vs. Right-Handers	266	60	8	1	0	13	39	96	.226	.263	.327
Home	204	45	8	1	1	14	23	63	.221	.284	.300
Road	190	37	5	1	0	5	29	61	.195	.232	.305
Grass	337	75	11	2	1	19	46	105	.223	.276	.316
Artificial Turf	57	7	2	0	0	0	6	19	.123	.158	.219
April	87	22	7	0	1	4	6	23	.253	.368	.309
May	95	21	3	0	0	6	10	30	.221	.253	.295
June	82	16	2	1	0	2	19	24	.195	.244	.347
July	69	11	0	1	0	2	10	31	.159	.188	.266
August	21	2	1	0	0	2	3	7	.095	.143	.208
Sept./Oct.	40	10	0	0	0	3	4	9	.250	.250	.318
Leading Off Inn.	107	25	7	0	1		16	33	.234	.327	.333
Runners On	158	28	3	1	0	18	22	53	.177	.209	.278
Runners/Scor. Pos.	99	14	2	0	0	17	14	34	.141	.162	.248
Runners On/2 Out	67	11	2	1	0	5	6	22	.164	.224	.233
Scor. Pos./2 Out	38	2	1	0	0	4	4	16	.053	.079	.143
Late Inning Pressure	58	12	1	0	0	4	5	20	.207	.224	.281
Leading Off	15	5	1	0	0	0	0	5	.333	.400	.333
Runners On	30	5	0	0	0	4	2	11	.167	.167	.219
Runners/Scor. Pos.	17	2	0	0	0	4	2	8	.118	.118	.211

DRIVING IN RUNS	From 1B	From 2B	From 3B	Scoring Position
Totals	1/113	7/72	10/40	17/112
Percentage	1%	10%	25%	15%
Driving In Runners from 3B with Less than Two Out:	8/18			44%

Loves to face: Richard Dotson (.450, 9-for-20, 1 HR)
Hates to face: Ted Higuera (0-for-15)
Angels had a record of 46–52 with Pettis starting in center field and Devon White in right; 19–33 after White was shifted to center in place of Pettis. ... Averaged 3.15 putouts per nine innings last season, highest rate among major-league center fielders (minimum: 500 innings). ... Slugging average in road games was the lowest among 162 A.L. qualifiers. ... Home run off Curt Young on April 22 is one of three career HR against southpaws. The other two were both hit off Mike Mason. ... Career ratio of 2.25 ground outs for every fly out is the highest of any active A.L. player (minimum: 1,000 PA). ... Career average of .440 (11-for-25, 1 HR) with the bases loaded.

Ken Phelps

Seattle Mariners — Bats Left

	AB	H	2B	3B	HR	RRF	BB	SO	BA	SA	OBA
Season	332	86	13	1	27	70	80	75	.259	.548	.410
vs. Left-Handers	37	10	4	0	3	8	11	8	.270	.622	.451
vs. Right-Handers	295	76	9	1	24	62	69	67	.258	.539	.405
Home	164	38	6	1	15	38	42	34	.232	.555	.394
Road	168	48	7	0	12	32	38	41	.286	.542	.427
Grass	129	36	6	0	9	24	25	32	.279	.535	.405
Artificial Turf	203	50	7	1	18	46	55	43	.246	.557	.414
April	58	19	1	0	7	19	14	15	.328	.707	.452
May	66	17	4	0	7	16	15	14	.258	.636	.390
June	55	10	0	0	0	3	11	9	.182	.182	.348
July	36	8	2	0	1	4	4	13	.222	.361	.333
August	53	15	4	1	6	15	19	9	.283	.736	.473
Sept./Oct.	64	17	2	0	6	13	17	15	.266	.569	.429
Leading Off Inn.	83	21	3	0	9	9	13	17	.253	.614	.367
Runners On	153	39	5	1	11	54	51	36	.255	.516	.438
Runners/Scor. Pos.	84	20	4	0	4	39	32	20	.238	.429	.443
Runners On/2 Out	74	16	2	1	3	19	29	17	.216	.392	.437
Scor. Pos./2 Out	47	10	1	0	2	16	18	13	.213	.362	.431
Late Inning Pressure	30	5	2	0	2	5	10	12	.167	.433	.375
Leading Off	6	1	1	0	0	0	3	3	.167	.333	.444
Runners On	14	2	0	0	1	4	6	6	.143	.357	.400
Runners/Scor. Pos.	7	1	0	0	1	4	3	4	.143	.571	.400

DRIVING IN RUNS	From 1B	From 2B	From 3B	Scoring Position
Totals	11/119	12/59	20/43	32/102
Percentage	9%	20%	47%	31%
Driving In Runners from 3B with Less than Two Out:	12/24			50%

Loves to face: Gene Nelson (3-for-3, 2 2B, 1 HR)
Hates to face: Jack Morris (0-for-26, 13 SO)
Averaged one walk per 5.3 plate appearances last season, 2d-highest rate in A.L. (minimum: 50 BB). ... Hit 26 home runs as a DH last season, tied for most in A.L. ... Started 103 of 113 games in which Seattle faced a right-handed starter, but only two of 49 games against southpaws. ... Equalled his previous career total with three HR vs. lefties. Career average of one home run per 12.6 at bats vs. right-handed pitchers is highest rate over the last 13 seasons (minimum: 40 HR). ... Four hits in 28 career at bats at Yankee Stadium, but three of the hits were HR. ... Career breakdown: .248 with bases empty, .234 with runners on base, .217 with runners in scoring position, .152 with two outs and runners in scoring position.

Tony Phillips

Oakland As — Bats Left and Right

	AB	H	2B	3B	HR	RRF	BB	SO	BA	SA	OBA
Season	379	91	20	0	10	48	57	76	.240	.372	.337
vs. Left-Handers	128	37	3	0	3	17	25	17	.289	.383	.403
vs. Right-Handers	251	54	17	0	7	31	32	59	.215	.367	.302
Home	175	44	8	0	5	19	28	40	.251	.383	.351
Road	204	47	12	0	5	29	29	36	.230	.363	.325
Grass	314	78	16	0	9	45	46	63	.248	.385	.342
Artificial Turf	65	13	4	0	1	3	11	13	.200	.308	.316
April	79	21	4	0	2	6	17	11	.266	.392	.396
May	85	20	6	0	2	10	11	21	.235	.376	.323
June	97	24	4	0	4	17	15	17	.247	.412	.348
July	33	10	3	0	0	4	4	9	.303	.394	.378
August	11	2	1	0	0	0	3	3	.182	.273	.357
Sept./Oct.	74	14	2	0	2	11	7	15	.189	.297	.250
Leading Off Inn.	95	18	5	0	0		12	16	.189	.242	.280
Runners On	143	41	11	0	6	44	24	24	.287	.490	.382
Runners/Scor. Pos.	80	22	5	0	3	33	12	10	.275	.413	.358
Runners On/2 Out	64	18	3	0	3	19	11	15	.281	.469	.387
Scor. Pos./2 Out	38	11	2	0	1	14	7	8	.289	.421	.400
Late Inning Pressure	56	9	2	0	2	9	7	13	.161	.304	.250
Leading Off	9	0	0	0	0	0	2	2	.000	.000	.182
Runners On	25	4	2	0	2	9	3	4	.160	.480	.241
Runners/Scor. Pos.	17	1	1	0	0	5	3	2	.059	.118	.190

DRIVING IN RUNS	From 1B	From 2B	From 3B	Scoring Position
Totals	11/103	12/61	15/31	27/92
Percentage	11%	20%	48%	29%
Driving In Runners from 3B with Less than Two Out:	11/15			73%

Loves to face: Rich Yett (.429, 9-for-21)
Hates to face: Ed Correa (0-for-9)
A switch hitter whose batting average vs. right-handers has declined in every season since 1983: .277, .245, .233, .228, .215. Career averages: .284 vs. left-handers, .238 vs. right-handers. ... A's allowed an average of 4.59 runs per nine innings with Phillips at second base, 5.25 with other second basemen. That's the fourth straight season in which Oakland has been stingier on defense with Phillips at second than at other times. ... Career batting average of .282 with runners on base, .236 with the bases empty. ... Has batted .211 during the past five Junes, 2d-lowest in majors to Dick Schofield's .195 (minimum: 300 AB). ... Has maintained or increased his home run total in each of his six seasons in the majors.

Luis Polonia
Oakland As   Bats Left

	AB	H	2B	3B	HR	RRF	BB	SO	BA	SA	OBA
Season	435	125	16	10	4	53	32	64	.287	.398	.335
vs. Left-Handers	89	21	2	3	0	8	7	17	.236	.326	.292
vs. Right-Handers	346	104	14	7	4	45	25	47	.301	.416	.347
Home	217	56	12	4	1	23	17	31	.258	.364	.312
Road	218	69	4	6	3	30	15	33	.317	.431	.359
Grass	373	109	15	7	2	45	29	53	.292	.386	.343
Artificial Turf	62	16	1	3	2	8	3	11	.258	.468	.288
April	24	5	0	1	1	4	3	2	.208	.417	.296
May	59	24	4	1	2	11	5	13	.407	.610	.453
June	90	26	3	1	0	8	8	9	.289	.344	.347
July	111	36	6	2	0	16	2	15	.324	.414	.336
August	70	13	2	4	0	7	0	14	.186	.329	.183
Sept./Oct.	81	21	1	1	1	7	14	11	.259	.333	.368
Leading Off Inn.	164	42	4	3	2	2	16	30	.256	.354	.322
Runners On	171	57	9	2	2	51	6	17	.333	.444	.354
Runners/Scor. Pos.	111	37	6	2	0	46	4	15	.333	.423	.353
Runners On/2 Out	60	16	2	2	0	18	2	9	.267	.367	.290
Scor. Pos./2 Out	47	14	1	2	0	17	2	8	.298	.404	.327
Late Inning Pressure	53	15	2	0	0	7	4	11	.283	.321	.333
Leading Off	10	3	0	0	0	0	1	1	.300	.300	.364
Runners On	29	9	2	0	0	7	2	6	.310	.379	.355
Runners/Scor. Pos.	22	7	2	0	0	7	1	5	.318	.409	.348

DRIVING IN RUNS	From 1B	From 2B	From 3B	Scoring Position
Totals	3/114	19/77	27/54	46/131
Percentage	3%	25%	50%	35%
Driving In Runners from 3B with Less than Two Out:			16/27	59%

Loves to face: Kirk McCaskill (3-for-3)
Hates to face: Mike Moore (0-for-6)
Started 103 games last season, 92 as the A's leadoff batter, and 11 in the 9th slot in the batting order. ... Batted .319 before the All-Star break, .257 afterwards. ... Tied for second in the A.L. with 10 triples (Willie Wilson led with 15). ... Had hits in six consecutive at bats with runners on base (June 20–22), one short of longest streak in majors last season. ... Batted .226 in day games, .318 at night. ... Successful on 20 consecutive stolen base attempts from May 27 to August 21. ... Led visiting players with a .500 average at Tiger Stadium last season. ... Born October 12, 1964, the day that Tim McCarver's three-run, 10th-inning homer gave the Cards a 5–2 win over the Yankees in Game 5 of the World Series.

Jim Presley
Seattle Mariners   Bats Right

	AB	H	2B	3B	HR	RRF	BB	SO	BA	SA	OBA
Season	575	142	23	6	24	90	38	157	.247	.433	.296
vs. Left-Handers	190	51	13	1	5	25	12	41	.268	.426	.310
vs. Right-Handers	385	91	10	5	19	65	26	116	.236	.436	.289
Home	288	74	16	4	11	44	13	80	.257	.455	.295
Road	287	68	7	2	13	46	25	77	.237	.411	.297
Grass	221	57	6	1	11	40	19	59	.258	.443	.317
Artificial Turf	354	85	17	5	13	50	19	98	.240	.427	.283
April	88	23	2	1	4	16	4	22	.261	.443	.309
May	101	28	3	2	6	22	7	34	.277	.525	.321
June	104	25	3	2	4	13	5	32	.240	.423	.277
July	90	21	3	0	2	7	1	25	.233	.333	.247
August	109	25	8	1	5	18	9	27	.229	.459	.288
Sept./Oct.	83	20	4	0	3	14	12	17	.241	.398	.337
Leading Off Inn.	119	25	2	2	6	6	7	34	.210	.412	.260
Runners On	268	68	14	3	13	79	20	74	.254	.474	.308
Runners/Scor. Pos.	167	45	10	2	7	66	14	40	.269	.479	.326
Runners On/2 Out	121	36	7	1	9	45	10	31	.298	.595	.356
Scor. Pos./2 Out	84	27	6	1	5	37	8	16	.321	.595	.387
Late Inning Pressure	67	14	0	1	3	9	7	18	.209	.403	.284
Leading Off	15	4	0	0	2	2	2	4	.267	.667	.353
Runners On	28	6	0	1	1	7	3	6	.214	.393	.290
Runners/Scor. Pos.	17	3	0	1	1	7	3	4	.176	.471	.300

DRIVING IN RUNS	From 1B	From 2B	From 3B	Scoring Position
Totals	11/195	32/128	22/69	54/197
Percentage	6%	25%	32%	27%
Driving In Runners from 3B with Less than Two Out:			12/32	38%

Loves to face: Rich Yett (.667, 4-for-6, 2 HR)
Hates to face: Gene Nelson (.071, 1-for-14, 7 SO)
Had his poorest year in the field with career-high 21 errors and career-low .953 fielding percentage. ... But his average of 2.22 assists per nine innings last season was 2d-highest among A.L. third basemen (minimum: 500 innings). ... Homered against every A.L. team except the Royals last season. ... Batting average and HR have declined in every season since 1985: .275, 28 HR; .265, 27 HR; .247, 24 HR. ... Career batting average of .227 in April, .266 thereafter. ... Career average of .329 (27-for-82, 8 HR) at Arlington Stadium. ... Left Tennessee 30 years after another Presley. (No, not Priscilla.) One of his stops on the road to the majors was in Chattanooga, where the Mariners have their AA team.

Kirby Puckett
Minnesota Twins   Bats Right

	AB	H	2B	3B	HR	RRF	BB	SO	BA	SA	OBA
Season	624	207	32	5	28	106	32	91	.332	.534	.367
vs. Left-Handers	177	60	10	4	11	32	11	24	.339	.627	.377
vs. Right-Handers	447	147	22	1	17	74	21	67	.329	.497	.363
Home	309	93	15	2	18	65	19	44	.301	.537	.343
Road	315	114	17	3	10	41	13	47	.362	.530	.390
Grass	241	81	11	1	5	28	10	41	.336	.452	.365
Artificial Turf	383	126	21	4	23	78	22	50	.329	.585	.368
April	82	29	2	1	6	16	6	13	.354	.622	.407
May	115	37	4	0	4	22	4	17	.322	.461	.345
June	102	39	9	2	4	14	8	17	.382	.627	.423
July	98	24	3	1	2	12	6	13	.245	.357	.295
August	112	38	10	0	5	18	4	17	.339	.563	.361
Sept./Oct.	115	40	4	1	7	24	4	14	.348	.583	.374
Leading Off Inn.	113	49	7	0	5	5	4	11	.434	.628	.462
Runners On	285	91	16	3	8	86	18	45	.319	.481	.355
Runners/Scor. Pos.	165	48	6	1	3	70	12	32	.291	.394	.328
Runners On/2 Out	83	27	4	1	2	26	7	16	.325	.470	.378
Scor. Pos./2 Out	60	16	2	0	0	19	2	13	.267	.300	.290
Late Inning Pressure	68	22	4	1	6	15	4	9	.324	.676	.365
Leading Off	19	7	0	0	2	2	1	2	.368	.684	.400
Runners On	29	10	2	1	2	11	3	5	.345	.690	.394
Runners/Scor. Pos.	15	2	0	0	1	8	2	4	.133	.333	.222

DRIVING IN RUNS	From 1B	From 2B	From 3B	Scoring Position
Totals	15/183	23/115	40/78	63/193
Percentage	8%	20%	51%	33%
Driving In Runners from 3B with Less than Two Out:			30/49	61%

Loves to face: Juan Nieves (.684, 13-for-19, 1 HR)
Hates to face: Bob James (0-for-8)
Only major leaguer with 200+ hits and 25+ home runs in both 1986 and 1987. ... Majors' leading hitter on Sundays (.431). ... Set major-league one-season record with 21 indoor home runs in 1987: 18 in Metrodome, three in Kingdome. ... Led majors in batting average on the road. ... Leading hitter against left-handers of any major-league regular since 1975. His .339 mark in 1987 lifted career average to .335. ... Career batting average of .337 with runners on base and two outs. ... Career average of .387 (41-for-106) at Cleveland Stadium is his highest at any ballpark, but it is the only A.L. park in which he has not homered. ... Don't be misled by his 1987 figures. Career average of .330 at Metrodome, .292 on road.

Rey Quinones
Seattle Mariners   Bats Right

	AB	H	2B	3B	HR	RRF	BB	SO	BA	SA	OBA
Season	478	132	18	2	12	57	26	71	.276	.397	.317
vs. Left-Handers	131	38	6	1	4	18	10	19	.290	.443	.345
vs. Right-Handers	347	94	12	1	8	39	16	52	.271	.380	.306
Home	221	73	7	1	7	35	12	25	.330	.466	.372
Road	257	59	11	1	5	22	14	46	.230	.339	.268
Grass	195	47	8	0	4	17	11	34	.241	.344	.280
Artificial Turf	283	85	10	2	8	40	15	37	.300	.435	.342
April	81	24	3	0	2	8	3	10	.296	.407	.318
May	84	22	2	0	4	11	8	14	.262	.429	.323
June	53	13	2	0	1	6	2	8	.245	.340	.273
July	88	28	5	0	3	15	5	12	.318	.477	.358
August	95	23	3	0	0	4	3	15	.242	.274	.273
Sept./Oct.	77	22	3	2	2	13	5	12	.286	.455	.345
Leading Off Inn.	125	34	7	1	5	5	7	26	.272	.464	.311
Runners On	187	59	5	1	4	49	16	21	.316	.417	.367
Runners/Scor. Pos.	112	34	1	1	2	43	12	7	.304	.384	.367
Runners On/2 Out	96	31	2	1	2	24	6	11	.323	.427	.369
Scor. Pos./2 Out	63	19	1	1	0	20	6	3	.302	.349	.371
Late Inning Pressure	67	21	0	1	5	16	6	18	.313	.567	.360
Leading Off	16	2	0	0	0	0	4	6	.125	.125	.300
Runners On	26	14	0	1	3	14	2	5	.538	.962	.533
Runners/Scor. Pos.	15	8	0	1	2	12	2	3	.533	1.067	.526

DRIVING IN RUNS	From 1B	From 2B	From 3B	Scoring Position
Totals	6/131	19/86	20/49	39/135
Percentage	5%	22%	41%	29%
Driving In Runners from 3B with Less than Two Out:			12/18	67%

Loves to face: Charlie Hough (.500, 5-for-10, 4 2B)
Hates to face: Mark Eichhorn (0-for-8)
Started more games in the 8th spot in the batting order than any other player in the A.L. (126). ... Committed 25 errors last season, most in A.L. Fielding percentage over the last two seasons is 2d-lowest among major-league shortstops with at least 150 games (.952). Mariano Duncan ranks last at .943. ... Grounded into 14 double plays in 75 DP situations, 6th-highest rate in A.L. (minimum: 40 opp's). ... Batted 101 points higher at home than on the road, 5th-largest difference in A.L. last season (minimum: 100 AB each way). ... Batting average with runners on base in Late-Inning Pressure Situations is the 4th-highest single-season average under those conditions over the last 13 years. He was 1-for-18 in 1986.

Jamie Quirk
Kansas City Royals — Bats Left

	AB	H	2B	3B	HR	RRF	BB	SO	BA	SA	OBA
Season	296	70	17	0	5	37	28	56	.236	.345	.307
vs. Left-Handers	17	4	1	0	0	2	1	4	.235	.294	.316
vs. Right-Handers	279	66	16	0	5	35	27	52	.237	.348	.307
Home	147	32	11	0	0	13	14	24	.218	.293	.279
Road	149	38	6	0	5	24	14	32	.255	.396	.335
Grass	114	32	5	0	4	23	14	24	.281	.430	.379
Artificial Turf	182	38	12	0	1	14	14	32	.209	.291	.260
April	21	2	2	0	0	4	5	1	.095	.190	.286
May	52	16	2	0	0	2	7	4	.308	.346	.393
June	69	15	3	0	2	6	0	12	.217	.348	.217
July	16	3	1	0	0	0	1	3	.188	.250	.278
August	66	23	6	0	2	19	9	17	.348	.530	.429
Sept./Oct.	72	11	3	0	1	6	6	19	.153	.236	.215
Leading Off Inn.	67	11	3	0	2	2	8	13	.164	.299	.263
Runners On	116	33	10	0	2	34	12	20	.284	.422	.351
Runners/Scor. Pos.	59	16	6	0	2	33	9	8	.271	.475	.347
Runners On/2 Out	58	19	6	0	1	17	6	10	.328	.483	.391
Scor. Pos./2 Out	35	9	4	0	1	17	6	4	.257	.457	.366
Late Inning Pressure	39	13	6	0	0	6	2	6	.333	.487	.381
Leading Off	8	4	3	0	0	0	0	1	.500	.875	.500
Runners On	14	3	2	0	0	6	1	1	.214	.357	.313
Runners/Scor. Pos.	10	3	2	0	0	6	1	1	.300	.500	.364

DRIVING IN RUNS	From 1B	From 2B	From 3B	Scoring Position
Totals	7/92	12/48	13/22	25/70
Percentage	8%	25%	59%	36%
Driving In Runners from 3B with Less than Two Out:		9/10		90%

Loves to face: Moose Haas (.545, 6-for-11)
Hates to face: Dave Stieb (.091, 2-for-22)
Started 88 games, all against right-handed pitchers.... Opponents were successful on 70 percent of stolen base attempts. Larry Owen, who platooned with Quirk, allowed a success rate of only 58 percent.... Three base runners had their only steals of the season with Quirk catching: Larry Herndon, Cecil Cooper, and Rance Mulliniks.... Not a Dome fan: .195 career mark at the Metrodome, .167 at the Kingdome. He did hit a three-run HR off Mike Scott at the Astrodome while with Cardinals in 1983.... Percentage of runners driven in from third base with less than two out was the highest among 301 major-league qualifiers last season. Over the past two seasons, he's driven in 17 of 19 runners in that situation.

Willie Randolph
New York Yankees — Bats Right

	AB	H	2B	3B	HR	RRF	BB	SO	BA	SA	OBA
Season	449	137	24	2	7	68	82	25	.305	.414	.411
vs. Left-Handers	133	44	8	0	3	22	34	7	.331	.459	.467
vs. Right-Handers	316	93	16	2	4	46	48	18	.294	.396	.385
Home	253	74	14	2	3	33	44	12	.292	.399	.395
Road	196	63	10	0	4	35	38	13	.321	.434	.430
Grass	398	117	21	2	6	59	72	23	.294	.402	.400
Artificial Turf	51	20	3	0	1	9	10	2	.392	.510	.492
April	75	21	0	0	0	9	15	3	.280	.333	.407
May	107	32	5	1	3	22	16	6	.299	.449	.386
June	97	36	9	1	1	15	22	9	.371	.515	.487
July	38	9	1	0	0	2	5	1	.237	.263	.326
August	20	4	0	0	0	0	1	2	.200	.200	.238
Sept./Oct.	112	35	5	0	3	20	23	4	.313	.438	.423
Leading Off Inn.	91	26	6	1	0	0	15	6	.286	.374	.387
Runners On	187	61	14	1	5	66	39	9	.326	.492	.430
Runners/Scor. Pos.	114	36	8	1	3	60	27	6	.316	.482	.435
Runners On/2 Out	65	22	4	1	2	21	15	3	.338	.523	.463
Scor. Pos./2 Out	54	17	4	1	2	21	12	3	.315	.537	.439
Late Inning Pressure	55	20	4	0	0	11	10	3	.364	.436	.462
Leading Off	11	2	1	0	0	0	0	0	.182	.273	.182
Runners On	30	11	2	0	0	11	6	2	.367	.433	.472
Runners/Scor. Pos.	20	9	1	0	0	11	3	1	.450	.500	.522

DRIVING IN RUNS	From 1B	From 2B	From 3B	Scoring Position
Totals	7/133	24/102	30/48	54/150
Percentage	5%	24%	63%	36%
Driving In Runners from 3B with Less than Two Out:		23/31		74%

Loves to face: Steve Trout (.406, 13-for-32)
Hates to face: Mike Moore (.111, 2-for-18)
Toughest batter to strike out in A.L. last season, averaging one whiff every 21.7 plate appearances.... Had the best strikeout-to-walk ratio in his career, and he's had some good ones in the past.... Batted over .300 for the first time in his career, but batted under .300 leading off innings for the first time since 1983.... Career average of .320 at Fenway Park.... One of two players in majors to hit .300 or better vs. left-handed pitchers in each of the past four seasons (minimum: 100 AB in each). The other: Kirby Puckett.... Total of 1,638 hits ranks 10th in team history, just ahead of the Scooter. Only five players in Yankees history have reached the 2,000 mark: Gehrig, Ruth, Mantle, DiMaggio, and Berra.

Gary Redus
Chicago White Sox — Bats Right

	AB	H	2B	3B	HR	RRF	BB	SO	BA	SA	OBA
Season	475	112	26	6	12	49	69	90	.236	.392	.328
vs. Left-Handers	201	54	14	3	7	20	35	27	.269	.473	.372
vs. Right-Handers	274	58	12	3	5	29	34	63	.212	.332	.295
Home	238	58	13	3	4	31	34	41	.244	.374	.331
Road	237	54	13	3	8	18	35	49	.228	.409	.326
Grass	395	93	21	5	7	41	56	71	.235	.367	.325
Artificial Turf	80	19	5	1	5	8	13	19	.238	.513	.344
April	73	15	4	1	0	4	14	19	.205	.288	.333
May	95	24	4	2	4	11	14	21	.253	.463	.345
June	51	10	2	0	2	4	7	12	.196	.353	.288
July	80	20	3	2	1	5	9	15	.250	.375	.322
August	91	23	8	1	2	13	14	11	.253	.429	.346
Sept./Oct.	85	20	5	0	3	12	11	12	.235	.400	.316
Leading Off Inn.	134	40	14	1	4	4	20	18	.299	.507	.390
Runners On	171	39	8	0	3	40	27	41	.228	.327	.322
Runners/Scor. Pos.	98	25	6	0	3	39	15	24	.255	.408	.333
Runners On/2 Out	65	18	6	0	2	19	15	13	.277	.462	.413
Scor. Pos./2 Out	47	15	5	0	2	19	5	10	.319	.553	.429
Late Inning Pressure	67	19	3	0	2	6	10	14	.284	.418	.372
Leading Off	17	6	2	0	0	0	4	1	.353	.471	.476
Runners On	29	8	1	0	2	6	4	9	.276	.517	.353
Runners/Scor. Pos.	14	4	0	0	2	6	1	5	.286	.714	.313

DRIVING IN RUNS	From 1B	From 2B	From 3B	Scoring Position
Totals	3/105	12/80	22/41	34/121
Percentage	3%	15%	54%	28%
Driving In Runners from 3B with Less than Two Out:		13/23		57%

Loves to face: Steve Trout (.571, 8-for-14, 1 HR)
Hates to face: Gary Lavelle (0-for-7)
Started 58 of 60 games in which Chicago faced a southpaw starter, 62 of 102 games vs. right-handers.... Established a personal record for stolen bases (52). Batting average leading off innings was also a career high.... Had a higher batting average on artificial turf than on grass fields in each of his six seasons in the majors. Career average: .230 on grass, .256 on plastic.... Has hit between .236 and .254 in each of his five full seasons in majors. That 18-point gap is the narrowest range of any player with at least 250 plate appearances in each of those years. The next four are all N.L. players: Keith Hernandez (23), Mookie Wilson (23), Leon Durham (24), and Ken Oberkfell (25).

Harold Reynolds
Seattle Mariners — Bats Left and Right

	AB	H	2B	3B	HR	RRF	BB	SO	BA	SA	OBA
Season	530	146	31	8	1	43	39	34	.275	.370	.325
vs. Left-Handers	162	45	8	2	1	13	10	14	.278	.370	.320
vs. Right-Handers	368	101	23	6	0	30	29	20	.274	.370	.327
Home	257	60	11	4	1	16	22	15	.233	.319	.296
Road	273	86	20	4	0	27	17	19	.315	.418	.353
Grass	206	66	15	3	0	24	16	11	.320	.422	.366
Artificial Turf	324	80	16	5	1	19	23	23	.247	.336	.298
April	75	22	5	1	0	10	4	6	.293	.387	.325
May	88	25	4	1	0	8	6	3	.284	.352	.326
June	81	19	5	1	0	3	8	6	.235	.321	.311
July	80	21	5	2	1	9	8	7	.263	.413	.333
August	100	34	10	2	0	4	8	4	.340	.480	.385
Sept./Oct.	106	25	2	1	0	9	5	8	.236	.274	.268
Leading Off Inn.	130	34	9	1	0	0	12	10	.262	.346	.329
Runners On	212	55	11	2	0	42	12	10	.259	.330	.296
Runners/Scor. Pos.	111	27	3	1	0	40	7	6	.243	.288	.282
Runners On/2 Out	88	21	4	1	0	14	4	7	.239	.307	.272
Scor. Pos./2 Out	50	10	0	1	0	14	3	5	.200	.240	.245
Late Inning Pressure	73	20	6	1	0	7	6	7	.274	.384	.325
Leading Off	21	5	1	0	0	0	3	3	.238	.286	.333
Runners On	29	8	3	0	0	7	1	2	.276	.379	.290
Runners/Scor. Pos.	17	4	0	0	0	7	0	2	.235	.235	.222

DRIVING IN RUNS	From 1B	From 2B	From 3B	Scoring Position
Totals	2/148	17/88	23/50	40/138
Percentage	1%	19%	46%	29%
Driving In Runners from 3B with Less than Two Out:		16/27		59%

Loves to face: Mike Boddicker (.467, 7-for-15)
Hates to face: Greg Harris (0-for-13)
Broke Rickey Henderson's 7-year reign as A.L. stolen base king. Stole 16 straight without being caught from August 18 to Sept. 15.... Averaged one strikeout every 17.2 plate appearances last season, 2d-best in A.L.... Only A.L. player to increase his batting average by more than 50 points in each of the past two seasons.... Career average of .261 in road games, but only .218 in Seattle. His two career HR were both hit batting right-handed at the Kingdome.... Career average of .160 (8-for-50, 0 XBH) at Comiskey Park.... Started 156 games in the 9th spot in the batting order. That sounded like an all-time record to us, but we found that Alfredo Griffin started 158 games at the bottom of the lineup in 1983. Who knows?

Jim Rice

Boston Red Sox — Bats Right

	AB	H	2B	3B	HR	RRF	BB	SO	BA	SA	OBA
Season	404	112	14	0	13	64	45	77	.277	.408	.357
vs. Left-Handers	123	35	2	0	4	17	16	19	.285	.398	.371
vs. Right-Handers	281	77	12	0	9	47	29	58	.274	.413	.351
Home	190	58	6	0	7	33	24	36	.305	.447	.391
Road	214	54	8	0	6	31	21	41	.252	.374	.326
Grass	330	98	14	0	11	58	36	63	.297	.439	.374
Artificial Turf	74	14	0	0	2	6	9	14	.189	.270	.282
April	70	15	4	0	3	5	8	16	.214	.400	.329
May	58	19	4	0	0	10	8	10	.328	.397	.403
June	103	28	4	0	2	20	10	21	.272	.369	.342
July	93	35	2	0	5	15	6	17	.376	.559	.414
August	32	6	0	0	1	6	4	7	.188	.281	.289
Sept./Oct.	48	9	0	0	2	8	9	6	.188	.313	.322
Leading Off Inn.	100	28	0	0	4	4	12	18	.280	.420	.363
Runners On	215	59	8	0	4	55	24	40	.274	.367	.356
Runners/Scor. Pos.	125	34	4	0	2	49	18	27	.272	.352	.369
Runners On/2 Out	101	24	2	0	1	18	6	19	.238	.287	.294
Scor. Pos./2 Out	64	13	2	0	0	15	4	15	.203	.234	.261
Late Inning Pressure	60	16	1	0	1	8	5	13	.267	.333	.333
Leading Off	11	2	0	0	0	0	1	2	.182	.182	.250
Runners On	30	8	0	0	0	7	3	8	.267	.267	.353
Runners/Scor. Pos.	18	7	0	0	0	7	3	5	.389	.389	.476

DRIVING IN RUNS	From 1B	From 2B	From 3B	Scoring Position
Totals	7/164	19/97	25/53	44/150
Percentage	4%	20%	47%	29%
Driving In Runners from 3B with Less than Two Out:		18/24		75%

Loves to face: Scott McGregor (.429, 18-for-42, 2 HR)
Hates to face: Bill Caudill (0-for-11)

Batting average in July was highest in A.L. . . . Grounded into 22 double plays in 108 double-play situations, 2d-highest rate (.204) in A.L. (minimum: 40 opportunities). . . . Batting average in Late-Inning Pressure Situations has been lower than his overall average in each of the last nine seasons, the longest streak among currently active players. . . . Has hit for a higher average at Fenway than he has in road games in each of his 14 seasons in the majors. Career averages: .325 (one HR per 18.9 AB) at home; .280 (one HR per 22.8 AB) on the road. . . . Only active player with 300+ home runs and career .300+ batting average. Of the 14 other players in history who have done that, all are in the Hall of Fame.

Ernest Riles

Milwaukee Brewers — Bats Left

	AB	H	2B	3B	HR	RRF	BB	SO	BA	SA	OBA
Season	276	72	11	1	4	40	30	47	.261	.351	.329
vs. Left-Handers	57	10	3	0	0	6	6	18	.175	.228	.250
vs. Right-Handers	219	62	8	1	4	34	24	29	.283	.384	.349
Home	133	38	7	1	1	18	19	22	.286	.376	.365
Road	143	34	4	0	3	22	11	25	.238	.329	.293
Grass	244	66	10	1	4	36	25	43	.270	.369	.333
Artificial Turf	32	6	1	0	0	4	5	4	.188	.219	.297
April	0	0	0	0	0	0	0	0	—	—	—
May	0	0	0	0	0	0	0	0	—	—	—
June	8	1	0	0	0	0	0	3	.125	.125	.125
July	99	24	5	0	2	16	13	15	.242	.354	.325
August	78	24	2	0	1	17	4	11	.308	.372	.341
Sept./Oct.	91	23	4	1	1	7	13	18	.253	.352	.340
Leading Off Inn.	54	11	3	1	0	4	4	10	.204	.296	.259
Runners On	134	36	2	0	1	37	11	19	.269	.306	.316
Runners/Scor. Pos.	76	22	1	0	1	37	8	10	.289	.342	.341
Runners On/2 Out	62	23	1	0	1	21	5	7	.371	.435	.418
Scor. Pos./2 Out	44	16	1	0	1	21	3	6	.364	.455	.404
Late Inning Pressure	42	12	4	1	0	4	1	6	.286	.429	.302
Leading Off	12	6	3	1	0	0	1	0	.500	.917	.500
Runners On	21	5	1	0	0	4	1	3	.238	.286	.273
Runners/Scor. Pos.	8	3	0	0	0	4	1	1	.375	.375	.444

DRIVING IN RUNS	From 1B	From 2B	From 3B	Scoring Position
Totals	1/96	13/58	22/39	35/97
Percentage	1%	22%	56%	36%
Driving In Runners from 3B with Less than Two Out:		13/17		76%

Loves to face: Gene Nelson (.556, 5-for-9)
Hates to face: Ed Correa (0-for-9)

Batted 108 points higher against right-handers than he did against southpaws, 4th-largest difference in A.L. last season (minimum: 50 AB each way). Career average of .217 vs. lefties, .283 vs. right-handers. . . . Had played 257 games in the field prior to 1987, all at shortstop. But last season he played 65 games at third base, only 21 at short. . . . Fielding percentage (.935) was 2d-worst of any A.L. third baseman (minimum: 50 games). The Brewskies have now committed 68 errors at third base over the past two seasons. . . . Averaged 1.80 assists per nine innings last season, lowest rate of any A.L. third baseman (minimum: 500 innings). . . . Career batting average of .293 at County Stadium, .241 on the road.

Billy Ripken

Baltimore Orioles — Bats Right

	AB	H	2B	3B	HR	RRF	BB	SO	BA	SA	OBA
Season	234	72	9	0	2	21	21	23	.308	.372	.363
vs. Left-Handers	89	31	4	0	1	8	7	7	.348	.427	.392
vs. Right-Handers	145	41	5	0	1	13	14	16	.283	.338	.346
Home	115	33	3	0	0	6	6	14	.287	.313	.322
Road	119	39	6	0	2	15	15	9	.328	.429	.400
Grass	197	59	7	0	0	11	18	20	.299	.335	.358
Artificial Turf	37	13	2	0	2	10	3	3	.351	.568	.390
April	0	0	0	0	0	0	0	0	—	—	
May	0	0	0	0	0	0	0	0	—	—	
June	0	0	0	0	0	0	0	0	—	—	
July	71	19	3	0	1	7	6	6	.268	.352	.333
August	117	41	4	0	1	12	8	16	.350	.410	.389
Sept./Oct.	46	12	2	0	0	6	6	1	.261	.304	.346
Leading Off Inn.	47	13	2	0	0	4	3	7	.277	.319	.333
Runners On	96	31	2	0	2	21	6	6	.323	.406	.359
Runners/Scor. Pos.	42	13	0	0	2	19	4	5	.310	.452	.362
Runners On/2 Out	38	10	0	0	1	9	2	4	.263	.342	.300
Scor. Pos./2 Out	19	6	0	0	1	9	2	3	.316	.474	.381
Late Inning Pressure	29	6	0	0	0	1	2	4	.207	.207	.258
Leading Off	11	2	0	0	0	0	0	1	.182	.182	.182
Runners On	11	2	0	0	0	1	0	1	.182	.182	.182
Runners/Scor. Pos.	5	0	0	0	0	1	0	0	.000	.000	.000

DRIVING IN RUNS	From 1B	From 2B	From 3B	Scoring Position
Totals	4/77	5/35	10/18	15/53
Percentage	5%	14%	56%	28%
Driving In Runners from 3B with Less than Two Out:		4/6		67%

Loves to face: Paul Kilgus (.750, 3-for-4, 1 BB)
Hates to face: Mike Moore (0-for-4)

One of four A.L. rookies to bat over .300 (minimum: 200 PA). . . . Hitless in his first two games (July 11–12), then wasn't held hitless in consecutive games again until Sept. 11–12. . . . Batted .207 in Late-Inning Pressure Situations, .322 in other situations. . . . Far short of qualification for fielding title, but his percentage (.990) was better than that of A.L. leader Marty Barrett (.988). . . . Only one iron man in this family: Billy missed the Orioles' last 18 games with an ankle injury. . . . One thing in common with big brother: If he ain't startin', he ain't departin'—the bench, that is. Billy played 58 games, all as starting second baseman. Cal hasn't come into a game off the bench since April 18, 1982.

Cal Ripken

Baltimore Orioles — Bats Right

	AB	H	2B	3B	HR	RRF	BB	SO	BA	SA	OBA
Season	624	157	28	3	27	103	81	77	.252	.436	.333
vs. Left-Handers	211	51	15	2	7	25	23	18	.242	.431	.311
vs. Right-Handers	413	106	13	1	20	78	58	59	.257	.438	.344
Home	310	77	12	2	17	54	31	32	.248	.465	.313
Road	314	80	16	1	10	49	50	45	.255	.408	.352
Grass	531	129	20	2	24	90	64	66	.243	.424	.320
Artificial Turf	93	28	8	1	3	13	17	11	.301	.505	.409
April	82	28	6	1	6	23	13	11	.341	.659	.423
May	116	29	6	1	7	18	12	21	.250	.500	.320
June	111	30	4	0	4	12	12	11	.270	.414	.339
July	97	21	4	0	2	16	17	12	.216	.320	.333
August	110	23	3	1	4	20	12	11	.209	.364	.280
Sept./Oct.	108	26	5	0	4	14	15	11	.241	.398	.325
Leading Off Inn.	123	32	4	1	4	4	12	16	.260	.407	.331
Runners On	283	75	15	0	17	93	35	36	.265	.498	.334
Runners/Scor. Pos.	149	42	6	0	14	86	24	20	.282	.604	.359
Runners On/2 Out	100	26	2	0	7	32	12	13	.260	.490	.339
Scor. Pos./2 Out	67	17	2	0	6	30	11	11	.254	.552	.359
Late Inning Pressure	91	18	1	1	1	7	5	14	.198	.264	.237
Leading Off	28	8	0	1	1	1	0	3	.286	.464	.286
Runners On	33	6	0	0	0	6	3	7	.182	.182	.243
Runners/Scor. Pos.	20	3	0	0	0	6	2	4	.150	.150	.217

DRIVING IN RUNS	From 1B	From 2B	From 3B	Scoring Position
Totals	12/213	26/120	38/69	64/189
Percentage	6%	22%	55%	34%
Driving In Runners from 3B with Less than Two Out:		29/41		71%

Loves to face: Gene Nelson (.409, 9-for-22, 2 HR)
Hates to face: Scott Bailes (0-for-10)

Has hit at least 25 HR in each of his six full seasons in the majors, but never more than 28. No other A.L. player has a streak of more than four seasons with 25+ HR. . . . Think it doesn't help to bat in front of Eddie Murray? How often is a 98-RBI man not walked intentionally even once in an entire season? The last time was 1983, when Ripken drove in 102 runs batting in front of Murray. . . . Yearly batting averages since 1983: .318, .304, .282, .282, .252. . . . Streak of 8,243 consecutive innings was ended when he was replaced at shortstop by Ron Washington on September 14. In the following game brother Billy's season was ended with a torn ligament. Do you believe in jinxes?

Ed Romero

Boston Red Sox — Bats Right

	AB	H	2B	3B	HR	RRF	BB	SO	BA	SA	OBA
Season	235	64	5	0	0	15	18	22	.272	.294	.322
vs. Left-Handers	72	11	1	0	0	5	7	9	.153	.167	.225
vs. Right-Handers	163	53	4	0	0	10	11	13	.325	.350	.366
Home	108	32	3	0	0	7	10	10	.296	.324	.353
Road	127	32	2	0	0	8	8	12	.252	.268	.294
Grass	193	55	4	0	0	11	15	18	.285	.306	.335
Artificial Turf	42	9	1	0	0	4	3	4	.214	.238	.261
April	56	16	2	0	0	3	6	7	.286	.321	.355
May	48	14	1	0	0	0	7	5	.292	.313	.382
June	18	6	0	0	0	3	2	0	.333	.333	.400
July	30	9	1	0	0	2	1	4	.300	.333	.323
August	10	1	0	0	0	0	0	1	.100	.100	.100
Sept./Oct.	73	18	1	0	0	7	2	5	.247	.260	.260
Leading Off Inn.	47	11	0	0	0	0	5	6	.234	.234	.308
Runners On	106	29	2	0	0	15	5	7	.274	.292	.301
Runners/Scor. Pos.	56	14	0	0	0	15	3	3	.250	.250	.279
Runners On/2 Out	35	8	0	0	0	10	2	1	.229	.229	.270
Scor. Pos./2 Out	28	8	0	0	0	10	1	1	.286	.286	.310
Late Inning Pressure	40	17	2	0	0	5	1	4	.425	.475	.429
Leading Off	14	3	0	0	0	0	0	2	.214	.214	.214
Runners On	12	6	0	0	0	5	0	2	.500	.500	.462
Runners/Scor. Pos.	9	3	0	0	0	5	0	2	.333	.333	.300

DRIVING IN RUNS	From 1B	From 2B	From 3B	Scoring Position
Totals	0/82	4/43	11/26	15/69
Percentage	0%	9%	42%	22%
Driving In Runners from 3B with Less than Two Out:		4/9		44%

Loves to face: Steve Ontiveros (.667, 4-for-6)
Hates to face: Pete Filson (0-for-12)
Only A.L. player to start at least one game at all four infield positions. . . . Batted 172 points higher against right-handers than he did against southpaws, largest such difference in A.L. last season (minimum: 50 AB each way). He and Cubs' Paul Noce were the only two right-handed batters to hit 100 points higher against right-handed pitchers than they did against lefties. . . . Has hit for a higher average on grass fields than he has on artificial surfaces in each of his nine seasons in the bigs. Career averages: .261 on grass, .204 on the rug. . . . Only active player with sub-.200 batting average at each A.L. dome (minimum: 25 AB in each): .143 at Kingdome, .137 at Metrodome.

Jerry Royster

White Sox/Yankees — Bats Right

	AB	H	2B	3B	HR	RRF	BB	SO	BA	SA	OBA
Season	196	52	13	0	7	28	23	32	.265	.439	.342
vs. Left-Handers	145	39	10	0	5	21	13	19	.269	.441	.325
vs. Right-Handers	51	13	3	0	2	7	10	13	.255	.431	.387
Home	110	30	9	0	3	16	13	16	.273	.436	.349
Road	86	22	4	0	4	12	10	16	.256	.442	.333
Grass	179	48	12	0	7	26	23	29	.268	.453	.351
Artificial Turf	17	4	1	0	0	2	0	3	.235	.294	.235
April	16	3	1	0	0	1	0	2	.188	.250	.278
May	19	5	2	0	2	3	5	5	.263	.684	.400
June	53	14	4	0	2	10	8	10	.264	.453	.355
July	29	9	0	0	2	6	3	3	.310	.517	.375
August	50	10	4	0	1	5	4	9	.200	.340	.259
Sept./Oct.	29	11	2	0	0	4	2	3	.379	.448	.419
Leading Off Inn.	53	17	5	0	2	2	9	8	.321	.528	.419
Runners On	67	16	3	0	1	22	9	10	.239	.328	.321
Runners/Scor. Pos.	34	10	2	0	0	19	8	5	.294	.353	.409
Runners On/2 Out	17	6	2	0	0	7	2	2	.353	.471	.421
Scor. Pos./2 Out	9	4	1	0	0	6	2	1	.444	.556	.545
Late Inning Pressure	31	11	3	0	0	4	4	4	.355	.452	.417
Leading Off	9	6	2	0	0	2	1	1	.667	.889	.727
Runners On	11	3	0	0	0	4	1	1	.273	.273	.308
Runners/Scor. Pos.	6	2	0	0	0	4	0	1	.333	.333	.286

DRIVING IN RUNS	From 1B	From 2B	From 3B	Scoring Position
Totals	2/46	9/28	10/17	19/45
Percentage	4%	32%	59%	42%
Driving In Runners from 3B with Less than Two Out:		8/13		62%

Loves to face: Jeff Reardon (.556, 5-for-9)
Hates to face: Tom Niedenfuer (0-for-9)
Batted .357 (15-for-42) in 18 games with the Yankees. Career average of .395 (17-for-43, 2 HR) at Yankee Stadium. . . . Had batted for a higher average with runners on base than with the bases empty in each of the previous 11 seasons. . . . Nevertheless, last season he drove in more runs (27) in fewer games (73) than he had averaged over the seven-year period from 1980 through 1986 (23 RBI, 93 games per season). Percentage of runners driven in from scoring position was highest of his career. . . . Has played for five different clubs over last 13 years, has hit much better in home games (.272) than road games (.232) during that time. . . . Career average of .260 on grass fields, .228 on artificial surfaces.

Argenis Salazar

Kansas City Royals — Bats Right

	AB	H	2B	3B	HR	RRF	BB	SO	BA	SA	OBA
Season	317	65	7	0	2	21	6	46	.205	.246	.219
vs. Left-Handers	91	18	2	0	2	7	1	15	.198	.286	.207
vs. Right-Handers	226	47	5	0	0	14	5	31	.208	.230	.224
Home	132	24	3	0	1	10	3	12	.182	.227	.200
Road	185	41	4	0	1	11	3	34	.222	.259	.233
Grass	138	32	2	0	1	10	2	21	.232	.268	.241
Artificial Turf	179	33	5	0	1	11	4	25	.184	.229	.202
April	44	13	3	0	0	3	0	3	.295	.364	.289
May	103	23	2	0	2	12	1	15	.223	.301	.231
June	91	13	1	0	0	1	1	13	.143	.154	.152
July	74	15	1	0	0	5	4	13	.203	.216	.244
August	1	1	0	0	0	0	0	0	1.000	1.000	1.000
Sept./Oct.	4	0	0	0	0	0	0	2	.000	.000	.000
Leading Off Inn.	92	16	5	0	0	0	1	10	.174	.228	.183
Runners On	130	26	1	0	1	20	2	18	.200	.231	.211
Runners/Scor. Pos.	77	18	1	0	1	20	1	12	.234	.286	.241
Runners On/2 Out	62	12	1	0	0	7	2	8	.194	.210	.219
Scor. Pos./2 Out	42	8	0	0	0	7	1	6	.190	.214	.209
Late Inning Pressure	28	5	1	0	0	0	0	9	.179	.214	.179
Leading Off	5	1	1	0	0	0	0	2	.200	.400	.200
Runners On	15	2	0	0	0	0	0	4	.133	.133	.133
Runners/Scor. Pos.	7	0	0	0	0	0	0	1	.000	.000	.000

DRIVING IN RUNS	From 1B	From 2B	From 3B	Scoring Position
Totals	0/92	11/62	8/29	19/91
Percentage	0%	18%	28%	21%
Driving In Runners from 3B with Less than Two Out:		7/14		50%

Loves to face: Ken Dayley (3-for-3)
Hates to face: Al Nipper (0-for-8)
Didn't draw his first walk of the 1987 season until May 31, after 150 plate appearances. Only one player in either league had a longer streak at any time last season: his new teammate, Bo Diaz (159). . . . Averaged 3.60 assists per nine innings last season, highest rate of any major-league shortstop (minimum: 500 innings). Royals allowed an average of 4.22 runs per nine innings with Salazar at shortstop, 4.58 with other shortstops. . . . Slugging percentage in home games was the lowest among 162 A.L. qualifiers. On-base average in leadoff situations was also the lowest in A.L. . . . Didn't start for the Royals after July 30. . . . Career average of .253 (and both career HR) vs. left-handed pitchers, .190 vs. right-handers.

Dick Schofield

California Angels — Bats Right

	AB	H	2B	3B	HR	RRF	BB	SO	BA	SA	OBA
Season	479	120	17	3	9	48	37	63	.251	.355	.305
vs. Left-Handers	161	43	8	2	2	14	14	13	.267	.379	.324
vs. Right-Handers	318	77	9	1	7	34	23	50	.242	.343	.296
Home	257	66	6	1	4	26	21	34	.257	.335	.310
Road	222	54	11	2	5	22	16	29	.243	.378	.300
Grass	402	96	12	2	7	39	31	56	.239	.331	.295
Artificial Turf	77	24	5	1	2	9	6	7	.312	.481	.361
April	82	21	1	0	2	10	6	13	.256	.341	.311
May	102	19	4	1	2	9	5	13	.186	.304	.224
June	97	21	3	0	3	15	8	11	.216	.340	.283
July	44	16	1	0	1	4	7	3	.364	.455	.442
August	63	20	6	0	1	7	5	9	.317	.460	.362
Sept./Oct.	91	23	2	2	0	3	6	14	.253	.319	.299
Leading Off Inn.	115	32	2	3	3	8	8	12	.278	.409	.325
Runners On	195	49	7	0	4	43	12	28	.251	.349	.297
Runners/Scor. Pos.	111	29	4	0	4	41	6	19	.261	.405	.298
Runners On/2 Out	86	21	1	0	2	17	5	15	.244	.326	.301
Scor. Pos./2 Out	57	14	0	0	2	17	1	11	.246	.351	.271
Late Inning Pressure	66	11	1	0	0	1	5	9	.167	.182	.233
Leading Off	23	4	0	0	0	0	1	1	.174	.174	.208
Runners On	20	2	0	0	0	1	1	5	.100	.100	.174
Runners/Scor. Pos.	9	0	0	0	0	1	0	2	.000	.000	.091

DRIVING IN RUNS	From 1B	From 2B	From 3B	Scoring Position
Totals	4/126	15/85	20/54	35/139
Percentage	3%	18%	37%	25%
Driving In Runners from 3B with Less than Two Out:		13/26		50%

Loves to face: Charlie Leibrandt (.440, 11-for-25)
Hates to face: Mark Gubicza (0-for-16)
Started in every batting-order slot except the cleanup spot. . . . Ended the season with 41 consecutive errorless games at shortstop. . . . Led A.L. shortstops in fielding percentage (.984); ranked next-to-last in assists per nine innings (2.70). . . . Hitless in 28 straight at bats vs. right-handed pitchers, tying Steve Balboni for longest streak in A.L. last season. . . . Look out Lou Gehrig: Schofield has hit four grand slams over last three seasons. . . . Has homered at every A.L. ballpark except Arlington Stadium (78 career AB) and Exhibition Stadium (65 AB). . . . One of two players to hit below .200 in Late-Inning Pressure Situations in each of last three seasons (minimum: 25 BA in each). The other: Darrell Porter.

Bill Schroeder

Milwaukee Brewers   Bats Right

Milwaukee Brewers	AB	H	2B	3B	HR	RRF	BB	SO	BA	SA	OBA
Season	250	83	12	0	14	42	16	56	.332	.548	.379
vs. Left-Handers	131	45	3	0	8	22	4	38	.344	.550	.368
vs. Right-Handers	119	38	9	0	6	20	12	18	.319	.546	.391
Home	120	42	7	0	5	21	6	28	.350	.533	.386
Road	130	41	5	0	9	21	10	28	.315	.562	.373
Grass	205	68	12	0	9	33	12	47	.332	.522	.377
Artificial Turf	45	15	0	0	5	9	4	9	.333	.667	.388
April	40	13	4	0	1	2	3	9	.325	.500	.357
May	26	5	1	0	1	2	1	8	.192	.346	.222
June	39	18	1	0	2	9	2	6	.462	.641	.512
July	49	17	3	0	4	11	5	13	.347	.653	.407
August	44	14	2	0	2	9	2	8	.318	.500	.362
Sept./Oct.	52	16	1	0	4	9	4	12	.308	.558	.357
Leading Off Inn.	60	18	1	0	4	4	3	14	.300	.517	.333
Runners On	115	40	4	0	8	36	6	25	.348	.591	.390
Runners/Scor. Pos.	71	25	4	0	6	32	5	15	.352	.662	.410
Runners On/2 Out	48	16	2	0	2	12	3	8	.333	.500	.396
Scor. Pos./2 Out	31	11	2	0	2	12	3	5	.355	.613	.444
Late Inning Pressure	27	11	1	0	3	9	4	6	.407	.778	.515
Leading Off	8	5	0	0	2	2	2	2	.625	1.375	.700
Runners On	11	4	0	0	1	7	1	2	.364	.636	.462
Runners/Scor. Pos.	9	3	0	0	0	5	1	2	.333	.333	.455

DRIVING IN RUNS	From 1B	From 2B	From 3B	Scoring Position
Totals	5/79	12/52	11/33	23/85
Percentage	6%	23%	33%	27%
Driving In Runners from 3B with Less than Two Out:		6/14		43%

Loves to face: Steve Farr (.667, 4-for-6, 2 2B, 2 HR)
Hates to face: Bert Blyleven (0-for-10)
Batted 120 points higher in 1987 than in 1986, largest increase of any player in the majors (minimum: 200 AB in both years). . . . Batted .373 in day games, highest average among 162 A.L. qualifiers. But career mark is higher at night (.263) than in the day (.246). . . . Started 42 of 54 games in which the Brewers faced left-handers, 24 of 108 vs. right-handers. . . . Bunt single in sixth inning was Brewers' only hit against Charlie Leibrandt on May 16. . . . Brewers pitchers allowed 5.29 runs per nine innings with Schroeder behind the plate, 4.87 with Surhoff catching. . . . Has homered at every A.L. ballpark except Oakland Coliseum (20 career AB). . . . Career breakdown: .272 with bases empty, .239 with runners on base.

Kevin Seitzer

Kansas City Royals   Bats Right

Kansas City Royals	AB	H	2B	3B	HR	RRF	BB	SO	BA	SA	OBA
Season	641	207	33	8	15	84	80	85	.323	.470	.399
vs. Left-Handers	175	54	6	5	2	13	22	20	.309	.434	.386
vs. Right-Handers	466	153	27	3	13	71	58	65	.328	.483	.404
Home	319	107	21	7	7	48	42	33	.335	.511	.413
Road	322	100	12	1	8	36	38	52	.311	.429	.386
Grass	241	77	8	1	6	29	32	36	.320	.436	.404
Artificial Turf	400	130	25	7	9	55	48	49	.325	.490	.396
April	76	29	3	5	1	13	10	7	.382	.592	.453
May	101	27	4	0	1	11	19	17	.267	.337	.388
June	114	32	3	0	2	9	9	16	.281	.360	.333
July	107	37	13	0	3	16	10	14	.346	.551	.402
August	119	47	5	1	6	21	15	14	.395	.605	.467
Sept./Oct.	124	35	5	2	2	14	17	17	.282	.403	.366
Leading Off Inn.	138	43	5	1	4	12	21	13	.312	.449	.371
Runners On	264	81	14	4	7	76	37	40	.307	.470	.391
Runners/Scor. Pos.	145	45	10	3	2	61	28	25	.310	.462	.420
Runners On/2 Out	87	32	10	1	3	34	17	12	.368	.609	.471
Scor. Pos./2 Out	55	20	7	1	1	27	11	9	.364	.582	.470
Late Inning Pressure	76	26	8	0	0	14	8	10	.342	.447	.400
Leading Off	19	5	2	0	0	1	3	2	.263	.368	.300
Runners On	39	15	5	0	0	14	6	6	.385	.513	.457
Runners/Scor. Pos.	26	10	4	0	0	13	3	5	.385	.538	.433

DRIVING IN RUNS	From 1B	From 2B	From 3B	Scoring Position
Totals	16/169	27/111	26/59	53/170
Percentage	9%	24%	44%	31%
Driving In Runners from 3B with Less than Two Out:		17/36		47%

Loves to face: Richard Dotson (.500, 6-for-12)
Hates to face: Paul Kilgus (0-for-6, 6 ground outs)
First rookie with 200 hits since 1964 when both Tony Oliva (217) and Richie Allen (201) broke in with a bang. . . . Had three hits in four at bats on opening day. His average slipped below .300 only once all year (June 14). . . . Led major-league rookies with a .399 on-base percentage (minimum: 200 PA). . . . Ranked fourth in A.L. with 59 multiple-hit games. . . . Batting average in August was highest in A.L. . . . On the negative side: committed 24 errors, 3d-most in A.L. Royals allowed 4.47 runs per nine innings with Seitzer at third, 3.83 with other third basemen. . . . Career average of .340 leading off innings. . . . Batted .318 during his minor-league career, then hit .323 with the Royals in September 1986.

Larry Sheets

Baltimore Orioles   Bats Left

Baltimore Orioles	AB	H	2B	3B	HR	RRF	BB	SO	BA	SA	OBA
Season	469	148	23	0	31	95	31	67	.316	.563	.358
vs. Left-Handers	145	44	4	0	10	29	8	22	.303	.538	.348
vs. Right-Handers	324	104	19	0	21	66	23	45	.321	.574	.363
Home	241	78	10	0	21	57	20	29	.324	.627	.371
Road	228	70	13	0	10	38	11	38	.307	.496	.344
Grass	411	130	19	0	29	83	26	59	.316	.574	.358
Artificial Turf	58	18	4	0	2	12	5	8	.310	.483	.359
April	28	10	1	0	0	5	3	5	.357	.393	.424
May	81	28	3	0	10	22	5	13	.346	.753	.379
June	78	21	5	0	4	18	6	8	.269	.487	.329
July	78	23	5	0	3	13	4	12	.295	.474	.325
August	93	31	4	0	9	20	7	14	.333	.667	.376
Sept./Oct.	111	35	5	0	5	17	6	15	.315	.495	.353
Leading Off Inn.	113	38	4	0	5	5	6	15	.336	.504	.375
Runners On	208	62	11	0	13	77	9	34	.298	.538	.326
Runners/Scor. Pos.	99	32	4	0	5	57	2	25	.323	.515	.321
Runners On/2 Out	86	26	7	0	3	27	2	17	.302	.488	.318
Scor. Pos./2 Out	49	15	3	0	1	21	1	11	.306	.429	.320
Late Inning Pressure	71	20	2	0	4	15	2	13	.282	.479	.303
Leading Off	20	8	0	0	1	1	0	4	.400	.550	.400
Runners On	28	6	1	0	2	13	0	5	.214	.464	.226
Runners/Scor. Pos.	14	5	0	0	2	12	0	3	.357	.786	.313

DRIVING IN RUNS	From 1B	From 2B	From 3B	Scoring Position
Totals	15/168	22/77	27/53	49/130
Percentage	9%	29%	51%	38%
Driving In Runners from 3B with Less than Two Out:		17/28		61%

Loves to face: Bill Long (.800, 4-for-5, 1 2B, 2 HR)
Hates to face: Walt Terrell (.077, 1-for-13)
Career total of 206 RBI in 1,250 plate appearances. Among active players with 1,000+ PA, only Mattingly and Canseco have more RBI per 100 plate appearances than Sheets. . . . One of six .300-hitters to top the 30-HR mark last season. The others: George Bell, Will Clark, Dwight Evans, Brook Jacoby, and Danny Tartabull. . . . Led the A.L. with a .486 mark (17-for-35) in 10 games vs. White Sox, and with a .406 average (13-for-32) in 10 games vs. Texas. . . . Yearly averages vs. left-handed pitchers since 1985: .118, .154, .303. Prior to 1987, he'd hit 35 HR vs. righties, only one vs. a lefty. . . . Ranks 3d in majors with a .333 batting average during month of May over past three seasons (minimum: 200 AB).

Pat Sheridan

Detroit Tigers   Bats Left

Detroit Tigers	AB	H	2B	3B	HR	RRF	BB	SO	BA	SA	OBA
Season	421	109	19	3	6	51	44	90	.259	.361	.327
vs. Left-Handers	77	15	3	0	0	6	5	24	.195	.234	.250
vs. Right-Handers	344	94	16	3	6	45	39	66	.273	.390	.344
Home	187	52	11	1	3	27	15	45	.278	.396	.324
Road	234	57	8	2	3	24	29	45	.244	.333	.330
Grass	375	98	16	2	6	47	32	82	.261	.363	.317
Artificial Turf	46	11	3	1	0	4	12	8	.239	.348	.397
April	67	19	0	1	0	6	4	7	.284	.313	.324
May	85	26	3	1	2	16	6	24	.306	.435	.351
June	77	22	5	0	1	10	11	18	.286	.390	.371
July	72	17	4	0	0	3	6	16	.236	.292	.295
August	73	20	5	1	3	11	9	17	.274	.493	.349
Sept./Oct.	47	5	2	0	0	5	8	8	.106	.149	.232
Leading Off Inn.	108	28	3	2	3	3	11	20	.259	.407	.333
Runners On	196	53	11	1	2	47	18	45	.270	.367	.324
Runners/Scor. Pos.	116	34	6	0	1	42	15	27	.293	.371	.360
Runners On/2 Out	86	23	4	0	2	25	12	23	.267	.384	.357
Scor. Pos./2 Out	64	18	3	0	1	22	10	15	.281	.375	.378
Late Inning Pressure	44	8	1	0	1	3	2	7	.182	.273	.229
Leading Off	14	4	0	0	1	1	0	1	.286	.500	.333
Runners On	16	3	1	0	0	2	1	4	.188	.250	.222
Runners/Scor. Pos.	9	1	0	0	0	1	1	3	.111	.111	.182

DRIVING IN RUNS	From 1B	From 2B	From 3B	Scoring Position
Totals	6/148	15/92	24/57	39/149
Percentage	4%	16%	42%	26%
Driving In Runners from 3B with Less than Two Out:		14/25		56%

Loves to face: Oil Can Boyd (.429, 9-for-21, 1 HR)
Hates to face: Witts (0-for-10, 8 SO vs. Bobby; 2-for-27, 9 SO vs. Mike)
Caught stealing 13 times in 31 attempts. Career average prior to 1987 was 78 percent (51-for-65). . . . Batted .302 in day games, .238 at night. Career figures: .291 by day, .249 by night. . . . Started 98 of 110 games vs. right-handed pitchers, three of 52 games vs. left-handers. . . . Career batting average of .195 vs. left-handers, .270 vs. right-handers. That 75-point difference is the 4th largest over the last 10 years. Has hit 29 of 30 career HR against right-handers. Only home run vs. a southpaw was hit off Scott McGregor in 1984. . . . Has homered at every A.L. ballpark except Comiskey Park (73 career AB). . . . Played in three of the last four A.L.C.S.

Ruben Sierra

Texas Rangers — Bats Left and Right

	AB	H	2B	3B	HR	RRF	BB	SO	BA	SA	OBA
Season	643	169	35	4	30	111	39	114	.263	.470	.302
vs. Left-Handers	237	59	11	1	12	36	8	32	.249	.456	.267
vs. Right-Handers	406	110	24	3	18	75	31	82	.271	.478	.321
Home	315	87	18	4	15	66	21	54	.276	.502	.323
Road	328	82	17	0	15	45	18	60	.250	.439	.282
Grass	536	141	30	4	25	99	32	93	.263	.474	.301
Artificial Turf	107	28	5	0	5	12	7	21	.262	.449	.304
April	70	15	2	1	3	15	4	15	.214	.400	.263
May	108	31	5	1	4	17	10	25	.287	.463	.342
June	116	32	9	0	3	11	10	16	.276	.431	.336
July	118	35	10	2	8	28	4	20	.297	.619	.317
August	118	30	5	0	9	24	7	22	.254	.525	.287
Sept./Oct.	113	26	4	0	3	16	4	16	.230	.345	.250
Leading Off Inn.	108	28	4	0	3		6	14	.259	.380	.298
Runners On	316	84	23	3	15	96	17	55	.266	.500	.295
Runners/Scor. Pos.	188	45	12	1	10	81	9	41	.239	.473	.262
Runners On/2 Out	116	33	9	0	5	33	4	18	.284	.491	.308
Scor. Pos./2 Out	83	21	3	0	5	30	4	13	.253	.470	.287
Late Inning Pressure	91	22	2	1	4	13	5	17	.242	.418	.281
Leading Off	12	4	1	0	0		1	0	.333	.417	.385
Runners On	50	11	1	1	4	13	2	12	.220	.520	.250
Runners/Scor. Pos.	30	6	1	0	2	8	2	7	.200	.433	.250

DRIVING IN RUNS	From 1B	From 2B	From 3B	Scoring Position
Totals	17/218	26/147	38/86	64/233
Percentage	8%	18%	44%	27%
Driving In Runners from 3B with Less than Two Out:		28/50		56%

Loves to face: Bud Black (.667, 6-for-9, 2 HR)
Hates to face: Juan Berenguer (0-for-8)

The start of his 14-game hitting streak in May coincided with his shift to the 3d slot in the batting order, a spot he occupied virtually for the remainder of the season. . . . Tied George Bell, Jose Canseco, and Gary Gaetti for A.L. lead with 58 RBI after the All-Star break. . . . Tied Jesse Barfield for lead among A.L. outfielders with 17 assists. Recorded at least one assist in four consecutive games (June 9–13). . . . Successful in only 14 of his 33 career stolen base attempts before he found the knack and finished the season with nine straight thefts. . . . Born October 6, 1965. The Twins beat Don Drysdale and the Dodgers that day in the opening game of the World Series. The game's hero was Don Mincher.

Don Slaught

Texas Rangers — Bats Right

	AB	H	2B	3B	HR	RRF	BB	SO	BA	SA	OBA
Season	237	53	15	2	8	16	24	51	.224	.405	.298
vs. Left-Handers	135	32	8	2	6	11	14	28	.237	.459	.313
vs. Right-Handers	102	21	7	0	2	5	10	23	.206	.333	.277
Home	125	32	5	1	5	8	9	21	.256	.432	.311
Road	112	21	10	1	3	8	15	30	.188	.375	.283
Grass	207	46	11	2	8	13	22	41	.222	.411	.300
Artificial Turf	30	7	4	0	0	3	2	10	.233	.367	.281
April	56	15	3	0	3	3	6	12	.268	.482	.339
May	65	12	3	0	3	6	7	18	.185	.369	.264
June	23	3	1	0	0	1	1	6	.130	.174	.167
July	26	6	4	0	2	2	5	5	.231	.385	.286
August	14	3	1	1	0	1	4	4	.214	.429	.389
Sept./Oct.	53	14	3	1	2	3	4	6	.264	.472	.328
Leading Off Inn.	53	15	4	0	4	4	4	12	.283	.585	.333
Runners On	102	19	6	0	1	9	11	21	.186	.275	.272
Runners/Scor. Pos.	56	9	3	0	0	5		16	.161	.214	.254
Runners On/2 Out	43	5	2	0	1	5	7	9	.116	.233	.255
Scor. Pos./2 Out	28	2	1	0	0	2	4	9	.071	.107	.212
Late Inning Pressure	47	12	3	0	1	5	5	10	.255	.383	.327
Leading Off	13	6	1	0	1		1	2	.462	.769	.500
Runners On	23	3	0	0	0	3		6	.130	.130	.231
Runners/Scor. Pos.	12	1	0	0	0	3		5	.083	.083	.267

DRIVING IN RUNS	From 1B	From 2B	From 3B	Scoring Position
Totals	3/77	4/46	1/20	5/66
Percentage	4%	9%	5%	8%
Driving In Runners from 3B with Less than Two Out:		1/7		14%

Loves to face: Matt Young (.571, 12-for-21)
Hates to face: Bert Blyleven (.036, 1-for-28)

Career batting average of .234 with runners in scoring position, 49 points lower than at other times, for the 2d-largest negative margin over last 10 years (minimum: 300 AB with RISP). . . . Rangers allowed 5.03 runs per nine innings with Slaught catching, 5.34 with Geno Petralli behind the plate, and 5.54 with Mike Stanley back there. . . . Drove in only five runners from scoring position in 66 opportunities, lowest rate of the past 13 years (minimum: 50 opp's). . . . Hit for a higher average at home than on the road in each of six major-league seasons. Has hit better vs. lefties than righties in each of the last five. . . . Beaned by Oil Can Boyd on May 17, 1986. Career average of .283 before the beaning, .237 since.

Roy Smalley

Minnesota Twins — Bats Left and Right

	AB	H	2B	3B	HR	RRF	BB	SO	BA	SA	OBA
Season	309	85	16	1	8	34	36	52	.275	.411	.352
vs. Left-Handers	24	6	0	0	1	6	1	4	.250	.375	.280
vs. Right-Handers	285	79	16	1	7	28	35	48	.277	.414	.357
Home	140	38	8	0	5	17	14	26	.271	.436	.342
Road	169	47	8	1	3	17	22	26	.278	.391	.359
Grass	137	38	7	0	3	17	19	21	.277	.394	.363
Artificial Turf	172	47	9	1	5	17	17	31	.273	.424	.342
April	62	17	7	1	2	8	4	9	.274	.516	.313
May	47	14	2	0	0	2	5	9	.298	.340	.377
June	76	29	6	0	3	16	8	7	.382	.579	.440
July	54	9	1	0	0	4	6	12	.167	.185	.250
August	36	7	0	0	3	9	8	7	.194	.444	.356
Sept./Oct.	34	9	0	0	0	1	4	7	.265	.265	.342
Leading Off Inn.	67	22	3	1	2	2	6	7	.328	.493	.384
Runners On	125	30	8	0	3	29	17	21	.240	.376	.329
Runners/Scor. Pos.	67	15	3	0	2	24	12	15	.224	.358	.338
Runners On/2 Out	51	10	4	0	2	16	10	11	.196	.392	.328
Scor. Pos./2 Out	34	7	2	0	2	15	8	8	.206	.441	.357
Late Inning Pressure	46	7	2	0	0	0	4	8	.152	.196	.220
Leading Off	7	3	1	0	0		0	0	.429	.571	.429
Runners On	20	2	1	0	0	2		4	.100	.150	.182
Runners/Scor. Pos.	9	0	0	0	0	2		4	.000	.000	.182

DRIVING IN RUNS	From 1B	From 2B	From 3B	Scoring Position
Totals	7/97	9/53	10/26	19/79
Percentage	7%	17%	38%	24%
Driving In Runners from 3B with Less than Two Out:		4/12		33%

Loves to face: Bob Stanley (.378, 14-for-37, 2 HR)
Hates to face: Walt Terrell (.045, 1-for-22)

Hitless in 25 consecutive at bats with runners on base (July 10 to Sept. 2), 2d-longest streak of its kind in A.L. last season. . . . Started 76 of 110 games in which the Twins faced a right-handed starter, but only one of their 52 games against southpaws. Plate appearances vs. left-handers, year by year since 1982: 223, 221, 92, 86, 69, 26. . . . Played 73 games as a designated hitter, batting .269 in that role. Twins had a 2–8 record in the 10 games that Smalley started in the field (all at third base). . . . Batting average leading off innings was the highest of his career. Career average: .256. . . . Twins' all-time leaders in games played: Killebrew (1,939), Oliva (1,676), Carew (1,635), Allison (1,236), Smalley (1,148).

Cory Snyder

Cleveland Indians — Bats Right

	AB	H	2B	3B	HR	RRF	BB	SO	BA	SA	OBA
Season	577	136	24	2	33	82	31	166	.236	.456	.273
vs. Left-Handers	163	36	12	1	5	19	12	55	.221	.399	.271
vs. Right-Handers	414	100	12	1	28	63	19	111	.242	.478	.274
Home	276	59	12	0	17	42	17	76	.214	.442	.255
Road	301	77	12	2	16	40	14	90	.256	.468	.290
Grass	488	115	22	1	28	66	25	129	.236	.457	.270
Artificial Turf	89	21	2	1	5	16	6	37	.236	.449	.289
April	86	23	5	1	5	11	6	24	.267	.523	.300
May	96	16	2	0	5	14	3	33	.167	.344	.190
June	83	22	2	0	3	11	7	25	.265	.398	.315
July	108	29	8	0	9	25	4	28	.269	.593	.295
August	107	25	5	1	8	15	9	29	.234	.523	.288
Sept./Oct.	97	21	2	0	3	6	4	27	.216	.330	.252
Leading Off Inn.	147	45	7	0	12	12	6	38	.306	.599	.333
Runners On	232	50	12	0	10	59	17	67	.216	.397	.266
Runners/Scor. Pos.	136	26	9	0	3	45	11	42	.191	.324	.242
Runners On/2 Out	117	21	5	0	3	23	7	38	.179	.299	.226
Scor. Pos./2 Out	79	14	4	0	2	14	4	26	.177	.304	.217
Late Inning Pressure	90	25	5	0	7	21	1	23	.278	.567	.283
Leading Off	25	6	0	0	1	1	0	10	.240	.360	.240
Runners On	33	11	3	0	4	18	0	6	.333	.788	.324
Runners/Scor. Pos.	19	6	3	0	1	12	0	5	.316	.632	.300

DRIVING IN RUNS	From 1B	From 2B	From 3B	Scoring Position
Totals	12/172	21/112	16/54	37/166
Percentage	7%	19%	30%	22%
Driving In Runners from 3B with Less than Two Out:		12/24		50%

Loves to face: Mark Williamson (.667, 4-for-6, 1 HR)
Hates to face: Roger Clemens (0-for-9, 9 SO)

Had 43 consecutive hitless at bats with runners on base (Aug. 22–Sept. 22), the longest streak in the majors last season. Was 14-for-53 with bases empty during the streak. . . . Overall batting average dropped 36 points from his rookie season. Breakdown shows a drop of only 10 points vs. right-handers, but a whopping 101-point slide (from .322 in 1986) vs. left-handers. . . . Grounded into three double plays in 98 double-play situations, 4th-lowest rate in A.L. (minimum: 40 opportunities). . . . Career batting average of .198 with two outs and runners in scoring position. . . . Career average of .487 (19-for-39, with five HR) at Memorial Stadium.

Mike Stanley

Bats Right

Texas Rangers	AB	H	2B	3B	HR	RRF	BB	SO	BA	SA	OBA
Season	216	59	8	1	6	38	31	48	.273	.403	.361
vs. Left-Handers	99	28	6	0	2	13	11	20	.283	.404	.354
vs. Right-Handers	117	31	2	1	4	25	20	28	.265	.402	.367
Home	109	35	6	0	3	24	15	21	.321	.459	.402
Road	107	24	2	1	3	14	16	27	.224	.346	.320
Grass	176	51	7	0	6	37	24	35	.290	.432	.371
Artificial Turf	40	8	1	1	0	1	7	13	.200	.275	.319
April	0	0	0	0	0	0	0	0	—	—	—
May	0	0	0	0	0	0	0	0	—	—	—
June	71	23	0	0	2	11	7	14	.324	.408	.385
July	59	17	6	0	2	16	13	13	.288	.492	.419
August	60	14	1	1	2	10	8	16	.233	.383	.310
Sept./Oct.	26	5	1	0	0	1	3	5	.192	.231	.276
Leading Off Inn.	47	12	2	0	1	1	4	10	.255	.362	.314
Runners On	99	29	5	1	3	35	19	22	.293	.455	.393
Runners/Scor. Pos.	54	16	2	1	2	32	15	9	.296	.481	.425
Runners On/2 Out	42	12	2	1	0	10	10	14	.286	.381	.423
Scor. Pos./2 Out	25	8	1	1	0	10	8	6	.320	.440	.485
Late Inning Pressure	20	8	1	0	1	7	2	4	.400	.600	.435
Leading Off	5	2	0	0	0	0	0	0	.400	.400	.400
Runners On	10	5	1	0	1	7	2	3	.500	.900	.538
Runners/Scor. Pos.	3	2	1	0	1	7	2	0	.667	2.000	.667

DRIVING IN RUNS	From 1B	From 2B	From 3B	Scoring Position
Totals	6/66	11/42	15/28	26/70
Percentage	9%	26%	54%	37%
Driving In Runners from 3B with Less than Two Out:			12/16	75%

Loves to face: Frank Viola (.417, 5-for-12, 1 HR)
Hates to face: Ted Higuera (0-for-4)

Opponents stole 76 bases in 86 attempts, a rate of 88.4 percent, the highest against any catcher in majors (minimum: 20 attempts). Of the 10 caught stealing, five were picked off by pitchers, and two others were caught stealing third, leaving only three thrown out by Stanley while trying to steal second: Brian Downing, Paul Molitor, and Ozzie Guillen. Shame on you! . . .Opponents were 16-for-16 against Guzman-Stanley battery, the same against Witt-Stanley. . . . Tied a major-league record by hitting two grand slams in his rookie season. Singled in his only other at bat with bases loaded. . . . Four hits (including a slam) in six at bats as a pinch-hitter. . . . Career average of .310 vs. left-handers, .254 vs. right-handers.

Terry Steinbach

Bats Right

Oakland As	AB	H	2B	3B	HR	RRF	BB	SO	BA	SA	OBA
Season	391	111	16	3	16	58	32	66	.284	.463	.349
vs. Left-Handers	137	40	8	3	5	17	12	22	.292	.504	.359
vs. Right-Handers	254	71	8	0	11	41	20	44	.280	.441	.344
Home	175	41	4	0	6	22	17	24	.234	.360	.308
Road	216	70	12	3	10	36	15	42	.324	.546	.384
Grass	332	98	13	2	16	52	28	55	.295	.491	.358
Artificial Turf	59	13	3	1	0	6	4	11	.220	.305	.303
April	49	11	2	1	2	9	6	10	.224	.429	.304
May	47	19	2	1	2	10	5	5	.404	.617	.472
June	61	14	2	0	2	7	8	10	.230	.361	.319
July	82	24	7	1	4	12	2	15	.293	.549	.310
August	77	23	2	0	2	12	4	14	.299	.403	.356
Sept./Oct.	75	20	1	0	4	8	7	12	.267	.440	.360
Leading Off Inn.	85	24	5	0	3	3	7	14	.282	.447	.358
Runners On	171	54	10	2	6	48	12	30	.316	.503	.368
Runners/Scor. Pos.	88	22	5	0	2	36	9	16	.250	.375	.337
Runners On/2 Out	72	15	2	0	1	14	3	14	.208	.278	.250
Scor. Pos./2 Out	47	9	2	0	1	14	3	8	.191	.298	.255
Late Inning Pressure	61	16	1	0	3	7	6	11	.262	.426	.338
Leading Off	15	5	1	0	0	0	1	4	.333	.400	.412
Runners On	20	6	0	0	1	5	4	2	.300	.450	.417
Runners/Scor. Pos.	9	2	0	0	1	5	4	1	.222	.556	.462

DRIVING IN RUNS	From 1B	From 2B	From 3B	Scoring Position
Totals	11/139	17/70	14/38	31/108
Percentage	8%	24%	37%	29%
Driving In Runners from 3B with Less than Two Out:			11/17	65%

Loves to face: Chris Bosio (.500, 5-for-10, 1 HR)
Hates to face: Jose DeLeon (0-for-8)

Opponents succeeded on only 62 percent of stolen base attempts, compared to 77 percent against Mickey Tettleton. A's allowed 5.31 runs per nine innings with Steinbach behind the plate, 4.36 with Mickey Tettleton catching. . . . Batted .325 in day games, .265 at night. . . . Batted 90 points higher on the road than he did in home games, 4th-largest difference in the league (minimum: 100 AB each way). . . . Hit four HR in 14 at bats at Arlington Stadium. . . . Batted .522 (12-for-23) at County Stadium; .478 (11-for-23, two HR) at Yankee Stadium. . . . Four hits (including two home runs) in seven at bats as a pinch-hitter last season. . . . Drove in 132 runs in 138 games for Huntsville of Southern Association in 1986.

B.J. Surhoff

Bats Left

Milwaukee Brewers	AB	H	2B	3B	HR	RRF	BB	SO	BA	SA	OBA
Season	395	118	22	3	7	68	36	30	.299	.423	.350
vs. Left-Handers	85	27	3	0	2	17	9	6	.318	.424	.379
vs. Right-Handers	310	91	19	3	5	51	27	24	.294	.423	.342
Home	194	61	10	2	5	41	15	13	.314	.464	.355
Road	201	57	12	1	2	27	21	17	.284	.383	.345
Grass	350	107	20	2	6	64	33	25	.306	.426	.358
Artificial Turf	45	11	2	1	1	4	3	5	.244	.400	.286
April	43	11	2	0	2	8	5	6	.256	.442	.327
May	48	12	2	0	0	7	0	6	.250	.292	.245
June	74	26	6	1	3	17	7	5	.351	.581	.402
July	73	21	4	2	1	11	4	3	.288	.438	.316
August	72	22	2	0	0	9	13	5	.306	.333	.407
Sept./Oct.	85	26	6	0	1	16	7	5	.306	.412	.347
Leading Off Inn.	76	20	5	1	2	2	4	5	.263	.434	.300
Runners On	180	60	10	1	4	65	17	14	.333	.467	.374
Runners/Scor. Pos.	106	34	3	1	3	58	13	10	.321	.453	.367
Runners On/2 Out	73	29	3	0	3	31	11	3	.397	.562	.476
Scor. Pos./2 Out	48	19	2	0	2	27	9	2	.396	.563	.491
Late Inning Pressure	67	20	4	0	2	14	5	8	.299	.448	.338
Leading Off	10	4	3	0	1	1	1	2	.400	1.000	.455
Runners On	31	11	0	0	1	13	1	3	.355	.452	.353
Runners/Scor. Pos.	20	7	0	0	1	13	1	2	.350	.500	.348

DRIVING IN RUNS	From 1B	From 2B	From 3B	Scoring Position
Totals	11/146	20/84	30/57	50/141
Percentage	8%	24%	53%	35%
Driving In Runners from 3B with Less than Two Out:			18/30	60%

Loves to face: Jimmy Key (.800, 4-for-5, 1 HR)
Hates to face: Mike Moore (0-for-10)

Opponents were successful on 65 percent of their stolen base attempts. Bill Schroeder, his alternate, allowed a rate of 79 percent. . . . But B. J. committed eight throwing errors on stolen bases, most by any A.L. catcher. . . . How common are throwing errors on stolen bases? In the A.L., 4.6 percent of all stolen-base attempts resulted in SB-E2; in N.L., 4.2 percent. . . . One of five players with six consecutive hits with two outs and runners on base last season; his batting average under those conditions was 2d-highest among 164 A.L. qualifiers. . . . Stole more than twice as many bases as any other A.L. catcher last season (11). The runner-up was teammate Schroeder (5). Benito Santiago led N.L. (21).

Dale Sveum

Bats Left and Right

Milwaukee Brewers	AB	H	2B	3B	HR	RRF	BB	SO	BA	SA	OBA
Season	535	135	27	3	25	98	40	133	.252	.454	.303
vs. Left-Handers	185	53	11	1	11	35	16	46	.286	.535	.338
vs. Right-Handers	350	82	16	2	14	63	24	87	.234	.411	.284
Home	257	67	14	2	9	38	20	68	.261	.436	.314
Road	278	68	13	1	16	60	20	65	.245	.471	.292
Grass	452	118	25	3	23	89	39	112	.261	.482	.318
Artificial Turf	83	17	2	0	2	9	1	21	.205	.301	.214
April	76	21	6	0	2	16	7	22	.276	.434	.337
May	80	16	1	0	3	9	2	28	.200	.325	.214
June	83	18	6	0	2	13	6	21	.217	.361	.267
July	81	21	3	0	7	21	9	15	.259	.556	.337
August	100	26	5	2	5	22	10	20	.260	.510	.322
Sept./Oct.	115	33	5	1	6	17	6	27	.287	.504	.322
Leading Off Inn.	132	31	3	1	6	6	9	36	.235	.409	.289
Runners On	243	68	18	2	14	87	19	53	.276	.539	.322
Runners/Scor. Pos.	145	42	12	1	9	76	15	33	.290	.572	.345
Runners On/2 Out	105	32	9	1	6	38	9	17	.305	.581	.360
Scor. Pos./2 Out	73	22	6	1	5	36	8	14	.301	.616	.370
Late Inning Pressure	81	23	5	0	6	19	3	21	.284	.568	.310
Leading Off	20	3	0	0	1	1	1	7	.150	.300	.190
Runners On	42	14	4	0	4	17	2	12	.333	.714	.364
Runners/Scor. Pos.	23	8	3	0	1	9	2	8	.348	.478	.400

DRIVING IN RUNS	From 1B	From 2B	From 3B	Scoring Position
Totals	15/165	31/116	27/61	58/177
Percentage	8%	27%	44%	33%
Driving In Runners from 3B with Less than Two Out:			17/28	61%

Loves to face: Bill Gullickson (.800, 4-for-5, 2 HR)
Hates to face: Walt Terrell (0-for-10)

Accounted for 58 of Brewers' major-league leading 83 RBI's from the 9th spot in the batting order. Sveum started only 88 games in the nine hole, but his RBI total there was greater than that of 19 teams. . . . Hit six ninth-inning HR, most in majors. . . . Averaged 2.65 assists per nine innings last season, lowest rate among major-league third basemen (minimum: 500 innings). . . . Committed 23 errors, 4th-highest total in A.L. . . . Batted .182 in day games, .284 at night. That 102-point margin was the 3d largest in the A.L. (minimum: 50 AB each way). . . . Career breakdown: .234 with bases empty, .270 with runners on base, .288 with runners in scoring position, .318 with two outs and runners in scoring position.

Pat Tabler

Cleveland Indians   Bats Right

	AB	H	2B	3B	HR	RBI	BB	SO	BA	SA	OBA
Season	553	170	34	3	11	89	51	84	.307	.439	.369
vs. Left-Handers	172	63	14	1	6	35	13	12	.366	.564	.412
vs. Right-Handers	381	107	20	2	5	54	38	72	.281	.383	.350
Home	285	95	21	3	5	48	27	37	.333	.481	.394
Road	268	75	13	0	6	41	24	47	.280	.396	.342
Grass	477	152	33	3	10	82	41	72	.319	.463	.376
Artificial Turf	76	18	1	0	1	7	10	12	.237	.289	.330
April	80	27	8	0	3	14	7	16	.338	.550	.404
May	109	36	9	0	3	20	3	12	.330	.495	.348
June	96	25	6	0	1	13	11	14	.260	.354	.339
July	90	32	4	2	1	9	16	15	.356	.478	.463
August	116	38	6	1	3	28	11	17	.328	.474	.382
Sept./Oct.	62	12	1	0	0	5	3	10	.194	.210	.227
Leading Off Inn.	99	22	7	2	0	0	4	14	.222	.333	.252
Runners On	270	96	13	0	5	83	30	42	.356	.459	.421
Runners/Scor. Pos.	162	62	9	0	4	80	26	25	.383	.512	.459
Runners On/2 Out	113	46	7	0	4	44	11	21	.407	.575	.464
Scor. Pos./2 Out	75	33	5	0	3	42	11	15	.440	.627	.517
Late Inning Pressure	78	25	1	1	0	7	10	13	.321	.359	.400
Leading Off	18	6	1	0	0	0	0	1	.333	.389	.333
Runners On	37	13	0	0	0	7	6	7	.351	.351	.444
Runners/Scor. Pos.	22	8	0	0	0	7	6	3	.364	.364	.483

DRIVING IN RUNS	From 1B	From 2B	From 3B	Scoring Position
Totals	7/172	31/123	40/72	71/195
Percentage	4%	25%	56%	36%

Driving In Runners from 3B with Less than Two Out: 21/30   70%

Loves to face: John Candelaria (5-for-5, 1 HR)
Hates to face: Steve Crawford (0-for-9)

Batted .306 as a designated hitter. Only one other DH cracked the .300 mark (minimum: 100 AB): Paul Molitor.... Hit safely in eight consecutive at bats (Aug. 21–22), longest streak in majors last season.... Yearly batting averages vs. left-handed pitchers since 1984: .283, .312, .333, .366.... Career breakdown: .272 with bases empty, .315 with runners on base, .338 with runners in scoring position. Career average of .527 (29-for-55) with the bases loaded is the highest in baseball over the last 13 years.... One of five major leaguers to have driven in better than 30 percent of runners from scoring position in each of the last five seasons (minimum: 100 opportunities). The others: Brett, Hrbek, Murray, and Winfield.

Danny Tartabull

Kansas City Royals   Bats Right

	AB	H	2B	3B	HR	RBI	BB	SO	BA	SA	OBA
Season	582	180	27	3	34	105	79	136	.309	.541	.390
vs. Left-Handers	149	43	7	2	7	24	25	39	.289	.503	.389
vs. Right-Handers	433	137	20	1	27	81	54	97	.316	.554	.390
Home	282	82	13	2	15	46	42	57	.291	.511	.381
Road	300	98	14	1	19	59	37	79	.327	.570	.398
Grass	233	76	10	0	14	44	27	65	.326	.549	.395
Artificial Turf	349	104	17	3	20	61	52	71	.298	.536	.387
April	76	22	2	0	1	6	5	17	.289	.355	.337
May	88	28	1	0	6	18	10	16	.318	.534	.384
June	94	32	4	1	4	16	13	20	.340	.532	.417
July	98	21	5	1	3	10	14	24	.214	.378	.310
August	111	33	7	0	9	27	17	34	.297	.604	.388
Sept./Oct.	115	44	8	1	11	28	20	25	.383	.757	.474
Leading Off Inn.	136	41	7	2	9	10	14	27	.301	.581	.367
Runners On	288	87	12	1	16	86	38	65	.302	.517	.378
Runners/Scor. Pos.	168	47	7	1	7	68	26	41	.280	.458	.367
Runners On/2 Out	115	25	3	0	8	31	24	28	.217	.452	.353
Scor. Pos./2 Out	73	14	2	0	4	23	19	21	.192	.384	.359
Late Inning Pressure	73	20	5	0	4	14	4	17	.274	.507	.312
Leading Off	18	1	1	0	0	0	1	6	.056	.111	.105
Runners On	38	13	3	0	3	13	2	7	.342	.658	.375
Runners/Scor. Pos.	23	7	1	0	2	11	2	4	.304	.609	.360

DRIVING IN RUNS	From 1B	From 2B	From 3B	Scoring Position
Totals	15/211	19/125	35/76	54/201
Percentage	7%	15%	46%	27%

Driving In Runners from 3B with Less than Two Out: 27/48   56%

Loves to face: Bill Wegman (.500, 8-for-16, 2 HR)
Hates to face: Tom Henke (0-for-8, 5 SO)

Stands tall with Mattingly, Bell, and Dwight Evans as the only .300 hitters with 30+ HR and 100+ RBI last season.... Incentive clauses or what? Batted .405 (15-for-37) with five HR and 14 RBI over the last 10 games of the season. Batting average after September 1 was 2d highest in A.L.... Led the A.L. with 20 home runs after the All-Star break.... Averaged 1.59 putouts per nine innings last season, lowest rate among A.L. right fielders (minimum: 500 innings).... Homered vs. every A.L. ballclub except the Orioles last season. Memorial Stadium is the only A.L. ballpark in which he's never homered.... Career average of one home run per 17.1 at bats vs. right-handed pitchers, one for every 27.5 at bats vs. left-handers.

Mickey Tettleton

Oakland As   Bats Left and Right

	AB	H	2B	3B	HR	RBI	BB	SO	BA	SA	OBA
Season	211	41	3	0	8	26	30	65	.194	.322	.292
vs. Left-Handers	84	18	2	0	2	7	14	19	.214	.310	.323
vs. Right-Handers	127	23	1	0	6	19	16	46	.181	.331	.271
Home	105	23	2	0	5	14	15	35	.219	.381	.311
Road	106	18	1	0	3	12	15	30	.170	.264	.273
Grass	171	35	3	0	7	21	25	54	.205	.345	.303
Artificial Turf	40	6	0	0	1	5	5	11	.150	.225	.244
April	34	3	0	0	0	5	4	15	.088	.088	.184
May	41	10	1	0	1	5	7	12	.244	.341	.354
June	36	6	2	0	1	1	2	10	.167	.306	.211
July	28	9	0	0	2	5	5	9	.321	.536	.412
August	30	7	0	0	3	8	7	8	.233	.533	.368
Sept./Oct.	42	6	0	0	1	2	5	11	.143	.214	.234
Leading Off Inn.	51	11	0	0	1	1	4	9	.216	.275	.273
Runners On	87	19	1	0	4	22	18	27	.218	.368	.346
Runners/Scor. Pos.	51	7	0	0	3	20	12	18	.137	.314	.292
Runners On/2 Out	36	8	0	0	3	11	10	12	.222	.472	.391
Scor. Pos./2 Out	22	4	0	0	3	11	7	8	.182	.591	.379
Late Inning Pressure	23	5	0	0	1	2	4	8	.217	.348	.321
Leading Off	6	2	0	0	0	0	1	2	.333	.333	.429
Runners On	6	1	0	0	0	1	0	2	.167	.167	.143
Runners/Scor. Pos.	2	0	0	0	0	0	0	1	.000	.000	.000

DRIVING IN RUNS	From 1B	From 2B	From 3B	Scoring Position
Totals	3/68	5/40	10/21	15/61
Percentage	4%	13%	48%	25%

Driving In Runners from 3B with Less than Two Out: 6/11   55%

Loves to face: Joel Davis (.600, 3-for-5)
Hates to face: Bert Blyleven (0-for-11)

Every season, the story's the same: Oakland's pitchers perform far better with Tettleton behind the plate than with their other catchers. Over the past four seasons, the A's have allowed an average of 4.32 runs per nine innings with Tettleton, 5.21 with other catchers including Heath, Bathe, Steinbach, and Willard, among others.... Batted .253 in day games, .143 at night. Batting average at night was the lowest among 299 major-league qualifiers. His 70-point difference in career averages (.262 day, .192 night) is the 6th largest in the majors over the last 10 years (minimum: 200 AB each way).... Hitless in 12 career at bats with the bases loaded, but has forced in a run with a walk six times.

Wayne Tolleson

New York Yankees   Bats Left and Right

	AB	H	2B	3B	HR	RBI	BB	SO	BA	SA	OBA
Season	349	77	4	0	1	23	43	72	.221	.241	.306
vs. Left-Handers	106	21	1	0	0	5	18	31	.198	.208	.315
vs. Right-Handers	243	56	3	0	1	18	25	41	.230	.255	.302
Home	152	32	3	0	0	11	23	31	.211	.230	.314
Road	197	45	1	0	1	12	20	41	.228	.249	.300
Grass	290	64	3	0	0	18	36	60	.221	.231	.307
Artificial Turf	59	13	1	0	1	5	7	12	.220	.288	.303
April	66	23	3	0	0	4	6	11	.348	.394	.403
May	90	18	1	0	1	9	13	19	.200	.244	.301
June	85	18	0	0	0	6	12	16	.212	.212	.309
July	76	15	0	0	0	4	7	11	.197	.197	.265
August	22	2	0	0	0	0	4	6	.091	.091	.231
Sept./Oct.	10	1	0	0	0	0	1	3	.100	.100	.182
Leading Off Inn.	85	16	0	0	0	0	12	21	.188	.188	.289
Runners On	133	34	1	0	0	22	17	26	.256	.263	.340
Runners/Scor. Pos.	76	21	1	0	0	22	12	15	.276	.289	.375
Runners On/2 Out	58	10	1	0	0	6	8	12	.172	.190	.273
Scor. Pos./2 Out	33	7	1	0	0	6	6	9	.212	.242	.333
Late Inning Pressure	47	16	0	0	0	5	4	10	.340	.404	.392
Leading Off	16	5	0	0	0	0	4	4	.313	.313	.450
Runners On	16	5	0	0	0	4	0	2	.313	.313	.313
Runners/Scor. Pos.	6	3	0	0	0	4	0	1	.500	.500	.500

DRIVING IN RUNS	From 1B	From 2B	From 3B	Scoring Position
Totals	0/92	9/62	13/34	22/96
Percentage	0%	15%	38%	23%

Driving In Runners from 3B with Less than Two Out: 10/19   53%

Loves to face: Mike Flanagan (.471, 8-for-17, 1 HR)
Hates to face: Mark Langston (.067, 1-for-15)

Begins the 1988 season with a streak of 204 consecutive at bats without an extra-base hit. He's the first player to reach the 200-at bat mark in one season in at least six years.... Has hit for a higher average on grass fields than he has on artificial surfaces in each of the last five seasons. Career figures: .256 on grass, .213 on the rug. ... Career averages of .192 at the Metrodome, .205 at the Kingdome.... Career breakdown: .259 with bases empty, .232 with runners on base, .216 with runners in scoring position, .195 with two out and runners in scoring position.... Most career plate appearances (2,302) of any active player without an intentional walk. Next on that list: Greg Gagne (1,355).

Alan Trammell — Bats Right

Detroit Tigers	AB	H	2B	3B	HR	RRF	BB	SO	BA	SA	OBA
Season	597	205	34	3	28	108	60	47	.343	.551	.402
vs. Left-Handers	214	77	11	1	11	48	24	19	.360	.575	.419
vs. Right-Handers	383	128	23	2	17	60	36	28	.334	.538	.393
Home	296	103	16	0	13	55	27	20	.348	.534	.404
Road	301	102	18	3	15	53	33	27	.339	.568	.401
Grass	506	178	29	1	25	96	49	39	.352	.561	.407
Artificial Turf	91	27	5	2	3	12	11	8	.297	.495	.375
April	51	17	2	0	1	8	2	3	.333	.431	.358
May	103	34	4	0	3	16	7	10	.330	.456	.375
June	109	41	8	1	9	22	12	13	.376	.716	.438
July	94	25	4	0	2	18	8	9	.266	.372	.320
August	113	35	6	1	6	24	12	4	.310	.540	.377
Sept./Oct.	127	53	10	1	7	20	19	8	.417	.677	.490
Leading Off Inn.	132	52	7	1	7	7	9	5	.394	.621	.433
Runners On	298	96	16	2	10	90	35	25	.322	.490	.388
Runners/Scor. Pos.	182	54	10	0	6	77	27	23	.297	.451	.380
Runners On/2 Out	136	46	9	0	6	36	19	10	.338	.537	.419
Scor. Pos./2 Out	73	22	6	0	4	29	14	8	.301	.548	.414
Late Inning Pressure	65	28	3	0	3	18	6	7	.431	.615	.466
Leading Off	15	7	0	0	0	0	1	3	.467	.467	.500
Runners On	36	16	2	0	3	18	2	1	.444	.750	.450
Runners/Scor. Pos.	22	12	1	0	1	13	2	1	.545	.727	.538

DRIVING IN RUNS	From 1B	From 2B	From 3B	Scoring Position
Totals	15/216	32/150	33/65	65/215
Percentage	7%	21%	51%	30%
Driving In Runners from 3B with Less than Two Out:		27/46		59%

Loves to face: Roger Clemens (.440, 11-for-25, 2 HR)
Hates to face: Rob Woodward (0-for-7)

Batted cleanup in every game he started last season after never having batted fourth prior to 1987. Only two other A.L. shortstops batted cleanup even once last season (Ripken and Presley).... Had batting streaks of 18 and 21 games, the only major leaguer to have two separate streaks of 15+ games.... Successful in 21 of 23 stolen base attempts.... Batting average vs. left-handers was highest of his career.... Wasn't this the season the Tigers always expected of Kirk Gibson?... Has batted .330 in Late-Inning Pressure Situations over the past five seasons.... Top career fielding percentages among shortstops active in 1987 (min.: 1,000 games): Ozzie .979, Trammell .975, Burleson .971, Concepcion .970.

Willie Upshaw — Bats Left

Toronto Blue Jays	AB	H	2B	3B	HR	RRF	BB	SO	BA	SA	OBA
Season	512	125	22	4	15	60	58	78	.244	.391	.324
vs. Left-Handers	144	30	6	2	2	18	19	30	.208	.319	.305
vs. Right-Handers	368	95	16	2	13	42	39	48	.258	.418	.332
Home	236	53	9	2	7	26	32	36	.225	.369	.319
Road	276	72	13	2	8	34	26	42	.261	.409	.329
Grass	207	50	8	2	7	25	25	31	.242	.401	.329
Artificial Turf	305	75	14	2	8	35	33	47	.246	.384	.321
April	75	20	3	2	4	12	10	10	.267	.520	.353
May	88	25	6	0	8	13	8	13	.284	.444	.344
June	100	25	7	1	4	14	6	13	.250	.460	.299
July	71	16	2	0	1	6	8	19	.225	.296	.313
August	93	18	1	1	1	9	10	14	.194	.258	.279
Sept./Oct.	85	21	3	0	3	9	16	9	.247	.388	.363
Leading Off Inn.	110	20	3	0	3	3	10	16	.182	.291	.250
Runners On	212	54	11	2	7	52	30	32	.255	.425	.351
Runners/Scor. Pos.	118	31	7	1	3	42	20	21	.263	.415	.367
Runners On/2 Out	90	19	2	0	3	22	20	16	.211	.333	.355
Scor. Pos./2 Out	52	12	1	0	2	19	14	10	.231	.365	.394
Late Inning Pressure	76	20	2	2	0	4	15	12	.263	.342	.391
Leading Off	22	3	0	0	0		3	3	.136	.136	.240
Runners On	27	8	0	1	0	4	6	4	.296	.370	.424
Runners/Scor. Pos.	14	4	0	0	0	3	5	3	.286	.286	.474

DRIVING IN RUNS	From 1B	From 2B	From 3B	Scoring Position
Totals	9/155	18/93	18/46	36/139
Percentage	6%	19%	39%	26%
Driving In Runners from 3B with Less than Two Out:		10/23		43%

Loves to face: Ken Schrom (.379, 11-for-29, 5 HR)
Hates to face: Ron Guidry (.088, 3-for-34)

Started at least one game in every batting-order slot except the cleanup position.... Stole 23 of 28 bases in 1986 (.821), but only 10 of 21 (.476) last season.... Batting average and RBI have decreased in each season since 1983: .306 (104), .278 (84), .275 (65), .251 (60), .244 (58).... Has hit for a higher average on artificial surfaces than he has on grass fields in each of the last seven seasons, longest streak of any active player.... One of three players with at least 500 AB in each of the last five seasons not to ground into 10 DP in any of those years. The others: Brett Butler and Willie Wilson.... Has hit 112 career home runs: 36 with runners on base, 76 with the bases empty.

Dave Valle — Bats Right

Seattle Mariners	AB	H	2B	3B	HR	RRF	BB	SO	BA	SA	OBA
Season	324	83	16	3	12	53	15	46	.256	.435	.292
vs. Left-Handers	148	45	10	3	7	33	9	18	.304	.554	.340
vs. Right-Handers	176	38	6	0	5	20	6	28	.216	.335	.251
Home	180	44	10	0	8	28	8	23	.244	.433	.285
Road	144	39	6	3	4	25	7	23	.271	.438	.301
Grass	111	32	6	1	4	21	6	14	.288	.468	.319
Artificial Turf	213	51	10	2	8	32	9	32	.239	.418	.278
April	32	8	1	0	3	5	2	6	.250	.563	.294
May	43	14	3	0	2	16	2	4	.326	.535	.354
June	42	14	5	3	1	8	4	5	.333	.667	.391
July	61	13	4	0	4	9	3	7	.213	.475	.242
August	76	21	2	0	2	8	0	7	.276	.382	.286
Sept./Oct.	70	13	1	0	0	7	4	17	.186	.200	.240
Leading Off Inn.	66	16	5	0	3	3	2	8	.242	.455	.265
Runners On	145	43	4	1	5	46	9	20	.297	.441	.338
Runners/Scor. Pos.	89	29	4	1	4	44	5	14	.326	.528	.354
Runners On/2 Out	67	22	3	1	2	22	2	9	.328	.493	.348
Scor. Pos./2 Out	46	15	3	1	2	22	1	7	.326	.565	.340
Late Inning Pressure	57	14	3	0	3	6	1	7	.246	.456	.259
Leading Off	11	2	0	0	1	1	0	1	.182	.455	.182
Runners On	21	4	0	0	1	4	0	2	.190	.333	.190
Runners/Scor. Pos.	15	2	0	0	0	4	0	2	.133	.333	.133

DRIVING IN RUNS	From 1B	From 2B	From 3B	Scoring Position
Totals	3/104	20/72	18/42	38/114
Percentage	3%	28%	43%	33%
Driving In Runners from 3B with Less than Two Out:		12/20		60%

Loves to face: Jeff Ballard (.750, 6-for-8, 1 HR)
Hates to face: Jimmy Key (0-for-7)

Drove in the winning run in three consecutive games that he played (May 27–30), something no other A.L. player did last season.... Grounded into 13 double plays in 64 double-play situations, 3d-highest rate (.203) in A.L. (minimum: 40 opportunities).... Batted .209 in day games, .273 at night.... Opponents were successful on only 63 percent of stolen-base attempts, compared with 76 percent rate against his alternate, Scott Bradley.... Career batting average of .297 with runners on base, .216 with bases empty. That 81-point difference is the largest over the last 10 years of any currently active A.L. player.... Career average of .293 vs. left-handers, .223 vs. right-handers.

Greg Walker — Bats Left

Chicago White Sox	AB	H	2B	3B	HR	RRF	BB	SO	BA	SA	OBA
Season	566	145	33	2	27	97	75	112	.256	.465	.346
vs. Left-Handers	210	50	9	0	13	43	22	50	.238	.467	.324
vs. Right-Handers	356	95	24	2	14	54	53	62	.267	.463	.358
Home	273	68	15	1	12	51	43	43	.249	.443	.352
Road	293	77	18	1	15	46	32	69	.263	.485	.339
Grass	477	125	26	1	26	88	65	89	.262	.484	.352
Artificial Turf	89	20	7	1	1	9	10	23	.225	.360	.310
April	70	7	2	1	2	10	7	22	.100	.243	.182
May	96	30	7	1	6	18	10	18	.313	.594	.367
June	89	23	6	0	7	17	16	16	.258	.562	.385
July	90	22	4	0	4	12	12	19	.244	.422	.340
August	102	28	7	0	4	15	17	16	.275	.461	.375
Sept./Oct.	119	35	7	0	4	25	13	21	.294	.454	.368
Leading Off Inn.	111	30	8	0	3	3	17	20	.270	.423	.377
Runners On	257	70	17	2	13	83	42	56	.272	.506	.373
Runners/Scor. Pos.	147	36	8	1	4	62	30	31	.245	.395	.363
Runners On/2 Out	120	33	8	0	6	39	21	22	.275	.492	.387
Scor. Pos./2 Out	74	17	3	0	3	32	16	14	.230	.392	.367
Late Inning Pressure	74	17	5	0	2	11	13	14	.230	.378	.356
Leading Off	9	3	1	0	0	0	2	0	.333	.444	.500
Runners On	37	9	1	0	2	11	6	6	.243	.432	.383
Runners/Scor. Pos.	22	2	0	0	0	7	6	6	.091	.091	.276

DRIVING IN RUNS	From 1B	From 2B	From 3B	Scoring Position
Totals	17/183	24/108	29/69	53/177
Percentage	9%	22%	42%	30%
Driving In Runners from 3B with Less than Two Out:		18/29		62%

Loves to face: Bob Stanley (.615, 8-for-13, 2 2B, 1 3B, 2 HR)
Hates to face: John Cerutti (0-for-10)

Averaged 0.54 assists per nine innings last season, 2d-lowest among A.L. first basemen (minimum: 500 innings).... Drove in 21 runs vs. Texas last season, matching the most by any A.L. player against any particular club. (Jose Canseco drove in 21 vs. Cleveland.).... Started all but 10 games for Chicago last season, including all 102 in which they faced a right-handed starting pitcher.... Career average of .227 (one HR per 29.0 AB) vs. left-handers, .286 (one HR per 20.2 AB) vs. right-handers.... Has hit 50 career HR at Comiskey, 50 HR on the road. Seventh player in White Sox' history to reach the 100-home run plateau.... Career batting average of .261 from April through August, .307 thereafter.

Gary Ward

Bats Right

New York Yankees	AB	H	2B	3B	HR	RRF	BB	SO	BA	SA	OBA
Season	529	131	22	1	16	82	33	101	.248	.384	.291
vs. Left-Handers	197	55	7	0	4	37	12	28	.279	.376	.321
vs. Right-Handers	332	76	15	1	12	45	21	73	.229	.389	.274
Home	259	73	10	0	7	46	15	47	.282	.402	.320
Road	270	58	12	1	9	36	18	54	.215	.367	.263
Grass	454	113	17	0	14	73	25	92	.249	.379	.287
Artificial Turf	75	18	5	1	2	9	8	9	.240	.413	.313
April	78	24	8	0	1	17	4	10	.308	.449	.341
May	99	29	4	0	6	20	9	19	.293	.515	.358
June	111	24	2	0	3	21	4	24	.216	.315	.239
July	78	16	1	0	2	9	9	17	.205	.295	.284
August	86	15	3	0	2	7	1	18	.174	.279	.182
Sept./Oct.	77	23	4	1	2	8	6	13	.299	.455	.349
Leading Off Inn.	119	29	4	0	5	5	7	24	.244	.403	.286
Runners On	244	70	13	0	6	72	15	39	.287	.414	.326
Runners/Scor. Pos.	140	40	7	0	2	61	11	25	.286	.379	.333
Runners On/2 Out	115	26	5	0	2	28	8	16	.226	.322	.282
Scor. Pos./2 Out	74	19	4	0	0	24	7	11	.257	.311	.329
Late Inning Pressure	65	19	4	0	4	12	4	16	.292	.538	.333
Leading Off	16	3	1	0	2	2	0	5	.188	.625	.188
Runners On	25	11	2	0	1	9	0	4	.440	.640	.429
Runners/Scor. Pos.	14	6	1	0	1	9	0	4	.429	.714	.412

DRIVING IN RUNS	From 1B	From 2B	From 3B	Scoring Position
Totals	9/188	28/118	29/63	57/181
Percentage	5%	24%	46%	31%
Driving In Runners from 3B with Less than Two Out:		19/28		68%

Loves to face: Ed Vande Berg (.769, 10-for-13)
Hates to face: Dennis Eckersley (.111, 2-for-18)
For those who thought that the Yankees' depth chart at first base started and ended with Mattingly, it should be noted that New York's backups fielded 242 chances without an error last season. Ward had the most errorless chances (126) of any first baseman in the A.L.... Started at five different positions last season.... Seven consecutive hits in at bats with runners on base (April 13–19) tied three others for longest streak in majors last season.... Career average of .331 at Royals Stadium is his highest at any ballpark.... Batted .266 with 10 HR and 61 RBI before the All-Star break; .218 with six HR and 17 RBI in the second half.... Career averages: April–May, .254; June-July, .282; Aug.–Oct., .304.

Claudell Washington

Bats Left

New York Yankees	AB	H	2B	3B	HR	RRF	BB	SO	BA	SA	OBA
Season	312	87	17	0	9	46	27	54	.279	.420	.336
vs. Left-Handers	61	22	4	0	1	3	8	12	.361	.475	.435
vs. Right-Handers	251	65	13	0	8	43	19	42	.259	.406	.311
Home	144	43	7	0	5	21	14	20	.299	.451	.361
Road	168	44	10	0	4	25	13	34	.262	.393	.315
Grass	255	70	12	0	8	42	25	42	.275	.416	.339
Artificial Turf	57	17	5	0	1	4	2	12	.298	.439	.322
April	25	7	1	0	1	4	3	6	.280	.440	.357
May	44	17	4	0	2	12	1	5	.386	.614	.400
June	57	13	2	0	1	9	8	7	.228	.316	.323
July	83	23	5	0	4	14	8	20	.277	.482	.341
August	72	17	3	0	0	3	6	12	.236	.278	.295
Sept./Oct.	31	10	2	0	1	4	1	4	.323	.484	.344
Leading Off Inn.	97	16	3	0	2	2	5	14	.165	.258	.206
Runners On	122	43	8	0	5	42	13	18	.352	.541	.415
Runners/Scor. Pos.	69	25	5	0	3	36	9	11	.362	.565	.436
Runners On/2 Out	59	22	4	0	2	23	5	7	.373	.542	.422
Scor. Pos./2 Out	41	16	4	0	2	23	4	6	.390	.634	.444
Late Inning Pressure	42	10	0	0	0	1	2	12	.238	.238	.273
Leading Off	8	1	0	0	0	0	1	1	.125	.125	.222
Runners On	12	3	0	0	0	1	1	5	.250	.250	.308
Runners/Scor. Pos.	3	2	0	0	0	1	1	1	.667	.667	.750

DRIVING IN RUNS	From 1B	From 2B	From 3B	Scoring Position
Totals	8/88	18/51	11/27	29/78
Percentage	9%	35%	41%	37%
Driving In Runners from 3B with Less than Two Out:		6/12		50%

Loves to face: Bob Stanley (.529, 9-for-17)
Hates to face: Steve Ontiveros (0-for-7)
Has played 1,438 major-league games in the outfield, and none at any other position. Games in the field, year by year since 1982: 139, 128, 107, 99, 77, 72.... Batting average vs. left-handed pitchers was a career high.... Percentage of runners driven in from scoring position was his highest since 1981.... Stole 10 of 11 bases last season, 4th-best percentage (.909) in A.L. (minimum: 10 SB).... Batted .290 in 73 starts, .190 (4-for-21, one HR) as a pinch-hitter. ... Career average of one home run per 24.3 at bats at Yankee Stadium, his highest rate at any A.L. ballpark.... Has hit 125 of his 139 career home runs against right-handed pitchers. Has never hit a grand slam.

Lou Whitaker

Bats Left

Detroit Tigers	AB	H	2B	3B	HR	RRF	BB	SO	BA	SA	OBA
Season	604	160	38	6	16	63	71	108	.265	.427	.341
vs. Left-Handers	226	49	9	2	4	24	19	47	.217	.327	.279
vs. Right-Handers	378	111	29	4	12	39	52	61	.294	.487	.376
Home	283	74	17	1	10	29	34	50	.261	.435	.341
Road	321	86	21	5	6	34	37	58	.268	.421	.342
Grass	506	133	31	5	14	58	64	90	.263	.427	.345
Artificial Turf	98	27	7	1	2	5	7	18	.276	.429	.321
April	72	18	3	0	1	5	9	14	.250	.333	.333
May	94	26	4	0	7	13	10	20	.277	.543	.346
June	106	28	5	2	1	7	11	19	.264	.377	.331
July	88	22	5	0	2	12	13	14	.250	.375	.343
August	116	33	12	2	3	15	14	20	.284	.500	.361
Sept./Oct.	128	33	9	2	2	11	14	21	.258	.406	.331
Leading Off Inn.	242	81	19	4	5	5	28	43	.335	.508	.406
Runners On	213	44	11	0	7	54	24	40	.207	.357	.282
Runners/Scor. Pos.	124	20	7	0	4	44	14	20	.161	.315	.239
Runners On/2 Out	96	19	5	0	3	19	13	18	.198	.344	.294
Scor. Pos./2 Out	64	9	3	0	2	15	8	13	.141	.281	.236
Late Inning Pressure	69	20	6	0	2	5	3	17	.290	.464	.319
Leading Off	18	9	5	0	1	1	0	3	.500	.944	.500
Runners On	30	5	1	0	0	3	2	10	.167	.200	.219
Runners/Scor. Pos.	17	3	1	0	0	3	1	4	.176	.235	.222

DRIVING IN RUNS	From 1B	From 2B	From 3B	Scoring Position
Totals	9/150	14/94	24/60	38/154
Percentage	6%	15%	40%	25%
Driving In Runners from 3B with Less than Two Out:		20/33		61%

Loves to face: Dave Stewart (.700, 7-for-10, 6 BB)
Hates to face: Ray Searage (0-for-10)
Batted 130 points lower with runners in scoring position than otherwise, largest decrease in the majors last season (minimum: 100 AB each way).... Overall average has declined in every season since 1983: .320, .289, .279, .269, .265. That's true of only three other A.L. players: Jackie Gutierrez, Andre Thornton, and Willie Upshaw.... Batting average leading off innings was highest of his career. Batting averages with runners on base and with runners in scoring position were both career lows.... Career total of 1,412 games played at second base, but not an inning at any other position. Same is true of Alan Trammell's 1,407 games at shortstop.... Whitaker's middle name is Rodman. Can he shoot free throws?

Devon White

Bats Left and Right

California Angels	AB	H	2B	3B	HR	RRF	BB	SO	BA	SA	OBA
Season	639	168	33	5	24	91	39	135	.263	.443	.306
vs. Left-Handers	199	49	9	2	11	27	13	36	.246	.477	.296
vs. Right-Handers	440	119	24	3	13	64	26	99	.270	.427	.311
Home	314	78	14	3	11	42	19	67	.248	.417	.293
Road	325	90	19	2	13	49	20	68	.277	.468	.320
Grass	528	141	26	5	20	78	30	112	.267	.449	.308
Artificial Turf	111	27	7	0	4	13	9	23	.243	.414	.300
April	93	26	4	2	7	14	8	18	.280	.591	.343
May	109	28	6	1	1	8	2	23	.257	.358	.270
June	107	36	7	1	7	25	8	25	.336	.617	.385
July	114	30	7	0	4	22	4	26	.263	.430	.288
August	108	20	5	1	2	14	9	26	.185	.306	.242
Sept./Oct.	108	28	4	0	3	8	8	17	.259	.380	.310
Leading Off Inn.	105	30	7	1	3	3	6	21	.286	.457	.324
Runners On	292	73	12	2	9	76	17	63	.250	.397	.294
Runners/Scor. Pos.	182	46	7	1	6	67	12	40	.253	.401	.299
Runners On/2 Out	110	24	4	1	1	26	6	24	.218	.300	.265
Scor. Pos./2 Out	87	19	3	1	1	26	6	18	.218	.310	.277
Late Inning Pressure	109	25	3	0	7	21	6	27	.229	.450	.276
Leading Off	26	4	2	0	2	2	0	7	.154	.462	.154
Runners On	51	14	0	0	3	17	3	13	.275	.451	.327
Runners/Scor. Pos.	35	12	0	0	3	17	3	9	.343	.600	.410

DRIVING IN RUNS	From 1B	From 2B	From 3B	Scoring Position
Totals	11/195	25/135	31/67	56/202
Percentage	6%	19%	46%	28%
Driving In Runners from 3B with Less than Two Out:		18/30		60%

Loves to face: Greg Harris (.500, 5-for-10)
Hates to face: Rich Yett (0-for-9)
Only player in majors with 20+ home runs and 10+ sacrifice bunts. He had 14 sac bunts.... Became the first player to hit 20 home runs and steal 20 bases in his rookie season since Mitchell Page in 1977. Ellis Burks also did it last season.... Tied for fourth among major-league outfielders with 16 assists. White played only 119 games in right field last season. The three players with more assists (Wilson, Barfield, and Sierra) all had the advantage of playing 150+ games in right field.... Hit one home run per 15.6 AB in Late-Inning Pressure Situations, one homer per 31.2 AB in unpressured at bats. Went 21 consecutive at bats in LIPS without a hit (Aug. 18–Sept. 8), the longest streak in the A.L. last season.

Frank White

Kansas City Royals — Bats Right

	AB	H	2B	3B	HR	RRF	BB	SO	BA	SA	OBA
Season	563	138	32	2	17	83	51	86	.245	.400	.308
vs. Left-Handers	148	42	10	0	5	22	15	18	.284	.453	.352
vs. Right-Handers	415	96	22	2	12	61	36	68	.231	.381	.292
Home	256	70	19	0	6	42	33	33	.273	.418	.355
Road	307	68	13	2	11	41	18	53	.221	.384	.267
Grass	242	55	11	1	10	34	16	38	.227	.405	.277
Artificial Turf	321	83	21	1	7	49	35	48	.259	.396	.331
April	73	15	2	0	2	11	9	8	.205	.315	.293
May	93	23	8	0	3	14	10	15	.247	.430	.320
June	94	24	3	1	1	16	8	18	.255	.340	.302
July	93	21	4	0	2	8	10	17	.226	.333	.301
August	108	30	9	0	5	21	8	15	.278	.500	.333
Sept./Oct.	102	25	6	1	4	13	6	13	.245	.441	.294
Leading Off Inn.	127	28	5	0	5	5	10	18	.220	.378	.277
Runners On	264	71	19	1	6	72	27	37	.269	.417	.334
Runners/Scor. Pos.	158	41	14	0	4	66	19	24	.259	.424	.331
Runners On/2 Out	114	25	6	1	2	28	15	17	.219	.342	.310
Scor. Pos./2 Out	79	18	6	0	2	27	12	12	.228	.380	.330
Late Inning Pressure	65	12	2	0	2	7	8	7	.185	.308	.274
Leading Off	18	2	0	0	0	0	2	2	.111	.111	.200
Runners On	27	6	1	0	1	6	4	2	.222	.370	.323
Runners/Scor. Pos.	20	4	1	0	1	6	3	2	.200	.400	.304

DRIVING IN RUNS	From 1B	From 2B	From 3B	Scoring Position
Totals	12/204	22/119	32/74	54/193
Percentage	6%	18%	43%	28%
Driving In Runners from 3B with Less than Two Out:		20/35		57%

Loves to face: Mike Morgan (.500, 14-for-28, 1 HR)
Hates to face: Dennis Eckersley (.091, 4-for-44)
Lowest batting average since 1976. . . . Committed 10 errors last season, but made six during a 22-game stretch (Aug. 30–Sept. 22). . . . For fourth straight season, set a new career high in walks. . . . Compare last season's totals to 88 strikeouts in 566 at bats in 1986; 86 in 563 in 1985. . . . Hits in seven consecutive at bats with runners on base (May 15–19) tied him for longest streak in majors last season. . . . The only A.L. player to have hit a grand slam in each of the last four seasons. . . . Career average of .478 (11-for-23, one HR) at Fenway Park. . . . Only one home run in 231 AB at Yankee Stadium. . . . Royals' all-time leader in games played (1,957). He passed Hal McRae and Amos Otis in 1987 to earn that distinction.

Ernie Whitt

Toronto Blue Jays — Bats Left

	AB	H	2B	3B	HR	RRF	BB	SO	BA	SA	OBA
Season	446	120	24	1	19	76	44	50	.269	.455	.334
vs. Left-Handers	63	15	3	0	0	8	6	15	.238	.286	.314
vs. Right-Handers	383	105	21	1	19	68	38	35	.274	.483	.337
Home	214	56	12	1	11	44	25	29	.262	.481	.337
Road	232	64	12	0	8	32	19	21	.276	.431	.329
Grass	177	45	7	0	4	21	13	16	.254	.362	.304
Artificial Turf	269	75	17	1	15	55	31	34	.279	.517	.353
April	49	13	3	0	1	7	9	3	.265	.388	.367
May	83	22	8	0	2	9	6	7	.265	.434	.315
June	66	14	3	0	2	12	6	12	.212	.348	.278
July	70	20	2	0	3	11	6	14	.286	.443	.342
August	93	32	5	1	3	16	8	7	.344	.516	.402
Sept./Oct.	85	19	3	0	8	21	9	7	.224	.541	.295
Leading Off Inn.	92	27	7	0	4	4	2	11	.293	.500	.309
Runners On	212	56	11	1	10	67	24	24	.264	.467	.335
Runners/Scor. Pos.	125	34	7	1	6	57	16	17	.272	.488	.347
Runners On/2 Out	89	23	4	1	3	28	12	11	.258	.427	.347
Scor. Pos./2 Out	64	16	4	1	2	26	8	9	.250	.438	.333
Late Inning Pressure	67	16	5	0	1	10	8	10	.239	.358	.312
Leading Off	13	3	1	0	0	0	0	1	.231	.308	.231
Runners On	33	6	3	0	0	9	5	5	.182	.273	.275
Runners/Scor. Pos.	15	4	3	0	0	9	3	2	.267	.467	.350

DRIVING IN RUNS	From 1B	From 2B	From 3B	Scoring Position
Totals	11/152	18/91	28/57	46/148
Percentage	7%	20%	49%	31%
Driving In Runners from 3B with Less than Two Out:		16/26		62%

Loves to face: Richard Dotson (.362, 17-for-47, 4 HR)
Hates to face: Tommy John (.077, 1-for-13)
Opponents succeeded on only 64 percent of stolen-base tries. Against Blue Jays backups Moore and Stark, the rate was 82 percent, but Jeff DeWillis threw out four of nine. . . . Started 110 of 112 games in which the Blue Jays faced right-handed starters, but only three of 50 games against southpaws. . . . Career average of .229 (one HR per 65.5 AB) vs. left-handers, .255 (one HR per 23.8 AB) vs. right-handers. . . . Has hit at least 10 but never 20 home runs in each of last six years, tying Carney Lansford for longest current streak of its kind in majors. . . . Career average of .349 (30-for-86, 4 HR) at Yankee Stadium. . . . Has caught in 929 games, and never played an inning at another position.

Alan Wiggins

Baltimore Orioles — Bats Left and Right

	AB	H	2B	3B	HR	RRF	BB	SO	BA	SA	OBA
Season	306	71	4	2	1	15	28	34	.232	.268	.298
vs. Left-Handers	130	30	2	0	0	6	6	15	.231	.246	.268
vs. Right-Handers	176	41	2	2	1	9	22	19	.233	.284	.318
Home	117	27	2	0	0	5	9	13	.231	.248	.286
Road	189	44	2	2	1	10	19	21	.233	.280	.305
Grass	231	58	3	2	1	10	17	26	.251	.294	.302
Artificial Turf	75	13	1	0	0	5	11	8	.173	.187	.284
April	70	22	2	0	1	5	8	9	.314	.386	.385
May	78	19	1	2	0	4	6	4	.244	.308	.294
June	59	11	1	0	0	3	4	9	.186	.203	.226
July	71	13	0	0	0	6	10	14	.183	.183	.284
August	28	6	0	0	0	1	3	.214	.214	.267
Sept./Oct.	0	0	0	0	0	0	0	—	—	—
Leading Off Inn.	115	20	1	0	0	0	10	13	.174	.183	.246
Runners On	116	27	1	2	0	14	8	13	.233	.276	.280
Runners/Scor. Pos.	61	13	1	1	0	13	3	6	.213	.262	.246
Runners On/2 Out	40	10	0	1	0	4	4	5	.250	.300	.318
Scor. Pos./2 Out	22	6	0	1	0	4	2	2	.273	.364	.333
Late Inning Pressure	41	11	0	0	0	0	2	4	.268	.268	.302
Leading Off	9	4	0	0	0	0	0	1	.444	.444	.444
Runners On	17	3	0	0	0	0	1	3	.176	.176	.222
Runners/Scor. Pos.	4	1	0	0	0	0	0	0	.250	.250	.250

DRIVING IN RUNS	From 1B	From 2B	From 3B	Scoring Position
Totals	1/85	4/47	9/22	13/69
Percentage	1%	9%	41%	19%
Driving In Runners from 3B with Less than Two Out:		6/13		46%

Loves to face: Frank Viola (.450, 9-for-20)
Hates to face: Tom Candiotti (0-for-10)
Wiggins started only 14 games (13 as DH, one in LF) after the All-Star break, playing his last game for Baltimore on August 28. He was suspended by the Commissioner on August 31. . . . Didn't start a game at second base after Billy Ripken joined the Orioles. . . . Played five games in the outfield, his first since 1983 when he played 108 games there. . . . Hitless in 25 consecutive at bats with runners on base (May 9 to June 16), 2d-longest streak in A.L. last season. . . . Lone 1987 home run was hit off of Cleveland's Doug Jones. It was only the fifth of Wiggins's career, and his first against a right-handed pitcher. . . . One hit in 19 career at bats at Fenway Park.

Ken Williams

Chicago White Sox — Bats Right

	AB	H	2B	3B	HR	RRF	BB	SO	BA	SA	OBA
Season	391	110	18	2	11	53	10	83	.281	.422	.314
vs. Left-Handers	159	47	7	1	8	24	3	39	.296	.503	.319
vs. Right-Handers	232	63	11	1	3	29	7	44	.272	.366	.310
Home	193	63	13	1	4	29	5	37	.326	.466	.358
Road	198	47	5	1	7	24	4	46	.237	.379	.271
Grass	345	100	17	2	10	52	8	75	.290	.438	.319
Artificial Turf	46	10	1	0	1	1	2	8	.217	.304	.280
April	0	0	0	0	0	0	0	0			
May	32	9	2	0	1	3	0	5	.281	.438	.324
June	78	25	6	0	2	13	2	17	.321	.474	.354
July	83	18	3	1	2	12	3	18	.217	.349	.258
August	94	32	5	0	3	16	1	14	.340	.489	.354
Sept./Oct.	104	26	2	1	3	9	4	29	.250	.375	.291
Leading Off Inn.	74	14	3	0	3	3	1	11	.189	.351	.211
Runners On	177	49	9	2	5	47	7	46	.277	.435	.317
Runners/Scor. Pos.	97	26	5	1	1	35	6	30	.268	.371	.321
Runners On/2 Out	80	22	4	1	3	24	3	22	.275	.463	.318
Scor. Pos./2 Out	52	14	3	0	0	16	2	15	.269	.327	.309
Late Inning Pressure	48	11	3	0	1	5	1	18	.229	.354	.269
Leading Off	12	2	1	0	1	1	0	3	.167	.500	.231
Runners On	24	3	2	0	0	4	1	12	.125	.208	.154
Runners/Scor. Pos.	20	3	2	0	0	4	0	10	.150	.250	.143

DRIVING IN RUNS	From 1B	From 2B	From 3B	Scoring Position
Totals	9/126	18/74	15/40	33/114
Percentage	7%	24%	38%	29%
Driving In Runners from 3B with Less than Two Out:		10/18		56%

Loves to face: Bruce Hurst (.500, 5-for-10)
Hates to face: Ron Guidry (0-for-6, 4 SO)
Averaged 2.86 putouts per nine innings last season, 3d-highest rate in A.L. (minimum: 500 innings). . . . Struck out 20 times last season before drawing his first walk on June 20. . . . One of five players to collect six consecutive hits with two outs and runners on base (Aug. 18–30) last season. . . . Nine rookies (eight of them in the A.L.) started more games than Williams (107) last season. . . . Career average of .328 (five HR) at Comiskey Park, .219 (7 HR) on the road. . . . Tied for sixth among A.L. rookies with 21 stolen bases. . . . First Williams with a neck to wear a White Sox uniform since Claude ("Lefty") Williams who pitched for the Sox from 1916 through 1920.

Willie Wilson
Kansas City Royals — Bats Left and Right

	AB	H	2B	3B	HR	RRF	BB	SO	BA	SA	OBA
Season	610	170	18	15	4	31	32	88	.279	.377	.320
vs. Left-Handers	170	41	5	2	1	11	7	35	.241	.312	.270
vs. Right-Handers	440	129	13	13	3	20	25	53	.293	.402	.340
Home	321	95	13	10	0	19	17	40	.296	.399	.334
Road	289	75	5	5	4	12	15	48	.260	.353	.305
Grass	214	54	4	3	3	10	13	36	.252	.341	.304
Artificial Turf	396	116	14	12	1	21	19	52	.293	.396	.329
April	77	18	2	2	0	3	2	8	.234	.312	.272
May	79	28	2	3	1	4	4	11	.354	.494	.400
June	119	32	3	0	2	3	3	18	.269	.345	.287
July	103	28	4	6	0	4	5	17	.272	.427	.306
August	107	29	3	1	1	5	11	16	.271	.346	.304
Sept./Oct.	125	35	4	3	0	12	7	18	.280	.360	.321
Leading Off Inn.	238	72	3	7	2	2	15	38	.303	.399	.349
Runners On	199	54	9	5	0	27	11	24	.271	.367	.318
Runners/Scor. Pos.	97	24	5	4	0	26	8	14	.247	.381	.308
Runners On/2 Out	97	23	3	5	0	12	5	12	.237	.371	.282
Scor. Pos./2 Out	57	12	1	4	0	11	4	8	.211	.368	.274
Late Inning Pressure	72	25	3	4	0	5	4	11	.347	.500	.382
Leading Off	17	4	0	0	0		2	5	.235	.235	.316
Runners On	36	12	2	2	0	5	1	3	.333	.500	.351
Runners/Scor. Pos.	18	5	1	1	0	4	1	2	.278	.444	.316

DRIVING IN RUNS	From 1B	From 2B	From 3B	Scoring Position
Totals	2/149	16/78	9/30	25/108
Percentage	1%	21%	30%	23%
Driving In Runners from 3B with Less than Two Out:			7/11	64%

Loves to face: Storm Davis (.452, 14-for-31)
Hates to face: Steve Ontiveros (0-for-11)
Has the most hits (1,387) of anyone in the 1980s. Closest pursuers: Robin Yount, 1,346; Keith Hernandez, 1,334; Bill Buckner, 1,328; Eddie Murray, 1,324. . . . Started 144 games as the Royals' leadoff batter. . . . Averaged one walk per 20.4 plate appearances, 5th-lowest rate in A.L. . . . Hit safely in six consecutive at bats in Late-Inning Pressure Situations (Apr. 29–May 13), tying Tony Fernandez for longest streak in A.L. last season. . . . Hitless in six at bats with the bases loaded; career average: .206. . . . Led A.L. in steals only once, but is one of five players in baseball history to have stolen 30 or more bases in 10 consecutive years: Brock (14 years), Cobb (12), Wagner (11), Campaneris (10), Wilson (10).

Dave Winfield
New York Yankees — Bats Right

	AB	H	2B	3B	HR	RRF	BB	SO	BA	SA	OBA
Season	575	158	22	1	27	104	76	96	.275	.457	.358
vs. Left-Handers	177	61	10	0	13	38	35	26	.345	.621	.449
vs. Right-Handers	398	97	12	1	14	66	41	70	.244	.384	.314
Home	269	76	12	0	11	48	41	39	.283	.450	.374
Road	306	82	10	1	16	56	35	57	.268	.464	.343
Grass	481	133	19	1	23	85	68	76	.277	.464	.364
Artificial Turf	94	25	3	0	4	19	8	20	.266	.426	.324
April	73	25	2	0	4	17	19	11	.342	.534	.478
May	104	26	4	1	7	23	11	21	.250	.510	.322
June	102	32	6	0	7	25	14	14	.314	.578	.397
July	89	21	3	0	3	14	11	18	.236	.371	.317
August	94	23	3	0	2	11	11	12	.245	.340	.321
Sept./Oct.	113	31	4	0	4	14	10	20	.274	.416	.331
Leading Off Inn.	139	33	3	0	8	8	13	23	.237	.432	.303
Runners On	259	83	13	0	10	87	38	39	.320	.486	.403
Runners/Scor. Pos.	152	54	8	0	7	78	24	17	.355	.546	.436
Runners On/2 Out	114	35	5	0	7	41	20	18	.307	.535	.410
Scor. Pos./2 Out	72	24	3	0	5	35	10	9	.333	.583	.415
Late Inning Pressure	77	20	3	0	3	18	7	10	.260	.416	.321
Leading Off	20	2	0	0	0	0	1	3	.100	.100	.143
Runners On	30	13	2	0	3	18	6	3	.433	.800	.528
Runners/Scor. Pos.	16	8	2	0	2	16	5	1	.500	1.000	.619

DRIVING IN RUNS	From 1B	From 2B	From 3B	Scoring Position
Totals	10/187	36/112	31/70	67/182
Percentage	5%	32%	44%	37%
Driving In Runners from 3B with Less than Two Out:			24/40	60%

Loves to face: Mike Moore (.647, 11-for-17, 2 HR)
Hates to face: Bobby Witt (0-for-8)
Fell three RBI short of his sixth consecutive 100-RBI season. Blame it on Mattingly, whose six grand salamis meant 12 runners in scoring position that Winny never saw. . . . Batted 109 points higher with runners in scoring position than he did otherwise. He's batted .300 or better with RISP in six of the last nine seasons. . . . Batted 101 points higher against left-handers than against righties, 2d-largest difference among everyday players in A.L. last season. . . . Career assist leaders among active outfielders: Winfield 146, Dwight Evans 142, Parker 140. . . . Batting average in Late-Inning Pressure Situations has been lower than his overall average in each of his last seven seasons with the Yankees.

Mike Young
Baltimore Orioles — Bats Left and Right

	AB	H	2B	3B	HR	RRF	BB	SO	BA	SA	OBA
Season	363	87	10	1	16	40	46	91	.240	.405	.328
vs. Left-Handers	144	34	2	0	5	14	21	37	.236	.354	.341
vs. Right-Handers	219	53	8	1	11	26	25	54	.242	.438	.318
Home	190	45	4	1	11	27	24	43	.237	.442	.327
Road	173	42	6	0	5	13	22	48	.243	.364	.328
Grass	318	77	8	1	15	38	42	82	.242	.415	.333
Artificial Turf	45	10	2	0	1	2	4	9	.222	.333	.286
April	0	0	0	0	0	0	0	0	—		
May	33	8	0	0	2	3	9	12	.242	.424	.405
June	101	29	2	1	5	16	12	21	.287	.475	.365
July	74	16	1	0	5	10	8	15	.216	.432	.293
August	82	18	3	0	1	4	10	23	.220	.293	.312
Sept./Oct.	73	16	4	0	3	7	7	20	.219	.397	.288
Leading Off Inn.	103	23	1	0	2	2	11	25	.223	.291	.310
Runners On	155	36	4	0	8	32	22	40	.232	.413	.326
Runners/Scor. Pos.	70	10	3	0	3	22	11	17	.143	.314	.256
Runners On/2 Out	62	10	1	0	1	6	10	20	.161	.226	.278
Scor. Pos./2 Out	35	3	0	0	0	4	7	10	.086	.086	.238
Late Inning Pressure	60	16	2	0	4	9	5	17	.267	.500	.323
Leading Off	19	7	1	0	1	1	1	4	.368	.579	.400
Runners On	22	6	1	0	2	7	2	5	.273	.591	.333
Runners/Scor. Pos.	9	2	1	0	1	5	2	2	.222	.667	.364

DRIVING IN RUNS	From 1B	From 2B	From 3B	Scoring Position
Totals	6/117	9/62	9/20	18/82
Percentage	5%	15%	45%	22%
Driving In Runners from 3B with Less than Two Out:			6/9	67%

Loves to face: Curt Young (.438, 7-for-16, 3 HR)
Hates to face: Doyle Alexander (0-for-11)
Loves the great outdoors: Has homered at every outdoor ballpark in A.L., but not at either the Kingdome (61 career AB) or the Metrodome (54). . . . Hit 60 points better in day games (.288) than at night (.228) last season. Previous career marks: day, 229; night, .269. . . . Didn't have a single assist in 60 games in the outfield last season; has now thrown out one base runner in his last 291 games. . . . Percentage of runners driven in from scoring position has declined in every season since 1984. . . . Batting averages with two outs and runners in scoring position, year by year since 1984: .225, .215, .182, .086. Career mark: .181. . . . If you're not getting the picture, his star is not exactly on the rise is what we mean.

Robin Yount
Milwaukee Brewers — Bats Right

	AB	H	2B	3B	HR	RRF	BB	SO	BA	SA	OBA
Season	635	198	25	9	21	105	76	94	.312	.479	.384
vs. Left-Handers	195	53	9	2	2	22	20	28	.272	.369	.336
vs. Right-Handers	440	145	16	7	19	83	56	66	.330	.527	.404
Home	311	110	13	6	12	64	37	47	.354	.550	.422
Road	324	88	12	3	9	41	39	47	.272	.410	.347
Grass	531	170	21	7	20	96	66	76	.320	.499	.393
Artificial Turf	104	28	4	2	1	9	10	18	.269	.375	.333
April	86	24	3	1	2	16	10	13	.279	.407	.354
May	92	27	5	1	4	6	12	21	.293	.500	.371
June	97	31	4	1	3	18	12	16	.320	.474	.391
July	114	41	5	3	6	23	12	19	.360	.614	.422
August	116	35	3	1	1	16	13	14	.302	.371	.366
Sept./Oct.	130	40	5	2	5	26	17	17	.308	.492	.388
Leading Off Inn.	118	30	6	2	0	0	11	22	.254	.339	.318
Runners On	290	109	14	5	12	96	41	40	.376	.583	.448
Runners/Scor. Pos.	185	60	11	4	6	82	33	31	.324	.524	.417
Runners On/2 Out	102	35	2	4	3	37	24	13	.343	.529	.468
Scor. Pos./2 Out	80	25	2	4	2	35	20	12	.313	.513	.450
Late Inning Pressure	84	25	1	0	1	13	9	11	.298	.345	.354
Leading Off	19	5	1	0	0	0	2	1	.263	.316	.333
Runners On	42	16	0	0	1	13	7	6	.381	.452	.442
Runners/Scor. Pos.	28	8	0	0	0	11	5	4	.286	.286	.361

DRIVING IN RUNS	From 1B	From 2B	From 3B	Scoring Position
Totals	13/170	43/146	28/60	71/206
Percentage	8%	29%	47%	34%
Driving In Runners from 3B with Less than Two Out:			18/30	60%

Loves to face: Mike Flanagan (.418, 28-for-67, 2 HR)
Hates to face: Mark Langston (.103, 3-for-29)
Does anyone realize he's still one of baseball's best hitters? Yount has hit .300+ in four of the last six seasons, and missed by two hits in 1984. . . . Set career highs in walks and strikeouts last season; ranked fourth in majors, with 62 multiple-hit games. . . . Drove in 20 runs over his last 14 games to top the 100 RBI mark for the second time in his career. . . . Drove in 103 runs, and it wasn't just opportunity, it was efficiency as well. Yount drove in 34 percent of the 206 runners in scoring position when he batted, the highest average of his career. But that total of 206 was 86 more than the number of opportunities he had in 1986, when he drove in only 46 runs.

Baltimore Orioles

	AB	H	2B	3B	HR	RRF	BB	SO	BA	SA	OBA
Season	5576	1437	219	20	211	722	524	939	.258	.418	.322
vs. Left-Handers	2088	508	78	8	68	237	171	361	.243	.386	.302
vs. Right-Handers	3488	929	141	12	143	485	353	578	.266	.437	.334
Home	2722	681	99	8	110	347	255	463	.250	.414	.315
Road	2854	756	120	12	101	375	269	476	.265	.422	.330
Grass	4715	1203	173	13	190	619	453	809	.255	.418	.321
Artificial Turf	861	234	46	7	21	103	71	130	.272	.415	.328
April	721	189	35	4	20	100	79	127	.262	.405	.338
May	997	269	35	6	58	154	96	156	.270	.491	.334
June	972	245	42	3	35	113	85	163	.252	.409	.313
July	881	223	31	4	33	124	90	130	.253	.410	.322
August	988	261	32	2	40	128	87	182	.264	.422	.325
Sept./Oct.	1017	250	44	1	25	103	87	181	.246	.365	.307
Leading Off Inn.	1347	356	50	6	49	49	101	212	.264	.419	.319
Runners On	2387	607	94	11	95	606	243	410	.254	.422	.321
Runners/Scor. Pos.	1227	314	47	7	50	498	152	242	.256	.428	.331
Runners On/2 Out	966	218	31	4	37	231	111	195	.226	.381	.306
Scor. Pos./2 Out	564	129	18	4	18	186	83	131	.229	.371	.329
Late Inning Pressure	823	204	23	2	27	102	65	154	.248	.379	.304
Leading Off	210	53	5	1	7	7	7	39	.252	.386	.276
Runners On	336	82	14	1	12	87	37	63	.244	.399	.317
Runners/Scor. Pos.	172	41	8	1	7	75	23	37	.238	.419	.320

DRIVING IN RUNS	From 1B	From 2B	From 3B	Scoring Position
Totals	100/1829	195/989	216/520	411/1509
Percentage	5%	20%	42%	27%
Driving In Runners from 3B with Less than Two Out:			140/263	53%

Love to face: Steve Trout (6–1 against him)
Hate to face: Roger Clemens (1–5 against him)
Set an all-time major-league record for home runs in one month with 58 during May.... Lost eight straight games that were decided by one run, longest streak in the majors last season. Also equalled the longest streak in team history; franchise mark of 15 was set by the Browns in 1937.... Ranked last in A.L. in stolen bases (69) for first time since 1954.... Have hit for a higher batting average in road games than at home in each of the past nine seasons, currently the longest such streak in the majors.... Cleanup hitters drove in only 91 runs, tying California for lowest total by number-four hitters in A.L.... Hit six home runs on May 28, most ever hit by Orioles in one game at Memorial Stadium.

Boston Red Sox

	AB	H	2B	3B	HR	RRF	BB	SO	BA	SA	OBA
Season	5586	1554	273	26	174	832	606	825	.278	.430	.352
vs. Left-Handers	1583	471	75	5	49	254	160	224	.298	.444	.364
vs. Right-Handers	4003	1083	198	21	125	578	446	601	.271	.424	.347
Home	2710	796	153	18	86	431	302	373	.294	.459	.367
Road	2876	758	120	8	88	401	304	452	.264	.403	.337
Grass	4716	1322	230	24	142	716	529	689	.280	.430	.356
Artificial Turf	870	232	43	2	32	116	77	136	.267	.431	.329
April	722	170	33	2	20	86	79	118	.235	.370	.317
May	891	224	43	1	29	130	87	131	.251	.400	.322
June	976	294	53	7	29	170	122	140	.301	.459	.384
July	942	287	47	5	33	130	82	125	.305	.470	.359
August	915	259	41	6	36	156	112	146	.283	.459	.365
Sept./Oct.	1140	320	56	5	27	160	124	165	.281	.410	.350
Leading Off Inn.	1320	372	65	0	47	47	114	192	.282	.438	.343
Runners On	2485	719	123	17	82	740	330	369	.289	.452	.373
Runners/Scor. Pos.	1448	414	66	9	48	649	243	241	.286	.443	.383
Runners On/2 Out	1030	267	46	6	28	278	139	172	.259	.397	.356
Scor. Pos./2 Out	681	179	29	3	21	253	107	123	.263	.407	.372
Late Inning Pressure	784	199	27	4	17	96	89	127	.254	.364	.332
Leading Off	191	45	4	0	2	2	18	32	.236	.288	.305
Runners On	338	93	16	3	9	88	49	55	.275	.420	.368
Runners/Scor. Pos.	195	46	4	2	3	74	36	33	.236	.323	.355

DRIVING IN RUNS	From 1B	From 2B	From 3B	Scoring Position
Totals	108/1867	243/1199	306/650	549/1849
Percentage	6%	20%	47%	30%
Driving In Runners from 3B with Less than Two Out:			214/353	61%

Love to face: Jim Clancy (16–5)
Hate to face: Ron Guidry (6–14)
First team in major-league history to produce grand slams in same game from first and second slot in batting order (Burks and Barrett, June 10).... Lost the opening game of 11 of 12 road trips last season, bringing four-year totals to 14 wins, 32 losses in road-trip openers.... Led A.L. in batting average for fifth time in past nine years. Compiled highest home-game mark for seventh time in past 12 seasons.... Came within one hit of the highest batting average vs. left-handed pitchers in the 13 years we've compiled that figure; 1986 Indians hold the mark.... Starting catchers batted .195 (two points better than Minnesota's catchers).... Didn't steal a base until 16th game of season.

California Angels

	AB	H	2B	3B	HR	RRF	BB	SO	BA	SA	OBA
Season	5570	1406	257	26	172	748	590	926	.252	.401	.326
vs. Left-Handers	1785	452	83	11	52	235	189	259	.253	.399	.325
vs. Right-Handers	3785	954	174	15	120	513	401	667	.252	.401	.326
Home	2743	700	114	14	88	364	300	447	.255	.403	.330
Road	2827	706	143	12	84	384	290	479	.250	.398	.322
Grass	4614	1154	198	21	144	620	494	758	.250	.396	.325
Artificial Turf	956	252	59	5	28	128	96	168	.264	.424	.332
April	785	213	38	3	32	114	93	132	.271	.450	.350
May	893	202	37	4	28	99	88	169	.226	.371	.297
June	914	222	39	6	33	135	128	177	.243	.407	.339
July	914	228	42	5	22	133	98	150	.249	.379	.322
August	1012	266	56	3	28	124	89	154	.263	.407	.324
Sept./Oct.	1052	275	45	5	29	143	94	144	.261	.396	.326
Leading Off Inn.	1314	332	63	5	49	49	144	187	.253	.420	.330
Runners On	2435	634	121	13	63	639	278	422	.260	.398	.337
Runners/Scor. Pos.	1477	360	72	6	40	564	192	278	.244	.382	.328
Runners On/2 Out	1012	231	49	6	20	217	112	181	.228	.341	.309
Scor. Pos./2 Out	673	140	22	3	15	194	84	127	.208	.316	.301
Late Inning Pressure	894	219	32	3	28	118	97	154	.245	.381	.323
Leading Off	222	53	14	0	5	5	19	31	.239	.369	.302
Runners On	386	98	11	2	12	102	48	71	.254	.386	.342
Runners/Scor. Pos.	231	56	6	2	8	92	40	42	.242	.390	.357

DRIVING IN RUNS	From 1B	From 2B	From 3B	Scoring Position
Totals	92/1696	210/1121	271/643	481/1764
Percentage	5%	19%	42%	27%
Driving In Runners from 3B with Less than Two Out:			196/325	60%

Love to face: Mike Moore (8–2)
Hate to face: Dave Stewart (1–8)
Ranked last in A.L. in batting average for second time in past three seasons, but pinch-hitters compiled a .327 mark, highest in either league, with an A.L.-leading nine home runs in 147 AB.... Batting average with two outs and runners in scoring position was lowest in A.L. since 1981.... Led A.L. in sacrifice bunts for fifth time in past six seasons. Gene Mauch's teams have led their leagues 13 times in his 21 full seasons as manager.... Starting center fielders and left fielders batted .214 and .224 respectively, both the lowest marks at their positions in the A.L.... Second-place hitters struck out 126 times, highest total by number-two hitters on any team in majors.

Chicago White Sox

	AB	H	2B	3B	HR	RRF	BB	SO	BA	SA	OBA
Season	5538	1427	283	36	173	726	487	971	.258	.415	.319
vs. Left-Handers	1990	498	98	10	76	250	176	393	.250	.424	.313
vs. Right-Handers	3548	929	185	26	97	476	311	578	.262	.411	.322
Home	2719	744	152	22	72	382	259	436	.274	.425	.336
Road	2819	683	131	14	101	344	228	535	.242	.406	.302
Grass	4718	1247	244	29	150	635	421	822	.264	.424	.325
Artificial Turf	820	180	39	7	23	91	66	149	.220	.368	.280
April	623	134	29	5	10	62	67	121	.215	.326	.294
May	889	220	42	5	35	112	90	182	.247	.424	.320
June	948	230	50	5	36	130	76	167	.243	.420	.302
July	953	260	40	7	29	124	73	155	.273	.421	.323
August	1028	285	62	6	32	146	94	174	.277	.443	.337
Sept./Oct.	1097	298	60	8	31	152	87	172	.272	.426	.325
Leading Off Inn.	1341	363	89	5	36	36	108	219	.271	.425	.328
Runners On	2313	587	115	11	72	625	233	439	.254	.406	.319
Runners/Scor. Pos.	1333	342	64	7	34	524	171	268	.257	.392	.332
Runners On/2 Out	975	231	49	4	28	241	117	202	.237	.382	.322
Scor. Pos./2 Out	622	150	30	2	15	201	88	132	.241	.368	.338
Late Inning Pressure	793	199	36	3	15	79	86	164	.251	.361	.326
Leading Off	205	58	13	1	2	2	15	33	.283	.385	.338
Runners On	338	77	13	1	10	74	43	87	.228	.361	.311
Runners/Scor. Pos.	195	42	8	1	5	63	27	55	.215	.344	.299

DRIVING IN RUNS	From 1B	From 2B	From 3B	Scoring Position
Totals	89/1567	210/1052	254/560	464/1612
Percentage	6%	20%	45%	29%
Driving In Runners from 3B with Less than Two Out:			184/303	61%

Love to face: Bob Stanley (11–4)
Hate to face: Mark Clear (0–7)
Led A.L. in doubles for only the second time in the team's 87-year history. The first time was in 1960.... Won on opening day with a lineup including Karkovice (c), Walker (1b), Hill (2b), Hulett (3b), Guillen (ss), Calderon (lf), Redus (cf), Baines (rf), and Fisk (dh), and never used that combination again.... Batting average in road games was the lowest in the A.L. last season, average at home was 5th-best in league.... Batting average on artificial turf was the 3d-lowest in the majors in the last 10 years. (Lower: Angels, .218 in 1984; Cubs, .203 in 1981).... Batters in the number-two position in the lineup batted .223 (lowest in majors), while 8th-spot hitters sported the highest average in the majors (.282).

Cleveland Indians

	AB	H	2B	3B	HR	RRF	BB	SO	BA	SA	OBA
Season	5606	1476	267	30	187	720	489	977	.263	.422	.324
vs. Left-Handers	1495	397	88	6	44	194	165	271	.266	.421	.338
vs. Right-Handers	4111	1079	179	24	143	526	324	706	.262	.422	.318
Home	2759	735	139	18	94	362	259	449	.266	.432	.330
Road	2847	741	128	12	93	358	230	528	.260	.412	.318
Grass	4771	1259	231	25	159	616	417	804	.264	.423	.324
Artificial Turf	835	217	36	5	28	104	72	173	.260	.416	.322
April	750	179	42	2	27	92	69	140	.239	.408	.305
May	936	234	36	6	30	104	86	178	.250	.397	.314
June	853	220	34	8	27	113	75	140	.258	.411	.322
July	946	255	50	5	33	119	80	146	.270	.438	.326
August	1061	295	56	2	32	144	99	188	.278	.425	.340
Sept./Oct.	1060	293	49	7	38	148	80	185	.276	.443	.328
Leading Off Inn.	1357	362	73	7	59	59	93	218	.267	.461	.315
Runners On	2399	608	103	7	57	590	237	435	.253	.373	.320
Runners/Scor. Pos.	1411	338	55	5	30	518	171	270	.240	.349	.318
Runners On/2 Out	1011	235	41	3	26	230	94	205	.232	.356	.302
Scor. Pos./2 Out	668	145	24	2	15	202	74	140	.217	.326	.301
Late Inning Pressure	784	207	29	3	32	95	62	137	.264	.431	.319
Leading Off	199	53	7	0	9	9	10	39	.266	.437	.301
Runners On	308	82	9	1	12	75	32	51	.266	.419	.335
Runners/Scor. Pos.	174	39	6	0	6	60	26	32	.224	.362	.319

DRIVING IN RUNS	From 1B	From 2B	From 3B	Scoring Position
Totals	78/1646	212/1111	243/597	455/1708
Percentage	5%	19%	41%	27%
Driving In Runners from 3B with Less than Two Out:		167/304		55%

Love to face: Floyd Bannister (9–3)
Hate to face: Jack Morris (7–20)

First team in A.L. history with three different players each of whom hit three home runs in a game in the same season (Carter, Jacoby, and Snyder). The 1950 Dodgers (Brown, Campanella, Hodges, and Snider) and 1956 Reds (Bailey, Bell, Kluszewski, and Thurman) hold major-league mark of four players. . . . Swept only two series last season, fewest in either league. . . . Led A.L. in errors for third time in past four seasons. . . . Ninth-place hitters batted .204, 2d-lowest mark of any batting slot in majors, except for ninth position on nine N.L. teams. . . . Pinch-hitters batted .186, lowest mark in A.L. . . . Lowest road-game winning percentage in majors for 2d time in past three seasons (.272 in 1985, .321 last season).

Detroit Tigers

	AB	H	2B	3B	HR	RRF	BB	SO	BA	SA	OBA
Season	5649	1535	274	32	225	871	653	913	.272	.451	.349
vs. Left-Handers	2023	533	98	6	69	304	225	347	.263	.420	.338
vs. Right-Handers	3626	1002	176	26	156	567	428	566	.276	.468	.355
Home	2715	733	122	9	125	432	318	461	.270	.460	.348
Road	2934	802	152	23	100	439	335	452	.273	.443	.350
Grass	4789	1324	229	24	202	760	553	767	.276	.461	.352
Artificial Turf	860	211	45	8	23	111	100	146	.245	.397	.329
April	703	176	30	6	18	88	88	86	.250	.387	.335
May	925	256	38	2	41	151	114	162	.277	.455	.358
June	949	279	55	7	48	163	104	152	.294	.518	.364
July	871	221	31	0	38	132	88	154	.254	.420	.326
August	1051	298	69	8	38	176	124	174	.284	.473	.362
Sept./Oct.	1150	305	51	9	42	161	135	185	.265	.435	.343
Leading Off Inn.	1303	382	71	12	57	57	128	198	.293	.497	.362
Runners On	2582	705	119	8	96	741	306	425	.273	.437	.348
Runners/Scor. Pos.	1487	381	73	3	47	620	211	251	.256	.404	.341
Runners On/2 Out	1093	287	53	2	39	300	149	182	.263	.422	.355
Scor. Pos./2 Out	706	174	39	1	21	252	106	118	.246	.394	.347
Late Inning Pressure	642	170	31	0	20	77	66	112	.265	.407	.336
Leading Off	159	50	9	0	8	8	12	19	.314	.522	.374
Runners On	289	71	14	0	6	63	36	53	.246	.356	.324
Runners/Scor. Pos.	158	42	8	0	2	51	25	26	.266	.354	.356

DRIVING IN RUNS	From 1B	From 2B	From 3B	Scoring Position
Totals	121/1905	240/1186	284/658	524/1844
Percentage	6%	20%	43%	28%
Driving In Runners from 3B with Less than Two Out:		207/364		57%

Love to face: Mike Boddicker (8–2)
Hate to face: Dennis Lamp (0–9)

Led majors with 531 extra-base hits, highest total in either league since 1982 Brewers (537). . . . Led majors in home runs for third time in past four seasons. . . . Highest on-base average leading off innings in A.L. over past 13 seasons. . . . Had a losing record (22–29) vs. left-handers, while playing 41 games above .500 against right-handers (76–35). . . . Won 67 games in which they never trailed, highest total in A.L. over past seven seasons. . . . Outscored their opponents by 181 runs over first five innings, were outscored by 20 runs thereafter. . . . Lowest ground outs-to-air outs ratio in A.L. (1.00) for third straight season. . . . Grounded into one DP for every 11.7 opportunities, lowest rate in A.L.

Kansas City Royals

	AB	H	2B	3B	HR	RRF	BB	SO	BA	SA	OBA
Season	5499	1443	239	40	168	700	523	1034	.262	.412	.328
vs. Left-Handers	1484	391	61	12	47	182	140	286	.263	.416	.327
vs. Right-Handers	4015	1052	178	28	121	518	383	748	.262	.411	.328
Home	2686	720	141	28	73	365	274	427	.268	.423	.335
Road	2813	723	98	12	95	335	249	607	.257	.402	.320
Grass	2159	565	73	8	73	269	202	461	.262	.404	.328
Artificial Turf	3340	878	166	32	95	431	321	573	.263	.417	.327
April	627	164	27	7	14	82	67	101	.262	.394	.334
May	920	252	37	5	30	122	79	167	.274	.423	.334
June	942	236	35	2	28	99	57	173	.251	.381	.295
July	937	228	44	10	20	100	91	199	.243	.376	.309
August	1012	285	46	4	43	154	123	203	.282	.462	.362
Sept./Oct.	1061	278	50	12	33	143	106	191	.262	.425	.329
Leading Off Inn.	1324	332	40	10	49	50	97	255	.251	.407	.305
Runners On	2405	636	121	17	64	595	243	437	.264	.409	.329
Runners/Scor. Pos.	1340	346	70	11	33	506	170	269	.258	.401	.334
Runners On/2 Out	1030	260	48	12	32	252	127	184	.252	.416	.336
Scor. Pos./2 Out	654	153	34	8	17	212	91	135	.234	.388	.329
Late Inning Pressure	688	182	35	6	16	82	66	138	.265	.403	.329
Leading Off	169	31	7	0	2	2	11	38	.183	.260	.233
Runners On	296	85	18	2	8	74	34	53	.287	.443	.357
Runners/Scor. Pos.	173	43	10	1	5	64	25	35	.249	.405	.335

DRIVING IN RUNS	From 1B	From 2B	From 3B	Scoring Position
Totals	102/1766	193/1048	235/561	428/1609
Percentage	6%	18%	42%	27%
Driving In Runners from 3B with Less than Two Out:		166/287		58%

Love to face: Dan Schatzeder (5–0)
Hate to face: Don Aase (0–7)

Shut out six times during April, tying major-league record shared by 1962 Cubs, 1973 Indians, and 1978 Mariners. . . . Ranked last in A.L. in runs for first time since 1970, the second season in the team's history. . . . 1987 on-base average leading off innings was 2d-lowest in majors during the past 13 years. . . . Won 29 of 32 home games in which they scored the first run. . . . Royals' starting short-stops had a composite batting average of .222, lowest in the A.L. . . . 14–6 record on west coast (at California, Oakland, and Seattle) was best in club history. . . . Royals' catchers were charged with interference five times, most in A.L., with three different players contributing: Owen (once), Quirk, and Madison (twice each).

Milwaukee Brewers

	AB	H	2B	3B	HR	RRF	BB	SO	BA	SA	OBA
Season	5625	1552	272	46	163	851	598	1040	.276	.428	.346
vs. Left-Handers	1836	503	85	12	47	262	185	356	.274	.410	.340
vs. Right-Handers	3789	1049	187	34	116	589	413	684	.277	.436	.349
Home	2729	800	134	29	72	436	292	506	.293	.443	.362
Road	2896	752	138	17	91	415	306	534	.260	.413	.331
Grass	4765	1351	236	41	140	757	511	876	.284	.438	.354
Artificial Turf	860	201	36	5	23	94	87	164	.234	.367	.304
April	738	218	40	5	29	134	81	136	.295	.481	.367
May	811	195	41	4	23	79	72	164	.240	.386	.302
June	943	259	43	8	22	145	101	176	.275	.407	.346
July	1005	284	47	12	38	173	99	177	.283	.467	.348
August	1025	285	48	8	23	164	126	172	.278	.408	.358
Sept./Oct.	1103	311	53	9	28	156	119	215	.282	.422	.351
Leading Off Inn.	1326	352	65	12	39	39	122	252	.265	.421	.331
Runners On	2536	756	125	19	83	771	277	469	.298	.461	.365
Runners/Scor. Pos.	1518	453	81	11	50	680	214	300	.298	.465	.378
Runners On/2 Out	1096	321	56	13	34	331	150	207	.293	.461	.382
Scor. Pos./2 Out	736	215	41	8	23	297	128	146	.292	.463	.401
Late Inning Pressure	769	237	35	5	20	120	75	143	.308	.445	.368
Leading Off	194	60	15	1	6	6	13	36	.309	.490	.356
Runners On	347	120	14	1	11	111	42	60	.346	.487	.408
Runners/Scor. Pos.	209	71	10	1	5	99	34	42	.340	.469	.416

DRIVING IN RUNS	From 1B	From 2B	From 3B	Scoring Position
Totals	114/1747	274/1172	299/645	573/1817
Percentage	7%	23%	46%	32%
Driving In Runners from 3B with Less than Two Out:		197/322		61%

Love to face: Charlie Hough (7–1)
Hate to face: Bert Blyleven (13–21)

First team in modern major-league history with streaks of 12 consecutive wins and 12 consecutive losses in the same season. . . . Highest batting average with runners on base in the past 13 seasons. . . . Hit for a higher batting average at home than on the road for ninth consecutive season, currently the longest such streak in A.L. . . . First Milwaukee team, Brewers or otherwise, to lead its league in stolen bases (176). . . . Starting catchers batted .319, 83 points higher than the composite average of the other 13 A.L. clubs' catchers. . . . Batted .309 (34 for 110) with bases loaded last season, highest in A.L. . . . Won seven games in which they trailed after eight innings, highest total in A.L.

Minnesota Twins

	AB	H	2B	3B	HR	RRF	BB	SO	BA	SA	OBA
Season	5441	1422	258	35	196	762	523	898	.261	.430	.328
vs. Left-Handers	1570	418	77	17	48	214	142	247	.266	.429	.326
vs. Right-Handers	3871	1004	181	18	148	548	381	651	.259	.430	.329
Home	2678	717	129	25	106	398	287	443	.268	.453	.341
Road	2763	705	129	10	90	364	236	455	.255	.407	.316
Grass	2143	550	96	7	73	294	195	365	.257	.410	.321
Artificial Turf	3298	872	162	28	123	468	328	533	.264	.442	.333
April	703	183	31	5	25	102	66	127	.260	.425	.326
May	949	253	37	4	37	142	89	150	.267	.431	.330
June	954	265	52	6	40	148	100	145	.278	.471	.346
July	896	215	42	9	26	105	82	126	.240	.394	.304
August	953	258	55	7	37	145	94	178	.271	.460	.337
Sept./Oct.	986	248	41	4	31	120	92	172	.252	.396	.323
Leading Off Inn.	1303	350	63	7	51	51	118	201	.269	.445	.335
Runners On	2316	617	119	19	74	640	249	363	.266	.430	.336
Runners/Scor. Pos.	1308	343	72	11	42	543	171	226	.262	.430	.343
Runners On/2 Out	941	236	46	9	33	253	121	166	.251	.424	.340
Scor. Pos./2 Out	616	148	28	6	20	215	83	111	.240	.403	.336
Late Inning Pressure	650	165	25	5	27	89	68	130	.254	.432	.326
Leading Off	170	46	4	0	11	11	15	34	.271	.488	.337
Runners On	268	67	10	4	7	69	35	54	.250	.396	.332
Runners/Scor. Pos.	135	33	4	1	4	58	28	26	.244	.378	.365

DRIVING IN RUNS	From 1B	From 2B	From 3B	Scoring Position
Totals	105/1610	207/1019	253/564	460/1583
Percentage	7%	20%	45%	29%
Driving In Runners from 3B with Less than Two Out:		172/295	58%	

Love to face: Dave Stewart (7–1)
Hate to face: Roger Clemens (1–9)
Hit home runs in first seven games of season, one short of A.L. record, set by 1932 Yankees. . . . Led A.L. in fielding percentage (.984) for first time in team history. Old Washington Senators led five times, most recently in 1934. . . . Ranked last in A.L. in singles, but seventh with 489 extra-base hits, only six fewer than the 3d-place Oakland A's. . . . Hit for a higher average vs. left-handed pitchers than vs. right-handers in each of the past eight seasons. . . . Starting catchers batted .193, lowest average by starters at any position other than pitcher on any team in majors. . . . Only team in A.L. not to win more than three consecutive road games last season.

New York Yankees

	AB	H	2B	3B	HR	RRF	BB	SO	BA	SA	OBA
Season	5511	1445	239	16	196	778	604	949	.262	.418	.336
vs. Left-Handers	1847	509	83	3	60	278	222	323	.276	.421	.354
vs. Right-Handers	3664	936	156	13	136	500	382	626	.255	.416	.327
Home	2673	720	111	9	98	397	319	449	.269	.428	.349
Road	2838	725	128	7	98	381	285	500	.255	.409	.324
Grass	4648	1213	188	14	164	656	513	791	.261	.413	.336
Artificial Turf	863	232	51	2	32	122	91	158	.269	.444	.338
April	701	187	37	4	19	112	98	115	.267	.412	.357
May	965	258	44	4	43	148	121	156	.267	.455	.351
June	954	257	37	2	32	151	111	182	.269	.413	.347
July	881	225	37	1	34	120	102	141	.255	.415	.334
August	949	228	38	1	36	104	57	162	.240	.396	.284
Sept./Oct.	1061	290	46	4	32	143	115	193	.273	.415	.344
Leading Off Inn.	1314	323	49	6	49	49	124	223	.246	.404	.313
Runners On	2345	646	109	2	85	667	299	392	.275	.432	.356
Runners/Scor. Pos.	1320	360	61	1	45	569	204	228	.273	.423	.366
Runners On/2 Out	953	236	41	1	31	243	142	177	.248	.390	.350
Scor. Pos./2 Out	614	150	30	1	18	213	103	115	.244	.384	.357
Late Inning Pressure	708	192	27	1	24	103	83	136	.271	.414	.350
Leading Off	178	42	4	0	8	8	20	37	.236	.393	.313
Runners On	294	85	13	1	11	90	39	47	.289	.452	.376
Runners/Scor. Pos.	144	48	7	0	7	80	30	21	.333	.528	.451

DRIVING IN RUNS	From 1B	From 2B	From 3B	Scoring Position
Totals	96/1760	219/1039	266/590	485/1629
Percentage	5%	21%	45%	30%
Driving In Runners from 3B with Less than Two Out:		198/328	60%	

Love to face: Mike Morgan (7–0)
Hate to face: Teddy Higuera (1–7)
Won first 10 home games of season, tying the 2d-longest start-of-season streak in this century. The modern record: 12, by the 1911 Detroit Tigers. . . . Led A.L. in batting average in Late-Inning Pressure Situations with two out and runners in scoring position—whew!—for first time in 13 years we've had to deal with that monster. . . . Hit 14 consecutive home runs with the bases empty, from August 18 to August 29. . . . Tied major-league record with 10 grand-slam home runs. . . . Eighth-place hitters batted .191, lowest mark of any batting slot in A.L., and lower than the ninth positions of nine N.L. teams. . . . Started 113 different combinations of players, highest total in majors.

Oakland A's

	AB	H	2B	3B	HR	RRF	BB	SO	BA	SA	OBA
Season	5511	1432	263	33	199	791	593	1056	.260	.428	.333
vs. Left-Handers	1845	487	82	12	70	264	216	338	.264	.435	.341
vs. Right-Handers	3666	945	181	21	129	527	377	718	.258	.424	.329
Home	2645	665	134	14	88	356	304	511	.251	.412	.330
Road	2866	767	129	19	111	435	289	545	.268	.442	.336
Grass	4637	1220	225	23	170	668	496	885	.263	.432	.336
Artificial Turf	874	212	38	10	29	123	97	171	.243	.408	.320
April	767	189	37	6	25	108	89	176	.246	.408	.326
May	848	223	36	6	38	121	108	156	.263	.454	.347
June	926	245	42	3	42	146	105	159	.265	.452	.341
July	964	277	53	5	35	137	60	195	.287	.462	.331
August	965	242	46	0	28	149	110	185	.251	.406	.330
Sept./Oct.	1041	256	49	3	31	130	121	185	.246	.388	.324
Leading Off Inn.	1309	340	64	6	53	53	133	246	.260	.408	.330
Runners On	2325	658	117	14	84	676	271	420	.283	.454	.355
Runners/Scor. Pos.	1369	359	64	11	42	560	192	257	.262	.417	.347
Runners On/2 Out	991	264	51	8	29	270	122	194	.266	.462	.350
Scor. Pos./2 Out	650	164	28	8	18	234	93	135	.252	.403	.349
Late Inning Pressure	764	197	34	1	28	114	86	165	.258	.415	.334
Leading Off	192	56	14	0	11	11	27	40	.292	.536	.382
Runners On	318	92	12	0	11	97	37	55	.289	.431	.362
Runners/Scor. Pos.	199	58	8	0	6	85	28	33	.291	.422	.373

DRIVING IN RUNS	From 1B	From 2B	From 3B	Scoring Position
Totals	115/1692	219/1034	256/612	475/1646
Percentage	7%	21%	42%	29%
Driving In Runners from 3B with Less than Two Out:		166/312	53%	

Love to face John Cerutti (3–0)
Hate to face: Mike Flanagan (5–15)
One of two teams to hit for a higher batting average with runners on base than with the bases empty in each of the last 13 years. The other: St. Louis. . . . A's have also hit better with runners in scoring position than overall for seven straight seasons, more than double the streak of any other team in majors. . . . Made fewest double plays in A.L. for eighth time in past 13 seasons. . . . Batted .207 with bases loaded, lowest in A.L. . . . Designated hitters batted .203 (Reggie .179, others .219), lowest of any team in history. . . . Started 16 different players in the leadoff position, most of any A.L. club. . . . Only team in majors with final records within a range of five wins in each of the past four seasons (77–85, 77–85, 76–86, 81–81).

Seattle Mariners

	AB	H	2B	3B	HR	RRF	BB	SO	BA	SA	OBA
Season	5508	1499	282	48	161	746	500	863	.272	.428	.335
vs. Left-Handers	1742	462	96	12	51	230	149	272	.265	.422	.324
vs. Right-Handers	3766	1037	186	36	110	516	351	591	.275	.431	.340
Home	2704	740	141	26	103	395	257	418	.274	.459	.340
Road	2804	759	141	22	58	351	243	445	.271	.399	.329
Grass	2171	611	116	14	50	298	183	338	.281	.417	.337
Artificial Turf	3337	888	166	34	111	448	317	525	.266	.434	.333
April	772	206	31	6	22	106	79	130	.267	.408	.337
May	898	254	42	13	24	135	78	157	.283	.439	.337
June	884	221	47	12	18	102	81	137	.250	.391	.319
July	884	248	47	6	32	116	56	133	.281	.456	.325
August	995	274	65	4	36	138	99	130	.275	.457	.344
Sept./Oct.	1075	296	50	7	29	149	107	176	.275	.416	.344
Leading Off Inn.	1325	363	81	11	43	43	106	200	.274	.449	.331
Runners On	2358	642	113	18	75	660	261	364	.272	.431	.343
Runners/Scor. Pos.	1435	381	65	11	39	565	180	231	.266	.408	.343
Runners On/2 Out	996	271	50	10	34	271	128	156	.272	.445	.357
Scor. Pos./2 Out	673	175	31	6	20	233	96	111	.260	.413	.355
Late Inning Pressure	679	182	28	9	22	95	73	137	.268	.433	.337
Leading Off	163	40	8	1	5	5	17	36	.245	.399	.317
Runners On	297	85	11	5	12	85	39	50	.286	.478	.365
Runners/Scor. Pos.	189	50	5	5	8	77	26	33	.265	.471	.347

DRIVING IN RUNS	From 1B	From 2B	From 3B	Scoring Position
Totals	94/1566	230/1134	260/594	490/1728
Percentage	6%	20%	44%	28%
Driving In Runners from 3B with Less than Two Out:		183/310	59%	

Love to face: Bill Wegman (5–0)
Hate to face: Jimmy Key (0–5)
Ranked last in A.L. in home runs with 161, a total that would have led the league in every season from 1972 through 1976. . . . Ranked second in A.L. with a .283 batting average in night games, but next-to-last with a .244 mark in day games. . . . Ninth consecutive season with a lower batting average in Late-Inning Pressure Situations than overall. . . . Have hit better with runners on base than with the bases empty in every season of their 11-year history. . . . Highest ground outs-to-air outs ratio in A.L. (1.33) for second consecutive season. . . . Grounded into one double play for every 8.1 opportunities, highest rate in majors. . . . Used 62 different starting lineup combinations, fewest in A.L.

Texas Rangers

	AB	H	2B	3B	HR	RRF	BB	SO	BA	SA	OBA
Season	5564	1478	264	35	194	803	567	1081	.266	.430	.333
vs. Left-Handers	1928	534	92	9	77	279	186	370	.277	.454	.340
vs. Right-Handers	3636	944	172	26	117	524	381	711	.260	.418	.330
Home	2753	767	134	20	93	414	297	521	.279	.443	.349
Road	2811	711	130	15	101	389	270	560	.253	.418	.317
Grass	4679	1263	225	30	161	694	467	883	.270	.434	.336
Artificial Turf	885	215	39	5	33	109	100	198	.243	.410	.321
April	658	173	24	5	25	87	71	142	.263	.429	.337
May	917	233	43	4	35	140	108	187	.254	.424	.331
June	990	276	58	7	40	152	96	206	.279	.473	.342
July	921	263	56	8	33	155	101	152	.286	.429	.353
August	998	254	43	7	29	137	87	191	.255	.399	.314
Sept./Oct.	1080	279	40	4	32	132	104	203	.258	.392	.325
Leading Off Inn.	1325	351	61	5	48	48	126	239	.265	.427	.332
Runners On	2402	662	118	19	77	686	267	454	.276	.437	.344
Runners/Scor. Pos.	1347	373	60	12	46	584	180	269	.277	.442	.352
Runners On/2 Out	1009	273	41	9	30	276	131	200	.271	.418	.357
Scor. Pos./2 Out	659	184	25	7	22	248	94	130	.279	.439	.372
Late Inning Pressure	795	205	33	3	25	110	115	151	.258	.401	.353
Leading Off	197	55	7	0	6	6	24	31	.279	.406	.360
Runners On	356	91	14	1	13	98	69	69	.256	.410	.371
Runners/Scor. Pos.	205	51	6	0	8	83	52	40	.249	.395	.391

DRIVING IN RUNS	From 1B	From 2B	From 3B	Scoring Position
Totals	110/1698	220/1041	276/613	496/1654
Percentage	6%	21%	45%	30%
Driving In Runners from 3B with Less than Two Out:		188/315		60%

Love to face: Dennis Eckersley (13–6)
Hate to face: Ken Dixon (0–4)
Have been shut out only once in their last 223 home games, by John Candelaria and Vern Ruhle on the final Saturday of the 1986 season. . . . Led A.L. in strikeouts for first time in team's history. . . . Tied major-league record by using four catchers in one game (Stanley, Petralli, Slaught, and Porter on Aug. 28). . . . Tied major-league record with four pinch-runners in one inning (9th inning, Sept. 10 at California). . . . Used 62 pinch-runners last season, most in either league. Edged Blue Jays by one. . . . Record of 14–5 in home games decided by one run, 4–16 in one-run decisions on the road. . . . Hit 28 1st-inning HR last season, tied with the Reds and the Tigers for the most in the majors.

Toronto Blue Jays

	AB	H	2B	3B	HR	RRF	BB	SO	BA	SA	OBA
Season	5635	1514	277	38	215	822	555	970	.269	.446	.336
vs. Left-Handers	1769	462	82	17	63	248	181	339	.261	.434	.331
vs. Right-Handers	3866	1052	195	21	152	574	374	631	.272	.451	.339
Home	2777	743	147	26	101	413	298	476	.268	.448	.341
Road	2858	771	130	12	114	409	257	494	.270	.443	.332
Grass	2209	582	95	9	86	313	211	377	.263	.431	.329
Artificial Turf	3426	932	182	29	129	509	344	593	.272	.455	.341
April	681	170	34	6	22	86	80	104	.250	.414	.331
May	929	254	46	3	36	137	86	170	.273	.446	.337
June	981	270	47	8	46	162	94	172	.275	.480	.339
July	923	245	39	5	34	129	97	183	.265	.429	.339
August	1028	283	55	6	39	153	88	175	.275	.454	.336
Sept./Oct.	1093	292	56	10	38	155	110	166	.267	.441	.336
Leading Off Inn.	1341	353	74	8	47	47	100	233	.263	.435	.318
Runners On	2416	656	122	17	89	696	279	395	.272	.447	.347
Runners/Scor. Pos.	1401	398	81	13	49	597	200	238	.284	.465	.369
Runners On/2 Out	1014	256	42	7	39	256	141	182	.252	.423	.348
Scor. Pos./2 Out	636	158	28	7	24	237	105	120	.248	.428	.358
Late Inning Pressure	884	237	41	8	26	135	112	162	.268	.421	.351
Leading Off	223	60	13	2	6	6	20	39	.269	.426	.329
Runners On	386	101	19	4	11	120	58	64	.262	.417	.357
Runners/Scor. Pos.	223	62	14	2	5	103	46	36	.278	.426	.394

DRIVING IN RUNS	From 1B	From 2B	From 3B	Scoring Position
Totals	108/1704	235/1076	264/606	499/1682
Percentage	6%	22%	44%	30%
Driving In Runners from 3B with Less than Two Out:		184/325		57%

Love to face: Frank Viola (10–2)
Hate to face: Frank Tanana (6–10, 0–3 last season)
Set an all-time major-league record with 10 home runs in one game (Sept. 14 vs. Baltimore). . . . Won 15 games in which they trailed after six innings, highest total in majors. . . . Won 55 of 74 games in which they scored the first run, highest average in A.L. (.743). . . . Fell 140 points to a .262 batting average with the bases loaded, after hitting .402 in 1986, the highest mark in either league over the past 13 years. . . . Record of 17–10 (.630) vs. left-handed pitchers at Exhibition Stadium, 10–15 (.400) against southpaws on the road. . . . Only three of their original 30 players selected in the 1976 expansion draft were active in 1987, and all three were still with the Blue Jays: Jim Clancy, Garth Iorg, and Ernie Whitt.

American League

	AB	H	2B	3B	HR	RRF	BB	SO	BA	SA	OBA
Season	77819	20620	3667	461	2634	10872	7812	13442	.265	.425	.333
vs. Left-Handers	24985	6625	1178	140	821	3431	2507	4386	.265	.422	.333
vs. Right-Handers	52834	13995	2489	321	1813	7441	5305	9056	.265	.427	.334
Home	38013	10261	1850	266	1309	5492	4021	6380	.270	.436	.341
Road	39806	10359	1817	195	1325	5380	3791	7062	.260	.416	.326
Grass	55734	14864	2559	282	1904	7915	5645	9625	.267	.425	.335
Artificial Turf	22085	5756	1108	179	730	2957	2167	3817	.261	.426	.329
April	9951	2551	468	66	308	1359	1106	1755	.256	.410	.333
May	12768	3327	557	67	487	1774	1302	2285	.261	.429	.330
June	13186	3519	634	84	476	1929	1335	2289	.267	.436	.336
July	12918	3459	606	82	440	1797	1199	2166	.268	.430	.330
August	13980	3773	712	74	477	2018	1389	2414	.270	.434	.337
Sept./Oct.	15016	3991	690	88	446	1995	1481	2533	.266	.413	.333
Leading Off Inn.	18549	4931	908	100	676	677	1614	3075	.266	.435	.328
Runners On	33704	9133	1619	192	1096	9332	3773	5794	.271	.428	.343
Runners/Scor. Pos.	19421	5162	931	118	595	7977	2651	3568	.266	.418	.348
Runners On/2 Out	14117	3586	637	94	440	3669	1784	2603	.254	.406	.341
Scor. Pos./2 Out	9152	2264	407	66	267	3177	1335	1774	.247	.394	.347
Late Inning Pressure	10657	2795	436	53	327	1415	1143	2010	.262	.405	.335
Leading Off	2672	702	124	6	88	88	228	484	.263	.412	.323
Runners On	4557	1229	188	26	145	1233	598	832	.270	.418	.352
Runners/Scor. Pos.	2602	682	104	16	79	1064	446	491	.262	.405	.364

DRIVING IN RUNS	From 1B	From 2B	From 3B	Scoring Position
Totals	1432/24053	3107/15221	3683/8413	6790/23634
Percentage	6%	20%	44%	29%
Driving In Runners from 3B with Less than Two Out:		2562/4406		58%

National League

Luis Aguayo
Philadelphia Phillies — Bats Right

	AB	H	2B	3B	HR	RRF	BB	SO	BA	SA	OBA
Season	209	43	9	1	12	22	15	56	.206	.431	.273
vs. Left-Handers	76	21	5	1	7	12	2	18	.276	.645	.304
vs. Right-Handers	133	22	4	0	5	10	13	38	.165	.308	.257
Home	92	19	4	1	5	10	3	21	.207	.435	.245
Road	117	24	5	0	7	12	12	35	.205	.427	.293
Grass	55	12	2	0	4	6	3	17	.218	.473	.295
Artificial Turf	154	31	7	1	8	16	12	39	.201	.416	.265
April	27	7	2	0	1	5	2	6	.259	.444	.300
May	70	14	3	1	8	9	7	12	.200	.614	.300
June	33	7	1	0	0	2	0	9	.212	.242	.229
July	39	8	2	0	0	1	5	14	.205	.256	.295
August	18	3	0	0	0	1	0	4	.167	.167	.211
Sept./Oct.	22	4	1	0	3	4	1	11	.182	.636	.217
Leading Off Inn.	43	13	4	0	7	7	2	6	.302	.884	.348
Runners On	86	14	3	0	1	11	4	19	.163	.233	.204
Runners/Scor. Pos.	51	6	3	0	0	9	3	12	.118	.176	.175
Runners On/2 Out	36	4	1	0	0	3	2	8	.111	.139	.179
Scor. Pos./2 Out	25	3	1	0	0	3	1	4	.120	.160	.185
Late Inning Pressure	41	11	2	0	3	5	1	12	.268	.537	.302
Leading Off	9	3	1	0	1	1	1	1	.333	.778	.400
Runners On	18	3	1	0	0	2	0	5	.167	.222	.167
Runners/Scor. Pos.	11	2	1	0	0	2	0	3	.182	.273	.182

DRIVING IN RUNS	From 1B	From 2B	From 3B	Scoring Position
Totals	1/65	4/45	5/18	9/63
Percentage	2%	9%	28%	14%
Driving In Runners from 3B with Less than Two Out:			3/7	43%

Loves to face: Tom Browning (.556, 5-for-9, 2 HR)
Hates to face: Ron Darling (0-for-9)
First player in baseball history with as few as 21 RBI in a season in which he hit 12+ homers. . . . Last three hits of 1987 were all home runs, capped by 10th-inning pinch-hit game winner off Jesse Orosco on Sept. 30, a blow that set up Cardinals' pennant clinching the next night. Aguayo had been 1-for-17 as a pinch hitter before that. . . . Eleven of his 12 home runs were solo shots; the other came with one on. . . . Collected nine hits from April 29 to May 21, all of them for extra bases. . . . Career batting average of .308 in Late-Inning Pressure Situations. Batting average in LIP Situations has been higher than overall average in each of last five seasons. . . . Hitless in his last nine at bats with the bases loaded.

Mike Aldrete
San Francisco Giants — Bats Left

	AB	H	2B	3B	HR	RRF	BB	SO	BA	SA	OBA
Season	357	116	18	2	9	53	43	50	.325	.462	.396
vs. Left-Handers	70	22	5	2	0	6	3	7	.314	.443	.342
vs. Right-Handers	287	94	13	0	9	47	40	43	.328	.467	.407
Home	176	59	7	1	7	25	26	24	.335	.506	.421
Road	181	57	11	1	2	28	17	26	.315	.420	.370
Grass	242	74	10	1	7	34	34	41	.306	.442	.390
Artificial Turf	115	42	8	1	2	19	9	9	.365	.504	.408
April	24	9	1	0	0	2	2	5	.375	.417	.407
May	51	17	3	0	0	6	5	8	.333	.392	.393
June	26	7	0	0	1	3	2	4	.269	.385	.321
July	90	28	5	1	3	14	7	12	.311	.489	.357
August	91	32	5	1	3	15	10	7	.352	.527	.416
Sept./Oct.	75	23	4	0	2	13	17	14	.307	.440	.435
Leading Off Inn.	85	22	5	0	2	2	7	9	.259	.388	.315
Runners On	143	58	6	1	4	48	16	23	.406	.545	.460
Runners/Scor. Pos.	86	36	4	0	3	44	14	13	.419	.570	.490
Runners On/2 Out	48	20	2	0	1	19	7	12	.417	.521	.491
Scor. Pos./2 Out	37	14	2	0	1	19	7	9	.378	.514	.477
Late Inning Pressure	54	12	3	0	2	8	7	7	.222	.389	.311
Leading Off	13	3	0	0	1	1	2	0	.231	.462	.333
Runners On	23	4	3	0	1	7	3	5	.174	.435	.269
Runners/Scor. Pos.	14	2	1	0	1	6	2	3	.143	.429	.250

DRIVING IN RUNS	From 1B	From 2B	From 3B	Scoring Position
Totals	6/90	21/67	17/32	38/99
Percentage	7%	31%	53%	38%
Driving In Runners from 3B with Less than Two Out:			10/14	71%

Loves to face: Jeff Heathcock (.800, 4-for-5)
Hates to face: David Palmer (.077, 1-for-13)
Had hits in seven consecutive at bats (May 4–6) to tie Terry Pendleton and Dave Collins for longest streak in N.L. last year. . . . One of two N.L. players to start 10+ games at each outfield position (other: Tracy Jones); one of two N.L. players to start 10+ games at four positions overall (other: Casey Candaele). . . . Led N.L. last season in batting with runners on base (.406) and in percentage of runners driven in from scoring position (38.4). . . . Career breakdown: .321 (eight HR) at Candlestick, .271 (three HR) on road. . . . Ground-ball hitter: 2.08 ground outs-to-air outs ratio was 7th-highest in N.L. . . . Batting average improved 75 points from 1986 to 1987, largest leap among N.L. players with 200+ at bats each year.

Dave Anderson
Los Angeles Dodgers — Bats Right

	AB	H	2B	3B	HR	RRF	BB	SO	BA	SA	OBA
Season	265	62	12	3	1	13	24	43	.234	.313	.299
vs. Left-Handers	72	18	2	2	0	6	7	8	.250	.333	.316
vs. Right-Handers	193	44	10	1	1	7	17	35	.228	.306	.292
Home	140	35	6	2	0	6	14	24	.250	.321	.316
Road	125	27	6	1	1	7	10	19	.216	.304	.279
Grass	187	42	8	2	0	8	18	32	.225	.289	.295
Artificial Turf	78	20	4	1	1	5	6	11	.256	.372	.310
April	18	3	0	0	0	1	1	3	.167	.167	.211
May	14	5	2	0	0	1	0	0	.357	.500	.357
June	83	22	5	3	1	3	8	10	.265	.434	.330
July	90	20	2	0	0	6	7	14	.222	.244	.276
August	32	10	2	0	0	1	5	7	.313	.375	.421
Sept./Oct.	28	2	1	0	0	1	3	9	.071	.107	.161
Leading Off Inn.	97	21	2	2	1	1	7	13	.216	.309	.269
Runners On	92	27	6	1	0	12	4	17	.293	.380	.327
Runners/Scor. Pos.	50	10	0	0	0	8	3	11	.200	.200	.255
Runners On/2 Out	40	13	4	0	0	5	1	9	.325	.425	.341
Scor. Pos./2 Out	22	3	0	0	0	3	1	7	.136	.136	.174
Late Inning Pressure	41	13	5	1	0	4	3	9	.317	.488	.356
Leading Off	12	4	0	1	0	0	0	2	.333	.500	.333
Runners On	19	6	3	0	0	4	0	4	.316	.474	.300
Runners/Scor. Pos.	9	2	0	0	0	3	0	3	.222	.222	.200

DRIVING IN RUNS	From 1B	From 2B	From 3B	Scoring Position
Totals	4/59	2/38	6/24	8/62
Percentage	7%	5%	25%	13%
Driving In Runners from 3B with Less than Two Out:			4/13	31%

Loves to face: Bob Knepper (.500, 9-for-18)
Hates to face: Mark Davis (0-for-13, 5 SO)
Clark Kent hitter who heads for the phone booth when chips are down: Batted .245 and .234 overall in last two seasons, but .310 and .317 in Late-Inning Pressure Situations. . . . Had streak of 20 consecutive hitless at bats in June. . . . Has only four hits (all singles) in 31 career at bats with the bases loaded. . . . Committed seven errors last season, including four vs. Atlanta. . . . Batting average with runners in scoring position has been lower than overall average in each of five seasons in majors. . . . One of four N.L. players who, in each of past three seasons, has had at least 200 at bats but never a .250 batting average. Others: L.A. infield partner Mariano Duncan, and power-hitting catchers Jody Davis and Ozzie Virgil.

Alan Ashby
Houston Astros — Bats Left and Right

	AB	H	2B	3B	HR	RRF	BB	SO	BA	SA	OBA
Season	386	111	16	0	14	63	50	52	.288	.438	.367
vs. Left-Handers	141	36	3	0	0	10	13	12	.255	.277	.318
vs. Right-Handers	245	75	13	0	14	53	37	40	.306	.531	.394
Home	200	67	8	0	8	40	26	29	.335	.495	.412
Road	186	44	8	0	6	23	24	23	.237	.376	.319
Grass	102	22	3	0	2	10	15	16	.216	.304	.311
Artificial Turf	284	89	13	0	12	53	35	36	.313	.486	.388
April	56	15	2	0	1	7	5	4	.268	.357	.328
May	77	26	5	0	2	12	12	6	.338	.481	.427
June	36	9	1	0	3	8	7	9	.250	.528	.372
July	83	26	6	0	3	14	14	10	.313	.494	.414
August	90	26	1	0	3	17	11	16	.289	.400	.359
Sept./Oct.	44	9	1	0	2	5	1	7	.205	.364	.217
Leading Off Inn.	87	29	3	0	7	7	10	12	.333	.609	.402
Runners On	180	49	8	0	5	54	25	25	.272	.400	.354
Runners/Scor. Pos.	104	31	4	0	5	52	18	13	.298	.481	.389
Runners On/2 Out	70	19	5	0	0	18	14	7	.271	.343	.393
Scor. Pos./2 Out	43	13	2	0	0	16	10	3	.302	.349	.434
Late Inning Pressure	70	23	1	0	4	8	7	11	.329	.514	.385
Leading Off	21	10	1	0	4	4	1	3	.476	1.095	.500
Runners On	29	7	0	0	0	4	3	6	.241	.241	.303
Runners/Scor. Pos.	19	3	0	0	0	4	1	5	.158	.158	.190

DRIVING IN RUNS	From 1B	From 2B	From 3B	Scoring Position
Totals	5/119	22/75	22/52	44/127
Percentage	4%	29%	42%	35%
Driving In Runners from 3B with Less than Two Out:			17/28	61%

Loves to face: Jamie Moyer (.636, 7-for-11)
Hates to face: Fernando Valenzuela (.093, 4-for-43)
Opponents stole on 80.1 percent of attempts with Ashby catching (121 of 151). Sure, Ryan and Scott don't give catchers a chance, but even with other guys pitching, rate vs. Ashby was still 76 percent. Top ten stealers in N.L. were a combined 28-for-29 against him. . . . But, only 7 of 13 stole third with Ash on duty; rate of 54 percent was lowest in majors among catchers who faced at least 10 attempted steals of third. . . . Astros were three games above .500 with Ashby in lineup, 11 below without him. . . . Involved in eight of the 15 catcher's interference plays in N.L. in '87: six as a batter (he led majors), two as a catcher. . . . Has homered at every current N.L. stadium except Busch (88 at bats there).

Wally Backman
New York Mets — Bats Left and Right

	AB	H	2B	3B	HR	RRF	BB	SO	BA	SA	OBA
Season	300	75	6	1	1	27	25	43	.250	.287	.307
vs. Left-Handers	35	3	0	0	0	3	3	5	.086	.086	.158
vs. Right-Handers	265	72	6	1	1	24	22	38	.272	.313	.326
Home	169	48	5	0	0	17	10	15	.284	.314	.322
Road	131	27	1	1	1	10	15	28	.206	.252	.288
Grass	243	66	6	0	1	20	16	32	.272	.309	.315
Artificial Turf	57	9	0	1	0	7	9	11	.158	.193	.273
April	49	11	2	0	0	6	5	5	.224	.265	.296
May	79	21	2	0	0	4	1	10	.266	.291	.275
June	23	6	0	0	0	3	3	6	.261	.261	.346
July	56	14	0	1	0	9	5	9	.250	.286	.306
August	68	13	1	0	1	5	9	9	.191	.250	.286
Sept./Oct.	25	10	1	0	0	3	2	4	.400	.440	.444
Leading Off Inn.	51	12	3	0	0	0	7	5	.235	.294	.328
Runners On	116	38	2	0	0	26	12	15	.328	.345	.388
Runners/Scor. Pos.	68	19	0	0	0	24	9	10	.279	.279	.359
Runners On/2 Out	46	19	2	0	0	15	5	7	.413	.457	.471
Scor. Pos./2 Out	31	11	0	0	0	13	4	5	.355	.355	.429
Late Inning Pressure	24	5	0	0	0	1	7	4	.208	.208	.387
Leading Off	6	2	0	0	0	0	2	0	.333	.333	.500
Runners On	9	1	0	0	0	1	4	2	.111	.111	.385
Runners/Scor. Pos.	6	0	0	0	0	1	2	1	.000	.000	.250

DRIVING IN RUNS	From 1B	From 2B	From 3B	Scoring Position
Totals	2/68	12/59	12/18	24/77
Percentage	3%	20%	67%	31%
Driving In Runners from 3B with Less than Two Out:	7/12			58%

Loves to face: Rick Mahler (.526, 20-for-38)
Hates to face: Bob Sebra (0-for-15)

Led major-league batters in 1987 with ground outs-to-air outs ratio of 2.94. He's second on career list among active players (Milt Thompson, 2.69; Backman, 2.55).... Batted 114 points higher on grass fields than on rugs, 2d-largest difference in N.L. (minimum: 50 at bats each way).... Career figures: .306 vs. right-handers, .138 vs. lefties. That 168-point gap is largest such imbalance over last 10 years by *any player* in majors, switch hitter or no (minimum: 200 at bats each way).... Had 76 starts vs. right-handers last year, only one against a lefty.... Has hit above .300 with runners on base in each of last three years.... Only major leaguer with one home run—no more, no less—in each of last four seasons.

Kevin Bass
Houston Astros — Bats Left and Right

	AB	H	2B	3B	HR	RRF	BB	SO	BA	SA	OBA
Season	592	168	31	5	19	87	53	77	.284	.449	.344
vs. Left-Handers	227	64	13	4	10	39	10	31	.282	.507	.315
vs. Right-Handers	365	104	18	1	9	48	43	46	.285	.414	.361
Home	302	86	17	2	10	53	30	45	.285	.454	.348
Road	290	82	14	3	9	34	23	32	.283	.445	.340
Grass	179	52	10	1	6	25	14	20	.291	.458	.342
Artificial Turf	413	116	21	4	13	62	39	57	.281	.446	.345
April	84	25	6	0	3	13	5	14	.298	.476	.344
May	99	26	5	2	3	13	9	10	.263	.414	.330
June	102	28	6	2	3	22	11	16	.275	.461	.339
July	94	26	3	1	2	7	4	10	.277	.394	.310
August	98	28	4	0	3	13	13	17	.286	.418	.372
Sept./Oct.	115	35	7	0	6	19	11	10	.304	.522	.362
Leading Off Inn.	146	45	10	0	6	6	11	18	.308	.500	.361
Runners On	259	73	13	2	10	78	29	40	.282	.463	.350
Runners/Scor. Pos.	151	42	7	1	6	68	23	19	.278	.457	.363
Runners On/2 Out	114	29	4	1	5	32	19	21	.254	.439	.361
Scor. Pos./2 Out	77	19	2	1	4	30	16	13	.247	.455	.376
Late Inning Pressure	99	31	7	0	4	20	8	13	.313	.505	.364
Leading Off	24	7	2	0	1		0	4	.292	.500	.292
Runners On	41	13	4	0	1	17	6	9	.317	.488	.400
Runners/Scor. Pos.	24	8	3	0	0	15	6	5	.333	.458	.438

DRIVING IN RUNS	From 1B	From 2B	From 3B	Scoring Position
Totals	10/187	34/124	24/52	58/176
Percentage	5%	27%	46%	33%
Driving In Runners from 3B with Less than Two Out:	16/24			67%

Loves to face: Kent Tekulve (.700, 7-for-10)
Hates to face: Pascual Perez (0-for-11)

One of two players to hit three extra-inning home runs last season (other: Jack Clark); Tigers' Charlie Maxwell set record of five in 1960.... Career rate of 4.00 strikeouts for every walk as right-handed batter, 1.6 SO/BB batting lefty; career batting averages: .279 right-handed, .274 lefty.... Has batted over .300 in Late-Inning Pressure Situations in each of last three seasons.... Has come to plate with bases loaded 51 times in his career, and has never walked.... Percentage of runners driven in from scoring position was a career high.... Has homered at every N.L. park except Veterans Stadium, the ballpark in which he has his highest career batting average (.365, 27-for-74).

Buddy Bell
Cincinnati Reds — Bats Right

	AB	H	2B	3B	HR	RRF	BB	SO	BA	SA	OBA
Season	522	148	19	2	17	71	71	39	.284	.425	.369
vs. Left-Handers	142	37	3	0	7	18	24	12	.261	.430	.367
vs. Right-Handers	380	111	16	2	10	53	47	27	.292	.424	.370
Home	262	78	10	1	8	41	41	10	.298	.435	.395
Road	260	70	9	1	9	30	30	29	.269	.415	.342
Grass	169	45	6	1	6	22	21	16	.266	.420	.344
Artificial Turf	353	103	13	1	11	49	50	23	.292	.428	.381
April	82	22	7	1	1	10	12	7	.268	.415	.358
May	54	18	1	0	2	8	4	6	.333	.463	.379
June	84	22	6	0	3	12	9	8	.262	.440	.330
July	97	29	0	0	2	10	12	3	.299	.361	.376
August	100	26	3	0	2	12	21	8	.260	.350	.388
Sept./Oct.	105	31	2	1	7	19	13	7	.295	.533	.378
Leading Off Inn.	126	29	1	0	3	3	12	9	.230	.310	.297
Runners On	216	61	9	2	8	62	30	21	.282	.454	.369
Runners/Scor. Pos.	139	40	7	1	4	53	26	16	.288	.439	.399
Runners On/2 Out	102	30	6	0	4	33	14	13	.294	.471	.379
Scor. Pos./2 Out	77	24	5	0	3	31	12	12	.312	.494	.404
Late Inning Pressure	67	18	3	1	2	9	8	6	.269	.433	.347
Leading Off	18	3	0	0	1	1	2	3	.167	.333	.250
Runners On	32	8	1	1	0	7	3	2	.250	.344	.314
Runners/Scor. Pos.	22	6	0	1	0	7	3	1	.273	.364	.360

DRIVING IN RUNS	From 1B	From 2B	From 3B	Scoring Position
Totals	11/142	24/116	19/55	43/171
Percentage	8%	21%	35%	25%
Driving In Runners from 3B with Less than Two Out:	9/19			47%

Loves to face: Kevin Gross (.500, 9-for-18)
Hates to face: Danny Cox (.105, 2-for-19)

Buddy and daddy Gus are only father-son pair in history of majors to have 100+ home runs apiece. But with one more homer, Bob Boone would put his name, and that of his father Ray, alongside Bells.... Bells' trump card: with just six more homers, Buddy will have career total of 200, and Bells would have unique distinction of being only father-son tandem with 200 each (Gus hit 206).... That one should be safe even from Pete and Petey Rose, but watch out for Bondses.... Has played in 2,276 games in regular season, but none in post-season.... Has homered in every current major league ballpark except Olympic Stadium (52 career AB there); also homered in old Minnesota park, giving him 26 notches on belt.

Rafael Belliard
Pittsburgh Pirates — Bats Right

	AB	H	2B	3B	HR	RRF	BB	SO	BA	SA	OBA
Season	203	42	4	3	1	15	20	25	.207	.271	.286
vs. Left-Handers	75	16	2	2	0	2	8	10	.213	.293	.306
vs. Right-Handers	128	26	2	1	1	13	12	15	.203	.258	.275
Home	91	17	1	1	0	6	12	11	.187	.220	.299
Road	112	25	3	2	1	9	8	14	.223	.313	.275
Grass	69	18	2	1	1	6	3	9	.261	.362	.292
Artificial Turf	134	24	2	2	0	9	17	16	.179	.224	.284
April	44	6	0	2	0	1	5	8	.136	.227	.240
May	77	20	3	0	1	9	7	9	.260	.338	.333
June	70	10	0	0	0	3	7	8	.143	.143	.221
July	2	0	0	0	0	0	1	0	.000	.000	.333
August	10	6	1	1	0	2	0	0	.600	.900	.600
Sept./Oct.	0	0	0	0	0	0	0	0	—	—	—
Leading Off Inn.	46	13	1	1	0	0	5	4	.283	.348	.353
Runners On	92	19	2	2	1	15	11	13	.207	.304	.302
Runners/Scor. Pos.	50	10	1	1	1	13	9	6	.200	.320	.317
Runners On/2 Out	38	9	2	2	0	5	8	5	.237	.395	.370
Scor. Pos./2 Out	19	4	1	1	0	3	7	1	.211	.368	.423
Late Inning Pressure	19	4	0	0	0	0	3	1	.211	.211	.348
Leading Off	7	2	0	0	0	0	1	0	.286	.286	.375
Runners On	2	2	0	0	0	0	1	0	1.000	1.000	1.000
Runners/Scor. Pos.	1	1	0	0	0	0	0	0	1.000	1.000	1.000

DRIVING IN RUNS	From 1B	From 2B	From 3B	Scoring Position
Totals	3/72	2/36	9/23	11/59
Percentage	4%	6%	39%	19%
Driving In Runners from 3B with Less than Two Out:	8/14			57%

Loves to face: Orel Hershiser (.417, 5-for-12)
Hates to face: Bob Forsch (0-for-7)

One of nine shortstops the Bucs used last season, he was replaced as the starter by Felix Fermin in July.... 2.40 ground outs-to-air outs ratio in 1987, 4th-highest in N.L. among players with 200 plate appearances.... Six hits in 14 career at bats with the bases loaded, but has .217 career batting average at less critical times.... Hit his only career home run off Eric Show on May 5th.... Hit three home runs in his minor-league career; they still talk about the two that he hit while with Lynn (that's a city, not a lady) in 1983.... Five extra-base hits in 263 career at bats at Three Rivers Stadium.... Career batting breakdown: .194 on artificial surfaces, .288 on grass fields, and .542 (13-for-24) at Dodger Stadium!

Barry Bonds
Pittsburgh Pirates — Bats Left

	AB	H	2B	3B	HR	RRF	BB	SO	BA	SA	OBA
Season	551	144	34	9	25	61	54	88	.261	.492	.329
vs. Left-Handers	206	47	13	5	8	22	20	42	.228	.456	.303
vs. Right-Handers	345	97	21	4	17	39	34	46	.281	.513	.345
Home	268	71	15	6	12	31	22	50	.265	.500	.324
Road	283	73	19	3	13	30	32	38	.258	.484	.333
Grass	154	40	10	2	7	14	17	25	.260	.487	.335
Artificial Turf	397	104	24	7	18	47	37	63	.262	.494	.326
April	65	15	3	2	2	8	11	11	.231	.431	.338
May	98	29	7	3	4	12	12	16	.296	.551	.378
June	116	27	5	1	6	13	8	16	.233	.448	.280
July	92	25	6	1	4	7	8	18	.272	.489	.337
August	79	22	8	1	6	12	8	13	.278	.633	.348
Sept./Oct.	101	26	5	1	3	9	7	14	.257	.416	.306
Leading Off Inn.	213	61	15	4	9	9	18	30	.286	.521	.350
Runners On	195	50	11	2	10	46	26	39	.256	.487	.339
Runners/Scor. Pos.	113	18	4	1	4	30	22	27	.159	.319	.290
Runners On/2 Out	102	26	6	2	5	24	13	21	.255	.500	.339
Scor. Pos./2 Out	67	10	2	1	2	16	11	14	.149	.299	.269
Late Inning Pressure	71	17	3	2	4	9	9	13	.239	.507	.321
Leading Off	17	4	0	1	0	0	1	2	.235	.353	.278
Runners On	29	6	1	0	2	7	7	6	.207	.448	.351
Runners/Scor. Pos.	18	1	0	0	0	2	6	6	.056	.056	.280

DRIVING IN RUNS	From 1B	From 2B	From 3B	Scoring Position
Totals	15/137	10/91	11/47	21/138
Percentage	11%	11%	23%	15%
Driving In Runners from 3B with Less than Two Out:		6/20		30%

Loves to face: Jimmy Jones (6-for-6)
Hates to face: Dennis Martinez (.045, 1-for-22)

Career batting average of .182 with runners in scoring position, .262 in all other situations.... Hitless in 21 consecutive at bats (June 18 to July 18) with runners in scoring position, longest such streak in N.L. last year.... Averaged 2.53 putouts per nine innings in left field last season, highest rate in majors (minimum: 500 innings).... Had N.L.'s 2d-lowest percentage of runners driven in from third base with less than two out last season.... Apparently has sought revenge on teams his father never played for: he hit four home runs at Riverfront Stadium last season, and was N.L.'s leading hitter (.447, 21-for-47) vs. San Diego. But are there enough such teams for Barry to make a living at that?

Bobby Bonilla
Pittsburgh Pirates — Bats Left and Right

	AB	H	2B	3B	HR	RRF	BB	SO	BA	SA	OBA
Season	466	140	33	3	15	80	39	64	.300	.481	.351
vs. Left-Handers	234	72	14	2	7	43	14	21	.308	.474	.345
vs. Right-Handers	232	68	19	1	8	37	25	43	.293	.487	.357
Home	223	59	14	1	7	35	20	27	.265	.430	.327
Road	243	81	19	2	8	45	19	37	.333	.527	.374
Grass	113	38	11	1	2	15	14	22	.336	.504	.405
Artificial Turf	353	102	22	2	13	65	25	42	.289	.473	.333
April	57	13	3	0	0	6	1	6	.228	.281	.241
May	46	12	0	0	3	8	7	6	.261	.457	.370
June	81	28	10	1	0	11	2	12	.346	.494	.356
July	86	23	3	1	5	13	12	8	.267	.500	.350
August	102	34	9	0	4	22	5	19	.333	.539	.355
Sept./Oct.	94	30	8	1	3	20	12	13	.319	.521	.396
Leading Off Inn.	95	26	4	0	3	8		10	.274	.411	.330
Runners On	241	72	21	2	6	71	23	39	.299	.477	.352
Runners/Scor. Pos.	139	39	12	1	5	64	15	22	.281	.489	.337
Runners On/2 Out	103	30	9	1	2	26	14	13	.291	.456	.381
Scor. Pos./2 Out	61	17	4	1	2	23	9	9	.279	.475	.380
Late Inning Pressure	79	22	8	1	1	12	9	14	.278	.443	.352
Leading Off	19	5	0	0	0		1	2	.263	.263	.300
Runners On	40	13	7	1	0	11	6	8	.325	.550	.413
Runners/Scor. Pos.	22	6	4	0	0	9	3	5	.273	.455	.360

DRIVING IN RUNS	From 1B	From 2B	From 3B	Scoring Position
Totals	13/164	13/100	39/72	52/172
Percentage	8%	13%	54%	30%
Driving In Runners from 3B with Less than Two Out:		30/42		71%

Loves to face: Bruce Ruffin (.438, 7-for-16)
Hates to face: John Tudor (.071, 1-for-14)

Home run total increased from three in 426 at bats in 1986 to 15 in 466 last season.... Played 89 games at third base, 34 in left field, 17 in right field, and six at first base, but was used exclusively at third base after August 5.... Averaged 1.80 assists per nine innings at third base, 3d-lowest rate in N.L. (minimum: 500 innings).... Led N.L. with a .403 average (27-for-67) vs. Expos.... Started 58 of 71 games in which Pirates faced a lefty, most of anyone on team. ... Over last 51 games of season, never went two straight games without a hit.... Raised average to .301 with 5-for-10 series vs. Mets, Sept. 25–27; then batted just once, as a pinch-hitter, over Bucs' last six games to finish at .300429.

Sid Bream
Pittsburgh Pirates — Bats Left

	AB	H	2B	3B	HR	RRF	BB	SO	BA	SA	OBA
Season	516	142	25	3	13	66	49	69	.275	.411	.336
vs. Left-Handers	193	53	9	1	8	27	12	29	.275	.456	.314
vs. Right-Handers	323	89	16	2	5	39	37	40	.276	.384	.348
Home	259	73	14	2	10	44	27	28	.282	.467	.347
Road	257	69	11	1	3	22	22	41	.268	.354	.324
Grass	142	41	7	1	2	14	13	23	.289	.394	.346
Artificial Turf	374	101	18	2	11	52	36	46	.270	.417	.332
April	60	19	3	1	4	8	9	12	.317	.600	.406
May	104	30	5	2	4	17	8	16	.288	.490	.339
June	79	21	3	0	1	6	9	8	.266	.342	.337
July	85	22	5	0	1	11	7	7	.259	.353	.315
August	95	24	4	0	1	8	12	8	.253	.326	.336
Sept./Oct.	93	26	5	0	2	16	4	18	.280	.398	.300
Leading Off Inn.	123	37	7	1	2	2	3	17	.301	.423	.317
Runners On	245	65	13	0	6	59	32	32	.265	.392	.345
Runners/Scor. Pos.	147	30	7	0	2	48	24	20	.204	.293	.309
Runners On/2 Out	115	29	8	0	2	29	14	15	.252	.374	.333
Scor. Pos./2 Out	74	16	4	0	1	24	11	10	.216	.311	.318
Late Inning Pressure	59	15	3	1	3	5	9	6	.254	.492	.353
Leading Off	15	4	1	0	1	1	0	1	.267	.533	.267
Runners On	25	6	1	0	0	2	7	3	.240	.280	.406
Runners/Scor. Pos.	12	1	0	0	0	1	6	2	.083	.083	.389

DRIVING IN RUNS	From 1B	From 2B	From 3B	Scoring Position
Totals	9/176	20/106	24/72	44/178
Percentage	5%	19%	33%	25%
Driving In Runners from 3B with Less than Two Out:		15/32		47%

Loves to face: Mike Scott (.400, 10-for-25, 2 HR)
Hates to face: Scott Sanderson (.105, 2-for-19)

A hot starter: career average of one home run every 14.4 at bats in April, one every 45.3 at bats after that.... An improving hitter against left-handers. Annual batting averages since 1985: .171, .224, .275; eight of his 13 homers last year were hit off southpaws.... Cleanup hitter in 62 games last year, but lost that spot to Bonilla in August.... Has homered in every N.L. stadium except Atlanta (45 AB) and Riverfront (43 AB).... Averaged 0.96 assists per nine innings last season, 2d-highest among N.L. first basemen (minimum: 500 innings).... Has been hit by a pitch only once in 1,405 plate appearances in majors; Craig McMurtry plunked him in June '86. No, Bream didn't charge the mound.

Bob Brenly
San Francisco Giants — Bats Right

	AB	H	2B	3B	HR	RRF	BB	SO	BA	SA	OBA
Season	375	100	19	1	18	53	47	85	.267	.467	.348
vs. Left-Handers	101	24	7	1	7	20	11	22	.238	.535	.304
vs. Right-Handers	274	76	12	0	11	33	36	63	.277	.442	.364
Home	173	52	10	0	10	32	25	31	.301	.532	.389
Road	202	48	9	1	8	21	22	54	.238	.411	.311
Grass	260	70	13	0	14	40	39	50	.269	.481	.364
Artificial Turf	115	30	6	1	4	13	8	35	.261	.435	.310
April	33	6	2	0	0	1	5	11	.182	.242	.289
May	42	13	3	0	1	10	9	11	.310	.452	.442
June	55	13	3	0	5	9	9	10	.236	.564	.338
July	86	31	5	1	6	11	6	16	.360	.651	.404
August	85	21	3	0	4	13	9	23	.247	.424	.320
Sept./Oct.	74	16	3	0	2	9	9	14	.216	.338	.294
Leading Off Inn.	79	23	2	0	7	7	10	18	.291	.582	.371
Runners On	145	39	8	0	4	39	20	32	.269	.407	.349
Runners/Scor. Pos.	103	23	6	0	3	37	16	24	.223	.369	.312
Runners On/2 Out	60	15	4	0	2	18	8	10	.250	.417	.348
Scor. Pos./2 Out	45	9	3	0	1	16	4	9	.200	.333	.265
Late Inning Pressure	70	22	3	1	6	12	9	13	.314	.643	.400
Leading Off	22	7	1	0	3	1	3	4	.318	.773	.348
Runners On	21	7	1	0	2	8	2	3	.333	.667	.391
Runners/Scor. Pos.	14	5	1	0	1	6	1	1	.357	.643	.400

DRIVING IN RUNS	From 1B	From 2B	From 3B	Scoring Position
Totals	4/95	16/81	15/50	31/131
Percentage	4%	20%	30%	24%
Driving In Runners from 3B with Less than Two Out:		11/27		41%

Loves to face: Andy Hawkins (.643, 9-for-14, 2 HR)
Hates to face: Andy McGaffigan (0-for-9)

The 30/30 Club is for other positions; catchers try for the 10/10 Club (home runs and stolen bases). Brenly's been in it each of the past two years, although in '86 he was helped by 64 games at other positions; there was no other member in 1986, but in '87, Benito Santiago joined up.... Career batting average of .256, but only .238 with runners in scoring position, .200 with runners in scoring position and two outs. ... Has homered in every N.L. park except Dodger Stadium (127 career AB).... His power is often overlooked when discussing catchers, but with 73 homers over last four years, he's in neighborhood with Jody Davis (76) and Ozzie Virgil (79), and those guys play in parks more conducive to home runs.

Hubie Brooks

Bats Right

Montreal Expos	AB	H	2B	3B	HR	RRF	BB	SO	BA	SA	OBA
Season	430	113	22	3	14	74	24	72	.263	.426	.301
vs. Left-Handers	121	40	10	1	5	34	5	18	.331	.554	.354
vs. Right-Handers	309	73	12	2	9	40	19	54	.236	.375	.280
Home	228	66	14	1	9	39	16	38	.289	.478	.333
Road	202	47	8	2	5	35	8	34	.233	.366	.263
Grass	87	21	3	0	2	11	4	12	.241	.345	.272
Artificial Turf	343	92	19	3	12	63	20	60	.268	.446	.308
April	11	1	0	0	0	0	0	3	.091	.091	.167
May	16	5	0	0	0	2	1	1	.313	.313	.353
June	85	27	5	1	5	23	6	19	.318	.576	.359
July	101	28	8	1	3	11	6	18	.277	.465	.315
August	95	14	1	0	2	7	8	13	.147	.221	.214
Sept./Oct.	122	38	8	1	4	31	3	18	.311	.492	.323
Leading Off Inn.	102	22	1	0	5	5	2	14	.216	.373	.231
Runners On	211	63	14	3	4	64	9	31	.299	.450	.324
Runners/Scor. Pos.	140	42	9	3	2	58	7	21	.300	.450	.325
Runners On/2 Out	76	23	6	2	1	27	4	13	.303	.474	.338
Scor. Pos./2 Out	53	17	5	2	1	26	3	9	.321	.547	.357
Late Inning Pressure	64	14	3	0	3	11	2	13	.219	.406	.239
Leading Off	15	4	0	0	1	1	0	0	.267	.467	.267
Runners On	25	5	1	0	1	9	1	4	.200	.360	.222
Runners/Scor. Pos.	18	3	1	0	1	9	1	3	.167	.389	.200

DRIVING IN RUNS	From 1B	From 2B	From 3B	Scoring Position
Totals	9/129	29/115	22/49	51/164
Percentage	7%	25%	45%	31%
Driving In Runners from 3B with Less than Two Out:		15/29		52%

Loves to face: Bob Knepper (.489, 23-for-47, 1 HR)
Hates to face: Steve Bedrosian (.107, 3-for-28, 14 SO)
Career average of .354 (29-for-82) with the bases loaded; it's .450 (18-for-40, four HRs) in three years with the Expos. Only other N.L. player to hit a grand slam in each of past three seasons is Gary Carter, who has done it in five consecutive years (longest streak in majors). . . . Career batting average of .300 in Late-Inning Pressure Situations; last year was the first since he became a starter in which he has not hit better in LIPS than overall. . . . Averaged only 2.65 assists per nine innings last season, lowest rate among N.L. short-stops (minimum: 500 innings). . . . Fielding percentage of .911 on grass fields, .962 on artificial turf. . . . Expos had a record of 0–6 with Hubie in cleanup spot.

Chris Brown

Bats Right

Giants/Padres	AB	H	2B	3B	HR	RRF	BB	SO	BA	SA	OBA
Season	287	68	9	0	12	40	20	46	.237	.394	.299
vs. Left-Handers	98	26	3	0	5	14	10	14	.265	.449	.339
vs. Right-Handers	189	42	6	0	7	26	10	32	.222	.365	.278
Home	137	30	6	0	5	18	10	20	.219	.372	.280
Road	150	38	3	0	7	22	10	26	.253	.413	.317
Grass	249	61	9	0	11	36	16	39	.245	.414	.300
Artificial Turf	38	7	0	0	1	4	4	7	.184	.263	.295
April	73	21	5	0	4	11	5	9	.288	.521	.350
May	8	0	0	0	0	0	3	2	.000	.000	.333
June	40	5	0	0	0	1	0	5	.125	.125	.125
July	60	18	2	0	3	11	3	10	.300	.483	.333
August	77	16	1	0	2	7	4	11	.208	.299	.262
Sept./Oct.	29	8	1	0	3	10	5	9	.276	.621	.400
Leading Off Inn.	52	8	0	0	2	2	4	8	.154	.269	.214
Runners On	132	34	8	0	7	35	11	25	.258	.477	.331
Runners/Scor. Pos.	81	21	4	0	4	28	9	14	.259	.457	.358
Runners On/2 Out	52	11	1	0	3	13	2	12	.212	.404	.268
Scor. Pos./2 Out	39	9	1	0	3	13	1	8	.231	.487	.286
Late Inning Pressure	48	11	3	0	0	5	5	6	.229	.292	.327
Leading Off	13	2	0	0	0	0	0	3	.154	.154	.154
Runners On	21	6	2	0	0	3	4	1	.286	.381	.444
Runners/Scor. Pos.	14	3	1	0	0	3	3	1	.214	.286	.421

DRIVING IN RUNS	From 1B	From 2B	From 3B	Scoring Position
Totals	6/88	10/63	12/31	22/94
Percentage	7%	16%	39%	23%
Driving In Runners from 3B with Less than Two Out:		7/15		47%

Loves to face: Mark Thurmond (.625, 5-for-8, 2 HR)
Hates to face: Zane Smith (.080, 2-for-25)
One of four players to hit .300 or better at both the Astrodome and Dodger Stadium over past 10 seasons (minimum: 25 AB at each). The others: David Green, Tony Gwynn, and Albert Hall. . . . Grounded into 14 double plays in 68 opportunities, 4th-highest rate in N.L. (minimum: 40 opportunities). . . . Welcome home: Brown faced ex-mates only once after trade to Padres. His first time up, he suffered a broken right hand when hit by a Mike Krukow pitch (Sept. 14). . . . Last season was first in which he hit less than .337 with runners in scoring position; career mark in those situations is .329, .264 at other times. . . . Fielding percentage of .929 at third base over last two seasons after leading N.L. with .971 mark in 1985.

Ken Caminiti

Bats Left and Right

Houston Astros	AB	H	2B	3B	HR	RRF	BB	SO	BA	SA	OBA
Season	203	50	7	1	3	25	12	44	.246	.335	.287
vs. Left-Handers	100	31	6	0	2	13	6	19	.310	.430	.349
vs. Right-Handers	103	19	1	1	1	12	6	25	.184	.243	.227
Home	90	24	3	1	2	13	6	20	.267	.389	.313
Road	113	26	4	0	1	12	6	24	.230	.292	.267
Grass	76	18	4	0	1	9	5	17	.237	.329	.280
Artificial Turf	127	32	3	1	2	16	7	27	.252	.339	.291
April	0	0	0	0	0	0	0	0	—	—	—
May	0	0	0	0	0	0	0	0	—	—	—
June	0	0	0	0	0	0	0	0	—	—	—
July	54	15	2	1	2	6	1	6	.278	.463	.286
August	86	20	3	0	1	14	7	25	.233	.302	.290
Sept./Oct.	63	15	2	0	0	5	4	13	.238	.270	.284
Leading Off Inn.	34	9	1	1	1	1	2	4	.265	.441	.306
Runners On	97	23	4	0	1	23	5	23	.237	.309	.272
Runners/Scor. Pos.	61	15	4	0	0	21	4	13	.246	.311	.288
Runners On/2 Out	47	12	1	0	1	12	5	13	.255	.340	.327
Scor. Pos./2 Out	34	8	1	0	0	10	4	8	.235	.265	.316
Late Inning Pressure	38	14	2	0	0	6	2	5	.368	.500	.390
Leading Off	8	2	0	0	0	0	0	0	.250	.250	.250
Runners On	16	2	1	0	0	5	1	3	.125	.188	.167
Runners/Scor. Pos.	13	2	1	0	0	5	1	3	.154	.231	.200

DRIVING IN RUNS	From 1B	From 2B	From 3B	Scoring Position
Totals	3/73	12/51	7/18	19/69
Percentage	4%	24%	39%	28%
Driving In Runners from 3B with Less than Two Out:		6/9		67%

Loves to face: Dave Dravecky (.625, 5-for-8, 1 HR)
Hates to face: Don Robinson (0-for-6, 3 SO)
Recalled by Astros at All-Star Break and went 7-for-14 with a double, triple, and two homers in his first four games. . . . Named N.L. Player of the Week after his first week in majors, before Chris Berman even had a nickname for him. . . . Two home runs in his first 14 at bats, one in his last 189. . . . Started all 27 post-break games in which a left-handed pitcher started vs. Houston; started 24 of 48 against right-handers. . . . Born on April 21, 1963; that's marked on your Houston baseball calendar as the day of John Bateman's first career home run.

Casey Candaele

Bats Left and Right

Montreal Expos	AB	H	2B	3B	HR	RRF	BB	SO	BA	SA	OBA
Season	449	122	23	4	1	24	38	28	.272	.347	.330
vs. Left-Handers	113	35	9	1	0	4	8	2	.310	.407	.352
vs. Right-Handers	336	87	14	3	1	20	30	26	.259	.327	.322
Home	244	66	9	3	1	13	16	16	.270	.344	.321
Road	205	56	14	1	0	11	22	12	.273	.351	.341
Grass	119	34	9	1	0	8	9	10	.286	.378	.331
Artificial Turf	330	88	14	3	1	16	29	18	.267	.336	.330
April	60	19	4	0	0	2	11	1	.317	.383	.423
May	110	35	6	2	0	5	6	9	.318	.409	.356
June	101	22	5	0	0	5	8	5	.218	.267	.275
July	82	26	5	1	1	5	5	6	.317	.439	.356
August	57	11	0	1	0	3	8	5	.193	.228	.288
Sept./Oct.	39	9	3	0	0	4	0	2	.231	.308	.250
Leading Off Inn.	175	44	7	2	0	0	14	17	.251	.314	.311
Runners On	137	36	3	1	0	23	12	6	.263	.299	.322
Runners/Scor. Pos.	83	17	1	0	0	21	9	6	.205	.217	.277
Runners On/2 Out	62	16	1	1	0	9	5	4	.258	.306	.313
Scor. Pos./2 Out	46	10	0	0	0	7	3	4	.217	.217	.265
Late Inning Pressure	64	21	4	1	1	3	4	4	.328	.469	.362
Leading Off	21	6	2	1	0	0	2	2	.286	.476	.348
Runners On	19	6	0	0	0	2	2	1	.316	.316	.364
Runners/Scor. Pos.	8	1	0	0	0	2	1	1	.125	.125	.200

DRIVING IN RUNS	From 1B	From 2B	From 3B	Scoring Position
Totals	2/90	11/69	10/34	21/103
Percentage	2%	16%	29%	20%
Driving In Runners from 3B with Less than Two Out:		8/15		53%

Loves to face: Rick Mahler (.625, 5-for-8, his only HR)
Hates to face: Terry Leach (0-for-8)
Would Casey Stengel have loved this guy? He's one of two N.L. rookies to start at least 100 games (Santiago 140, Candaele 102); one of two N.L. players to start at five different positions (Oquendo started at seven); one of two N.L. players to start 10+ games at four positions (other: Mike Aldrete). . . . Played at least two different positions in same game 32 times last season, including three games in which he played three positions. . . . Stole only seven bases in 17 attempts last season, 3d-worst percentage (.412) in majors; he was 0-for-3 testing Mike Scioscia's arm. . . . However, he did lead N.L. with .444 batting average (16-for-36) vs. Dodgers.

John Cangelosi
Pittsburgh Pirates — Bats Left and Right

	AB	H	2B	3B	HR	RRF	BB	SO	BA	SA	OBA
Season	182	50	8	3	4	18	46	33	.275	.418	.427
vs. Left-Handers	103	29	7	1	4	15	19	15	.282	.485	.400
vs. Right-Handers	79	21	1	2	0	3	27	18	.266	.329	.458
Home	102	30	4	2	2	13	20	21	.294	.431	.411
Road	80	20	4	1	2	5	26	12	.250	.400	.444
Grass	44	9	2	1	1	1	9	8	.205	.364	.340
Artificial Turf	138	41	6	2	3	17	37	25	.297	.435	.453
April	22	6	1	0	0	1	10	4	.273	.318	.500
May	19	3	1	0	0	2	14	6	.158	.211	.543
June	26	8	0	0	0	1	9	4	.308	.308	.486
July	36	12	2	0	1	1	4	6	.333	.472	.400
August	41	12	3	2	2	8	3	5	.293	.610	.341
Sept./Oct.	38	9	1	1	1	5	6	8	.237	.395	.348
Leading Off Inn.	82	19	2	1	3	3	27	13	.232	.390	.422
Runners On	45	14	2	2	1	15	11	10	.311	.511	.467
Runners/Scor. Pos.	32	12	1	2	1	14	6	6	.375	.625	.488
Runners On/2 Out	15	5	2	0	1	8	4	3	.333	.667	.500
Scor. Pos./2 Out	12	4	1	0	1	7	3	2	.333	.667	.467
Late Inning Pressure	42	10	0	0	1	1	13	11	.238	.310	.418
Leading Off	20	4	0	0	1	1	7	5	.200	.350	.407
Runners On	8	2	0	0	0		3	3	.250	.250	.455
Runners/Scor. Pos.	5	2	0	0	0	0	2	2	.400	.400	.571

DRIVING IN RUNS	From 1B	From 2B	From 3B	Scoring Position
Totals	4/29	4/26	6/12	10/38
Percentage	14%	15%	50%	26%
Driving In Runners from 3B with Less than Two Out:			4/6	67%

Loves to face: Neal Heaton (.353, 6-for-17)
Hates to face: Don Carman (0-for-6)

Sure, he had only 18 RBI for the season, but he came up only 42 times with a runner on second or third. At one point, he went 38 consecutive plate appearances without a runner in scoring position, from July 6 to August 1 (longest such streak in majors last season). Thirteen of those 38 plate appearances were as a pinch-hitter.... Struck out 19 times as a pinch-hitter last season, most in majors.... Batted .294 in his 38 starts.... Sixty-two percent of his career plate appearances have been as a left-handed batter, but 24 of his 36 extra-base hits, and all six of his home runs, have come from the right side.... Played all three outfield positions last season, committing one error at each.

Gary Carter
New York Mets — Bats Right

	AB	H	2B	3B	HR	RRF	BB	SO	BA	SA	OBA
Season	523	123	18	2	20	88	42	73	.235	.392	.290
vs. Left-Handers	183	44	9	0	7	27	24	15	.240	.404	.322
vs. Right-Handers	340	79	9	2	13	61	18	58	.232	.385	.271
Home	255	59	8	1	9	45	24	39	.231	.376	.294
Road	268	64	10	1	11	43	18	34	.239	.407	.286
Grass	366	89	12	1	13	60	34	55	.243	.388	.305
Artificial Turf	157	34	6	1	7	28	8	18	.217	.401	.254
April	79	19	2	1	3	14	4	7	.241	.405	.271
May	79	17	2	1	2	13	10	14	.215	.342	.308
June	86	23	3	0	4	13	9	12	.267	.442	.333
July	85	22	4	0	4	16	3	10	.259	.447	.284
August	91	19	4	0	5	20	9	13	.209	.418	.277
Sept./Oct.	103	23	3	0	2	12	7	17	.223	.311	.270
Leading Off Inn.	114	22	4	0	5	5	6	15	.193	.360	.233
Runners On	261	63	10	1	10	78	23	40	.241	.402	.297
Runners/Scor. Pos.	163	40	5	1	6	68	14	25	.245	.399	.295
Runners On/2 Out	132	35	5	0	3	32	12	19	.265	.371	.326
Scor. Pos./2 Out	83	24	3	0	2	28	8	14	.289	.398	.352
Late Inning Pressure	74	17	0	1	3	6	5	16	.230	.378	.288
Leading Off	21	4	0	0	1	1	1	3	.190	.333	.227
Runners On	31	4	0	0	1	4	4	9	.129	.226	.229
Runners/Scor. Pos.	18	2	0	0	1	4	3	6	.111	.278	.238

DRIVING IN RUNS	From 1B	From 2B	From 3B	Scoring Position
Totals	14/184	27/120	27/75	54/195
Percentage	8%	23%	36%	28%
Driving In Runners from 3B with Less than Two Out:			20/38	53%

Loves to face: Joe Price (.500, 10-for-20, 4 HR)
Hates to face: Rick Sutcliffe (.135, 5-for-37, 1 HR)

Started 133 games last season; in starts that followed an off-day or a rest-day, he batted .285; in starts that followed a game that he had started, he hit .216.... Batted .272 in day games, .220 at night.... Had only one hit in 15 at bats with the bases loaded last season, but that hit was a home run, giving him at least one grand slam in each of last five seasons, longest current streak in majors. Major league record is nine, by Willie McCovey (1964–72).... Yearly batting averages with runners in scoring position since joining Mets: .331, .282, .245.; overall averages in those seasons: .281, .255, .236.... Has six opening-day home runs, one shy of National League mark shared by Willie Mays and Ed Mathews.

Jack Clark
St. Louis Cardinals — Bats Right

	AB	H	2B	3B	HR	RRF	BB	SO	BA	SA	OBA
Season	419	120	23	1	35	107	136	139	.286	.597	.459
vs. Left-Handers	138	36	9	0	10	33	59	45	.261	.543	.480
vs. Right-Handers	281	84	14	1	25	74	77	94	.299	.623	.447
Home	202	59	10	1	17	51	63	66	.292	.604	.457
Road	217	61	13	0	18	56	73	73	.281	.590	.460
Grass	123	34	8	0	10	34	43	41	.276	.585	.461
Artificial Turf	296	86	15	1	25	73	93	98	.291	.601	.458
April	68	21	4	0	6	13	13	23	.309	.662	.420
May	94	32	8	0	9	36	23	22	.340	.713	.470
June	95	26	5	0	8	24	26	30	.274	.579	.426
July	71	19	3	0	6	19	41	28	.268	.563	.531
August	67	16	2	0	5	11	27	26	.239	.493	.453
Sept./Oct.	24	6	1	0	1	4	6	10	.250	.417	.400
Leading Off Inn.	94	20	3	1	6	6	29	37	.213	.457	.398
Runners On	227	75	16	0	20	92	80	66	.330	.665	.500
Runners/Scor. Pos.	148	45	10	0	13	76	60	47	.304	.635	.498
Runners On/2 Out	93	29	6	0	9	36	42	32	.312	.667	.526
Scor. Pos./2 Out	59	17	2	0	6	29	33	22	.288	.627	.543
Late Inning Pressure	67	18	2	1	9	20	17	24	.269	.731	.412
Leading Off	19	4	0	1	2	2	2	7	.211	.632	.286
Runners On	30	8	0	0	4	15	13	11	.267	.667	.477
Runners/Scor. Pos.	18	3	0	0	1	9	13	8	.167	.333	.500

DRIVING IN RUNS	From 1B	From 2B	From 3B	Scoring Position
Totals	14/141	30/108	28/64	58/172
Percentage	10%	28%	44%	34%
Driving In Runners from 3B with Less than Two Out:			21/38	55%

Loves to face: Lee Smith (.500, 11-for-22, 2 HR)
Hates to face: Greg Harris (0-for-8, 5 SO)

Averaged one home run every 12 at bats last season, best in N.L. (minimum: 10 HR). Also stood number one with one walk every 4.1 times up.... Joins Mike Hargrove as only major leaguers since 1975 to walk six times with bases loaded in one season.... Giants walked him 19 times, the most walks by any team against any batter in majors last season—and Giants only faced Cards 12 times.... Has played only 13 games in outfield over past three seasons, but has 94 assists in 1,008 career games out there, highest rate among 34 active 1,000-game outfielders.... Batted cleanup in 314 of 315 starts with Cards; hasn't hit lower than fourth in 606 starts since June 12, 1982. ... Career average of .307 in New York City.

Will Clark
San Francisco Giants — Bats Left

	AB	H	2B	3B	HR	RRF	BB	SO	BA	SA	OBA
Season	529	163	29	5	35	93	49	98	.308	.580	.371
vs. Left-Handers	173	55	16	2	7	35	5	33	.318	.555	.341
vs. Right-Handers	356	108	13	3	28	58	44	65	.303	.593	.385
Home	274	93	17	2	22	55	24	46	.339	.657	.393
Road	255	70	12	3	13	38	25	52	.275	.498	.347
Grass	405	126	22	3	28	71	39	75	.311	.588	.373
Artificial Turf	124	37	7	2	7	22	10	23	.298	.556	.365
April	79	21	3	2	3	7	8	17	.266	.468	.330
May	70	24	3	2	6	13	3	9	.343	.700	.378
June	99	35	6	0	5	18	4	18	.354	.566	.385
July	91	22	2	0	4	13	7	15	.242	.396	.303
August	98	28	7	1	9	21	13	19	.286	.653	.366
Sept./Oct.	92	33	8	0	8	21	14	20	.359	.707	.454
Leading Off Inn.	137	38	9	1	8	8	11	30	.277	.533	.336
Runners On	198	67	9	3	15	73	23	35	.338	.641	.412
Runners/Scor. Pos.	119	37	4	2	7	55	18	21	.311	.555	.400
Runners On/2 Out	87	23	2	0	7	25	17	13	.264	.529	.396
Scor. Pos./2 Out	59	15	1	0	4	18	13	8	.254	.475	.389
Late Inning Pressure	79	21	5	1	3	10	9	17	.266	.468	.348
Leading Off	21	7	1	1	0	0	1	4	.333	.476	.364
Runners On	27	9	2	0	1	8	5	4	.333	.519	.455
Runners/Scor. Pos.	16	4	1	0	1	7	5	3	.250	.500	.429

DRIVING IN RUNS	From 1B	From 2B	From 3B	Scoring Position
Totals	14/142	25/95	19/47	44/142
Percentage	10%	26%	40%	31%
Driving In Runners from 3B with Less than Two Out:			16/26	62%

Loves to face: Rob Murphy (.556, 5-for-9)
Hates to face: Orel Hershiser (.143, 2-for-14, 7 SO)

One of two N.L. left-handed batters to hit for higher average vs. left-handers than vs. righties in 1987 (minimum: 50 at bats each way); he's the only one of the three who also did it in '86.... Grounded into only two double plays in 88 DP situations, 3d-lowest rate in N.L. (minimum: 40 opportunities).... Only player in N.L. to start 10+ games in both leadoff and cleanup slots.... Stole five bases in 22 attempts last season, worst rate in majors (minimum: 10 CS).... Hit .362 (one HR every 11.1 AB) in day games, .273 (one HR every 19.9 AB) at night.... Nine homers and 23 RBI vs. Reds were most by any N.L. player vs. any club. Nearly won Triple Crown vs. Reds, but trailed Ozzie Smith's .444 by a single point.

Vince Coleman

St. Louis Cardinals   Bats Left and Right

	AB	H	2B	3B	HR	RRF	BB	SO	BA	SA	OBA
Season	623	180	14	10	3	46	70	126	.289	.358	.363
vs. Left-Handers	209	56	8	7	3	17	29	46	.268	.416	.361
vs. Right-Handers	414	124	6	3	0	29	41	80	.300	.329	.364
Home	287	79	8	6	3	29	29	59	.275	.376	.348
Road	336	101	6	4	0	17	41	67	.301	.342	.376
Grass	173	58	1	0	0	11	23	35	.335	.341	.413
Artificial Turf	450	122	13	10	3	35	47	91	.271	.364	.343
April	75	18	1	0	0	6	14	16	.240	.253	.367
May	98	30	1	3	0	7	13	22	.306	.378	.393
June	117	37	1	3	0	12	10	23	.316	.376	.370
July	92	22	2	0	0	6	12	21	.239	.261	.333
August	121	37	6	2	1	7	9	19	.306	.413	.351
Sept./Oct.	120	36	3	2	2	8	12	25	.300	.408	.364
Leading Off Inn.	249	74	6	5	1		35	54	.297	.373	.390
Runners On	217	69	6	3	1	44	19	39	.318	.387	.371
Runners/Scor. Pos.	137	41	3	2	1	40	13	28	.299	.372	.358
Runners On/2 Out	105	31	3	3	1	23	9	24	.295	.410	.351
Scor. Pos./2 Out	76	20	2	2	1	21	8	19	.263	.382	.333
Late Inning Pressure	90	35	4	0	0	9	8	17	.389	.433	.439
Leading Off	21	8	2	0	0		3	6	.381	.476	.458
Runners On	44	16	2	0	0	9	2	9	.364	.409	.391
Runners/Scor. Pos.	26	7	0	0	0	6	1	6	.269	.269	.296

DRIVING IN RUNS	From 1B	From 2B	From 3B	Scoring Position
Totals	6/128	13/104	24/59	37/163
Percentage	5%	13%	41%	23%
Driving In Runners from 3B with Less than Two Out:			14/29	48%

Loves to face: Jeff D. Robinson (.625, 5-for-8)
Hates to face: Tom Browning (0-for-13)
326 career stolen bases in 456 games in majors. Through his first 456 games, Lou Brock had 159 stolen bases; Rickey Henderson, 285.... Stole third base 24 times, more than 23 other teams.... Career: two hits in 23 at bats with bases loaded.... Stole 15 bases in 15 tries vs. Mets last year, now 30-for-30 in career vs. Mets.... Stole 20 bases vs. Phillies, most by any player vs. any club last season.... Committed five of his nine errors in 12 games vs. Dodgers last season.... Batted .347 in day games, .259 at night.... Career breakdown: .263 with bases empty, .263 with runners on base, .262 with runners in scoring position.... Walked 50 times in 1985, 60 in '86, 70 in '87. At that rate, he will tie Ruth's record of 170 in 1997.

Dave Concepcion

Cincinnati Reds   Bats Right

	AB	H	2B	3B	HR	RRF	BB	SO	BA	SA	OBA
Season	279	89	15	0	1	34	28	24	.319	.384	.377
vs. Left-Handers	150	51	9	0	1	18	14	11	.340	.420	.392
vs. Right-Handers	129	38	6	0	0	16	14	13	.295	.341	.361
Home	133	42	9	0	1	14	10	7	.316	.406	.361
Road	146	47	6	0	0	20	18	17	.322	.363	.392
Grass	77	21	4	0	0	6	10	7	.273	.325	.348
Artificial Turf	202	68	11	0	1	28	18	17	.337	.406	.389
April	37	13	1	0	0	7	5	2	.351	.378	.409
May	64	19	3	0	0	5	6	6	.297	.344	.357
June	38	11	3	0	0	5	4	2	.289	.368	.349
July	52	14	1	0	0	4	4	5	.269	.288	.321
August	43	11	2	0	1	4	6	7	.256	.372	.347
Sept./Oct.	45	21	5	0	0	9	3	2	.467	.578	.500
Leading Off Inn.	68	17	2	0	0		8	6	.250	.279	.329
Runners On	130	45	6	0	0	33	13	8	.346	.392	.397
Runners/Scor. Pos.	76	28	4	0	0	31	12	7	.368	.421	.440
Runners On/2 Out	64	18	3	0	0	15	7	4	.281	.328	.352
Scor. Pos./2 Out	42	13	3	0	0	15	7	4	.310	.381	.408
Late Inning Pressure	43	16	3	0	0	3	4	5	.372	.442	.426
Leading Off	14	3	1	0	0	0	0	2	.214	.286	.214
Runners On	18	9	1	0	0	3	3	1	.500	.556	.571
Runners/Scor. Pos.	10	5	1	0	0	3	3	1	.500	.600	.615

DRIVING IN RUNS	From 1B	From 2B	From 3B	Scoring Position
Totals	2/80	16/59	15/35	31/94
Percentage	3%	27%	43%	33%
Driving In Runners from 3B with Less than Two Out:			7/14	50%

Loves to face: John Tudor (.471, 8-for-17,
Hates to face: Orel Hershiser (.050, 1-for-20)
One of four major leaguers to start at every infield position last season.... Grounded into 10 double plays in only 48 DP situations, 2d-highest rate (20.8 percent) in N.L. (minimum: 40 opportunities). ... Batted .388 in day games, highest in majors.... Last 10 errors have all been committed in road games. Last error at Riverfront was June 30, 1986.... Yearly batting averages in Late-Inning Pressure Situations since 1984: .180, .210, .311, .372.... Started 46 of 47 games in which Reds faced left-handers, but only 20 of 115 against right-handers.... Most games at shortstop: Aparicio 2,581, Bowa 2,222, Appling 2,218, Concepcion 2,165, Maranville 2,154; three of them are in Hall of Fame, with Bowa not yet eligible.

Joey Cora

San Diego Padres   Bats Left and Right

	AB	H	2B	3B	HR	RRF	BB	SO	BA	SA	OBA
Season	241	57	7	2	0	15	28	26	.237	.282	.317
vs. Left-Handers	98	24	2	1	0	6	9	10	.245	.286	.308
vs. Right-Handers	143	33	5	1	0	9	19	16	.231	.280	.323
Home	111	23	2	0	0	5	16	14	.207	.225	.310
Road	130	34	5	2	0	10	12	12	.262	.331	.324
Grass	165	38	4	0	0	8	24	21	.230	.255	.330
Artificial Turf	76	19	3	2	0	7	4	5	.250	.342	.288
April	70	17	4	0	0	6	14	9	.243	.300	.376
May	106	24	3	1	0	8	12	12	.226	.274	.303
June	8	2	0	1	0	0	0	1	.250	.500	.250
July	0	0	0	0	0	0	0	0	—	—	—
August	0	0	0	0	0	0	0	0	—	—	—
Sept./Oct.	57	14	0	0	0	1	2	4	.246	.246	.271
Leading Off Inn.	80	14	1	1	0		10	6	.175	.213	.267
Runners On	78	17	2	1	0	15	7	8	.218	.269	.279
Runners/Scor. Pos.	55	9	1	0	0	12	6	7	.164	.182	.242
Runners On/2 Out	33	9	1	0	0	8	4	2	.273	.303	.351
Scor. Pos./2 Out	26	7	1	0	0	8	4	2	.269	.308	.367
Late Inning Pressure	41	6	0	0	0	0	5	7	.146	.146	.239
Leading Off	12	1	0	0	0	0	2	1	.083	.083	.214
Runners On	14	2	0	0	0	0	1	4	.143	.143	.200
Runners/Scor. Pos.	10	0	0	0	0	0	1	4	.000	.000	.091

DRIVING IN RUNS	From 1B	From 2B	From 3B	Scoring Position
Totals	2/43	5/42	7/26	12/68
Percentage	5%	12%	27%	18%
Driving In Runners from 3B with Less than Two Out:			4/10	40%

Loves to face: Orel Hershiser (.444, 4-for-9)
Hates to face: Kelly Downs (0-for-6)
Padres' opening day second baseman, became their leadoff hitter one week into the season, started 46 of their first 51 games, and was in Las Vegas (AAA) by the second week of June.... Averaged 3.38 assists per nine innings last season, 2d-highest rate among major league second basemen (minimum: 500 innings).... Batted .292 in day games, .204 at night.... Failed in 13 tries to drive a runner home from scoring position in Late-Inning Pressure Situations. Drove in 22 percent of runners from scoring position in non-pressure situations.... Statistics that Cora will *not* use in salary negotiations: Padres had 20–57 record in games in which Cora played; they were 45–40 without him.

Jose Cruz

Houston Astros   Bats Left

	AB	H	2B	3B	HR	RRF	BB	SO	BA	SA	OBA
Season	365	88	17	4	11	39	36	65	.241	.400	.307
vs. Left-Handers	128	29	3	1	4	13	8	25	.227	.359	.270
vs. Right-Handers	237	59	14	3	7	26	28	40	.249	.422	.326
Home	180	48	10	2	6	22	15	31	.267	.444	.320
Road	185	40	7	2	5	17	21	34	.216	.357	.295
Grass	100	19	3	1	3	10	12	19	.190	.330	.277
Artificial Turf	265	69	14	3	8	29	24	46	.260	.426	.318
April	62	15	4	0	2	6	6	10	.242	.403	.309
May	85	23	4	2	2	10	9	12	.271	.435	.337
June	80	20	3	0	3	8	8	14	.250	.400	.318
July	62	13	4	1	1	6	3	13	.210	.355	.242
August	31	7	0	1	2	6	5	6	.226	.484	.333
Sept./Oct.	45	10	2	0	1	3	5	10	.222	.333	.294
Leading Off Inn.	89	21	2	2	2	2	5	14	.236	.371	.277
Runners On	161	37	11	1	2	30	20	33	.230	.348	.310
Runners/Scor. Pos.	88	21	7	1	2	29	15	20	.239	.409	.340
Runners On/2 Out	70	17	5	1	0	14	4	13	.243	.343	.284
Scor. Pos./2 Out	45	13	4	1	0	14	4	8	.289	.422	.347
Late Inning Pressure	73	17	3	1	2	7	7	14	.233	.384	.296
Leading Off	21	4	0	1	0	0	1	4	.190	.286	.227
Runners On	29	6	2	0	0	5	3	5	.207	.276	.273
Runners/Scor. Pos.	14	5	2	0	0	5	3	2	.357	.500	.444

DRIVING IN RUNS	From 1B	From 2B	From 3B	Scoring Position
Totals	5/112	11/69	12/30	23/99
Percentage	4%	16%	40%	23%
Driving In Runners from 3B with Less than Two Out:			7/15	47%

Loves to face: Shane Rawley (.471, 8-for-17, 1 HR)
Hates to face: Frank Williams, (0-for-9, 4 SO)
Averaged 2.06 putouts per nine innings last season, 4th-highest rate among N.L. left fielders (minimum: 500 innings).... Has played more games in outfield (2,148) than any player who was active in 1987.... Yearly batting averages with runners in scoring position since 1983: .317, .331, .331, .389, .239.... With bases loaded, he has hit .463 (19-for-41) during that five-year span.... Batting average was his lowest since 1973, when he hit .227 for St. Louis; he started only 19 of Houston's 75 games after the All-Star Break.... Batted .172 (5-for-29) as pinch-hitter last season.... Has .285 career batting average, 2,235 hits, 1,070 RBI, 1,027 runs scored, one All-Star Game at bat.

Kal Daniels
Cincinnati Reds — Bats Left

	AB	H	2B	3B	HR	RRF	BB	SO	BA	SA	OBA
Season	368	123	24	1	26	65	60	62	.334	.617	.429
vs. Left-Handers	76	15	4	0	1	6	9	17	.197	.289	.291
vs. Right-Handers	292	108	20	1	25	59	51	45	.370	.702	.464
Home	175	54	12	0	13	30	25	29	.309	.600	.398
Road	193	69	12	1	13	35	35	33	.358	.632	.456
Grass	136	44	6	1	9	25	25	19	.324	.581	.429
Artificial Turf	232	79	18	0	17	40	35	43	.341	.638	.429
April	70	21	6	1	7	16	6	14	.300	.714	.355
May	67	24	2	0	3	9	13	13	.358	.522	.463
June	80	21	3	0	6	10	15	13	.263	.525	.379
July	11	6	4	0	1	3	1	1	.545	1.182	.583
August	65	25	5	0	3	11	13	8	.385	.600	.487
Sept./Oct.	75	26	4	0	6	16	12	13	.347	.640	.443
Leading Off Inn.	150	56	12	0	15	15	21	29	.373	.753	.450
Runners On	127	39	10	1	5	44	26	21	.307	.520	.429
Runners/Scor. Pos.	76	24	8	1	2	38	21	15	.316	.526	.464
Runners On/2 Out	46	9	2	1	3	10	18	9	.196	.478	.431
Scor. Pos./2 Out	31	5	1	1	2	8	16	6	.161	.452	.447
Late Inning Pressure	51	19	3	0	1	6	15	10	.373	.490	.522
Leading Off	19	10	2	0	1	1	5	5	.526	.789	.625
Runners On	20	5	1	0	0	5	7	4	.250	.300	.464
Runners/Scor. Pos.	10	2	1	0	0	5	5	3	.200	.300	.467

DRIVING IN RUNS	From 1B	From 2B	From 3B	Scoring Position
Totals	5/83	14/56	20/34	34/90
Percentage	6%	25%	59%	38%
Driving In Runners from 3B with Less than Two Out:		17/21		81%

Loves to face: Mike Krukow (.556, 5-for-9, 2 HR)
Hates to face: Ron Darling (0-for-7)

How's this for keepin' company? Daniels is one of six guys to hit .320+ in each of last two years. The others are Boggs, Gwynn, Mattingly, Puckett, Raines; they all did it as everyday players, but Daniels has .194 career average in 108 at bats vs. southpaws. . . . Gulf of 172 points between batting average vs. right-handers and left-handers was widest in majors last year (minimum: 50 at bats each way). Led majors with .702 slugging average vs. right-handers. . . . Only major leaguer to drive in more than 50 percent of runners from scoring position with less than two outs last year (minimum: 15 RRF). . . . Career on-base average (.444) leading off innings is best of any active player (minimum: 200 leadoff PA).

Chili Davis
San Francisco Giants — Bats Left and Right

	AB	H	2B	3B	HR	RRF	BB	SO	BA	SA	OBA
Season	500	125	22	1	24	77	72	109	.250	.442	.344
vs. Left-Handers	183	48	6	1	14	34	20	48	.262	.536	.337
vs. Right-Handers	317	77	16	0	10	43	52	61	.243	.388	.349
Home	223	54	7	1	9	28	38	50	.242	.404	.352
Road	277	71	15	0	15	49	34	59	.256	.473	.338
Grass	365	95	16	1	17	54	52	81	.260	.449	.352
Artificial Turf	135	30	6	0	7	23	20	28	.222	.422	.325
April	86	26	4	0	3	14	9	16	.302	.453	.365
May	101	23	5	0	2	11	11	25	.228	.337	.301
June	90	18	3	0	6	14	13	20	.200	.300	.301
July	87	24	5	1	6	19	11	18	.276	.563	.360
August	78	13	2	0	1	7	14	18	.167	.231	.298
Sept./Oct.	58	21	3	0	6	12	14	12	.362	.724	.486
Leading Off Inn.	103	26	3	0	8	8	12	17	.252	.515	.330
Runners On	208	58	8	1	12	65	45	45	.279	.500	.403
Runners/Scor. Pos.	121	33	5	1	9	56	37	26	.273	.554	.432
Runners On/2 Out	86	17	1	0	5	21	25	18	.198	.384	.378
Scor. Pos./2 Out	56	13	1	0	5	21	21	13	.232	.518	.442
Late Inning Pressure	76	16	3	0	4	12	18	18	.211	.408	.358
Leading Off	20	7	2	0	2	2	2	4	.350	.750	.409
Runners On	29	5	1	0	2	10	13	7	.172	.414	.419
Runners/Scor. Pos.	17	4	1	0	1	7	11	5	.235	.471	.517

DRIVING IN RUNS	From 1B	From 2B	From 3B	Scoring Position
Totals	10/142	22/93	21/48	43/141
Percentage	7%	24%	44%	30%
Driving In Runners from 3B with Less than Two Out:		15/25		60%

Loves to face: Rick Honeycutt (.450, 9-for-20, 4 HR)
Hates to face: Joe Niekro (.170, 8-for-47, 1 HR)

One of two players to post double-figures in both home runs and steals in each of last six years; other: Andre Dawson, who has done it 11 years in a row. . . . Good news for Angels in his career batting breakdown: .246 on artificial turf, .268 on Candlestick's grass, .286 on other grass fields. . . . Averaged 2.19 putouts per nine innings last year, 2d-lowest rate among N.L. center fielders (minimum: 500 innings). . . . Has homered from both sides of plate in the same game three times in career (N.L. record). In fact, he did it twice in 1987! Until 1987, only Mantle had done that twice in one year (in both 1955 & 1956). Chili, Kevin Bass, and Eddie Murray all did it twice last season.

Eric Davis
Cincinnati Reds — Bats Right

	AB	H	2B	3B	HR	RRF	BB	SO	BA	SA	OBA
Season	474	139	23	4	37	103	84	134	.293	.593	.399
vs. Left-Handers	147	50	8	0	17	39	27	36	.340	.741	.440
vs. Right-Handers	327	89	15	4	20	64	57	98	.272	.526	.380
Home	232	65	10	2	17	43	44	64	.280	.560	.394
Road	242	74	13	2	20	60	40	70	.306	.624	.403
Grass	147	45	8	1	10	30	31	37	.306	.578	.425
Artificial Turf	327	94	15	3	27	73	53	97	.287	.599	.386
April	77	28	5	1	7	16	10	19	.364	.727	.437
May	82	27	6	0	12	37	11	21	.329	.841	.404
June	76	19	3	1	4	13	18	22	.250	.474	.394
July	92	32	5	2	6	17	14	27	.348	.641	.434
August	104	26	4	0	6	15	19	30	.250	.462	.363
Sept./Oct.	43	7	0	0	2	5	12	15	.163	.302	.351
Leading Off Inn.	88	30	7	0	8	8	16	14	.341	.693	.442
Runners On	203	58	14	3	15	81	45	65	.286	.606	.410
Runners/Scor. Pos.	118	33	9	2	10	68	30	42	.280	.644	.417
Runners On/2 Out	73	19	7	0	5	27	16	21	.260	.562	.393
Scor. Pos./2 Out	47	10	6	0	3	23	11	15	.213	.532	.362
Late Inning Pressure	59	12	2	0	5	19	15	20	.203	.492	.360
Leading Off	12	3	1	0	1	1	3	1	.250	.583	.400
Runners On	32	7	1	0	4	18	11	11	.219	.625	.409
Runners/Scor. Pos.	25	6	1	0	3	15	8	8	.240	.640	.412

DRIVING IN RUNS	From 1B	From 2B	From 3B	Scoring Position
Totals	18/146	27/94	20/51	47/145
Percentage	12%	29%	39%	32%
Driving In Runners from 3B with Less than Two Out:		14/29		48%

Loves to face: Don Carman (.600, 3-for-5, 3 HR)
Hates to face: Mike Scott (.095, 2-for-21, 1 HR, 9 SO)

14-for-14 stealing third base last season, the "most perfect" thief of third in majors. . . . Averaged 3.12 putouts per nine innings; he and Gary Pettis (3.15) had top rates in majors among center fielders. They probably also led in over-the-wall putouts. . . . Ended season with 0-for-17 slump to drop final average below .300. . . . Only major-leaguer to boost his batting average by 15+ points in each of last three years (minimum: 100 at bats each year): .224, .246, .277, .293; over .300 in '88? . . . Slugging average vs. left-handers (.741) was highest in majors. . . . Joined 30/30 Club at earliest date ever (Aug. 2). Bobby Bonds did it on Aug. 5, 1973. . . . Career at Veterans Stadium: batting .385, slugging .942 (8 HR in 52 AB).

Glenn Davis
Houston Astros — Bats Right

	AB	H	2B	3B	HR	RRF	BB	SO	BA	SA	OBA
Season	578	145	35	2	27	97	47	84	.251	.458	.310
vs. Left-Handers	193	47	13	1	10	29	20	30	.244	.477	.323
vs. Right-Handers	385	98	22	1	17	68	27	54	.255	.449	.304
Home	285	71	16	1	12	47	24	41	.249	.439	.312
Road	293	74	19	1	15	50	23	43	.253	.478	.308
Grass	182	49	13	0	11	36	14	24	.269	.522	.323
Artificial Turf	396	96	22	2	16	61	33	60	.242	.429	.304
April	89	22	4	0	3	9	1	13	.247	.393	.256
May	96	28	7	0	7	21	14	17	.292	.583	.375
June	92	29	10	0	3	14	8	12	.315	.522	.376
July	94	21	3	1	4	17	6	12	.223	.404	.272
August	99	18	7	0	4	14	5	16	.182	.374	.226
Sept./Oct.	108	27	4	1	6	22	13	14	.250	.472	.341
Leading Off Inn.	143	38	7	0	11	11	4	19	.266	.545	.291
Runners On	278	69	19	1	11	81	32	44	.248	.442	.327
Runners/Scor. Pos.	159	39	13	1	5	65	22	28	.245	.434	.332
Runners On/2 Out	134	35	11	1	4	37	19	24	.261	.448	.357
Scor. Pos./2 Out	78	21	6	1	3	32	13	12	.269	.487	.360
Late Inning Pressure	95	16	3	0	4	14	12	20	.168	.326	.266
Leading Off	22	5	0	0	3	3	0	4	.227	.636	.261
Runners On	46	8	1	0	1	11	10	9	.174	.261	.316
Runners/Scor. Pos.	29	6	1	0	1	11	8	7	.207	.345	.368

DRIVING IN RUNS	From 1B	From 2B	From 3B	Scoring Position
Totals	17/187	23/115	30/78	53/193
Percentage	9%	20%	38%	27%
Driving In Runners from 3B with Less than Two Out:		17/39		44%

Loves to face: Tim Burke (.750, 6-for-8, 2 HR)
Hates to face: Lance McCullers (0-for-18)

N.L.'s leading hitter (.395, 15-for-38) in 11 games vs. Pirates last season. . . . Astros' cleanup hitter in 78 of 87 games before All-Star break, but in only 26 of 75 games after break. Houston used five different players in cleanup spot, but had a winning record with only one of them, Alan Ashby (19–15). . . . Finished season with career-high 32 consecutive errorless games at first base. . . . Career batting average of only .208 in Late-Inning Pressure Situations. . . . Has had three straight 20-homer seasons; Houston record is four by Jim Wynn (1967–70). . . . Career average of .173 at Jack Murphy Stadium is his lowest anywhere, but he had three–home run game there on Sept. 10.

Jody Davis

Chicago Cubs   Bats Right

	AB	H	2B	3B	HR	RRF	BB	SO	BA	SA	OBA
Season	428	106	12	2	19	53	52	91	.248	.418	.331
vs. Left-Handers	107	27	2	1	5	12	11	19	.252	.430	.325
vs. Right-Handers	321	79	10	1	14	41	41	72	.246	.414	.332
Home	207	53	9	1	7	21	28	41	.256	.411	.347
Road	221	53	3	1	12	32	24	50	.240	.425	.315
Grass	304	78	10	1	15	38	40	64	.257	.444	.345
Artificial Turf	124	28	2	1	4	15	12	27	.226	.355	.295
April	60	20	4	0	4	10	5	10	.333	.600	.385
May	96	24	1	1	6	16	8	14	.250	.469	.308
June	83	15	3	0	0	3	10	21	.181	.217	.274
July	60	15	1	1	2	7	11	11	.250	.400	.366
August	77	23	2	0	6	15	12	21	.299	.558	.389
Sept./Oct.	52	9	1	0	1	2	6	14	.173	.250	.271
Leading Off Inn.	84	23	5	0	4	4	12	15	.274	.476	.371
Runners On	190	39	5	1	4	38	24	36	.205	.305	.292
Runners/Scor. Pos.	115	23	1	1	2	33	17	24	.200	.278	.299
Runners On/2 Out	83	14	1	1	3	17	11	18	.169	.313	.266
Scor. Pos./2 Out	57	11	1	1	2	15	9	13	.193	.351	.303
Late Inning Pressure	57	18	1	0	4	9	5	14	.316	.544	.381
Leading Off	16	6	1	0	1	1	2	2	.375	.625	.444
Runners On	18	4	0	0	1	6	1	5	.222	.389	.263
Runners/Scor. Pos.	10	3	0	0	0	4	0	3	.300	.300	.300

DRIVING IN RUNS	From 1B	From 2B	From 3B	Scoring Position
Totals	4/137	15/82	15/49	30/131
Percentage	3%	18%	31%	23%
Driving In Runners from 3B with Less than Two Out:			11/22	50%

Loves to face: Bryn Smith (.364, 16-for-44, 3 HR)
Hates to face: John Tudor (.045, 1-for-22)
Had eight home runs by May 9th; had seven home runs after August 9th; in the three months in between, he had only four homers in 229 at bats. . . . Caught 123 games last season, his sixth straight season with 120+ games caught, but his lowest total during that span. . . . Last season marked first time in career that he hit more home runs on road than he did at home. Career breakdown: .265, one homer every 22.2 at bats at home; .241, one every 32.6 on road. . . . Batting average has been under .200 with two out and runners on base in each of last three seasons. . . . Homered vs. every opposing N.L. club last season. . . . Batted 4th-5th-6th during first 10 weeks of season, 6th-7th-8th thereafter.

Andre Dawson

Chicago Cubs   Bats Right

	AB	H	2B	3B	HR	RRF	BB	SO	BA	SA	OBA
Season	621	178	24	2	49	139	32	103	.287	.568	.328
vs. Left-Handers	141	42	5	0	9	30	10	22	.298	.525	.348
vs. Right-Handers	480	136	19	2	40	109	22	81	.283	.581	.321
Home	292	97	13	2	27	71	16	47	.332	.668	.373
Road	329	81	11	0	22	68	16	56	.246	.480	.288
Grass	423	129	15	2	38	101	21	68	.305	.619	.343
Artificial Turf	198	49	9	0	11	38	11	35	.247	.460	.296
April	81	24	5	1	6	20	7	13	.296	.605	.360
May	110	30	3	0	8	22	4	18	.273	.518	.302
June	112	33	3	1	6	23	1	15	.295	.500	.304
July	87	24	4	0	8	23	4	13	.276	.598	.315
August	110	34	2	0	15	28	9	16	.309	.736	.361
Sept./Oct.	121	33	7	0	6	23	7	28	.273	.479	.328
Leading Off Inn.	103	27	3	0	11	11	4	16	.262	.612	.290
Runners On	310	96	18	1	23	113	13	45	.310	.597	.341
Runners/Scor. Pos.	180	59	11	1	15	93	12	26	.328	.650	.376
Runners On/2 Out	119	39	8	1	9	45	5	20	.328	.639	.355
Scor. Pos./2 Out	73	26	5	1	5	36	5	11	.356	.658	.397
Late Inning Pressure	84	23	1	0	9	25	4	14	.274	.607	.307
Leading Off	17	4	0	0	3	3	0	3	.235	.765	.235
Runners On	42	13	1	0	4	20	1	4	.310	.619	.356
Runners/Scor. Pos.	27	9	1	0	3	18	3	4	.333	.704	.400

DRIVING IN RUNS	From 1B	From 2B	From 3B	Scoring Position
Totals	21/210	27/137	42/76	69/213
Percentage	10%	20%	55%	32%
Driving In Runners from 3B with Less than Two Out:			26/40	65%

Loves to face: Jesse Orosco (.545, 12-for-22, 2 HR)
Hates to face: Atlee Hammaker (.130, 3-for-23)
You got it right: 49 homers, 32 walks (including seven intentional), the biggest surplus of home runs over walks by any 40-homer man in baseball history. Other 40-homer men with more HR than BB: Hal Trosky (42 HR, 36 BB) in 1936; Orlando Cepeda (46, 39) in 1961; Dave Kingman (48, 45) in 1979; Tony Armas (43, 32) in 1984; George Bell (47, 39) last year. . . . Batted .315 in daylight, only .238 at night last season, making it 12 straight years that he has hit better in day games. . . . Career figures at Wrigley Field: batting .340, slugging .629, with 38 doubles, 10 triples, 43 home runs in 645 at bats. . . . Has 11 straight seasons in double figures in both home runs and steals, tying all-time record set by Bobby Bonds (1969–79).

Bob Dernier

Chicago Cubs   Bats Right

	AB	H	2B	3B	HR	RRF	BB	SO	BA	SA	OBA
Season	199	63	4	4	8	21	19	19	.317	.497	.379
vs. Left-Handers	141	48	3	3	7	16	15	12	.340	.553	.408
vs. Right-Handers	58	15	1	1	1	5	4	7	.259	.362	.306
Home	99	31	2	1	4	9	8	9	.313	.475	.364
Road	100	32	2	3	4	12	11	10	.320	.520	.393
Grass	140	43	3	1	4	12	12	11	.307	.429	.366
Artificial Turf	59	20	1	3	4	9	7	8	.339	.661	.409
April	20	9	0	1	2	4	1	0	.450	.850	.476
May	39	12	1	1	1	4	1	2	.308	.462	.325
June	28	11	0	0	0	3	5	3	.393	.393	.485
July	35	12	1	0	1	2	4	3	.343	.457	.425
August	35	11	0	1	2	4	2	2	.314	.543	.351
Sept./Oct.	42	8	2	1	2	4	6	9	.190	.429	.292
Leading Off Inn.	82	22	2	1	4	4	6	7	.268	.463	.318
Runners On	65	19	0	1	1	14	6	5	.292	.369	.361
Runners/Scor. Pos.	45	12	0	1	0	12	3	4	.267	.311	.327
Runners On/2 Out	29	9	0	1	1	8	2	3	.310	.483	.355
Scor. Pos./2 Out	20	6	0	1	0	6	1	2	.300	.400	.333
Late Inning Pressure	36	14	0	0	2	4	5	5	.389	.556	.463
Leading Off	12	3	0	0	1	1	0	1	.250	.500	.250
Runners On	9	5	0	0	0	2	2	1	.556	.556	.636
Runners/Scor. Pos.	4	2	0	0	0	2	2	1	.500	.500	.667

DRIVING IN RUNS	From 1B	From 2B	From 3B	Scoring Position
Totals	2/40	4/34	7/14	11/48
Percentage	5%	12%	50%	23%
Driving In Runners from 3B with Less than Two Out:			3/6	50%

Loves to face: John Franco (.545, 6-for-11, 1 HR)
Hates to face: Bryn Smith (.125, 3-for-24)
Batted .226 as a pinch-hitter, .313 in his starts, and a sneaky .476 (10-for-21) as a late-game defensive sub or after pinch-hitting and staying in. . . . Ended season with 13 consecutive hitless at bats. . . . Platooned for the first time in career and responded well. 1987 average vs. right-handed pitchers was well above career mark of .244, and average vs. southpaws was a career high. . . . Started 37 of 38 games in which Cubs faced a southpaw, but only three of 123 games vs. righties. . . . Career batting average of .167 (5-for-30) with the bases loaded. . . . Has hit for a higher average with bases empty than with runners on base in each of the last four seasons; 17 of 21 career homers have been solo shots.

Bo Diaz

Cincinnati Reds   Bats Right

	AB	H	2B	3B	HR	RRF	BB	SO	BA	SA	OBA
Season	496	134	28	1	15	82	19	73	.270	.421	.300
vs. Left-Handers	138	49	12	0	4	24	7	20	.355	.529	.383
vs. Right-Handers	358	85	16	1	11	58	12	53	.237	.380	.268
Home	252	77	20	1	8	52	10	34	.306	.488	.338
Road	244	57	8	0	7	30	9	39	.234	.352	.261
Grass	139	34	7	0	4	19	7	20	.245	.381	.275
Artificial Turf	357	100	21	1	11	63	12	53	.280	.437	.310
April	71	20	4	0	1	17	4	15	.282	.380	.325
May	93	19	2	0	2	9	2	13	.204	.290	.229
June	91	32	12	0	2	13	7	13	.352	.549	.404
July	94	33	5	1	5	23	0	16	.351	.585	.357
August	99	19	4	0	3	15	4	8	.192	.323	.219
Sept./Oct.	48	11	1	0	2	5	2	8	.229	.375	.255
Leading Off Inn.	105	31	6	0	3	3	3	13	.295	.438	.315
Runners On	217	63	16	1	10	77	11	26	.290	.512	.322
Runners/Scor. Pos.	122	39	9	1	6	65	9	14	.320	.557	.350
Runners On/2 Out	85	27	5	0	7	37	7	12	.318	.624	.376
Scor. Pos./2 Out	59	19	4	0	4	30	6	8	.322	.593	.385
Late Inning Pressure	61	11	2	0	1	5	3	14	.180	.262	.227
Leading Off	16	5	1	0	0	0	1	3	.313	.375	.353
Runners On	20	2	0	0	1	5	1	6	.100	.250	.136
Runners/Scor. Pos.	14	1	0	0	0	3	1	6	.071	.071	.125

DRIVING IN RUNS	From 1B	From 2B	From 3B	Scoring Position
Totals	12/150	26/94	29/59	55/153
Percentage	8%	28%	49%	36%
Driving In Runners from 3B with Less than Two Out:			20/26	77%

Loves to face: Zane Smith (.529, 9-for-17)
Hates to face: Nolan Ryan (.069, 2-for-29)
Averaged one walk every 27.9 times up last season, 2d-lowest rate in majors. . . . Had eight consecutive hits in at bats with runners in scoring position (June 26 to July 7), the longest such streak in majors last season. . . . Batted 118 points higher vs. southpaws than vs. right-handers, 3d-largest such difference in N.L. (minimum: 50 at bats each way). . . . Has played for four teams, but has never had a year in which he hit more home runs on road than he did at home. . . . Leads N.L. catchers in games caught over last two seasons (271). . . . Has hit 64 home runs in five seasons in N.L., but you can't regard a guy as a power hitter when he has been shut out in 115 at bats at The Launching Pad in Atlanta.

Mike Diaz

Pittsburgh Pirates — Bats Right

	AB	H	2B	3B	HR	RRF	BB	SO	BA	SA	OBA
Season	241	58	8	2	16	50	31	42	.241	.490	.326
vs. Left-Handers	168	43	6	2	14	30	24	26	.256	.565	.350
vs. Right-Handers	73	15	2	0	2	20	7	16	.205	.315	.271
Home	121	28	4	2	9	29	17	18	.231	.521	.317
Road	120	30	4	0	7	21	14	24	.250	.458	.336
Grass	55	17	2	0	4	12	7	16	.309	.564	.409
Artificial Turf	186	41	6	2	12	38	24	26	.220	.468	.301
April	41	10	2	0	4	11	3	5	.244	.585	.289
May	35	8	1	0	2	4	2	11	.229	.429	.256
June	53	13	2	0	4	9	10	5	.245	.509	.369
July	35	8	1	0	2	8	6	10	.229	.429	.364
August	33	5	0	1	1	7	5	7	.152	.303	.263
Sept./Oct.	44	14	2	1	3	11	5	4	.318	.614	.373
Leading Off Inn.	69	18	2	0	11	11	3	13	.261	.768	.292
Runners On	104	24	4	1	3	37	20	19	.231	.375	.351
Runners/Scor. Pos.	64	19	3	1	3	37	15	13	.297	.516	.402
Runners On/2 Out	48	9	2	0	1	11	8	11	.188	.292	.328
Scor. Pos./2 Out	27	8	2	0	1	11	7	6	.296	.481	.457
Late Inning Pressure	53	11	2	0	2	14	5	12	.208	.358	.274
Leading Off	7	1	0	0	0	0	0	2	.143	.143	.143
Runners On	30	8	1	0	2	14	5	7	.267	.500	.306
Runners/Scor. Pos.	22	7	1	0	2	14	1	5	.318	.636	.308

DRIVING IN RUNS	From 1B	From 2B	From 3B	Scoring Position
Totals	5/83	12/49	17/33	29/82
Percentage	6%	24%	52%	35%
Driving In Runners from 3B with Less than Two Out:		14/21		67%

Loves to face: John Tudor (.467, 7-for-15, 4 HR)
Hates to face: Bob Ojeda (.067, 1-for-15)
Has hit two homers in a game twice in his career, victimizing Tudor both times. . . . Batted .219 (7-for-32) as a pinch-hitter, but was the only pinch-hitter in majors to get four game-winning RBI last season. . . . Two of those pinch-hit game-winners came on home runs, both against the Mets. . . . Career batting average of .292 in Late-Inning Pressure Situations, .240 at other times. . . . Started at four different positions (RF-LF-C-1B) within a one-week span in June. . . . Made 57 starts vs. left-handed pitchers, only five vs. right-handers. . . . Has averaged one home run every 16 at bats over past two years, about the same rate as George Bell, Dale Murphy, Andre Dawson, and Darrell Evans have had over that span.

Bill Doran

Houston Astros — Bats Left and Right

	AB	H	2B	3B	HR	RRF	BB	SO	BA	SA	OBA
Season	625	177	23	3	16	85	82	64	.283	.406	.365
vs. Left-Handers	223	65	5	1	7	35	39	19	.291	.417	.395
vs. Right-Handers	402	112	18	2	9	50	43	45	.279	.400	.348
Home	292	89	9	1	7	40	55	31	.305	.414	.412
Road	333	88	14	2	9	45	27	33	.264	.399	.320
Grass	194	53	9	1	6	33	18	22	.273	.423	.335
Artificial Turf	431	124	14	2	10	52	64	42	.288	.399	.378
April	85	17	1	0	5	14	9	12	.200	.388	.274
May	110	30	5	0	0	12	13	10	.273	.318	.350
June	103	33	3	1	5	14	14	16	.320	.515	.392
July	108	31	5	0	4	13	12	11	.287	.444	.361
August	114	41	5	1	2	22	15	8	.360	.474	.431
Sept./Oct.	105	25	4	1	0	10	19	7	.238	.295	.362
Leading Off Inn.	135	40	6	1	5	5	16	12	.296	.467	.371
Runners On	256	81	13	0	7	76	30	20	.316	.449	.385
Runners/Scor. Pos.	158	47	7	0	3	63	23	16	.297	.399	.399
Runners On/2 Out	96	24	5	0	2	20	12	9	.250	.365	.339
Scor. Pos./2 Out	68	17	3	0	1	16	10	9	.250	.338	.354
Late Inning Pressure	97	30	3	0	1	15	14	8	.309	.371	.393
Leading Off	25	9	1	0	0	0	8	1	.360	.400	.515
Runners On	45	14	2	0	0	14	3	3	.311	.356	.347
Runners/Scor. Pos.	28	9	1	0	0	13	3	3	.321	.357	.375

DRIVING IN RUNS	From 1B	From 2B	From 3B	Scoring Position
Totals	14/167	26/131	28/64	54/195
Percentage	8%	20%	44%	28%
Driving In Runners from 3B with Less than Two Out:		22/35		63%

Loves to face: Craig Lefferts (.522, 12-for-23)
Hates to face: Mike LaCoss (0-for-10)
The only player in majors last season to play in 162 games without the benefit of having his dad make out the lineup card. Became only second Houston player to play 162 games; and you thought we wouldn't get Enos Cabell's name in the book this year. . . . Career batting average of .214 with runners on base in Late-Inning Pressure Situations. . . . Ranked fourth in N.L. with 54 multiple-hit games. . . . Could be another Dawson: career average is .409 (38-for-93) with five home runs at Wrigley Field. . . . How's this progression: Batted .218 in 30 games batting leadoff, .285 in 82 games batting second, and .323 in 50 games batting third. Could Lanier be considering him as cleanup hitter in '88?

Mariano Duncan

Los Angeles Dodgers — Bats Left and Right

	AB	H	2B	3B	HR	RRF	BB	SO	BA	SA	OBA
Season	261	56	8	1	6	18	17	62	.215	.322	.267
vs. Left-Handers	91	25	4	0	4	9	4	19	.275	.451	.305
vs. Right-Handers	170	31	4	1	2	9	13	43	.182	.253	.247
Home	110	25	3	0	3	9	7	27	.227	.336	.277
Road	151	31	5	1	3	9	10	35	.205	.311	.259
Grass	190	42	6	1	4	14	12	44	.221	.326	.273
Artificial Turf	71	14	2	0	2	4	5	18	.197	.310	.250
April	85	24	3	0	2	6	7	22	.282	.388	.347
May	93	15	2	0	1	6	3	23	.161	.215	.188
June	16	4	1	0	0	0	1	6	.250	.313	.294
July	42	8	2	1	2	4	5	7	.190	.429	.277
August	25	5	0	0	1	2	1	4	.200	.320	.231
Sept./Oct.	0	0	0	0	0	0	0	0	—	—	—
Leading Off Inn.	84	15	2	0	1	1	7	25	.179	.238	.250
Runners On	96	20	3	1	1	13	4	20	.208	.292	.238
Runners/Scor. Pos.	53	9	0	1	1	12	4	13	.170	.264	.224
Runners On/2 Out	43	8	1	0	1	6	4	6	.186	.279	.255
Scor. Pos./2 Out	26	4	0	0	1	5	4	4	.154	.269	.267
Late Inning Pressure	34	11	3	1	0	3	6	9	.324	.471	.439
Leading Off	9	3	1	0	0	0	3	3	.333	.444	.538
Runners On	17	6	1	1	0	3	2	4	.353	.529	.421
Runners/Scor. Pos.	5	2	0	1	0	2	2	1	.400	.800	.571

DRIVING IN RUNS	From 1B	From 2B	From 3B	Scoring Position
Totals	1/61	6/43	5/20	11/63
Percentage	2%	14%	25%	17%
Driving In Runners from 3B with Less than Two Out:		4/11		36%

Loves to face: Lance McCullers (5-for-5)
Hates to face: Bob Forsch (0-for-14, 6 SO)
One of two N.L. players with at least 200 at bats in both 1986 and 1987, but a sub-.230 batting average each year; the other: Bob Melvin. . . . Stole 11 bases in 12 attempts in '87, 3d-best rate (.917) in N.L. (minimum: 10 SB); he was caught by Downs-Melvin battery on April 10. . . . Career breakdown: .274, one home run every 37.1 at bats vs. lefties; .209, one every 98 vs. right-handers. . . . Hit 10 triples in 1986 spring training, but has one in 668 at bats in the two regular seasons since. . . . Led N.L. shortstops with 21 errors last season, despite playing only 67 games there; he got it done quickly, with 12 errors over an in-and-out-of-the-lineup 11-game span from July 11 to August 13.

Shawon Dunston

Chicago Cubs — Bats Right

	AB	H	2B	3B	HR	RRF	BB	SO	BA	SA	OBA
Season	346	85	18	3	5	24	10	68	.246	.358	.267
vs. Left-Handers	78	18	2	1	1	3	0	12	.231	.321	.238
vs. Right-Handers	268	67	16	2	4	21	10	56	.250	.369	.276
Home	181	40	8	2	3	16	5	32	.221	.337	.239
Road	165	45	10	1	2	8	5	36	.273	.382	.298
Grass	233	53	12	2	4	21	7	43	.227	.348	.248
Artificial Turf	113	32	6	1	1	3	3	25	.283	.381	.308
April	77	15	5	0	0	2	2	13	.195	.260	.215
May	110	28	9	1	3	13	2	29	.255	.436	.265
June	53	19	1	1	2	4	2	10	.358	.528	.382
July	0	0	0	0	0	0	0	0	—	—	—
August	19	6	1	0	0	1	2	4	.316	.368	.381
Sept./Oct.	87	17	2	1	0	4	2	12	.195	.241	.220
Leading Off Inn.	94	25	4	2	0	5	0	20	.266	.351	.303
Runners On	131	30	8	0	2	21	1	16	.229	.336	.237
Runners/Scor. Pos.	62	15	3	0	2	20	1	7	.242	.387	.246
Runners On/2 Out	48	12	2	0	1	13	1	5	.250	.354	.280
Scor. Pos./2 Out	31	10	2	0	1	13	1	2	.323	.484	.344
Late Inning Pressure	64	20	3	1	0	2	3	13	.313	.391	.338
Leading Off	20	8	1	1	0	0	2	4	.400	.550	.455
Runners On	21	5	1	0	0	2	0	4	.238	.286	.227
Runners/Scor. Pos.	9	1	0	0	0	2	0	1	.111	.111	.100

DRIVING IN RUNS	From 1B	From 2B	From 3B	Scoring Position
Totals	3/112	6/45	10/31	16/76
Percentage	3%	13%	32%	21%
Driving In Runners from 3B with Less than Two Out:		5/17		29%

Loves to face: Don Robinson (.556, 5-for-9, 1 HR)
Hates to face: Sid Fernandez (.071, 1-for-14, 5 SO)
Not only did he bat 50+ points lower at Wrigley Field than he did in road games, he also committed 10 of his 14 errors at home. His fielding percentage was 25 points higher on artificial turf than it was on grass fields. . . . Did not draw a walk in 80 plate appearances against left-handers last season; he has walked six times in 289 career plate appearances vs. lefties. . . . Walked twice in a game only once last season, and that was with the aid of an intentional pass. . . . Had N.L.'s lowest percentage of runners driven in from third base with less than two outs last season (minimum: 15 opportunities). . . . Hitless in 19 at bats vs. Giants last season. . . . Career average of .065 (2-for-31) at San Diego Stadium.

Leon Durham

Chicago Cubs	AB	H	2B	3B	HR	RRF	BB	SO	BA	SA	OBA
Season	439	120	22	1	27	64	51	92	.273	.513	.348
vs. Left-Handers	74	19	3	0	2	8	3	19	.257	.378	.286
vs. Right-Handers	365	101	19	1	25	56	48	73	.277	.540	.359
Home	236	70	12	0	16	42	30	48	.297	.551	.375
Road	203	50	10	1	11	22	21	44	.246	.468	.316
Grass	327	89	16	0	20	49	37	69	.272	.505	.345
Artificial Turf	112	31	6	1	7	15	14	23	.277	.536	.354
April	74	23	1	0	6	10	9	9	.311	.568	.381
May	94	28	5	0	6	10	11	17	.298	.543	.371
June	75	22	6	0	3	8	7	19	.293	.493	.354
July	70	15	6	0	2	11	5	15	.214	.386	.267
August	65	16	2	0	5	12	10	17	.246	.508	.342
Sept./Oct.	61	16	2	1	5	13	9	15	.262	.574	.357
Leading Off Inn.	116	33	6	0	8	8	7	31	.284	.543	.325
Runners On	182	45	9	0	8	45	33	38	.247	.429	.359
Runners/Scor. Pos.	93	19	4	0	2	32	23	22	.204	.312	.356
Runners On/2 Out	74	15	2	0	1	12	18	16	.203	.270	.359
Scor. Pos./2 Out	35	6	1	0	1	11	14	9	.171	.286	.408
Late Inning Pressure	51	13	1	0	1	2	4	10	.255	.333	.309
Leading Off	18	3	0	0	0	0	1	5	.167	.167	.211
Runners On	13	3	0	0	0	1	3	4	.231	.231	.375
Runners/Scor. Pos.	6	1	0	0	0	1	2	1	.167	.167	.375

Bats Left

DRIVING IN RUNS	From 1B	From 2B	From 3B	Scoring Position
Totals	8/138	14/69	15/42	29/111
Percentage	6%	20%	36%	26%
Driving In Runners from 3B with Less than Two Out:			10/26	38%

Loves to face: Andy Hawkins (.474, 9-for-19, 1 HR)
Hates to face: Bruce Ruffin (0-for-10, 7 SO)
May take advantage of his home park better than anyone in N.L.: in seven years with Cubs, has hit .304 with 89 home runs at Wrigley Field; .255 with 46 home runs on road. The players who most closely typify that difference: at home he's Jim Rice; on the road, he's Brian Dayett. ... Batting average with runners in scoring position declined for fifth straight season, to the lowest mark of his career. ... It seems strange, then, but Cubs had a winning record (22–21) with Durham in the cleanup spot. ... Homered vs. every opposing N.L. club last season except his former mates from St. Louis. ... Had three sacrifice bunts as rookie with Cardinals in 1980, but has had none in seven seasons with Chicago.

Len Dykstra

New York Mets	AB	H	2B	3B	HR	RRF	BB	SO	BA	SA	OBA
Season	431	123	37	3	10	44	40	67	.285	.455	.352
vs. Left-Handers	74	15	6	0	1	8	8	13	.203	.324	.289
vs. Right-Handers	357	108	31	3	9	36	32	54	.303	.482	.365
Home	212	62	17	1	7	27	19	27	.292	.481	.359
Road	219	61	20	2	3	17	21	40	.279	.429	.344
Grass	306	92	25	2	8	33	24	46	.301	.474	.359
Artificial Turf	125	31	12	1	2	11	16	21	.248	.408	.333
April	56	14	3	1	2	5	7	10	.250	.446	.333
May	67	24	7	1	4	11	6	7	.358	.672	.419
June	77	19	4	0	0	1	4	17	.247	.299	.284
July	68	20	4	0	2	9	6	9	.294	.441	.351
August	81	21	7	1	1	6	9	12	.259	.407	.355
Sept./Oct.	82	25	12	0	1	12	8	12	.305	.488	.367
Leading Off Inn.	189	53	16	3	4	4	18	33	.280	.460	.346
Runners On	132	40	12	0	4	38	15	16	.303	.485	.387
Runners/Scor. Pos.	82	22	7	0	1	31	13	14	.268	.390	.381
Runners On/2 Out	56	17	4	0	1	15	8	9	.304	.429	.400
Scor. Pos./2 Out	37	11	4	0	0	13	7	8	.297	.405	.409
Late Inning Pressure	50	11	3	0	2	6	6	7	.220	.400	.304
Leading Off	11	1	0	0	0	2	2	2	.091	.091	.231
Runners On	23	4	2	0	1	5	2	3	.174	.391	.240
Runners/Scor. Pos.	17	3	2	0	0	3	1	3	.176	.294	.222

Bats Left

DRIVING IN RUNS	From 1B	From 2B	From 3B	Scoring Position
Totals	6/76	17/71	11/22	28/93
Percentage	8%	24%	50%	30%
Driving In Runners from 3B with Less than Two Out:			9/12	75%

Loves to face: Randy O'Neal (.667, 6-for-9, 1 HR)
Hates to face: Bob Forsch (0-for-14)
The fallout from his 1986 post-season power hitting? Extra-base hits increased from 42 in '86 to 50 in '87, but there was corresponding increase in strikeouts (55 to 67) and decline in walks (58 to 40). ... Grounded into only one double play in 50 double-play situations, 2d-lowest rate (.020) in N.L. (minimum: 40 opportunities). ... Batted .323 in day games, .261 at night. ... Annual batting averages vs. left-handed pitchers since 1985: .268, .233, .203. ... Started 95 of 102 games in which the Mets faced a right-handed starter, but only five of 60 games against southpaws. ... Career figures for California native's games on West Coast: .215 batting average, no home runs.

Nick Esasky

Cincinnati Reds	AB	H	2B	3B	HR	RRF	BB	SO	BA	SA	OBA
Season	346	94	19	2	22	59	29	76	.272	.529	.327
vs. Left-Handers	91	23	5	0	6	15	17	22	.253	.505	.370
vs. Right-Handers	255	71	14	2	16	44	12	54	.278	.537	.310
Home	191	47	9	1	10	31	19	42	.246	.461	.313
Road	155	47	10	1	12	28	10	34	.303	.613	.345
Grass	96	28	4	1	10	23	5	21	.292	.667	.327
Artificial Turf	250	66	15	1	12	36	24	55	.264	.476	.327
April	0	0	0	0	0	0	0	0	—	—	—
May	34	8	3	0	2	6	4	7	.235	.500	.308
June	54	13	1	1	6	16	4	14	.241	.630	.293
July	75	20	5	0	5	18	6	15	.267	.533	.321
August	91	26	1	0	5	8	8	22	.286	.462	.343
Sept./Oct.	92	27	9	1	4	11	7	18	.293	.543	.343
Leading Off Inn.	77	20	3	0	4	4	4	14	.260	.455	.296
Runners On	148	44	10	2	12	49	17	34	.297	.635	.367
Runners/Scor. Pos.	75	21	5	0	6	35	12	21	.280	.587	.375
Runners On/2 Out	61	18	2	2	5	23	10	15	.295	.639	.394
Scor. Pos./2 Out	38	10	1	0	4	19	8	11	.263	.605	.391
Late Inning Pressure	49	14	1	0	2	8	7	13	.286	.429	.375
Leading Off	14	2	0	0	0	0	3	3	.143	.143	.294
Runners On	18	7	0	0	2	8	2	5	.389	.722	.450
Runners/Scor. Pos.	12	5	0	0	2	8	0	4	.417	.917	.417

Bats Right

DRIVING IN RUNS	From 1B	From 2B	From 3B	Scoring Position
Totals	15/111	13/63	9/25	22/88
Percentage	14%	21%	36%	25%
Driving In Runners from 3B with Less than Two Out:			6/13	46%

Loves to face: Steve Bedrosian (.571, 8-for-14, 1 HR)
Hates to face: Jeff D. Robinson (0-for-15)
Career-high marks in home runs and RBI despite playing fewest games (100) since his rookie season. ... Also had lowest strikeout rate of career (one every five times up). ... Averaged 0.45 assists per nine innings last year, lowest rate among major league first basemen (minimum: 500 innings). ... Hit home runs in three games in a row before All-Star break, then added another in his first game after break. ... Career batting average of .230 at Riverfront, .260 on the road. ... .271 vs. left-handers, .233 vs. right-handers. ... Don't give him this "friendly confines" stuff: Esasky has only one home run in 69 career at bats at Wrigley Field, the majors' best home-run park over the five years that he's been around.

Mike Fitzgerald

Montreal Expos	AB	H	2B	3B	HR	RRF	BB	SO	BA	SA	OBA
Season	287	69	11	0	3	36	42	54	.240	.310	.338
vs. Left-Handers	126	27	4	0	2	14	20	30	.214	.294	.327
vs. Right-Handers	161	42	7	0	1	22	22	24	.261	.323	.348
Home	154	39	8	0	1	26	26	25	.253	.325	.363
Road	133	30	3	0	2	10	16	29	.226	.293	.309
Grass	77	21	2	0	1	7	9	18	.273	.338	.349
Artificial Turf	210	48	9	0	2	29	33	36	.229	.300	.335
April	15	4	1	0	0	1	1	3	.267	.333	.313
May	67	13	2	0	1	6	9	16	.194	.269	.286
June	56	15	2	0	2	13	8	6	.268	.411	.359
July	44	14	1	0	0	7	9	4	.318	.341	.434
August	44	10	1	0	0	4	7	12	.227	.250	.333
Sept./Oct.	61	13	4	0	0	5	8	13	.213	.279	.314
Leading Off Inn.	71	19	3	0	1	1	7	12	.268	.352	.333
Runners On	139	33	6	0	1	34	25	29	.237	.302	.355
Runners/Scor. Pos.	87	23	3	0	1	32	17	20	.264	.333	.387
Runners On/2 Out	64	12	1	0	0	11	14	15	.188	.203	.333
Scor. Pos./2 Out	42	9	0	0	0	10	11	10	.214	.214	.377
Late Inning Pressure	44	11	1	0	0	5	4	8	.250	.273	.313
Leading Off	9	3	0	0	0	0	0	1	.333	.333	.333
Runners On	23	6	1	0	0	5	2	5	.261	.304	.320
Runners/Scor. Pos.	16	5	1	0	0	4	0	4	.313	.313	.313

Bats Right

DRIVING IN RUNS	From 1B	From 2B	From 3B	Scoring Position
Totals	5/98	14/74	14/39	28/113
Percentage	5%	19%	36%	25%
Driving In Runners from 3B with Less than Two Out:			12/19	63%

Loves to face: Joe Price (.625, 5-for-8)
Hates to face: Joe Magrane (0-for-10)
Opponents succeeded on 83.9 percent of stolen-base tries, highest rate against any primary catcher in majors: 137 tried, 115 made it; rate against other Expos' catchers was 78.6, meaning there were no Whitey Fords on the staff. ... Batted .300 in day games, .213 at night. ... Two of his three HR last season were hit against his former mates, the Mets. ... Rate of runners driven in from scoring position last season was a career-low, following a career-high 40 percent in 1986. ... Which Expos player will miss Vance Law the most? Our man Fitz, who would replace Law in the field when Vance would pitch mop-up relief. That's how Fitz was mop-up first baseman on June 27, and mop-up second baseman on Aug. 1.

Tim Flannery

San Diego Padres — Bats Left

	AB	H	2B	3B	HR	RRF	BB	SO	BA	SA	OBA
Season	276	63	5	1	0	21	42	30	.228	.254	.332
vs. Left-Handers	41	10	1	0	0	2	4	4	.244	.268	.311
vs. Right-Handers	235	53	4	1	0	19	38	26	.226	.251	.336
Home	122	30	3	0	0	11	21	9	.246	.270	.361
Road	154	33	2	1	0	10	21	21	.214	.240	.309
Grass	199	48	3	1	0	16	32	18	.241	.266	.349
Artificial Turf	77	15	2	0	0	5	10	12	.195	.221	.287
April	21	3	1	0	0	0	5	0	.143	.190	.333
May	16	5	1	1	0	2	1	2	.313	.500	.353
June	84	22	0	0	0	5	11	2	.262	.262	.347
July	53	12	2	0	0	6	7	9	.226	.264	.311
August	63	19	1	0	0	6	12	10	.302	.317	.413
Sept./Oct.	39	2	0	0	0	2	6	7	.051	.051	.191
Leading Off Inn.	59	9	3	0	0	0	12	7	.153	.203	.306
Runners On	106	33	2	1	0	21	14	9	.311	.349	.385
Runners/Scor. Pos.	67	21	2	1	0	21	9	3	.313	.373	.385
Runners On/2 Out	44	12	1	0	0	12	10	5	.273	.295	.407
Scor. Pos./2 Out	36	11	1	0	0	12	7	1	.306	.333	.419
Late Inning Pressure	53	7	1	0	0	3	7	9	.132	.151	.233
Leading Off	12	1	0	0	0	0	3	3	.083	.083	.267
Runners On	24	5	1	0	0	3	2	3	.208	.250	.269
Runners/Scor. Pos.	16	3	1	0	0	3	2	1	.188	.250	.278

DRIVING IN RUNS	From 1B	From 2B	From 3B	Scoring Position
Totals	0/60	12/54	9/24	21/78
Percentage	0%	22%	38%	27%
Driving In Runners from 3B with Less than Two Out:		5/11		45%

Loves to face: Ed Lynch (.500, 7-for-14, 1 HR)
Hates to face: Rick Sutcliffe (.143, 4-for-28, 1 HR)
Batted .350, .345 and .346 in minors in first three years in organized ball; then again, George Brett never hit .300 in bushes. . . . Flan's batting average vs. left-handed pitchers was *above .200* for first time in nine years in majors. His career average vs. lefties is now .161, compared to .271 vs. righties. The 110-point difference is 2d-largest of its kind in majors over last 10 years (minimum: 200 at bats each way). . . . Had one hit in last 36 at bats of 1987, dropping his final mark to .228, a full-season career low. . . . Had N.L.'s lowest slugging average (.251) vs. right-handers last season. . . . Born on Sept. 29, 1957, the day the Brooklyn Dodgers and New York Giants played their last games.

Tom Foley

Montreal Expos — Bats Left

	AB	H	2B	3B	HR	RRF	BB	SO	BA	SA	OBA
Season	280	82	18	3	5	30	11	40	.293	.432	.322
vs. Left-Handers	21	4	1	0	0	0	0	5	.190	.238	.190
vs. Right-Handers	259	78	17	3	5	30	11	35	.301	.448	.332
Home	121	38	7	2	3	9	5	21	.314	.479	.346
Road	159	44	11	1	2	21	6	19	.277	.396	.303
Grass	105	31	7	1	2	19	3	14	.295	.438	.315
Artificial Turf	175	51	11	2	3	11	8	26	.291	.429	.326
April	37	6	1	0	0	4	2	5	.162	.189	.225
May	38	10	3	0	2	7	3	3	.263	.500	.317
June	29	10	2	1	0	0	2	6	.345	.483	.387
July	32	9	4	0	0	2	1	8	.281	.406	.303
August	70	27	7	1	2	11	1	10	.386	.600	.394
Sept./Oct.	74	20	1	1	1	6	2	8	.270	.351	.289
Leading Off Inn.	52	19	4	0	2	2	2	8	.365	.558	.389
Runners On	117	30	7	1	2	27	0	21	.256	.385	.256
Runners/Scor. Pos.	63	16	5	1	2	26	0	11	.254	.460	.254
Runners On/2 Out	47	10	2	1	0	11	0	10	.213	.298	.213
Scor. Pos./2 Out	29	6	2	1	0	11	0	4	.207	.345	.207
Late Inning Pressure	43	17	3	1	1	4	3	4	.395	.581	.435
Leading Off	3	2	0	0	0	0	0	1	.667	.667	.667
Runners On	18	8	1	0	1	4	0	2	.444	.667	.444
Runners/Scor. Pos.	6	4	1	0	1	4	0	1	.667	1.333	.667

DRIVING IN RUNS	From 1B	From 2B	From 3B	Scoring Position
Totals	6/92	9/50	10/27	19/77
Percentage	6%	18%	37%	25%
Driving In Runners from 3B with Less than Two Out:		5/12		42%

Loves to face: Brian Fisher (.545, 6-for-11, 1 HR)
Hates to face: Dwight Gooden (.091, 2-for-22, 7 SO)
Quietly batted .293 last season, as Rodgers had him batting everywhere in the order from first through eighth, except cleanup. . . . Averaged one extra-base hit every 10.8 at bats, the same rate that a shortstop named Ripken had. . . . Stole only six bases in 16 tries last season, 2d-lowest rate (.375) in majors (minimum: 10 CS). . . . Finished season with 0-for-12 slump, his longest drought of year. . . . Made 65 starts vs. right-handed pitchers, two vs. lefties. . . . Had his first regular-season hit-by-pitch experience last year, when ex-teammate Kevin Gross scuffed him; in '86, Roger McDowell broke Foley's wrist with a spring-training pitch, but that doesn't count, despite what Foley might say about it.

Curt Ford

St. Louis Cardinals — Bats Left

	AB	H	2B	3B	HR	RRF	BB	SO	BA	SA	OBA
Season	228	65	9	5	3	28	14	32	.285	.408	.325
vs. Left-Handers	21	6	1	0	0	2	2	5	.286	.333	.348
vs. Right-Handers	207	59	8	5	3	26	12	27	.285	.415	.323
Home	104	29	4	2	1	14	6	15	.279	.385	.316
Road	124	36	5	3	2	14	8	17	.290	.427	.333
Grass	87	24	2	3	0	8	6	11	.276	.368	.323
Artificial Turf	141	41	7	2	3	20	8	21	.291	.433	.327
April	22	9	2	1	0	5	3	3	.409	.591	.480
May	69	22	4	3	1	8	3	11	.319	.507	.347
June	43	14	2	0	2	8	2	4	.326	.512	.348
July	65	15	1	1	0	6	5	8	.231	.277	.292
August	16	3	0	0	0	1	1	3	.188	.188	.222
Sept./Oct.	13	2	0	0	0	0	0	3	.154	.154	.154
Leading Off Inn.	63	19	2	1	1	4	4	8	.302	.413	.353
Runners On	100	30	5	3	1	26	6	13	.300	.440	.330
Runners/Scor. Pos.	65	20	3	2	1	25	3	8	.308	.462	.324
Runners On/2 Out	42	8	1	0	0	7	2	5	.190	.214	.227
Scor. Pos./2 Out	29	6	1	0	0	7	1	2	.207	.241	.233
Late Inning Pressure	52	15	3	0	0	8	4	7	.288	.346	.333
Leading Off	18	4	1	0	0	0	1	1	.222	.278	.263
Runners On	17	6	1	0	0	8	2	1	.353	.412	.400
Runners/Scor. Pos.	12	3	1	0	0	8	1	1	.250	.333	.286

DRIVING IN RUNS	From 1B	From 2B	From 3B	Scoring Position
Totals	1/68	9/49	15/32	24/81
Percentage	1%	18%	47%	30%
Driving In Runners from 3B with Less than Two Out:		9/15		60%

Loves to face: Orel Hershiser (.800, 4-for-5)
Hates to face: Roger McDowell (0-for-9)
Only player in majors last year who hit more home runs in one game (two at Montreal, June 27) than in the rest of the season combined. . . . Started 54 games against right-handed pitchers, but started only twice against southpaws. . . . One of four Cardinals who hit .300+ in both 1987 Championship Series and World Series. . . . Started 50 games in right field, most by any of the 12 right fielders that the Cards used last year. Percentage of playing time in right field: Ford played 29 percent of innings; Lindeman, 23.2; Morris, 20.3; Oquendo, 11.2; Lance Johnson, 6.3; Landrum, 4.3; David Green, 3.5; Pena, 1.0; Lawless, 0.5; Clark, 0.4; Ricky Horton, one inning; Todd Worrell, one-third of an inning.

Terry Francona

Cincinnati Reds — Bats Left

	AB	H	2B	3B	HR	RRF	BB	SO	BA	SA	OBA
Season	207	47	5	0	3	13	10	12	.227	.295	.266
vs. Left-Handers	19	1	0	0	0	2	2	2	.053	.053	.143
vs. Right-Handers	188	46	5	0	3	11	8	10	.245	.319	.279
Home	110	25	1	0	2	10	5	8	.227	.291	.261
Road	97	22	4	0	1	3	5	4	.227	.299	.272
Grass	50	10	2	0	0	0	2	3	.200	.240	.245
Artificial Turf	157	37	3	0	3	13	8	9	.236	.312	.273
April	56	10	0	0	1	5	5	4	.179	.232	.246
May	41	10	2	0	0	1	1	1	.244	.293	.262
June	29	6	2	0	0	0	0	1	.207	.276	.207
July	34	8	0	0	2	5	2	1	.235	.412	.278
August	25	5	1	0	0	2	1	3	.200	.240	.259
Sept./Oct.	22	8	0	0	0	2	1	2	.364	.364	.391
Leading Off Inn.	45	12	1	0	2	2	1	2	.267	.422	.283
Runners On	94	19	0	0	1	11	5	4	.202	.234	.250
Runners/Scor. Pos.	48	9	0	0	0	9	4	1	.188	.188	.264
Runners On/2 Out	41	5	0	0	0	3	3	0	.122	.122	.200
Scor. Pos./2 Out	26	3	0	0	0	3	2	0	.115	.115	.207
Late Inning Pressure	35	8	1	0	1	3	2	2	.229	.343	.270
Leading Off	9	2	1	0	1	1	1	1	.222	.667	.300
Runners On	19	5	0	0	0	2	1	1	.263	.263	.300
Runners/Scor. Pos.	10	2	0	0	0	2	1	0	.200	.200	.273

DRIVING IN RUNS	From 1B	From 2B	From 3B	Scoring Position
Totals	1/68	5/41	4/17	9/58
Percentage	1%	12%	24%	16%
Driving In Runners from 3B with Less than Two Out:		2/4		50%

Loves to face: Ed Whitson (.625, 5-for-8)
Hates to face: Mike LaCoss (0-for-13)
Led the Reds in pinch-hit appearances (44) last season, while Francona himself was pinch-hit for eight times. . . . Started 42 games, all against right-handed pitchers. . . . Has never had more than 41 at bats against left-handed pitchers in any season, and even with 1-for-19 performance last season, his average vs. southpaws (.293, 44-for-150) is still better than his average against right-handers (.274). . . . Career batting average of .207 (6-for-29, no XBH) with the bases loaded. . . . Yearly batting averages since 1984: .346, .267, .250, .227. . . . Career average of .235 in Late-Inning Pressure Situations, .286 at other times. . . . Terry and his dad Tito have now played for 12 of the 26 teams in the majors.

Andres Galarraga

Bats Right

Montreal Expos	AB	H	2B	3B	HR	RRF	BB	SO	BA	SA	OBA
Season	551	168	40	3	13	91	41	127	.305	.459	.361
vs. Left-Handers	164	53	15	0	7	28	17	33	.323	.543	.385
vs. Right-Handers	387	115	25	3	6	63	24	94	.297	.424	.351
Home	264	83	24	1	7	49	24	59	.314	.492	.385
Road	287	85	16	2	6	42	17	68	.296	.429	.339
Grass	139	40	7	0	3	19	11	36	.288	.403	.344
Artificial Turf	412	128	33	3	10	72	30	91	.311	.478	.367
April	72	23	7	0	1	15	9	13	.319	.458	.367
May	89	33	8	0	3	21	13	18	.371	.562	.447
June	94	32	11	1	3	18	8	22	.340	.574	.410
July	79	21	5	1	1	11	3	19	.266	.392	.310
August	103	30	3	1	2	12	6	22	.291	.398	.336
Sept./Oct.	114	29	6	0	3	14	8	33	.254	.386	.304
Leading Off Inn.	113	37	6	1	3	3	7	22	.327	.478	.367
Runners On	262	90	25	1	6	84	28	68	.344	.515	.415
Runners/Scor. Pos.	157	52	11	1	2	70	22	49	.331	.452	.423
Runners On/2 Out	104	39	10	0	4	36	13	25	.375	.587	.458
Scor. Pos./2 Out	70	25	5	0	2	29	11	18	.357	.514	.464
Late Inning Pressure	78	22	6	1	2	12	3	18	.282	.462	.321
Leading Off	19	6	1	1	0	0	0	4	.316	.474	.316
Runners On	31	7	2	0	1	11	3	8	.226	.387	.324
Runners/Scor. Pos.	19	4	0	0	0	9	2	4	.211	.211	.304

DRIVING IN RUNS	From 1B	From 2B	From 3B	Scoring Position
Totals	14/180	37/124	27/61	64/185
Percentage	8%	30%	44%	35%
Driving In Runners from 3B with Less than Two Out:		20/35		57%

Loves to face: Todd Worrell (.556, 5-for-9)
Hates to face: Ron Robinson (0-for-6)
One of three players in majors last season—and the only non-Cardinal—who drove in 90+ runs while hitting less than 15 home runs. The others: Willie McGee and Terry Pendleton.... How'd he do it? Check those batting averages in clutch situations.... Hit by a pitch 10 times last season, most in N.L.... Stole only seven bases in 17 attempts last season, 3d-worst percentage in majors.... Career average of .259 with the bases empty, .313 with runners on base, .328 with runners on base and two outs.... Batted .406 (28-for-69) with three homers and 13 RBI in 18 games against the Cardinals last season.... Raised his batting average above .300 on April 20 and kept it there for rest of year.

Ken Griffey

Bats Left

Atlanta Braves	AB	H	2B	3B	HR	RRF	BB	SO	BA	SA	OBA
Season	399	114	24	1	14	68	46	54	.286	.456	.358
vs. Left-Handers	87	22	2	0	2	13	6	9	.253	.345	.298
vs. Right-Handers	312	92	22	1	12	55	40	45	.295	.487	.374
Home	223	65	15	1	8	43	24	30	.291	.475	.355
Road	176	49	9	0	6	25	22	24	.278	.432	.362
Grass	324	91	20	1	8	55	39	43	.281	.423	.356
Artificial Turf	75	23	4	0	6	13	7	11	.307	.600	.366
April	62	22	4	0	4	14	9	9	.355	.613	.431
May	50	17	5	1	2	15	3	3	.340	.600	.382
June	93	26	5	0	4	13	8	15	.280	.462	.333
July	77	16	1	0	2	12	10	11	.208	.299	.295
August	71	19	3	0	2	7	13	8	.268	.394	.381
Sept./Oct.	46	14	6	0	0	7	3	8	.304	.435	.347
Leading Off Inn.	92	28	1	0	5	5	7	14	.304	.478	.354
Runners On	190	46	16	0	1	55	27	27	.242	.342	.330
Runners/Scor. Pos.	115	29	7	0	1	49	19	15	.252	.339	.348
Runners On/2 Out	75	18	5	0	0	13	18	15	.240	.307	.387
Scor. Pos./2 Out	47	11	2	0	0	11	14	9	.234	.277	.410
Late Inning Pressure	79	18	6	0	1	10	2	13	.228	.342	.247
Leading Off	25	7	1	0	1	0	0	4	.280	.440	.280
Runners On	40	8	3	0	0	9	2	7	.200	.275	.238
Runners/Scor. Pos.	23	5	1	0	0	7	1	4	.217	.261	.250

DRIVING IN RUNS	From 1B	From 2B	From 3B	Scoring Position
Totals	10/152	22/99	22/43	44/142
Percentage	7%	22%	51%	31%
Driving In Runners from 3B with Less than Two Out:		20/32		63%

Loves to face: Al Nipper (.538, 7-for-13, 1 HR)
Hates to face: Bob Walk (0-for-14)
Batted .611 (11-for-18) as a pinch-hitter last season; the Braves' other pinch-hitters batted a composite .188.... Six of his 14 home runs were hit against his ex-mates from Cincinnati.... Career batting average has once again dropped below .300 to .2993. Batted .285 in A.L.; N.L. career average stands at .306.... Home run rate has increased through the years. At bats per home run: 64.3 with Cincinnati ('73–'81), 40.3 with the Yankees ('82–'86), 26.6 with Atlanta ('86–'87).... Has batted .448 (26-for-58) with the bases loaded since 1984.... Has played for only three managers (Anderson, McNamara, Tanner) in 10 1/2 seasons in N.L., but played for six in his 4 1/2-year tour of duty with Yankees.

Phil Garner

Bats Right

Astros/Dodgers	AB	H	2B	3B	HR	RRF	BB	SO	BA	SA	OBA
Season	238	49	9	0	5	24	28	44	.206	.307	.285
vs. Left-Handers	143	33	6	0	4	17	18	23	.231	.357	.311
vs. Right-Handers	95	16	3	0	1	7	10	21	.168	.232	.245
Home	111	22	3	0	0	7	15	17	.198	.225	.291
Road	127	27	6	0	5	17	13	27	.213	.378	.280
Grass	113	25	6	0	2	7	19	23	.221	.327	.331
Artificial Turf	125	24	3	0	3	17	9	21	.192	.288	.241
April	48	14	2	0	2	11	2	5	.292	.458	.308
May	51	9	3	0	1	4	5	9	.176	.294	.250
June	25	3	0	0	0	1	4	8	.120	.120	.233
July	29	6	0	0	1	2	5	5	.207	.310	.314
August	41	7	1	0	0	2	3	6	.171	.195	.227
Sept./Oct.	44	10	3	0	1	4	9	11	.227	.364	.358
Leading Off Inn.	63	15	3	0	0	0	6	12	.238	.286	.304
Runners On	95	20	3	0	2	21	18	15	.211	.305	.325
Runners/Scor. Pos.	65	15	3	0	1	19	13	12	.231	.323	.341
Runners On/2 Out	40	6	1	0	1	7	10	4	.150	.250	.320
Scor. Pos./2 Out	26	3	1	0	0	5	9	4	.115	.154	.343
Late Inning Pressure	43	12	2	0	1	5	4	11	.279	.395	.340
Leading Off	9	4	0	0	0	0	1	2	.444	.444	.500
Runners On	16	4	1	0	0	4	3	4	.250	.313	.368
Runners/Scor. Pos.	10	3	1	0	0	4	2	3	.300	.400	.417

DRIVING IN RUNS	From 1B	From 2B	From 3B	Scoring Position
Totals	2/61	5/51	12/23	17/74
Percentage	3%	10%	52%	23%
Driving In Runners from 3B with Less than Two Out:		9/12		75%

Loves to face: Ed Lynch (.458, 11-for-24)
Hates to face: Tom Hume (.097, 3-for-31)
Astros played .552 ball (16–13) with Garner starting at third last season, but .451 (60–73) in their other games.... Played nine innings at shortstop for Dodgers last season, his first action there since 1980.... Used as a pinch-hitter 32 times last season, but was taken out for a hitter 16 times.... Batting average in Late-Inning Pressure Situations has been higher than his overall average in each of the last five seasons.... Over last 13 seasons, has batted .303 in LIPS with runners in scoring position.... First major-league game: Sept. 10, 1973, with A's. Only two other players from that world champion Oakland team were still active last year: Reggie Jackson and Manny Trillo.

Pedro Guerrero

Bats Right

Los Angeles Dodgers	AB	H	2B	3B	HR	RRF	BB	SO	BA	SA	OBA
Season	545	184	25	2	27	90	74	85	.338	.539	.416
vs. Left-Handers	167	61	7	2	8	26	27	21	.365	.575	.451
vs. Right-Handers	378	123	18	0	19	64	47	64	.325	.524	.400
Home	275	89	11	0	12	44	34	44	.324	.495	.397
Road	270	95	14	2	15	46	40	41	.352	.585	.434
Grass	415	138	16	1	21	70	56	69	.333	.528	.414
Artificial Turf	130	46	9	1	6	20	18	16	.354	.577	.421
April	72	24	4	2	5	18	9	13	.333	.653	.410
May	97	37	4	0	9	22	9	20	.381	.701	.426
June	101	24	2	0	2	8	13	19	.238	.317	.325
July	82	34	4	0	6	16	19	12	.415	.683	.520
August	94	24	5	0	1	6	8	12	.255	.340	.317
Sept./Oct.	99	41	6	0	4	20	16	9	.414	.596	.500
Leading Off Inn.	111	33	7	2	5	5	16	19	.297	.532	.391
Runners On	243	82	10	0	11	74	38	39	.337	.514	.421
Runners/Scor. Pos.	125	43	3	0	7	64	31	21	.344	.536	.457
Runners On/2 Out	87	25	1	0	4	24	15	18	.287	.437	.398
Scor. Pos./2 Out	47	15	0	0	2	19	14	8	.319	.447	.475
Late Inning Pressure	78	20	5	0	1	9	15	12	.256	.359	.376
Leading Off	22	3	0	0	0	0	4	4	.136	.273	.269
Runners On	33	10	2	0	1	9	10	4	.303	.455	.465
Runners/Scor. Pos.	14	7	0	0	1	9	9	0	.500	.714	.696

DRIVING IN RUNS	From 1B	From 2B	From 3B	Scoring Position
Totals	11/169	20/89	31/55	51/144
Percentage	7%	22%	56%	35%
Driving In Runners from 3B with Less than Two Out:		25/39		64%

Loves to face: Todd Worrell (5-for-5, 2 HR)
Hates to face: Dwight Gooden (.150, 3-for-20, 2 HR, 10 SO)
Had highest batting average by a Dodgers player since Tommy Davis hit .346 in 1962; only difference is that Davis broke his ankle three years *after* his career-high season; Guerrero broke his the year before.... Averaged only 1.62 putouts per nine innings last season, lowest rate of any left fielder in majors (minimum: 500 innings).... Batting average in July was highest in majors.... Career average of .311 vs. left-handers, .309 vs. right-handers.... Ranked second in N.L. with 56 multiple-hit games.... Played three consecutive games without a hit only once last season.... Ended the season with a career-high 17-game hitting streak, the longest of his career. Look out, Willie Keeler!

Tony Gwynn

San Diego Padres — Bats Left

	AB	H	2B	3B	HR	RRF	BB	SO	BA	SA	OBA
Season	589	218	36	13	7	58	82	35	.370	.511	.447
vs. Left-Handers	249	90	12	3	3	24	30	10	.361	.470	.433
vs. Right-Handers	340	128	24	10	4	34	52	25	.376	.541	.457
Home	282	110	15	11	5	27	44	19	.390	.574	.473
Road	307	108	21	2	2	31	38	16	.352	.453	.423
Grass	425	159	24	12	6	44	58	26	.374	.529	.452
Artificial Turf	164	59	12	1	1	14	24	9	.360	.463	.435
April	90	30	4	1	2	8	7	6	.333	.467	.381
May	95	32	9	1	1	9	17	5	.337	.484	.447
June	93	44	5	5	1	10	11	3	.473	.667	.524
July	96	28	5	1	1	10	15	9	.292	.396	.381
August	117	47	9	3	1	10	13	7	.402	.556	.466
Sept./Oct.	98	37	4	2	1	5	19	5	.378	.490	.475
Leading Off Inn.	135	47	4	2	3	3	10	12	.348	.474	.397
Runners On	230	78	17	7	0	51	47	7	.339	.474	.447
Runners/Scor. Pos.	126	38	7	2	0	43	41	6	.302	.389	.465
Runners On/2 Out	94	28	7	2	0	16	24	4	.298	.415	.441
Scor. Pos./2 Out	56	15	4	1	0	14	22	4	.268	.375	.474
Late Inning Pressure	89	30	6	2	0	6	13	10	.337	.449	.417
Leading Off	26	7	0	1	0	0	2	6	.269	.346	.321
Runners On	34	10	3	0	0	6	7	2	.294	.382	.405
Runners/Scor. Pos.	18	4	1	0	0	5	7	2	.222	.278	.423

DRIVING IN RUNS	From 1B	From 2B	From 3B	Scoring Position
Totals	11/163	12/94	28/49	40/143
Percentage	7%	13%	57%	28%
Driving In Runners from 3B with Less than Two Out:			22/27	81%

Loves to face: Ron Darling (.500, 18-for-36)
Hates to face: Scott Garrelts (.143, 4-for-28)
Did not go more than eight at bats without a hit at any time last season. . . . Moved into batting lead on June 24 and held it for rest of season. . . . Batted .466 vs. Atlanta last season, with 34 hits, the most by any player vs. any team last year. . . . Hit a career-high .361 vs. left-handers last season, lifting career mark vs. southpaws to .318. That's 2d-best by any player in majors over last 13 years (minimum: 150 hits vs. LHP), behind Kirby Puckett's .335. . . . A wart: Had only one hit in nine at bats with bases loaded last season, but not to worry. His career average in those situations is still a cool .390. . . . Only player in majors with 100+ runs, 200+, hits and 300+ total bases in both 1986 and 1987.

Albert Hall

Atlanta Braves — Bats Left and Right

	AB	H	2B	3B	HR	RRF	BB	SO	BA	SA	OBA
Season	292	83	20	4	3	26	38	36	.284	.411	.369
vs. Left-Handers	122	35	8	0	1	9	13	16	.287	.377	.358
vs. Right-Handers	170	48	12	4	2	17	25	20	.282	.435	.378
Home	136	40	7	2	3	14	23	19	.294	.441	.401
Road	156	43	13	2	0	12	15	17	.276	.385	.339
Grass	180	51	8	3	3	17	31	24	.283	.411	.393
Artificial Turf	112	32	12	1	0	9	7	12	.286	.411	.328
April	11	2	2	0	0	0	1	2	.182	.364	.250
May	69	23	7	2	1	10	11	5	.333	.536	.425
June	36	9	1	0	0	2	9	2	.250	.278	.400
July	45	9	3	0	0	4	3	9	.200	.267	.245
August	38	12	1	0	0	2	4	5	.316	.342	.395
Sept./Oct.	93	28	6	2	2	8	10	13	.301	.473	.375
Leading Off Inn.	113	42	11	3	1	1	10	13	.372	.549	.423
Runners On	92	20	5	0	0	23	19	8	.217	.272	.354
Runners/Scor. Pos.	61	16	5	0	0	23	17	4	.262	.344	.425
Runners On/2 Out	42	9	2	0	0	11	10	4	.214	.262	.365
Scor. Pos./2 Out	27	7	2	0	0	11	8	3	.259	.333	.429
Late Inning Pressure	56	18	5	2	0	4	6	7	.321	.482	.397
Leading Off	12	4	0	2	0	0	1	3	.333	.667	.385
Runners On	20	5	2	0	0	4	2	1	.250	.350	.318
Runners/Scor. Pos.	13	3	2	0	0	4	2	1	.231	.385	.333

DRIVING IN RUNS	From 1B	From 2B	From 3B	Scoring Position
Totals	0/56	7/49	15/30	22/79
Percentage	0%	14%	50%	28%
Driving In Runners from 3B with Less than Two Out:			8/14	57%

Loves to face: Mike LaCoss (.571, 4-for-7)
Hates to face: Mark Davis (0-for-8)
Had outstanding leading-off-innings numbers; Braves properly used him as leadoff batter in 63 of 65 games that he started. . . . Batted 98 points lower with runners on base than he did with the bases empty, 2d-largest such difference in N.L. last season (minimum: 75 at bats both ways). . . . Hit safely in his first 14 starts last season. . . . Had 43 more at bats last season than he had in parts of six previous seasons with Braves. . . . Stole six bases in four games last October; unfortunately for Braves, it wasn't in a post-season series, but in a play-out-the-string sequence against the Astros and Giants. . . . Bob Horner, he's not: Hall has driven in only one of 120 runners from first base in his career.

Billy Hatcher

Houston Astros — Bats Right

	AB	H	2B	3B	HR	RRF	BB	SO	BA	SA	OBA
Season	564	167	28	3	11	66	42	70	.296	.415	.352
vs. Left-Handers	202	56	12	1	4	30	17	29	.277	.406	.335
vs. Right-Handers	362	111	16	2	7	36	25	41	.307	.420	.361
Home	259	79	11	0	3	27	20	43	.305	.382	.358
Road	305	88	17	3	8	39	22	27	.289	.443	.346
Grass	189	52	8	1	6	24	15	17	.275	.423	.340
Artificial Turf	375	115	20	2	5	42	27	53	.307	.411	.358
April	87	34	7	1	3	12	4	11	.391	.598	.424
May	103	29	5	1	0	11	11	13	.282	.350	.350
June	113	33	4	0	4	13	11	21	.292	.434	.360
July	55	13	1	0	1	4	4	7	.236	.309	.311
August	120	40	8	1	3	19	8	9	.333	.492	.385
Sept./Oct.	86	18	3	0	0	7	4	9	.209	.244	.250
Leading Off Inn.	166	49	11	0	1	1	17	20	.295	.380	.371
Runners On	191	60	8	2	5	60	20	25	.314	.455	.370
Runners/Scor. Pos.	112	36	6	2	5	51	15	14	.321	.464	.386
Runners On/2 Out	90	27	3	1	2	27	4	16	.300	.422	.330
Scor. Pos./2 Out	60	18	2	1	1	24	4	11	.300	.417	.344
Late Inning Pressure	81	29	7	2	1	12	6	14	.358	.531	.409
Leading Off	17	6	1	0	0	0	0	4	.353	.412	.353
Runners On	39	10	1	1	1	12	6	6	.256	.410	.356
Runners/Scor. Pos.	21	7	1	1	1	12	5	5	.333	.619	.462

DRIVING IN RUNS	From 1B	From 2B	From 3B	Scoring Position
Totals	12/135	20/90	23/50	43/140
Percentage	9%	22%	46%	31%
Driving In Runners from 3B with Less than Two Out:			15/23	65%

Loves to face: Fernando Valenzuela (.393, 11-for-28, 1 HR)
Hates to face: Ed Whitson (0-for-10)
8-for-8 on steals of third last season, leading Astros' perfect 14-for-14 team total. . . . Averaged only 2.12 putouts per nine innings last season, lowest rate among N.L. center fielders (minimum: 500 innings). . . . Career average of .322 in Late-Inning Pressure Situations, .266 at other times. . . . Led N.L. with .391 batting average in April. . . . Batted .275 in 72 games in leadoff spot, .317 in 67 games batting second. . . . Took .311 batting average to sidelines as he sat out 10-game suspension for doctored bat in early September; batted only .203 in 21 games after his return. . . . That left his post-September 1 career batting average at .210, compared to .294 career average from April through August.

Mickey Hatcher

Los Angeles Dodgers — Bats Right

	AB	H	2B	3B	HR	RRF	BB	SO	BA	SA	OBA
Season	287	81	19	1	7	44	20	19	.282	.429	.328
vs. Left-Handers	125	41	13	0	4	22	12	6	.328	.528	.384
vs. Right-Handers	162	40	6	1	3	22	8	13	.247	.352	.283
Home	137	35	8	0	3	23	8	8	.255	.401	.301
Road	150	46	11	1	3	21	12	11	.307	.453	.352
Grass	209	52	12	0	5	34	14	15	.249	.378	.296
Artificial Turf	78	29	7	1	2	10	6	4	.372	.564	.412
April	16	3	2	0	0	3	2	5	.188	.313	.263
May	47	16	4	0	2	5	1	0	.340	.553	.354
June	60	17	4	0	0	7	3	2	.283	.350	.313
July	82	32	5	1	4	16	3	3	.390	.622	.419
August	68	11	3	0	1	11	10	6	.162	.250	.266
Sept./Oct.	14	2	1	0	0	2	1	3	.143	.214	.200
Leading Off Inn.	78	23	6	0	2	2	2	6	.295	.449	.313
Runners On	119	35	7	1	3	40	14	8	.294	.445	.365
Runners/Scor. Pos.	71	21	4	0	0	31	9	6	.296	.352	.369
Runners On/2 Out	52	14	3	0	1	18	7	3	.269	.385	.367
Scor. Pos./2 Out	37	9	2	0	0	15	5	3	.243	.297	.349
Late Inning Pressure	48	9	0	0	1	4	4	8	.188	.250	.250
Leading Off	19	6	0	0	1	1	0	4	.316	.474	.316
Runners On	20	2	0	0	0	3	4	3	.100	.100	.250
Runners/Scor. Pos.	13	1	0	0	0	3	2	2	.077	.077	.200

DRIVING IN RUNS	From 1B	From 2B	From 3B	Scoring Position
Totals	7/84	17/59	13/27	30/86
Percentage	8%	29%	48%	35%
Driving In Runners from 3B with Less than Two Out:			8/11	73%

Loves to face: Danny Jackson (.414, 12-for-29)
Hates to face: Greg Maddux (0-for-6)
Batted 123 points higher on artificial surfaces than on grass fields, largest such difference in N.L. (minimum: 50 at bats each way). Career average is 51 points higher on artificial surfaces (.307 to .256 on grass) and that's the largest difference of any player over the last 10 years with at least 1,000 at bats both ways. . . . Has batted .300+ vs. left-handed pitchers in four of the last five seasons. . . . Batted .063 (1-for-16) as a pinch-hitter last season; the one hit came in his last pinch-hit appearance of the year, Sept. 19. . . . Yearly batting averages in Late-Inning Pressure Situations since 1983: .431, .348, .218, .170, .188. . . . Has drawn 138 walks in nine years in majors, or two less than Jack Clark had last year alone.

Batters: National League

Von Hayes
Philadelphia Phillies — Bats Left

	AB	H	2B	3B	HR	RRF	BB	SO	BA	SA	OBA
Season	556	154	36	5	21	88	121	77	.277	.473	.404
vs. Left-Handers	168	39	8	1	3	22	35	31	.232	.345	.361
vs. Right-Handers	388	115	28	4	18	66	86	46	.296	.528	.422
Home	278	70	14	3	14	54	71	30	.252	.475	.401
Road	278	84	22	2	7	34	50	47	.302	.471	.407
Grass	142	39	9	1	2	14	25	24	.275	.394	.383
Artificial Turf	414	115	27	4	19	74	96	53	.278	.500	.411
April	65	16	3	0	1	9	19	12	.246	.338	.417
May	75	18	0	2	2	12	23	16	.240	.373	.410
June	87	29	12	1	5	14	17	5	.333	.667	.442
July	98	33	9	1	8	25	24	14	.337	.694	.463
August	114	34	7	1	3	27	14	14	.298	.456	.433
Sept./Oct.	117	24	5	0	2	11	11	16	.205	.299	.271
Leading Off Inn.	97	32	4	0	5	5	18	10	.330	.526	.435
Runners On	248	74	21	4	8	75	58	27	.298	.512	.426
Runners/Scor. Pos.	158	41	8	3	4	62	45	19	.259	.424	.415
Runners On/2 Out	71	22	5	2	3	26	25	9	.310	.563	.490
Scor. Pos./2 Out	55	16	4	2	3	25	22	7	.291	.600	.494
Late Inning Pressure	82	24	7	0	2	10	17	9	.293	.451	.410
Leading Off	23	8	2	0	1	1	1	2	.348	.565	.375
Runners On	31	10	3	0	0	8	10	1	.323	.419	.476
Runners/Scor. Pos.	16	6	2	0	0	8	7	0	.375	.500	.542

DRIVING IN RUNS	From 1B	From 2B	From 3B	Scoring Position
Totals	15/155	27/128	25/52	52/180
Percentage	10%	21%	48%	29%
Driving In Runners from 3B with Less than Two Out:		21/34	62%	

Loves to face: Mike Krukow (.471, 16-for-34, 1 HR)
Hates to face: Mike Bielecki (.077, 1-for-13)

A player who provides both power and on-base ability: Over past two years, he has 82 doubles to lead N.L., and .442 on-base average when leading off innings. . . . Averaged one walk every 5.6 times up, 2d-best rate in N.L. (minimum: 50 BB). . . . Has hit 50 home runs at the Vet, 25 home runs on road, since joining Phillies in 1983. . . . Averaged 29 stolen bases per year from '82 to '86, but swiped only 16 in '87. . . . Has homered at every N.L. ballpark except Dodger Stadium (101 career at bats). . . . Career batting average of .290 (one home run every 32.2 at bats) vs. right-handers, .238 (one every 57.7) vs. left-handers. Hasn't hit above .240 vs. lefties in any of the five seasons in which he has 100+ at bats against them.

Keith Hernandez
New York Mets — Bats Left

	AB	H	2B	3B	HR	RRF	BB	SO	BA	SA	OBA
Season	587	170	28	2	18	91	81	104	.290	.436	.377
vs. Left-Handers	252	64	10	1	6	31	32	51	.254	.373	.343
vs. Right-Handers	335	106	18	1	12	60	49	53	.316	.484	.403
Home	281	81	13	1	6	39	42	52	.288	.406	.386
Road	306	89	15	1	12	52	39	52	.291	.464	.369
Grass	414	120	17	1	13	65	54	79	.290	.430	.375
Artificial Turf	173	50	11	1	5	26	27	25	.289	.451	.383
April	74	22	4	0	4	12	11	13	.297	.514	.391
May	100	34	3	1	1	8	12	21	.340	.420	.411
June	99	25	4	1	5	17	8	17	.253	.465	.315
July	100	31	5	0	0	10	20	13	.310	.360	.421
August	107	32	10	0	3	21	14	21	.299	.477	.387
Sept./Oct.	107	26	2	0	5	23	16	19	.243	.402	.339
Leading Off Inn.	92	24	1	0	4	10	20	10	.261	.402	.333
Runners On	284	85	14	1	7	80	48	45	.299	.430	.399
Runners/Scor. Pos.	171	44	10	0	6	72	34	27	.257	.421	.379
Runners On/2 Out	92	21	5	0	3	18	17	18	.228	.380	.355
Scor. Pos./2 Out	64	12	5	0	2	16	14	12	.188	.359	.342
Late Inning Pressure	78	21	1	0	2	7	9	19	.269	.359	.352
Leading Off	15	4	0	0	1	1		5	.267	.467	.313
Runners On	42	10	1	0	0	5	6	11	.238	.262	.347
Runners/Scor. Pos.	22	3	1	0	0	5	2	6	.136	.182	.240

DRIVING IN RUNS	From 1B	From 2B	From 3B	Scoring Position
Totals	13/189	32/131	28/62	60/193
Percentage	7%	24%	45%	31%
Driving In Runners from 3B with Less than Two Out:		26/39	67%	

Loves to face: Dave Smith (.600, 9-for-15)
Hates to face: Bob McClure (.067, 1-for-15)

One of seven players in majors with 80+ runs scored and 80+ RBI in each of last four years; Keith's the only one of them who hasn't had a 20-HR season in there. . . . Did set a career high with 18 home runs, but strikeouts exceeded walks for first time since 1977. . . . Those 289 plate appearances vs. left-handers were most *by a righty or lefty* in majors. . . . Batting average with runners in scoring position was his lowest in any full year in majors. . . . Only N.L. first baseman to average more than one assist per nine innings (minimum: 500 innings). . . . Has more career assists (1,554) than any first baseman in history of baseball; he broke George Sisler's record last year. . . . Led N.L. with .382 batting average in Sunday games.

Tom Herr
St. Louis Cardinals — Bats Left and Right

	AB	H	2B	3B	HR	RRF	BB	SO	BA	SA	OBA
Season	510	134	29	0	2	85	68	62	.263	.331	.346
vs. Left-Handers	191	57	13	0	2	36	29	16	.298	.398	.386
vs. Right-Handers	319	77	16	0	0	49	39	46	.241	.292	.322
Home	246	69	12	0	1	34	34	25	.280	.341	.368
Road	264	65	17	0	1	51	34	37	.246	.322	.325
Grass	121	27	5	0	0	25	16	16	.223	.264	.307
Artificial Turf	389	107	24	0	2	60	52	46	.275	.352	.358
April	52	15	7	0	1	13	8	5	.288	.481	.393
May	58	17	1	0	0	2	7	12	.293	.310	.379
June	104	32	5	0	0	17	15	11	.308	.356	.393
July	95	19	6	0	0	19	13	11	.200	.263	.288
August	95	32	9	0	1	20	9	11	.337	.463	.380
Sept./Oct.	106	19	1	0	0	14	16	12	.179	.189	.280
Leading Off Inn.	82	21	4	0	0		8	7	.256	.305	.322
Runners On	266	73	17	0	2	85	39	34	.274	.361	.357
Runners/Scor. Pos.	160	43	11	0	1	77	32	21	.269	.356	.368
Runners On/2 Out	79	22	7	0	1	28	13	10	.278	.405	.382
Scor. Pos./2 Out	53	15	5	0	1	26	12	7	.283	.434	.415
Late Inning Pressure	76	22	3	0	1	21	8	15	.289	.368	.349
Leading Off	19	6	1	0	0	0	2	3	.316	.368	.381
Runners On	42	12	1	0	1	21	3	10	.286	.381	.319
Runners/Scor. Pos.	29	10	1	0	1	21	3	6	.345	.483	.382

DRIVING IN RUNS	From 1B	From 2B	From 3B	Scoring Position
Totals	9/161	23/126	51/81	74/207
Percentage	6%	18%	63%	36%
Driving In Runners from 3B with Less than Two Out:		40/53	75%	

Loves to face: Mike Scott (.415, 17-for-41, 7 BBs)
Hates to face: Ron Darling (.081, 3-for-37, 1 HR)

Tied for major-league lead with a dozen "scoring fly balls" last season. He drove in Coleman on six of those. . . . Drove in N.L.-high 17 runs in 13 games vs. Mets last season. . . . Has batted .306 with runners on base, .244 with bases empty over last three years. . . . Averaged 2.69 assists per nine innings last season, lowest average among N.L. second basemen (minimum: 500 innings). . . . Committed six errors in 42 day games, one error in 96 games at night. . . . Career batting average of .213 at Atlanta Stadium is his lowest at any N.L. ballpark. . . . Those knees really must ache: Became first Cardinals player since Ken Reitz in 1980 to have a 500–at bat season and not hit a single triple.

Glenn Hubbard
Atlanta Braves — Bats Right

	AB	H	2B	3B	HR	RRF	BB	SO	BA	SA	OBA
Season	443	117	33	2	5	40	77	57	.264	.381	.378
vs. Left-Handers	104	30	9	0	2	13	24	12	.288	.433	.419
vs. Right-Handers	339	87	24	2	3	27	53	45	.257	.366	.365
Home	222	56	12	2	3	20	45	32	.252	.365	.383
Road	221	61	21	0	2	20	32	25	.276	.398	.373
Grass	312	84	20	2	4	26	63	40	.269	.385	.397
Artificial Turf	131	33	13	0	1	14	14	17	.252	.374	.329
April	65	21	7	0	0	10	17	6	.323	.431	.476
May	82	25	6	0	3	11	12	12	.305	.488	.394
June	75	22	5	2	1	7	23	10	.293	.453	.465
July	88	22	7	0	1	4	10	8	.250	.364	.333
August	90	21	8	0	0	6	12	12	.233	.322	.324
Sept./Oct.	43	6	0	0	0	2	3	9	.140	.140	.196
Leading Off Inn.	109	31	11	0	1	1	18	10	.284	.413	.386
Runners On	177	49	10	0	2	37	43	28	.277	.367	.423
Runners/Scor. Pos.	88	24	6	0	0	33	30	18	.273	.341	.451
Runners On/2 Out	76	18	2	0	0	13	25	12	.237	.263	.426
Scor. Pos./2 Out	42	10	2	0	0	13	19	9	.238	.286	.475
Late Inning Pressure	71	18	4	0	1	4	6	11	.254	.352	.321
Leading Off	19	4	2	0	0	0	2	3	.211	.316	.286
Runners On	24	6	2	0	0	3	1	4	.250	.333	.308
Runners/Scor. Pos.	12	3	1	0	0	3	0	2	.250	.333	.250

DRIVING IN RUNS	From 1B	From 2B	From 3B	Scoring Position
Totals	4/140	10/71	21/41	31/112
Percentage	3%	14%	51%	28%
Driving In Runners from 3B with Less than Two Out:		14/20	70%	

Loves to face: Dave Stewart (.538, 7-for-13, 1 HR)
Hates to face: Steve Trout (.105, 2-for-19)

Averaged 3.63 assists per nine innings last season, giving him highest rate of any second basemen in majors (minimum: 500 innings) for second year in a row. He must have fielded all the balls hit to right of Gerald Perry, who ranked near bottom among first basemen in same category. . . . Had best strikeout to walk ratio of his career. . . . Overall batting average and average in Late-Inning Pressure Situations were also career highs. . . . Should like A.L.: he's one of two active players (the other: Andre Dawson) to have hit for a higher average on grass fields than on artificial turf in each of last nine seasons. Career averages: .252 on grass, .224 on rug. . . . Started 136 games last season, all in 8th-spot in lineup.

Chris James
Philadelphia Phillies — Bats Right

	AB	H	2B	3B	HR	RRF	BB	SO	BA	SA	OBA
Season	358	105	20	6	17	54	27	67	.293	.525	.344
vs. Left-Handers	149	42	10	3	9	26	11	26	.282	.570	.327
vs. Right-Handers	209	63	10	3	8	28	16	41	.301	.493	.355
Home	172	52	10	3	9	31	18	33	.302	.552	.366
Road	186	53	10	3	8	23	9	34	.285	.500	.322
Grass	85	20	2	0	7	14	2	17	.235	.506	.247
Artificial Turf	273	85	18	6	10	40	25	50	.311	.531	.372
April	27	7	1	1	0	0	3	10	.259	.370	.333
May	16	4	1	0	0	1	1	3	.250	.313	.294
June	56	19	3	0	6	15	3	11	.339	.714	.377
July	88	31	8	2	4	11	3	13	.352	.625	.380
August	102	27	5	2	7	19	10	20	.265	.559	.330
Sept./Oct.	69	17	2	1	0	8	7	10	.246	.304	.308
Leading Off Inn.	73	25	5	0	2	2	4	13	.342	.493	.385
Runners On	158	39	7	3	7	44	13	35	.247	.462	.299
Runners/Scor. Pos.	103	24	5	2	6	40	7	23	.233	.495	.274
Runners On/2 Out	71	18	2	2	3	15	5	14	.254	.465	.303
Scor. Pos./2 Out	48	10	1	2	2	13	3	12	.208	.438	.255
Late Inning Pressure	49	15	1	0	2	3	5	9	.306	.449	.370
Leading Off	12	4	1	0	1	1	3	1	.333	.667	.467
Runners On	23	4	0	0	0	1	2	6	.174	.174	.240
Runners/Scor. Pos.	14	1	0	0	0	1	2	4	.071	.071	.188

DRIVING IN RUNS	From 1B	From 2B	From 3B	Scoring Position
Totals	6/114	16/79	15/37	31/116
Percentage	5%	20%	41%	27%
Driving In Runners from 3B with Less than Two Out:				11/18 61%

Loves to face: Neal Heaton (.462, 6-for-13, 1 HR)
Hates to face: Mike Dunne (0-for-8)
Hit all 17 home runs over span of 240 at bats between June 2 and Aug. 29, an average of one homer every 14.1 at bats during that period. . . . Homered in consecutive games three times in a three-week period in August. . . . Averaged 2.21 putouts per nine innings last season, 2d-highest rate among N.L. left fielders (minimum: 500 innings). . . . Born on day that 1962 World Series opened: Whitey Ford beat Giants for his 10th Series victory. . . . Career average of .467 (7-for-15, one HR) as a pinch-hitter. . . . Started 45 of 49 games in which Phils faced a left-handed starter, but only 45 of 113 in which they faced a right-hander. He may have earned more time against righties with that .301 average against them.

Dion James
Atlanta Braves — Bats Left

	AB	H	2B	3B	HR	RRF	BB	SO	BA	SA	OBA
Season	494	154	37	6	10	64	70	63	.312	.472	.397
vs. Left-Handers	89	27	7	1	1	14	22	14	.303	.438	.442
vs. Right-Handers	405	127	30	5	9	50	48	49	.314	.479	.386
Home	237	89	21	4	5	37	39	20	.376	.561	.466
Road	257	65	16	2	5	27	31	43	.253	.389	.331
Grass	381	125	29	5	10	55	53	49	.328	.509	.410
Artificial Turf	113	29	8	1	0	9	17	14	.257	.345	.354
April	74	24	8	0	1	9	15	16	.324	.473	.440
May	92	23	7	2	2	12	14	15	.250	.435	.349
June	75	22	4	0	2	6	14	10	.293	.427	.404
July	65	23	2	2	2	9	15	4	.354	.538	.475
August	91	26	5	2	3	17	4	10	.286	.484	.309
Sept./Oct.	97	36	11	0	0	11	8	8	.371	.485	.425
Leading Off Inn.	196	67	18	2	6	6	22	26	.342	.546	.411
Runners On	173	55	13	3	4	58	30	26	.318	.497	.415
Runners/Scor. Pos.	113	36	8	3	3	53	20	19	.319	.522	.416
Runners On/2 Out	72	20	5	1	1	21	13	17	.278	.417	.388
Scor. Pos./2 Out	49	14	2	1	1	19	7	13	.286	.429	.375
Late Inning Pressure	82	22	3	0	0	5	11	9	.268	.305	.362
Leading Off	22	5	2	0	0	0	2	2	.227	.318	.292
Runners On	31	8	0	0	0	5	4	4	.258	.258	.361
Runners/Scor. Pos.	15	4	0	0	0	5	1	1	.267	.267	.353

DRIVING IN RUNS	From 1B	From 2B	From 3B	Scoring Position
Totals	11/105	20/91	23/46	43/137
Percentage	10%	22%	50%	31%
Driving In Runners from 3B with Less than Two Out:				17/27 63%

Loves to face: Mike Krukow (.545, 6-for-11, 1 HR)
Hates to face: Dennis Martinez (0-for-8)
Batted 123 points higher in home games than he did on road, largest such difference in N.L. in 1987 (minimum: 50 at bats each way). . . . Career batting average of .376 (89-for-237) in Atlanta Stadium. . . . Career batting average of .245 in day games, .319 at night. That 74-point gap is 2d-largest in majors over last 10 years (minimum: 200 at bats each way). . . . Left-handed batter who has higher career batting and slugging averages vs. left-handed pitchers (.314, .421) than vs. right-handers (.292, .412). . . . Even so, started 104 of 113 games in which the Braves faced a right-handed starter, but only 14 of 48 games vs. lefties. . . . Tied for 4th in N.L. with 37 doubles, including one that killed a bird at Shea Stadium.

Stan Jefferson
San Diego Padres — Bats Left and Right

	AB	H	2B	3B	HR	RRF	BB	SO	BA	SA	OBA
Season	422	97	8	7	8	33	39	92	.230	.339	.296
vs. Left-Handers	154	37	2	0	1	4	15	30	.240	.273	.310
vs. Right-Handers	268	60	6	7	7	29	24	62	.224	.377	.288
Home	213	45	5	3	5	19	25	59	.211	.333	.298
Road	209	52	3	4	3	14	14	33	.249	.344	.295
Grass	309	68	8	6	7	30	32	75	.220	.353	.295
Artificial Turf	113	29	0	1	1	3	7	17	.257	.301	.300
April	21	6	0	1	0	2	1	1	.286	.381	.318
May	67	16	2	2	1	6	13	19	.239	.373	.366
June	57	11	2	0	0	2	6	22	.193	.228	.266
July	81	24	1	1	2	7	7	19	.296	.407	.352
August	115	31	2	2	4	9	4	20	.270	.426	.294
Sept./Oct.	81	9	1	1	1	7	8	13	.111	.185	.198
Leading Off Inn.	159	42	2	4	3	3	11	39	.264	.384	.316
Runners On	143	24	2	2	2	27	14	22	.168	.252	.238
Runners/Scor. Pos.	94	14	2	1	1	24	11	13	.149	.223	.231
Runners On/2 Out	70	12	1	1	1	12	5	7	.171	.257	.227
Scor. Pos./2 Out	53	8	1	0	1	11	5	5	.151	.226	.224
Late Inning Pressure	67	8	1	0	1	4	5	22	.119	.179	.178
Leading Off	13	1	0	0	0	0	1	6	.077	.077	.143
Runners On	34	3	0	0	0	3	2	4	.088	.088	.135
Runners/Scor. Pos.	24	3	0	0	0	1	1	2	.125	.125	.154

DRIVING IN RUNS	From 1B	From 2B	From 3B	Scoring Position
Totals	3/90	8/80	14/37	22/117
Percentage	3%	10%	38%	19%
Driving In Runners from 3B with Less than Two Out:				9/13 69%

Loves to face: Rick Mahler (.400, 4-for-10, 2 HR)
Hates to face: Don Robinson (0-for-5, 4 SO)
Led N.L. rookies in triples (7), walks (39), and stolen bases (34). . . . Batting average of .168 with runners on base left him 134th among 136 N.L. qualifiers; average with runners in scoring position (.149) ranked 133d out of 137 players. . . . Finished the season with only one hit (a solo home run) in his last 31 at bats, and carries a streak of 27 consecutive hitless at bats with runners on base, which tied for longest in N.L. last year, into 1988. . . . Had only one hit in nine at bats with the bases loaded, and one less than that in nine at bats as a pinch-hitter. . . . Hit three of hit eight home runs against Atlanta. . . . Stole 10 bases in May, 4th-best in N.L.; season total of 34 steals was second on team to Gwynn's 56.

Steve Jeltz
Philadelphia Phillies — Bats Left and Right

	AB	H	2B	3B	HR	RRF	BB	SO	BA	SA	OBA
Season	293	68	9	6	0	12	39	54	.232	.304	.324
vs. Left-Handers	80	14	3	2	0	7	9	16	.175	.263	.258
vs. Right-Handers	213	54	6	4	0	5	30	38	.254	.319	.348
Home	163	34	4	3	0	9	22	33	.209	.270	.303
Road	130	34	5	3	0	3	17	21	.262	.346	.351
Grass	80	21	4	1	0	2	12	15	.263	.338	.366
Artificial Turf	213	47	5	5	0	10	27	39	.221	.291	.308
April	44	6	0	0	0	1	4	12	.136	.136	.208
May	18	3	0	0	0	0	7	2	.167	.167	.400
June	50	11	1	1	0	3	5	8	.220	.280	.291
July	30	7	2	1	0	2	3	4	.233	.367	.303
August	97	28	4	2	0	4	12	15	.289	.371	.373
Sept./Oct.	54	13	2	2	0	2	8	13	.241	.352	.339
Leading Off Inn.	69	21	3	2	0	0	13	10	.304	.406	.415
Runners On	128	22	6	2	0	12	17	26	.172	.250	.274
Runners/Scor. Pos.	69	7	1	1	0	11	12	16	.101	.145	.235
Runners On/2 Out	45	4	1	1	0	3	8	13	.089	.156	.226
Scor. Pos./2 Out	34	2	0	0	0	2	7	9	.059	.059	.220
Late Inning Pressure	31	9	1	2	0	1	4	5	.290	.452	.389
Leading Off	11	4	0	0	0	0	1	1	.364	.364	.417
Runners On	8	3	1	1	0	1	3	2	.375	.750	.583
Runners/Scor. Pos.	3	0	0	0	0	0	1	1	.000	.000	.250

DRIVING IN RUNS	From 1B	From 2B	From 3B	Scoring Position
Totals	3/100	5/53	4/21	9/74
Percentage	3%	9%	19%	12%
Driving In Runners from 3B with Less than Two Out:				4/11 36%

Loves to face: Danny Cox (.455, 10-for-22)
Hates to face: Bob Forsch (.056, 1-for-18)
"Your attention please, ladies and gentlemen": Jeltz was yanked for a pinch-hitter 35 times last season, the most by any non-pitcher in N.L. . . . And for good reason: Jeltz batted a league-low .101 with runners in scoring position, a league-low .059 with runners in scoring position and two outs, and a league-low .089 with runners on base and two outs. . . . Ground-ball hitter: 2.22 ground outs-to-air outs ratio was 6th-highest in N.L. . . . Averaged 2.90 assists per nine innings last season, 3d-lowest rate among N.L. shortstops (minimum: 500 innings). . . . Started 95 games, all in 8th-spot in lineup; Phils' 8th-place hitters hit a combined .208; you guessed it, a league low. . . . Has not had a three-hit game since June 28, 1986.

Howard Johnson
New York Mets — Bats Left and Right

	AB	H	2B	3B	HR	RRF	BB	SO	BA	SA	OBA
Season	554	147	22	1	36	102	83	113	.265	.504	.364
vs. Left-Handers	194	56	6	0	15	41	26	39	.289	.552	.376
vs. Right-Handers	360	91	16	1	21	61	57	74	.253	.478	.358
Home	271	71	10	1	13	42	42	62	.262	.450	.364
Road	283	76	12	0	23	60	41	51	.269	.555	.365
Grass	380	107	16	1	21	64	61	78	.282	.495	.384
Artificial Turf	174	40	6	0	15	38	22	35	.230	.523	.320
April	63	15	1	0	3	12	11	16	.238	.397	.347
May	88	20	4	0	5	13	10	26	.227	.443	.310
June	96	31	4	0	7	16	9	16	.323	.583	.393
July	99	29	2	0	10	22	11	17	.293	.616	.366
August	93	28	4	1	8	25	23	21	.301	.624	.440
Sept./Oct.	115	24	7	0	3	14	19	17	.209	.348	.326
Leading Off Inn.	134	29	5	0	10	10	14	26	.216	.478	.291
Runners On	248	76	13	1	15	81	41	50	.306	.548	.405
Runners/Scor. Pos.	137	38	6	0	9	65	35	30	.277	.518	.424
Runners On/2 Out	105	29	7	0	7	38	22	18	.276	.543	.406
Scor. Pos./2 Out	66	14	3	0	4	31	20	14	.212	.439	.402
Late Inning Pressure	79	25	4	0	6	20	12	17	.316	.595	.398
Leading Off	15	3	1	0	2	2	2	3	.200	.667	.294
Runners On	35	15	2	0	4	18	6	9	.429	.829	.488
Runners/Scor. Pos.	18	6	0	0	2	14	5	6	.333	.667	.440

DRIVING IN RUNS	From 1B	From 2B	From 3B	Scoring Position
Totals	18/177	20/99	28/70	48/169
Percentage	10%	20%	40%	28%
Driving In Runners from 3B with Less than Two Out:		16/34		47%

Loves to face: Jim Acker (.600, 6-for-10, 2 HR)
Hates to face: Tom Browning (0-for-17)
Batted .255 from left side (.254 in 1986), but right-side average jumped dramatically: .227 in 1984, .156 in 1985, .213 in 1986, .289 in 1987. Before '87, had only seven homers in 245 right-handed at bats.... Had seven successive hits with runners on base (June 29 to July 2), longest such streak in N.L. in 1987.... Led N.L. with 23 homers in road games; has hit for higher average on road than at home in each of last five years.... Had one home run every 13.7 at bats before Herzog challenged his bat, July 30; one every 19.3 at bats afterwards.... Hit four home runs in Astrodome last season, most by any visitor.... Has homered in every N.L. ballpark except Dodger Stadium, where he doesn't even have an extra-base hit.

Tracy Jones
Cincinnati Reds — Bats Right

	AB	H	2B	3B	HR	RRF	BB	SO	BA	SA	OBA
Season	359	104	17	3	10	45	23	40	.290	.437	.333
vs. Left-Handers	169	59	10	2	5	21	17	17	.349	.521	.405
vs. Right-Handers	190	45	7	1	5	24	6	23	.237	.363	.265
Home	160	48	9	2	4	13	14	10	.300	.456	.364
Road	199	56	8	1	6	32	9	30	.281	.422	.308
Grass	113	25	5	0	3	10	4	16	.221	.345	.252
Artificial Turf	246	79	12	3	7	35	19	24	.321	.480	.369
April	37	12	4	1	2	5	3	4	.324	.649	.395
May	64	22	2	1	3	12	7	4	.344	.547	.403
June	86	26	6	0	4	13	1	15	.302	.512	.315
July	73	18	2	0	1	4	7	5	.247	.315	.313
August	44	10	0	0	0	3	4	5	.227	.227	.292
Sept./Oct.	55	16	3	1	0	8	1	7	.291	.382	.293
Leading Off Inn.	100	28	2	1	3	3	7	11	.280	.410	.327
Runners On	130	40	5	0	3	38	8	18	.308	.415	.345
Runners/Scor. Pos.	80	27	3	0	3	37	8	10	.338	.488	.389
Runners On/2 Out	60	17	1	0	0	6	6	9	.283	.450	.348
Scor. Pos./2 Out	38	11	1	0	3	16	6	4	.289	.553	.386
Late Inning Pressure	54	15	1	0	1	8	2	9	.278	.352	.322
Leading Off	14	3	0	0	1	1	0	3	.214	.214	.214
Runners On	17	6	0	0	0	7	1	4	.353	.353	.429
Runners/Scor. Pos.	14	6	0	0	0	7	1	4	.429	.429	.500

DRIVING IN RUNS	From 1B	From 2B	From 3B	Scoring Position
Totals	3/88	14/66	18/37 ·	32/103
Percentage	3%	21%	49%	31%
Driving In Runners from 3B with Less than Two Out:		13/22		59%

Loves to face: Neal Heaton (.625, 5-for-8 , 1 HR)
Hates to face: Bob Ojeda (0-for-6)
Only Reds player to start all 47 games in which team faced a left handed starter; started only 32 of 115 vs. right-handers.... One of two N.L. players to start at least 10 games at each of the outfield positions (other: Mike Aldrete).... Grounded into 10 double plays in 50 DP situations, 7th-highest rate in N.L. (minimum: 40 opportunities).... Batted 100 points higher on carpets than on grass fields, 3d-largest such difference in N.L. (minimum: 50 at bats each way).... Drove in 11 runs at the Astrodome last season, most among visitors there.... Here's a guy who must get jacked up by that omnipresent Budweiser theme: Jones has a career average of .552 (16-for-29) at Busch Stadium.

John Kruk
San Diego Padres — Bats Left

	AB	H	2B	3B	HR	RRF	BB	SO	BA	SA	OBA
Season	447	140	14	2	20	93	73	93	.313	.488	.406
vs. Left-Handers	137	35	3	1	4	28	16	38	.255	.380	.329
vs. Right-Handers	310	105	11	1	16	65	57	55	.339	.535	.439
Home	215	64	6	0	8	39	45	51	.298	.437	.416
Road	232	76	8	2	12	54	28	42	.328	.534	.397
Grass	328	99	6	0	15	67	56	71	.302	.457	.401
Artificial Turf	119	41	8	2	5	26	17	22	.345	.571	.423
April	42	11	2	0	2	3	10	8	.262	.452	.404
May	74	30	4	0	3	17	15	17	.405	.581	.506
June	73	23	0	1	1	15	15	18	.315	.384	.432
July	76	25	3	0	5	16	10	10	.329	.566	.402
August	97	31	3	1	7	30	11	19	.320	.588	.382
Sept./Oct.	85	20	2	0	2	12	12	21	.235	.329	.327
Leading Off Inn.	116	33	2	0	4	4	15	16	.284	.405	.366
Runners On	207	63	9	2	10	83	38	52	.304	.512	.406
Runners/Scor. Pos.	136	45	8	0	7	72	30	34	.331	.544	.441
Runners On/2 Out	90	28	3	1	5	35	18	22	.311	.533	.402
Scor. Pos./2 Out	63	22	3	0	4	31	16	12	.349	.587	.481
Late Inning Pressure	87	28	1	0	3	12	15	18	.322	.437	.422
Leading Off	25	4	0	0	1	1	3	4	.160	.280	.250
Runners On	35	12	0	0	0	9	10	10	.343	.343	.489
Runners/Scor. Pos.	25	9	0	0	0	9	9	5	.360	.360	.529

DRIVING IN RUNS	From 1B	From 2B	From 3B	Scoring Position
Totals	13/137	29/104	31/65	60/169
Percentage	9%	28%	48%	36%
Driving In Runners from 3B with Less than Two Out:		20/37		54%

Loves to face: Ron Darling (.571, 8-for-14, 2 HR)
Hates to face: Mike LaCoss (0-for-8, 3 SO)
When the situation gets hotter, so does Kruk: .312 career batting average is good enough, but he has hit .335 with runners on base, .361 with runners on base and two outs, .375 in Late-Inning Pressure Situations with runners on base, and .400 in LIPS with runners in scoring position.... Led N.L. with 21 RBI vs. Braves last season, and was only visitor to hit four home runs at Atlanta Stadium.... Batting average in May was highest in majors.... Led N.L. with 30 RBI in August despite Dawson's 15 home runs that month.... Batting average at season's end was at its lowest point since mid-May.... Batted .500 (6-for-12) as pinch-hitter.... Had never hit more than 11 HR in any of six previous years in organized ball.

Ken Landreaux
Los Angeles Dodgers — Bats Left

	AB	H	2B	3B	HR	RRF	BB	SO	BA	SA	OBA
Season	182	37	4	0	6	25	16	28	.203	.324	.269
vs. Left-Handers	20	4	1	0	0	2	1	4	.200	.250	.238
vs. Right-Handers	162	33	3	0	6	23	15	24	.204	.333	.272
Home	91	27	3	0	4	16	6	11	.297	.462	.343
Road	91	10	1	0	2	9	10	17	.110	.187	.196
Grass	126	29	3	0	5	20	10	22	.230	.373	.288
Artificial Turf	56	8	1	0	1	5	6	6	.143	.214	.226
April	29	4	0	0	1	1	5	3	.138	.138	.265
May	50	13	2	0	2	7	4	8	.260	.420	.321
June	11	2	0	0	0	1	2	1	.182	.182	.308
July	26	8	1	0	2	6	0	4	.308	.577	.308
August	52	8	1	0	2	8	5	9	.154	.288	.224
Sept./Oct.	14	2	0	0	0	2	0	3	.143	.143	.143
Leading Off Inn.	40	7	1	0	1	1	3	5	.175	.275	.233
Runners On	80	21	2	0	4	23	5	15	.263	.438	.299
Runners/Scor. Pos.	47	10	1	0	1	15	3	10	.213	.298	.250
Runners On/2 Out	32	8	0	0	2	8	0	7	.250	.438	.250
Scor. Pos./2 Out	21	4	0	0	0	4	0	4	.190	.190	.190
Late Inning Pressure	45	8	1	0	0	4	6	6	.178	.200	.275
Leading Off	13	2	0	0	0	0	2	0	.154	.154	.267
Runners On	20	4	1	0	0	4	2	4	.200	.250	.273
Runners/Scor. Pos.	13	2	0	0	0	3	2	2	.154	.154	.267

DRIVING IN RUNS	From 1B	From 2B	From 3B	Scoring Position
Totals	7/58	5/35	7/22	12/57
Percentage	12%	14%	32%	21%
Driving In Runners from 3B with Less than Two Out:		5/10		50%

Loves to face: Andy McGaffigan (.500, 8-for-16, 1 HR)
Hates to face: Andy Hawkins (.091, 2-for-22)
Plate appearances over last three years have declined from 527 to 310 to 204.... Dodgers' most frequently used pinch-hitter in 1987 (55 games). Batted .200 (10-for-50), but that was *good* on a team that had worst pinch-hitting (.165) in majors.... Played the field for total of only two innings after August 26.... Started 32 games against right-handed pitching, two games against lefties.... Batted 33 consecutive times without a runner in scoring position, May 2–17, but he can't use that as an excuse for total of only 23 RBI: The percentage of runners he drove in from scoring position was his lowest since 1978.... Has only one hit in 16 at bats with the bases loaded since 1985.

Barry Larkin
Cincinnati Reds — Bats Right

	AB	H	2B	3B	HR	RRF	BB	SO	BA	SA	OBA
Season	439	107	16	2	12	47	36	52	.244	.371	.306
vs. Left-Handers	131	36	4	2	5	16	14	12	.275	.450	.349
vs. Right-Handers	308	71	12	0	7	31	22	40	.231	.338	.288
Home	241	57	9	0	6	31	24	32	.237	.349	.306
Road	198	50	7	2	6	16	12	20	.253	.399	.307
Grass	107	29	3	1	5	9	8	12	.271	.458	.339
Artificial Turf	332	78	13	1	7	38	28	40	.235	.343	.296
April	16	5	0	0	1	3	2	4	.313	.500	.389
May	83	16	4	0	3	7	4	7	.193	.349	.247
June	49	9	4	0	2	8	7	7	.184	.388	.286
July	97	27	3	1	1	8	7	12	.278	.361	.346
August	96	23	1	0	1	4	4	10	.240	.281	.267
Sept./Oct.	98	27	4	1	4	17	12	12	.276	.459	.348
Leading Off Inn.	102	26	3	0	5	5	10	18	.255	.431	.327
Runners On	183	53	8	1	6	41	17	13	.290	.443	.354
Runners/Scor. Pos.	103	25	4	0	5	38	11	9	.243	.427	.319
Runners On/2 Out	72	20	0	1	1	10	7	7	.278	.347	.350
Scor. Pos./2 Out	42	8	0	0	0	7	7	5	.190	.190	.320
Late Inning Pressure	61	15	0	0	1	4	1	10	.246	.295	.258
Leading Off	13	3	0	0	0	0	0	3	.231	.231	.231
Runners On	24	7	0	0	1	4	1	2	.292	.417	.320
Runners/Scor. Pos.	15	2	0	0	1	4	1	2	.133	.333	.188

DRIVING IN RUNS	From 1B	From 2B	From 3B	Scoring Position
Totals	3/125	16/88	15/41	31/129
Percentage	2%	18%	37%	24%
Driving In Runners from 3B with Less than Two Out:			12/24	50%

Loves to face: Jesse Orosco (2-for-2)
Hates to face: Atlee Hammaker (0-for-7)
More day games, please: Larkin batted .282 during day, .226 at night in 1987, following .356-day, .240-night season in 1986. Career totals: .303 in day games, .229 at night; that 74-point difference is 4th-largest in majors over last 10 seasons (minimum: 200 at bats each way).... Batted .264 in 44 games started in 8th slot in lineup; Reds' number eight hitters had highest collective batting average (.265) in N.L.... Career average of .311 with runners on base, .216 with the bases empty.... What would Woody Hayes have said about an athlete who was born in Cincinnati and attended renowned Moeller High School there, but then went to play college ball at the University of Michigan?

Mike LaValliere
Pittsburgh Pirates — Bats Left

	AB	H	2B	3B	HR	RRF	BB	SO	BA	SA	OBA
Season	340	102	19	0	1	36	43	32	.300	.365	.377
vs. Left-Handers	77	17	4	0	0	6	9	13	.221	.273	.302
vs. Right-Handers	263	85	15	0	1	30	34	19	.323	.392	.399
Home	174	53	8	0	1	21	21	16	.305	.368	.378
Road	166	49	11	0	0	15	22	16	.295	.361	.377
Grass	84	23	5	0	0	7	12	10	.274	.333	.361
Artificial Turf	256	79	14	0	1	29	31	22	.309	.375	.383
April	35	12	3	0	0	3	7	4	.343	.429	.452
May	70	20	3	0	0	8	8	8	.286	.329	.359
June	62	17	4	0	0	7	11	7	.274	.339	.387
July	61	13	3	0	0	5	7	5	.213	.262	.290
August	63	25	5	0	1	8	7	4	.397	.524	.451
Sept./Oct.	49	15	1	0	0	5	3	4	.306	.327	.346
Leading Off Inn.	75	21	6	0	0		4	8	.280	.360	.325
Runners On	142	41	7	0	0	35	33	12	.289	.338	.416
Runners/Scor. Pos.	93	27	5	0	0	33	24	11	.290	.344	.425
Runners On/2 Out	64	15	2	0	0	14	15	5	.234	.266	.380
Scor. Pos./2 Out	46	12	2	0	0	14	12	4	.261	.304	.414
Late Inning Pressure	42	14	3	0	0	3	4	5	.333	.405	.391
Leading Off	10	4	1	0	0	0	0	2	.400	.500	.400
Runners On	15	4	1	0	0	3	1	2	.267	.333	.313
Runners/Scor. Pos.	10	2	1	0	0	3	1	2	.200	.300	.273

DRIVING IN RUNS	From 1B	From 2B	From 3B	Scoring Position
Totals	4/94	17/75	14/31	31/106
Percentage	4%	23%	45%	29%
Driving In Runners from 3B with Less than Two Out:			12/16	75%

Loves to face: Kelly Downs (.615, 8-for-13)
Hates to face: Mike Krukow (0-for-6)
Opponents were successful on only 54.8 percent of stolen-base attempts (68 of 124), lowest success rate vs. any No. 1 catcher in N.L. ... Batted 102 points higher vs. right-handers than vs. lefties, 4th-largest such difference in N.L. (minimum: 50 at bats each way); started 85 of 91 games in which Pirates faced right-handers, 14 of 71 vs. lefties. ... Had only two passed balls, fewest among 21 catchers in majors who caught 100+ games last season.... What does he have in common with Jerry Narron and Sal Butera? They're the only three non pitchers who played in majors in 1987 who have 700+ career plate appearances and no stolen bases. Narron & Butera have never even tried; Lav was 0 for 1 with Cards in '86.

Vance Law
Montreal Expos — Bats Right

	AB	H	2B	3B	HR	RRF	BB	SO	BA	SA	OBA
Season	436	119	27	1	12	59	51	62	.273	.422	.347
vs. Left-Handers	153	44	10	0	3	19	24	21	.288	.412	.384
vs. Right-Handers	283	75	17	1	9	40	27	41	.265	.428	.326
Home	209	56	18	0	3	32	24	29	.268	.397	.339
Road	227	63	9	1	9	27	27	33	.278	.445	.354
Grass	118	31	2	0	2	14	15	18	.263	.331	.346
Artificial Turf	318	88	25	1	10	45	36	44	.277	.456	.347
April	73	20	4	0	4	10	5	13	.274	.493	.316
May	93	29	8	0	1	14	18	16	.312	.430	.423
June	64	16	3	0	1	9	8	7	.250	.344	.329
July	78	29	10	1	4	10	9	7	.372	.679	.437
August	74	14	1	0	1	9	7	11	.189	.243	.256
Sept./Oct.	54	11	1	0	1	7	4	8	.204	.278	.259
Leading Off Inn.	97	25	7	0	4	4		13	.258	.454	.287
Runners On	192	51	12	0	3	50	32	26	.266	.375	.366
Runners/Scor. Pos.	119	33	7	0	2	46	26	17	.277	.387	.399
Runners On/2 Out	88	22	3	0	1	18	21	12	.250	.318	.394
Scor. Pos./2 Out	62	17	2	0	1	18	19	10	.274	.355	.444
Late Inning Pressure	58	15	3	0	1	10	7	6	.259	.362	.338
Leading Off	12	3	1	0	0	0	1	2	.250	.333	.308
Runners On	28	7	1	0	1	10	4	1	.250	.393	.344
Runners/Scor. Pos.	15	5	1	0	1	10	2	1	.333	.600	.412

DRIVING IN RUNS	From 1B	From 2B	From 3B	Scoring Position
Totals	5/132	17/97	25/51	42/148
Percentage	4%	18%	49%	28%
Driving In Runners from 3B with Less than Two Out:			17/28	61%

Loves to face: Jim Deshaies (4-for-4, 4 BB)
Hates to face: Ron Darling (.059, 1-for-17)
N.L.'s leading hitter (.425, 17-for-40) vs. Astros last year.... Started 50 of 51 games in which Expos faced a lefty starter, 68 of 111 vs. right-handers. ... Cubs will be his fourth club in nine-year career. Papa Vern played for only one club, Pittsburgh, in 16 years in majors.... Has pitched in six games over last two seasons. Other active position players who have pitched in majors: Sal Butera, Rick Cerone, Luis Salazar (twice each); Jim Gantner, Greg Gross, Rick Leach, Paul O'Neill, Jose Oquendo, Craig Reynolds, Ray Shines, Tim Wallach, Glenn Wilson.... Opponents have batted .276 (8-for-29) vs. Law, but he has retired Eric Davis, Howard Johnson, and Tony Gwynn, among others.

Jeffrey Leonard
San Francisco Giants — Bats Right

	AB	H	2B	3B	HR	RRF	BB	SO	BA	SA	OBA
Season	503	141	29	4	19	65	21	68	.280	.467	.309
vs. Left-Handers	145	41	11	0	5	15	6	17	.283	.462	.306
vs. Right-Handers	358	100	18	4	14	50	15	51	.279	.469	.310
Home	225	63	14	1	9	27	11	37	.280	.471	.311
Road	278	78	15	3	10	38	10	31	.281	.464	.307
Grass	365	101	21	1	15	43	17	51	.277	.463	.309
Artificial Turf	138	40	8	3	4	22	4	17	.290	.478	.308
April	82	29	6	1	5	15	5	10	.354	.634	.391
May	113	43	14	3	7	19	4	13	.381	.743	.403
June	97	19	3	0	2	7	3	15	.196	.289	.223
July	102	23	6	0	2	9	8	18	.225	.343	.279
August	75	20	0	0	1	11	1	11	.267	.307	.273
Sept./Oct.	34	7	0	0	2	4	0	1	.206	.382	.206
Leading Off Inn.	79	25	6	1	4	4	2	6	.316	.570	.333
Runners On	220	57	8	1	6	51	12	32	.259	.386	.297
Runners/Scor. Pos.	134	33	3	0	4	44	10	24	.246	.358	.293
Runners On/2 Out	73	15	2	0	3	17	6	12	.205	.356	.266
Scor. Pos./2 Out	52	12	2	0	2	15	4	8	.231	.385	.286
Late Inning Pressure	74	19	3	2	2	9	6	10	.257	.432	.305
Leading Off	16	5	1	1	1	1	0	2	.313	.688	.313
Runners On	34	6	1	0	0	6	5	6	.176	.206	.268
Runners/Scor. Pos.	23	4	1	0	0	6	5	6	.174	.217	.300

DRIVING IN RUNS	From 1B	From 2B	From 3B	Scoring Position
Totals	7/142	15/101	23/55	38/156
Percentage	5%	15%	42%	24%
Driving In Runners from 3B with Less than Two Out:			19/37	51%

Loves to face: Danny Cox (.429, 9-for-21)
Hates to face: Kent Tekulve (.100, 2-for-20)
Has not been caught stealing on artificial turf since July 24, 1984. Since then he is a perfect 19-for-19 on the rug, but only 35-for-52 (.673) on grass fields. ... Averaged only 1.68 putouts per nine innings last season, 2d-lowest rate among major-league left fielders (minimum: 500 innings). ... Averaged one walk every 25.3 plate appearances last season, 4th-lowest rate in N.L. ... Batted .545 (6-for-11, two HR) as a pinch-hitter. ... First player in history to hit home runs in four consecutive League Championship games.... Seven hits in 14 at bats with the bases loaded over last two years. ... Career batting average: .299 vs. left-handers, .260 vs. right-handers, but variance was minimal (.283, .279) last season.

Jim Lindeman
St. Louis Cardinals   Bats Right

	AB	H	2B	3B	HR	RRF	BB	SO	BA	SA	OBA
Season	207	43	13	0	8	28	11	56	.208	.386	.253
vs. Left-Handers	101	21	4	0	4	13	7	27	.208	.366	.252
vs. Right-Handers	106	22	9	0	4	15	4	29	.208	.406	.254
Home	112	22	7	0	2	15	5	33	.196	.313	.233
Road	95	21	6	0	6	13	6	23	.221	.474	.276
Grass	35	7	3	0	0	2	1	6	.200	.286	.222
Artificial Turf	172	36	10	0	8	26	10	50	.209	.407	.259
April	54	13	7	0	3	11	2	14	.241	.537	.263
May	18	2	0	0	0	3	0	7	.111	.111	.105
June	2	0	0	0	0	0	0	2	.000	.000	.000
July	38	8	2	0	0	1	2	10	.211	.263	.268
August	69	17	4	0	4	12	6	14	.246	.478	.316
Sept./Oct.	26	3	0	0	1	1	1	9	.115	.231	.148
Leading Off Inn.	53	16	5	0	4	4	3	6	.302	.623	.362
Runners On	94	17	3	0	2	22	6	27	.181	.277	.221
Runners/Scor. Pos.	58	11	2	0	2	22	4	14	.190	.328	.227
Runners On/2 Out	43	7	1	0	1	7	3	12	.163	.256	.217
Scor. Pos./2 Out	29	6	1	0	1	7	2	7	.207	.345	.258
Late Inning Pressure	34	6	1	0	0	0	1	10	.176	.206	.200
Leading Off	14	5	1	0	0	0	0	3	.357	.429	.357
Runners On	8	0	0	0	0	0	0	1	.000	.000	.000
Runners/Scor. Pos.	5	0	0	0	0	0	0	0	.000	.000	.000

DRIVING IN RUNS	From 1B	From 2B	From 3B	Scoring Position
Totals	2/70	7/42	11/35	18/77
Percentage	3%	17%	31%	23%
Driving In Runners from 3B with Less than Two Out:			7/21	33%

Loves to face: Bob Kipper (.400, 2-for-5, 2 HR)
Hates to face: Rick Reuschel (0-for-10, 4 SO)
When will you learn not to pay through the nose for a "promising" rookie in your rotisserie league? Even if Whitey did say that he'd play every day. Even if he did bat .351 with six home runs in spring training. ... Cardinals had a record of 7–0 in games in which he homered during regular season; he then homered in Game Three of playoffs with Cards trailing, 4–0, but sure enough, they came back to win. ... Hit five of his eight home runs vs. Pirates, including a two-HR game. ... Started 33 of 58 games in which Cardinals faced a left-handed starter, 24 of 104 games against right-handers; started only 12 games at first base during regular season. ... Batted .321 (9-for-28) with team-high seven RBI in post season play.

Shane Mack
San Diego Padres   Bats Right

	AB	H	2B	3B	HR	RRF	BB	SO	BA	SA	OBA
Season	238	57	11	3	4	27	18	47	.239	.361	.299
vs. Left-Handers	132	35	4	2	4	20	7	24	.265	.417	.313
vs. Right-Handers	106	22	7	1	0	7	11	23	.208	.292	.282
Home	111	25	7	3	2	16	10	26	.225	.396	.293
Road	127	32	4	0	2	11	8	21	.252	.331	.304
Grass	171	45	9	3	3	24	15	34	.263	.404	.323
Artificial Turf	67	12	2	0	1	3	3	13	.179	.254	.236
April	0	0	0	0	0	0	0	0	—	—	—
May	20	6	2	0	0	1	2	5	.300	.400	.364
June	74	18	4	0	1	9	4	13	.243	.338	.282
July	54	13	2	1	2	4	4	15	.241	.426	.305
August	42	12	1	1	1	8	2	8	.286	.429	.304
Sept./Oct.	48	8	2	1	0	5	6	6	.167	.250	.286
Leading Off Inn.	52	11	2	0	2	2	7	7	.212	.365	.305
Runners On	111	33	7	3	1	24	4	24	.297	.441	.328
Runners/Scor. Pos.	61	13	4	3	0	20	2	13	.213	.377	.254
Runners On/2 Out	54	19	4	2	0	11	2	13	.352	.500	.375
Scor. Pos./2 Out	32	9	3	2	0	10	1	7	.281	.500	.303
Late Inning Pressure	42	8	2	0	0	1	4	7	.190	.238	.261
Leading Off	8	0	0	0	0	0	1	1	.000	.000	.111
Runners On	20	6	1	0	0	1	0	4	.300	.350	.300
Runners/Scor. Pos.	8	0	0	0	0	0	1	0	.000	.000	.000

DRIVING IN RUNS	From 1B	From 2B	From 3B	Scoring Position
Totals	5/82	6/51	12/21	18/72
Percentage	6%	12%	57%	25%
Driving In Runners from 3B with Less than Two Out:			6/10	60%

Loves to face: Neal Heaton (.444, 4-for-9)
Hates to face: Floyd Youmans (0-for-4, 2 SO)
Grounded into 11 double plays in 54 double-play situations, 5th-highest rate in N.L. (minimum: 40 opportunities); league averages: one every 9.4 situations in N.L., one every 9.5 in A.L. ... Averaged 2.70 putouts per nine innings last season, 3d-highest rate among N.L. center fielders (minimum: 500 innings). ... Starting right fielder in his first two major-league games, did not appear there again the rest of the season. ... Batted .150 (3-for-20) as a pinch-hitter. ... Started 38 of 65 games in which the Padres faced a southpaw starter, but only 15 of 97 games vs. right-handers. ... Padres were 25–28 in 53 games that he started. Whaddya mean, so what? They were 40–69 in 109 other games.

Dave Magadan
New York Mets   Bats Left

	AB	H	2B	3B	HR	RRF	BB	SO	BA	SA	OBA
Season	192	61	13	1	3	24	22	22	.318	.443	.386
vs. Left-Handers	48	21	3	0	2	14	5	4	.438	.625	.481
vs. Right-Handers	144	40	10	1	1	10	17	18	.278	.382	.354
Home	89	34	8	0	2	16	12	10	.382	.539	.451
Road	103	27	5	1	1	8	10	12	.262	.359	.327
Grass	130	44	9	0	2	19	16	14	.338	.454	.408
Artificial Turf	62	17	4	1	1	5	6	8	.274	.419	.338
April	10	3	1	0	2	2	2	1	.300	1.000	.417
May	52	17	5	0	2	7	8	8	.327	.423	.410
June	31	6	2	0	0	4	2	3	.194	.258	.242
July	22	10	2	0	0	1	3	2	.455	.545	.520
August	35	12	1	1	0	5	5	3	.343	.429	.425
Sept./Oct.	42	13	2	0	1	5	2	5	.310	.429	.341
Leading Off Inn.	38	12	2	0	0	4	4	4	.316	.368	.381
Runners On	90	28	6	1	0	21	12	11	.311	.400	.388
Runners/Scor. Pos.	54	14	2	0	0	18	11	8	.259	.296	.379
Runners On/2 Out	41	9	3	0	0	9	7	7	.220	.293	.333
Scor. Pos./2 Out	29	6	2	0	0	9	7	5	.207	.276	.361
Late Inning Pressure	39	11	3	0	2	4	3	6	.282	.513	.333
Leading Off	4	1	0	0	0	0	1	0	.250	.250	.400
Runners On	23	4	1	0	0	2	1	5	.174	.217	.208
Runners/Scor. Pos.	14	1	0	0	0	1	1	4	.071	.071	.133

DRIVING IN RUNS	From 1B	From 2B	From 3B	Scoring Position
Totals	5/60	9/40	7/22	16/62
Percentage	8%	23%	32%	26%
Driving In Runners from 3B with Less than Two Out:			4/8	50%

Loves to face: Scott Sanderson (3-for-3)
Hates to face: Orel Hershiser (0-for-6)
Batted .344 in 42 starts last season, but Mets were a sub-.500 team in those games: 19 wins, 23 losses. (To be fair, keep in mind that HoJo played shortstop in 26 of those games). ... Started only nine games vs. left-handed pitchers, despite being only player in majors with 25+ plate appearances vs. lefties to bat .400+ against them. ... Led N.L. rookies with a .386 on-base average. ... Has now hit above .300 in each of five seasons in pro ball. ... Homered in first at bat and 10th at bat of 1987, after hitting only one in his last three years in minors. ... Born on September 30, 1962, the day that Mets ended their inaugural season by losing their 120th game, as Joe Pignatano hit into a triple play at Chicago.

Candy Maldonado
San Francisco Giants   Bats Right

	AB	H	2B	3B	HR	RRF	BB	SO	BA	SA	OBA
Season	442	129	28	4	20	89	34	78	.292	.509	.346
vs. Left-Handers	132	39	9	1	6	23	17	21	.295	.515	.371
vs. Right-Handers	310	90	19	3	14	66	17	57	.290	.506	.334
Home	228	55	9	1	14	48	14	44	.241	.474	.288
Road	214	74	19	3	6	41	20	34	.346	.547	.406
Grass	335	93	15	3	17	74	25	61	.278	.493	.328
Artificial Turf	107	36	13	1	3	15	9	17	.336	.561	.400
April	89	29	8	0	2	14	8	15	.326	.483	.378
May	99	31	7	2	5	20	6	16	.313	.576	.376
June	89	32	7	0	5	16	4	14	.360	.607	.394
July	0	0	0	0	0	0	0	0	—	—	—
August	75	14	3	1	4	16	7	19	.187	.413	.253
Sept./Oct.	90	23	3	1	4	23	9	14	.256	.444	.317
Leading Off Inn.	116	36	7	0	8	8	10	18	.310	.578	.375
Runners On	218	62	15	3	6	75	16	37	.284	.463	.335
Runners/Scor. Pos.	135	40	9	2	4	64	14	22	.296	.481	.354
Runners On/2 Out	103	29	6	2	3	27	9	18	.282	.466	.345
Scor. Pos./2 Out	63	18	3	1	3	23	7	11	.286	.508	.366
Late Inning Pressure	71	27	8	0	3	16	2	10	.380	.620	.405
Leading Off	22	7	2	0	2	2	1	2	.318	.682	.348
Runners On	34	13	5	0	0	13	1	6	.382	.529	.417
Runners/Scor. Pos.	24	10	3	0	0	11	1	5	.417	.542	.462

DRIVING IN RUNS	From 1B	From 2B	From 3B	Scoring Position
Totals	11/135	30/103	27/60	57/163
Percentage	8%	29%	45%	35%
Driving In Runners from 3B with Less than Two Out:			21/36	58%

Loves to face: Frank DiPino (.667, 6-for-9, 1 HR)
Hates to face: Shane Rawley (.080, 2-for-25)
Has outstanding career clutch figures: .238 with bases empty, but .283 with runners on base, .290 with runners in scoring position, and .371 (13-for-35, three HR) with the bases loaded. ... Annual batting averages in Late-Inning Pressure Situations since 1984: .227, .214, .330, .380. ... Did not play in more than three consecutive games without collecting an RBI last season. ... In two seasons with Giants he has batting average of .235 at Candlestick, .310 on road; but 14 of last year's 20 home runs came at the 'Stick. ... Batted .344 in day games, .256 at night. ... Has homered at every N.L. ballpark except the Astrodome (74 career at bats).

Mike Marshall

Los Angeles Dodgers — Bats Right

	AB	H	2B	3B	HR	RRF	BB	SO	BA	SA	OBA
Season	402	118	19	0	16	75	18	79	.294	.460	.327
vs. Left-Handers	125	35	8	0	5	19	5	20	.280	.464	.313
vs. Right-Handers	277	83	11	0	11	56	13	59	.300	.458	.333
Home	183	52	7	0	5	24	10	34	.284	.404	.327
Road	219	66	12	0	11	51	8	45	.301	.507	.328
Grass	301	86	13	0	11	55	15	59	.286	.439	.325
Artificial Turf	101	32	6	0	5	20	3	20	.317	.525	.333
April	72	21	3	0	3	15	3	21	.292	.458	.338
May	30	4	0	0	0	3	1	5	.133	.133	.161
June	92	34	7	0	5	18	5	17	.370	.609	.402
July	76	18	4	0	3	11	2	18	.237	.408	.266
August	35	13	3	0	2	12	0	12	.371	.629	.371
Sept./Oct.	97	28	2	0	3	16	7	16	.289	.402	.330
Leading Off Inn.	91	27	1	0	5	5	4	21	.297	.473	.333
Runners On	210	69	14	0	10	69	10	33	.329	.538	.358
Runners/Scor. Pos.	122	40	10	0	6	59	7	19	.328	.557	.358
Runners On/2 Out	97	29	7	0	4	28	5	14	.299	.495	.340
Scor. Pos./2 Out	62	20	5	0	3	24	3	9	.323	.548	.354
Late Inning Pressure	56	11	2	0	2	11	1	19	.196	.339	.220
Leading Off	9	2	0	0	0	0	1	4	.222	.222	.300
Runners On	24	7	2	0	2	11	0	6	.292	.625	.280
Runners/Scor. Pos.	13	5	1	0	2	10	0	6	.385	.923	.357

DRIVING IN RUNS	From 1B	From 2B	From 3B	Scoring Position
Totals	10/157	31/96	18/47	49/143
Percentage	6%	32%	38%	34%
Driving In Runners from 3B with Less than Two Out:			12/28	43%

Loves to face: Scott Garrelts (.524, 11-for-21, 4 HR)
Hates to face: Pascual Perez (.130, 3-for-23)
With 79 strikeouts and only 18 walks, this was his third consecutive season with strikeout/walk ratio of more than 3.00; among N.L. players with 100+ at bats each season, Jeffrey Leonard is the only other one to do that each year, 1985–87.... Averaged 1.51 putouts per nine innings last season, lowest rate among major-league right fielders (minimum: 500 innings).... No stolen bases, five caught stealing. Who gave this guy the green light? ... Percentage of runners driven in from scoring position (34.3) was a career high.... Yearly total of games played since 1983: 140, 134, 135, 103, 104; for second year in a row, played in fewer games than the other Mike Marshall pitched in for '74 Dodgers (106).

Carmelo Martinez

San Diego Padres — Bats Right

	AB	H	2B	3B	HR	RRF	BB	SO	BA	SA	OBA
Season	447	122	21	2	15	72	70	82	.273	.430	.372
vs. Left-Handers	184	50	11	0	9	33	37	30	.272	.478	.395
vs. Right-Handers	263	72	10	2	6	39	33	52	.274	.395	.355
Home	216	61	8	1	10	43	37	40	.282	.468	.390
Road	231	61	13	1	5	29	33	42	.264	.394	.355
Grass	323	92	15	2	15	63	50	58	.285	.483	.383
Artificial Turf	124	30	6	0	0	9	20	24	.242	.290	.345
April	65	13	4	1	1	7	5	13	.200	.338	.257
May	77	23	1	0	3	14	14	14	.299	.429	.419
June	62	19	4	0	5	20	16	10	.306	.613	.443
July	75	21	5	0	2	14	14	15	.280	.427	.385
August	78	17	1	1	0	5	10	11	.218	.256	.315
Sept./Oct.	90	29	6	0	4	12	11	19	.322	.522	.392
Leading Off Inn.	98	25	2	0	8	8	9	18	.255	.520	.324
Runners On	229	71	14	2	4	61	42	39	.310	.441	.415
Runners/Scor. Pos.	129	38	6	0	3	54	33	24	.295	.411	.431
Runners On/2 Out	100	24	4	1	3	21	20	23	.240	.390	.367
Scor. Pos./2 Out	63	12	2	0	2	17	14	14	.190	.317	.338
Late Inning Pressure	72	15	4	0	1	10	8	17	.208	.306	.288
Leading Off	16	5	0	0	1	1	3	5	.313	.500	.421
Runners On	31	7	2	0	0	9	5	4	.226	.290	.333
Runners/Scor. Pos.	14	3	0	0	0	8	4	1	.214	.214	.389

DRIVING IN RUNS	From 1B	From 2B	From 3B	Scoring Position
Totals	12/156	16/92	29/65	45/157
Percentage	8%	17%	45%	29%
Driving In Runners from 3B with Less than Two Out:			26/39	67%

Loves to face: Atlee Hammaker (.455, 5-for-11, 3 HR, 7 BB)
Hates to face: Ron Robinson (0-for-13)
Not exactly a "two-out hitter": Martinez has career average of .311 with runners in scoring position and *less than* two out, but only .174 with runners in scoring position *and* two out; .144 (13-for-90) in latter situation over past two years.... Another weird breakdown: .331 career average with a runner on first base only, but only .247 in other situations with runners on base.... Hit six of his 15 home runs against Giants, and was only visiting player to hit four home runs at Candlestick last season. Career average of .327 (32 for 98, 7 HR) there.... Yearly batting averages in Late-Inning Pressure Situations are headed down the chute; since 1983: .273, .267, .253, .226, .197.

Dave Martinez

Chicago Cubs — Bats Left

	AB	H	2B	3B	HR	RRF	BB	SO	BA	SA	OBA
Season	459	134	18	8	8	37	57	96	.292	.418	.372
vs. Left-Handers	23	6	0	0	1	1	2	8	.261	.391	.320
vs. Right-Handers	436	128	18	8	7	36	55	88	.294	.420	.374
Home	231	65	10	5	5	18	30	42	.281	.433	.366
Road	228	69	8	3	3	19	27	54	.303	.404	.377
Grass	326	94	13	6	6	24	43	67	.288	.420	.373
Artificial Turf	133	40	5	2	2	13	14	29	.301	.414	.369
April	50	12	0	1	1	7	9	5	.240	.340	.356
May	70	19	2	0	0	5	12	11	.271	.300	.373
June	86	31	6	3	1	5	13	9	.360	.535	.450
July	71	23	2	1	3	6	6	14	.324	.507	.385
August	98	26	6	1	3	9	9	28	.265	.439	.327
Sept./Oct.	84	23	2	2	0	5	8	29	.274	.345	.337
Leading Off Inn.	152	44	7	2	4	4	14	29	.289	.441	.353
Runners On	158	44	5	2	1	30	24	41	.278	.354	.372
Runners/Scor. Pos.	94	26	4	2	0	28	20	24	.277	.362	.400
Runners On/2 Out	78	17	2	0	0	11	15	22	.218	.244	.344
Scor. Pos./2 Out	51	11	2	0	0	11	13	13	.216	.255	.375
Late Inning Pressure	62	23	2	1	0	5	4	14	.371	.435	.409
Leading Off	12	5	0	0	0	0	0	4	.417	.417	.417
Runners On	28	9	1	0	0	5	3	6	.321	.357	.387
Runners/Scor. Pos.	16	5	1	0	0	5	3	4	.313	.375	.421

DRIVING IN RUNS	From 1B	From 2B	From 3B	Scoring Position
Totals	2/104	16/78	10/30	26/108
Percentage	2%	21%	33%	24%
Driving In Runners from 3B with Less than Two Out:			6/12	50%

Loves to face: Terry Leach (.556, 5-for-9, 1 HR)
Hates to face: Ron Darling (.050, 1-for-20)
Batted .371 in Late-Inning Pressure Situations last season, which was 10th best in league, but only third best among Cubs' outfielders behind league leader Jerry Mumphrey (.409) and Bob Dernier (.389); no other N.L. team placed three players among top ten in this category.... Started 119 of 123 games in which Cubs faced a right-handed starter, but did not start any games against lefties.... Began season batting low in lineup, was elevated to leadoff spot in June, and hit .297 from that spot.... New York native had 22 hits vs. Mets last season, most by any opposing player.... That didn't help him any in Pittsburgh, though; career figures at Three Rivers Stadium: two hits, both singles, in 33 at bats.

Willie McGee

St. Louis Cardinals — Bats Left and Right

	AB	H	2B	3B	HR	RRF	BB	SO	BA	SA	OBA
Season	620	177	37	11	11	106	24	90	.285	.434	.312
vs. Left-Handers	208	60	16	5	6	42	8	35	.288	.500	.309
vs. Right-Handers	412	117	21	6	5	64	16	55	.284	.400	.313
Home	300	89	20	5	6	54	10	45	.297	.457	.316
Road	320	88	17	6	5	52	14	45	.275	.413	.308
Grass	157	42	7	2	4	26	10	26	.268	.414	.316
Artificial Turf	463	135	30	9	7	80	14	64	.292	.441	.310
April	61	18	3	1	1	13	4	9	.295	.426	.333
May	109	27	4	1	3	25	3	20	.248	.385	.278
June	101	34	6	3	1	18	3	13	.337	.485	.352
July	117	38	9	1	3	20	4	20	.325	.496	.347
August	125	33	8	2	1	19	5	12	.264	.384	.292
Sept./Oct.	107	27	7	3	2	11	5	16	.252	.430	.281
Leading Off Inn.	119	31	9	1	0	0	4	15	.261	.353	.285
Runners On	322	95	17	5	9	104	16	47	.295	.463	.328
Runners/Scor. Pos.	211	52	10	3	4	89	12	31	.246	.379	.287
Runners On/2 Out	150	42	5	4	6	40	6	24	.280	.487	.312
Scor. Pos./2 Out	105	23	1	4	3	30	6	17	.219	.352	.268
Late Inning Pressure	96	23	8	1	0	10	4	18	.240	.344	.277
Leading Off	23	3	2	0	0	1	1	7	.130	.217	.167
Runners On	40	11	5	0	0	10	3	7	.275	.400	.341
Runners/Scor. Pos.	26	6	4	0	0	10	3	5	.231	.385	.333

DRIVING IN RUNS	From 1B	From 2B	From 3B	Scoring Position
Totals	17/254	32/165	46/95	78/260
Percentage	7%	19%	48%	30%
Driving In Runners from 3B with Less than Two Out:			36/53	68%

Loves to face: Mike Scott (.560, 14-for-25)
Hates to face: Bob Sebra (0-for-7)
How can he finish with career-high 105 RBI despite career-low .246 with runners in scoring position? He batted with 260 runners in scoring position, most in majors since 1975. ... Third-highest ground outs-to-air outs ratio in N.L. (2.41); led N.L. with 24 DP grounders.... Career strikeout/walk ratio vs. left-handers (4.6) is worst among active N.L.ers (minimum: 500 AB vs. LHP). ... Late-Inning Pressure Situations batting average has been lower than overall average all six years in majors.... Batted with bases loaded 33 times in '87 to lead majors; had 10 hits, six for extra bases and was hit by two pitches, which no other NLer did even once. Not as great as Mattingly's six slams, but not too shabby.

Kevin McReynolds

New York Mets — Bats Right

	AB	H	2B	3B	HR	RBI	BB	SO	BA	SA	OBA
Season	590	163	32	5	29	98	39	70	.276	.495	.318
vs. Left-Handers	221	64	14	2	12	37	11	25	.290	.534	.325
vs. Right-Handers	369	99	18	3	17	61	28	45	.268	.472	.314
Home	298	82	12	1	18	52	22	37	.275	.503	.324
Road	292	81	20	4	11	46	17	33	.277	.486	.312
Grass	426	116	23	2	22	70	27	49	.272	.491	.312
Artificial Turf	164	47	9	3	7	28	12	21	.287	.506	.333
April	61	19	2	0	5	11	7	11	.311	.590	.377
May	102	24	8	0	2	13	8	9	.235	.373	.291
June	99	31	7	0	7	19	6	8	.313	.596	.346
July	104	31	6	2	5	22	6	13	.298	.538	.333
August	110	29	3	1	4	15	6	17	.264	.418	.297
Sept./Oct.	114	29	6	2	6	18	6	12	.254	.500	.292
Leading Off Inn.	110	43	8	1	5	5	7	8	.391	.618	.432
Runners On	279	62	11	4	11	80	23	43	.222	.409	.274
Runners/Scor. Pos.	183	39	8	4	6	69	15	28	.213	.399	.262
Runners On/2 Out	117	29	4	4	7	42	11	21	.248	.530	.313
Scor. Pos./2 Out	83	22	4	4	5	37	7	13	.265	.590	.322
Late Inning Pressure	87	19	2	0	1	12	8	6	.218	.276	.278
Leading Off	21	6	0	0	1	1	1	0	.286	.429	.318
Runners On	39	7	2	0	0	11	6	5	.179	.231	.277
Runners/Scor. Pos.	28	6	1	0	0	11	5	2	.214	.250	.314

DRIVING IN RUNS	From 1B	From 2B	From 3B	Scoring Position
Totals	14/206	24/153	31/70	55/223
Percentage	7%	16%	44%	25%
Driving In Runners from 3B with Less than Two Out:			19/35	54%

Loves to face: Jay Tibbs (.560, 14-for-25, 4 HR)
Hates to face: Mark Davis (.050, 1-for-20)

One of 11 players in majors with 25+ home runs and 95+ RBI in each of last two seasons, but in typical low-key style, Mac is the only one of the 11 not to reach the glamour levels (30 home runs, 100 RBI) in either year. . . . Batted only .200, no homers, two RBI in 11 games vs. old San Diego mates. . . . Annual batting averages with runners in scoring position since 1984: .303, .311, .270, .213. . . . Hit 103 points higher with bases empty (.325) than with runners on base (.222), biggest difference on Mets. . . . Stole 14 bases in 15 tries last season, tied with R. J. Reynolds for top percentage (.933) in majors (minimum: 10 SB). . . . Batted .236 in day games, .299 at night. And they said he would shy away from New York night life!

Bob Melvin

San Francisco Giants — Bats Right

	AB	H	2B	3B	HR	RBI	BB	SO	BA	SA	OBA
Season	246	49	8	0	11	32	17	44	.199	.366	.249
vs. Left-Handers	99	24	2	0	5	16	4	8	.242	.414	.272
vs. Right-Handers	147	25	6	0	6	16	13	36	.170	.333	.235
Home	114	20	3	0	6	16	7	15	.175	.360	.221
Road	132	29	5	0	5	16	10	29	.220	.371	.273
Grass	176	37	6	0	8	24	11	29	.210	.381	.255
Artificial Turf	70	12	2	0	3	8	6	15	.171	.329	.234
April	55	14	1	0	4	7	2	10	.255	.491	.281
May	69	17	7	0	3	10	9	9	.246	.478	.333
June	45	6	0	0	1	4	2	11	.133	.200	.167
July	25	4	0	0	1	4	1	6	.160	.160	.185
August	22	0	0	0	0	0	0	4	.000	.000	.000
Sept./Oct.	30	8	0	0	3	7	3	4	.267	.567	.333
Leading Off Inn.	50	8	3	0	2	2	1	14	.160	.340	.176
Runners On	111	26	5	0	2	23	10	15	.234	.333	.293
Runners/Scor. Pos.	70	15	3	0	1	20	9	14	.214	.300	.296
Runners On/2 Out	43	10	3	0	0	10	3	9	.233	.302	.283
Scor. Pos./2 Out	30	7	2	0	0	9	3	8	.233	.300	.303
Late Inning Pressure	42	12	1	0	2	5	3	10	.286	.452	.333
Leading Off	9	3	0	0	2	2	0	0	.333	1.000	.333
Runners On	21	8	1	0	0	3	2	5	.381	.429	.435
Runners/Scor. Pos.	12	4	0	0	0	3	2	4	.333	.333	.429

DRIVING IN RUNS	From 1B	From 2B	From 3B	Scoring Position
Totals	4/76	9/60	8/23	17/83
Percentage	5%	15%	35%	20%
Driving In Runners from 3B with Less than Two Out:			6/14	43%

Loves to face: Rick Aguilera (.750, 3-for-4)
Hates to face: Orel Hershiser (0-for-9)

One of two N.L. players with at least 200 at bats in both 1986 and 1987, but a sub-.230 batting average each year; the other: Mariano Duncan. . . . Career batting average of .274 vs. left-handers, .172 vs. right-handers, 2d-largest such difference in majors over last 10 years (minimum: 200 at bats each way). Largest difference (103 points) belongs to Sal Butera. . . . Made only one error last season, but caught only 78 games, three shy of minimum qualification for fielding average leadership. His percentage of .998 was superior to Alan Ashby's (.993), which led N.L. . . . Opponents stole only 48 bases in 84 attempts (57 percent); among catchers facing at least 50 attempts, only Mike LaValliere did better (55 percent).

Eddie Milner

San Francisco Giants — Bats Left

	AB	H	2B	3B	HR	RBI	BB	SO	BA	SA	OBA
Season	214	54	14	0	4	21	24	33	.252	.374	.328
vs. Left-Handers	32	5	0	0	0	0	3	12	.156	.156	.229
vs. Right-Handers	182	49	14	0	4	21	21	21	.269	.412	.345
Home	110	26	6	0	4	8	13	13	.236	.400	.317
Road	104	28	8	0	0	13	11	20	.269	.346	.339
Grass	161	40	9	0	4	16	17	23	.248	.379	.320
Artificial Turf	53	14	5	0	0	5	7	10	.264	.358	.350
April	18	4	0	0	0	2	1	2	.222	.222	.263
May	0	0	0	0	0	0	0	0	—	—	—
June	31	6	1	0	1	2	1	9	.194	.323	.219
July	49	9	2	0	0	4	6	6	.184	.224	.273
August	44	12	6	0	1	4	5	9	.273	.477	.347
Sept./Oct.	72	23	5	0	2	9	11	7	.319	.472	.410
Leading Off Inn.	84	19	2	0	3	3	10	13	.226	.357	.309
Runners On	69	20	6	0	0	17	7	11	.290	.377	.355
Runners/Scor. Pos.	39	11	1	0	0	14	7	9	.282	.308	.391
Runners On/2 Out	27	5	3	0	0	6	2	4	.185	.296	.241
Scor. Pos./2 Out	18	3	1	0	0	5	2	4	.167	.222	.250
Late Inning Pressure	37	10	4	0	1	3	6	7	.270	.459	.372
Leading Off	11	3	0	0	1	1	2	3	.273	.545	.385
Runners On	15	3	2	0	0	2	1	2	.200	.333	.250
Runners/Scor. Pos.	9	1	0	0	0	1	1	2	.111	.111	.200

DRIVING IN RUNS	From 1B	From 2B	From 3B	Scoring Position
Totals	3/49	6/29	7/14	13/43
Percentage	6%	21%	50%	30%
Driving In Runners from 3B with Less than Two Out:			4/8	50%

Loves to face: Danny Darwin (.538, 7-for-13, 1 HR)
Hates to face: Dave Smith (0-for-9)

Stuck in the fifties: no, not Elvis, hula hoops, and DA haircuts, we mean the .250s; Milner is the only player in the majors whose batting average has been in the .250s in each of the past three years. Career batting average: .255. . . . Started 40 games for Giants last season, all against right-handed pitchers, all as center fielder, all as leadoff batter. . . . Career average of .263 (40 home runs) vs. right-handed pitchers, .220 (two homers) vs. left-handers; last home run off a lefty came in 1984. . . . Batted .211 (4-for-19) as a pinch-hitter. . . . Had one of the 18 five-hit games in majors last season (the first five-hit game of his career); the other 17 were all turned in by guys who hit higher than .252.

Kevin Mitchell

Padres/Giants — Bats Right

	AB	H	2B	3B	HR	RBI	BB	SO	BA	SA	OBA
Season	464	130	20	2	22	73	48	88	.280	.474	.350
vs. Left-Handers	139	47	11	1	10	24	19	20	.338	.647	.418
vs. Right-Handers	325	83	9	1	12	49	29	68	.255	.400	.319
Home	227	66	11	2	9	38	23	43	.291	.476	.360
Road	237	64	9	0	13	35	25	45	.270	.473	.340
Grass	335	98	16	2	14	54	41	63	.293	.478	.372
Artificial Turf	129	32	4	0	8	19	7	25	.248	.465	.287
April	78	21	4	1	2	9	5	16	.269	.423	.313
May	52	10	0	0	1	7	7	10	.192	.250	.288
June	55	14	3	0	2	7	8	10	.255	.418	.344
July	97	26	7	0	6	18	9	19	.268	.526	.324
August	84	32	2	1	5	12	6	14	.381	.607	.429
Sept./Oct.	98	27	4	0	6	20	14	19	.276	.500	.372
Leading Off Inn.	85	24	4	1	5	5	8	20	.282	.529	.344
Runners On	213	68	8	0	11	62	23	40	.319	.512	.384
Runners/Scor. Pos.	123	37	4	0	8	56	21	28	.301	.528	.400
Runners On/2 Out	79	24	5	0	1	28	6	11	.304	.405	.353
Scor. Pos./2 Out	59	22	4	0	1	28	6	11	.373	.492	.431
Late Inning Pressure	71	16	1	0	1	12	5	16	.225	.282	.276
Leading Off	14	2	0	0	0	0	3	4	.143	.143	.294
Runners On	37	10	0	0	1	12	1	9	.270	.378	.289
Runners/Scor. Pos.	24	8	1	0	1	12	1	7	.333	.500	.360

DRIVING IN RUNS	From 1B	From 2B	From 3B	Scoring Position
Totals	9/138	23/91	19/57	42/148
Percentage	7%	25%	33%	28%
Driving In Runners from 3B with Less than Two Out:			8/19	42%

Loves to face: John Tudor (.667, 6-for-9, 2 HR)
Hates to face: Guy Hoffman (0-for-8)

Riches to rags and back to riches again: Went from World Champion Mets to last-place Padres to Division Champion Giants in less than a year. . . . Homered vs. every opposing club last season except the Mets. . . . Batted .245 in 62 games with San Diego, hitting from third to seventh in lineup; batted .306 in 69 games with Giants, including .326 with 38 RBI in 58 games batting second in lineup. . . . Batted .308 in day games, .264 at night. . . . Two hits in 14 career at bats with the bases loaded. . . . Career batting average of .350 with two out and runners in scoring position. . . . Started 115 games at third base, four in left field last year, after nomadic existence with '86 Mets, when he started at six different positions.

Keith Moreland

Chicago Cubs	AB	H	2B	3B	HR	RRF	BB	SO	BA	SA	OBA
Season	563	150	29	1	27	91	39	66	.266	.465	.309
vs. Left-Handers	122	36	10	0	3	18	15	15	.295	.451	.362
vs. Right-Handers	441	114	19	1	24	73	24	51	.259	.469	.294
Home	272	79	11	1	19	56	22	29	.290	.548	.338
Road	291	71	18	0	8	35	17	37	.244	.388	.282
Grass	390	112	16	1	23	69	31	41	.287	.510	.335
Artificial Turf	173	38	13	0	4	22	8	25	.220	.364	.250
April	73	12	2	0	1	9	3	9	.164	.233	.192
May	105	24	4	0	2	8	8	8	.229	.324	.283
June	107	30	5	0	10	31	5	15	.280	.607	.302
July	86	30	2	1	6	14	8	14	.349	.605	.404
August	102	25	7	0	4	14	11	10	.245	.431	.313
Sept./Oct.	90	29	9	0	4	15	4	10	.322	.556	.347
Leading Off Inn.	134	36	6	0	5	5	4	16	.269	.425	.290
Runners On	251	66	13	0	12	76	23	28	.263	.458	.314
Runners/Scor. Pos.	145	33	6	0	5	57	11	17	.228	.372	.267
Runners On/2 Out	119	28	7	0	3	26	11	16	.235	.370	.300
Scor. Pos./2 Out	77	16	4	0	2	21	5	12	.208	.338	.256
Late Inning Pressure	72	17	3	0	2	3	4	10	.236	.361	.276
Leading Off	27	7	2	0	1	1	0	3	.259	.444	.259
Runners On	24	6	0	0	1	2	3	6	.250	.375	.333
Runners/Scor. Pos.	9	1	0	0	0	0	2	3	.111	.111	.273

DRIVING IN RUNS	From 1B	From 2B	From 3B	Scoring Position
Totals	14/188	21/110	29/74	50/184
Percentage	7%	19%	39%	27%
Driving In Runners from 3B with Less than Two Out:			22/36	61%

Loves to face: Bob Knepper (.441, 15-for-34, 2 HR)
Hates to face: Scott Garrelts (0-for-15)
Averaged 2.17 assists per nine innings in 1987 (3d-highest rate among N.L. third basemen) in first year as regular third baseman; but he led majors with 28 errors at that position. . . . Cubs won only two of the 12 games that Moreland didn't start last year. . . . Ten home runs in June tied him with Dale Murphy for most in N.L. . . . Career batting average of .314 vs. left-handers is second-best to Gwynn's .318 among active N.L. players (minimum: 150 hits vs. LHP). . . . Since joining Cubs he has hit 67 homers at Wrigley Field, 33 on road. . . . Batted for higher average the lower he hit in the order: Hit .164 in 19 a starts batting 4th; .245 in 42 starts batting 5th; .294 in 83 starts batting 6th; .391 in five starts batting 7th.

Jim Morrison

Pittsburgh Pirates	AB	H	2B	3B	HR	RRF	BB	SO	BA	SA	OBA
Season	348	92	22	1	9	46	27	57	.264	.411	.315
vs. Left-Handers	142	41	9	1	5	21	20	19	.289	.472	.370
vs. Right-Handers	206	51	13	0	4	25	7	38	.248	.379	.273
Home	175	53	12	1	6	24	14	25	.303	.486	.354
Road	173	39	10	0	3	22	13	32	.225	.335	.275
Grass	100	27	6	0	3	17	10	18	.270	.420	.327
Artificial Turf	248	65	16	1	6	29	17	39	.262	.407	.310
April	72	24	6	0	4	13	8	8	.333	.583	.395
May	106	23	8	1	1	13	0	24	.217	.340	.220
June	94	23	6	0	2	11	11	14	.245	.372	.321
July	64	18	1	0	2	8	6	10	.281	.391	.343
August	12	4	1	0	0	1	2	1	.333	.417	.400
Sept./Oct.	0	0	0	0	0	0	0	0	—	—	—
Leading Off Inn.	77	21	5	0	1	1	4	11	.273	.377	.309
Runners On	158	44	9	0	4	41	14	27	.278	.411	.331
Runners/Scor. Pos.	89	25	6	0	1	32	8	19	.281	.382	.330
Runners On/2 Out	71	21	2	0	3	19	8	8	.296	.451	.367
Scor. Pos./2 Out	43	13	2	0	1	15	4	6	.302	.419	.362
Late Inning Pressure	52	12	2	1	1	4	6	11	.231	.365	.310
Leading Off	12	2	0	0	0	0	0	2	.167	.167	.167
Runners On	24	5	0	0	1	4	2	7	.208	.333	.269
Runners/Scor. Pos.	14	1	0	0	0	2	1	6	.071	.071	.133

DRIVING IN RUNS	From 1B	From 2B	From 3B	Scoring Position
Totals	7/130	10/64	20/41	30/105
Percentage	5%	16%	49%	29%
Driving In Runners from 3B with Less than Two Out:			14/24	58%

Loves to face: Steve Trout (.458, 11-for-24)
Hates to face: Ron Guidry (.130, 3-for-23, 7 SO)
Figures *above* are for N.L. only. . . . He switches leagues and becomes Jose Oquendo: Morrison started at six different positions (2B-3B-SS-RF-LF-DH) for Sparky after being traded to Tigers. . . . Batting average in Late-Inning Pressure Situations has been lower than overall average in each of last six seasons. . . . Batted .059 (1-for-17) with bases loaded last season (combined leagues). . . . Has hit 76 of 110 career HR with the bases empty. . . . Had three hits in his first six at bats at Tiger Stadium, 1-for-35 (.029) thereafter. . . . Will have to return to N.L. to finish his HR cycle: Has homered at every current stadium in major leagues except the Astrodome. Favorite A.L. ballpark: County Stadium (.396, 19-for-48, 2 HR).

Jerry Mumphrey

Chicago Cubs	AB	H	2B	3B	HR	RRF	BB	SO	BA	SA	OBA
Season	309	103	19	2	13	48	35	47	.333	.534	.400
vs. Left-Handers	7	1	1	0	0	0	1	1	.143	.286	.250
vs. Right-Handers	302	102	18	2	13	48	34	46	.338	.540	.404
Home	156	45	8	1	7	23	19	23	.288	.487	.366
Road	153	58	11	1	6	25	16	24	.379	.582	.435
Grass	223	71	14	1	8	32	27	31	.318	.498	.390
Artificial Turf	86	32	5	1	5	16	8	16	.372	.628	.426
April	7	3	0	0	1	4	3	0	.429	.857	.600
May	69	26	5	0	1	10	6	10	.377	.493	.421
June	70	19	3	0	3	12	8	13	.271	.443	.346
July	57	17	1	0	4	8	6	9	.298	.526	.365
August	62	22	6	1	3	6	6	8	.355	.629	.412
Sept./Oct.	44	16	4	1	1	8	6	7	.364	.568	.440
Leading Off Inn.	64	21	2	0	4	4	4	4	.328	.547	.368
Runners On	134	38	6	1	3	38	21	24	.284	.410	.378
Runners/Scor. Pos.	76	23	2	1	1	31	17	11	.303	.395	.426
Runners On/2 Out	61	18	3	1	1	13	11	8	.295	.426	.403
Scor. Pos./2 Out	38	11	1	1	0	10	9	5	.289	.368	.426
Late Inning Pressure	44	18	2	1	2	9	7	4	.409	.636	.490
Leading Off	10	4	0	0	0	0	0	0	.400	.400	.400
Runners On	21	7	1	1	1	8	3	2	.333	.619	.417
Runners/Scor. Pos.	13	4	0	1	0	5	1	1	.308	.462	.357

DRIVING IN RUNS	From 1B	From 2B	From 3B	Scoring Position
Totals	7/90	17/64	11/27	28/91
Percentage	8%	27%	41%	31%
Driving In Runners from 3B with Less than Two Out:			9/14	64%

Loves to face: Kevin Gross (.455, 10-for-22, 4 HR)
Hates to face: Andy McGaffigan (.053, 1-for-19, 7 SO)
Batted .409 in Late-Inning Pressure Situations in 1987 to lead N.L. . . . Also led N.L. players who were at least semi-regulars in batting average in night games (.410), on artificial turf (.372) and, not surprisingly given the first two, in road games (.379). . . . Despite all that, was 0-for-10 with bases loaded, biggest 0-for in majors. . . . When did Gene Michael discover that he was a switch-hitter? Mumphrey's first 183 plate appearances last season were from left side of plate. Career average of .307 batting left, .256 batting right; all 76 starts came vs. right-handers. . . . Has been hit by a pitch four times in his career, only once (by Renie Martin in 1983) in 4,108 plate appearances over last nine years!

Dale Murphy

Atlanta Braves	AB	H	2B	3B	HR	RRF	BB	SO	BA	SA	OBA
Season	566	167	27	1	44	109	115	136	.295	.580	.417
vs. Left-Handers	150	48	8	0	14	31	60	32	.320	.653	.512
vs. Right-Handers	416	119	19	1	30	78	55	104	.286	.553	.376
Home	269	93	11	1	25	64	77	52	.346	.673	.493
Road	297	74	16	0	19	45	38	84	.249	.495	.338
Grass	411	129	16	1	37	92	94	94	.314	.628	.445
Artificial Turf	155	38	11	0	7	17	21	42	.245	.452	.337
April	83	27	7	1	3	10	11	23	.325	.542	.404
May	97	31	3	0	11	21	33	25	.320	.691	.492
June	97	30	5	0	10	24	19	21	.309	.670	.427
July	91	19	2	0	4	14	15	18	.209	.363	.321
August	101	33	5	0	8	19	15	27	.327	.614	.410
Sept./Oct.	97	27	5	0	8	21	22	22	.278	.577	.425
Leading Off Inn.	157	51	11	0	11	11	15	38	.325	.605	.384
Runners On	259	68	10	0	19	84	70	68	.263	.521	.424
Runners/Scor. Pos.	153	38	4	0	14	71	59	45	.248	.549	.462
Runners On/2 Out	126	29	7	0	8	32	36	38	.230	.476	.405
Scor. Pos./2 Out	79	18	3	0	6	25	32	25	.228	.494	.455
Late Inning Pressure	83	20	3	0	4	7	20	25	.241	.482	.394
Leading Off	21	6	1	0	1	1	2	6	.286	.476	.348
Runners On	35	8	2	0	0	3	10	11	.229	.286	.413
Runners/Scor. Pos.	18	1	0	0	0	2	8	8	.056	.056	.370

DRIVING IN RUNS	From 1B	From 2B	From 3B	Scoring Position
Totals	13/162	25/117	27/64	52/181
Percentage	8%	21%	42%	29%
Driving In Runners from 3B with Less than Two Out:			21/33	64%

Loves to face: Bob Knepper (.419, 31-for-74, 7 HR)
Hates to face: Jeff D. Robinson (.077, 2-for-26, 7 SO)
Has played the most games (1,227) and has struck out the most times (1,001) of any player in the '80s; stands second in '80s home runs (264 to Schmidt's 295) and '80s runs scored (801 to Henderson's 891). . . . Career average of one home run every 15.7 at bats at Atlanta Stadium, one every 20.9 at bats on road. Best home run rate is at Candlestick (one every 13.9 at bats), worst is at Olympic Stadium (one every 49.3). . . . Had highest home-game slugging average (.673) of any player in majors last season; also led majors with 29 intentional walks. . . . Reached base safely in 73 of first 74 games, including streak of 48 in a row. (DiMaggio reached base in 74 straight games surrounding his 56-game hitting streak in 1941.)

Graig Nettles

Atlanta Braves — Bats Left

	AB	H	2B	3B	HR	RRF	BB	SO	BA	SA	OBA
Season	177	37	8	1	5	34	22	25	.209	.350	.294
vs. Left-Handers	48	11	2	1	0	8	5	7	.229	.313	.291
vs. Right-Handers	129	26	6	0	5	26	17	18	.202	.364	.295
Home	82	19	4	1	2	23	13	10	.232	.378	.330
Road	95	18	4	0	3	11	9	15	.189	.326	.260
Grass	141	29	5	1	5	32	19	19	.206	.362	.296
Artificial Turf	36	8	3	0	0	2	3	6	.222	.306	.282
April	14	3	0	0	1	4	3	4	.214	.429	.353
May	49	10	2	0	1	13	6	7	.204	.306	.286
June	31	5	0	0	2	5	6	4	.161	.355	.297
July	42	10	4	1	0	4	3	3	.238	.381	.289
August	19	6	2	0	0	2	1	2	.316	.421	.350
Sept./Oct.	22	3	0	0	1	6	3	5	.136	.273	.231
Leading Off Inn.	37	3	0	0	0	0	3	4	.081	.081	.150
Runners On	91	23	7	0	4	33	15	15	.253	.462	.352
Runners/Scor. Pos.	56	11	3	0	3	30	10	7	.196	.411	.309
Runners On/2 Out	40	12	2	0	3	15	8	8	.300	.575	.417
Scor. Pos./2 Out	27	7	1	0	3	15	6	4	.259	.630	.394
Late Inning Pressure	52	13	2	0	2	10	7	9	.250	.404	.333
Leading Off	16	1	0	0	0	0	1	4	.063	.063	.118
Runners On	16	8	2	0	2	10	6	2	.500	1.000	.609
Runners/Scor. Pos.	11	4	1	0	1	8	3	2	.364	.727	.467

DRIVING IN RUNS	From 1B	From 2B	From 3B	Scoring Position
Totals	4/71	11/43	14/30	25/73
Percentage	6%	26%	47%	34%
Driving In Runners from 3B with Less than Two Out:		10/17		59%

Loves to face: Jeff D. Robinson (.526, 10-for-19, 3 HR)
Hates to face: John Tudor (.143, 4-for-28)

Let's hope he gets a chance to face Robinson, now with Pirates, at Three Rivers Stadium, the only current major-league park in which he has not homered (50 career at bats). . . . Invited to '87 spring camp by Braves; hit .404 with seven home runs in 20 games. . . . Led major-league pinch-hitters in games (82) and RBI (23); RBI were two shy of major-league mark shared by Joe Cronin, Jerry Lynch, Rusty Staub. . . . Has hit for higher average with runners on base than with bases empty in each of 13 seasons since we started keeping track in '75. Hope Hall-of-Fame electors keep fact in mind when he becomes eligible. Overall career average is .248; no nonpitcher elected for playing ability has had career average below .250.

Ken Oberkfell

Atlanta Braves — Bats Left

	AB	H	2B	3B	HR	RRF	BB	SO	BA	SA	OBA
Season	508	142	29	2	3	49	48	29	.280	.362	.342
vs. Left-Handers	142	44	11	2	0	17	8	10	.310	.415	.349
vs. Right-Handers	366	98	18	0	3	32	40	19	.268	.342	.340
Home	259	76	15	1	2	30	29	13	.293	.382	.363
Road	249	66	14	1	1	19	19	16	.265	.341	.320
Grass	358	101	17	1	3	37	37	19	.282	.360	.349
Artificial Turf	150	41	12	1	0	12	11	10	.273	.367	.325
April	73	24	3	0	0	6	11	3	.329	.370	.417
May	117	38	13	1	0	10	9	6	.325	.453	.367
June	60	15	4	1	0	9	6	2	.250	.350	.324
July	70	16	4	0	1	7	5	0	.229	.329	.280
August	96	26	2	0	1	10	7	7	.271	.323	.327
Sept./Oct.	92	23	3	0	1	7	10	11	.250	.315	.324
Leading Off Inn.	112	33	8	1	0	0	4	5	.295	.384	.319
Runners On	211	56	11	1	1	47	28	14	.265	.341	.347
Runners/Scor. Pos.	129	32	7	1	0	42	18	11	.248	.318	.333
Runners On/2 Out	81	19	5	0	1	20	12	9	.235	.333	.333
Scor. Pos./2 Out	60	13	5	0	0	18	9	8	.217	.300	.319
Late Inning Pressure	76	17	4	0	0	4	8	7	.224	.276	.294
Leading Off	21	5	1	0	0	0	0	1	.238	.286	.238
Runners On	33	5	0	0	0	4	7	5	.152	.152	.293
Runners/Scor. Pos.	21	3	0	0	0	4	5	3	.143	.143	.296

DRIVING IN RUNS	From 1B	From 2B	From 3B	Scoring Position
Totals	5/146	15/95	26/59	41/154
Percentage	3%	16%	44%	27%
Driving In Runners from 3B with Less than Two Out:		17/25		68%

Loves to face: Bob Walk (.469, 15-for-32)
Hates to face: Dave Smith (.091, 2-for-22)

Batted 42 points higher against left-handers than vs. right-handers, largest such difference among left-handed N.L. batters last year (minimum: 50 at bats each way), and first time in his career that he has hit higher "the wrong way." Career numbers are along more traditional lines: .292 vs. right-handers, .255 vs. left-handers. . . . Averaged one strikeout every 19.5 plate appearances, 3d-best rate in N.L. . . . Went 157 consecutive plate appearances between strikeouts from June 9 to August 12, but hit only .255 during that stretch. . . . In nine full seasons in majors, his lowest average is .269, but he has hit only 23 home runs. . . . Career average of .311 at Dodger Stadium, the only park where he's a .300 hitter.

Ron Oester

Cincinnati Reds — Bats Left and Right

	AB	H	2B	3B	HR	RRF	BB	SO	BA	SA	OBA
Season	237	60	9	6	2	23	22	51	.253	.367	.317
vs. Left-Handers	60	12	1	0	0	1	5	20	.200	.217	.262
vs. Right-Handers	177	48	8	6	2	22	17	31	.271	.418	.335
Home	125	29	4	2	0	10	13	25	.232	.296	.304
Road	112	31	5	4	2	13	9	26	.277	.446	.331
Grass	60	20	2	3	1	5	5	9	.333	.517	.385
Artificial Turf	177	40	7	3	1	18	17	42	.226	.316	.294
April	78	22	2	3	1	7	10	20	.282	.423	.364
May	75	12	3	1	0	7	6	16	.160	.227	.222
June	66	20	3	2	1	5	5	13	.303	.455	.352
July	18	6	1	0	0	4	1	2	.333	.389	.368
August	0	0	0	0	0	0	0	0	—	—	—
Sept./Oct.	0	0	0	0	0	0	0	0	—	—	—
Leading Off Inn.	45	12	0	3	0	0	5	10	.267	.400	.340
Runners On	109	29	7	2	1	22	14	22	.266	.394	.350
Runners/Scor. Pos.	55	15	5	2	1	22	11	12	.273	.491	.394
Runners On/2 Out	43	12	2	1	1	10	7	10	.279	.442	.380
Scor. Pos./2 Out	22	7	2	1	1	10	4	6	.318	.636	.423
Late Inning Pressure	35	9	3	0	1	8	1	6	.257	.429	.278
Leading Off	4	0	0	0	0	0	0	1	.000	.000	.000
Runners On	20	9	3	0	1	8	1	3	.450	.750	.476
Runners/Scor. Pos.	10	4	3	0	1	8	1	1	.400	1.000	.455

DRIVING IN RUNS	From 1B	From 2B	From 3B	Scoring Position
Totals	2/79	7/36	12/25	19/61
Percentage	3%	19%	48%	31%
Driving In Runners from 3B with Less than Two Out:		7/16		44%

Loves to face: Kevin Gross (.524, 11-for-21)
Hates to face: Fernando Valenzuela (.118, 6-for-51)

Last year was first time since 1980 that he failed to play in 90 percent of team's games, and Reds missed him; they were 10 games over .500 with Oester in the starting lineup, four games below .500 without him. . . . Career average of .292 in Late-Inning Pressure Situations, and .306 in such situations with runners on base. . . . Charged with an error on his final chance in the field, making a wild throw as Mookie Wilson bowled him over on pivot at second base. . . . Had hit .310 in last 24 games before that season-ending injury, and finished up with season-high nine-game hitting streak. Since Reds didn't offer him a contract, he'll have to carry it with him somewhere else.

Jose Oquendo

St. Louis Cardinals — Bats Left and Right

	AB	H	2B	3B	HR	RRF	BB	SO	BA	SA	OBA
Season	248	71	9	0	1	30	54	29	.286	.335	.408
vs. Left-Handers	112	31	4	0	1	13	20	11	.277	.339	.375
vs. Right-Handers	136	40	5	0	0	17	34	18	.294	.331	.435
Home	111	33	5	0	0	13	26	16	.297	.342	.424
Road	137	38	4	0	1	17	28	13	.277	.328	.395
Grass	71	22	3	0	1	9	15	5	.310	.394	.425
Artificial Turf	177	49	6	0	0	21	39	24	.277	.311	.402
April	29	13	4	0	0	1	6	2	.448	.586	.528
May	53	16	2	0	0	8	11	3	.302	.340	.415
June	52	14	2	0	0	8	13	2	.269	.308	.409
July	44	13	1	0	1	6	7	5	.295	.386	.392
August	45	10	0	0	0	5	9	7	.222	.222	.352
Sept./Oct.	25	5	0	0	0	2	8	10	.200	.200	.382
Leading Off Inn.	65	17	2	0	0	0	15	7	.262	.292	.400
Runners On	104	31	5	0	1	30	24	12	.298	.375	.417
Runners/Scor. Pos.	61	17	2	0	1	27	14	6	.279	.361	.392
Runners On/2 Out	46	12	2	0	0	10	9	4	.261	.304	.382
Scor. Pos./2 Out	31	7	0	0	0	9	6	3	.226	.226	.351
Late Inning Pressure	62	14	3	0	1	6	15	10	.226	.323	.377
Leading Off	20	3	1	0	0	0	4	4	.150	.200	.292
Runners On	24	6	1	0	1	6	6	3	.250	.417	.400
Runners/Scor. Pos.	13	4	1	0	1	6	2	0	.308	.615	.400

DRIVING IN RUNS	From 1B	From 2B	From 3B	Scoring Position
Totals	3/74	7/47	19/35	26/82
Percentage	4%	15%	54%	32%
Driving In Runners from 3B with Less than Two Out:		15/18		83%

Loves to face: Dave Dravecky (.467, 7-for-15)
Hates to face: Kent Tekulve (0-for-8)

First player to start at seven different positions in one season since Jack Rothrock of 1928 Red Sox; Oquendo didn't catch, and pitched only in relief. . . . Batted .380 in day games, .223 at night. That difference of 157 points was largest in majors in '87 (minimum: 50 at bats each way). . . . An 0-for-13 slump from Sept. 9 to Oct. 2 dropped his batting average below .300 for season. . . . Batted .385 (10-for-26, one HR) as a pinch-hitter. . . . Has hit two regular-season home runs in career, both off left-handed pitchers (Lavelle and Lefferts) at Candlestick Park. Then in Game Seven of 1987 N.L.C.S., he tagged another Giants' lefty, Atlee Hammaker, this time at Busch. Has no HR in 596 career AB vs. right-handers.

Junior Ortiz
Pittsburgh Pirates — Bats Right

	AB	H	2B	3B	HR	RRF	BB	SO	BA	SA	OBA
Season	192	52	8	1	1	22	15	23	.271	.339	.322
vs. Left-Handers	160	44	8	0	0	16	10	17	.275	.325	.316
vs. Right-Handers	32	8	0	1	1	6	5	6	.250	.406	.351
Home	96	26	3	1	0	15	10	13	.271	.323	.336
Road	96	26	5	0	1	7	5	10	.271	.354	.307
Grass	54	16	2	0	0	3	2	4	.296	.333	.321
Artificial Turf	138	36	6	1	1	19	13	19	.261	.341	.322
April	31	7	1	1	0	5	4	3	.226	.323	.314
May	23	4	0	0	0	1	4	1	.174	.174	.208
June	34	11	1	0	1	6	0	6	.324	.441	.324
July	30	7	0	0	0		4	5	.233	.233	.324
August	35	11	3	0	0	5	3	3	.314	.400	.359
Sept./Oct.	39	12	3	0	0	5	3	5	.308	.385	.357
Leading Off Inn.	41	9	3	0	0		3	8	.220	.293	.273
Runners On	71	23	2	1	0	21	6	6	.324	.380	.372
Runners/Scor. Pos.	48	14	1	1	0	21	6	6	.292	.354	.364
Runners On/2 Out	34	11	1	1	0	11	3	4	.324	.412	.378
Scor. Pos./2 Out	25	8	0	1	0	11	3	4	.320	.400	.393
Late Inning Pressure	24	5	0	0	0	2	1	2	.208	.208	.240
Leading Off	5	1	0	0	0	0	0	0	.200	.200	.200
Runners On	10	3	0	0	0	2	0	1	.300	.300	.300
Runners/Scor. Pos.	9	3	0	0	0	2	0	1	.333	.333	.333

DRIVING IN RUNS	From 1B	From 2B	From 3B	Scoring Position
Totals	1/51	8/39	12/24	20/63
Percentage	2%	21%	50%	32%
Driving In Runners from 3B with Less than Two Out:		8/12		67%

Loves to face: Zane Smith (.636, 7-for-11)
Hates to face: Don Carman (0-for-10, 5 SO)

Syd Thrift must like him: he's one of two players on Bucs' roster on Aug. 31, 1985, who were still there at close of 1987 season; the other: Bob Walk. . . . And what's not to like: .232 career average with bases empty, but .316 with runners on base. . . . A ground-ball hitter: 2.33 ground outs-to-air outs ratio was 5th-highest in N.L. . . . Started 54 of 71 games in which the Pirates faced a southpaw, but had only one start against a right-hander. . . . Opponents were successful on 70 percent of stolen-base attempts (compared with 55 percent for teammate Mike LaValliere), but it was Ortiz who was the only Bucs' catcher to throw out Vince Coleman last season, on August 1, in ninth inning of a tied game, no less!

Rafael Palmeiro
Chicago Cubs — Bats Left

	AB	H	2B	3B	HR	RRF	BB	SO	BA	SA	OBA
Season	221	61	15	1	14	32	20	26	.276	.543	.336
vs. Left-Handers	26	3	0	0	1	3	4	3	.115	.231	.226
vs. Right-Handers	195	58	15	1	13	29	16	23	.297	.585	.352
Home	88	24	3	1	5	14	9	12	.273	.500	.333
Road	133	37	12	0	9	18	11	14	.278	.571	.338
Grass	142	34	5	1	7	20	14	18	.239	.437	.304
Artificial Turf	79	27	10	0	7	12	6	8	.342	.734	.395
April	0	0	0	0	0	0	0	0	———	———	———
May	0	0	0	0	0	0	0	0	———	———	———
June	34	9	2	1	2	7	5	2	.265	.559	.350
July	39	11	1	0	2	5	1	3	.282	.462	.300
August	72	20	6	0	5	10	3	11	.278	.569	.307
Sept./Oct.	76	21	6	0	5	10	11	10	.276	.553	.371
Leading Off Inn.	49	15	5	0	5	5	2	7	.306	.714	.333
Runners On	94	23	5	1	5	23	13	7	.245	.479	.330
Runners/Scor. Pos.	46	9	3	0	2	16	8	6	.196	.391	.304
Runners On/2 Out	34	7	3	0	1	7	7	2	.206	.382	.341
Scor. Pos./2 Out	20	4	2	0	1	7	5	2	.200	.450	.360
Late Inning Pressure	35	12	3	0	1	4	4	8	.343	.514	.410
Leading Off	8	0	0	0	0	0	0	4	.000	.000	.000
Runners On	12	5	0	0	1	4	4	1	.417	.667	.563
Runners/Scor. Pos.	7	2	0	0	0	2	3	2	.286	.286	.500

DRIVING IN RUNS	From 1B	From 2B	From 3B	Scoring Position
Totals	5/71	7/40	6/14	13/54
Percentage	7%	18%	43%	24%
Driving In Runners from 3B with Less than Two Out:		5/8		63%

Loves to face: Bob Forsch (.500, 6-for-12, 1 HR)
Hates to face: Brian Fisher (.091, 1-for-11)

Recalled from Iowa, June 16, and started 47 games for Cubs, all vs. right-handers. . . . He did hit a HR off left-hander Bob McClure on June 30. . . . Had highest slugging average (.543) among N.L. rookies with 200+ plate appearances. . . . Career average of one home run per 15.2 at bats in road games, one per 21.0 at bats at Wrigley Field. . . . Belted five home runs during final two weeks of 1987 season, during a 14-for-36 tear that included only two strikeouts. . . . One of 10 players who have hit two (or more) home runs off Dwight Gooden; others: Jody Davis and Mike Schmidt (three each); Bob Brenly, Jack Clark, Pedro Guerrero, Kevin McReynolds, Rick Schu, Tim Wallach, and Denny Walling (two each).

Dave Parker
Cincinnati Reds — Bats Left

	AB	H	2B	3B	HR	RRF	BB	SO	BA	SA	OBA
Season	589	149	28	0	26	99	44	104	.253	.433	.311
vs. Left-Handers	205	49	11	0	8	44	9	45	.239	.410	.285
vs. Right-Handers	384	100	17	0	18	55	35	59	.260	.445	.324
Home	291	82	15	0	14	54	23	38	.282	.478	.339
Road	298	67	13	0	12	45	21	66	.225	.389	.284
Grass	173	36	8	0	7	25	12	37	.208	.376	.262
Artificial Turf	416	113	20	0	19	74	32	67	.272	.457	.331
April	94	28	5	0	8	18	5	22	.298	.606	.333
May	102	29	5	0	4	14	10	23	.284	.451	.357
June	105	24	3	0	6	20	8	17	.229	.429	.296
July	104	25	6	0	3	22	7	16	.240	.385	.296
August	96	21	5	0	1	9	6	13	.219	.302	.276
Sept./Oct.	88	22	4	0	4	16	8	13	.250	.432	.306
Leading Off Inn.	143	39	8	0	6	6	5	23	.273	.455	.302
Runners On	278	78	13	0	15	88	28	50	.281	.489	.350
Runners/Scor. Pos.	164	40	10	0	6	68	23	40	.244	.415	.343
Runners On/2 Out	109	21	1	0	4	16	15	22	.193	.312	.307
Scor. Pos./2 Out	63	7	0	0	1	9	12	19	.111	.159	.282
Late Inning Pressure	75	18	2	0	2	8	1	21	.240	.347	.253
Leading Off	22	6	2	0	1	1	0	8	.273	.500	.304
Runners On	29	8	0	0	0	6	1	10	.276	.276	.281
Runners/Scor. Pos.	20	4	0	0	0	6	1	9	.200	.200	.217

DRIVING IN RUNS	From 1B	From 2B	From 3B	Scoring Position
Totals	20/194	27/133	26/68	53/201
Percentage	10%	20%	38%	26%
Driving In Runners from 3B with Less than Two Out:		24/40		60%

Loves to face: Greg Minton (.550, 11-for-20)
Hates to face: Tommy John (.208, 5-for-24, 1 XBH, 9 SO)

Has driven in 432 runs in the past four years; only Mattingly has more. . . . Only player in majors who has hit 60+ points higher with runners on base (.312) than with bases empty (.252) over past five years. . . . Led N.L. with eight HR in April; for the season, Reds won 20 of the 24 games in which he hit a home run. . . . Overall batting average (.253) was the lowest of his career. . . . Batting average with runners on base and two outs fell from .412 in 1986 to .193 last year. . . . Bay Area Blues? Has hit only four career homers at Candlestick Park, the fewest he has at any N.L. stadium. . . . Batted .184 in day games, .288 at night; for 1988, Oakland has more home day games scheduled (41) than any team in A.L.

Lance Parrish
Philadelphia Phillies — Bats Right

	AB	H	2B	3B	HR	RRF	BB	SO	BA	SA	OBA
Season	466	114	21	0	17	71	47	104	.245	.399	.313
vs. Left-Handers	138	42	4	0	6	16	21	30	.304	.464	.391
vs. Right-Handers	328	72	17	0	11	55	26	74	.220	.372	.278
Home	234	59	17	0	5	37	24	59	.252	.389	.322
Road	232	55	4	0	12	34	23	45	.237	.409	.305
Grass	114	28	3	0	5	16	17	24	.246	.404	.341
Artificial Turf	352	86	18	0	12	55	30	80	.244	.398	.304
April	64	12	0	0	3	15	6	18	.188	.328	.257
May	74	19	4	0	1	8	8	13	.257	.351	.329
June	78	16	3	0	3	11	4	18	.205	.359	.247
July	80	21	4	0	2	11	5	16	.263	.388	.306
August	93	27	7	0	5	16	15	16	.290	.527	.389
Sept./Oct.	77	19	3	0	3	10	9	23	.247	.403	.322
Leading Off Inn.	96	17	4	0	1	1	11	22	.177	.250	.262
Runners On	236	61	14	0	11	65	19	54	.258	.458	.310
Runners/Scor. Pos.	133	32	5	0	7	49	7	34	.241	.436	.273
Runners On/2 Out	114	31	7	0	8	33	7	28	.272	.544	.314
Scor. Pos./2 Out	71	14	2	0	4	21	3	19	.197	.394	.230
Late Inning Pressure	76	16	1	0	4	12	10	18	.211	.382	.302
Leading Off	13	2	1	0	1	1	1	3	.154	.462	.214
Runners On	39	7	0	0	1	9	2	11	.179	.256	.220
Runners/Scor. Pos.	26	6	0	0	1	9	0	7	.231	.346	.231

DRIVING IN RUNS	From 1B	From 2B	From 3B	Scoring Position
Totals	17/172	18/105	19/52	37/157
Percentage	10%	17%	37%	24%
Driving In Runners from 3B with Less than Two Out:		13/20		65%

Loves to face: Jamie Moyer (.462, 6-for-13, 2 HR)
Hates to face: Dennis Martinez (.156, 5-for-32)

In April, opponents stole 23 bases in 27 tries (and the four caught included a pitcher's pickoff and a failed steal of home), and the boo birds were out. But Parrish rebounded and finished season with opponents' stolen-base rate of only 72 percent. We say "only" because N.L. average was 71 percent, and average against other Phillies' catchers was 82 percent. . . . Grounded into only three double plays with Tigers in 1986, but in '87 he grounded into 23 in 123 DP situations, highest rate in majors (minimum: 40 opportunities). . . . Batted .185 in day games, .265 at night, his second consecutive year under .200 in daylight. . . . Had just one hit in 10 at bats with the bases loaded last season: a grand slam off Rick Reuschel.

Al Pedrique

Mets/Pirates — Bats Right

	AB	H	2B	3B	HR	RRF	BB	SO	BA	SA	OBA
Season	252	74	10	1	1	28	19	29	.294	.353	.349
vs. Left-Handers	135	40	4	0	0	10	11	12	.296	.326	.351
vs. Right-Handers	117	34	6	1	1	18	8	17	.291	.385	.346
Home	133	41	5	0	0	13	9	14	.308	.346	.361
Road	119	33	5	1	1	15	10	15	.277	.361	.336
Grass	49	13	3	0	1	7	5	7	.265	.388	.345
Artificial Turf	203	61	7	1	0	21	14	22	.300	.345	.350
April	5	0	0	0	0	0	1	2	.000	.000	.167
May	3	0	0	0	0	0	0	1	.000	.000	.000
June	36	9	1	1	0	4	2	8	.250	.333	.289
July	47	13	2	0	1	8	3	6	.277	.383	.333
August	104	40	6	0	0	13	8	6	.385	.442	.430
Sept./Oct.	57	12	1	0	0	3	5	6	.211	.228	.286
Leading Off Inn.	59	17	1	0	0	0	6	9	.288	.305	.364
Runners On	107	40	6	1	1	28	8	7	.374	.477	.419
Runners/Scor. Pos.	59	27	4	1	1	26	6	6	.458	.610	.500
Runners On/2 Out	47	20	4	1	1	18	5	5	.426	.617	.491
Scor. Pos./2 Out	28	14	3	1	1	17	5	4	.500	.786	.576
Late Inning Pressure	40	9	2	0	0	3	1	6	.225	.275	.262
Leading Off	13	2	0	0	0	0	1	2	.154	.154	.267
Runners On	15	6	1	0	0	3	0	2	.400	.467	.400
Runners/Scor. Pos.	9	3	0	0	0	2	0	2	.333	.333	.333

DRIVING IN RUNS	From 1B	From 2B	From 3B	Scoring Position
Totals	4/79	11/49	12/21	23/70
Percentage	5%	22%	57%	33%
Driving In Runners from 3B with Less than Two Out:			7/11	64%

Loves to face: Neal Heaton (.615, 8-for-13)
Hates to face: Greg Mathews (0-for-6)

This is not a test, this is an actual emergency: Pedrique's batting average with runners in scoring position (.458, we swear) was highest in majors last season. It gets worse: He also led the majors in hitting with runners on base and two outs (.426) and with runners in scoring position and two outs (.500). Please return to your homes and stand by for further information. . . . At one point last August, he had eight consecutive hits vs. left-handed pitchers, the longest streak in the majors last season. . . . Batted .301 in 88 games for Pirates, but six hitless at bats with Mets in April cost him his .300 status for season. . . . Or was it his seven hitless at bats as a pinch-hitter?

Tony Pena

St. Louis Cardinals — Bats Right

	AB	H	2B	3B	HR	RRF	BB	SO	BA	SA	OBA
Season	384	82	13	4	5	46	36	54	.214	.307	.281
vs. Left-Handers	137	31	4	0	3	17	11	15	.226	.321	.280
vs. Right-Handers	247	51	9	4	2	29	25	39	.206	.300	.282
Home	187	42	7	3	1	21	13	25	.225	.310	.274
Road	197	40	6	1	4	25	23	29	.203	.305	.288
Grass	90	15	2	1	0	10	11	18	.167	.211	.257
Artificial Turf	294	67	11	3	5	36	25	36	.228	.337	.289
April	10	1	0	0	0	0	2	5	.100	.100	.308
May	28	8	1	1	0	7	2	5	.286	.393	.333
June	96	28	4	1	1	12	7	7	.292	.385	.337
July	81	16	3	2	0	9	10	12	.198	.284	.283
August	85	14	3	0	2	7	10	7	.165	.271	.253
Sept./Oct.	84	15	2	0	2	11	5	20	.179	.274	.225
Leading Off Inn.	93	20	3	1	1	1	5	15	.215	.301	.263
Runners On	162	34	6	1	4	45	19	16	.210	.333	.290
Runners/Scor. Pos.	91	19	3	1	2	40	15	9	.209	.330	.315
Runners On/2 Out	47	10	2	1	2	13	9	7	.213	.426	.339
Scor. Pos./2 Out	32	5	1	1	0	9	7	3	.156	.250	.308
Late Inning Pressure	73	16	3	1	1	4	6	11	.219	.329	.288
Leading Off	15	5	2	0	0	0	2	3	.333	.467	.444
Runners On	33	4	0	0	1	4	3	3	.121	.212	.194
Runners/Scor. Pos.	14	1	0	0	0	2	1	0	.071	.071	.133

DRIVING IN RUNS	From 1B	From 2B	From 3B	Scoring Position
Totals	7/122	10/63	24/46	34/109
Percentage	6%	16%	52%	31%
Driving In Runners from 3B with Less than Two Out:			20/33	61%

Loves to face: Pascual Perez (.438, 7-for-16, 2 HR)
Hates to face: Kent Tekulve (.071, 1-for-14)

Batting average with runners in scoring position in each of last five years: .318, .306, .267, .223, .209. . . . Opponents were successful on 72.4 percent of stolen-base attempts (71 of 98), compared with 56.8 percent (25 of 44) against Steve Lake. . . . Grounded into 19 double plays in 94 DP situations, 6th-highest rate in N.L. (minimum: 40 opportunities). . . . Hitless in 26 consecutive at bats with runners on base (Aug. 10 to Sept. 4). . . . Batting average after the All-Star Break (.183) was lowest in majors (minimum: 150 plate appearances). . . . Class, what is next number in this sequence: 15, 15, 10, 10, 5. Right, "5"; those are his yearly home-run totals since 1983. . . . Please send any *positive* notes to Elias Sports Bureau.

Terry Pendleton

St. Louis Cardinals — Bats Left and Right

	AB	H	2B	3B	HR	RRF	BB	SO	BA	SA	OBA
Season	583	167	29	4	12	100	70	74	.286	.412	.360
vs. Left-Handers	208	70	9	1	4	41	18	19	.337	.447	.386
vs. Right-Handers	375	97	20	3	8	59	52	55	.259	.392	.346
Home	293	78	15	1	5	47	28	32	.266	.375	.331
Road	290	89	14	3	7	53	42	42	.307	.448	.388
Grass	158	50	8	0	6	29	19	28	.316	.481	.381
Artificial Turf	425	117	21	4	6	71	51	46	.275	.386	.352
April	81	25	6	0	1	9	3	7	.309	.420	.333
May	103	34	5	0	1	20	14	9	.330	.408	.397
June	99	28	2	0	3	15	14	16	.283	.394	.374
July	101	31	6	1	3	19	12	16	.307	.475	.383
August	94	26	6	3	2	26	19	10	.277	.468	.391
Sept./Oct.	105	23	4	0	2	11	8	16	.219	.314	.272
Leading Off Inn.	119	32	8	1	2	2	18	13	.269	.403	.365
Runners On	275	88	16	3	7	95	37	35	.320	.476	.393
Runners/Scor. Pos.	167	54	9	3	2	85	28	20	.323	.449	.408
Runners On/2 Out	99	35	5	3	2	42	13	11	.354	.525	.434
Scor. Pos./2 Out	73	28	4	3	0	38	11	7	.384	.521	.471
Late Inning Pressure	89	28	7	2	3	16	9	19	.315	.539	.384
Leading Off	16	5	2	0	0	0	3	3	.313	.438	.421
Runners On	40	16	4	2	3	16	5	9	.400	.825	.478
Runners/Scor. Pos.	20	8	2	2	1	12	5	6	.400	.850	.538

DRIVING IN RUNS	From 1B	From 2B	From 3B	Scoring Position
Totals	11/193	32/128	45/81	77/209
Percentage	6%	25%	56%	37%
Driving In Runners from 3B with Less than Two Out:			30/47	64%

Loves to face: Zane Smith (.522, 12-for-23)
Hates to face: Mike LaCoss (.063, 1-for-16)

Mets fans need no convincing of his prowess in Late-Inning Pressure Situations with runners on base, but there it is in black and white: .400 batting average, .825 slugging average. His 9th-inning HR off Roger McDowell in such a situation on Sept. 11 was Cardinals' key hit of season, preventing a loss that would have reduced Cards' lead to one-half game. . . . Rate of runners driven in from scoring position was highest of his career and 4th-highest in N.L. last season. . . . Averaged 2.40 assists per nine innings last season, 2d-highest rate among N.L. third basemen (minimum: 500 innings). . . . Has never batted in cleanup position during regular season, but did bat there in Game Two of 1987 N.L.C.S.

Gerald Perry

Atlanta Braves — Bats Left

	AB	H	2B	3B	HR	RRF	BB	SO	BA	SA	OBA
Season	533	144	35	2	12	76	48	63	.270	.411	.329
vs. Left-Handers	125	32	11	1	5	18	11	21	.256	.480	.321
vs. Right-Handers	408	112	24	1	7	58	37	42	.275	.390	.331
Home	255	66	20	1	2	32	28	23	.259	.369	.331
Road	278	78	15	1	10	44	20	40	.281	.450	.327
Grass	403	110	28	2	7	50	37	46	.273	.404	.332
Artificial Turf	130	34	7	0	5	26	11	17	.262	.431	.319
April	62	13	2	0	1	8	4	10	.210	.290	.254
May	87	21	3	0	2	16	8	12	.241	.345	.305
June	81	22	6	1	1	11	10	10	.272	.407	.348
July	76	26	5	0	1	10	6	9	.342	.447	.390
August	107	31	9	1	5	15	9	12	.290	.533	.342
Sept./Oct.	120	31	10	0	2	16	11	10	.258	.392	.321
Leading Off Inn.	94	23	4	1	1	1	7	9	.245	.340	.297
Runners On	246	69	15	1	7	71	22	26	.280	.435	.336
Runners/Scor. Pos.	147	42	9	0	4	61	12	13	.286	.429	.333
Runners On/2 Out	78	20	3	0	2	23	6	5	.256	.372	.310
Scor. Pos./2 Out	55	15	1	0	1	20	4	3	.273	.345	.322
Late Inning Pressure	83	24	6	0	1	13	5	15	.289	.398	.326
Leading Off	21	7	1	0	0	0	1	4	.333	.381	.364
Runners On	37	11	3	0	1	13	3	7	.297	.459	.341
Runners/Scor. Pos.	23	8	1	0	1	12	3	4	.348	.522	.407

DRIVING IN RUNS	From 1B	From 2B	From 3B	Scoring Position
Totals	10/163	23/110	31/60	54/170
Percentage	6%	21%	52%	32%
Driving In Runners from 3B with Less than Two Out:			22/41	54%

Loves to face: Danny Cox (.579, 11-for-19)
Hates to face: Scott Sanderson (.105, 2-for-19)

Stole 42 bases, the most by a Braves player since Ol' Hap Myers swiped 57 in 1913—74 years and two cities ago. . . . Led N.L. with nine stolen bases vs. Astros; one was a steal of home as he led only successful triple steal in majors all season. . . . Started 111 of 113 games in which Braves faced right-handed starters, 20 of 48 games against lefties. . . . Strange home run stats: hit only two of his 12 at home, and hit five of 12 off lefties, despite only 23 percent of at bats coming vs. southpaws. . . . Ground-ball hitter in a fly-ball park: 1.98 ground outs-to-air outs ratio was 9th-highest in N.L. . . . Averaged 0.58 assists per nine innings last season, 3d-lowest rate among N.L. first basemen (minimum: 500 innings).

Tim Raines
Montreal Expos — Bats Left and Right

	AB	H	2B	3B	HR	RRF	BB	SO	BA	SA	OBA
Season	530	175	34	8	18	69	90	52	.330	.526	.429
vs. Left-Handers	164	65	13	4	5	23	21	18	.396	.616	.471
vs. Right-Handers	366	110	21	4	13	46	69	34	.301	.486	.411
Home	276	93	15	5	9	32	49	29	.337	.525	.437
Road	254	82	19	3	9	37	41	23	.323	.528	.420
Grass	144	49	12	2	5	21	25	14	.340	.556	.439
Artificial Turf	386	126	22	6	13	48	65	38	.326	.516	.425
April	0	0	0	0	0	0	0	0	—	—	—
May	106	37	9	1	4	18	17	14	.349	.566	.444
June	103	40	8	0	3	19	14	7	.388	.553	.462
July	90	24	5	0	3	8	13	8	.267	.422	.349
August	115	37	6	4	6	17	18	15	.322	.600	.418
Sept./Oct.	116	37	6	3	2	7	28	8	.319	.474	.459
Leading Off Inn.	154	55	9	5	5	5	17	10	.357	.578	.431
Runners On	194	63	12	1	7	58	51	25	.325	.505	.460
Runners/Scor. Pos.	119	40	5	0	3	47	42	17	.336	.454	.500
Runners On/2 Out	65	18	2	0	4	21	23	13	.277	.492	.466
Scor. Pos./2 Out	42	12	1	0	1	14	19	8	.286	.381	.508
Late Inning Pressure	71	28	6	3	3	13	13	6	.394	.690	.482
Leading Off	27	13	3	1	2	2	1	1	.481	.889	.500
Runners On	20	9	3	1	1	11	9	5	.450	.850	.600
Runners/Scor. Pos.	14	6	2	0	1	9	9	4	.429	.786	.625

DRIVING IN RUNS	From 1B	From 2B	From 3B	Scoring Position
Totals	11/122	23/98	17/40	40/138
Percentage	9%	23%	43%	29%
Driving In Runners from 3B with Less than Two Out:		13/23		57%

Loves to face: Orel Hershiser (.438, 14-for-32)
Hates to face: Rick Aguilera (.083, 2-for-24)
As you look at those statistics for May, remember that he did not attend spring training last year.... His .396 average vs. left-handers was highest in majors among everyday players.... Career batting average of .352 in Late-Inning Pressure Situations is highest among anyone since we invented that category in 1975; his .394 mark in LIPS in 1987 stood 3d in N.L. behind part-timers Jerry Mumphrey (.409) and Tom Foley (.395).... Of eight major leaguers with 50+ stolen bases in '87, only Raines was successful more than 90 percent of time (50 of 55).... Didn't steal a base in last 11 games, his longest drought all season.... Career batting average of .217 at the Astrodome, the only place he has a career average under .280.

Johnny Ray
Pittsburgh Pirates — Bats Left and Right

	AB	H	2B	3B	HR	RRF	BB	SO	BA	SA	OBA
Season	472	129	19	3	5	58	41	36	.273	.358	.328
vs. Left-Handers	191	49	6	0	2	17	19	17	.257	.319	.322
vs. Right-Handers	281	80	13	3	3	41	22	19	.285	.384	.332
Home	228	69	8	1	5	38	23	17	.303	.412	.361
Road	244	60	11	2	0	20	18	19	.246	.307	.297
Grass	134	33	6	0	0	11	10	10	.246	.291	.297
Artificial Turf	338	96	13	3	5	47	31	26	.284	.385	.340
April	78	20	2	0	3	15	7	6	.256	.397	.318
May	109	28	6	1	0	14	7	12	.257	.330	.297
June	107	29	3	1	1	12	8	9	.271	.346	.316
July	83	24	5	0	0	7	10	4	.289	.349	.366
August	95	28	3	1	1	10	9	5	.295	.379	.352
Sept./Oct.	0	0	0	0	0	0	0	0	—	—	—
Leading Off Inn.	81	20	3	0	0	0	4	2	.247	.284	.282
Runners On	222	59	10	2	3	56	24	20	.266	.369	.331
Runners/Scor. Pos.	140	35	6	1	1	49	18	15	.250	.329	.325
Runners On/2 Out	64	17	3	0	0	17	10	8	.266	.313	.365
Scor. Pos./2 Out	50	12	2	0	0	16	10	6	.240	.280	.367
Late Inning Pressure	66	20	5	0	2	8	6	4	.303	.470	.361
Leading Off	21	7	2	0	0	2	0	.333	.429	.391	
Runners On	30	10	3	0	1	7	1	4	.333	.533	.355
Runners/Scor. Pos.	18	4	0	0	1	6	1	2	.222	.389	.263

DRIVING IN RUNS	From 1B	From 2B	From 3B	Scoring Position
Totals	7/132	20/103	26/66	46/169
Percentage	5%	19%	39%	27%
Driving In Runners from 3B with Less than Two Out:		19/40		48%

Loves to face: Steve Trout (.313, 10-for-32)
Hates to face: Tom Niedenfuer (.077, 1-for-13)
Has never set foot on a major-league diamond at any position other than second base, but he's being talked about as left-field material for Angels.... Had never batted in cleanup position, either, before Gene Mauch put him there for nine games in September; Angels lost eight of those nine games.... Averaged 3.15 assists per nine innings with the Pirates last season, 3d-highest rate among N.L. second basemen (minimum: 500 innings).... Career average of .301 batting left-handed, .256 batting right-handed.... One of only three major leaguers to play in 150+ games in each of last six years, but because he didn't have a long consecutive-game streak, he gets a lot less pub than Dale Murphy or Cal Ripken.

Randy Ready
San Diego Padres — Bats Right

	AB	H	2B	3B	HR	RRF	BB	SO	BA	SA	OBA
Season	350	108	26	6	12	57	67	44	.309	.520	.423
vs. Left-Handers	175	58	15	4	6	26	46	18	.331	.566	.473
vs. Right-Handers	175	50	11	2	6	31	21	26	.286	.474	.367
Home	171	58	12	4	7	35	30	20	.339	.579	.443
Road	179	50	14	2	5	22	37	24	.279	.464	.404
Grass	254	85	20	5	9	45	42	31	.335	.559	.433
Artificial Turf	96	23	6	1	3	12	25	13	.240	.417	.398
April	24	6	5	0	0	3	4	4	.250	.458	.357
May	55	15	4	1	0	6	10	4	.273	.382	.385
June	77	29	4	0	1	15	10	9	.377	.468	.448
July	59	15	3	1	2	9	14	10	.254	.441	.392
August	49	14	5	3	1	8	11	7	.286	.571	.435
Sept./Oct.	86	29	5	1	8	16	18	10	.337	.698	.457
Leading Off Inn.	79	21	4	2	3	3	15	8	.266	.481	.383
Runners On	158	54	12	2	4	49	27	17	.342	.519	.439
Runners/Scor. Pos.	92	30	7	1	0	36	17	11	.326	.424	.427
Runners On/2 Out	65	26	7	1	2	26	17	4	.400	.631	.524
Scor. Pos./2 Out	39	15	5	1	0	19	11	3	.385	.564	.520
Late Inning Pressure	54	14	3	0	1	5	16	10	.259	.370	.437
Leading Off	11	3	0	0	0	0	5	3	.273	.273	.500
Runners On	22	4	0	0	0	4	9	2	.182	.182	.438
Runners/Scor. Pos.	16	3	0	0	0	4	7	1	.188	.188	.435

DRIVING IN RUNS	From 1B	From 2B	From 3B	Scoring Position
Totals	12/116	18/75	15/32	33/107
Percentage	10%	24%	47%	31%
Driving In Runners from 3B with Less than Two Out:		10/17		59%

Loves to face: Bob Knepper (.714, 5-for-7, 1 HR)
Hates to face: Orel Hershiser (0-for-6)
Only N.L. player to start at least one game in each spot in lineup (excluding 9th) last season.... 1987 was his first full major-league season; compiled a .343 average in six seasons in minors.... Batting average in June was 3d-highest in N.L.... Started 58 of 65 games in which Pads faced left-handed starters, 31 of 97 games against right-handers.... Batting average in Late-Inning Pressure Situations has been lower than overall average in each of five seasons in majors. Career figures: .213 in LIPS, .283 in non-LIPS.... A junior-grade Eddie Murray, judging by these career numbers: .253 with bases empty, .294 with runners on base, .313 with runners in scoring position, .341 with two out and runners in scoring position.

Jeff Reed
Montreal Expos — Bats Left

	AB	H	2B	3B	HR	RRF	BB	SO	BA	SA	OBA
Season	207	44	11	0	1	22	12	20	.213	.280	.254
vs. Left-Handers	31	8	4	0	0	7	2	4	.258	.387	.294
vs. Right-Handers	176	36	7	0	1	15	10	16	.205	.261	.247
Home	86	14	3	0	1	10	5	9	.163	.233	.204
Road	121	30	8	0	0	12	7	11	.248	.314	.290
Grass	57	12	2	0	0	4	4	6	.211	.246	.266
Artificial Turf	150	32	9	0	1	18	8	14	.213	.293	.250
April	30	4	2	0	0	3	3	2	.133	.200	.212
May	12	2	1	0	0	0	1	3	.167	.250	.286
June	33	6	1	0	0	2	1	5	.182	.212	.206
July	36	10	4	0	1	7	4	5	.278	.472	.341
August	55	9	0	0	0	3	1	1	.164	.164	.207
Sept./Oct.	41	13	3	0	0	9	0	4	.317	.390	.295
Leading Off Inn.	49	12	3	0	0	0	2	4	.245	.306	.275
Runners On	84	19	5	0	1	22	7	7	.226	.321	.281
Runners/Scor. Pos.	51	12	4	0	1	21	6	4	.235	.373	.295
Runners On/2 Out	36	8	3	0	1	10	4	1	.222	.389	.300
Scor. Pos./2 Out	27	5	2	0	1	9	4	1	.185	.370	.290
Late Inning Pressure	19	4	1	0	0	1	2	1	.211	.263	.286
Leading Off	4	1	0	0	0	0	0	0	.250	.250	.250
Runners On	6	1	1	0	0	1	1	1	.167	.333	.286
Runners/Scor. Pos.	3	1	1	0	0	1	1	0	.333	.667	.500

DRIVING IN RUNS	From 1B	From 2B	From 3B	Scoring Position
Totals	3/60	8/36	10/29	18/65
Percentage	5%	22%	34%	28%
Driving In Runners from 3B with Less than Two Out:		7/12		58%

Loves to face: Jim Acker (.667, 2-for-3, 1 HR)
Hates to face: Brian Fisher (0-for-7)
Ugh, Canada: .163 batting average at Olympic Stadium was worst by any N.L. player in his home park last season.... Started 56 of 111 games in which Montreal faced right-handed starters, five of 51 games against left-handers; has .262 career average in 42 at bats vs. lefties.... Hit .303 with eight RBI in 13 games vs. Cardinals.... Committed 12 errors last season, tying teammate Fitzgerald for 2d most among N.L. catchers, behind Santiago's 22. Fitz caught 52 percent of Expos' innings, Reed 38 percent.... Expos' starting catchers batted only .224 to rank 11th in N.L.; then again, the two teams whose starting catchers had worst batting averages in their respective leagues met in the World Series!

Craig Reynolds

Houston Astros — Bats Left

	AB	H	2B	3B	HR	RRF	BB	SO	BA	SA	OBA
Season	374	95	17	3	4	29	30	44	.254	.348	.303
vs. Left-Handers	43	6	0	0	0	0	3	10	.140	.140	.196
vs. Right-Handers	331	89	17	3	4	29	27	34	.269	.375	.317
Home	189	49	8	2	0	11	17	19	.259	.323	.316
Road	185	46	9	1	4	18	13	25	.249	.373	.291
Grass	122	32	5	0	4	15	8	17	.262	.402	.303
Artificial Turf	252	63	12	3	0	14	22	27	.250	.321	.304
April	47	14	3	0	0	3	6	6	.298	.362	.370
May	46	13	3	1	0	7	3	3	.283	.391	.320
June	66	20	3	0	2	7	2	6	.303	.439	.319
July	73	15	4	0	0	3	8	10	.205	.260	.274
August	61	17	1	1	2	5	6	6	.279	.426	.338
Sept./Oct.	81	16	3	1	0	4	5	13	.198	.259	.241
Leading Off Inn.	76	22	3	1	1	1	6	7	.289	.395	.341
Runners On	163	34	5	1	2	27	16	23	.209	.288	.267
Runners/Scor. Pos.	84	11	2	0	1	22	13	12	.131	.190	.229
Runners On/2 Out	71	13	0	0	1	7	13	8	.183	.225	.310
Scor. Pos./2 Out	43	4	0	0	0	5	11	5	.093	.093	.278
Late Inning Pressure	62	16	0	0	1	1	4	9	.258	.306	.303
Leading Off	14	5	0	0	1	1	0	1	.357	.571	.357
Runners On	28	4	0	0	0	0	1	6	.143	.143	.172
Runners/Scor. Pos.	14	0	0	0	0	0	0	3	.000	.000	.000

DRIVING IN RUNS	From 1B	From 2B	From 3B	Scoring Position
Totals	5/125	5/68	15/41	20/109
Percentage	4%	7%	37%	18%
Driving In Runners from 3B with Less than Two Out:		13/19		68%

Loves to face: Pascual Perez (.500, 8-for-16, 3 HR)
Hates to face: Mark Davis (0-for-13)

Hit all four of his home runs at Candlestick Park last season. Has career average of .312 there, his best at any N.L. park, with seven homers in 157 at bats. . . . Grounded into only four double plays in 87 DP situations, 7th-lowest rate in N.L. (minimum: 40 opportunities). . . . Batted .131 with runners in scoring position to rank 135th out of 137 N.L. qualifiers, ahead of only Steve Jeltz and Luis Aguayo; Reynolds hit .355 in those situations in 1986. . . . Started 105 of 107 games in which Astros faced a right-handed starter, but only three of 55 games against lefties. . . . Ironic note to Thon tragedy: Reynolds, who has taken Thon's job, has not been hit by a pitch in 1,925 plate appearances since May 9, 1982.

R.J. Reynolds

Pittsburgh Pirates — Bats Left and Right

	AB	H	2B	3B	HR	RRF	BB	SO	BA	SA	OBA
Season	335	87	24	1	7	54	34	80	.260	.400	.323
vs. Left-Handers	57	20	2	0	0	12	5	2	.351	.386	.391
vs. Right-Handers	278	67	22	1	7	42	29	78	.241	.403	.309
Home	172	46	15	1	2	26	15	40	.267	.401	.318
Road	163	41	9	0	5	28	19	40	.252	.399	.328
Grass	96	22	3	0	4	15	10	28	.229	.385	.302
Artificial Turf	239	65	21	1	3	39	24	52	.272	.406	.331
April	28	11	4	0	0	2	1	2	.393	.536	.414
May	69	20	6	1	1	12	7	16	.290	.449	.355
June	76	24	5	0	3	14	10	16	.316	.500	.395
July	56	4	1	0	0	2	6	20	.071	.089	.156
August	63	14	5	0	1	13	6	13	.222	.349	.278
Sept./Oct.	43	14	3	0	2	11	4	13	.326	.535	.375
Leading Off Inn.	76	23	5	0	2	2	3	16	.303	.447	.329
Runners On	162	43	11	1	4	51	20	42	.265	.420	.335
Runners/Scor. Pos.	97	23	5	0	0	40	16	24	.237	.289	.328
Runners On/2 Out	70	15	3	0	1	15	7	21	.214	.300	.286
Scor. Pos./2 Out	51	10	1	0	0	13	6	15	.196	.216	.281
Late Inning Pressure	49	13	2	0	1	11	8	15	.265	.367	.356
Leading Off	8	1	0	0	0	0	0	2	.125	.125	.125
Runners On	31	8	0	0	1	11	4	10	.258	.387	.324
Runners/Scor. Pos.	20	5	0	0	0	9	4	7	.250	.250	.346

DRIVING IN RUNS	From 1B	From 2B	From 3B	Scoring Position
Totals	9/125	16/80	22/41	38/121
Percentage	7%	20%	54%	31%
Driving In Runners from 3B with Less than Two Out:		16/21		76%

Loves to face: Rick Aguilera (.500, 8-for-16, 5 2B)
Hates to face: Nolan Ryan (.111, 2-for-18, 9 SO)

His batting average with runners on base (.265) looks nondescript, but it's good stuff considering that he was hitless in 27 consecutive runners-on-base at bats from July 1 to August 6, tying Stan Jefferson for longest such streak in N.L. last season. . . . Started 79 of 91 games in which Pirates faced a right-handed pitcher, but made no starts against left-handers; made 60 starts in right field, 19 in left. . . . Only homer of career off a left-handed pitcher was hit off Pete Falcone in 1984. . . . Stole 14 bases in 15 attempts last season, tied with Kevin McReynolds for top rate (.933) in majors in 1987 (minimum: 10 SB); R.J. was caught on first try of year, vs. Leach-Carter on April 20, then stole 14 straight.

Luis Salazar

San Diego Padres — Bats Right

	AB	H	2B	3B	HR	RRF	BB	SO	BA	SA	OBA
Season	189	48	5	0	3	18	14	30	.254	.328	.302
vs. Left-Handers	97	25	4	0	2	8	4	18	.258	.361	.287
vs. Right-Handers	92	23	1	0	1	10	10	12	.250	.293	.317
Home	95	27	1	0	1	7	4	16	.284	.326	.310
Road	94	21	4	0	2	11	10	14	.223	.330	.295
Grass	130	36	2	0	2	10	9	20	.277	.338	.321
Artificial Turf	59	12	3	0	1	8	5	10	.203	.305	.262
April	13	1	0	0	0	0	0	1	.077	.077	.077
May	46	15	1	0	0	4	4	7	.326	.348	.373
June	43	13	1	0	2	5	4	7	.302	.465	.362
July	23	4	0	0	1	3	1	4	.174	.304	.208
August	33	8	2	0	0	2	3	5	.242	.303	.306
Sept./Oct.	31	7	1	0	0	4	2	6	.226	.258	.265
Leading Off Inn.	46	7	0	0	0	0	3	9	.152	.152	.204
Runners On	87	23	3	0	2	17	7	13	.264	.368	.313
Runners/Scor. Pos.	53	12	3	0	1	14	5	9	.226	.340	.283
Runners On/2 Out	38	9	1	0	1	8	4	4	.237	.342	.310
Scor. Pos./2 Out	26	6	1	0	1	8	3	4	.231	.385	.310
Late Inning Pressure	37	6	0	0	0	6	1	10	.162	.216	.179
Leading Off	11	1	0	0	0	0	0	4	.091	.091	.091
Runners On	19	4	1	0	0	6	1	5	.211	.263	.238
Runners/Scor. Pos.	11	4	1	0	0	5	1	3	.364	.455	.385

DRIVING IN RUNS	From 1B	From 2B	From 3B	Scoring Position
Totals	3/61	3/35	9/28	12/63
Percentage	5%	9%	32%	19%
Driving In Runners from 3B with Less than Two Out:		5/14		36%

Loves to face: Bob Knepper (.400, 18-for-45, 2 HR)
Hates to face: Tom Browning (0-for-11)

Played seven positions last season, all except second base and catcher, leaving him one position behind league leader Jose Oquendo. . . . Unlike W.C. Fields, this fellow will take Philadelphia any day: His career batting average at the Vet is .365, with .622 slugging average; elsewhere on the planet, his averages are .260 and .367. . . . Owns a career average of .208 (10-for-48) with the bases loaded: he's 7 for 20 with less than two outs, but 3-for-28 for all those managers (are you listening, Larry Bowa?) who have let him bat with the bases loaded *and* two outs. . . . Threw a wild pitch in each of his two pitching appearances; he's now one behind Dan Quisenberry's career total, in 892.1 fewer innings.

Juan Samuel

Philadelphia Phillies — Bats Right

	AB	H	2B	3B	HR	RRF	BB	SO	BA	SA	OBA
Season	655	178	37	15	28	104	60	162	.272	.502	.335
vs. Left-Handers	181	45	9	4	9	25	25	47	.249	.492	.344
vs. Right-Handers	474	133	28	11	19	79	35	115	.281	.506	.331
Home	320	92	22	10	15	56	40	73	.288	.559	.367
Road	335	86	15	5	13	48	20	89	.257	.448	.302
Grass	172	42	4	2	7	24	11	48	.244	.413	.298
Artificial Turf	483	136	33	13	21	80	49	114	.282	.534	.348
April	81	22	7	2	1	10	8	24	.272	.444	.333
May	105	28	5	1	7	22	8	16	.267	.533	.316
June	107	28	4	3	4	14	11	23	.262	.467	.336
July	108	30	4	2	8	22	16	33	.278	.574	.375
August	125	35	9	5	2	18	15	33	.280	.480	.357
Sept./Oct.	129	35	8	2	6	18	2	33	.271	.504	.288
Leading Off Inn.	203	55	16	5	9	9	19	53	.271	.532	.342
Runners On	251	78	13	8	11	87	21	56	.311	.558	.358
Runners/Scor. Pos.	162	52	9	7	9	82	15	33	.321	.630	.366
Runners On/2 Out	97	25	5	2	0	27	15	29	.258	.351	.357
Scor. Pos./2 Out	74	20	5	2	0	27	10	20	.270	.392	.357
Late Inning Pressure	87	28	5	2	3	16	14	25	.322	.529	.412
Leading Off	18	3	0	0	0	0	3	6	.167	.167	.286
Runners On	41	16	3	1	2	15	7	9	.390	.659	.469
Runners/Scor. Pos.	21	6	1	0	2	14	4	7	.286	.619	.385

DRIVING IN RUNS	From 1B	From 2B	From 3B	Scoring Position
Totals	7/144	32/126	37/65	69/191
Percentage	5%	25%	57%	36%
Driving In Runners from 3B with Less than Two Out:		27/35		77%

Loves to face: Jamie Moyer (.440, 11-for-25, 1 HR)
Hates to face: Sid Fernandez (.121, 4-for-33, 12 SO)

Has hit 10+ triples for four straight years; no other player has done it in the last two. Last major leaguer to hit 10+ triples for four years was Roberto Clemente's six straight, 1965–70. . .Last year's monthly averages (above) are as consistent as his yearly averages: .277, .272, .264, 266, .272; he's the only major leaguer in the .260s or .270s in each of the last five years. . . . 17 consecutive errorless games to finish the season matched his longest streak of season. . . . Batted leadoff only once in 61 games under Felske (through June 17), but in 92 of 100 games for Elia. . . . Percentage of runners driven in from scoring position has increased in each of his seasons in the majors: 23.1, 24.1, 26.9, 28.5, 36.1.

Ryne Sandberg

Chicago Cubs   Bats Right

	AB	H	2B	3B	HR	RRF	BB	SO	BA	SA	OBA
Season	523	154	25	2	16	62	59	79	.294	.442	.367
vs. Left-Handers	114	35	9	0	2	14	21	16	.307	.439	.412
vs. Right-Handers	409	119	16	2	14	48	38	63	.291	.443	.353
Home	257	77	14	2	8	34	23	39	.300	.463	.357
Road	266	77	11	0	8	28	36	40	.289	.421	.376
Grass	377	111	18	2	13	51	37	56	.294	.456	.357
Artificial Turf	146	43	7	0	3	11	22	23	.295	.404	.391
April	74	20	7	0	1	7	12	10	.270	.405	.379
May	118	33	6	1	8	19	15	21	.280	.551	.361
June	42	14	4	0	2	9	5	4	.333	.571	.404
July	61	21	2	0	1	4	4	6	.344	.426	.379
August	117	38	1	0	3	14	11	18	.325	.410	.385
Sept./Oct.	111	28	5	1	1	9	12	20	.252	.342	.325
Leading Off Inn.	116	35	9	0	4	4	8	19	.302	.483	.347
Runners On	214	61	7	0	4	50	25	33	.285	.374	.362
Runners/Scor. Pos.	128	30	4	0	2	45	19	22	.234	.313	.333
Runners On/2 Out	91	22	4	0	3	27	9	18	.242	.385	.317
Scor. Pos./2 Out	66	14	2	0	2	24	6	12	.212	.333	.288
Late Inning Pressure	64	19	2	0	1	12	13	10	.297	.375	.416
Leading Off	9	3	0	0	0	0	1	1	.333	.333	.400
Runners On	38	13	0	0	1	12	9	8	.342	.421	.468
Runners/Scor. Pos.	23	7	0	0	1	12	7	4	.304	.435	.467

DRIVING IN RUNS	From 1B	From 2B	From 3B	Scoring Position
Totals	4/145	19/98	23/56	42/154
Percentage	3%	19%	41%	27%
Driving In Runners from 3B with Less than Two Out:			13/26	50%

Loves to face: Dennis Rasmussen (.714, 5-for-7)
Hates to face: Bryn Smith (.071, 3-for-42)
Will he ever get off to a hot start? Career batting average is .227 in April, .297 in later months. ... Stole 21 bases in 23 attempts last season, 4th-best percentage in N.L. (minimum: 10 SB); one of his two times caught was an attempted steal of home on double steal. ... Played 132 games in '87 after averaging 155 over the previous five years. ... Despite 43 extra-base hits, drove in only four runners from first base last season. ... Has batted .300 or better at Wrigley Field in five of six seasons with Cubs. Career figures: .309 with 53 home runs at Wrigley, .268 with 37 home runs elsewhere. ... One of nine players with 20+ stolen bases in each of last six years. ... Batting average over the past four years is .2999.

Rafael Santana

New York Mets   Bats Right

	AB	H	2B	3B	HR	RRF	BB	SO	BA	SA	OBA
Season	439	112	21	2	5	47	29	57	.255	.346	.302
vs. Left-Handers	168	44	6	1	3	23	14	16	.262	.363	.322
vs. Right-Handers	271	68	15	1	2	24	15	41	.251	.336	.289
Home	221	54	13	0	2	22	17	31	.244	.330	.297
Road	218	58	8	2	3	25	12	26	.266	.362	.307
Grass	314	80	18	1	3	35	23	39	.255	.347	.305
Artificial Turf	125	32	3	1	2	12	6	18	.256	.344	.295
April	61	12	1	0	1	5	4	9	.197	.262	.246
May	57	19	3	0	1	7	3	10	.333	.439	.367
June	70	18	2	1	2	14	8	10	.257	.400	.333
July	85	25	8	0	0	6	3	8	.294	.388	.318
August	81	21	5	1	1	10	4	10	.259	.383	.291
Sept./Oct.	85	17	2	0	0	5	7	10	.200	.224	.269
Leading Off Inn.	99	23	6	0	1	1	4	12	.232	.323	.262
Runners On	188	53	10	2	2	44	19	22	.282	.388	.346
Runners/Scor. Pos.	114	29	6	2	1	41	15	15	.254	.368	.338
Runners On/2 Out	81	23	5	1	1	19	13	12	.284	.407	.383
Scor. Pos./2 Out	48	12	3	1	0	17	12	8	.250	.354	.400
Late Inning Pressure	48	11	3	1	0	7	1	7	.229	.333	.245
Leading Off	16	4	2	0	0	0	0	1	.250	.375	.250
Runners On	16	5	1	1	0	7	0	2	.313	.500	.313
Runners/Scor. Pos.	12	4	1	1	0	7	0	2	.333	.583	.333

DRIVING IN RUNS	From 1B	From 2B	From 3B	Scoring Position
Totals	6/131	16/93	20/45	36/138
Percentage	5%	17%	44%	26%
Driving In Runners from 3B with Less than Two Out:			12/24	50%

Loves to face: Gary Lucas (.800, 4-for-5)
Hates to face: Mike Jackson (0-for-8)
What do Kevin Gross, Orel Hershiser, Mike Krukow, Nolan Ryan, and Rick Reuschel have in common? Each has three stolen bases in majors, or one more than Santana has in his 513-game career. (Yes, *that* Rick Reuschel.) Oh yeah, Joaquin Andujar has seven steals. ... Removed for pinch-hitter 32 times last season, second among N.L. nonpitchers to Steve Jeltz's 35. ... Led N.L. with a .450 average (18-for-40) in 12 games vs. Giants. ... Started year with 16 hitless at bats, and ended it with 13 hitless at bats; in between he batted .273. ... Career batting averages by month: April .188, May .247, June .248, July .266, August .286, and .220 after September 1. Have patience, George and Billy!

Benito Santiago

San Diego Padres   Bats Right

	AB	H	2B	3B	HR	RRF	BB	SO	BA	SA	OBA
Season	546	164	33	2	18	81	16	112	.300	.467	.324
vs. Left-Handers	182	62	17	1	8	30	6	32	.341	.577	.363
vs. Right-Handers	364	102	16	1	10	51	10	80	.280	.412	.304
Home	274	77	17	1	11	47	10	50	.281	.471	.307
Road	272	87	16	1	7	34	6	62	.320	.463	.342
Grass	394	112	21	1	13	56	11	84	.284	.442	.308
Artificial Turf	152	52	12	1	5	25	5	28	.342	.533	.365
April	78	22	4	1	3	7	1	16	.282	.474	.291
May	93	26	1	0	2	9	2	23	.280	.355	.306
June	73	18	4	0	1	10	4	20	.247	.342	.291
July	83	25	7	0	2	15	4	20	.301	.458	.337
August	106	35	7	0	6	26	5	13	.330	.566	.357
Sept./Oct.	113	38	10	1	4	14	0	20	.336	.549	.342
Leading Off Inn.	123	36	8	0	0	0	1	34	.293	.358	.304
Runners On	255	79	14	1	11	74	10	40	.310	.502	.333
Runners/Scor. Pos.	137	40	11	1	4	58	9	27	.292	.474	.327
Runners On/2 Out	106	37	10	1	4	34	3	16	.349	.575	.373
Scor. Pos./2 Out	71	23	8	1	1	27	3	14	.324	.507	.351
Late Inning Pressure	103	39	6	1	3	18	1	27	.379	.544	.385
Leading Off	28	11	2	0	0	0	0	10	.393	.464	.393
Runners On	47	19	4	1	2	17	1	9	.404	.660	.417
Runners/Scor. Pos.	27	11	4	1	0	13	1	6	.407	.630	.429

DRIVING IN RUNS	From 1B	From 2B	From 3B	Scoring Position
Totals	12/200	23/112	28/61	51/173
Percentage	6%	21%	46%	29%
Driving In Runners from 3B with Less than Two Out:			17/28	61%

Loves to face: Guy Hoffman (.667, 6-for-9)
Hates to face: John Mitchell (0-for-6, 3 SO)
Averaged one walk every 35.8 plate appearances, lowest rate in majors last season; walked twice during 34-game hitting streak (including one in Game One of streak, and an intentional walk in Game Seven). ... Batted only .346 during 34-game streak, lowest average during any one-season streak of 30+ games. ... That streak is a club record, a rookie record, a record for catchers, etc. ... Raised season average to .300 with two hits in season finale. ... Led major-league catchers with 22 errors; 12 were on throws trying to prevent stolen bases. ... Led N.L. with 22 passed balls, most in N.L. since Ted Simmons (28) in 1975. ... Loves that Keystone State: 9-for-17 at Philadelphia and 9-for-20 at Pittsburgh.

Steve Sax

Los Angeles Dodgers   Bats Right

	AB	H	2B	3B	HR	RRF	BB	SO	BA	SA	OBA
Season	610	171	22	7	6	48	44	61	.280	.369	.331
vs. Left-Handers	205	57	10	2	2	15	15	14	.278	.376	.330
vs. Right-Handers	405	114	12	5	4	33	29	47	.281	.365	.332
Home	289	75	9	2	2	16	19	28	.260	.325	.310
Road	321	96	13	5	4	32	25	33	.299	.408	.351
Grass	439	123	13	4	4	30	31	45	.280	.355	.331
Artificial Turf	171	48	9	3	2	18	13	16	.281	.404	.333
April	91	18	4	1	0	4	7	10	.198	.264	.263
May	106	34	4	2	2	7	8	16	.321	.453	.368
June	109	29	3	0	1	15	9	10	.266	.321	.322
July	77	19	1	1	0	4	3	5	.247	.286	.272
August	111	31	7	1	0	5	7	10	.279	.346	.328
Sept./Oct.	116	40	3	2	3	13	10	10	.345	.483	.402
Leading Off Inn.	218	63	7	3	4	4	11	21	.289	.404	.326
Runners On	209	55	8	2	1	43	20	24	.263	.335	.326
Runners/Scor. Pos.	130	35	6	2	0	40	13	18	.269	.346	.333
Runners On/2 Out	85	19	2	0	0	20	11	10	.224	.294	.313
Scor. Pos./2 Out	59	16	2	0	0	20	9	8	.271	.373	.368
Late Inning Pressure	94	33	6	1	1	12	9	11	.351	.468	.408
Leading Off	25	9	2	1	0	1	3	3	.360	.520	.385
Runners On	41	14	3	0	0	11	6	5	.341	.415	.426
Runners/Scor. Pos.	31	9	2	0	0	10	5	5	.290	.355	.389

DRIVING IN RUNS	From 1B	From 2B	From 3B	Scoring Position
Totals	3/129	17/105	22/50	39/155
Percentage	2%	16%	44%	25%
Driving In Runners from 3B with Less than Two Out:			14/29	48%

Loves to face: Zane Smith (.455, 15-for-33)
Hates to face: Terry Leach (0-for-12)
Led Dodgers with .351 batting average in Late-Inning Pressure Situations; his LIPS average has been higher than overall average in each of last five seasons. Career: .318 in LIPS, .278 at other times. ... One of five players with 25+ SB in each of last six seasons; others: Henderson, Raines, Ozzie, Willie Wilson. ... Has only one extra-base hit in 70 career AB (15-for-70, .214) with the bases loaded; at least he went for the gusto, with a grand-slam off Jay Baller in 1986. ... Reached base safely in each of his last 25 starts, including a 19-game hitting streak that was completely overshadowed by Santiago's concurrent 34-game streak; in 1986, Sax reached base safely in his last 34 games, including 25-game hitting streak.

Mike Schmidt

Philadelphia Phillies — Bats Right

	AB	H	2B	3B	HR	RRF	BB	SO	BA	SA	OBA
Season	522	153	28	0	35	118	83	80	.293	.548	.388
vs. Left-Handers	133	44	9	0	7	27	28	11	.331	.556	.442
vs. Right-Handers	389	109	19	0	28	91	55	69	.280	.545	.368
Home	260	89	18	0	15	70	43	38	.342	.585	.433
Road	262	64	10	0	20	48	40	42	.244	.511	.343
Grass	128	33	6	0	5	16	15	15	.258	.422	.338
Artificial Turf	394	120	22	0	30	102	68	65	.305	.589	.404
April	67	19	0	0	6	19	15	12	.284	.552	.410
May	70	20	3	0	7	19	3	18	.286	.629	.311
June	70	21	5	0	4	13	11	10	.300	.543	.402
July	95	29	6	0	5	21	23	11	.305	.526	.433
August	113	37	9	0	6	22	21	12	.327	.566	.434
Sept./Oct.	107	27	5	0	7	24	10	17	.252	.495	.314
Leading Off Inn.	127	37	5	0	7		20	19	.291	.496	.388
Runners On	270	81	17	0	17	100	43	40	.300	.552	.393
Runners/Scor. Pos.	161	50	14	0	9	81	29	27	.311	.565	.406
Runners On/2 Out	125	43	10	0	11	51	25	22	.344	.688	.457
Scor. Pos./2 Out	80	28	9	0	5	37	17	14	.350	.650	.469
Late Inning Pressure	87	23	4	0	4	14	16	14	.264	.448	.379
Leading Off	26	4	1	0	1	1	4	5	.154	.308	.267
Runners On	43	14	2	0	1	11	8	6	.326	.442	.431
Runners/Scor. Pos.	25	8	2	0	1	11	7	4	.320	.520	.469

DRIVING IN RUNS	From 1B	From 2B	From 3B	Scoring Position
Totals	20/186	33/122	30/65	63/187
Percentage	11%	27%	46%	34%
Driving In Runners from 3B with Less than Two Out:			20/34	59%

Loves to face: Bob Knepper (.403, 29-for-72, 8 HR)
Hates to face: Danny Darwin (0-for-7)

Has hit 35+ HR in 11 seasons; only Aaron (11) and Ruth (12) have done that.... Stands third in N.L. history with 530 homers, ranks 8th with 1,505 RBI. This season he could pass some pretty fair names: Stargell (1,540), Hornsby (1,550), McCovey (1,555), Banks (1,636).... Hit five homers at Busch Stadium last season, only Jack Clark (17) and Willie McGee (six) hit more.... Has not hit a grand-slam homer since Aug. 15, 1983; that's 154 home runs ago. Schmidt has hit only seven slams in his career, the same number as Puddinhead Jones, and one less than Andy Seminick.... Averaged 2.45 assists per nine innings last season, highest rate among major-league third basemen (minimum: 500 innings).

Rick Schu

Philadelphia Phillies — Bats Right

	AB	H	2B	3B	HR	RRF	BB	SO	BA	SA	OBA
Season	196	46	6	3	7	25	20	36	.235	.403	.311
vs. Left-Handers	102	27	4	1	5	14	10	14	.265	.471	.330
vs. Right-Handers	94	19	2	2	2	11	10	22	.202	.330	.290
Home	100	25	3	2	5	14	10	19	.250	.470	.324
Road	96	21	3	1	2	11	10	17	.219	.333	.296
Grass	56	8	0	1	2	9	6	12	.143	.286	.234
Artificial Turf	140	38	6	2	5	16	14	24	.271	.450	.342
April	11	1	0	0	1	1	0	3	.091	.364	.091
May	36	6	0	0	2	4	3	11	.167	.333	.262
June	55	19	2	1	2	7	4	9	.345	.527	.390
July	17	5	1	2	0	7	1	2	.294	.588	.333
August	36	10	2	0	2	6	3	4	.278	.500	.333
Sept./Oct.	41	5	1	0	0	0	9	7	.122	.146	.280
Leading Off Inn.	53	15	1	1		4	4	9	.283	.566	.333
Runners On	77	17	2	1	3	21	13	18	.221	.390	.337
Runners/Scor. Pos.	52	7	2	1	1	17	10	17	.135	.269	.281
Runners On/2 Out	29	5	1	0		6	5	8	.172	.207	.294
Scor. Pos./2 Out	22	2	1	0	0	6	3	8	.091	.136	.200
Late Inning Pressure	30	5	1	1	0	5	1	7	.167	.267	.194
Leading Off	7	1	0	0	0	0	0	3	.143	.143	.143
Runners On	15	3	1	1	0	5	1	3	.200	.400	.250
Runners/Scor. Pos.	10	3	1	1	0	5	1	3	.300	.600	.364

DRIVING IN RUNS	From 1B	From 2B	From 3B	Scoring Position
Totals	5/50	8/46	5/16	13/62
Percentage	10%	17%	31%	21%
Driving In Runners from 3B with Less than Two Out:			3/5	60%

Loves to face: Greg Mathews (.500, 7-for-14, 1 HR)
Hates to face: Andy Hawkins (0-for-11)

One of 10 players who have hit two or more home runs off Dwight Gooden; Schu has done it in only eight at bats, the fewest among the 10 players.... Bet you thought his scoring-position batting average couldn't get any worse than .189 in 1986; he got you with a .135 mark in '87. He's the only player in majors with sub-.200 average with runners in scoring position in each of last two years (minimum: 50 at bats each year).... Career breakdown: .268 with bases empty, .233 with runners on base, .198 with runners in scoring position; .189 on grass fields, .281 on artificial surfaces.... Had two hits, both singles, in 24 at bats as a pinch-hitter.... Fielding average at third base has declined every year: .952, .933, .913, .905.

Mike Scioscia

Los Angeles Dodgers — Bats Left

	AB	H	2B	3B	HR	RRF	BB	SO	BA	SA	OBA
Season	461	122	26	1	6	42	55	23	.265	.364	.343
vs. Left-Handers	132	36	8	1	0	12	16	11	.273	.348	.356
vs. Right-Handers	329	86	18	0	6	30	39	12	.261	.371	.338
Home	219	57	6	0	2	18	29	5	.260	.315	.345
Road	242	65	20	1	4	24	26	18	.269	.409	.341
Grass	336	94	18	0	4	28	44	13	.280	.369	.362
Artificial Turf	125	28	8	1	2	14	11	10	.224	.352	.290
April	78	25	5	0	2	9	12	5	.321	.462	.411
May	85	22	3	0	1	7	11	3	.259	.329	.344
June	40	6	1	0	0	1	5	3	.150	.175	.244
July	75	17	8	0	1	8	6	4	.227	.373	.280
August	89	28	6	1	1	9	9	3	.315	.438	.374
Sept./Oct.	94	24	3	0	1	8	12	5	.255	.319	.346
Leading Off Inn.	99	26	6	0	3	3	8	3	.263	.414	.318
Runners On	187	48	7	0	0	36	23	8	.257	.294	.335
Runners/Scor. Pos.	105	28	3	0	0	33	21	6	.267	.295	.383
Runners On/2 Out	72	14	1	0	0	11	18	4	.194	.208	.356
Scor. Pos./2 Out	46	9	1	0	0	11	17	4	.196	.217	.413
Late Inning Pressure	73	18	5	0	2	8	9	5	.247	.397	.329
Leading Off	19	4	1	0	1	1	1	0	.211	.421	.250
Runners On	22	4	1	0	0	6	4	2	.182	.227	.308
Runners/Scor. Pos.	11	4	1	0	0	6	4		.364	.455	.533

DRIVING IN RUNS	From 1B	From 2B	From 3B	Scoring Position
Totals	2/127	13/80	20/42	33/122
Percentage	2%	16%	48%	27%
Driving In Runners from 3B with Less than Two Out:			13/20	65%

Loves to face: Ed Lynch (.550, 11-for-20, 2 HR)
Hates to face: Larry Andersen (0-for 7, 7 ground outs)

Toughest batter to strike out in majors last year, averaging one strikeout every 22.7 plate appearances.... Hitless in 28 consecutive at bats vs. right-handed pitchers, July 24 to Sept. 8, longest streak by N.L. nonpitcher last season. (Rick Sutcliffe was hitless in 37 at bats vs. RHP).... One of three left-handed N.L. batters to hit for a higher average against southpaws than he did against right-handers last season (minimum: 50 at bats each way; others: Will Clark, Ken Oberkfell).... Has hit for higher average on grass fields than on artificial turf in each of eight seasons in majors; similarly, batting average in Late-Inning Pressure Situations has been lower than his overall average every year.

John Shelby

Los Angeles Dodgers — Bats Left and Right

	AB	H	2B	3B	HR	RRF	BB	SO	BA	SA	OBA
Season	476	132	26	0	21	70	31	97	.277	.464	.317
vs. Left-Handers	158	53	11	0	10	30	10	30	.335	.595	.366
vs. Right-Handers	318	79	15	0	11	40	21	67	.248	.399	.293
Home	239	58	8	0	8	34	15	48	.243	.377	.284
Road	237	74	18	0	13	36	16	49	.312	.553	.352
Grass	349	94	16	0	16	57	25	73	.269	.453	.314
Artificial Turf	127	38	10	0	5	13	6	24	.299	.496	.326
April	0	0	0	0	0	0	0	0	—	—	—
May	36	9	1	0	2	4	3	7	.250	.444	.308
June	114	27	8	0	6	18	7	20	.237	.465	.276
July	104	26	5	0	3	13	7	24	.250	.385	.292
August	113	37	5	0	7	16	6	23	.327	.558	.355
Sept./Oct.	109	33	7	0	3	19	8	23	.303	.450	.347
Leading Off Inn.	90	24	6	0	3	3	5	12	.267	.433	.313
Runners On	209	58	12	0	8	57	11	52	.278	.450	.301
Runners/Scor. Pos.	116	30	8	0	2	44	9	37	.259	.379	.291
Runners On/2 Out	95	26	6	0	5	32	4	21	.274	.495	.303
Scor. Pos./2 Out	61	17	5	0	1	23	3	14	.279	.410	.313
Late Inning Pressure	71	12	1	0	1	7	6	20	.169	.268	.234
Leading Off	15	2	0	0	1	1	2	4	.133	.333	.235
Runners On	27	3	1	0	0	5	4	9	.111	.148	.226
Runners/Scor. Pos.	20	3	1	0	0	5	3	7	.150	.200	.261

DRIVING IN RUNS	From 1B	From 2B	From 3B	Scoring Position
Totals	9/144	16/88	24/59	40/147
Percentage	6%	18%	41%	27%
Driving In Runners from 3B with Less than Two Out:			12/25	48%

Loves to face: Bob Knepper (.571, 4-for-7, 1 HR)
Hates to face: Tim Conroy (0-for-8, 5 SO)

Figures *above* are for N.L. only.... Home run total has increased in each season in majors: 0, 1, 5, 6, 7, 11, 22. If he hits 23 or more homers in 1988 he will become the first player in major league history to increase his home run output in seven consecutive seasons (others with six-year streaks: Cy Williams, Eddie Robinson, Tim McCarver, and Jimmy Piersall).... L.A.'s brunch crowd may have missed it, but he hit .367 on Sundays after joining Dodgers, 3rd-highest in N.L.... Batted cleanup for first time in career in 1987, but Dodgers spoiled his fun by going 4–14 in those games.... Played center field in every inning of every Dodgers game from his May 22 arrival until July 24. Stop snickering, Cal Jr!

Ted Simmons

Atlanta Braves   Bats Left and Right

	AB	H	2B	3B	HR	RRF	BB	SO	BA	SA	OBA
Season	177	49	8	0	4	32	21	23	.277	.390	.350
vs. Left-Handers	91	24	7	0	3	22	6	16	.264	.440	.306
vs. Right-Handers	86	25	1	0	1	10	15	7	.291	.337	.392
Home	79	22	4	0	1	20	8	7	.278	.367	.337
Road	98	27	4	0	3	12	13	16	.276	.408	.360
Grass	120	31	6	0	1	21	16	11	.258	.333	.341
Artificial Turf	57	18	2	0	3	11	5	12	.316	.509	.371
April	24	4	2	0	0	0	1	7	.167	.250	.200
May	37	12	1	0	2	11	6	4	.324	.514	.419
June	31	8	3	0	1	7	3	4	.258	.452	.314
July	30	7	0	0	0	3	3	2	.233	.233	.294
August	28	8	1	0	0	5	2	4	.286	.321	.333
Sept./Oct.	27	10	1	0	1	6	6	2	.370	.519	.485
Leading Off Inn.	30	3	0	0	0	0	2	3	.100	.100	.156
Runners On	94	34	7	0	3	31	13	14	.362	.532	.431
Runners/Scor. Pos.	52	22	6	0	2	27	10	7	.423	.654	.500
Runners On/2 Out	45	15	2	0	1	13	7	9	.333	.444	.423
Scor. Pos./2 Out	29	13	1	0	1	12	5	6	.448	.586	.529
Late Inning Pressure	42	13	0	0	1	7	5	5	.310	.381	.383
Leading Off	8	1	0	0	0	0	1	1	.125	.125	.222
Runners On	24	10	0	0	1	7	2	3	.417	.542	.462
Runners/Scor. Pos.	15	8	0	0	1	6	1	2	.533	.733	.563

DRIVING IN RUNS	From 1B	From 2B	From 3B	Scoring Position
Totals	6/77	13/44	9/24	22/68
Percentage	8%	30%	38%	32%
Driving In Runners from 3B with Less than Two Out:	5/10		50%	

Loves to face: Bob Ojeda (.417, 10-for-24)
Hates to face: Ed Whitson (.111, 3-for-27, 1 HR)
Last of a dying breed: One of two nonpitchers active in 1987 who played in N.L. prior to division play. (The other, Hal McRae, didn't make it through 1987.). ... Batted .423 with runners in scoring position to rank second in N.L.; Al Pedrique was number one. Repeat: Al Pedrique was number one. ... Nine hits in 29 pinch-hit AB, but was hitless in last 12. ... Career comparison with Hall-of-Famer Yogi Berra: Batting average: Ted .286, Yogi .285; Home Runs: Yogi, 358 to 246 (but Ted played almost all of his career in poor home-run parks); RBI: Yogi 1,430; Ted 1,378. If Ted doesn't make Hall, blame bias against Midwest teams and limited post-season exposure (.183 in 17 games, including mini-playoffs).

Ozzie Smith

St. Louis Cardinals   Bats Left and Right

	AB	H	2B	3B	HR	RRF	BB	SO	BA	SA	OBA
Season	600	182	40	4	0	79	89	36	.303	.383	.392
vs. Left-Handers	220	55	15	0	0	33	33	12	.250	.318	.346
vs. Right-Handers	380	127	25	4	0	46	56	24	.334	.421	.419
Home	286	82	20	2	0	38	41	16	.287	.371	.375
Road	314	100	20	2	0	41	48	20	.318	.395	.408
Grass	164	52	12	1	0	25	23	11	.317	.402	.399
Artificial Turf	436	130	28	3	0	54	66	25	.298	.376	.389
April	65	12	2	0	0	6	12	5	.185	.215	.308
May	99	34	9	0	0	19	19	5	.343	.434	.445
June	107	33	7	1	0	20	13	4	.308	.393	.380
July	102	30	6	1	0	14	15	7	.294	.373	.390
August	114	36	8	1	0	13	16	5	.316	.404	.397
Sept./Oct.	113	37	8	1	0	7	14	10	.327	.416	.402
Leading Off Inn.	120	43	9	0	0	0	25	4	.358	.433	.469
Runners On	260	80	16	4	0	79	34	16	.308	.400	.385
Runners/Scor. Pos.	174	52	10	2	0	71	26	12	.299	.379	.382
Runners On/2 Out	94	26	5	0	0	29	16	6	.277	.330	.382
Scor. Pos./2 Out	73	19	3	0	0	26	15	6	.260	.301	.386
Late Inning Pressure	91	27	4	0	0	15	15	2	.297	.341	.396
Leading Off	17	7	1	0	0	0	4	1	.412	.471	.524
Runners On	53	14	2	0	0	15	7	1	.264	.302	.350
Runners/Scor. Pos.	37	10	1	0	0	15	6	1	.270	.297	.372

DRIVING IN RUNS	From 1B	From 2B	From 3B	Scoring Position
Totals	11/149	31/134	37/72	68/206
Percentage	7%	23%	51%	33%
Driving In Runners from 3B with Less than Two Out:	25/38		66%	

Loves to face: Andy McGaffigan (.450, 9-for-20)
Hates to face: David Palmer (.107, 3-for-28)
Career batting breakdown: .231 from 1978 to 1981; .249 from 1982 to 1984; .287 since 1985. Batting average has increased in each of last four seasons. ... Led majors in 1987 with .469 on-base average when leading off innings; that on the heels of .440 mark in 1986. ... Shares with Willie Wilson the longest current streak of 20-steal seasons (10); Lou Brock had 15 straight, 1963–77. ... Has 12 hits in 23 at bats with bases loaded over last two seasons. ... *He* would be Mr. October if month were only two weeks long: has career batting average of .351 in League Championship Series, but .173 in World Series. ... The best get better: Ozzie's 1987 fielding average (.987) was the best of his career.

Chris Speier

San Francisco Giants   Bats Right

	AB	H	2B	3B	HR	RRF	BB	SO	BA	SA	OBA
Season	317	79	13	0	11	43	42	51	.249	.394	.342
vs. Left-Handers	92	25	2	0	4	13	9	15	.272	.424	.337
vs. Right-Handers	225	54	11	0	7	30	33	36	.240	.382	.344
Home	159	36	4	0	6	18	24	23	.226	.365	.332
Road	158	43	9	0	5	25	18	28	.272	.424	.352
Grass	211	46	7	0	6	27	35	32	.218	.336	.331
Artificial Turf	106	33	6	0	5	16	7	19	.311	.509	.365
April	37	14	2	0	2	5	9	4	.378	.595	.500
May	54	11	1	0	2	11	7	4	.204	.333	.302
June	85	21	5	0	3	10	6	15	.247	.412	.304
July	39	8	2	0	1	6	4	6	.205	.333	.279
August	59	14	1	0	2	6	9	11	.237	.356	.348
Sept./Oct.	43	11	2	0	1	5	7	11	.256	.372	.360
Leading Off Inn.	78	22	2	0	2	2	7	10	.282	.385	.341
Runners On	127	31	7	0	3	35	17	19	.244	.370	.331
Runners/Scor. Pos.	75	18	5	0	3	34	13	15	.240	.427	.348
Runners On/2 Out	51	11	4	0	2	17	10	9	.216	.412	.344
Scor. Pos./2 Out	34	8	3	0	2	16	8	7	.235	.500	.381
Late Inning Pressure	79	18	3	0	2	12	5	13	.228	.342	.274
Leading Off	16	4	1	0	0	0	2	3	.250	.313	.333
Runners On	42	8	0	0	0	10	1	6	.190	.214	.209
Runners/Scor. Pos.	25	5	1	0	0	10	1	3	.200	.240	.231

DRIVING IN RUNS	From 1B	From 2B	From 3B	Scoring Position
Totals	4/80	15/64	13/29	28/93
Percentage	5%	23%	45%	30%
Driving In Runners from 3B with Less than Two Out:	9/13		69%	

Loves to face: Dwight Gooden (.438, 7-for-16)
Hates to face: Kent Tekulve (.083, 3-for-36)
Grand slam on May 5 was second of career; first was off Tommy John on Sept. 23, 1972. 15-year gap between slams is 2d-longest in major-league history, behind Max Carey's 15+ years (June 25, 1912 to Sept. 14, 1927). Others who have gone more than 10 years between slams: Alan Ashby, Kurt Bevacqua, Bob Boone, Thomas Corcoran, Eddie Joost, Al Kaline, Deacon McGuire, and Cy Williams. ... Decided not to wait *another* 15 years; hit another on May 9. ... Has played 1,004 games for the Giants by the Bay. If he plays in 111 more (his total in 1987) he will trail only McCovey (2,256), Mays (2,095), and Davenport (1,501). ... Pinch-hit batting averages in each of last three years: .417, .412, .357.

Kurt Stillwell

Cincinnati Reds   Bats Left and Right

	AB	H	2B	3B	HR	RRF	BB	SO	BA	SA	OBA
Season	395	102	20	7	4	38	32	50	.258	.375	.316
vs. Left-Handers	97	22	2	2	0	10	6	16	.227	.289	.286
vs. Right-Handers	298	80	18	5	4	28	26	34	.268	.403	.325
Home	150	39	9	4	3	14	14	22	.260	.433	.323
Road	245	63	11	3	1	24	18	28	.257	.339	.311
Grass	129	29	7	1	1	13	11	16	.225	.318	.294
Artificial Turf	266	73	13	6	3	25	21	34	.274	.402	.326
April	70	22	4	1	2	13	6	8	.314	.486	.377
May	66	19	2	0	0	4	7	7	.288	.318	.360
June	76	16	3	1	1	9	3	11	.211	.316	.238
July	60	15	3	2	0	3	2	7	.250	.367	.274
August	89	20	5	2	1	7	11	12	.225	.360	.310
Sept./Oct.	34	10	3	1	0	2	3	5	.294	.441	.351
Leading Off Inn.	80	20	4	0	1	1	10	6	.250	.338	.333
Runners On	157	47	12	2	3	37	13	25	.299	.459	.353
Runners/Scor. Pos.	85	23	5	0	1	28	8	17	.271	.365	.333
Runners On/2 Out	55	16	4	1	1	15	7	13	.291	.455	.371
Scor. Pos./2 Out	35	11	3	0	0	12	5	9	.314	.400	.400
Late Inning Pressure	62	15	2	0	0	7	5	9	.242	.274	.290
Leading Off	9	4	1	0	0	0	3	1	.444	.556	.583
Runners On	29	8	1	0	0	7	0	5	.276	.310	.258
Runners/Scor. Pos.	16	3	0	0	0	6	0	5	.188	.188	.167

DRIVING IN RUNS	From 1B	From 2B	From 3B	Scoring Position
Totals	8/100	13/73	13/31	26/104
Percentage	8%	18%	42%	25%
Driving In Runners from 3B with Less than Two Out:	8/15		53%	

Loves to face: Rick Honeycutt (.333, 3-for-9)
Hates to face: Lee Smith (0-for-4, 2 SO)
.914 fielding average was lowest among 35 shortstops who played 50+ games there; it was .929 in 18 games on the Cincinnati rug, .920 in 20 games on grass fields, and .882 on carpets other than the one at Riverfront. Not the best of signs for someone who'll be playing on the K.C. carpet in '88. Kurt: check with Frank White about the official scorer there. ... Youngest nonpitcher on an N.L. opening day roster in 1987. ... Led visiting N.L. players with 13 hits at Astrodome last season. ... Only four career homers, but one was a grand slam, tying him with Bob Horner in that category. ... Started 26 games in 8th spot in lineup, where he hit .306; hit .242 when batting elsewhere in lineup.

Darryl Strawberry

New York Mets — Bats Left

	AB	H	2B	3B	HR	RRF	BB	SO	BA	SA	OBA
Season	532	151	32	5	39	108	97	122	.284	.583	.398
vs. Left-Handers	230	57	10	2	16	51	25	58	.248	.517	.330
vs. Right-Handers	302	94	22	3	23	57	72	64	.311	.632	.446
Home	264	85	17	2	20	56	40	57	.322	.629	.418
Road	268	66	15	3	19	52	57	65	.246	.537	.380
Grass	375	112	20	4	28	71	66	80	.299	.597	.408
Artificial Turf	157	39	12	1	11	37	31	42	.248	.548	.375
April	75	23	7	1	5	16	8	14	.307	.627	.369
May	85	22	2	0	10	17	24	24	.259	.635	.422
June	79	19	6	1	5	16	13	18	.241	.532	.358
July	89	26	4	2	3	12	21	21	.292	.483	.432
August	98	27	3	1	8	19	15	25	.276	.571	.379
Sept./Oct.	106	34	10	0	8	28	16	20	.321	.642	.416
Leading Off Inn.	160	39	9	1	10	10	17	39	.244	.500	.328
Runners On	236	74	17	2	23	92	58	51	.314	.695	.447
Runners/Scor. Pos.	135	36	8	1	13	68	40	30	.267	.630	.428
Runners On/2 Out	112	33	6	2	11	41	26	20	.295	.679	.432
Scor. Pos./2 Out	67	17	3	1	6	29	19	11	.254	.597	.425
Late Inning Pressure	75	16	1	1	2	3	14	19	.213	.333	.344
Leading Off	25	4	1	0	1	1	2	5	.160	.320	.250
Runners On	30	8	0	0	1	2	9	8	.267	.367	.436
Runners/Scor. Pos.	14	2	0	0	0	0	6	4	.143	.143	.400

DRIVING IN RUNS	From 1B	From 2B	From 3B	Scoring Position
Totals	23/182	30/114	16/42	46/156
Percentage	13%	26%	38%	29%
Driving In Runners from 3B with Less than Two Out:			10/18	56%

Loves to face: Bob Forsch (.450, 9-for-20, 5 HR)
Hates to face: Zane Smith (.059, 1-for-17, 7 SO)
Only player to average 25+ homers and 25+ steals over last five years.... Has hit 51 points higher with runners on base than with bases empty over past five years; among those with 1,000 at bats in each situation, only Dave Parker (60 points) is ahead of him.... Grounded into only four double plays in 127 DP situations, 4th-lowest rate in N.L. (minimum: 40 opportunities).... Led majors with 12 first-inning homers.... Career slugging average vs. right-handers (.575) is best in majors over last 13 years (minimum: 300 TB); home run rate vs. righties (one every 14.3 at bats) is second to Ken Phelps in same span (minimum: 40 HR vs. RHP). Career: .283 vs. right-handers; .234, one HR every 20 AB, vs. lefties.

Franklin Stubbs

Los Angeles Dodgers — Bats Left

	AB	H	2B	3B	HR	RRF	BB	SO	BA	SA	OBA
Season	386	90	16	3	16	53	31	85	.233	.415	.290
vs. Left-Handers	86	16	0	0	0	5	1	22	.186	.186	.205
vs. Right-Handers	300	74	16	3	16	48	30	63	.247	.480	.313
Home	209	35	7	0	6	22	14	49	.167	.287	.221
Road	177	55	9	3	10	31	17	36	.311	.565	.371
Grass	297	61	11	1	13	40	25	69	.205	.380	.268
Artificial Turf	89	29	5	2	3	13	6	16	.326	.528	.368
April	83	25	4	0	7	17	6	24	.301	.602	.348
May	83	23	4	0	1	6	6	18	.277	.361	.326
June	74	15	4	0	3	13	7	15	.203	.378	.268
July	77	17	2	2	4	9	7	10	.221	.455	.294
August	29	1	1	0	0	1	2	8	.034	.069	.094
Sept./Oct.	40	9	1	1	1	7	3	10	.225	.375	.279
Leading Off Inn.	84	16	3	1	3	3	7	18	.190	.357	.261
Runners On	159	46	8	1	8	45	16	30	.289	.503	.350
Runners/Scor. Pos.	94	26	5	1	5	38	11	23	.277	.511	.346
Runners On/2 Out	73	21	3	0	4	22	8	13	.288	.493	.358
Scor. Pos./2 Out	48	13	2	0	3	19	7	11	.271	.500	.364
Late Inning Pressure	59	10	2	0	3	7	9	17	.169	.356	.279
Leading Off	17	3	0	0	2	2	3	3	.176	.529	.263
Runners On	20	5	2	0	1	5	5	7	.250	.500	.400
Runners/Scor. Pos.	12	2	1	0	0	3	4	6	.167	.250	.375

DRIVING IN RUNS	From 1B	From 2B	From 3B	Scoring Position
Totals	8/113	16/73	13/38	29/111
Percentage	7%	22%	34%	26%
Driving In Runners from 3B with Less than Two Out:			7/18	39%

Loves to face: Bryn Smith (.500, 8-for-16, 4 HR)
Hates to face: Ron Darling (.083, 2-for-24, 1 HR, 14 SO)
Had highest fielding average (.994) among N.L. first basemen last season, even though Gold Glove went to Hernandez.... Had no extra-base hits vs. left-handed pitchers last year; has hit 42 of 47 career home runs off right-handers.... Batted 120 points higher on artificial turf than on grass fields, 2d-largest such difference in N.L. last season (minimum: 50 at bats each way).... Career average of .254 before the All-Star Break, .174 after the break.... Fly-ball hitter: averaged only 0.58 ground outs-per-fly out, third-lowest rate in majors (minimum: 200 plate appearances).... If the dog days hit in August, then Stubbs wins the 1987 Spuds MacKenzie Award: he hit .034 that month, lowest in majors (minimum: 25 AB).

Garry Templeton

San Diego Padres — Bats Left and Right

	AB	H	2B	3B	HR	RRF	BB	SO	BA	SA	OBA
Season	510	113	13	5	5	51	42	92	.222	.296	.281
vs. Left-Handers	189	44	6	1	2	23	14	33	.233	.307	.284
vs. Right-Handers	321	69	7	4	3	28	28	59	.215	.290	.278
Home	250	51	7	4	2	23	21	52	.204	.288	.267
Road	260	62	6	1	3	28	21	40	.238	.304	.293
Grass	371	78	8	5	3	35	32	72	.210	.283	.274
Artificial Turf	139	35	5	0	2	16	10	20	.252	.331	.298
April	73	18	3	0	0	3	8	11	.247	.288	.321
May	87	16	3	1	0	7	5	13	.184	.241	.234
June	72	13	1	1	1	8	9	22	.181	.264	.268
July	85	26	2	3	1	5	4	15	.306	.435	.337
August	87	17	2	0	0	9	9	14	.195	.218	.268
Sept./Oct.	106	23	2	0	3	19	7	17	.217	.321	.265
Leading Off Inn.	131	36	6	0	1	1	8	17	.275	.344	.317
Runners On	222	46	6	3	3	49	21	42	.207	.302	.275
Runners/Scor. Pos.	134	25	3	1	2	44	20	25	.187	.269	.291
Runners On/2 Out	103	19	1	2	2	22	15	24	.184	.291	.294
Scor. Pos./2 Out	71	12	0	1	1	18	15	17	.169	.239	.322
Late Inning Pressure	92	20	1	1	3	7	10	19	.217	.348	.294
Leading Off	30	8	1	0	1	1	3	6	.267	.400	.333
Runners On	34	5	0	1	1	5	4	9	.147	.294	.237
Runners/Scor. Pos.	19	1	0	0	0	2	4	6	.053	.053	.217

DRIVING IN RUNS	From 1B	From 2B	From 3B	Scoring Position
Totals	5/162	16/109	25/53	41/162
Percentage	9%	15%	47%	25%
Driving In Runners from 3B with Less than Two Out:			17/26	65%

Loves to face: Dickie Noles (.429, 12-for-28)
Hates to face: Don Carman (0-for-12)
Erred for the cycle last season: Only player in majors to commit at least one error vs. every opposing club in his league last season: On the plus side, he finished season with only one error in his last 32 games.... Has hit for a higher average in road games than at home in each of last six seasons, longest streak of any active player. These happen to be his six years at San Diego Jack Murphy Stadium, a park that's good for HR but bad for batting average, and the stadium where Tempy has his lowest career average (.239).... Career average of .301 with runners on base, .265 with the bases empty.... The perks of batting eighth: Templeton has been intentionally walked 79 times, most in majors, over past four years.

Tim Teufel

New York Mets — Bats Right

	AB	H	2B	3B	HR	RRF	BB	SO	BA	SA	OBA
Season	299	92	29	0	14	64	44	53	.308	.545	.398
vs. Left-Handers	190	61	22	0	8	36	30	27	.321	.563	.412
vs. Right-Handers	109	31	7	0	6	28	14	26	.284	.514	.373
Home	132	43	16	0	4	21	22	18	.326	.538	.419
Road	167	49	13	0	10	43	22	35	.293	.551	.380
Grass	200	57	17	0	8	35	27	34	.285	.490	.367
Artificial Turf	99	35	12	0	6	29	17	19	.354	.657	.458
April	31	12	3	0	0	5	5	8	.387	.484	.472
May	38	12	5	0	1	8	9	7	.316	.526	.438
June	37	10	3	0	3	11	3	10	.270	.595	.341
July	54	20	7	0	4	13	7	8	.370	.722	.444
August	46	16	6	0	2	10	9	6	.348	.609	.455
Sept./Oct.	93	22	5	0	4	17	11	14	.237	.419	.317
Leading Off Inn.	51	19	5	0	3	3	4	6	.373	.647	.429
Runners On	142	41	15	0	8	58	22	26	.289	.563	.380
Runners/Scor. Pos.	95	35	13	0	7	54	18	21	.368	.726	.461
Runners On/2 Out	54	14	4	0	2	20	9	9	.259	.444	.365
Scor. Pos./2 Out	40	13	4	0	2	20	6	6	.325	.575	.413
Late Inning Pressure	41	14	4	0	2	12	9	5	.341	.561	.460
Leading Off	8	3	1	0	0	0	1	0	.375	.500	.444
Runners On	22	7	2	0	1	11	5	3	.318	.545	.444
Runners/Scor. Pos.	14	6	2	0	1	11	5	3	.429	.786	.579

DRIVING IN RUNS	From 1B	From 2B	From 3B	Scoring Position
Totals	7/81	25/76	18/39	43/115
Percentage	9%	33%	46%	37%
Driving In Runners from 3B with Less than Two Out:			10/17	59%

Loves to face: Tom Browning (.563, 9-for-16, 3 HR)
Hates to face: Jamie Moyer (.071, 1-for-14)
Collected 30 extra-base hits vs. left-handed pitchers. Believe it or not, he and Jose Canseco shared the major-league lead in that category.... Hit four home runs at Chicago, tying teammate Howard Johnson for most among visitors there last season.... Started 52 of 60 games in which Mets faced lefty starters, 19 of 102 games vs. right-handers. Hits both types of pitching. Career batting average of .272 (.424 slugging average) vs. left-handers, .268 (.429) vs. righties.... Eight hits in 20 at bats against Reds were all for extra bases (five doubles, three homers).... Drove in 10 of 17 runners from scoring position in Late-Inning Pressure Situations; that rate of 58.8 percent tied Marvell Wynne for N.L. lead.

Andres Thomas
Atlanta Braves — Bats Right

	AB	H	2B	3B	HR	RRF	BB	SO	BA	SA	OBA
Season	324	75	11	0	5	42	14	50	.231	.312	.268
vs. Left-Handers	96	22	4	0	1	9	3	8	.229	.302	.260
vs. Right-Handers	228	53	7	0	4	33	11	42	.232	.316	.271
Home	174	45	4	0	4	24	5	29	.259	.351	.283
Road	150	30	7	0	1	18	9	21	.200	.267	.250
Grass	246	61	10	0	5	35	9	38	.248	.350	.280
Artificial Turf	78	14	1	0	0	7	5	12	.179	.192	.229
April	41	10	4	0	1	6	3	6	.244	.415	.311
May	70	14	3	0	0	6	3	13	.200	.243	.233
June	77	21	0	0	3	11	7	10	.273	.390	.341
July	107	23	4	0	0	13	1	17	.215	.252	.222
August	29	7	0	0	1	6	0	4	.241	.345	.241
Sept./Oct.	0	0	0	0	0	0	0	0	—	—	—
Leading Off Inn.	59	14	1	0	0	0	3	12	.237	.254	.274
Runners On	157	40	6	0	3	40	6	20	.255	.350	.287
Runners/Scor. Pos.	93	24	4	0	1	36	5	10	.258	.333	.303
Runners On/2 Out	71	21	3	0	1	23	1	9	.296	.380	.315
Scor. Pos./2 Out	48	15	2	0	0	21	1	7	.313	.354	.340
Late Inning Pressure	45	6	0	0	0	1	4	8	.133	.133	.204
Leading Off	7	0	0	0	0	0	1	1	.000	.000	.125
Runners On	20	3	0	0	0	1	1	5	.150	.150	.190
Runners/Scor. Pos.	7	1	0	0	0	1	1	2	.143	.143	.250

DRIVING IN RUNS	From 1B	From 2B	From 3B	Scoring Position
Totals	4/115	15/71	18/45	33/116
Percentage	3%	21%	40%	28%
Driving In Runners from 3B with Less than Two Out:		8/18		44%

Loves to face: Eric Show (.571, 4-for-7, 1 HR)
Hates to face: Bill Dawley (0-for-6)

Led N.L. shortstops (minimum: 500 innings) with average of 3.53 assists per nine innings. Could be tough to repeat in '88: major-league leader Argenis Salazar (3.60 with K.C. last year) is now with Reds. ... Thomas is bustin' out all over: he has career average of one home run every 22.2 at bats during June, one homer every 112.4 at bats in other months. ... His season ended on August 9 when he suffered ligament damage in his knee while breaking up a double play in Los Angeles. ... Hit five of six homers on the road in 1986, four of five homers in Atlanta last season. ... Has walked 22 times in 199 major-league games, or three more walks than Jack Clark had in 12 regular-season games vs. Giants last season.

Milt Thompson
Philadelphia Phillies — Bats Left

	AB	H	2B	3B	HR	RRF	BB	SO	BA	SA	OBA
Season	527	159	26	9	7	44	42	87	.302	.425	.351
vs. Left-Handers	84	18	3	0	0	3	8	14	.214	.250	.283
vs. Right-Handers	443	141	23	9	7	41	34	73	.318	.458	.365
Home	270	89	16	7	3	25	24	48	.330	.474	.382
Road	257	70	10	2	4	19	18	39	.272	.374	.319
Grass	131	33	6	0	2	6	8	19	.252	.344	.295
Artificial Turf	396	126	20	9	5	38	34	68	.318	.452	.370
April	70	22	3	1	0	3	4	10	.314	.386	.351
May	105	22	3	3	1	6	13	14	.210	.324	.297
June	79	21	5	1	1	4	4	18	.266	.392	.301
July	76	31	6	3	3	10	7	10	.408	.684	.452
August	108	45	6	1	2	17	3	15	.417	.546	.425
Sept./Oct.	89	18	3	0	0	4	11	20	.202	.236	.290
Leading Off Inn.	154	47	6	0	3	3	9	23	.305	.403	.344
Runners On	176	55	7	5	2	39	18	29	.313	.443	.371
Runners/Scor. Pos.	100	27	5	3	0	33	12	17	.270	.380	.339
Runners On/2 Out	68	18	3	1	1	15	11	14	.265	.382	.367
Scor. Pos./2 Out	52	12	3	1	0	13	9	10	.231	.327	.344
Late Inning Pressure	74	22	0	1	2	5	3	20	.297	.405	.325
Leading Off	18	10	0	0	2	2	1	2	.556	.889	.579
Runners On	27	7	0	0	0	3	2	5	.259	.259	.310
Runners/Scor. Pos.	12	4	0	0	0	3	1	2	.333	.333	.385

DRIVING IN RUNS	From 1B	From 2B	From 3B	Scoring Position
Totals	8/119	9/79	20/38	29/117
Percentage	7%	11%	53%	25%
Driving In Runners from 3B with Less than Two Out:		12/16		75%

Loves to face: Ed Lynch (.600, 6-for-10, 1 HR)
Hates to face: Charlie Kerfeld (0-for-8)

Has highest career rate of ground outs-to-air outs among major leaguers with 1,000 plate appearances since 1975 (2.69); his 1987 rate of 2.60 was third in majors behind Wally Backman and Julio Franco. (The guy he replaced in Phils' outfield, Gary Redus, is among 10 players with the *lowest* ratios). ... Averaged 2.86 putouts per nine innings last season, 2d-highest among N.L. center fielders (minimum: 500 innings). ... Batted 105 points higher against right-handers than vs. lefties, 3d-largest such difference in N.L. (minimum: 50 at bats each way). ... July batting average (.408) was 2d-highest in majors; came back to hit .417 in August to lead majors. ... Career: .247 before All-Star Break, .320 after break.

Rob Thompson
San Francisco Giants — Bats Right

	AB	H	2B	3B	HR	RRF	BB	SO	BA	SA	OBA
Season	420	110	26	5	10	46	40	91	.262	.419	.338
vs. Left-Handers	129	40	7	2	3	16	10	18	.310	.465	.382
vs. Right-Handers	291	70	19	3	7	30	30	73	.241	.399	.318
Home	205	54	11	3	7	23	20	40	.263	.449	.346
Road	215	56	15	2	3	23	20	51	.260	.391	.329
Grass	316	84	18	3	9	38	31	64	.266	.427	.343
Artificial Turf	104	26	8	2	1	8	9	27	.250	.394	.322
April	53	11	2	0	2	8	7	14	.208	.358	.311
May	45	17	4	0	2	8	2	11	.378	.600	.417
June	85	19	5	0	3	6	7	20	.224	.388	.290
July	78	17	2	2	1	10	5	15	.218	.333	.265
August	99	30	10	1	0	7	9	20	.303	.424	.367
Sept./Oct.	60	16	3	2	2	7	10	11	.267	.483	.405
Leading Off Inn.	148	34	13	3	2	2	14	29	.230	.399	.305
Runners On	136	39	5	1	4	40	12	24	.287	.426	.366
Runners/Scor. Pos.	84	28	3	0	3	36	9	14	.333	.476	.423
Runners On/2 Out	57	22	2	0	3	26	4	9	.386	.579	.453
Scor. Pos./2 Out	42	19	1	0	3	25	3	6	.452	.690	.511
Late Inning Pressure	61	14	5	0	1	10	8	15	.230	.361	.329
Leading Off	23	2	0	0	0	0	2	6	.087	.087	.160
Runners On	17	6	1	0	1	10	4	3	.353	.588	.476
Runners/Scor. Pos.	12	5	1	0	1	10	3	2	.417	.750	.533

DRIVING IN RUNS	From 1B	From 2B	From 3B	Scoring Position
Totals	6/90	15/63	15/36	30/99
Percentage	7%	24%	42%	30%
Driving In Runners from 3B with Less than Two Out:		6/18		33%

Loves to face: Jim Acker (.571, 4-for-7, 2 HR)
Hates to face: David Palmer (0-for-11)

Batted .320 in day games, .222 at night last season; career averages: .300 in day games, .243 at night. ... Led N.L. with .415 average (17-for-41) in 11 games vs. Mets; owns .429 career batting average (18-for-42) at Shea Stadium. ... Has only three hits in 15 career at bats with the bases loaded, but all three of them have gone for extra bases (one double, two grand-slam home runs). ... Giants' starting leadoff hitter in 35 games: team was 24–11 (.686) in those games, 66–61 (.520) with other leadoff hitters. Thompson batted .361 in 20 games batting leadoff after August 1; Giants' record in those games: 17–3. ... Committed four errors during final week of season to match his 1986 total of 17.

Manny Trillo
Chicago Cubs — Bats Right

	AB	H	2B	3B	HR	RRF	BB	SO	BA	SA	OBA
Season	214	63	8	0	8	27	25	37	.294	.444	.367
vs. Left-Handers	94	28	2	0	4	11	10	18	.298	.447	.362
vs. Right-Handers	120	35	6	0	4	16	15	19	.292	.442	.370
Home	112	39	5	0	6	14	13	16	.348	.554	.416
Road	102	24	3	0	2	13	12	21	.235	.324	.313
Grass	153	52	7	0	7	22	17	23	.340	.523	.404
Artificial Turf	61	11	1	0	1	5	8	14	.180	.246	.275
April	16	2	0	0	0	0	2	2	.125	.125	.222
May	36	8	1	0	3	8	3	5	.222	.500	.282
June	44	15	3	0	1	6	6	6	.341	.477	.420
July	37	15	2	0	3	7	9	9	.405	.703	.522
August	45	14	2	0	1	5	5	9	.311	.422	.373
Sept./Oct.	36	9	0	0	0	1	0	6	.250	.250	.250
Leading Off Inn.	59	20	7	0	2	2	5	6	.339	.559	.391
Runners On	84	26	0	0	4	23	14	12	.310	.452	.404
Runners/Scor. Pos.	48	14	0	0	0	15	10	4	.292	.292	.407
Runners On/2 Out	28	6	0	0	2	8	4	4	.214	.429	.313
Scor. Pos./2 Out	18	3	0	0	0	4	4	1	.167	.167	.318
Late Inning Pressure	52	11	1	0	3	9	10	8	.212	.404	.333
Leading Off	16	2	0	0	0	0	1	1	.125	.125	.176
Runners On	18	3	0	0	1	7	8	3	.167	.333	.407
Runners/Scor. Pos.	9	2	0	0	0	5	7	0	.222	.222	.529

DRIVING IN RUNS	From 1B	From 2B	From 3B	Scoring Position
Totals	4/62	6/40	9/21	15/61
Percentage	6%	15%	43%	25%
Driving In Runners from 3B with Less than Two Out:		7/13		54%

Loves to face: Mike Krukow (.458, 11-for-24, 1 HR)
Hates to face: Mike Scott (.045, 1-for-22)

One of four players in majors to start at least one game at every infield position last season. ... Batted 157 points higher on grass fields than on carpets, largest such difference in N.L. last season (minimum: 50 at bats each way). ... Batting average in Late-Inning Pressure Situations has been lower than his overall average in each of last five seasons. ... Batted .318 (7-for-22) as a pinch hitter last season, after bringing .172 career pinch-hit average into year. ... Hit career-high eight home runs in only 214 at bats last year, but opposing pitchers and managers still haven't given him an intentional walk since 1983. Only two players have more plate appearances over that span without an IBB: Lonnie Smith and Wayne Tolleson.

Jose Uribe

San Francisco Giants — Bats Left and Right

	AB	H	2B	3B	HR	RRF	BB	SO	BA	SA	OBA
Season	309	90	16	5	5	31	24	35	.291	.424	.343
vs. Left-Handers	96	25	5	0	3	13	6	10	.260	.406	.311
vs. Right-Handers	213	65	11	5	2	18	18	25	.305	.432	.358
Home	155	49	11	3	4	19	7	16	.316	.503	.346
Road	154	41	5	2	1	12	17	19	.266	.344	.341
Grass	204	66	14	5	4	24	11	21	.324	.500	.361
Artificial Turf	105	24	2	0	1	7	13	14	.229	.276	.311
April	18	6	2	0	0	1	1	4	.333	.444	.368
May	29	9	0	0	1	3	2	2	.310	.414	.355
June	0	0	0	0	0	0	0	0	—	—	—
July	81	21	5	0	1	5	8	12	.259	.358	.326
August	87	23	6	2	0	10	8	10	.264	.379	.323
Sept./Oct.	94	31	3	3	3	12	5	7	.330	.521	.370
Leading Off Inn.	77	25	6	2	1	1	4	8	.325	.494	.358
Runners On	124	38	8	2	3	28	15	12	.306	.476	.383
Runners/Scor. Pos.	71	17	4	0	0	19	13	7	.239	.296	.353
Runners On/2 Out	54	12	2	0	1	8	12	5	.222	.315	.364
Scor. Pos./2 Out	34	5	1	0	0	6	12	4	.147	.176	.370
Late Inning Pressure	42	14	1	0	1	3	6	4	.333	.429	.417
Leading Off	8	5	1	0	0	0	2	0	.625	.750	.700
Runners On	14	4	0	0	0	2	1	2	.286	.286	.333
Runners/Scor. Pos.	11	4	0	0	0	2	0	1	.364	.364	.364

DRIVING IN RUNS	From 1B	From 2B	From 3B	Scoring Position
Totals	6/91	9/57	10/28	19/85
Percentage	7%	16%	36%	22%
Driving In Runners from 3B with Less than Two Out:		7/14	50%	

Loves to face: Rick Mahler (.556, 10-for-18)
Hates to face: Zane Smith (.063, 1-for-16)
Grounded into only one double play in 57 DP situations, lowest rate in N.L. (minimum: 40 opportunities). . . . Yearly batting averages since 1984: .211, .237, .223, .291. . . . Overlooked cog in Giants' lineup was injured for most of first half of season; Giants were 56–34 (.622) with Uribe starting at shortstop, only 34–38 (.472) with others filling in. . . . Has been up 55 times (excluding walks, hit by pitch) with a runner on third and less than two out, but has only one sacrifice fly to his name(s). Until he got that one, last August 1, he had been the leader among players active in 1987 in career plate appearances without a sac fly, but the king is dead, long live the new king: Buddy Biancalana, 607 plate appearances.

Andy Van Slyke

Pittsburgh Pirates — Bats Left

	AB	H	2B	3B	HR	RRF	BB	SO	BA	SA	OBA
Season	564	165	36	11	21	84	56	122	.293	.507	.359
vs. Left-Handers	229	53	10	5	3	26	18	56	.231	.358	.292
vs. Right-Handers	335	112	26	6	18	58	38	66	.334	.609	.403
Home	278	76	15	4	11	48	35	56	.273	.475	.353
Road	286	89	21	7	10	36	21	66	.311	.538	.365
Grass	149	43	8	5	7	21	13	32	.289	.550	.346
Artificial Turf	415	122	28	6	14	63	43	90	.294	.492	.363
April	52	14	3	2	0	8	8	11	.269	.404	.371
May	82	20	3	0	4	13	5	22	.244	.427	.284
June	100	33	7	2	7	20	11	21	.330	.650	.402
July	104	28	8	2	3	12	12	24	.269	.471	.345
August	117	38	9	1	5	19	9	21	.325	.547	.373
Sept./Oct.	109	32	6	4	2	12	11	23	.294	.477	.366
Leading Off Inn.	104	36	10	3	4	4	5	19	.346	.615	.376
Runners On	233	67	13	3	10	73	26	50	.288	.489	.360
Runners/Scor. Pos.	157	48	8	3	7	66	18	35	.306	.529	.374
Runners On/2 Out	96	29	5	2	5	35	6	20	.302	.552	.350
Scor. Pos./2 Out	75	22	4	2	3	31	3	16	.293	.520	.329
Late Inning Pressure	75	20	5	0	5	16	2	21	.267	.533	.278
Leading Off	18	6	2	0	1	1	1	3	.333	.611	.368
Runners On	35	8	2	0	3	14	1	13	.229	.543	.237
Runners/Scor. Pos.	25	7	2	0	2	12	1	9	.280	.600	.286

DRIVING IN RUNS	From 1B	From 2B	From 3B	Scoring Position
Totals	7/134	32/120	24/71	56/191
Percentage	5%	27%	34%	29%
Driving In Runners from 3B with Less than Two Out:		13/34	38%	

Loves to face: Roger McDowell (.467, 7-for-15, 2 HR)
Hates to face: Mike Scott (.045, 1-for-22)
Saw everyday duty vs. left-handers for first time in his career; Leyland kept him in even through 29 consecutive hitless at bats vs. lefties from July 11 to July 31, longest such streak in N.L. last season. . . . Career batting average of .284 vs. right-handers, .215 vs. lefties; that 69-point difference is 6th-largest over last 10 seasons (minimum: 200 at bats each way). He has hit 56 of 62 home runs off right-handers. . . . Led N.L. with .769 slugging average vs. Cubs in '87; related fact: batted .343 in day games, .276 at night. . . . Yearly batting averages since 1984: .244, .259, .270, .293; he's one of only three players whose average has increased by 10+ points in each of those years (minimum: 100 at bats each year).

Ozzie Virgil

Atlanta Braves — Bats Right

	AB	H	2B	3B	HR	RRF	BB	SO	BA	SA	OBA
Season	429	106	13	1	27	74	47	81	.247	.471	.331
vs. Left-Handers	110	24	2	0	7	18	16	20	.218	.427	.328
vs. Right-Handers	319	82	11	1	20	56	31	61	.257	.486	.331
Home	213	55	8	1	15	45	29	38	.258	.516	.354
Road	216	51	5	0	12	29	18	43	.236	.426	.307
Grass	310	78	10	1	17	57	37	54	.252	.455	.340
Artificial Turf	119	28	3	0	10	17	10	27	.235	.513	.305
April	52	12	2	0	3	6	4	14	.231	.442	.333
May	84	21	1	0	13	19	14	21	.250	.726	.364
June	81	20	3	0	4	16	4	12	.247	.432	.291
July	60	10	3	0	1	3	8	8	.167	.267	.275
August	76	24	4	1	3	17	5	13	.316	.513	.358
Sept./Oct.	76	19	0	0	3	13	12	13	.250	.368	.348
Leading Off Inn.	89	17	3	0	5	15	5	17	.191	.393	.321
Runners On	194	48	6	1	7	54	19	30	.247	.397	.326
Runners/Scor. Pos.	121	32	2	1	3	45	12	21	.264	.372	.343
Runners On/2 Out	81	16	3	0	3	18	12	12	.198	.346	.316
Scor. Pos./2 Out	57	11	2	0	1	14	6	8	.193	.281	.292
Late Inning Pressure	68	16	0	0	5	15	7	13	.235	.456	.307
Leading Off	14	2	0	0	1	1	1	4	.143	.357	.200
Runners On	35	9	0	0	0	10	4	4	.257	.257	.333
Runners/Scor. Pos.	21	8	0	0	0	10	4	4	.381	.381	.480

DRIVING IN RUNS	From 1B	From 2B	From 3B	Scoring Position
Totals	8/136	18/86	21/57	39/143
Percentage	6%	21%	37%	27%
Driving In Runners from 3B with Less than Two Out:		15/33	45%	

Loves to face: Kelly Downs (.400, 4-for-10, 3 HR)
Hates to face: Sid Fernandez (0-for-21)
Hit 13 HR in a 61–at bat span from April 27 to May 20; had 14 other homers in 368 other at bats last year. Led N.L. in May (13). . . . Career rate of one homer every 17.5 AB before All-Star break, one every 31.2 AB after break. . . . Grounded into 18 double plays in 87 DP situations, 3d-highest rate in N.L. (minimum: 40 opportunities). . . . Career rate of runners driven in from scoring position is 37.3 in Late-Inning Pressure Situations, 23.8 at other times. . . . Made key tag at plate, despite a high knee from Winfield, in memorable collision in 1987 All-Star Game. . . . Has sub-.200 career batting average at four different parks across the U.S. and Canada: Olympic (.196), Wrigley (.189), Shea (.181), Candlestick (.177).

Tim Wallach

Montreal Expos — Bats Right

	AB	H	2B	3B	HR	RRF	BB	SO	BA	SA	OBA
Season	593	177	42	4	26	131	37	98	.298	.514	.343
vs. Left-Handers	160	49	17	1	1	28	11	28	.306	.444	.353
vs. Right-Handers	433	128	25	3	25	103	26	70	.296	.540	.340
Home	290	87	26	4	13	68	19	45	.300	.552	.349
Road	303	90	16	0	13	63	18	53	.297	.479	.337
Grass	154	47	5	0	8	33	8	29	.305	.494	.343
Artificial Turf	439	130	37	4	18	98	29	69	.296	.522	.343
April	59	16	4	0	1	11	3	9	.271	.390	.302
May	117	36	8	0	5	33	5	19	.308	.504	.346
June	103	31	13	0	5	26	11	13	.301	.573	.368
July	96	32	7	2	5	21	5	15	.333	.604	.373
August	100	32	5	1	6	23	7	15	.320	.570	.364
Sept./Oct.	118	30	5	1	4	17	6	27	.254	.415	.296
Leading Off Inn.	143	49	8	2	7	7	2	30	.343	.573	.361
Runners On	299	86	25	2	10	115	28	44	.288	.485	.351
Runners/Scor. Pos.	211	59	18	0	7	102	20	31	.280	.464	.343
Runners On/2 Out	161	49	12	2	7	56	12	21	.304	.534	.360
Scor. Pos./2 Out	111	31	8	0	4	45	8	15	.279	.459	.339
Late Inning Pressure	73	22	3	0	6	17	2	18	.301	.589	.320
Leading Off	20	6	0	0	2	2	0	5	.300	.600	.300
Runners On	34	13	2	0	2	13	2	6	.382	.618	.417
Runners/Scor. Pos.	22	8	2	0	1	11	1	4	.364	.591	.391

DRIVING IN RUNS	From 1B	From 2B	From 3B	Scoring Position
Totals	18/178	43/153	44/95	87/248
Percentage	10%	28%	46%	35%
Driving In Runners from 3B with Less than Two Out:		30/50	60%	

Loves to face: Shane Rawley (.404, 19-for-47)
Hates to face: Alejandro Pena (.050, 1-for-20)
Did club-record 123 RBI derive from increased opportunities or improved execution? It's baseball version of social sciences' heredity-vs.-environment debate. Answer: You're both right. He batted with 247 runners in scoring position, and he drove in 35.2 percent of them. (His average over five previous seasons: 176 and 27.3). . . . Led majors with 41 "go-aheads" in 1987; what are they? See Cubs essay on page 118. . . . Had averaged 13.2 road homers, 1982 to 1986, but only once had he reached double figures at the Big O in its pre-dome days. . . . One of last year's surprises: of 26 home runs, Wallach hit only one, in 160 at bats no less, against left-handers. Did lift his batting average vs. LHP from .215 in 1986 to .306 in 1987.

Denny Walling

Bats Left

Houston Astros	AB	H	2B	3B	HR	RRF	BB	SO	BA	SA	OBA
Season	325	92	21	4	5	33	39	37	.283	.418	.356
vs. Left-Handers	35	7	1	0	1	3	1	10	.200	.314	.222
vs. Right-Handers	290	85	20	4	4	30	38	27	.293	.431	.370
Home	156	45	7	0	2	19	19	18	.288	.372	.364
Road	169	47	14	4	3	14	20	19	.278	.462	.349
Grass	98	25	7	2	2	7	17	10	.255	.429	.365
Artificial Turf	227	67	14	2	3	26	22	27	.295	.414	.352
April	33	9	1	0	1	2	1	2	.273	.394	.294
May	56	19	6	0	0	4	4	11	.339	.446	.371
June	65	16	2	1	2	8	10	6	.246	.400	.347
July	74	23	7	3	0	7	10	7	.311	.486	.388
August	44	11	3	0	0	4	4	5	.250	.318	.306
Sept./Oct.	53	14	2	0	2	8	10	6	.264	.415	.381
Leading Off Inn.	59	20	6	0	0	0	4	8	.339	.441	.381
Runners On	151	35	7	1	4	32	18	18	.232	.371	.306
Runners/Scor. Pos.	96	21	2	1	2	26	11	13	.219	.323	.288
Runners On/2 Out	50	10	3	1	0	12	12	5	.200	.300	.355
Scor. Pos./2 Out	39	8	1	1	0	10	6	4	.205	.282	.311
Late Inning Pressure	39	11	2	0	0	3	7	6	.282	.333	.391
Leading Off	13	4	0	0	0	0	1	2	.308	.308	.357
Runners On	16	6	2	0	0	3	5	2	.375	.500	.524
Runners/Scor. Pos.	7	3	1	0	0	3	4	1	.429	.571	.636

DRIVING IN RUNS	From 1B	From 2B	From 3B	Scoring Position
Totals	5/93	11/72	12/41	23/113
Percentage	5%	15%	29%	20%
Driving In Runners from 3B with Less than Two Out:		8/19		42%

Loves to face: Jeff D. Robinson (.667, 6-for-12, 1 HR)
Hates to face: Floyd Youmans (.056, 1-for-18)
N.L.'s answer to Pat Tabler: owns a career batting average of .396 with bases loaded, tops among active N.L. players (minimum: 15 BL hits); but he has never hit a grand-slam home run. ... Hit 96 points lower with runners on base than with bases empty, 3d-largest such difference in N.L. last season (minimum: 75 at bats each way). ... Made only one start against a left-hander; HR off Ray Hayward was his first off a lefty since 1983. ... Averaged only 1.68 assists per nine innings last season, lowest in majors among third basemen (minimum: 500 innings). ... Pinch-hitting: .533 (8-for-15) in 1987, .387 (12-for-31) in 1986. ... Broke into majors with Oakland in 1975, as pinch-hitter for Gaylen (ZaSu) Pitts.

Mitch Webster

Bats Left and Right

Montreal Expos	AB	H	2B	3B	HR	RRF	BB	SO	BA	SA	OBA
Season	588	165	30	8	15	68	70	95	.281	.435	.361
vs. Left-Handers	200	57	11	1	7	26	17	29	.285	.455	.344
vs. Right-Handers	388	108	19	7	8	42	53	66	.278	.425	.369
Home	285	76	14	4	9	36	36	43	.267	.439	.353
Road	303	89	16	4	6	32	34	52	.294	.432	.368
Grass	158	47	10	2	2	19	21	25	.297	.424	.379
Artificial Turf	430	118	20	6	13	49	49	70	.274	.440	.354
April	77	22	4	1	1	8	8	11	.286	.403	.368
May	106	32	9	0	1	13	11	14	.302	.415	.368
June	98	29	5	2	2	10	13	12	.296	.449	.378
July	91	26	4	2	3	11	3	11	.286	.473	.320
August	101	26	3	1	4	10	24	21	.257	.426	.394
Sept./Oct.	115	30	5	2	4	16	11	26	.261	.443	.333
Leading Off Inn.	90	24	5	2	2	2	8	11	.267	.433	.340
Runners On	249	71	16	2	6	59	36	38	.285	.438	.372
Runners/Scor. Pos.	129	37	7	2	4	49	22	21	.287	.465	.385
Runners On/2 Out	88	18	1	1	4	25	16	15	.205	.375	.333
Scor. Pos./2 Out	53	14	1	1	3	23	11	8	.264	.491	.400
Late Inning Pressure	71	20	2	0	2	8	7	15	.282	.394	.341
Leading Off	14	3	0	0	0	1	1	2	.214	.214	.313
Runners On	33	12	2	0	0	6	4	9	.364	.424	.400
Runners/Scor. Pos.	23	9	0	0	0	6	4	6	.391	.391	.433

DRIVING IN RUNS	From 1B	From 2B	From 3B	Scoring Position
Totals	13/176	22/108	18/43	40/151
Percentage	7%	20%	42%	26%
Driving In Runners from 3B with Less than Two Out:		12/26		46%

Loves to face: Mike Dunne (.444, 8-for-18, 3 HR)
Hates to face: Terry Leach (.071, 1-for-14)
One of two players in majors to hit for cycle with the bases loaded last season; the other: teammate Hubie Brooks. Career average with the bases loaded: .458 (11-for-24). ... Grounded into only six double plays in 133 DP situations, 6th-lowest rate in N.L. (minimum: 40 opportunities). ... Led N.L. with 23 hits vs. Phillies; scored 11 runs in nine games at the Vet, most among visiting players, including one on a steal of home. ... Played exclusively in right field last season, after having started 114 games in center field in 1986. ... Career batting average of .322 on grass fields, .267 on artificial surfaces. ... Has homered at every N.L. ballpark except Dodger Stadium, where he has hit .340 in 47 career at bats.

Matt Williams

Bats Right

San Francisco Giants	AB	H	2B	3B	HR	RRF	BB	SO	BA	SA	OBA
Season	245	46	9	2	8	23	16	68	.188	.339	.240
vs. Left-Handers	78	15	1	1	4	7	5	19	.192	.385	.241
vs. Right-Handers	167	31	8	1	4	16	11	49	.186	.317	.239
Home	112	20	5	0	5	11	7	31	.179	.357	.227
Road	133	26	4	2	3	12	9	37	.195	.323	.250
Grass	192	38	6	1	7	18	11	55	.198	.349	.240
Artificial Turf	53	8	3	1	1	5	5	13	.151	.302	.237
April	58	9	0	1	2	5	5	28	.155	.293	.219
May	87	20	5	1	1	10	5	15	.230	.345	.272
June	74	14	3	0	5	7	5	19	.189	.432	.241
July	5	0	0	0	0	0	0	2	.000	.000	.000
August	0	0	0	0	0	0	0	0	—	—	—
Sept./Oct.	21	3	1	0	0	1	1	4	.143	.190	.217
Leading Off Inn.	52	12	1	1	1	1	3	12	.231	.346	.273
Runners On	101	16	4	0	2	17	9	27	.158	.257	.225
Runners/Scor. Pos.	69	11	3	0	1	15	8	21	.159	.246	.244
Runners On/2 Out	49	6	1	0	2	9	6	16	.122	.265	.218
Scor. Pos./2 Out	35	4	1	0	1	7	6	12	.114	.229	.244
Late Inning Pressure	22	3	0	1	1	4	2	8	.136	.364	.200
Leading Off	4	1	0	1	0	0	0	1	.250	.750	.250
Runners On	10	0	0	0	0	3	1	3	.000	.000	.083
Runners/Scor. Pos.	7	0	0	0	0	3	1	2	.000	.000	.111

DRIVING IN RUNS	From 1B	From 2B	From 3B	Scoring Position
Totals	1/69	6/58	8/27	14/85
Percentage	1%	10%	30%	16%
Driving In Runners from 3B with Less than Two Out:		5/16		31%

Loves to face: Jim Deshaies (.400, 2-for-5, 2 HR)
Hates to face: Fernando Valenzuela (0-for-6, 5 SO)
Those two home runs off Deshaies were his only hits in 15 at bats (including 10 strikeouts) vs. Astros last season. ... Filled in at shortstop for injured Uribe before All-Star break; averaged 3.51 assists per nine innings last season, 2d-highest rate among N.L. shortstops. And no, Ozzie does not rank number one, he's third, behind Williams and Andres Thomas. ... Giants won only 35 of the 73 games that he started. ... Recalled from minors in September, but started only once before division title was clinched. ... Struck out 14 times in his first 23 at bats. ... Had highest rate of strikeouts in N.L. last season, one every 3.9 plate appearances; no fewer than 11 A.L. players had worse rates than N.L. leader.

Glenn Wilson

Bats Right

Philadelphia Phillies	AB	H	2B	3B	HR	RRF	BB	SO	BA	SA	OBA
Season	569	150	21	2	14	58	38	82	.264	.381	.308
vs. Left-Handers	155	42	7	0	2	14	9	15	.271	.355	.307
vs. Right-Handers	414	108	14	2	12	44	29	67	.261	.391	.308
Home	278	70	8	1	5	28	28	37	.252	.342	.315
Road	291	80	13	1	9	30	10	45	.275	.419	.300
Grass	158	46	9	0	5	15	6	26	.291	.443	.319
Artificial Turf	411	104	12	2	9	43	32	56	.253	.358	.304
April	65	16	0	1	3	5	4	9	.246	.415	.290
May	95	25	5	1	4	13	5	15	.263	.463	.297
June	106	36	5	0	3	12	6	15	.340	.472	.372
July	103	24	3	0	2	10	9	13	.233	.320	.292
August	111	25	4	0	0	13	9	15	.225	.261	.282
Sept./Oct.	89	24	4	0	2	5	5	15	.270	.382	.309
Leading Off Inn.	136	43	6	1	3	3	7	19	.316	.441	.350
Runners On	266	65	10	0	3	47	17	39	.244	.316	.284
Runners/Scor. Pos.	145	35	5	0	0	39	8	24	.241	.276	.270
Runners On/2 Out	120	28	5	0	1	17	8	18	.233	.300	.281
Scor. Pos./2 Out	77	16	4	0	0	15	4	11	.208	.260	.247
Late Inning Pressure	95	22	1	0	1	7	8	16	.232	.274	.291
Leading Off	24	7	0	0	0	0	3	3	.292	.292	.370
Runners On	47	11	1	0	0	6	4	7	.234	.255	.294
Runners/Scor. Pos.	26	9	1	0	0	6	3	4	.346	.385	.414

DRIVING IN RUNS	From 1B	From 2B	From 3B	Scoring Position
Totals	5/203	21/112	18/57	39/169
Percentage	2%	19%	32%	23%
Driving In Runners from 3B with Less than Two Out:		15/24		63%

Loves to face: John Candelaria (.500, 7-for-14, 2 HR)
Hates to face: Ted Power (.063, 1-for-16, 1 HR)
And good riddance to Dwight Gooden, who through 1987 had struck out Wilson 15 times, more than he got any other batter in N.L. ... Led major-league outfielders with 18 assists, and also had highest average of putouts per nine innings (2.15) among N.L. right fielders (minimum: 500 innings). With all those chances, should it be surprising that he also led N.L. outfielders with 11 errors? ... Has 57 outfield assists over last three years, second in majors to Jesse Barfield's 59; no other player has more than 46 over that span. ... Hit 12 homers in his first 294 at bats last season, but only two homers in 275 at bats thereafter. ... Has grounded into 57 DP in last three years; N.L. leader during that time: Tony Pena, 59.

Mookie Wilson

New York Mets — Bats Left and Right

	AB	H	2B	3B	HR	RRF	BB	SO	BA	SA	OBA
Season	385	115	19	7	9	37	35	85	.299	.455	.359
vs. Left-Handers	225	61	13	4	3	15	19	46	.271	.404	.329
vs. Right-Handers	160	54	6	3	6	22	16	39	.338	.525	.401
Home	176	47	7	2	5	18	18	42	.267	.415	.337
Road	209	68	12	5	4	19	17	43	.325	.488	.379
Grass	253	77	12	6	6	28	26	58	.304	.470	.370
Artificial Turf	132	38	7	1	3	9	9	27	.288	.424	.338
April	48	18	3	2	2	5	3	12	.375	.646	.412
May	65	21	5	2	2	8	7	12	.323	.554	.397
June	74	20	3	2	2	9	5	16	.270	.446	.325
July	67	14	2	0	0	3	7	15	.209	.239	.284
August	59	20	4	1	1	8	4	12	.339	.492	.375
Sept./Oct.	72	22	2	0	2	4	9	18	.306	.417	.383
Leading Off Inn.	142	48	10	3	3	3	9	33	.338	.514	.386
Runners On	136	36	6	3	2	30	18	29	.265	.397	.348
Runners/Scor. Pos.	87	21	2	3	2	27	15	18	.241	.402	.350
Runners On/2 Out	55	11	2	1	1	11	12	13	.200	.327	.343
Scor. Pos./2 Out	40	8	1	1	1	11	12	8	.200	.350	.385
Late Inning Pressure	61	17	2	1	1	8	4	17	.279	.393	.333
Leading Off	21	7	2	0	0	0	0	7	.333	.429	.364
Runners On	26	8	0	1	0	7	2	6	.308	.385	.357
Runners/Scor. Pos.	15	6	0	1	0	6	2	3	.400	.533	.471

DRIVING IN RUNS	From 1B	From 2B	From 3B	Scoring Position
Totals	4/81	12/74	12/31	24/105
Percentage	5%	16%	39%	23%
Driving In Runners from 3B with Less than Two Out:		8/14		57%

Loves to face: Greg Mathews (.636, 14-for-22)
Hates to face: Ricky Horton (.042, 1-for-24)
One of those hits off Mathews came leading off last game of '87 season, lifting average to .301. But after Mathews left game, Mook went 0-for-3, and average fell to .299, his 6th straight year hitting at least .275 but never .300, longest such streak in majors. . . . Grounded into only two double plays in 55 DP situations, 5th-lowest rate in N.L. (minimum: 40 opportunities). Mets had three of N.L.'s top five in that category (Strawberry, Dykstra, Wilson). . . . Led Mets in starts vs. left-handers (59 of 60 games); started only 17 of 102 against right-handers despite hitting .338 (5th in N.L.) against them. . . . One of five players with 20+ SB in each of last five seasons; others: Henderson, Raines, W. Wilson, and Ozzie.

Herm Winningham

Montreal Expos — Bats Left

	AB	H	2B	3B	HR	RRF	BB	SO	BA	SA	OBA
Season	347	83	20	3	4	43	34	68	.239	.349	.304
vs. Left-Handers	29	10	3	0	0	4	3	9	.345	.448	.394
vs. Right-Handers	318	73	17	3	4	39	31	59	.230	.340	.295
Home	180	49	9	1	2	29	16	38	.272	.367	.332
Road	167	34	11	2	2	14	18	30	.204	.329	.275
Grass	88	22	8	2	2	8	11	16	.250	.455	.330
Artificial Turf	259	61	12	1	2	35	23	52	.236	.313	.295
April	25	3	1	0	0	0	2	5	.120	.160	.185
May	54	19	5	3	2	17	8	13	.352	.667	.429
June	65	21	3	0	1	8	8	12	.323	.415	.392
July	54	9	0	0	0	3	4	13	.167	.167	.224
August	73	12	5	0	0	5	4	11	.164	.233	.205
Sept./Oct.	76	19	6	0	1	10	8	14	.250	.368	.318
Leading Off Inn.	95	16	6	0	0	0	2	19	.168	.232	.186
Runners On	138	39	7	2	4	43	19	27	.283	.449	.360
Runners/Scor. Pos.	85	27	4	2	4	41	17	13	.318	.553	.415
Runners On/2 Out	51	16	1	0	3	18	7	13	.314	.510	.397
Scor. Pos./2 Out	35	12	1	0	3	18	7	7	.343	.629	.452
Late Inning Pressure	50	8	1	0	1	6	9	18	.160	.240	.288
Leading Off	13	1	0	0	0	0	0	3	.077	.077	.077
Runners On	17	5	0	0	1	6	6	6	.294	.471	.478
Runners/Scor. Pos.	13	5	0	0	1	6	5	4	.385	.615	.556

DRIVING IN RUNS	From 1B	From 2B	From 3B	Scoring Position
Totals	5/92	12/68	22/34	34/102
Percentage	5%	18%	65%	33%
Driving In Runners from 3B with Less than Two Out:		15/18		83%

Loves to face: Doug Drabek (.500, 5-for-10)
Hates to face: Andy Hawkins (.100, 2-for-20)
Drove in 15 of 18 runners from third base with less than two outs; that rate of 83.3 percent put him second in N.L., behind Lee Mazzilli (85.7 percent). . . . Started 82 games last season, all against right-handed pitchers. Perhaps Expos should reconsider his limited role vs. left-handers; career averages: .291 (30-for-103) vs. left-handers, .232 vs. right-handers. . . . Batting average after the All-Star break (.205) was 2d-lowest in N.L. (minimum: 150 plate appearances). . . . Career breakdown: .229 with bases empty, .254 with runners on base, .262 with runners in scoring position. . . . Struck out in six of his last eight at bats as a pinch-hitter. . . . Batted under .200 with runners in scoring position in both 1985 and 1986.

Marvell Wynne

San Diego Padres — Bats Left

	AB	H	2B	3B	HR	RRF	BB	SO	BA	SA	OBA
Season	188	47	8	2	2	25	20	37	.250	.346	.321
vs. Left-Handers	39	9	1	0	0	2	5	15	.231	.256	.318
vs. Right-Handers	149	38	7	2	2	23	15	22	.255	.369	.321
Home	80	13	1	2	2	13	7	17	.163	.300	.230
Road	108	34	7	0	0	12	13	20	.315	.380	.385
Grass	138	31	3	2	2	20	10	26	.225	.319	.277
Artificial Turf	50	16	5	0	0	5	10	11	.320	.420	.426
April	44	11	1	0	1	6	3	7	.250	.341	.298
May	44	11	3	0	0	6	7	11	.250	.318	.353
June	19	7	1	0	0	2	4	3	.368	.421	.458
July	23	9	2	1	0	5	1	3	.391	.565	.417
August	30	4	0	1	1	5	1	7	.133	.300	.161
Sept./Oct.	28	5	1	0	0	1	4	6	.179	.214	.281
Leading Off Inn.	47	9	0	1	1	1	5	13	.191	.298	.269
Runners On	81	23	5	1	1	24	10	13	.284	.407	.359
Runners/Scor. Pos.	43	15	3	1	0	22	9	10	.349	.465	.453
Runners On/2 Out	31	13	1	1	1	13	7	4	.419	.613	.526
Scor. Pos./2 Out	20	9	1	1	0	11	7	4	.450	.600	.593
Late Inning Pressure	48	14	3	0	0	10	5	9	.292	.354	.352
Leading Off	7	1	0	0	0	0	1	2	.143	.143	.250
Runners On	21	5	3	0	0	10	4	4	.238	.381	.346
Runners/Scor. Pos.	11	4	2	0	0	10	3	3	.364	.545	.467

DRIVING IN RUNS	From 1B	From 2B	From 3B	Scoring Position
Totals	1/61	9/31	13/24	22/55
Percentage	2%	29%	54%	40%
Driving In Runners from 3B with Less than Two Out:		6/12		50%

Loves to face: Rick Sutcliffe (.409, 9-for-22)
Hates to face: Dwight Gooden (0-for-19)
Drove in 10 of 17 runners from scoring position in Late-Inning Pressure Situations; that rate of 58.8 percent tied Tim Teufel for N.L. lead. . . . Furthermore, he ranked second in N.L. in batting average with runners on base and two outs (.419), and ranked third in league in batting with runners in scoring position and two outs (.450). . . . Is this Marvell or the Toy Cannon? . . . Batted 152 points higher in road games than at home, largest such difference in majors last season (minimum: 50 at bats each way). . . . Career batting average of .309 during June, .235 in all other months combined. . . . Batting average in Late-Inning Pressure Situations has been higher than his overall average in each of the last four seasons.

Gerald Young

Houston Astros — Bats Left and Right

	AB	H	2B	3B	HR	RRF	BB	SO	BA	SA	OBA
Season	274	88	9	2	1	16	26	27	.321	.380	.380
vs. Left-Handers	105	41	5	0	1	7	6	12	.390	.467	.425
vs. Right-Handers	169	47	4	2	0	9	20	15	.278	.325	.353
Home	145	52	8	2	0	9	16	14	.359	.441	.423
Road	129	36	1	0	1	7	10	13	.279	.310	.329
Grass	91	28	0	0	1	3	7	9	.308	.341	.357
Artificial Turf	183	60	9	2	0	13	19	18	.328	.399	.390
April	0	0	0	0	0	0	0	0	—	—	—
May	0	0	0	0	0	0	0	0	—	—	—
June	0	0	0	0	0	0	0	0	—	—	—
July	65	17	3	0	0	6	5	6	.262	.308	.306
August	114	33	3	2	0	4	11	11	.289	.351	.357
Sept./Oct.	95	38	3	0	1	6	10	10	.400	.463	.457
Leading Off Inn.	116	37	3	1	0	0	11	13	.319	.362	.383
Runners On	78	27	2	1	0	14	10	9	.346	.397	.411
Runners/Scor. Pos.	43	14	1	0	0	13	8	3	.326	.349	.415
Runners On/2 Out	32	8	1	1	0	6	7	4	.250	.344	.385
Scor. Pos./2 Out	20	5	1	0	0	5	7	2	.250	.300	.444
Late Inning Pressure	49	15	3	0	0	4	5	5	.306	.367	.370
Leading Off	11	4	1	0	0	0	0	1	.364	.455	.364
Runners On	21	7	1	0	0	4	4	3	.333	.381	.440
Runners/Scor. Pos.	10	4	0	0	0	4	4	1	.400	.400	.571

DRIVING IN RUNS	From 1B	From 2B	From 3B	Scoring Position
Totals	1/60	4/38	9/17	13/55
Percentage	2%	11%	53%	24%
Driving In Runners from 3B with Less than Two Out:		8/12		67%

Loves to face: Eric Nolte (.571, 4-for-7)
Hates to face: Lance McCullers (0-for-6)
Had highest batting average (.321) among N.L. rookies with at least 200 plate appearances. . . . Stole 12 bases in 12 attempts on artificial turf, but only 14 of 23 on grass fields. . . . His .390 batting average vs. left-handers was 3rd-best in N.L. among players with 50+ plate appearances vs. lefties. . . . He also hit .373 in day games, but he's playing in the wrong place to take advantage of that. . . . Reached base safely in 37 of 38 games from August 9 to Sept. 20. . . . All four guys on this page are outfielders who grew up in Mets' organization. We're already studying this end-of-the-alphabet trend for next year's *Analyst*, but somewhere, there's a youngster named Zygmunt catching flies and practicing curtain calls.

Atlanta Braves

	AB	H	2B	3B	HR	RRF	BB	SO	BA	SA	OBA
Season	5428	1401	284	24	152	726	641	834	.258	.403	.339
vs. Left-Handers	1577	405	87	7	48	231	215	240	.257	.412	.347
vs. Right-Handers	3851	996	197	17	104	495	426	594	.259	.400	.335
Home	2668	739	143	17	82	408	371	373	.277	.436	.367
Road	2760	662	141	7	70	318	270	461	.240	.372	.310
Grass	3982	1042	194	21	115	557	507	600	.262	.408	.347
Artificial Turf	1446	359	90	3	37	169	134	234	.248	.391	.314
April	707	190	46	1	16	91	94	127	.269	.405	.361
May	1012	275	59	6	38	169	130	155	.272	.455	.354
June	898	226	40	4	30	120	119	131	.252	.405	.342
July	867	207	42	4	16	92	88	115	.239	.352	.310
August	920	247	45	4	29	127	91	136	.268	.421	.334
Sept./Oct.	1024	256	52	5	23	127	119	170	.250	.378	.333
Leading Off Inn.	1313	355	76	7	34	34	124	196	.270	.417	.336
Runners On	2365	602	123	7	60	634	333	376	.255	.389	.347
Runners/Scor. Pos.	1432	372	73	5	36	560	241	229	.260	.393	.365
Runners On/2 Out	1002	235	42	2	26	244	165	182	.235	.358	.345
Scor. Pos./2 Out	666	159	25	1	15	212	124	120	.239	.347	.361
Late Inning Pressure	851	204	37	2	16	90	96	146	.240	.344	.320
Leading Off	214	47	10	2	3	3	16	41	.220	.327	.274
Runners On	356	87	15	0	4	78	47	61	.244	.320	.337
Runners/Scor. Pos.	206	54	7	0	3	71	32	39	.262	.340	.366

DRIVING IN RUNS	From 1B	From 2B	From 3B	Scoring Position
Totals	83/1653	216/1124	274/620	490/1744
Percentage	5%	19%	44%	28%
Driving In Runners from 3B with Less than Two Out:		189/331		57%

Love to face: Mike Scott (10–3 against him)
Hate to face: Ron Darling (0–8 against him)
Ranked last in N.L. in strikeouts for second season in a row.... Ranked next-to-last in N.L. in stolen-base percentage (.665). Tanner's teams had ranked last in three of the four previous seasons.... First of Tanner's teams ever to lead a league in sac bunts (86).... Ranked 2d in N.L. in batting average at home, last on the road.... Have won 26 of their last 29 one-run home games, while posting a 7–29 record in one-run road games during that time.... Only team in majors to hit better vs. left-handers than right-handers in each of the past five seasons.... Used only 21 pinch runners, fewest in N.L.... Braves' leadoff hitters (first slot in batting order) outhit those of every other N.L. team (.307).

Chicago Cubs

	AB	H	2B	3B	HR	RRF	BB	SO	BA	SA	OBA
Season	5583	1475	244	33	209	708	504	1064	.264	.432	.326
vs. Left-Handers	1283	346	54	5	42	154	126	245	.270	.418	.335
vs. Right-Handers	4300	1129	190	28	167	554	378	819	.263	.436	.323
Home	2752	750	123	21	114	376	249	503	.273	.457	.333
Road	2831	725	121	12	95	332	255	561	.256	.408	.319
Grass	3899	1038	164	22	154	517	360	729	.266	.438	.329
Artificial Turf	1684	437	80	11	55	191	144	335	.260	.418	.319
April	684	175	31	3	24	88	67	107	.256	.415	.323
May	1006	262	42	4	41	128	91	179	.260	.432	.321
June	984	269	46	8	34	132	81	187	.273	.440	.330
July	858	240	31	4	37	116	76	179	.280	.455	.340
August	1011	278	46	5	47	133	96	189	.275	.470	.337
Sept./Oct.	1040	251	48	9	26	111	93	223	.241	.380	.307
Leading Off Inn.	1351	367	70	6	54	54	90	243	.272	.452	.319
Runners On	2367	603	96	10	75	574	248	430	.255	.399	.324
Runners/Scor. Pos.	1356	324	47	8	35	475	179	263	.239	.363	.324
Runners On/2 Out	1014	235	38	6	28	222	119	203	.232	.364	.314
Scor. Pos./2 Out	647	141	22	5	15	188	91	136	.218	.337	.316
Late Inning Pressure	773	218	23	4	27	97	73	158	.282	.427	.344
Leading Off	197	51	6	1	7	7	8	37	.259	.406	.291
Runners On	305	90	6	2	11	81	45	64	.295	.436	.384
Runners/Scor. Pos.	170	44	3	1	5	67	34	38	.259	.376	.379

DRIVING IN RUNS	From 1B	From 2B	From 3B	Scoring Position
Totals	85/1699	188/1044	225/579	413/1623
Percentage	5%	18%	39%	25%
Driving In Runners from 3B with Less than Two Out:		153/297		52%

Love to face: Mark Davis (8–1)
Hate to face: John Tudor (1–8)
Tied major-league record with their 42d consecutive season without winning a league title. St. Louis Browns also went 42 years without a pennant (1902 through 1943). Best move Cubs made may have been hiring Jim Frey instead of ex-Blackhawk Phil Esposito to lead them out of the wilderness.... Led N.L. in HR for third consecutive season. Hit HR in 14 consecutive games (Aug. 9 through Aug. 23), tying a team record set in 1961.... Batting average in Late-Inning Pressure Situations was highest in N.L. since 1982.... Faced fewer southpaw starters (38) than any other team in majors, despite nearly identical winning percentages when facing left-handed (17–21, .447) and right-handed (59–64, .480) starters.

Cincinnati Reds

	AB	H	2B	3B	HR	RRF	BB	SO	BA	SA	OBA
Season	5560	1478	262	29	192	767	514	928	.266	.427	.330
vs. Left-Handers	1629	438	79	6	55	225	166	293	.269	.426	.339
vs. Right-Handers	3931	1040	183	23	137	542	348	635	.265	.427	.326
Home	2728	732	135	13	94	388	267	409	.268	.431	.335
Road	2832	746	127	16	98	379	247	519	.263	.423	.324
Grass	1651	421	76	10	61	212	163	288	.255	.424	.323
Artificial Turf	3909	1057	186	19	131	555	351	640	.270	.428	.332
April	761	215	41	8	32	125	75	144	.283	.484	.348
May	923	239	39	2	35	130	79	155	.259	.419	.320
June	912	230	52	5	35	128	83	168	.252	.435	.316
July	951	265	40	6	29	140	70	140	.279	.425	.331
August	964	236	36	2	26	105	105	152	.245	.367	.320
Sept./Oct.	1049	293	54	6	35	139	102	169	.279	.442	.344
Leading Off Inn.	1338	364	56	5	51	51	112	216	.272	.436	.330
Runners On	2335	653	128	14	86	661	256	385	.280	.457	.350
Runners/Scor. Pos.	1345	373	80	7	47	558	194	257	.277	.452	.365
Runners On/2 Out	956	237	42	6	35	245	135	175	.248	.414	.345
Scor. Pos./2 Out	621	147	33	2	21	210	111	128	.237	.398	.357
Late Inning Pressure	764	193	31	1	19	105	74	151	.253	.370	.320
Leading Off	193	50	11	0	6	6	20	40	.259	.409	.332
Runners On	331	93	12	1	10	96	37	65	.281	.414	.352
Runners/Scor. Pos.	210	55	8	1	8	89	29	51	.262	.424	.347

DRIVING IN RUNS	From 1B	From 2B	From 3B	Scoring Position
Totals	111/1606	231/1082	231/561	462/1643
Percentage	7%	21%	41%	28%
Driving In Runners from 3B with Less than Two Out:		158/286		55%

Love to face: David Palmer (8–1)
Hate to face: Rick Mahler (2–11)
Batted .336 (37-for-110) with bases loaded last season, highest in majors.... Ninth-place hitters drove in nine more runs (57) than eighth-place hitters (48).... Outscored opponents by 31 runs despite 54-run deficit over first three innings.... First N.L. team in past six seasons with more multi run innings (206) than one-run innings (201).... Led N.L. in batting average in night games for second consecutive season, and have compiled the league's lowest day-game mark during that period (.248 by day, .266 by night since 1986).... Reds' hitters in the second slot in the batting order had a composite batting average of .248, lowest in the league. League average for number-two hitters was .283 last season.

Houston Astros

	AB	H	2B	3B	HR	RRF	BB	SO	BA	SA	OBA
Season	5485	1386	238	28	122	630	526	936	.253	.373	.318
vs. Left-Handers	1990	489	81	9	45	218	193	363	.246	.363	.314
vs. Right-Handers	3495	897	157	19	77	412	333	573	.257	.379	.321
Home	2717	714	114	11	51	321	281	479	.263	.369	.332
Road	2768	672	124	17	71	309	245	457	.243	.377	.305
Grass	1662	406	72	6	46	196	160	272	.244	.378	.312
Artificial Turf	3823	980	166	22	76	434	366	664	.256	.371	.321
April	721	187	34	1	20	84	53	122	.259	.393	.311
May	901	236	50	7	16	111	102	145	.262	.386	.336
June	912	224	35	4	26	111	94	185	.246	.378	.315
July	899	225	41	7	18	93	78	132	.250	.372	.310
August	1000	265	41	6	20	121	101	167	.265	.378	.333
Sept./Oct.	1052	249	37	3	22	110	98	185	.237	.340	.303
Leading Off Inn.	1340	359	58	6	35	35	104	210	.268	.399	.323
Runners On	2342	591	106	10	53	560	261	410	.252	.374	.323
Runners/Scor. Pos.	1370	338	63	7	30	487	193	255	.247	.369	.330
Runners On/2 Out	1030	237	45	7	16	223	144	195	.230	.334	.326
Scor. Pos./2 Out	674	154	28	6	10	198	114	131	.228	.332	.342
Late Inning Pressure	905	250	38	4	19	108	92	152	.276	.390	.343
Leading Off	228	65	7	1	9	9	14	39	.285	.443	.329
Runners On	399	103	16	2	3	92	51	71	.258	.331	.338
Runners/Scor. Pos.	224	62	11	2	2	88	40	43	.277	.371	.376

DRIVING IN RUNS	From 1B	From 2B	From 3B	Scoring Position
Totals	89/1638	193/1085	224/558	417/1643
Percentage	5%	18%	40%	25%
Driving In Runners from 3B with Less than Two Out:		155/273		57%

Love to face: Mike Krukow (6–13)
Hate to face: Dwight Gooden (1–9)
Made the fewest double plays in N.L. (113) for second consecutive season.... Starting center fielders outhit those of any other team in N.L. (.314).... Ninth-place hitters drove in 27 runs and eighth-place hitters 34, respectively the lowest and 3d-lowest totals of any batting-order positions in either league last season.... Only team in majors not to hit a pinch-hit HR last season. They hit seven in 1986.... Lowest winning percentage in majors on grass fields (17–31, .354).... Batted .308 in 18 games vs. the Braves, highest batting average by any club against any N.L. opponent last season.... Day-game batting average was lowest in the majors.... 28 triples tied club mark for fewest in a season, set by the 1968 edition.

Los Angeles Dodgers

	AB	H	2B	3B	HR	RRF	BB	SO	BA	SA	OBA
Season	5517	1389	236	23	125	624	445	923	.252	.371	.309
vs. Left-Handers	1807	479	92	9	38	206	146	277	.265	.389	.322
vs. Right-Handers	3710	910	144	14	87	418	299	646	.245	.362	.303
Home	2649	637	90	5	52	274	208	416	.240	.337	.297
Road	2868	752	146	18	73	350	237	507	.262	.402	.320
Grass	4021	1001	154	12	93	455	339	671	.249	.363	.309
Artificial Turf	1496	388	82	11	32	169	106	252	.259	.393	.308
April	803	200	36	5	20	96	69	172	.249	.381	.312
May	868	222	33	4	24	96	63	150	.256	.386	.307
June	893	220	42	4	19	95	73	140	.246	.366	.303
July	884	226	37	5	28	105	68	132	.256	.404	.309
August	996	247	44	2	15	100	70	151	.248	.341	.300
Sept./Oct.	1073	274	44	3	19	132	102	178	.255	.355	.322
Leading Off Inn.	1364	335	58	8	33	34	95	215	.246	.372	.298
Runners On	2288	600	97	11	50	548	208	396	.262	.380	.322
Runners/Scor. Pos.	1312	329	49	6	22	463	156	264	.251	.348	.325
Runners On/2 Out	990	238	35	3	22	221	103	175	.240	.348	.315
Scor. Pos./2 Out	622	145	19	2	10	184	89	126	.233	.318	.332
Late Inning Pressure	856	190	39	5	12	86	94	173	.222	.321	.300
Leading Off	213	45	7	2	5	5	24	40	.211	.333	.294
Runners On	364	77	20	3	4	78	49	79	.212	.316	.304
Runners/Scor. Pos.	207	45	9	2	3	70	42	55	.217	.324	.347

DRIVING IN RUNS	From 1B	From 2B	From 3B	Scoring Position
Totals	81/1585	186/997	229/578	415/1575
Percentage	5%	19%	40%	26%
Driving In Runners from 3B with Less than Two Out:		155/307		50%

Love to face: Bob Knepper (17–7)
Hate to face: Craig Lefferts (0–7)
No team in N.L. history has played a season without scoring five runs in an inning, but the Dodgers made it to August 2 without one. . . . Stopped one at bat short of the lowest batting average in N.L. in Late-Inning Pressure Situations since 1975; 1984 Reds retained the honor by .00008. . . . Ranked last in N.L. in batting, slugging, on-base average, and runs (635). . . . Pinch-hitters batted .166, lowest average in majors. . . . Ranked last in league in walks for second consecutive season. . . . First team to lead N.L. in errors for three seasons in a row since the Pirates of 1954–1957. Major-league record: 7, by Phillies (1930–1936). . . . Have batted .111 (12-for-108) with two outs and the bases loaded over the past two seasons.

Montreal Expos

	AB	H	2B	3B	HR	RRF	BB	SO	BA	SA	OBA
Season	5527	1467	310	39	120	725	501	918	.265	.401	.328
vs. Left-Handers	1622	463	110	10	35	227	150	263	.285	.430	.346
vs. Right-Handers	3905	1004	200	29	85	498	351	655	.257	.388	.321
Home	2723	742	163	23	62	393	266	430	.272	.418	.339
Road	2804	725	147	16	58	332	235	488	.259	.384	.317
Grass	1468	392	76	8	29	180	131	260	.267	.389	.328
Artificial Turf	4059	1075	234	31	91	545	370	658	.265	.405	.328
April	664	157	35	2	10	70	57	119	.236	.340	.302
May	982	285	64	6	21	149	97	169	.290	.432	.356
June	942	271	61	5	24	152	93	138	.288	.439	.351
July	875	239	57	8	21	102	64	137	.273	.429	.324
August	997	243	37	10	24	114	102	161	.244	.373	.314
Sept./Oct.	1067	272	56	8	20	138	88	194	.255	.379	.314
Leading Off Inn.	1362	363	67	12	31	31	78	213	.267	.402	.310
Runners On	2348	648	144	14	48	653	270	403	.276	.411	.350
Runners/Scor. Pos.	1440	399	81	10	31	582	204	259	.277	.412	.363
Runners On/2 Out	1009	265	50	8	28	282	131	190	.263	.411	.351
Scor. Pos./2 Out	681	182	32	5	18	245	105	127	.267	.408	.370
Late Inning Pressure	734	207	38	6	22	104	60	126	.282	.440	.335
Leading Off	190	56	8	3	5	5	7	24	.295	.447	.323
Runners On	294	91	16	1	8	90	35	56	.310	.452	.378
Runners/Scor. Pos.	179	60	10	0	6	83	27	37	.335	.492	.409

DRIVING IN RUNS	From 1B	From 2B	From 3B	Scoring Position
Totals	101/1566	250/1142	253/591	503/1733
Percentage	6%	22%	43%	29%
Driving In Runners from 3B with Less than Two Out:		177/317		56%

Love to face: Mario Soto (11–4)
Hate to face: Fernando Valenzuela (4–11)
Batting average with two outs and runners in scoring position was highest in N.L. since 1982. . . . Batting average vs. left-handed pitchers was league's highest since 1979. 'Spos have led N.L. in that category in three of last four seasons. . . . Only team in majors to hit better in Late-Inning Pressure Situations than overall in each of the past three seasons. . . . Shut out in both ends of a doubleheader at St. Louis on Sept. 29. That hadn't happened to them since June 21, 1974, when Giants shut Montreal down behind Jim Barr and John D'Acquisto at Candlestick. . . . Hit only seven first-inning homers, lowest total in the majors last season. . . . Hit fewer home runs against left-handers (35) than any team in the majors last season.

New York Mets

	AB	H	2B	3B	HR	RRF	BB	SO	BA	SA	OBA
Season	5601	1499	287	34	192	806	592	1012	.268	.434	.339
vs. Left-Handers	2102	554	105	12	76	313	218	367	.264	.433	.335
vs. Right-Handers	3499	945	182	22	116	493	374	645	.270	.434	.341
Home	2716	754	139	11	93	399	295	485	.278	.440	.350
Road	2885	745	148	23	99	407	297	527	.258	.428	.328
Grass	3910	1073	192	21	133	557	411	701	.274	.436	.344
Artificial Turf	1691	426	95	13	59	249	181	311	.252	.428	.326
April	674	179	32	5	28	96	74	127	.266	.453	.336
May	924	248	51	7	30	116	105	187	.268	.436	.345
June	974	262	47	7	36	140	85	175	.269	.443	.331
July	939	264	49	5	28	136	102	160	.281	.433	.351
August	976	256	49	7	35	155	114	184	.262	.434	.342
Sept./Oct.	1114	290	59	3	35	163	112	179	.260	.413	.329
Leading Off Inn.	1329	357	77	8	45	45	109	237	.269	.440	.328
Runners On	2456	663	129	17	85	699	317	441	.270	.440	.351
Runners/Scor. Pos.	1503	382	77	12	54	606	240	286	.254	.429	.352
Runners On/2 Out	1053	269	53	9	37	283	155	198	.255	.428	.354
Scor. Pos./2 Out	690	165	37	7	23	245	127	132	.239	.413	.361
Late Inning Pressure	755	197	28	4	22	100	90	144	.261	.396	.341
Leading Off	184	47	9	0	6	6	18	30	.255	.402	.328
Runners On	344	85	13	2	8	86	49	79	.247	.366	.338
Runners/Scor. Pos.	205	46	9	2	4	76	34	45	.224	.346	.331

DRIVING IN RUNS	From 1B	From 2B	From 3B	Scoring Position
Totals	117/1666	250/1204	246/593	496/1797
Percentage	7%	21%	41%	28%
Driving In Runners from 3B with Less than Two Out:		170/302		56%

Love to face: Rick Reuschel (23–10)
Hate to face: Don Sutton (11–18)
First team to lead the N.L. in slugging average in consecutive seasons since the Pirates of 1971 and 1972. Also led league in runs and batting average in each of last two seasons, after never having led in any of those three categories prior to 1986. . . . Also led N.L in extra-base hits last season for first time in team history, breaking Philadelphia's three-year hold on that title. . . . Batting average on grass surfaces was highest in N.L. since 1983. . . . Only team in majors whose eighth-place hitters didn't execute a sacrifice bunt last season. . . . First N.L. team in past six seasons to score three or more runs in an inning at least 100 times. . . . Ground outs-to-air outs ratio of 1.10 was lowest in N.L. since 1984.

Phila. Phillies

	AB	H	2B	3B	HR	RRF	BB	SO	BA	SA	OBA
Season	5475	1390	248	51	169	690	587	1109	.254	.410	.327
vs. Left-Handers	1501	375	72	13	51	186	174	290	.250	.417	.328
vs. Right-Handers	3974	1015	176	38	118	504	413	819	.255	.408	.326
Home	2707	711	136	32	80	381	331	537	.263	.425	.343
Road	2768	679	112	19	89	309	256	572	.245	.396	.311
Grass	1414	341	56	6	43	147	137	293	.241	.380	.312
Artificial Turf	4061	1049	192	45	126	543	450	816	.258	.421	.332
April	671	156	20	5	17	77	71	153	.232	.353	.305
May	856	204	29	8	36	116	96	178	.238	.417	.317
June	933	251	50	8	31	116	76	181	.269	.439	.326
July	917	254	51	13	33	139	114	179	.277	.469	.357
August	1070	298	58	11	27	135	129	187	.279	.429	.356
Sept./Oct.	1028	227	40	6	25	107	101	231	.221	.344	.291
Leading Off Inn.	1316	366	65	10	45	45	133	247	.278	.445	.347
Runners On	2377	600	113	26	66	587	268	481	.252	.405	.326
Runners/Scor. Pos.	1438	338	65	19	37	502	178	316	.235	.384	.314
Runners On/2 Out	985	233	46	8	28	232	136	228	.237	.385	.332
Scor. Pos./2 Out	673	148	35	7	14	195	97	157	.220	.355	.322
Late Inning Pressure	834	217	30	6	25	94	115	177	.260	.400	.351
Leading Off	204	61	10	0	9	9	27	30	.299	.480	.384
Runners On	376	93	14	3	5	74	62	83	.247	.340	.353
Runners/Scor. Pos.	216	55	9	1	5	72	44	57	.255	.375	.376

DRIVING IN RUNS	From 1B	From 2B	From 3B	Scoring Position
Totals	100/1641	208/1132	213/544	421/1676
Percentage	6%	18%	39%	25%
Driving In Runners from 3B with Less than Two Out:		150/265		57%

Love to face: Joe Hesketh (4–0)
Hate to face: Pasqual Perez (1–8)
Led the majors in strikeouts for fourth consecutive season. . . . Eighth-place hitters batted .208, lowest mark of any batting slot in N.L. with exception of ninth positions. In fact, Cardinals' number-nine hitters had a higher average (.210). . . . Batted .171 (14-for-82) with bases loaded last season, 3d-lowest in N.L. over past 13 seasons. . . . Compiled N.L.'s lowest batting averages during months of April, May, and September. . . . Batted .201 in 12 games vs. the Giants, lowest batting average by any club against any N.L. opponent last season. . . . No left-handed batter homered for the Phils from Aug. 14 to Sept. 14. . . . Batting average on grass fields was lowest in the majors last season.

Pittsburgh Pirates

	AB	H	2B	3B	HR	RBI	BB	SO	BA	SA	OBA
Season	5536	1464	282	45	131	710	535	914	.264	.403	.330
vs. Left-Handers	2424	624	112	22	60	294	226	379	.257	.396	.322
vs. Right-Handers	3112	840	170	23	71	416	309	535	.270	.408	.336
Home	2744	744	138	24	71	397	280	426	.271	.417	.339
Road	2792	720	144	21	60	313	255	488	.258	.389	.321
Grass	1455	375	71	11	36	158	137	280	.258	.396	.322
Artificial Turf	4081	1089	211	34	95	552	398	634	.267	.405	.332
April	648	168	36	8	17	82	77	100	.259	.418	.338
May	917	232	45	8	22	122	80	171	.253	.391	.315
June	1012	261	48	6	26	122	104	165	.258	.394	.327
July	895	219	37	4	19	91	92	155	.245	.359	.318
August	990	293	63	8	23	148	90	137	.296	.445	.353
Sept./Oct.	1074	291	53	11	24	145	92	186	.271	.408	.328
Leading Off Inn.	1338	362	73	11	38	38	104	205	.271	.427	.326
Runners On	2394	655	126	19	56	635	286	404	.274	.412	.348
Runners/Scor. Pos.	1446	377	66	14	30	547	214	265	.261	.388	.348
Runners On/2 Out	1036	277	55	11	23	266	130	181	.267	.408	.352
Scor. Pos./2 Out	685	174	30	9	13	231	102	130	.254	.381	.353
Late Inning Pressure	756	191	38	5	22	96	88	140	.253	.403	.331
Leading Off	190	47	7	1	3	3	17	27	.247	.342	.313
Runners On	332	92	20	1	10	84	41	70	.277	.434	.351
Runners/Scor. Pos.	207	47	8	0	5	67	30	52	.227	.338	.314

DRIVING IN RUNS	From 1B	From 2B	From 3B	Scoring Position
Totals	106/1692	198/1087	274/657	472/1744
Percentage	6%	18%	42%	27%
Driving In Runners from 3B with Less than Two Out:		193/348		55%

Love to face: Greg Maddux (4–0)
Hate to face: Bill Dawley (0–6)

Made 32d triple play in team history, highest total of any major-league team past or present, and did it the hard way. It was the first TP since 1972 without a runner on first base. . . . Starting catchers batted .284, highest average at that position in N.L. St. Louis, which traded LaValliere for Pena, ranked last with a .220 mark. . . . Second-place hitters batted .314, 2d-highest mark by any batting slot in N.L., behind St. Louis's number-two hitters (.317). . . . Cleanup hitters drove in only 90 runs, lowest total by number-four hitters on any team in majors. . . . Faced more left-handed starters (71) than any other team in majors, compiled a 32–39 mark in those games, compared to 48–43 when facing right-handed starters.

St. Louis Cardinals

	AB	H	2B	3B	HR	RBI	BB	SO	BA	SA	OBA
Season	5500	1449	252	49	94	782	644	933	.263	.378	.340
vs. Left-Handers	1896	498	97	14	38	289	238	315	.263	.389	.342
vs. Right-Handers	3604	951	155	35	56	493	406	618	.264	.373	.339
Home	2675	707	128	26	42	378	285	444	.264	.379	.335
Road	2825	742	124	23	52	404	359	489	.263	.378	.345
Grass	1460	390	59	10	26	217	188	264	.267	.375	.349
Artificial Turf	4040	1059	193	39	68	565	456	669	.262	.380	.336
April	677	186	40	4	15	97	80	120	.275	.412	.352
May	909	267	44	10	17	162	105	150	.294	.420	.366
June	954	273	35	10	15	155	111	192	.286	.391	.360
July	929	235	42	8	17	127	128	173	.253	.370	.344
August	993	255	54	9	17	134	122	149	.257	.381	.336
Sept./Oct.	1038	233	37	8	13	107	98	200	.224	.313	.289
Leading Off Inn.	1293	344	58	13	20	20	158	215	.266	.377	.350
Runners On	2490	704	124	21	52	740	319	397	.283	.412	.359
Runners/Scor. Pos.	1570	421	68	15	31	664	240	257	.268	.390	.357
Runners On/2 Out	1024	278	49	12	25	286	141	178	.271	.416	.361
Scor. Pos./2 Out	713	180	24	9	15	250	118	124	.252	.374	.360
Late Inning Pressure	889	235	41	5	17	123	102	174	.264	.379	.341
Leading Off	217	59	14	1	2	2	25	43	.272	.373	.350
Runners On	396	107	16	2	12	118	53	72	.270	.412	.356
Runners/Scor. Pos.	241	59	10	2	5	101	44	45	.245	.365	.361

DRIVING IN RUNS	From 1B	From 2B	From 3B	Scoring Position
Totals	95/1671	232/1185	361/749	593/1934
Percentage	6%	20%	48%	31%
Driving In Runners from 3B with Less than Two Out:		254/413		62%

Love to face: Tom Hume (11–2)
Hate to face: Steve Bedrosian (1–7)

Scored in their first 112 games, the longest start-of-season streak in N.L. history. Combined with last 33 games of 1986 season, Cards fell five games short of overall N.L. mark, set by Pirates in 1924 and 1925. . . . Only N.L. team to hit better with runners on base than with the bases empty in each of the past 13 years. . . . Led N.L. in stolen bases for sixth straight season (248). . . . Led league in fielding percentage (.982) for fourth season in a row, tying longest streak in modern N.L. history, set by Tinker, Evers, Chance, and Cubs teammates from 1905 through 1908. . . . Won nine games in which they trailed after eight innings, most in majors. . . . Ground outs-to-air outs ratio of 1.51 was by far the highest in majors since 1975.

San Diego Padres

	AB	H	2B	3B	HR	RBI	BB	SO	BA	SA	OBA
Season	5456	1419	209	48	113	650	577	992	.260	.378	.332
vs. Left-Handers	2040	552	88	15	50	245	221	351	.271	.402	.343
vs. Right-Handers	3416	867	121	33	63	405	356	641	.254	.364	.325
Home	2627	669	96	31	60	330	304	505	.255	.383	.333
Road	2829	750	113	17	53	320	273	487	.265	.373	.330
Grass	3996	1038	141	40	89	494	423	749	.260	.382	.332
Artificial Turf	1460	381	68	8	24	156	154	243	.261	.368	.331
April	757	178	33	6	12	66	66	127	.235	.342	.299
May	936	246	35	7	12	105	117	173	.263	.354	.348
June	903	246	31	8	16	125	110	181	.272	.378	.349
July	841	229	35	8	22	108	87	164	.272	.411	.339
August	973	265	35	12	23	128	91	158	.272	.404	.336
Sept./Oct.	1046	255	40	7	28	118	106	189	.244	.376	.316
Leading Off Inn.	1326	319	37	10	28	28	121	243	.241	.347	.306
Runners On	2351	631	103	27	50	587	275	407	.268	.399	.343
Runners/Scor. Pos.	1406	355	63	11	27	503	221	261	.252	.371	.349
Runners On/2 Out	1041	278	46	12	22	262	141	193	.267	.398	.356
Scor. Pos./2 Out	709	182	34	7	13	230	118	129	.257	.379	.364
Late Inning Pressure	917	220	33	5	12	94	101	200	.240	.326	.315
Leading Off	227	48	3	1	3	3	26	58	.211	.273	.292
Runners On	387	93	16	3	3	85	52	79	.240	.320	.330
Runners/Scor. Pos.	233	53	9	1	0	74	45	43	.227	.275	.349

DRIVING IN RUNS	From 1B	From 2B	From 3B	Scoring Position
Totals	90/1633	182/1077	264/628	446/1705
Percentage	6%	17%	42%	26%
Driving In Runners from 3B with Less than Two Out:		167/298		56%

Love to face: Atlee Hammaker (8–3)
Hate to face: Kelly Downs (0–4)

Here we go again: San Diego's first 10 games of the 1986 season all were decided by one run. Last season, San Diego became second team in modern N.L. history to start a season with three one-run losses (the other: 1975 Dodgers). The 1905 Red Sox hold the major-league mark (4). . . . First team in major-league history to lead off a game with three home runs (Wynne, Gwynn, and Kruk, Apr. 13). . . . Padres outscored their opponents 98–80 in first inning, were outscored by 113 runs thereafter. . . . Led N.L. in batting average in road games, ranked next-to-last in home games. . . . Have hit better with runners on base than with the bases empty in each of the past 10 seasons.

San Francisco Giants

	AB	H	2B	3B	HR	RBI	BB	SO	BA	SA	OBA
Season	5608	1458	274	32	205	762	511	1094	.260	.430	.324
vs. Left-Handers	1672	439	85	10	67	227	133	316	.263	.446	.319
vs. Right-Handers	3936	1019	189	22	138	535	378	778	.259	.423	.326
Home	2703	700	127	13	118	368	250	508	.259	.447	.324
Road	2905	758	147	19	87	394	261	586	.261	.414	.324
Grass	4079	1067	192	21	160	567	382	788	.262	.437	.327
Artificial Turf	1529	391	82	11	45	195	129	306	.256	.412	.318
April	788	213	40	5	27	100	70	174	.270	.437	.330
May	926	257	59	8	32	133	77	170	.278	.462	.339
June	919	215	38	0	40	112	60	191	.234	.406	.284
July	966	245	45	5	30	125	81	174	.254	.404	.313
August	999	251	48	7	32	130	94	203	.251	.409	.317
Sept./Oct.	1010	277	44	7	44	162	129	182	.274	.462	.360
Leading Off Inn.	1356	347	68	10	58	58	107	257	.256	.449	.313
Runners On	2303	640	112	12	76	631	237	418	.278	.436	.346
Runners/Scor. Pos.	1418	384	65	5	49	548	190	281	.271	.427	.354
Runners On/2 Out	954	227	41	2	33	249	123	183	.238	.389	.330
Scor. Pos./2 Out	654	162	29	1	26	225	98	130	.248	.414	.349
Late Inning Pressure	889	237	51	5	31	129	93	174	.267	.440	.338
Leading Off	226	66	11	3	14	14	19	40	.292	.553	.347
Runners On	383	103	26	0	8	105	44	70	.269	.399	.345
Runners/Scor. Pos.	246	67	15	0	6	94	36	47	.272	.407	.363

DRIVING IN RUNS	From 1B	From 2B	From 3B	Scoring Position
Totals	91/1540	237/1126	224/569	461/1695
Percentage	6%	21%	39%	27%
Driving In Runners from 3B with Less than Two Out:		156/314		50%

Love to face: Mark Thurmond (6–1)
Hate to face: Zane Smith (1–5)

Started the season with wins in each of their first 10 games that were decided by one run. That was the longest one-run-game winning streak in the majors last season, and the 2d-longest ever to start an N.L. season. The 1972 Mets won their first 11 one-run games. . . . Led N.L. in double plays for first time since leaving Manhattan. Set an N.L. record with 15 double plays over a six-game period (Apr. 24 through Apr. 27). . . . Hit 58 home runs leading off innings, most in the N.L. . . . Ranked third in N.L. with a .278 batting average in day games, last with a .248 mark under the lights. . . . Giants and Dodgers were the only teams in the majors not to score more than six runs in any inning last season.

National League

	AB	H	2B	3B	HR	RRF	BB	SO	BA	SA	OBA
Season	66276	17275	3126	435	1824	8580	6577	11657	.261	.404	.328
vs. Left-Handers	21543	5662	1062	132	605	2815	2206	3699	.263	.409	.332
vs. Right-Handers	44733	11613	2064	303	1219	5765	4371	7958	.260	.401	.327
Home	32409	8599	1532	227	919	4413	3387	5515	.265	.412	.336
Road	33867	8676	1594	208	905	4167	3190	6142	.256	.396	.321
Grass	32997	8584	1447	188	985	4257	3338	5895	.260	.405	.329
Artificial Turf	33279	8691	1679	247	839	4323	3239	5762	.261	.402	.327
April	8555	2204	424	53	238	1072	853	1592	.258	.403	.326
May	11160	2973	550	77	324	1537	1142	1982	.266	.417	.336
June	11236	2948	525	69	332	1508	1089	1983	.262	.410	.328
July	10821	2848	507	77	298	1374	1048	1840	.263	.407	.329
August	11889	3134	556	83	318	1530	1205	1974	.264	.405	.332
Sept./Oct.	12615	3168	564	76	314	1559	1240	2286	.251	.383	.320
Leading Off Inn.	16026	4238	763	106	472	473	1335	2697	.264	.414	.324
Runners On	28416	7591	1401	188	757	7509	3278	4948	.267	.410	.341
Runners/Scor. Pos.	17036	4392	797	119	429	6495	2450	3193	.258	.394	.346
Runners On/2 Out	12094	3009	542	86	323	3015	1623	2281	.249	.388	.340
Scor. Pos./2 Out	8035	1939	348	61	193	2613	1294	1570	.241	.372	.349
Late Inning Pressure	9923	2559	427	52	244	1226	1078	1915	.258	.385	.331
Leading Off	2483	642	103	15	72	72	221	449	.259	.399	.322
Runners On	4267	1114	190	20	86	1067	565	843	.261	.375	.346
Runners/Scor. Pos.	2544	647	108	12	52	952	437	552	.254	.368	.359

DRIVING IN RUNS	From 1B	From 2B	From 3B	Scoring Position
Totals	1149/19590	2571/13285	3018/7227	5589/20512
Percentage	6%	19%	42%	27%
Driving In Runners from 3B with Less than Two Out:		2077/3751		55%

IV
Pitcher Section

Pitcher Section

The Pitcher Section is an alphabetical listing of every pitcher who faced at least 300 batters in either the American or the National League last season. Also included are several key pitchers who did not face the required 300 batters, including all those who finished at least 20 games in relief. Pitchers are listed alphabetically within each league, followed by the totals for each team and the league as a whole.

Column Headings Information

Don Aase

Baltimore Orioles	W-L	ERA	AB	H	HR	BB	SO	BA	SA	OBA

W-L	Won-Lost Record
ERA	Earned-Run Average
AB	At Bats
H	Hits
HR	Home Runs
BB	Bases on Balls
SO	Strikeouts
BA	Batting Average
SA	Slugging Average
OBA	On-Base Average

In addition to the expected categories for pitchers (won-lost record, ERA, walks, and strikeouts), this book includes a unique perspective on each pitcher's season: the batting performance of the league against him. While this method may be unfamiliar at first, it enables us to look at the pitcher and his abilities in fascinating detail.

By compiling pitching statistics in this way, we can examine a pitcher's performance in the same "within the game" contexts we've used to look at batters. To take one example, we're all familiar with platoon differentials for batters; we know that some right-handed batters are far more effective against left-handed pitchers than they are against righties. The same must be true of pitchers, but because the specific information was never available before, who knew how big those differences were? Well, we know now, and the differences can be huge: to take one example, Kent Tekulve of Philadelphia last season allowed a .309 average to left-handed batters, while limiting right-handed hitters to a .197 average—a whopping 112-point difference. Given that large a variance, a manager should think twice about letting him face a lefty hitter in a clutch situation.

Moreover, by looking at the opponents' batting figures with runners on base or in scoring position, we can show conclusively for the first time who are those underrated pitchers who may give up a lot of hits or home runs, but rarely give them up with men on or in clutch situations. And we can also see those pitchers who (whisper the word, please) fold under the same pressure. (Bear in mind that overall batting averages increase with men on base. This makes any pitcher who holds opponents to a lower average with runners on all the more impressive.)

Season Summary Information

	W-L	ERA	AB	H	HR	BB	SO	BA	SA	OBA
Season	19-7	2.87	910	204	19	74	170	.224	.330	.285
vs. Left-Handed Batters			475	95	7	42	93	.200	.282	.269
vs. Right-Handed Batters			435	109	12	32	77	.251	.382	.302
Home	10-2	3.23	468	118	10	30	86	.252	.357	.297
Road	9-5	2.50	442	86	9	44	84	.195	.301	.272
Grass	14-6	3.06	702	163	16	59	128	.232	.343	.291
Artificial Turf	5-1	2.22	208	41	3	15	42	.197	.284	.264
April	3-1	3.00	132	32	2	11	31	.242	.364	.301
May	1-1	4.26	103	29	1	13	20	.282	.379	.356
June	2-1	3.26	114	25	4	10	15	.219	.342	.291
July	4-1	2.93	163	32	7	16	30	.196	.337	.269
August	5-1	2.51	173	38	2	14	27	.220	.277	.282
Sept./Oct.	4-2	2.23	225	48	3	10	47	.213	.316	.249

Each pitcher's seasonal performance is broken down into a variety of special categories. The first line for each pitcher gives his totals for the whole season. This is followed by breakdowns of his performance against left- and right-handed hitters, in home and road games, on grass fields and on artificial turf, and by month. (For pitchers who pitched for more than one team within a league, all totals are combined. The "home" totals for Dave Dravecky, for example, include all games he pitched in San Diego while with the Padres, and all games he pitched in San Francisco while with the Giants.)

Leading Off Inn.	240	59	6	14	37	.246	.367	.287
Runners On	350	79	8	32	63	.226	.343	.290
Runners/Scor. Pos.	178	40	4	21	41	.225	.343	.301
Runners On/2 Out	152	30	3	14	31	.197	.309	.278
Scor. Pos./2 Out	89	20	2	9	20	.225	.371	.310

Following these breakdowns, each pitcher's performance is divided into specific game situations. Totals are given for each pitcher against batters who led off an inning, and against players batting with runners on base. These are followed by his performance with runners in scoring position (on second or third base, or both), with runners on base and two out, and with runners in scoring position and two out.

Late Inning Pressure	79	19	2	11	19	.241	.342	.333
Leading Off	24	7	1	3	5	.292	.458	.370
Runners On	26	7	1	3	4	.269	.385	.345
Runners/Scor. Pos.	10	1	0	3	2	.100	.100	.308

The next group shows the pitcher's performance in late-inning pressure situations, which are defined a little differently for pitchers than they are for batters. For pitchers, late-inning pressure is defined as any situation occurring in the seventh inning or later with the score tied, or with his team leading or trailing by one or two runs.

Each pitcher's totals are listed for all late-inning pressure situations, then broken out for his performance when facing a leadoff batter, with runners on base, and with runners in scoring position.

First 9 Batters	240	50	2	27	44	.208	.288	.288
Second 9 Batters	362	81	8	23	75	.224	.340	.272
All Batters Thereafter	308	73	9	24	51	.237	.351	.297

The last set of breakdowns tracks a pitcher's performance throughout each appearance by listing the opponents' batting record according to the number of batters he has faced, regardless of when he entered the game. This allows us to spotlight those pitchers who get stronger as the game progresses, and to pick out those who can breeze through the order once, but falter the second or third time around.

Following the statistics for each pitcher are a series of comments, beginning with the batter each pitcher loves to face and hates to face. The statistics listed for each individual match-up are from regular season games in the last ten years. Contained within the comments for each pitcher is his "Ground outs-to-air outs" ratio, which consists of his total of ground outs divided by outs on balls hit in the air. (Also included are plays in which the batter reaches base on an error.) An average figure is roughly 1.15. Pitchers with ratios below 0.75 have their games charted by NASA; those above 1.50 receive hate mail from burrowing animals.

American League

Darrel Akerfelds
Throws Right

Cleveland Indians	W–L	ERA	AB	H	HR	BB	SO	BA	SA	OBA
Season	2-6	6.75	296	84	18	38	42	.284	.530	.374
vs. Left-Handers			150	45	12	18	21	.300	.613	.383
vs. Right-Handers			146	39	6	20	21	.267	.445	.365
Home	0-1	7.63	127	39	8	13	15	.307	.551	.390
Road	2-5	6.14	169	45	10	25	27	.266	.515	.362
Grass	2-3	5.98	254	69	12	28	36	.272	.472	.357
Artificial Turf	0-3	11.70	42	15	6	10	6	.357	.881	.463
April			0	0	0	0	0	—	—	—
May			0	0	0	0	0	—	—	—
June			0	0	0	0	0	—	—	—
July	0-1	4.61	54	14	3	7	7	.259	.500	.339
August	1-3	9.53	115	33	7	16	15	.287	.557	.385
Sept./Oct.	1-2	5.23	127	37	8	15	20	.291	.520	.378
Leading Off Inn.			71	22	4	8	7	.310	.535	.388
Runners On			129	32	6	17	22	.248	.450	.344
Runners/Scor. Pos.			62	18	4	10	12	.290	.565	.392
Runners On/2 Out			51	10	2	9	10	.196	.392	.317
Scor. Pos./2 Out			28	4	1	6	7	.143	.321	.294
Late Inning Pressure			22	6	0	0	3	.273	.273	.304
Leading Off			6	1	0	0	0	.167	.167	.286
Runners On			8	1	0	0	2	.125	.125	.125
Runners/Scor. Pos.			3	1	0	0	1	.333	.333	.333
First 9 Batters			116	30	6	24	19	.259	.440	.394
Second 9 Batters			104	27	9	8	15	.260	.606	.316
All Batters Thereafter			76	27	3	6	8	.355	.566	.419

Loves to face: Glenn Braggs (.125, 1-for-8)
Hates to face: Terry Steinbach (2-for-2, 1 HR, 1 BB, 1 HBP)
Ground outs-to-air outs ratio: 0.63, 6th–lowest in A.L. last season (minimum: 200 BFP), 0.64 for career. . . . Additional statistics: 6 double-play ground outs in 72 opportunities, 13 doubles, 3 triples in 74.2 innings last season. . . . Allowed 8 first-inning runs in 13 starts. . . . Batting support: 4.54 runs per start. . . . Started 13 games, averaging 5.13 innings per start. Longest stint was an 8-inning complete-game loss to Milwaukee. Record as a starter: 2–6, 7.29 ERA. . . . Allowed 12 earned runs in 5.1 innings in two starts vs. Toronto. . . . Allowed 10 home runs in his first 26.2 innings. . . . Has unleashed nine wild pitches in his 80 innings in the big leagues. . . . Anyone ever had a 6.75 ERA for three consecutive seasons? Akerfelds goes for the hat trick in '88.

Neil Allen
Throws Right

White Sox/Yankees	W–L	ERA	AB	H	HR	BB	SO	BA	SA	OBA
Season	0-8	5.93	298	97	8	36	42	.326	.477	.399
vs. Left-Handers			165	50	7	17	23	.303	.485	.368
vs. Right-Handers			133	47	1	19	19	.353	.466	.436
Home	0-5	4.93	181	59	5	20	19	.326	.481	.395
Road	0-3	7.53	117	38	3	16	23	.325	.470	.406
Grass	0-8	6.35	274	91	8	35	37	.332	.496	.409
Artificial Turf	0-0	1.42	24	6	0	1	5	.250	.250	.280
April	0-1	13.50	16	7	2	3	1	.438	1.000	.526
May			0	0	0	0	0	—	—	—
June	0-2	8.78	56	21	2	7	11	.375	.518	.444
July	0-2	3.78	63	20	0	6	8	.317	.349	.386
August	0-2	7.71	68	26	2	10	6	.382	.544	.457
Sept./Oct.	0-1	3.65	95	23	2	10	16	.242	.400	.314
Leading Off Inn.			67	19	3	7	11	.284	.478	.360
Runners On			142	51	4	22	16	.359	.514	.443
Runners/Scor. Pos.			82	29	2	16	8	.354	.500	.455
Runners On/2 Out			48	14	1	6	3	.292	.438	.370
Scor. Pos./2 Out			30	8	1	6	1	.267	.400	.389
Late Inning Pressure			19	6	0	4	2	.316	.316	.435
Leading Off			4	1	0	1	1	.250	.250	.400
Runners On			11	3	0	3	1	.273	.273	.429
Runners/Scor. Pos.			6	2	0	1	0	.333	.333	.429
First 9 Batters			152	53	4	20	24	.349	.526	.425
Second 9 Batters			90	29	2	11	11	.322	.422	.398
All Batters Thereafter			56	15	2	5	7	.268	.429	.328

Loves to face: Jim Morrison (0-for-10)
Hates to face: Julio Franco (.500, 6-for-12)
Ground outs-to-air outs ratio: 1.23 last season, 1.22 for career. . . . Additional statistics: 9 double-play ground outs in 91 opportunities, 15 doubles, 3 triples in 74.1 innings last season. . . . Allowed 12 first-inning runs in 11 starts. . . . Batting support: 2.58 runs per start. . . . Robin Yount was the only right-handed batter to homer against Allen last season. . . . Opponents' overall batting average for 1987 was by far the highest of his career. Previous high was .269 in 1983. . . . Yankees haven't had the greatest luck with former Chicago pitchers: George and Gracie won as many games for them as Burns and Allen.

Doyle Alexander
Throws Right

Detroit Tigers	W–L	ERA	AB	H	HR	BB	SO	BA	SA	OBA
Season	9-0	1.53	313	63	3	26	44	.201	.262	.263
vs. Left-Handers			151	30	1	19	21	.199	.258	.288
vs. Right-Handers			162	33	2	7	23	.204	.265	.237
Home	5-0	1.14	140	31	1	15	25	.221	.279	.297
Road	4-0	1.84	173	32	2	11	19	.185	.249	.234
Grass	8-0	0.84	225	43	2	18	36	.191	.244	.251
Artificial Turf	1-0	3.38	88	20	1	8	8	.227	.307	.292
April			0	0	0	0	0	—	—	—
May			0	0	0	0	0	—	—	—
June			0	0	0	0	0	—	—	—
July			0	0	0	0	0	—	—	—
August	3-0	2.37	108	22	1	6	14	.204	.278	.246
Sept./Oct.	6-0	1.09	205	41	2	20	30	.200	.254	.271
Leading Off Inn.			87	20	1	4	14	.230	.276	.264
Runners On			103	22	1	15	15	.214	.291	.314
Runners/Scor. Pos.			53	10	1	10	11	.189	.264	.317
Runners On/2 Out			40	8	0	6	5	.200	.250	.304
Scor. Pos./2 Out			24	4	0	4	4	.167	.208	.286
Late Inning Pressure			29	6	0	4	4	.207	.276	.303
Leading Off			9	2	0	1	3	.222	.222	.300
Runners On			8	3	0	3	0	.375	.625	.545
Runners/Scor. Pos.			4	2	0	1	0	.500	.500	.600
First 9 Batters			92	23	1	7	19	.250	.315	.303
Second 9 Batters			93	16	2	9	9	.172	.258	.222
All Batters Thereafter			128	24	0	13	16	.188	.227	.262

Loves to face: Curtis Wilkerson (0-for-13)
Hates to face: Brook Jacoby (.556, 10-for-18, 1 HR)
Figures *above* are for A.L. only. . . . Ground outs-to-air outs ratio: 0.83 last season, 0.93 for career. . . . Additional statistics: 18 double-play ground outs in 122 opportunities, 26 doubles, 2 triples in 206.0 innings last season. . . . Allowed 16 first-inning runs in 27 starts. . . . Batting support: 4.48 runs per start (3.56 with Atlanta, 5.82 with Detroit). . . . August ERA was 4th-best in A.L., and September ERA (0.71) led the majors. . . . Made 11 starts for Detroit. He won nine; Tigers also won the other two. . . . Combined September–October record of 24–5 since 1982. . . . Career record of 44–21, including 20 wins in his last 24 decisions, following complete games. . . . Has won nine consecutive decisions vs. the Angels since losing to them on June 26, 1977, while pitching for Texas.

Joaquin Andujar
Throws Right

Oakland As	W–L	ERA	AB	H	HR	BB	SO	BA	SA	OBA
Season	3-5	6.08	234	63	11	26	32	.269	.449	.348
vs. Left-Handers			116	31	3	16	15	.267	.397	.356
vs. Right-Handers			118	32	8	10	17	.271	.500	.341
Home	1-4	6.02	156	40	8	20	24	.256	.436	.348
Road	2-1	6.20	78	23	3	6	8	.295	.474	.349
Grass	3-5	6.08	234	63	11	26	32	.269	.449	.348
Artificial Turf			0	0	0	0	0	—	—	—
April	0-0	0.00	3	0	0	0	1	.000	.000	.250
May	1-0	4.00	32	8	0	6	5	.250	.250	.368
June	1-1	5.68	48	12	2	7	3	.250	.458	.351
July	1-3	6.27	146	40	8	13	22	.274	.473	.338
August	0-1	40.50	5	3	1	0	1	.600	1.200	.600
Sept./Oct.			0	0	0	0	0	—	—	—
Leading Off Inn.			54	15	3	10	7	.278	.481	.400
Runners On			95	27	7	14	12	.284	.547	.378
Runners/Scor. Pos.			56	15	3	11	6	.268	.500	.391
Runners On/2 Out			31	8	3	3	6	.258	.677	.324
Scor. Pos./2 Out			21	6	2	3	4	.286	.762	.375
Late Inning Pressure			15	5	2	1	1	.333	.733	.375
Leading Off			2	1	0	1	0	.500	.500	.667
Runners On			6	3	2	0	0	.500	1.500	.500
Runners/Scor. Pos.			2	0	0	0	0	.000	.000	.000
First 9 Batters			89	20	3	15	13	.225	.348	.346
Second 9 Batters			81	24	4	6	11	.296	.469	.345
All Batters Thereafter			64	19	4	5	8	.297	.563	.357

Loves to face: Keith Moreland (.111, 4-for-36)
Hates to face: Gerald Perry (.450, 9-for-20)
Ground outs-to-air outs ratio: 1.24 last season, 1.33 career. . . . Additional statistics: 9 double-play ground outs in 62 opportunities, 7 doubles, 1 triple in 60.2 innings last season. . . . Allowed 12 first-inning runs in 13 starts. . . . Batting support: 5.46 runs per start. . . . Yearly batting averages by opposing right-handed batters since 1982: .228, .222, .223, .223, .222, .271. . . . Danny Cox had better watch out. St. Louis sent Andujar packing after his ejection from Game 7 of the 1985 World Series. . . . Career strikeout-to-walk ratio of 0.95 vs. left-handed batters, 1.89 vs. right-handers. . . . One of six players in major-league history to pitch more than 2,000 innings and not allow a grand-slam home run. The others: Old Hoss Radbourn, Jim McCormick, Eddie Plank, Jim Palmer, and Herb Pennock.

Keith Atherton

Minnesota Twins — Throws Right

	W–L	ERA	AB	H	HR	BB	SO	BA	SA	OBA
Season	7-5	4.54	309	81	10	30	51	.262	.424	.332
vs. Left-Handers			162	43	6	17	28	.265	.444	.339
vs. Right-Handers			147	38	4	13	23	.259	.401	.325
Home	5-1	2.89	141	32	1	13	26	.227	.291	.299
Road	2-4	6.00	168	49	9	17	25	.292	.536	.360
Grass	2-3	6.89	124	35	8	13	22	.282	.556	.357
Artificial Turf	5-2	3.00	185	46	2	17	29	.249	.335	.316
April	1-0	2.92	47	11	1	5	7	.234	.404	.308
May	1-1	5.84	48	10	0	8	7	.208	.229	.321
June	2-1	3.57	68	17	1	7	16	.250	.353	.338
July	0-2	5.40	39	12	1	3	3	.308	.410	.349
August	1-0	4.05	53	14	2	4	13	.264	.434	.328
Sept./Oct.	2-1	5.93	54	17	5	3	5	.315	.704	.351
Leading Off Inn.			53	9	1	7	8	.170	.245	.267
Runners On			167	42	4	16	29	.251	.407	.323
Runners/Scor. Pos.			91	27	3	13	13	.297	.505	.391
Runners On/2 Out			83	26	3	8	11	.313	.530	.387
Scor. Pos./2 Out			48	16	2	8	4	.333	.583	.448
Late Inning Pressure			136	33	4	17	14	.243	.412	.323
Leading Off			24	3	0	7	2	.125	.167	.323
Runners On			71	16	2	7	8	.225	.394	.288
Runners/Scor. Pos.			36	9	2	6	3	.250	.500	.341
First 9 Batters			293	76	10	28	50	.259	.430	.328
Second 9 Batters			16	5	0	2	1	.313	.313	.400
All Batters Thereafter			0	0	0	0	0	—	—	—

Loves to face: Tim Hulett (0-for-9, 5 SO)
Hates to face: Wade Boggs (.571, 8-for-14, 1 HR)
Ground outs-to-air outs ratio: 0.68 last season, 0.54 for career....
Additional statistics: 3 double-play ground outs in 71 opportunities, 14 doubles, 3 triples in 79.1 innings last season.... Would have had 13 saves under the rules as they existed in 1969, but settled for two under the current rules.... Was the winning pitcher in three consecutive appearances (Aug. 30 to Sept. 5).... Opponents stole eight bases in 10 attempts in '87.... Career record of 0–6 vs. Toronto. ... Opponents' career batting averages: .229 leading off innings, .190 with the bases loaded.... Winner of Claude Rains Award— he's always there but you never see him. Did you know that he's pitched at least 56 games in each of the last four seasons? Only one other A.L. pitcher has done that (Dave Righetti).

Scott Bailes

Cleveland Indians — Throws Left

	W–L	ERA	AB	H	HR	BB	SO	BA	SA	OBA
Season	7-8	4.64	490	145	21	47	65	.296	.484	.358
vs. Left-Handers			99	27	4	6	17	.273	.394	.321
vs. Right-Handers			391	118	17	41	48	.302	.506	.367
Home	3-5	5.43	226	72	11	21	36	.319	.509	.376
Road	4-3	4.01	264	73	10	26	29	.277	.462	.343
Grass	5-7	4.93	378	115	16	33	52	.304	.489	.358
Artificial Turf	2-1	3.72	112	30	5	14	13	.268	.464	.359
April	1-0	2.22	91	21	1	15	14	.231	.363	.339
May	1-0	2.35	57	14	3	4	8	.246	.404	.290
June	0-1	7.50	58	21	3	2	11	.362	.569	.383
July	1-3	5.97	119	35	5	8	10	.294	.479	.341
August	3-3	4.41	137	42	8	14	21	.307	.526	.373
Sept./Oct.	1-1	8.59	28	12	1	4	1	.429	.679	.500
Leading Off Inn.			110	34	5	15	11	.309	.536	.392
Runners On			232	60	7	24	35	.259	.388	.326
Runners/Scor. Pos.			117	29	4	15	17	.248	.376	.329
Runners On/2 Out			103	27	3	11	16	.262	.369	.345
Scor. Pos./2 Out			61	17	3	7	10	.279	.426	.371
Late Inning Pressure			84	28	2	3	13	.333	.440	.356
Leading Off			20	4	0	1	4	.200	.200	.238
Runners On			39	14	2	2	7	.359	.538	.390
Runners/Scor. Pos.			20	8	2	0	5	.400	.750	.400
First 9 Batters			253	74	10	19	42	.292	.470	.342
Second 9 Batters			137	39	9	20	13	.285	.533	.379
All Batters Thereafter			100	32	2	8	10	.320	.450	.369

Loves to face: Dick Schofield (0-for-10)
Hates to face: Tom Brunansky (4-for-4)
Ground outs-to-air outs ratio: 0.97 last season, 1.05 for career....
Additional statistics: 8 double-play ground outs in 112 opportunities, 23 doubles, 3 triples in 120.1 innings last season.... Allowed 7 first-inning runs in 17 starts.... Batting support: 5.00 runs per start.... Earned six saves in nine opportunities. Was seven-for-22 in 1986.... April ERA was 5th-best in A.L.... Compiled similar stats in each of his two seasons in majors: wins-losses, 10–10 in 1986, 7–8 in 1987; ERA: 4.95, 4.64; walks: 43, 47; strikeouts: 60, 65.... Record of 5–7 with a 4.68 ERA in 17 starts; 2–1, 4.50 ERA in 22 relief appearances.... Has made 27 career starts, and never completed one.... Opponents' career batting averages: .287 by left-handed batters, .287 by right-handers.

Jeff Ballard

Baltimore Orioles — Throws Left

	W–L	ERA	AB	H	HR	BB	SO	BA	SA	OBA
Season	2-8	6.59	291	100	15	35	27	.344	.560	.413
vs. Left-Handers			42	15	2	7	5	.357	.571	.449
vs. Right-Handers			249	85	13	28	22	.341	.558	.406
Home	0-7	7.62	174	61	7	25	15	.351	.534	.432
Road	2-1	5.08	117	39	8	10	12	.333	.598	.383
Grass	1-8	6.75	264	92	13	32	23	.348	.561	.418
Artificial Turf	1-0	5.14	27	8	2	3	4	.296	.556	.367
April			0	0	0	0	0	—	—	—
May	2-1	6.31	104	36	9	8	11	.346	.644	.393
June	0-2	5.87	30	8	1	10	3	.267	.500	.450
July			0	0	0	0	0	—	—	—
August			0	0	0	0	0	—	—	—
Sept./Oct.	0-5	6.94	157	56	5	17	13	.357	.516	.417
Leading Off Inn.			73	30	5	6	4	.411	.671	.456
Runners On			127	43	6	17	10	.339	.528	.414
Runners/Scor. Pos.			73	29	4	13	3	.397	.630	.483
Runners On/2 Out			43	11	1	6	4	.256	.326	.347
Scor. Pos./2 Out			27	9	1	6	1	.333	.444	.455
Late Inning Pressure			14	3	0	2	1	.214	.286	.313
Leading Off			5	2	0	1	0	.400	.600	.500
Runners On			4	1	0	0	0	.250	.250	.250
Runners/Scor. Pos.			1	1	0	0	0	1.000	1.000	1.000
First 9 Batters			116	39	4	10	8	.336	.474	.389
Second 9 Batters			100	36	6	13	11	.360	.620	.434
All Batters Thereafter			75	25	5	12	8	.333	.613	.420

Loves to face: Dave Winfield (0-for-6)
Hates to face: Dave Valle (.750, 6-for-8, 1 HR)
Ground outs-to-air outs ratio: 1.51 last season, his first in majors. ... Additional statistics: 11 double-play ground outs in 70 opportunities, 18 doubles, 0 triples in 69.2 innings last season.... Allowed 9 first-inning runs in 14 starts.... Batting support: 5.71 runs per start.... Lost his last eight decisions over a span of 10 starts after a 2–0 record in his first four games.... Opponents' batting average was the highest among 239 major-league qualifiers last season.... More hits than innings pitched and more walks than strikeouts—a deadly parlay. Forty-five other pitchers hit that exacta in 1987, and with only slightly more success than Ballard. They posted a combined record of 56–86, with a 5.92 ERA. Only Jimmy Jones of San Diego had a winning record with more than three wins.

Scott Bankhead

Seattle Mariners — Throws Right

	W–L	ERA	AB	H	HR	BB	SO	BA	SA	OBA
Season	9-8	5.42	593	168	35	37	95	.283	.530	.326
vs. Left-Handers			328	98	12	17	45	.299	.506	.332
vs. Right-Handers			265	70	23	20	50	.264	.558	.317
Home	5-3	4.58	283	73	17	17	51	.258	.502	.306
Road	4-5	6.22	310	95	18	20	44	.306	.555	.343
Grass	3-5	7.21	242	78	14	17	35	.322	.579	.361
Artificial Turf	6-3	4.27	351	90	21	20	60	.256	.496	.301
April	4-1	2.94	126	31	5	8	27	.246	.429	.294
May	1-2	7.06	127	38	11	10	16	.299	.614	.350
June	2-2	4.70	118	30	4	6	21	.254	.407	.288
July	0-1	9.00	58	22	5	1	11	.379	.724	.377
August	0-2	7.98	62	22	5	8	11	.355	.726	.437
Sept./Oct.	2-0	4.33	102	25	5	4	9	.245	.461	.275
Leading Off Inn.			153	41	11	3	20	.268	.536	.282
Runners On			207	67	10	13	33	.324	.556	.360
Runners/Scor. Pos.			103	35	4	9	17	.340	.563	.378
Runners On/2 Out			95	29	5	8	17	.305	.568	.359
Scor. Pos./2 Out			54	17	3	6	9	.315	.611	.383
Late Inning Pressure			28	10	1	1	5	.357	.500	.379
Leading Off			8	2	1	0	1	.250	.625	.250
Runners On			8	4	0	0	1	.500	.625	.500
Runners/Scor. Pos.			3	2	0	0	0	.667	.667	.667
First 9 Batters			221	68	10	15	33	.308	.525	.349
Second 9 Batters			205	54	16	12	39	.263	.566	.309
All Batters Thereafter			167	46	9	10	23	.275	.491	.315

Loves to face: Cal Ripken (0-for-7, 4 SO)
Hates to face: George Bell (.533, 8-for-15, 4 HR)
Ground outs-to-air outs ratio: 0.70 last season, 0.75 for career....
Additional statistics: 6 double-play ground outs in 97 opportunities, 29 doubles, 6 triples in 149.1 innings last season.... Allowed 15 first-inning runs in 25 starts.... Batting support: 5.08 runs per start. ... Averaged 5.73 innings per start, lowest among Mariners' regular starters.... At the end of April, Higuera and Saberhagen were 4–0, and among the pitchers at 4–1 was Bankhead.... Allowed nine home runs in 45 at bats to the A.L.'s top seven home run hitters. ... Career average of one walk per 40.3 leadoff batters faced, one walk per 13.1 batters faced in other situations.... One of five members of 1984 U.S. Olympic baseball team to pitch in majors last season. Others: Mike Dunne, Pat Pacillo, Billy Swift, Bobby Witt.

Floyd Bannister

Chicago White Sox — Throws Left

	W–L	ERA	AB	H	HR	BB	SO	BA	SA	OBA
Season	16-11	3.58	878	216	38	49	124	.246	.426	.285
vs. Left-Handers			125	30	3	14	18	.240	.376	.314
vs. Right-Handers			753	186	35	35	106	.247	.434	.280
Home	6-5	3.93	362	99	12	27	53	.273	.412	.323
Road	10-6	3.35	516	117	26	22	71	.227	.436	.257
Grass	13-9	3.36	701	174	26	42	98	.248	.408	.290
Artificial Turf	3-2	4.44	177	42	12	7	26	.237	.497	.265
April	1-1	4.74	99	25	5	5	15	.253	.515	.288
May	2-2	2.84	148	35	5	12	19	.236	.392	.294
June	0-4	7.89	117	35	12	9	13	.299	.650	.344
July	3-1	2.20	156	41	5	10	18	.263	.410	.307
August	4-2	4.75	162	42	8	7	14	.259	.451	.288
Sept./Oct.	6-1	1.34	196	38	3	6	45	.194	.265	.218
Leading Off Inn.			222	50	8	15	33	.225	.360	.274
Runners On			306	76	10	18	44	.248	.386	.287
Runners/Scor. Pos.			154	34	4	12	27	.221	.331	.272
Runners On/2 Out			129	28	3	12	17	.217	.302	.284
Scor. Pos./2 Out			79	15	2	8	12	.190	.278	.264
Late Inning Pressure			76	17	3	5	10	.224	.408	.272
Leading Off			20	1	0	0	3	.050	.050	.050
Runners On			16	3	0	3	3	.188	.188	.316
Runners/Scor. Pos.			9	1	0	2	2	.111	.111	.273
First 9 Batters			285	71	11	15	58	.249	.435	.285
Second 9 Batters			285	70	13	16	34	.246	.418	.285
All Batters Thereafter			308	75	14	18	32	.244	.425	.285

Loves to face: Darrell Porter (0-for-17)
Hates to face: Gary Gaetti (.471, 16-for-34, 7 HR)
Ground outs-to-air outs ratio: 0.84 last season, 0.90 for career. . . . Additional statistics: 15 double-play ground outs in 144 opportunities, 34 doubles, 5 triples in 228.2 innings last season. . . . Allowed 14 first-inning runs in 34 starts. . . . Batting support: 4.53 runs per start. . . . Most home runs allowed to right-handed batters in the past 13 years. . . . Tied Clemens for most wins in A.L. after the All-Star break (12), and ranked fourth in ERA during that time (2.62). . . . Allowed an average of 1.93 walks per nine innings, 4th-lowest rate among A.L. pitchers. . . . Defeated every opposing A.L. club except the Indians last season. . . . Has won seven decisions in a row vs. Detroit since 1984. . . . Opponents' career batting average of .199 with two outs and runners in scoring position.

Juan Berenguer

Minnesota Twins — Throws Right

	W–L	ERA	AB	H	HR	BB	SO	BA	SA	OBA
Season	8-1	3.94	420	100	10	47	110	.238	.374	.312
vs. Left-Handers			223	62	8	29	50	.278	.462	.360
vs. Right-Handers			197	38	2	18	60	.193	.274	.257
Home	5-0	2.31	226	46	3	19	56	.204	.296	.264
Road	3-1	5.98	194	54	7	28	54	.278	.464	.364
Grass	3-1	6.39	169	47	7	27	44	.278	.485	.372
Artificial Turf	5-0	2.37	251	53	3	20	66	.211	.299	.268
April	1-0	2.08	47	9	0	4	22	.191	.298	.255
May	2-0	2.25	116	23	2	11	26	.198	.302	.268
June	2-0	4.08	112	30	2	15	36	.268	.366	.354
July	0-0	9.00	36	10	4	5	4	.278	.667	.357
August	0-0	5.40	34	6	2	6	10	.176	.353	.293
Sept./Oct.	3-1	4.66	75	22	0	6	12	.293	.413	.337
Leading Off Inn.			96	20	3	10	31	.208	.354	.283
Runners On			177	47	4	23	47	.266	.412	.343
Runners/Scor. Pos.			117	29	4	18	33	.248	.419	.338
Runners On/2 Out			88	23	2	8	26	.261	.420	.323
Scor. Pos./2 Out			58	14	2	7	17	.241	.431	.323
Late Inning Pressure			123	26	1	15	30	.211	.301	.291
Leading Off			33	6	0	4	9	.182	.273	.270
Runners On			42	10	1	7	12	.238	.357	.327
Runners/Scor. Pos.			27	6	1	6	9	.222	.333	.333
First 9 Batters			290	71	7	36	83	.245	.386	.325
Second 9 Batters			87	22	2	5	17	.253	.379	.290
All Batters Thereafter			43	7	1	6	10	.163	.279	.265

Loves to face: Mike Heath (0-for-14)
Hates to face: Rickey Henderson (.444, 8-for-18, 2 2B, 3 3B)
Ground outs-to-air outs ratio: 0.60, 2d-lowest in A.L. last season (minimum: 200 BFP), 0.62 for career. . . . Additional statistics: 3 double-play ground outs in 70 opportunities, 23 doubles, 2 triples in 112.0 innings last season. . . . Earned four saves in 10 opportunities; faced only 55 batters protecting leads of three runs or less in the eighth inning or later. . . . May ERA was 2d lowest in A.L. . . . Strikeout-to-walk ratio in 1987 was the best of his career. . . . Hasn't lost a night game since Sept. 13, 1985. Since then: 7–0 in night games, 4–5 in day games. . . . Has never allowed a grand slam home run (faced 82 batters with bases loaded). . . . Lost last nine starts to finish 1981 season with career record of 3–17 and 5.06 ERA; he's gone 35–25 with a 3.74 ERA in six seasons since then.

Eric Bell

Baltimore Orioles — Throws Left

	W–L	ERA	AB	H	HR	BB	SO	BA	SA	OBA
Season	10-13	5.45	643	174	32	78	111	.271	.495	.350
vs. Left-Handers			86	28	4	9	11	.326	.523	.389
vs. Right-Handers			557	146	28	69	100	.262	.490	.344
Home	3-6	5.95	249	70	17	27	47	.281	.566	.350
Road	7-7	5.16	394	104	15	51	64	.264	.449	.350
Grass	8-11	5.60	526	147	27	68	90	.279	.511	.363
Artificial Turf	2-2	4.80	117	27	5	10	21	.231	.419	.291
April	2-1	4.58	72	19	3	9	17	.264	.500	.354
May	3-1	4.05	122	27	2	19	18	.221	.388	.329
June	1-3	9.78	86	31	6	18	10	.360	.663	.471
July	3-2	2.85	151	34	5	10	30	.225	.384	.273
August	0-4	7.25	143	44	11	14	17	.308	.622	.369
Sept./Oct.	1-2	6.62	69	19	5	8	19	.275	.551	.346
Leading Off Inn.			160	42	8	17	34	.263	.463	.337
Runners On			239	73	12	39	40	.305	.527	.400
Runners/Scor. Pos.			136	42	5	28	22	.309	.485	.422
Runners On/2 Out			91	20	3	20	16	.220	.385	.360
Scor. Pos./2 Out			58	12	1	15	9	.207	.310	.370
Late Inning Pressure			44	9	0	5	7	.205	.250	.286
Leading Off			13	2	0	1	2	.154	.231	.214
Runners On			13	2	0	2	2	.154	.154	.267
Runners/Scor. Pos.			5	2	0	1	1	.400	.400	.500
First 9 Batters			245	56	9	34	50	.229	.404	.323
Second 9 Batters			213	71	15	28	36	.333	.634	.413
All Batters Thereafter			185	47	8	16	25	.254	.454	.313

Loves to face: Henry Cotto (0-for-7)
Hates to face: Wally Joyner (.625, 5-for-8, 1 HR)
Ground outs-to-air outs ratio: 1.10 last season, 1.15 for career (2.62 vs. left-handed batters, 0.98 vs. right-handers). . . . Additional statistics: 17 double-play ground outs in 123 opportunities, 40 doubles, 4 triples in 165.0 innings last season. . . . Allowed 18 first-inning runs in 29 starts. . . . Batting support: 4.17 runs per start, 8th-lowest average in A.L. (minimum: 15 GS). . . . Started more games (29) than any rookie pitcher in the majors, but also led A.L. rookies with 13 losses. . . . Only complete games last season were in back-to-back victories in July. Failed to complete five innings in 11 starts. Only one A.L. pitcher had a higher total: Ken Schrom (14). . . . Allowed 12 extra-base hits with no singles during a stretch from Aug. 25 through Sept. 5.

Bud Black

Kansas City Royals — Throws Left

	W–L	ERA	AB	H	HR	BB	SO	BA	SA	OBA
Season	8-6	3.60	475	126	16	35	61	.265	.432	.320
vs. Left-Handers			117	27	4	8	19	.231	.393	.278
vs. Right-Handers			358	99	12	27	42	.277	.444	.334
Home	5-1	3.14	238	57	7	10	33	.239	.403	.273
Road	3-5	4.10	237	69	9	25	28	.291	.460	.366
Grass	1-3	5.63	159	52	8	19	17	.327	.516	.409
Artificial Turf	7-3	2.68	316	74	8	16	44	.234	.389	.273
April	0-0	2.35	28	6	0	4	7	.214	.286	.313
May	2-1	2.55	94	23	2	6	14	.245	.404	.290
June	1-1	2.61	38	7	1	2	5	.184	.342	.225
July	1-4	4.08	117	35	3	7	12	.299	.436	.339
August	2-0	5.70	128	42	8	12	12	.328	.563	.400
Sept./Oct.	2-0	2.14	70	13	2	4	11	.186	.329	.234
Leading Off Inn.			117	33	3	8	10	.282	.470	.339
Runners On			207	47	7	16	26	.227	.353	.288
Runners/Scor. Pos.			116	26	4	11	18	.224	.353	.290
Runners On/2 Out			86	23	4	6	10	.267	.419	.323
Scor. Pos./2 Out			54	13	4	5	7	.241	.463	.305
Late Inning Pressure			39	12	1	5	9	.308	.538	.386
Leading Off			12	4	0	1	1	.333	.500	.385
Runners On			16	3	1	2	5	.188	.438	.278
Runners/Scor. Pos.			10	1	0	2	5	.100	.100	.250
First 9 Batters			205	47	7	17	36	.229	.395	.293
Second 9 Batters			157	45	5	8	14	.287	.433	.325
All Batters Thereafter			113	34	4	10	11	.301	.496	.363

Loves to face: Ozzie Guillen (0-for-12)
Hates to face: Ruben Sierra (.667, 6-for-9, 2 HR)
Ground outs-to-air outs ratio: 1.18 last season, 1.07 for career. . . . Additional statistics: 12 double-play ground outs in 89 opportunities, 19 doubles, 6 triples in 122.1 innings last season. . . . Allowed 14 first-inning runs in 18 starts. . . . Batting support: 5.44 runs per start. . . . Averaged 5.48 innings per start, lowest among Royals' regular starters. . . . Record of 7–5, with a 4.01 ERA in 18 starts; 1–1, 1.90 ERA in 11 relief appearances. Career figures: 49–48, 3.92 as a starter; 5–8, 2.32 in relief. . . . Earned 10 saves in 19 opportunities over past two seasons. . . . Opponents batted 93 points higher on grass fields than on artificial surfaces, largest such difference in A.L. (minimum: 100 AB each way). . . . Has lost his last seven decisions to the Yankees.

Bert Blyleven

Minnesota Twins   Throws Right

	W-L	ERA	AB	H	HR	BB	SO	BA	SA	OBA
Season	15-12	4.01	1002	249	46	101	196	.249	.433	.321
vs. Left-Handers			555	130	32	61	114	.234	.447	.313
vs. Right-Handers			447	119	14	40	82	.266	.416	.331
Home	9-6	3.83	608	144	25	66	134	.237	.413	.315
Road	6-6	4.31	394	105	21	35	62	.266	.464	.330
Grass	4-4	5.08	281	79	18	26	42	.281	.512	.346
Artificial Turf	11-8	3.61	721	170	28	75	154	.236	.402	.311
April	1-1	4.24	130	35	8	10	22	.269	.492	.324
May	3-3	5.05	199	49	13	13	36	.246	.482	.299
June	3-2	2.83	154	36	5	16	25	.234	.364	.314
July	3-2	4.50	174	47	6	22	39	.270	.431	.355
August	3-2	5.26	154	44	5	17	30	.286	.448	.360
Sept./Oct.	2-2	2.47	191	38	9	23	44	.199	.387	.284
Leading Off Inn.			253	65	16	20	52	.257	.490	.316
Runners On			381	94	12	41	73	.247	.386	.322
Runners/Scor. Pos.			209	51	7	30	47	.244	.407	.333
Runners On/2 Out			165	43	6	18	43	.261	.424	.337
Scor. Pos./2 Out			104	25	4	12	31	.240	.433	.319
Late Inning Pressure			105	23	1	18	29	.219	.333	.336
Leading Off			30	6	0	5	9	.200	.300	.314
Runners On			37	12	1	5	6	.324	.486	.409
Runners/Scor. Pos.			20	8	1	5	2	.400	.700	.500
First 9 Batters			302	76	12	26	59	.252	.424	.315
Second 9 Batters			297	82	17	26	56	.276	.505	.338
All Batters Thereafter			403	91	17	49	81	.226	.387	.313

Loves to face: Don Slaught (.036, 1-for-28)
Hates to face: Oddibe McDowell (.417, 10-for-24, 5 HR)
Ground outs-to-air outs ratio: 1.51 last season, 1.22 for career....
Additional statistics: 31 double-play ground outs in 187 opportunities, 3d-highest rate in A.L. (minimum: 20 GS), 45 doubles, 1 triple in 267.0 innings last season.... Led majors with 92 extra-base hits allowed, eight fewer than in 1986.... Batting support: 5.00 runs per start.... Failed to strike out two batters per walk for the third time in 18-year career.... Loss in Game 5 of World Series ended string of five post-season wins in a row, two shy of Bob Gibson's record. ... Has won last seven decisions vs. Milwaukee, last six vs. Oakland. ... Career record of 48-30 in August.... First major-league start (June 5, 1970) was microcosm of career: Gave up a home run to first batter he faced (Lee Maye), but won the game.

Mike Boddicker

Baltimore Orioles   Throws Right

	W-L	ERA	AB	H	HR	BB	SO	BA	SA	OBA
Season	10-12	4.18	854	212	29	78	152	.248	.413	.315
vs. Left-Handers			485	116	18	40	75	.239	.416	.303
vs. Right-Handers			369	96	11	38	77	.260	.409	.330
Home	5-6	4.24	436	105	17	33	78	.241	.427	.301
Road	5-6	4.12	418	107	12	45	74	.256	.400	.329
Grass	7-10	4.35	685	176	25	60	127	.257	.428	.321
Artificial Turf	3-2	3.52	169	36	4	18	25	.213	.355	.291
April	2-0	1.50	123	25	2	9	23	.203	.276	.269
May	2-1	3.57	145	34	5	15	28	.234	.386	.309
June	1-3	3.38	173	40	5	14	34	.231	.364	.291
July	2-0	6.15	109	32	7	9	16	.294	.587	.347
August	2-3	6.57	151	40	5	19	26	.265	.450	.355
Sept./Oct.	1-5	4.54	153	41	5	12	25	.268	.444	.321
Leading Off Inn.			219	57	9	17	37	.260	.434	.319
Runners On			331	81	10	37	62	.245	.402	.321
Runners/Scor. Pos.			192	45	5	26	42	.234	.385	.326
Runners On/2 Out			137	33	2	23	26	.241	.372	.350
Scor. Pos./2 Out			94	24	1	17	21	.255	.383	.369
Late Inning Pressure			87	22	1	11	14	.253	.379	.333
Leading Off			26	11	0	3	3	.423	.615	.483
Runners On			35	6	0	5	8	.171	.229	.268
Runners/Scor. Pos.			19	4	0	5	4	.211	.211	.360
First 9 Batters			272	58	10	18	52	.213	.360	.272
Second 9 Batters			260	70	9	30	44	.269	.450	.349
All Batters Thereafter			322	84	10	30	56	.261	.429	.322

Loves to face: Ernest Riles (.100, 2-for-20)
Hates to face: Carney Lansford (.424, 14-for-33, 4 HR)
Ground outs-to-air outs ratio: 1.17 last season, 1.43 for career....
Additional statistics: 19 double-play ground outs in 157 opportunities, 38 doubles, 8 triples in 226.0 innings last season.... Allowed 13 first-inning runs in 33 starts.... Batting support: 4.24 runs per start.... Led the Orioles' staff with an average of 6.85 innings pitched per start.... April ERA was 2d-best in A.L.... Has ended the last three seasons with losing streaks of five, seven, and four games. He has started those years with records of 5-1, 10-1, and 6-1, respectively.... Opponents have hit for a lower average in Memorial Stadium than they have in road games in each of the last seven seasons.... Career record of 40-23 in starts following wins, 19-26 following losses. ...

Chris Bosio

Milwaukee Brewers   Throws Right

	W-L	ERA	AB	H	HR	BB	SO	BA	SA	OBA
Season	11-8	5.24	677	187	18	50	150	.276	.415	.326
vs. Left-Handers			356	94	11	30	79	.264	.424	.322
vs. Right-Handers			321	93	7	20	71	.290	.405	.329
Home	4-4	6.23	297	84	8	20	73	.283	.434	.330
Road	7-4	4.48	380	103	10	30	77	.271	.400	.322
Grass	9-8	5.54	585	166	15	42	132	.284	.424	.331
Artificial Turf	2-0	3.42	92	21	3	8	18	.228	.359	.290
April	3-0	3.94	63	16	2	3	20	.254	.381	.288
May	0-1	5.93	59	19	1	5	14	.322	.407	.369
June	0-1	7.52	82	24	2	9	17	.293	.500	.363
July	4-0	3.51	125	33	2	5	32	.264	.368	.288
August	1-3	6.19	150	45	5	11	36	.300	.440	.352
Sept./Oct.	3-3	5.01	198	50	6	17	31	.253	.404	.312
Leading Off Inn.			162	49	3	10	35	.302	.426	.343
Runners On			293	85	6	27	56	.290	.406	.347
Runners/Scor. Pos.			185	52	3	20	43	.281	.400	.346
Runners On/2 Out			107	27	2	8	20	.252	.355	.304
Scor. Pos./2 Out			75	21	1	4	15	.280	.387	.316
Late Inning Pressure			126	33	2	8	26	.262	.381	.304
Leading Off			32	6	1	1	8	.188	.313	.212
Runners On			46	14	0	5	5	.304	.370	.365
Runners/Scor. Pos.			31	9	0	5	4	.290	.387	.378
First 9 Batters			315	82	5	25	83	.260	.371	.315
Second 9 Batters			182	49	8	14	37	.269	.445	.321
All Batters Thereafter			180	56	5	11	30	.311	.461	.349

Loves to face: Randy Bush (0-for-7, 4 SO)
Hates to face: Mike Kingery (4-for-4, 1 HR)
Ground outs-to-air outs ratio: 1.48 last season, 1.53 for career....
Additional statistics: 16 double-play ground outs in 140 opportunities, 32 doubles, 4 triples in 170.0 innings last season.... Allowed 8 first-inning runs in 19 starts.... Batting support: 5.21 runs per start.... Led all rookie pitchers with 150 strikeouts, and tied for third among rookies with 11 wins.... Average of 7.94 strikeouts per nine innings was 4th highest among A.L. pitchers.... Record of 1-5 (5.69 ERA) in day games, 10-3 (5.02) at night.... Record of 8-7 (5.22 ERA) in 19 starts, 3-1 (5.29 ERA) in 27 relief appearances.... Faced 22 batters with the bases loaded, allowing three walks and one grand slam.... Career record of 0-4 vs. Detroit.... Has allowed only three unearned runs in 204.2 innings.

DeWayne Buice

California Angels   Throws Right

	W-L	ERA	AB	H	HR	BB	SO	BA	SA	OBA
Season	6-7	3.39	408	87	12	40	109	.213	.348	.285
vs. Left-Handers			192	42	6	25	54	.219	.349	.309
vs. Right-Handers			216	45	6	15	55	.208	.347	.264
Home	3-3	2.33	198	35	4	17	58	.177	.273	.248
Road	3-4	4.50	210	52	8	23	51	.248	.419	.321
Grass	5-6	2.78	355	70	9	31	94	.197	.315	.265
Artificial Turf	1-1	7.90	53	17	3	9	15	.321	.566	.413
April	1-0	3.38	28	7	1	4	9	.250	.393	.333
May	1-3	3.63	82	17	4	7	21	.207	.378	.278
June	1-0	2.18	68	11	4	5	27	.162	.338	.227
July	1-0	1.90	81	10	0	6	16	.123	.173	.184
August	1-2	3.86	73	18	1	9	21	.247	.356	.329
Sept./Oct.	1-2	5.89	76	24	2	9	15	.316	.487	.388
Leading Off Inn.			92	18	5	5	20	.196	.380	.237
Runners On			175	44	5	16	45	.251	.400	.318
Runners/Scor. Pos.			108	29	2	11	23	.269	.417	.336
Runners On/2 Out			82	21	0	4	25	.256	.329	.299
Scor. Pos./2 Out			57	16	0	2	13	.281	.386	.317
Late Inning Pressure			245	55	6	24	64	.224	.363	.295
Leading Off			56	11	2	4	12	.196	.339	.250
Runners On			104	27	4	11	27	.260	.452	.333
Runners/Scor. Pos.			66	19	2	8	15	.288	.500	.360
First 9 Batters			349	71	9	35	97	.203	.332	.279
Second 9 Batters			59	16	3	5	12	.271	.441	.323
All Batters Thereafter			0	0	0	0	0	—	—	—

Loves to face: Ellis Burks (0-for-6, 3 SO)
Hates to face: Willie Wilson (3-for-3, 1 2B, 1 HR)
Ground outs-to-air outs ratio: 1.23 last season, his first in majors.
... Additional statistics: 11 double-play ground outs in 81 opportunities, 17 doubles, 1 triple in 114.0 innings last season.... Ranked third among A.L. rookie pitchers with 57 appearances, but led all rookies with 17 saves (22 opportunities).... Faced 41 consecutive right-handed batters without allowing a hit (May 20-June 20), longest streak in majors last season.... Walked four of 17 batters faced with the bases loaded.... This is no "wet behind the ears" rookie. He spent the last nine seasons in the Oakland and San Francisco organizations, playing for eight different minor league clubs. But he pitched more innings for the Angels in 1987 than he had in any single season in the minors.

John Candelaria

Throws Left

California Angels	W–L	ERA	AB	H	HR	BB	SO	BA	SA	OBA
Season	8-6	4.71	455	127	17	20	74	.279	.444	.308
vs. Left-Handers			71	24	2	5	16	.338	.465	.377
vs. Right-Handers			384	103	15	15	58	.268	.440	.295
Home	6-3	4.72	286	78	12	15	48	.273	.427	.309
Road	2-3	4.68	169	49	5	5	26	.290	.473	.305
Grass	7-4	4.93	339	95	14	18	54	.280	.442	.314
Artificial Turf	1-2	4.03	116	32	3	2	20	.276	.448	.288
April	3-0	2.51	122	33	2	6	21	.270	.344	.302
May	1-2	6.86	82	26	5	5	10	.317	.585	.348
June	1-1	6.62	75	25	4	4	13	.333	.560	.370
July			0	0	0	0	0	—	—	—
August	2-2	4.10	137	31	4	4	25	.226	.358	.248
Sept./Oct.	1-1	6.52	39	12	2	1	5	.308	.538	.317
Leading Off Inn.			118	28	3	4	13	.237	.347	.262
Runners On			169	56	10	9	29	.331	.586	.355
Runners/Scor. Pos.			88	29	5	5	16	.330	.614	.347
Runners On/2 Out			73	26	6	5	15	.356	.712	.397
Scor. Pos./2 Out			41	14	2	4	7	.341	.610	.400
Late Inning Pressure			24	4	0	2	5	.167	.167	.231
Leading Off			7	2	0	1	2	.286	.286	.375
Runners On			10	1	0	0	0	.100	.100	.100
Runners/Scor. Pos.			1	0	0	0	0	.000	.000	.000
First 9 Batters			174	48	8	5	28	.276	.466	.294
Second 9 Batters			164	44	4	9	29	.268	.390	.305
All Batters Thereafter			117	35	5	6	17	.299	.487	.331

Loves to face: Jim Rice (0-for-7)
Hates to face: Pat Tabler (5-for-5, 1 2B, 1 HR)
Figures *above* are for A.L. only. . . . Ground outs-to-air outs ratio: 0.95 last season, 0.87 for career. . . . Additional statistics: 7 double-play ground outs in 89 opportunities, 21 doubles, 6 triples in 129.0 innings last season. . . . Allowed 22 first-inning runs in 23 starts. . . . Batting support: 5.17 runs per start. . . . Has held opposing left-handed batters to an average under .200 in four of the last five seasons. . . . Has allowed only two home runs to left-handed batters since 1985; both were hit in the same game by the same player: Fred Lynn (Aug. 20, 1987). . . . Career record of 33–14 during the month of July, including 18 wins in 21 decisions over past six seasons. . . . Hasn't walked more than five left-handed batters in any season since 1982.

Tom Candiotti

Throws Right

Cleveland Indians	W–L	ERA	AB	H	HR	BB	SO	BA	SA	OBA
Season	7-18	4.78	773	193	28	93	111	.250	.406	.330
vs. Left-Handers			388	92	12	49	45	.237	.366	.319
vs. Right-Handers			385	101	16	44	66	.262	.447	.340
Home	5-11	4.39	518	126	17	47	70	.243	.375	.307
Road	2-7	5.56	255	67	11	46	41	.263	.471	.371
Grass	7-15	4.71	703	171	24	87	101	.243	.390	.326
Artificial Turf	0-3	5.51	70	22	4	6	10	.314	.671	.368
April	1-4	6.75	105	33	5	11	9	.314	.552	.381
May	0-2	4.78	128	32	5	14	23	.250	.398	.324
June	1-3	4.85	95	22	5	23	13	.232	.484	.383
July	1-2	5.09	136	32	4	15	20	.235	.353	.303
August	4-2	2.86	157	32	5	13	17	.204	.318	.263
Sept./Oct.	0-5	5.31	152	42	4	17	29	.276	.401	.351
Leading Off Inn.			196	48	7	18	26	.245	.403	.312
Runners On			309	74	8	53	44	.239	.366	.347
Runners/Scor. Pos.			187	50	6	39	31	.267	.412	.380
Runners On/2 Out			127	32	5	26	20	.252	.441	.383
Scor. Pos./2 Out			92	25	4	22	18	.272	.467	.417
Late Inning Pressure			106	26	4	16	16	.245	.396	.350
Leading Off			30	11	2	4	3	.367	.600	.441
Runners On			46	9	2	9	6	.196	.348	.339
Runners/Scor. Pos.			26	5	2	6	4	.192	.423	.364
First 9 Batters			246	61	7	25	39	.248	.370	.318
Second 9 Batters			225	56	12	25	29	.249	.467	.320
All Batters Thereafter			302	76	9	43	43	.252	.391	.346

Loves to face: Spike Owen (.040, 1-for-25)
Hates to face: George Bell (.588, 10-for-17, 1 HR)
Ground outs-to-air outs ratio: 1.21 last season, 1.20 for career. . . . Additional statistics: 17 double-play ground outs in 151 opportunities, 33 doubles, 2 triples in 201.2 innings last season. . . . Allowed 26 first-inning runs in 32 starts. . . . Batting support: 3.69 runs per start, 2d-lowest A.L. (min.: 15 GS). . . . Led A.L. in losses in home games (11) and in day games (10). . . . August ERA was 5th best in A.L. . . . Over the last 40 years, 20 pitchers have pitched two one-hitters in one season. Of those 20, Candiotti had the highest ERA and the most losses. Honorable mention: Skip Lockwood (8–15 in 1972) and Denny McLain (3.92 ERA in 1966). . . . First pitcher since Mike Torrez in 1983 to walk 10 batters in a game, and the first since who-knows-when to win a 10-walk performance.

Steve Carlton

Throws Left

Indians/Twins	W–L	ERA	AB	H	HR	BB	SO	BA	SA	OBA
Season	6-14	5.74	592	165	24	86	91	.279	.461	.372
vs. Left-Handers			113	29	2	13	19	.257	.389	.336
vs. Right-Handers			479	136	22	73	72	.284	.478	.380
Home	3-7	5.02	320	85	13	39	52	.266	.453	.344
Road	3-7	6.65	272	80	11	47	39	.294	.471	.402
Grass	5-12	6.69	455	133	21	65	72	.292	.495	.381
Artificial Turf	1-2	3.00	137	32	3	21	19	.234	.350	.340
April	2-2	5.09	65	16	4	10	7	.246	.477	.342
May	1-2	6.04	100	28	3	18	21	.280	.410	.397
June	2-1	2.56	115	23	1	14	22	.200	.322	.287
July	0-4	7.60	138	44	9	21	21	.319	.565	.404
August	1-4	8.78	123	45	5	14	10	.366	.569	.435
Sept./Oct.	0-1	2.93	51	9	2	9	10	.176	.314	.311
Leading Off Inn.			144	40	6	14	17	.278	.458	.346
Runners On			263	80	11	46	39	.304	.498	.406
Runners/Scor. Pos.			163	48	7	30	32	.294	.485	.396
Runners On/2 Out			102	30	7	22	12	.294	.549	.424
Scor. Pos./2 Out			67	20	3	16	11	.299	.493	.434
Late Inning Pressure			60	21	2	7	6	.350	.517	.412
Leading Off			14	4	0	1	1	.286	.357	.333
Runners On			28	12	2	4	0	.429	.750	.485
Runners/Scor. Pos.			16	5	1	4	0	.313	.500	.429
First 9 Batters			220	57	8	33	41	.259	.414	.357
Second 9 Batters			180	47	6	27	21	.261	.428	.355
All Batters Thereafter			192	61	10	26	29	.318	.547	.405

Loves to face: Willie Randolph (0-for-8)
Hates to face: Ray Knight (.356, 31-for-87, 6 2B, 3 3B, 4 HR)
Ground outs-to-air outs ratio: 1.14 last season, 1.09 for career. . . . Additional statistics: 19 double-play ground outs in 147 opportunities, 28 doubles, 4 triples in 152.0 innings last season. . . . Allowed 17 first-inning runs in 21 starts. . . . Batting support: 4.67 runs per start. . . . Why wasn't he on the Twins post-season roster? Maybe the club's 1–8 record in games in which he appeared had something to do with it. Nahhhh! . . . Made major-league debut on Apr. 12, 1965, in relief of Barney Schultz. Walked the first batter he faced (George Altman), and was replaced by Bob Purkey. . . . The first hit vs. Carlton: Pete Rose; the first home run: Doug Clemens; first strikeout victim: Dick Ellsworth. . . . What were the odds Ellsworth would get his name in this book twice?

John Cerutti

Throws Left

Toronto Blue Jays	W–L	ERA	AB	H	HR	BB	SO	BA	SA	OBA
Season	11-4	4.40	573	144	30	59	92	.251	.476	.321
vs. Left-Handers			137	34	6	13	26	.248	.438	.313
vs. Right-Handers			436	110	24	46	66	.252	.489	.324
Home	3-2	5.99	258	66	17	34	41	.256	.512	.341
Road	8-2	3.12	315	78	13	25	51	.248	.448	.304
Grass	7-2	3.25	226	56	11	21	34	.248	.447	.313
Artificial Turf	4-2	5.18	347	88	19	38	58	.254	.496	.326
April	1-0	4.09	40	10	1	5	10	.250	.400	.333
May	1-2	4.23	100	20	6	12	17	.200	.440	.283
June	3-0	6.14	113	30	7	12	11	.265	.487	.339
July	1-0	4.01	91	21	5	12	16	.231	.473	.320
August	4-1	2.33	147	37	4	10	22	.252	.449	.299
Sept./Oct.	1-1	6.75	82	26	7	8	16	.317	.598	.378
Leading Off Inn.			145	37	7	14	21	.255	.476	.321
Runners On			221	49	12	22	37	.222	.430	.290
Runners/Scor. Pos.			118	21	5	11	23	.178	.347	.244
Runners On/2 Out			96	20	4	8	17	.208	.417	.269
Scor. Pos./2 Out			55	10	2	4	10	.182	.364	.237
Late Inning Pressure			39	9	2	5	8	.231	.436	.318
Leading Off			10	3	1	2	2	.300	.600	.417
Runners On			12	2	1	1	2	.167	.417	.231
Runners/Scor. Pos.			5	0	0	1	1	.000	.000	.167
First 9 Batters			280	68	16	29	55	.243	.461	.315
Second 9 Batters			171	44	7	19	22	.257	.474	.330
All Batters Thereafter			122	32	7	11	15	.262	.516	.323

Loves to face: Carmen Castillo (0-for-9)
Hates to face: Jim Rice (.625, 5-for-8, 2 2B, 2 HR)
Ground outs-to-air outs ratio: 0.62, 4th lowest in A.L. last season (minimum: 200 BFP), 0.75 for career. . . . Additional statistics: 13 double-play ground outs in 102 opportunities, 27 doubles, 6 triples in 151.1 innings last season. . . . Allowed 16 first-inning runs in 21 starts, including 7 HR, most in the A.L. . . . Batting support: 5.90 runs per start, 5th-highest average in A.L. (min.: 15 GS). . . . Road-game ERA ranked fourth in the A.L. . . . Record of 9–4 with a 4.75 ERA in 21 starts; 2–0, 3.53 ERA, in 23 relief appearances. Career average of 4.85 strikeouts per nine innings as a starter, 7.48 in relief. . . . Career record of 14–5 in night games, 6–5 in day games. . . . Opponents' career breakdown: .273 with bases empty, .244 with runners on base, .222 with runners in scoring position.

Jim Clancy
Toronto Blue Jays — Throws Right

	W–L	ERA	AB	H	HR	BB	SO	BA	SA	OBA
Season	15-11	3.54	918	234	24	80	180	.255	.401	.314
vs. Left-Handers			508	143	12	42	98	.281	.433	.335
vs. Right-Handers			410	91	12	38	82	.222	.361	.288
Home	7-5	3.00	455	114	13	35	80	.251	.404	.305
Road	8-6	4.08	463	120	11	45	100	.259	.397	.323
Grass	5-5	4.45	339	93	9	38	74	.274	.428	.345
Artificial Turf	10-6	3.01	579	141	15	42	106	.244	.385	.295
April	2-2	4.13	112	31	4	15	11	.277	.464	.359
May	5-1	1.71	169	31	2	8	40	.183	.249	.220
June	1-2	2.89	163	45	5	17	25	.276	.448	.349
July	2-1	5.26	150	44	6	8	35	.293	.493	.329
August	2-4	4.71	161	41	1	17	33	.255	.360	.328
Sept./Oct.	3-1	3.19	163	42	6	15	36	.258	.423	.318
Leading Off Inn.			240	71	11	19	46	.296	.496	.347
Runners On			366	87	7	33	64	.238	.374	.298
Runners/Scor. Pos.			194	49	5	24	37	.253	.392	.329
Runners On/2 Out			147	31	0	18	36	.211	.293	.297
Scor. Pos./2 Out			91	18	0	13	24	.198	.242	.298
Late Inning Pressure			64	23	0	5	8	.359	.469	.406
Leading Off			21	6	0	0	3	.286	.429	.286
Runners On			23	10	0	3	2	.435	.565	.500
Runners/Scor. Pos.			15	7	0	3	0	.467	.667	.556
First 9 Batters			298	79	8	30	58	.265	.403	.331
Second 9 Batters			294	68	9	21	60	.231	.395	.280
All Batters Thereafter			326	87	7	29	62	.267	.405	.329

Loves to face: Larry Herndon (0-for-18)
Hates to face: Ron Kittle (.500, 8-for-16, 4 HR)
Ground outs-to-air outs ratio: 1.20 last season, 1.03 for career. . . . Additional statistics: 19 double-play ground outs in 160 opportunities, 52 doubles, 5 triples in 241.1 innings last season. . . . Allowed 19 first-inning runs in 37 starts. . . . Batting support: 5.16 runs per start. . . . One of three pitchers to win five games in May. His ERA that month was the best in A.L. . . . Record of 5–8 vs. the Eastern Division, 10–3 vs. the West. . . . Balked on June 22 for first time in his major-league career. . . . Hasn't defeated Boston since Sept. 24, 1984; hasn't beaten Detroit since Sept. 14, 1984. He's dropped six consecutive decisions to the Red Sox and eight straight to the Tigers. . . . Has made 264 consecutive appearances as a starter since his last relief appearance on Aug. 4, 1979.

Mark Clear
Milwaukee Brewers — Throws Right

	W–L	ERA	AB	H	HR	BB	SO	BA	SA	OBA
Season	8-5	4.48	293	70	9	55	81	.239	.403	.363
vs. Left-Handers			140	35	5	32	37	.250	.464	.394
vs. Right-Handers			153	35	4	23	44	.229	.346	.333
Home	4-1	4.50	148	35	6	19	40	.236	.412	.329
Road	4-4	4.46	145	35	3	36	41	.241	.393	.394
Grass	7-3	4.50	258	65	9	46	69	.252	.434	.369
Artificial Turf	1-2	4.35	35	5	0	9	12	.143	.171	.326
April	2-0	5.00	34	9	1	7	6	.265	.529	.390
May	2-1	2.19	44	11	0	5	16	.250	.318	.333
June	1-2	7.59	85	23	3	18	21	.271	.424	.417
July	0-2	6.75	59	17	4	10	12	.288	.542	.380
August	1-0	1.64	39	8	1	7	13	.205	.410	.319
Sept./Oct.	2-0	0.00	32	2	0	8	13	.063	.063	.250
Leading Off Inn.			66	20	3	8	21	.303	.545	.378
Runners On			160	36	4	32	46	.225	.375	.352
Runners/Scor. Pos.			109	21	2	20	30	.193	.312	.311
Runners On/2 Out			66	13	1	13	21	.197	.288	.338
Scor. Pos./2 Out			50	9	0	8	17	.180	.220	.293
Late Inning Pressure			115	27	3	32	30	.235	.374	.393
Leading Off			27	7	2	5	7	.259	.556	.375
Runners On			63	13	1	17	20	.206	.302	.361
Runners/Scor. Pos.			39	9	0	11	11	.231	.282	.377
First 9 Batters			267	63	9	52	77	.236	.408	.364
Second 9 Batters			24	6	0	3	4	.250	.333	.321
All Batters Thereafter			2	1	0	0	0	.500	.500	.667

Loves to face: Tom Brunansky (.071, 1-for-14, 8 SO)
Hates to face: Pete O'Brien (.600, 6-for-10, 1 HR)
Ground outs-to-air outs ratio: 0.89 last season, 0.87 for career. . . . Additional statistics: 4 double-play ground outs in 85 opportunities, 15 doubles, 3 triples in 78.1 innings last season. . . . Lasted only 3.1 innings and lost his only major-league start on June 30 vs. Detroit, breaking a string of 425 relief appearances. . . . Allowed only one home run to a left-handed batter in three seasons prior to 1987. . . . Earned 22 saves in 32 opportunities in two seasons with Milwaukee (69 percent). . . . Career record of 7–0 vs. the Chisox. . . . Has won his last seven decisions against the Mariners. . . . Opponents' batting average with two outs and runners in scoring position was his *highest* in last four years. Only one other pitcher held opponents below .200 in each of those seasons (Dave Smith).

Roger Clemens
Boston Red Sox — Throws Right

	W–L	ERA	AB	H	HR	BB	SO	BA	SA	OBA
Season	20-9	2.97	1055	248	19	83	256	.235	.348	.295
vs. Left-Handers			603	142	6	50	133	.235	.332	.299
vs. Right-Handers			452	106	13	33	123	.235	.369	.290
Home	11-6	2.75	594	130	12	38	135	.219	.337	.270
Road	9-3	3.26	461	118	7	45	121	.256	.362	.327
Grass	17-8	3.09	928	218	17	74	227	.235	.345	.295
Artificial Turf	3-1	2.10	127	30	2	9	29	.236	.370	.297
April	1-2	2.86	108	25	2	10	28	.231	.306	.308
May	3-2	2.54	176	41	3	15	40	.233	.335	.297
June	2-2	5.53	161	41	5	19	38	.255	.404	.339
July	5-1	2.26	226	51	3	14	38	.226	.363	.277
August	3-1	4.07	169	48	4	12	42	.284	.432	.335
Sept./Oct.	6-1	1.51	215	42	2	13	70	.195	.256	.240
Leading Off Inn.			267	81	3	15	57	.303	.408	.350
Runners On			443	91	9	49	112	.205	.312	.289
Runners/Scor. Pos.			271	54	6	31	71	.199	.310	.285
Runners On/2 Out			176	36	3	22	51	.205	.324	.296
Scor. Pos./2 Out			120	24	1	15	35	.200	.292	.294
Late Inning Pressure			107	28	5	12	23	.262	.430	.336
Leading Off			29	7	1	2	5	.241	.345	.290
Runners On			38	9	2	6	9	.237	.395	.341
Runners/Scor. Pos.			22	7	1	4	5	.318	.455	.423
First 9 Batters			291	61	3	27	94	.210	.296	.286
Second 9 Batters			294	66	5	24	67	.224	.320	.283
All Batters Thereafter			470	121	11	32	95	.257	.398	.310

Loves to face: Cory Snyder (0-for-9, 9 SO)
Hates to face: Alvin Davis (.526, 10-for-19, 4 2B, 2 HR)
Ground outs-to-air outs ratio: 1.00 last season, 0.93 for career. . . . Additional statistics: 14 double-play ground outs in 207 opportunities, 52 doubles, 5 triples in 281.2 innings last season. . . . Allowed 16 first-inning runs in 36 starts. . . . Batting support: 5.56 runs per start. . . . One of three players to pitch a complete-game victory without a single strikeout last season, and he did it twice. The others: Mike Morgan and Danny Cox. . . . Career mark of 7–0 against Cleveland, with complete games in each of last five wins. . . . Opponents' batting average with runners in scoring position has been under .200 in each of the last three seasons. . . . No pitcher has won 20 games in three consecutive seasons since Jim Palmer did it for four straight years from 1975 through 1978.

Pat Clements
New York Yankees — Throws Left

	W–L	ERA	AB	H	HR	BB	SO	BA	SA	OBA
Season	3-3	4.95	304	91	4	30	36	.299	.398	.364
vs. Left-Handers			84	14	1	8	21	.167	.250	.255
vs. Right-Handers			220	77	3	22	15	.350	.455	.405
Home	1-1	3.46	158	47	3	11	21	.297	.399	.345
Road	2-2	6.57	146	44	1	19	15	.301	.397	.383
Grass	2-3	4.08	258	75	3	18	32	.291	.380	.338
Artificial Turf	1-0	10.03	46	16	1	12	4	.348	.500	.483
April	1-0	12.46	17	7	0	6	3	.412	.529	.565
May	0-0	0.77	35	6	0	6	6	.171	.171	.286
June	0-0	1.98	48	9	0	3	7	.188	.250	.231
July	1-2	5.89	74	27	1	8	5	.365	.486	.422
August	0-0	9.00	40	18	1	3	4	.450	.600	.477
Sept./Oct.	1-1	5.25	90	24	2	4	11	.267	.378	.320
Leading Off Inn.			63	20	1	6	7	.317	.460	.377
Runners On			161	48	1	18	21	.298	.379	.364
Runners/Scor. Pos.			102	33	0	14	16	.324	.363	.397
Runners On/2 Out			72	23	1	6	11	.319	.417	.372
Scor. Pos./2 Out			49	17	0	5	9	.347	.367	.407
Late Inning Pressure			81	27	1	5	8	.333	.457	.364
Leading Off			19	7	0	2	0	.368	.526	.429
Runners On			40	14	1	1	5	.350	.500	.349
Runners/Scor. Pos.			23	9	0	1	4	.391	.435	.385
First 9 Batters			256	82	2	26	29	.320	.410	.382
Second 9 Batters			45	8	2	4	6	.178	.333	.260
All Batters Thereafter			3	1	0	0	1	.333	.333	.333

Loves to face: Bill Buckner (0-for-8)
Hates to face: George Brett (.750, 3-for-4, 1 2B, 1 HR)
Ground outs-to-air outs ratio: 3.16, highest in A.L. last season (minimum: 200 BFP), 1.76 for career. . . . Additional statistics: 17 double-play ground outs in 80 opportunities, highest rate in A.L. (minimum: 40 opp.), 18 doubles, 0 triples in 80.0 innings last season. . . . Earned seven saves (four vs. Baltimore) in 13 opportunities. . . . Career record of 7–1 vs. A.L. East opponents, 1–2 vs. the Western Division; 8–3 in the American League, 0–6 in the National. . . . George Brett was the only left-handed batter to homer off Clements last season. . . . Opposing left-handers had outhit right-handers in his two previous major-league seasons. . . . Opponents have hit .313 with runners in scoring position over past three seasons, but only .130 (3-for-23) with the bases loaded.

Edwin Correa

Texas Rangers — Throws Right

	W–L	ERA	AB	H	HR	BB	SO	BA	SA	OBA
Season	3-5	7.59	279	83	17	52	61	.297	.552	.412
vs. Left-Handers			136	33	5	22	30	.243	.404	.350
vs. Right-Handers			143	50	12	30	31	.350	.692	.469
Home	2-1	8.49	123	39	10	16	30	.317	.610	.404
Road	1-4	6.92	156	44	7	36	31	.282	.506	.418
Grass	3-4	8.55	221	71	17	37	46	.321	.620	.425
Artificial Turf	0-1	4.41	58	12	0	15	15	.207	.293	.368
April	1-1	3.24	91	22	2	11	22	.242	.374	.337
May	0-4	11.45	93	33	7	25	17	.355	.688	.492
June	2-0	8.69	81	24	7	12	21	.296	.593	.387
July	0-0	8.10	14	4	1	4	1	.286	.571	.444
August			0	0	0	0	0	—	—	—
Sept./Oct.			0	0	0	0	0	—	—	—
Leading Off Inn.			66	20	5	9	11	.303	.591	.395
Runners On			118	32	9	32	22	.271	.568	.425
Runners/Scor. Pos.			79	20	5	24	13	.253	.532	.419
Runners On/2 Out			51	15	5	17	9	.294	.686	.471
Scor. Pos./2 Out			40	11	3	13	7	.275	.625	.453
Late Inning Pressure			14	6	1	0	3	.429	.714	.429
Leading Off			4	0	0	0	1	.000	.000	.000
Runners On			3	2	0	0	1	.667	1.000	.667
Runners/Scor. Pos.			0	0	0	0	0			
First 9 Batters			109	32	6	21	24	.294	.523	.412
Second 9 Batters			101	32	8	18	22	.317	.673	.426
All Batters Thereafter			69	19	3	13	15	.275	.420	.393

Loves to face: Ernest Riles (0-for-9)
Hates to face: Cal Ripken (.714, 5-for-7)
Ground outs-to-air outs ratio: 0.97 last season, 1.05 for career. . . . Additional statistics: 2 double-play ground outs in 55 opportunities, 16 doubles, 2 triples in 70.0 innings last season. . . . Opponents averaged 12.54 extra-base hits per 100 at bats, highest rate among 139 qualifying pitchers in the majors. . . . Allowed 18 first-inning runs in 15 starts, 2d-highest average in A.L. (minimum: 15 GS). . . . Batting support: 5.47 runs per start. . . . Opposing right-handers outhit lefties by 107 points, 2d-largest such difference in A.L. last season (minimum: 100 AB each way). . . . Stress fracture in his right shoulder ended his season on July 5. . . . Yearly opponents' batting averages leading off innings: .143, .230, .303. . . . Youngest player on a major-league opening-day roster in 1987.

Steve Crawford

Boston Red Sox — Throws Right

	W–L	ERA	AB	H	HR	BB	SO	BA	SA	OBA
Season	5-4	5.33	290	91	13	32	43	.314	.524	.386
vs. Left-Handers			132	44	6	16	17	.333	.538	.405
vs. Right-Handers			158	47	7	16	26	.297	.513	.369
Home	5-1	4.54	146	44	6	14	21	.301	.507	.366
Road	0-3	6.17	144	47	7	18	22	.326	.542	.405
Grass	5-4	5.06	235	72	11	23	37	.306	.528	.371
Artificial Turf	0-0	6.43	55	19	2	9	6	.345	.509	.446
April	0-1	7.02	68	20	3	1	17	.294	.529	.324
May	2-0	2.13	48	12	1	9	8	.250	.396	.368
June	2-1	10.32	49	20	4	9	9	.408	.755	.500
July	0-0	0.96	34	7	1	3	3	.206	.324	.270
August	1-1	7.00	39	15	2	6	3	.385	.615	.467
Sept./Oct.	0-1	3.95	52	17	2	4	3	.327	.481	.375
Leading Off Inn.			59	18	3	8	9	.305	.492	.397
Runners On			145	51	9	15	20	.352	.634	.416
Runners/Scor. Pos.			86	30	8	12	15	.349	.721	.429
Runners On/2 Out			62	24	4	6	9	.387	.710	.449
Scor. Pos./2 Out			42	18	4	5	9	.429	.857	.489
Late Inning Pressure			23	6	1	5	4	.261	.435	.393
Leading Off			6	3	1	2	1	.500	.625	
Runners On			6	1	0	2	1	.167	.333	.375
Runners/Scor. Pos.			1	0	0	2	1	.000	.000	.667
First 9 Batters			203	63	9	24	32	.310	.527	.383
Second 9 Batters			80	26	4	8	11	.325	.525	.400
All Batters Thereafter			7	2	0	0	0	.286	.429	.286

Loves to face: Pat Tabler (0-for-9)
Hates to face: Jesse Barfield (.357, 5-for-14, 1 2B, 4 HR)
Ground outs-to-air outs ratio: 2.19 last season, 1.68 for career. . . . Additional statistics: 13 double-play ground outs in 72 opportunities, 20 doubles, 1 triple in 72.2 innings last season. . . . Faced 324 batters, only two while protecting leads of three runs or less in the eighth inning or later. . . . Didn't appear in a save situation last season; earned 16 saves in 29 opportunities over two previous seasons. . . . Career record of 12–6 at Fenway, 7–10 on the road. . . . Yearly opponents' batting averages (and ERAs) since 1984: .286 (3.34), .289 (3.76), .308 (3.92), .314 (5.33). . . . Has faced 63 batters with the bases loaded, never walked in a run or allowed a grand slam. . . . Most innings pitched of any active pitcher with an opponents' career batting average of over .300.

Chuck Crim

Milwaukee Brewers — Throws Right

	W–L	ERA	AB	H	HR	BB	SO	BA	SA	OBA
Season	6-8	3.67	500	133	15	39	56	.266	.390	.322
vs. Left-Handers			227	65	9	24	27	.286	.436	.357
vs. Right-Handers			273	68	6	15	29	.249	.352	.292
Home	4-4	3.19	263	71	4	21	31	.270	.357	.324
Road	2-4	4.19	237	62	11	18	25	.262	.426	.320
Grass	6-6	3.39	424	113	9	35	49	.267	.363	.326
Artificial Turf	0-2	5.40	76	20	6	4	7	.263	.539	.300
April	2-1	4.08	65	17	2	6	8	.262	.400	.333
May	0-0	2.89	73	17	1	3	7	.233	.315	.263
June	1-4	5.63	128	40	6	12	13	.313	.500	.373
July	1-0	1.15	59	14	1	4	7	.237	.288	.286
August	1-1	3.96	93	24	2	11	10	.258	.376	.343
Sept./Oct.	1-2	2.57	82	21	3	3	11	.256	.366	.282
Leading Off Inn.			112	31	7	8	15	.277	.518	.331
Runners On			228	59	6	24	28	.259	.377	.331
Runners/Scor. Pos.			125	31	3	18	17	.248	.368	.345
Runners On/2 Out			100	23	0	14	11	.230	.240	.325
Scor. Pos./2 Out			62	12	0	10	9	.194	.210	.306
Late Inning Pressure			150	40	3	13	20	.267	.347	.326
Leading Off			37	8	1	4	7	.216	.324	.293
Runners On			62	18	2	9	10	.290	.403	.380
Runners/Scor. Pos.			33	7	2	7	7	.212	.394	.350
First 9 Batters			361	93	9	26	46	.258	.363	.313
Second 9 Batters			116	34	6	10	9	.293	.474	.346
All Batters Thereafter			23	6	0	3	1	.261	.391	.346

Loves to face: Darrell Evans (0-for-5, 3 SO)
Hates to face: Jerry Browne (2-for-2, 1 BB)
Ground outs-to-air outs ratio: 1.38 last season, his first in majors. . . . Additional statistics: 17 double-play ground outs in 109 opportunities, 15 doubles, 1 triple in 130.0 innings last season. . . . Ranked third among major-league rookies with 12 saves (in 15 opportunities). Didn't record his first save until July 30, but ranked fifth in the A.L. after the All-Star break. . . . Record of 1–4 with a 5.19 ERA in five starts; 5–4, 3.29 ERA, in 48 relief appearances. . . . Allowed five hits in 14 at bats (.357) with the bases loaded. . . . Was born July 23, 1961, the day of the longest doubleheader in major-league baseball history. Detroit and Kansas City took six hours and 50 minutes to play two games, including a 17–14 nightcap.

John Davis

Kansas City Royals — Throws Right

	W–L	ERA	AB	H	HR	BB	SO	BA	SA	OBA
Season	5-2	2.27	149	29	0	26	24	.195	.248	.315
vs. Left-Handers			66	16	0	13	11	.242	.288	.358
vs. Right-Handers			83	13	0	13	13	.157	.217	.280
Home	2-1	1.83	67	15	0	10	9	.224	.313	.325
Road	3-1	2.63	82	14	0	16	15	.171	.195	.307
Grass	2-1	2.37	63	10	0	12	14	.159	.175	.295
Artificial Turf	3-1	2.19	86	19	0	14	10	.221	.302	.330
April			0	0	0	0	0	—	—	—
May			0	0	0	0	0	—	—	—
June			0	0	0	0	0	—	—	—
July	0-0	4.91	11	1	0	6	3	.091	.182	.389
August	3-0	1.67	67	15	0	10	10	.224	.284	.329
Sept./Oct.	2-2	2.66	71	13	0	10	11	.183	.225	.284
Leading Off Inn.			33	3	0	4	5	.091	.121	.189
Runners On			70	16	0	15	10	.229	.286	.356
Runners/Scor. Pos.			44	10	0	14	6	.227	.295	.397
Runners On/2 Out			33	11	0	9	6	.333	.424	.476
Scor. Pos./2 Out			22	8	0	9	4	.364	.455	.548
Late Inning Pressure			79	16	0	14	13	.203	.253	.319
Leading Off			18	1	0	1	2	.056	.056	.105
Runners On			34	9	0	10	5	.265	.353	.422
Runners/Scor. Pos.			22	6	0	9	3	.273	.364	.469
First 9 Batters			128	25	0	24	21	.195	.242	.318
Second 9 Batters			16	3	0	2	2	.188	.313	.316
All Batters Thereafter			5	1	0	0	0	.200	.200	.200

Loves to face: Ruben Sierra (0-for-3, 2 SO)
Hates to face: Pat Sheridan (.500, 1-for-2, 1 2B, 1 BB)
Ground outs-to-air outs ratio: 2.18 last season, his first in majors. . . Additional statistics: 5 double-play ground outs in 32 opportunities, 6 doubles, 1 triple in 43.2 innings last season. . . . Earned two saves in seven opportunities. . . . Faced 181 batters, but only 19 protecting leads of three runs or less in the eighth inning or later. . . . Spent six years in the minors with a winning record only once, a 7–1 mark in 1982, when he compiled a 6.14 ERA for Butte, allowing the most earned runs in the Pioneer League (55). . . . Career total of 43.2 innings pitched is the most of any active pitcher who hasn't allowed a home run. . . . Was born January 5, 1963, the day Charlie Hough turned 15 and Rogers Hornsby died. . . . You think it's easy writing notes about John Davis?

Jose DeLeon

Throws Right

Chicago White Sox	W–L	ERA	AB	H	HR	BB	SO	BA	SA	OBA
Season	11-12	4.02	770	177	24	97	153	.230	.370	.322
vs. Left-Handers			397	101	13	59	64	.254	.393	.351
vs. Right-Handers			373	76	11	38	89	.204	.346	.290
Home	3-7	5.12	364	87	9	46	79	.239	.368	.329
Road	8-5	3.08	406	90	15	51	74	.222	.372	.315
Grass	7-10	4.50	610	148	17	79	112	.243	.369	.331
Artificial Turf	4-2	2.35	160	29	7	18	41	.181	.375	.284
April	2-2	2.60	93	13	2	20	24	.140	.247	.304
May	2-1	3.58	142	31	6	19	20	.218	.401	.311
June	1-4	5.64	117	30	5	16	17	.256	.410	.346
July	0-2	4.15	114	27	3	16	18	.237	.360	.336
August	3-2	5.35	138	39	0	12	33	.283	.341	.354
Sept./Oct.	3-1	3.02	166	37	8	14	41	.223	.416	.286
Leading Off Inn.			194	48	7	20	34	.247	.402	.330
Runners On			312	73	4	49	62	.234	.321	.336
Runners/Scor. Pos.			189	47	4	30	33	.249	.376	.345
Runners On/2 Out			133	33	2	23	31	.248	.338	.359
Scor. Pos./2 Out			90	25	2	18	17	.278	.400	.398
Late Inning Pressure			79	20	2	12	12	.253	.392	.359
Leading Off			21	6	1	4	3	.286	.476	.423
Runners On			28	7	0	5	6	.250	.393	.364
Runners/Scor. Pos.			18	6	0	2	3	.333	.444	.400
First 9 Batters			263	62	11	23	61	.236	.395	.303
Second 9 Batters			237	54	3	27	42	.228	.312	.310
All Batters Thereafter			270	61	10	47	50	.226	.396	.348

Loves to face: Nick Esasky (0-for-14, 8 SO)
Hates to face: Craig Reynolds (.471, 8-for-17, 1 HR)
Ground outs-to-air outs ratio: 0.83 last season, 0.82 for career. . . .
Additional statistics: 12 double-play ground outs in 154 opportunities, 28 doubles, 4 triples in 206.0 innings last season. . . . Allowed 16 first-inning runs in 31 starts. . . . Batting support: 4.55 runs per start. . . . Road-game ERA ranked 2d in A.L. last season. . . . Willie Wilson led off DeLeon's season with a bunt single. DeLeon didn't allow a hit to the next 39 batters he faced, longest streak in the A.L. last season. . . . Of 13 pitchers in baseball history with 100+ starts and more strikeouts than hits allowed, only DeLeon has a losing record. The other five active pitchers who meet those criteria (Clemens, Fernandez, Gooden, Ryan, Soto) have a composite winning percentage of .569; DeLeon's is .368 (32–55).

Ken Dixon

Throws Right

Baltimore Orioles	W–L	ERA	AB	H	HR	BB	SO	BA	SA	OBA
Season	7-10	6.43	439	128	31	27	91	.292	.565	.333
vs. Left-Handers			214	60	14	17	40	.280	.556	.332
vs. Right-Handers			225	68	17	10	51	.302	.573	.333
Home	3-6	6.59	239	72	18	15	55	.301	.590	.341
Road	4-4	6.26	200	56	13	12	36	.280	.535	.322
Grass	6-7	6.31	367	107	26	23	78	.292	.556	.333
Artificial Turf	1-3	7.00	72	21	5	4	13	.292	.611	.329
April	1-2	6.66	103	30	7	6	23	.291	.524	.330
May	2-1	4.57	83	19	3	8	23	.229	.410	.293
June	0-4	10.24	91	32	10	7	17	.352	.791	.398
July	0-1	6.55	50	18	2	3	7	.360	.500	.400
August	4-0	2.67	100	22	5	1	19	.220	.420	.228
Sept./Oct.	0-2	43.20	12	7	4	2	2	.583	1.750	.643
Leading Off Inn.			101	36	12	5	15	.356	.792	.387
Runners On			174	53	12	14	43	.305	.552	.356
Runners/Scor. Pos.			117	34	7	9	32	.291	.504	.341
Runners On/2 Out			81	29	6	9	16	.358	.642	.422
Scor. Pos./2 Out			56	19	3	6	14	.339	.554	.403
Late Inning Pressure			107	26	5	10	28	.243	.430	.308
Leading Off			21	5	1	2	3	.238	.429	.304
Runners On			50	15	2	7	14	.300	.460	.386
Runners/Scor. Pos.			35	9	1	6	10	.257	.343	.366
First 9 Batters			232	64	13	19	63	.276	.509	.329
Second 9 Batters			143	36	12	6	20	.252	.566	.280
All Batters Thereafter			64	28	6	2	8	.438	.766	.463

Loves to face: Chris Bando (0-for-11)
Hates to face: Dave Winfield (.583, 7-for-12, 4 HR)
Ground outs-to-air outs ratio: 0.76 last season, 0.73 for career. . . .
Additional statistics: 7 double-play ground outs in 59 opportunities, 21 doubles, 3 triples in 105.0 innings last season. . . . Allowed 13 first-inning runs in 15 starts, 4th-highest average in A.L. (minimum: 15 GS). . . . Batting support: 5.27 runs per start. . . . Record of 5–6 in 15 starts; he averaged less than five innings per start. . . . Losing pitcher in three consecutive relief appearances (June 1–9). . . . Recorded five saves, all in the month of May. . . . Career record of 4–11 with a 5.95 ERA in day games; 22–17, 4.20 ERA at night. . . . Career record of 1–9 in June, 25–19 in all other months combined. . . . Opponents' slugging percentage was the highest among 239 qualifying pitchers in the majors last season.

Richard Dotson

Throws Right

Chicago White Sox	W–L	ERA	AB	H	HR	BB	SO	BA	SA	OBA
Season	11-12	4.17	807	201	24	86	114	.249	.399	.320
vs. Left-Handers			430	108	15	48	63	.251	.419	.326
vs. Right-Handers			377	93	9	38	51	.247	.377	.314
Home	6-8	4.35	421	109	14	40	58	.259	.409	.323
Road	5-4	3.99	386	92	10	46	56	.238	.389	.318
Grass	9-11	4.07	706	174	22	72	101	.246	.395	.315
Artificial Turf	2-1	4.91	101	27	2	14	13	.267	.426	.357
April	1-2	4.99	118	35	1	13	21	.297	.424	.364
May	2-2	3.43	138	27	5	15	21	.196	.362	.275
June	2-1	4.32	160	40	6	13	28	.250	.425	.306
July	3-2	4.57	168	38	8	19	21	.226	.411	.303
August	2-4	3.45	181	48	3	20	20	.265	.348	.337
Sept./Oct.	1-1	5.40	42	13	1	6	3	.310	.524	.396
Leading Off Inn.			199	42	4	24	20	.211	.332	.296
Runners On			333	92	9	33	53	.276	.429	.339
Runners/Scor. Pos.			151	44	5	22	24	.291	.457	.375
Runners On/2 Out			129	33	3	15	22	.256	.403	.333
Scor. Pos./2 Out			70	14	2	12	14	.200	.343	.317
Late Inning Pressure			107	32	6	5	14	.299	.533	.330
Leading Off			30	8	1	0	3	.267	.500	.267
Runners On			35	11	1	3	4	.314	.457	.368
Runners/Scor. Pos.			17	5	1	3	3	.294	.529	.400
First 9 Batters			233	55	7	37	38	.236	.399	.339
Second 9 Batters			244	52	5	19	37	.213	.316	.268
All Batters Thereafter			330	94	12	30	39	.285	.461	.344

Loves to face: Donnie Hill (0-for-10)
Hates to face: Ernie Whitt (.362, 17-for-47, 4 HR)
Ground outs-to-air outs ratio: 1.11 last season, 1.32 for career. . . .
Additional statistics: 19 double-play ground outs in 181 opportunities, 35 doubles, 7 triples in 211.1 innings last season. . . . Allowed 13 first-inning runs in 31 starts. . . . Batting support: 3.97 runs per start, 4th-lowest average in A.L. (minimum: 15 GS). . . . Led the White Sox' staff with an average of 6.82 innings per start. . . . Opponents stole only two bases in 10 attempts, lowest success rate of any A.L. pitcher (minimum: 10 attempts). . . . Only pitcher to shut out the Blue Jays at Exhibition Stadium last season. . . . Hasn't had a winning season since he went 22–7 in 1983; only two other pitchers have had losing records in each of last four seasons: Jose DeLeon and Ernie Camacho (who's done it for five years).

Dennis Eckersley

Throws Right

Oakland As	W–L	ERA	AB	H	HR	BB	SO	BA	SA	OBA
Season	6-8	3.03	434	99	11	17	113	.228	.362	.260
vs. Left-Handers			184	50	5	11	32	.272	.429	.313
vs. Right-Handers			250	49	6	6	81	.196	.312	.220
Home	6-3	1.31	214	33	4	10	69	.154	.248	.191
Road	0-5	5.03	220	66	7	7	44	.300	.473	.328
Grass	6-8	3.18	359	81	10	14	94	.226	.365	.257
Artificial Turf	0-0	2.33	75	18	1	3	19	.240	.347	.278
April	1-1	2.81	55	11	0	3	12	.200	.236	.241
May	2-3	4.33	108	28	4	4	22	.259	.435	.296
June	2-0	1.11	90	18	0	4	22	.200	.222	.234
July	1-1	3.55	46	10	2	2	13	.217	.391	.245
August	0-1	2.49	80	17	3	2	26	.213	.388	.241
Sept./Oct.	0-2	4.50	55	15	2	2	18	.273	.509	.293
Leading Off Inn.			104	24	3	1	28	.231	.365	.245
Runners On			177	35	5	11	43	.198	.322	.245
Runners/Scor. Pos.			110	19	1	8	28	.173	.236	.230
Runners On/2 Out			85	17	3	7	22	.200	.329	.261
Scor. Pos./2 Out			60	10	1	4	17	.167	.233	.219
Late Inning Pressure			176	42	6	8	50	.239	.386	.270
Leading Off			47	11	1	0	10	.234	.298	.234
Runners On			64	13	3	8	20	.203	.391	.288
Runners/Scor. Pos.			38	7	0	5	14	.184	.211	.273
First 9 Batters			324	74	9	13	91	.228	.373	.259
Second 9 Batters			91	17	2	2	20	.187	.275	.213
All Batters Thereafter			19	8	0	2	2	.421	.579	.478

Loves to face: Frank White (.091, 4-for-44,)
Hates to face: Kent Hrbek (.429, 9-for-21, 2 HR)
Ground outs-to-air outs ratio: 1.02 last season, 0.71 for career. . . .
Additional statistics: 6 double-play ground outs in 66 opportunities, 23 doubles, 1 triple in 115.2 innings last season. . . . Earned 16 saves in 19 opportunities. . . . Allowed an average of 1.38 walks per nine innings, lowest rate among major league relievers (minimum: 30 games). . . . Opponents' batting average with runners in scoring position was the lowest of his 13-year career. . . . Natural for relief role: has held opponents to lower batting averages with two outs and runners in scoring position than at other times in 11 consecutive seasons. . . . Opponents' career batting averages: .275 by left-handed batters, .224 by right-handers. . . . Opponents were 0-for-11 with the bases loaded last season.

Mark Eichhorn

Toronto Blue Jays — Throws Right

	W–L	ERA	AB	H	HR	BB	SO	BA	SA	OBA
Season	10-6	3.17	471	110	14	52	96	.234	.374	.315
vs. Left-Handers			183	47	6	25	30	.257	.410	.350
vs. Right-Handers			288	63	8	27	66	.219	.351	.292
Home	6-1	2.27	248	54	4	16	48	.218	.310	.268
Road	4-5	4.18	223	56	10	36	48	.251	.444	.362
Grass	3-3	4.74	165	45	10	24	39	.273	.509	.369
Artificial Turf	7-3	2.36	306	65	4	28	57	.212	.301	.284
April	3-1	2.19	91	18	2	10	20	.198	.330	.277
May	3-1	2.57	74	15	1	12	18	.203	.297	.326
June	2-1	5.40	100	31	7	6	21	.310	.570	.361
July	1-2	3.07	57	13	0	13	10	.228	.263	.371
August	1-1	2.55	86	18	4	6	14	.209	.384	.263
Sept./Oct.	0-0	3.06	63	15	0	5	13	.238	.302	.300
Leading Off Inn.			108	22	1	5	23	.204	.296	.239
Runners On			204	49	7	36	41	.240	.392	.354
Runners/Scor. Pos.			145	25	3	32	31	.172	.269	.322
Runners On/2 Out			102	23	2	22	26	.225	.373	.363
Scor. Pos./2 Out			78	13	1	20	20	.167	.256	.337
Late Inning Pressure			170	39	4	20	46	.229	.353	.309
Leading Off			44	12	1	2	11	.273	.455	.304
Runners On			60	13	1	14	15	.217	.300	.360
Runners/Scor. Pos.			43	8	1	12	12	.186	.279	.357
First 9 Batters			420	98	12	46	92	.233	.367	.312
Second 9 Batters			51	12	2	6	4	.235	.431	.339
All Batters Thereafter			0	0	0	0	0	—	—	—

Loves to face: Pete Incaviglia (0-for-8, 4 SO)
Hates to face: Ruppert Jones (.714, 5-for-7, 2 2B, 1 HR)
Ground outs-to-air outs ratio: 1.46 last season, 1.67 for career. . . .
Additional statistics: 7 double-play ground outs in 84 opportunities, 20 doubles, 2 triples in 127.2 innings last season. . . . Faced 540 batters, the most by an A.L. reliever (and same number as N.L. leader, Lance McCullers), but only 24 while protecting leads of three runs or less in the eighth inning or later. . . . Career batting average of .253 by opposing left-handers, .189 by right-handers. . . . Opponents' batting averages with runners in scoring position (1982, 1986, 1987): .227, .194, .172. (He didn't pitch in the majors from 1983-85). . . . Has walked eight of the 58 batters faced with the bases loaded. . . . ERA of 2.09 on artificial turf is lowest in majors over past three seasons (minimum: 150 IP).

Steve Farr

Kansas City Royals — Throws Right

	W–L	ERA	AB	H	HR	BB	SO	BA	SA	OBA
Season	4-3	4.15	358	97	9	44	88	.271	.416	.351
vs. Left-Handers			146	40	4	22	34	.274	.432	.369
vs. Right-Handers			212	57	5	22	54	.269	.406	.339
Home	2-1	4.37	175	45	3	30	43	.257	.394	.364
Road	2-2	3.94	183	52	6	14	45	.284	.437	.338
Grass	1-2	4.67	115	36	5	10	29	.313	.504	.375
Artificial Turf	3-1	3.94	243	61	4	34	59	.251	.374	.341
April	0-1	8.53	57	22	1	6	12	.386	.544	.455
May	2-0	1.93	71	16	1	7	22	.224	.313	.297
June	0-1	3.54	78	23	2	5	22	.295	.462	.333
July	1-1	5.40	77	22	5	10	13	.286	.506	.368
August	0-0	11.57	20	8	0	7	5	.400	.700	.536
Sept./Oct.	1-0	0.55	59	7	0	9	14	.119	.136	.235
Leading Off Inn.			76	21	1	6	15	.276	.421	.329
Runners On			197	52	4	19	52	.264	.381	.327
Runners/Scor. Pos.			121	33	3	13	34	.273	.405	.341
Runners On/2 Out			83	16	0	9	28	.193	.229	.272
Scor. Pos./2 Out			56	12	0	7	19	.214	.250	.302
Late Inning Pressure			110	36	6	13	21	.327	.564	.395
Leading Off			26	8	0	4	5	.308	.462	.400
Runners On			53	17	3	4	10	.321	.547	.362
Runners/Scor. Pos.			25	10	2	3	6	.400	.680	.448
First 9 Batters			277	79	8	38	68	.285	.455	.373
Second 9 Batters			80	18	1	6	20	.225	.288	.276
All Batters Thereafter			1	0	0	0	0	.000	.000	.000

Loves to face: Dwayne Murphy (0-for-7)
Hates to face: Bill Schroeder (.667, 4-for-6, 2 2B, 2 HR)
Ground outs-to-air outs ratio: 0.91 last season, 1.13 for career. . . .
Additional statistics: 5 double-play ground outs in 86 opportunities, 19 doubles, 3 triples in 91.0 innings last season. . . . Faced 408 batters, but only 28 while protecting leads of three runs or less in the eighth inning or later. . . . Earned only one save in six opportunities, compared to 8-for-10 in 1986. . . . Opponents were 7-for-16 with the bases loaded, including two doubles, a triple, and a grand slam. The only other A.L. pitcher whose opponents hit for the cycle with the bags full was Steve Carlton. . . . Career record of 5–15 with a 4.52 ERA on grass fields; 12–4, 3.17 ERA, on artificial turf. . . . Opponents' career average of .282 in Late-Inning Pressure Situations, .235 in unpressured situations.

Chuck Finley

California Angels — Throws Left

	W–L	ERA	AB	H	HR	BB	SO	BA	SA	OBA
Season	2-7	4.67	355	102	7	43	63	.287	.411	.367
vs. Left-Handers			135	35	1	8	29	.259	.356	.299
vs. Right-Handers			220	67	6	35	34	.305	.445	.405
Home	2-4	5.23	162	45	3	19	36	.278	.420	.357
Road	0-3	4.20	193	57	4	24	27	.295	.404	.376
Grass	2-6	4.52	315	85	7	39	60	.270	.397	.354
Artificial Turf	0-1	6.00	40	17	0	4	3	.425	.525	.477
April	0-2	3.46	49	12	0	9	13	.245	.286	.362
May	0-0	6.97	44	15	0	8	9	.341	.432	.442
June	0-1	4.66	41	14	1	5	7	.341	.488	.404
July	2-1	4.97	96	26	3	6	23	.271	.438	.314
August	0-2	2.20	64	17	1	5	5	.266	.375	.338
Sept./Oct.	0-1	6.19	61	18	2	10	6	.295	.443	.397
Leading Off Inn.			82	26	2	6	13	.317	.427	.378
Runners On			164	50	2	26	32	.305	.439	.399
Runners/Scor. Pos.			91	27	1	20	17	.297	.451	.421
Runners On/2 Out			59	14	0	16	14	.237	.305	.400
Scor. Pos./2 Out			36	8	0	14	10	.222	.250	.440
Late Inning Pressure			73	17	1	9	14	.233	.329	.317
Leading Off			20	3	0	1	2	.150	.150	.190
Runners On			27	10	0	5	4	.370	.519	.469
Runners/Scor. Pos.			19	7	0	3	3	.368	.579	.455
First 9 Batters			217	61	5	35	43	.281	.406	.385
Second 9 Batters			121	35	1	6	17	.289	.397	.323
All Batters Thereafter			17	6	1	2	3	.353	.588	.421

Loves to face: Bill Madlock (0-for-4, 3 SO)
Hates to face: Mike Heath (.800, 4-for-5)
Ground outs-to-air outs ratio: 1.15 last season, 1.16 for career. . . .
Additional statistics: 10 double-play ground outs in 85 opportunities, 23 doubles, 0 triples in 90.2 innings last season. . . . Led A.L. with 0.61 ERA in four games vs. Orioles. . . . Allowed only one stolen base in seven attempts last season, lowest rate in A.L. (minimum: 5 attempts). . . . If you want to get something done you've got to do it yourself: Angels had 2–30 record in games in which Finley relieved; he was personally credited with both victories. . . . That doesn't leave many chances for saves: Finley is one of three pitchers in majors with 20+ relief appearances in each of last two seasons but no saves in either; the others: Nate Snell and Ed Vande Berg. What do you mean, "Who are they?" . . . .No relation to the Mule.

Mike Flanagan

Orioles/Blue Jays — Throws Left

	W–L	ERA	AB	H	HR	BB	SO	BA	SA	OBA
Season	6-8	4.06	561	148	12	51	93	.264	.408	.325
vs. Left-Handers			100	25	0	9	16	.250	.270	.312
vs. Right-Handers			461	123	12	42	77	.267	.438	.327
Home	5-3	3.32	315	82	5	26	58	.260	.384	.317
Road	1-5	5.03	246	66	7	25	35	.268	.439	.335
Grass	2-5	4.37	357	89	8	35	57	.249	.401	.316
Artificial Turf	4-3	3.47	204	59	4	16	36	.289	.422	.341
April	0-3	5.40	95	21	5	10	14	.221	.484	.295
May	0-2	8.27	70	24	1	6	7	.343	.486	.395
June			0	0	0	0	0	—	—	—
July	1-0	2.89	75	22	0	5	12	.293	.360	.333
August	2-1	4.15	127	35	3	15	17	.276	.433	.352
Sept./Oct.	3-2	2.37	194	46	3	15	43	.237	.345	.292
Leading Off Inn.			139	36	5	16	24	.259	.453	.335
Runners On			237	62	3	15	41	.262	.359	.304
Runners/Scor. Pos.			128	30	2	10	24	.234	.352	.288
Runners On/2 Out			95	22	2	6	17	.232	.358	.277
Scor. Pos./2 Out			58	11	2	4	12	.190	.379	.242
Late Inning Pressure			67	19	2	7	10	.284	.433	.351
Leading Off			20	4	1	2	3	.200	.450	.273
Runners On			22	8	0	2	1	.364	.409	.417
Runners/Scor. Pos.			10	5	0	2	0	.500	.600	.583
First 9 Batters			177	52	3	18	36	.294	.429	.359
Second 9 Batters			179	46	5	14	23	.257	.413	.309
All Batters Thereafter			205	50	4	19	34	.244	.385	.308

Loves to face: Bob Boone (.091, 2-for-22)
Hates to face: Wayne Tolleson (.471, 8-for-17, 1 HR)
Ground outs-to-air outs ratio: 1.06 last season, 1.29 for career. . . .
Additional statistics: 10 double-play ground outs in 112 opportunities, 39 doubles, 3 triples in 144.0 innings last season. . . . Allowed 12 first-inning runs in 23 starts. . . . Batting support: 4.65 runs per start. . . . Fifth straight season with a winning record. . . . Pitched 11 innings in final appearance of season, his longest outing since August 15, 1979, when he tossed a 12-inning, complete-game victory over Chicago. . . . Career winning percentage of .672 (80–39) at Memorial Stadium, .463 (62–72) elsewhere. . . . Career batting average of .230 by opposing left-handed batters, .272 by right-handers. Has allowed only one home run to a left-handed batter over the last three seasons: Greg Walker, July 24, 1986.

Willie Fraser
California Angels   Throws Right

	W–L	ERA	AB	H	HR	BB	SO	BA	SA	OBA
Season	10-10	3.92	666	160	26	63	106	.240	.414	.310
vs. Left-Handers			324	81	12	37	44	.250	.423	.331
vs. Right-Handers			342	79	14	26	62	.231	.406	.290
Home	2-6	4.48	269	64	11	34	48	.238	.383	.324
Road	8-4	3.54	397	96	15	29	58	.242	.436	.300
Grass	7-9	4.25	540	132	21	51	85	.244	.419	.314
Artificial Turf	3-1	2.60	126	28	5	12	21	.222	.397	.290
April	1-1	3.38	76	18	4	12	13	.237	.408	.356
May	1-1	3.07	109	24	5	10	14	.220	.376	.283
June	3-3	3.88	174	38	7	13	22	.218	.420	.279
July	1-2	4.74	70	15	4	11	13	.214	.443	.325
August	3-1	5.48	82	22	5	7	15	.268	.524	.326
Sept./Oct.	1-2	3.66	155	43	1	10	29	.277	.368	.323
Leading Off Inn.			157	34	4	17	19	.217	.357	.305
Runners On			284	69	9	21	50	.243	.396	.296
Runners/Scor. Pos.			160	38	3	13	31	.238	.331	.292
Runners On/2 Out			125	30	4	11	19	.240	.384	.301
Scor. Pos./2 Out			80	18	2	8	12	.225	.338	.295
Late Inning Pressure			61	14	2	6	13	.230	.361	.319
Leading Off			16	3	1	1	2	.188	.438	.278
Runners On			26	7	0	3	6	.269	.308	.345
Runners/Scor. Pos.			18	6	0	2	5	.333	.333	.400
First 9 Batters			271	62	10	33	51	.229	.387	.315
Second 9 Batters			211	58	10	17	31	.275	.479	.335
All Batters Thereafter			184	40	6	13	24	.217	.380	.274

Loves to face: Steve Balboni (0-for-9)
Hates to face: Oddibe McDowell (.750, 3-for-4, 1 2B, 1 HR)
Ground outs-to-air outs ratio: 0.65, 10th-lowest in A.L. last season (minimum: 200 BFP), 0.66 for career. . . . Additional statistics: 10 double-play ground outs in 130 opportunities, 34 doubles, 2 triples in 176.2 innings last season. . . . Allowed 4 first-inning runs in 23 starts, lowest average in A.L. (minimum: 15 GS). . . . Batting support: 4.70 runs per start. . . . One of three rookies to complete five games last season. The others: Bill Long and Mike Dunne. . . . Pitched the most innings of any rookie in majors. . . . Record of 7–9 (4.34 ERA) in 23 starts, 3–1 (2.27 ERA) in 13 relief appearances. . . . Allowed one home run for every 6.8 inning for the season, but surrendered only one in his last 47.2 innings. . . . One of five A.L. pitchers to be credited with both a save and a shutout last season.

George Frazier
Minnesota Twins   Throws Right

	W–L	ERA	AB	H	HR	BB	SO	BA	SA	OBA
Season	5-5	4.98	299	77	9	51	58	.258	.398	.359
vs. Left-Handers			169	42	5	26	32	.249	.402	.345
vs. Right-Handers			130	35	4	25	26	.269	.392	.377
Home	4-1	4.15	145	34	4	20	28	.234	.366	.329
Road	1-4	5.74	154	43	5	31	30	.279	.429	.385
Grass	1-3	5.29	126	37	4	23	25	.294	.429	.386
Artificial Turf	4-2	4.75	173	40	5	28	33	.231	.376	.338
April	2-2	3.86	41	10	0	5	8	.244	.268	.319
May	3-0	4.82	69	18	1	9	17	.261	.362	.341
June	0-1	6.92	47	12	4	15	13	.255	.532	.422
July	0-2	7.24	50	14	1	10	8	.280	.420	.381
August	0-0	1.84	50	11	1	7	6	.220	.320	.322
Sept./Oct.	0-0	5.59	42	12	2	5	6	.286	.500	.362
Leading Off Inn.			65	15	1	10	15	.231	.308	.333
Runners On			158	43	7	21	28	.272	.462	.342
Runners/Scor. Pos.			100	21	4	17	23	.210	.370	.305
Runners On/2 Out			68	14	2	6	10	.206	.324	.280
Scor. Pos./2 Out			49	10	1	5	8	.204	.286	.291
Late Inning Pressure			89	25	1	15	19	.281	.337	.377
Leading Off			20	4	0	4	3	.200	.250	.333
Runners On			46	13	1	9	11	.283	.348	.386
Runners/Scor. Pos.			36	8	1	8	10	.222	.306	.348
First 9 Batters			273	69	9	47	53	.253	.396	.356
Second 9 Batters			26	8	0	4	5	.308	.423	.387
All Batters Thereafter			0	0	0	0	0			

Loves to face: Pete O'Brien (0-for-8)
Hates to face: Garth Iorg (.600, 6-for-10)
Ground outs-to-air outs ratio: 1.00 last season, 1.38 for career. . . . Additional statistics: 7 double-play ground outs in 130 opportunities, 15 doubles, 0 triples in 81.1 innings last season. . . . Twins lost 25 of the last 27 games in which he appeared. . . . Has made 415 relief appearances, but never started a game in the majors. . . . He's nothing if not a survivor. Only nine other pitchers have at least one save in every season during the 1980s, but his career-high is eight (1983). . . . Opponents' yearly batting averages with runners in scoring position since 1984: .303, .293, .253, .210. . . . Opposing batters have hit .329 with the bases loaded but only one grand slam in 85 at bats. . . . Complete this progression: Frazier has appeared in post-season play in 1981, 1984, 1987. . . .

Wes Gardner
Boston Red Sox   Throws Right

	W–L	ERA	AB	H	HR	BB	SO	BA	SA	OBA
Season	3-6	5.42	351	98	17	42	70	.279	.493	.358
vs. Left-Handers			162	51	8	28	29	.315	.549	.414
vs. Right-Handers			189	47	9	14	41	.249	.444	.306
Home	2-1	3.10	188	51	4	15	34	.271	.399	.324
Road	1-5	8.26	163	47	13	27	36	.288	.601	.394
Grass	3-4	4.79	276	76	10	34	54	.275	.449	.357
Artificial Turf	0-2	7.85	75	22	7	8	16	.293	.653	.361
April	0-1	3.86	54	15	2	4	14	.278	.444	.328
May	0-1	6.75	44	14	4	6	11	.318	.682	.400
June	0-1	12.27	35	12	4	4	3	.343	.714	.425
July	0-2	5.04	98	27	3	9	18	.276	.439	.343
August	1-0	1.96	62	13	1	7	15	.210	.323	.286
Sept./Oct.	2-1	7.53	58	17	3	12	9	.293	.534	.408
Leading Off Inn.			74	19	3	5	14	.257	.446	.304
Runners On			174	48	9	22	27	.276	.483	.357
Runners/Scor. Pos.			106	24	5	18	16	.226	.396	.333
Runners On/2 Out			74	20	5	7	12	.270	.527	.341
Scor. Pos./2 Out			48	10	4	5	8	.208	.458	.283
Late Inning Pressure			144	41	6	22	34	.285	.465	.377
Leading Off			31	10	1	2	7	.323	.452	.364
Runners On			74	19	3	14	17	.257	.432	.371
Runners/Scor. Pos.			36	8	1	12	8	.222	.306	.408
First 9 Batters			279	78	15	30	59	.280	.498	.351
Second 9 Batters			50	16	2	10	9	.320	.580	.433
All Batters Thereafter			22	4	0	2	2	.182	.227	.250

Loves to face: Larry Parrish (0-for-5, 4 SO)
Hates to face: Tom Brunansky (.600, 3-for-5, 3 HR)
Ground outs-to-air outs ratio: 0.74 last season, 0.86 for career. . . . Additional statistics: 8 double-play ground outs in 87 opportunities, 24 doubles, 0 triples in 89.2 innings last season. . . . Started one game last season, his first start at any level of organized ball since he started seven games for Little Falls of the N.Y.-Penn. League in 1982. . . . Led Bosox with 10 saves (in 14 opportunities). . . . Faced 69 batters while protecting leads of three runs or less in the eighth inning or later, highest total on team (eight more than Schiraldi). . . . Allowed the most home runs of any relief pitcher in the majors last season. . . . Struck out six consecutive right-handed batters on April 15. . . . Opponents' career breakdown: .329 by left-handed batters, .273 by right-handers.

Jerry Don Gleaton
Kansas City Royals   Throws Left

	W–L	ERA	AB	H	HR	BB	SO	BA	SA	OBA
Season	4-4	4.26	176	38	4	28	44	.216	.324	.319
vs. Left-Handers			62	13	1	7	16	.210	.306	.286
vs. Right-Handers			114	25	3	21	28	.219	.333	.336
Home	0-2	3.91	82	15	2	16	22	.183	.317	.313
Road	4-2	4.62	94	23	2	12	22	.245	.330	.324
Grass	3-1	4.35	75	17	2	8	17	.227	.333	.298
Artificial Turf	1-3	4.20	101	21	2	20	27	.208	.317	.333
April			0	0	0	0	0			
May	1-1	3.46	44	7	1	6	10	.159	.250	.260
June	0-1	5.79	35	7	1	5	11	.200	.343	.300
July	0-1	5.40	28	8	0	7	8	.286	.321	.417
August	2-1	4.30	54	13	2	7	13	.241	.407	.328
Sept./Oct.	1-0	1.69	15	3	0	3	2	.200	.200	.300
Leading Off Inn.			36	9	2	3	8	.250	.500	.308
Runners On			86	18	2	15	26	.209	.314	.317
Runners/Scor. Pos.			55	14	2	12	15	.255	.382	.371
Runners On/2 Out			41	10	2	7	11	.244	.439	.354
Scor. Pos./2 Out			31	8	2	5	6	.258	.452	.361
Late Inning Pressure			93	21	1	14	21	.226	.290	.327
Leading Off			19	6	0	0	1	.316	.526	.316
Runners On			49	10	0	9	16	.204	.224	.328
Runners/Scor. Pos.			35	7	0	7	12	.200	.229	.333
First 9 Batters			169	37	4	27	43	.219	.331	.322
Second 9 Batters			7	1	0	1	1	.143	.143	.250
All Batters Thereafter			0	0	0	0	0			

Loves to face: Dale Sveum (0-for-3, 3 SO)
Hates to face: Fred Lynn (.625, 5-for-8, 1 HR)
Ground outs-to-air outs ratio: 0.98 last season, 1.00 for career. . . . Additional statistics: 3 double-play ground outs in 42 opportunities, 5 doubles, 1 triple in 50.2 innings last season. . . . Earned five saves in 11 opportunities, including three against the Blue Jays but none after August 11. . . . Who knows the way to Wrigley Field? Career record of 2–2 with a 2.35 ERA in day games (opponents' batting average: .208); 8–12, 5.31 ERA (.283 BA) in night games. He's allowed 22 home runs, all in night games. . . . Has been a major leaguer in parts of seven years, but has never spent an entire season in the bigs. . . . Has lost all four decisions to the Yankees. . . . Didn't he play one of the daughters on Petticoat Junction? Or was that Joe Don Looney?

Mike Griffin

Baltimore Orioles — Throws Right

	W–L	ERA	AB	H	HR	BB	SO	BA	SA	OBA
Season	3–5	4.36	290	78	9	33	42	.269	.445	.347
vs. Left-Handers			150	40	5	18	17	.267	.467	.347
vs. Right-Handers			140	38	4	15	25	.271	.421	.346
Home	2–2	3.95	167	42	6	18	29	.251	.431	.326
Road	1–3	4.94	123	36	3	15	13	.293	.463	.373
Grass	3–5	4.37	264	71	8	30	41	.269	.451	.347
Artificial Turf	0–0	4.26	26	7	1	3	1	.269	.385	.345
April			0	0	0	0	0	—	—	—
May			0	0	0	0	0	—	—	—
June	0–1	4.50	22	5	1	4	2	.227	.409	.333
July	2–2	3.33	92	25	3	10	12	.272	.457	.346
August	1–2	3.70	95	26	2	10	17	.274	.421	.355
Sept./Oct.	0–0	6.41	81	22	3	9	11	.272	.469	.341
Leading Off Inn.			66	19	2	5	8	.288	.455	.347
Runners On			135	38	4	15	17	.281	.474	.351
Runners/Scor. Pos.			69	19	2	12	8	.275	.464	.369
Runners On/2 Out			57	15	2	10	6	.263	.456	.373
Scor. Pos./2 Out			36	9	2	7	3	.250	.528	.372
Late Inning Pressure			39	8	0	2	6	.205	.256	.279
Leading Off			11	2	0	0	0	.182	.182	.182
Runners On			14	4	0	1	2	.286	.429	.375
Runners/Scor. Pos.			5	2	0	1	0	.400	.600	.500
First 9 Batters			167	46	5	17	26	.275	.443	.348
Second 9 Batters			78	20	2	10	8	.256	.410	.341
All Batters Thereafter			45	12	2	6	8	.267	.511	.352

Loves to face: Harold Reynolds (0-for-4)
Hates to face: Darrell Evans (.571, 4-for-7, 1 HR)
Ground outs-to-air outs ratio: 1.03 last season, 1.16 for career. . . .
Additional statistics: 4 double-play ground outs in 66 opportunities, 16 doubles, 4 triples in 74.1 innings last season. . . . Record of 3–3 (3.25 ERA) in six starts, 0–2 (5.40 ERA) in 17 relief appearances. . . . Last appeared in the majors in 1982 for the Padres. His last major-league victory had been in 1981 for the Cubs. Made his major-league debut in 1979 for the Yankees. . . . Opposing left-handed batters have a career average of .303. . . . Credited with a win in rain-shortened game of July 20, despite pitching only four innings as the starting pitcher. Against the rules? Nope. Rule 10.19b states that the "must pitch five complete innings" rule in respect to the starting pitcher applies only to games of six or more innings.

Mark Gubicza

Kansas City Royals — Throws Right

	W–L	ERA	AB	H	HR	BB	SO	BA	SA	OBA
Season	13–18	3.98	893	231	18	120	166	.259	.384	.347
vs. Left-Handers			512	133	10	72	83	.260	.385	.350
vs. Right-Handers			381	98	8	48	83	.257	.383	.342
Home	7–10	3.75	458	118	7	53	71	.258	.378	.332
Road	6–8	4.22	435	113	11	67	95	.260	.391	.361
Grass	5–7	4.41	364	94	9	58	73	.258	.393	.363
Artificial Turf	8–11	3.68	529	137	9	62	93	.259	.378	.335
April	1–3	4.74	95	23	2	12	11	.242	.400	.324
May	2–2	4.29	135	36	5	21	23	.267	.474	.363
June	3–3	3.94	158	37	2	25	32	.234	.335	.339
July	2–2	2.70	168	45	2	16	31	.268	.339	.330
August	1–5	6.02	152	43	5	26	27	.283	.474	.395
Sept./Oct.	4–3	2.94	185	47	2	20	42	.254	.319	.325
Leading Off Inn.			224	60	1	30	39	.268	.371	.357
Runners On			380	92	11	55	73	.242	.376	.334
Runners/Scor. Pos.			227	48	7	35	50	.211	.357	.309
Runners On/2 Out			154	36	6	28	37	.234	.396	.352
Scor. Pos./2 Out			109	22	5	22	26	.202	.394	.336
Late Inning Pressure			93	29	3	11	21	.312	.441	.381
Leading Off			27	6	0	3	5	.222	.296	.300
Runners On			30	14	3	3	4	.467	.800	.500
Runners/Scor. Pos.			15	5	3	3	3	.333	.933	.421
First 9 Batters			264	70	4	42	43	.265	.371	.367
Second 9 Batters			270	71	5	33	52	.263	.396	.342
All Batters Thereafter			359	90	9	45	71	.251	.384	.334

Loves to face: Dick Schofield (0-for-16)
Hates to face: Greg Walker (.421, 8-for-19, 2 HR)
Ground outs-to-air outs ratio: 1.78, 4th highest in A.L. last season (minimum: 20 GS), 1.52 for career. . . . Additional statistics: 35 double-play ground outs (tied for most in majors) in 191 opportunities, 2d-highest rate in A.L. (minimum: 20 GS), 38 doubles, 10 triples in 241.2 innings last season. . . . Allowed 20 first-inning runs in 35 starts. . . . Batting support: 4.09 runs per start, 7th-lowest average in A.L. (minimum: 15 GS). . . . Career record of 1–9 in April, 48–39 in other months. . . . Only A.L pitcher to lose six consecutive starts last season. . . . Set career-highs in starts (35), complete games (10), and innings pitched. . . . Pitched two complete games vs. Rangers last season, but went 0–3 against them. . . . Opponents have career average of .160 (8-for-50) with the bases loaded.

Lee Guetterman

Seattle Mariners — Throws Left

	W–L	ERA	AB	H	HR	BB	SO	BA	SA	OBA
Season	11–4	3.81	439	117	13	35	42	.267	.419	.320
vs. Left-Handers			75	12	0	6	7	.160	.213	.220
vs. Right-Handers			364	105	13	29	35	.288	.462	.341
Home	6–0	3.64	210	56	8	19	23	.267	.448	.330
Road	5–4	3.97	229	61	5	16	19	.266	.393	.310
Grass	4–2	4.29	156	39	4	9	15	.250	.372	.286
Artificial Turf	7–2	3.53	283	78	9	26	27	.276	.445	.339
April			0	0	0	0	0	—	—	—
May	2–0	4.82	35	9	0	1	3	.257	.343	.278
June	3–1	2.83	137	35	2	7	12	.255	.336	.297
July	4–1	5.35	141	43	5	13	13	.305	.468	.359
August	0–2	3.95	56	17	3	7	6	.304	.607	.379
Sept./Oct.	2–0	2.25	70	13	3	7	8	.186	.371	.256
Leading Off Inn.			112	32	8	6	12	.286	.571	.322
Runners On			179	48	4	17	16	.268	.408	.327
Runners/Scor. Pos.			99	20	0	14	11	.202	.263	.288
Runners On/2 Out			76	20	0	6	6	.263	.342	.317
Scor. Pos./2 Out			47	7	0	6	3	.149	.213	.245
Late Inning Pressure			12	1	0	2	3	.083	.083	.200
Leading Off			2	0	0	1	1	.000	.000	.333
Runners On			7	0	0	1	2	.000	.000	.111
Runners/Scor. Pos.			4	0	0	1	2	.000	.000	.167
First 9 Batters			171	45	5	19	25	.263	.421	.337
Second 9 Batters			133	32	4	9	7	.241	.368	.288
All Batters Thereafter			135	40	4	7	10	.296	.467	.331

Loves to face: Ray Knight (0-for-5)
Hates to face: Gary Gaetti (.778, 7-for-9)
Ground outs-to-air outs ratio: 1.40 last season, 1.46 for career. . . .
Additional statistics: 8 double-play ground outs in 81 opportunities, 22 doubles, 3 triples in 113.1 innings last season. . . . Allowed 12 first-inning runs in 17 starts. . . . Batting support: 5.53 runs per start. . . . Averaged only 3.34 strikeouts per nine innings, 2d-lowest rate among A.L. starters. (minimum: 15 GS). . . . Has allowed 20 home runs in his career, but only two of them to left-handed batters (Lou Whitaker and Wade Boggs, both in 1986). Opponents' career breakdown: .262 by left-handers, .317 by right-handers. . . . At 6'8", he may be asked to fill pivot left vacant by Dennis Rasmussen (Creighton) on Yankees' front line between forwards Dave Winfield (Minnesota) and Tim Stoddard (N.C. State).

Ron Guidry

New York Yankees — Throws Left

	W–L	ERA	AB	H	HR	BB	SO	BA	SA	OBA
Season	5–8	3.67	448	111	14	38	96	.248	.417	.307
vs. Left-Handers			86	26	3	7	19	.302	.453	.362
vs. Right-Handers			362	85	11	31	77	.235	.409	.294
Home	2–4	2.58	219	49	7	17	50	.224	.379	.282
Road	3–4	4.78	229	62	7	21	46	.271	.454	.331
Grass	4–7	3.79	363	91	12	33	76	.251	.427	.313
Artificial Turf	1–1	3.18	85	20	2	5	20	.235	.376	.278
April			0	0	0	0	0	—	—	—
May	0–1	2.84	25	7	0	1	6	.280	.400	.296
June	1–2	3.03	114	30	4	7	24	.263	.430	.311
July	2–1	2.34	157	37	7	12	35	.236	.427	.288
August	1–4	5.79	130	33	2	15	31	.254	.408	.331
Sept./Oct.	1–0	5.40	22	4	1	3	0	.182	.364	.280
Leading Off Inn.			112	22	4	10	19	.196	.366	.262
Runners On			176	43	3	11	44	.244	.386	.289
Runners/Scor. Pos.			102	27	1	8	22	.265	.422	.313
Runners On/2 Out			85	24	1	6	21	.282	.471	.330
Scor. Pos./2 Out			56	16	0	5	13	.286	.464	.344
Late Inning Pressure			56	17	2	3	9	.304	.518	.339
Leading Off			17	2	1	0	2	.118	.353	.118
Runners On			22	5	0	1	3	.227	.364	.261
Runners/Scor. Pos.			12	3	0	1	1	.250	.500	.308
First 9 Batters			159	48	9	18	32	.302	.566	.371
Second 9 Batters			137	32	2	13	34	.234	.365	.303
All Batters Thereafter			152	31	3	7	30	.204	.309	.239

Loves to face: Willie Upshaw (.088, 3-for-34)
Hates to face: Jim Rice (.360, 27-for-75, 6 HR)
Ground outs-to-air outs ratio: 0.63, 7th lowest in A.L. last season (minimum: 200 BFP), 0.90 for career. . . . Additional statistics: 6 double-play ground outs in 67 opportunities, 26 doubles, 4 triples in 117.2 innings last season. . . . Allowed 21 first-inning runs in 17 starts. . . . Batting support: 4.18 runs per start, 9th-lowest average in A.L. (minimum: 15 GS). . . . July ERA was 5th-best in A.L. . . . Had a 2.34 ERA in his five wins, but a *better* ERA (2.00) in nine no-decision starts. . . . Has walked only three of the 98 batters he's faced with the bases full. . . . Exactly half of his career wins have been managed by Billy Martin. But look at the losses! 84–26 (.764) under Billy, 84–62 (.575) for other managers. . . . Needs 211 strikeouts to pass Whitey Ford as Yankees' all-time leader.

Jose Guzman
Texas Rangers — Throws Right

	W–L	ERA	AB	H	HR	BB	SO	BA	SA	OBA
Season	14-14	4.67	781	196	30	82	143	.251	.420	.322
vs. Left-Handers			408	98	11	34	72	.240	.363	.300
vs. Right-Handers			373	98	19	48	71	.263	.483	.344
Home	9-9	4.98	405	105	18	39	68	.259	.447	.322
Road	5-5	4.32	376	91	12	43	75	.242	.391	.321
Grass	13-12	4.53	684	172	28	71	121	.251	.430	.320
Artificial Turf	1-2	5.61	97	24	2	11	22	.247	.351	.330
April	1-1	5.50	69	18	3	5	7	.261	.449	.316
May	1-4	8.54	113	41	6	12	18	.363	.566	.429
June	4-1	2.48	131	26	4	4	29	.198	.405	.221
July	2-4	5.40	148	40	9	12	21	.270	.493	.323
August	2-1	4.59	117	27	2	26	24	.231	.325	.363
Sept./Oct.	4-3	3.54	203	44	6	23	44	.217	.340	.297
Leading Off Inn.			200	42	4	18	44	.210	.320	.279
Runners On			304	87	14	28	49	.286	.470	.340
Runners/Scor. Pos.			176	47	7	20	32	.267	.403	.332
Runners On/2 Out			116	25	3	15	27	.216	.319	.311
Scor. Pos./2 Out			80	16	2	10	19	.200	.300	.297
Late Inning Pressure			58	15	2	4	13	.259	.466	.306
Leading Off			20	4	1	0	6	.200	.400	.200
Runners On			14	3	0	1	1	.214	.357	.267
Runners/Scor. Pos.			6	1	0	1	1	.167	.167	.286
First 9 Batters			282	64	6	36	59	.227	.330	.313
Second 9 Batters			234	70	12	18	31	.299	.530	.350
All Batters Thereafter			265	62	12	28	53	.234	.419	.306

Loves to face: Rickey Henderson (.111, 2-for-18)
Hates to face: Kent Hrbek (.727, 8-for-11, 2 2B, 2 HR)
Ground outs-to-air outs ratio: 1.26 last season, 1.32 for career.... Additional statistics: 23 double-play ground outs in 146 opportunities, 40 doubles, 1 triple in 208.1 innings last season.... Allowed 23 first-inning runs in 30 starts. ERA of 5.86 over first four innings, 3.35 thereafter.... Batting support: 4.67 runs per start.... Record of 11–14 with a 4.97 ERA in 30 starts; 3–0, 1.80 ERA in seven relief appearances.... Only pitcher in majors to strike out six consecutive left-handed batters last season.... Balked in four consecutive games (June 28 to July 12).... Career record of 1–7 with a 5.37 ERA in day games; 25–24, 4.31 ERA at night.... Triple by Dan Gladden on Sept. 23 last season was the first of Guzman's career, and came just four outs short of the 400-inning mark.

John Habyan
Baltimore Orioles — Throws Right

	W–L	ERA	AB	H	HR	BB	SO	BA	SA	OBA
Season	6-7	4.80	443	110	20	40	64	.248	.447	.311
vs. Left-Handers			256	65	9	24	29	.254	.441	.318
vs. Right-Handers			187	45	11	16	35	.241	.455	.301
Home	3-5	6.00	226	63	15	14	26	.279	.553	.316
Road	3-2	3.64	217	47	5	26	38	.217	.336	.306
Grass	6-7	4.90	402	103	19	29	55	.256	.460	.305
Artificial Turf	0-0	3.86	41	7	1	11	9	.171	.317	.358
April			0	0	0	0	0			
May	1-1	5.54	50	14	3	6	6	.280	.600	.339
June	0-1	5.84	98	27	5	16	13	.276	.531	.383
July	2-1	2.19	42	7	1	4	7	.167	.238	.239
August	1-0	3.42	93	14	4	6	21	.151	.333	.202
Sept./Oct.	2-4	5.63	160	48	7	8	17	.300	.469	.335
Leading Off Inn.			117	35	6	8	14	.299	.538	.344
Runners On			151	36	5	23	23	.238	.397	.339
Runners/Scor. Pos.			99	24	1	17	20	.242	.313	.341
Runners On/2 Out			64	13	1	14	14	.203	.344	.354
Scor. Pos./2 Out			48	10	1	11	13	.208	.313	.367
Late Inning Pressure			29	6	2	0	4	.207	.483	.207
Leading Off			10	3	0	0	1	.300	.300	.300
Runners On			3	1	0	0	0	.333	1.000	.333
Runners/Scor. Pos.			0	0	0	0	0	—	—	—
First 9 Batters			215	49	10	20	42	.228	.419	.295
Second 9 Batters			149	36	6	12	15	.242	.450	.301
All Batters Thereafter			79	25	4	8	7	.316	.519	.371

Loves to face: Carney Lansford (0-for-7)
Hates to face: John Moses (.800, 4-for-5)
Ground outs-to-air outs ratio: 0.85 last season, 0.89 for career.... Additional statistics: 4 double-play ground outs in 60 opportunities, 18 doubles, 5 triples in 116.1 innings last season.... Allowed 5 first-inning runs in 13 starts.... Batting support: 4.00 runs per start. ... Record of 2–7 with a 5.93 ERA in 13 starts; 4–0, 3.19 ERA (and a save in the only opportunity of his major-league career) in 14 relief appearances.... Opponents' overall batting average hasn't varied much in his three seasons in the majors: .250, .250, .248.... Opponents' career breakdown: .255 on grass fields, .171 on artificial surfaces, .223 in day games, .258 at night.... Career record of 57–33 in the minors.... That concludes the Habyan corpus.

Greg Harris
Texas Rangers — Throws Right

	W–L	ERA	AB	H	HR	BB	SO	BA	SA	OBA
Season	5-10	4.86	559	157	18	56	106	.281	.440	.349
vs. Left-Handers			270	69	4	26	50	.256	.363	.319
vs. Right-Handers			289	88	14	30	56	.304	.512	.377
Home	3-2	4.65	316	84	10	27	61	.266	.418	.329
Road	2-8	5.16	243	73	8	29	45	.300	.469	.373
Grass	4-8	4.70	482	133	14	47	94	.276	.419	.343
Artificial Turf	1-2	6.00	77	24	4	9	12	.312	.571	.384
April	1-2	4.02	57	14	3	7	15	.246	.439	.323
May	0-2	5.50	76	23	2	7	23	.303	.434	.376
June	1-3	6.58	111	40	1	9	21	.360	.495	.418
July	2-1	2.48	114	28	1	7	15	.246	.333	.287
August	1-1	6.38	72	18	4	9	16	.250	.458	.329
Sept./Oct.	0-1	4.81	129	34	7	17	16	.264	.481	.349
Leading Off Inn.			133	37	2	12	21	.278	.398	.342
Runners On			251	76	10	26	47	.303	.498	.367
Runners/Scor. Pos.			139	37	2	16	24	.266	.374	.340
Runners On/2 Out			99	27	5	11	18	.273	.505	.345
Scor. Pos./2 Out			62	13	1	7	13	.210	.339	.290
Late Inning Pressure			72	23	3	10	15	.319	.528	.405
Leading Off			17	4	1	2	4	.235	.471	.316
Runners On			33	14	1	4	6	.424	.667	.487
Runners/Scor. Pos.			22	7	0	4	5	.318	.409	.429
First 9 Batters			273	74	11	32	65	.271	.451	.352
Second 9 Batters			166	46	3	15	24	.277	.373	.341
All Batters Thereafter			120	37	4	9	17	.308	.508	.354

Loves to face: Jose Canseco (0-for-10, 7 SO)
Hates to face: Gary Gaetti (.667, 8-for-12, 1 HR)
Ground outs-to-air outs ratio: 1.26 last season, 1.29 for career.... Additional statistics: 11 double-play ground outs in 135 opportunities, 29 doubles, 3 triples in 140.2 innings last season.... Allowed 9 first-inning runs in 19 starts.... Batting support: 6.16 runs per start, 2d-highest average in A.L. (minimum: 15 GS).... Lost all six decisions with a 7.26 ERA in day games; 5–4 (4.19) at night.... Career record of 10–16 with a 4.88 ERA as a starter; 17–19 with 36 saves and a 3.05 ERA in relief.... Yearly batting averages of opposing right-handers since 1984: .179, .199, .251, .304.... Opponents' career average of .191 (13-for-68) with the bases loaded. Has never allowed a grand slam.... Appeared in 173 games over the last three seasons, 5th-highest total among A.L. pitchers.

Tom Henke
Toronto Blue Jays — Throws Right

	W–L	ERA	AB	H	HR	BB	SO	BA	SA	OBA
Season	0-6	2.49	330	62	10	25	128	.188	.330	.242
vs. Left-Handers			163	28	3	12	59	.172	.288	.225
vs. Right-Handers			167	34	7	13	69	.204	.371	.258
Home	0-2	1.62	170	28	6	11	67	.165	.294	.213
Road	0-4	3.48	160	34	4	14	61	.213	.369	.271
Grass	0-3	2.83	127	25	3	8	51	.197	.331	.244
Artificial Turf	0-3	2.29	203	37	7	17	77	.182	.330	.240
April	0-0	0.00	39	7	0	2	13	.179	.205	.220
May	0-1	1.84	49	6	1	4	21	.122	.286	.182
June	0-2	6.32	62	17	4	8	26	.274	.500	.357
July	0-1	1.86	62	8	1	5	24	.129	.210	.188
August	0-1	2.00	63	12	2	4	23	.190	.365	.235
Sept./Oct.	0-1	2.40	55	12	2	2	21	.218	.364	.246
Leading Off Inn.			74	14	2	4	29	.189	.297	.231
Runners On			139	28	7	16	52	.201	.410	.275
Runners/Scor. Pos.			88	18	6	13	32	.205	.477	.292
Runners On/2 Out			70	16	3	12	24	.229	.400	.341
Scor. Pos./2 Out			56	12	3	9	17	.214	.429	.323
Late Inning Pressure			219	38	4	20	82	.174	.269	.239
Leading Off			52	11	1	3	19	.212	.308	.255
Runners On			83	16	2	13	26	.193	.313	.290
Runners/Scor. Pos.			53	11	2	10	15	.208	.358	.313
First 9 Batters			323	60	10	22	128	.186	.331	.234
Second 9 Batters			7	2	0	3	0	.286	.286	.500
All Batters Thereafter								—	—	

Loves to face: Dwayne Murphy (0-for-8, 7 SO)
Hates to face: Reggie Jackson (.571, 4-for-7)
Ground outs-to-air outs ratio: 0.61, 3d lowest in A.L. last season (minimum: 200 BFP), 0.66 for career.... Additional statistics: 2 double-play ground outs in 56 opportunities, 13 doubles, 2 triples in 94.0 innings last season.... Averaged 12.26 strikeouts per nine innings, highest rate in majors (minimum: 30 relief appearances).... Struck out seven consecutive batters over two games (Aug. 20–22).... Only A.L. pitcher with more strikeouts than innings in each of last three years.... Yearly opponents' batting averages since 1984: .313, .206, .191, .188.... Hurled 21.2 scoreless innings to start the season.... Most appearances in a winless season by any pitcher in baseball history (72).... First pitcher to be named to All-Star squad without a win since Dave LaRoche in 1976.

Mike Henneman — Throws Right

Detroit Tigers	W–L	ERA	AB	H	HR	BB	SO	BA	SA	OBA
Season	11-3	2.98	362	86	8	30	75	.238	.351	.300
vs. Left-Handers			170	41	6	20	29	.241	.412	.328
vs. Right-Handers			192	45	2	10	46	.234	.297	.273
Home	7-0	1.65	169	30	5	7	41	.178	.290	.210
Road	4-3	4.34	193	56	3	23	34	.290	.404	.371
Grass	10-2	2.87	301	72	7	25	62	.239	.342	.298
Artificial Turf	1-1	3.60	61	14	1	5	13	.230	.393	.309
April			0	0	0	0	0	—		
May	2-0	1.15	52	9	0	0	14	.173	.308	.185
June	1-0	4.11	62	18	1	8	8	.290	.403	.371
July	5-1	2.05	79	18	2	6	18	.228	.329	.279
August	1-0	2.14	82	21	0	6	17	.256	.317	.307
Sept./Oct.	2-2	5.16	87	20	3	10	18	.230	.391	.323
Leading Off Inn.			77	19	3	5	13	.247	.455	.301
Runners On			176	37	3	18	37	.210	.290	.284
Runners/Scor. Pos.			103	19	2	13	25	.184	.262	.277
Runners On/2 Out			80	13	0	10	18	.163	.213	.256
Scor. Pos./2 Out			53	9	0	9	16	.170	.208	.290
Late Inning Pressure			113	20	2	9	27	.177	.274	.250
Leading Off			26	3	1	0	5	.115	.269	.115
Runners On			43	10	1	7	11	.233	.326	.353
Runners/Scor. Pos.			26	7	1	7	7	.269	.423	.441
First 9 Batters			280	67	7	24	61	.239	.371	.302
Second 9 Batters			77	19	1	4	13	.247	.299	.293
All Batters Thereafter			5	0	0	2	1	.000	.000	.286

Loves to face: Joe Carter (0-for-9)
Hates to face: B.J. Surhoff (.750, 3-for-4, 1 2B, 1 3B)
Ground outs-to-air outs ratio: 1.40 last season, his first in majors. . . . Additional statistics: 9 double-play ground outs in 86 opportunities, 13 doubles, 2 triples in 96.2 innings last season. . . . Ranked 5th among A.L. rookie pitchers with 55 appearances. He was the majors' 3d-winningest rookie, behind Dunne (13) and Musselman (12). . . . Winning pitcher in five of six appearances (July 11 - 25); could have been five in a row, but Sparky used him to allow Reggie to face a right-hander in his last at bat at Tiger Stadium. What a guy. ..Gary Ward's 2-run game-winning homer on July 31 handed Henneman his first loss. He was just one win shy of the A.L. record of nine wins at the start of a career, set by Joe Pate in 1926 and equalled by Whitey Ford in 1950.

Willie Hernandez — Throws Left

Detroit Tigers	W–L	ERA	AB	H	HR	BB	SO	BA	SA	OBA
Season	3-4	3.67	192	53	8	20	30	.276	.469	.340
vs. Left-Handers			70	17	2	5	10	.243	.386	.286
vs. Right-Handers			122	36	6	15	20	.295	.516	.370
Home	2-2	4.76	70	21	5	4	8	.300	.529	.338
Road	1-2	3.09	122	32	3	16	22	.262	.434	.340
Grass	3-3	3.63	175	47	8	17	26	.269	.440	.330
Artificial Turf	0-1	4.15	17	6	0	3	4	.353	.765	.429
April	0-1	18.00	5	2	0	2	0	.400	.400	.571
May	0-0	10.13	12	4	2	0	2	.333	.833	.333
June	1-0	2.00	69	17	0	4	9	.246	.362	.284
July	0-1	2.00	29	5	1	4	7	.172	.276	.265
August	1-0	2.84	51	15	3	4	6	.294	.510	.339
Sept./Oct.	1-2	7.94	26	10	2	6	6	.385	.731	.500
Leading Off Inn.			37	10	1	3	5	.270	.486	.325
Runners On			96	32	5	13	13	.333	.531	.402
Runners/Scor. Pos.			61	18	2	13	9	.295	.443	.403
Runners On/2 Out			46	16	2	5	7	.348	.500	.412
Scor. Pos./2 Out			31	9	1	5	6	.290	.419	.389
Late Inning Pressure			96	26	3	13	17	.271	.448	.355
Leading Off			18	4	0	1	3	.222	.222	.263
Runners On			51	17	3	9	10	.333	.588	.426
Runners/Scor. Pos.			31	10	0	9	6	.323	.419	.463
First 9 Batters			188	52	8	19	29	.277	.473	.338
Second 9 Batters			4	1	0	1	1	.250	.250	.400
All Batters Thereafter			0	0	0	0	0	—		

Loves to face: Pete O'Brien (0-for-17)
Hates to face: Greg Brock (3-for-3, 2 BB)
Ground outs-to-air outs ratio: 0.71 last season, 1.07 for career. . . . Additional statistics: 4 double-play ground outs in 45 opportunities, 7 doubles, 3 triples in 49.0 innings last season. . . . Earned eight saves in 17 opportunities, raising his three-year totals to 63-for-88 (72 percent) since his 32-for-33 performance in 1984. . . . Despite his screwball, opposing right-handers had a higher batting average than lefties in each of his 11 seasons in the majors, longest current streak in baseball. . . . But Hernandez is one of four southpaws to strike out opposing right-handers at a higher rate than left-handers in each of the past three seasons. The others: Eric Bell, Mike Mason, and Pat Perry. . . . Yearly opponents' batting averages since joining the Tigers: .194, .210, .251, .276.

Ted Higuera — Throws Left

Milwaukee Brewers	W–L	ERA	AB	H	HR	BB	SO	BA	SA	OBA
Season	18-10	3.85	980	236	24	87	240	.241	.368	.301
vs. Left-Handers			163	45	4	8	40	.276	.393	.310
vs. Right-Handers			817	191	20	79	200	.234	.364	.300
Home	12-4	3.50	557	134	11	44	146	.241	.348	.294
Road	6-6	4.33	423	102	13	43	94	.241	.395	.311
Grass	16-9	3.95	852	210	21	75	212	.246	.373	.305
Artificial Turf	2-1	3.25	128	26	3	12	28	.203	.336	.280
April	4-0	3.25	133	33	4	14	34	.248	.391	.315
May	0-5	6.59	165	46	7	11	47	.279	.461	.320
June	2-2	6.08	149	47	5	14	35	.315	.490	.378
July	4-1	3.77	182	51	2	13	36	.280	.368	.325
August	3-1	1.64	148	23	1	14	39	.155	.209	.226
Sept./Oct.	5-1	2.62	203	36	5	21	49	.177	.305	.257
Leading Off Inn.			243	55	7	25	68	.226	.346	.301
Runners On			402	107	6	33	79	.266	.383	.315
Runners/Scor. Pos.			203	62	1	16	38	.305	.419	.342
Runners On/2 Out			158	31	2	15	39	.196	.297	.266
Scor. Pos./2 Out			93	24	0	10	19	.258	.355	.330
Late Inning Pressure			139	27	4	7	30	.194	.317	.233
Leading Off			40	6	1	0	10	.150	.250	.150
Runners On			38	11	2	3	3	.289	.500	.341
Runners/Scor. Pos.			18	4	1	2	2	.222	.444	.300
First 9 Batters			274	64	5	35	71	.234	.332	.318
Second 9 Batters			284	67	4	25	79	.236	.342	.295
All Batters Thereafter			422	105	15	27	90	.249	.410	.294

Loves to face: Gary Pettis (0-for-15)
Hates to face: Jesse Barfield (.435, 10-for-23, 2 HR)
Ground outs-to-air outs ratio: 0.79 last season, 0.79 for career. . . . Additional statistics: 23 double-play ground outs in 216 opportunities, 47 doubles, 3 triples in 261.2 innings last season. . . . Allowed 14 first-inning runs in 35 starts. . . . Batting support: 5.51 runs per start. . . . Tied for A.L. lead in wins for April and September, tied for most losses in May. Career record of 6–10 in May, 47–19 in other months. . . . Pitched the only complete-game extra-inning shutout in the A.L. last season. . . . Last season's winning percentage (.643) was the *lowest* of his three seasons in majors. No other A.L. pitcher has reached that level in every season since 1975. . . . Another Ray Searage record bites the dust: Higuera set new team record with 32-inning scoreless streak.

Charlie Hough — Throws Right

Texas Rangers	W–L	ERA	AB	H	HR	BB	SO	BA	SA	OBA
Season	18-13	3.79	1069	238	36	124	223	.223	.372	.311
vs. Left-Handers			509	122	17	71	93	.240	.375	.336
vs. Right-Handers			560	116	19	53	130	.207	.370	.288
Home	11-8	4.40	585	139	24	65	138	.238	.403	.323
Road	7-5	3.07	484	99	12	59	85	.205	.335	.296
Grass	17-10	3.62	876	192	31	98	192	.219	.373	.304
Artificial Turf	1-3	4.53	193	46	5	26	31	.238	.368	.341
April	1-1	4.41	123	30	1	13	24	.244	.341	.326
May	4-0	3.50	165	41	5	15	31	.248	.370	.315
June	3-2	3.51	173	33	4	29	24	.191	.306	.316
July	3-4	5.29	190	46	11	23	50	.242	.468	.326
August	3-3	3.52	197	41	9	24	49	.208	.391	.298
Sept./Oct.	4-3	2.90	221	47	6	20	45	.213	.344	.294
Leading Off Inn.			271	66	9	24	49	.244	.402	.312
Runners On			420	86	11	54	104	.205	.314	.305
Runners/Scor. Pos.			261	49	6	43	76	.188	.280	.315
Runners On/2 Out			190	41	6	25	53	.216	.342	.329
Scor. Pos./2 Out			132	30	4	23	40	.227	.348	.370
Late Inning Pressure			123	27	5	6	30	.220	.374	.273
Leading Off			35	9	4	0	6	.257	.600	.278
Runners On			30	7	0	2	8	.233	.333	.324
Runners/Scor. Pos.			19	5	0	2	6	.263	.368	.391
First 9 Batters			300	70	9	46	66	.233	.383	.343
Second 9 Batters			294	63	9	40	62	.214	.361	.314
All Batters Thereafter			475	105	18	38	95	.221	.373	.287

Loves to face: Butch Wynegar (.115, 3-for-26)
Hates to face: Garth Iorg (.481, 13-for-27, 2 HR)
Ground outs-to-air outs ratio: 1.02 last season, 1.04 for career. . . . Additional statistics: 12 double-play ground outs in 161 opportunities, 42 doubles, 5 triples in 285.1 innings last season. . . . Allowed 27 first-inning runs in 40 starts. . . . Batting support: 5.25 runs per start. . . . Road-game ERA was the best in A.L. last season. Opponents have batted under .210 in road games in each of the last three seasons. . . . Has won last 12 decisions vs. Cleveland, lost seven in a row vs. Milwaukee. . . . One of three pitchers to work 200+ innings in each of the past six seasons. The others: Morris and Valenzuela. . . . Made his major-league debut on Aug. 12, 1970, in relief of Pete Mikkelsen. His catcher in that game was Jeff Torborg. . . . Oldest opening-day pitcher in the majors in 1987.

Steve Howe

Texas Rangers   Throws Left

	W-L	ERA	AB	H	HR	BB	SO	BA	SA	OBA
Season	3-3	4.31	118	33	2	8	19	.280	.398	.341
vs. Left-Handers			35	7	0	2	6	.200	.314	.282
vs. Right-Handers			83	26	2	6	13	.313	.434	.367
Home	2-0	2.76	59	14	1	4	10	.237	.322	.308
Road	1-3	6.00	59	19	1	4	9	.322	.475	.375
Grass	2-3	4.55	105	30	2	7	16	.286	.419	.348
Artificial Turf	1-0	2.45	13	3	0	1	3	.231	.231	.286
April			0	0	0	0	0	—	—	—
May			0	0	0	0	0	—	—	—
June			0	0	0	0	0	—	—	—
July			0	0	0	0	0	—	—	—
August	1-2	5.52	61	23	0	5	10	.377	.492	.433
Sept./Oct.	2-1	3.24	57	10	2	3	9	.175	.298	.242
Leading Off Inn.			26	5	0	1	8	.192	.231	.222
Runners On			59	20	0	3	7	.339	.441	.371
Runners/Scor. Pos.			32	9	0	3	5	.281	.406	.343
Runners On/2 Out			32	9	0	2	3	.281	.344	.324
Scor. Pos./2 Out			18	5	0	2	3	.278	.389	.350
Late Inning Pressure			47	13	1	5	7	.277	.404	.358
Leading Off			9	0	0	1	3	.000	.000	.100
Runners On			24	9	0	3	1	.375	.500	.444
Runners/Scor. Pos.			14	4	0	3	1	.286	.429	.412
First 9 Batters			115	32	2	8	19	.278	.400	.341
Second 9 Batters			3	1	0	0	0	.333	.333	.333
All Batters Thereafter			0	0	0	0	0	—	—	—

Loves to face: Johnny Ray (0-for-9)
Hates to face: Alvin Davis (3-for-3, 1 BB)
Ground outs-to-air outs ratio: 1.59 last season, 1.50 for career (2.53 vs. left-handed batters, 1.21 vs. right-handers). ... Additional statistics: 2 double-play ground outs in 21 opportunities, 6 doubles, 1 triple in 31.1 innings last season. ... Has pitched in majors only in odd-numbered years since 1983. Is it just a coincidence that the rock group Yes has toured only in even-numbered years? ... The last home run allowed to a left-handed batter was hit by Lloyd Moseby in 1985. ... Opposing batters have hit .303 with runners in scoring position. ... Record of 6–7 with a 4.98 ERA and four saves in 10 opportunities since returning from his full-season suspension in 1984. Allowed 91 hits in 72.1 innings during that time.

Jay Howell

Oakland As   Throws Right

	W-L	ERA	AB	H	HR	BB	SO	BA	SA	OBA
Season	3-4	5.89	173	48	6	21	35	.277	.474	.355
vs. Left-Handers			83	21	1	10	15	.253	.373	.340
vs. Right-Handers			90	27	5	11	20	.300	.567	.369
Home	1-1	5.03	76	16	4	7	21	.211	.382	.277
Road	2-3	6.57	97	32	2	14	14	.330	.546	.412
Grass	2-3	5.26	152	38	6	16	32	.250	.441	.324
Artificial Turf	1-1	10.80	21	10	0	5	3	.476	.714	.556
April	2-1	6.75	53	16	2	4	10	.302	.528	.345
May	0-0	5.14	28	7	2	4	2	.250	.500	.344
June	0-0	0.00	31	4	0	5	13	.129	.129	.250
July	1-3	12.96	35	13	1	8	8	.371	.657	.489
August	0-0	4.50	26	8	1	0	2	.308	.500	.308
Sept./Oct.			0	0	0	0	0	—	—	—
Leading Off Inn.			31	10	2	6	5	.323	.613	.432
Runners On			97	26	3	10	21	.268	.423	.330
Runners/Scor. Pos.			55	16	2	9	12	.291	.455	.379
Runners On/2 Out			42	13	2	5	6	.310	.548	.383
Scor. Pos./2 Out			25	10	1	5	2	.400	.640	.500
Late Inning Pressure			121	33	2	15	25	.273	.421	.355
Leading Off			20	6	1	4	3	.300	.550	.417
Runners On			72	18	1	8	18	.250	.361	.321
Runners/Scor. Pos.			41	12	1	8	10	.293	.439	.400
First 9 Batters			171	48	6	19	34	.281	.480	.352
Second 9 Batters			2	0	0	2	1	.000	.000	.500
All Batters Thereafter			0	0	0	0	0	—	—	—

Loves to face: Gary Carter (0-for-4)
Hates to face: Luis Salazar (2-for-2, 1 HR)
Ground outs-to-air outs ratio: 1.31 last season, 1.12 for career. ... Additional statistics: 2 double-play ground outs in 44 opportunities, 10 doubles, 3 triples in 44.1 innings last season. ... Earned 16 saves in 25 opportunities, raising his three-year total with Oakland to 61-for-83 (73 percent). ... Home run by Mike Easler in Howell's final appearance (Aug. 23) was the only one he allowed to a left-handed batter last season. ... Opponents' career breakdown: .247 with bases empty, .285 with runners on base, .302 with runners in scoring position. ... Last win on artificial turf was May 1, 1985. Since then he has a 12–14 record on grass fields, 0–8 on rugs. ... Yearly opponents' batting averages since 1984: .223, .261, .262, .277. ... Has pitched only 97.2 innings over the past two seasons.

Charles Hudson

New York Yankees   Throws Right

	W-L	ERA	AB	H	HR	BB	SO	BA	SA	OBA
Season	11-7	3.61	573	137	19	57	100	.239	.391	.308
vs. Left-Handers			250	67	7	36	35	.268	.424	.354
vs. Right-Handers			323	70	12	21	65	.217	.365	.270
Home	4-4	4.09	266	66	11	27	48	.248	.417	.313
Road	7-3	3.18	307	71	8	30	52	.231	.368	.304
Grass	8-7	3.90	508	123	18	52	93	.242	.398	.312
Artificial Turf	3-0	1.45	65	14	1	5	7	.215	.338	.282
April	3-0	2.38	121	23	4	11	27	.190	.322	.263
May	3-1	3.86	119	34	2	11	11	.286	.429	.348
June	1-1	5.60	74	22	3	8	15	.297	.514	.361
July	0-1	5.56	43	12	1	2	13	.279	.395	.298
August	2-1	2.66	87	18	4	11	19	.207	.356	.296
Sept./Oct.	2-3	3.58	129	28	5	14	15	.217	.372	.295
Leading Off Inn.			138	28	3	18	23	.203	.312	.299
Runners On			229	54	7	19	41	.236	.367	.290
Runners/Scor. Pos.			114	26	4	11	23	.228	.351	.282
Runners On/2 Out			100	22	3	4	17	.220	.370	.250
Scor. Pos./2 Out			58	10	2	4	12	.172	.293	.226
Late Inning Pressure			63	14	1	4	9	.222	.286	.269
Leading Off			19	4	0	1	0	.211	.211	.250
Runners On			21	6	1	1	6	.286	.476	.318
Runners/Scor. Pos.			9	3	1	1	3	.333	.778	.400
First 9 Batters			245	50	7	30	47	.204	.335	.293
Second 9 Batters			180	43	8	17	36	.239	.433	.302
All Batters Thereafter			148	44	4	10	17	.297	.432	.344

Loves to face: Dwight Evans (0-for-8)
Hates to face: Darrell Porter (.409, 9-for-22, 1 HR, 5 BB)
Ground outs-to-air outs ratio: 0.68 last season, 0.86 for career. ... Additional statistics: 13 double-play ground outs in 120 opportunities, 20 doubles, 5 triples in 154.2 innings last season. ... Allowed 5 first-inning runs in 16 starts. ... Batting support: 5.31 runs per start. ... Record of 5-1 with a 2.15 ERA in day games; 6-6, 4.22 ERA at night. Career records: 20–8 under the sun, 23–41 under the lights. ... Sent to Columbus in June despite a 7–2 record. ... Opponents' career batting average of .274 by left-handers, .242 by right-handers. ... Career record of 37–45 with a 4.06 ERA as a starter; 6–4 with a 2.78 ERA in 41 relief appearances. ... Only pitcher with 10+ starts and 10+ relief games in each of last three years. Is he versatile, or can't he hold a job?

Bruce Hurst

Boston Red Sox   Throws Left

	W-L	ERA	AB	H	HR	BB	SO	BA	SA	OBA
Season	15-13	4.41	911	239	35	76	190	.262	.432	.317
vs. Left-Handers			129	32	4	16	32	.248	.419	.333
vs. Right-Handers			782	207	31	60	158	.265	.435	.314
Home	12-4	4.30	517	137	14	37	113	.265	.400	.313
Road	3-9	4.56	394	102	21	39	77	.259	.475	.323
Grass	14-11	4.41	783	205	26	65	166	.262	.418	.317
Artificial Turf	1-2	4.41	128	34	9	11	24	.266	.523	.321
April	2-3	4.45	126	31	4	12	21	.246	.397	.307
May	3-1	2.27	166	33	4	11	43	.199	.301	.247
June	4-1	3.54	185	51	4	14	33	.276	.400	.325
July	2-1	6.00	144	42	10	10	33	.292	.576	.338
August	3-3	3.99	179	44	8	15	42	.246	.430	.299
Sept./Oct.	1-4	8.33	111	38	4	14	18	.342	.541	.417
Leading Off Inn.			231	61	11	19	52	.264	.437	.320
Runners On			360	98	13	25	66	.272	.447	.315
Runners/Scor. Pos.			159	49	4	19	34	.308	.459	.366
Runners On/2 Out			148	34	0	9	28	.230	.284	.274
Scor. Pos./2 Out			73	19	0	7	14	.260	.329	.325
Late Inning Pressure			98	30	6	9	15	.306	.561	.364
Leading Off			29	9	3	2	6	.310	.655	.355
Runners On			31	10	2	3	1	.323	.581	.378
Runners/Scor. Pos.			15	3	0	3	0	.200	.267	.300
First 9 Batters			273	70	11	23	73	.256	.429	.314
Second 9 Batters			266	60	8	22	51	.226	.361	.282
All Batters Thereafter			372	109	16	31	66	.293	.487	.345

Loves to face: Eddie Murray (.088, 3-for-34, 2 HR)
Hates to face: Tom Brunansky (.577, 15-for-26, 1 HR)
Ground outs-to-air outs ratio: 1.37 last season, 1.14 for career. ... Additional statistics: 27 double-play ground outs in 178 opportunities, 44 doubles, 3 triples in 238.2 innings last season. ... Allowed 11 first-inning runs in 33 starts. ... Batting support: 4.79 runs per start. ... May ERA was 3d-lowest in A.L. ... Losing pitcher in seven of his last eight starts. ... Has allowed 10 hits in last 19 at bats with the bases loaded, including five doubles and a home run. ... Fantasy-league draft alert. Hurst has similar career stats (70-67, 4.33 ERA) to those of two other A.L. southpaws also burdened by pitching in hitters' parks: Mark Langston (55-51, 4.24) and Frank Viola (80-74, 4.10). After last season, Hurst will come a lot cheaper than the other two.

Danny Jackson
Kansas City Royals — Throws Left

	W–L	ERA	AB	H	HR	BB	SO	BA	SA	OBA
Season	9-18	4.02	849	219	11	109	152	.258	.364	.345
vs. Left-Handers			161	45	1	14	45	.280	.348	.333
vs. Right-Handers			688	174	10	95	107	.253	.368	.347
Home	6-9	4.30	460	117	6	57	86	.254	.365	.340
Road	3-9	3.68	389	102	5	52	66	.262	.362	.350
Grass	3-7	2.93	309	76	3	37	58	.246	.327	.326
Artificial Turf	6-11	4.66	540	143	8	72	94	.265	.385	.355
April	0-4	4.35	120	33	0	18	13	.275	.342	.370
May	2-2	3.15	147	33	4	17	46	.224	.374	.317
June	2-4	5.35	141	40	3	23	24	.284	.433	.389
July	0-3	3.69	123	30	1	9	20	.244	.358	.293
August	3-3	3.35	176	38	2	19	31	.216	.295	.296
Sept./Oct.	2-2	4.54	142	45	1	23	18	.317	.394	.405
Leading Off Inn.			207	53	1	29	38	.256	.348	.350
Runners On			388	103	7	45	68	.265	.387	.344
Runners/Scor. Pos.			226	60	4	25	43	.265	.381	.337
Runners On/2 Out			159	35	3	22	33	.220	.346	.319
Scor. Pos./2 Out			109	26	3	12	25	.239	.376	.314
Late Inning Pressure			104	24	1	9	21	.231	.308	.289
Leading Off			30	9	0	3	5	.300	.367	.364
Runners On			38	9	1	2	10	.237	.368	.268
Runners/Scor. Pos.			19	4	0	1	6	.211	.263	.238
First 9 Batters			259	56	2	42	56	.216	.297	.333
Second 9 Batters			258	76	1	37	37	.295	.388	.386
All Batters Thereafter			332	87	8	30	59	.262	.398	.321

Loves to face: Reid Nichols (.091, 1-for-11)
Hates to face: Gary Roenicke (.500, 5-for-10, 2 HR, 5 BB)
Ground outs-to-air outs ratio: 1.53 last season, 1.54 for career. . . . Additional statistics: 21 double-play ground outs in 199 opportunities, 37 doubles, 10 triples in 224.0 innings last season. . . . Allowed 13 first-inning runs in 34 starts. . . . Batting support: 3.35 runs per start, lowest average in A.L. for 2d consecutive season (min.: 15 GS). Over the last four seasons the Royals have scored 4.2 runs per game overall, less than 3.5 in Jackson's starts. . . . Toughest pitcher in the majors to take deep. Allowed an average of one homer per 20.4 innings. The good news for Cincinnati is that he had equally impressive numbers on the road as he did in Royals Stadium, not exactly a HR haven. . . . Record of 1–8 in day games, 8-10 at night. . . . Now in same division as his buddy, Brett Butler.

Bob James
Chicago White Sox — Throws Right

	W–L	ERA	AB	H	HR	BB	SO	BA	SA	OBA
Season	4-6	4.67	211	54	10	17	34	.256	.474	.321
vs. Left-Handers			91	26	6	7	13	.286	.560	.333
vs. Right-Handers			120	28	4	10	21	.233	.408	.311
Home	3-2	4.65	123	31	7	10	21	.252	.472	.326
Road	1-4	4.70	88	23	3	7	13	.261	.477	.313
Grass	4-6	4.28	185	45	10	14	31	.243	.454	.309
Artificial Turf	0-0	7.94	26	9	0	3	3	.346	.615	.400
April	1-2	10.38	19	7	2	4	0	.368	.684	.458
May	1-0	1.83	72	13	4	3	14	.181	.417	.213
June	0-1	4.15	35	7	3	3	3	.200	.514	.263
July	1-1	3.38	42	13	1	2	9	.310	.452	.370
August			0	0	0	0	0	—	—	—
Sept./Oct.	1-2	9.28	43	14	0	5	8	.326	.465	.412
Leading Off Inn.			46	16	4	2	7	.348	.717	.375
Runners On			92	23	2	12	14	.250	.413	.355
Runners/Scor. Pos.			73	15	1	11	13	.205	.342	.326
Runners On/2 Out			51	14	1	6	7	.275	.471	.362
Scor. Pos./2 Out			42	11	0	6	7	.262	.429	.367
Late Inning Pressure			102	26	5	10	17	.255	.451	.328
Leading Off			24	9	3	1	5	.375	.792	.400
Runners On			42	12	1	6	5	.286	.452	.385
Runners/Scor. Pos.			33	9	1	6	4	.273	.455	.381
First 9 Batters			197	52	9	17	30	.264	.482	.326
Second 9 Batters			14	2	1	0	4	.143	.357	.250
All Batters Thereafter			0	0	0	0	0	—	—	—

Loves to face: Kirby Puckett (0-for-8)
Hates to face: Randy Bush (.800, 4-for-5, 1 HR)
Ground outs-to-air outs ratio: 0.81 last season, 1.00 for career. . . . Additional statistics: 5 double-play ground outs in 34 opportunities, 6 doubles, 5 triples in 54.0 innings last season. . . . Earned 10 saves in 14 opportunities, raising totals over past five years to 73 saves in 103 opportunities (71 percent). . . . Shared A.L. lead with six saves in May, but had none after the All-Star break. . . . First losing record since 1982. . . . Faced the Angels twice last season: lost both games, retired only one batter, and allowed three earned runs for an 81.00 ERA. . . . Has struck out only 5.29 batters per nine innings over the past two seasons, compared to a previous career rate of 8.37. . . . Career record of 20–15 on grass fields, 4–11 on artificial turf (although ERAs are nearly identical).

Tommy John
New York Yankees — Throws Left

	W–L	ERA	AB	H	HR	BB	SO	BA	SA	OBA
Season	13-6	4.03	736	212	12	47	63	.288	.387	.335
vs. Left-Handers			123	25	1	8	18	.203	.260	.258
vs. Right-Handers			613	187	11	39	45	.305	.413	.351
Home	6-3	4.38	355	108	9	25	29	.304	.431	.351
Road	7-3	3.70	381	104	3	22	34	.273	.346	.321
Grass	11-6	4.40	620	183	12	37	57	.295	.400	.339
Artificial Turf	2-0	2.10	116	29	0	10	6	.250	.319	.315
April	1-0	2.55	63	12	1	5	7	.190	.238	.261
May	4-1	4.22	126	41	3	4	10	.325	.452	.351
June	2-2	6.58	112	35	2	7	6	.313	.393	.353
July	3-0	2.43	155	36	3	10	15	.232	.355	.283
August	2-1	3.94	113	31	2	9	10	.274	.372	.339
Sept./Oct.	1-2	4.54	167	57	1	12	15	.341	.431	.387
Leading Off Inn.			191	55	7	9	18	.288	.466	.323
Runners On			307	87	4	28	28	.283	.368	.348
Runners/Scor. Pos.			181	47	2	22	20	.260	.326	.348
Runners On/2 Out			116	33	3	16	12	.284	.414	.381
Scor. Pos./2 Out			80	20	1	12	10	.250	.325	.362
Late Inning Pressure			37	11	0	2	1	.297	.324	.333
Leading Off			12	3	0	0	0	.250	.333	.250
Runners On			11	3	0	2	0	.273	.273	.385
Runners/Scor. Pos.			3	0	0	1	0	.000	.000	.250
First 9 Batters			268	78	3	16	23	.291	.366	.343
Second 9 Batters			250	72	7	19	19	.288	.432	.339
All Batters Thereafter			218	62	2	12	21	.284	.362	.322

Loves to face: Joe Carter (0-for-9)
Hates to face: Mark McGwire (.500, 5-for-10, 2 2B, 2 HR)
Ground outs-to-air outs ratio: 2.66, highest in majors last season (minimum: 20 GS), 2.50 for career. . . . Additional statistics: 27 double-play ground outs in 147 opportunities, highest rate in A.L. (minimum: 20 GS), 31 doubles, 3 triples in 187.2 innings last season. . . . Batting support: 5.82 runs per start, 7th-highest average in A.L. (minimum: 15 GS). . . . Average of 3.02 strikeouts per nine innings was lowest in majors (minimum: 15 GS). . . . Opposing right-handers have hit above .300 in four of last five seasons. . . . Complete-game win on July 20 was first in more than four years. In that game, Don Mattingly tied modern major-league record for first basemen with 22 putouts. That mark was set by Ernie Banks in 1963 with Dick Ellsworth on the mound.

Doug Jones
Cleveland Indians — Throws Right

	W–L	ERA	AB	H	HR	BB	SO	BA	SA	OBA
Season	6-5	3.15	360	101	4	24	87	.281	.353	.332
vs. Left-Handers			185	50	1	12	40	.270	.319	.312
vs. Right-Handers			175	51	3	12	47	.291	.389	.352
Home	5-1	3.76	213	63	3	14	51	.296	.376	.345
Road	1-4	2.33	147	38	1	10	36	.259	.320	.313
Grass	6-5	3.43	325	95	4	22	77	.292	.366	.344
Artificial Turf	0-0	0.90	35	6	0	2	10	.171	.229	.216
April	0-1	5.79	65	21	2	9	15	.323	.477	.408
May			0	0	0	0	0	—	—	—
June	0-0	54.00	6	4	1	0	1	.667	1.167	.714
July	3-2	2.22	107	24	1	6	25	.224	.280	.272
August	0-1	1.11	84	17	0	5	21	.202	.214	.263
Sept./Oct.	3-1	3.38	98	35	0	4	25	.357	.418	.379
Leading Off Inn.			76	23	0	3	21	.303	.329	.338
Runners On			189	59	3	18	40	.312	.413	.372
Runners/Scor. Pos.			118	37	3	14	24	.314	.441	.377
Runners On/2 Out			71	18	0	7	17	.254	.310	.321
Scor. Pos./2 Out			50	12	0	5	10	.240	.300	.309
Late Inning Pressure			150	44	1	14	39	.293	.340	.363
Leading Off			35	10	0	1	10	.286	.314	.324
Runners On			76	25	1	11	17	.329	.408	.407
Runners/Scor. Pos.			43	13	1	8	9	.302	.395	.389
First 9 Batters			303	82	2	20	75	.271	.330	.323
Second 9 Batters			56	19	2	4	12	.339	.482	.381
All Batters Thereafter			1	0	0	0	0	.000	.000	.000

Loves to face: Jesse Barfield (0-for-4, 3 SO)
Hates to face: Ernie Whitt (3-for-3, 1 HR)
Ground outs-to-air outs ratio: 1.58 last season, 1.65 for career. . . . Additional statistics: 9 double-play ground outs in 114 opportunities, 14 doubles, 0 triples in 91.1 innings last season. . . . Averaged 22.8 innings pitched per home run allowed, 2d-best rate among 239 qualifying pitchers in the majors. . . . July ERA was 3d-best in A.L. . . . Led the Indians with eight saves (in 12 opportunities), lowest total to lead a team. (Garber and Quisenberry led K.C., also with eight). . . . Opponents' career batting average of .297 on grass fields (3.64 ERA), .175 on artificial surfaces (1.00 ERA). . . . Has walked four of 25 career batters faced with the bases loaded. . . . Spent eight seasons in Brewers organization, but pitched only 2.2 innings for big club (in 1982).

Jimmy Key
Toronto Blue Jays — Throws Left

	W–L	ERA	AB	H	HR	BB	SO	BA	SA	OBA
Season	17-8	2.76	951	210	24	66	161	.221	.344	.272
vs. Left-Handers			157	39	4	9	35	.248	.382	.290
vs. Right-Handers			794	171	20	57	126	.215	.336	.268
Home	10-4	2.36	554	107	15	37	100	.193	.310	.245
Road	7-4	3.36	397	103	9	29	61	.259	.390	.309
Grass	5-3	3.28	321	82	8	27	50	.255	.383	.313
Artificial Turf	12-5	2.51	630	128	16	39	111	.203	.324	.251
April	4-1	3.03	128	25	6	16	15	.195	.359	.285
May	2-2	3.97	181	46	5	7	35	.254	.392	.284
June	2-2	1.55	138	23	0	9	26	.167	.217	.215
July	4-1	2.87	189	38	6	14	40	.201	.339	.260
August	3-0	3.21	107	26	5	5	17	.243	.449	.277
Sept./Oct.	2-2	2.10	208	52	2	15	28	.250	.327	.300
Leading Off Inn.			258	54	2	10	41	.209	.271	.242
Runners On			331	87	8	27	57	.263	.408	.316
Runners/Scor. Pos.			173	43	3	17	27	.249	.370	.311
Runners On/2 Out			126	26	3	17	22	.206	.349	.301
Scor. Pos./2 Out			80	16	1	9	13	.200	.325	.281
Late Inning Pressure			115	25	4	12	24	.217	.357	.295
Leading Off			31	5	0	3	6	.161	.161	.235
Runners On			41	9	1	5	7	.220	.341	.298
Runners/Scor. Pos.			19	3	0	4	4	.158	.263	.292
First 9 Batters			303	65	7	17	54	.215	.320	.256
Second 9 Batters			300	64	8	18	52	.213	.343	.257
All Batters Thereafter			348	81	9	31	55	.233	.365	.298

Loves to face: Eddie Murray (.095, 2-for-21)
Hates to face: B. J. Surhoff (.800, 4-for-5, 1 HR)
Ground outs-to-air outs ratio: 1.74, 5th highest in A.L. last season (minimum: 20 GS), 1.44 for career. . . . Additional statistics: 24 double-play ground outs in 164 opportunities, 29 doubles, 8 triples in 261.0 innings last season. . . . Allowed 18 first-inning runs in 36 starts. . . . Batting support: 4.61 runs per start. . . . Led Blue Jays' staff with an average of 7.25 innings per start. . . . Could have won 20. Had 17 wins with four starts remaining. Jays had been victorious with Key on the mound in 12 consecutive starts, but were 0-for-2 in the final week of the season. . . . Only visiting pitcher to win two games at Fenway Park last season. . . . Yearly averages with two out and runners on base: .397, .263, .210, .206. . . . Opponents' career average of .121 (4-for-33, no XBH, 4 BB) with bases loaded.

Paul Kilgus
Texas Rangers — Throws Left

	W–L	ERA	AB	H	HR	BB	SO	BA	SA	OBA
Season	2-7	4.13	350	95	14	31	42	.271	.454	.334
vs. Left-Handers			76	19	6	7	11	.250	.539	.313
vs. Right-Handers			274	76	8	24	31	.277	.431	.340
Home	0-4	4.67	134	36	7	11	17	.269	.493	.329
Road	2-3	3.79	216	59	7	20	25	.273	.431	.338
Grass	2-6	4.61	279	77	12	26	34	.276	.466	.342
Artificial Turf	0-1	2.37	71	18	2	5	8	.254	.408	.303
April			0	0	0	0	0	—	—	—
May			0	0	0	0	0	—	—	—
June	0-1	1.64	45	14	1	2	2	.311	.467	.354
July	1-1	3.52	85	19	3	9	10	.224	.388	.305
August	1-3	5.40	138	43	6	16	23	.312	.522	.383
Sept./Oct.	0-2	4.09	82	19	4	4	7	.232	.402	.267
Leading Off Inn.			88	28	1	7	12	.318	.443	.368
Runners On			157	36	5	10	19	.229	.382	.284
Runners/Scor. Pos.			75	19	3	7	10	.253	.427	.333
Runners On/2 Out			65	17	2	5	8	.262	.415	.333
Scor. Pos./2 Out			37	12	2	5	5	.324	.541	.432
Late Inning Pressure			26	6	3	4	5	.231	.654	.333
Leading Off			8	0	0	0	3	.000	.000	.000
Runners On			5	2	0	0	0	.400	.800	.400
Runners/Scor. Pos.			1	1	0	0	0	1.000	1.000	1.000
First 9 Batters			161	40	6	16	20	.248	.398	.324
Second 9 Batters			109	30	2	6	11	.275	.394	.313
All Batters Thereafter			80	25	6	9	11	.313	.650	.382

Loves to face: Steve Balboni (0-for-4, 2 SO)
Hates to face: Larry Sheets (.800, 4-for-5, 2 HR)
Ground outs-to-air outs ratio: 1.45 last season, his first in majors. . . . Additional statistics: 9 double-play ground outs in 75 opportunities, 20 doubles, 1 triple in 89.1 innings last season. . . . Allowed 9 first-inning runs in 12 starts. . . . Batting support: 4.25 runs per start. . . . Record of 2–5 with a 4.59 ERA in 12 starts; 0–2, 2.61 ERA in 13 relief appearances. . . . Record of 2–0 with a 2.76 ERA in day games; 0–7, 4.44 ERA at night. . . . Allowed one home run per 12.7 AB by opposing left-handers, highest rate by a southpaw over the past 13 years (minimum: 5 HR), except for teammate Ron Meridith last season (five home runs in 37 at bats). . . . You never know. Kilgus was drafted in the 43d round of the June 1984 free-agent draft.

Eric King
Detroit Tigers — Throws Right

	W–L	ERA	AB	H	HR	BB	SO	BA	SA	OBA
Season	6-9	4.89	443	111	15	60	89	.251	.393	.343
vs. Left-Handers			229	55	5	31	47	.240	.358	.332
vs. Right-Handers			214	56	10	29	42	.262	.430	.355
Home	2-4	5.95	221	62	9	30	39	.281	.457	.374
Road	4-5	3.90	222	49	6	30	50	.221	.329	.312
Grass	5-7	5.12	395	100	15	55	76	.253	.410	.348
Artificial Turf	1-2	2.92	48	11	0	5	13	.229	.250	.302
April	2-1	2.45	54	12	0	8	14	.222	.259	.323
May	0-3	5.40	113	28	3	16	18	.248	.372	.344
June	1-2	3.20	65	10	2	8	15	.154	.262	.257
July	2-1	3.15	74	16	2	7	17	.216	.338	.280
August	1-2	7.88	67	24	6	12	10	.358	.672	.457
Sept./Oct.	0-0	7.27	70	21	2	9	15	.300	.443	.388
Leading Off Inn.			102	24	4	8	19	.235	.382	.297
Runners On			196	51	6	33	41	.260	.403	.365
Runners/Scor. Pos.			109	26	3	23	20	.239	.358	.368
Runners On/2 Out			79	18	3	16	20	.228	.405	.365
Scor. Pos./2 Out			49	11	2	13	10	.224	.408	.397
Late Inning Pressure			161	43	2	21	31	.267	.335	.353
Leading Off			36	10	1	3	6	.278	.361	.333
Runners On			78	23	1	13	18	.295	.385	.398
Runners/Scor. Pos.			44	11	1	11	11	.250	.364	.404
First 9 Batters			317	83	8	48	71	.262	.372	.359
Second 9 Batters			88	19	4	8	11	.216	.409	.296
All Batters Thereafter			38	9	3	4	7	.237	.526	.310

Loves to face: Eddie Murray (0-for-17, 0 SO)
Hates to face: Dan Pasqua (.750, 3-for-4, 2 HR)
Ground outs-to-air outs ratio: 1.11 last season, 1.12 for career. . . . Additional statistics: 10 double-play ground outs in 115 opportunities, 16 doubles, 1 triple in 116.0 innings last season. . . . Earned nine saves in 18 opportunities. . . . Changing of the guard: King faced 86 batters while protecting leads of three runs or less in the eighth inning or later. That's seven more than rookie Mike Henneman, and 19 more than Willie Hernandez. . . . Owes his fielders a dinner or two: He's allowed 121 runs in two seasons with Detroit; only four were unearned. . . . Opponents' career breakdown: .217 at Tiger Stadium, .246 in road games. . . . Acquired from Giants in the same deal that landed Matt Nokes. . . . Was born four days before Shea Stadium opened.

Mark Langston
Seattle Mariners — Throws Left

	W–L	ERA	AB	H	HR	BB	SO	BA	SA	OBA
Season	19-13	3.84	1015	242	30	114	262	.238	.383	.317
vs. Left-Handers			147	29	4	14	42	.197	.293	.265
vs. Right-Handers			868	213	26	100	220	.245	.399	.325
Home	7-8	4.29	472	111	15	52	126	.235	.383	.313
Road	12-5	3.45	543	131	15	62	136	.241	.383	.320
Grass	11-2	3.33	429	102	11	48	104	.238	.373	.315
Artificial Turf	8-11	4.22	586	140	19	66	158	.239	.391	.318
April	3-2	3.66	148	35	2	15	36	.236	.365	.311
May	3-2	4.11	184	43	6	19	53	.234	.386	.306
June	4-2	4.17	182	39	6	18	48	.214	.374	.286
July	1-3	5.35	139	36	6	14	29	.259	.439	.331
August	4-1	2.14	171	41	3	23	41	.240	.327	.332
Sept./Oct.	4-3	3.83	191	48	7	25	55	.251	.414	.336
Leading Off Inn.			249	61	10	30	60	.245	.438	.329
Runners On			451	115	12	36	114	.255	.404	.310
Runners/Scor. Pos.			233	66	7	23	59	.283	.433	.342
Runners On/2 Out			180	41	6	18	41	.228	.372	.305
Scor. Pos./2 Out			105	25	3	11	25	.238	.371	.316
Late Inning Pressure			101	24	1	5	21	.238	.317	.274
Leading Off			26	5	0	1	4	.192	.231	.222
Runners On			39	10	0	1	10	.256	.308	.275
Runners/Scor. Pos.			19	7	0	0	3	.368	.421	.368
First 9 Batters			277	66	8	34	69	.238	.383	.322
Second 9 Batters			269	59	9	32	76	.219	.357	.306
All Batters Thereafter			469	117	13	48	117	.249	.399	.320

Loves to face: Cory Snyder (.091, 2-for-22, 15 SO)
Hates to face: Tom Brookens (.458, 11-for-24)
Ground outs-to-air outs ratio: 1.10 last season, 1.04 for career. . . . Additional statistics: 20 double-play ground outs in 220 opportunities, 45 doubles, 6 triples in 272.0 innings last season. . . . Allowed 19 first-inning runs in 35 starts. . . . Batting support: 4.57 runs per start. . . . Won 12 road games last season, two more than any other pitcher in the majors. . . . August ERA was 2d-best in the A.L. . . . Led Mariners' staff with an average of 7.77 innings per start. . . . Strikeout-to-walk ratio has improved dramatically over past three seasons: 0.79 in 1985, 1.99 in 1986, 2.29 last season. . . . Career batting average of .195 by opposing left-handers, .253 by right-handers. . . . Opponents' career breakdown: .229 with bases empty, .261 with runners on base, .269 with runners in scoring position.

Dave LaPoint — Chicago White Sox — Throws Left

	W–L	ERA	AB	H	HR	BB	SO	BA	SA	OBA
Season	6-3	2.94	308	69	7	31	43	.224	.334	.297
vs. Left-Handers			40	9	0	5	6	.225	.250	.311
vs. Right-Handers			268	60	7	26	37	.224	.347	.295
Home	4-1	3.24	193	48	3	22	27	.249	.347	.329
Road	2-2	2.48	115	21	4	9	16	.183	.313	.242
Grass	6-2	2.92	289	67	6	30	41	.232	.339	.306
Artificial Turf	0-1	3.18	19	2	1	1	2	.105	.263	.150
April			0	0	0	0	0	—	—	—
May			0	0	0	0	0	—	—	—
June			0	0	0	0	0	—	—	—
July			0	0	0	0	0	—	—	—
August	2-2	4.89	139	38	4	16	24	.273	.424	.353
Sept./Oct.	4-1	1.51	169	31	3	15	19	.183	.260	.250
Leading Off Inn.			80	20	2	6	6	.250	.400	.310
Runners On			134	27	3	12	28	.201	.291	.267
Runners/Scor. Pos.			65	12	1	7	13	.185	.246	.264
Runners On/2 Out			57	12	1	9	11	.211	.263	.318
Scor. Pos./2 Out			35	6	0	5	6	.171	.171	.275
Late Inning Pressure			15	4	2	0	1	.267	.733	.267
Leading Off			5	2	1	0	0	.400	1.000	.400
Runners On			5	2	1	0	0	.400	1.200	.400
Runners/Scor. Pos.			3	0	0	0	1	.000	.000	.000
First 9 Batters			103	22	2	11	18	.214	.311	.296
Second 9 Batters			96	16	2	11	15	.167	.250	.252
All Batters Thereafter			109	31	3	9	10	.284	.431	.339

Loves to face: Ray Knight (.129, 4-for-31, 1 HR)
Hates to face: Scott Fletcher (.700, 7-for-10, 2 BB)
Figures *above* are for A.L. only.... Ground outs-to-air outs ratio: 1.69 last season, 1.34 for career.... Additional statistics: 8 double-play ground outs in 74 opportunities, 16 doubles, 1 triple in 98.2 innings last season.... Allowed 4 first-inning runs in 14 starts.... Batting support: 5.43 runs per start.... Ranked seventh in the league with a 2.94 mark after the All-Star break.... Combined-league record of 7-4 last season, career record now stands at .500 (53–53).... Has not allowed a home run to a left-handed batter since Mike Scioscia connected on Sept. 29, 1986.... Has pitched for five different teams in the last three years. White Sox were his sixth team in seven years. (Cardinals count only once, even though he had two tours of duty with them.)

Jack Lazorko — California Angels — Throws Right

	W–L	ERA	AB	H	HR	BB	SO	BA	SA	OBA
Season	5-6	4.59	435	108	20	44	55	.248	.439	.318
vs. Left-Handers			190	55	12	25	7	.289	.553	.369
vs. Right-Handers			245	53	8	19	48	.216	.351	.277
Home	4-3	6.27	246	65	18	30	34	.264	.524	.346
Road	1-3	2.44	189	43	2	14	21	.228	.328	.279
Grass	5-4	4.53	364	88	18	38	52	.242	.429	.315
Artificial Turf	0-2	4.91	71	20	2	6	3	.282	.493	.333
April			0	0	0	0	0	—	—	—
May	0-2	3.91	91	18	5	8	12	.198	.385	.263
June	2-2	5.28	109	29	7	11	15	.266	.505	.336
July	2-1	3.38	90	23	4	8	9	.256	.411	.323
August	0-0	16.20	34	15	2	8	1	.441	.824	.535
Sept./Oct.	1-1	2.90	111	23	2	9	18	.207	.324	.264
Leading Off Inn.			113	35	5	6	15	.310	.522	.350
Runners On			155	44	9	20	24	.284	.510	.363
Runners/Scor. Pos.			84	28	6	13	12	.333	.595	.410
Runners On/2 Out			64	20	4	7	10	.313	.578	.380
Scor. Pos./2 Out			36	12	2	6	4	.333	.556	.429
Late Inning Pressure			64	13	1	5	6	.203	.281	.261
Leading Off			21	8	1	1	1	.381	.619	.409
Runners On			17	4	0	2	2	.235	.235	.316
Runners/Scor. Pos.			8	3	0	2	0	.375	.375	.500
First 9 Batters			196	46	12	24	28	.235	.485	.321
Second 9 Batters			136	35	5	11	14	.257	.404	.311
All Batters Thereafter			103	27	3	9	13	.262	.398	.321

Loves to face: George Bell (0-for-7)
Hates to face: Kent Hrbek (3-for-3, 2 HR)
Ground outs-to-air outs ratio: 0.97 last season, 1.23 for career.... Additional statistics: 10 double-play ground outs in 85 opportunities, 17 doubles, 3 triples in 117.2 innings last season.... Record of 3-5 (5.17 ERA) as a starter, 2-1 (3.69 ERA) in 15 relief appearances. Angels had a 2-13 record in his relief outings.... Has pitched for a different club in each of the last four seasons (Milwaukee, Seattle, Detroit, and California). Has also been in the Houston, San Francisco, and Texas organizations.... Had started only one game prior to the 1987 season, but pitched in Angels' rotation from May 20 until All-Star break.... Opponents batted .600 (6-for-10) with bases loaded last season, highest average allowed by any pitcher in majors (minimum: 10 at bats).

Charlie Leibrandt — Kansas City Royals — Throws Left

	W–L	ERA	AB	H	HR	BB	SO	BA	SA	OBA
Season	16-11	3.41	929	235	23	74	151	.253	.392	.307
vs. Left-Handers			155	36	2	9	23	.232	.310	.273
vs. Right-Handers			774	199	21	65	128	.257	.408	.314
Home	8-4	3.28	430	102	8	34	68	.237	.363	.293
Road	8-7	3.52	499	133	15	40	83	.267	.417	.320
Grass	7-4	3.41	352	96	8	27	58	.273	.406	.323
Artificial Turf	9-7	3.40	577	139	15	47	93	.241	.383	.298
April	3-1	2.37	130	33	1	12	21	.254	.354	.322
May	3-2	2.48	146	31	5	5	28	.212	.370	.238
June	2-3	3.08	192	49	6	14	28	.255	.422	.306
July	2-2	3.00	131	29	2	12	23	.221	.305	.285
August	3-1	3.43	172	49	4	13	27	.285	.390	.330
Sept./Oct.	3-2	5.90	158	44	7	18	24	.278	.481	.350
Leading Off Inn.			237	62	8	10	33	.262	.451	.291
Runners On			362	89	6	42	56	.246	.340	.322
Runners/Scor. Pos.			215	43	4	29	33	.200	.288	.292
Runners On/2 Out			153	38	3	30	28	.248	.366	.375
Scor. Pos./2 Out			98	21	2	23	17	.214	.327	.369
Late Inning Pressure			76	18	2	9	14	.237	.408	.314
Leading Off			19	4	0	2	1	.211	.316	.286
Runners On			29	5	0	4	8	.172	.241	.265
Runners/Scor. Pos.			14	1	0	3	2	.071	.071	.222
First 9 Batters			286	70	9	22	51	.245	.399	.298
Second 9 Batters			279	70	6	19	42	.251	.369	.297
All Batters Thereafter			364	95	8	33	58	.261	.404	.323

Loves to face: Bob Boone (.083, 2-for-24)
Hates to face: Brian Downing (.609, 14-for-23, 2 HR, 5 BB)
Ground outs-to-air outs ratio: 1.27 last season, 1.19 for career.... Additional statistics: 9 double-play ground outs in 154 opportunities, 50 doubles, 3 triples in 240.1 innings last season.... Allowed 18 first-inning runs in 35 starts.... Batting support: 4.63 runs per start.... Only pitcher to defeat all 13 opposing A.L. clubs last season.... Struck out an average of 5.65 batters per nine innings, 56 percent higher than his prior career rate (3.64).... Opponents' batting average with runners in scoring position was lowest of eight-year career.... Has an April record of 10-1 in four seasons with the Royals.... Since joining K.C., has allowed 25 HR at Royals Stadium, 44 on road.... Earliest recollection is Larsen's perfect game, four days after his birth. Honest.

Bill Long — Chicago White Sox — Throws Right

	W–L	ERA	AB	H	HR	BB	SO	BA	SA	OBA
Season	8-8	4.37	659	179	20	28	72	.272	.434	.303
vs. Left-Handers			344	96	10	13	39	.279	.439	.307
vs. Right-Handers			315	83	10	15	33	.263	.429	.298
Home	2-5	5.14	271	78	10	13	28	.288	.469	.323
Road	6-3	3.84	388	101	10	15	44	.260	.410	.289
Grass	8-6	4.11	569	149	19	23	65	.262	.425	.292
Artificial Turf	0-2	6.04	90	30	1	5	7	.333	.489	.367
April			0	0	0	0	0	—	—	—
May	1-1	3.45	107	24	5	2	11	.224	.411	.239
June	3-3	4.28	156	47	5	11	23	.301	.474	.353
July	1-2	4.24	124	26	6	5	11	.210	.411	.240
August	3-0	2.89	140	36	2	6	20	.257	.393	.289
Sept./Oct.	0-2	7.45	132	46	2	4	7	.348	.470	.368
Leading Off Inn.			172	39	3	5	22	.227	.314	.253
Runners On			226	73	9	15	18	.323	.531	.363
Runners/Scor. Pos.			132	39	5	12	14	.295	.515	.347
Runners On/2 Out			92	27	4	7	9	.293	.478	.343
Scor. Pos./2 Out			60	15	2	5	6	.250	.417	.308
Late Inning Pressure			81	22	1	5	15	.272	.383	.314
Leading Off			24	6	0	0	6	.250	.333	.250
Runners On			23	7	1	3	2	.304	.522	.385
Runners/Scor. Pos.			12	3	1	3	1	.250	.500	.400
First 9 Batters			248	69	7	6	31	.278	.440	.298
Second 9 Batters			200	49	7	7	20	.245	.400	.276
All Batters Thereafter			211	61	6	15	21	.289	.460	.333

Loves to face: Ruben Sierra (.077, 1-for-13, 1 HR)
Hates to face: Larry Sheets (.800, 4-for-5, 1 2B, 2 HR)
Ground outs-to-air outs ratio: 1.31 last season, 1.32 for career.... Additional statistics: 15 double-play ground outs in 99 opportunities, 37 doubles, 5 triples in 169.0 innings last season.... Allowed 12 first-inning runs in 23 starts.... Batting support: 5.70 runs per start, 10th-highest average in A.L. (minimum: 15 GS).... Led all major-league pitchers with an average of 1.49 walks per nine innings. Made 10 starts in which he didn't walk a batter, highest total in majors.... Tied for major-league lead among rookies in both complete games (5) and shutouts (2).... Season debut was a 2-hit shutout of the Yankees on May 5.... One of five A.L. pitchers with both a save and a shutout last season.... Career ERA of 5.45 in 26 starts, 1.30 in seven relief appearances.

Mike Loynd
Texas Rangers   Throws Right

	W–L	ERA	AB	H	HR	BB	SO	BA	SA	OBA
Season	1-5	6.10	286	82	14	38	48	.287	.486	.370
vs. Left-Handers			134	42	8	17	16	.313	.522	.392
vs. Right-Handers			152	40	6	21	32	.263	.454	.351
Home	1-3	6.26	189	54	8	28	32	.286	.450	.377
Road	0-2	5.79	97	28	6	10	16	.289	.557	.355
Grass	1-4	6.27	250	73	13	35	39	.292	.496	.378
Artificial Turf	0-1	5.00	36	9	1	3	9	.250	.417	.308
April	1-0	2.70	40	11	2	4	3	.275	.450	.341
May	0-2	4.34	75	21	5	11	16	.280	.520	.379
June	0-2	5.24	85	19	3	15	15	.224	.400	.337
July	0-1	10.57	35	11	2	3	5	.314	.543	.368
August	0-0	9.00	46	17	2	3	8	.370	.565	.400
Sept./Oct.	0-0	40.50	5	3	0	2	1	.600	.600	.714
Leading Off Inn.			64	16	5	8	9	.250	.516	.333
Runners On			142	39	4	15	25	.275	.415	.340
Runners/Scor. Pos.			81	26	2	7	16	.321	.481	.367
Runners On/2 Out			61	17	1	9	14	.279	.426	.371
Scor. Pos./2 Out			37	12	1	4	10	.324	.541	.390
Late Inning Pressure			1	0	0	1	0	.000	.000	.500
Leading Off			0	0	0	1	0	—	—	1.000
Runners On			1	0	0	0	0	.000	.000	.000
Runners/Scor. Pos.			0	0	0	0	0	—	—	—
First 9 Batters			163	45	9	23	35	.276	.497	.367
Second 9 Batters			83	22	3	14	8	.265	.386	.367
All Batters Thereafter			40	15	2	1	5	.375	.650	.390

Loves to face: Cal Ripken (0-for-7)
Hates to face: Julio Franco (2-for-2, 3 BB)
Ground outs-to-air outs ratio: 1.04 last season, 1.10 for career.... Additional statistics: 4 double-play ground outs in 64 opportunities, 13 doubles, 1 triple in 69.1 innings last season.... Averaged 3.88 innings pitched in eight games started.... Has faced 521 batters in two seasons, but only two in Late-Inning Pressure Situations. Made 18 relief appearances last season, but didn't face a single batter while protecting a lead of three runs or less in the seventh inning or later.... Record of 0–5 with a 6.97 ERA in eight starts; 1–0, 5.40 ERA in 18 relief appearances.... Two-year ERA of 5.82 is 3d highest in majors during that time, behind John Butcher (6.56) and Jerry Reuss (5.92) (minimum: 100 innings).... Has allowed four hits in seven career at bats with the bases loaded.

Gary Lucas
California Angels   Throws Left

	W–L	ERA	AB	H	HR	BB	SO	BA	SA	OBA
Season	1-5	3.63	274	66	7	35	44	.241	.365	.329
vs. Left-Handers			96	27	3	16	16	.281	.448	.383
vs. Right-Handers			178	39	4	19	28	.219	.320	.298
Home	1-2	2.58	156	30	2	16	27	.192	.282	.270
Road	0-3	5.28	118	36	5	19	17	.305	.475	.403
Grass	1-5	3.42	247	57	5	30	40	.231	.340	.314
Artificial Turf	0-0	6.00	27	9	2	5	4	.333	.593	.455
April	0-1	10.57	33	12	2	3	6	.364	.636	.417
May	1-1	8.74	45	17	2	8	5	.378	.578	.463
June	0-0	1.04	30	5	0	1	3	.167	.167	.194
July	0-0	0.96	63	9	0	6	9	.143	.206	.225
August	0-1	2.08	67	17	2	6	12	.254	.388	.324
Sept./Oct.	0-2	2.53	36	6	1	11	9	.167	.250	.362
Leading Off Inn.			62	19	4	4	9	.306	.565	.348
Runners On			128	36	3	22	20	.281	.414	.382
Runners/Scor. Pos.			78	24	3	20	8	.308	.462	.440
Runners On/2 Out			56	19	2	11	10	.339	.571	.448
Scor. Pos./2 Out			34	13	2	10	6	.382	.618	.523
Late Inning Pressure			92	20	3	22	16	.217	.370	.365
Leading Off			24	6	1	2	4	.250	.417	.308
Runners On			47	11	2	14	10	.234	.447	.403
Runners/Scor. Pos.			28	7	2	13	6	.250	.500	.476
First 9 Batters			233	53	5	30	39	.227	.339	.320
Second 9 Batters			41	13	2	5	5	.317	.512	.383
All Batters Thereafter			0	0	0	0	0	—	—	—

Loves to face: Claudell Washington (.111, 2-for-18)
Hates to face: Rafael Santana (.800, 4-for-5)
Ground outs-to-air outs ratio: 1.71 last season, 1.44 for career.... Additional statistics: 10 double-play ground outs in 68 opportunities, 11 doubles, 1 triple in 74.1 innings last season.... Faced 33 consecutive batters without allowing a hit (July 2–July 10).... Faced only one batter in a game five times, something no other Angels pitcher was asked to do even once.... Has held opposing batters to a lower average in home games than he has in road games in each of his eight major league seasons. During that time he has called three different cities "home": San Diego, Montreal, and Anaheim.... Opponents' batting averages with runners in scoring position since 1984: .232, .281, .289, .308.... Opponents' career batting average of .213 with the bases loaded, including four slams.

Kirk McCaskill
California Angels   Throws Right

	W–L	ERA	AB	H	HR	BB	SO	BA	SA	OBA
Season	4-6	5.67	294	84	14	34	56	.286	.463	.363
vs. Left-Handers			156	49	9	16	21	.314	.532	.382
vs. Right-Handers			138	35	5	18	35	.254	.384	.342
Home	1-1	5.02	111	31	4	12	19	.279	.423	.352
Road	3-5	6.07	183	53	10	22	37	.290	.486	.369
Grass	2-5	6.75	219	69	10	26	39	.315	.489	.389
Artificial Turf	2-1	2.95	75	15	4	8	17	.200	.387	.286
April	2-0	2.57	71	13	3	3	22	.183	.310	.213
May			0	0	0	0	0	—	—	—
June			0	0	0	0	0	—	—	—
July	0-3	9.64	64	27	2	10	10	.422	.547	.507
August	2-2	5.15	145	39	7	20	22	.269	.469	.361
Sept./Oct.	0-1	15.00	14	5	2	1	2	.357	.786	.400
Leading Off Inn.			74	26	3	5	11	.351	.554	.407
Runners On			122	36	7	16	21	.295	.484	.374
Runners/Scor. Pos.			63	18	4	7	8	.286	.492	.352
Runners On/2 Out			47	12	4	10	8	.255	.553	.386
Scor. Pos./2 Out			27	6	3	4	4	.222	.593	.323
Late Inning Pressure			8	4	0	1	0	.500	.500	.556
Leading Off			3	1	0	0	0	.333	.333	.333
Runners On			2	2	0	0	0	1.000	1.000	1.000
Runners/Scor. Pos.			1	1	0	0	0	1.000	1.000	1.000
First 9 Batters			107	29	5	14	22	.271	.449	.363
Second 9 Batters			105	31	5	14	21	.295	.457	.378
All Batters Thereafter			82	24	4	6	13	.293	.488	.341

Loves to face: Oddibe McDowell (.095, 2-for-21)
Hates to face: Rickey Henderson (.556, 5-for-9, 2 HR)
Ground outs-to-air outs ratio: 0.84 last season, 1.06 for career.... Additional statistics: 4 double-play ground outs in 69 opportunities, 10 doubles, 0 triples in 74.2 innings last season.... Allowed 11 first-inning runs in 13 starts.... Batting support: 3.69 runs per start.... Compiled a 6.88 ERA after returning on July 11 from elbow surgery.... Allowed one home run per 5.3 innings, nearly double his prior career rate (one per 10.4 innings).... Opponents were 2-for-6 with the bases loaded last season, and both hits were grand slams (Kingery and Pagliarulo).... Opposing left-handers have outhit right-handers in all three seasons in majors.... Born on April 9, 1961, two days before the Los Angeles Angels made their major-league debut.

Scott McGregor
Baltimore Orioles   Throws Left

	W–L	ERA	AB	H	HR	BB	SO	BA	SA	OBA
Season	2-7	6.64	344	112	15	35	39	.326	.509	.388
vs. Left-Handers			62	15	2	7	8	.242	.339	.324
vs. Right-Handers			282	97	13	28	31	.344	.546	.403
Home	0-5	6.43	170	57	7	19	26	.335	.518	.394
Road	2-2	6.85	174	55	8	16	13	.316	.500	.381
Grass	1-7	7.53	313	109	15	32	37	.348	.550	.406
Artificial Turf	1-0	0.00	31	3	0	3	2	.097	.097	.200
April	0-3	4.74	94	27	3	7	13	.287	.426	.327
May	2-2	6.16	117	35	6	14	8	.299	.487	.376
June	0-2	10.69	73	30	3	9	9	.411	.603	.482
July	0-0	2.57	27	8	1	1	4	.296	.481	.321
August	0-0	18.90	17	7	2	2	3	.412	.941	.474
Sept./Oct.	0-0	2.45	16	5	0	2	2	.313	.313	.389
Leading Off Inn.			79	26	3	12	8	.329	.468	.424
Runners On			156	55	9	16	18	.353	.564	.404
Runners/Scor. Pos.			87	32	5	9	11	.368	.575	.406
Runners On/2 Out			57	20	3	6	7	.351	.579	.413
Scor. Pos./2 Out			34	12	1	3	4	.353	.500	.405
Late Inning Pressure			19	11	1	2	2	.579	.789	.591
Leading Off			6	5	1	0	1	.833	1.333	.833
Runners On			11	6	0	1	0	.545	.636	.538
Runners/Scor. Pos.			6	3	0	1	0	.500	.667	.500
First 9 Batters			156	48	5	18	22	.308	.442	.385
Second 9 Batters			108	36	6	10	9	.333	.565	.387
All Batters Thereafter			80	28	4	7	8	.350	.563	.393

Loves to face: Rick Cerone (.125, 4-for-32)
Hates to face: Larry Herndon (.469, 15-for-32, 4 HR)
Ground outs-to-air outs ratio: 0.70 last season, 0.79 for career.... Additional statistics: 6 double-play ground outs in 87 opportunities, 14 doubles, 2 triples in 85.1 innings last season.... Allowed 10 first-inning runs in 15 starts.... Batting support: 4.40 runs per start.... Opposing right-handers hit .353 at Memorial Stadium, with six HR in 139 AB. ..Allowed more than a hit an inning for eighth straight season, longest current streak in majors.... Has won eight straight decisions vs. Oakland, lost eight to Cleveland.... Cleveland?... Yearly batting averages by opposing right-handed batters since 1983: .282, .289, .289, .283, .344.... One of 14 pitchers with 100 wins in 1980s, but the only one of them whose ERA is above 4.00 during that time (107–80, 4.07).

Greg Minton

Throws Right

California Angels	W–L	ERA	AB	H	HR	BB	SO	BA	SA	OBA
Season	5-4	3.08	276	71	4	29	35	.257	.333	.328
vs. Left-Handers			127	34	3	14	10	.268	.378	.338
vs. Right-Handers			149	37	1	15	25	.248	.295	.319
Home	3-1	2.85	147	39	2	14	17	.265	.340	.329
Road	2-3	3.34	129	32	2	15	18	.248	.326	.326
Grass	4-3	3.31	238	61	4	25	33	.256	.345	.327
Artificial Turf	1-1	1.69	38	10	0	4	2	.263	.263	.333
April			0	0	0	0	0	—	—	—
May			0	0	0	0	0	—	—	—
June	1-0	1.56	60	12	0	4	14	.200	.233	.262
July	2-1	3.22	83	21	3	7	7	.253	.373	.311
August	0-1	3.26	70	21	0	8	8	.300	.329	.363
Sept./Oct.	2-2	4.24	63	17	1	10	6	.270	.381	.370
Leading Off Inn.			64	17	1	9	6	.266	.328	.356
Runners On			127	32	1	14	18	.252	.323	.326
Runners/Scor. Pos.			67	13	0	9	9	.194	.209	.282
Runners On/2 Out			50	8	0	10	11	.160	.180	.300
Scor. Pos./2 Out			35	6	0	7	6	.171	.171	.310
Late Inning Pressure			140	39	2	17	15	.279	.350	.361
Leading Off			34	10	0	3	1	.294	.324	.351
Runners On			64	17	0	10	9	.266	.313	.373
Runners/Scor. Pos.			37	7	0	7	6	.189	.216	.318
First 9 Batters			236	56	4	26	29	.237	.318	.313
Second 9 Batters			40	15	0	3	6	.375	.425	.419
All Batters Thereafter			0	0	0	0	0	—	—	—

Loves to face: Bill Madlock (.087, 2-for-23)
Hates to face: Dave Parker (.550, 11-for-20)
Figures *above* are for A.L. only. . . . Ground outs-to-air outs ratio: 2.23, 5th highest in A.L. last season (minimum: 200 BFP), 2.39 for career. . . . Additional statistics: 23 double-play ground outs in 96 opportunities, highest rate in majors (minimum: 40 opportunities), 15 doubles, 1 triple in 99.1 innings last season. . . . Earned 11 saves in 15 opportunities, after going 9-for-20 over two previous seasons. . . . Combined league record of 0–3 with a 4.78 ERA in day games; 6–1, 2.41 ERA at night. . . . Allowed only four home runs over the first 341.2 innings of his career; has surrendered 33 in 605 innings since then. . . . Was part of history in his major-league debut on Sept. 7, 1975. He relieved Pete Falcone against Cincinnati as Reds beat Giants for earliest pennant clinching in N.L. history.

Dale Mohorcic

Throws Right

Texas Rangers	W–L	ERA	AB	H	HR	BB	SO	BA	SA	OBA
Season	7-6	2.99	359	88	11	19	48	.245	.368	.285
vs. Left-Handers			151	45	5	8	16	.298	.444	.335
vs. Right-Handers			208	43	6	11	32	.207	.313	.249
Home	4-3	3.53	186	47	7	8	25	.253	.392	.282
Road	3-3	2.42	173	41	4	11	23	.237	.341	.289
Grass	6-5	3.14	301	74	10	12	40	.246	.372	.275
Artificial Turf	1-1	2.20	58	14	1	7	8	.241	.345	.333
April	1-1	3.31	57	13	1	5	8	.228	.298	.302
May	3-1	2.63	96	22	2	5	11	.229	.313	.272
June	1-0	1.29	70	12	2	3	13	.171	.286	.205
July	1-0	4.24	64	18	2	4	9	.281	.422	.319
August	0-2	3.68	27	6	2	0	1	.222	.444	.222
Sept./Oct.	1-2	4.35	45	17	2	2	6	.378	.578	.404
Leading Off Inn.			69	18	2	2	11	.261	.362	.292
Runners On			185	41	7	13	23	.222	.357	.270
Runners/Scor. Pos.			109	28	3	11	15	.257	.358	.320
Runners On/2 Out			73	12	2	3	15	.164	.274	.197
Scor. Pos./2 Out			45	7	0	2	10	.156	.178	.191
Late Inning Pressure			184	57	7	13	23	.310	.473	.352
Leading Off			36	11	2	0	4	.306	.472	.306
Runners On			97	26	4	9	11	.268	.433	.324
Runners/Scor. Pos.			57	16	1	8	7	.281	.368	.358
First 9 Batters			343	84	11	16	48	.245	.370	.281
Second 9 Batters			16	4	0	3	0	.250	.313	.368
All Batters Thereafter			0	0	0	0	0	—	—	—

Loves to face: Cal Ripken (0-for-8)
Hates to face: Brook Jacoby (.667, 4-for-6)
Ground outs-to-air outs ratio: 2.21 last season, 2.15 for career. . . . Additional statistics: 14 double-play ground outs in 95 opportunities, 9 doubles, 1 triple in 99.1 innings last season. . . . Allowed 1.72 walks per nine innings, 3d-lowest rate among major league relievers (min.: 30 games). . . . Opponents' career average of .302 in Late-Inning Pressure Situations, .220 in unpressured situations. Difference of 82 points is largest over last 10 years (min.: 250 AB each way). . . . Made major-league debut on May 31, 1986, four months and change past 30th birthday. Others to debut past the big three-oh since 1970: Ubaldo Heredia (1987), Bill Early (1986), Ernesto Escarrega (1982), Steve Stroughter (1982), Gerry Pritle (1978), Damaso Blanco (1972), Minnie Mendoza (1970).

Mike Moore

Throws Right

Seattle Mariners	W–L	ERA	AB	H	HR	BB	SO	BA	SA	OBA
Season	9-19	4.71	919	268	29	84	115	.292	.460	.348
vs. Left-Handers			547	163	15	49	58	.298	.463	.353
vs. Right-Handers			372	105	14	35	57	.282	.457	.341
Home	4-8	4.12	425	116	16	36	58	.273	.445	.328
Road	5-11	5.25	494	152	13	48	57	.308	.474	.366
Grass	5-8	5.04	386	118	11	36	45	.306	.466	.361
Artificial Turf	4-11	4.48	533	150	18	48	70	.281	.456	.339
April	1-3	4.76	129	36	2	17	16	.279	.380	.356
May	1-3	5.28	124	39	6	18	14	.315	.516	.401
June	1-3	5.83	123	40	5	7	19	.325	.537	.356
July	0-4	5.94	136	42	7	13	14	.309	.522	.367
August	3-4	3.39	228	62	5	14	32	.272	.421	.313
Sept./Oct.	3-2	4.37	179	49	4	15	20	.274	.430	.328
Leading Off Inn.			227	72	10	16	22	.317	.555	.362
Runners On			403	120	10	39	46	.298	.432	.353
Runners/Scor. Pos.			243	73	4	30	24	.300	.420	.367
Runners On/2 Out			155	46	7	20	22	.297	.484	.377
Scor. Pos./2 Out			96	26	1	16	12	.271	.375	.375
Late Inning Pressure			82	21	4	12	12	.256	.463	.351
Leading Off			25	5	2	1	4	.200	.520	.231
Runners On			31	8	1	6	4	.258	.355	.378
Runners/Scor. Pos.			17	5	1	5	1	.294	.471	.455
First 9 Batters			278	82	6	20	32	.295	.450	.341
Second 9 Batters			254	76	8	28	21	.299	.476	.362
All Batters Thereafter			387	110	15	36	62	.284	.457	.344

Loves to face: Mike Young (.103, 3-for-29)
Hates to face: Dan Pasqua (.579, 11-for-19, 2 HR)
Ground outs-to-air outs ratio: 1.46 last season, 1.32 for career. . . . Additional statistics: 30 double-play ground outs in 184 opportunities, 54 doubles, 7 triples in 231.0 innings last season. . . . Allowed 22 first-inning runs in 33 starts. . . . Batting support: 4.06 runs per start, 6th-lowest average in A.L. (minimum: 15 GS). . . . Only pitcher in either league to complete six consecutive starts last season. . . . Led the A.L. with 11 losses in road games. . . . Record of 1–7 (6.52 ERA) in day games, 8–12 (4.24 ERA) at night. . . . Record of 3–12 vs. Eastern Division clubs, 6–7 vs. the West. . . . Minus his great 1985 season (17–10, 3.46 ERA), his career stats look like those of another enigma, Jose Rijo. Moore: 40–61 (.396), 4.75 ERA; Rijo: 19–30 (.387), 4.74 ERA.

Mike Morgan

Throws Right

Seattle Mariners	W–L	ERA	AB	H	HR	BB	SO	BA	SA	OBA
Season	12-17	4.65	827	245	25	53	85	.296	.455	.340
vs. Left-Handers			447	135	13	31	49	.302	.468	.345
vs. Right-Handers			380	110	12	22	36	.289	.439	.335
Home	7-10	4.79	509	148	16	24	55	.291	.446	.325
Road	5-7	4.42	318	97	9	29	30	.305	.469	.364
Grass	4-4	3.45	237	69	5	22	26	.291	.435	.352
Artificial Turf	8-13	5.14	590	176	20	31	59	.298	.463	.335
April	1-3	7.36	100	32	7	4	11	.320	.610	.343
May	4-2	2.70	185	44	3	10	26	.238	.314	.279
June	1-3	4.37	148	46	5	9	14	.311	.507	.348
July	2-3	6.84	101	32	3	12	6	.317	.505	.393
August	2-4	4.86	157	47	6	8	15	.299	.478	.337
Sept./Oct.	2-2	4.91	136	44	1	10	13	.324	.412	.374
Leading Off Inn.			199	62	6	16	13	.312	.467	.366
Runners On			369	103	9	20	34	.279	.415	.317
Runners/Scor. Pos.			213	52	4	18	20	.244	.366	.303
Runners On/2 Out			138	34	3	12	16	.246	.362	.311
Scor. Pos./2 Out			89	22	3	11	11	.247	.404	.337
Late Inning Pressure			34	10	2	3	3	.294	.500	.368
Leading Off			10	1	0	1	0	.100	.100	.250
Runners On			11	4	0	1	1	.364	.364	.417
Runners/Scor. Pos.			8	3	0	0	1	.375	.375	.375
First 9 Batters			264	71	5	21	34	.269	.413	.325
Second 9 Batters			248	86	9	13	17	.347	.536	.380
All Batters Thereafter			315	88	11	19	34	.279	.425	.322

Loves to face: New teammates (see below)
Hates to face: Bo Jackson (.750, 6-for-8) even more than Brian Bosworth does
Cal Ripken and Eddie Murray are a combined 10-for-72 vs. Morgan. . . . Ground outs-to-air outs ratio: 1.93 last season, 1.60 for career. . . . Additional statistics: 26 double-play ground outs in 175 opportunities, 42 doubles, 7 triples in 207.0 innings last season. . . . Allowed 21 first-inning runs in 31 starts. . . . Batting support: 4.77 runs per start. . . . Faced 61 consecutive batters without a strikeout (July 20 to Aug. 3), 2d-longest streak in A.L. last season (the longest was 64 by Moose Haas). . . . Career record of 0–6 vs. the Red Sox, 0–7 vs. the Yankees. . . . Has spent all or part of seven seasons in the majors, but has never had a winning record. . . . Cal Sr. will be Morgan's ninth manager in his eighth big-league season.

Jack Morris
Detroit Tigers — Throws Right

Detroit Tigers	W–L	ERA	AB	H	HR	BB	SO	BA	SA	OBA
Season	18-11	3.38	996	227	39	93	208	.228	.391	.293
vs. Left-Handers			533	126	28	61	94	.236	.441	.313
vs. Right-Handers			463	101	11	32	114	.218	.333	.269
Home	8-7	3.15	577	127	29	38	120	.220	.404	.268
Road	10-4	3.73	419	100	10	55	88	.239	.372	.326
Grass	15-10	3.46	868	193	37	82	178	.222	.392	.289
Artificial Turf	3-1	2.81	128	34	2	11	30	.266	.383	.324
April	3-2	3.43	158	37	6	17	28	.234	.373	.309
May	3-0	4.91	125	32	10	6	27	.256	.528	.291
June	5-1	2.79	176	34	5	18	37	.193	.313	.268
July	1-2	3.69	152	38	5	8	24	.250	.428	.286
August	3-2	2.98	154	29	7	14	41	.188	.364	.256
Sept./Oct.	3-4	3.08	231	57	6	30	51	.247	.381	.331
Leading Off Inn.			246	48	8	26	60	.195	.346	.272
Runners On			364	82	12	43	70	.225	.368	.305
Runners/Scor. Pos.			210	37	4	31	49	.176	.252	.276
Runners On/2 Out			152	29	6	16	31	.191	.336	.268
Scor. Pos./2 Out			98	8	3	14	24	.082	.184	.196
Late Inning Pressure			136	32	7	11	26	.235	.434	.291
Leading Off			37	7	1	1	8	.189	.297	.211
Runners On			41	11	4	7	4	.268	.634	.367
Runners/Scor. Pos.			18	4	1	5	1	.222	.444	.375
First 9 Batters			279	63	11	32	77	.226	.384	.306
Second 9 Batters			280	53	8	21	57	.189	.311	.245
All Batters Thereafter			437	111	20	40	74	.254	.446	.315

Loves to face: Ken Phelps (0-for-26, 13 SO)
Hates to face: Mark McGwire (2-for-2, 2 HR)
Ground outs-to-air outs ratio: 0.94 last season, 1.15 for career. . . .
Additional statistics: 11 double-play ground outs in 169 opportunities, 29 doubles, 8 triples in 266.0 innings last season. . . . Batting support: 5.18 runs per start. . . . Didn't throw a shutout last season after tossing six in his last 18 starts of 1986. . . . Pitched 7+ innings in 12 straight starts, longest streak in majors last season, but far short of his 26-game streak in 1983, which no one has approached since. . . . Opponents' career batting average is .201 with two outs and runners in scoring position; 1987 figure was the lowest of the past 13 seasons. . . . Has allowed only four (singles) in 40 AB with the bases loaded since allowing grand slams in consecutive innings to Tony Armas and Bill Buckner in 1984.

Jeff Musselman
Toronto Blue Jays — Throws Left

Toronto Blue Jays	W–L	ERA	AB	H	HR	BB	SO	BA	SA	OBA
Season	12-5	4.15	316	75	7	54	54	.237	.373	.353
vs. Left-Handers			109	18	2	11	23	.165	.275	.252
vs. Right-Handers			207	57	5	43	31	.275	.425	.402
Home	10-2	4.20	136	29	3	27	23	.213	.338	.355
Road	2-3	4.10	180	46	4	27	31	.256	.400	.351
Grass	2-3	4.89	146	38	4	22	28	.260	.411	.355
Artificial Turf	10-2	3.58	170	37	3	32	26	.218	.341	.351
April	1-0	1.42	42	6	1	3	8	.143	.262	.217
May	1-1	3.94	55	13	0	8	6	.236	.327	.328
June	4-0	3.43	68	12	1	15	14	.176	.221	.333
July	3-3	7.20	43	14	1	9	5	.326	.488	.442
August	1-0	5.29	65	19	1	8	14	.292	.508	.370
Sept./Oct.	2-1	4.38	43	11	3	11	7	.256	.465	.418
Leading Off Inn.			67	18	2	14	10	.269	.403	.395
Runners On			166	37	4	27	30	.223	.349	.333
Runners/Scor. Pos.			98	25	4	21	17	.255	.449	.388
Runners On/2 Out			61	15	2	10	9	.246	.426	.352
Scor. Pos./2 Out			43	12	2	8	5	.279	.512	.392
Late Inning Pressure			157	42	4	31	24	.268	.427	.398
Leading Off			35	11	1	7	4	.314	.457	.429
Runners On			85	19	2	19	15	.224	.353	.371
Runners/Scor. Pos.			51	11	2	15	8	.216	.412	.403
First 9 Batters			282	67	7	52	49	.238	.379	.361
Second 9 Batters			34	8	0	2	5	.235	.324	.278
All Batters Thereafter			—	—	—	—	—	—	—	—

Loves to face: Harold Baines (0-for-4, 3 SO)
Hates to face: Mike Felder (3-for-3)
Ground outs-to-air outs ratio: 2.13 last season, 2.32 for career. . . .
Additional statistics: 18 double-play ground outs in 95 opportunities, 2d-highest rate in A.L. (minimum: 40 opp.), 18 doubles, 2 triples in 89.0 innings last season. . . . Led rookie pitchers with 68 appearances last season, 5th-highest total in A.L.; that top five is composed of three Blue Jays and two Rangers. . . . His total of 12 wins led A.L. rookies; rookie record for relief wins is 15 by Hoyt Wilhelm in 1952. . . . Right-handed batters outhit left-handed batters by 110 points, largest such difference against any A.L. pitcher last season (minimum: 100 AB each way). Even more of a difference in his career averages: right-handed batters have hit .282, lefties .175.

Gene Nelson
Oakland As — Throws Right

Oakland As	W–L	ERA	AB	H	HR	BB	SO	BA	SA	OBA
Season	6-5	3.93	482	120	12	35	94	.249	.411	.304
vs. Left-Handers			239	62	4	15	43	.259	.393	.300
vs. Right-Handers			243	58	8	20	51	.239	.428	.307
Home	4-2	3.36	262	60	4	20	58	.229	.370	.288
Road	2-3	4.67	220	60	8	15	36	.273	.459	.322
Grass	6-4	3.34	408	99	7	30	82	.243	.385	.297
Artificial Turf	0-1	7.23	74	21	5	5	12	.284	.554	.337
April	0-1	7.11	50	17	2	6	7	.340	.520	.424
May	2-0	1.50	69	16	0	7	18	.232	.362	.303
June	1-0	2.61	81	20	2	5	15	.247	.358	.284
July	1-1	2.13	95	19	1	5	16	.200	.326	.245
August	2-1	3.04	88	17	3	5	21	.193	.352	.253
Sept./Oct.	0-2	8.10	99	31	4	7	17	.313	.566	.355
Leading Off Inn.			109	29	1	4	16	.266	.385	.292
Runners On			216	55	8	20	45	.255	.435	.314
Runners/Scor. Pos.			129	33	3	15	26	.256	.395	.322
Runners On/2 Out			96	18	1	13	19	.188	.281	.291
Scor. Pos./2 Out			58	13	0	10	10	.224	.293	.338
Late Inning Pressure			121	26	4	6	22	.215	.364	.256
Leading Off			30	8	0	0	4	.267	.367	.267
Runners On			53	11	3	2	10	.208	.377	.232
Runners/Scor. Pos.			28	6	1	2	5	.214	.321	.258
First 9 Batters			340	80	8	22	65	.235	.379	.285
Second 9 Batters			114	34	4	9	21	.298	.518	.360
All Batters Thereafter			28	6	0	4	8	.214	.357	.303

Loves to face: Darrell Evans (.059, 1-for-17, 1 HR)
Hates to face: George Brett (.421, 8-for-19, 4 HR)
Ground outs-to-air outs ratio: 0.91 last season, 1.20 for career. . . .
Additional statistics: 1 double-play ground out in 88 opportunities, lowest rate in A.L. (minimum: 40 opp.), 28 doubles, 7 triples in 123.2 innings last season. . . . Record of 1–3 (5.34 ERA) in six starts, 5–2 (3.51 ERA) in 48 relief appearances. . . . Career record of 0–6 in starts following relief appearances. . . . Opponents' career batting average of .238 in Late-Inning Pressure Situations, .270 at other times. . . . Pitched 15 scoreless innings with a 2–0 record in four games vs. Yankees last season. . . . Faced 31 batters with the bases loaded last season, tying Mark Eichhorn for most in the majors; held opponents to .143 average (4-for-28) with seven strikeouts.

Tom Niedenfuer
Baltimore Orioles — Throws Right

Baltimore Orioles	W–L	ERA	AB	H	HR	BB	SO	BA	SA	OBA
Season	3-5	4.99	206	55	11	22	37	.267	.495	.336
vs. Left-Handers			108	33	8	11	17	.306	.602	.370
vs. Right-Handers			98	22	3	11	20	.224	.378	.301
Home	2-0	4.71	112	30	6	10	17	.268	.500	.328
Road	1-5	5.32	94	25	5	12	20	.266	.489	.346
Grass	3-3	5.10	185	48	10	19	32	.259	.492	.327
Artificial Turf	0-2	3.86	21	7	1	3	5	.333	.524	.417
April			0	0	0	0	0	—	—	—
May	0-0	7.94	23	8	2	8	3	.348	.652	.516
June	1-0	5.27	53	14	5	5	10	.264	.623	.317
July	1-3	4.05	49	10	1	4	12	.204	.347	.259
August	0-0	5.40	35	11	1	1	4	.314	.429	.351
Sept./Oct.	1-2	3.97	46	12	2	4	8	.261	.478	.320
Leading Off Inn.			35	7	3	5	6	.200	.543	.292
Runners On			109	29	2	13	22	.266	.385	.341
Runners/Scor. Pos.			78	20	0	11	18	.256	.308	.337
Runners On/2 Out			58	19	1	8	10	.328	.466	.418
Scor. Pos./2 Out			45	15	0	7	8	.333	.400	.423
Late Inning Pressure			130	34	7	13	27	.262	.492	.326
Leading Off			22	4	1	4	5	.182	.409	.308
Runners On			60	15	1	7	15	.250	.367	.324
Runners/Scor. Pos.			36	8	0	6	12	.222	.250	.326
First 9 Batters			196	51	11	21	36	.260	.500	.330
Second 9 Batters			10	4	0	1	1	.400	.400	.455
All Batters Thereafter			0	0	0	0	0	—	—	—

Loves to face: Johnny Ray (.077, 1-for-13)
Hates to face: Paul Molitor (2-for-2, 1 2B, 1 HR)
Figures *above* for A.L. only. . . . Ground outs-to-air outs ratio: 0.63, 9th-lowest in majors last season (minimum: 200 BFP), 0.55 for career. . . . Additional statistics: 2 double-play ground outs in 57 opportunities, 11 doubles, 2 triples in 68.2 innings last season. . . . Ranked sixth in A.L. with 11 saves after the All-Star break. . . . Record of 1–2 with a 9.39 ERA in day games last season; 3–3, 3.06 ERA in night games. . . . Earned run average has risen every season since his 1.90 mark in 1983 through his combined-leagues figure of 4.46 last season. . . . Opponents' career batting average of .211 on artificial surfaces, .244 on grass fields. . . . Opposing left-handers have outhit right-handers in all seven seasons in majors. Career averages: left-handers, .261; right-handers, .214.

Joe Niekro

Throws Right

Yankees/Twins	W–L	ERA	AB	H	HR	BB	SO	BA	SA	OBA
Season	7-13	5.33	574	155	15	64	84	.270	.420	.351
vs. Left-Handers			306	88	11	38	41	.288	.484	.367
vs. Right-Handers			268	67	4	26	43	.250	.347	.332
Home	4-4	4.50	208	54	7	26	28	.260	.428	.355
Road	3-9	5.81	366	101	8	38	56	.276	.415	.348
Grass	3-6	4.63	302	77	8	31	43	.255	.407	.329
Artificial Turf	4-7	6.15	272	78	7	33	41	.287	.434	.374
April	1-1	4.35	37	9	0	6	4	.243	.243	.356
May	2-2	2.75	130	25	2	12	24	.192	.285	.276
June	2-1	5.75	83	24	2	12	16	.289	.482	.379
July	0-4	5.59	150	42	8	10	18	.280	.520	.333
August	1-2	6.64	77	20	0	17	11	.260	.338	.404
Sept./Oct.	1-3	7.83	97	35	3	7	11	.361	.526	.402
Leading Off Inn.			148	41	3	12	23	.277	.432	.340
Runners On			234	71	6	27	33	.303	.474	.380
Runners/Scor. Pos.			139	43	3	24	20	.309	.489	.406
Runners On/2 Out			90	23	1	15	16	.256	.389	.380
Scor. Pos./2 Out			54	14	1	13	10	.259	.444	.420
Late Inning Pressure			21	4	0	1	3	.190	.286	.227
Leading Off			8	2	0	0	1	.250	.375	.250
Runners On			3	1	0	0	0	.333	.333	.333
Runners/Scor. Pos.			2	1	0	0	0	.500	.500	.500
First 9 Batters			207	52	4	26	35	.251	.353	.338
Second 9 Batters			200	62	8	21	25	.310	.515	.376
All Batters Thereafter			167	41	3	17	24	.246	.389	.337

Loves to face: Tim Hulett (0-for-15)
Hates to face: Dwight Evans (.800, 4-for-5, 2 HR)
Ground outs-to-air outs ratio: 1.09 last season, 1.11 for career.... Additional statistics: 10 double-play ground outs in 92 opportunities, 33 doubles, 4 triples in 147.0 innings last season.... Allowed 9 first-inning runs in 26 starts.... Batting support: 3.88 runs per start, 3d-lowest average in A.L. (minimum: 15 GS).... Has defeated every major-league team except the Blue Jays (0–3).... Didn't allow a home run in his first 43.2 innings pitched last season.... Only pitcher in majors with 25+ starts in each of last two years, but without 10+ wins in either season.... Has never struck out 10 or more batters in a game.... Traded from first-place Yanks to the second-place Twins on June 6. By June 11 the Twins had moved into first place, while the Yanks had relinquished their lead.

Phil Niekro

Throws Right

Indians/Blue Jays	W–L	ERA	AB	H	HR	BB	SO	BA	SA	OBA
Season	7-13	6.10	546	157	22	60	64	.288	.487	.359
vs. Left-Handers			300	94	11	35	28	.313	.507	.387
vs. Right-Handers			246	63	11	25	36	.256	.463	.325
Home	2-6	7.79	219	70	8	26	19	.320	.534	.392
Road	5-7	5.06	327	87	14	34	45	.266	.456	.337
Grass	3-11	6.92	371	111	16	44	45	.299	.512	.374
Artificial Turf	4-2	4.36	175	46	6	16	19	.263	.434	.328
April	1-0	6.50	73	21	5	10	8	.288	.562	.381
May	1-5	5.82	131	36	6	13	19	.275	.466	.338
June	4-2	3.43	152	38	4	17	20	.250	.368	.333
July	1-3	9.36	109	36	1	11	7	.330	.505	.388
August	0-3	7.45	81	26	6	9	10	.321	.654	.385
Sept./Oct.			0	0	0	0	0	—	—	—
Leading Off Inn.			138	38	7	9	12	.275	.507	.324
Runners On			218	62	7	37	25	.284	.468	.388
Runners/Scor. Pos.			125	36	4	26	13	.288	.472	.409
Runners On/2 Out			93	24	2	18	9	.258	.409	.384
Scor. Pos./2 Out			64	18	2	13	5	.281	.453	.410
Late Inning Pressure			41	8	0	8	5	.195	.244	.333
Leading Off			14	1	0	0	1	.071	.143	.071
Runners On			11	3	0	3	1	.273	.273	.438
Runners/Scor. Pos.			4	1	0	2	1	.250	.250	.500
First 9 Batters			198	72	11	20	25	.364	.611	.423
Second 9 Batters			182	37	3	16	20	.203	.346	.270
All Batters Thereafter			166	48	8	24	19	.289	.494	.378

Loves to face: Reggie Jackson (.059, 1-for-17)
Hates to face: Andre Dawson (.418, 23-for-55)
Figures *above* are for A.L. only.... Ground outs-to-air outs ratio: 0.79 last season, 1.06 for career.... Additional statistics: 4 double-play ground outs in 106 opportunities, 33 doubles, 6 triples in 138.2 innings last season.... Allowed 27 first-inning runs in 26 starts.... Batting support: 4.15 runs per start.... Five losses in May tied Ted Higuera for most in A.L.... Has put on a side show for the season finale in two of the last three seasons. In 1985 he defeated a squad of Triple-A players in Blue Jays' uniforms for his 300th victory, a game in which he allegedly did not throw a knuckleball. His appearance in the Braves' home finale last season was not as successful. In three innings he allowed five runs, six hits and walked six batters. Tanner lifted him before he could be tagged with the loss.

Juan Nieves

Throws Left

Milwaukee Brewers	W–L	ERA	AB	H	HR	BB	SO	BA	SA	OBA
Season	14-8	4.88	755	199	24	100	163	.264	.420	.348
vs. Left-Handers			126	23	3	22	40	.183	.286	.302
vs. Right-Handers			629	176	21	78	123	.280	.447	.358
Home	4-4	6.22	250	72	11	38	61	.288	.484	.381
Road	10-4	4.23	505	127	13	62	102	.251	.388	.332
Grass	12-6	5.13	597	159	20	84	128	.266	.430	.356
Artificial Turf	2-2	3.92	158	40	4	16	35	.253	.380	.320
April	2-0	4.88	91	21	2	13	12	.231	.363	.324
May	2-2	3.72	135	31	1	19	28	.230	.319	.323
June	1-3	5.90	109	30	6	22	29	.275	.459	.394
July	2-1	7.58	118	36	4	14	20	.305	.534	.376
August	4-0	4.66	161	46	7	16	38	.286	.472	.350
Sept./Oct.	3-2	3.32	141	35	4	16	36	.248	.369	.327
Leading Off Inn.			181	45	7	26	36	.249	.420	.346
Runners On			328	89	9	42	73	.271	.418	.349
Runners/Scor. Pos.			186	48	6	20	42	.258	.398	.322
Runners On/2 Out			133	33	4	19	30	.248	.406	.344
Scor. Pos./2 Out			84	19	3	10	23	.226	.369	.316
Late Inning Pressure			30	7	1	9	5	.233	.467	.410
Leading Off			7	2	0	3	1	.286	.429	.500
Runners On			16	3	1	5	3	.188	.500	.381
Runners/Scor. Pos.			9	2	1	3	2	.222	.556	.417
First 9 Batters			264	67	7	31	67	.254	.383	.332
Second 9 Batters			238	63	6	30	57	.265	.395	.342
All Batters Thereafter			253	69	11	39	39	.273	.482	.371

Loves to face: Chet Lemon (.059, 1-for-17)
Hates to face: Kirby Puckett (.684, 13-for-19, 1 HR)
Ground outs-to-air outs ratio: 0.64, 8th-lowest in A.L. last season (minimum: 200 BFP), 0.77 for career.... Additional statistics: 14 double-play ground outs in 163 opportunities, 42 doubles, 2 triples in 195.2 innings last season.... Allowed 17 first-inning runs in 33 starts.... Batting support: 5.76 runs per start, 8th-highest average in A.L. (minimum: 15 GS).... Winless in five consecutive starts after his April 15 no-hitter against the Orioles.... Didn't lose a game from July 7 to Sept. 15, a span of 12 starts.... Faced 42 consecutive left-handed batters without allowing a hit (May 20–June 18), longest streak in majors last season.... In 1986, left-handed batters hit .308 with only one home run.... Opponents' career batting average of .304 at County Stadium, .267 on the road.

Al Nipper

Throws Right

Boston Red Sox	W–L	ERA	AB	H	HR	BB	SO	BA	SA	OBA
Season	11-12	5.43	691	196	30	62	89	.284	.498	.345
vs. Left-Handers			374	100	16	28	43	.267	.471	.318
vs. Right-Handers			317	96	14	34	46	.303	.530	.375
Home	5-4	4.07	293	85	10	25	35	.290	.485	.346
Road	6-8	6.42	398	111	20	37	54	.279	.508	.344
Grass	9-9	5.41	591	169	24	55	81	.286	.492	.349
Artificial Turf	2-3	5.54	100	27	6	7	8	.270	.530	.318
April	3-0	2.86	133	34	5	10	19	.256	.436	.310
May	1-4	8.18	133	43	7	14	8	.323	.602	.391
June	3-2	3.93	137	29	4	11	22	.212	.409	.272
July	0-3	8.50	76	25	3	10	9	.329	.539	.414
August	1-1	5.29	76	28	2	5	7	.368	.513	.410
Sept./Oct.	3-2	5.45	136	37	9	12	24	.272	.515	.329
Leading Off Inn.			170	50	7	12	23	.294	.524	.351
Runners On			284	79	11	34	35	.278	.454	.350
Runners/Scor. Pos.			174	43	10	27	23	.247	.471	.336
Runners On/2 Out			109	27	7	12	13	.248	.505	.328
Scor. Pos./2 Out			73	16	6	9	11	.219	.507	.305
Late Inning Pressure			48	14	3	2	8	.292	.542	.314
Leading Off			16	9	2	0	1	.563	1.125	.563
Runners On			10	2	0	2	3	.200	.200	.308
Runners/Scor. Pos.			6	0	0	2	3	.000	.000	.222
First 9 Batters			233	63	8	26	29	.270	.481	.346
Second 9 Batters			222	67	12	15	28	.302	.541	.351
All Batters Thereafter			236	66	10	21	32	.280	.475	.337

Loves to face: Argenis Salazar (0-for-8)
Hates to face: Mickey Hatcher (.571, 8-for-14)
Ground outs-to-air outs ratio: 1.16 last season, 1.13 for career.... Additional statistics: 13 double-play ground outs in 134 opportunities, 46 doubles, 6 triples in 174.0 innings last season.... Allowed 19 first-inning runs in 30 starts.... Batting support: 5.53 runs per start.... Averaged only 5.80 innings per start, lowest among Boston's regular starters last season.... Drilled Darryl Strawberry with a fastball during 1987 spring training game in retaliation for the Straw Man's home run strut in Game 7 of the 1986 World Series. Will Nipper dare to plunk him this season with his own name penciled into the Cubs' batting order?... Has spent parts of the last three seasons on the disabled list.... ERAs year by year, starting with his three appearances in 1983: 2.25, 3.89, 4.06, 5.38, 5.43.

Edwin Nunez

Seattle Mariners · Throws Right

	W–L	ERA	AB	H	HR	BB	SO	BA	SA	OBA
Season	3-4	3.80	172	45	7	18	34	.262	.424	.328
vs. Left-Handers			98	28	5	8	17	.286	.490	.343
vs. Right-Handers			74	17	2	10	17	.230	.338	.310
Home	2-2	4.66	101	23	6	10	21	.228	.436	.296
Road	1-2	2.45	71	22	1	8	13	.310	.408	.375
Grass	1-1	2.63	55	19	1	6	8	.345	.455	.403
Artificial Turf	2-3	4.28	117	26	6	12	26	.222	.410	.293
April	1-1	4.09	37	7	2	4	9	.189	.351	.279
May	0-0	3.86	18	6	0	5	2	.333	.389	.478
June	1-0	1.50	19	3	1	0	4	.158	.316	.158
July	1-1	0.90	36	10	1	1	8	.278	.389	.297
August	0-0	9.82	31	10	2	4	7	.323	.581	.389
Sept./Oct.	0-2	3.24	31	9	1	4	4	.290	.484	.351
Leading Off Inn.			38	10	1	2	5	.263	.368	.300
Runners On			70	21	4	12	18	.300	.529	.384
Runners/Scor. Pos.			46	13	3	7	11	.283	.543	.351
Runners On/2 Out			33	8	2	3	7	.242	.455	.306
Scor. Pos./2 Out			24	6	2	1	5	.250	.500	.280
Late Inning Pressure			87	30	4	11	15	.345	.552	.406
Leading Off			16	5	0	2	1	.313	.375	.389
Runners On			43	15	3	7	9	.349	.628	.415
Runners/Scor. Pos.			31	10	2	6	8	.323	.613	.400
First 9 Batters			171	44	7	18	34	.257	.421	.325
Second 9 Batters			1	1	0	0	0	1.000	1.000	1.000
All Batters Thereafter			0	0	0	0	0	—	—	—

Loves to face: Pete O'Brien (0-for-9)
Hates to face: Don Mattingly (.556, 5-for-9, 3 HR)
Ground outs-to-air outs ratio: 0.84 last season, 0.73 for career. . . .
Additional statistics: 3 double-play ground outs in 44 opportunities,
5 doubles, 1 triple in 47.1 innings last season. . . . Earned 12 saves
in 21 opportunities, raising his career totals to 35-for-55 (64%). All
but two of last season's saves occurred before the All-Star break. . . .
Lost the Battle of the Nunezes to Jose on Sept. 6 at Toronto. . . .
Opponents have hit for a higher average in road games than at home
in each of the last four seasons. During that time: .220 in the Pacific
Northwest, .262 elsewhere. . . . Opponents' career batting average
of .276 in Late-Inning Pressure Situations, .232 in nonpressure
situations. . . . Has pitched for the Mariners in each of the last six
seasons, but will celebrate only his 25th birthday this May.

Jose Nunez

Toronto Blue Jays · Throws Right

	W–L	ERA	AB	H	HR	BB	SO	BA	SA	OBA
Season	5-2	5.01	356	91	12	58	99	.256	.430	.356
vs. Left-Handers			149	47	5	25	28	.315	.503	.409
vs. Right-Handers			207	44	7	33	71	.213	.377	.317
Home	4-1	5.10	176	43	5	22	55	.244	.415	.325
Road	1-1	4.93	180	48	7	36	44	.267	.444	.384
Grass	1-1	4.46	130	34	4	30	28	.262	.423	.395
Artificial Turf	4-1	5.34	226	57	8	28	71	.252	.434	.331
April	0-0	4.32	33	8	2	4	13	.242	.455	.324
May	0-0	2.57	46	12	1	11	12	.261	.370	.397
June	0-0	4.09	42	9	2	3	10	.214	.429	.267
July	1-0	6.75	110	31	4	13	32	.282	.491	.352
August	1-1	5.31	77	17	1	16	21	.221	.338	.351
Sept./Oct.	3-1	4.70	48	14	2	11	11	.292	.479	.417
Leading Off Inn.			84	30	4	9	18	.357	.631	.419
Runners On			167	41	7	32	47	.246	.413	.358
Runners/Scor. Pos.			98	28	3	25	29	.286	.429	.414
Runners On/2 Out			78	26	5	16	24	.333	.577	.447
Scor. Pos./2 Out			54	20	3	12	20	.370	.593	.485
Late Inning Pressure			33	7	0	10	7	.212	.333	.395
Leading Off			10	2	0	1	1	.200	.400	.273
Runners On			14	4	0	5	3	.286	.429	.474
Runners/Scor. Pos.			9	4	0	5	2	.444	.667	.643
First 9 Batters			206	51	7	32	60	.248	.422	.346
Second 9 Batters			98	27	3	19	25	.276	.429	.383
All Batters Thereafter			52	13	2	7	14	.250	.462	.339

Loves to face: Dave Winfield (0-for-4, 4 SO)
Hates to face: Joe Carter (2-for-2, 2 HR, 1 BB)
Ground outs-to-air outs ratio: 0.65, 9th-lowest in A.L. last season
(minimum: 200 BFP), his first in majors. . .Additional statistics: 8
double-play ground outs in 83 opportunities, 16 doubles, 5 triples
in 97.0 innings last season. . . . Averaged 9.19 strikeouts per nine
innings, highest among A.L. rookies (minimum: 50 IP). . . . Averaged 4.59 innings pitched in nine starts. Failed to complete five
innings in five consecutive starts, tying Ken Schrom and Mike
Krukow for the longest streak of the season. . . . Opposing left-
handers outhit right-handers by 103 points, 2d-largest difference in
the A.L. last season (minimum: 100 AB each way). . . . Faced 427
batters, only four while protecting leads of three runs or less in the
eighth inning or later.

Steve Ontiveros

Oakland As · Throws Right

	W–L	ERA	AB	H	HR	BB	SO	BA	SA	OBA
Season	10-8	4.00	583	141	19	50	97	.242	.381	.305
vs. Left-Handers			290	70	11	34	57	.241	.400	.323
vs. Right-Handers			293	71	8	16	40	.242	.362	.287
Home	5-4	3.50	306	75	6	26	53	.245	.343	.309
Road	5-4	4.56	277	66	13	24	44	.238	.422	.301
Grass	8-7	4.11	489	125	15	40	78	.256	.393	.316
Artificial Turf	2-1	3.46	94	16	4	10	19	.170	.319	.250
April	0-0	0.00	8	2	0	1	0	.250	.250	.333
May	0-1	5.14	86	22	3	9	23	.256	.395	.333
June	5-0	0.66	97	14	1	6	23	.144	.196	.194
July	0-4	4.11	141	37	4	12	16	.262	.383	.325
August	2-1	6.14	116	30	10	10	20	.259	.552	.323
Sept./Oct.	3-2	4.29	135	36	1	12	15	.267	.363	.327
Leading Off Inn.			147	32	4	13	28	.218	.354	.281
Runners On			228	59	7	20	37	.259	.382	.319
Runners/Scor. Pos.			124	27	3	14	27	.218	.315	.298
Runners On/2 Out			94	21	1	12	18	.223	.277	.318
Scor. Pos./2 Out			59	9	0	11	13	.153	.169	.296
Late Inning Pressure			87	25	2	10	18	.287	.414	.380
Leading Off			26	7	0	0	8	.269	.385	.269
Runners On			33	11	2	7	4	.333	.545	.463
Runners/Scor. Pos.			14	4	1	7	2	.286	.500	.545
First 9 Batters			266	59	8	18	62	.222	.342	.273
Second 9 Batters			184	53	7	22	21	.288	.457	.365
All Batters Thereafter			133	29	4	10	14	.218	.353	.283

Loves to face: George Brett (0-for-14)
Hates to face: Danny Tartabull (.500, 5-for-10)
Ground outs-to-air outs ratio: 1.91, 3d-highest in A.L. last season
(minimum: 20 GS), 1.60 for career. . . . Additional statistics: 11
double-play ground outs in 107 opportunities, 20 doubles, 2 triples
in 150.2 innings last season. . . . Allowed 7 first-inning runs in 22
starts. . . . Batting support: 5.41 runs per start. . . . One of four
pitchers to win five games in June, when his ERA was the lowest
in the majors. Career record of 5–0 with a 1.21 ERA during June;
8–13, 4.27 ERA in other months. . . . Career record of 9–6 with a
3.96 ERA in 22 starts; 4–7 with a 3.45 ERA and 19 saves in 98 relief
appearances. . . . Career breakdown: .250 by left-handed batters,
.213 by right-handers. . . . Opponents' career average of .115 (3-for-
26, two BB) with the bases loaded.

Dan Petry

Detroit Tigers · Throws Right

	W–L	ERA	AB	H	HR	BB	SO	BA	SA	OBA
Season	9-7	5.61	531	148	22	76	93	.279	.463	.375
vs. Left-Handers			254	69	8	39	41	.272	.433	.367
vs. Right-Handers			277	79	14	37	52	.285	.491	.383
Home	4-4	5.95	241	66	12	32	44	.274	.473	.371
Road	5-3	5.33	290	82	10	44	49	.283	.455	.378
Grass	7-6	5.82	432	119	19	68	75	.275	.465	.381
Artificial Turf	2-1	4.63	99	29	3	8	18	.293	.455	.349
April	0-3	5.61	98	27	4	17	18	.276	.459	.390
May	2-0	2.95	83	17	4	9	21	.205	.398	.280
June	3-1	7.40	96	29	5	20	16	.302	.542	.429
July	1-0	8.44	62	20	2	10	10	.323	.468	.413
August	2-2	5.47	115	36	5	4	19	.313	.513	.350
Sept./Oct.	1-1	4.29	77	19	2	16	9	.247	.364	.385
Leading Off Inn.			121	33	4	18	19	.273	.421	.380
Runners On			258	71	13	34	43	.275	.484	.366
Runners/Scor. Pos.			150	38	6	24	30	.253	.427	.353
Runners On/2 Out			101	26	8	14	14	.257	.535	.364
Scor. Pos./2 Out			71	16	4	10	10	.225	.437	.345
Late Inning Pressure			34	10	3	5	5	.294	.647	.400
Leading Off			10	3	1	1	1	.300	.700	.364
Runners On			12	3	1	2	1	.250	.500	.400
Runners/Scor. Pos.			9	2	1	1	0	.222	.556	.300
First 9 Batters			221	62	7	27	36	.281	.443	.367
Second 9 Batters			181	50	10	29	34	.276	.519	.381
All Batters Thereafter			129	36	5	20	23	.279	.419	.380

Loves to face: Charlie Moore (.037, 1-for-27)
Hates to face: Jerry Hairston (.467, 7-for-15, 2 2B, 3 HR)
Ground outs-to-air outs ratio: 1.21 last season, 1.46 for career. . . .
Additional statistics: 13 double-play ground outs in 132 opportunities, 26 doubles, 3 triples in 134.2 innings last season. . . . Allowed
16 first-inning runs in 21 starts. . . . Batting support: 6.95 runs per
start, highest average in majors (minimum: 15 GS). That explains
his 9–7 record despite a 5.61 ERA. . . . Record of 7–7 with a 6.31
ERA in 21 starts; 2–0, 2.93 ERA in relief. . . . Won't be sorry to
leave Tiger Stadium. Over past five seasons, only two pitchers in
majors have higher winning percentages in road games than Petry's
.667 mark (38–19): Clemens and Gooden. During those five seasons,
Petry has a 28–30 record at home. . . . Career statistics: one HR per
33.9 at bats at Tiger Stadium, one per 41.5 elsewhere.

Dan Plesac

Milwaukee Brewers — Throws Left

	W–L	ERA	AB	H	HR	BB	SO	BA	SA	OBA
Season	5-6	2.61	296	63	8	23	89	.213	.318	.275
vs. Left-Handers			57	8	2	6	20	.140	.281	.219
vs. Right-Handers			239	55	6	17	69	.230	.326	.288
Home	2-2	3.31	137	30	5	6	43	.219	.358	.253
Road	3-4	2.05	159	33	3	17	46	.208	.283	.292
Grass	5-4	2.75	256	52	7	20	80	.203	.313	.264
Artificial Turf	0-2	1.69	40	11	1	3	9	.275	.350	.341
April	0-0	0.66	49	7	1	3	14	.143	.204	.208
May	0-0	0.96	37	8	1	5	13	.216	.297	.310
June	4-0	1.89	65	12	1	5	26	.185	.246	.254
July	1-4	4.91	71	18	3	7	18	.254	.437	.321
August	0-0	1.35	47	7	2	1	14	.149	.277	.163
Sept./Oct.	0-2	7.94	27	11	0	2	4	.407	.481	.452
Leading Off Inn.			59	9	1	4	20	.153	.254	.219
Runners On			143	36	7	12	41	.252	.427	.310
Runners/Scor. Pos.			81	21	4	6	20	.259	.444	.311
Runners On/2 Out			67	17	2	5	21	.254	.358	.315
Scor. Pos./2 Out			40	10	0	4	11	.250	.275	.333
Late Inning Pressure			214	51	6	17	59	.238	.355	.301
Leading Off			41	8	1	2	13	.195	.341	.250
Runners On			109	30	5	9	26	.275	.450	.331
Runners/Scor. Pos.			62	17	2	6	13	.274	.419	.338
First 9 Batters			283	62	8	21	87	.219	.329	.278
Second 9 Batters			13	1	0	2	2	.077	.077	.200
All Batters Thereafter			0	0	0	0	0	—	—	—

Loves to face: Brook Jacoby (0-for-7, 4 SO)
Hates to face: Willie Randolph (.667, 4-for-6)
Ground outs-to-air outs ratio: 1.00 last season, 0.84 for career. . . . Additional statistics: 7 double-play ground outs in 66 opportunities, 7 doubles, 0 triples in 79.1 innings last season. . . . Averaged 10.10 strikeouts per nine innings, 3d-highest rate among A.L. relievers. (minimum: 30 games). . . . Earned 23 saves, including a major-league-leading total of seven in April, in 36 opportunities. Was 14-for-20 in 1986. . . . Made only one relief appearance in three minor-league seasons before his debut with the Brewers in 1986. In two seasons with Milwaukee he has made 108 appearances, all in relief. . . . Only five active pitchers (minimum: 150 innings pitched) have a better career ratio of strikeouts to walks: Henke, Gooden, Saberhagen, DeLeon, and Clemens.

Eric Plunk

Oakland As — Throws Right

	W–L	ERA	AB	H	HR	BB	SO	BA	SA	OBA
Season	4-6	4.74	359	91	8	62	90	.253	.368	.362
vs. Left-Handers			192	53	2	30	43	.276	.365	.371
vs. Right-Handers			167	38	6	32	47	.228	.371	.353
Home	2-3	4.86	173	41	4	36	43	.237	.341	.366
Road	2-3	4.62	186	50	4	26	47	.269	.392	.358
Grass	3-5	5.11	285	72	7	51	74	.253	.372	.364
Artificial Turf	1-1	3.26	74	19	1	11	16	.257	.351	.356
April	0-1	4.67	105	27	3	21	17	.257	.400	.383
May	1-1	3.24	98	28	2	12	20	.286	.367	.357
June	0-2	15.83	39	12	2	13	16	.308	.615	.491
July			0	0	0	0	0	—	—	—
August	1-0	1.29	23	3	0	3	9	.130	.174	.231
Sept./Oct.	2-2	3.08	94	21	1	13	28	.223	.277	.312
Leading Off Inn.			82	19	2	13	22	.232	.341	.344
Runners On			185	43	4	28	48	.232	.341	.329
Runners/Scor. Pos.			102	22	4	22	28	.216	.363	.346
Runners On/2 Out			78	20	3	11	22	.256	.410	.356
Scor. Pos./2 Out			50	13	3	8	13	.260	.480	.373
Late Inning Pressure			74	13	2	13	22	.176	.284	.295
Leading Off			20	4	1	3	7	.200	.400	.304
Runners On			36	6	0	3	10	.167	.194	.225
Runners/Scor. Pos.			19	2	0	2	6	.105	.105	.182
First 9 Batters			208	48	2	30	59	.231	.303	.328
Second 9 Batters			87	25	4	17	18	.287	.448	.396
All Batters Thereafter			64	18	2	15	13	.281	.469	.420

Loves to face: Darrell Evans (0-for-9)
Hates to face: Harold Baines (.833, 5-for-6)
Ground outs-to-air outs ratio: 1.01 last season, 0.91 for career. . . . Additional statistics: 7 double-play ground outs in 98 opportunities, 17 doubles, 0 triples in 95.0 innings last season. . . . Allowed 4 first-inning runs in 11 starts. . . . Batting support: 4.27 runs per start. . . . Averaged only 5.03 innings in 11 games started. . . . Record of 1–4 with a 5.53 ERA in his starts; 3–2, 3.63 ERA in 21 relief appearances last season. Career total of 69 strikeouts in 71.1 innings in relief. . . . Allowed only one home run over his last 33 innings pitched. . . . Has walked only one of 25 career batters faced with the bases loaded (compared to one per six batters faced overall). But maybe he's being too fine: Opponents have 10 hits in 22 at bats with the bags full, including three grand slams.

Dan Quisenberry

Kansas City Royals — Throws Right

	W–L	ERA	AB	H	HR	BB	SO	BA	SA	OBA
Season	4-1	2.76	202	58	3	10	17	.287	.421	.322
vs. Left-Handers			103	33	2	7	11	.320	.466	.364
vs. Right-Handers			99	25	1	3	6	.253	.374	.279
Home	4-0	0.99	101	23	0	4	11	.228	.297	.255
Road	0-1	4.98	101	35	3	6	6	.347	.545	.389
Grass	0-1	5.59	91	32	3	6	5	.352	.549	.398
Artificial Turf	4-0	0.91	111	26	0	4	12	.234	.315	.259
April	1-0	0.00	26	7	0	2	4	.269	.308	.321
May	1-0	2.51	58	16	0	1	3	.276	.328	.300
June	0-0	4.05	29	7	2	0	4	.241	.517	.241
July	2-1	1.69	39	9	1	4	4	.231	.385	.302
August	0-0	5.14	33	12	0	3	2	.364	.515	.417
Sept./Oct.	0-0	4.91	17	7	0	0	0	.412	.647	.389
Leading Off Inn.			38	6	0	1	5	.158	.184	.179
Runners On			105	36	3	6	7	.343	.543	.375
Runners/Scor. Pos.			68	24	0	6	6	.353	.515	.400
Runners On/2 Out			62	22	1	3	3	.355	.516	.385
Scor. Pos./2 Out			41	15	0	3	3	.366	.512	.409
Late Inning Pressure			87	27	2	3	6	.310	.460	.341
Leading Off			15	3	0	0	1	.200	.200	.200
Runners On			47	16	2	3	3	.340	.574	.380
Runners/Scor. Pos.			30	9	0	3	3	.300	.467	.364
First 9 Batters			196	54	2	10	17	.276	.398	.313
Second 9 Batters			6	4	1	0	0	.667	1.167	.667
All Batters Thereafter			0	0	0	0	0	—	—	—

Loves to face: Julio Franco (0-for-16)
Hates to face: Kent Hrbek (.611, 11-for-18, 2 HR)
Ground outs-to-air outs ratio: 2.38, 4th-highest in A.L. last season (minimum: 200 BFP), 2.31 for career. . . . Additional statistics: 3 double-play ground outs in 35 opportunities, 14 doubles, 2 triples in 49.0 innings last season. . . . Only home run by an opposing right-hander was hit by Joe Carter. . . . Had seven saves by June 6, but earned only one after that. . . . Yearly saves totals since 1983: 45 (in 51 opportunities), 44 (53), 37 (49), 12 (17), 8 (12). . . . Opponents' yearly batting averages in LIP situations since 1983: .234, .265, .277, .309, .310. . . . Opposing left-handers have hit .300 or better in each of the last three seasons. . . . Long live King Quis: More innings than any other active pitcher without a balk (894.1). Jim Clancy was nabbed last June 22, after 1,873 innings.

Dennis Rasmussen

New York Yankees — Throws Left

	W–L	ERA	AB	H	HR	BB	SO	BA	SA	OBA
Season	9-7	4.75	558	145	31	55	89	.260	.504	.328
vs. Left-Handers			99	31	5	9	19	.313	.535	.370
vs. Right-Handers			459	114	26	46	70	.248	.497	.319
Home	6-3	4.06	246	62	6	28	46	.252	.398	.332
Road	3-4	5.29	312	83	25	27	43	.266	.587	.325
Grass	8-7	4.88	466	122	24	46	78	.262	.500	.330
Artificial Turf	1-0	4.07	92	23	7	9	11	.250	.522	.317
April	2-1	2.82	146	34	9	9	27	.233	.486	.277
May	1-3	5.12	122	32	8	15	21	.262	.557	.343
June	3-0	4.78	118	28	6	11	18	.237	.432	.313
July	2-0	5.40	56	16	2	9	11	.286	.518	.379
August	1-3	6.52	116	35	6	11	12	.302	.534	.362
Sept./Oct.			0	0	0	0	0	—	—	—
Leading Off Inn.			140	40	9	14	16	.286	.564	.363
Runners On			215	47	7	21	42	.219	.405	.285
Runners/Scor. Pos.			106	21	3	11	20	.198	.387	.268
Runners On/2 Out			89	20	4	12	17	.225	.461	.324
Scor. Pos./2 Out			52	11	2	7	10	.212	.481	.317
Late Inning Pressure			36	8	1	3	2	.222	.389	.275
Leading Off			11	3	0	1	0	.273	.364	.333
Runners On			11	3	0	0	0	.273	.455	.250
Runners/Scor. Pos.			4	0	0	0	0	.000	.000	.000
First 9 Batters			209	53	9	21	40	.254	.455	.322
Second 9 Batters			184	52	10	13	29	.283	.543	.338
All Batters Thereafter			165	40	12	21	20	.242	.521	.324

Loves to face: Dave Engle (.071, 1-for-14)
Hates to face: Ryne Sandberg (.714, 5-for-7, 3 2B)
Figures above are for A.L. only. . . . Ground outs-to-air outs ratio: 0.67 last season, 0.68 for career. . . . Additional statistics: 9 double-play ground outs in 129 opportunities, 41 doubles, 6 triples in 191.1 innings last season. . . . Allowed 23 first-inning runs in 32 starts. . . . Batting support: 5.78 runs per start (5.84 with Yankees was 6th-highest average in A.L. [minimum: 15 GS]). . . . Leadoff batters reached base safely in nine consecutive innings (May 24–June 7), longest streak in majors last season. . . . Hello, Riverfront: Career record of 13–5 on artificial turf, 7–9 in road games on grass surfaces. . . . Career record of 11–1 during month of July. So when did Yankees send him to Columbus despite an 8–4 record? . . . Opponents have 10 hits, including five slams, in 25 AB with bases loaded.

Jeff Reardon
Minnesota Twins — Throws Right

	W–L	ERA	AB	H	HR	BB	SO	BA	SA	OBA
Season	8-8	4.48	302	70	14	28	83	.232	.417	.301
vs. Left-Handers			156	47	9	16	30	.301	.532	.364
vs. Right-Handers			146	23	5	12	53	.158	.295	.231
Home	5-2	3.48	160	36	5	14	47	.225	.369	.282
Road	3-6	5.70	142	34	9	14	36	.239	.472	.321
Grass	3-4	5.93	117	25	8	13	34	.214	.453	.303
Artificial Turf	5-4	3.60	185	45	6	15	49	.243	.395	.299
April	1-1	7.27	37	11	1	5	3	.297	.459	.409
May	1-2	7.36	60	16	5	10	19	.267	.533	.380
June	2-1	4.20	58	15	4	2	18	.259	.500	.279
July	1-1	2.13	46	11	2	2	13	.239	.391	.271
August	1-2	5.54	46	9	1	6	14	.196	.348	.283
Sept./Oct.	2-1	1.65	55	8	1	3	16	.145	.255	.186
Leading Off Inn.			60	8	1	4	20	.133	.217	.200
Runners On			142	36	10	13	41	.254	.500	.319
Runners On/Scor. Pos.			93	26	8	11	27	.280	.548	.358
Runners On/2 Out			71	20	5	6	15	.282	.507	.354
Scor. Pos./2 Out			51	18	5	5	11	.353	.667	.431
Late Inning Pressure			216	53	10	22	61	.245	.426	.315
Leading Off			42	7	1	4	14	.167	.262	.239
Runners On			113	29	8	11	30	.257	.504	.323
Runners On/Scor. Pos.			76	21	6	10	19	.276	.513	.360
First 9 Batters			291	66	14	28	79	.227	.416	.296
Second 9 Batters			11	4	0	0	0	.364	.455	.417
All Batters Thereafter			0	0	0	0	0	—	—	—

Loves to face: Terry Kennedy (.087, 2-for-23)
Hates to face: Thad Bosley (.600, 3-for-5, 2 HR)
Ground outs-to-air outs ratio: 0.43, lowest in majors since 1984 when Bill Caudill established 13-year low of 0.34 (minimum: 200 BFP), 0.57 for career. ... Additional statistics: 4 double-play ground outs in 51 opportunities, 14 doubles, 0 triples in 80.1 innings last season. ... Opponents' batting average declined steadily in each month, from .297 in April to .145 in Sept./October. ... Opponents stole eight bases in eight tries. ... Allowed 10 home runs in 9th inning to lead majors. ... Opposing left-handers outhit right-handers by 144 points, largest difference in majors (minimum: 100 AB each way). ... Has never balked in 746 career innings. ... Opponents had seven hits (including three home runs) in 14 at bats with the bases loaded last season.

Jerry Reed
Seattle Mariners — Throws Right

	W–L	ERA	AB	H	HR	BB	SO	BA	SA	OBA
Season	1-2	3.42	310	79	7	24	51	.255	.365	.314
vs. Left-Handers			137	36	3	11	18	.263	.358	.320
vs. Right-Handers			173	43	4	13	33	.249	.370	.309
Home	1-1	2.85	157	38	3	12	35	.242	.338	.300
Road	0-1	3.98	153	41	4	12	16	.268	.392	.327
Grass	0-1	4.19	131	38	4	9	13	.290	.435	.343
Artificial Turf	1-1	2.85	179	41	3	15	38	.229	.313	.292
April	0-0	5.63	31	8	2	3	6	.258	.452	.361
May	0-0	2.81	61	18	2	5	8	.295	.426	.348
June	0-0	4.30	57	15	1	1	8	.263	.368	.288
July	0-1	3.00	67	16	2	6	11	.239	.418	.297
August	1-0	0.00	13	3	0	0	3	.231	.231	.231
Sept./Oct.	0-1	3.38	81	19	0	9	15	.235	.259	.311
Leading Off Inn.			67	15	2	4	13	.224	.313	.278
Runners On			138	33	3	13	20	.239	.362	.307
Runners On/Scor. Pos.			81	17	2	10	17	.210	.346	.293
Runners On/2 Out			64	15	0	9	8	.234	.328	.338
Scor. Pos./2 Out			43	10	0	7	7	.233	.302	.340
Late Inning Pressure			112	24	2	8	19	.214	.304	.267
Leading Off			27	6	0	2	5	.222	.222	.276
Runners On			42	7	1	5	4	.167	.262	.255
Runners On/Scor. Pos.			24	3	1	4	3	.125	.250	.250
First 9 Batters			240	57	7	20	47	.238	.363	.303
Second 9 Batters			68	22	0	4	4	.324	.382	.361
All Batters Thereafter			2	0	0	0	0	.000	.000	.000

Loves to face: Tom Brookens (0-for-7)
Hates to face: Paul Molitor (.462, 6-for-13, 2 HR)
Ground outs-to-air outs ratio: 1.05 last season, 1.12 for career. ... Additional statistics: 8 double-play ground outs in 61 opportunities, 11 doubles, 1 triple in 81.2 innings last season. ... Four of his seven saves were recorded after Sept. 1. ... Did not allow a home run in his last 28 innings pitched. ... Has earned 15 saves in 25 opportunities over past three seasons. ... Opponents' career on-base average of .262 leading off innings. Only five active pitchers who've started as many innings as Reed have a lower average. ... Survived the entire 1987 season with the Mariners (including a few weeks on the disabled list) after spending parts of five seasons on the Triple-A shuttle. ... Born four days after the Brooklyn Dodgers won their only World Championship.

Jerry Reuss
California Angels — Throws Left

	W–L	ERA	AB	H	HR	BB	SO	BA	SA	OBA
Season	4-5	5.25	343	112	16	17	37	.327	.525	.361
vs. Left-Handers			66	24	3	3	8	.364	.530	.391
vs. Right-Handers			277	88	13	14	29	.318	.523	.354
Home	2-2	3.83	182	61	8	8	20	.335	.505	.365
Road	2-3	6.93	161	51	8	9	17	.317	.547	.357
Grass	4-5	4.93	332	108	15	16	36	.325	.515	.359
Artificial Turf	0-0	18.00	11	4	1	1	1	.364	.818	.417
April			0	0	0	0	0	—	—	—
May			0	0	0	0	0	—	—	—
June	2-0	0.52	62	14	0	2	9	.226	.226	.250
July	1-1	7.43	106	40	8	3	9	.377	.679	.394
August	1-1	3.86	49	14	2	1	7	.286	.469	.300
Sept./Oct.	0-3	6.82	126	44	6	11	12	.349	.563	.407
Leading Off Inn.			86	23	4	3	6	.267	.453	.292
Runners On			136	48	8	7	18	.353	.610	.382
Runners On/Scor. Pos.			67	25	3	5	9	.373	.612	.411
Runners On/2 Out			51	16	3	3	9	.314	.588	.352
Scor. Pos./2 Out			29	11	1	2	5	.379	.655	.419
Late Inning Pressure			21	9	0	0	2	.429	.571	.409
Leading Off			6	3	0	0	0	.500	.500	.500
Runners On			10	2	0	0	2	.200	.300	.182
Runners On/Scor. Pos.			4	0	0	0	1	.000	.000	.000
First 9 Batters			136	41	9	9	12	.301	.544	.349
Second 9 Batters			119	40	4	6	14	.336	.521	.368
All Batters Thereafter			88	31	3	2	11	.352	.500	.370

Loves to face: Willie Wilson (0-for-7)
Hates to face: Todd Benzinger (3-for-3)
Figures *above* are for A.L. only. ... Ground outs-to-air outs ratio: 2.13, 6th-highest in majors last season (minimum: 20 GS), 1.92 for career. ... Additional statistics: 18 DP ground outs in 105 opportunities, 22 doubles, 6 triples in 119.0 innings last season. ... Allowed 21 first-inning runs in 23 starts. ... Batting support: 4.74 runs per start. ... Has lost eight straight decisions on artificial turf. Last win on a rug: July 10, 1985. Since then; 13–12 on grass. ... Believers in N.L. superiority pointed to Reuss's A.L. debut for support. After compiling an 0-5 record (7.61 ERA) in seven N.L. starts, Reuss shut out the Royals, then won next two starts before losing five of last six decisions. ... He's old, but he's not that old. Nine pitchers active in '87 actually blew out more candles than Reuss.

Rick Rhoden
New York Yankees — Throws Right

	W–L	ERA	AB	H	HR	BB	SO	BA	SA	OBA
Season	16-10	3.86	687	184	22	61	107	.268	.419	.327
vs. Left-Handers			363	100	14	37	47	.275	.455	.342
vs. Right-Handers			324	84	8	24	60	.259	.380	.311
Home	10-3	3.29	340	90	10	28	50	.265	.409	.322
Road	6-7	4.47	347	94	12	33	57	.271	.429	.332
Grass	16-5	3.16	526	127	14	44	87	.241	.373	.299
Artificial Turf	0-5	6.69	161	57	8	17	20	.354	.571	.417
April	2-2	3.60	95	24	1	9	16	.253	.316	.314
May	4-1	4.02	152	40	4	11	25	.263	.388	.315
June	3-2	3.68	128	30	5	12	19	.234	.414	.301
July	4-1	2.45	138	36	3	16	22	.261	.384	.335
August	2-3	4.50	138	43	6	12	23	.312	.500	.368
Sept./Oct.	1-1	8.00	36	11	3	1	2	.306	.667	.316
Leading Off Inn.			176	45	5	13	28	.256	.415	.311
Runners On			263	68	9	27	46	.259	.399	.324
Runners On/Scor. Pos.			147	32	4	24	28	.218	.333	.322
Runners On/2 Out			112	25	2	17	19	.223	.313	.326
Scor. Pos./2 Out			71	13	2	16	12	.183	.296	.333
Late Inning Pressure			52	10	2	3	7	.192	.346	.236
Leading Off			14	1	0	2	1	.071	.071	.188
Runners On			14	0	0	1	3	.000	.000	.067
Runners On/Scor. Pos.			9	0	0	0	1	.000	.000	.000
First 9 Batters			246	56	5	16	43	.228	.325	.275
Second 9 Batters			227	66	9	20	32	.291	.471	.344
All Batters Thereafter			214	62	8	25	32	.290	.472	.366

Loves to face: Pat Tabler (0-for-7, 4 SO)
Hates to face: Jamie Quirk (.571, 4-for-7, 3 2B)
Ground outs-to-air outs ratio: 1.25 last season, 1.34 for career. ... Additional statistics: 15 double-play ground outs in 118 opportunities, 30 doubles, 4 triples in 181.2 innings last season. ... Allowed 9 first-inning runs in 29 starts. ... Batting support: 4.03 runs per start, 5th-lowest average in A.L. (minimum: 15 GS). ... Opposing batters hit 113 points higher on artificial surfaces than on grass fields, largest difference in A.L. (minimum: 100 AB each way). ... Has thrown only one complete-game shutout in 98 starts since blanking the Phillies in his final appearance of 1984. ... Has committed only six errors in his 14-year career, three of them on wild pick-off attempts. ... Last pitcher to get an extra-base hit in a World Series game, a double off Ron Guidry in Game 4 of 1977 Series.

Dave Righetti
New York Yankees

Throws Left

	W-L	ERA	AB	H	HR	BB	SO	BA	SA	OBA
Season	8-6	3.51	362	95	9	44	77	.262	.362	.341
vs. Left-Handers			96	26	3	9	19	.271	.396	.324
vs. Right-Handers			266	69	6	35	58	.259	.350	.348
Home	5-2	2.79	179	39	7	17	38	.218	.358	.288
Road	3-4	4.24	183	56	2	27	39	.306	.366	.391
Grass	7-5	3.61	294	78	8	32	61	.265	.367	.336
Artificial Turf	1-1	3.06	68	17	1	12	16	.250	.338	.363
April	2-1	4.80	55	14	1	12	10	.255	.345	.394
May	1-0	3.52	56	14	3	4	16	.250	.446	.295
June	2-2	4.66	81	25	2	6	17	.309	.420	.352
July	1-0	1.76	56	14	1	9	9	.250	.304	.348
August	0-0	2.03	47	10	1	9	7	.213	.298	.339
Sept./Oct.	2-3	3.78	67	18	1	4	18	.269	.328	.310
Leading Off Inn.			67	20	3	7	20	.299	.448	.373
Runners On			201	56	5	27	40	.279	.383	.356
Runners/Scor. Pos.			121	35	3	17	23	.289	.388	.364
Runners On/2 Out			91	27	2	17	22	.297	.385	.407
Scor. Pos./2 Out			65	19	2	12	16	.292	.415	.403
Late Inning Pressure			254	67	5	35	56	.264	.346	.347
Leading Off			51	16	1	4	17	.314	.392	.364
Runners On			133	37	3	23	26	.278	.368	.373
Runners/Scor. Pos.			85	25	2	14	14	.294	.388	.375
First 9 Batters			316	83	8	35	69	.263	.361	.336
Second 9 Batters			44	11	1	8	8	.250	.364	.358
All Batters Thereafter			2	1	0	1	0	.500	.500	.667

Loves to face: Mike Young (.063, 1-for-16)
Hates to face: Paul Molitor (.382, 13-for-34, 1 HR)
Ground outs-to-air outs ratio: 1.23 last season, 1.06 for career. . . .
Additional statistics: 9 double-play ground outs in 109 opportunities, 9 doubles, 0 triples in 95.0 innings last season. . . . Opponents' batting average of .206 in day games, .286 at night. . . . Allowed as many home runs to left-handed batters in 1987 as in previous three seasons combined. . . . Opposing left-handers had a higher extra-base hit percentage (per at bat) than right-handers in each of the last three seasons. Only one other southpaw can say that: Fernando Valenzuela. . . . Yankees' all-time leaders in saves: Gossage 150, Lyle 141, Righetti 138. . . . Career records: 33–22, 3.31 ERA as a starter; 33–27, 2.73 ERA in relief. . . . 38–16, 2.68 ERA at Yankee Stadium; 20–29, 3.72 on the road.

Jose Rijo
Oakland As

Throws Right

	W-L	ERA	AB	H	HR	BB	SO	BA	SA	OBA
Season	2-7	5.90	347	106	10	41	67	.305	.455	.379
vs. Left-Handers			175	53	6	25	37	.303	.491	.387
vs. Right-Handers			172	53	4	16	30	.308	.419	.370
Home	2-3	4.35	168	51	4	18	39	.304	.446	.372
Road	0-4	7.46	179	55	6	23	28	.307	.464	.385
Grass	2-4	4.87	280	82	6	33	55	.293	.411	.369
Artificial Turf	0-3	10.93	67	24	4	8	12	.358	.642	.421
April	0-2	5.85	83	26	2	14	21	.313	.446	.414
May	0-0	0.00	11	3	0	0	1	.273	.273	.273
June	0-2	7.43	55	17	1	5	10	.309	.400	.367
July	1-1	4.50	68	20	1	6	11	.294	.382	.360
August	1-2	6.84	109	34	5	14	19	.312	.541	.387
Sept./Oct.	0-0	5.40	21	6	1	2	5	.286	.524	.333
Leading Off Inn.			80	21	2	8	10	.263	.375	.330
Runners On			172	48	4	23	40	.279	.413	.365
Runners/Scor. Pos.			101	30	2	18	26	.297	.426	.393
Runners On/2 Out			75	18	1	12	21	.240	.360	.352
Scor. Pos./2 Out			51	13	1	11	16	.255	.392	.387
Late Inning Pressure			18	6	2	4	3	.333	.722	.455
Leading Off			7	3	0	0	0	.429	.571	.429
Runners On			7	3	2	2	1	.429	1.286	.556
Runners/Scor. Pos.			4	1	1	1	1	.250	1.000	.400
First 9 Batters			149	39	3	15	37	.262	.376	.329
Second 9 Batters			102	35	2	13	16	.343	.480	.417
All Batters Thereafter			96	32	5	13	14	.333	.552	.414

Loves to face: Brett Butler (.125, 2-for-16)
Hates to face: Lance Parrish (.571, 4-for-7, 1 HR)
Ground outs-to-air outs ratio: 1.21 last season, 1.03 for career. . . .
Additional statistics: 2 double-play ground outs in 83 opportunities, 2d-lowest rate in A.L. (minimum: 40 opp.), 16 doubles, 3 triples in 82.1 innings last season. . . . Allowed 6 first-inning runs in 14 starts. . . . Batting support: 3.93 runs per start. . . . Averaged only 5.14 innings per start. . . . Be patient, Reds fans: career record of 6–21 before the All-Star break (including 1–9, 7.07 ERA during June), 13–9 after the All-Star break. . . . Opposing batters have hit .378 with runners in scoring position in Late-Inning Pressure Situations. . . . Career total of 68 strikeouts in 68.2 innings as a reliever. But his ERA is only slightly lower in relief (4.59) than as a starter (4.78).

Jeff M. Robinson
Detroit Tigers

Throws Right

	W-L	ERA	AB	H	HR	BB	SO	BA	SA	OBA
Season	9-6	5.37	504	132	16	54	98	.262	.413	.340
vs. Left-Handers			277	63	9	35	47	.227	.397	.312
vs. Right-Handers			227	69	7	19	51	.304	.432	.375
Home	2-2	5.40	233	52	8	30	51	.223	.386	.317
Road	7-4	5.35	271	80	8	24	47	.295	.435	.361
Grass	6-4	5.36	403	104	12	45	77	.258	.407	.342
Artificial Turf	3-2	5.40	101	28	4	9	21	.277	.436	.333
April	1-1	3.68	84	20	4	8	15	.238	.452	.304
May	2-1	4.63	88	19	4	11	18	.216	.398	.300
June	1-2	8.76	100	29	3	21	20	.290	.470	.418
July	3-0	2.83	109	24	1	4	22	.220	.275	.267
August	2-1	6.05	82	26	2	8	15	.317	.427	.385
Sept./Oct.	0-1	8.68	41	14	2	2	8	.341	.561	.391
Leading Off Inn.			130	24	4	7	21	.185	.300	.226
Runners On			197	69	9	29	34	.350	.579	.437
Runners/Scor. Pos.			112	41	4	17	22	.366	.598	.455
Runners On/2 Out			83	31	6	17	16	.373	.723	.495
Scor. Pos./2 Out			55	20	3	10	12	.364	.691	.485
Late Inning Pressure			37	7	1	3	7	.189	.270	.250
Leading Off			10	1	0	1	1	.100	.100	.182
Runners On			10	3	1	0	1	.300	.600	.300
Runners/Scor. Pos.			7	2	0	0	1	.286	.286	.286
First 9 Batters			205	45	7	24	43	.220	.346	.302
Second 9 Batters			165	45	5	18	33	.273	.424	.351
All Batters Thereafter			134	42	4	12	22	.313	.500	.387

Loves to face: Jose Canseco (0-for-8)
Hates to face: Pete Incaviglia (3-for-3)
Ground outs-to-air outs ratio: 1.19 last season, his first in majors. . . . Additional statistics: 9 double-play ground outs in 99 opportunities, 22 doubles, 3 triples in 127.1 innings last season. . . . Allowed 5 first-inning runs in 21 starts, 4th-lowest average in A.L. (minimum: 15 GS). . . . Batting support: 5.71 runs per start, 9th-highest average in A.L. (minimum: 15 GS). Maybe that's why only four pitchers in either league had as many wins as Robinson with as high an ERA (Scott Bankhead, Eric Bell, Al Nipper, and Dan Petry). . . . Ranked 5th among A.L. rookies with 21 games started. . . . Faced 316 left-handed batters, didn't hit any with pitches. But he plunked seven right-handers, or one for every 36 he faced.

Jeff Russell
Texas Rangers

Throws Right

	W-L	ERA	AB	H	HR	BB	SO	BA	SA	OBA
Season	5-4	4.44	383	109	9	52	56	.285	.418	.369
vs. Left-Handers			182	53	7	22	27	.291	.467	.362
vs. Right-Handers			201	56	2	30	29	.279	.373	.374
Home	1-2	5.71	164	52	4	27	17	.317	.470	.408
Road	4-2	3.51	219	57	5	25	39	.260	.379	.337
Grass	5-3	4.27	330	93	8	47	52	.282	.418	.368
Artificial Turf	0-1	5.54	53	16	1	5	4	.302	.415	.373
April			0	0	0	0	0	—	—	—
May	0-0	3.21	57	19	1	4	9	.333	.421	.371
June	1-1	2.78	88	24	1	12	13	.273	.364	.363
July	3-0	3.86	69	19	1	11	12	.275	.362	.370
August	0-3	8.51	105	33	4	19	18	.314	.524	.413
Sept./Oct.	1-0	2.55	64	14	2	6	4	.219	.375	.296
Leading Off Inn.			81	22	3	7	14	.272	.407	.344
Runners On			193	50	4	35	26	.259	.378	.365
Runners/Scor. Pos.			117	37	3	29	19	.316	.479	.437
Runners On/2 Out			87	29	3	9	7	.333	.506	.396
Scor. Pos./2 Out			60	24	3	7	7	.400	.633	.463
Late Inning Pressure			82	23	1	11	15	.280	.378	.372
Leading Off			20	5	1	2	4	.250	.400	.348
Runners On			31	11	0	8	3	.355	.452	.487
Runners/Scor. Pos.			21	10	0	7	3	.476	.619	.607
First 9 Batters			283	78	7	36	45	.276	.413	.356
Second 9 Batters			85	28	1	12	10	.329	.424	.412
All Batters Thereafter			15	3	1	4	1	.200	.467	.368

Loves to face: Carlton Fisk (0-for-6, 3 SO)
Hates to face: Dave Winfield (.833, 5-for-6, 2 2B, 1 BB)
Ground outs-to-air outs ratio: 1.33 last season, 1.11 for career. . . .
Additional statistics: 14 double-play ground outs in 107 opportunities, 22 doubles, 1 triple in 97.1 innings last season. . . . We're convinced that Russell would make a fine stopper. First, opposing batters have a career batting average of .205 in Late-Inning Pressure Situations, .279 in unpressured situations. That 75-point difference is the largest in the majors over the last 10 years (minimum: 100 AB each way). . . . Second, in limited opportunities, he's been successful, earning five saves in six save situations. . . . Finally, his career record in relief is 10–5 with a 3.68 ERA; he's 13–30 with a 4.80 ERA as a starter. . . . Allowed only two hits in 19 at bats with the bases loaded last season, but forced in four runs with walks.

Bret Saberhagen

Throws Right

Kansas City Royals	W–L	ERA	AB	H	HR	BB	SO	BA	SA	OBA
Season	18-10	3.36	975	246	27	53	163	.252	.400	.294
vs. Left-Handers			512	124	14	34	103	.242	.391	.290
vs. Right-Handers			463	122	13	19	60	.263	.410	.298
Home	11-4	3.58	529	138	14	20	90	.261	.420	.290
Road	7-6	3.11	446	108	13	33	73	.242	.377	.298
Grass	5-5	3.22	327	82	11	19	49	.251	.401	.293
Artificial Turf	13-5	3.43	648	164	16	34	114	.253	.400	.294
April	4-0	1.32	118	22	0	6	14	.186	.237	.230
May	5-1	3.06	175	45	7	10	36	.257	.406	.301
June	4-1	1.85	158	29	2	10	29	.184	.278	.232
July	2-4	5.23	170	51	8	4	25	.300	.518	.314
August	1-1	5.67	138	42	8	9	24	.304	.587	.347
Sept./Oct.	2-3	3.21	216	57	2	14	35	.264	.361	.316
Leading Off Inn.			256	71	10	6	47	.277	.465	.297
Runners On			363	85	8	27	57	.234	.361	.287
Runners/Scor. Pos.			200	47	5	16	36	.235	.365	.285
Runners On/2 Out			164	38	1	13	30	.232	.299	.296
Scor. Pos./2 Out			103	20	0	10	20	.194	.233	.265
Late Inning Pressure			104	30	4	5	16	.288	.462	.324
Leading Off			31	9	1	0	8	.290	.419	.290
Runners On			32	9	0	4	3	.281	.313	.368
Runners/Scor. Pos.			20	4	0	4	3	.200	.200	.320
First 9 Batters			275	71	12	14	51	.258	.444	.297
Second 9 Batters			278	68	2	16	48	.245	.353	.288
All Batters Thereafter			422	107	13	23	64	.254	.403	.295

Loves to face: Gary Gaetti (.059, 1-for-17)
Hates to face: Wade Boggs (.500, 11-for-22, 1 HR)
Ground outs-to-air outs ratio: 1.17 last season, 1.20 for career. . . .
Additional statistics: 19 double-play ground outs in 150 opportunities, 49 doubles, 7 triples in 257.0 innings last season. . . . Allowed 16 first-inning runs in 33 starts. . . . Batting support: 5.27 runs per start, compared to 3.32 in 1986. . . . Allowed 1.86 walks per nine innings, 2d-lowest rate among A.L. pitchers. . . . Won six consecutive starts twice, one short of his personal longest streak, and two short of Rich Gale's team record. . . . Faced 29 consecutive left-handed batters without allowing a hit (Aug. 27–Sept. 1). . . . Despite four years in majors and 55 wins, Saberhagen was youngest player on Royals roster last season until recall of Gary Thurman in August. Saberhagen is 16 months younger than Bo Jackson.

Calvin Schiraldi

Throws Right

Boston Red Sox	W–L	ERA	AB	H	HR	BB	SO	BA	SA	OBA
Season	8-5	4.41	313	75	15	40	93	.240	.422	.326
vs. Left-Handers			142	40	9	27	32	.282	.514	.392
vs. Right-Handers			171	35	6	13	61	.205	.345	.265
Home	4-0	3.27	158	33	6	21	39	.209	.361	.302
Road	4-5	5.67	155	42	9	19	54	.271	.484	.351
Grass	6-3	4.34	237	55	12	38	62	.232	.426	.338
Artificial Turf	2-2	4.66	76	20	3	2	31	.263	.408	.282
April	0-2	9.00	30	9	4	11	9	.300	.700	.476
May	2-1	4.09	39	8	2	6	14	.205	.385	.311
June	2-1	1.93	68	13	2	5	13	.191	.309	.247
July	2-1	8.18	44	13	4	5	15	.295	.591	.367
August	2-0	5.79	56	16	2	7	21	.286	.464	.375
Sept./Oct.	0-0	2.14	76	16	1	6	21	.211	.303	.265
Leading Off Inn.			59	11	0	7	18	.186	.186	.273
Runners On			170	42	13	18	54	.247	.524	.316
Runners/Scor. Pos.			103	27	7	12	34	.262	.515	.333
Runners On/2 Out			78	15	3	7	25	.192	.372	.259
Scor. Pos./2 Out			54	12	3	5	18	.222	.463	.288
Late Inning Pressure			151	34	7	26	47	.225	.391	.339
Leading Off			28	3	0	3	9	.107	.107	.194
Runners On			85	19	7	13	29	.224	.482	.327
Runners/Scor. Pos.			55	13	3	10	21	.236	.418	.354
First 9 Batters			285	70	14	39	83	.246	.432	.337
Second 9 Batters			22	5	1	1	6	.227	.409	.250
All Batters Thereafter			6	0	0	0	4	.000	.000	.000

Loves to face: Andy Van Slyke (0-for-5)
Hates to face: Tony Gwynn (.600, 3-for-5, 1 3B, 1 HR)
Ground outs-to-air outs ratio: 0.69 last season, 0.78 for career. . . .
Additional statistics: 3 double-play ground outs in 81 opportunities, 12 doubles, 0 triples in 83.2 innings last season. . . . Earned six saves in 11 opportunities, all but one after the All-Star break. . . . Allowed five extra-inning homers, most in the majors last season. . . . Struck out 11 batters in his only start, on Sept. 3 at Minnesota. Red Sox infielders didn't have an assist in that entire 10-inning game. . . . Opponents' career batting average of .224 in Late-Inning Pressure Situations, .274 in unpressured situations. He'll need more than that to overcome his reputation. . . . Opponents' career average of .211 with the bases loaded. . . . Pitched three scoreless innings in 1984 in his only previous Wrigley experience.

Dave Schmidt

Throws Right

Baltimore Orioles	W–L	ERA	AB	H	HR	BB	SO	BA	SA	OBA
Season	10-5	3.77	487	128	13	26	70	.263	.411	.301
vs. Left-Handers			217	68	7	15	29	.313	.484	.358
vs. Right-Handers			270	60	6	11	41	.222	.352	.254
Home	4-2	3.39	308	78	8	15	51	.253	.380	.290
Road	6-3	4.47	179	50	5	11	19	.279	.464	.319
Grass	9-3	3.44	404	104	10	22	61	.257	.389	.297
Artificial Turf	1-2	5.59	83	24	3	4	9	.289	.518	.322
April	2-1	2.84	69	14	2	4	9	.203	.391	.247
May	4-0	1.64	83	21	1	3	11	.253	.349	.276
June	2-1	4.05	131	37	6	7	21	.282	.458	.319
July	2-0	3.21	131	30	1	8	22	.229	.344	.273
August	0-3	8.44	73	26	3	4	7	.356	.534	.397
Sept./Oct.			0	0	0	0	0	—	—	—
Leading Off Inn.			117	24	4	4	13	.205	.359	.231
Runners On			207	54	5	12	31	.261	.415	.300
Runners/Scor. Pos.			123	29	3	8	15	.236	.390	.280
Runners On/2 Out			88	19	3	5	12	.216	.375	.258
Scor. Pos./2 Out			57	11	1	4	5	.193	.298	.246
Late Inning Pressure			80	25	0	5	7	.313	.400	.353
Leading Off			23	3	0	0	2	.130	.174	.130
Runners On			29	12	0	0	2	.414	.552	.414
Runners/Scor. Pos.			17	3	0	0	1	.176	.235	.176
First 9 Batters			250	69	6	12	35	.276	.432	.311
Second 9 Batters			135	35	6	9	22	.259	.444	.306
All Batters Thereafter			102	24	1	5	13	.235	.314	.271

Loves to face: Gary Pettis (0-for-12)
Hates to face: Spike Owen (.563, 9-for-16, 1 HR)
Ground outs-to-air outs ratio: 1.51 last season, 1.46 for career. . . .
Additional statistics: 11 double-play ground outs in 81 opportunities, 21 doubles, 6 triples in 124.0 innings last season. . . . Allowed 9 first-inning runs in 14 starts. . . . Batting support: 4.86 runs per start. . . . The only one of 17 Orioles pitchers who threw 20+ innings last season to have an ERA below 4.00. . . . Batting average by opposing left-handers was the highest of his career, but .222 by opposing right-handers was his career-best. . . . Best day-game ERA in the majors last season (1.73). Career records: 10–6 in day games, 23–27 at night. . . . ERA of 4.35 in 28 career starts, 2.90 in 228 relief appearances. . . . Retired the leadoff batter in at least 70 percent of the innings he's started in six of his seven seasons.

Ken Schrom

Throws Right

Cleveland Indians	W–L	ERA	AB	H	HR	BB	SO	BA	SA	OBA
Season	6-13	6.50	620	185	29	57	61	.298	.508	.357
vs. Left-Handers			323	102	17	27	30	.316	.548	.363
vs. Right-Handers			297	83	12	30	31	.279	.465	.350
Home	3-8	6.70	399	127	16	36	44	.318	.511	.373
Road	3-5	6.16	221	58	13	21	17	.262	.502	.328
Grass	5-12	7.13	561	175	27	55	58	.312	.526	.373
Artificial Turf	1-1	1.56	59	10	2	2	3	.169	.339	.197
April	1-2	6.52	73	21	1	6	5	.288	.411	.338
May	3-2	4.60	163	38	6	14	15	.233	.399	.291
June	0-3	10.20	76	33	4	4	7	.434	.724	.457
July	0-0	5.46	106	28	4	15	11	.264	.434	.352
August	1-4	10.31	87	30	6	9	12	.345	.621	.406
Sept./Oct.	1-2	6.11	115	35	8	9	11	.304	.565	.367
Leading Off Inn.			152	47	10	13	17	.309	.566	.364
Runners On			252	84	11	29	25	.333	.544	.400
Runners/Scor. Pos.			158	53	7	21	13	.335	.551	.406
Runners On/2 Out			95	30	4	10	7	.316	.547	.381
Scor. Pos./2 Out			69	21	4	9	5	.304	.609	.385
Late Inning Pressure			45	12	1	5	2	.267	.400	.333
Leading Off			15	6	1	0	0	.400	.667	.400
Runners On			15	2	0	3	1	.133	.267	.263
Runners/Scor. Pos.			7	0	0	3	1	.000	.000	.273
First 9 Batters			249	72	6	25	33	.289	.430	.353
Second 9 Batters			209	66	13	15	14	.316	.589	.362
All Batters Thereafter			162	47	10	17	14	.290	.525	.357

Loves to face: Carlton Fisk (.077, 2-for-26)
Hates to face: Wally Joyner (.571, 8-for-14, 2 HR)
Ground outs-to-air outs ratio: 0.73 last season, 0.79 for career. . . .
Additional statistics: 10 double-play ground outs in 133 opportunities, 37 doubles, 3 triples in 153.2 innings last season. . . . Allowed 18 first-inning runs in 29 starts. . . . Batting support: 4.55 runs per start. . . . Averaged only 3.57 strikeouts per nine innings, 3d-lowest rate among A.L. starters. (minimum: 15 GS). . . . Record of 1–7 with a 8.31 ERA in day games; 5–6, 5.89 at night. . . . Averaged 5.01 innings per start, lowest among Cleveland's regular starters. Failed to complete five innings in five consecutive starts, tying Jose Nunez and Mike Krukow for the longest streak of the season. . . . Opponents' average of .087 (4-for-46) with the bases loaded through 1986; .545 (6-for-11) in 1987.

Jeff Sellers

Boston Red Sox — Throws Right

Boston Red Sox	W-L	ERA	AB	H	HR	BB	SO	BA	SA	OBA
Season	7-8	5.28	539	161	10	61	99	.299	.438	.368
vs. Left-Handers			289	88	4	33	42	.304	.436	.372
vs. Right-Handers			250	73	6	28	57	.292	.440	.364
Home	4-3	5.04	271	80	5	23	55	.295	.421	.348
Road	3-5	5.53	268	81	5	38	44	.302	.455	.388
Grass	5-7	5.52	428	131	6	42	80	.306	.430	.364
Artificial Turf	2-1	4.45	111	30	4	19	19	.270	.468	.383
April	1-1	8.16	61	23	1	4	7	.377	.590	.415
May	1-0	6.92	50	18	1	10	9	.360	.500	.484
June	0-0	14.29	27	11	0	7	7	.407	.556	.529
July	1-2	3.96	95	22	1	15	20	.232	.326	.336
August	2-3	5.50	131	38	5	9	26	.290	.496	.333
Sept./Oct.	2-2	3.42	175	49	2	16	30	.280	.366	.332
Leading Off Inn.			133	35	2	18	25	.263	.406	.351
Runners On			244	76	4	21	49	.311	.467	.360
Runners/Scor. Pos.			132	42	1	11	33	.318	.470	.359
Runners On/2 Out			107	32	1	6	24	.299	.458	.342
Scor. Pos./2 Out			65	20	0	2	16	.308	.477	.338
Late Inning Pressure			76	27	0	6	11	.355	.434	.398
Leading Off			21	7	0	1	3	.333	.429	.364
Runners On			38	12	0	3	7	.316	.395	.357
Runners/Scor. Pos.			23	5	0	0	6	.217	.304	.208
First 9 Batters			188	57	6	27	44	.303	.473	.388
Second 9 Batters			171	53	2	13	27	.310	.421	.362
All Batters Thereafter			180	51	2	21	28	.283	.417	.353

Loves to face: Ken Phelps (0-for-7)
Hates to face: George Bell (.625, 5-for-8)
Ground outs-to-air outs ratio: 1.12 last season, 1.20 for career (1.65 vs. left-handed batters, 0.73 vs. right-handers). . . . Additional statistics: 8 double-play ground outs in 120 opportunities, 37 doubles, 4 triples in 139.2 innings last season. . . . Allowed 8 first-inning runs in 22 starts. . . . Batting support: 5.00 runs per start. . . . Opponents have batted over .300 with runners in scoring position and in Late-Inning Pressure Situations in each of his three seasons in the majors. . . . All of his decisions were recorded in his 22 starts. Had an ERA of 14.54 in his three relief appearances. . . . Opponents' batting average has increased in each season since 1985: .273, .282, .299. . . . One of his two shutouts last season was a 5-hitter against the soon to be World Champion Twins on Sept. 1.

Mike Smithson

Minnesota Twins — Throws Right

Minnesota Twins	W-L	ERA	AB	H	HR	BB	SO	BA	SA	OBA
Season	4-7	5.94	441	126	17	38	53	.286	.469	.351
vs. Left-Handers			253	81	17	21	30	.320	.593	.371
vs. Right-Handers			188	45	0	17	23	.239	.303	.326
Home	2-1	4.71	196	52	7	18	20	.265	.449	.332
Road	2-6	6.98	245	74	10	20	33	.302	.486	.366
Grass	1-4	8.42	154	51	6	14	26	.331	.513	.398
Artificial Turf	3-3	4.71	287	75	11	24	27	.261	.446	.325
April	3-1	3.48	131	29	3	8	11	.221	.366	.271
May	0-2	9.00	31	12	2	4	3	.387	.645	.474
June	1-1	6.67	109	33	5	9	16	.303	.486	.366
July	0-2	8.86	94	32	5	8	14	.340	.585	.406
August			0	0	0	0	0	—	—	—
Sept./Oct.	0-1	4.95	76	20	2	9	9	.263	.408	.337
Leading Off Inn.			107	28	5	10	11	.262	.430	.336
Runners On			188	65	10	14	18	.346	.617	.396
Runners/Scor. Pos.			107	31	6	9	13	.290	.542	.341
Runners On/2 Out			77	26	4	7	9	.338	.636	.407
Scor. Pos./2 Out			53	14	2	5	7	.264	.472	.328
Late Inning Pressure			24	7	0	3	1	.292	.333	.393
Leading Off			8	3	0	0	0	.375	.375	.375
Runners On			11	4	0	1	1	.364	.455	.462
Runners/Scor. Pos.			8	2	0	1	1	.250	.375	.333
First 9 Batters			168	45	2	15	21	.268	.351	.344
Second 9 Batters			162	41	8	11	21	.253	.444	.307
All Batters Thereafter			111	40	7	12	11	.360	.685	.424

Loves to face: Ivan Calderon (.048, 1-for-21)
Hates to face: George Brett (.607, 17-for-28, 2 HR)
Ground outs-to-air outs ratio: 1.22 last season, 1.22 for career (0.99 vs. left-handed batters, 1.61 vs. right-handers). . . . Additional statistics: 7 double-play ground outs in 86 opportunities, 24 doubles, 3 triples in 109.0 innings last season. . . . Allowed 14 first-inning runs in 20 starts. . . . Batting support: 6.00 runs per start, 3d-highest average in A.L. (minimum:m: 15 GS). . . . Allowed all 17 home runs to left-handed batters. No other pitcher over the last 13 years allowed as many as 10 home runs without surrendering at least one to both left- and right-handed batters. . . . Last home run allowed to a right-hander was hit by Robin Yount on Sept. 3, 1986. . . . Opponents stole 22 bases in 22 attempts. . . . Won his first three starts with an ERA of 2.01; 1–7, 6.96 thereafter.

Bob Stanley

Boston Red Sox — Throws Right

Boston Red Sox	W-L	ERA	AB	H	HR	BB	SO	BA	SA	OBA
Season	4-15	5.01	616	198	17	42	67	.321	.468	.363
vs. Left-Handers			299	107	8	29	28	.358	.522	.413
vs. Right-Handers			317	91	9	13	39	.287	.416	.314
Home	3-5	4.28	284	85	4	14	30	.299	.405	.329
Road	1-10	5.70	332	113	13	28	37	.340	.521	.392
Grass	4-12	4.53	534	163	13	36	59	.305	.446	.347
Artificial Turf	0-3	8.66	82	35	4	6	8	.427	.610	.467
April	2-3	4.05	134	40	2	9	11	.299	.448	.340
May	0-4	5.26	154	48	5	8	14	.312	.474	.346
June	1-1	5.19	108	39	4	7	12	.361	.528	.397
July	0-2	8.10	29	10	1	1	5	.345	.517	.355
August	1-3	4.68	133	42	4	10	18	.316	.429	.366
Sept./Oct.	0-2	5.52	58	19	1	7	7	.328	.448	.400
Leading Off Inn.			147	61	4	8	16	.415	.599	.445
Runners On			294	84	9	22	29	.286	.429	.333
Runners/Scor. Pos.			169	49	6	17	21	.290	.432	.347
Runners On/2 Out			119	33	6	11	10	.277	.487	.338
Scor. Pos./2 Out			75	20	5	9	8	.267	.520	.345
Late Inning Pressure			86	33	2	9	8	.384	.547	.438
Leading Off			23	13	1	2	1	.565	.870	.600
Runners On			45	14	1	6	4	.311	.467	.385
Runners/Scor. Pos.			29	11	1	4	3	.379	.586	.441
First 9 Batters			250	77	4	23	32	.308	.416	.366
Second 9 Batters			170	59	5	8	15	.347	.488	.372
All Batters Thereafter			196	62	8	11	20	.316	.515	.353

Loves to face: George Bell (.130, 3-for-23)
Hates to face Boston; Daryl, that is (.556, 5-for-9, 1 HR)
Ground outs-to-air outs ratio: 1.64 last season, 2.25 for career. . . . Additional statistics: 23 double-play ground outs in 142 opportunities, 33 doubles, 3 triples in 152.2 innings last season. . . . Allowed 5 first-inning runs in 20 starts, 5th-lowest average in A.L. (min.: 15 GS). . . . Batting support: 4.25 runs per start. . . . Has lost his last six decisions to White Sox. . . . Record of 4-12 (5.08 ERA) in 20 starts, 0–3 (4.68 ERA) in 14 relief appearances. . . . Batting average by opposing left-handers was the 2d–highest among 240 qualifying pitchers in the majors last season. Len Barker had the highest (.360). . . . Only pitcher in majors whose opponents have batted .300+ in each of last two years (min.: 75 IP each season).

Dave Stewart

Oakland As — Throws Right

Oakland As	W-L	ERA	AB	H	HR	BB	SO	BA	SA	OBA
Season	20-13	3.68	980	224	24	105	205	.229	.357	.306
vs. Left-Handers			554	129	13	67	119	.233	.357	.314
vs. Right-Handers			426	95	11	38	86	.223	.357	.294
Home	11-6	2.84	489	105	7	53	109	.215	.303	.294
Road	9-7	4.56	491	119	17	52	96	.242	.411	.318
Grass	17-11	3.36	862	197	17	91	178	.229	.342	.304
Artificial Turf	3-2	6.10	118	27	7	14	27	.229	.466	.321
April	3-2	4.11	131	34	1	20	27	.260	.359	.355
May	3-2	3.93	124	27	3	14	30	.218	.363	.300
June	3-3	3.72	145	29	7	14	34	.200	.379	.273
July	4-0	2.58	168	34	2	19	36	.202	.292	.286
August	5-2	3.78	191	46	5	15	44	.241	.372	.301
Sept./Oct.	2-4	4.03	221	54	6	23	34	.244	.376	.318
Leading Off Inn.			249	55	9	23	51	.221	.398	.289
Runners On			385	89	8	49	78	.231	.348	.321
Runners/Scor. Pos.			230	52	3	27	53	.226	.309	.309
Runners On/2 Out			168	34	2	18	37	.202	.262	.283
Scor. Pos./2 Out			110	20	0	12	28	.182	.200	.268
Late Inning Pressure			115	31	5	16	21	.270	.443	.356
Leading Off			32	10	4	3	7	.313	.750	.371
Runners On			42	10	0	10	7	.238	.286	.377
Runners/Scor. Pos.			21	7	0	6	3	.333	.381	.464
First 9 Batters			289	53	5	37	76	.183	.304	.283
Second 9 Batters			302	72	7	25	61	.238	.358	.298
All Batters Thereafter			389	99	12	43	68	.254	.396	.329

Loves to face: Rance Mulliniks (.059, 1-for-17)
Hates to face: Lou Whitaker (.700, 7-for-10, 6 BB)
Ground outs-to-air outs ratio: 0.79 last season, 0.87 for career. . . . Additional statistics: 14 double-play ground outs in 175 opportunities, 48 doubles, 3 triples in 261.1 innings last season. . . . Allowed 12 first-inning runs in 37 starts. . . . Batting support: 4.73 runs per start. . . . Allowed one home run per 19.0 innings at the Oakland Coliseum (2d-best rate for an A.L. pitcher in home games). But on the road he allowed one per 7.5 innings. . . . Career record of 5–0 vs. the Brewers. . . . Career record of 4–12 in April, 55–41 in all other months combined. . . . Who could have predicted a 20-win season for a 7-year journeyman? Certainly not the Dodgers, Phillies, or Rangers, who all gave up on him. Sudden success last season was comparable to that of Mike Krukow in 1986.

Dave Stieb

Throws Right

Toronto Blue Jays	W–L	ERA	AB	H	HR	BB	SO	BA	SA	OBA
Season	13-9	4.09	685	164	16	87	115	.239	.377	.329
vs. Left-Handers			364	88	10	53	57	.242	.390	.338
vs. Right-Handers			321	76	6	34	58	.237	.361	.319
Home	5-4	4.98	292	70	7	40	51	.240	.387	.333
Road	8-5	3.44	393	94	9	47	64	.239	.369	.326
Grass	6-4	3.28	307	77	7	37	55	.251	.368	.339
Artificial Turf	7-5	4.73	378	87	9	50	60	.230	.384	.321
April	0-2	6.63	77	25	2	12	16	.325	.455	.429
May	3-1	4.09	125	33	3	16	15	.264	.400	.348
June	3-2	4.00	103	24	2	16	12	.233	.320	.342
July	3-0	2.61	135	26	2	10	25	.193	.304	.247
August	4-2	3.32	154	34	5	12	33	.221	.383	.281
Sept./Oct.	0-2	5.84	91	22	2	21	14	.242	.440	.391
Leading Off Inn.			173	39	7	23	28	.225	.428	.320
Runners On			280	76	4	34	41	.271	.386	.355
Runners/Scor. Pos.			161	45	1	21	26	.280	.385	.360
Runners On/2 Out			108	27	3	17	19	.250	.389	.362
Scor. Pos./2 Out			70	17	1	10	12	.243	.357	.346
Late Inning Pressure			36	2	0	2	9	.056	.056	.105
Leading Off			11	0	0	1	3	.000	.000	.083
Runners On			4	1	0	1	0	.250	.250	.400
Runners/Scor. Pos.			2	1	0	0	0	.500	.500	.500
First 9 Batters			261	61	7	27	46	.234	.360	.308
Second 9 Batters			227	60	5	38	30	.264	.419	.372
All Batters Thereafter			197	43	4	22	39	.218	.350	.305

Loves to face: Mark Salas (.063, 1-for-16)
Hates to face: Larry Parrish (.485, 16-for-33, 3 HR)
Ground outs-to-air outs ratio: 1.06 last season, 1.14 for career. . . .
Additional statistics: 13 double-play ground outs in 141 opportunities, 38 doubles, 4 triples in 185.0 innings last season. . . . Allowed 17 first-inning runs in 31 starts. . . . Batting support: 5.97 runs per start, 4th-highest average in A.L. (minimum: 15 GS). . . . Average of one home run per 28.0 innings in night games, lowest rate in majors. . . . Compiled highest ERA in majors (7.43) over first four weeks (minimum: 5 GS), and didn't win after August 18. But in between, he was 13-3 with a 3.07 ERA. . . . Faced 28 consecutive batters in Late-Inning Pressure Situations without allowing a hit (July 5–Sept. 21), longest A.L. streak of season. . . . Has lost his last six decisions to the Brewers.

Tim Stoddard

Throws Right

New York Yankees	W–L	ERA	AB	H	HR	BB	SO	BA	SA	OBA
Season	4-3	3.50	353	83	13	30	78	.235	.391	.293
vs. Left-Handers			145	40	6	14	18	.276	.448	.340
vs. Right-Handers			208	43	7	16	60	.207	.351	.260
Home	3-1	2.91	196	46	6	18	42	.235	.378	.296
Road	1-2	4.28	157	37	7	12	36	.236	.408	.288
Grass	3-1	3.50	315	75	11	27	70	.238	.387	.296
Artificial Turf	1-2	3.48	38	8	2	3	8	.211	.421	.268
April	0-0	3.60	16	2	0	4	4	.125	.125	.300
May	0-1	3.57	65	16	4	5	10	.246	.462	.300
June	1-0	3.71	66	15	2	6	18	.227	.364	.292
July	2-1	3.52	61	15	1	7	15	.246	.344	.324
August	1-0	2.82	85	18	3	3	25	.212	.376	.236
Sept./Oct.	0-1	4.11	60	17	3	5	6	.283	.483	.328
Leading Off Inn.			80	16	2	3	18	.200	.300	.229
Runners On			152	35	5	17	34	.230	.375	.302
Runners/Scor. Pos.			94	21	1	10	24	.223	.319	.290
Runners On/2 Out			70	12	1	8	19	.171	.257	.256
Scor. Pos./2 Out			47	9	1	7	15	.191	.298	.296
Late Inning Pressure			128	35	4	11	21	.273	.406	.329
Leading Off			34	9	1	1	5	.265	.412	.286
Runners On			52	14	1	7	10	.269	.365	.350
Runners/Scor. Pos.			35	8	0	5	7	.229	.286	.317
First 9 Batters			321	76	11	30	69	.237	.389	.299
Second 9 Batters			30	6	2	0	9	.200	.400	.200
All Batters Thereafter			2	1	0	0	0	.500	.500	.500

Loves to face: Carney Lansford (0-for-15)
Hates to face: Ruben Sierra (.800, 4-for-5, 2 2B, 1 HR)
Ground outs-to-air outs ratio: 0.69 last season, 1.08 for career. . . .
Additional statistics: 4 double-play ground outs in 75 opportunities, 10 doubles, 3 triples in 92.2 innings last season. . . . Saved as many games last season as in three previous years combined (8). . . . Has made 463 consecutive relief appearances without a start. . . . Has defeated every A.L. club except the Blue Jays. . . . Has faced more batters over the past three seasons than any other pitcher who hasn't hit at least one batter with a pitch. In fact, Stoddard has faced 1,155 left-handers in his career and never plunked one. . . . Made big-league debut with the Chisox in 1975, pitching one inning and allowed a home run to Steve Brye. Wasn't heard from again until he surfaced with the Orioles in 1978.

Les Straker

Throws Right

Minnesota Twins	W–L	ERA	AB	H	HR	BB	SO	BA	SA	OBA
Season	8-10	4.37	583	150	24	59	76	.257	.443	.325
vs. Left-Handers			321	85	16	36	45	.265	.489	.338
vs. Right-Handers			262	65	8	23	31	.248	.385	.308
Home	6-3	4.12	262	67	8	22	39	.256	.416	.315
Road	2-7	4.57	321	83	16	37	37	.259	.464	.332
Grass	2-6	3.89	251	61	11	27	30	.243	.426	.313
Artificial Turf	6-4	4.76	332	89	13	32	46	.268	.455	.333
April	1-0	2.08	46	9	1	7	9	.196	.326	.302
May	1-2	4.81	93	24	5	14	13	.258	.473	.361
June	1-3	4.20	113	33	2	8	14	.292	.434	.331
July	2-1	4.94	105	26	4	11	13	.248	.429	.319
August	1-3	5.40	108	29	5	10	9	.269	.454	.328
Sept./Oct.	2-1	3.73	118	29	7	9	18	.246	.475	.300
Leading Off Inn.			151	40	5	15	16	.265	.411	.331
Runners On			219	51	10	25	31	.233	.420	.307
Runners/Scor. Pos.			121	26	6	16	20	.215	.421	.294
Runners On/2 Out			91	17	5	10	13	.187	.374	.267
Scor. Pos./2 Out			55	10	3	5	9	.182	.364	.250
Late Inning Pressure			39	14	4	3	3	.359	.821	.395
Leading Off			11	4	1	1	0	.364	.727	.417
Runners On			12	5	1	1	1	.417	.750	.429
Runners/Scor. Pos.			8	3	1	1	1	.375	.750	.400
First 9 Batters			236	53	5	24	37	.225	.318	.295
Second 9 Batters			211	52	12	21	25	.246	.493	.313
All Batters Thereafter			136	45	7	14	14	.331	.581	.392

Loves to face: Harold Reynolds (0-for-9)
Hates to face: Frank White (.800, 4-for-5, 1 HR)
Ground outs-to-air outs ratio: 1.20 last season, his first in majors. . . . Additional statistics: 11 double-play ground outs in 102 opportunities, 22 doubles, 7 triples in 154.1 innings last season. . . . Allowed 5 first-inning runs in 26 starts, 3d-lowest average in A.L. (minimum: 15 GS). . . . Batting support: 4.38 runs per start. . . . Spent 10 seasons in minors before making his major-league debut last season. Was teammate of Gary Redus and Nick Esasky at Billings of the Pioneer League in 1978. . . . Had 1–6 record vs. teams that finished above .500, but was 7–4 against teams below .500. . . . Opponents batted .420 (21-for-50) from 7th inning on; his ERA during that part of game was 10.80. But will that satisfy critics of Kelly's move to lift him in Game 3 of World Series? Of course not.

Don Sutton

Throws Right

California Angels	W–L	ERA	AB	H	HR	BB	SO	BA	SA	OBA
Season	11-11	4.70	740	199	38	41	99	.269	.458	.311
vs. Left-Handers			369	86	16	24	46	.233	.398	.286
vs. Right-Handers			371	113	22	17	53	.305	.518	.338
Home	3-6	4.28	356	92	20	23	56	.258	.447	.310
Road	8-5	5.10	384	107	18	18	43	.279	.469	.313
Grass	9-9	4.72	610	156	34	33	84	.256	.452	.299
Artificial Turf	2-2	4.60	130	43	4	8	15	.331	.485	.370
April	1-3	4.23	108	33	6	6	12	.306	.500	.350
May	1-2	5.35	132	39	6	11	15	.295	.485	.352
June	3-3	3.06	141	38	3	2	20	.270	.369	.280
July	2-1	4.88	99	19	10	8	15	.192	.505	.273
August	2-1	3.58	138	31	7	9	19	.225	.399	.268
Sept./Oct.	2-1	7.58	122	39	6	5	18	.320	.525	.349
Leading Off Inn.			189	55	10	9	29	.291	.487	.327
Runners On			275	80	17	11	36	.291	.524	.322
Runners/Scor. Pos.			144	37	11	7	25	.257	.514	.296
Runners On/2 Out			103	21	6	5	20	.204	.398	.248
Scor. Pos./2 Out			59	9	4	3	14	.153	.356	.206
Late Inning Pressure			41	9	3	1	7	.220	.463	.238
Leading Off			13	4	2	0	2	.308	.846	.308
Runners On			10	2	1	0	2	.200	.500	.200
Runners/Scor. Pos.			3	1	1	0	1	.333	1.333	.333
First 9 Batters			297	83	18	15	42	.279	.502	.318
Second 9 Batters			273	83	13	14	35	.304	.487	.339
All Batters Thereafter			170	33	7	12	22	.194	.335	.257

Loves to face: Keith Hernandez (.154, 8-for-52)
Hates to face: Andre Dawson (.344, 11-for-32, 4 HR)
Ground outs-to-air outs ratio: 0.77 last season, 0.88 for career. . . . Additional statistics: 16 double-play ground outs in 134 opportunities, 24 doubles, 1 triple in 191.2 innings last season. . . . Allowed 16 first-inning runs in 34 starts. . . . Batting support: 4.91 runs per start. . . . Allowed an average of 1.93 walks per nine innings, 3d-lowest rate among A.L. starters. . . . Opposing batters hit 75 points higher on artificial surfaces than on grass fields, 2d-largest difference in A.L. (minimum: 100 AB each way). . . . ERA of 2.47 during month of June over past three seasons is 6th-lowest in majors (minimum: 75 IP). . . . Has started 20+ games in 22 consecutive seasons. That's not just an oddity, its a record. Others with streaks of 20+ years: Phil Niekro (21), Tom Seaver (20), and Cy Young (20).

Greg Swindell

Cleveland Indians — Throws Left

	W–L	ERA	AB	H	HR	BB	SO	BA	SA	OBA
Season	3-8	5.10	396	112	18	37	97	.283	.467	.343
vs. Left-Handers			68	21	4	3	13	.309	.574	.333
vs. Right-Handers			328	91	14	34	84	.277	.445	.345
Home	2-3	3.80	180	46	7	15	44	.256	.411	.316
Road	1-5	6.22	216	66	11	22	53	.306	.514	.365
Grass	3-6	4.28	340	93	14	31	85	.274	.435	.335
Artificial Turf	0-2	10.29	56	19	4	6	12	.339	.661	.391
April	1-3	4.76	124	29	6	11	29	.234	.387	.296
May	2-2	3.61	192	57	8	15	51	.297	.469	.346
June	0-3	9.00	80	26	4	11	17	.325	.588	.404
July			0	0	0	0	0	—	—	—
August			0	0	0	0	0	—	—	—
Sept./Oct.			0	0	0	0	0	—	—	—
Leading Off Inn.			97	25	3	9	21	.258	.381	.321
Runners On			160	49	9	14	32	.306	.544	.360
Runners/Scor. Pos.			91	25	6	10	17	.275	.549	.337
Runners On/2 Out			71	21	4	6	19	.296	.535	.351
Scor. Pos./2 Out			51	17	4	3	11	.333	.647	.370
Late Inning Pressure			57	17	2	7	13	.298	.456	.375
Leading Off			12	2	0	3	2	.167	.250	.333
Runners On			30	10	2	1	6	.333	.567	.355
Runners/Scor. Pos.			21	6	1	1	4	.286	.476	.318
First 9 Batters			122	28	3	12	38	.230	.352	.299
Second 9 Batters			121	41	6	9	22	.339	.537	.386
All Batters Thereafter			153	43	9	16	37	.281	.503	.345

Loves to face: Ruben Sierra (0-for-3, 3 SO)
Hates to face: Dave Winfield (.600, 3-for-5, 3 HR)
Ground outs-to-air outs ratio: 0.72 last season, 0.76 for career (0.93 vs. left-handers, 0.73 vs. right-handers). . . . Additional statistics: 6 double-play ground outs in 84 opportunities, 17 doubles, 1 triple in 102.1 innings last season. . . . Allowed 8 first-inning runs in 15 starts. . . . Batting support: 4.47 runs per start. . . . Led the Indians' staff with an average of 6.80 innings per start (minimum: 10 GS). . . . Lost five of his last six starts. . . . Last appearance was June 29 due to ligament damage in his left elbow. . . . Career total of four walks to the 99 left-handed batters he's faced; he walked one right-handed batters for every 12 he's faced. . . . Were Forest Gregory Swindell's parents disappointed when their son chose *base*ball?

Frank Tanana

Detroit Tigers — Throws Left

	W–L	ERA	AB	H	HR	BB	SO	BA	SA	OBA
Season	15-10	3.91	844	216	27	56	146	.256	.410	.302
vs. Left-Handers			140	33	4	11	32	.236	.364	.296
vs. Right-Handers			704	183	23	45	114	.260	.419	.304
Home	10-5	3.06	413	94	10	25	75	.228	.358	.273
Road	5-5	4.76	431	122	17	31	71	.283	.459	.330
Grass	14-9	3.85	699	177	22	45	129	.253	.405	.300
Artificial Turf	1-1	4.19	145	39	5	11	17	.269	.434	.313
April	2-1	2.57	99	16	3	9	17	.162	.293	.231
May	2-2	4.71	149	43	7	11	25	.289	.503	.344
June	3-1	2.40	148	28	1	12	25	.189	.270	.256
July	3-3	4.17	156	42	6	9	26	.269	.449	.304
August	3-2	5.23	170	56	7	8	30	.329	.494	.352
Sept./Oct.	2-1	4.11	122	31	3	7	23	.254	.393	.298
Leading Off Inn.			212	56	6	15	36	.264	.415	.319
Runners On			332	89	6	26	56	.268	.367	.315
Runners/Scor. Pos.			187	47	3	21	37	.251	.332	.317
Runners On/2 Out			132	31	1	15	20	.235	.303	.318
Scor. Pos./2 Out			86	20	1	12	16	.233	.291	.333
Late Inning Pressure			77	21	0	2	12	.273	.377	.291
Leading Off			21	4	0	0	7	.190	.333	.190
Runners On			26	7	0	1	2	.269	.308	.296
Runners/Scor. Pos.			16	4	0	1	1	.250	.313	.294
First 9 Batters			274	65	8	18	54	.237	.361	.281
Second 9 Batters			268	75	13	19	52	.280	.493	.333
All Batters Thereafter			302	76	6	19	40	.252	.381	.294

Loves to face: Fred Lynn (.122, 5-for-41)
Hates to face: Paul Mol (.460, 23-for-50, 1 HR)
Ground outs-to-air outs ratio: 1.00 last season, 0.99 for career. . . . Additional statistics: 18 double-play ground outs in 164 opportunities, 37 doubles, 6 triples in 218.2 innings last season. . . . Batting support: 5.44 runs per start. . . . Opponents stole third base eight times (most in majors), without anyone getting caught. . . . Everyone will remember the masterpiece he threw against Toronto to win A.L. East in the regular-season finale, but he also whitewashed Jays on June 22, under a little bit less pressure. Was 3–0 vs. Jays last season, and you know what each of those wins meant. . . . Opponents' batting average was his lowest since 1977, when he led A.L. in ERA. . . . Struck out more batters from 1974 through 1978 (1,052) than he has in nine seasons since then (997).

Walt Terrell

Detroit Tigers — Throws Right

	W–L	ERA	AB	H	HR	BB	SO	BA	SA	OBA
Season	17-10	4.05	947	254	30	94	143	.268	.424	.333
vs. Left-Handers			475	122	15	49	69	.257	.419	.326
vs. Right-Handers			472	132	15	45	74	.280	.430	.340
Home	13-2	2.47	515	118	14	45	79	.229	.355	.290
Road	4-8	6.09	432	136	16	49	64	.315	.507	.383
Grass	16-7	3.72	809	211	26	74	122	.261	.412	.322
Artificial Turf	1-3	6.03	138	43	4	20	21	.312	.500	.394
April	1-3	3.07	114	34	2	9	14	.298	.447	.344
May	3-2	3.33	171	38	7	22	36	.222	.368	.308
June	2-2	4.85	118	31	4	14	20	.263	.424	.343
July	2-1	5.09	181	53	6	16	23	.293	.464	.352
August	3-2	4.36	168	45	5	18	25	.268	.411	.333
Sept./Oct.	6-0	3.58	195	53	6	15	25	.272	.436	.325
Leading Off Inn.			238	63	13	17	35	.265	.487	.316
Runners On			386	99	11	47	64	.256	.415	.331
Runners/Scor. Pos.			199	51	5	27	38	.256	.417	.331
Runners On/2 Out			166	39	2	18	36	.235	.313	.314
Scor. Pos./2 Out			95	18	2	10	24	.189	.295	.267
Late Inning Pressure			99	30	6	10	11	.303	.535	.364
Leading Off			25	7	2	1	2	.280	.600	.308
Runners On			37	10	2	5	5	.270	.459	.349
Runners/Scor. Pos.			18	6	2	5	3	.333	.722	.458
First 9 Batters			287	61	7	34	46	.213	.324	.294
Second 9 Batters			275	81	10	24	41	.295	.484	.352
All Batters Thereafter			385	112	13	36	56	.291	.457	.349

Loves to face: Roy Smalley (.045, 1-for-22)
Hates to face: Steve Balboni (.500, 12-for-24, 4 HR)
Ground outs-to-air outs ratio: 1.25 last season, 1.31 for career. . . . Additional statistics: 25 double-play ground outs in 192 opportunities, 50 doubles, 4 triples in 244.2 innings last season. . . . Allowed 26 first-inning runs in 35 starts. . . . Batting support: 5.37 runs per start. . . . Led majors in wins in home games. . . . During three seasons with Detroit: 32–7, 2.87 ERA at Tiger Stadium; 15–25, 5.64 ERA in road games. . . . Allowed hits to seven right-handed batters in a row (Sept. 26–Oct. 1), tying Ken Schrom for longest streak in majors last season. . . . As valuable as HoJo has been to the Mets, where would '87 Tigers have been without Terrell's eight straight wins down the stretch? A trade that helped both clubs? Where'd we put our cliche repellent?

Bobby Thigpen

Chicago White Sox — Throws Right

	W–L	ERA	AB	H	HR	BB	SO	BA	SA	OBA
Season	7-5	2.73	336	86	10	24	52	.256	.372	.311
vs. Left-Handers			177	49	4	16	25	.277	.367	.340
vs. Right-Handers			159	37	6	8	27	.233	.377	.278
Home	4-2	2.78	212	57	8	12	38	.269	.396	.311
Road	3-3	2.65	124	29	2	12	14	.234	.331	.312
Grass	6-5	3.39	275	73	10	18	48	.265	.400	.315
Artificial Turf	1-0	0.00	61	13	0	6	4	.213	.246	.294
April	0-1	3.79	72	20	4	6	6	.278	.458	.333
May	2-1	3.14	52	13	2	5	6	.250	.365	.316
June			0	0	0	0	0	—	—	—
July	1-0	4.00	40	14	0	1	7	.350	.475	.395
August	0-2	1.89	72	16	1	3	15	.222	.264	.263
Sept./Oct.	4-1	1.95	100	23	3	9	18	.230	.301	.294
Leading Off Inn.			75	26	3	4	8	.347	.547	.380
Runners On			158	36	4	16	25	.228	.323	.307
Runners/Scor. Pos.			89	20	2	11	15	.225	.326	.317
Runners On/2 Out			73	17	1	9	11	.233	.301	.317
Scor. Pos./2 Out			47	9	0	6	9	.191	.234	.283
Late Inning Pressure			197	47	6	15	29	.239	.350	.299
Leading Off			47	16	2	2	4	.340	.532	.367
Runners On			84	15	1	11	15	.179	.226	.281
Runners/Scor. Pos.			47	11	1	8	6	.234	.319	.345
First 9 Batters			305	78	10	21	48	.256	.384	.310
Second 9 Batters			31	8	0	3	4	.258	.258	.324
All Batters Thereafter			0	0	0	0	0	—	—	—

Loves to face: Dale Sveum (0-for-5)
Hates to face: Randy Bush (3-for-3, 1 HR)
Ground outs-to-air outs ratio: 0.87 last season, 0.82 for career. . . . Additional statistics: 5 double-play ground outs in 83 opportunities, 7 doubles, 1 triple in 89.0 innings last season. . . . Earned 16 saves in 22 opportunities, after going seven for 11 in 1986. . . . All but one of his saves came after the All-Star break. Only one A.L. pitcher had more during the second half (Tom Henke, 17). . . . Led all rookies with a 2.73 ERA (minimum: 50 IP). . . . Opponents' career batting average of .227 in Late-Inning Pressure Situations, .265 in unpressured situations. . . . Has faced 141 batters with runners on base in Late-Inning Pressure Situations, and allowed only one home run. . . . Bill Schroeder was one-for-two against Thigpen in their *Peanuts* battles last season.

Mark Thurmond

Detroit Tigers — Throws Left

	W–L	ERA	AB	H	HR	BB	SO	BA	SA	OBA
Season	0-1	4.23	251	83	5	24	21	.331	.466	.384
vs. Left-Handers			91	25	1	9	10	.275	.363	.330
vs. Right-Handers			160	58	4	15	11	.363	.525	.415
Home	0-1	4.03	120	39	3	12	8	.325	.467	.381
Road	0-0	4.41	131	44	2	12	13	.336	.466	.386
Grass	0-1	4.37	243	82	5	24	20	.337	.477	.391
Artificial Turf	0-0	0.00	8	1	0	0	1	.125	.125	.125
April	0-0	0.00	12	2	0	2	2	.167	.167	.286
May	0-1	4.20	59	20	2	5	5	.339	.492	.385
June	0-0	2.84	54	16	1	8	5	.296	.389	.381
July	0-0	8.31	39	18	1	3	1	.462	.718	.477
August	0-0	3.55	48	11	1	4	5	.229	.375	.288
Sept./Oct.	0-0	5.00	39	16	0	2	3	.410	.487	.439
Leading Off Inn.			44	16	0	7	5	.364	.409	.451
Runners On			153	48	3	13	13	.314	.451	.359
Runners/Scor. Pos.			91	28	1	13	8	.308	.418	.380
Runners On/2 Out			65	21	2	5	5	.323	.477	.371
Scor. Pos./2 Out			43	14	1	5	4	.326	.465	.396
Late Inning Pressure			43	13	2	5	3	.302	.465	.367
Leading Off			7	2	0	2	0	.286	.286	.444
Runners On			25	5	1	3	2	.200	.360	.276
Runners/Scor. Pos.			17	3	1	3	2	.176	.412	.286
First 9 Batters			199	64	3	21	18	.322	.442	.379
Second 9 Batters			46	16	1	1	2	.348	.478	.362
All Batters Thereafter			6	3	1	2	1	.500	1.167	.625

Loves to face: Dan Pasqua (0-for-5)
Hates to face: Bob Boone (2-for-2, 1 HR, 1 BB)
Ground outs-to-air outs ratio: 1.43 last season, 1.38 for career. . . . Additional statistics: 13 double-play ground outs in 73 opportunities, 15 doubles, 2 triples in 61.2 innings last season. . . . Only home run allowed to a left-handed batter was hit by B.J. Surhoff. . . . Used exclusively as a reliever for the first time in his career. 1983–85 with San Diego: 106 games, 85 as a starter; 1986–87 with Detroit: 73 games, four starts. Career record: 32–28, 3.39 ERA in 89 starts; 3–3, 3.48 ERA, 10 saves in relief. . . . His season starts in July: career record of 13–20 with a 4.62 ERA before the All-Star break; 22–11, 2.69 ERA thereafter. . . . Yearly opponents' batting averages since 1983: .248, .256, .291, .290, .331. . . . Opponents' career BA of .190 (8-for-42) with the bases loaded.

Ed Vande Berg

Cleveland Indians — Throws Left

	W–L	ERA	AB	H	HR	BB	SO	BA	SA	OBA
Season	1-0	5.10	295	96	9	21	40	.325	.468	.364
vs. Left-Handers			136	38	0	9	18	.279	.324	.322
vs. Right-Handers			159	58	9	12	22	.365	.591	.400
Home	1-0	6.25	171	56	8	11	21	.327	.526	.368
Road	0-0	3.66	124	40	1	10	19	.323	.387	.360
Grass	1-0	4.68	273	89	9	17	38	.326	.480	.359
Artificial Turf	0-0	10.80	22	7	0	4	2	.318	.318	.423
April	0-0	9.39	33	13	1	3	5	.394	.606	.410
May	0-0	1.13	28	6	1	0	5	.214	.321	.214
June	0-0	6.16	80	25	3	4	11	.313	.463	.345
July	0-0	4.09	46	18	2	4	4	.391	.609	.431
August	0-0	7.43	58	20	2	4	7	.345	.448	.381
Sept./Oct.	1-0	2.03	50	14	0	6	8	.280	.360	.357
Leading Off Inn.			57	18	2	1	9	.316	.474	.328
Runners On			163	52	4	12	21	.319	.429	.356
Runners/Scor. Pos.			104	32	3	6	16	.308	.433	.330
Runners On/2 Out			70	21	1	5	9	.300	.343	.347
Scor. Pos./2 Out			49	13	1	2	8	.265	.327	.294
Late Inning Pressure			54	16	0	9	8	.296	.370	.391
Leading Off			13	2	0	1	4	.154	.231	.214
Runners On			24	9	0	5	1	.375	.458	.467
Runners/Scor. Pos.			16	5	0	3	1	.313	.375	.400
First 9 Batters			246	80	6	21	33	.325	.447	.371
Second 9 Batters			40	15	3	0	4	.375	.675	.375
All Batters Thereafter			9	1	0	0	3	.111	.111	.111

Loves to face: Dwayne Murphy (.045, 1-for-22)
Hates to face: Alan Trammell (.563, 9-for-16, 4 HR)
Ground outs-to-air outs ratio: 1.68 last season, 1.47 for career. . . . Additional statistics: 10 double-play ground outs in 80 opportunities, 11 doubles, 2 triples in 72.1 innings last season. . . . Has appeared 115 times in relief over the past two seasons but has only two wins without a single save to show for it. No other pitcher in the majors has relieved more than 57 times since 1986 without registering a save. . . . Faced only 10 batters while protecting leads of three runs or less in the eighth inning or later. . . . The Dodgers have now acquired a left-handed reliever in each of the last three off-seasons: Vande Berg, Young, and Orosco. . . . Last 18 home runs he's allowed have been hit by right-handed batters. Last lefty to homer: Darrell Evans, Aug. 26, 1986.

Frank Viola

Minnesota Twins — Throws Left

	W–L	ERA	AB	H	HR	BB	SO	BA	SA	OBA
Season	17-10	2.90	955	230	29	66	197	.241	.378	.293
vs. Left-Handers			163	40	5	12	35	.245	.374	.305
vs. Right-Handers			792	190	24	54	162	.240	.379	.291
Home	11-3	2.69	526	129	18	33	113	.245	.394	.295
Road	6-7	3.14	429	101	11	33	84	.235	.359	.292
Grass	5-5	2.74	328	78	6	23	58	.238	.335	.290
Artificial Turf	12-5	2.98	627	152	23	43	139	.242	.400	.295
April	1-3	3.55	122	30	3	16	27	.246	.336	.333
May	2-2	4.43	157	37	8	9	27	.236	.452	.281
June	3-1	1.96	159	40	4	4	28	.252	.390	.268
July	5-0	1.88	174	36	5	10	44	.207	.310	.250
August	3-2	3.94	181	50	6	14	34	.276	.414	.340
Sept./Oct.	3-2	1.88	162	37	3	13	37	.228	.358	.290
Leading Off Inn.			246	59	9	16	46	.240	.398	.292
Runners On			366	85	11	28	80	.232	.369	.287
Runners/Scor. Pos.			187	40	5	12	46	.214	.337	.259
Runners On/2 Out			159	33	4	14	40	.208	.327	.276
Scor. Pos./2 Out			90	17	1	7	24	.189	.267	.247
Late Inning Pressure			114	28	1	4	14	.246	.316	.283
Leading Off			33	10	1	1	1	.303	.455	.361
Runners On			42	9	0	2	7	.214	.238	.250
Runners/Scor. Pos.			17	6	0	1	1	.353	.412	.389
First 9 Batters			299	48	7	20	87	.161	.284	.220
Second 9 Batters			299	84	10	22	51	.281	.428	.329
All Batters Thereafter			357	98	12	24	59	.275	.415	.325

Loves to face: Don Slaught (.053, 1-for-19)
Hates to face: Greg Brock (.800, 4-for-5, 1 BB)
Ground outs-to-air outs ratio: 0.89 last season, 0.80 for career. . . . Additional statistics: 13 double-play ground outs in 175 opportunities, 44 doubles, 0 triples in 251.2 innings last season. . . . Allowed 9 first-inning runs in 36 starts. . . . Batting support: 4.31 runs per start. . . . Opponents stole only six bases in 15 attempts; base stealers were successful on 81 percent of tries vs. other Twins pitchers. . . . Began 1987 season by striking out first six batters he faced: Davis, Phillips, Lansford, Canseco, Cey, McGwire. . . . Later in season, faced 96 batters in a row without issuing a walk. . . . Lost four consecutive starts after his first victory. Record of 16–6, 2.69 ERA after May 2. . . . Only pitcher in majors with 35+ starts in each of last four years.

Bill Wegman

Milwaukee Brewers — Throws Right

	W–L	ERA	AB	H	HR	BB	SO	BA	SA	OBA
Season	12-11	4.24	865	229	31	53	102	.265	.425	.310
vs. Left-Handers			467	120	16	33	54	.257	.420	.308
vs. Right-Handers			398	109	15	20	48	.274	.432	.311
Home	7-5	3.66	538	134	15	26	67	.249	.379	.287
Road	5-6	5.25	327	95	16	27	35	.291	.502	.345
Grass	9-8	4.09	716	190	25	39	87	.265	.425	.306
Artificial Turf	3-3	4.97	149	39	6	14	15	.262	.430	.327
April	2-1	3.18	127	30	3	11	15	.236	.331	.297
May	1-4	5.29	136	35	6	7	19	.257	.463	.292
June	3-2	4.53	176	51	7	12	18	.290	.466	.333
July	2-2	2.87	177	47	5	3	20	.266	.429	.288
August	0-1	6.43	85	27	3	4	14	.318	.459	.352
Sept./Oct.	4-1	4.36	164	39	7	16	16	.238	.402	.310
Leading Off Inn.			221	61	10	14	23	.276	.457	.322
Runners On			325	85	14	20	46	.262	.443	.303
Runners/Scor. Pos.			174	44	8	8	30	.253	.443	.280
Runners On/2 Out			135	32	6	10	18	.237	.407	.290
Scor. Pos./2 Out			81	17	3	7	11	.210	.358	.273
Late Inning Pressure			75	20	1	5	6	.267	.373	.309
Leading Off			24	5	0	1	1	.208	.208	.240
Runners On			20	5	0	1	3	.250	.400	.273
Runners/Scor. Pos.			8	1	0	0	3	.125	.125	.111
First 9 Batters			273	65	12	21	43	.238	.429	.300
Second 9 Batters			276	79	13	14	30	.286	.482	.323
All Batters Thereafter			316	85	6	18	29	.269	.373	.307

Loves to face: Wally Joyner (.105, 2-for-19, 1 HR)
Hates to face: Ellis Burks (4-for-4, 1 HR)
Ground outs-to-air outs ratio: 0.78 last season, 0.88 for career. . . . Additional statistics: 15 double-play ground outs in 156 opportunities, 40 doubles, 3 triples in 225.0 innings last season. . . . Allowed 13 first-inning runs in 33 starts. . . . Batting support: 5.06 runs per start. . . . Averaged 6.80 innings per start, more than any Milwaukee pitcher except Higuera. . . . Allowed an average of 2.12 walks per nine innings, 6th-lowest rate among A.L. pitchers. . . . Record of 8–2 vs. East Division opponents, 4–9 vs. the West. Only pitcher to defeat the Tigers three times last season. . . . Career record of 0–5 vs. the Mariners. . . . Figure this: Career strikeout-to-walk ratio of 2.84 at County Stadium, 1.21 in road games. Opponents' career batting: .264 home, .281 road.

Bill Wilkinson

Seattle Mariners — Throws Left

	W–L	ERA	AB	H	HR	BB	SO	BA	SA	OBA
Season	3-4	3.66	274	61	8	21	73	.223	.350	.272
vs. Left-Handers			104	20	6	7	29	.192	.394	.243
vs. Right-Handers			170	41	2	14	44	.241	.324	.289
Home	3-3	5.21	147	40	3	10	36	.272	.401	.313
Road	0-1	2.11	127	21	5	11	37	.165	.291	.227
Grass	0-1	2.60	90	15	5	10	29	.167	.344	.245
Artificial Turf	3-3	4.25	184	46	3	11	44	.250	.353	.286
April	0-0	1.50	22	5	0	1	4	.227	.273	.250
May	0-1	8.31	54	19	1	5	8	.352	.519	.400
June	1-1	4.35	33	5	0	3	9	.152	.273	.211
July	1-0	1.17	55	10	2	4	16	.182	.291	.237
August	0-1	2.70	55	9	3	2	15	.164	.327	.186
Sept./Oct.	1-1	3.60	55	13	2	6	21	.236	.345	.311
Leading Off Inn.			55	12	4	4	14	.218	.527	.271
Runners On			130	36	2	8	34	.277	.369	.306
Runners/Scor. Pos.			75	19	1	6	18	.253	.360	.287
Runners On/2 Out			58	18	1	3	10	.310	.379	.344
Scor. Pos./2 Out			36	11	1	3	5	.306	.417	.359
Late Inning Pressure			139	28	3	12	42	.201	.295	.263
Leading Off			30	6	2	2	10	.200	.433	.250
Runners On			64	15	0	4	18	.234	.281	.275
Runners/Scor. Pos.			33	5	0	2	9	.152	.212	.194
First 9 Batters			252	59	8	20	69	.234	.369	.285
Second 9 Batters			22	2	0	1	4	.091	.136	.125
All Batters Thereafter			0	0	0	0	0	—	—	—

Loves to face: Wade Boggs (0-for-4)
Hates to face: Mark Davidson (2-for-2)
Ground outs-to-air outs ratio: 1.44 last season, 1.48 for career. . . . Additional statistics: 6 DP ground outs in 68 opportunities, 9 doubles, 1 triple in 76.1 innings last season. . . . Earned 10 saves in 18 opportunities. Four of his 10 saves were against the Texas Rangers. . . . Ranked 4th among A.L. rookie pitchers with 56 appearances. . . . Opposing batters hit .305 through June 12, .178 thereafter. His ERA, before and after: 6.66, 2.25. . . . Used exclusively in relief in 1987 after starting two games in June 1985. In four years of professional ball prior to 1987, Wilkinson had started 74 games and relieved only once. . . . Special for Curt Gowdy Sr.: only two players born in Wyoming were on a major–league 40-man roster last spring: Wilkinson and Tom Browning.

Mitch Williams

Texas Rangers — Throws Left

	W–L	ERA	AB	H	HR	BB	SO	BA	SA	OBA
Season	8-6	3.23	361	63	9	94	129	.175	.280	.353
vs. Left-Handers			123	18	3	25	50	.146	.244	.309
vs. Right-Handers			238	45	6	69	79	.189	.298	.374
Home	6-2	2.84	188	34	4	50	67	.181	.282	.364
Road	2-4	3.66	173	29	5	44	62	.168	.277	.339
Grass	7-3	3.09	319	56	7	83	113	.176	.273	.354
Artificial Turf	1-3	4.26	42	7	2	11	16	.167	.333	.340
April	2-1	4.38	41	8	0	8	15	.195	.195	.370
May	1-1	4.20	50	9	2	14	22	.180	.320	.364
June	2-1	3.31	53	8	1	16	18	.151	.226	.357
July	1-0	2.29	64	12	1	19	22	.188	.313	.376
August	1-0	2.29	66	8	3	20	27	.121	.303	.326
Sept./Oct.	1-3	3.51	87	18	2	17	25	.207	.287	.337
Leading Off Inn.			72	13	1	20	25	.181	.236	.379
Runners On			183	33	5	55	64	.180	.290	.373
Runners/Scor. Pos.			117	19	2	40	38	.162	.248	.373
Runners On/2 Out			85	17	2	29	31	.200	.306	.404
Scor. Pos./2 Out			64	12	0	25	23	.188	.234	.416
Late Inning Pressure			169	31	4	27	59	.183	.278	.314
Leading Off			39	10	1	7	11	.256	.333	.408
Runners On			69	11	2	16	30	.159	.261	.333
Runners/Scor. Pos.			37	5	1	9	13	.135	.243	.306
First 9 Batters			333	57	8	93	121	.171	.276	.359
Second 9 Batters			28	6	1	1	8	.214	.321	.26?
All Batters Thereafter			—	—	—	—	—	—	—	—

Loves to face: Mike Pagliarulo (0-for-8, 6 SO)
Hates to face: Devon White (.600, 3-for-5, 2 BB)
Ground outs-to-air outs ratio: 0.67 last season, 0.78 for career. . . . Additional statistics: 8 double-play ground outs in 102 opportunities, 7 doubles, 2 triples in 108.2 innings last season. . . . Averaged 10.58 strikeouts per nine innings, 2d-highest rate among A.L. relievers. (minimum: 30 games). The other side of the coin? He had the highest rate of walks per nine innings (7.82) among major-league relievers. . . . Has most appearances (165 games, 164 in relief) of any pitcher in majors over last two seasons. . . . Opponents' career average is .143 (5-for-35) with the bases loaded, but he has walked 11 batters to force in runs, including a major-league high of seven last season. . . . Was the pitcher in a 9–1 double play (as in right fielder to pitcher) on May 3 at Toronto.

Mark Williamson

Baltimore Orioles — Throws Right

	W–L	ERA	AB	H	HR	BB	SO	BA	SA	OBA
Season	8-9	4.03	468	122	12	41	73	.261	.387	.322
vs. Left-Handers			210	57	5	20	33	.271	.395	.338
vs. Right-Handers			258	65	7	21	40	.252	.380	.310
Home	5-5	4.43	230	60	6	21	30	.261	.383	.324
Road	3-4	3.66	238	62	6	20	43	.261	.391	.321
Grass	8-9	4.58	399	105	11	38	63	.263	.391	.330
Artificial Turf	0-0	0.95	69	17	1	3	10	.246	.362	.278
April	1-2	6.43	54	14	2	10	9	.259	.500	.375
May	1-1	3.22	82	18	2	9	15	.220	.305	.297
June	0-3	5.22	116	37	3	6	15	.319	.431	.363
July	3-1	2.16	58	13	1	4	9	.224	.345	.270
August	3-2	3.00	85	21	3	5	16	.247	.365	.293
Sept./Oct.	0-0	4.34	73	19	1	7	9	.260	.384	.321
Leading Off Inn.			100	19	0	7	20	.190	.260	.243
Runners On			213	60	5	27	23	.282	.385	.358
Runners/Scor. Pos.			135	37	4	26	14	.274	.393	.384
Runners On/2 Out			94	28	4	13	12	.298	.457	.383
Scor. Pos./2 Out			66	21	4	13	7	.318	.545	.430
Late Inning Pressure			198	63	8	24	27	.318	.500	.394
Leading Off			45	8	0	1	7	.178	.222	.196
Runners On			89	29	3	19	7	.326	.483	.436
Runners/Scor. Pos.			60	16	2	18	6	.267	.417	.425
First 9 Batters			356	90	8	32	57	.253	.368	.318
Second 9 Batters			91	26	4	6	15	.286	.484	.327
All Batters Thereafter			21	6	0	3	1	.286	.286	.375

Loves to face: Devon White (0-for-5, 3 SO)
Hates to face: Willie Wilson (4-for-4, 1 3B)
Ground outs-to-air outs ratio: 1.84 last season, his first in majors (1.21 vs. left-handed batters, 2.62 vs. right-handers). . . . Additional statistics: 17 double-play ground outs in 101 opportunities, 17 doubles, 3 triples in 125.0 innings last season. . . . Walked only one of the 46 batters he faced leading off in Late-Inning Pressure Situations. . . . The bad news: He allowed eight hits (in 19 at bats) with the bases loaded, tying Rick Mahler for most in majors. The good news: They were all singles. . . . What does he have in common with Bo Belinsky, Luis Tiant, and Fred Hutchinson? All led the Pacific Coast League in winning percentage (Williamson in 1986, the others in '69, '64, and '38, respectively). . . . Thanks to our buddy, Bill Weiss, for that one.

Jim Winn

Chicago White Sox — Throws Right

	W–L	ERA	AB	H	HR	BB	SO	BA	SA	OBA
Season	4-6	4.79	350	95	10	62	44	.271	.397	.390
vs. Left-Handers			152	40	2	35	10	.263	.336	.401
vs. Right-Handers			198	55	8	27	34	.278	.444	.381
Home	2-1	5.63	178	50	1	37	28	.281	.354	.413
Road	2-5	3.97	172	45	9	25	16	.262	.442	.365
Grass	4-2	4.66	287	76	6	54	40	.265	.366	.390
Artificial Turf	0-4	5.40	63	19	4	8	4	.302	.540	.389
April	0-0	4.63	45	14	1	9	7	.311	.511	.404
May	2-1	4.19	67	13	1	20	7	.194	.269	.393
June	0-3	3.79	70	18	2	10	7	.257	.386	.318
July	2-1	3.57	64	18	5	9	8	.281	.531	.370
August	0-0	11.68	57	22	0	14	9	.386	.421	.521
Sept./Oct.	0-1	2.57	47	10	1	2	4	.213	.277	.260
Leading Off Inn.			70	20	3	12	5	.286	.414	.405
Runners On			203	53	3	31	30	.261	.335	.367
Runners/Scor. Pos.			123	34	2	20	19	.276	.341	.386
Runners On/2 Out			90	25	2	18	13	.278	.367	.409
Scor. Pos./2 Out			63	18	1	12	9	.286	.349	.416
Late Inning Pressure			144	42	6	22	14	.292	.438	.396
Leading Off			34	10	2	3	2	.294	.471	.368
Runners On			74	24	2	11	7	.324	.446	.425
Runners/Scor. Pos.			43	15	1	8	5	.349	.442	.472
First 9 Batters			307	82	8	50	40	.267	.381	.378
Second 9 Batters			42	12	2	12	4	.286	.500	.455
All Batters Thereafter			1	1	0	0	0	1.000	1.000	1.000

Loves to face: Rafael Santana (0-for-6)
Hates to face: Tim Laudner (.667, 2-for-3, 2 HR)
Ground outs-to-air outs ratio: 2.67, 2d-highest in A.L. last season (minimum: 200 BFP), 2.11 for career. . . . Additional statistics: 14 double-play ground outs in 97 opportunities, 12 doubles, 1 triple in 94.0 innings last season. . . . Earned six saves in 12 opportunities. . . . Three of his six defeats were at the hands of Minnesota. . . . Lost three consecutive relief appearances (June 16–21). . . . Four of his six saves were within an eight-day span (July 18–25). . . . The only home run he allowed at Comiskey was hit by Cal Ripken Jr. . . . Strikeout-to-walk ratio of 1.84 in 1986, 0.71 in 1987. . . . Opponents' career batting average is .249 on grass fields, .278 on artificial surfaces. . . . Opposing batters have hit .356 with runners on in Late-Inning Pressure Situations.

Bobby Witt

Texas Rangers | | | | | | | | | | Throws Right

	W–L	ERA	AB	H	HR	BB	SO	BA	SA	OBA
Season	8-10	4.91	520	114	10	140	160	.219	.325	.385
vs. Left-Handers			292	67	6	74	74	.229	.332	.387
vs. Right-Handers			228	47	4	66	86	.206	.316	.382
Home	4-3	3.89	290	61	6	76	89	.210	.303	.372
Road	4-7	6.24	230	53	4	64	71	.230	.352	.400
Grass	7-8	4.69	455	101	9	124	144	.222	.327	.387
Artificial Turf	1-2	6.38	65	13	1	16	16	.200	.308	.369
April	0-1	4.41	52	12	1	20	22	.231	.346	.432
May	1-2	6.35	64	14	2	18	19	.219	.344	.398
June	2-0	2.08	40	3	0	12	11	.075	.100	.302
July	1-2	4.00	103	21	1	21	27	.204	.301	.344
August	3-2	4.66	134	29	4	39	48	.216	.321	.389
Sept./Oct.	1-3	6.55	127	35	2	30	33	.276	.402	.411
Leading Off Inn.			115	25	4	42	42	.217	.374	.427
Runners On			281	64	5	54	80	.228	.331	.351
Runners/Scor. Pos.			178	37	2	34	57	.208	.287	.333
Runners On/2 Out			112	18	1	20	34	.161	.205	.293
Scor. Pos./2 Out			81	9	0	14	30	.111	.136	.250
Late Inning Pressure			38	8	0	13	12	.211	.263	.423
Leading Off			12	3	0	5	4	.250	.250	.471
Runners On			18	1	0	5	8	.056	.056	.261
Runners/Scor. Pos.			9	0	0	3	4	.000	.000	.250
First 9 Batters			175	38	4	48	71	.217	.349	.388
Second 9 Batters			167	35	4	42	48	.210	.329	.365
All Batters Thereafter			178	41	2	50	41	.230	.298	.400

Loves to face: Pat Sheridan (0-for-10, 8 SO)
Hates to face: Fellow Olympian B. J. Surhoff (.667, 4-for-6, 3 BB)
Ground outs-to-air outs ratio: 0.87 last season, 0.88 for career. . . .
Additional statistics: 10 double-play ground outs in 148 opportunities, 21 doubles, 2 triples in 143.0 innings last season. . . . Allowed 17 first-inning runs in 25 starts. . . . Batting support: 4.40 runs per start. . . . Only A.L. starter with more strikeouts than innings in each of last two years. . . . Led majors in walks last season; averaged 8.81 walks per nine innings, 2.12 more than closest competitor, Ed Correa. (Valenzuela led N.L. with 4.45). . . . First complete game came in his 56th career start, his final start of 1987 season. . . . Opponents batted .067 (1-for-15) with bases loaded last season; he fanned an A.L.-high eight batters with the bags full, and he walked in only one run!

Mike Witt

California Angels | | | | | | | | | | Throws Right

	W–L	ERA	AB	H	HR	BB	SO	BA	SA	OBA
Season	16-14	4.01	965	252	34	84	192	.261	.435	.321
vs. Left-Handers			525	143	22	52	90	.272	.463	.338
vs. Right-Handers			440	109	12	32	102	.248	.402	.300
Home	9-8	4.05	525	128	23	48	98	.244	.429	.309
Road	7-6	3.95	440	124	11	36	94	.282	.443	.336
Grass	15-11	4.06	810	208	32	73	169	.257	.437	.319
Artificial Turf	1-3	3.72	155	44	2	11	23	.284	.426	.331
April	2-2	5.18	128	29	4	11	31	.227	.391	.286
May	3-2	3.93	142	38	6	21	29	.268	.465	.358
June	4-1	1.60	163	31	3	15	40	.190	.294	.258
July	4-1	4.34	155	47	7	8	34	.303	.503	.341
August	2-3	4.73	156	46	4	17	19	.295	.455	.362
Sept./Oct.	1-5	4.58	221	61	10	12	39	.276	.484	.319
Leading Off Inn.			238	76	7	20	34	.319	.496	.372
Runners On			413	102	19	42	84	.247	.429	.314
Runners/Scor. Pos.			213	52	6	29	43	.244	.394	.327
Runners On/2 Out			161	38	5	18	25	.236	.385	.313
Scor. Pos./2 Out			96	22	2	15	16	.229	.375	.333
Late Inning Pressure			131	34	5	14	19	.260	.420	.331
Leading Off			36	13	0	3	6	.361	.472	.410
Runners On			55	17	4	5	6	.309	.545	.367
Runners/Scor. Pos.			28	6	1	5	6	.214	.357	.333
First 9 Batters			300	78	10	20	73	.260	.443	.310
Second 9 Batters			286	82	11	25	48	.287	.493	.345
All Batters Thereafter			379	92	13	39	71	.243	.385	.312

Loves to face: Pat Sheridan (.074, 2-for-27)
Hates to face: Matt Nokes (.833, 5-for-6, 1 2B, 2 HR)
Ground outs-to-air outs ratio: 1.14 last season, 1.45 for career. . . .
Additional statistics: 19 double-play ground outs in 214 opportunities, 48 doubles, 9 triples in 247.0 innings last season. . . . Total of 91 extra-base hits was one fewer than major-league leader Bert Blyleven, 26 more than Witt's previous career high. . . . Allowed 20 first-inning runs in 36 starts. . . . Batting support: 4.42 runs per start. . . . Opponents' career average of .229 in Late-Inning Pressure Situations, .254 in unpressured at bats. . . . June ERA was third-best in A.L. Mark of 2.54 during past three Augusts is best in majors during that time (minimum: 75 IP). . . . Winning records in six of his seven seasons in majors. . . . Only other pitcher to lead the Angels in wins for four seasons in a row: Dean Chance (1962–65).

Rich Yett

Cleveland Indians | | | | | | | | | | Throws Right

	W–L	ERA	AB	H	HR	BB	SO	BA	SA	OBA
Season	3-9	5.25	373	96	21	49	59	.257	.488	.347
vs. Left-Handers			175	42	5	24	29	.240	.377	.333
vs. Right-Handers			198	54	16	25	30	.273	.586	.358
Home	2-1	4.97	159	38	10	19	28	.239	.491	.326
Road	1-8	5.46	214	58	11	30	31	.271	.486	.362
Grass	3-6	5.22	309	78	16	43	50	.252	.469	.347
Artificial Turf	0-3	5.40	64	18	5	6	9	.281	.578	.343
April	1-0	2.95	63	10	1	6	16	.159	.286	.232
May	0-3	8.25	43	10	4	9	7	.233	.535	.370
June	0-2	7.41	73	22	5	9	13	.301	.589	.381
July			0	0	0	0	0	—	—	—
August	2-0	0.72	89	18	1	9	14	.202	.258	.276
Sept./Oct.	0-4	8.53	105	36	10	16	9	.343	.714	.434
Leading Off Inn.			90	30	6	9	12	.333	.611	.394
Runners On			160	40	11	23	31	.250	.500	.344
Runners/Scor. Pos.			83	19	3	18	17	.229	.410	.359
Runners On/2 Out			71	15	6	12	15	.211	.479	.325
Scor. Pos./2 Out			45	10	2	10	8	.222	.378	.364
Late Inning Pressure			54	13	2	10	10	.241	.370	.359
Leading Off			13	5	1	2	2	.385	.615	.467
Runners On			30	7	1	6	5	.233	.333	.361
Runners/Scor. Pos.			15	2	0	6	3	.133	.133	.381
First 9 Batters			212	45	14	35	42	.212	.458	.325
Second 9 Batters			103	35	5	6	10	.340	.573	.384
All Batters Thereafter			58	16	2	8	7	.276	.448	.364

Loves to face: Devon White (0-for-9)
Hates to face: Jim Presley (.667, 4-for-6, 1 2B, 2 HR)
Ground outs-to-air outs ratio: 1.14 last season, 0.94 for career. . . .
Additional statistics: 7 double-play ground outs in 80 opportunities, 17 doubles, 3 triples in 97.2 innings last season. . . . Allowed 5 first-inning runs in 11 starts. . . . Batting support: 4.91 runs per start. . . . Record of 2–2 with a 3.12 ERA in day games; 1–7, 6.96 ERA at night. . . . Faced 30 consecutive left-handed batters without allowing a hit (Apr. 14–May 17). . . . Record of 2–4 with a 4.77 ERA in 11 starts; 1–5, 5.86 ERA, in 26 relief appearances. Used exclusively as a starter (10 games) after his recall from Buffalo of the American Association on Aug. 10. . . . Born October 6, 1962, the day that Billy Pierce 3-hit the Yankees to pull Giants even at three games apiece in the 1962 Series.

Curt Young

Oakland As | | | | | | | | | | Throws Left

	W–L	ERA	AB	H	HR	BB	SO	BA	SA	OBA
Season	13-7	4.08	771	194	38	44	124	.252	.453	.293
vs. Left-Handers			147	32	5	3	19	.218	.361	.243
vs. Right-Handers			624	162	33	41	105	.260	.474	.304
Home	5-3	3.67	333	78	15	20	59	.234	.405	.281
Road	8-4	4.41	438	116	23	24	65	.265	.489	.303
Grass	12-5	3.86	651	161	31	37	98	.247	.433	.290
Artificial Turf	1-2	5.34	120	33	7	7	26	.275	.558	.308
April	3-1	2.79	139	30	5	9	26	.216	.388	.262
May	3-2	2.53	165	37	5	10	22	.224	.358	.271
June	3-2	5.45	140	33	11	6	24	.236	.529	.272
July	1-0	5.79	37	11	2	2	9	.297	.514	.333
August	1-2	7.34	143	46	8	5	17	.322	.566	.342
Sept./Oct.	2-0	2.61	147	37	7	12	26	.252	.422	.311
Leading Off Inn.			197	45	9	13	32	.228	.411	.283
Runners On			277	72	15	13	38	.260	.484	.292
Runners/Scor. Pos.			134	36	4	7	19	.269	.455	.301
Runners On/2 Out			108	24	6	8	15	.222	.435	.276
Scor. Pos./2 Out			58	12	1	5	7	.207	.345	.270
Late Inning Pressure			63	16	3	5	7	.254	.397	.314
Leading Off			18	4	1	1	1	.222	.389	.300
Runners On			19	9	2	0	1	.474	.789	.450
Runners/Scor. Pos.			6	4	0	0	0	.667	.667	.571
First 9 Batters			270	63	6	14	41	.233	.374	.273
Second 9 Batters			257	71	16	17	39	.276	.514	.320
All Batters Thereafter			244	60	16	13	44	.246	.475	.287

Loves to face: Eddie Murray (.048, 1-for-21)
Hates to face: Mike Heath (.600, 6-for-10, 2 HR)
Ground outs-to-air outs ratio: 0.89 last season, 0.79 for career. . . .
Additional statistics: 13 double-play ground outs in 133 opportunities, 35 doubles, 3 triples in 203.0 innings last season. . . . Allowed 5 first-inning runs in 31 starts, lowest average in A.L. (minimum: 15 GS). . . . Batting support: 5.52 runs per start. . . . Allowed home runs in 19 consecutive games. We don't know if that's a record, but we do know it's five games more than the next longest streak of the past six seasons. . . . Allowed an average of 1.95 walks per nine innings, 5th-lowest rate among A.L. pitchers. . . . Born April 16, 1960, the day that Gene Mauch made his major-league managerial debut as the Phillies were routed by the Braves, 13–3.

Baltimore Orioles

	W–L	ERA	AB	H	HR	BB	SO	BA	SA	OBA
Season	67-95	5.01	5623	1555	226	547	870	.277	.465	.341
vs. Left-Handers			2195	604	90	215	306	.275	.469	.341
vs. Right-Handers			3428	951	136	332	564	.277	.461	.342
Home	31-51	4.99	2905	797	125	269	454	.274	.469	.336
Road	36-44	5.03	2718	758	101	278	416	.279	.460	.347
Grass	57-81	5.04	4797	1332	191	474	749	.278	.464	.343
Artificial Turf	10-14	4.83	826	223	35	73	121	.270	.469	.331
April	9-12	4.22	710	179	27	67	126	.252	.435	.318
May	17-11	4.80	981	266	38	111	151	.271	.442	.345
June	5-23	6.20	1000	304	50	114	142	.304	.526	.377
July	16-10	3.94	884	229	27	71	147	.259	.422	.314
August	13-15	5.11	964	259	41	79	156	.269	.466	.328
Sept./Oct.	7-24	5.47	1084	318	43	105	148	.293	.481	.354
Leading Off Inn.			1321	372	61	119	194	.282	.495	.343
Runners On			2396	681	87	276	367	.284	.455	.356
Runners/Scor. Pos.			1443	413	49	210	238	.286	.450	.370
Runners On/2 Out			991	259	36	137	150	.261	.433	.352
Scor. Pos./2 Out			663	177	23	107	107	.267	.434	.370
Late Inning Pressure			924	255	33	98	151	.276	.447	.346
Leading Off			226	56	4	20	29	.248	.376	.309
Runners On			380	114	10	51	60	.300	.447	.380
Runners/Scor. Pos.			227	63	6	45	40	.278	.401	.389
First 9 Batters			2905	770	98	289	501	.265	.427	.334
Second 9 Batters			1563	458	79	156	211	.293	.522	.357
All Batters Thereafter			1155	327	49	102	158	.283	.481	.340

Starting pitchers: 42–70, 5.26 ERA
Relief pitchers: 25–25, 4.59 ERA
Ground outs-to-air outs ratio: 1.15. . . . Opponents grounded into one double play for every 8.2 opportunities, highest rate in A.L. . . . Set major-league record for home runs allowed (226) since someone got bright idea to keep track of such things in 1950. . . . How did we survive all those years without it? . . . Were swept in 15 series, highest total in majors last season. . . . June ERA was highest by any team in majors during any month of 1987 season. Also had highest mark in A.L. in August, as well as after September 1. . . . Opposing right-handed batters outhit left-handers for eighth straight season, longest current streak in majors. . . . Lowest home-game winning percentage in majors (31–51, .378), but a perfect record (25–0) when leading after eight innings at Memorial Stadium.

Boston Red Sox

	W–L	ERA	AB	H	HR	BB	SO	BA	SA	OBA
Season	78-84	4.77	5608	1584	190	517	1034	.282	.451	.344
vs. Left-Handers			2546	730	70	262	427	.287	.446	.353
vs. Right-Handers			3062	854	120	255	607	.279	.455	.336
Home	50-30	4.35	2857	798	75	223	514	.279	.426	.331
Road	28-54	5.21	2751	786	115	294	520	.286	.477	.356
Grass	68-69	4.75	4777	1347	149	434	879	.282	.442	.342
Artificial Turf	10-15	4.91	831	237	41	83	155	.285	.502	.353
April	9-13	4.49	759	208	27	66	138	.274	.453	.334
May	13-14	4.41	902	246	31	85	168	.273	.441	.338
June	15-12	5.47	973	281	36	97	181	.289	.464	.355
July	11-15	4.78	903	244	33	82	154	.270	.462	.333
August	14-13	4.82	940	276	33	81	188	.294	.459	.349
Sept./Oct.	16-17	4.61	1131	329	30	106	205	.291	.431	.349
Leading Off Inn.			1329	398	45	107	245	.299	.467	.355
Runners On			2525	696	91	252	455	.276	.450	.339
Runners/Scor. Pos.			1441	387	55	179	286	.269	.448	.342
Runners On/2 Out			1034	256	32	105	202	.248	.413	.320
Scor. Pos./2 Out			653	160	25	78	139	.245	.432	.327
Late Inning Pressure			829	246	34	104	174	.297	.480	.373
Leading Off			209	70	12	17	42	.335	.569	.385
Runners On			371	102	16	56	78	.275	.441	.366
Runners/Scor. Pos.			214	55	6	43	51	.257	.397	.371
First 9 Batters			2498	693	87	278	538	.277	.447	.351
Second 9 Batters			1496	425	49	113	238	.284	.440	.335
All Batters Thereafter			1614	466	54	126	258	.289	.467	.340

Starting pitchers: 59–60, 4.55 ERA
Relief pitchers: 19–24, 5.45 ERA (highest in majors)
Ground outs-to-air outs ratio: 1.19, 2d-highest in A.L. . . . Led the majors with 47 complete games, 13 shutouts (tied for highest in majors). . . . Opponents' batting average leading off innings was highest in A.L. over 13 years we've compiled those figures. . . . Annual batting averages of opposing left-handed batters since 1984: .263, .268, .279, .287. . . . Bullpen didn't finish any shutouts last season. League-leading 13 shutouts were all complete games. . . . Worst extra-inning record in the majors. Lost 12 of 15 games that were tied after nine, outscored 31–6 during the extra frames. They lost all seven extra-inning *road* games last season, as well as the infamous Game 6 in the 1986 Series since their miraculous overtime win at Anaheim in Game 5 of that year's A.L.C.S.

California Angels

	W–L	ERA	AB	H	HR	BB	SO	BA	SA	OBA
Season	75-87	4.38	5600	1481	212	504	941	.264	.430	.327
vs. Left-Handers			2442	659	96	245	364	.270	.442	.337
vs. Right-Handers			3158	822	116	259	577	.260	.421	.319
Home	38-43	4.33	2854	732	116	268	496	.256	.418	.322
Road	37-44	4.43	2746	749	96	236	445	.273	.442	.332
Grass	63-72	4.40	4681	1223	183	423	799	.261	.426	.324
Artificial Turf	12-15	4.25	919	258	29	81	142	.281	.452	.339
April	12-11	4.45	788	202	29	84	159	.256	.409	.329
May	9-17	4.87	907	248	43	97	145	.273	.463	.343
June	17-11	3.18	926	219	29	64	171	.237	.376	.284
July	15-11	4.37	924	243	41	75	150	.263	.444	.323
August	13-16	4.34	1015	271	35	94	154	.267	.430	.330
Sept./Oct.	9-21	5.06	1040	298	35	90	162	.287	.454	.346
Leading Off Inn.			1354	383	50	100	190	.283	.449	.336
Runners On			2354	658	101	230	416	.280	.463	.342
Runners/Scor. Pos.			1293	357	53	156	229	.276	.459	.349
Runners On/2 Out			954	249	38	106	181	.261	.442	.336
Scor. Pos./2 Out			588	152	20	79	107	.259	.422	.348
Late Inning Pressure			1008	248	28	119	176	.246	.377	.327
Leading Off			259	71	9	21	36	.274	.429	.331
Runners On			429	116	13	59	77	.270	.417	.359
Runners/Scor. Pos.			248	67	8	47	47	.270	.431	.383
First 9 Batters			2779	707	105	287	514	.254	.420	.327
Second 9 Batters			1653	475	61	125	249	.287	.454	.338
All Batters Thereafter			1168	299	46	92	178	.256	.420	.312

Starting pitchers: 52–60, 4.78 ERA
Relief pitchers: 23–27, 3.64 ERA
Ground outs-to-air outs ratio: 1.07. . . . Lowest ERA in majors during June. . . . Have held opposing batters to a lower batting average in Late-Inning Pressure Situations than overall in each of the past four seasons, tying Detroit for the longest current streak in A.L. . . . Used relief pitchers for three innings or more 73 times, highest total in either league. . . . Record of 36–0 when leading after eight innings on the road was the best in the majors last season. . . . Starting pitchers were called for only one balk in 953 innings pitched last season. (Chuck Finley) . . . More than twice as many starts by left-handers in 1987 (39) as they had in 1986 (16). . . . Relievers had a losing record despite the second-best ERA in the league.

Chicago White Sox

	W–L	ERA	AB	H	HR	BB	SO	BA	SA	OBA
Season	77-85	4.30	5537	1436	189	537	792	.259	.416	.327
vs. Left-Handers			2329	625	78	256	315	.268	.422	.341
vs. Right-Handers			3208	811	111	281	477	.253	.412	.317
Home	38-43	4.68	2851	769	90	291	416	.270	.418	.340
Road	39-42	3.90	2686	667	99	246	376	.248	.414	.313
Grass	67-71	4.29	4747	1229	157	465	686	.259	.409	.327
Artificial Turf	10-14	4.33	790	207	32	72	106	.262	.458	.328
April	6-12	4.02	602	151	19	79	92	.251	.420	.337
May	14-13	3.90	916	204	38	101	128	.223	.400	.301
June	7-21	5.73	948	271	45	100	133	.286	.482	.355
July	14-13	3.92	927	246	35	84	120	.265	.424	.330
August	14-16	4.80	1056	296	25	94	150	.280	.407	.343
Sept./Oct.	22-10	3.42	1088	268	27	79	169	.246	.373	.300
Leading Off Inn.			1328	336	43	118	167	.253	.401	.319
Runners On			2331	646	71	253	343	.277	.426	.348
Runners/Scor. Pos.			1299	363	39	167	194	.279	.435	.358
Runners On/2 Out			980	267	27	122	149	.272	.409	.355
Scor. Pos./2 Out			628	159	14	90	98	.253	.379	.350
Late Inning Pressure			936	257	38	97	130	.275	.450	.347
Leading Off			233	66	11	14	29	.283	.481	.329
Runners On			370	108	12	56	48	.292	.457	.389
Runners/Scor. Pos.			224	70	8	42	29	.313	.491	.423
First 9 Batters			2656	712	91	259	425	.268	.430	.336
Second 9 Batters			1465	348	47	140	200	.238	.373	.306
All Batters Thereafter			1416	376	51	138	167	.266	.435	.333

Starting pitchers: 57–61, 4.21 ERA
Relief pitchers: 20–24, 4.51 ERA
Ground outs-to-air outs ratio: 1.12. . . . Opponents grounded into one double play for every 8.9 opportunities, 2d-highest rate in A.L. . . . Opposing batters have hit better in Late-Inning Pressure Situations than overall in each of the past three seasons, tying the Mets for the longest current streak in majors. . . . What do Jim Fregosi and Cyril Ritchard have in common? The White Sox manager used his relief pitchers to face a single batter 31 times, most in either league. . . . Started a pitcher on three days' rest only four times last year, fewest in majors. . . . July ERA was best in the A.L. . . . Bullpen didn't commit a balk in 427.1 innings pitched last season. . . . Opponents' average with runners in scoring position was the highest by Chisox' staff since 1976.

Cleveland Indians

	W–L	ERA	AB	H	HR	BB	SO	BA	SA	OBA
Season	61-101	5.28	5622	1566	219	606	849	.279	.455	.351
vs. Left-Handers			2389	657	75	252	323	.275	.432	.345
vs. Right-Handers			3233	909	144	354	526	.281	.472	.355
Home	35-46	5.41	2963	843	118	292	442	.285	.459	.351
Road	26-55	5.15	2659	723	101	314	407	.272	.450	.350
Grass	53-85	5.34	4837	1354	184	523	740	.280	.450	.352
Artificial Turf	8-16	4.92	785	212	35	83	109	.270	.485	.342
April	8-14	5.60	751	203	28	95	121	.270	.451	.354
May	8-20	4.92	919	246	38	93	161	.268	.437	.334
June	10-15	5.59	878	250	36	98	136	.285	.481	.359
July	10-17	5.87	955	268	34	108	130	.281	.446	.351
August	15-15	4.56	1044	269	40	104	148	.258	.420	.330
Sept./Oct.	10-20	5.33	1075	330	43	108	153	.307	.491	.375
Leading Off Inn.			1311	368	55	110	191	.281	.465	.340
Runners On			2530	721	89	332	373	.285	.449	.367
Runners/Scor. Pos.			1507	432	56	235	229	.287	.459	.376
Runners On/2 Out			1066	280	37	156	166	.263	.422	.361
Scor. Pos./2 Out			731	198	27	119	116	.271	.438	.379
Late Inning Pressure			889	254	22	117	149	.286	.406	.370
Leading Off			217	60	8	17	36	.276	.433	.335
Runners On			426	128	14	70	65	.300	.441	.395
Runners/Scor. Pos.			251	74	11	52	42	.295	.454	.406
First 9 Batters			2848	784	89	316	502	.275	.425	.350
Second 9 Batters			1491	420	79	137	172	.282	.508	.343
All Batters Thereafter			1283	362	51	153	175	.282	.458	.360

Starting pitchers: 39–75, 5.37 ERA (highest in majors)
Relief pitchers: 22–26, 5.11 ERA
Ground outs-to-air outs ratio: 1.02, 2d–lowest in A.L. . . . Opponents grounded into one double play for every 12.5 opportunities, lowest rate in majors. . . . Had highest ERA in majors, first team to top the 5.00-mark since the 1956 Senators. . . . Led majors with 74 wild pitches, despite meager contribution of 22 by knuckle-twins Niekro and Candiotti. . . . Played doubleheader vs. Boston on Aug. 29 in which all four starters (Stanley and Candiotti, Hurst and Yett) pitched complete games, the first such occurrence since June 12, 1983, when Blyleven and Barker, Wilcox and Morris did it for Tribe and Bengals. . . . Starters failed to complete five innings in 51 games, highest total in majors last season. . . . Allowed four or more runs in an inning a major–league–high 55 times.

Detroit Tigers

	W–L	ERA	AB	H	HR	BB	SO	BA	SA	OBA
Season	98-64	4.02	5588	1430	180	563	976	.256	.407	.325
vs. Left-Handers			2482	608	85	295	405	.245	.407	.325
vs. Right-Handers			3106	822	95	268	571	.265	.407	.326
Home	54-27	3.58	2792	662	101	253	500	.237	.390	.303
Road	44-37	4.49	2796	768	79	310	476	.275	.424	.347
Grass	85-52	4.00	4724	1195	159	479	822	.253	.404	.323
Artificial Turf	13-12	4.18	864	235	21	84	154	.272	.421	.335
April	9-12	3.47	693	168	22	78	121	.242	.390	.320
May	15-11	4.24	922	229	44	96	175	.248	.435	.319
June	17-9	4.20	906	219	22	116	156	.242	.375	.330
July	17-9	4.18	881	234	26	67	148	.266	.414	.317
August	19-11	4.21	1045	285	37	84	182	.273	.429	.327
Sept./Oct.	21-12	3.77	1141	295	29	122	194	.259	.394	.333
Leading Off Inn.			1339	325	46	114	237	.243	.400	.306
Runners On			2364	627	72	291	400	.265	.415	.344
Runners/Scor. Pos.			1333	333	34	208	260	.250	.379	.345
Runners On/2 Out			992	247	32	129	179	.249	.396	.341
Scor. Pos./2 Out			635	139	19	99	132	.219	.354	.332
Late Inning Pressure			882	221	26	93	151	.251	.396	.323
Leading Off			215	46	6	12	38	.214	.344	.256
Runners On			353	96	14	58	58	.272	.448	.375
Runners/Scor. Pos.			202	55	7	51	36	.272	.441	.415
First 9 Batters			2507	631	72	277	481	.252	.387	.326
Second 9 Batters			1506	383	56	137	254	.254	.424	.320
All Batters Thereafter			1575	416	52	149	241	.264	.423	.328

Starting pitchers: 74–46, 4.05 ERA
Relief pitchers: 24–18, 3.94 ERA
Ground outs-to-air outs ratio: 1.11. . . . Opposing left-handed batters compiled lowest mark in A.L. for fourth consecutive season. During that period, left-handers have hit .242; right-handers have hit 11 points higher. . . . Opposing batters have hit for a higher average in road games than at Tigers Stadium in each of the past seven seasons. . . . Staff's fielding percentage (.975) was the highest in the A.L. last season. . . . In 12 games vs. Oakland last season Sparky had his pitchers intentionally walk 10 batters, the most free passes handed out by any team against any A.L. opponent last season. . . . Opponents' batting average in Late-Inning Pressure Situations has increased in every year since 1984: .204, .221, .247, .251.

Kansas City Royals

	W–L	ERA	AB	H	HR	BB	SO	BA	SA	OBA
Season	83-79	3.86	5448	1424	128	548	923	.261	.398	.330
vs. Left-Handers			2022	527	43	210	365	.261	.389	.329
vs. Right-Handers			3426	897	85	338	558	.262	.404	.331
Home	46-35	3.88	2785	718	57	260	462	.258	.395	.322
Road	37-44	3.83	2663	706	71	288	461	.265	.402	.339
Grass	28-34	3.95	2045	552	56	219	347	.270	.409	.343
Artificial Turf	55-45	3.80	3403	872	72	329	576	.256	.392	.323
April	9-10	3.86	657	176	7	66	94	.268	.382	.338
May	18-9	3.16	901	216	27	77	188	.240	.388	.303
June	12-16	4.10	912	228	26	99	167	.250	.406	.326
July	10-18	3.95	941	259	24	81	148	.275	.405	.331
August	16-13	4.46	991	275	27	115	159	.277	.438	.355
Sept./Oct.	18-13	3.60	1046	270	17	110	167	.258	.367	.329
Leading Off Inn.			1319	347	31	101	211	.263	.414	.319
Runners On			2386	616	55	269	401	.258	.384	.332
Runners/Scor. Pos.			1422	351	33	181	258	.247	.373	.327
Runners On/2 Out			1040	265	23	145	197	.255	.379	.350
Scor. Pos./2 Out			703	171	18	109	134	.243	.373	.346
Late Inning Pressure			810	219	20	86	142	.270	.406	.339
Leading Off			203	52	2	14	29	.256	.355	.304
Runners On			343	95	10	43	64	.277	.420	.353
Runners/Scor. Pos.			201	47	5	37	43	.234	.358	.343
First 9 Batters			2367	608	61	268	428	.257	.399	.334
Second 9 Batters			1462	392	25	137	227	.268	.391	.333
All Batters Thereafter			1619	424	42	143	268	.262	.404	.322

Starting pitchers: 64–66, 3.80 ERA (lowest in A.L.)
Relief pitchers: 19–13, 4.07 ERA
Ground outs-to-air outs ratio: 1.38, highest in A.L. since 1983. . . . Opponents grounded into one double play for every 8.9 opportunities, 3d-highest rate in A.L. . . . Allowed fewest home runs in A.L. for third consecutive season. . . . Pitchers were involved in 25 double plays as fielders, most of any staff in the majors. . . . Allowed 29 innings of four runs or more, fewest by any A.L. staff. . . . Eleven shutouts last season were all complete games by the starting pitcher. . . . In 12 games vs. Boston last season, Royals' pitchers hit 10 batters, the most batters hit by any staff against any A.L. club. . . . First team to have two pitchers lose at least 18 games (Gubicza and Jackson) since the 1977 Oakland A's (Blue and Langford, 19 apiece).

Milwaukee Brewers

	W–L	ERA	AB	H	HR	BB	SO	BA	SA	OBA
Season	91-71	4.62	5702	1548	169	529	1039	.271	.415	.333
vs. Left-Handers			2158	585	67	220	377	.271	.422	.339
vs. Right-Handers			3544	963	102	309	662	.272	.411	.330
Home	48-33	4.74	2916	810	79	241	552	.278	.416	.332
Road	43-38	4.50	2786	738	90	288	487	.265	.415	.335
Grass	80-57	4.64	4868	1336	141	447	902	.274	.417	.335
Artificial Turf	11-14	4.55	834	212	28	82	137	.254	.409	.324
April	18-3	4.17	735	187	22	75	128	.254	.392	.323
May	6-18	5.33	835	231	25	80	171	.277	.432	.338
June	13-15	5.90	979	295	35	108	176	.301	.473	.373
July	15-13	4.82	1017	292	27	71	171	.287	.432	.332
August	18-11	4.32	1048	286	31	89	195	.273	.409	.329
Sept./Oct.	21-11	3.43	1088	257	29	106	198	.236	.358	.306
Leading Off Inn.			1346	360	48	118	255	.267	.429	.329
Runners On			2521	708	72	258	452	.281	.428	.344
Runners/Scor. Pos.			1435	399	38	156	278	.278	.422	.341
Runners On/2 Out			1028	252	22	105	198	.245	.374	.318
Scor. Pos./2 Out			642	161	13	71	132	.251	.369	.328
Late Inning Pressure			1005	249	22	107	197	.248	.358	.321
Leading Off			249	53	7	16	53	.213	.345	.263
Runners On			418	111	11	61	79	.266	.390	.357
Runners/Scor. Pos.			236	59	6	46	47	.250	.369	.368
First 9 Batters			2823	751	77	273	569	.266	.402	.332
Second 9 Batters			1494	417	48	138	260	.279	.428	.338
All Batters Thereafter			1385	380	44	118	210	.274	.430	.331

Starting pitchers: 60–51, 4.78 ERA
Relief pitchers: 31–20, 4.29 ERA
Ground outs-to-air outs ratio: 0.97, lowest in A.L. . . . Lowest ERA in A.L. during September (3.42). . . . Lowest fielding percentage (.924) of any major league pitching staff last season. The main culprits? Nieves (5 errors), Bosio (4), and Crim (4). . . . They were the only undefeated team in the majors last season when leading after seven innings at home (42–0). . . . ERA in May was the worst in the A.L., September ERA (3.42) was the best in the league. . . . Most walks allowed by Brewers' pitchers since 1977, the year before George ("Get the Ball Over") Bamberger arrived. . . . Walked 15 of 146 batters (one per 9.7) with the bases loaded. That's the highest rate by a Brewers' staff in the 13 years of The Player Analysis. . . . Relievers recorded 24 saves in road games, highest total in the A.L.

Thank you for purchasing the 1988 Elias Baseball Analyst. In order that we may continue to create, in future editions, the most useful and entertaining book possible, please take a few moments to fill out the survey questionnaire below.

We appreciate your help.

I purchased my copy of the 1988 Analyst at

- ☐ B. Dalton's
- ☐ WaldenBooks
- ☐ Crown Books
- ☐ Another bookstore
- ☐ A supermarket
- ☐ I received it as a gift
- ☐ _____ (other)

The month in which I purchased or received the 1988 Analyst was

- ☐ January   ☐ July
- ☐ February   ☐ August
- ☐ March   ☐ September
- ☐ April   ☐ October
- ☐ May   ☐ November
- ☐ June   ☐ December

I have purchased previous editions of the Analyst

- ☐ Once
- ☐ Twice
- ☐ Three times or more
- ☐ Never

I *first* heard of the Analyst

- ☐ Reading about it in a sports publication
- ☐ From a friend or acquaintance
- ☐ Hearing it mentioned on TV or radio
- ☐ In an advertisement
- ☐ By seeing it on display in a store

In order of preference, my favorite sections of the Analyst are the

- ___ Team Essays
- ___ Won-Lost Record by Starting Position
- ___ Batting Comparisons
- ___ Pitching Comparisons
- ___ Batter/Pitcher Section Tables
- ___ Batter/Pitcher Section Notes (i.e. "Loves to Face, Hates to Face" etc.)
- ___ Batting/Pitching Rankings
- ___ Single Season and Career Leaders
- ___ Batter-Pitcher Matchups
- ___ Ballparks
  Please fill in a number from 1-10 for each of the sections above

Have you purchased any of the titles below during the past two years? (check as many as apply)

- ☐ The Baseball Encyclopedia or Encyclopedia Update
- ☐ Bill James Baseball Abstract
- ☐ The Scouting Report

What is your level of interest in any of the titles listed below?

Not Interested; Would Not Purchase	Somewhat Interested; Would Probably Purchase	Very Interested; Would Definitely Purchase
☐	☐	☐ The Elias College Football Analyst
☐	☐	☐ The Elias Pro Football Analyst
☐	☐	☐ The Elias College Basketball Analyst
☐	☐	☐ The Elias Pro Basketball Analyst

We would like some personal information about you, as well:

Your age

- ☐ Under 15   ☐ 35-44
- ☐ 15-17   ☐ 45-54
- ☐ 18-24   ☐ 55+
- ☐ 25-34

Your gender

- ☐ Male   ☐ Female

Your educational level

- ☐ High School graduate
- ☐ Some college
- ☐ College graduate
- ☐ Graduate degree
- ☐ Still in High School
- ☐ Still in College

Magazines you read regularly (check as many as apply)

- ☐ Sports Illustrated
- ☐ Sport
- ☐ The Sporting News
- ☐ Baseball America
- ☐ Playboy
- ☐ Rolling Stone

Thanks again for your help.

FOLD ALONG DOTTED LINE AND STAPLE. NO POSTAGE IS NECESSARY.

Minnesota Twins

	W–L	ERA	AB	H	HR	BB	SO	BA	SA	OBA
Season	85-77	4.63	5514	1465	210	564	990	.266	.438	.337
vs. Left-Handers			2536	699	122	280	449	.276	.485	.349
vs. Right-Handers			2978	766	88	284	541	.257	.398	.326
Home	56-25	3.86	2833	716	92	276	546	.253	.407	.323
Road	29-52	5.46	2681	749	118	288	444	.279	.471	.351
Grass	24-38	5.58	2062	578	94	228	349	.280	.473	.354
Artificial Turf	61-39	4.07	3452	887	116	336	641	.257	.417	.326
April	12-9	4.10	705	179	24	73	128	.254	.411	.326
May	14-14	5.18	970	258	47	101	172	.266	.463	.339
June	17-11	4.45	956	257	30	108	192	.269	.425	.346
July	13-14	4.93	919	248	39	87	168	.270	.453	.336
August	13-15	5.06	948	263	31	102	149	.277	.431	.352
Sept./Oct.	16-14	3.99	1016	260	39	93	181	.256	.439	.319
Leading Off Inn.			1303	335	53	120	234	.257	.431	.325
Runners On			2392	656	94	252	430	.274	.457	.343
Runners/Scor. Pos.			1368	361	55	186	273	.264	.451	.346
Runners On/2 Out			1019	264	40	111	203	.259	.442	.338
Scor. Pos./2 Out			641	163	23	83	135	.254	.429	.345
Late Inning Pressure			891	222	25	105	177	.249	.394	.329
Leading Off			213	46	5	27	40	.216	.343	.310
Runners On			393	105	15	47	78	.267	.433	.343
Runners/Scor. Pos.			237	66	12	40	46	.278	.464	.370
First 9 Batters			2767	692	92	304	563	.250	.404	.327
Second 9 Batters			1468	416	64	130	225	.283	.479	.343
All Batters Thereafter			1279	357	54	130	202	.279	.466	.350

Starting pitchers: 55–54, 4.47 ERA
Relief pitchers: 30–23, 5.11 ERA
Ground outs-to-air outs ratio: 1.05, 3d–lowest in A.L.... First A.L. champion to finish last in league in complete games since the 1913 Philadelphia A's.... Highest road-game ERA in majors.... Lost 14 games in which they led after six innings, more than any major-league team except the Indians, who also lost 14.... Outscored opponents 15–2 in extra innings last season, but those two runs they allowed were both translated into losses. Record of 9–2 in extra-inning games was the best in the A.L.... Opponents scored seven or more runs in an inning six times last season, most in the majors.... Three of the four A.L. teams who play their home games on artificial turf ranked one-two-three in ERA on the rug: Toronto (ranked 1st), Kansas City (2d), Minnesota (3d), Seattle (7th).

New York Yankees

	W–L	ERA	AB	H	HR	BB	SO	BA	SA	OBA
Season	89-73	4.36	5552	1475	179	542	900	.266	.418	.332
vs. Left-Handers			1868	497	59	195	285	.266	.415	.335
vs. Right-Handers			3684	978	120	347	615	.265	.419	.330
Home	51-30	3.84	2801	723	88	254	471	.258	.404	.324
Road	38-43	4.90	2751	752	91	288	429	.273	.433	.344
Grass	78-60	4.25	4708	1230	146	443	784	.261	.409	.325
Artificial Turf	11-13	4.98	844	245	33	99	116	.290	.467	.367
April	14-7	3.82	693	170	20	77	115	.245	.375	.322
May	17-11	3.91	941	243	32	84	147	.258	.418	.321
June	17-11	4.38	977	257	34	76	165	.263	.422	.317
July	15-11	4.03	912	247	28	90	155	.271	.422	.334
August	11-17	5.02	971	269	32	112	164	.277	.442	.353
Sept./Oct.	15-16	4.79	1058	289	33	103	154	.273	.418	.339
Leading Off Inn.			1326	339	45	115	209	.256	.411	.319
Runners On			2382	638	65	257	405	.268	.406	.336
Runners/Scor. Pos.			1365	364	30	179	245	.267	.390	.345
Runners On/2 Out			1028	271	26	132	179	.264	.403	.350
Scor. Pos./2 Out			668	170	16	101	122	.254	.389	.357
Late Inning Pressure			850	227	25	76	146	.267	.395	.324
Leading Off			214	58	4	16	33	.271	.379	.322
Runners On			364	96	10	39	65	.264	.385	.325
Runners/Scor. Pos.			209	56	4	24	35	.268	.368	.327
First 9 Batters			2798	732	78	287	507	.262	.396	.331
Second 9 Batters			1578	429	61	153	226	.272	.453	.336
All Batters Thereafter			1176	314	40	102	167	.267	.423	.327

Starting pitchers: 62–54, 4.37 ERA
Relief pitchers: 27–19, 4.43 ERA
Ground outs-to-air outs ratio: 1.09.... First team ever to lead the A.L. in saves for three consecutive seasons.... Walked only three of the 145 batters faced with the bases loaded.... Ranking of ERA within the A.L. by months: April (3d), May (5th), June (7th), July (4th), August (11th), September (12th).... Fewer innings pitched by rookies (46.2) than any club in the A.L. last season.... Through May 1 of last season: 22 of 23 home runs allowed were solo shots; only two of 23 were hit by a left-handed batter (both by Mel Hall).... Lost 20–3 at Texas on July 19, only the second time in team history that it allowed 20 runs. The other: Cleveland 24, New York 6 on July 29, 1928 (must have been the Browns).... Faced 66 batters with two outs and the bases loaded without walking any.

Oakland A's

	W–L	ERA	AB	H	HR	BB	SO	BA	SA	OBA
Season	81-81	4.32	5580	1442	176	531	1042	.258	.412	.324
vs. Left-Handers			2555	660	64	274	474	.258	.391	.330
vs. Right-Handers			3025	782	112	257	568	.259	.430	.320
Home	42-39	3.69	2786	666	75	263	580	.239	.367	.306
Road	39-42	4.99	2794	776	101	268	462	.278	.457	.342
Grass	70-66	4.14	4702	1202	141	434	882	.256	.401	.320
Artificial Turf	11-15	5.33	878	240	35	97	160	.273	.474	.348
April	9-14	4.65	764	205	17	105	135	.268	.402	.359
May	15-10	3.66	872	223	25	74	166	.256	.399	.316
June	16-11	4.24	912	219	33	79	182	.240	.398	.302
July	12-15	4.51	953	246	28	84	172	.258	.401	.321
August	15-14	4.55	1011	265	42	84	190	.262	.451	.322
Sept./Oct.	14-17	4.32	1068	284	31	105	197	.266	.416	.330
Leading Off Inn.			1324	332	43	121	234	.251	.405	.316
Runners On			2412	633	77	259	446	.262	.415	.332
Runners/Scor. Pos.			1388	357	36	182	277	.257	.391	.338
Runners On/2 Out			1004	242	28	120	199	.241	.375	.327
Scor. Pos./2 Out			645	148	13	89	134	.229	.340	.327
Late Inning Pressure			974	245	33	104	200	.252	.399	.325
Leading Off			248	67	8	18	47	.270	.419	.322
Runners On			417	105	18	55	84	.252	.420	.335
Runners/Scor. Pos.			221	55	5	43	50	.249	.344	.361
First 9 Batters			2933	715	72	275	614	.244	.379	.310
Second 9 Batters			1506	421	55	145	246	.280	.449	.344
All Batters Thereafter			1141	306	49	111	182	.268	.450	.335

Starting pitchers: 54–58, 4.55 ERA
Relief pitchers: 27–23, 4.10 ERA
Ground outs-to-air outs ratio: 1.12.... Opponents grounded into one double play for every 11.7 opportunities, 2d-lowest rate in majors.... Allowed the fewest 1st-inning runs (62) and the fewest 1st-inning home runs (9) in the majors last season.... Pitchers were involved in only six double plays as fielders last season, fewest of any staff in the majors.... Only the third team in A.L. history with a pair of relievers each of whom saved at least 16 games in the same season. (Eckersley and Howell each had 16.) The other two: 1973 White Sox (Cy Acosta and Terry Forster), 1971 Royals (Ted Abernathy and Tom Burgmeier).... One of three major-league teams with a winning record (11–10) in road games decided by one run. The others: Montreal (10–8) and Seattle (11–10).

Seattle Mariners

	W–L	ERA	AB	H	HR	BB	SO	BA	SA	OBA
Season	78-84	4.49	5533	1503	199	497	919	.272	.439	.332
vs. Left-Handers			2342	652	79	200	347	.278	.444	.333
vs. Right-Handers			3191	851	120	297	572	.267	.436	.331
Home	40-41	4.51	2837	752	115	243	500	.265	.442	.324
Road	38-43	4.46	2696	751	84	254	419	.279	.437	.339
Grass	34-28	4.47	2067	581	65	191	324	.281	.438	.340
Artificial Turf	44-56	4.50	3466	922	134	306	595	.266	.440	.327
April	12-11	4.74	768	198	28	68	144	.258	.426	.322
May	14-12	4.77	910	257	37	87	147	.282	.459	.344
June	13-14	4.44	918	246	32	57	151	.268	.436	.311
July	10-16	5.38	879	257	39	89	131	.292	.485	.356
August	12-17	3.93	996	272	34	93	162	.273	.445	.335
Sept./Oct.	17-14	3.87	1062	273	29	103	184	.257	.393	.321
Leading Off Inn.			1327	375	65	102	195	.283	.497	.336
Runners On			2383	673	75	213	377	.282	.440	.338
Runners/Scor. Pos.			1360	371	39	155	222	.273	.424	.337
Runners On/2 Out			979	253	32	111	160	.258	.413	.336
Scor. Pos./2 Out			616	154	19	83	100	.250	.401	.341
Late Inning Pressure			729	194	22	70	143	.266	.402	.330
Leading Off			181	44	6	14	35	.243	.387	.301
Runners On			304	83	8	37	59	.273	.391	.349
Runners/Scor. Pos.			179	48	7	30	35	.268	.430	.364
First 9 Batters			2513	667	85	236	455	.265	.429	.328
Second 9 Batters			1434	402	56	129	204	.280	.459	.340
All Batters Thereafter			1586	434	58	132	260	.274	.439	.329

Starting pitchers: 62–69, 4.61 ERA
Relief pitchers: 16–15, 4.27 ERA
Ground outs-to-air outs ratio: 1.19, 3d–highest in A.L.... Starters failed to complete five innings in 30 games, lowest total in A.L. last season.... Lost seven games (37-7) in front of the home fans in which they were leading after seven innings (most in majors), but were the only team with a perfect record in road games in which they led after seven innings (31-0).... Mariners' pitchers have allowed exactly 1,000 home runs at the Kingdome, while surrendering 706 on the road over the last 11 years.... White Sox were shut out four times last season, three times by the Mariners.... Only major-league staff that did not allow a grand slam homer in 1987. Opponents hit three slams in May of 1986, none since.... Allowed fewest walks in A.L. for first time in team's 10-year history.

Texas Rangers

	W–L	ERA	AB	H	HR	BB	SO	BA	SA	OBA
Season	75-87	4.63	5486	1388	199	760	1103	.253	.415	.347
vs. Left-Handers			2467	621	86	335	469	.252	.403	.344
vs. Right-Handers			3019	767	113	425	634	.254	.425	.350
Home	43-38	4.64	2841	723	111	386	584	.254	.419	.347
Road	32-49	4.62	2645	665	88	374	519	.251	.411	.347
Grass	68-69	4.54	4668	1181	174	644	951	.253	.416	.346
Artificial Turf	7-18	5.13	818	207	25	116	152	.253	.406	.352
April	8-11	4.65	644	165	16	95	134	.256	.388	.361
May	11-16	5.32	921	261	40	131	195	.283	.457	.377
June	16-12	4.31	958	231	36	121	173	.241	.420	.331
July	14-13	4.39	922	228	33	116	177	.247	.411	.332
August	12-17	5.08	987	252	40	166	227	.255	.431	.361
Sept./Oct.	14-18	4.13	1054	251	34	131	197	.238	.379	.327
Leading Off Inn.			1276	314	43	159	263	.246	.398	.336
Runners On			2485	625	84	357	499	.252	.404	.346
Runners/Scor. Pos.			1472	361	42	257	324	.245	.379	.356
Runners On/2 Out			1056	257	36	160	235	.243	.396	.349
Scor. Pos./2 Out			708	167	21	122	179	.236	.377	.357
Late Inning Pressure			839	219	27	98	183	.261	.414	.346
Leading Off			206	47	10	20	46	.228	.388	.312
Runners On			337	92	7	50	70	.273	.445	.372
Runners/Scor. Pos.			194	52	2	39	41	.268	.361	.393
First 9 Batters			2797	691	96	419	613	.247	.400	.349
Second 9 Batters			1397	372	51	181	244	.266	.433	.353
All Batters Thereafter			1292	325	52	160	246	.252	.428	.337

Starting pitchers: 46–63, 4.94 ERA
Relief pitchers: 29–24, 4.04 ERA
Ground outs-to-air outs ratio: 1.17. . . . Opponents grounded into one double play for every 9.9 opportunities, 3d-lowest rate in A.L. . . . Third team in major-league history without a complete-game shutout for an entire season. The others: 1981 Yankees and 1986 Cardinals. . . . Pitched only three shutouts, fewest in A.L. since Seattle tossed only one in 1977. . . . Led A.L. in walks for second consecutive season. Ditto, strikeouts. . . . Walked the leadoff batter in 159 innings, 2d-highest total in A.L. over past 13 years, but 10 fewer than the 1986 Rangers. . . . Committed 26 balks, seven more than the 1986 A's, who set an A.L. record a year earlier. . . . Started a pitcher on three days' rest 32 times last season, most in A.L. . . . Pitchers combined for 24 errors, tied for most in the majors.

Toronto Blue Jays

	W–L	ERA	AB	H	HR	BB	SO	BA	SA	OBA
Season	96-66	3.74	5426	1323	158	567	1064	.244	.395	.316
vs. Left-Handers			2108	536	56	223	409	.254	.402	.326
vs. Right-Handers			3318	787	102	344	655	.237	.391	.310
Home	52-29	3.54	2785	650	83	272	545	.233	.384	.303
Road	44-37	3.96	2641	673	75	295	519	.255	.407	.330
Grass	35-28	3.95	2051	524	64	241	411	.255	.411	.334
Artificial Turf	61-38	3.62	3375	799	94	326	653	.237	.386	.305
April	12-8	3.65	682	160	22	78	120	.235	.389	.317
May	16-11	3.47	871	199	22	85	171	.228	.365	.297
June	17-11	4.03	943	242	32	98	164	.257	.413	.328
July	15-12	4.20	901	218	26	94	195	.242	.396	.313
August	17-12	3.87	964	235	29	92	190	.244	.421	.310
Sept./Oct.	19-12	3.28	1065	269	27	120	224	.253	.385	.329
Leading Off Inn.			1346	347	48	110	250	.258	.428	.315
Runners On			2243	555	63	274	430	.247	.395	.328
Runners/Scor. Pos.			1295	313	36	200	255	.242	.388	.339
Runners On/2 Out			946	224	26	145	205	.237	.389	.341
Scor. Pos./2 Out			631	145	16	105	136	.230	.374	.342
Late Inning Pressure			958	221	19	121	234	.231	.348	.317
Leading Off			244	57	5	22	57	.234	.357	.297
Runners On			374	92	7	70	76	.246	.356	.361
Runners/Scor. Pos.			228	52	5	56	46	.228	.364	.373
First 9 Batters			2828	681	81	311	626	.241	.382	.317
Second 9 Batters			1406	342	40	142	227	.243	.408	.312
All Batters Thereafter			1192	300	37	114	211	.252	.413	.319

Starting pitchers: 62–44, 3.89 ERA
Relief pitchers: 34–22, 3.45 ERA (lowest in A.L.)
Ground outs-to-air outs ratio: 1.17. . . . Led the A.L. in ERA for second time in past three seasons. . . . Opposing batters hit .186 with the bases loaded, 3d-lowest mark in A.L. over past 13 years. Jays hold 13-year A.L. low as well: Opponents batted .150 in 1977, the first season of the team's existence. . . . Opponents scored three or more runs in an inning 64 times last season, lowest total in the majors, (Houston staff ranked second with 68 such innings). . . . The only active pitcher with 15 or more career wins against Toronto is now a member of their staff: Mike Flanagan (17–7 career vs. Blue Jays). . . . Good defense helped their pitchers. Jays allowed the fewest unearned runs (50) in their history, also the fewest in the majors last season.

American League

	W–L	ERA	AB	H	HR	BB	SO	BA	SA	OBA
Season	1134-1134	4.46	77819	20620	2634	7812	13442	.265	.425	.333
vs. Left-Handers			32439	8660	1070	3462	5315	.267	.427	.338
vs. Right-Handers			45380	11960	1564	4350	8127	.264	.424	.330
Home	624-510	4.29	39806	10359	1325	3791	7062	.260	.416	.326
Road	510-624	4.63	38013	10261	1309	4021	6380	.270	.436	.341
Grass	810-810	4.53	55734	14864	1904	5645	9625	.267	.425	.335
Artificial Turf	324-324	4.27	22085	5756	730	2167	3817	.261	.426	.329
April	147-147	4.29	9951	2551	308	1106	1755	.256	.410	.333
May	187-187	4.42	12768	3327	487	1302	2285	.261	.429	.330
June	192-192	4.72	13186	3519	476	1335	2289	.267	.436	.336
July	187-187	4.52	12918	3459	440	1199	2166	.268	.430	.330
August	202-202	4.57	13980	3773	477	1389	2414	.270	.434	.337
Sept./Oct.	219-219	4.20	15016	3991	446	1481	2533	.266	.413	.333
Leading Off Inn.			18549	4931	676	1614	3075	.266	.435	.328
Runners On			33704	9133	1096	3773	5794	.271	.428	.343
Runners/Scor. Pos.			19421	5162	595	2651	3568	.266	.418	.348
Runners On/2 Out			14117	3586	440	1784	2603	.254	.406	.341
Scor. Pos./2 Out			9152	2264	267	1335	1774	.247	.394	.347
Late Inning Pressure			12524	3277	374	1395	2353	.262	.404	.337
Leading Off			3117	793	97	248	550	.254	.400	.312
Runners On			5279	1443	165	752	961	.273	.420	.362
Runners/Scor. Pos.			3071	819	92	595	588	.267	.406	.378
First 9 Batters			38019	9834	1184	4079	7336	.259	.409	.332
Second 9 Batters			20919	5700	771	1963	3183	.272	.445	.336
All Batters Thereafter			18881	5086	679	1770	2923	.269	.438	.333

National League

Jim Acker
Atlanta Braves — Throws Right

	W–L	ERA	AB	H	HR	BB	SO	BA	SA	OBA
Season	4-9	4.16	430	109	11	51	68	.253	.384	.336
vs. Left-Handers			231	55	3	27	31	.238	.329	.317
vs. Right-Handers			199	54	8	24	37	.271	.447	.358
Home	4-1	4.50	227	56	6	25	35	.247	.374	.324
Road	0-8	3.79	203	53	5	26	33	.261	.394	.349
Grass	4-3	4.70	315	80	10	36	49	.254	.397	.334
Artificial Turf	0-6	2.78	115	29	1	15	19	.252	.348	.341
April	0-1	5.52	56	15	1	8	11	.268	.393	.364
May	0-2	3.60	117	34	3	11	11	.291	.453	.357
June	0-0	4.76	63	15	1	7	8	.238	.317	.319
July	0-2	7.94	50	17	2	2	8	.340	.560	.365
August	1-1	3.33	83	16	3	14	21	.193	.325	.313
Sept./Oct.	3-3	2.08	61	12	1	9	9	.197	.246	.300
Leading Off Inn.			99	27	5	7	13	.273	.495	.321
Runners On			207	52	3	24	34	.251	.353	.333
Runners/Scor. Pos.			141	34	1	19	27	.241	.312	.337
Runners On/2 Out			95	27	3	13	18	.284	.411	.376
Scor. Pos./2 Out			69	20	1	10	13	.290	.377	.388
Late Inning Pressure			196	58	5	25	24	.296	.439	.382
Leading Off			53	16	2	2	8	.302	.472	.327
Runners On			88	26	1	12	10	.295	.409	.394
Runners/Scor. Pos.			56	17	1	11	7	.304	.411	.437
First 9 Batters			368	91	8	46	61	.247	.361	.336
Second 9 Batters			62	18	3	5	7	.290	.516	.338
All Batters Thereafter			0	0	0	0	0	—	—	—

Loves to face: Garry Templeton (0-for-7)
Hates to face: Howard Johnson (.600, 6-for-10, 2 HR)
Ground outs-to-air outs ratio: 1.70 last season, 2.01 for career. . . . Additional statistics: 16 double-play ground outs in 85 opportunities, 3d-highest rate in N.L. (minimum: 40 opp.), 21 doubles, 1 triple in 114.2 innings last season. . . . Recorded six of his 14 saves after September 1. . . . Faced 39 consecutive batters without allowing a hit (Aug. 15–Aug. 27), longest streak in majors last season. . . . Lowest winning percentage in majors over past three seasons among pitchers with 25 or more decisions (9–21, .300). . . . Has forced in five runs with bases-loaded walks over the past two years. . . . Opponents' career batting averages: left-handers .284, right-handers .258. . . . Born on Sept. 24, 1958, three days after the Braves clinched their last league title.

Rick Aguilera
New York Mets — Throws Right

	W–L	ERA	AB	H	HR	BB	SO	BA	SA	OBA
Season	11-3	3.60	449	124	12	33	77	.276	.421	.329
vs. Left-Handers			219	66	6	19	31	.301	.447	.361
vs. Right-Handers			230	58	6	14	46	.252	.396	.297
Home	6-2	3.82	261	71	7	19	48	.272	.429	.322
Road	5-1	3.28	188	53	5	14	29	.282	.410	.338
Grass	8-2	3.49	325	85	9	23	57	.262	.415	.313
Artificial Turf	3-1	3.90	124	39	3	10	20	.315	.435	.370
April	2-1	4.06	124	35	3	11	24	.282	.435	.341
May	2-1	4.00	108	35	2	8	20	.324	.444	.371
June			0	0	0	0	0	—	—	—
July			0	0	0	0	0	—	—	—
August	2-0	1.65	60	13	2	3	8	.217	.383	.266
Sept./Oct.	5-1	3.76	157	41	5	11	25	.261	.408	.314
Leading Off Inn.			114	37	1	6	16	.325	.430	.364
Runners On			198	45	6	16	40	.227	.379	.286
Runners/Scor. Pos.			113	23	2	9	31	.204	.327	.258
Runners On/2 Out			82	18	4	8	17	.220	.427	.289
Scor. Pos./2 Out			52	10	2	6	14	.192	.346	.276
Late Inning Pressure			35	11	0	3	8	.314	.343	.368
Leading Off			10	5	0	0	2	.500	.600	.500
Runners On			16	4	0	1	4	.250	.250	.294
Runners/Scor. Pos.			12	2	0	1	4	.167	.167	.231
First 9 Batters			145	44	2	14	27	.303	.441	.363
Second 9 Batters			140	29	5	10	22	.207	.336	.263
All Batters Thereafter			164	51	5	9	28	.311	.476	.354

Loves to face: Tim Raines (.083, 2-for-24)
Hates to face: Kal Daniels (.636, 7-for-11)
Ground outs-to-air outs ratio: 1.61 last season, 1.28 for career. . . . Additional statistics: 14 double-play ground outs in 91 opportunities, 23 doubles, 3 triples in 115.0 innings last season. . . . Allowed 10 first-inning runs in 17 starts. . . . Batting support: 5.53 runs per start, 4th-highest average in N.L. (minimum: 15 GS). . . . Record of 31–17 (.646) over last three seasons is 4th-best in N.L., behind Gooden (56–17, .767), Tudor (44–17, .721), and Darling (43–20, .683). . . . Last season was the first in which opposing batters hit for a lower average with runners on base than with the bases empty. . . . Annual batting averages by opposing left-handers since 1985: .241, .290, .301. . . . Opponents have only one hit (a single) in 11 career at bats with the bases loaded. Never forced in a run with a walk.

Larry Andersen
Houston Astros — Throws Right

	W–L	ERA	AB	H	HR	BB	SO	BA	SA	OBA
Season	9-5	3.45	385	95	7	41	94	.247	.366	.319
vs. Left-Handers			189	44	3	26	40	.233	.344	.326
vs. Right-Handers			196	51	4	15	54	.260	.388	.313
Home	4-4	2.56	193	47	2	20	52	.244	.337	.316
Road	5-1	4.41	192	48	5	21	42	.250	.396	.323
Grass	3-0	2.87	122	29	4	8	27	.238	.393	.282
Artificial Turf	6-5	3.71	263	66	3	33	67	.251	.354	.336
April	2-1	2.61	37	7	0	3	11	.189	.216	.250
May	1-1	5.63	61	15	2	11	19	.246	.410	.373
June	2-2	1.86	69	14	0	7	17	.203	.232	.276
July	1-0	3.44	76	21	1	11	12	.276	.408	.360
August	2-0	3.15	73	18	2	5	20	.247	.397	.295
Sept./Oct.	1-1	4.08	69	20	2	4	15	.290	.464	.324
Leading Off Inn.			86	19	1	9	24	.221	.314	.295
Runners On			167	40	3	26	36	.240	.353	.338
Runners/Scor. Pos.			103	26	3	20	20	.252	.408	.362
Runners On/2 Out			82	24	2	12	18	.293	.439	.383
Scor. Pos./2 Out			55	17	2	9	12	.309	.491	.406
Late Inning Pressure			263	67	4	25	66	.255	.365	.321
Leading Off			64	14	0	6	19	.219	.266	.286
Runners On			102	27	2	15	19	.265	.382	.355
Runners/Scor. Pos.			58	17	2	13	10	.293	.483	.405
First 9 Batters			361	87	6	38	88	.241	.346	.314
Second 9 Batters			24	8	1	3	6	.333	.667	.407
All Batters Thereafter			0	0	0	0	0	—	—	—

Loves to face: Mike Scioscia (0-for-7, 7 ground outs)
Hates to face: Ozzie Smith (.600, 6-for-10, 8 BB)
Ground outs-to-air outs ratio: 2.01 last season, 1.28 for career. . . . Additional statistics: 7 double-play ground outs in 77 opportunities, 19 doubles, 3 triples in 101.2 innings last season. . . . Reached the 100-inning level for the first time in 10 major-league seasons. . . . Earned five saves in 16 opportunities. . . . Averaged 8.32 strikeouts per nine innings; previous career mark was 5.00. . . . Struck out five consecutive left-handed batters (Aug. 8-11). . . . Opponents batted .250 (4-for-16) with the bases loaded last season, but did hit for the cycle. The grand-slam was hit by Andy Van Slyke. . . . Born May 6, 1953, the day that Bobo Holloman of the Browns pitched a no-hitter in his first major league start. It was the only complete game of Holloman's 3–7 career.

Steve Bedrosian
Philadelphia Phillies — Throws Right

	W–L	ERA	AB	H	HR	BB	SO	BA	SA	OBA
Season	5-3	2.83	334	79	11	28	74	.237	.362	.297
vs. Left-Handers			193	48	8	19	45	.249	.394	.315
vs. Right-Handers			141	31	3	9	29	.220	.319	.272
Home	2-2	3.38	167	42	6	11	39	.251	.407	.302
Road	3-1	2.33	167	37	5	17	35	.222	.317	.292
Grass	1-0	1.54	87	20	2	12	20	.230	.310	.323
Artificial Turf	4-3	3.29	247	59	9	16	54	.239	.381	.287
April	2-1	7.84	42	11	4	7	7	.262	.571	.373
May	1-0	1.04	60	9	1	6	21	.150	.233	.227
June	0-0	0.69	48	12	0	5	11	.250	.313	.321
July	0-1	1.96	68	16	1	2	10	.235	.279	.257
August	1-0	3.52	60	18	3	4	13	.300	.483	.344
Sept./Oct.	1-1	3.68	56	13	2	4	12	.232	.357	.283
Leading Off Inn.			71	16	4	6	18	.225	.423	.286
Runners On			150	33	3	16	32	.220	.313	.293
Runners/Scor. Pos.			90	14	2	12	24	.156	.233	.252
Runners On/2 Out			71	14	2	10	17	.197	.324	.296
Scor. Pos./2 Out			47	7	1	7	14	.149	.213	.259
Late Inning Pressure			249	62	7	18	55	.249	.357	.300
Leading Off			52	14	3	3	13	.269	.481	.309
Runners On			117	24	2	12	25	.205	.291	.279
Runners/Scor. Pos.			70	12	2	9	17	.171	.271	.266
First 9 Batters			326	78	11	27	69	.239	.368	.299
Second 9 Batters			8	1	0	1	5	.125	.125	.222
All Batters Thereafter			0	0	0	0	0	—	—	—

Loves to face: Hubie Brooks (.107, 3-for-28, 14 SO)
Hates to face: Nick Esasky (.571, 8-for-14, 1 HR)
Ground outs-to-air outs ratio: 0.78 last season, 0.84 for career. . . . Additional statistics: 6 double-play ground outs in 63 opportunities, 5 doubles, 2 triples in 89.0 innings last season. . . . Record streak of saves in 13 consecutive appearances was established under two different managers. . . . Completed 30 relief appearances in a row, longest N.L. streak over past six seasons. . . . Career average of 8.20 strikeouts per nine innings in relief, compared to 5.85 in 46 starts. . . . Opponents batted only .237 last season, but the top 15 batters in the league hit .419 (13-for-31) against him, with eight walks and only two strikeouts. . . . Opponents' batting average with runners in scoring position has been under .200 in five of six full seasons in majors (career average: .193).

Tom Browning

Cincinnati Reds — Throws Left

	W–L	ERA	AB	H	HR	BB	SO	BA	SA	OBA
Season	10-13	5.02	708	201	27	61	117	.284	.472	.342
vs. Left-Handers			116	31	4	15	21	.267	.431	.351
vs. Right-Handers			592	170	23	46	96	.287	.480	.340
Home	6-6	4.92	377	99	17	36	67	.263	.472	.332
Road	4-7	5.14	331	102	10	25	50	.308	.471	.354
Grass	2-4	4.04	219	63	7	16	31	.288	.438	.336
Artificial Turf	8-9	5.44	489	138	20	45	86	.282	.487	.344
April	2-3	6.16	119	36	6	9	22	.303	.546	.352
May	2-3	10.23	100	36	6	9	11	.360	.620	.411
June	0-0	7.20	40	12	1	6	5	.300	.425	.404
July	1-2	4.75	120	39	4	6	20	.325	.533	.354
August	1-3	4.38	138	33	7	17	22	.239	.442	.321
Sept./Oct.	4-2	2.29	191	45	3	14	37	.236	.340	.293
Leading Off Inn.			176	57	7	12	35	.324	.534	.370
Runners On			298	77	10	30	41	.258	.426	.327
Runners/Scor. Pos.			174	50	9	24	27	.287	.511	.367
Runners On/2 Out			120	26	4	16	23	.217	.367	.314
Scor. Pos./2 Out			80	18	4	12	16	.225	.425	.326
Late Inning Pressure			28	10	1	3	3	.357	.536	.419
Leading Off			8	4	0	0	0	.500	.625	.500
Runners On			15	3	0	1	3	.200	.200	.250
Runners/Scor. Pos.			11	2	0	0	3	.182	.182	.182
First 9 Batters			257	82	6	20	50	.319	.475	.365
Second 9 Batters			240	61	12	23	41	.254	.483	.322
All Batters Thereafter			211	58	9	18	26	.275	.455	.336

Loves to face: Howard Johnson (0-for-17)
Hates to face: Tim Teufel (.563, 9-for-16, 3 2B, 3 HR)
Ground outs-to-air outs ratio: 0.65, 6th lowest in N.L. last season (minimum: 200 BFP), 0.67 for career. . . . Additional statistics: 15 double-play ground outs in 141 opportunities, 46 doubles, 3 triples in 183.0 innings last season. . . . Allowed 25 first-inning runs in 31 starts. . . . Batting support: 4.29 runs per start. . . . Leadoff batters reached base safely in seven consecutive innings (Aug. 18–24), tying Bob Sebra and Mike LaCoss for longest streak in N.L. last season. In the 189 innings he started, 23 leadoff batters hit extra-base hits, the 2d-highest rate in N.L. (minimum: 100 PA). . . . Career record of 20–21 (4.64 ERA) before the All-Star break, 25–14 (3.38 ERA) after the break. . . . Has walked only one of 46 batters faced with the bases loaded.

Tim Burke

Montreal Expos — Throws Right

	W–L	ERA	AB	H	HR	BB	SO	BA	SA	OBA
Season	7-0	1.19	327	64	3	17	58	.196	.254	.234
vs. Left-Handers			170	37	2	11	22	.218	.288	.264
vs. Right-Handers			157	27	1	6	36	.172	.217	.201
Home	5-0	0.97	159	32	1	11	24	.201	.258	.250
Road	2-0	1.41	168	32	2	6	34	.190	.250	.218
Grass	2-0	0.34	96	16	0	4	21	.167	.198	.200
Artificial Turf	5-0	1.53	231	48	3	13	37	.208	.277	.248
April	0-0	6.23	17	5	1	1	4	.294	.471	.333
May	0-0	0.00	65	11	0	4	7	.169	.185	.217
June	0-0	3.00	64	15	2	6	6	.234	.344	.292
July	2-0	0.54	60	12	0	2	11	.200	.250	.226
August	5-0	0.52	63	12	0	2	12	.190	.270	.215
Sept./Oct.	0-0	0.57	58	9	0	2	18	.155	.155	.183
Leading Off Inn.			76	16	1	4	7	.211	.289	.250
Runners On			139	25	1	10	26	.180	.223	.232
Runners/Scor. Pos.			87	17	1	10	14	.195	.253	.273
Runners On/2 Out			59	8	0	5	12	.136	.153	.203
Scor. Pos./2 Out			37	6	0	5	6	.162	.189	.262
Late Inning Pressure			180	34	1	7	39	.189	.239	.218
Leading Off			43	10	0	2	5	.233	.302	.267
Runners On			71	10	0	5	16	.141	.155	.195
Runners/Scor. Pos.			48	7	0	5	9	.146	.167	.222
First 9 Batters			307	64	3	16	55	.208	.270	.246
Second 9 Batters			20	0	0	1	3	.000	.000	.048
All Batters Thereafter			0	0	0	0	0	—	—	—

Loves to face: Kevin McReynolds (0-for-12)
Hates to face: Glenn Davis (.750, 6-for-8, 2 HR)
Ground outs-to-air outs ratio: 1.74 last season, 1.70 for career. . . . Additional statistics: 7 double-play ground outs in 67 opportunities, 8 doubles, 1 triple in 91.0 innings last season. . . . Earned 18 saves in 24 opportunities, including seven after Aug. 30. . . . Allowed an average of 1.68 walks per nine innings, lowest rate among N.L. relievers (minimum: 30 games). . . . One of four N.L. pitchers to win five games in August. . . . Won first eight decisions of his three-year major-league career, as well as the last eight; was 9–11 in between. That adds up to 25–11, or the 3d-highest winning percentage in the N.L. during that time (.694), behind Gooden and Tudor (minimum: 25 decisions). . . . Career breakdown: .260 by left-handed batters, .181 by right-handers.

Jeff Calhoun

Philadelphia Phillies — Throws Left

	W–L	ERA	AB	H	HR	BB	SO	BA	SA	OBA
Season	3-1	1.48	149	25	1	26	31	.168	.255	.292
vs. Left-Handers			52	13	1	8	6	.250	.404	.349
vs. Right-Handers			97	12	0	18	25	.124	.175	.261
Home	3-0	0.00	88	9	0	8	19	.102	.170	.177
Road	0-1	3.94	61	16	1	18	12	.262	.377	.427
Grass	0-1	6.30	36	11	1	16	5	.306	.472	.519
Artificial Turf	3-0	0.00	113	14	0	10	26	.124	.186	.194
April			0	0	0	0	0	—	—	—
May			0	0	0	0	0	—	—	—
June	0-0	4.91	15	4	1	3	3	.267	.600	.368
July	0-0	0.00	12	2	0	2	1	.167	.250	.286
August	1-1	0.98	55	4	0	8	11	.073	.109	.203
Sept./Oct.	2-0	1.56	67	15	0	13	16	.224	.299	.346
Leading Off Inn.			33	7	1	6	7	.212	.364	.333
Runners On			67	10	0	17	12	.149	.194	.322
Runners/Scor. Pos.			42	8	0	14	11	.190	.262	.390
Runners On/2 Out			27	2	0	6	3	.074	.074	.242
Scor. Pos./2 Out			18	2	0	5	3	.111	.111	.304
Late Inning Pressure			96	15	0	17	23	.156	.229	.281
Leading Off			22	3	0	5	6	.136	.136	.296
Runners On			42	6	0	9	9	.143	.190	.288
Runners/Scor. Pos.			25	5	0	8	8	.200	.280	.382
First 9 Batters			148	25	1	26	30	.169	.257	.294
Second 9 Batters			1	0	0	0	1	.000	.000	.000
All Batters Thereafter			0	0	0	0	0	—	—	—

Loves to face: Ozzie Smith (0-for-9)
Hates to face: Junior Ortiz (2-for-2)
Ground outs-to-air outs ratio: 0.77 last season, 1.08 for career. . . . Additional statistics: 1 double-play ground out in 36 opportunities, 8 doubles, 1 triple in 42.2 innings last season. . . . Allowed an average of 5.27 hits per nine innings, lowest rate among N.L. relievers (minimum: 30 games). . . . Faced 27 consecutive batters in Late-Inning Pressure Situations without allowing a hit (June 26–Aug. 18), 3d-longest streak in majors last season. . . . Doesn't love to face just Ozzie: He held N.L.'s top 15 batters, a group that batted a collective .311, to just one hit (a double by Tony Gwynn) in 18 at bats. . . . Only two left-handed batters have ever homered against Calhoun: Dave Parker (1985) and Dave Martinez (1987). . . . Opponents' career batting average of .167 leading off innings.

Don Carman

Philadelphia Phillies — Throws Left

	W–L	ERA	AB	H	HR	BB	SO	BA	SA	OBA
Season	13-11	4.22	796	194	34	69	125	.244	.431	.306
vs. Left-Handers			109	34	3	6	14	.312	.468	.364
vs. Right-Handers			687	160	31	63	111	.233	.425	.297
Home	6-7	4.72	379	92	16	30	69	.243	.435	.305
Road	7-4	3.76	417	102	18	39	56	.245	.427	.308
Grass	4-3	3.67	186	46	10	20	27	.247	.452	.319
Artificial Turf	9-8	4.39	610	148	24	49	98	.243	.425	.302
April	1-1	1.89	70	14	3	5	15	.200	.343	.263
May	2-2	3.60	146	31	3	11	27	.212	.322	.273
June	1-3	7.31	135	41	13	11	14	.304	.667	.354
July	3-1	6.21	114	35	4	16	15	.307	.544	.389
August	1-2	3.32	153	40	3	11	21	.261	.366	.311
Sept./Oct.	5-2	3.22	178	33	8	15	33	.185	.360	.255
Leading Off Inn.			200	49	9	19	31	.245	.455	.311
Runners On			289	81	12	31	42	.280	.457	.353
Runners/Scor. Pos.			160	44	7	27	26	.275	.456	.379
Runners On/2 Out			130	41	6	20	15	.315	.515	.414
Scor. Pos./2 Out			83	26	3	19	9	.313	.470	.447
Late Inning Pressure			46	11	1	6	6	.239	.348	.327
Leading Off			10	2	0	2	0	.200	.200	.333
Runners On			24	6	1	2	3	.250	.417	.308
Runners/Scor. Pos.			15	2	0	2	1	.133	.133	.235
First 9 Batters			277	61	8	29	62	.220	.372	.297
Second 9 Batters			276	70	13	18	39	.254	.438	.305
All Batters Thereafter			243	63	13	22	24	.259	.490	.318

Loves to face: Bill Almon (0-for-13)
Hates to face: Eric Davis (.600, 3-for-5, 3 HR)
Ground outs-to-air outs ratio: 0.57, 3d-lowest in majors last season (minimum: 200 BFP), 0.57 for career. . . . Additional statistics: 6 double-play ground outs in 126 opportunities, 37 doubles, 5 triples in 211.0 innings last season. . . . Allowed 14 first-inning runs in 35 starts. . . . Batting support: 4.54 runs per start. . . . Five wins in September were the 2d-most in the N.L. . . . Allowed the gopher ball in 1987 at almost twice his prior career rate: one per 43.8 at bats through 1986, one per 23.4 at bats last season. . . . Surrendered home runs in nine consecutive appearances (June 1–July 11), longest streak in N.L. last season. . . . Has dropped five straight decisions against Cardinals. . . . Yearly batting averages by opposing left-handed batters since 1984: .176, .218, .233, .312.

David Cone

New York Mets — Throws Right

	W-L	ERA	AB	H	HR	BB	SO	BA	SA	OBA
Season	5-6	3.71	364	87	11	44	68	.239	.387	.327
vs. Left-Handers			189	44	5	28	26	.233	.376	.338
vs. Right-Handers			175	43	6	16	42	.246	.400	.314
Home	3-3	3.94	174	46	4	22	30	.264	.420	.350
Road	2-3	3.52	190	41	7	22	38	.216	.358	.306
Grass	4-4	3.77	264	65	7	34	51	.246	.390	.338
Artificial Turf	1-2	3.58	100	22	4	10	17	.220	.380	.297
April	0-2	7.36	60	18	3	11	12	.300	.517	.403
May	2-0	3.34	118	29	3	16	18	.246	.415	.333
June			0	0	0	0	0	—	—	—
July			0	0	0	0	0	—	—	—
August	1-1	3.75	44	10	2	3	10	.227	.409	.292
Sept./Oct.	2-3	2.68	142	30	3	14	28	.211	.303	.298
Leading Off Inn.			89	24	3	10	11	.270	.393	.356
Runners On			150	34	5	24	29	.227	.393	.328
Runners/Scor. Pos.			78	16	2	14	15	.205	.333	.316
Runners On/2 Out			65	15	1	8	13	.231	.308	.315
Scor. Pos./2 Out			42	9	1	4	9	.214	.286	.283
Late Inning Pressure			27	9	0	4	8	.333	.444	.419
Leading Off			5	1	0	2	2	.200	.200	.429
Runners On			14	5	0	2	4	.357	.500	.438
Runners/Scor. Pos.			5	3	0	1	1	.600	.600	.667
First 9 Batters			157	38	5	21	31	.242	.401	.339
Second 9 Batters			109	27	1	15	19	.248	.312	.339
All Batters Thereafter			98	22	5	8	18	.224	.449	.294

Loves to face: Will Clark (0-for-6)
Hates to face: Rob Thompson (.667, 4-for-6)
Ground outs-to-air outs ratio: 0.96 last season, 0.93 for career. . . . Additional statistics: 4 double-play ground outs in 80 opportunities, 15 doubles, 3 triples in 99.1 innings last season. . . . Allowed 9 first-inning runs in 13 starts. . . . Batting support: 3.77 runs per start. . . . Career average of one walk allowed per 9.3 batters faced, but ended last season with a streak of good control, walking only one of the last 30 batters he faced. . . . Compiled 2.92 ERA after three-month layoff that followed broken right pinky finger. . . . Future considerations: Has made 19 career relief appearances, striking out 42 batters in 43.1 innings. . . . Will Frank Cashen's subliminal craving for ice cream ultimately destroy the Mets? First Strawberry, then HoJo, now Cone. What's next? A comeback by Gene Freese?

Danny Cox

St. Louis Cardinals — Throws Right

	W-L	ERA	AB	H	HR	BB	SO	BA	SA	OBA
Season	11-9	3.88	772	224	17	71	101	.290	.421	.351
vs. Left-Handers			380	120	7	42	35	.316	.450	.382
vs. Right-Handers			392	104	10	29	66	.265	.393	.319
Home	6-3	3.40	474	136	9	32	54	.287	.403	.332
Road	5-6	4.64	298	88	8	39	47	.295	.450	.379
Grass	3-3	3.88	172	48	5	24	30	.279	.430	.371
Artificial Turf	8-6	3.88	600	176	12	47	71	.293	.418	.345
April	3-0	3.38	125	31	3	14	18	.248	.368	.324
May	2-2	5.02	154	51	2	12	13	.331	.461	.379
June	2-1	3.51	152	42	4	10	27	.276	.421	.327
July	1-0	1.20	58	16	1	10	12	.276	.345	.382
August	1-1	3.56	115	36	2	7	7	.313	.426	.352
Sept./Oct.	2-5	4.78	168	48	5	18	24	.286	.446	.353
Leading Off Inn.			190	57	5	18	23	.300	.442	.364
Runners On			342	94	5	30	50	.275	.365	.332
Runners/Scor. Pos.			189	46	4	21	30	.243	.354	.316
Runners On/2 Out			140	36	2	17	17	.257	.336	.342
Scor. Pos./2 Out			89	22	1	12	11	.247	.326	.343
Late Inning Pressure			60	18	2	5	7	.300	.467	.348
Leading Off			17	5	0	2	2	.294	.353	.368
Runners On			21	5	1	2	3	.238	.381	.292
Runners/Scor. Pos.			11	2	0	2	2	.182	.182	.286
First 9 Batters			250	72	6	20	35	.288	.428	.342
Second 9 Batters			249	64	3	23	41	.257	.373	.321
All Batters Thereafter			273	88	8	28	25	.322	.458	.385

Loves to face: Rob Thompson (0-for-9)
Hates to face: Gerald Perry (.579, 11-for-19)
Ground outs-to-air outs ratio: 1.33 last season, 1.39 for career. . . . Additional statistics: 25 double-play ground outs in 167 opportunities, 36 doubles, 7 triples in 199.1 innings last season. . . . Allowed 15 first-inning runs in 31 starts. . . . Batting support: 4.87 runs per start. . . . Lost five of six starts in September before earning "money pitcher" tag by being on the mound for division clincher and Championship Series clincher. Then he lost Game 7 of the Series. . . . Batting average by opposing left-handers was the highest of his career. . . . Career record of 14-23 in starts following winning starts, 21-11 following losing starts. . . . Has walked only one of 47 batters faced with the bases loaded in his career. . . . Has lost his last four decisions against Mets.

Ron Darling

New York Mets — Throws Right

	W-L	ERA	AB	H	HR	BB	SO	BA	SA	OBA
Season	12-8	4.29	784	183	24	96	167	.233	.380	.318
vs. Left-Handers			444	99	10	48	91	.223	.356	.299
vs. Right-Handers			340	84	14	48	76	.247	.412	.343
Home	4-6	3.86	334	79	10	34	74	.237	.377	.307
Road	8-2	4.61	450	104	14	62	93	.231	.382	.326
Grass	7-7	4.19	515	119	20	62	111	.231	.392	.316
Artificial Turf	5-1	4.48	269	64	4	34	56	.238	.357	.323
April	2-1	6.28	121	39	1	11	21	.322	.471	.376
May	0-2	4.82	145	37	9	19	23	.255	.476	.349
June	0-2	3.82	136	23	4	23	39	.169	.324	.289
July	4-2	4.10	158	42	2	9	23	.266	.392	.308
August	5-1	3.72	179	37	4	28	47	.207	.307	.313
Sept./Oct.	1-0	2.57	45	5	2	6	14	.111	.244	.216
Leading Off Inn.			193	46	8	23	45	.238	.404	.323
Runners On			329	77	10	44	60	.234	.392	.324
Runners/Scor. Pos.			192	47	7	33	29	.245	.427	.354
Runners On/2 Out			137	32	7	20	32	.234	.431	.335
Scor. Pos./2 Out			93	24	5	17	18	.258	.484	.378
Late Inning Pressure			70	24	5	7	13	.343	.586	.397
Leading Off			20	6	1	1	3	.300	.450	.333
Runners On			26	9	1	3	5	.346	.538	.400
Runners/Scor. Pos.			15	5	1	1	3	.333	.533	.353
First 9 Batters			254	49	6	31	64	.193	.303	.280
Second 9 Batters			254	63	8	28	50	.248	.409	.324
All Batters Thereafter			276	71	10	37	53	.257	.424	.348

Loves to face: Dave Martinez (.050, 1-for-20)
Hates to face: John Kruk (.571, 8-for-14, 2 HR)
Ground outs-to-air outs ratio: 1.13 last season, 1.15 for career. . . . Additional statistics: 15 double-play ground outs in 152 opportunities, 31 doubles, 6 triples in 207.2 innings last season. . . . Allowed 18 first-inning runs in 32 starts. . . . Batting support: 5.03 runs per start. . . . Opponents stole 33 bases in 37 attempts; with Carter catching, it was 25 of 27, and the only two guys who were caught (Stubbs and Guerrero) were actually picked off, not thrown out at the next base by the catcher. . . . You want consistency? Yearly opponents' batting average since 1984: .235, .235, .234, .233. Career batting averages: .235 by left-handers, .235 by right-handed batters. . . . Career record of 8-0 vs. the Braves.

Danny Darwin

Houston Astros — Throws Right

	W-L	ERA	AB	H	HR	BB	SO	BA	SA	OBA
Season	9-10	3.59	748	184	17	69	134	.246	.374	.313
vs. Left-Handers			373	100	11	41	57	.268	.434	.342
vs. Right-Handers			375	84	6	28	77	.224	.315	.283
Home	5-4	3.09	371	92	6	40	74	.248	.340	.324
Road	4-6	4.10	377	92	11	29	60	.244	.408	.301
Grass	1-1	3.38	178	38	4	15	33	.213	.309	.281
Artificial Turf	8-9	3.66	570	146	13	54	101	.256	.395	.323
April	1-1	2.89	107	27	1	11	21	.252	.383	.333
May	1-3	4.99	125	37	3	11	23	.296	.432	.353
June	2-0	2.33	139	29	3	14	24	.209	.288	.279
July	3-3	3.49	179	38	4	10	35	.212	.352	.258
August	1-2	4.65	131	42	4	12	20	.321	.481	.378
Sept./Oct.	1-1	3.44	67	11	2	11	11	.164	.284	.291
Leading Off Inn.			188	39	4	16	32	.207	.303	.277
Runners On			304	81	4	29	54	.266	.355	.331
Runners/Scor. Pos.			177	42	1	22	36	.237	.299	.320
Runners On/2 Out			135	30	1	20	24	.222	.311	.327
Scor. Pos./2 Out			90	16	1	16	20	.178	.256	.308
Late Inning Pressure			64	19	0	5	10	.297	.422	.357
Leading Off			13	3	0	2	1	.231	.308	.375
Runners On			34	8	0	2	7	.235	.294	.278
Runners/Scor. Pos.			17	6	0	2	3	.353	.471	.421
First 9 Batters			257	63	8	25	52	.245	.397	.317
Second 9 Batters			235	53	2	22	46	.226	.294	.291
All Batters Thereafter			256	68	7	22	36	.266	.426	.329

Loves to face: Bo Diaz (0-for-9)
Hates to face: Eddie Milner (.538, 7-for-13, 1 HR)
Ground outs-to-air outs ratio: 0.97 last season, 0.87 for career. . . . Additional statistics: 9 double-play ground outs in 133 opportunities, 35 doubles, 5 triples in 195.2 innings last season. . . . Allowed 16 first-inning runs in 30 starts. . . . Batting support: 4.43 runs per start. . . . June ERA was 5th-best in N.L. . . . Struck out 40 times last season as a batter, most by an N.L. pitcher. . . . Career records: 53-72, 3.86 ERA as a starter; 28-16, 2.53 ERA in relief. . . . Opponents have batted for a higher average with runners on base than they have with the bases empty in each of his ten seasons in the majors, the longest streak by a currently active pitcher. Since we've been keeping track, only Steve Rogers has had a longer streak (11 years).

Mark Davis

Giants/Padres — Throws Left

	W–L	ERA	AB	H	HR	BB	SO	BA	SA	OBA
Season	9–8	3.99	492	123	14	59	98	.250	.390	.336
vs. Left-Handers			113	25	3	11	20	.221	.345	.302
vs. Right-Handers			379	98	11	48	78	.259	.404	.346
Home	4–4	3.00	227	50	7	27	51	.220	.370	.307
Road	5–4	4.89	265	73	7	32	47	.275	.408	.361
Grass	7–4	3.51	374	89	10	43	81	.238	.369	.322
Artificial Turf	2–4	5.64	118	34	4	16	17	.288	.458	.382
April	3–0	2.19	91	22	0	7	16	.242	.275	.311
May	0–3	8.84	68	21	7	11	14	.309	.647	.405
June	1–2	4.39	103	29	2	10	21	.282	.437	.351
July	1–1	4.19	70	14	0	12	18	.200	.229	.333
August	3–0	2.53	75	15	2	10	12	.200	.360	.294
Sept./Oct.	1–2	2.78	85	22	3	9	17	.259	.412	.330
Leading Off Inn.			113	29	4	13	25	.257	.416	.344
Runners On			227	56	8	28	45	.247	.414	.335
Runners/Scor. Pos.			127	33	3	17	26	.260	.409	.356
Runners On/2 Out			98	27	6	14	26	.276	.541	.372
Scor. Pos./2 Out			61	15	3	9	15	.246	.508	.352
Late Inning Pressure			135	29	4	22	31	.215	.363	.333
Leading Off			34	9	1	1	11	.265	.441	.306
Runners On			56	12	2	15	13	.214	.393	.380
Runners/Scor. Pos.			26	6	0	11	7	.231	.308	.459
First 9 Batters			334	79	9	43	68	.237	.368	.328
Second 9 Batters			103	28	4	8	23	.272	.456	.333
All Batters Thereafter			55	16	1	8	7	.291	.400	.391

Loves to face: Dave Anderson (0-for-13)
Hates to face: Ryne Sandberg (.458, 11-for-24)
Ground outs-to-air outs ratio: 1.12 last season, 0.91 for career. . . .
Additional statistics: 14 double-play ground outs in 111 opportunities, 21 doubles, 3 triples in 133.0 innings last season. . . . Allowed 5 first-inning runs in 11 starts. . . . Batting support: 5.09 runs per start. . . . April ERA was 4th-best in N.L. . . . Career marks: 13–28, 5.12 ERA as a starter; 18–24, 3.29 ERA in relief. . . . Opposing left-handers have hit .183 over past three seasons, 15 points lower than vs. any other pitcher in majors during that time (minimum: 250 BFP). . . . Opponents' career batting average is .202 in Late-Inning Pressure Situations. . . . Been around longer than you think. Made major-league debut in 1980, three days before Fernando.

Bill Dawley

St. Louis Cardinals — Throws Right

	W–L	ERA	AB	H	HR	BB	SO	BA	SA	OBA
Season	5–8	4.47	359	93	15	38	65	.259	.457	.330
vs. Left-Handers			130	33	3	20	14	.254	.377	.353
vs. Right-Handers			229	60	12	18	51	.262	.502	.316
Home	4–6	4.82	209	57	6	23	34	.273	.435	.345
Road	1–2	3.98	150	36	9	15	31	.240	.487	.310
Grass	1–2	4.44	91	22	6	8	24	.242	.495	.310
Artificial Turf	4–6	4.48	268	71	9	30	41	.265	.444	.337
April	0–2	4.30	50	9	3	4	9	.180	.380	.241
May	1–2	5.29	69	19	2	6	10	.275	.493	.333
June	3–1	2.52	89	21	3	7	21	.236	.371	.299
July	0–2	4.66	73	23	2	10	18	.315	.479	.398
August	1–0	2.84	45	10	2	8	5	.222	.444	.333
Sept./Oct.	0–1	11.25	33	11	3	3	2	.333	.697	.378
Leading Off Inn.			86	28	3	6	10	.326	.523	.370
Runners On			150	42	4	27	30	.280	.440	.385
Runners/Scor. Pos.			109	28	3	23	23	.257	.413	.381
Runners On/2 Out			63	20	3	18	11	.317	.508	.469
Scor. Pos./2 Out			54	16	2	15	8	.296	.463	.449
Late Inning Pressure			138	43	5	18	24	.312	.493	.391
Leading Off			35	12	0	5	2	.343	.400	.425
Runners On			57	19	1	12	14	.333	.474	.449
Runners/Scor. Pos.			40	12	1	10	11	.300	.425	.440
First 9 Batters			308	82	11	32	54	.266	.448	.335
Second 9 Batters			47	10	3	6	10	.213	.468	.302
All Batters Thereafter			4	1	1	0	1	.250	1.000	.250

Loves to face: Andres Thomas (0-for-6)
Hates to face: Mike Marshall (.500, 6-for-12, 1 HR)
Ground outs-to-air outs ratio: 0.92 last season, 0.77 for career. . . .
Additional statistics: 6 double-play ground outs in 63 opportunities, 22 doubles, 2 triples in 96.2 innings last season. . . . Earned 14 saves in 16 opportunities as a rookie in 1983; only 11-for-34 since then. . . . Has made 263 relief appearances without a start in five-year career. . . . Opponents' yearly batting averages in Late-Inning Pressure Situations since 1983: .169, .200, .241 .267, .312. . . . Opponents have hit for a higher average in day games than in night games in each of his five seasons in the majors. Career averages: .280 in day games (8–8, 5.00 ERA), .223 at night (19–20, 2.60 ERA). . . . Opponents' career batting average is .436 (24-for-55, 3 BB) with the bases loaded. . . . Career record of 6–0 vs. Pittsburgh.

Ken Dayley

St. Louis Cardinals — Throws Left

	W–L	ERA	AB	H	HR	BB	SO	BA	SA	OBA
Season	9–5	2.66	222	52	2	33	63	.234	.338	.337
vs. Left-Handers			73	18	0	9	26	.247	.301	.337
vs. Right-Handers			149	34	2	24	37	.228	.356	.337
Home	3–1	4.56	104	33	1	13	26	.317	.462	.393
Road	6–4	1.27	118	19	1	20	37	.161	.229	.291
Grass	4–1	0.56	50	7	0	6	16	.140	.140	.246
Artificial Turf	5–4	3.40	172	45	2	27	47	.262	.395	.363
April			0	0	0	0	0	—	—	—
May	0–0	0.00	18	3	0	1	3	.167	.167	.211
June	1–0	3.12	35	9	0	8	10	.257	.314	.409
July	5–1	1.56	57	11	0	5	23	.193	.263	.258
August	2–3	3.12	67	16	1	9	19	.239	.358	.333
Sept./Oct.	1–1	4.50	45	13	1	10	8	.289	.489	.418
Leading Off Inn.			42	6	0	5	16	.143	.238	.250
Runners On			117	26	1	21	30	.222	.316	.343
Runners/Scor. Pos.			68	19	0	18	21	.279	.382	.432
Runners On/2 Out			55	14	1	11	16	.255	.418	.388
Scor. Pos./2 Out			35	10	0	9	11	.286	.457	.444
Late Inning Pressure			178	43	1	28	57	.242	.348	.349
Leading Off			34	6	0	5	14	.176	.294	.300
Runners On			92	20	0	18	26	.217	.293	.348
Runners/Scor. Pos.			52	15	0	16	18	.288	.404	.457
First 9 Batters			212	49	1	31	60	.231	.321	.333
Second 9 Batters			10	3	1	2	3	.300	.700	.417
All Batters Thereafter			0	0	0	0	0			

Loves to face: Bruce Bochy (0-for-9)
Hates to face: Argenis Salazar (3-for-3)
Ground outs-to-air outs ratio: 1.19 last season, 1.13 for career. . . .
Additional statistics: 7 double-play ground outs in 57 opportunities, 9 doubles, 4 triples in 61.0 innings last season. . . . Hasn't allowed a regular-season homer to a left-handed batter since Strawberry clocked him on Oct. 1, 1985. Post-season? Kent Hrbek, Game 6. . . . Held opposing left-handed batters below .300 batting average for first time in his career, as precursor to Hrbek's Series slam. . . . One of four N.L. pitchers to win five games in July. . . . Opponents' career batting average is higher on grass fields (.278, 4.40 ERA) than it is on artificial surfaces (.269, 3.39 ERA) despite the 1987 numbers listed above. . . . Has pitched 364.2 innings in career without committing a balk.

Jeff Dedmon

Atlanta Braves — Throws Right

	W–L	ERA	AB	H	HR	BB	SO	BA	SA	OBA
Season	3–4	3.91	334	82	8	42	40	.246	.368	.327
vs. Left-Handers			158	35	4	22	14	.222	.323	.311
vs. Right-Handers			176	47	4	20	26	.267	.409	.342
Home	2–1	3.83	168	43	3	20	21	.256	.375	.335
Road	1–3	4.00	166	39	5	22	19	.235	.361	.319
Grass	2–3	3.65	259	63	7	32	33	.243	.378	.327
Artificial Turf	1–1	4.79	75	19	1	10	7	.253	.333	.330
April	0–0	6.75	41	10	2	4	4	.244	.488	.311
May	2–1	2.25	68	15	0	6	7	.221	.235	.280
June	0–1	1.42	68	12	1	7	12	.176	.265	.253
July	1–1	1.35	47	11	0	9	4	.234	.255	.362
August	0–1	8.00	76	24	5	12	9	.316	.566	.396
Sept./Oct.	0–0	5.19	34	10	0	4	4	.294	.412	.368
Leading Off Inn.			71	19	1	13	6	.268	.338	.381
Runners On			164	44	5	23	20	.268	.439	.349
Runners/Scor. Pos.			102	25	2	20	14	.245	.382	.354
Runners On/2 Out			75	26	2	11	10	.347	.520	.430
Scor. Pos./2 Out			54	19	2	10	6	.352	.574	.453
Late Inning Pressure			96	25	1	16	13	.260	.365	.357
Leading Off			25	7	0	4	3	.280	.320	.379
Runners On			42	13	0	9	3	.310	.452	.407
Runners/Scor. Pos.			23	6	0	8	2	.261	.348	.412
First 9 Batters			287	69	7	34	34	.240	.366	.316
Second 9 Batters			43	11	0	6	5	.256	.279	.360
All Batters Thereafter			4	2	1	2	1	.500	1.500	.667

Loves to face: Glenn Davis (0-for-9)
Hates to face: Tim Raines (.583, 7-for-12, 1 HR)
Ground outs-to-air outs ratio: 1.75 last season, 2.41 for career. . . .
Additional statistics: 10 double-play ground outs in 68 opportunities, 13 doubles, 2 triples in 89.2 innings last season. . . . Opponents stole 18 bases in 20 tries, 2nd-highest rate vs. any N.L. pitcher with 20+ attempts; only runners caught stealing: Bob Melvin, Steve Sax. . . . Faced opposing pitchers 18 times last season; they had only two hits in 13 at bats, but he walked his fraternity brothers five times, 2d-most in N.L.; Sid Fernandez, who faced 53 pitchers, led with six walks. . . . Batting average by opposing left-handed batters was a career low. . . . Has made between 53 and 60 appearances, pitching between 80 and 100 innings, in each of the past four seasons.

Jim Deshaies

Houston Astros — Throws Left

	W–L	ERA	AB	H	HR	BB	SO	BA	SA	OBA
Season	11-6	4.62	579	149	22	57	104	.257	.427	.322
vs. Left-Handers			99	26	2	13	15	.263	.404	.345
vs. Right-Handers			480	123	20	44	89	.256	.431	.317
Home	6-0	2.75	274	59	4	18	53	.215	.299	.263
Road	5-6	6.46	305	90	18	39	51	.295	.541	.373
Grass	4-3	6.14	173	49	12	22	31	.283	.578	.362
Artificial Turf	7-3	4.00	406	100	10	35	73	.246	.362	.305
April	2-0	2.51	50	10	2	10	18	.200	.380	.333
May	2-2	5.30	134	31	4	16	22	.231	.381	.313
June	4-0	2.04	128	26	4	6	21	.203	.320	.239
July	1-2	5.19	100	27	3	7	16	.270	.410	.318
August	1-1	7.62	57	20	5	4	6	.351	.632	.387
Sept./Oct.	1-1	6.18	110	35	4	14	21	.318	.536	.389
Leading Off Inn.			150	35	4	10	21	.233	.360	.281
Runners On			221	58	10	23	49	.262	.457	.328
Runners/Scor. Pos.			121	30	5	17	30	.248	.438	.333
Runners On/2 Out			105	26	5	9	24	.248	.448	.307
Scor. Pos./2 Out			63	14	4	9	17	.222	.476	.319
Late Inning Pressure			13	4	0	0	3	.308	.308	.308
Leading Off			6	3	0	0	0	.500	.500	.500
Runners On			1	0	0	0	0	.000	.000	.000
Runners/Scor. Pos.			0	0	0	0	0	—	—	—
First 9 Batters			199	50	9	27	50	.251	.462	.339
Second 9 Batters			196	54	5	17	28	.276	.393	.332
All Batters Thereafter			184	48	8	13	26	.245	.424	.293

Loves to face: Mookie Wilson (.100, 2-for-20, 11 SO)
Hates to face: Vance Law (4-for-4, 4 BB)
Ground outs-to-air outs ratio: 0.67, 7th-lowest in N.L. last season (minimum: 200 BFP), 0.63 for career. . . . Additional statistics: 5 double-play ground outs in 103 opportunities, 26 doubles, 3 triples in 152.0 innings last season. . . . Allowed 19 first-inning runs in 25 starts. . . . Batting support: 4.64 runs per start. . . . June ERA was 2d-best in N.L. . . . Walked seven times (as a batter) last season, tied for most among N.L. pitchers. . . . Career record of 12–3 at the Astrodome, where opposing batters have hit .221, compared to .271 at other stadiums. . . . Opponents' career breakdown: .262 with bases empty, .231 with runners on base, .207 with runners in scoring position. . . . Has allowed 39 career home runs, only four with more than one runner on base.

Frank DiPino

Chicago Cubs — Throws Left

	W–L	ERA	AB	H	HR	BB	SO	BA	SA	OBA
Season	3-3	3.15	297	75	7	34	61	.253	.367	.327
vs. Left-Handers			94	23	2	5	23	.245	.340	.284
vs. Right-Handers			203	52	5	29	38	.256	.379	.346
Home	3-2	2.68	154	33	4	21	40	.214	.331	.311
Road	0-1	3.72	143	42	3	13	21	.294	.406	.346
Grass	3-3	3.03	217	51	6	26	51	.235	.350	.317
Artificial Turf	0-0	3.48	80	24	1	8	10	.300	.413	.356
April	0-0	0.00	17	3	0	4	5	.176	.294	.318
May	1-0	3.00	57	14	3	4	12	.246	.421	.290
June	0-1	3.38	50	14	1	7	10	.280	.380	.379
July	0-1	6.75	24	7	0	2	8	.292	.375	.346
August	2-1	3.13	81	19	2	10	17	.235	.346	.319
Sept./Oct.	0-0	2.60	68	18	1	7	11	.265	.353	.325
Leading Off Inn.			63	11	1	4	14	.175	.238	.235
Runners On			144	38	2	19	30	.264	.361	.341
Runners/Scor. Pos.			86	24	0	15	19	.279	.326	.371
Runners On/2 Out			68	16	1	12	16	.235	.324	.350
Scor. Pos./2 Out			46	12	0	9	10	.261	.326	.382
Late Inning Pressure			134	30	2	13	30	.224	.291	.293
Leading Off			33	5	0	1	9	.152	.152	.200
Runners On			55	12	0	7	11	.218	.236	.297
Runners/Scor. Pos.			36	10	0	5	7	.278	.278	.349
First 9 Batters			285	71	7	32	60	.249	.368	.324
Second 9 Batters			12	4	0	2	1	.333	.333	.400
All Batters Thereafter			0	0	0	0	0			

Loves to face: Joel Youngblood (0-for-10)
Hates to face: Candy Maldonado (.667, 6-for-9, 1 HR)
Ground outs-to-air outs ratio: 1.27 last season, 1.22 for career. . . . Additional statistics: 5 double-play ground outs in 71 opportunities, 11 doubles, 1 triple in 80.0 innings last season. . . . What happens to a pitcher's home/road stats when he's traded from the Astrodome to Wrigley Field? Wrong! Opponents batting average in home games last season was his lowest since 1983. . . . Last season's record marked the first time that he'd won as many games as he lost since 1982 when he recorded the first decisions of his major-league career. Only two other pitchers who were active last season have streaks of at least six seasons without a winning record: Ron Davis and Gene Garber. . . . Career record is 0–6 vs. the Dodgers.

Kelly Downs

San Francisco Giants — Throws Right

	W–L	ERA	AB	H	HR	BB	SO	BA	SA	OBA
Season	12-9	3.63	718	185	14	67	137	.258	.365	.324
vs. Left-Handers			425	118	5	38	75	.278	.367	.339
vs. Right-Handers			293	67	9	29	62	.229	.362	.302
Home	5-5	3.48	324	77	6	31	68	.238	.343	.307
Road	7-4	3.75	394	108	8	36	69	.274	.383	.338
Grass	10-7	3.83	531	130	13	46	106	.245	.362	.308
Artificial Turf	2-2	3.04	187	55	1	21	31	.294	.374	.368
April	2-0	3.91	92	23	2	7	20	.250	.359	.310
May	2-2	3.06	134	34	2	14	29	.254	.388	.329
June	2-2	4.88	129	37	4	9	22	.287	.426	.333
July	2-2	3.60	141	37	3	14	27	.262	.348	.331
August	2-2	4.68	130	37	3	11	15	.285	.415	.345
Sept./Oct.	2-1	1.37	92	17	0	12	24	.185	.207	.279
Leading Off Inn.			176	46	4	17	33	.261	.381	.326
Runners On			310	86	8	31	63	.277	.416	.348
Runners/Scor. Pos.			191	46	4	26	39	.241	.361	.333
Runners On/2 Out			129	34	1	16	27	.264	.349	.354
Scor. Pos./2 Out			89	20	0	13	19	.225	.281	.330
Late Inning Pressure			71	17	1	13	12	.239	.310	.353
Leading Off			15	3	1	4	3	.200	.400	.368
Runners On			31	10	0	7	7	.323	.387	.436
Runners/Scor. Pos.			15	5	0	7	4	.333	.467	.522
First 9 Batters			288	63	1	26	69	.219	.267	.286
Second 9 Batters			221	60	7	17	44	.271	.425	.332
All Batters Thereafter			209	62	6	24	24	.297	.435	.368

Loves to face: Mike Marshall (0-for-7)
Hates to face: Ken Griffey (.462, 6-for-13, 2 HR)
Ground outs-to-air outs ratio: 1.40 last season, 1.42 for career. . . . Additional statistics: 15 double-play ground outs in 132 opportunities, 33 doubles, 1 triple in 186.0 innings last season. . . . Allowed 8 first-inning runs in 28 starts, 4th-lowest average in N.L. (minimum: 15 GS). . . . Batting support: 4.00 runs per start. . . . Record of 11–8, 3.81 ERA in 28 games as a starter; 1–1, 1.96 ERA in 13 relief appearances. . . . Beat the Padres three times in San Diego last season. He was the only major league pitcher to beat an opposing team three times in their own ballpark. . . . Career record of 53–69 in seven minor league seasons, 16–13 in two seasons with the Giants. . . . Opponents have only one hit in 12 at bats with the bases loaded, but the hit was a grand slam by Barry Lyons.

Doug Drabek

Pittsburgh Pirates — Throws Right

	W–L	ERA	AB	H	HR	BB	SO	BA	SA	OBA
Season	11-12	3.88	668	165	22	46	120	.247	.415	.294
vs. Left-Handers			349	96	15	30	54	.275	.479	.332
vs. Right-Handers			319	69	7	16	66	.216	.345	.251
Home	6-5	3.66	305	78	10	16	63	.256	.423	.291
Road	5-7	4.05	363	87	12	30	57	.240	.408	.296
Grass	2-3	3.52	141	32	6	11	21	.227	.404	.283
Artificial Turf	9-9	3.98	527	133	16	35	99	.252	.417	.297
April	1-2	3.91	88	21	4	4	19	.239	.443	.269
May	0-1	5.23	40	10	1	7	4	.250	.400	.362
June	0-4	5.09	140	43	9	9	24	.307	.443	.344
July	1-3	4.13	101	23	5	10	15	.228	.436	.297
August	5-0	2.79	152	30	3	9	29	.197	.368	.241
Sept./Oct.	4-2	3.38	147	38	4	7	29	.259	.408	.292
Leading Off Inn.			170	48	6	15	27	.282	.453	.341
Runners On			248	67	11	9	47	.270	.488	.291
Runners/Scor. Pos.			118	32	6	8	26	.271	.508	.308
Runners On/2 Out			103	26	3	5	23	.252	.437	.287
Scor. Pos./2 Out			56	14	2	4	11	.250	.446	.300
Late Inning Pressure			25	11	1	1	1	.440	.600	.462
Leading Off			9	4	0	0	0	.444	.556	.444
Runners On			6	2	1	1	0	.333	.833	.429
Runners/Scor. Pos.			0	0	0	1	0	—	—	1.000
First 9 Batters			238	57	6	18	52	.239	.391	.292
Second 9 Batters			228	42	3	19	37	.184	.303	.246
All Batters Thereafter			202	66	13	9	31	.327	.569	.352

Loves to face: Eric Davis (0-for-9)
Hates to face: Tim Raines (.556, 5-for-9, 3 HR)
Ground outs-to-air outs ratio: 1.07 last season, 0.90 for career. . . . Additional statistics: 8 double-play ground outs in 111 opportunities, 34 doubles, 6 triples in 176.1 innings last season. . . . Allowed 20 first-inning runs in 28 starts. . . . Batting support: 4.39 runs per start. . . . Lost eight of his first nine decisions, but led the N.L. with 10 wins after the All-Star break. . . . Allowed an average of 2.35 walks per nine innings last season, 5th-lowest rate in the N.L. . . . Allowed only two hits in 49 at bats to opposing pitchers; right-handed-hitting pitchers went 0-for-35 against him. . . . Opponents' career breakdown: .276 by left-handed batters, .219 by right-handers. . . . Opponents have five hits in eight at bats with the bases loaded.

Dave Dravecky
Padres/Giants — Throws Left

	W–L	ERA	AB	H	HR	BB	SO	BA	SA	OBA
Season	10-12	3.43	719	186	18	64	138	.259	.378	.321
vs. Left-Handers			106	15	3	11	34	.142	.245	.222
vs. Right-Handers			613	171	15	53	104	.279	.401	.338
Home	6-6	2.92	371	89	10	29	77	.240	.369	.299
Road	4-6	4.01	348	97	8	35	61	.279	.388	.345
Grass	8-8	2.96	489	117	14	39	97	.239	.368	.300
Artificial Turf	2-4	4.53	230	69	4	25	41	.300	.400	.366
April	0-3	4.80	63	21	1	6	17	.333	.444	.403
May	1-2	4.39	97	23	7	15	16	.237	.495	.339
June	2-2	2.89	136	27	2	10	27	.199	.279	.253
July	2-2	3.49	140	37	3	16	26	.264	.371	.335
August	3-0	2.08	161	43	2	10	29	.267	.335	.310
Sept./Oct.	2-3	4.45	122	35	3	7	23	.287	.426	.333
Leading Off Inn.			180	48	5	12	33	.267	.406	.316
Runners On			288	77	7	29	61	.267	.378	.332
Runners/Scor. Pos.			168	43	2	20	40	.256	.345	.328
Runners On/2 Out			125	32	3	16	27	.256	.360	.340
Scor. Pos./2 Out			80	22	0	12	16	.275	.313	.370
Late Inning Pressure			41	11	3	7	12	.268	.488	.375
Leading Off			11	2	1	1	3	.182	.455	.250
Runners On			13	4	0	2	3	.308	.308	.400
Runners/Scor. Pos.			5	2	0	2	0	.400	.400	.571
First 9 Batters			322	77	5	27	71	.239	.332	.299
Second 9 Batters			224	58	9	17	39	.259	.429	.320
All Batters Thereafter			173	51	4	20	28	.295	.399	.362

Loves to face: Sid Bream (0-for-11)
Hates to face: Gary Carter (.429, 9-for-21, 4 HR)
Ground outs-to-air outs ratio: 1.29 last season, 1.11 for career. . . . Additional statistics: 18 double-play ground outs in 135 opportunities, 30 doubles, 1 triple in 191.1 innings last season. . . . Allowed 8 first-inning runs in 28 starts. . . . Batting support: 4.29 runs per start. . . . Opponents were 9 for 11 stealing while with Padres, but only 11 of 19 after trade to Giants. . . . Record of 10–8 in 28 starts last season, 0–4 in 20 relief games. Career marks: 46–27 as a starter, 9–10 in relief. . . . Opposing left-handers batted 137 points lower than right-handers, largest such difference in majors (minimum: 100 AB each way). . . . Career record of 25–12 (2.45 ERA) in day games, 35–43 (3.45 ERA) at night. . . . Only player in majors with 50+ at bats in '87 (actually 56) and no RBI.

Mike Dunne
Pittsburgh Pirates — Throws Right

	W–L	ERA	AB	H	HR	BB	SO	BA	SA	OBA
Season	13-6	3.03	596	143	10	68	72	.240	.337	.317
vs. Left-Handers			324	89	8	46	23	.275	.407	.366
vs. Right-Handers			272	54	2	22	49	.199	.254	.256
Home	6-2	2.42	249	55	5	25	36	.221	.317	.292
Road	7-4	3.50	347	88	5	43	36	.254	.352	.334
Grass	3-2	2.88	131	33	1	11	16	.252	.321	.308
Artificial Turf	10-4	3.07	465	110	9	57	56	.237	.342	.319
April			0	0	0	0	0	—	—	—
May			0	0	0	0	0	—	—	—
June	3-3	3.86	151	39	2	25	20	.258	.377	.360
July	3-1	2.06	135	33	0	8	20	.244	.259	.285
August	3-1	2.45	164	34	6	16	17	.207	.341	.280
Sept./Oct.	4-1	3.72	146	37	2	19	15	.253	.363	.339
Leading Off Inn.			157	40	4	11	21	.255	.376	.304
Runners On			240	53	2	35	28	.221	.283	.315
Runners/Scor. Pos.			137	28	0	26	18	.204	.248	.323
Runners On/2 Out			95	19	1	8	17	.200	.274	.262
Scor. Pos./2 Out			57	12	0	6	10	.211	.281	.286
Late Inning Pressure			72	18	2	4	7	.250	.375	.289
Leading Off			21	6	1	1	1	.286	.429	.318
Runners On			21	6	0	2	2	.286	.333	.348
Runners/Scor. Pos.			12	3	0	1	1	.250	.333	.308
First 9 Batters			182	41	0	20	25	.225	.302	.302
Second 9 Batters			174	43	3	25	28	.247	.333	.338
All Batters Thereafter			240	59	7	23	19	.246	.367	.312

Loves to face: Vance Law (0-for-8)
Hates to face: Mitch Webster (.444, 8-for-18, 3 HR)
Ground outs-to-air outs ratio: 1.86 last season, his first in majors. . . . Additional statistics: 24 double-play ground outs in 133 opportunities, 2d-highest rate in N.L. (minimum: 20 GS), 18 doubles, 5 triples in 163.1 innings last season. . . . Allowed 17 first-inning runs in 23 starts. . . . Batting support: 3.96 runs per start. . . . Qualified for ERA championship by pitching eight innings in Bucs' season finale. Finished second to Nolan Ryan. . . . Led rookies in wins, complete games, and ERA. . . . Led N.L. with a 2.47 ERA in day games. . . . Record is 6–1 (2.47 ERA) in day games, 7–5 (3.28) at night. . . . Faced 61 batters in a row without a strikeout (Aug. 9–Aug. 20), longest N.L. streak of season. . . . Major-league debut matched him against Dwight Gooden in Doc's return from rehab.

Sid Fernandez
New York Mets — Throws Left

	W–L	ERA	AB	H	HR	BB	SO	BA	SA	OBA
Season	12-8	3.81	581	130	16	67	134	.224	.363	.310
vs. Left-Handers			71	16	2	7	14	.225	.408	.291
vs. Right-Handers			510	114	14	60	120	.224	.357	.312
Home	9-3	2.98	334	66	6	39	89	.198	.311	.292
Road	3-5	5.05	247	64	10	28	45	.259	.433	.333
Grass	10-5	3.09	406	82	8	50	103	.202	.315	.298
Artificial Turf	2-3	5.74	175	48	8	17	31	.274	.474	.337
April	4-1	2.18	124	24	2	15	35	.194	.290	.286
May	2-1	2.06	117	23	1	17	36	.197	.282	.304
June	3-2	5.65	112	29	4	7	22	.259	.420	.306
July	1-2	4.34	112	27	3	14	17	.241	.411	.341
August	0-2	9.00	25	8	2	3	4	.320	.600	.379
Sept./Oct.	2-0	4.44	91	19	4	11	20	.209	.374	.295
Leading Off Inn.			145	31	8	14	33	.214	.414	.292
Runners On			234	55	6	29	54	.235	.376	.320
Runners/Scor. Pos.			128	28	2	23	30	.219	.305	.329
Runners On/2 Out			107	23	3	17	21	.215	.383	.328
Scor. Pos./2 Out			65	14	1	13	12	.215	.292	.354
Late Inning Pressure			44	8	0	4	12	.182	.205	.265
Leading Off			13	3	0	0	3	.231	.231	.286
Runners On			18	1	0	0	6	.056	.056	.056
Runners/Scor. Pos.			4	1	0	0	1	.250	.250	.250
First 9 Batters			217	45	7	23	66	.207	.341	.288
Second 9 Batters			191	41	4	26	34	.215	.335	.303
All Batters Thereafter			173	44	5	18	34	.254	.434	.333

Loves to face: Ozzie Virgil (0-for-21)
Hates to face: Graig Nettles (.467, 7-for-15, 1 HR)
Ground outs-to-air outs ratio: 0.46, lowest in N.L. last season (minimum: 200 BFP), 0.48 for career. . . . Additional statistics: 2 double-play ground outs in 102 opportunities, lowest rate in majors (minimum: 20 GS), 25 doubles, 4 triples in 156.0 innings last season. . . . Allowed 8 first-inning runs in 27 starts. . . . Batting support: 5.22 runs per start, 8th-highest average in N.L. (minimum: 15 GS). . . . Averaged 5.70 innings per start, lowest average among Mets' regular starters. . . . Walked opposing pitchers six times last season, most in N.L.; meanwhile, he held top 15 N.L. batters to a .187 average. . . . Career record of 24–12 with a 2.91 ERA before the All-Star break; 19–18, 3.88 ERA after the break. . . . Opponents have hit .200 or less at Shea Stadium in each of his four seasons with Mets.

Brian Fisher
Pittsburgh Pirates — Throws Right

	W–L	ERA	AB	H	HR	BB	SO	BA	SA	OBA
Season	11-9	4.52	705	185	27	72	117	.262	.458	.332
vs. Left-Handers			377	100	9	50	56	.265	.438	.350
vs. Right-Handers			328	85	18	22	61	.259	.482	.311
Home	4-5	5.79	333	108	10	28	48	.324	.547	.375
Road	7-4	3.50	372	77	17	44	69	.207	.379	.294
Grass	4-2	3.69	169	35	10	24	28	.207	.414	.309
Artificial Turf	7-7	4.79	536	150	17	48	89	.280	.472	.340
April	0-0	7.71	47	13	0	6	12	.277	.426	.370
May	2-1	3.64	112	31	1	15	18	.277	.375	.362
June	2-3	5.73	139	46	7	14	22	.331	.583	.396
July	2-2	3.93	127	31	5	10	18	.244	.472	.298
August	1-2	4.71	133	32	7	12	18	.241	.459	.301
Sept./Oct.	4-1	3.57	147	32	7	15	29	.218	.395	.293
Leading Off Inn.			176	51	8	17	25	.290	.500	.359
Runners On			290	73	9	30	49	.252	.455	.317
Runners/Scor. Pos.			179	40	7	19	33	.223	.419	.291
Runners On/2 Out			109	18	1	12	21	.165	.229	.248
Scor. Pos./2 Out			72	9	1	9	15	.125	.181	.222
Late Inning Pressure			54	13	2	5	10	.241	.426	.317
Leading Off			15	2	0	3	2	.133	.200	.316
Runners On			14	8	2	0	2	.571	1.214	.571
Runners/Scor. Pos.			9	5	2	0	1	.556	1.444	.556
First 9 Batters			260	68	11	39	54	.262	.462	.361
Second 9 Batters			217	63	8	15	31	.290	.525	.339
All Batters Thereafter			228	54	8	18	32	.237	.390	.290

Loves to face: Jeff Reed (0-for-7)
Hates to face: Tom Foley (.545, 6-for-11, 1 HR)
Ground outs-to-air outs ratio: 0.94 last season, 0.97 for career. . . . Additional statistics: 10 double-play ground outs in 126 opportunities, 39 doubles, 9 triples in 185.1 innings last season. . . . Allowed 13 first-inning runs in 26 starts. . . . Batting support: 4.58 runs per start. . . . Drabek, Easley, and Fisher had a combined record of 6–15 before the All-Star break, 16–5 after the break. Meanwhile, Clements, Guante, and Rhoden were a combined 16–8 before the break, 6–7 thereafter. . . . Won all four starts vs. Cubs, with 1.45 ERA, and was only pitcher to shut them out twice. . . . Also was the only pitcher to shut out Cardinals in St. Louis. . . . One of two pitchers to hit two HR last season. . . . Opponents' career batting average is .406 (13-for-32, 6 XBH, 2 HR) with the bases loaded.

Bob Forsch
St. Louis Cardinals — Throws Right

	W–L	ERA	AB	H	HR	BB	SO	BA	SA	OBA
Season	11-7	4.32	693	189	15	45	89	.273	.410	.318
vs. Left-Handers			375	99	4	28	45	.264	.363	.313
vs. Right-Handers			318	90	11	17	44	.283	.465	.324
Home	3-4	4.54	267	72	6	24	49	.270	.419	.331
Road	8-3	4.19	426	117	9	21	40	.275	.404	.310
Grass	5-2	4.10	247	67	6	14	26	.271	.413	.312
Artificial Turf	6-5	4.45	446	122	9	31	63	.274	.408	.322
April	2-1	4.43	89	27	1	4	11	.303	.438	.340
May	2-0	5.79	120	40	3	6	9	.333	.492	.365
June	2-2	5.46	118	35	2	7	16	.297	.449	.333
July	3-0	2.93	142	30	3	14	14	.211	.324	.288
August	1-1	3.86	113	30	3	10	15	.265	.416	.325
Sept./Oct.	1-3	4.08	111	27	3	4	24	.243	.360	.267
Leading Off Inn.			183	50	3	8	28	.273	.404	.304
Runners On			267	81	8	20	28	.303	.457	.349
Runners/Scor. Pos.			153	43	3	16	16	.281	.412	.341
Runners On/2 Out			116	33	4	7	11	.284	.474	.336
Scor. Pos./2 Out			74	18	2	7	7	.243	.419	.317
Late Inning Pressure			33	8	0	4	8	.242	.303	.324
Leading Off			10	2	0	1	4	.200	.200	.273
Runners On			12	3	0	3	2	.250	.417	.400
Runners/Scor. Pos.			8	2	0	3	1	.250	.500	.455
First 9 Batters			260	68	5	14	37	.262	.385	.301
Second 9 Batters			235	65	5	14	33	.277	.404	.316
All Batters Thereafter			198	56	5	17	19	.283	.449	.343

Loves to face: Len Dykstra (0-for-14)
Hates to face: Darryl Strawberry (.450, 9-for-20, 5 HR)
Ground outs-to-air outs ratio: 1.05 last season, 1.43 for career.... Additional statistics: 11 double-play ground outs in 126 opportunities, 38 doubles, 6 triples in 179.0 innings last season.... Allowed 19 first-inning runs in 30 starts.... Batting support: 5.63 runs per start, 3d-highest average in N.L. (minimum: 15 GS).... ERA was 2d highest of his career to a 6.02 mark in 1984.... Averaged 5.82 innings per start, lowest among Cards' regular starters.... One of two pitchers to hit two home runs last season. Also led pitchers with eight extra-base hits (as a batter).... Over the last four seasons, he's walked an average of one out of 12.3 batters leading off innings, one per 22.6 batters faced at other times.

John Franco
Cincinnati Reds — Throws Left

	W–L	ERA	AB	H	HR	BB	SO	BA	SA	OBA
Season	8-5	2.52	310	76	6	27	61	.245	.345	.304
vs. Left-Handers			46	11	0	3	11	.239	.283	.280
vs. Right-Handers			264	65	6	24	50	.246	.356	.308
Home	4-2	4.14	142	44	4	12	25	.310	.444	.359
Road	4-3	1.20	168	32	2	15	36	.190	.262	.257
Grass	2-2	1.33	102	19	2	12	20	.186	.275	.272
Artificial Turf	6-3	3.11	208	57	4	15	41	.274	.380	.320
April	1-0	0.00	24	0	0	0	3	.000	.000	.000
May	1-1	1.59	44	11	1	3	10	.250	.386	.298
June	3-1	0.52	64	14	1	7	10	.219	.313	.296
July	2-1	4.30	53	12	2	6	9	.226	.396	.305
August	0-2	5.19	77	29	2	5	16	.377	.494	.410
Sept./Oct.	1-0	2.03	48	10	0	6	13	.208	.229	.291
Leading Off Inn.			72	20	4	2	12	.278	.500	.297
Runners On			140	36	1	18	29	.257	.321	.338
Runners/Scor. Pos.			81	16	0	17	20	.198	.235	.330
Runners On/2 Out			69	20	0	10	14	.290	.362	.380
Scor. Pos./2 Out			47	14	0	9	11	.298	.362	.411
Late Inning Pressure			205	48	3	24	39	.234	.322	.313
Leading Off			44	12	2	2	8	.273	.477	.304
Runners On			104	25	0	16	22	.240	.279	.339
Runners/Scor. Pos.			65	13	0	15	16	.200	.246	.346
First 9 Batters			296	70	6	25	60	.236	.338	.294
Second 9 Batters			14	6	0	2	1	.429	.500	.500
All Batters Thereafter			0	0	0	0	0			

Loves to face: Alan Ashby (0-for-9)
Hates to face: Andre Dawson (.714, 5-for-7)
Ground outs-to-air outs ratio: 1.54 last season, 1.77 for career.... Additional statistics: 8 double-play ground outs in 69 opportunities, 13 doubles, 0 triples in 82.0 innings last season.... Earned 32 saves in 41 opportunities.... Retired the first 32 batters he faced in 1987. In Franco's 12th appearance, Vance Law doubled to snap the streak.... ERA was below 1.00 as late as July 6.... Opposing Mets batters were hitless in 12 at bats last season.... Only pitcher to work at least 75 innings with an ERA below 3.00 in each of the last four seasons.... Hasn't allowed a home run to a left-handed batter since Apr. 13, 1985, during which time he's allowed 16 to right-handers.... Career record of 6–0 vs. San Diego.

Gene Garber
Atlanta Braves — Throws Right

	W–L	ERA	AB	H	HR	BB	SO	BA	SA	OBA
Season	8-10	4.41	280	87	7	28	48	.311	.450	.372
vs. Left-Handers			129	36	2	14	26	.279	.380	.350
vs. Right-Handers			151	51	5	14	22	.338	.510	.391
Home	7-3	3.83	168	50	5	16	31	.298	.452	.355
Road	1-7	5.33	112	37	2	12	17	.330	.446	.397
Grass	8-6	4.31	219	68	6	21	37	.311	.466	.369
Artificial Turf	0-4	4.80	61	19	1	7	11	.311	.393	.382
April	3-2	6.92	55	20	3	5	4	.364	.600	.410
May	4-1	2.40	54	11	1	7	12	.204	.296	.290
June	1-3	2.93	59	17	1	5	11	.288	.424	.344
July	0-1	3.21	55	16	1	5	16	.291	.382	.344
August	0-3	7.50	57	23	1	6	5	.404	.544	.469
Sept./Oct.			0	0	0	0	0	—	—	—
Leading Off Inn.			57	18	1	2	12	.316	.491	.339
Runners On			161	46	4	19	29	.286	.391	.359
Runners/Scor. Pos.			117	29	3	19	25	.248	.350	.350
Runners On/2 Out			76	24	2	12	15	.316	.447	.409
Scor. Pos./2 Out			61	17	2	12	13	.279	.426	.397
Late Inning Pressure			207	65	4	22	37	.314	.435	.378
Leading Off			46	16	1	2	10	.348	.565	.375
Runners On			115	33	2	15	20	.287	.348	.366
Runners/Scor. Pos.			87	20	1	15	18	.230	.276	.340
First 9 Batters			260	80	6	27	44	.308	.442	.371
Second 9 Batters			20	7	1	1	4	.350	.550	.381
All Batters Thereafter			0	0	0	0	0	—	—	—

Loves to face: Lee Lacy (.050, 1-for-20)
Hates to face: Terry Kennedy (.421, 8-for-19, 1 HR)
Figures *above* are for N.L. only.... Ground outs-to-air outs ratio: 2.48 last season, 2.19 for career.... Additional statistics: 9 double-play ground outs in 72 opportunities, 18 doubles, 2 triples in 83.2 innings last season.... Earned 18 saves in 26 opportunities. Tied for A.L. lead with seven in September.... Failed to post a winning record for 10th season in a row, the longest streak among currently active players.... Four-decade candidate has made only nine starts among his 905 appearances: his major-league debut on June 17, 1969 (in which he allowed home runs in the same inning to Willie Smith, Billy Williams, and Don Kessinger), and eight more for Royals in 1973.... Returned to K.C. after 13-year absence. Was a teammate of Orlando Cepeda last time around.

Scott Garrelts
San Francisco Giants — Throws Right

	W–L	ERA	AB	H	HR	BB	SO	BA	SA	OBA
Season	11-7	3.22	364	70	10	55	127	.192	.310	.297
vs. Left-Handers			194	35	4	28	67	.180	.284	.283
vs. Right-Handers			170	35	6	27	60	.206	.341	.313
Home	5-3	3.86	145	29	5	18	51	.200	.359	.287
Road	6-4	2.80	219	41	5	37	76	.187	.279	.304
Grass	9-5	3.21	246	44	8	37	84	.179	.317	.284
Artificial Turf	2-2	3.24	118	26	2	18	43	.220	.297	.324
April	3-2	4.12	68	14	3	14	22	.206	.368	.341
May	2-1	1.69	69	15	1	9	30	.217	.333	.308
June	1-2	3.72	68	13	1	9	25	.191	.294	.282
July	3-2	3.66	67	12	3	7	26	.179	.328	.253
August	2-0	2.08	63	13	0	8	20	.206	.222	.296
Sept./Oct.	0-0	5.00	29	3	2	8	4	.103	.310	.297
Leading Off Inn.			79	17	1	16	23	.215	.304	.347
Runners On			164	33	7	26	53	.201	.354	.307
Runners/Scor. Pos.			93	19	3	22	32	.204	.344	.350
Runners On/2 Out			68	13	4	14	28	.191	.382	.329
Scor. Pos./2 Out			42	8	2	12	17	.190	.357	.370
Late Inning Pressure			251	49	6	36	95	.195	.307	.294
Leading Off			54	13	1	11	18	.241	.352	.369
Runners On			117	22	4	15	42	.188	.308	.276
Runners/Scor. Pos.			66	14	2	14	25	.212	.333	.341
First 9 Batters			341	64	9	54	117	.188	.299	.297
Second 9 Batters			23	6	1	1	10	.261	.478	.292
All Batters Thereafter			0	0	0	0	0	—	—	—

Loves to face: Keith Moreland (0-for-15)
Hates to face: Mike Marshall (.524, 11-for-21, 4 HR)
Ground outs-to-air outs ratio: 1.51 last season, 1.30 for career.... Additional statistics: 10 double-play ground outs in 83 opportunities, 7 doubles, 3 triples in 106.1 innings last season.... Earned 12 saves, all before the All-Star break, in 26 opportunities.... Averaged 10.75 strikeouts per nine innings, 3d-highest rate among N.L. relievers (minimum: 30 games).... Career averages: 9.41 in relief, 5.03 as a starter.... Was the winning pitcher in three consecutive appearances for the first time in his career (July 19–26).... Career records: 23–13, 2.80 ERA at Candlestick Park; 14–14, 3.53 ERA on the road. 23–11, 2.84 in day games; 14–16, 3.50 ERA at night.... Opponents' career breakdown: .232 by left-handed batters, .211 by right-handers.

Dwight Gooden

New York Mets — Throws Right

	W–L	ERA	AB	H	HR	BB	SO	BA	SA	OBA
Season	15-7	3.21	665	162	11	53	148	.244	.344	.299
vs. Left-Handers			368	88	5	35	77	.239	.318	.304
vs. Right-Handers			297	74	6	18	71	.249	.377	.293
Home	8-5	3.41	345	85	6	34	73	.246	.336	.313
Road	7-2	2.98	320	77	5	19	75	.241	.353	.284
Grass	12-5	3.13	495	122	9	41	106	.246	.347	.303
Artificial Turf	3-2	3.43	170	40	2	12	42	.235	.335	.290
April			0	0	0	0	0	—	—	—
May			0	0	0	0	0	—	—	—
June	5-1	2.12	164	35	3	16	43	.213	.329	.280
July	3-2	3.30	164	43	2	10	24	.262	.366	.311
August	4-1	3.24	158	40	3	15	32	.253	.354	.318
Sept./Oct.	3-3	4.15	179	44	3	12	49	.246	.330	.290
Leading Off Inn.			169	45	4	13	34	.266	.379	.322
Runners On			273	63	3	21	57	.231	.311	.283
Runners/Scor. Pos.			164	36	0	18	36	.220	.262	.293
Runners On/2 Out			114	25	2	8	24	.219	.333	.276
Scor. Pos./2 Out			74	15	0	8	15	.203	.284	.289
Late Inning Pressure			88	24	2	8	19	.273	.398	.337
Leading Off			26	8	0	1	5	.308	.346	.333
Runners On			28	7	0	5	6	.250	.321	.371
Runners/Scor. Pos.			14	4	0	3	1	.286	.286	.421
First 9 Batters			198	53	2	19	37	.268	.323	.329
Second 9 Batters			203	48	5	11	45	.236	.365	.274
All Batters Thereafter			264	61	4	23	66	.231	.345	.296

Loves to face: Marvell Wynne (0-for-19)
Hates to face: Bo Diaz (.714, 5-for-7)
Ground outs-to-air outs ratio: 1.54 last season, 1.14 for career. . . .
Additional statistics: 19 double-play ground outs in opportunities, 26 doubles, 4 triples in 179.2 innings last season. . . . Allowed 14 first-inning runs in 25 starts. . . . Batting support: 5.04 runs per start, 10th-highest average in N.L. (minimum: 15 GS). . . . Only pitcher in majors with 10+ wins and sub-3.50 ERA in each of last four seasons. . . . Night-game ERA of 2.29 was best in majors. Career breakdown: 20–15, 3.64 ERA in day games; 53–11, 1.90 ERA at night. . . . Annual batting averages by opposing right-handed batters since 1984: .170, .198, .221, .249. . . . Opponents have only three hits in 44 career at bats with two out and runners in scoring position in Late-Inning Pressure Situations (.068).

Rich Gossage

San Diego Padres — Throws Right

	W–L	ERA	AB	H	HR	BB	SO	BA	SA	OBA
Season	5-4	3.12	193	47	4	19	44	.244	.383	.307
vs. Left-Handers			101	25	2	16	21	.248	.396	.342
vs. Right-Handers			92	22	2	3	23	.239	.370	.263
Home	3-1	3.20	93	21	3	6	22	.226	.387	.270
Road	2-3	3.04	100	26	1	13	22	.260	.380	.339
Grass	3-2	3.79	130	30	3	15	31	.231	.385	.304
Artificial Turf	2-2	1.65	63	17	1	4	13	.270	.381	.313
April			0	0	0	0	0	—	—	—
May	0-0	3.97	42	11	1	6	11	.262	.429	.347
June	0-0	0.00	34	7	0	2	10	.206	.265	.243
July	2-3	3.97	44	14	2	6	11	.318	.568	.400
August	2-0	3.18	47	11	1	0	6	.234	.340	.234
Sept./Oct.	1-1	4.70	26	4	0	5	6	.154	.231	.281
Leading Off Inn.			43	8	0	3	13	.186	.209	.239
Runners On			88	21	2	14	17	.239	.398	.333
Runners/Scor. Pos.			57	11	0	11	12	.193	.298	.310
Runners On/2 Out			45	12	1	7	8	.267	.511	.365
Scor. Pos./2 Out			35	9	0	6	7	.257	.429	.366
Late Inning Pressure			125	29	3	16	27	.232	.384	.313
Leading Off			32	5	0	2	11	.156	.188	.206
Runners On			47	10	1	13	6	.213	.362	.365
Runners/Scor. Pos.			33	6	0	10	5	.182	.273	.348
First 9 Batters			187	46	4	19	44	.246	.385	.311
Second 9 Batters			6	1	0	0	0	.167	.333	.167
All Batters Thereafter			0	0	0	0	0			

Loves to face: Dale Murphy (.056, 1-for-18)
Hates to face: Kevin Bass (.625, 5-for-8)
Ground outs-to-air outs ratio: 0.87 last season, 0.83 for career. . . .
Additional statistics: 5 double-play ground outs in 44 opportunities, 13 doubles, 1 triple in 52.0 innings last season. . . . Earned 11 saves in 17 opportunities, raising totals to 83-for-119 (.697) during four seasons with Padres. . . . Bitched that Yankees brought him into too many tight spots. Entered only 12 games last season with runners in scoring position, started innings 26 times in 40 appearances. . . . Opponents' batting average leading off innings has been under .200 in nine of the last 11 seasons. . . . It's official. Goose was the pitcher for Pete Rose's final at bat, a pinch-hit strikeout on Aug. 17, 1986. . . . Has defeated every major–league team except Atlanta and Seattle.

Jim Gott

Giants/Pirates — Throws Right

	W–L	ERA	AB	H	HR	BB	SO	BA	SA	OBA
Season	1-2	3.41	337	81	4	40	90	.240	.315	.324
vs. Left-Handers			161	47	4	29	47	.292	.422	.401
vs. Right-Handers			176	34	0	11	43	.193	.216	.245
Home	0-1	3.15	152	34	1	18	44	.224	.276	.306
Road	1-1	3.64	185	47	3	22	46	.254	.346	.338
Grass	1-0	3.65	172	39	1	25	54	.227	.279	.328
Artificial Turf	0-2	3.16	165	42	3	15	36	.255	.352	.319
April	1-0	3.38	31	9	0	4	8	.290	.387	.389
May	0-0	6.75	59	16	0	7	16	.271	.356	.353
June	0-0	3.98	74	16	3	14	22	.216	.365	.341
July	0-0	3.46	53	12	1	7	17	.226	.283	.317
August	0-1	2.08	53	14	0	3	10	.264	.283	.304
Sept./Oct.	0-1	1.00	67	14	0	5	17	.209	.239	.264
Leading Off Inn.			72	15	1	8	19	.208	.264	.296
Runners On			174	45	1	18	46	.259	.328	.326
Runners/Scor. Pos.			107	23	1	16	31	.215	.299	.315
Runners On/2 Out			76	15	0	6	23	.197	.211	.256
Scor. Pos./2 Out			49	7	0	6	15	.143	.163	.236
Late Inning Pressure			107	23	1	13	26	.215	.271	.300
Leading Off			20	3	0	4	5	.150	.200	.292
Runners On			60	14	1	6	13	.233	.300	.303
Runners/Scor. Pos.			36	6	1	6	9	.167	.278	.286
First 9 Batters			290	68	2	30	78	.234	.293	.307
Second 9 Batters			34	8	1	8	10	.235	.382	.395
All Batters Thereafter			13	5	1	2	2	.385	.615	.467

Loves to face: Ryne Sandberg (.067, 1-for-15)
Hates to face: Leon Durham (.500, 5-for-10, 2 HR)
Ground outs-to-air outs ratio: 1.82 last season, 1.37 for career. . . .
Additional statistics: 3 double-play ground outs in 82 opportunities, 9 doubles, 2 triples in 87.0 innings last season. . . . Earned 13 saves in 16 opportunities. . . . No saves in 27 relief appearances for the Giants, 13 in 25 games for the Bucs. . . . Faced 189 right-handed batters without allowing a home run, highest total in N.L. Last HR by an opposing right-hander was hit by Kevin Gross in 1985. . . . Has walked only one of 56 batters faced with the bases loaded. . . . Gott and Jeff Robinson, the relievers acquired from Giants, have superb career marks in the ultimate category: two outs and runners in scoring position in Late-Inning Pressure Situations. Opposing batters are 4-for-40 vs. Robinson, 5-for-46 vs. Gott.

Mark Grant

Giants/Padres — Throws Right

	W–L	ERA	AB	H	HR	BB	SO	BA	SA	OBA
Season	7-9	4.24	630	170	22	73	90	.270	.433	.346
vs. Left-Handers			367	95	7	48	47	.259	.379	.344
vs. Right-Handers			263	75	15	25	43	.285	.510	.349
Home	4-5	3.94	357	87	11	35	52	.244	.398	.312
Road	3-4	4.65	273	83	11	38	38	.304	.480	.389
Grass	5-6	3.87	472	118	16	51	66	.250	.409	.324
Artificial Turf	2-3	5.50	158	52	6	22	24	.329	.506	.411
April	1-0	2.42	83	23	2	9	13	.277	.386	.355
May	0-1	5.32	94	29	3	9	12	.309	.447	.365
June	0-1	2.40	57	14	1	3	7	.246	.404	.283
July	1-3	5.52	121	34	6	16	8	.281	.512	.365
August	3-2	4.63	141	40	4	14	22	.284	.433	.348
Sept./Oct.	2-2	3.96	134	30	6	22	28	.224	.396	.333
Leading Off Inn.			158	45	8	11	24	.285	.513	.335
Runners On			268	71	13	38	38	.265	.463	.355
Runners/Scor. Pos.			158	39	8	30	22	.247	.443	.365
Runners On/2 Out			115	31	6	21	17	.270	.487	.382
Scor. Pos./2 Out			73	17	3	18	9	.233	.411	.385
Late Inning Pressure			40	16	2	5	3	.400	.625	.467
Leading Off			11	6	0	1	1	.545	.636	.583
Runners On			21	6	2	3	2	.286	.619	.375
Runners/Scor. Pos.			13	4	1	1	2	.308	.538	.357
First 9 Batters			230	50	11	33	46	.217	.417	.314
Second 9 Batters			220	61	5	17	27	.277	.395	.332
All Batters Thereafter			180	59	6	23	17	.328	.500	.404

Loves to face: Rafael Ramirez (0-for-10)
Hates to face: Andre Dawson (.727, 8-for-11, 3 HR)
Ground outs-to-air outs ratio: 1.20 last season, 1.14 for career. . . .
Additional statistics: 14 double-play ground outs in 128 opportunities, 33 doubles, 2 triples in 163.1 innings last season. . . . Allowed 11 first-inning runs in 25 starts. . . . Batting support: 3.88 runs per start, 9th-lowest average in N.L. (minimum: 15 GS). . . . Made seven consecutive starts without a decision (Apr. 19–June 24) longest streak in majors last season. . . . ERA of 1.80 in 35 innings pitched vs. Atlanta last season; led the league with a 0.71 ERA against Pirates. . . . In two previous seasons, opponents hit .370 with runners on, .189 with bases empty. . . . Fourth pitcher selected in June 1981 free-agent draft, after Mike Moore, Matt Williams (who's pitched just 34 innings in majors), and Ron Darling.

Kevin Gross

Philadelphia Phillies   Throws Right

	W–L	ERA	AB	H	HR	BB	SO	BA	SA	OBA
Season	9-16	4.35	767	205	26	87	110	.267	.429	.347
vs. Left-Handers			424	118	12	58	52	.278	.432	.369
vs. Right-Handers			343	87	14	29	58	.254	.426	.318
Home	5-11	3.85	438	110	15	51	66	.251	.409	.331
Road	4-5	5.09	329	95	11	36	44	.289	.456	.369
Grass	1-4	6.97	182	59	7	12	24	.324	.522	.382
Artificial Turf	8-12	3.67	585	146	19	75	86	.250	.400	.337
April	0-3	3.68	80	21	1	9	11	.263	.350	.348
May	3-1	3.48	128	35	6	12	17	.273	.461	.338
June	3-3	5.21	145	40	4	16	20	.276	.434	.360
July	0-2	4.29	133	36	5	18	12	.271	.451	.359
August	2-3	4.91	150	43	7	15	24	.287	.473	.355
Sept./Oct.	1-4	4.15	131	30	3	17	26	.229	.366	.320
Leading Off Inn.			180	52	8	25	27	.289	.506	.393
Runners On			354	87	3	35	50	.246	.345	.312
Runners/Scor. Pos.			203	53	2	28	29	.261	.365	.347
Runners On/2 Out			133	28	1	19	23	.211	.278	.318
Scor. Pos./2 Out			89	20	0	16	14	.225	.292	.355
Late Inning Pressure			59	16	4	8	9	.271	.525	.358
Leading Off			18	4	1	0	3	.222	.444	.222
Runners On			22	5	1	3	4	.227	.364	.320
Runners/Scor. Pos.			11	1	0	2	3	.091	.091	.231
First 9 Batters			263	71	10	25	39	.270	.445	.338
Second 9 Batters			254	72	7	29	34	.283	.433	.360
All Batters Thereafter			250	62	9	33	37	.248	.408	.344

Loves to face: Dave Martinez (.053, 1-for-19)
Hates to face: Jerry Mumphrey (.455, 10-for-22, 4 HR)
Ground outs-to-air outs ratio: 0.99 last season, 1.04 for career. . . . Additional statistics: 14 double-play ground outs in 156 opportunities, 30 doubles, 8 triples in 200.2 innings last season. . . . Allowed 16 first-inning runs in 33 starts. . . . Batting support: 3.58 runs per start, 5th-lowest average in N.L. (minimum: 15 GS). . . . Only N.L. pitcher to lose 11 home games. . . . Failed to complete five innings 10 times, one fewer than N.L. co-leaders Mike Krukow and Floyd Youmans. . . . One of five N.L. pitchers to throw more than 200 innings in each of the past three seasons. The others: Darling, Hershiser, Scott, and Valenzuela. . . . One of two N.L. pitchers (Bob Forsch is the other) to have hit a home run in each of the last three seasons.

Atlee Hammaker

San Francisco Giants   Throws Left

	W–L	ERA	AB	H	HR	BB	SO	BA	SA	OBA
Season	10-10	3.58	640	159	22	57	107	.248	.386	.312
vs. Left-Handers			107	18	1	11	24	.168	.215	.258
vs. Right-Handers			533	141	21	46	83	.265	.420	.322
Home	9-2	2.73	369	80	12	32	53	.217	.352	.280
Road	1-8	4.91	271	79	10	25	54	.292	.432	.353
Grass	9-7	3.55	479	121	17	39	74	.253	.401	.312
Artificial Turf	1-3	3.67	161	38	5	18	33	.236	.342	.311
April			0	0	0	0	0	—	—	—
May	2-1	1.86	107	24	1	8	18	.224	.280	.284
June	2-4	4.25	137	32	6	12	27	.234	.409	.291
July	2-3	3.62	140	41	4	16	19	.293	.393	.367
August	3-1	4.25	137	30	5	12	23	.219	.380	.282
Sept./Oct.	1-1	4.80	119	32	6	9	20	.269	.454	.326
Leading Off Inn.			162	40	8	13	25	.247	.426	.303
Runners On			252	68	8	26	49	.270	.397	.342
Runners/Scor. Pos.			143	31	4	20	34	.217	.329	.315
Runners On/2 Out			104	29	3	11	19	.279	.404	.348
Scor. Pos./2 Out			70	16	2	10	16	.229	.343	.325
Late Inning Pressure			41	13	1	4	8	.317	.415	.370
Leading Off			13	5	1	0	2	.385	.615	.385
Runners On			15	4	0	2	4	.267	.333	.333
Runners/Scor. Pos.			9	2	0	0	3	.222	.333	.200
First 9 Batters			242	55	6	21	46	.227	.335	.291
Second 9 Batters			223	56	7	19	34	.251	.390	.316
All Batters Thereafter			175	48	9	17	27	.274	.451	.335

Loves to face: Von Hayes (.105, 2-for-19)
Hates to face: Dale Murphy (.556, 15-for-27, 5 HR)
Ground outs-to-air outs ratio: 1.43 last season, 1.39 for career. . . . Additional statistics: 18 double-play ground outs in 127 opportunities, 22 doubles, 0 triples in 168.1 innings last season. . . . Allowed 13 first-inning runs in 27 starts. . . . Batting support: 4.85 runs per start. . . . Career record of 26–10 with a 2.89 ERA at Candlestick; 14–32, 4.09 ERA elsewhere. Home-game ERA of 2.56 is 5th lowest in majors over past five seasons (minimum: 250 IP). . . . Opponents' career batting averages: .184 by left-handed batters, .266 by right-handers. Allowed only three RBI by left-handers last season (a single by Keith Hernandez, a 2-run HR by Darryl Strawberry). . . . Averaged 1.68 walks per nine innings prior to 1984, 2.48 in 1985, 3.05 last season.

Bill Gullickson

Cincinnati Reds   Throws Right

	W–L	ERA	AB	H	HR	BB	SO	BA	SA	OBA
Season	10-11	4.85	645	172	33	39	89	.267	.487	.308
vs. Left-Handers			336	88	17	22	35	.262	.479	.305
vs. Right-Handers			309	84	16	17	54	.272	.495	.311
Home	5-5	5.63	309	87	15	16	43	.282	.508	.314
Road	5-6	4.18	336	85	18	23	46	.253	.467	.302
Grass	2-4	4.78	161	41	11	11	21	.255	.503	.306
Artificial Turf	8-7	4.88	484	131	22	28	68	.271	.481	.308
April	3-1	2.41	117	26	3	4	18	.222	.385	.248
May	4-1	4.54	155	40	7	7	28	.258	.458	.291
June	0-3	7.76	124	39	13	8	14	.315	.702	.358
July	3-2	3.74	132	33	5	11	14	.250	.409	.303
August	0-4	6.52	117	34	5	9	15	.291	.487	.339
Sept./Oct.			0	0	0	0	0	—	—	—
Leading Off Inn.			162	43	4	8	20	.265	.395	.300
Runners On			243	66	11	14	28	.272	.494	.307
Runners/Scor. Pos.			147	37	7	9	19	.252	.476	.288
Runners On/2 Out			104	27	6	13	15	.260	.519	.347
Scor. Pos./2 Out			74	18	5	9	12	.243	.514	.333
Late Inning Pressure			28	9	0	1	2	.321	.393	.345
Leading Off			9	5	0	0	0	.556	.667	.556
Runners On			10	3	0	0	0	.300	.400	.300
Runners/Scor. Pos.			5	0	0	0	0	.000	.000	.000
First 9 Batters			222	54	5	14	35	.243	.369	.283
Second 9 Batters			218	56	14	13	31	.257	.518	.300
All Batters Thereafter			205	62	14	12	23	.302	.580	.342

Loves to face: George Vukovich (.182, 2-for-11)
Hates to face: Gary Rajsich (.600, 3-for-5, 1 BB, 1 HBP)
Figures *above* are for N.L. only. . . . Ground outs-to-air outs ratio: 0.77 last season, 0.91 for career. . . . Additional statistics: 9 double-play ground outs in 123 opportunities, 43 doubles, 5 triples in 213.0 innings last season. . . . Allowed 15 first-inning runs in 27 starts. . . . Batting support: 4.70 runs per start. . . . Opponents' batting average with runners in scoring position (.279) was the highest of his career. . . . Made nine starts in which he didn't issue a walk, most in N.L. . . . Had combined-leagues record of 14–13, his fifth winning season; only Morris (9), Tudor, (8) and Candelaria (6) have streaks that long. Curiously, in last four of those years, Gully allowed more hits than innings. . . . Heads for the Land of the Rising Sun with 29 day-game wins over past five seasons, 3d-most in majors.

Andy Hawkins

San Diego Padres   Throws Right

	W–L	ERA	AB	H	HR	BB	SO	BA	SA	OBA
Season	3-10	5.05	457	131	16	49	51	.287	.468	.356
vs. Left-Handers			229	77	7	33	17	.336	.515	.415
vs. Right-Handers			228	54	9	16	34	.237	.421	.293
Home	1-5	5.55	234	72	11	20	30	.308	.530	.363
Road	2-5	4.55	223	59	5	29	21	.265	.404	.349
Grass	2-7	5.19	310	94	13	28	41	.303	.510	.362
Artificial Turf	1-3	4.76	147	37	3	21	10	.252	.381	.345
April	0-2	3.94	107	25	6	11	22	.234	.458	.305
May	2-4	6.43	141	43	4	17	12	.305	.511	.384
June	1-1	4.13	110	30	3	11	6	.273	.418	.339
July	0-2	7.24	54	19	2	8	8	.352	.519	.429
August			0	0	0	0	0	—	—	—
Sept./Oct.	0-1	3.27	45	14	1	2	3	.311	.422	.340
Leading Off Inn.			108	33	4	14	10	.306	.509	.385
Runners On			202	50	5	22	22	.248	.391	.320
Runners/Scor. Pos.			117	28	3	13	11	.239	.402	.313
Runners On/2 Out			88	24	2	11	9	.273	.455	.360
Scor. Pos./2 Out			55	15	2	9	6	.273	.491	.385
Late Inning Pressure			26	7	1	4	5	.269	.462	.367
Leading Off			6	0	0	2	1	.000	.000	.250
Runners On			8	1	0	0	3	.125	.250	.125
Runners/Scor. Pos.			1	0	0	0	1	.000	.000	.000
First 9 Batters			183	51	5	19	19	.279	.426	.348
Second 9 Batters			159	44	6	13	18	.277	.459	.335
All Batters Thereafter			115	36	5	17	14	.313	.548	.396

Loves to face: Mookie Wilson (0-for-16, 8 SO)
Hates to face: Bob Brenly (.643, 9-for-14, 2 HR)
Ground outs-to-air outs ratio: 1.10 last season, 1.01 for career. . . . Additional statistics: 11 double-play ground outs in 88 opportunities, 31 doubles, 2 triples in 117.2 innings last season. . . . Allowed 14 first-inning runs in 20 starts. . . . Batting support: 4.90 runs per start. . . . Opponents were 5 for 13 (38 percent) on stolen-base attempts; only two other N.L. pitchers (minimum: 10 attempts) held potential base stealers below 40 percent (Mahler and Reuschel). . . . Struck out an average of 3.90 batters per nine innings, 3d-lowest rate among N.L. pitchers (minimum: 15 GS). . . . Opposing pitchers hit .297 (11-for-36) against the Hawk, highest average against any N.L. pitcher (minimum: 20 AB). . . . Yearly opponents' batting averages since 1983: .244, .255, .267, .268, .287.

Neal Heaton
Montreal Expos   Throws Left

	W–L	ERA	AB	H	HR	BB	SO	BA	SA	OBA
Season	13-10	4.52	756	207	25	37	105	.274	.426	.308
vs. Left-Handers			123	30	4	4	24	.244	.415	.266
vs. Right-Handers			633	177	21	33	81	.280	.428	.316
Home	7-4	3.87	428	112	14	18	60	.262	.423	.291
Road	6-6	5.36	328	95	11	19	45	.290	.430	.330
Grass	3-2	5.63	159	47	5	11	23	.296	.428	.343
Artificial Turf	10-8	4.23	597	160	20	26	82	.268	.425	.299
April	3-1	4.18	105	23	3	5	17	.219	.362	.255
May	3-1	3.95	162	37	6	7	24	.228	.377	.263
June	4-1	4.91	146	41	5	7	20	.281	.466	.312
July	2-1	3.06	123	32	6	4	18	.260	.439	.283
August	0-2	6.16	136	50	2	4	18	.368	.463	.387
Sept./Oct.	1-4	5.24	84	24	3	10	8	.286	.452	.361
Leading Off Inn.			198	46	5	3	23	.232	.338	.248
Runners On			268	82	14	19	37	.306	.515	.348
Runners/Scor. Pos.			154	47	8	16	25	.305	.500	.360
Runners On/2 Out			106	22	4	10	21	.208	.387	.276
Scor. Pos./2 Out			65	11	2	8	15	.169	.292	.260
Late Inning Pressure			49	17	0	3	6	.347	.429	.396
Leading Off			13	1	0	0	2	.077	.077	.077
Runners On			18	10	0	1	0	.556	.611	.600
Runners/Scor. Pos.			11	6	0	1	0	.545	.545	.583
First 9 Batters			263	64	9	14	25	.243	.380	.281
Second 9 Batters			257	72	8	10	44	.280	.420	.310
All Batters Thereafter			236	71	8	13	36	.301	.483	.337

Loves to face: Ken Griffey (0-for-12)
Hates to face: Al Pedrique (.615, 8-for-13)
Ground outs-to-air outs ratio: 0.96 last season, 0.93 for career. . . . Additional statistics: 11 double-play ground outs in 120 opportunities, 34 doubles, 3 triples in 193.1 innings last season. . . . Allowed 21 first-inning runs in 32 starts. . . . Batting support: 4.81 runs per start. . . . Allowed an average of 1.72 walks per nine innings, 3d-lowest rate in the majors last season. . . . Won his last start of the season after going 0–6 in his previous 10 starts. Career record of 8–17 with a 5.59 ERA in September and October. . . . Opponents' career batting average is .414 (24-for-58, 3 HR) with the bases loaded. . . . Has faced 108 batters leading off innings in Late-Inning Pressure Situations and walked only one, the lowest average of the past 13 seasons (minimum: 100 BFP).

Orel Hershiser
Los Angeles Dodgers   Throws Right

	W–L	ERA	AB	H	HR	BB	SO	BA	SA	OBA
Season	16-16	3.06	1000	247	17	74	190	.247	.352	.304
vs. Left-Handers			589	160	10	49	91	.272	.385	.330
vs. Right-Handers			411	87	7	25	99	.212	.304	.266
Home	9-6	2.42	505	119	6	32	104	.236	.311	.286
Road	7-10	3.71	495	128	11	42	86	.259	.394	.322
Grass	12-9	2.71	712	176	11	47	134	.247	.346	.298
Artificial Turf	4-7	3.94	288	71	6	27	56	.247	.368	.320
April	2-3	3.00	172	46	2	16	32	.267	.349	.333
May	2-3	3.65	142	39	0	7	28	.275	.373	.311
June	5-1	0.90	183	38	2	11	42	.208	.279	.253
July	2-2	2.97	134	31	2	12	24	.231	.284	.299
August	2-3	2.96	174	41	5	15	34	.236	.391	.304
Sept./Oct.	3-4	4.97	195	52	6	13	30	.267	.421	.324
Leading Off Inn.			254	61	3	18	49	.240	.335	.296
Runners On			397	101	6	33	76	.254	.353	.317
Runners/Scor. Pos.			218	49	3	24	56	.225	.294	.310
Runners On/2 Out			154	35	2	14	36	.227	.312	.296
Scor. Pos./2 Out			97	19	2	10	29	.196	.289	.278
Late Inning Pressure			143	45	3	18	21	.315	.469	.395
Leading Off			36	13	2	5	4	.361	.611	.439
Runners On			68	20	0	7	11	.294	.382	.360
Runners/Scor. Pos.			39	10	0	5	10	.256	.282	.341
First 9 Batters			308	77	5	15	62	.250	.360	.289
Second 9 Batters			289	63	2	16	64	.218	.270	.266
All Batters Thereafter			403	107	10	43	64	.266	.404	.341

Loves to face: Jeff Stone (0-for-18)
Hates to face: Kal Daniels (.571, 8-for-14, 2 HR)
Ground outs-to-air outs ratio: 2.35, 3d-highest in N.L. last season (minimum: 20 GS), 2.24 for career. . . . Additional statistics: 30 double-play ground outs in 200 opportunities, 40 doubles, 7 triples in 264.2 innings last season. . . . Allowed 11 first-inning runs in 35 starts. . . . Batting support: 4.06 runs per start. . . . June ERA was best in N.L., but Steve Ontiveros led the majors. . . . Led all pitchers with 19 hits as a batter, and was the only pitcher to steal two bases. . . . Career record of 35-16 with a 2.43 ERA at Dodger Stadium; 25–25, 3.47 ERA on the road. . . . Yearly batting averages by left-handed batters since 1985: .222, .252, .272. Career breakdown: .249 by left-handers, .210 by right-handers. . . . Only pitcher in majors to finish at .500 in each of last two years.

Guy Hoffman
Cincinnati Reds   Throws Left

	W–L	ERA	AB	H	HR	BB	SO	BA	SA	OBA
Season	9-10	4.37	602	160	20	49	87	.266	.449	.323
vs. Left-Handers			101	31	2	13	17	.307	.446	.388
vs. Right-Handers			501	129	18	36	70	.257	.449	.309
Home	5-5	4.46	302	80	13	24	41	.265	.467	.321
Road	4-5	4.27	300	80	7	25	46	.267	.430	.324
Grass	2-4	4.20	194	56	5	15	29	.289	.464	.340
Artificial Turf	7-6	4.45	408	104	15	34	58	.255	.441	.315
April	1-1	2.08	65	16	1	3	5	.246	.323	.279
May	1-0	3.06	68	20	3	6	9	.294	.515	.347
June	4-1	4.32	125	31	5	9	26	.248	.448	.297
July	1-4	5.94	131	40	4	8	14	.305	.519	.343
August	1-3	4.88	106	28	4	12	9	.264	.472	.345
Sept./Oct.	1-1	4.30	107	25	3	11	24	.234	.374	.317
Leading Off Inn.			150	40	5	12	20	.267	.440	.325
Runners On			232	66	10	23	30	.284	.534	.350
Runners/Scor. Pos.			121	35	5	17	15	.289	.529	.372
Runners On/2 Out			101	26	4	10	20	.257	.495	.324
Scor. Pos./2 Out			57	16	2	6	9	.281	.509	.349
Late Inning Pressure			32	7	1	0	8	.219	.406	.219
Leading Off			10	1	0	0	2	.100	.200	.100
Runners On			3	2	0	0	1	.667	1.000	.667
Runners/Scor. Pos.			1	1	0	0	0	1.000	2.000	1.000
First 9 Batters			277	76	10	23	49	.274	.451	.330
Second 9 Batters			188	44	5	15	23	.234	.394	.293
All Batters Thereafter			137	40	5	11	15	.292	.518	.349

Loves to face: Gary Roenicke (0-for-11)
Hates to face: Benito Santiago (.667, 6-for-9)
Ground outs-to-air outs ratio: 1.30 last season, 1.32 for career. . . . Additional statistics: 12 double-play ground outs in 107 opportunities, 40 doubles, 5 triples in 158.2 innings last season. . . . Allowed 8 first-inning runs in 22 starts. . . . Batting support: 4.95 runs per start. . . . Averaged 5.80 innings pitched in 22 starts, lowest IP/GS among Reds' regular starters. . . . Record of 6-10, 4.72 ERA in 22 starts; 3–0, 2.90 in 14 relief appearances, raising his career record as a reliever to 8–0. . . . Hitless in 36 career at bats with the bases empty, but, like Devon White, has hit .250 with runners on. . . . Allowed only one hit in 11 at bats with the bases loaded last season, but the hit was a grand slam by Tom Pagnozzi. . . . Opponents' career batting average is .305 with runners in scoring position.

Brian Holton
Los Angeles Dodgers   Throws Right

	W–L	ERA	AB	H	HR	BB	SO	BA	SA	OBA
Season	3-2	3.89	323	87	11	32	58	.269	.427	.332
vs. Left-Handers			158	43	4	22	16	.272	.392	.361
vs. Right-Handers			165	44	7	10	42	.267	.461	.303
Home	2-0	2.48	153	39	2	16	28	.255	.314	.324
Road	1-2	5.19	170	48	9	16	30	.282	.529	.340
Grass	2-1	4.04	214	56	8	23	36	.262	.402	.332
Artificial Turf	1-1	3.58	109	31	3	9	22	.284	.477	.333
April	1-0	4.02	60	14	3	5	10	.233	.467	.292
May	1-0	1.93	51	12	1	4	14	.235	.333	.286
June	0-1	4.26	46	11	1	4	9	.239	.348	.300
July	1-0	5.40	68	19	2	8	12	.279	.412	.351
August	0-0	2.76	61	16	2	8	9	.262	.426	.348
Sept./Oct.	0-1	5.63	37	15	2	3	4	.405	.622	.439
Leading Off Inn.			75	23	4	1	13	.307	.480	.316
Runners On			155	37	4	20	33	.239	.374	.320
Runners/Scor. Pos.			90	23	3	17	17	.256	.444	.364
Runners On/2 Out			69	17	3	12	16	.246	.435	.358
Scor. Pos./2 Out			49	11	3	9	10	.224	.490	.345
Late Inning Pressure			89	22	3	11	16	.247	.416	.324
Leading Off			24	7	2	0	5	.292	.542	.292
Runners On			38	6	0	7	6	.158	.211	.277
Runners/Scor. Pos.			23	5	0	6	1	.217	.304	.355
First 9 Batters			290	77	9	28	55	.266	.407	.327
Second 9 Batters			30	9	2	3	3	.300	.600	.364
All Batters Thereafter			3	1	0	1	0	.333	.667	.500

Loves to face: Carmelo Martinez (0-for-5)
Hates to face: Eddie Milner (.714, 5-for-7)
Ground outs-to-air outs ratio: 1.18 last season, 1.26 for career. . . . Additional statistics: 7 double-play ground outs in 78 opportunities, 14 doubles, 2 triples in 83.1 innings last season. . . . Spent eight seasons in minors before making major-league debut with Dodgers in 1985. . . . Ranked fourth among N.L. rookie pitchers with 53 appearances. . . . Has made 64 relief appearances in parts of three seasons with the Dodgers, but only five in save situations (two saves). . . . Opponents' career breakdown: .300 with bases empty, .264 with runners on base, .246 with runners in scoring position, .224 with two out and runners in scoring position. . . . Has walked the leadoff batter in only two of the 105 innings he's started (0-for-31 in Late-Inning Pressure Situations).

Rick Honeycutt

Los Angeles Dodgers — Throws Left

	W–L	ERA	AB	H	HR	BB	SO	BA	SA	OBA
Season	2-12	4.59	478	133	10	45	92	.278	.416	.343
vs. Left-Handers			87	19	2	4	17	.218	.333	.253
vs. Right-Handers			391	114	8	41	75	.292	.435	.362
Home	2-7	3.92	267	75	8	18	49	.281	.442	.331
Road	0-5	5.44	211	58	2	27	43	.275	.384	.357
Grass	2-9	4.41	339	95	8	28	58	.280	.422	.339
Artificial Turf	0-3	5.03	139	38	2	17	34	.273	.403	.353
April	0-1	0.69	53	14	0	2	11	.264	.340	.304
May	2-3	2.18	166	40	2	13	39	.241	.349	.296
June	0-3	5.19	102	26	3	14	17	.255	.392	.345
July	0-4	8.63	109	38	4	8	19	.349	.569	.398
August	0-1	7.94	48	15	1	8	6	.313	.438	.411
Sept./Oct.			0	0	0	0	0	—	—	—
Leading Off Inn.			113	28	1	8	21	.248	.363	.298
Runners On			206	60	5	27	40	.291	.447	.379
Runners/Scor. Pos.			125	34	3	21	24	.272	.408	.381
Runners On/2 Out			90	25	2	13	16	.278	.444	.375
Scor. Pos./2 Out			55	13	1	11	11	.236	.382	.373
Late Inning Pressure			8	4	0	2	1	.500	.625	.600
Leading Off			3	1	0	0	1	.333	.333	.333
Runners On			2	2	0	2	0	1.000	1.500	1.000
Runners/Scor. Pos.			1	1	0	1	0	1.000	1.000	1.000
First 9 Batters			195	49	4	17	42	.251	.390	.318
Second 9 Batters			163	45	1	16	29	.276	.368	.341
All Batters Thereafter			120	39	5	12	21	.325	.525	.386

Loves to face: Tom Brookens (.100, 2-for-20)
Hates to face: Chili Davis (.450, 9-for-20, 4 HR)
Figures *above* are for N.L. only. . . . Ground outs-to-air outs ratio: 1.80 last season, 1.89 for career. . . . Additional statistics: 8 double-play ground outs in 109 opportunities, 37 doubles, 4 triples in 115.2 innings last season. . . . Allowed 6 first-inning runs in 24 starts. . . . Batting support: 2.83 runs per start, lowest average in majors (minimum: 15 GS). Was the losing pitcher in three games in which he didn't allow an earned run. . . . Won only one of last 18 starts, and victory was over Indians. We're checking to see if that counts. . . . Has defeated every A.L. team except the Orioles (0–5). . . . Opposing left-handed batters have a career batting average of .239, compared with a .277 mark by right-handers. . . . Strikeouts per nine innings, year by year since 1983: 3.12, 3.68, 4.25, 5.26, 6.59.

Ricky Horton

St. Louis Cardinals — Throws Left

	W–L	ERA	AB	H	HR	BB	SO	BA	SA	OBA
Season	8-3	3.82	481	127	15	42	55	.264	.443	.321
vs. Left-Handers			120	27	1	11	21	.225	.333	.288
vs. Right-Handers			361	100	14	31	34	.277	.479	.332
Home	4-1	3.22	220	56	6	16	25	.255	.409	.305
Road	4-2	4.34	261	71	9	26	30	.272	.471	.334
Grass	1-1	4.78	104	28	3	15	11	.269	.423	.358
Artificial Turf	7-2	3.56	377	99	12	27	44	.263	.448	.310
April	0-0	1.13	57	12	0	3	15	.211	.281	.250
May	2-0	3.38	71	17	3	5	5	.239	.423	.289
June	1-0	4.35	81	24	2	6	7	.296	.444	.341
July	2-1	4.60	124	33	4	14	11	.266	.460	.338
August	1-1	4.12	78	20	3	8	7	.256	.474	.326
Sept./Oct.	2-1	4.34	70	21	3	6	10	.300	.529	.351
Leading Off Inn.			114	33	6	4	12	.289	.500	.314
Runners On			206	53	4	22	29	.257	.427	.325
Runners/Scor. Pos.			129	30	1	19	16	.233	.341	.325
Runners On/2 Out			98	20	1	14	14	.204	.357	.304
Scor. Pos./2 Out			64	11	0	12	8	.172	.250	.303
Late Inning Pressure			145	37	5	14	24	.255	.414	.319
Leading Off			38	11	2	3	5	.289	.474	.341
Runners On			55	12	2	9	13	.218	.436	.323
Runners/Scor. Pos.			28	6	0	7	8	.214	.250	.361
First 9 Batters			359	93	12	26	44	.259	.440	.308
Second 9 Batters			81	23	2	8	5	.284	.457	.344
All Batters Thereafter			41	11	1	8	6	.268	.439	.380

Loves to face: Mookie Wilson (.042, 1-for-24)
Hates to face: Pedro Guerrero (.714, 5-for-7, 2 HR)
Ground outs-to-air outs ratio: 1.52 last season, 1.42 for career. . . . Additional statistics: 7 double-play ground outs in 87 opportunities, 25 doubles, 8 triples in 125.0 innings last season. . . . Earned seven saves in 15 opportunities, none after June 27. . . . Had allowed only one career home run in Late-Inning Pressure Situations before the 1987 season. . . . Only home run surrendered to a lefty last season was hit by Kal Daniels (the only one he's ever hit off a southpaw). . . . Career record of 7–0 in nine starts following relief appearances. . . . Ranks sixth in majors with an ERA of 3.11 in road games over the past three seasons (minimum: 150 IP). . . . Opponents' career batting average of .162 (6-for-37, one HR) with the bases loaded. Even better (.053, 1-for-19) with two out and the bags full.

Tom Hume

Phillies/Reds — Throws Right

	W–L	ERA	AB	H	HR	BB	SO	BA	SA	OBA
Season	2-4	5.36	319	89	10	43	33	.279	.451	.369
vs. Left-Handers			151	51	3	26	10	.338	.490	.433
vs. Right-Handers			168	38	7	17	23	.226	.417	.309
Home	2-2	4.61	203	58	4	24	22	.286	.433	.358
Road	0-2	6.75	116	31	6	19	11	.267	.483	.387
Grass	0-2	8.06	88	25	6	17	9	.284	.557	.409
Artificial Turf	2-2	4.38	231	64	4	26	24	.277	.411	.352
April	0-0	6.75	46	13	2	9	5	.283	.500	.431
May	0-0	3.60	39	7	1	1	4	.179	.333	.220
June	0-0	5.63	66	20	3	11	6	.303	.485	.392
July	1-2	4.09	84	23	2	4	13	.274	.393	.307
August	0-2	6.88	65	22	2	17	3	.338	.585	.476
Sept./Oct.	1-0	4.76	19	4	0	1	2	.211	.263	.261
Leading Off Inn.			75	27	2	7	7	.360	.533	.415
Runners On			158	37	4	26	14	.234	.392	.352
Runners/Scor. Pos.			103	24	3	18	9	.233	.398	.346
Runners On/2 Out			60	6	1	9	7	.100	.183	.229
Scor. Pos./2 Out			43	6	1	7	5	.140	.256	.260
Late Inning Pressure			39	15	0	7	2	.385	.538	.500
Leading Off			12	8	0	1	0	.667	1.000	.692
Runners On			19	4	0	6	2	.211	.316	.448
Runners/Scor. Pos.			11	2	0	4	1	.182	.273	.444
First 9 Batters			235	62	7	32	28	.264	.438	.360
Second 9 Batters			57	16	1	5	3	.281	.404	.339
All Batters Thereafter			27	11	2	6	2	.407	.667	.500

Loves to face: Phil Garner (.097, 3-for-31)
Hates to face: Leon Durham (.550, 11-for-20, 1 HR)
Ground outs-to-air outs ratio: 1.26 last season, 1.34 for career (1.61 vs. left-handed batters, 1.16 vs. right-handers). . . . Additional statistics: 9 double-play ground outs in 88 opportunities, 19 doubles, 3 triples in 84.0 innings last season. . . . Made 49 relief appearances last season for two different teams under three different managers, none in a save situation. Earned 10 saves in 22 opportunities over three previous seasons. . . . Opposing left-handers batted 112 points higher than right-handers, 2d-largest difference in N.L. (minimum: 100 AB each way), and the 10th time in 11 seasons that lefties outhit righties. . . . Ratio of walks to strikeouts by left-handed batters was highest in N.L. among pitchers who faced as many lefties as Hume did since 1985.

Mike Jackson

Philadelphia Phillies — Throws Right

	W–L	ERA	AB	H	HR	BB	SO	BA	SA	OBA
Season	3-10	4.20	402	88	16	56	93	.219	.378	.316
vs. Left-Handers			189	50	6	40	31	.265	.407	.397
vs. Right-Handers			213	38	10	16	62	.178	.352	.236
Home	2-3	2.13	185	28	2	28	48	.151	.222	.266
Road	1-7	6.29	217	60	14	28	45	.276	.512	.360
Grass	0-1	7.52	111	33	11	16	23	.297	.622	.386
Artificial Turf	3-9	3.14	291	55	5	40	70	.189	.285	.290
April	0-1	1.86	65	9	0	12	20	.138	.200	.278
May	0-2	8.03	43	11	2	14	6	.256	.419	.431
June	2-3	5.34	113	29	8	13	23	.257	.504	.336
July	1-2	2.61	75	16	0	8	20	.213	.267	.298
August	0-0	4.35	39	9	3	2	7	.231	.487	.262
Sept./Oct.	0-2	4.00	67	14	3	7	17	.209	.373	.284
Leading Off Inn.			95	20	2	13	18	.211	.326	.312
Runners On			177	40	10	24	40	.226	.429	.312
Runners/Scor. Pos.			100	20	5	21	26	.200	.390	.328
Runners On/2 Out			77	14	4	14	20	.182	.390	.308
Scor. Pos./2 Out			53	9	1	12	17	.170	.302	.323
Late Inning Pressure			96	24	2	12	17	.250	.354	.345
Leading Off			25	5	1	2	4	.200	.360	.286
Runners On			40	11	1	6	7	.275	.425	.370
Runners/Scor. Pos.			18	4	0	6	4	.222	.278	.417
First 9 Batters			303	60	9	40	78	.198	.330	.295
Second 9 Batters			72	19	6	11	12	.264	.542	.361
All Batters Thereafter			27	9	1	5	3	.333	.481	.424

Loves to face: Rafael Santana (0-for-8)
Hates to face: Marvell Wynne (1-for-1, 1 HR, 2 BB, 1 HBP)
Ground outs-to-air outs ratio: 0.62, 4th-lowest in N.L. last season (minimum: 200 BFP), 0.66 for career. . . . Additional statistics: 5 double-play ground outs in 78 opportunities, 14 doubles, 1 triple in 109.1 innings last season. . . . Ranked second among N.L. rookie pitchers with 55 appearances. . . . Record of 1–4, 6.68 ERA in seven starts; 2–6, 3.09 ERA in 48 relief appearances. . . . Entered only four games in save situations in the seventh inning or later. . . . Opponents batted 108 points higher on grass fields than on artificial surfaces, highest such difference in the majors last season (minimum: 100 AB each way). . . . Lefty/righty breakdown was even wider in nine games in 1986 (.320 and .174, respectively).

Jimmy Jones — San Diego Padres — Throws Right

	W–L	ERA	AB	H	HR	BB	SO	BA	SA	OBA
Season	9-7	4.14	570	154	14	54	51	.270	.386	.336
vs. Left-Handers			306	82	6	32	27	.268	.366	.338
vs. Right-Handers			264	72	8	22	24	.273	.409	.333
Home	4-5	3.62	307	80	9	26	29	.261	.381	.320
Road	5-2	4.72	263	74	5	28	22	.281	.392	.354
Grass	8-5	3.52	416	106	10	37	36	.255	.356	.320
Artificial Turf	1-2	5.87	154	48	4	17	15	.312	.468	.377
April			0	0	0	0	0	——	——	——
May	0-2	9.00	70	26	1	12	6	.371	.486	.465
June	2-1	2.86	108	23	3	9	7	.213	.315	.280
July	1-1	4.82	115	34	4	10	11	.296	.461	.354
August	3-1	3.13	116	30	2	8	15	.259	.328	.312
Sept./Oct.	3-2	3.46	161	41	4	15	12	.255	.379	.315
Leading Off Inn.			141	36	4	14	10	.255	.369	.327
Runners On			243	77	8	24	24	.317	.465	.376
Runners/Scor. Pos.			142	46	6	17	16	.324	.507	.388
Runners On/2 Out			102	34	3	17	7	.333	.451	.433
Scor. Pos./2 Out			69	23	2	14	5	.333	.464	.446
Late Inning Pressure			32	8	1	1	4	.250	.375	.273
Leading Off			9	3	1	1	1	.333	.778	.400
Runners On			10	3	0	0	2	.300	.300	.300
Runners/Scor. Pos.			7	3	0	0	2	.429	.429	.429
First 9 Batters			226	47	6	17	30	.208	.323	.264
Second 9 Batters			192	46	2	20	11	.240	.313	.318
All Batters Thereafter			152	61	6	17	10	.401	.572	.462

Loves to face: Sid Bream (0-for-8)
Hates to face: Barry Bonds (6-for-6)
Ground outs-to-air outs ratio: 1.78 last season, 1.71 for career.... Additional statistics: 14 double-play ground outs in 108 opportunities, 20 doubles, 2 triples in 145.2 innings last season.... Allowed 6 first-inning runs in 22 starts, 3d-lowest average in N.L. (minimum: 15 GS).... Batting support: 5.00 runs per start.... Padres lost first seven games in which he appeared.... Appeared in eight games as a reliever, but none after June 29.... Averaged only 3.15 strikeouts per nine innings, lowest rate of any N.L. pitcher (minimum: 15 GS).... Opponents' career breakdown: .217 with bases empty, .322 with runners on base.... One of two pitchers drafted before Dwight Gooden in June 1982 free agent draft. The other, of course, was Bryan Oelkers.

Bob Kipper — Pittsburgh Pirates — Throws Left

	W–L	ERA	AB	H	HR	BB	SO	BA	SA	OBA
Season	5-9	5.94	432	117	25	52	83	.271	.516	.350
vs. Left-Handers			79	16	0	3	16	.203	.241	.241
vs. Right-Handers			353	101	25	49	67	.286	.578	.372
Home	2-5	5.57	249	67	13	32	53	.269	.498	.352
Road	3-4	6.46	183	50	12	20	30	.273	.541	.346
Grass	2-4	6.56	144	39	9	17	24	.271	.514	.350
Artificial Turf	3-5	5.64	288	78	16	35	59	.271	.517	.350
April	2-2	4.43	90	23	4	7	18	.256	.467	.309
May	1-3	7.30	99	30	7	12	14	.303	.586	.378
June	1-1	4.98	128	29	7	18	29	.227	.461	.324
July	1-3	7.23	92	29	6	13	17	.315	.587	.398
August			0	0	0	0	0	——	——	——
Sept./Oct.	0-0	6.35	23	6	1	2	5	.261	.435	.320
Leading Off Inn.			104	28	5	12	19	.269	.462	.345
Runners On			177	51	11	20	31	.288	.582	.355
Runners/Scor. Pos.			98	28	5	15	20	.286	.551	.371
Runners On/2 Out			71	16	2	8	14	.225	.408	.304
Scor. Pos./2 Out			42	9	2	7	10	.214	.452	.327
Late Inning Pressure			14	2	0	4	6	.143	.143	.333
Leading Off			5	0	0	0	3	.000	.000	.000
Runners On			3	0	0	2	1	.000	.000	.400
Runners/Scor. Pos.			1	0	0	0	0	.000	.000	.000
First 9 Batters			177	44	9	20	36	.249	.458	.323
Second 9 Batters			158	52	10	18	26	.329	.627	.398
All Batters Thereafter			97	21	6	14	21	.216	.443	.321

Loves to face: Ryne Sandberg (.077, 1-for-13)
Hates to face: Bruce Bochy (3-for-3, 1 2B, 2 HR, 2 BB)
Ground outs-to-air outs ratio: 0.69, 8th lowest in N.L. last season (minimum: 200 BFP), 0.69 for career (1.49 vs. left-handers, 0.58 vs. right-handers).... Additional statistics: 6 double-play ground outs in 76 opportunities, 25 doubles, 3 triples in 110.2 innings last season.... Allowed 7 first-inning runs in 20 starts.... Batting support: 4.05 runs per start.... Average of 4.23 walks per nine innings was 4th highest among N.L. pitchers (minimum: 15 GS).... Career record of 0–8 in starts following winning starts, 9–3 following losing starts.... Has never allowed a home run to a left-handed batter (168 career AB), while allowing a career rate of one per 17.6 at bats to right-handers.... Yearly batting averages by opposing left-handers since 1985: .278, .268, .203.

Bob Knepper — Houston Astros — Throws Left

	W–L	ERA	AB	H	HR	BB	SO	BA	SA	OBA
Season	8-17	5.27	723	226	26	54	76	.313	.502	.362
vs. Left-Handers			117	33	3	5	17	.282	.419	.317
vs. Right-Handers			606	193	23	49	59	.318	.518	.370
Home	5-7	4.30	387	111	14	21	43	.287	.463	.324
Road	3-10	6.47	336	115	12	33	33	.342	.548	.403
Grass	2-6	7.29	181	69	10	23	17	.381	.652	.451
Artificial Turf	6-11	4.64	542	157	16	31	59	.290	.452	.330
April	1-2	6.04	120	40	3	8	15	.333	.483	.382
May	1-3	6.43	84	27	5	6	8	.321	.560	.363
June	1-3	7.27	111	38	9	4	11	.342	.667	.362
July	1-4	4.81	142	43	4	11	14	.303	.479	.359
August	3-2	4.14	158	44	4	10	16	.278	.462	.321
Sept./Oct.	1-3	3.95	108	34	1	15	12	.315	.398	.398
Leading Off Inn.			177	47	6	9	22	.266	.441	.301
Runners On			306	101	8	27	30	.330	.497	.383
Runners/Scor. Pos.			184	53	5	21	18	.288	.424	.360
Runners On/2 Out			141	52	2	14	16	.369	.504	.433
Scor. Pos./2 Out			93	31	2	10	9	.333	.473	.410
Late Inning Pressure			53	15	0	5	9	.283	.358	.356
Leading Off			15	3	0	0	1	.200	.200	.200
Runners On			20	7	0	3	5	.350	.500	.435
Runners/Scor. Pos.			9	3	0	2	0	.333	.444	.455
First 9 Batters			264	78	12	21	37	.295	.508	.346
Second 9 Batters			251	76	9	15	22	.303	.478	.345
All Batters Thereafter			208	72	5	18	17	.346	.524	.402

Loves to face: Jose Uribe (.105, 2-for-19)
Hates to face: Dale Murphy (.419, 31-for-74, 7 HR, 21 BB)
Ground outs-to-air outs ratio: 1.71 last season, 1.30 for career.... Additional statistics: 21 double-play ground outs in 123 opportunities, 37 doubles, 11 triples (most in majors) in 177.2 innings last season.... Allowed 31 first-inning runs in 31 starts, 4th-highest average in N.L. (minimum: 15 GS).... Batting support: 4.13 runs per start.... Average of 3.85 strikeouts per nine innings was 2d-lowest rate among N.L. pitchers (minimum: 15 GS).... Losing pitcher in six consecutive starts (May 17 to June 13) for the first time in his career.... Dropped a decision to every opposing team except the Giants last season.... Next-to-last loss of season made him first to reach 100 during 1980s. Jim Clancy (99), Rick Honeycutt (97), and Frank Tanana (97) shouldn't be too long getting there.

Mike Krukow — San Francisco Giants — Throws Right

	W–L	ERA	AB	H	HR	BB	SO	BA	SA	OBA
Season	5-6	4.80	633	182	24	46	104	.288	.463	.334
vs. Left-Handers			348	109	13	34	50	.313	.486	.371
vs. Right-Handers			285	73	11	12	54	.256	.435	.286
Home	1-3	4.26	324	89	11	24	58	.275	.423	.326
Road	4-3	5.42	309	93	13	22	46	.301	.505	.342
Grass	5-5	4.50	500	141	22	35	80	.282	.472	.328
Artificial Turf	0-1	6.00	133	41	2	11	24	.308	.429	.356
April	1-3	3.16	137	35	5	7	19	.255	.431	.293
May	0-2	10.87	112	45	3	11	15	.402	.616	.448
June	0-1	7.11	53	21	3	5	8	.396	.585	.433
July	1-0	3.77	110	29	4	7	23	.264	.464	.308
August	1-0	3.99	106	25	7	5	19	.236	.443	.268
Sept./Oct.	2-0	2.43	115	27	2	11	20	.235	.313	.305
Leading Off Inn.			160	54	12	12	27	.338	.650	.384
Runners On			256	77	8	23	43	.301	.457	.351
Runners/Scor. Pos.			152	39	3	18	31	.257	.375	.324
Runners On/2 Out			90	22	2	12	16	.244	.378	.340
Scor. Pos./2 Out			61	14	1	11	10	.230	.344	.356
Late Inning Pressure			49	19	3	2	7	.388	.653	.404
Leading Off			14	5	1	0	1	.357	.714	.357
Runners On			22	8	2	2	4	.364	.636	.400
Runners/Scor. Pos.			18	5	2	2	4	.278	.611	.333
First 9 Batters			226	59	8	26	45	.261	.429	.339
Second 9 Batters			213	63	7	12	33	.296	.474	.328
All Batters Thereafter			194	60	9	8	26	.309	.490	.335

Loves to face: Keith Moreland (.079, 3-for-38)
Hates to face: Kal Daniels (.556, 5-for-9, 2 HR)
Ground outs-to-air outs ratio: 1.06 last season, 1.21 for career.... Additional statistics: 14 double-play ground outs in 125 opportunities, 31 doubles, 4 triples in 163.0 innings last season.... Allowed 25 first-inning runs in 28 starts.... Batting support: 5.64 runs per start, 2d-highest average in N.L. (minimum: 15 GS).... Led N.L. in home-game wins in 1986 (12), but won only once at Candlestick last season.... Won his last four decisions (plus an N.L.C.S. victory) after a 1–6 start, and ranked 6th in N.L. with a 2.97 ERA after the All-Star break.... Yearly averages of opposing right-handers since 1985: .189, .219, .256.... Last N.L. pitcher to win five or fewer games following a 20-win season was also a member of the Giants: Ron Bryant was 24–12 in 1973 and 3–15 a year later.

Mike LaCoss

San Francisco Giants — Throws Right

	W–L	ERA	AB	H	HR	BB	SO	BA	SA	OBA
Season	13–10	3.68	651	184	16	63	79	.283	.419	.346
vs. Left-Handers			367	111	11	41	41	.302	.466	.371
vs. Right-Handers			284	73	5	22	38	.257	.359	.314
Home	7–8	3.23	376	100	10	37	52	.266	.394	.333
Road	6–2	4.33	275	84	6	26	27	.305	.455	.365
Grass	7–9	3.72	450	128	12	49	57	.284	.424	.355
Artificial Turf	6–1	3.61	201	56	4	14	22	.279	.408	.327
April	1–1	5.19	71	20	1	10	5	.282	.437	.366
May	4–1	3.34	119	33	3	7	21	.277	.437	.317
June	1–2	6.12	96	33	4	13	9	.344	.542	.418
July	2–2	3.28	103	36	1	13	12	.350	.427	.427
August	3–2	2.22	154	31	4	9	19	.201	.305	.245
Sept./Oct.	2–2	3.64	108	31	3	11	13	.287	.435	.355
Leading Off Inn.			167	55	5	15	21	.329	.473	.385
Runners On			274	74	7	35	33	.270	.409	.351
Runners/Scor. Pos.			167	41	5	25	22	.246	.383	.342
Runners On/2 Out			103	29	5	12	12	.282	.476	.357
Scor. Pos./2 Out			72	17	3	10	9	.236	.375	.329
Late Inning Pressure			65	18	3	16	8	.277	.508	.415
Leading Off			16	5	2	4	1	.313	.750	.450
Runners On			27	7	1	7	3	.259	.407	.400
Runners/Scor. Pos.			18	5	1	6	3	.278	.500	.440
First 9 Batters			270	77	5	30	36	.285	.415	.360
Second 9 Batters			201	47	4	16	24	.234	.323	.289
All Batters Thereafter			180	60	7	17	19	.333	.533	.389

Loves to face: Terry Francona (.643, 9-for-14, 3 3B)
Hates to face: Tom Foley (0-for-13)
Ground outs-to-air outs ratio: 1.86 last season, 1.89 for career.... Additional statistics: 23 double-play ground outs in 141 opportunities, 29 doubles, 6 triples in 171.0 innings last season.... Allowed 9 first-inning runs in 26 starts.... Batting support: 4.35 runs per start.... August ERA was 4th-lowest in N.L.... Day-game ERA of 2.74 was 3d-lowest (7–3 in day games, 6–7 at night).... LaCoss aux Foldes: record of 21–8 (.724) before the All-Star break over past four seasons, 10–21(.323) 30–45 (.400) after the break.... Faced 30 consecutive right-handed batters without allowing a hit, one fewer than Nolan Ryan's longest N.L. streak last season.... LaCoss concluded an 11-for-23 streak by hitting HRs in consecutive games in June 1986, but has only six hits in 76 AB since then.

Les Lancaster

Chicago Cubs — Throws Right

	W–L	ERA	AB	H	HR	BB	SO	BA	SA	OBA
Season	8–3	4.90	515	138	14	51	78	.268	.406	.332
vs. Left-Handers			264	84	8	28	31	.318	.481	.379
vs. Right-Handers			251	54	6	23	47	.215	.327	.280
Home	6–2	4.78	271	69	7	28	37	.255	.399	.321
Road	2–1	5.03	244	69	7	23	41	.283	.414	.343
Grass	6–2	4.74	378	95	12	37	59	.251	.407	.315
Artificial Turf	2–1	5.35	137	43	2	14	19	.314	.401	.377
April	0–0	2.84	24	6	0	4	7	.250	.250	.357
May	0–0	6.00	11	2	1	0	2	.182	.455	.182
June	1–0	2.84	46	11	0	6	8	.239	.261	.321
July	1–1	5.96	85	18	5	12	21	.212	.459	.306
August	3–0	6.29	179	52	6	16	25	.291	.480	.343
Sept./Oct.	3–2	3.74	170	49	2	13	15	.288	.359	.341
Leading Off Inn.			125	35	3	14	19	.280	.424	.353
Runners On			220	58	8	25	32	.264	.423	.333
Runners/Scor. Pos.			136	32	4	16	21	.235	.353	.304
Runners On/2 Out			95	19	4	8	18	.200	.368	.262
Scor. Pos./2 Out			62	9	1	6	14	.145	.226	.221
Late Inning Pressure			34	8	1	5	2	.235	.353	.333
Leading Off			10	3	0	1	0	.300	.300	.364
Runners On			13	2	0	2	2	.154	.154	.267
Runners/Scor. Pos.			9	2	0	1	1	.222	.222	.300
First 9 Batters			202	61	6	23	38	.302	.446	.370
Second 9 Batters			159	28	4	13	26	.176	.296	.241
All Batters Thereafter			154	49	4	15	14	.318	.468	.372

Loves to face: Billy Hatcher (0-for-7)
Hates to face: Kevin Mitchell (.600, 3-for-5, 1 2B, 2 HR)
Ground outs-to-air outs ratio: 0.90 last season, his first in majors. ... Additional statistics: 6 double-play ground outs in 102 opportunities, 27 doubles, 1 triple in 132.1 innings last season.... Allowed 19 first-inning runs in 18 starts, 3d-highest average in N.L. (minimum: 15 GS).... Batting support: 4.78 runs per start.... Made Cubs' opening-day roster after being non-roster player in spring training. Hadn't pitched in Triple A ball before 1987.... Cubs lost the first six games in which he appeared.... Won four consecutive starts from Aug. 27 to Sept. 11.... Didn't complete any of his 18 starts.... Tied another rookie, Mike Jackson, for the league lead in balks (8).... Cubs opposed a right-handed starter in each of Lancaster's 18 starts.

Terry Leach

New York Mets — Throws Right

	W–L	ERA	AB	H	HR	BB	SO	BA	SA	OBA
Season	11–1	3.22	503	132	14	29	61	.262	.404	.303
vs. Left-Handers			240	66	6	17	19	.275	.429	.323
vs. Right-Handers			263	66	8	12	42	.251	.380	.285
Home	3–0	4.61	169	52	8	8	21	.308	.515	.343
Road	8–1	2.59	334	80	6	21	40	.240	.347	.284
Grass	7–1	3.67	325	95	12	19	37	.292	.471	.332
Artificial Turf	4–0	2.50	178	37	2	10	24	.208	.281	.250
April	0–0	0.96	31	6	0	0	5	.194	.290	.194
May	3–0	3.00	81	24	2	6	14	.296	.432	.352
June	3–0	2.54	114	27	4	1	10	.237	.377	.243
July	2–0	2.70	70	17	1	8	6	.243	.329	.321
August	2–1	5.45	143	44	5	10	13	.308	.503	.351
Sept./Oct.	1–0	2.00	64	14	2	4	13	.219	.328	.265
Leading Off Inn.			128	39	3	5	13	.305	.469	.336
Runners On			204	46	1	17	27	.225	.289	.284
Runners/Scor. Pos.			130	29	0	9	15	.223	.277	.271
Runners On/2 Out			81	16	0	7	12	.198	.222	.261
Scor. Pos./2 Out			57	9	0	2	9	.158	.193	.186
Late Inning Pressure			65	20	2	3	15	.308	.446	.338
Leading Off			17	3	0	1	5	.176	.176	.222
Runners On			24	7	1	2	5	.292	.500	.346
Runners/Scor. Pos.			14	3	0	2	4	.214	.286	.313
First 9 Batters			279	71	7	17	43	.254	.380	.299
Second 9 Batters			128	35	4	7	13	.273	.430	.311
All Batters Thereafter			96	26	3	5	5	.271	.438	.307

Loves to face: Steve Sax (0-for-12)
Hates to face: Dave Martinez (.556, 5-for-9, 1 HR)
Ground outs-to-air outs ratio: 1.66 last season, 1.64 for career.... Additional statistics: 11 double-play ground outs in 87 opportunities, 27 doubles, 1 triple in 131.1 innings last season.... Allowed 5 first-inning runs in 12 starts.... Batting support: 6.42 runs per start.... ERA in road games was the lowest in N.L.... Opposing pitchers batted better against Leach (.286) than did position players (.261).... And you thought Doc was unhittable at night? Career records: 3–6, 4.48 ERA in day games; 13–0, 2.70 ERA at night. Not to mention 9–0, 2.35 ERA before the All-Star break; 7–6, 4.15 ERA thereafter.... Has won all seven career starts following relief appearances.... Record is 11–2 with a 2.87 ERA in 18 career starts. ... Career record of 5–0 vs. Montreal.

Tim Leary

Los Angeles Dodgers — Throws Right

	W–L	ERA	AB	H	HR	BB	SO	BA	SA	OBA
Season	3–11	4.76	424	121	15	36	61	.285	.462	.343
vs. Left-Handers			204	59	5	16	18	.289	.451	.344
vs. Right-Handers			220	62	10	20	43	.282	.473	.343
Home	2–5	4.55	214	60	5	17	29	.280	.402	.332
Road	1–6	4.99	210	61	10	19	32	.290	.524	.355
Grass	3–7	4.78	295	82	10	23	43	.278	.454	.331
Artificial Turf	0–4	4.73	129	39	5	13	18	.302	.481	.371
April	0–1	5.40	48	14	3	4	9	.292	.583	.346
May	0–0	5.84	47	13	2	2	7	.277	.447	.306
June	1–2	4.01	97	28	2	8	13	.289	.423	.346
July	1–3	6.75	74	22	4	11	10	.297	.568	.395
August	1–4	3.57	89	24	2	8	15	.270	.382	.330
Sept./Oct.	0–1	4.08	69	20	2	3	7	.290	.435	.319
Leading Off Inn.			103	29	3	5	14	.282	.437	.321
Runners On			176	55	7	19	22	.313	.506	.381
Runners/Scor. Pos.			110	33	4	12	14	.300	.491	.391
Runners On/2 Out			82	28	4	11	12	.341	.573	.419
Scor. Pos./2 Out			54	17	2	11	9	.315	.500	.431
Late Inning Pressure			70	18	1	5	11	.257	.329	.307
Leading Off			19	3	0	1	2	.158	.158	.200
Runners On			22	10	1	2	2	.455	.682	.500
Runners/Scor. Pos.			8	4	0	1	0	.500	.500	.556
First 9 Batters			241	62	6	18	37	.257	.382	.309
Second 9 Batters			111	41	7	9	18	.369	.685	.423
All Batters Thereafter			72	18	2	9	6	.250	.389	.333

Loves to face: Ken Oberkfell (0-for-7)
Hates to face: Buddy Bell (.667, 6-for-9)
Ground outs-to-air outs ratio: 1.01 last season, 1.15 for career.... Additional statistics: 8 double-play ground outs in 71 opportunities, 24 doubles, 3 triples in 107.2 innings last season.... Allowed 7 first-inning runs in 12 starts.... Batting support: 3.50 runs per start.... Averaged 5.36 innings pitched per start.... Batted .304 (7-for-23) last season, highest average among N.L. pitchers (minimum: 20 AB). Also helped his own cause with five RBI.... Has six hits in 13 career at bats with runners on base.... Career record of 16–27 with a 4.57 ERA as a starter; 4–4, 3.05 ERA in relief.... Opponents' career batting average of .302 leading off innings.... ERA has increased in every season of his six-year major-league career.

Craig Lefferts

Padres/Giants — Throws Left

	W–L	ERA	AB	H	HR	BB	SO	BA	SA	OBA
Season	5-5	3.83	373	92	13	33	57	.247	.410	.310
vs. Left-Handers			114	26	5	5	25	.228	.412	.264
vs. Right-Handers			259	66	8	28	32	.255	.409	.329
Home	4-1	2.93	167	34	6	14	29	.204	.353	.262
Road	1-4	4.61	206	58	7	19	28	.282	.456	.348
Grass	4-1	3.15	253	56	9	22	37	.221	.379	.284
Artificial Turf	1-4	5.40	120	36	4	11	20	.300	.475	.364
April	0-0	2.11	75	17	1	8	16	.227	.347	.310
May	0-2	7.20	67	22	5	4	11	.328	.597	.375
June	2-0	4.80	64	17	3	3	12	.266	.484	.299
July	0-1	2.75	66	11	3	7	9	.167	.364	.247
August	1-2	5.02	56	16	1	1	3	.286	.375	.293
Sept./Oct.	2-0	2.03	45	9	0	10	6	.200	.244	.339
Leading Off Inn.			83	25	3	4	13	.301	.494	.333
Runners On			173	42	5	24	29	.243	.393	.335
Runners/Scor. Pos.			111	25	3	21	22	.225	.369	.348
Runners On/2 Out			73	13	2	11	12	.178	.274	.286
Scor. Pos./2 Out			46	7	1	10	8	.152	.239	.304
Late Inning Pressure			189	52	9	15	25	.275	.487	.330
Leading Off			47	17	3	1	5	.362	.660	.375
Runners On			85	22	3	11	15	.259	.435	.340
Runners/Scor. Pos.			54	12	2	11	11	.222	.389	.348
First 9 Batters			352	90	13	31	52	.256	.426	.318
Second 9 Batters			21	2	0	2	5	.095	.143	.174
All Batters Thereafter			0	0	0	0	0	—	—	—

Loves to face: Keith Moreland (0-for-11)
Hates to face: R. J. Reynolds (.625, 5-for-8)
Ground outs-to-air outs ratio: 0.94 last season, 0.81 for career. . . . Additional statistics: 8 double-play ground outs in 83 opportunities, 18 doubles, 2 triples in 98.2 innings last season. . . . What a difference a day makes! Career record of 0–10 during May, 10–1 in June. . . . Career record of 25–13, with a 2.50 ERA on grass fields; 2–14, 4.43 ERA on artificial surfaces. . . . Opponents' career batting averages: .214 by left-handers, .254 by right-handers. Last season's .228 mark by lefties was the *highest* of his five-year career. . . . Career record of 7–0 vs. Los Angeles. . . . Made 56 appearances as a rookie in 1983, and that total remains the lowest of his career. Only three other pitchers have made at least that many appearances in each of the past five seasons.

Ed Lynch

Chicago Cubs — Throws Right

	W–L	ERA	AB	H	HR	BB	SO	BA	SA	OBA
Season	2-9	5.38	441	130	17	48	80	.295	.488	.366
vs. Left-Handers			208	69	6	27	30	.332	.534	.411
vs. Right-Handers			233	61	11	21	50	.262	.446	.324
Home	0-3	4.55	227	67	8	22	41	.295	.476	.363
Road	2-6	6.22	214	63	9	26	39	.294	.500	.369
Grass	0-8	5.63	320	101	12	34	55	.316	.513	.384
Artificial Turf	2-1	4.81	121	29	5	14	25	.240	.421	.319
April	1-1	3.00	80	21	4	6	14	.263	.475	.322
May	0-4	5.68	104	31	2	12	11	.298	.433	.368
June	0-0	4.60	58	14	0	8	12	.241	.414	.333
July	0-1	5.40	73	27	4	7	13	.370	.589	.425
August	1-2	4.87	76	20	3	10	14	.263	.421	.349
Sept./Oct.	0-1	11.12	50	17	4	5	16	.340	.660	.411
Leading Off Inn.			94	26	4	8	19	.277	.500	.346
Runners On			210	60	8	30	33	.286	.486	.373
Runners/Scor. Pos.			126	37	6	20	21	.294	.532	.388
Runners On/2 Out			87	18	1	19	19	.207	.299	.349
Scor. Pos./2 Out			54	12	1	15	13	.222	.352	.391
Late Inning Pressure			77	28	5	8	9	.364	.675	.430
Leading Off			19	7	1	1	3	.368	.737	.429
Runners On			40	13	2	6	4	.325	.525	.413
Runners/Scor. Pos.			32	11	2	4	3	.344	.594	.417
First 9 Batters			328	89	12	37	64	.271	.454	.348
Second 9 Batters			84	27	3	7	12	.321	.476	.374
All Batters Thereafter			29	14	2	4	4	.483	.897	.545

Loves to face: Dave Concepcion (.050, 1-for-20)
Hates to face: Mike Scioscia (.550, 11-for-20, 2 HR)
Ground outs-to-air outs ratio: 0.98 last season, 0.96 for career. . . . Additional statistics: 9 double-play ground outs in 102 opportunities, 20 doubles, 7 triples in 110.1 innings last season. . . . Struck out 6.53 batters per nine innings, nearly double his previous career average (3.43). . . . Had a record of 2–4 as a starter, 0–5 in relief last season. Has split career appearances almost down the middle: 115 starts, 128 relief appearances. . . . Allowed four hits in 16 at bats with the bases loaded last season, including grand slams to Juan Samuel and Howard Johnson. . . . Yearly batting averages by opposing left-handed batters over the last three seasons: .274, .302, .332. . . . Has walked only one of 72 batters faced with the bases loaded.

Greg Maddux

Chicago Cubs — Throws Right

	W–L	ERA	AB	H	HR	BB	SO	BA	SA	OBA
Season	6-14	5.61	615	181	17	74	101	.294	.452	.373
vs. Left-Handers			341	110	8	46	49	.323	.487	.403
vs. Right-Handers			274	71	9	28	52	.259	.409	.336
Home	1-6	4.65	305	84	10	34	63	.275	.439	.351
Road	5-8	6.60	310	97	7	40	38	.313	.465	.395
Grass	4-8	5.23	425	122	13	51	78	.287	.447	.365
Artificial Turf	2-6	6.46	190	59	4	23	23	.311	.463	.391
April	1-2	5.96	104	31	1	12	19	.298	.404	.371
May	3-2	4.68	126	34	3	15	20	.270	.429	.357
June	0-3	4.24	130	35	7	14	22	.269	.477	.345
July	2-2	4.26	118	34	3	9	16	.288	.449	.344
August	0-2	13.91	49	18	3	12	8	.367	.612	.484
Sept./Oct.	0-3	6.53	88	29	0	12	16	.330	.420	.410
Leading Off Inn.			153	38	2	8	29	.248	.353	.290
Runners On			286	86	10	38	39	.301	.486	.383
Runners/Scor. Pos.			187	57	6	29	29	.305	.476	.396
Runners On/2 Out			110	32	6	18	13	.291	.509	.391
Scor. Pos./2 Out			78	25	4	17	9	.321	.526	.442
Late Inning Pressure			62	17	3	7	11	.274	.468	.348
Leading Off			17	4	0	1	3	.235	.353	.278
Runners On			28	8	2	3	7	.286	.536	.355
Runners/Scor. Pos.			20	8	2	3	6	.400	.750	.478
First 9 Batters			229	71	6	29	40	.310	.450	.391
Second 9 Batters			209	54	4	22	36	.258	.397	.335
All Batters Thereafter			177	56	7	23	25	.316	.520	.395

Loves to face: Buddy Bell (0-for-9)
Hates to face: Franklin Stubbs (.556, 5-for-9)
Ground outs-to-air outs ratio: 2.36, 2d-highest in N.L. last season (minimum: 20 GS), 2.23 for career. . . . Additional statistics: 17 double-play ground outs in 127 opportunities, 36 doubles, 5 triples in 155.2 innings last season. . . . Allowed 25 first-inning runs in 27 starts. . . . Batting support: 4.04 runs per start. . . . Led N.L. rookie pitchers with 27 starts, and had the most losses of any rookie in either league. . . . Average of 5.53 innings per start was lowest among Cubs' regular starters. . . . Average of 4.28 walks per nine innings was 3d-lowest among N.L. pitchers (minimum: 15 GS). . . . Opponents' career batting average is .302. . . . Had a record of 1–11 vs. Eastern Division opponents, 5–3 vs. the Western Division. . . . Youngest player on a National League opening-day roster in 1987.

Joe Magrane

St. Louis Cardinals — Throws Left

	W–L	ERA	AB	H	HR	BB	SO	BA	SA	OBA
Season	9-7	3.54	640	157	9	60	101	.245	.338	.318
vs. Left-Handers			93	21	1	9	21	.226	.312	.301
vs. Right-Handers			547	136	8	51	80	.249	.342	.321
Home	5-2	2.81	325	81	6	30	50	.249	.351	.326
Road	4-5	4.29	315	76	3	30	51	.241	.324	.311
Grass	3-0	3.18	163	38	1	15	30	.233	.288	.298
Artificial Turf	6-7	3.67	477	119	8	45	71	.249	.354	.325
April	1-0	3.00	21	5	0	1	7	.238	.238	.261
May	3-0	2.30	158	34	2	13	24	.215	.297	.275
June	1-1	5.27	54	15	1	5	6	.278	.426	.339
July	0-1	4.06	115	30	1	15	22	.261	.339	.348
August	2-4	4.81	131	38	2	14	15	.290	.374	.373
Sept./Oct.	2-1	2.93	161	35	3	12	27	.217	.329	.292
Leading Off Inn.			162	39	2	12	22	.241	.321	.305
Runners On			255	72	4	31	41	.282	.388	.361
Runners/Scor. Pos.			159	44	3	25	29	.277	.403	.372
Runners On/2 Out			108	27	1	19	19	.250	.333	.367
Scor. Pos./2 Out			70	20	1	16	12	.286	.400	.419
Late Inning Pressure			63	17	0	10	8	.270	.333	.378
Leading Off			14	5	0	3	1	.357	.429	.500
Runners On			29	7	0	7	6	.241	.345	.389
Runners/Scor. Pos.			16	3	0	6	4	.188	.313	.409
First 9 Batters			210	39	3	20	46	.186	.276	.271
Second 9 Batters			203	54	4	20	27	.266	.365	.338
All Batters Thereafter			227	64	2	20	28	.282	.370	.345

Loves to face: Mike Fitzgerald (0-for-10)
Hates to face: Ozzie Virgil (.600, 3-for-5, 1 HR)
Ground outs-to-air outs ratio: 2.05, 4th-highest in N.L. last season, his first in majors. . . . Additional statistics: 22 double-play ground outs in 116 opportunities, 28 doubles, 2 triples in 170.1 innings last season. . . . Allowed 9 first-inning runs in 26 starts. . . . Batting support: 4.15 runs per start. . . . First rookie pitcher since Joe Black in 1952 to start 1st and 7th games of World Series. First pitcher ever, rookie or no, to start 1st and 7th without pitching in between. . . . Opponents had 18 steals in 21 tries. . . . Only N.L. rookie to throw two shutouts. . . . Lost a steal of home when July 6 game was postponed before becoming official. Last pitchers in each league to steal home were both from St. Louis: Curt Simmons of the Cards in 1963, Harry Dorish of the Browns in 1950.

Rick Mahler
Atlanta Braves — Throws Right

	W–L	ERA	AB	H	HR	BB	SO	BA	SA	OBA
Season	8-13	4.98	750	212	24	85	95	.283	.437	.356
vs. Left-Handers			401	126	11	51	46	.314	.469	.391
vs. Right-Handers			349	86	13	34	49	.246	.401	.314
Home	6-6	4.18	422	112	11	43	53	.265	.393	.333
Road	2-7	6.07	328	100	13	42	42	.305	.494	.384
Grass	7-8	4.45	589	160	17	63	74	.272	.411	.340
Artificial Turf	1-5	7.09	161	52	7	22	21	.323	.534	.411
April	2-2	3.46	140	35	2	17	23	.250	.321	.331
May	0-4	6.29	175	54	6	24	18	.309	.457	.392
June	2-2	5.91	131	34	6	13	19	.260	.473	.322
July	2-3	3.65	143	43	4	15	20	.301	.462	.367
August	1-2	6.48	106	32	6	9	12	.302	.547	.364
Sept./Oct.	1-0	3.78	55	14	0	7	3	.255	.309	.339
Leading Off Inn.			185	57	6	17	26	.308	.470	.369
Runners On			309	93	8	45	38	.301	.456	.388
Runners/Scor. Pos.			185	57	6	30	27	.308	.454	.399
Runners On/2 Out			119	35	5	23	18	.294	.496	.408
Scor. Pos./2 Out			77	23	4	16	13	.299	.494	.419
Late Inning Pressure			72	25	3	11	7	.347	.542	.434
Leading Off			21	7	1	2	2	.333	.571	.391
Runners On			24	10	0	7	4	.417	.500	.548
Runners/Scor. Pos.			16	7	0	5	3	.438	.438	.571
First 9 Batters			287	74	5	32	41	.258	.359	.335
Second 9 Batters			249	67	10	25	35	.269	.438	.335
All Batters Thereafter			214	71	9	28	19	.332	.542	.407

Loves to face: Luis Quinones (0-for-9)
Hates to face: Greg Gross (.667, 10-for-15)
Ground outs-to-air outs ratio: 1.74 last season, 1.60 for career. . . .
Additional statistics: 22 double-play ground outs in 151 opportunities, 34 doubles, 5 triples in 197.0 innings last season. . . . Allowed 22 first-inning runs in 28 starts. . . . Batting support: 4.46 runs per start. . . . Opponents had only nine steals in 24 attempts, a success rate of 38 percent (2d lowest among N.L. pitchers). Against other Atlanta pitchers, that rate was 81 percent. . . . Opening-day shutout in 1987 was his third, tying Rip Sewell (1943, 1947, 1949) and Chris Short (1965, 1968, 1970) for modern N.L. record. . . . Losingest pitcher in majors over past three seasons (39–46). . . . Only N.L. pitcher against whom left-handers hit .300 or better in each of past two seasons (minimum: 100 AB in each).

Dennis Martinez
Montreal Expos — Throws Right

	W–L	ERA	AB	H	HR	BB	SO	BA	SA	OBA
Season	11-4	3.30	546	133	9	40	84	.244	.355	.301
vs. Left-Handers			344	82	5	28	54	.238	.343	.294
vs. Right-Handers			202	51	4	12	30	.252	.376	.312
Home	6-1	2.44	295	64	5	23	47	.217	.349	.283
Road	5-3	4.38	251	69	4	17	37	.275	.363	.322
Grass	3-1	2.53	122	30	1	5	17	.246	.320	.281
Artificial Turf	8-3	3.51	424	103	8	35	67	.243	.366	.306
April			0	0	0	0	0	—	—	—
May			0	0	0	0	0	—	—	—
June	3-0	2.86	133	29	1	9	23	.218	.301	.273
July	3-1	4.45	116	31	3	9	15	.267	.431	.328
August	1-2	3.19	160	43	2	14	22	.269	.350	.339
Sept./Oct.	4-1	2.89	137	30	3	8	24	.219	.350	.259
Leading Off Inn.			139	37	3	11	12	.266	.403	.325
Runners On			217	55	4	18	42	.253	.359	.318
Runners/Scor. Pos.			132	34	3	11	33	.258	.364	.318
Runners On/2 Out			99	29	1	10	19	.293	.364	.369
Scor. Pos./2 Out			70	21	1	7	17	.300	.386	.372
Late Inning Pressure			34	7	0	2	6	.206	.265	.250
Leading Off			9	4	0	1	0	.444	.667	.500
Runners On			15	3	0	1	5	.200	.200	.250
Runners/Scor. Pos.			11	3	0	0	4	.273	.273	.273
First 9 Batters			181	37	1	14	31	.204	.276	.264
Second 9 Batters			176	43	5	13	26	.244	.403	.307
All Batters Thereafter			189	53	3	13	27	.280	.386	.330

Loves to face: Barry Bonds (.045, 1-for-22)
Hates to face: Mickey Hatcher (.409, 9-for-22)
Ground outs-to-air outs ratio: 1.08 last season, 1.16 for career. . . .
Additional statistics: 7 double-play ground outs in 84 opportunities, 28 doubles, 3 triples in 144.2 innings last season. . . . Allowed 8 first-inning runs in 22 starts. . . . Batting support: 5.27 runs per start, 6th-highest average in N.L. (minimum: 15 GS). . . . Averaged 6.58 innings pitched in his 22 starts, highest among Expos' regular starters. . . . Did not appear in a day game last season. . . . Won all four starts vs. Mets, compiling a 0.64 ERA. . . . Only pitcher in majors with 100+ innings and ERA of 4.50 or higher every year from 1983 through 1986. . . . Strange but true: Opposing right-handed batters have outhit left-handers in each of the past seven seasons. No other active right-hander has a streak longer than four years.

Greg Mathews
St. Louis Cardinals — Throws Left

	W–L	ERA	AB	H	HR	BB	SO	BA	SA	OBA
Season	11-11	3.73	740	184	17	71	108	.249	.385	.314
vs. Left-Handers			125	30	2	15	14	.240	.336	.321
vs. Right-Handers			615	154	15	56	94	.250	.395	.312
Home	6-7	4.05	386	99	7	33	55	.256	.396	.314
Road	5-4	3.40	354	85	10	38	53	.240	.373	.313
Grass	4-3	2.86	226	50	4	21	27	.221	.319	.286
Artificial Turf	7-8	4.14	514	134	13	50	81	.261	.414	.326
April	2-2	5.47	98	27	2	18	14	.276	.398	.388
May	0-2	7.71	66	22	2	6	5	.333	.515	.384
June	3-2	2.17	161	31	2	17	24	.193	.280	.270
July	2-2	3.65	138	33	4	11	16	.239	.391	.293
August	2-0	4.74	148	43	6	10	27	.291	.480	.335
Sept./Oct.	2-3	1.75	129	28	1	9	22	.217	.326	.268
Leading Off Inn.			193	50	5	17	34	.259	.399	.319
Runners On			282	69	7	33	37	.245	.390	.322
Runners/Scor. Pos.			154	38	5	23	22	.247	.435	.341
Runners On/2 Out			123	28	4	19	17	.228	.455	.331
Scor. Pos./2 Out			79	17	2	15	12	.215	.443	.340
Late Inning Pressure			57	13	1	7	8	.228	.368	.313
Leading Off			14	3	0	5	1	.214	.286	.421
Runners On			24	7	0	1	5	.292	.417	.320
Runners/Scor. Pos.			11	4	0	0	3	.364	.545	.364
First 9 Batters			255	65	5	29	47	.255	.400	.331
Second 9 Batters			248	51	4	15	41	.206	.286	.249
All Batters Thereafter			237	68	8	27	20	.287	.473	.360

Loves to face: Dale Murphy (0-for-11)
Hates to face: Eric Davis (2-for-2, 2 HR)
Ground outs-to-air outs ratio: 1.00 last season, 1.06 for career. . . .
Additional statistics: 22 double-play ground outs in 135 opportunities, 44 doubles, 3 triples in 197.2 innings last season. . . . Allowed 18 first-inning runs in 32 starts. . . . Batting support: 4.09 runs per start. . . . Didn't win more than two decisions in a row, or lose more than two in a row, during the 1987 season. . . . Allowed five three-run homers to tie for N.L. lead. . . . June ERA was 4th-best in N.L., September ERA was the best. . . . Has allowed only four home runs to left-handed batters in his two seasons, but one was hit by Steve Carlton. . . . Has a career ERA of 2.95 on grass fields, compared to 4.02 on artificial turf. . . . Was originally drafted by, but didn't sign with, the team he faced in the 1987 World Series.

Lance McCullers
San Diego Padres — Throws Right

	W–L	ERA	AB	H	HR	BB	SO	BA	SA	OBA
Season	8-10	3.72	471	115	11	59	126	.244	.376	.330
vs. Left-Handers			239	54	2	42	66	.226	.301	.340
vs. Right-Handers			232	61	9	17	60	.263	.453	.317
Home	6-5	2.97	237	53	3	33	77	.224	.316	.319
Road	2-5	4.53	234	62	8	26	49	.265	.436	.341
Grass	7-8	3.40	333	81	7	43	98	.243	.363	.331
Artificial Turf	1-2	4.50	138	34	4	16	28	.246	.406	.327
April	2-2	5.68	52	16	0	7	17	.308	.423	.390
May	0-1	4.00	72	18	2	13	14	.250	.375	.368
June	2-2	4.26	94	23	2	8	25	.245	.372	.304
July	2-1	4.94	86	20	3	15	24	.233	.372	.347
August	1-1	2.31	89	18	1	7	26	.202	.292	.260
Sept./Oct.	1-3	1.77	78	20	3	9	20	.256	.449	.337
Leading Off Inn.			99	23	2	6	22	.232	.374	.276
Runners On			236	57	5	37	75	.242	.356	.347
Runners/Scor. Pos.			163	36	2	28	50	.221	.307	.338
Runners On/2 Out			108	25	1	20	34	.231	.296	.352
Scor. Pos./2 Out			85	17	0	15	28	.200	.235	.320
Late Inning Pressure			280	73	6	44	70	.261	.400	.362
Leading Off			66	15	1	3	19	.227	.394	.261
Runners On			130	33	2	28	35	.254	.354	.388
Runners/Scor. Pos.			94	22	0	21	23	.234	.277	.376
First 9 Batters			430	100	11	53	118	.233	.367	.318
Second 9 Batters			41	15	0	6	8	.366	.463	.447
All Batters Thereafter			0	0	0	0	0	—	—	—

Loves to face: Glenn Davis (0-for-18)
Hates to face: Mariano Duncan (5-for-5)
Ground outs-to-air outs ratio: 1.13 last season, 0.92 for career. . . .
Additional statistics: 5 double-play ground outs in 107 opportunities, 27 doubles, 1 triple in 123.1 innings last season. . . . Changing of the guard: McCullers entered 26 games in save situations last season, Gossage 17. In 1986, the tally was Goose 26, Lance 17. . . . Allowed only four hits in 25 at bats with the bases loaded last season, but one of those hits was a pinch-hit grand slam by Jim Sundberg. . . . Opponents' batting average in Late-Inning Pressure Situations has been higher than in unpressured situations in each of his three seasons in the majors. . . . Opponents' career breakdown: .235 with the bases empty, .215 with runners on base. . . . Other career averages: .250 by left-handed batters, .203 by right-handers.

Roger McDowell

New York Mets   Throws Right

	W–L	ERA	AB	H	HR	BB	SO	BA	SA	OBA
Season	7-5	4.16	344	95	7	28	32	.276	.366	.330
vs. Left-Handers			169	41	3	17	19	.243	.320	.314
vs. Right-Handers			175	54	4	11	13	.309	.411	.346
Home	5-3	4.53	196	50	7	12	19	.255	.383	.294
Road	2-2	3.65	148	45	0	16	13	.304	.345	.376
Grass	6-4	4.76	269	77	7	18	25	.286	.394	.330
Artificial Turf	1-1	2.18	75	18	0	10	7	.240	.267	.329
April			0	0	0	0	0	—	—	—
May	2-1	4.15	67	20	0	4	10	.299	.373	.342
June	2-2	5.68	79	27	4	7	7	.342	.506	.395
July	1-0	1.42	71	17	1	1	5	.239	.282	.253
August	2-2	4.74	72	16	1	4	3	.222	.292	.256
Sept./Oct.	0-0	5.02	55	15	1	12	7	.273	.364	.403
Leading Off Inn.			73	25	4	3	2	.342	.548	.368
Runners On			184	52	2	14	22	.283	.342	.332
Runners/Scor. Pos.			111	34	1	11	15	.306	.369	.359
Runners On/2 Out			85	28	1	6	9	.329	.388	.387
Scor. Pos./2 Out			58	20	0	5	8	.345	.379	.406
Late Inning Pressure			202	56	6	19	15	.277	.391	.339
Leading Off			44	15	3	1	1	.341	.568	.356
Runners On			102	29	2	12	8	.284	.373	.359
Runners/Scor. Pos.			62	21	1	9	7	.339	.435	.411
First 9 Batters			309	83	7	26	27	.269	.366	.326
Second 9 Batters			35	12	0	2	5	.343	.371	.368
All Batters Thereafter			0	0	0	0	0	—	—	—

Loves to face: Curt Ford (0-for-9)
Hates to face: Keith Moreland (.500, 8-for-16, 2 HR)
Ground outs-to-air outs ratio: 2.81, 3d-highest in N.L. last season (minimum: 200 BFP), 3.16 for career. . . . Additional statistics: 12 double-play ground outs in 90 opportunities, 10 doubles, 0 triples in 88.2 innings last season. . . . Struck out an average of 3.25 batters per nine innings, 2d-lowest rate among N.L. relievers (minimum: 30 games). . . . Earned 25 saves in 31 opportunities (81 percent), a much higher rate than over his two previous seasons (39-for-58, 67 percent). . . . No other pitcher has saved 15 or more games and posted winning records in each of McDowell's three seasons in the majors. . . . Career average against McDowell is virtually the same by left-handed batters (.241) and right-handers (.242). . . . Has faced 720 right-handed batters in his career without allowing a triple.

Andy McGaffigan

Montreal Expos   Throws Right

	W–L	ERA	AB	H	HR	BB	SO	BA	SA	OBA
Season	5-2	2.39	447	105	5	42	100	.235	.320	.303
vs. Left-Handers			240	65	4	26	51	.271	.392	.343
vs. Right-Handers			207	40	1	16	49	.193	.237	.254
Home	3-0	3.00	218	58	2	19	47	.266	.367	.328
Road	2-2	1.85	229	47	3	23	53	.205	.275	.280
Grass	1-1	1.13	113	21	1	9	34	.186	.230	.252
Artificial Turf	4-1	2.85	334	84	4	33	66	.251	.350	.320
April	0-0	0.64	50	9	0	4	13	.180	.200	.241
May	0-0	3.10	83	23	0	5	22	.277	.313	.326
June	0-1	3.15	69	16	1	7	12	.232	.304	.308
July	2-1	2.63	53	15	0	3	9	.283	.340	.321
August	2-0	1.80	90	21	2	12	22	.233	.356	.327
Sept./Oct.	1-0	2.63	102	21	2	11	22	.206	.353	.281
Leading Off Inn.			108	28	2	5	28	.259	.352	.292
Runners On			203	41	1	22	49	.202	.261	.283
Runners/Scor. Pos.			123	29	0	16	32	.236	.285	.322
Runners On/2 Out			95	16	0	10	25	.168	.211	.248
Scor. Pos./2 Out			62	13	0	8	19	.210	.258	.300
Late Inning Pressure			158	36	2	17	37	.228	.323	.303
Leading Off			42	8	1	0	13	.190	.286	.190
Runners On			58	13	0	11	15	.224	.293	.348
Runners/Scor. Pos.			38	10	0	8	11	.263	.342	.391
First 9 Batters			407	93	3	34	90	.229	.305	.291
Second 9 Batters			40	12	2	8	10	.300	.475	.417
All Batters Thereafter			0	0	0	0	0	—	—	—

Loves to face: Bob Brenly (0-for-9)
Hates to face: Bob Horner (.400, 6-for-15, 4 HR)
Ground outs-to-air outs ratio: 1.27 last season, 1.18 for career. . . . Additional statistics: 8 double-play ground outs in 92 opportunities, 17 doubles, 3 triples in 120.1 innings last season. . . . Opponents' career batting average of .186 (8-for-43) with the bases loaded. . . . Last season was his first full season in which he was used only in relief. Career record of 11–19 as a starting pitcher, 14–6 as a reliever. . . . Pitched three or more innings in 14 relief appearances last season, tying California's DeWayne Buice and Chuck Finley for major-league lead. . . . Only home run allowed to a right-handed batter was hit by Keith Moreland in the season finale. . . . Ranks sixth in majors with an ERA of 3.14 in road games over the past five seasons (minimum: 250 IP).

Dave Meads

Houston Astros   Throws Left

	W–L	ERA	AB	H	HR	BB	SO	BA	SA	OBA
Season	5-3	5.55	187	60	8	16	32	.321	.535	.372
vs. Left-Handers			56	15	2	4	11	.268	.411	.317
vs. Right-Handers			131	45	6	12	21	.344	.588	.395
Home	5-0	3.27	79	22	0	3	13	.278	.342	.301
Road	0-3	7.43	108	38	8	13	19	.352	.676	.419
Grass	0-2	10.34	68	29	8	10	13	.426	.868	.488
Artificial Turf	5-1	3.27	119	31	0	6	19	.261	.345	.299
April	1-0	7.20	19	5	0	1	5	.263	.632	.300
May	3-1	4.20	54	12	1	4	11	.222	.352	.288
June	1-0	9.35	39	18	3	4	3	.462	.795	.500
July	0-0	0.79	42	13	0	2	5	.310	.310	.333
August	0-2	11.57	11	4	2	2	2	.364	.909	.462
Sept./Oct.	0-0	8.53	22	8	2	3	6	.364	.682	.423
Leading Off Inn.			41	12	2	5	8	.293	.512	.370
Runners On			93	31	3	5	15	.333	.352	.356
Runners/Scor. Pos.			48	18	2	4	8	.375	.563	.400
Runners On/2 Out			40	13	1	3	9	.325	.475	.372
Scor. Pos./2 Out			25	10	1	2	6	.400	.640	.444
Late Inning Pressure			73	19	2	6	20	.260	.438	.325
Leading Off			20	4	1	1	5	.200	.450	.238
Runners On			31	9	0	3	11	.290	.323	.353
Runners/Scor. Pos.			19	6	0	3	6	.316	.368	.409
First 9 Batters			177	55	8	14	32	.311	.531	.359
Second 9 Batters			10	5	0	2	0	.500	.600	.583
All Batters Thereafter			0	0	0	0	0	—	—	—

Loves to face: Wally Backman (0-for-4, 4 ground outs)
Hates to face: Mike Marshall (2-for-2, 1 HR)
Ground outs-to-air outs ratio: 1.25 last season, his first in majors. . . . Additional statistics: 8 double-play ground outs in 47 opportunities, 8 doubles, 4 triples in 48.2 innings last season. . . . Entered only two games in save situations, and came up empty. . . . Allowed an average of 11.10 hits per nine innings, 3d-highest rate among N.L. relievers (minimum: 30 games). . . . After 28.1 innings he had an ERA of 6.35, but a record of 5–1. Meanwhile, Nolan Ryan couldn't buy a win. . . . Allowed only one run over 17 appearances (June 19 to Aug. 5). . . . Astros lost 15 of the last 19 games in which he appeared. . . . Of the 123 pitchers with winning records and at least as many innings pitched as Meads last season, only two had higher ERAs: Mike Mason (4–3, 5.64) and Dan Petry (9–7, 5.61).

John Mitchell

New York Mets   Throws Right

	W–L	ERA	AB	H	HR	BB	SO	BA	SA	OBA
Season	3-6	4.11	444	124	6	36	57	.279	.365	.333
vs. Left-Handers			240	71	2	24	24	.296	.363	.358
vs. Right-Handers			204	53	4	12	33	.260	.368	.301
Home	3-1	3.95	264	71	2	26	36	.269	.330	.336
Road	0-5	4.36	180	53	4	10	21	.294	.417	.328
Grass	3-3	4.18	327	91	3	29	46	.278	.349	.337
Artificial Turf	0-3	3.90	117	33	3	7	11	.282	.410	.320
April			0	0	0	0	0	—	—	—
May	0-1	5.40	89	29	1	5	14	.326	.416	.362
June	1-0	2.53	123	33	1	8	12	.268	.309	.313
July	1-2	5.54	107	31	2	10	8	.290	.402	.350
August	1-2	4.32	98	25	1	12	19	.255	.347	.336
Sept./Oct.	0-1	1.29	27	6	1	1	4	.222	.370	.241
Leading Off Inn.			108	28	0	7	15	.259	.296	.304
Runners On			199	56	4	20	26	.281	.402	.339
Runners/Scor. Pos.			116	34	3	13	19	.293	.457	.351
Runners On/2 Out			86	26	3	10	11	.302	.500	.375
Scor. Pos./2 Out			59	19	3	7	9	.322	.610	.394
Late Inning Pressure			26	10	1	2	1	.385	.538	.429
Leading Off			7	3	0	0	1	.429	.571	.429
Runners On			8	3	1	2	0	.375	.750	.500
Runners/Scor. Pos.			2	0	0	1	0	.000	.000	.333
First 9 Batters			162	39	2	11	26	.241	.315	.293
Second 9 Batters			141	41	0	13	17	.291	.348	.348
All Batters Thereafter			141	41	4	12	14	.312	.440	.361

Loves to face: Von Hayes (0-for-10)
Hates to face: Mitch Webster (3-for-3, 3 BB)
Ground outs-to-air outs ratio: 2.07 last season, 2.21 for career. . . . Additional statistics: 8 double-play ground outs in 100 opportunities, 18 doubles, 1 triple in 111.2 innings last season. . . . Allowed 10 first-inning runs in 19 starts. . . . Batting support: 4.79 runs per start. . . . Only N.L. rookie to allow less than three walks per nine innings (minimum: 50 IP). . . . June ERA was 7th-best in N.L. . . . Allowed only one hit to an opposing pitcher in 32 at bats; Kevin Gross spoiled the no-hitter with a single on August 5. . . . Career record of 48–34 with a 3.29 ERA in five seasons in minors. . . . Joined Mets along with Bob Ojeda in trade that sent Wes Gardner and Calvin Schiraldi to Boston, and Mitchell pitched more innings than any of them last season.

Jamie Moyer
Chicago Cubs   Throws Left

	W–L	ERA	AB	H	HR	BB	SO	BA	SA	OBA
Season	12-15	5.10	776	210	28	97	147	.271	.428	.353
vs. Left-Handers			108	24	5	18	15	.222	.398	.336
vs. Right-Handers			668	186	23	79	132	.278	.433	.355
Home	5-7	4.82	409	106	18	49	81	.259	.435	.341
Road	7-8	5.44	367	104	10	48	66	.283	.420	.366
Grass	6-10	5.35	524	141	23	62	98	.269	.447	.348
Artificial Turf	6-5	4.59	252	69	5	35	49	.274	.389	.361
April	2-1	3.38	99	23	0	11	30	.232	.273	.309
May	3-2	3.94	120	28	5	20	15	.233	.358	.352
June	3-2	4.71	155	39	6	20	27	.252	.419	.339
July	1-2	4.84	140	38	2	17	29	.271	.371	.352
August	1-4	9.00	111	35	8	18	16	.315	.604	.406
Sept./Oct.	2-4	5.00	151	47	7	11	30	.311	.517	.354
Leading Off Inn.			188	55	7	21	42	.293	.452	.367
Runners On			341	91	14	49	51	.267	.446	.358
Runners/Scor. Pos.			184	55	7	35	27	.299	.495	.406
Runners On/2 Out			149	45	8	26	21	.302	.510	.412
Scor. Pos./2 Out			94	29	3	23	14	.309	.468	.454
Late Inning Pressure			83	27	5	15	5	.325	.578	.434
Leading Off			20	6	2	3	1	.300	.600	.391
Runners On			41	13	3	7	3	.317	.659	.417
Runners/Scor. Pos.			23	6	1	5	1	.261	.478	.393
First 9 Batters			265	64	10	30	53	.242	.396	.315
Second 9 Batters			254	67	6	33	57	.264	.390	.352
All Batters Thereafter			257	79	12	34	37	.307	.498	.391

Loves to face: Bill Doran (0-for-9)
Hates to face: Lance Parrish (.462, 6-for-13, 2 HR)
Ground outs-to-air outs ratio: 1.38 last season, 1.43 for career....
Additional statistics: 16 double-play ground outs in 173 opportunities, 28 doubles, 5 triples in 201.0 innings last season.... Allowed 20 first-inning runs in 33 starts.... Batting support: 3.79 runs per start, 8th-lowest average in N.L. (minimum: 15 GS).... Allowed 4.34 walks per nine innings, 2d-highest rate among N.L. pitchers (minimum: 15 GS).... Only pitcher to defeat the Astros twice in Houston last season.... Struck out seven consecutive batters vs. Giants on July 3, three short of Tom Seaver's all-time major-league record. Two other pitchers had seven Ks in a row last season (Brian Fisher and Tom Henke), but both streaks spanned two games.... Opponents' career batting average of .310 leading off innings.

Rob Murphy
Cincinnati Reds   Throws Left

	W–L	ERA	AB	H	HR	BB	SO	BA	SA	OBA
Season	8-5	3.04	380	91	7	32	99	.239	.355	.297
vs. Left-Handers			120	28	1	9	33	.233	.308	.287
vs. Right-Handers			260	63	6	23	66	.242	.377	.302
Home	5-3	3.93	212	57	6	17	54	.269	.420	.320
Road	3-2	1.97	168	34	1	15	45	.202	.274	.268
Grass	2-2	2.92	98	26	1	9	26	.265	.388	.327
Artificial Turf	6-3	3.08	282	65	6	23	73	.230	.344	.287
April	3-1	1.86	64	10	2	10	18	.156	.266	.267
May	0-0	1.56	62	11	0	4	16	.177	.242	.227
June	1-2	6.75	52	18	1	4	9	.346	.481	.386
July	1-0	4.50	67	20	1	7	20	.299	.403	.365
August	1-2	3.60	76	18	3	4	19	.237	.461	.275
Sept./Oct.	2-0	1.13	59	14	0	3	17	.237	.271	.274
Leading Off Inn.			88	16	4	6	26	.182	.375	.234
Runners On			152	38	0	16	39	.250	.336	.318
Runners/Scor. Pos.			76	25	0	15	19	.329	.447	.430
Runners On/2 Out			77	17	0	14	20	.221	.299	.341
Scor. Pos./2 Out			39	9	0	13	12	.231	.308	.423
Late Inning Pressure			127	33	3	14	30	.260	.394	.331
Leading Off			30	6	2	2	8	.200	.433	.250
Runners On			48	14	0	10	10	.292	.417	.407
Runners/Scor. Pos.			25	9	0	10	4	.360	.560	.528
First 9 Batters			365	86	5	32	97	.236	.337	.296
Second 9 Batters			15	5	2	0	2	.333	.800	.333
All Batters Thereafter			0	0	0	0	0	—	—	—

Loves to face: Dale Murphy (0-for-9)
Hates to face: Will Clark (.556, 5-for-9, 3 2B)
Ground outs-to-air outs ratio: 1.20 last season, 1.21 for career....
Additional statistics: 5 double-play ground outs in 49 opportunities, 17 doubles, 3 triples in 100.2 innings last season.... Removed for a pinch-hitter 38 times last season, highest total in N.L.... Faced only one batter in 12 appearances, also a league high.... Career record of 5–0 (2.05 ERA) in day games, 6–0 (0.99 ERA) from September 1 on.... Allowed only seven homers last season, but three of them were surrendered in the same game (vs. Pittsburgh, Aug. 18).... Has allowed only one home run in his career outside of Riverfront Stadium (Kevin McReynolds at Shea, July 18).... One more home run note: Has faced 183 left-handed batters, and allowed only one home run (to Barry Bonds).

Randy Myers
New York Mets   Throws Left

	W–L	ERA	AB	H	HR	BB	SO	BA	SA	OBA
Season	3-6	3.96	271	61	6	30	92	.225	.343	.296
vs. Left-Handers			80	14	1	8	36	.175	.300	.244
vs. Right-Handers			191	47	5	22	56	.246	.361	.318
Home	1-0	4.37	129	30	2	12	46	.233	.357	.292
Road	2-6	3.60	142	31	4	18	46	.218	.331	.301
Grass	1-2	3.24	182	41	2	18	64	.225	.313	.291
Artificial Turf	2-4	5.40	89	20	4	12	28	.225	.404	.308
April	0-1	13.50	24	7	1	9	8	.292	.417	.485
May	0-0	5.40	17	3	0	4	7	.176	.235	.333
June	0-2	2.61	33	6	0	5	13	.182	.212	.282
July	2-1	4.57	85	22	5	4	21	.259	.494	.292
August	0-0	1.35	50	9	0	2	21	.180	.240	.208
Sept./Oct.	1-2	2.41	62	14	0	6	22	.226	.290	.278
Leading Off Inn.			60	13	2	9	21	.217	.367	.319
Runners On			124	26	3	11	47	.210	.306	.262
Runners/Scor. Pos.			69	14	2	7	29	.203	.304	.256
Runners On/2 Out			59	10	2	5	18	.169	.271	.234
Scor. Pos./2 Out			35	6	1	2	13	.171	.257	.216
Late Inning Pressure			86	17	3	14	29	.198	.326	.307
Leading Off			20	4	1	4	7	.200	.350	.333
Runners On			38	7	1	5	15	.184	.263	.273
Runners/Scor. Pos.			22	5	1	3	8	.227	.364	.308
First 9 Batters			249	58	5	28	87	.233	.349	.305
Second 9 Batters			22	3	1	2	5	.136	.273	.200
All Batters Thereafter			0	0	0	0	0	—	—	

Loves to face: Tom Foley (0-for-4, 4 SO)
Hates to face: Carmelo Martinez (2-for-2)
Ground outs-to-air outs ratio: 0.80 last season, 0.80 for career....
Additional statistics: 2 double-play ground outs in 58 opportunities, 10 doubles, 2 triples in 75.0 innings last season.... Led N.L. rookies with six saves. In the entire league last season, rookies registered only 29 saves.... Five of his six saves were after Aug. 1.... Led N.L. relievers with an average of 11.04 strikeouts per nine innings (minimum: 30 games).... Walked 14 batters while striking out 16 in his first 12 innings. After that, he walked only 16 while striking out 76.... Allowed a home run in four consecutive games in July, but allowed only one in 28 games thereafter.... Opposing left-handed batters have a career average of .169 with only one home run in 89 at bats (by Sid Bream).

Randy O'Neal
Braves/Cardinals   Throws Right

	W–L	ERA	AB	H	HR	BB	SO	BA	SA	OBA
Season	4-2	5.32	268	81	12	26	37	.302	.496	.366
vs. Left-Handers			135	46	3	19	18	.341	.489	.419
vs. Right-Handers			133	35	9	7	19	.263	.504	.308
Home	2-1	3.92	154	41	6	10	23	.266	.422	.317
Road	2-1	7.33	114	40	6	16	14	.351	.596	.427
Grass	3-2	4.99	194	60	9	20	24	.309	.505	.376
Artificial Turf	1-0	6.23	74	21	3	6	13	.284	.473	.338
April	2-0	4.82	79	26	5	5	11	.329	.633	.369
May	1-1	5.56	98	29	3	8	13	.296	.459	.355
June	0-0	5.40	18	5	1	3	1	.278	.611	.381
July	1-1	6.75	55	19	1	8	8	.345	.436	.424
August	0-0		0	0	0	0	0			
Sept./Oct.	0-0	1.80	18	2	0	2	4	.111	.167	.200
Leading Off Inn.			65	24	5	3	10	.369	.646	.406
Runners On			124	32	4	15	14	.258	.427	.333
Runners/Scor. Pos.			68	15	3	10	11	.221	.426	.313
Runners On/2 Out			51	14	3	8	7	.275	.490	.373
Scor. Pos./2 Out			37	9	3	6	6	.243	.514	.349
Late Inning Pressure			7	2	1	1	1	.286	.857	.375
Leading Off			3	1	1	1	0	.333	1.333	.333
Runners On			1	0	0	0	1	.000	.000	.000
Runners/Scor. Pos.			1	0	0	0	1	.000	.000	.000
First 9 Batters			123	37	7	15	16	.301	.528	.383
Second 9 Batters			83	27	2	6	9	.325	.458	.367
All Batters Thereafter			62	17	3	5	12	.274	.484	.328

Loves to face: Argenis Salazar (0-for-7)
Hates to face: Len Dykstra (.667, 6-for-9, 1 HR)
Ground outs-to-air outs ratio: 2.38 last season, 1.54 for career....
Additional statistics: 8 double-play ground outs in 63 opportunities, 12 doubles, 2 triples in 66.0 innings last season.... Averaged 5.21 innings pitched in his 11 starts.... Career record of 14–12 with a 4.12 ERA in 37 starts; 0–3, 4.20 ERA in 49 relief appearances.... Yearly opponents' batting averages have risen every season of his four-year career: .222, .240, .260, .302. But last season's average with runners in scoring position was a career low.... Opposing right-handers have outhit left-handers during his career, despite last season's 78-point spread in the other direction.... Opponents have only four hits in 22 career at bats (.182) with the bases loaded, and are 0-for-11 with two outs and the bases full.

Jesse Orosco

New York Mets — Throws Left

	W–L	ERA	AB	H	HR	BB	SO	BA	SA	OBA
Season	3-9	4.44	293	78	5	31	78	.266	.358	.336
vs. Left-Handers			74	17	0	5	21	.230	.243	.275
vs. Right-Handers			219	61	5	26	57	.279	.397	.356
Home	2-4	2.83	157	39	2	16	49	.248	.299	.320
Road	1-5	6.31	136	39	3	15	29	.287	.426	.355
Grass	3-7	4.20	230	61	2	22	67	.265	.326	.327
Artificial Turf	0-2	5.29	63	17	3	9	11	.270	.476	.370
April	0-1	5.79	36	9	1	4	10	.250	.361	.325
May	1-3	4.05	54	17	1	3	19	.315	.407	.345
June	0-2	6.97	43	14	1	10	9	.326	.419	.463
July	1-1	4.05	52	13	1	5	9	.250	.327	.316
August	1-0	4.61	47	11	0	6	16	.234	.340	.304
Sept./Oct.	0-2	2.65	61	14	1	3	15	.230	.311	.277
Leading Off Inn.			60	19	1	6	14	.317	.417	.379
Runners On			160	41	3	20	44	.256	.350	.335
Runners/Scor. Pos.			99	21	3	17	28	.212	.333	.322
Runners On/2 Out			67	15	2	10	20	.224	.358	.325
Scor. Pos./2 Out			48	11	2	9	12	.229	.396	.351
Late Inning Pressure			182	47	4	24	50	.258	.352	.344
Leading Off			39	9	0	4	12	.231	.282	.302
Runners On			91	26	3	16	23	.286	.396	.391
Runners/Scor. Pos.			61	15	3	14	16	.246	.410	.385
First 9 Batters			281	75	4	29	76	.267	.352	.335
Second 9 Batters			12	3	1	2	2	.250	.500	.357
All Batters Thereafter			0	0	0	0	0			

Loves to face: Barry Bonds (0-for-12, 6 SO)
Hates to face: Andre Dawson (.545, 12-for-22, 2 HR)
Ground outs-to-air outs ratio: 0.81 last season, 0.87 for career. . . .
Additional statistics: 4 double-play ground outs in 86 opportunities, 12 doubles, 0 triples in 77.0 innings last season. . . . Earned only 16 saves in 25 opportunities last season (64%), well below his rate of the previous four seasons (86 for 115, 75%). . . . Allowed grand slam home runs in extra innings on consecutive Saturdays to Tom Herr (Apr. 25) and Tim Raines (May 2). The only other pitcher ever to allow two extra-inning slams in one season: Sammy Stewart in 1980. Pitchers who allowed two extra-inning slams in their *careers*: Sheriff Blake, Bob Hogue, Tom Hume, Syl Johnson, Lindy McDaniel, Dale Murray, Ron Taylor. . . . Opponents hit better with bases empty than with runners on in each of the past seven seasons.

David Palmer

Atlanta Braves — Throws Right

	W–L	ERA	AB	H	HR	BB	SO	BA	SA	OBA
Season	8-11	4.90	602	169	17	64	111	.281	.429	.354
vs. Left-Handers			332	96	9	42	66	.289	.449	.371
vs. Right-Handers			270	73	8	22	45	.270	.404	.332
Home	4-7	6.21	304	93	8	35	54	.306	.461	.384
Road	4-4	3.62	298	76	9	29	57	.255	.396	.322
Grass	6-9	5.14	416	116	11	45	76	.279	.425	.355
Artificial Turf	2-2	4.37	186	53	6	19	35	.285	.435	.353
April	0-4	3.22	136	33	7	15	27	.243	.412	.322
May	4-0	5.19	140	42	5	13	32	.300	.479	.367
June	0-4	7.29	89	31	2	6	14	.348	.506	.378
July	1-0	0.00	21	2	0	4	4	.095	.143	.240
August	2-2	4.05	129	32	1	14	18	.248	.364	.331
Sept./Oct.	1-1	7.84	87	29	2	12	16	.333	.460	.420
Leading Off Inn.			150	42	5	11	26	.280	.453	.329
Runners On			261	74	9	32	53	.284	.444	.370
Runners/Scor. Pos.			172	46	3	25	42	.267	.360	.361
Runners On/2 Out			111	25	3	17	22	.225	.351	.348
Scor. Pos./2 Out			85	19	2	14	17	.224	.318	.347
Late Inning Pressure			24	5	1	3	3	.208	.333	.296
Leading Off			8	2	0	0	1	.250	.250	.250
Runners On			7	2	1	1	1	.286	.714	.375
Runners/Scor. Pos.			3	0	0	0	1	.000	.000	.000
First 9 Batters			224	51	5	23	48	.228	.348	.298
Second 9 Batters			210	57	6	25	35	.271	.419	.357
All Batters Thereafter			168	61	6	16	28	.363	.548	.423

Loves to face: Ozzie Smith (.107, 3-for-28)
Hates to face: Tim Wallach (.545, 6-for-11, 2 HR)
Ground outs-to-air outs ratio: 2.03, 5th-highest in N.L. last season (minimum: 20 GS), 2.10 for career (2.60 vs. left-handed batters, 1.72 vs. right-handers). . . . Additional statistics: 12 double-play ground outs in 120 opportunities, 28 doubles, 5 triples in 152.1 innings last season. . . . Allowed 15 first-inning runs in 28 starts. . . . Batting support: 4.96 runs per start. . . . Didn't complete any of his 28 starts. . . . Day-game ERA of 2.66 was 2d-lowest in N.L. Over the last six seasons, his record is 14–8 in day games, 25–30 at night. . . . Has lost eight decisions in a row to the Reds since beating them on Sept. 1, 1979. . . . ERA was below 3.00 in first three seasons in majors, and between 3.00 and 4.00 for four seasons after that before reaching career-high mark in 1987.

Jeff Parrett

Montreal Expos — Throws Right

	W–L	ERA	AB	H	HR	BB	SO	BA	SA	OBA
Season	7-6	4.21	231	53	8	30	56	.229	.385	.317
vs. Left-Handers			140	35	5	18	29	.250	.407	.333
vs. Right-Handers			91	18	3	12	27	.198	.352	.291
Home	3-4	3.93	133	26	4	17	32	.195	.346	.285
Road	4-2	4.62	98	27	4	13	24	.276	.439	.360
Grass	1-0	9.31	39	13	3	5	8	.333	.590	.409
Artificial Turf	6-6	3.27	192	40	5	25	48	.208	.344	.298
April	0-1	3.86	19	5	0	1	5	.263	.421	.300
May			0	0	0	0	0	—	—	—
June	1-1	2.45	38	8	2	6	13	.211	.395	.318
July	1-1	6.39	52	14	3	8	13	.269	.481	.367
August	3-2	2.45	74	11	1	8	14	.149	.216	.229
Sept./Oct.	2-1	6.94	48	15	2	7	11	.313	.521	.400
Leading Off Inn.			54	11	2	5	16	.204	.352	.271
Runners On			98	24	3	17	22	.245	.408	.353
Runners/Scor. Pos.			73	16	3	13	17	.219	.411	.333
Runners On/2 Out			47	10	0	9	12	.213	.319	.339
Scor. Pos./2 Out			37	5	0	8	10	.135	.243	.289
Late Inning Pressure			107	29	4	15	24	.271	.439	.358
Leading Off			25	7	1	3	7	.280	.440	.357
Runners On			49	13	2	8	9	.265	.469	.362
Runners/Scor. Pos.			34	6	2	6	8	.176	.412	.293
First 9 Batters			219	51	8	30	54	.233	.384	.324
Second 9 Batters			12	2	0	0	2	.167	.417	.167
All Batters Thereafter			0	0	0	0	0			

Loves to face: Garry Templeton (0-for-5)
Hates to face: John Kruk (.750, 3-for-4, 1 HR)
Ground outs-to-air outs ratio: 0.88 last season, 0.85 for career. . . .
Additional statistics: 2 double-play ground outs in 37 opportunities, 10 doubles, 1 triple in 62.0 innings last season. . . . Earned six saves in 12 opportunities. . . . Faced only 57 batters protecting leads of three runs or less in eighth inning or later, or 21% of his season's total. Other Expos relievers: Burke, 123; McGaffigan, 76; St. Claire, 27. . . . Opposing right-handed batters hit .172 at Olympic Stadium with one home run (Terry Francona) in 52 at bats. . . . Was just as good with two outs and runners in scoring position in 1986, when opposing batters had only one hit in 10 at bats. . . . No relation to Mike Parrott, who was 1–16 for the 1980 Seattle Mariners. Birds of a different feather.

Alejandro Pena

Los Angeles Dodgers — Throws Right

	W–L	ERA	AB	H	HR	BB	SO	BA	SA	OBA
Season	2-7	3.50	327	82	9	37	76	.251	.382	.325
vs. Left-Handers			177	42	2	23	39	.237	.305	.320
vs. Right-Handers			150	40	7	14	37	.267	.473	.331
Home	0-4	2.52	200	47	4	16	46	.235	.340	.294
Road	2-3	5.08	127	35	5	21	30	.276	.449	.371
Grass	0-6	2.98	238	57	7	22	55	.239	.370	.306
Artificial Turf	2-1	4.88	89	25	2	15	21	.281	.416	.374
April	0-1	1.72	59	15	2	2	16	.254	.407	.279
May	0-4	7.04	98	35	4	13	14	.357	.571	.422
June	1-1	2.79	37	8	1	8	11	.216	.324	.356
July	0-0	4.50	40	8	2	7	10	.200	.375	.313
August	1-0	6.75	11	2	0	2	2	.182	.273	.286
Sept./Oct.	0-1	0.39	82	14	0	5	23	.171	.183	.227
Leading Off Inn.			77	18	2	8	17	.234	.390	.306
Runners On			141	35	4	19	36	.248	.383	.333
Runners/Scor. Pos.			74	14	1	13	16	.189	.257	.305
Runners On/2 Out			63	15	1	6	14	.238	.349	.324
Scor. Pos./2 Out			35	5	0	5	8	.143	.171	.286
Late Inning Pressure			90	19	1	12	28	.211	.289	.301
Leading Off			19	7	0	3	6	.368	.474	.455
Runners On			46	6	1	8	17	.130	.239	.255
Runners/Scor. Pos.			24	4	0	6	6	.167	.208	.323
First 9 Batters			216	47	4	28	56	.218	.296	.309
Second 9 Batters			73	20	3	4	12	.274	.479	.308
All Batters Thereafter			38	15	2	5	8	.395	.684	.444

Loves to face: Tim Wallach (.050, 1-for-20)
Hates to face: Tony Pena (.440, 11-for-25)
Ground outs-to-air outs ratio: 0.88 last season, 1.16 for career. . . .
Additional statistics: 4 double-play ground outs in 75 opportunities, 14 doubles, 1 triple in 87.1 innings last season. . . . Led majors with eight saves in September. . . . Record of 0-5 with a 5.30 ERA in seven starts last season; 2-2, 2.26 ERA in 30 relief appearances. . . . Career figures: 23–20, 3.07 as a starter; 5–8, 3.53 in relief. . . . Career record of 4–0 with four no-decisions in starting assignments following relief appearances. . . . Averaged 5.95 strikeouts per nine innings before 1985 shoulder surgery, 6.98 since then. . . . Has split 30 decisions at Dodger Stadium and 24 in road games, but ERA is much lower at home (2.54) than on road (3.87). . . . Has faced 1,258 batters at Dodger Stadium and never allowed a triple.

Pascual Perez

Montreal Expos — Throws Right

	W–L	ERA	AB	H	HR	BB	SO	BA	SA	OBA
Season	7-0	2.30	252	52	5	16	58	.206	.298	.256
vs. Left-Handers			148	33	2	12	33	.223	.291	.286
vs. Right-Handers			104	19	3	4	25	.183	.308	.211
Home	3-0	2.97	124	32	3	11	28	.258	.379	.324
Road	4-0	1.70	128	20	2	5	30	.156	.219	.187
Grass	2-0	1.50	84	14	1	3	19	.167	.214	.193
Artificial Turf	5-0	2.72	168	38	4	13	39	.226	.339	.286
April			0	0	0	0	0	—	—	—
May			0	0	0	0	0	—	—	—
June			0	0	0	0	0	—	—	—
July			0	0	0	0	0	—	—	—
August	0-0	1.93	49	9	0	4	8	.184	.224	.245
Sept./Oct.	7-0	2.40	203	43	5	12	50	.212	.315	.258
Leading Off Inn.			70	19	1	2	15	.271	.371	.292
Runners On			82	20	3	6	15	.244	.378	.300
Runners/Scor. Pos.			46	12	2	3	9	.261	.413	.314
Runners On/2 Out			35	8	0	3	7	.229	.257	.289
Scor. Pos./2 Out			24	6	0	2	5	.250	.292	.308
Late Inning Pressure			32	7	1	0	4	.219	.344	.219
Leading Off			9	3	0	0	0	.333	.444	.333
Runners On			12	3	1	0	2	.250	.500	.250
Runners/Scor. Pos.			7	3	1	0	1	.429	.857	.429
First 9 Batters			81	14	0	7	21	.173	.198	.236
Second 9 Batters			82	20	3	6	18	.244	.402	.295
All Batters Thereafter			89	18	2	3	19	.202	.292	.237

Loves to face: Ozzie Virgil (0-for-12)
Hates to face: Craig Reynolds (.500, 8-for-16, 3 HR)
Ground outs-to-air outs ratio: 2.80, 4th-highest in N.L. last season (minimum: 200 BFP), 1.72 for career.... Additional statistics: 6 double-play ground outs in 39 opportunities, 8 doubles, 0 triples in 70.1 innings last season.... Allowed 4 first-inning runs in 10 starts.... Batting support: 5.60 runs per start.... When we last saw Perez, he was a 1–13 pitcher for the 1985 Braves.... One of two N.L. pitchers to win seven consecutive starts last season. The other: Rick Aguilera.... Seven wins in September were the most by any pitcher in any month last season.... Career record of 17–14 with a 3.15 ERA on artificial turf; 26–27, 4.21 ERA on grass fields.... If you can't beat 'em, etc.: Perez had a career record of 0–6 against the Expos.

Ted Power

Cincinnati Reds — Throws Right

	W–L	ERA	AB	H	HR	BB	SO	BA	SA	OBA
Season	10-13	4.50	798	213	28	71	133	.267	.439	.327
vs. Left-Handers			425	121	11	44	71	.285	.440	.347
vs. Right-Handers			373	92	17	27	62	.247	.437	.302
Home	3-5	5.72	342	98	16	35	56	.287	.512	.350
Road	7-8	3.63	456	115	12	36	77	.252	.384	.309
Grass	5-3	3.61	254	62	10	23	43	.244	.413	.310
Artificial Turf	5-10	4.94	544	151	18	48	90	.278	.450	.334
April	2-0	3.54	109	26	3	9	16	.239	.394	.294
May	2-2	3.95	156	38	5	14	31	.244	.391	.302
June	2-1	3.86	140	38	5	8	21	.271	.443	.309
July	2-2	6.03	129	38	6	9	22	.295	.535	.340
August	2-4	4.04	130	33	3	15	22	.254	.377	.340
Sept./Oct.	0-4	5.73	134	40	6	16	21	.299	.493	.371
Leading Off Inn.			194	51	4	16	28	.263	.407	.319
Runners On			341	91	12	36	64	.267	.428	.332
Runners/Scor. Pos.			202	56	7	20	39	.277	.441	.332
Runners On/2 Out			141	40	7	20	21	.284	.482	.373
Scor. Pos./2 Out			91	24	5	14	16	.264	.462	.362
Late Inning Pressure			41	12	0	5	5	.293	.366	.383
Leading Off			13	2	0	0	0	.154	.231	.154
Runners On			14	3	0	4	4	.214	.214	.421
Runners/Scor. Pos.			8	2	0	3	1	.250	.250	.455
First 9 Batters			273	77	10	27	49	.282	.454	.342
Second 9 Batters			268	68	8	24	42	.254	.396	.316
All Batters Thereafter			257	68	10	20	42	.265	.467	.320

Loves to face: Glenn Wilson (.063, 1-for-16, 1 HR)
Hates to face: Chili Davis (.571, 8-for-14)
Ground outs-to-air outs ratio: 0.86 last season, 0.86 for career.... Additional statistics: 12 double-play ground outs in 151 opportunities, 49 doubles, 2 triples in 204.0 innings last season.... Allowed 36 first-inning runs in 34 starts, 2d-highest rate in N.L. (minimum: 15 GS).... Batting support: 4.50 runs per start.... Lost his last six decisions, including five consecutive starts (Aug. 25 to Sept. 17). ... Allowed nearly as many home runs last season (28) as in previous six seasons combined (33).... Career record of 18–20 with a 4.25 ERA as a starter; 26–22, 3.66 ERA in relief.... Career strikeout-to-walk ratio is 1.16 vs. left-handed batters (.286 BA), 1.87 vs. right-handers (.232 BA).... Opponents have batted .346 (27-for-78, one HR) with the bases loaded.

Pat Perry

Cardinals/Reds — Throws Left

	W–L	ERA	AB	H	HR	BB	SO	BA	SA	OBA
Season	5-2	3.56	292	60	7	25	39	.205	.342	.274
vs. Left-Handers			92	22	1	2	10	.239	.370	.268
vs. Right-Handers			200	38	6	23	29	.190	.330	.277
Home	3-1	3.12	153	29	4	12	21	.190	.353	.256
Road	2-1	4.06	139	31	3	13	18	.223	.331	.294
Grass	0-1	4.02	60	14	2	3	10	.233	.383	.270
Artificial Turf	5-1	3.44	232	46	5	22	29	.198	.332	.275
April	1-0	1.47	64	12	1	2	13	.188	.281	.209
May	1-1	10.38	40	14	2	5	3	.350	.600	.422
June	0-0	2.45	38	5	1	3	4	.132	.263	.195
July	1-1	4.32	59	11	2	4	9	.186	.373	.250
August	1-0	5.54	49	14	1	8	6	.286	.429	.397
Sept./Oct.	1-0	0.00	42	4	0	3	4	.095	.119	.174
Leading Off Inn.			75	18	1	5	12	.240	.347	.296
Runners On			104	24	4	11	15	.231	.423	.302
Runners/Scor. Pos.			65	16	2	9	8	.246	.431	.333
Runners On/2 Out			41	4	0	8	8	.098	.195	.245
Scor. Pos./2 Out			28	3	0	6	5	.107	.250	.265
Late Inning Pressure			127	24	3	13	15	.189	.331	.275
Leading Off			37	7	1	2	6	.189	.324	.250
Runners On			32	8	1	6	5	.250	.469	.368
Runners/Scor. Pos.			19	5	0	6	3	.263	.421	.440
First 9 Batters			270	53	6	20	39	.196	.322	.259
Second 9 Batters			22	7	1	5	0	.318	.591	.444
All Batters Thereafter			0	0	0	0	0			

Loves to face: Kevin Bass (0-for-9)
Hates to face: Keith Moreland (3-for-3, 1 HR)
Ground outs-to-air outs ratio: 0.92 last season, 0.86 for career.... Additional statistics: 5 double-play ground outs in 44 opportunities, 15 doubles, 2 triples in 81.0 innings last season.... Only home run allowed to a left-handed batter last season was hit by Will Clark. ... Allowed no runs on 6 hits in 15.1 innings pitched after being traded to the Reds.... Has made 109 relief appearances in three seasons, but only 16 in save situations in the seventh inning or later. ... Left-handers have hit him for a higher average than right-handers in each of his three seasons in the majors. Only two southpaws have longer current streaks: Jim Deshaies and Frank Viola. ... Opponents' career breakdown: .172 with bases empty, .278 with runners on base, .283 with runners in scoring position.

Charlie Puleo

Atlanta Braves — Throws Right

	W–L	ERA	AB	H	HR	BB	SO	BA	SA	OBA
Season	6-8	4.23	465	122	11	40	99	.262	.391	.319
vs. Left-Handers			246	70	9	25	43	.285	.459	.347
vs. Right-Handers			219	52	2	15	56	.237	.315	.288
Home	4-2	3.88	212	52	6	16	48	.245	.387	.299
Road	2-6	4.52	253	70	5	24	51	.277	.395	.336
Grass	5-5	4.05	322	83	8	26	68	.258	.388	.310
Artificial Turf	1-3	4.66	143	39	3	14	31	.273	.399	.340
April	0-0	3.60	22	7	0	2	5	.318	.364	.400
May	0-0	4.56	98	26	4	4	20	.265	.439	.301
June	2-1	3.89	64	16	1	6	13	.250	.313	.315
July	2-2	4.13	121	29	3	11	28	.240	.380	.296
August	1-4	6.08	103	31	3	12	25	.301	.495	.364
Sept./Oct.	1-1	2.70	57	13	0	5	8	.228	.246	.286
Leading Off Inn.			112	30	2	11	21	.268	.393	.344
Runners On			207	59	6	18	39	.285	.415	.329
Runners/Scor. Pos.			129	34	5	13	27	.264	.411	.311
Runners On/2 Out			87	22	2	3	18	.253	.356	.278
Scor. Pos./2 Out			60	14	1	3	13	.233	.317	.270
Late Inning Pressure			42	10	0	2	9	.238	.333	.273
Leading Off			12	4	0	0	1	.333	.417	.333
Runners On			18	3	0	1	3	.167	.278	.211
Runners/Scor. Pos.			12	1	0	0	2	.083	.083	.083
First 9 Batters			226	63	6	25	47	.279	.407	.351
Second 9 Batters			140	33	2	8	32	.236	.350	.275
All Batters Thereafter			99	26	3	7	20	.263	.414	.303

Loves to face: Andre Dawson (.105, 2-for-19)
Hates to face: Will Clark (3-for-3, 1 HR, 2 BB)
Ground outs-to-air outs ratio: 0.86 last season, 0.92 for career (0.77 vs. left-handed batters, 1.08 vs. right-handers).... Additional statistics: 12 double-play ground outs in 102 opportunities, 21 doubles, 3 triples in 123.1 innings last season.... Allowed 19 first-inning runs in 16 starts, highest average in N.L. (minimum: 15 GS).... Batting support: 3.75 runs per start, 7th-lowest in N.L. (minimum: 15 GS).... Record of 4–8 (4.71 ERA) in 16 starts, 2–0 (2.84 ERA) in 19 relief appearances.... Struck out one more batter than his previous career best in 1982, when he pitched 47.2 more innings than in 1987.... Opposing right-handed batters have outhit left-handers in all six seasons in majors.... Has faced 40 batters with the bases loaded, never walked in a run.

Shane Rawley
Philadelphia Phillies   Throws Left

	W–L	ERA	AB	H	HR	BB	SO	BA	SA	OBA
Season	17-11	4.39	895	250	23	86	123	.279	.428	.343
vs. Left-Handers			102	30	3	10	11	.294	.471	.357
vs. Right-Handers			793	220	20	76	112	.277	.422	.341
Home	8-4	4.38	436	124	12	35	56	.284	.440	.338
Road	9-7	4.40	459	126	11	51	67	.275	.416	.348
Grass	4-4	3.47	219	59	5	27	38	.269	.397	.347
Artificial Turf	13-7	4.69	676	191	18	59	85	.283	.438	.341
April	1-1	3.64	117	35	2	18	11	.299	.427	.393
May	5-1	2.83	164	42	4	11	24	.256	.384	.305
June	2-3	5.85	131	44	2	8	16	.336	.481	.366
July	5-0	3.66	150	39	4	13	23	.260	.393	.321
August	4-1	3.33	196	51	4	15	27	.260	.372	.315
Sept./Oct.	0-5	7.82	137	39	7	21	22	.285	.547	.381
Leading Off Inn.			221	66	7	19	27	.299	.466	.360
Runners On			389	105	11	42	54	.270	.427	.336
Runners/Scor. Pos.			223	51	6	30	35	.229	.377	.312
Runners On/2 Out			169	43	5	22	24	.254	.438	.344
Scor. Pos./2 Out			106	23	3	20	17	.217	.396	.346
Late Inning Pressure			82	23	4	8	11	.280	.451	.344
Leading Off			21	5	2	1	3	.238	.524	.273
Runners On			29	9	2	4	4	.310	.586	.394
Runners/Scor. Pos.			10	3	1	3	1	.300	.800	.462
First 9 Batters			286	72	6	29	44	.252	.381	.326
Second 9 Batters			274	71	6	26	47	.259	.401	.323
All Batters Thereafter			335	107	11	31	32	.319	.490	.373

Loves to face: Candy Maldonado (.080, 2-for-25)
Hates to face: Andre Dawson (.444, 16-for-36, 5 HR)
Ground outs-to-air outs ratio: 0.91 last season, 1.23 for career. . . .
Additional statistics: 14 double-play ground outs in 179 opportunities, 56 doubles (most in majors), 4 triples in 229.2 innings last season. . . . Allowed 20 first-inning runs in 36 starts. . . . Batting support: 4.92 runs per start. . . . Led N.L. with five wins in May and tied for league lead with five in July. . . . Led the league with 17 wins at the end of August, but lost his last five decisions. . . . Career record of 9–21 in September and October. . . . Only pitcher to increase his ratio of home runs to innings pitched in each of the past six seasons. . . . Career record of 9–0 vs. Dodgers. . . . Since joining Phillies: 37–13 in night games on artificial turf, 14–19 in all other games. (Sorry 'bout that, but its *true*.)

Rick Reuschel
Pirates/Giants   Throws Right

	W–L	ERA	AB	H	HR	BB	SO	BA	SA	OBA
Season	13-9	3.09	854	207	13	42	107	.242	.350	.282
vs. Left-Handers			487	125	7	23	40	.257	.390	.293
vs. Right-Handers			367	82	6	19	67	.223	.297	.267
Home	7-4	3.42	416	99	9	17	47	.238	.365	.271
Road	6-5	2.80	438	108	4	25	60	.247	.336	.291
Grass	5-5	3.10	327	71	3	18	46	.217	.297	.264
Artificial Turf	8-4	3.09	527	136	10	24	61	.258	.383	.293
April	0-1	2.81	97	22	3	10	15	.227	.330	.299
May	3-1	1.67	159	41	1	10	22	.258	.333	.312
June	3-2	2.68	169	35	3	11	21	.207	.325	.261
July	2-1	2.43	136	32	4	3	16	.235	.368	.250
August	1-2	5.68	134	43	2	2	14	.321	.478	.326
Sept./Oct.	4-2	3.80	159	34	0	6	19	.214	.289	.251
Leading Off Inn.			220	59	4	7	32	.268	.395	.303
Runners On			337	86	6	19	33	.255	.365	.290
Runners/Scor. Pos.			178	44	4	13	16	.247	.343	.290
Runners On/2 Out			130	23	0	10	20	.177	.208	.236
Scor. Pos./2 Out			76	15	0	8	12	.197	.237	.274
Late Inning Pressure			76	17	2	6	14	.224	.342	.294
Leading Off			22	5	0	0	4	.227	.318	.261
Runners On			27	6	2	2	5	.222	.444	.267
Runners/Scor. Pos.			16	3	1	1	3	.188	.375	.222
First 9 Batters			285	78	6	8	37	.274	.428	.291
Second 9 Batters			259	62	1	15	28	.239	.320	.290
All Batters Thereafter			310	67	6	19	42	.216	.303	.266

Loves to face: Jim Lindeman (0-for-10)
Hates to face: Chris Brown (.462, 6-for-13, 2 HR)
Ground outs-to-air outs ratio: 1.28 last season, 2.04 for career. . . .
Additional statistics: 17 double-play ground outs in 161 opportunities, 33 doubles, 10 triples in 227.0 innings last season. . . . Allowed 21 first-inning runs in 25 starts. . . . Batting support: 4.44 runs per start. . . . Held opponents to lowest stolen-base percentage among N.L. pitchers (minimum: 10 attempts): only 5 of 15 were successful, and no one tried to steal in his 50 innings with Giants. . . . Average of 1.67 walks per nine innings was lowest in N.L. . . . Control was even better in leadoff situations: one walk per 33.0 leadoff batters, one per 19.7 batters faced at other times. . . . Led pitchers with 10 RBI last season. . . . Best ERA in majors during the month of May (1.83) over past three seasons (minimum: 75 IP).

Don Robinson
Pirates/Giants   Throws Right

	W–L	ERA	AB	H	HR	BB	SO	BA	SA	OBA
Season	11-7	3.42	410	105	7	40	79	.256	.378	.320
vs. Left-Handers			223	54	2	25	45	.242	.332	.317
vs. Right-Handers			187	51	5	15	34	.273	.433	.324
Home	6-2	3.72	186	48	4	19	33	.258	.392	.327
Road	5-5	3.17	224	57	3	21	46	.254	.366	.315
Grass	5-3	3.80	175	46	2	22	39	.263	.383	.343
Artificial Turf	6-4	3.14	235	59	5	18	40	.251	.374	.302
April	2-1	5.06	37	9	2	8	3	.243	.459	.378
May	2-1	3.60	77	20	0	6	19	.260	.312	.313
June	1-3	3.44	71	20	1	6	14	.282	.380	.333
July	1-1	3.86	62	17	3	2	17	.274	.468	.297
August	2-0	1.71	76	16	0	9	14	.211	.329	.287
Sept./Oct.	3-1	3.74	87	23	1	9	12	.264	.379	.333
Leading Off Inn.			93	24	2	8	14	.258	.366	.317
Runners On			198	54	3	20	40	.273	.404	.335
Runners/Scor. Pos.			131	34	2	15	25	.260	.412	.329
Runners On/2 Out			81	16	1	12	17	.198	.309	.301
Scor. Pos./2 Out			64	13	1	9	11	.203	.328	.301
Late Inning Pressure			243	66	6	26	49	.272	.416	.342
Leading Off			54	16	2	6	10	.296	.463	.367
Runners On			119	33	2	13	24	.277	.420	.348
Runners/Scor. Pos.			82	21	1	11	16	.256	.415	.344
First 9 Batters			363	92	7	34	71	.253	.380	.315
Second 9 Batters			45	13	0	6	8	.289	.378	.373
All Batters Thereafter			0	0	0	0	0	.000	.000	.000

Loves to face: Leon Durham (.100, 3-for-30)
Hates to face: Shawon Dunston (.556, 5-for-9, 1 HR)
Ground outs-to-air outs ratio: 0.87 last season, 0.89 for career. . . .
Additional statistics: 4 double-play ground outs in 90 opportunities, 23 doubles, 3 triples in 108.0 innings last season. . . . Earned 19 saves in 27 opportunities, after a 15-for-16 performance in 1986. . . . Record of 6–6 (3.86 ERA) with Pittsburgh, 5–1 (2.74 ERA) with the Giants. . . . Faced 31 consecutive batters in Late-Inning Pressure Situations without allowing a hit, longest streak in majors last season. . . . Home run by John Kruk on July 10 was first off Robinson by a left-handed batter in over three years. . . . Career records: 44–44, 4.15 ERA as a starter; 26–26, 3.24 ERA in relief. . . . Survived some lean years in Pittsburgh in between post-season appearances in 1979 and 1987.

Jeff D. Robinson
Giants/Pirates   Throws Right

	W–L	ERA	AB	H	HR	BB	SO	BA	SA	OBA
Season	8-9	2.85	426	89	11	54	101	.209	.336	.297
vs. Left-Handers			237	55	6	30	55	.232	.367	.319
vs. Right-Handers			189	34	5	24	46	.180	.296	.270
Home	4-3	2.39	211	44	5	23	51	.209	.332	.285
Road	4-6	3.29	215	45	6	31	50	.209	.340	.308
Grass	5-5	3.21	266	59	8	33	69	.222	.372	.308
Artificial Turf	3-4	2.27	160	30	3	21	32	.188	.275	.279
April	2-0	1.86	61	10	1	5	17	.164	.230	.235
May	1-4	4.43	74	21	2	14	16	.284	.459	.393
June	2-2	3.00	70	14	3	14	14	.200	.371	.333
July	1-0	1.88	81	14	1	13	20	.173	.235	.281
August	1-2	5.40	59	16	3	3	16	.271	.542	.306
Sept./Oct.	1-1	1.52	81	14	1	5	18	.173	.222	.221
Leading Off Inn.			101	27	4	10	24	.267	.465	.333
Runners On			177	37	4	30	41	.209	.316	.321
Runners/Scor. Pos.			118	19	2	24	30	.161	.254	.299
Runners On/2 Out			71	9	1	17	17	.127	.183	.295
Scor. Pos./2 Out			48	4	0	15	13	.083	.104	.302
Late Inning Pressure			271	57	8	34	67	.210	.347	.297
Leading Off			70	18	3	7	16	.257	.486	.325
Runners On			100	20	3	15	29	.200	.310	.302
Runners/Scor. Pos.			70	11	2	10	22	.157	.271	.259
First 9 Batters			398	83	9	52	96	.209	.327	.299
Second 9 Batters			28	6	2	2	5	.214	.464	.267
All Batters Thereafter			0	0	0	0	0	—	—	—

Loves to face: Nick Esasky (0-for-15)
Hates to face: Denny Walling (.667, 8-for-12, 1 HR)
Ground outs-to-air outs ratio: 1.85 last season, 1.72 for career. . . .
Additional statistics: 12 double-play ground outs in 92 opportunities, 21 doubles, 0 triples in 123.1 innings last season. . . . Earned 14 saves in 25 opportunities. . . . N.L.'s top 15 batters hit only .167 (9-for-54) against him, lowest against any pitcher (minimum: 50 AB). . . . Prior to 1987, had never walked a leadoff batter in Late-Inning Pressure Situations (56 BFP). . . . Career breakdown: .283 by left-handed batters, .222 by right-handers. . . . Opponents' batting average with two outs and runners in scoring position was 3d lowest of past 13 years among pitchers who faced as many batters in that situation as Robinson. . . . By the way, all the Robinsons thrive in that situation. Career marks: Don, .208; Jeff, .220; Ron, .207.

Ron Robinson

Cincinnati Reds	W–L	ERA	AB	H	HR	BB	SO	BA	SA	OBA
Season	7-5	3.68	579	148	14	43	99	.256	.411	.305
vs. Left-Handers			274	80	5	23	30	.292	.456	.341
vs. Right-Handers			305	68	9	20	69	.223	.370	.271
Home	2-5	4.56	293	83	7	23	47	.283	.454	.334
Road	5-0	2.85	286	65	7	20	52	.227	.367	.274
Grass	3-0	2.44	160	35	3	12	31	.219	.325	.270
Artificial Turf	4-5	4.19	419	113	11	31	68	.270	.444	.318
April	0-0	2.25	73	15	2	3	13	.205	.315	.234
May	1-1	3.60	76	21	2	7	18	.276	.421	.333
June	2-1	2.96	98	23	1	10	18	.235	.327	.300
July	1-1	6.21	115	36	4	9	16	.313	.565	.360
August	2-0	3.00	110	24	1	7	22	.218	.309	.263
Sept./Oct.	1-2	3.58	107	29	4	7	12	.271	.486	.319
Leading Off Inn.			148	44	5	7	23	.297	.459	.329
Runners On			221	61	4	26	31	.276	.448	.343
Runners/Scor. Pos.			133	33	2	24	20	.248	.398	.348
Runners On/2 Out			91	19	1	18	15	.209	.297	.339
Scor. Pos./2 Out			61	12	1	16	10	.197	.295	.364
Late Inning Pressure			129	38	5	14	24	.295	.465	.359
Leading Off			35	15	3	1	5	.429	.714	.444
Runners On			53	13	0	10	8	.245	.340	.354
Runners/Scor. Pos.			29	9	0	10	4	.310	.379	.463
First 9 Batters			324	74	7	22	65	.228	.352	.275
Second 9 Batters			149	49	3	12	20	.329	.497	.372
All Batters Thereafter			106	25	4	9	14	.236	.472	.299

Loves to face: Carmelo Martinez (0-for-13)
Hates to face: Steve Sax (.467, 14-for-30)
Ground outs-to-air outs ratio: 0.72, 10th-lowest in N.L. last season (minimum: 200 BFP), 0.96 for career. . . . Additional statistics: 5 double-play ground outs in 96 opportunities, 34 doubles, 7 triples in 154.0 innings last season. . . . Allowed 2 first-inning runs in 18 starts, 2d-lowest average in majors (minimum: 15 GS). . . . Batting support: 6.11 runs per start, highest average in N.L. (minimum: 15 GS). . . . Earned four saves in 14 opportunities. . . . First 30 appearances were out of the bullpen; started last 18 games from June 17 on. Career records: 11–11 as a starter, 14–6 in relief. . . . Career record of 10–12 with a 4.06 ERA at Riverfront Stadium; 15–5, 2.98 ERA on the road. . . . Career record of 15–3, 2.89 ERA, before the All-Star break; 10–14, 4.04 ERA thereafter.

Nolan Ryan

Houston Astros	W–L	ERA	AB	H	HR	BB	SO	BA	SA	OBA
Season	8-16	2.76	771	154	14	87	270	.200	.292	.284
vs. Left-Handers			402	85	6	51	133	.211	.289	.300
vs. Right-Handers			369	69	8	36	137	.187	.295	.266
Home	5-7	2.21	411	79	4	38	154	.192	.258	.264
Road	3-9	3.41	360	75	10	49	116	.208	.331	.306
Grass	3-6	3.65	278	58	7	35	86	.209	.324	.301
Artificial Turf	5-10	2.29	493	96	7	52	184	.195	.274	.274
April	1-2	2.45	90	17	2	10	36	.189	.289	.275
May	1-2	2.82	135	23	3	17	45	.170	.267	.263
June	2-4	4.68	131	35	3	8	43	.267	.389	.314
July	0-5	2.36	96	19	0	18	29	.198	.250	.325
August	1-1	2.15	133	21	3	13	51	.158	.263	.238
Sept./Oct.	3-2	2.31	186	39	3	21	66	.210	.285	.293
Leading Off Inn.			199	38	2	19	74	.191	.236	.265
Runners On			303	65	7	35	94	.215	.327	.295
Runners/Scor. Pos.			199	38	3	25	69	.191	.266	.280
Runners On/2 Out			139	30	2	13	40	.216	.288	.283
Scor. Pos./2 Out			98	22	1	11	30	.224	.286	.303
Late Inning Pressure			63	11	0	8	32	.175	.190	.268
Leading Off			16	3	0	3	6	.188	.188	.316
Runners On			23	5	0	4	12	.217	.217	.333
Runners/Scor. Pos.			14	3	0	3	6	.214	.214	.353
First 9 Batters			273	52	6	26	94	.190	.300	.266
Second 9 Batters			259	49	4	29	88	.189	.274	.273
All Batters Thereafter			239	53	4	32	88	.222	.301	.315

Loves to face: Bo Diaz (.069, 2-for-29)
Hates to face: Milt Thompson (.438, 7-for-16)
Ground outs-to-air outs ratio: 1.17 last season, 1.10 for career. . . . Additional statistics: 6 double-play ground outs in 121 opportunities, 23 doubles, 3 triples in 211.2 innings last season. . . . Allowed 10 first-inning runs in 34 starts. . . . Batting support: 3.35 runs per start, 3d-lowest average in N.L. (minimum: 15 GS). . . . Hasn't completed a game in 59 starts since April 25, 1986, but did pitch nine innings of 14-inning game vs. Padres on Sept. 19. . . . Lost eight straight starts (with an ERA of 4.01), the longest streak in the majors since 1984 (Britt Burns). . . . Struck out 61 batters in 33.1 innings vs. Giants last season. . . . Career total of 2,182 innings pitched in the American League, 2,145 innings pitched in the National League. Whose cap will he wear on his Cooperstown plaque?

Bruce Ruffin

Philadelphia Phillies	W–L	ERA	AB	H	HR	BB	SO	BA	SA	OBA
Season	11-14	4.35	790	236	17	73	93	.299	.425	.355
vs. Left-Handers			134	36	2	13	21	.269	.351	.333
vs. Right-Handers			656	200	15	60	72	.305	.441	.360
Home	7-3	5.13	348	106	7	35	43	.305	.434	.365
Road	4-11	3.77	442	130	10	38	50	.294	.419	.348
Grass	1-6	3.86	238	72	5	21	32	.303	.424	.360
Artificial Turf	10-8	4.57	552	164	12	52	61	.297	.426	.354
April	1-1	5.25	97	32	5	11	16	.330	.567	.394
May	2-3	7.39	116	37	3	11	17	.319	.483	.375
June	1-2	3.24	125	40	2	9	16	.320	.432	.365
July	5-1	1.81	163	40	3	12	11	.245	.344	.295
August	1-4	5.86	138	39	3	18	19	.283	.391	.358
Sept./Oct.	1-3	4.12	151	48	1	12	14	.318	.404	.367
Leading Off Inn.			193	61	3	22	21	.316	.446	.389
Runners On			336	94	7	37	46	.280	.393	.344
Runners/Scor. Pos.			178	55	4	20	28	.309	.433	.364
Runners On/2 Out			130	36	3	17	20	.277	.400	.365
Scor. Pos./2 Out			75	22	2	9	14	.293	.427	.376
Late Inning Pressure			39	12	2	2	4	.308	.513	.341
Leading Off			9	1	1	2	0	.111	.444	.273
Runners On			16	4	0	0	2	.250	.313	.250
Runners/Scor. Pos.			9	2	0	0	1	.222	.222	.222
First 9 Batters			282	78	5	27	41	.277	.379	.338
Second 9 Batters			274	83	3	15	29	.303	.387	.337
All Batters Thereafter			234	75	9	31	23	.321	.526	.396

Loves to face: Leon Durham (0-for-10, 7 SO)
Hates to face: Eric Davis (.538, 7-for-13, 1 HR)
Ground outs-to-air outs ratio: 2.58, highest in N.L. last season (minimum: 20 GS), 2.44 for career. . . . Additional statistics: 29 double-play ground outs in 177 opportunities, 35 doubles, 7 triples in 204.2 innings last season. . . . Allowed 21 first-inning runs in 35 starts. . . . Batting support: 2.89 runs per start. . . . Struck out an average of 4.09 batters per nine innings, 5th-lowest rate in N.L. (minimum: 15 GS). . . . Led N.L. with 11 road-game losses. . . . The slimmer of the two pitchers who allowed hits to seven batters in a row last season. His round partner: Charlie Kerfeld. . . . Only major-league shutout was at Wrigley Field. . . . Opponents' career batting average of .048 (1-for-21, 3 BB) leading off innings in Late-Inning Pressure Situations.

Randy St. Claire

Montreal Expos	W–L	ERA	AB	H	HR	BB	SO	BA	SA	OBA
Season	3-3	4.03	256	64	9	20	43	.250	.395	.304
vs. Left-Handers			126	35	2	8	20	.278	.373	.314
vs. Right-Handers			130	29	7	12	23	.223	.415	.294
Home	2-3	5.17	119	30	6	9	26	.252	.454	.300
Road	1-0	3.03	137	34	3	11	17	.248	.343	.307
Grass	1-0	2.25	74	15	3	8	9	.203	.324	.280
Artificial Turf	2-3	4.79	182	49	6	12	34	.269	.423	.313
April	1-0	4.38	48	14	1	4	7	.292	.396	.346
May	1-3	5.65	57	16	1	5	10	.281	.351	.333
June	0-0	5.14	29	10	2	2	4	.345	.586	.375
July	0-0	3.00	23	5	1	1	2	.217	.435	.250
August	1-0	3.86	34	7	2	2	6	.206	.382	.263
Sept./Oct.	0-0	2.50	65	12	2	6	14	.185	.338	.254
Leading Off Inn.			57	9	2	2	8	.158	.263	.186
Runners On			110	28	5	11	18	.255	.427	.320
Runners/Scor. Pos.			65	17	2	10	9	.262	.400	.354
Runners On/2 Out			49	11	3	7	12	.224	.469	.321
Scor. Pos./2 Out			33	9	1	6	7	.273	.455	.385
Late Inning Pressure			90	24	2	9	13	.267	.367	.333
Leading Off			20	4	0	1	3	.200	.200	.238
Runners On			43	11	2	5	8	.256	.442	.333
Runners/Scor. Pos.			25	6	1	5	4	.240	.440	.367
First 9 Batters			236	62	9	18	38	.263	.419	.314
Second 9 Batters			20	2	0	2	5	.100	.100	.182
All Batters Thereafter			0	0	0	0	0	—	—	—

Loves to face: Leon Durham (0-for-6, 3 SO)
Hates to face: Milt Thompson (3-for-3, 1 2B, 1 BB)
Ground outs-to-air outs ratio: 0.95 last season, 1.17 for career (0.76 vs. left-handed batters, 1.72 vs. right-handers). . . . Additional statistics: 7 double-play ground outs in 53 opportunities, 6 doubles, 2 triples in 67.0 innings last season. . . . Earned seven saves in just nine opportunities, after going one-for-one in 1986. . . . Undefeated in five career decisions on grass surfaces with a 3.20 ERA; 5–6, 4.05 ERA on artificial turf. . . . He's also 5–0 in day games, where key to success has been control: career average of 1.89 walks per nine innings in day games, 3.51 in night games. . . . Opponents' career batting average of .206 (29-for-141, 5 BB) leading off innings. . . . Opponents' career average of .237 in Late-Inning Pressure Situations, .262 in unpressured situations.

Scott Sanderson

Chicago Cubs — Throws Right

	W–L	ERA	AB	H	HR	BB	SO	BA	SA	OBA
Season	8-9	4.29	569	156	23	50	106	.274	.469	.333
vs. Left-Handers			324	95	11	37	45	.293	.472	.365
vs. Right-Handers			245	61	12	13	61	.249	.465	.289
Home	3-4	4.99	232	67	10	22	50	.289	.504	.350
Road	5-5	3.83	337	89	13	28	56	.264	.445	.322
Grass	7-5	3.86	415	107	18	35	86	.258	.463	.318
Artificial Turf	1-4	5.54	154	49	5	15	20	.318	.487	.374
April	1-0	3.38	21	6	0	2	3	.286	.333	.333
May	2-1	4.25	164	40	10	11	33	.244	.488	.294
June	0-3	7.71	68	29	3	5	16	.426	.676	.462
July	1-2	3.43	73	16	4	8	15	.219	.425	.298
August	3-1	2.89	109	29	3	11	20	.266	.413	.339
Sept./Oct.	1-2	4.76	134	36	3	13	19	.269	.433	.331
Leading Off Inn.			141	36	6	11	28	.255	.447	.309
Runners On			228	57	7	28	46	.250	.417	.328
Runners/Scor. Pos.			128	31	3	23	24	.242	.406	.346
Runners On/2 Out			93	16	3	14	23	.172	.312	.280
Scor. Pos./2 Out			58	9	0	12	13	.155	.207	.300
Late Inning Pressure			61	14	3	6	13	.230	.410	.304
Leading Off			16	4	1	2	2	.250	.438	.333
Runners On			21	5	0	2	5	.238	.333	.292
Runners/Scor. Pos.			13	3	0	1	3	.231	.385	.267
First 9 Batters			244	60	9	24	52	.246	.414	.313
Second 9 Batters			188	50	6	11	32	.266	.457	.310
All Batters Thereafter			137	46	8	15	22	.336	.584	.400

Loves to face: Rafael Ramirez (.111, 3-for-27)
Hates to face: Willie McGee (.435, 20-for-46, 2 HR)
Ground outs-to-air outs ratio: 0.89 last season, 0.83 for career....
Additional statistics: 11 double-play ground outs in 110 opportunities, 26 doubles, 8 triples in 144.2 innings last season.... Allowed 2 first-inning runs in 22 starts, lowest average in majors (minimum: 15 GS).... Batting support: 4.27 runs per start.... Hasn't completed a start since 5-hit shutout of St. Louis on April 23, 1986.... Career ERA of 2.16 in 25 relief appearances, 3.70 as a starter.... Opponents' batting average with two outs and runners in scoring position, year by year since 1984: .203, .190, .175, .155.... Incidentally, the Sanderson juggernaut rolls on: He's the only active player to hit better with runners in scoring position than overall in each of the last seven seasons.

Mike Scott

Houston Astros — Throws Right

	W–L	ERA	AB	H	HR	BB	SO	BA	SA	OBA
Season	16-13	3.23	916	199	21	79	233	.217	.331	.281
vs. Left-Handers			507	119	9	46	99	.235	.335	.300
vs. Right-Handers			409	80	12	33	134	.196	.325	.258
Home	10-3	2.20	443	87	9	35	131	.196	.293	.260
Road	6-10	4.26	473	112	12	44	102	.237	.366	.301
Grass	1-8	6.29	233	66	8	24	46	.283	.446	.349
Artificial Turf	15-5	2.29	683	133	13	55	187	.195	.291	.258
April	3-1	2.05	162	31	5	8	49	.191	.309	.229
May	2-2	2.97	128	22	2	17	33	.172	.273	.269
June	4-1	2.40	159	26	2	10	53	.164	.220	.216
July	2-3	4.26	124	36	3	17	34	.290	.444	.380
August	2-3	4.03	177	47	4	11	34	.266	.395	.311
Sept./Oct.	3-3	3.91	166	37	5	16	30	.223	.349	.293
Leading Off Inn.			244	51	9	7	59	.209	.352	.231
Runners On			329	87	7	41	83	.264	.374	.347
Runners/Scor. Pos.			216	52	3	31	64	.241	.315	.337
Runners On/2 Out			145	32	3	16	38	.221	.310	.302
Scor. Pos./2 Out			105	22	1	14	29	.210	.248	.308
Late Inning Pressure			95	24	1	3	31	.253	.326	.270
Leading Off			26	6	1	0	7	.231	.385	.231
Runners On			29	12	0	2	5	.414	.483	.424
Runners/Scor. Pos.			21	6	0	2	5	.286	.286	.320
First 9 Batters			287	64	7	31	77	.223	.342	.303
Second 9 Batters			289	62	7	26	69	.215	.322	.279
All Batters Thereafter			340	73	7	22	87	.215	.321	.264

Loves to face: Andy Van Slyke (.045, 1-for-22)
Hates to face: Willie McGee (.560, 14-for-25)
Ground outs-to-air outs ratio: 1.08 last season, 1.19 for career....
Additional statistics: 10 double-play ground outs in 149 opportunities, 33 doubles, 4 triples in 247.2 innings last season.... Allowed 19 first-inning runs in 36 starts.... Batting support: 3.67 runs per start, 6th-lowest average in N.L. (minimum: 15 GS).... ERA of 4.88 in day games, 2.56 at night.... Struck out nine consecutive batters in Late-Inning Pressure Situations, a 1987 major-league high.... Scott faced 122 consecutive batters without a walk (Aug. 22–Sept. 11), the longest streak in either league last season.... Fanned only one of 20 batters faced with the bases loaded; allowed grand slams to Jack Clark and Bob Brenly.... Opponents' batting average at the Astrodome, year by year since 1985: .195, .176, .196.

Bob Sebra

Montreal Expos — Throws Right

	W–L	ERA	AB	H	HR	BB	SO	BA	SA	OBA
Season	6-15	4.42	676	184	15	67	156	.272	.410	.337
vs. Left-Handers			374	97	8	39	79	.259	.398	.329
vs. Right-Handers			302	87	7	28	77	.288	.424	.347
Home	2-7	4.31	332	84	7	32	95	.253	.383	.320
Road	4-8	4.52	344	100	8	35	61	.291	.436	.354
Grass	2-3	5.44	176	51	5	21	30	.290	.420	.363
Artificial Turf	4-12	4.05	500	133	10	46	126	.266	.406	.328
April	1-3	3.86	85	25	4	12	15	.294	.518	.378
May	2-2	4.60	122	33	3	17	29	.270	.393	.357
June	1-3	4.67	105	29	1	4	32	.276	.381	.297
July	2-2	2.32	153	32	4	11	35	.209	.307	.267
August	0-4	4.98	138	41	1	12	28	.297	.420	.351
Sept./Oct.	0-1	8.20	73	24	2	11	17	.329	.548	.424
Leading Off Inn.			169	48	6	11	39	.284	.462	.335
Runners On			285	86	6	33	62	.302	.456	.386
Runners/Scor. Pos.			192	49	2	23	48	.255	.349	.324
Runners On/2 Out			125	37	1	12	29	.296	.432	.358
Scor. Pos./2 Out			94	24	1	8	25	.255	.351	.314
Late Inning Pressure			37	7	1	1	8	.189	.270	.211
Leading Off			11	2	0	0	2	.182	.182	.182
Runners On			7	3	0	1	1	.429	.429	.500
Runners/Scor. Pos.			5	3	0	0	0	.600	.600	.600
First 9 Batters			252	73	5	35	54	.290	.409	.376
Second 9 Batters			226	59	5	16	60	.261	.394	.309
All Batters Thereafter			198	52	5	16	42	.263	.429	.316

Loves to face: Wally Backman (0-for-15)
Hates to face: Jose Lind (2-for-2, 1 BB)
Ground outs-to-air outs ratio: 0.96 last season, 0.97 for career....
Additional statistics: 12 double-play ground outs in 122 opportunities, 42 doubles, 3 triples in 177.1 innings last season.... Allowed 22 first-inning runs in 27 starts.... Batting support: 3.33 runs per start, 2d-lowest average in N.L. (minimum: 15 GS).... Strikeout rate of 7.92 per nine innings puts him in baseball's high-rent district. N.L.'s top five: Ryan, Scott, Sebra, Gooden, Darling.... Had streaks of 30 consecutive right-handed batters faced (June 21–July 7) and 28 left-handers (July 7–July 17) without allowing a hit.... Opponents' career batting average of .159 in Late-Inning Pressure Situations.... How many Cornhuskers have names that are anagrams of *Nebraska*? Too bad Sebra's first name ain't Ank.

Eric Show

San Diego Padres — Throws Right

	W–L	ERA	AB	H	HR	BB	SO	BA	SA	OBA
Season	8-16	3.84	778	188	26	85	117	.242	.404	.322
vs. Left-Handers			424	105	12	53	67	.248	.401	.329
vs. Right-Handers			354	83	14	32	50	.234	.407	.312
Home	5-6	2.73	412	83	11	49	71	.201	.342	.291
Road	3-10	5.15	366	105	15	36	46	.287	.473	.357
Grass	8-10	3.16	621	129	19	70	99	.208	.357	.293
Artificial Turf	0-6	7.07	157	59	7	15	18	.376	.586	.437
April	1-1	3.24	119	22	5	9	19	.185	.353	.258
May	0-6	5.14	162	37	8	17	26	.228	.438	.300
June	2-2	2.93	100	23	1	11	10	.230	.340	.307
July	2-3	4.32	128	36	4	12	18	.281	.469	.357
August	1-3	4.78	143	37	5	24	21	.259	.413	.367
Sept./Oct.	2-1	1.95	126	33	3	12	23	.262	.381	.331
Leading Off Inn.			202	52	4	16	28	.257	.381	.312
Runners On			287	66	5	48	43	.230	.355	.343
Runners/Scor. Pos.			176	43	4	29	26	.244	.398	.346
Runners On/2 Out			123	23	1	22	22	.187	.252	.320
Scor. Pos./2 Out			83	17	0	13	16	.205	.253	.313
Late Inning Pressure			48	9	3	2	12	.188	.375	.235
Leading Off			18	4	0	0	3	.222	.222	.222
Runners On			2	1	0	1	0	.500	.500	.750
Runners/Scor. Pos.			0	0	0	0	0			
First 9 Batters			262	59	9	33	33	.225	.397	.318
Second 9 Batters			248	68	10	24	39	.274	.452	.345
All Batters Thereafter			268	61	7	28	45	.228	.366	.303

Loves to face: Steve Sax (.111, 4-for-36)
Hates to face: Darryl Strawberry (.500, 13-for-26, 4 HR)
Ground outs-to-air outs ratio: 0.84 last season, 0.95 for career....
Additional statistics: 14 double-play ground outs in 134 opportunities, 40 doubles, 4 triples in 206.1 innings last season.... Allowed 16 first-inning runs in 34 starts.... Batting support: 3.94 runs per start.... Home-game ERA was 6th best in N.L.... Six losses in May were the most by any pitcher in any month last season.... Hurled two complete-game shutouts at Dodger Stadium last season. ... Opponents hit 168 points higher on grass fields than on artificial turf, largest difference in majors (minimum: 100 AB each way).... Opponents' career batting average of .185 with two outs and runners in scoring position, .138 (9-for-65) with bases loaded.

Doug Sisk

New York Mets — Throws Right

	W–L	ERA	AB	H	HR	BB	SO	BA	SA	OBA
Season	3–1	3.46	307	83	5	22	37	.270	.378	.323
vs. Left-Handers			138	37	0	12	13	.268	.341	.325
vs. Right-Handers			169	46	5	10	24	.272	.408	.322
Home	0–0	3.79	143	43	1	11	17	.301	.392	.359
Road	3–1	3.19	164	40	4	11	20	.244	.366	.292
Grass	1–1	3.11	213	56	2	16	26	.263	.347	.322
Artificial Turf	2–0	4.30	94	27	3	6	11	.287	.447	.327
April	0–0	4.22	41	13	2	4	2	.317	.537	.391
May	1–0	3.86	50	15	0	4	5	.300	.340	.364
June	2–1	2.66	72	14	2	4	10	.194	.306	.247
July	0–0	6.00	41	15	1	4	4	.366	.537	.413
August	0–0	3.21	56	16	0	4	5	.286	.393	.328
Sept./Oct.	0–0	2.19	47	10	0	2	11	.213	.234	.245
Leading Off Inn.			71	18	0	4	8	.254	.352	.303
Runners On			141	45	5	13	13	.319	.489	.376
Runners/Scor. Pos.			89	27	3	8	5	.303	.461	.354
Runners On/2 Out			61	20	3	5	5	.328	.508	.379
Scor. Pos./2 Out			42	15	1	2	3	.357	.476	.386
Late Inning Pressure			125	36	2	10	14	.288	.368	.346
Leading Off			31	7	0	1	6	.226	.258	.250
Runners On			54	17	2	7	4	.315	.463	.393
Runners/Scor. Pos.			32	9	1	4	3	.281	.406	.361
First 9 Batters			285	77	4	21	36	.270	.372	.325
Second 9 Batters			22	6	1	1	1	.273	.455	.304
All Batters Thereafter			0	0	0	0	0	—	—	—

Loves to face: Jack Clark (.167, 2-for-12)
Hates to face: Lonnie Smith (.500, 2-for-4, 1 BB, 1 HBP)
Ground outs-to-air outs ratio: 3.34, highest in majors last season (minimum: 200 BFP), 2.85 for career. . . . Additional statistics: 10 double-play ground outs in 77 opportunities, 12 doubles, 3 triples in 78.0 innings last season. . . . Has allowed only 11 home runs in 412.1 career innings; that rate of one every 37.48 innings is lowest among active pitchers (minimum: 100 innings). . . . Last year we told you that Sisk had faced 364 right-handed batters at Shea without ever allowing a home run. Well, (Dale) Murphy's Law struck on April 12 while the ink on the *Analyst* was still wet. . . . Out Of Their League: The top 15 N.L. batters, who hit .311 overall last year, batted .556 (20 for 36) against Sisk, the best average by that top-15 group vs. any N.L. pitcher (minimum: 30 at bats).

Bryn Smith

Montreal Expos — Throws Right

	W–L	ERA	AB	H	HR	BB	SO	BA	SA	OBA
Season	10–9	4.37	598	164	16	31	94	.274	.410	.310
vs. Left-Handers			347	90	8	18	49	.259	.372	.293
vs. Right-Handers			251	74	8	13	45	.295	.462	.333
Home	6–3	4.50	327	89	8	23	58	.272	.388	.323
Road	4–6	4.21	271	75	8	8	36	.277	.435	.293
Grass	3–3	4.71	174	50	5	4	30	.287	.443	.302
Artificial Turf	7–6	4.24	424	114	11	27	64	.269	.396	.313
April			0	0	0	0	0	—	—	—
May	2–1	5.93	131	40	7	4	27	.305	.534	.326
June	3–2	5.52	117	37	1	11	17	.316	.402	.380
July	2–1	2.70	123	28	3	3	17	.228	.358	.246
August	1–2	4.82	113	32	5	8	17	.283	.460	.331
Sept./Oct.	2–3	3.07	114	27	0	5	16	.237	.281	.262
Leading Off Inn.			153	33	3	2	20	.216	.320	.226
Runners On			242	71	8	15	42	.293	.475	.328
Runners/Scor. Pos.			136	41	4	7	25	.301	.463	.324
Runners On/2 Out			108	29	4	8	21	.269	.463	.319
Scor. Pos./2 Out			66	16	3	5	13	.242	.439	.296
Late Inning Pressure			8	4	0	0	1	.500	.625	.500
Leading Off			3	2	0	0	1	.667	.667	.667
Runners On			3	2	0	0	0	.667	1.000	.667
Runners/Scor. Pos.			3	2	0	0	0	.667	1.000	.667
First 9 Batters			221	60	5	7	41	.271	.394	.299
Second 9 Batters			215	56	6	12	29	.260	.395	.297
All Batters Thereafter			162	48	5	12	24	.296	.451	.341

Loves to face: Rick Schu (0-for-10, 4 SO)
Hates to face: Franklin Stubbs (.500, 8-for-16, 3 2B, 4 HR)
Ground outs-to-air outs ratio: 1.62 last season, 1.79 for career. . . . Additional statistics: 12 double-play ground outs in 104 opportunities, 25 doubles, 4 triples in 150.1 innings last season. . . . Allowed 22 first-inning runs in 27 starts. . . . Batting support: 5.19 runs per start, 9th-highest average in N.L. (minimum: 15 GS), after marks of 4.53 and 5.44 in 1985 and 1986, compared to 3.95 per game for other Montreal starters during those three seasons. The result: 38–22 mark over last three years is 5th best in N.L. . . . Opponents' yearly batting averages with runners in scoring position since 1984: .177, .258, .258, .301; leading off innings since 1984: .309, .278, .268, .216. . . . Last season was first time since 1981 that opposing right-handers hit for higher average than left-handers.

John Smiley

Pittsburgh Pirates — Throws Left

	W–L	ERA	AB	H	HR	BB	SO	BA	SA	OBA
Season	5–5	5.76	283	69	7	50	58	.244	.389	.354
vs. Left-Handers			87	17	1	12	21	.195	.299	.287
vs. Right-Handers			196	52	6	38	37	.265	.429	.383
Home	5–3	2.77	167	27	3	30	36	.162	.281	.286
Road	0–2	11.28	116	42	4	20	22	.362	.543	.453
Grass	0–1	10.54	62	24	3	7	14	.387	.645	.449
Artificial Turf	5–4	4.70	221	45	4	43	44	.204	.317	.330
April	1–0	2.53	36	8	1	6	8	.222	.389	.333
May	2–1	6.75	82	21	5	10	18	.256	.488	.337
June	0–0	7.62	52	15	0	10	9	.288	.385	.391
July	0–1	1.62	53	7	1	9	12	.132	.245	.258
August	0–2	16.20	33	14	0	10	2	.424	.485	.558
Sept./Oct.	2–1	4.50	27	4	0	5	9	.148	.259	.273
Leading Off Inn.			65	12	0	11	17	.185	.262	.303
Runners On			126	35	3	27	22	.278	.421	.397
Runners/Scor. Pos.			84	26	1	20	19	.310	.417	.430
Runners On/2 Out			41	6	1	10	13	.146	.244	.314
Scor. Pos./2 Out			31	4	0	7	11	.129	.129	.289
Late Inning Pressure			135	33	2	31	28	.244	.378	.381
Leading Off			31	5	0	9	8	.161	.226	.350
Runners On			60	17	2	17	10	.283	.467	.430
Runners/Scor. Pos.			38	12	1	13	9	.316	.474	.472
First 9 Batters			275	69	7	49	57	.251	.400	.361
Second 9 Batters			8	0	0	1	1	.000	.000	.111
All Batters Thereafter			0	0	0	0	0	—	—	—

Loves to face: Len Dykstra (0-for-7)
Hates to face: Glenn Davis (2-for-2, 2 HR)
Ground outs-to-air outs ratio: 1.30 last season, 1.30 for career. . . . Additional statistics: 8 double-play ground outs in 68 opportunities, 16 doubles, 2 triples in 75.0 innings last season. . . . Led N.L. rookie pitchers with 63 appearances. . . . Allowed six home runs in his first 28 innings pitched, but only one over his last 47 innings pitched. . . . Opposing left-handed batters had only four hits in 47 at bats at Three Rivers Stadium, including a home run by Dave Magadan. . . . Opponents' career batting average of .338 on grass fields, .194 on artificial surfaces. . . . Great batting average in leadoff situations (both LIP and unpressured situations); but, oh, those bases on balls. . . . Has made 75 relief appearances without a start for Pirates, but talk is he'll get shot at rotation in spring.

Dave Smith

Houston Astros — Throws Right

	W–L	ERA	AB	H	HR	BB	SO	BA	SA	OBA
Season	2–3	1.65	214	39	0	21	73	.182	.229	.257
vs. Left-Handers			113	23	0	15	25	.204	.239	.297
vs. Right-Handers			101	16	0	6	48	.158	.218	.211
Home	1–2	1.47	128	22	0	14	44	.172	.203	.252
Road	1–1	1.93	86	17	0	7	29	.198	.267	.266
Grass	1–1	2.63	54	14	0	5	13	.259	.333	.333
Artificial Turf	1–2	1.36	160	25	0	16	60	.156	.194	.232
April	0–0	0.00	24	3	0	0	9	.125	.125	.120
May	0–0	0.00	33	2	0	2	15	.061	.091	.114
June	0–0	1.15	52	6	0	7	22	.115	.192	.233
July	2–0	2.16	33	8	0	4	13	.242	.303	.324
August	0–0	2.00	32	6	0	4	10	.188	.219	.278
Sept./Oct.	0–3	5.00	40	14	0	4	4	.350	.400	.409
Leading Off Inn.			47	9	0	3	13	.191	.277	.240
Runners On			98	20	0	14	31	.204	.235	.307
Runners/Scor. Pos.			67	14	0	13	26	.209	.239	.341
Runners On/2 Out			47	8	0	8	12	.170	.191	.291
Scor. Pos./2 Out			34	5	0	7	10	.147	.147	.293
Late Inning Pressure			146	28	0	15	45	.192	.233	.270
Leading Off			33	6	0	2	11	.182	.303	.229
Runners On			66	14	0	11	17	.212	.227	.329
Runners/Scor. Pos.			46	10	0	11	14	.217	.239	.373
First 9 Batters			212	39	0	21	72	.184	.231	.260
Second 9 Batters			2	0	0	0	1	.000	.000	.000
All Batters Thereafter										

Loves to face: Gary Carter (.067, 1-for-15)
Hates to face: Tony Gwynn (.700, 7-for-10)
Ground outs-to-air outs ratio: 1.40 last season, 1.40 for career. . . . Additional statistics: 2 double-play ground outs in 44 opportunities, 6 doubles, 2 triples in 60.0 innings last season. . . . Didn't allow a run in his first 27 2/3 innings. That was the longest streak without allowing an earned run at the start of a season ever accomplished entirely in relief. Smith broke the previous mark, set in 1953 by Hoyt Wilhelm, by the narrowest of margins—one-third of an inning. . . . Smith's streak of 22 consecutive scoreless appearances was the longest in the majors only since 1983, when—you won't believe this—Warren Brusstar went 25 games without being scored on. . . . One of two pitchers to appear in at least 30 games and not allow a home run last season. The other: Dickie Noles.

Lee Smith
Chicago Cubs — Throws Right

	W-L	ERA	AB	H	HR	BB	SO	BA	SA	OBA
Season	4-10	3.12	324	84	4	32	96	.259	.358	.326
vs. Left-Handers			178	48	3	25	47	.270	.399	.360
vs. Right-Handers			146	36	1	7	49	.247	.308	.281
Home	3-5	3.79	152	47	3	8	43	.309	.447	.344
Road	1-5	2.56	172	37	1	24	53	.215	.279	.311
Grass	3-7	2.89	218	61	3	15	60	.280	.381	.326
Artificial Turf	1-3	3.58	106	23	1	17	36	.217	.311	.325
April	0-2	2.45	42	10	0	5	19	.238	.333	.319
May	1-1	1.74	75	12	1	2	21	.160	.227	.182
June	1-2	5.02	61	22	1	6	17	.361	.475	.418
July	0-1	1.93	34	8	1	1	9	.235	.382	.257
August	2-1	1.47	71	19	0	13	17	.268	.310	.381
Sept./Oct.	0-3	8.10	41	13	1	5	13	.317	.512	.391
Leading Off Inn.			65	15	2	4	11	.231	.431	.275
Runners On			170	43	0	22	55	.253	.312	.339
Runners/Scor. Pos.			109	28	0	16	34	.257	.339	.352
Runners On/2 Out			77	17	0	12	26	.221	.326	.326
Scor. Pos./2 Out			54	10	0	9	18	.185	.241	.302
Late Inning Pressure			238	67	3	29	71	.282	.387	.360
Leading Off			47	10	1	2	9	.213	.362	.245
Runners On			127	36	0	21	41	.283	.362	.385
Runners/Scor. Pos.			79	24	0	15	24	.304	.418	.415
First 9 Batters			318	84	4	32	95	.264	.365	.331
Second 9 Batters			6	0	0	0	1	.000	.000	.000
All Batters Thereafter			0	0	0	0	0			

Loves to face: Darrell Evans (0-for-7)
Hates to face: Jack Clark (.500, 11-for-22, 2 3B, 2 HR)
Ground outs-to-air outs ratio: 1.49 last season, 1.24 for career.... Additional statistics: 4 double-play ground outs in 72 opportunities, 18 doubles, 1 triple in 83.2 innings last season.... Earned 36 saves in 48 opportunities; career-best rate was 29-for-34 in 1983.... Faced 223 batters protecting leads of three runs or less in the eighth inning or later. Only Bedrosian (254) and Worrell (226) faced more. ... Only home run allowed to a right-handed batter last season was hit by a pitcher (Jeff Robinson).... Opponents' batting average with runners in scoring position was the highest of his career.... Career record of 16-28 with a 3.06 ERA before the All-Star break; 19-18, 2.68 ERA afterwards.... He'll be glad to retire the lumber— 40 strikeouts in 60 career at bats.

Zane Smith
Atlanta Braves — Throws Left

	W-L	ERA	AB	H	HR	BB	SO	BA	SA	OBA
Season	15-10	4.09	922	245	19	91	130	.266	.377	.333
vs. Left-Handers			105	27	1	8	22	.257	.314	.310
vs. Right-Handers			817	218	18	83	108	.267	.386	.336
Home	6-6	5.69	440	136	14	46	60	.309	.473	.373
Road	9-4	2.74	482	109	5	45	70	.226	.290	.297
Grass	11-8	4.32	664	180	17	61	90	.271	.405	.333
Artificial Turf	4-2	3.52	258	65	2	30	40	.252	.306	.333
April	2-1	3.02	156	43	1	19	25	.276	.359	.318
May	3-2	5.08	175	51	1	24	26	.291	.360	.378
June	3-1	4.05	150	38	6	13	23	.253	.387	.317
July	1-2	4.75	117	31	2	12	13	.265	.376	.331
August	5-1	3.28	170	39	3	17	22	.229	.324	.303
Sept./Oct.	1-3	4.62	154	43	6	15	21	.279	.468	.347
Leading Off Inn.			224	50	4	23	28	.223	.308	.304
Runners On			392	108	13	43	54	.276	.421	.346
Runners/Scor. Pos.			203	58	6	30	34	.286	.429	.375
Runners On/2 Out			165	43	5	22	34	.261	.394	.348
Scor. Pos./2 Out			98	27	3	17	22	.276	.408	.383
Late Inning Pressure			68	21	2	1	7	.309	.456	.329
Leading Off			18	6	0	0	0	.333	.389	.333
Runners On			25	7	2	1	4	.280	.600	.333
Runners/Scor. Pos.			7	1	0	1	3	.143	.143	.333
First 9 Batters			286	59	4	28	58	.206	.280	.282
Second 9 Batters			286	80	4	33	30	.280	.374	.355
All Batters Thereafter			350	106	11	30	42	.303	.460	.358

Loves to face: Darryl Strawberry (.059, 1-for-17, 7 SO)
Hates to face: Reggie Williams (.714, 5-for-7, 2 2B, 2 BB)
Ground outs-to-air outs ratio: 1.77 last season, 2.04 for career.... Additional statistics: 35 double-play ground outs (tied for most in majors) in 202 opportunities, 40 doubles, 3 triples in 242.0 innings last season.... Allowed 15 first-inning runs in 36 starts.... Batting support: 5.22 runs per start, 7th-highest average in N.L. (minimum: 15 GS).... Road-game ERA was 2d lowest in N.L.... Record of 3-5 with a 4.54 ERA in day games; 12-5, 3.92 ERA at night.... Opponents' batting averages with runners in scoring position, year by year since 1984: .227, .241, .288, .286.... Has walked only one of 43 batters faced with the bases loaded.... Led N.L. with 14 sacrifice bunts (as a batter) last season.... Given name is Leroy Purdy Smith. (Thought you'd want to know.)

Rick Sutcliffe
Chicago Cubs — Throws Right

	W-L	ERA	AB	H	HR	BB	SO	BA	SA	OBA
Season	18-10	3.68	884	223	24	106	174	.252	.402	.332
vs. Left-Handers			500	131	13	72	99	.262	.420	.357
vs. Right-Handers			384	92	11	34	75	.240	.378	.299
Home	10-5	3.49	460	114	14	63	95	.248	.398	.338
Road	8-5	3.88	424	109	10	43	79	.257	.406	.326
Grass	15-6	3.28	652	158	17	82	131	.242	.382	.328
Artificial Turf	3-4	4.82	232	65	7	24	43	.280	.457	.345
April	3-2	4.11	110	25	3	19	21	.227	.345	.344
May	4-0	2.08	151	30	2	21	34	.199	.318	.299
June	3-2	4.73	147	37	5	19	29	.252	.401	.335
July	5-0	2.48	145	39	5	9	31	.269	.421	.314
August	0-2	5.82	129	43	4	20	22	.333	.543	.418
Sept./Oct.	3-4	3.40	202	49	5	18	37	.243	.391	.303
Leading Off Inn.			227	56	6	22	49	.247	.414	.313
Runners On			340	90	7	54	65	.265	.403	.361
Runners/Scor. Pos.			205	48	3	43	41	.234	.346	.355
Runners On/2 Out			146	39	2	29	33	.267	.384	.392
Scor. Pos./2 Out			103	29	1	25	23	.282	.408	.422
Late Inning Pressure			76	19	1	13	16	.250	.382	.363
Leading Off			22	5	1	2	4	.227	.409	.292
Runners On			28	7	0	7	5	.250	.357	.405
Runners/Scor. Pos.			20	4	0	6	5	.200	.300	.370
First 9 Batters			270	65	8	23	65	.241	.404	.299
Second 9 Batters			261	60	7	38	44	.230	.337	.327
All Batters Thereafter			353	98	9	45	65	.278	.448	.361

Loves to face: Tommy Herr (.129, 4-for-31)
Hates to face: Von Hayes (.412, 14-for-34, 6 2B, 1 3B, 3 HR)
Ground outs-to-air outs ratio: 1.20 last season, 0.90 for career.... Additional statistics: 14 double-play ground outs in 157 opportunities, 42 doubles, 9 triples in 237.1 innings last season.... Allowed 12 first-inning runs in 34 starts.... Batting support: 5.38 runs per start, 5th-highest average in N.L. (minimum: 15 GS).... A throwback to yesteryear: pitched three consecutive complete-game victories during September.... Set personal record for walks in a season. Previous high of 102 was set in 1983 with Cleveland.... Has lost six consecutive decisions to the Pirates since defeating them on June 7, 1985.... Has lost 17 of his last 29 decisions on artificial turf, while going 52-31 on grass fields during that time.... Walked seven times last season, tied for highest total among pitchers.

Kent Tekulve
Philadelphia Phillies — Throws Right

	W-L	ERA	AB	H	HR	BB	SO	BA	SA	OBA
Season	6-4	3.09	395	96	8	29	60	.243	.349	.293
vs. Left-Handers			165	51	5	18	15	.309	.467	.377
vs. Right-Handers			230	45	3	11	45	.196	.265	.230
Home	2-2	3.47	215	54	4	15	28	.251	.353	.300
Road	4-2	2.63	180	42	4	14	32	.233	.344	.284
Grass	2-2	2.40	117	30	3	7	24	.256	.376	.294
Artificial Turf	4-2	3.36	278	66	5	22	36	.237	.338	.292
April	1-0	3.00	56	15	2	3	6	.268	.411	.300
May	0-2	4.19	76	21	1	7	10	.276	.408	.337
June	1-1	3.57	68	16	1	5	12	.235	.324	.284
July	3-0	3.46	50	12	0	1	9	.240	.280	.255
August	1-1	1.40	66	14	1	6	11	.212	.288	.274
Sept./Oct.	0-0	3.05	79	18	3	7	12	.228	.367	.291
Leading Off Inn.			89	27	2	3	11	.303	.438	.326
Runners On			179	38	3	19	28	.212	.302	.284
Runners/Scor. Pos.			122	22	3	19	24	.180	.279	.285
Runners On/2 Out			75	14	2	9	13	.187	.333	.274
Scor. Pos./2 Out			53	8	2	9	11	.151	.302	.274
Late Inning Pressure			206	45	6	14	32	.218	.340	.266
Leading Off			53	17	2	1	6	.321	.472	.333
Runners On			84	15	2	9	14	.179	.274	.253
Runners/Scor. Pos.			57	9	2	9	11	.158	.281	.265
First 9 Batters			388	93	8	29	58	.240	.348	.290
Second 9 Batters			7	3	0	0	2	.429	.429	.429
All Batters Thereafter			0	0	0	0	0	—	—	—

Loves to face: Vince Coleman (0-for-10)
Hates to face: Kevin Bass (.700, 7-for-10, 2 3B)
Ground outs-to-air outs ratio: 2.02 last season, 2.25 for career.... Additional statistics: 10 double-play ground outs in 83 opportunities, 16 doubles, 1 triple in 105.0 innings last season.... Left-handed opponents outhit right-handers by 113 points, largest difference in N.L. (minimum: 100 AB each way).... Fewest saves of any pitcher to lead his league in appearances since saves were introduced in 1969. ... Oldest pitcher to lead his league in appearances since 40-year old Joe Berry of Philadelphia led the A.L. with 52 games in 1945. Tekulve is the oldest pitcher in this century to lead the N.L. ... Best ERA in majors from September 1 on over past five seasons (1.61).... Opponents' batting average with runners in scoring position was his lowest in 13 years of *The Player Analysis*.

Jay Tibbs

Throws Right

Montreal Expos	W–L	ERA	AB	H	HR	BB	SO	BA	SA	OBA
Season	4-5	4.99	329	95	10	34	54	.289	.450	.354
vs. Left-Handers			163	48	4	20	22	.294	.479	.370
vs. Right-Handers			166	47	6	14	32	.283	.422	.339
Home	2-2	4.11	136	37	3	14	23	.272	.397	.338
Road	2-3	5.63	193	58	7	20	31	.301	.487	.366
Grass	1-1	7.36	61	20	3	9	10	.328	.557	.414
Artificial Turf	3-4	4.48	268	75	7	25	44	.280	.425	.340
April	1-4	4.64	127	34	6	13	17	.268	.449	.336
May	3-0	5.74	108	34	1	12	20	.315	.426	.380
June	0-0	10.13	24	9	2	1	5	.375	.667	.400
July	0-0	3.86	30	9	0	4	4	.300	.433	.382
August			0	0	0	0	0	—	—	—
Sept./Oct.	0-1	2.45	40	9	1	4	8	.225	.400	.295
Leading Off Inn.			76	19	2	9	11	.250	.408	.329
Runners On			139	44	5	15	22	.317	.489	.381
Runners/Scor. Pos.			86	27	2	10	18	.314	.465	.381
Runners On/2 Out			57	16	3	6	7	.281	.474	.349
Scor. Pos./2 Out			42	10	1	4	7	.238	.357	.304
Late Inning Pressure			18	4	2	3	2	.222	.611	.333
Leading Off			4	0	0	1	0	.000	.000	.200
Runners On			8	1	1	1	2	.125	.500	.222
Runners/Scor. Pos.			5	1	1	0	2	.200	.800	.200
First 9 Batters			153	37	4	13	24	.242	.366	.301
Second 9 Batters			100	27	1	11	20	.270	.420	.342
All Batters Thereafter			76	31	5	10	10	.408	.658	.471

Loves to face: R. J. Reynolds (.083, 1-for-12)
Hates to face: Kevin McReynolds (.560, 14-for-25, 4 HR)
Ground outs-to-air outs ratio: 1.63 last season, 1.56 for career. . . .
Additional statistics: 9 double-play ground outs in 65 opportunities,
19 doubles, 2 triples in 83.0 innings last season. . . . Allowed 4
first-inning runs in 12 starts. . . . Batting support: 4.92 runs per start.
. . . Expos lost nine of the last 10 games in which he appeared. . . .
Three of his four victories came in consecutive starts (May 5–15).
. . . ERA has risen each season from a career low of 2.86 as a rookie
in 1984 to last season's 4.99 mark. . . . Career record of 3–10 with
a 5.08 ERA on grass fields; 24–22, 3.60 ERA on artificial turf. . . .
Yearly opponents' batting averages with runners on base: .239, .283,
.290, .317. . . . Has walked only one of the 45 batters he's faced with
the bases loaded.

Steve Trout

Throws Left

Chicago Cubs	W–L	ERA	AB	H	HR	BB	SO	BA	SA	OBA
Season	6-3	3.00	277	72	3	27	32	.260	.339	.326
vs. Left-Handers			29	9	0	2	6	.310	.448	.375
vs. Right-Handers			248	63	3	25	26	.254	.327	.320
Home	5-1	1.86	190	45	2	17	27	.237	.295	.301
Road	1-2	5.82	87	27	1	10	5	.310	.437	.378
Grass	5-2	2.53	208	54	2	22	27	.260	.317	.332
Artificial Turf	1-1	4.50	69	18	1	5	5	.261	.406	.307
April	1-1	2.79	109	28	3	7	12	.257	.394	.297
May	1-0	3.86	26	7	0	1	4	.269	.308	.321
June	2-2	5.57	82	27	0	16	8	.329	.402	.439
July	2-0	0.00	60	10	0	3	8	.167	.167	.206
August			0	0	0	0	0	—	—	—
Sept./Oct.			0	0	0	0	0	—	—	—
Leading Off Inn.			71	20	1	5	6	.282	.423	.338
Runners On			119	30	1	10	12	.252	.311	.305
Runners/Scor. Pos.			66	10	1	8	7	.152	.197	.237
Runners On/2 Out			48	14	0	3	7	.292	.333	.333
Scor. Pos./2 Out			31	6	0	2	4	.194	.194	.242
Late Inning Pressure			9	4	0	0	1	.444	.556	.400
Leading Off			4	3	0	0	0	.750	1.000	.750
Runners On			3	1	0	0	0	.333	.333	.250
Runners/Scor. Pos.			2	0	0	0	1	.000	.000	.000
First 9 Batters			90	22	1	9	11	.244	.300	.313
Second 9 Batters			85	26	0	10	10	.306	.388	.381
All Batters Thereafter			102	24	2	8	11	.235	.333	.288

Loves to face: Glenn Hubbard (.105, 2-for-19)
Hates to face: Gary Redus (.571, 8-for-14, 1 HR)
Figures *above* are for N.L. only. . . . Ground outs-to-air outs ratio:
2.37, 3d highest in majors last season (minimum: 20 GS), 2.07 for
career. . . . Additional statistics: 19 double-play ground outs in 107
opportunities, 20 doubles, 1 triple in 121.1 innings last season. . . .
Allowed 9 first-inning runs in 20 starts. . . . Batting support: 4.60
runs per start. . . . Opponents' batting average with runners in scoring position was lowest since his rookie season. . . . Left-handed
batters have hit .333 over the last two seasons, but only one lefty,
Harold Baines, has homered against him. . . . Only pitcher in majors
with 100+ innings in each of last three years, and with more walks
than strikeouts in each. . . . ERA by month for past six seasons,
April through September: 3.21, 3.80, 4.26, 4.35, 4.56, 4.93.

John Tudor

Throws Left

St. Louis Cardinals	W–L	ERA	AB	H	HR	BB	SO	BA	SA	OBA
Season	10-2	3.84	367	100	11	32	54	.272	.455	.331
vs. Left-Handers			65	16	2	6	18	.246	.446	.310
vs. Right-Handers			302	84	9	26	36	.278	.457	.335
Home	5-1	2.88	186	48	3	15	29	.258	.371	.312
Road	5-1	4.89	181	52	8	17	25	.287	.541	.350
Grass	2-0	4.60	62	19	2	7	9	.306	.516	.371
Artificial Turf	8-2	3.70	305	81	9	25	45	.266	.443	.322
April	2-1	6.06	70	26	1	7	8	.371	.557	.430
May			0	0	0	0	0	—	—	—
June			0	0	0	0	0	—	—	—
July			0	0	0	0	0	—	—	—
August	3-1	3.43	154	38	5	16	19	.247	.422	.316
Sept./Oct.	5-0	3.35	143	36	5	9	27	.252	.441	.296
Leading Off Inn.			96	29	2	3	15	.302	.500	.323
Runners On			141	33	4	17	21	.234	.383	.317
Runners/Scor. Pos.			80	21	2	12	11	.263	.400	.351
Runners On/2 Out			62	16	1	8	12	.258	.371	.343
Scor. Pos./2 Out			38	11	0	6	7	.289	.395	.386
Late Inning Pressure			16	6	0	2	0	.375	.563	.444
Leading Off			4	1	0	0	0	.250	.250	.250
Runners On			5	3	0	2	0	.600	1.000	.714
Runners/Scor. Pos.			3	2	0	2	0	.667	1.000	.800
First 9 Batters			129	34	4	12	20	.264	.434	.329
Second 9 Batters			128	33	5	12	27	.258	.414	.321
All Batters Thereafter			110	33	2	8	7	.300	.527	.345

Loves to face: Jody Davis (.045, 1-for-22)
Hates to face: Mike Diaz (.467, 7-for-15, 4 HR, 3 BB)
Ground outs-to-air outs ratio: 0.96 last season, 0.90 for career. . . .
Additional statistics: 6 double-play ground outs in 59 opportunities,
26 doubles, 4 triples in 96.0 innings last season. . . . Allowed 9
first-inning runs in 16 starts. . . . Batting support: 5.00 runs per start.
. . . Didn't allow a three-run or grand-slam home run. . . . Undefeated in night games last season (7–0). . . . Only pitcher to collect two
game-winning RBIs last season. . . . Regular-season record of 44–17
with the Cards, but 0–2 with Series title on the line. . . . Career
record of 36–35 (.507) before the All-Star break, 59–25 (.702) after
the break. . . . Has faced 84 batters with the bases loaded, but
walked in only two runs in his career. . . . Has won eight consecutive
decisions against the Cubs.

Lee Tunnell

Throws Right

St. Louis Cardinals	W–L	ERA	AB	H	HR	BB	SO	BA	SA	OBA
Season	4-4	4.84	293	90	5	34	49	.307	.430	.377
vs. Left-Handers			134	34	0	20	26	.254	.328	.348
vs. Right-Handers			159	56	5	14	23	.352	.516	.401
Home	4-2	4.09	171	45	2	16	33	.263	.351	.328
Road	0-2	5.93	122	45	3	18	16	.369	.541	.441
Grass	0-0	4.50	45	17	1	7	4	.378	.467	.462
Artificial Turf	4-4	4.91	248	73	4	27	45	.294	.423	.361
April			0	0	0	0	0	—	—	—
May	2-0	3.14	53	13	3	14	10	.245	.509	.293
June	1-2	5.40	126	42	2	10	20	.333	.460	.380
July	1-0	4.11	54	16	0	8	10	.296	.333	.391
August	0-1	15.75	20	9	0	4	2	.450	.500	.520
Sept./Oct.	0-1	2.53	40	10	0	8	7	.250	.325	.375
Leading Off Inn.			69	23	2	6	14	.333	.522	.395
Runners On			144	44	1	21	23	.306	.403	.385
Runners/Scor. Pos.			92	29	0	15	13	.315	.413	.396
Runners On/2 Out			54	13	0	10	13	.241	.352	.359
Scor. Pos./2 Out			38	10	0	6	8	.263	.421	.364
Late Inning Pressure			46	13	0	12	5	.283	.348	.441
Leading Off			12	2	0	2	1	.167	.167	.333
Runners On			22	7	0	7	2	.318	.455	.483
Runners/Scor. Pos.			13	3	0	5	2	.231	.385	.444
First 9 Batters			161	45	1	23	25	.280	.360	.362
Second 9 Batters			87	30	3	8	20	.345	.552	.406
All Batters Thereafter			45	15	1	3	4	.333	.444	.375

Loves to face: Dale Murphy (0-for-10, 4 SO)
Hates to face: Mariano Duncan (.833, 5-for-6)
Ground outs-to-air outs ratio: 2.11 last season, 1.85 for career. . . .
Additional statistics: 13 double-play ground outs in 75 opportunities, 15 doubles, 3 triples in 74.1 innings last season. . . . Whitey's
mop-up man: Cards lost 10 of the last 11 games in which he appeared. . . . Appeared in only one save situation from seventh inning
on last season, raising his career total to four in 56 relief appearances. . . . Career record of 0–5 with a 5.50 ERA during the month
of April. . . . Opposing left-handed batters had outhit right-handers
by 45 points prior to last season. . . . Hasn't allowed a home run to
a left-handed batter since Sept. 2, 1985, to Claudell Washington. . . .
Career strikeout-to-walk ratio of 0.92 vs. left-handed batters, 2.00
vs. right-handers.

Fernando Valenzuela

Los Angeles Dodgers — Throws Left

	W-L	ERA	AB	H	HR	BB	SO	BA	SA	OBA
Season	14-14	3.98	968	254	25	124	190	.262	.401	.348
vs. Left-Handers			167	38	4	13	43	.228	.377	.283
vs. Right-Handers			801	216	21	111	147	.270	.406	.361
Home	6-7	3.50	463	116	7	59	83	.251	.339	.336
Road	8-7	4.43	505	138	18	65	107	.273	.457	.359
Grass	13-8	3.46	769	193	22	97	155	.251	.391	.337
Artificial Turf	1-6	6.19	199	61	3	27	35	.307	.437	.390
April	3-1	2.92	141	38	1	12	36	.270	.355	.327
May	2-1	4.26	151	40	6	18	28	.265	.457	.351
June	2-3	3.77	167	40	3	17	28	.240	.347	.310
July	2-3	5.79	147	46	7	21	24	.313	.510	.406
August	2-4	4.27	174	43	0	34	45	.247	.305	.367
Sept./Oct.	3-2	3.10	188	47	8	22	29	.250	.441	.329
Leading Off Inn.			221	53	5	33	52	.240	.344	.339
Runners On			479	123	11	51	88	.257	.388	.330
Runners/Scor. Pos.			278	60	4	35	53	.216	.284	.304
Runners On/2 Out			207	53	9	21	39	.256	.430	.325
Scor. Pos./2 Out			136	31	4	17	24	.228	.338	.314
Late Inning Pressure			140	32	1	17	28	.229	.300	.312
Leading Off			36	7	1	4	9	.194	.306	.275
Runners On			55	12	0	9	7	.218	.273	.328
Runners/Scor. Pos.			32	6	0	7	3	.188	.188	.333
First 9 Batters			263	65	6	35	52	.247	.365	.340
Second 9 Batters			268	74	8	34	63	.276	.440	.358
All Batters Thereafter			437	115	11	55	75	.263	.398	.347

Loves to face: Wally Backman (0-for-16)
Hates to face: Bob Horner (.423, 22-52, 6 HR)
Ground outs-to-air outs ratio: 1.18 last season, 1.35 for career. . . . Additional statistics: 21 double-play ground outs in 233 opportunities, 49 doubles, 5 triples in 251.0 innings last season. . . . Allowed 15 first-inning runs in 34 starts. . . . Batting support: 4.03 runs per start. . . . Here's a screwball note: Despite 1987 figures, career figures show that left-handers have hit 'Nando for higher average (.244) than have right-handers (.230). . . . Allowed more hits than innings for first time in career; also allowed career-high total of walks. . . . Faced more batters with bases loaded (28) than any N.L. pitcher: allowed only two hits (both singles) in 26 at bats, with one walk and major-league high 11 strikeouts. . . . Five shutouts in first seven major-league starts, four in last 83 starts.

Bob Walk

Pittsburgh Pirates — Throws Right

	W-L	ERA	AB	H	HR	BB	SO	BA	SA	OBA
Season	8-2	3.31	435	107	11	51	78	.246	.377	.328
vs. Left-Handers			229	58	4	26	32	.253	.380	.331
vs. Right-Handers			206	49	7	25	46	.238	.374	.325
Home	6-0	3.05	273	64	7	32	48	.234	.370	.318
Road	2-2	3.74	162	43	4	19	30	.265	.389	.344
Grass	1-2	4.41	61	16	1	5	16	.262	.377	.328
Artificial Turf	7-0	3.13	374	91	10	46	62	.243	.377	.328
April	0-0	3.95	54	14	2	5	15	.259	.407	.322
May	2-1	4.19	66	14	3	13	11	.212	.424	.346
June	0-0	4.20	54	13	2	9	7	.241	.389	.349
July	0-0	2.53	39	10	0	4	7	.256	.282	.333
August	4-1	3.53	130	34	3	15	19	.262	.400	.342
Sept./Oct.	2-0	1.59	92	22	1	5	19	.239	.326	.278
Leading Off Inn.			100	23	2	13	17	.230	.330	.330
Runners On			195	51	5	20	39	.262	.385	.330
Runners/Scor. Pos.			116	28	3	12	23	.241	.388	.308
Runners On/2 Out			87	22	4	9	16	.253	.444	.323
Scor. Pos./2 Out			60	13	2	6	11	.217	.350	.288
Late Inning Pressure			24	8	1	3	6	.333	.583	.407
Leading Off			8	3	1	1	2	.375	.750	.444
Runners On			8	3	0	1	2	.375	.500	.444
Runners/Scor. Pos.			5	2	0	0	2	.400	.600	.400
First 9 Batters			243	59	7	34	53	.243	.383	.337
Second 9 Batters			109	24	1	13	16	.220	.284	.306
All Batters Thereafter			83	24	3	4	9	.289	.482	.330

Loves to face: Ken Griffey (0-for-14)
Hates to face: Kevin McReynolds (.714, 5-for-7, 2 2B)
Ground outs-to-air outs ratio: 1.41 last season, 1.22 for career. . . . Additional statistics: 11 double-play ground outs in 93 opportunities, 16 doubles, 4 triples in 117.0 innings last season. . . . Allowed 5 first-inning runs in 12 starts. . . . Batting support: 5.42 runs per start. . . . Only N.L. pitcher to make 10 starts and 10 relief appearances in each of the past two seasons. . . . Took a regular turn in Pirates' rotation from Aug. 7 to Sept. 2, going 5–1 record in six starts, before straining a hammy. . . . During that time, he shut out Cardinals to snap their 145-game streak without being shut out, five short of modern N.L. mark set by Bucs in 1924–1925. . . . Opponents have career batting average of .319 in Late-Inning Pressure Situations, .260 in unpressured situations.

Bob Welch

Los Angeles Dodgers — Throws Right

	W-L	ERA	AB	H	HR	BB	SO	BA	SA	OBA
Season	15-9	3.22	921	204	21	86	196	.221	.342	.289
vs. Left-Handers			533	126	10	50	100	.236	.345	.301
vs. Right-Handers			388	78	11	36	96	.201	.338	.273
Home	7-6	3.24	502	113	13	35	105	.225	.349	.278
Road	8-3	3.19	419	91	8	51	91	.217	.334	.302
Grass	13-7	2.87	748	162	17	59	158	.217	.330	.275
Artificial Turf	2-2	4.80	173	42	4	27	38	.243	.393	.345
April	3-1	2.23	132	25	3	12	27	.189	.311	.262
May	3-1	3.53	136	32	3	12	32	.235	.353	.297
June	2-2	4.60	159	40	7	18	33	.252	.421	.335
July	1-2	3.35	161	37	1	14	34	.230	.335	.288
August	2-3	2.64	164	38	5	20	37	.232	.372	.310
Sept./Oct.	4-0	2.93	169	32	2	10	33	.189	.260	.238
Leading Off Inn.			246	47	5	13	49	.191	.289	.232
Runners On			317	79	11	41	66	.249	.404	.332
Runners/Scor. Pos.			174	42	3	25	42	.241	.356	.330
Runners On/2 Out			146	32	3	17	38	.219	.329	.301
Scor. Pos./2 Out			91	18	2	12	26	.198	.319	.291
Late Inning Pressure			101	25	2	10	10	.248	.347	.315
Leading Off			27	7	0	2	2	.259	.370	.310
Runners On			37	8	1	6	6	.216	.324	.326
Runners/Scor. Pos.			19	4	0	2	1	.211	.263	.286
First 9 Batters			280	53	5	29	73	.189	.293	.267
Second 9 Batters			278	68	6	29	64	.245	.371	.313
All Batters Thereafter			363	83	10	28	59	.229	.358	.288

Loves to face: Terry Kennedy (.164, 9-for-55)
Hates to face: Bill Madlock (.381, 16-for-42, 4 HR)
Ground outs-to-air outs ratio: 1.06 last season, 0.91 for career. . . . Additional statistics: 10 double-play ground outs in 152 opportunities, 40 doubles, 4 triples in 251.2 innings last season. . . . Allowed 16 first-inning runs in 35 starts. . . . Batting support: 4.71 runs per start. . . . Record of 8–2 to start the season, 4–0 to end the season, but won only three of 19 starts in between. . . . Has a career total of 110 batters faced with the bases loaded, but has never allowed a grand slam. . . . Previous success by the Bay: career record of 19–4 against Giants. . . . A couple of things that he accomplished in 1987 but won't repeat in A.L. in '88: (1) walked seven times (as a batter), tied for most among N.L. pitchers; (2) struck out opposing pitchers 37 times, most in N.L.

Ed Whitson

San Diego Padres — Throws Right

	W-L	ERA	AB	H	HR	BB	SO	BA	SA	OBA
Season	10-13	4.73	784	197	36	64	135	.251	.443	.309
vs. Left-Handers			427	122	14	41	64	.286	.443	.351
vs. Right-Handers			357	75	22	23	71	.210	.443	.258
Home	5-7	4.96	406	101	24	36	75	.249	.478	.309
Road	5-6	4.47	378	96	12	28	60	.254	.405	.310
Grass	7-12	5.11	643	163	34	52	107	.253	.463	.309
Artificial Turf	3-1	3.05	141	34	2	12	28	.241	.348	.310
April	3-2	4.94	103	23	10	10	21	.223	.553	.298
May	2-4	5.18	155	40	6	18	29	.258	.439	.339
June	3-1	3.48	126	27	4	11	20	.214	.349	.277
July	2-0	5.30	150	43	5	11	22	.287	.453	.335
August	0-2	4.50	125	25	5	6	13	.238	.438	.279
Sept./Oct.	0-4	4.78	145	39	6	8	30	.269	.441	.308
Leading Off Inn.			193	46	12	21	30	.238	.446	.316
Runners On			293	81	14	14	53	.276	.505	.310
Runners/Scor. Pos.			147	43	7	9	25	.293	.524	.333
Runners On/2 Out			126	40	9	8	18	.317	.619	.363
Scor. Pos./2 Out			74	27	5	5	11	.365	.662	.413
Late Inning Pressure			60	20	6	3	13	.333	.650	.365
Leading Off			16	3	1	1	5	.188	.375	.235
Runners On			15	8	3	0	2	.533	1.133	.533
Runners/Scor. Pos.			5	4	1	0	0	.800	1.400	.800
First 9 Batters			285	72	16	25	59	.253	.474	.316
Second 9 Batters			261	60	10	18	34	.230	.383	.281
All Batters Thereafter			238	65	10	21	42	.273	.471	.332

Loves to face: Billy Hatcher (0-for-10)
Hates to face: Eric Davis (.500, 7-for-14, 1 HR)
Ground outs-to-air outs ratio: 1.17 last season, 0.98 for career. . . . Additional statistics: 17 double-play ground outs in 131 opportunities, 28 doubles, 7 triples in 205.2 innings last season. . . . Allowed 25 first-inning runs in 34 starts. . . . Batting support: 4.44 runs per start. . . . Through May 16, accounted for half of San Diego's wins, posting a 4–5 mark compared to 4–25 by his teammates. Shades of Carlton and the '72 Phillies. . . . Set personal record for strikeouts, and allowed 13 more home runs than in any other season of his 11-year career. . . . Opposing batters have hit .313 with runners on base over past three seasons, compared to .263 with the bases empty. . . . Has gone 11–20 since rejoining San Diego, compared to a 15–10 mark with the Yankees. So does he still hate New York?

Frank Williams

Cincinnati Reds — Throws Right

	W-L	ERA	AB	H	HR	BB	SO	BA	SA	OBA
Season	4-0	2.30	397	101	5	39	60	.254	.360	.322
vs. Left-Handers			170	40	0	21	25	.235	.271	.318
vs. Right-Handers			227	61	5	18	35	.269	.427	.325
Home	0-0	1.50	220	55	2	17	37	.250	.359	.301
Road	4-0	3.35	177	46	3	22	23	.260	.362	.347
Grass	3-0	3.42	104	30	1	17	7	.288	.385	.390
Artificial Turf	1-0	1.93	293	71	4	22	53	.242	.352	.296
April	0-0	2.03	49	14	1	7	7	.286	.388	.386
May	0-0	3.66	74	14	1	4	16	.189	.270	.231
June	0-0	2.41	73	20	0	7	8	.274	.370	.333
July	1-0	2.18	74	20	2	4	11	.270	.419	.313
August	1-0	0.95	73	19	1	9	10	.260	.370	.341
Sept./Oct.	2-0	2.51	54	14	0	8	8	.259	.352	.349
Leading Off Inn.			97	19	3	6	16	.196	.340	.243
Runners On			162	44	1	22	18	.272	.383	.360
Runners/Scor. Pos.			103	32	0	21	14	.311	.408	.417
Runners On/2 Out			82	25	0	14	9	.305	.427	.406
Scor. Pos./2 Out			57	20	0	13	7	.351	.474	.471
Late Inning Pressure			157	40	2	19	26	.255	.357	.335
Leading Off			43	11	2	2	7	.256	.488	.289
Runners On			66	17	0	11	7	.258	.333	.363
Runners/Scor. Pos.			45	14	0	11	5	.311	.400	.431
First 9 Batters			379	93	5	39	57	.245	.356	.317
Second 9 Batters			18	8	0	0	3	.444	.444	.444
All Batters Thereafter			0	0	0	0	0			

Loves to face: Jose Cruz (0-for-9, 4 SO)
Hates to face: Eddie Milner (.600, 6-for-10, 3 2B)
Ground outs-to-air outs ratio: 1.54 last season, 1.74 for career. . . .
Additional statistics: 10 double-play ground outs in 65 opportunities, 23 doubles, 2 triples in 105.2 innings last season. . . . Faced one batter in nine appearances. Only one N.L. pitcher had more one-batter appearances: teammate Rob Murphy. . . . Allowed one extra-base hit for every 9.5 at bats by opposing right-handed hitters, compared to prior career rate of one per 51 at bats. . . . Last left-hander to homer off Williams was Bob Knepper on June 29, 1985. . . . Only two active pitchers have pitched as many innings as Williams and compiled a higher winning percentage and a lower ERA: Dwight Gooden and John Franco. . . . Has never allowed a home run with runners on base in Late-Inning Pressure Situations.

Todd Worrell

St. Louis Cardinals — Throws Right

	W-L	ERA	AB	H	HR	BB	SO	BA	SA	OBA
Season	8-6	2.66	355	86	8	34	92	.242	.366	.307
vs. Left-Handers			146	34	3	23	43	.233	.315	.333
vs. Right-Handers			209	52	5	11	49	.249	.402	.286
Home	5-3	3.25	166	39	6	12	38	.235	.410	.285
Road	3-3	2.15	189	47	2	22	54	.249	.328	.325
Grass	1-3	3.24	99	26	2	8	31	.263	.343	.318
Artificial Turf	7-3	2.45	256	60	6	26	61	.234	.375	.303
April	0-0	5.40	18	5	1	5	4	.278	.444	.435
May	0-2	6.59	57	21	2	4	11	.368	.579	.403
June	3-1	0.89	70	12	0	6	22	.171	.229	.237
July	1-3	4.11	66	19	3	5	19	.288	.455	.338
August	3-0	0.79	82	19	1	8	16	.232	.341	.297
Sept./Oct.	1-0	2.04	62	10	1	6	20	.161	.242	.235
Leading Off Inn.			70	20	2	6	13	.286	.457	.342
Runners On			190	38	3	21	51	.200	.274	.277
Runners/Scor. Pos.			111	23	3	16	28	.207	.297	.302
Runners On/2 Out			98	21	1	13	27	.214	.286	.306
Scor. Pos./2 Out			63	13	1	11	15	.206	.270	.324
Late Inning Pressure			252	64	7	29	71	.254	.409	.329
Leading Off			50	14	2	5	11	.280	.520	.345
Runners On			131	30	3	19	37	.229	.328	.322
Runners/Scor. Pos.			82	18	3	15	20	.220	.341	.333
First 9 Batters			344	83	7	32	88	.241	.360	.304
Second 9 Batters			11	3	1	2	4	.273	.545	.385
All Batters Thereafter			0	0	0	0	0			

Loves to face: Lance Parrish (0-for-7)
Hates to face: Pedro Guerrero (5-for-5, 2 HR)
Ground outs-to-air outs ratio: 0.74 last season, 0.77 for career. . . .
Additional statistics: 7 double-play ground outs in 74 opportunities, 14 doubles, 3 triples in 94.2 innings last season. . . . Earned 33 saves in 49 opportunities (67 percent). Career rate (74-for-105, 70 percent) is well below those of N.L. top relievers of past three seasons: Lee Smith, 100-for-129 (78%); Dave Smith, 84-for-103 (82%); Steve Bedrosian, 69-for-87 (79%). . . . Opponents' career breakdown: .280 with bases empty, .192 with runners on base. . . . Difference of 87 points in Late-Inning Pressure Situations (.194 with runners on, .281 with bases empty) is largest among active pitchers (minimum: 100 AB each way). . . . Has faced 36 batters with the bases loaded: .194 (3-for-31), two grand slams, no walks, nine SO.

Floyd Youmans

Montreal Expos — Throws Right

	W-L	ERA	AB	H	HR	BB	SO	BA	SA	OBA
Season	9-8	4.64	446	112	13	47	94	.251	.415	.321
vs. Left-Handers			259	73	6	33	38	.282	.444	.361
vs. Right-Handers			187	39	7	14	56	.209	.374	.261
Home	4-3	4.78	204	55	3	25	43	.270	.402	.346
Road	5-5	4.52	242	57	10	22	51	.236	.426	.299
Grass	3-4	5.67	135	37	6	17	34	.274	.481	.359
Artificial Turf	6-4	4.23	311	75	7	30	60	.241	.386	.303
April	1-2	6.65	88	24	4	8	16	.273	.477	.323
May	2-1	3.92	80	20	5	10	25	.250	.475	.333
June	1-0	4.00	38	11	0	3	10	.289	.316	.341
July	4-1	1.13	130	20	1	11	25	.154	.208	.218
August	0-2	9.88	60	21	1	11	9	.350	.600	.452
Sept./Oct.	1-2	8.49	50	16	3	4	9	.320	.600	.370
Leading Off Inn.			110	25	3	15	23	.227	.364	.320
Runners On			176	50	4	19	40	.284	.472	.348
Runners/Scor. Pos.			106	25	1	15	28	.236	.349	.323
Runners On/2 Out			72	13	1	12	17	.181	.292	.298
Scor. Pos./2 Out			47	7	0	10	10	.149	.191	.191
Late Inning Pressure			27	4	0	6	7	.148	.185	.303
Leading Off			7	1	0	3	2	.143	.143	.400
Runners On			11	1	0	2	3	.091	.182	.231
Runners/Scor. Pos.			5	1	0	1	1	.200	.400	.333
First 9 Batters			182	41	4	17	47	.225	.363	.287
Second 9 Batters			161	48	6	18	28	.298	.509	.370
All Batters Thereafter			103	23	3	12	19	.223	.359	.302

Loves to face: Martinezes (Carmelo & Dave, both 0-for-8, 4 SO)
Hates to face: Bobby Bonilla (.625, 5-for-8, 1 HR)
Ground outs-to-air outs ratio: 0.60, 3d lowest in N.L. last season (minimum: 200 BFP), 0.79 for career. . . . Additional statistics: 3 double-play ground outs in 63 opportunities, 28 doubles, 3 triples in 116.1 innings last season. . . . Allowed 8 first-inning runs in 23 starts. . . . Batting support: 3.87 runs per start. . . . Opponents were 32-for-34 stealing, the highest rate vs. any N.L. pitcher (minimum: 20 attempts); only Maldonado and Perry were caught with Youmans on the mound. . . . Youngest opening-day starting pitcher in majors in 1987. . . . Hurled three shutouts in four starts (July 8–26). ERA of 1.69 in July over past three seasons is lowest in majors during that time (minimum: 75 IP). . . . Opponents' career batting average of .184 leading off innings.

Matt Young

Los Angeles Dodgers — Throws Left

	W-L	ERA	AB	H	HR	BB	SO	BA	SA	OBA
Season	5-8	4.47	215	62	3	17	42	.288	.381	.339
vs. Left-Handers			64	15	1	4	11	.234	.313	.279
vs. Right-Handers			151	47	2	13	31	.311	.411	.364
Home	4-2	2.10	111	27	1	6	22	.243	.297	.282
Road	1-6	7.40	104	35	2	11	20	.337	.471	.397
Grass	5-4	2.39	142	36	1	9	30	.254	.303	.298
Artificial Turf	0-4	9.18	73	26	2	8	12	.356	.534	.415
April	0-3	9.72	36	13	1	4	5	.361	.528	.425
May	1-2	5.00	37	11	1	4	16	.297	.459	.366
June	2-0	1.74	35	6	0	2	8	.171	.200	.211
July	2-1	4.11	60	18	1	5	6	.300	.383	.354
August	0-1	1.69	43	12	0	2	6	.279	.326	.311
Sept./Oct.	0-1	27.00	4	2	0	0	1	.500	.500	.500
Leading Off Inn.			41	13	0	3	9	.317	.390	.364
Runners On			125	39	2	12	24	.312	.416	.370
Runners/Scor. Pos.			90	24	1	11	18	.267	.344	.343
Runners On/2 Out			44	9	0	4	8	.205	.227	.271
Scor. Pos./2 Out			36	7	0	4	6	.194	.222	.275
Late Inning Pressure			155	49	2	13	32	.316	.406	.367
Leading Off			30	10	0	3	6	.333	.367	.394
Runners On			90	31	2	9	20	.344	.478	.400
Runners/Scor. Pos.			60	18	1	9	14	.300	.417	.386
First 9 Batters			205	62	3	17	41	.302	.400	.354
Second 9 Batters			10	0	0	0	1	.000	.000	.000
All Batters Thereafter			0	0	0	0	0			

Loves to face: Wade Boggs (.053, 1-for-19)
Hates to face: Chet Lemon (.529, 9-for-17, 4 HR)
Ground outs-to-air outs ratio: 2.49 last season, 1.72 for career. . . .
Additional statistics: 9 double-play ground outs in 68 opportunities, 11 doubles, 0 triples in 54.1 innings last season. . . . Eleven saves last season, but none after August 20. Dodgers used Pena as their stopper in September. . . . Career records: 31–45 with a 4.49 ERA (5.64 strikeouts per nine innings) as a starter; 11–11, 3.84 ERA (7.43 SO rate) in relief. . . . Career record 0–4 in starting assignments following relief appearances. . . . Opposing right-handed batters have hit over .300 in three of the last four seasons. Career breakdown: .225 (one HR per 88.8 AB) by left-handers, .284 (one HR per 37.7 AB) by right-handers. . . . Opponents' career batting average of .354 (29-for-82, one walk, four HR) with the bases loaded.

Atlanta Braves

	W–L	ERA	AB	H	HR	BB	SO	BA	SA	OBA
Season	69-92	4.63	5532	1529	163	587	837	.276	.421	.347
vs. Left-Handers			2322	669	66	271	338	.288	.433	.362
vs. Right-Handers			3210	860	97	316	499	.268	.413	.336
Home	42-39	4.90	2878	820	88	285	428	.285	.434	.350
Road	27-53	4.34	2654	709	75	302	409	.267	.408	.344
Grass	56-63	4.60	4140	1141	129	414	608	.276	.425	.343
Artificial Turf	13-29	4.70	1392	388	34	173	229	.279	.412	.360
April	9-12	4.07	721	199	24	70	116	.276	.426	.341
May	16-12	4.69	1037	293	26	108	155	.283	.414	.353
June	11-16	4.32	899	233	31	78	144	.259	.409	.317
July	9-17	4.43	873	239	23	88	137	.274	.416	.339
August	11-17	5.08	946	264	30	109	137	.279	.441	.356
Sept./Oct.	13-18	5.00	1056	301	29	134	148	.285	.423	.369
Leading Off Inn.			1317	365	44	109	175	.277	.434	.337
Runners On			2452	710	75	308	381	.290	.438	.367
Runners/Scor. Pos.			1502	426	43	221	280	.284	.419	.370
Runners On/2 Out			1047	296	34	157	190	.283	.431	.379
Scor. Pos./2 Out			725	206	24	119	142	.284	.426	.387
Late Inning Pressure			929	280	27	104	132	.301	.456	.372
Leading Off			243	76	11	11	32	.313	.519	.343
Runners On			400	126	7	60	55	.315	.435	.402
Runners/Scor. Pos.			255	71	2	49	43	.278	.345	.392
First 9 Batters			2873	746	77	320	489	.260	.391	.335
Second 9 Batters			1463	403	40	140	194	.275	.412	.340
All Batters Thereafter			1196	380	46	127	154	.318	.505	.384

Starting pitchers: 47–65, 4.82 ERA
Relief pitchers: 22–27, 4.26 ERA
Ground outs-to-air outs ratio: 1.47, highest in majors. . . . Highest ERA in N.L. since 4.85 by the 1977 Braves. . . . Best staff in the majors in at least one regard: Pitchers combined for a .982 fielding percentage. No pitcher committed more than one error. . . . First N.L. team in 13 years whose opponents topped the .300 mark in Late-Inning Pressure Situations. . . . Opponents also compiled highest batting average in N.L. with two outs and runners in scoring position and 2d-highest in N.L. with runners on base during that period. . . . Pitchers had 40 starts on three days' rest last season, most by any team in majors. . . . There were only three 1–0 games at Atlanta Stadium over past 11 seasons. Last time Braves and opponents played nine scoreless innings there was Sept. 17, 1976.

Chicago Cubs

	W–L	ERA	AB	H	HR	BB	SO	BA	SA	OBA
Season	76-85	4.55	5541	1524	159	628	1024	.275	.425	.349
vs. Left-Handers			2401	712	68	298	398	.297	.464	.374
vs. Right-Handers			3140	812	91	330	626	.259	.395	.330
Home	40-40	4.35	2816	758	90	322	548	.269	.426	.345
Road	36-45	4.77	2725	766	69	306	476	.281	.423	.354
Grass	54-59	4.52	3935	1070	124	445	745	.272	.427	.347
Artificial Turf	22-26	4.64	1606	454	35	183	279	.283	.420	.356
April	10-10	3.64	681	173	11	79	140	.254	.360	.331
May	18-10	3.77	979	235	28	110	178	.240	.379	.320
June	12-17	4.83	980	281	30	121	185	.287	.446	.367
July	12-13	4.34	846	235	29	80	166	.278	.442	.341
August	14-14	5.56	978	296	32	138	168	.303	.470	.387
Sept./Oct.	10-21	4.90	1077	304	29	100	187	.282	.434	.342
Leading Off Inn.			1309	351	37	124	248	.268	.426	.335
Runners On			2498	696	70	324	422	.279	.427	.359
Runners/Scor. Pos.			1511	415	37	241	261	.275	.416	.368
Runners On/2 Out			1045	267	32	161	202	.256	.401	.356
Scor. Pos./2 Out			699	176	14	134	136	.252	.375	.374
Late Inning Pressure			953	258	24	126	188	.271	.403	.357
Leading Off			233	60	7	20	38	.258	.408	.322
Runners On			441	120	7	68	91	.272	.379	.367
Runners/Scor. Pos.			288	83	5	50	59	.288	.410	.388
First 9 Batters			2904	783	78	336	604	.270	.410	.346
Second 9 Batters			1386	366	37	147	232	.264	.406	.336
All Batters Thereafter			1251	375	44	145	188	.300	.480	.372

Starting pitchers: 59–61, 4.72 ERA
Relief pitchers: 17–24, 4.24 ERA
Ground outs-to-air outs ratio: 1.33. . . . Sutcliffe and Smith became first Cubs pitchers to appear in same All-Star Game since Curt Davis and Lon Warneke in 1936. . . . Had the fewest complete games in either league since 1981, fewest in a full season since 1977, when San Diego had only six. . . . Opponents compiled highest batting average vs. left-handed pitchers in N.L. over past 13 years. . . . Allowed the N.L.'s highest batting average with the bases empty for ninth time in past 12 seasons, but have yielded highest mark with runners on only twice during that time. . . . Lowest ERA of any N.L. staff during May. . . . Sutcliffe has been Chicago's opening-day starter for three straight years (1985-87). The last to pitch four in a row: Ferguson Jenkins (7 years, 1967–73).

Cincinnati Reds

	W–L	ERA	AB	H	HR	BB	SO	BA	SA	OBA
Season	84-78	4.24	5558	1486	170	485	919	.267	.429	.326
vs. Left-Handers			2013	553	51	206	299	.275	.424	.340
vs. Right-Handers			3545	933	119	279	620	.263	.432	.318
Home	42-39	4.41	2861	780	97	239	477	.273	.451	.328
Road	42-39	4.07	2697	706	73	246	442	.262	.406	.323
Grass	24-24	4.06	1575	417	46	166	252	.265	.417	.335
Artificial Turf	60-54	4.32	3983	1069	124	319	667	.268	.434	.322
April	15-7	3.19	730	170	20	55	116	.233	.378	.286
May	13-14	4.83	938	256	33	69	158	.273	.443	.322
June	14-13	4.83	936	261	33	88	146	.279	.455	.340
July	13-14	4.87	967	286	31	80	151	.296	.482	.348
August	9-20	4.36	972	266	28	93	159	.274	.432	.337
Sept./Oct.	20-10	3.32	1015	247	25	100	189	.243	.375	.314
Leading Off Inn.			1356	373	46	97	214	.275	.445	.324
Runners On			2312	637	58	242	371	.276	.433	.341
Runners/Scor. Pos.			1352	381	36	190	235	.282	.446	.362
Runners On/2 Out			998	262	25	140	176	.263	.416	.355
Scor. Pos./2 Out			648	171	18	112	120	.264	.420	.374
Late Inning Pressure			936	241	19	103	165	.257	.379	.334
Leading Off			243	69	11	12	37	.284	.481	.318
Runners On			383	96	0	63	68	.251	.324	.354
Runners/Scor. Pos.			229	56	0	58	43	.245	.319	.388
First 9 Batters			3129	822	75	286	590	.263	.399	.323
Second 9 Batters			1362	362	50	116	193	.266	.446	.324
All Batters Thereafter			1067	302	45	83	136	.283	.497	.338

Starting pitchers: 51–63, 4.87 ERA (highest in N.L.)
Relief pitchers: 33–15, 3.10 ERA (lowest in majors)
Ground outs-to-air outs ratio: 0.99, lowest in N.L. since 1984, when San Diego established 13-year league low (0.91). . . . Set all-time major-league record for relief appearances; Rose made 392 pitching changes last season. . . . Have held opposing batters to a lower batting average in Late-Inning Pressure Situations than overall in each of the past five seasons, the longest current streak in either league. . . . Only the second team in the past 13 years not to allow a home run in Late-Inning Pressure Situations with runners on base. The other: San Francisco during strike-tainted 1981 season. . . . Only team in the majors that hasn't won a game by a 1–0 score in either of the last two seasons. Last 1–0 victory: August 30, 1985.

Houston Astros

	W–L	ERA	AB	H	HR	BB	SO	BA	SA	OBA
Season	76-86	3.84	5452	1363	141	525	1137	.250	.386	.317
vs. Left-Handers			2251	567	49	249	441	.252	.376	.328
vs. Right-Handers			3201	796	92	276	696	.249	.394	.309
Home	47-34	2.88	2771	645	46	234	619	.233	.332	.295
Road	29-52	4.89	2681	718	95	291	518	.268	.443	.340
Grass	17-31	5.17	1611	448	66	183	311	.278	.466	.352
Artificial Turf	59-55	3.31	3841	915	75	342	826	.238	.353	.302
April	12-9	3.46	708	170	18	62	181	.240	.384	.304
May	12-15	4.04	872	195	23	94	197	.224	.358	.302
June	16-11	3.92	931	229	30	77	205	.246	.387	.305
July	10-17	3.79	896	230	20	104	172	.257	.392	.335
August	15-14	3.72	1013	271	30	74	184	.268	.422	.317
Sept./Oct.	11-20	4.01	1032	268	20	114	198	.260	.373	.335
Leading Off Inn.			1348	299	32	93	281	.222	.338	.275
Runners On			2233	607	56	254	440	.272	.406	.344
Runners/Scor. Pos.			1375	357	33	196	294	.260	.383	.347
Runners On/2 Out			1026	273	23	117	200	.266	.390	.344
Scor. Pos./2 Out			689	177	18	97	142	.257	.383	.352
Late Inning Pressure			1008	250	14	96	241	.248	.316	.316
Leading Off			256	56	4	19	55	.219	.328	.278
Runners On			400	108	5	56	83	.270	.358	.355
Runners/Scor. Pos.			246	70	5	51	49	.285	.402	.397
First 9 Batters			2789	688	76	289	610	.247	.389	.318
Second 9 Batters			1382	345	29	126	271	.250	.366	.313
All Batters Thereafter			1281	330	36	110	256	.258	.403	.319

Starting pitchers: 53–65, 3.82 ERA
Relief pitchers: 23–21, 3.92 ERA
Ground outs-to-air outs ratio: 1.15. . . . Opponents grounded into one double play for every 11.6 opportunities, lowest rate in N.L. . . . Best ERA and fewest HR allowed in majors at home; worst ERA and most HR allowed in N.L. on the road. . . . Led N.L. in strikeouts for fifth time in past 10 years. Ryan and Scott became first teammates to rank one-two since Frank Tanana and Ryan for 1976 Angels. Drysdale and Koufax were last N.L. teammates to do it (1962). . . . There have been 29 1–0 games at the Astrodome during the 1980s, seven more than at any other stadium. . . . Astros pitchers were 5-for-5 batting against Shane Rawley last season. Danny Darwin had three hits, including a double and triple; Mike Scott had the other two hits.

Los Angeles Dodgers

	W-L	ERA	AB	H	HR	BB	SO	BA	SA	OBA
Season	73-89	3.72	5553	1415	130	565	1097	.255	.382	.325
vs. Left-Handers			2397	616	46	246	416	.257	.370	.326
vs. Right-Handers			3156	799	84	319	681	.253	.391	.324
Home	40-41	3.21	2868	715	56	245	555	.249	.351	.310
Road	33-48	4.26	2685	700	74	320	542	.261	.416	.341
Grass	62-58	3.37	4140	1032	99	390	813	.249	.373	.316
Artificial Turf	11-31	4.77	1413	383	31	175	284	.271	.410	.353
April	12-11	3.26	791	200	15	68	165	.253	.372	.314
May	11-15	3.90	893	238	21	88	195	.267	.410	.334
June	13-14	3.39	906	213	22	90	183	.235	.355	.306
July	10-16	4.58	901	242	25	100	170	.269	.410	.344
August	10-19	3.70	963	249	19	122	196	.259	.375	.341
Sept./Oct.	17-14	3.48	1099	273	28	97	188	.248	.374	.314
Leading Off Inn.			1344	333	27	114	259	.248	.361	.308
Runners On			2382	633	60	281	463	.266	.399	.344
Runners/Scor. Pos.			1395	347	31	210	295	.249	.363	.346
Runners On/2 Out			1021	254	29	129	211	.249	.389	.337
Scor. Pos./2 Out			660	148	19	107	146	.224	.359	.337
Late Inning Pressure			1041	275	15	120	197	.264	.363	.340
Leading Off			255	70	5	23	46	.275	.380	.335
Runners On			460	123	6	69	86	.267	.372	.360
Runners/Scor. Pos.			266	69	2	55	47	.259	.338	.379
First 9 Batters			2640	647	53	278	567	.245	.357	.319
Second 9 Batters			1382	359	33	127	281	.260	.397	.323
All Batters Thereafter			1531	409	44	160	249	.267	.412	.338

Starting pitchers: 57–68, 3.64 ERA (lowest in majors)
Relief pitchers: 16–21, 3.94 ERA
Ground outs-to-air outs ratio: 1.35. . . . Led N.L. in complete games for 4th consecutive season. . . . Starters completed at least five innings in 144 of 162 games last season, highest total in the majors. . . . Swept in doubleheaders by Cardinals on July 8 and 9, first time Dodgers had lost four games in two days to same team since 1935. . . . Tied N.L. record by using five pitchers in an inning (8th inning, Aug. 26), and it worked: Mets failed to score. . . . Lost 12 games in which they led after six innings, second consecutive year that they've led the N.L. in that category. . . . Best ERA in majors on grass fields, but 2d worst in N.L. on artificial surfaces. . . . Allowed only one grand slam to an opposing batter last season. Every other N.L. club allowed at least two.

New York Mets

	W-L	ERA	AB	H	HR	BB	SO	BA	SA	OBA
Season	92-70	3.84	5532	1407	135	510	1032	.254	.383	.319
vs. Left-Handers			2408	617	49	236	392	.256	.379	.323
vs. Right-Handers			3124	790	86	274	640	.253	.386	.315
Home	49-32	3.73	2790	709	63	257	543	.254	.378	.319
Road	43-38	3.96	2742	698	72	253	489	.255	.388	.319
Grass	67-47	3.71	3906	995	93	362	747	.255	.380	.320
Artificial Turf	25-23	4.17	1626	412	42	148	285	.253	.390	.316
April	11-9	4.56	698	186	19	74	133	.266	.420	.338
May	13-14	3.88	926	258	22	96	180	.279	.408	.349
June	16-12	3.64	935	229	26	86	176	.245	.373	.310
July	16-11	3.96	921	242	21	68	125	.263	.394	.317
August	18-11	3.97	1002	250	23	96	190	.250	.376	.314
Sept./Oct.	18-13	3.33	1050	242	24	90	228	.230	.341	.293
Leading Off Inn.			1335	358	37	114	230	.268	.407	.330
Runners On			2422	601	54	247	459	.248	.369	.315
Runners/Scor. Pos.			1426	346	28	176	277	.243	.356	.319
Runners On/2 Out			1044	257	32	113	201	.246	.390	.323
Scor. Pos./2 Out			688	171	18	82	136	.249	.382	.333
Late Inning Pressure			1018	279	27	107	196	.274	.390	.344
Leading Off			252	69	5	16	49	.274	.365	.320
Runners On			441	121	11	59	84	.274	.383	.359
Runners/Scor. Pos.			253	73	7	43	49	.289	.399	.387
First 9 Batters			2861	722	61	270	576	.252	.366	.318
Second 9 Batters			1392	346	34	124	230	.249	.377	.310
All Batters Thereafter			1279	339	40	116	226	.265	.428	.330

Starting pitchers: 70–44, 3.92
Relief pitchers: 22–26, 3.68
Ground outs-to-air outs ratio: 1.31. . . . Opposing batters have hit better in Late-Inning Pressure Situations than overall in each of the past three seasons, tying the White Sox for the longest current streak in the majors. . . . But the Mets have held their opponents to lower batting averages with runners in scoring position than overall for five years running, also currently the longest streak in the majors. . . . Have lost all 64 regular-season home games over past three years in which they trailed after eight innings. But, of course, Dave Smith could explain the irony to those who don't recall the details of Game 3 of the 1986 N.L.C.S. . . . Lost eight home games in which they led after six innings (most in the majors). . . . "Big Five" starters accounted for 148 starts in 1986, only 113 starts last season.

Montreal Expos

	W-L	ERA	AB	H	HR	BB	SO	BA	SA	OBA
Season	91-71	3.92	5565	1428	145	446	1012	.257	.393	.313
vs. Left-Handers			2748	713	62	247	469	.259	.393	.320
vs. Right-Handers			2817	715	83	199	543	.254	.394	.305
Home	48-33	3.93	2857	733	74	242	544	.257	.399	.316
Road	43-38	3.90	2708	695	71	204	468	.257	.388	.308
Grass	25-17	3.83	1425	360	39	110	267	.253	.384	.307
Artificial Turf	66-54	3.95	4140	1068	106	336	745	.258	.397	.314
April	8-12	4.55	668	177	25	57	107	.265	.439	.321
May	17-11	3.97	977	255	29	77	191	.261	.403	.316
June	15-12	4.94	961	276	28	72	163	.287	.436	.337
July	18-8	2.78	870	200	21	58	151	.230	.354	.280
August	15-14	3.72	1021	264	18	90	176	.259	.373	.322
Sept./Oct.	18-14	3.69	1068	256	24	92	224	.240	.369	.300
Leading Off Inn.			1367	337	38	79	223	.247	.381	.290
Runners On			2298	626	67	223	427	.272	.426	.335
Runners/Scor. Pos.			1422	369	35	164	298	.259	.393	.331
Runners On/2 Out			994	236	19	110	207	.237	.362	.316
Scor. Pos./2 Out			678	152	10	86	154	.224	.332	.314
Late Inning Pressure			863	201	16	76	171	.233	.336	.295
Leading Off			220	48	3	12	41	.218	.300	.259
Runners On			348	85	7	42	73	.244	.356	.326
Runners/Scor. Pos.			228	56	5	32	50	.246	.368	.336
First 9 Batters			3059	757	74	256	570	.247	.373	.306
Second 9 Batters			1434	372	40	109	263	.259	.408	.313
All Batters Thereafter			1072	299	31	81	179	.279	.431	.329

Starting pitchers: 62–57, 4.30
Relief pitchers: 29–14, 3.22
Ground outs-to-air outs ratio: 1.16. . . . Walked the leadoff batter only once for every 18.4 innings, lowest rate in majors since 1983. . . . Used a starter on three days' rest only seven times in 1987, fewest by any N.L. team. . . . Only team in majors without a game won by a rookie pitcher. Two rookies on staff (Fischer and Heredia) combined for only 23.2 innings pitched last season, lowest rookie total in the majors. . . . Worst ERA in N.L. during June, best ERA in majors for July. . . . Expos staff combined for a .939 fielding percentage, worst in the N.L. . . . Road-game ERA was the lowest in the N.L. . . . Number of batters faced while protecting leads of three runs or less in the eighth inning or later: Burke 123, McGaffigan 76, Parrett 57, St. Claire 27.

Phila. Phillies

	W-L	ERA	AB	H	HR	BB	SO	BA	SA	OBA
Season	80-82	4.18	5523	1453	167	587	877	.263	.414	.335
vs. Left-Handers			1763	502	48	239	258	.285	.431	.371
vs. Right-Handers			3760	951	119	348	619	.253	.406	.317
Home	43-38	4.09	2828	726	78	286	470	.257	.403	.326
Road	37-44	4.28	2695	727	89	301	407	.270	.425	.344
Grass	16-26	4.61	1420	403	56	165	228	.284	.456	.360
Artificial Turf	64-56	4.04	4103	1050	111	422	649	.256	.399	.326
April	7-13	4.34	677	181	22	94	108	.267	.425	.362
May	15-11	4.13	885	225	27	87	146	.254	.406	.322
June	13-15	4.91	941	267	34	89	142	.284	.461	.344
July	18-9	3.64	919	246	23	83	122	.268	.400	.329
August	15-15	3.91	870	279	31	118	166	.261	.399	.334
Sept./Oct.	12-19	4.25	1031	255	30	116	193	.247	.397	.324
Leading Off Inn.			1307	366	42	134	202	.280	.449	.351
Runners On			2418	615	63	307	379	.254	.391	.336
Runners/Scor. Pos.			1437	342	38	241	257	.238	.371	.342
Runners On/2 Out			1009	230	29	154	166	.228	.369	.335
Scor. Pos./2 Out			672	146	16	128	123	.217	.341	.347
Late Inning Pressure			978	246	31	99	165	.252	.387	.323
Leading Off			241	65	11	20	39	.270	.440	.328
Runners On			413	93	11	54	69	.225	.349	.319
Runners/Scor. Pos.			241	47	6	46	47	.195	.307	.325
First 9 Batters			3042	745	81	342	565	.245	.381	.323
Second 9 Batters			1326	367	39	114	188	.277	.425	.336
All Batters Thereafter			1155	341	47	131	124	.295	.487	.366

Starting pitchers: 53–64, 4.59 ERA
Relief pitchers: 27–18, 3.39 ERA
Ground outs-to-air outs ratio: 1.06, 2d-lowest in N.L. . . . Opponents grounded into one double play for every 10.8 opportunities, 2d-lowest rate in N.L. . . . Have held opposing batter to lowest batting average in Late-Inning Pressure Situations with runners in scoring position in N.L. in each of past two seasons. . . . One of three teams to hold opposing batters to lower batting averages with runners on base than with the bases empty in each of the past two seasons. The others: Mets and Red Sox. . . . Starters failed to complete five innings in 47 games, highest total in N.L. . . . Record of 65-3 when leading after seven innings was the best in the N.L. . . . Phillies scored total of eight runs in Joe Cowley's four starts. Cowley had a 13.91 ERA in those games.

Pittsburgh Pirates

	W–L	ERA	AB	H	HR	BB	SO	BA	SA	OBA
Season	80-82	4.20	5437	1377	164	562	914	.253	.407	.324
vs. Left-Handers			2595	669	62	273	365	.258	.402	.328
vs. Right-Handers			2842	708	102	289	549	.249	.412	.319
Home	47-34	3.91	2822	703	84	278	485	.249	.403	.317
Road	33-48	4.51	2615	674	80	284	429	.258	.412	.331
Grass	19-23	4.19	1345	335	44	140	241	.249	.405	.321
Artificial Turf	61-59	4.20	4092	1042	120	422	673	.255	.408	.324
April	8-11	4.58	649	165	25	73	129	.254	.436	.329
May	13-14	4.94	895	236	28	115	152	.264	.420	.349
June	13-17	4.57	999	269	29	114	161	.269	.432	.344
July	11-15	3.62	883	217	29	78	147	.246	.402	.307
August	15-14	4.10	949	242	29	86	128	.255	.407	.317
Sept./Oct.	20-11	3.59	1062	248	24	96	197	.234	.361	.298
Leading Off Inn.			1325	361	43	120	211	.272	.432	.336
Runners On			2300	608	72	252	372	.264	.430	.333
Runners/Scor. Pos.			1384	350	47	182	239	.253	.426	.333
Runners On/2 Out			893	186	21	103	179	.208	.327	.291
Scor. Pos./2 Out			588	118	15	80	114	.201	.327	.297
Late Inning Pressure			920	232	23	107	180	.252	.384	.331
Leading Off			228	59	7	27	44	.259	.408	.342
Runners On			388	104	12	52	71	.268	.423	.352
Runners/Scor. Pos.			247	61	8	39	52	.247	.417	.346
First 9 Batters			2824	712	77	322	541	.252	.400	.328
Second 9 Batters			1365	339	35	141	208	.248	.396	.321
All Batters Thereafter			1248	326	52	99	165	.261	.437	.316

Starting pitchers: 60–55, 4.05 ERA
Relief pitchers: 20–27, 4.54 ERA (highest in N.L.)
Ground outs-to-air outs ratio: 1.27. . . . Tied Houston for N.L. lead with 13 shutouts. . . . Opponents' batting average with two outs and runners on base was 4th-lowest in N.L. over past 13 years. . . . Used 12 rookie pitchers last season, highest total in majors over past six seasons. . . . Won eight consecutive road games from Sept. 9 through Sept. 21, the longest road winning streak in the N.L. last season. . . . Used 12 rookie pitchers last season, by far the most in the majors. Brewers used seven, most in the A.L., N.L. runners-up were Braves, Dodgers, and Mets with five each. Pirates' rookies pitched a total of 466.2 innings, no other N.L. team's rookies combined for more than 325 innings. . . . ERA of 6.30 in 18 games vs. the Mets was the highest of any team against any N.L. opponent.

St. Louis Cardinals

	W–L	ERA	AB	H	HR	BB	SO	BA	SA	OBA
Season	95-67	3.91	5589	1484	129	533	873	.266	.404	.331
vs. Left-Handers			1833	489	25	200	293	.267	.376	.338
vs. Right-Handers			3756	995	104	333	580	.265	.418	.327
Home	49-32	3.73	2846	754	60	250	442	.265	.398	.326
Road	46-35	4.09	2743	730	69	283	431	.266	.410	.336
Grass	26-16	3.71	1393	362	35	135	233	.260	.387	.327
Artificial Turf	69-51	3.98	4196	1122	94	398	640	.267	.410	.332
April	12-8	3.88	681	178	12	67	108	.261	.377	.328
May	17-9	4.69	922	272	24	75	111	.295	.453	.347
June	17-11	3.72	961	248	17	89	164	.258	.383	.323
July	16-11	3.72	936	240	24	99	159	.256	.394	.329
August	17-12	4.02	1025	283	26	104	140	.276	.422	.345
Sept./Oct.	16-16	3.49	1064	263	26	99	191	.247	.390	.313
Leading Off Inn.			1369	383	34	95	210	.280	.430	.330
Runners On			2392	635	48	275	382	.265	.392	.339
Runners/Scor. Pos.			1424	368	28	213	233	.258	.386	.350
Runners On/2 Out			1036	257	20	152	173	.248	.386	.348
Scor. Pos./2 Out			678	163	10	120	109	.240	.375	.358
Late Inning Pressure			1134	296	24	152	232	.261	.400	.350
Leading Off			272	72	5	33	49	.265	.393	.353
Runners On			497	125	8	89	116	.252	.382	.363
Runners/Scor. Pos.			292	73	4	73	74	.250	.370	.396
First 9 Batters			2976	755	65	290	533	.254	.389	.322
Second 9 Batters			1425	373	34	122	225	.262	.392	.321
All Batters Thereafter			1188	356	30	121	115	.300	.457	.365

Starting pitchers: 59–41, 4.01 ERA
Relief pitchers: 36–26, 3.78 ERA
Ground outs-to-air outs ratio: 1.21. . . . Opponents grounded into one double play for every 7.7 opportunities, highest rate in majors. . . . Home record of 41–0 when leading after eight innings was the best in the N.L. last season. . . . Allowed fewest homers in the majors. Before you cite Busch Stadium as the reason, we'll point out that they also allowed the fewest *road-game* home runs in the majors (69, tied with the Cubs). Cards' staff had ranked 10th in N.L. in home runs allowed on the road in each of the previous two seasons. . . . Allowed the fewest first-inning home runs in the N.L. (13). . . . Opponents scored four or more runs in an inning only 23 times last season, fewest "big innings" allowed by any team in the majors. Cards scored four or more runs an inning 45 times.

San Diego Padres

	W–L	ERA	AB	H	HR	BB	SO	BA	SA	OBA
Season	65-97	4.27	5476	1402	175	602	897	.256	.409	.332
vs. Left-Handers			2529	675	64	322	375	.267	.406	.350
vs. Right-Handers			2947	727	111	280	522	.247	.412	.316
Home	37-44	3.76	2799	676	97	300	514	.242	.401	.316
Road	28-53	4.81	2677	726	78	302	383	.271	.417	.348
Grass	51-69	4.03	4049	998	139	424	685	.246	.404	.320
Artificial Turf	14-28	4.98	1427	404	36	178	212	.283	.424	.365
April	6-17	4.40	774	203	29	75	150	.262	.439	.333
May	6-22	5.54	948	257	39	129	139	.271	.462	.360
June	15-12	3.67	882	205	23	83	131	.232	.361	.300
July	11-14	4.81	859	233	28	102	147	.271	.434	.352
August	16-12	3.69	952	233	25	104	155	.245	.374	.321
Sept./Oct.	11-20	3.68	1061	271	31	109	175	.255	.391	.325
Leading Off Inn.			1309	344	44	124	198	.263	.425	.328
Runners On			2349	608	70	299	397	.259	.410	.343
Runners/Scor. Pos.			1401	360	41	210	237	.257	.411	.351
Runners On/2 Out			1024	262	29	153	177	.256	.406	.356
Scor. Pos./2 Out			674	176	17	115	116	.261	.409	.371
Late Inning Pressure			945	247	35	124	208	.261	.436	.348
Leading Off			247	62	7	15	65	.251	.417	.294
Runners On			367	94	10	75	74	.256	.395	.381
Runners/Scor. Pos.			228	58	4	58	47	.254	.360	.401
First 9 Batters			3017	729	97	347	568	.242	.395	.323
Second 9 Batters			1391	366	42	133	173	.263	.405	.331
All Batters Thereafter			1068	307	36	122	156	.287	.455	.361

Starting pitchers: 41–71, 4.43 ERA
Relief pitchers: 24–26, 3.99 ERA
Ground outs-to-air outs ratio: 1.22. . . . The only team whose opponents have hit better with runners on base than with the bases empty in each of the 13 seasons we've compiled those figures. . . . Allowed most home runs in N.L. for fourth time in past six seasons. . . . Lowest winning percentage in majors in one-run games (19–34, .358). . . . Padres' staff allowed the fewest first-inning runs in the league (80). . . . Starting pitchers averaged 5.73 innings per start, lowest in the N.L. . . . Greg Booker was the only pitcher in the majors to hit two batters with pitches with the bases loaded last season. . . . Most shutouts (10) by a last place team since the 1984 Pirates (13), who finished last in the N.L. East while leading the league in ERA.

San Francisco Giants

	W–L	ERA	AB	H	HR	BB	SO	BA	SA	OBA
Season	90-72	3.68	5518	1407	146	547	1038	.255	.387	.323
vs. Left-Handers			2411	640	57	265	442	.265	.394	.338
vs. Right-Handers			3107	767	89	282	596	.247	.381	.311
Home	46-35	3.40	2731	657	72	252	517	.241	.369	.306
Road	44-37	3.96	2787	750	74	295	521	.269	.404	.340
Grass	68-52	3.67	4058	1023	115	404	765	.252	.388	.321
Artificial Turf	22-20	3.70	1460	384	31	143	273	.263	.384	.329
April	16-7	3.34	777	202	18	79	139	.260	.386	.332
May	11-15	4.79	888	253	24	94	180	.285	.441	.354
June	11-16	4.19	905	237	29	102	183	.262	.413	.335
July	14-13	3.33	950	238	24	108	193	.251	.362	.327
August	18-11	3.12	998	237	27	71	175	.237	.366	.287
Sept./Oct.	20-10	3.37	1000	240	24	93	168	.240	.361	.309
Leading Off Inn.			1340	368	48	132	246	.275	.438	.342
Runners On			2360	615	64	266	455	.261	.395	.334
Runners/Scor. Pos.			1407	331	32	206	287	.235	.357	.329
Runners On/2 Out			957	229	30	134	199	.239	.374	.335
Scor. Pos./2 Out			636	135	14	114	132	.212	.322	.335
Late Inning Pressure			1044	257	36	143	242	.246	.403	.336
Leading Off			254	69	12	35	50	.272	.480	.362
Runners On			442	113	19	67	114	.256	.428	.348
Runners/Scor. Pos.			268	64	11	57	72	.239	.414	.363
First 9 Batters			3006	710	70	342	655	.236	.359	.315
Second 9 Batters			1416	369	39	107	240	.261	.400	.317
All Batters Thereafter			1096	328	37	98	143	.299	.449	.355

Starting pitchers: 54–48, 3.96 ERA
Relief pitchers: 36–24, 3.23 ERA
Ground outs-to-air outs ratio: 1.35, 2d-highest in N.L. . . . Led N.L. in ERA for first time since 1967. . . . Opponents grounded into one double play for every 7.9 opportunities, 2d-highest rate in N.L. . . . Opposing left-handed batters outhit right-handers for 13th consecutive season. . . . Opposing batters hit .193 with the bases loaded, 3d-lowest mark in N.L. since 1975. . . . Roger Craig was noted for throwing to first base as often as to the plate. But last season's Giants committed as many balks by May 23 as Craig did in his entire career (12). . . . Pitchers were involved in 22 double plays as fielders last season, highest total of any N.L. staff. . . . Bullpen had the most decisions (60) of any team in the majors. . . . Lost seven games in which they led after eight innings (most in majors).

National League

	W–L	ERA	AB	H	HR	BB	SO	BA	SA	OBA
Season	971-971	4.08	66276	17275	1824	6577	11657	.261	.404	.328
vs. Left-Handers			27671	7422	647	3052	4486	.268	.404	.341
vs. Right-Handers			38605	9853	1177	3525	7171	.255	.403	.319
Home	530-441	3.86	33867	8676	905	3190	6142	.256	.396	.321
Road	441-530	4.32	32409	8599	919	3387	5515	.265	.412	.336
Grass	485-485	4.06	32997	8584	985	3338	5895	.260	.405	.329
Artificial Turf	486-486	4.10	33279	8691	839	3239	5762	.261	.402	.327
April	126-126	3.91	8555	2204	238	853	1592	.258	.403	.326
May	162-162	4.43	11160	2973	324	1142	1982	.266	.417	.336
June	166-166	4.25	11236	2948	332	1089	1983	.262	.410	.328
July	158-158	3.98	10821	2848	298	1048	1840	.263	.407	.329
August	173-173	4.06	11889	3134	318	1205	1974	.264	.405	.332
Sept./Oct.	186-186	3.84	12615	3168	314	1240	2286	.251	.383	.320
Leading Off Inn.			16026	4238	472	1335	2697	.264	.414	.324
Runners On			28416	7591	757	3278	4948	.267	.410	.341
Runners/Scor. Pos.			17036	4392	429	2450	3193	.258	.394	.346
Runners On/2 Out			12094	3009	323	1623	2281	.249	.388	.340
Scor. Pos./2 Out			8035	1939	193	1294	1570	.241	.372	.349
Late Inning Pressure			11769	3062	291	1357	2317	.260	.391	.337
Leading Off			2944	775	88	243	545	.263	.410	.322
Runners On			4980	1308	103	754	984	.263	.382	.358
Runners/Scor. Pos.			3041	781	59	611	632	.257	.372	.376
First 9 Batters			35120	8816	884	3678	6868	.251	.384	.323
Second 9 Batters			16724	4367	452	1506	2698	.261	.402	.324
All Batters Thereafter			14432	4092	488	1393	2091	.284	.452	.348

V
Rankings Section

Rankings Section

The Rankings Section consists of a series of lists ranking players in a wide variety of batting and pitching categories. Players are ranked in 24 batting categories and 24 pitching categories ranging from the simple (batting average, for example) to the more esoteric (like percentage of runners driven in from third base with less than two out). Listed are the players ranking in the top 20 and bottom 20 in each league.

The exact number of plate appearances required to qualify for ranking in each category varies. The number of eligible players for each ranking is determined by the number of players in each league who had 200 or more plate appearances, or who faced 200 or more batters. In the American League, the 162 players and 145 pitchers with the most plate appearances or batters faced in a given category are eligible for ranking; in the National League, the top 136 batters and 125 pitchers are eligible. (If there is a tie for the final position, all tied players are included.) In some categories, a large number of players tied for last place (as, for example, in Home Run Percentage vs. Left-Handed Pitchers). In such cases, a line indicating "42 players tied with 0.00" is used in place of the Bottom 20 list.

The intent here is to rank all players who qualify as at least semiregulars for the season. To do this properly, it is necessary to look at the number of plate appearances in each specific situation. Jamie Quirk and Larry Owen platooned at catcher for Kansas City last year, and both can be considered as at least "semiregulars." But the vast majority of Quirk's plate appearances were against right-handers, and Owen's were mostly against left-handers. Quirk was one of the 162 American League batters who faced righties most often, so he is ranked there, but he failed to meet this qualification against lefties, so he is not ranked in that category. Owen, of course, is ranked against lefties but not against righties.

The material in this section is generally based on the categories used in the Batter and Pitcher Sections. If any of the breakdowns are unfamiliar, detailed descriptions can be found in the introductions to the Batter and Pitcher Sections.

Batting Average vs. Left-Handed Pitchers

American League

Top 20			Bottom 20		
1. Tommy Hinzo	CLE	.391	163. Jack Howell	CAL	.123
2. Mike Greenwell	BOS	.378	162. Ed Romero	BOS	.153
3. Larry Herndon	DET	.373	161. Darnell Coles	DET	.156
4. Dwight Evans	BOS	.368	160. Dan Pasqua	NY	.164
5. Pat Tabler	CLE	.366	159. Stan Javier	OAK	.165
6. Claudell Washington	NY	.361	158. Gary Pettis	CAL	.172
7. Alan Trammell	DET	.360	157. Ernest Riles	MIL	.175
8. Billy Ripken	BAL	.348	156. Garth Iorg	TOR	.181
9. Marty Barrett	BOS	.347	155. Dwayne Murphy	OAK	.182
10. Phil Bradley	SEA	.347	154. Tim Laudner	MIN	.194
11. Dave Winfield	NY	.345	153. Steve Balboni	KC	.194
12. Bill Schroeder	MIL	.344	151. Rick Burleson	BAL	.195
13. George Bell	TOR	.343	151. Pat Sheridan	DET	.195
14. Pete Incaviglia	TEX	.341	150. Argenis Salazar	KC	.198
15. Kirby Puckett	MIN	.339	149. Wayne Tolleson	NY	.198
16. Wade Boggs	BOS	.331	148. Henry Cotto	NY	.200
17. Paul Molitor	MIL	.331	147. Ozzie Guillen	CHI	.201
18. Willie Randolph	NY	.331	146. Matt Nokes	DET	.207
19. Todd Benzinger	BOS	.325	145. Willie Upshaw	TOR	.208
20. Ellis Burks	BOS	.325	144. John Moses	SEA	.209

National League

Top 20			Bottom 20		
1. Dave Magadan	NY	.438	136. Paul Noce	CHI	.148
2. Tim Raines	MTL	.396	135. Joel Youngblood	SF	.169
3. Gerald Young	HOU	.390	134. Steve Jeltz	PHI	.175
4. Pedro Guerrero	LA	.365	133. Franklin Stubbs	LA	.186
5. Tony Gwynn	SD	.361	132. Matt Williams	SF	.192
6. Bo Diaz	CIN	.355	131. Dickie Thon	HOU	.196
7. R.J. Reynolds	PIT	.351	130. Kal Daniels	CIN	.197
8. Tracy Jones	CIN	.349	129. Ron Oester	CIN	.200
9. Jose Lind	PIT	.342	128. Len Dykstra	NY	.203
10. Benito Santiago	SD	.341	127. Gary Roenicke	ATL	.205
11. Bob Dernier	CHI	.340	126. Jim Lindeman	STL	.208
12. Eric Davis	CIN	.340	125. Rafael Belliard	PIT	.213
13. Dave Concepcion	CIN	.340	123. Milt Thompson	PHI	.214
14. Kevin Mitchell	SF	.338	123. Mike Fitzgerald	MTL	.214
15. Terry Pendleton	STL	.337	122. Ozzie Virgil	ATL	.218
16. John Shelby	LA	.335	121. Mike LaValliere	PIT	.221
17. Randy Ready	SD	.331	120. Alex Trevino	LA	.222
18. Mike Schmidt	PHI	.331	119. Glenn Hoffman	LA	.224
19. Brian Dayett	CHI	.331	118. Tony Pena	STL	.226
20. Hubie Brooks	MTL	.331	117. Jose Cruz	HOU	.227

Batting Average vs. Right-Handed Pitchers

American League

Top 20			Bottom 20		
1. Wade Boggs	BOS	.377	162. Al Newman	MIN	.178
2. Paul Molitor	MIL	.363	161. Mickey Tettleton	OAK	.181
3. Don Mattingly	NY	.341	160. Steve Buechele	TEX	.188
4. Alan Trammell	DET	.334	159. Tim Laudner	MIN	.189
5. Tony Fernandez	TOR	.334	158. Tim Hulett	CHI	.201
6. Robin Yount	MIL	.330	157. Doug DeCinces	CAL	.207
7. Kirby Puckett	MIN	.329	156. Argenis Salazar	KC	.208
8. Kevin Seitzer	KC	.328	155. Reggie Jackson	OAK	.208
9. Alvin Davis	SEA	.325	154. Gary Redus	CHI	.212
10. Ed Romero	BOS	.325	153. Steve Balboni	KC	.212
11. Julio Franco	CLE	.323	152. Steve Lombardozzi	MIN	.215
12. Larry Sheets	BAL	.321	151. Tony Phillips	OAK	.215
13. Mike Greenwell	BOS	.317	150. Dave Valle	SEA	.216
14. Danny Tartabull	KC	.316	149. Rick Burleson	BAL	.217
15. Harold Baines	CHI	.315	148. Rick Cerone	NY	.217
16. Brook Jacoby	CLE	.314	147. Bob Boone	CAL	.220
17. Mickey Brantley	SEA	.313	146. Dave Henderson	BOS	.220
18. Ozzie Guillen	CHI	.311	145. Fred Manrique	CHI	.221
19. Kent Hrbek	MIN	.310	144. Tommy Hinzo	CLE	.223
20. Matt Nokes	DET	.307	143. Gary Pettis	CAL	.226

National League

Top 20			Bottom 20		
1. Tony Gwynn	SD	.376	136. Luis Aguayo	PHI	.165
2. Kal Daniels	CIN	.370	135. Bob Melvin	SF	.170
3. John Kruk	SD	.339	134. Mariano Duncan	LA	.182
4. Jerry Mumphrey	CHI	.338	133. Matt Williams	SF	.186
5. Mookie Wilson	NY	.338	132. Jim Sundberg	CHI	.190
6. Andy Van Slyke	PIT	.334	131. Darren Daulton	PHI	.198
7. Ozzie Smith	STL	.334	130. Graig Nettles	ATL	.202
8. Mike Aldrete	SF	.328	129. Rafael Belliard	PIT	.203
9. Pedro Guerrero	LA	.325	128. Ken Landreaux	LA	.204
10. Mike LaValliere	PIT	.323	127. Jeff Reed	MTL	.205
11. Milt Thompson	PHI	.318	126. Tony Pena	STL	.206
12. Keith Hernandez	NY	.316	125. Shane Mack	SD	.208
13. Dion James	ATL	.314	124. Garry Templeton	SD	.215
14. Darryl Strawberry	NY	.311	123. Lance Parrish	PHI	.220
15. Billy Hatcher	HOU	.307	122. Chris Brown	SD	.222
16. Alan Ashby	HOU	.306	121. Stan Jefferson	SD	.224
17. Jose Uribe	SF	.305	120. Tim Flannery	SD	.226
18. Will Clark	SF	.303	119. Dave Anderson	LA	.228
19. Len Dykstra	NY	.303	118. Rafael Ramirez	ATL	.228
20. Chris James	PHI	.301	117. Jeff Blauser	ATL	.229

Slugging Average vs. Left-Handed Pitchers

American League

Top 20			Bottom 20		
1. Dwight Evans	BOS	.688	163. Ed Romero	BOS	.167
2. George Bell	TOR	.686	162. Dan Pasqua	NY	.200
3. Phil Bradley	SEA	.642	161. Wayne Tolleson	NY	.208
4. Pete Incaviglia	TEX	.632	160. Stan Javier	OAK	.212
5. Kirby Puckett	MIN	.627	159. Garth Iorg	TOR	.225
6. Mark McGwire	OAK	.626	158. Ernest Riles	MIL	.228
7. Dave Winfield	NY	.621	157. Pat Sheridan	DET	.234
8. Jose Canseco	OAK	.618	156. Ozzie Guillen	CHI	.238
9. Larry Herndon	DET	.593	155. Alan Wiggins	BAL	.246
10. Rickey Henderson	NY	.585	154. Gary Pettis	CAL	.250
11. Cecil Fielder	TOR	.582	153. John Moses	SEA	.256
12. Alan Trammell	DET	.575	152. Jack Howell	CAL	.260
13. Pat Tabler	CLE	.564	151. Darnell Coles	DET	.273
14. Dave Valle	SEA	.554	150. Jim Gantner	MIL	.279
15. Brian Downing	CAL	.554	147. Bill Buckner	CAL	.286
16. Ron Kittle	NY	.553	147. Ernie Whitt	TOR	.286
17. Bill Schroeder	MIL	.550	147. Argenis Salazar	KC	.286
18. Tommy Hinzo	CLE	.547	146. Dwayne Murphy	OAK	.288
19. Wade Boggs	BOS	.544	145. Mark Davidson	MIN	.291
20. Ivan Calderon	CHI	.542	144. Mark McLemore	CAL	.294

National League

Top 20			Bottom 20		
1. Eric Davis	CIN	.741	136. Paul Noce	CHI	.148
2. Dale Murphy	ATL	.653	135. Franklin Stubbs	LA	.186
3. Kevin Mitchell	SF	.647	134. Ron Oester	CIN	.217
4. Luis Aguayo	PHI	.645	132. Milt Thompson	PHI	.250
5. Dave Magadan	NY	.625	132. Dickie Thon	HOU	.250
6. Tim Raines	MTL	.616	131. Steve Jeltz	PHI	.263
7. John Shelby	LA	.595	129. Mike LaValliere	PIT	.273
8. Benito Santiago	SD	.577	129. Stan Jefferson	SD	.273
9. Pedro Guerrero	LA	.575	128. Tito Landrum	LA	.276
10. Chris James	PHI	.570	127. Alan Ashby	HOU	.277
11. Randy Ready	SD	.566	125. Glenn Hoffman	LA	.286
12. Mike Diaz	PIT	.565	125. Joey Cora	SD	.286
13. Tim Teufel	NY	.563	124. Joel Youngblood	SF	.288
14. Mike Schmidt	PHI	.556	123. Kurt Stillwell	CIN	.289
15. Will Clark	SF	.555	122. Kal Daniels	CIN	.289
16. Hubie Brooks	MTL	.554	121. Rafael Belliard	PIT	.293
17. Bob Dernier	CHI	.553	120. Mike Fitzgerald	MTL	.294
18. Howard Johnson	NY	.552	119. Andres Thomas	ATL	.302
19. Darnell Coles	PIT	.545	118. Garry Templeton	SD	.307
20. Jack Clark	STL	.543	117. Graig Nettles	ATL	.313

Slugging Average vs. Right-Handed Pitchers

American League

Top 20				Bottom 20			
1.	Kent Hrbek	MIN	.617	162.	Al Newman	MIN	.221
2.	Mark McGwire	OAK	.614	161.	Argenis Salazar	KC	.230
3.	Wade Boggs	BOS	.607	160.	Wayne Tolleson	NY	.255
4.	Paul Molitor	MIL	.606	159.	Gary Pettis	CAL	.263
5.	Alvin Davis	SEA	.591	158.	Fred Manrique	CHI	.279
6.	Mike Greenwell	BOS	.583	157.	Alan Wiggins	BAL	.284
7.	Don Mattingly	NY	.578	156.	Spike Owen	BOS	.294
8.	Matt Nokes	DET	.578	155.	Tommy Hinzo	CLE	.295
9.	Brook Jacoby	CLE	.575	154.	Tim Hulett	CHI	.302
10.	Larry Sheets	BAL	.574	153.	Mark McLemore	CAL	.303
11.	Sam Horn	BOS	.574	152.	Bob Boone	CAL	.306
12.	George Bell	TOR	.572	151.	Steve Buechele	TEX	.306
13.	Darrell Evans	DET	.570	150.	Jerry Browne	TEX	.310
14.	Wally Joyner	CAL	.556	149.	Steve Lombardozzi	MIN	.321
15.	Danny Tartabull	KC	.554	148.	Juan Castillo	MIL	.322
16.	Kirk Gibson	DET	.549	147.	Juan Beniquez	TOR	.324
17.	Ken Phelps	SEA	.539	146.	Marty Barrett	BOS	.325
18.	Alan Trammell	DET	.538	145.	Rick Burleson	BAL	.326
19.	George Brett	KC	.532	144.	Rick Cerone	NY	.329
20.	Mike Pagliarulo	NY	.530	143.	Mickey Tettleton	OAK	.331

National League

Top 20				Bottom 20			
1.	Kal Daniels	CIN	.702	136.	Tim Flannery	SD	.251
2.	Darryl Strawberry	NY	.632	135.	Mariano Duncan	LA	.253
3.	Jack Clark	STL	.623	134.	Rafael Belliard	PIT	.258
4.	Andy Van Slyke	PIT	.609	133.	Jeff Reed	MTL	.261
5.	Will Clark	SF	.593	132.	Jim Sundberg	CHI	.276
6.	Rafael Palmeiro	CHI	.585	131.	Joey Cora	SD	.280
7.	Andre Dawson	CHI	.581	130.	Jeff Blauser	ATL	.288
8.	Dale Murphy	ATL	.553	129.	Garry Templeton	SD	.290
9.	Mike Schmidt	PHI	.545	128.	Tom Herr	STL	.292
10.	Tony Gwynn	SD	.541	127.	Shane Mack	SD	.292
11.	Tim Wallach	MTL	.540	126.	Tony Pena	STL	.300
12.	Jerry Mumphrey	CHI	.540	125.	Dave Anderson	LA	.306
13.	Leon Durham	CHI	.540	124.	Luis Aguayo	PHI	.308
14.	Nick Esasky	CIN	.537	123.	Wally Backman	NY	.313
15.	John Kruk	SD	.535	122.	Darren Daulton	PHI	.314
16.	Alan Ashby	HOU	.531	120.	Rafael Ramirez	ATL	.316
17.	Von Hayes	PHI	.528	120.	Andres Thomas	ATL	.316
18.	Eric Davis	CIN	.526	119.	Matt Williams	SF	.317
19.	Mookie Wilson	NY	.525	118.	Terry Francona	CIN	.319
20.	Pedro Guerrero	LA	.524	117.	Steve Jeltz	PHI	.319

Home Run Percentage vs. Left-Handed Pitchers

American League

Top 20				Bottom 20			
1.	Mark McGwire	OAK	9.36	145.	Bill Buckner	CAL	0.00
2.	George Bell	TOR	9.14	145.	Daryl Boston	CHI	0.00
3.	Cecil Fielder	TOR	8.50	145.	Bob Boone	CAL	0.00
4.	Dwight Evans	BOS	8.33	145.	Greg Gagne	MIN	0.00
5.	Larry Parrish	TEX	7.37	145.	Mike Felder	MIL	0.00
6.	Jose Canseco	OAK	7.35	145.	Mark Davidson	MIN	0.00
7.	Dave Winfield	NY	7.34	145.	Rick Burleson	BAL	0.00
8.	Tim Laudner	MIN	7.14	145.	Al Newman	MIN	0.00
8.	Pete Incaviglia	TEX	7.14	145.	Charlie Moore	TOR	0.00
10.	Larry Sheets	BAL	6.90	145.	Ozzie Guillen	CHI	0.00
11.	Ivan Calderon	CHI	6.84	145.	Jim Gantner	MIL	0.00
12.	Ron Kittle	NY	6.38	145.	Ed Romero	BOS	0.00
13.	Tom Brunansky	MIN	6.33	145.	Ernest Riles	MIL	0.00
14.	Phil Bradley	SEA	6.25	145.	Luis Polonia	OAK	0.00
15.	Brian Downing	CAL	6.21	145.	Dan Pasqua	NY	0.00
15.	Kirby Puckett	MIN	6.21	145.	Alan Wiggins	BAL	0.00
17.	Bo Jackson	KC	6.19	145.	Ernie Whitt	TOR	0.00
18.	Greg Walker	CHI	6.19	145.	Wayne Tolleson	NY	0.00
19.	Bill Schroeder	MIL	6.11	145.	Pat Sheridan	DET	0.00
20.	Dave Henderson	BOS	6.06	144.	Alfredo Griffin	OAK	0.53

National League

Top 20				Bottom 20
1.	Eric Davis	CIN	11.56	24 players tied with .000
2.	Dale Murphy	ATL	9.33	
3.	Luis Aguayo	PHI	9.21	
4.	Mike Diaz	PIT	8.33	
5.	Darnell Coles	PIT	7.79	
6.	Howard Johnson	NY	7.73	
7.	Chili Davis	SF	7.65	
8.	Jack Clark	STL	7.25	
9.	Kevin Mitchell	SF	7.19	
10.	Darryl Strawberry	NY	6.96	
11.	Bob Brenly	SF	6.93	
12.	Gary Roenicke	ATL	6.84	
13.	Nick Esasky	CIN	6.59	
14.	Andre Dawson	CHI	6.38	
15.	Ozzie Virgil	ATL	6.36	
16.	John Shelby	LA	6.33	
17.	Chris James	PHI	6.04	
18.	Kevin McReynolds	NY	5.43	
19.	Mike Schmidt	PHI	5.26	
20.	Glenn Davis	HOU	5.18	

Home Run Percentage vs. Right-Handed Pitchers

American League

Top 20				Bottom 20			
1.	Mark McGwire	OAK	8.55	156.	Spike Owen	BOS	0.00
2.	Sam Horn	BOS	8.53	156.	Al Newman	MIN	0.00
3.	Darrell Evans	DET	8.26	156.	Jerry Browne	TEX	0.00
4.	Kent Hrbek	MIN	8.26	156.	Argenis Salazar	KC	0.00
5.	Ken Phelps	SEA	8.14	156.	Ed Romero	BOS	0.00
6.	Mike Pagliarulo	NY	7.57	156.	Harold Reynolds	SEA	0.00
7.	Matt Nokes	DET	7.49	156.	Gary Pettis	CAL	0.00
8.	Wally Joyner	CAL	7.16	155.	Marty Barrett	BOS	0.24
9.	George Bell	TOR	7.13	154.	Wayne Tolleson	NY	0.41
10.	Fred McGriff	TOR	7.06	153.	Ozzie Guillen	CHI	0.51
11.	Brook Jacoby	CLE	6.78	152.	Tommy Hinzo	CLE	0.52
12.	Cory Snyder	CLE	6.76	151.	Scott Fletcher	TEX	0.54
13.	Fred Lynn	BAL	6.64	150.	Alan Wiggins	BAL	0.57
14.	Kirk Gibson	DET	6.49	149.	Steve Lyons	CHI	0.60
15.	Larry Sheets	BAL	6.48	148.	Mark McLemore	CAL	0.65
16.	Dan Pasqua	NY	6.46	147.	Alfredo Griffin	OAK	0.65
17.	Ken Gerhart	BAL	6.45	146.	Willie Wilson	KC	0.68
17.	Alvin Davis	SEA	6.45	145.	Billy Ripken	BAL	0.69
19.	Steve Balboni	KC	6.36	144.	Phil Bradley	SEA	0.70
20.	Danny Tartabull	KC	6.24	143.	John Moses	SEA	0.77

National League

Top 20				Bottom 20			
1.	Jack Clark	STL	8.90	126.	Dave Concepcion	CIN	0.00
2.	Kal Daniels	CIN	8.56	126.	Vince Coleman	STL	0.00
3.	Andre Dawson	CHI	8.33	126.	Jeff Blauser	ATL	0.00
4.	Will Clark	SF	7.87	126.	Steve Jeltz	PHI	0.00
5.	Darryl Strawberry	NY	7.62	126.	Tom Herr	STL	0.00
6.	Dale Murphy	ATL	7.21	126.	Tim Flannery	SD	0.00
7.	Mike Schmidt	PHI	7.20	126.	Joey Cora	SD	0.00
8.	Leon Durham	CHI	6.85	125.	Gerald Young	HOU	0.00
9.	Rafael Palmeiro	CHI	6.67	125.	Ozzie Smith	STL	0.00
10.	Nick Esasky	CIN	6.27	125.	Jose Oquendo	STL	0.00
11.	Ozzie Virgil	ATL	6.27	125.	Shane Mack	SD	0.00
12.	Eric Davis	CIN	6.12	125.	Casey Candaele	MTL	0.30
13.	Howard Johnson	NY	5.83	124.	Wally Backman	NY	0.38
14.	Tim Wallach	MTL	5.77	123.	Mike LaValliere	PIT	0.38
15.	Alan Ashby	HOU	5.71	122.	Dave Anderson	LA	0.52
16.	Tim Teufel	NY	5.50	121.	Jeff Reed	MTL	0.57
17.	Keith Moreland	CHI	5.44	120.	Mike Fitzgerald	MTL	0.62
18.	Andy Van Slyke	PIT	5.37	119.	Dave Magadan	NY	0.69
19.	Franklin Stubbs	LA	5.33	118.	Rafael Santana	NY	0.74
20.	John Kruk	SD	5.16	117.	Rafael Belliard	PIT	0.78

Batting Average, Day Games

American League

Top 20				Bottom 20		
1. Bill Schroeder	MIL	.373		162. Tim Laudner	MIN	.137
2. Larry Herndon	DET	.373		161. Carmen Castillo	CLE	.141
3. Alan Trammell	DET	.371		160. Dale Sveum	MIL	.182
4. George Brett	KC	.367		159. Kelly Gruber	TOR	.183
5. Rickey Henderson	NY	.367		158. Jamie Quirk	KC	.185
6. Kirby Puckett	MIN	.362		157. Cory Snyder	CLE	.185
7. Kevin Seitzer	KC	.360		156. Tony Phillips	OAK	.186
8. Paul Molitor	MIL	.353		155. John Moses	SEA	.194
9. Mike Greenwell	BOS	.347		154. Juan Beniquez	TOR	.195
10. Robin Yount	MIL	.346		153. Garth Iorg	TOR	.196
11. Wade Boggs	BOS	.337		152. Gary Pettis	CAL	.202
12. Gene Larkin	MIN	.333		151. Jack Howell	CAL	.205
12. Don Mattingly	NY	.333		150. Dwayne Murphy	OAK	.207
14. Dave Bergman	DET	.329		149. Stan Javier	OAK	.208
15. Terry Steinbach	OAK	.325		148. Dave Valle	SEA	.209
16. Pete Incaviglia	TEX	.323		147. Steve Balboni	KC	.211
17. Ken Williams	CHI	.318		146. Larry Owen	KC	.212
18. Lonnie Smith	KC	.317		145. Argenis Salazar	KC	.213
19. Scott Fletcher	TEX	.313		144. Spike Owen	BOS	.216
19. Juan Castillo	MIL	.313		143. Doug DeCinces	CAL	.220

National League

Top 20				Bottom 20		
1. Dave Concepcion	CIN	.388		136. Bob Melvin	SF	.130
2. Jose Oquendo	STL	.380		135. Jim Sundberg	CHI	.162
3. Gerald Young	HOU	.373		134. Mike Brumley	CHI	.169
4. Will Clark	SF	.362		133. Rick Schu	PHI	.172
5. Jose Uribe	SF	.360		132. Dave Parker	CIN	.184
6. Vince Coleman	STL	.347		131. Lance Parrish	PHI	.185
7. Kal Daniels	CIN	.347		130. Luis Aguayo	PHI	.192
8. Pedro Guerrero	LA	.345		128. Mariano Duncan	LA	.198
9. Candy Maldonado	SF	.344		128. Matt Williams	SF	.198
10. Andy Van Slyke	PIT	.343		127. Ron Oester	CIN	.200
11. Ken Griffey	ATL	.339		126. Stan Jefferson	SD	.202
12. Tim Raines	MTL	.338		125. Paul Noce	CHI	.203
13. Mickey Hatcher	LA	.337		124. Chico Walker	CHI	.205
14. Bob Dernier	CHI	.336		123. Tim Flannery	SD	.205
15. Andres Galarraga	MTL	.335		122. Phil Garner	LA	.212
16. Randy Ready	SD	.333		121. Terry Francona	CIN	.213
17. Billy Hatcher	HOU	.328		120. Rafael Belliard	PIT	.214
18. Keith Hernandez	NY	.327		119. Paul O'Neill	CIN	.215
19. Len Dykstra	NY	.323		118. Tony Pena	STL	.216
20. Tony Gwynn	SD	.323		117. Chris Speier	SF	.219

Batting Average, Night Games

American League

Top 20				Bottom 20		
1. Wade Boggs	BOS	.375		162. Mickey Tettleton	OAK	.143
2. Julio Franco	CLE	.353		161. Juan Castillo	MIL	.177
3. Paul Molitor	MIL	.352		160. Tim Hulett	CHI	.189
4. Tony Fernandez	TOR	.337		159. Argenis Salazar	KC	.202
5. Alan Trammell	DET	.332		158. Reggie Jackson	OAK	.204
6. Rance Mulliniks	TOR	.330		156. Wayne Tolleson	NY	.204
7. Larry Sheets	BAL	.329		156. Chris Bando	CLE	.204
8. Billy Ripken	BAL	.328		155. Steve Balboni	KC	.206
9. Don Mattingly	NY	.324		154. John Marzano	BOS	.207
10. Mike Greenwell	BOS	.320		153. Al Newman	MIN	.208
11. Kirby Puckett	MIN	.319		152. Tim Laudner	MIN	.209
12. Marty Barrett	BOS	.319		151. Gary Pettis	CAL	.211
13. Luis Polonia	OAK	.318		150. Garth Iorg	TOR	.216
14. Pat Tabler	CLE	.314		149. Rick Burleson	BAL	.224
15. B.J. Surhoff	MIL	.312		148. Bo Jackson	KC	.224
16. Bill Schroeder	MIL	.311		147. Lee Lacy	BAL	.226
17. Brook Jacoby	CLE	.311		146. Mike Young	BAL	.228
18. Kevin Seitzer	KC	.310		145. Cecil Cooper	MIL	.228
19. Mickey Brantley	SEA	.310		144. Don Baylor	MIN	.230
20. Dwight Evans	BOS	.310		143. Mike Pagliarulo	NY	.231

National League

Top 20				Bottom 20		
1. Jerry Mumphrey	CHI	.410		137. Matt Williams	SF	.181
2. Tony Gwynn	SD	.388		136. Chris Brown	SD	.201
3. Mike Aldrete	SF	.341		135. Phil Garner	LA	.203
4. Pedro Guerrero	LA	.334		134. Rafael Belliard	PIT	.203
5. John Kruk	SD	.329		133. Joey Cora	SD	.204
6. Dion James	ATL	.328		132. Jim Lindeman	STL	.210
7. Tim Raines	MTL	.328		131. Tony Pena	STL	.213
8. Kal Daniels	CIN	.326		130. Mike Fitzgerald	MTL	.213
9. Dave Martinez	CHI	.318		129. Luis Aguayo	PHI	.213
10. Dave Magadan	NY	.316		128. Jeff Reed	MTL	.214
11. Ozzie Smith	STL	.311		127. Leon Durham	CHI	.216
12. Tim Teufel	NY	.311		126. Ken Landreaux	LA	.218
13. Mike LaValliere	PIT	.304		125. Garry Templeton	SD	.220
14. Tom Foley	MTL	.303		124. Steve Jeltz	PHI	.220
15. Denny Walling	HOU	.303		123. Gary Carter	NY	.220
16. Mike Marshall	LA	.302		122. Graig Nettles	ATL	.221
17. Gerald Young	HOU	.302		121. Rob Thompson	SF	.222
18. Alan Ashby	HOU	.300		120. Jose Oquendo	STL	.223
19. Kevin McReynolds	NY	.299		119. Franklin Stubbs	LA	.224
20. Benito Santiago	SD	.299		118. Mariano Duncan	LA	.225

Batting Average, Grass Surfaces

American League

Top 20				Bottom 20		
1. Paul Molitor	MIL	.376		162. Rick Dempsey	CLE	.154
2. Wade Boggs	BOS	.369		161. Bo Jackson	KC	.178
3. Alan Trammell	DET	.352		160. Marc Sullivan	BOS	.180
4. Kirby Puckett	MIN	.336		159. Stan Javier	OAK	.186
5. Bill Schroeder	MIL	.332		158. Tim Hulett	CHI	.191
6. Mickey Brantley	SEA	.329		157. Chris Bando	CLE	.200
7. Tony Fernandez	TOR	.329		156. Mickey Tettleton	OAK	.205
8. Danny Tartabull	KC	.326		155. George Hendrick	CAL	.211
9. George Brett	KC	.325		154. Rich Gedman	BOS	.215
10. Don Mattingly	NY	.323		153. Rick Burleson	BAL	.216
11. Harold Reynolds	SEA	.320		152. Tom Brunansky	MIN	.218
12. Robin Yount	MIL	.320		151. Gary Gaetti	MIN	.219
13. Brett Butler	CLE	.320		150. Reggie Jackson	OAK	.220
14. Kevin Seitzer	KC	.320		149. Wayne Tolleson	NY	.221
15. Pat Tabler	CLE	.319		148. Don Slaught	TEX	.222
16. Larry Sheets	BAL	.316		147. Gary Pettis	CAL	.223
17. Scott Fletcher	TEX	.315		146. Oddibe McDowell	TEX	.224
18. Geno Petralli	TEX	.313		145. Dwayne Murphy	OAK	.225
19. George Bell	TOR	.311		144. Dave Henderson	BOS	.226
20. Matt Nokes	DET	.309		143. Steve Balboni	KC	.226

National League

Top 20				Bottom 20		
1. Tony Gwynn	SD	.374		136. Bruce Benedict	ATL	.135
2. Lee Mazzilli	NY	.356		135. Tony Pena	STL	.167
3. Tim Raines	MTL	.340		134. Jose Cruz	HOU	.190
4. Manny Trillo	CHI	.340		133. Jim Sundberg	CHI	.194
5. Dave Magadan	NY	.338		132. Matt Williams	SF	.198
6. Bobby Bonilla	PIT	.336		131. Alex Trevino	LA	.204
7. Vince Coleman	STL	.335		130. Franklin Stubbs	LA	.205
8. Randy Ready	SD	.335		129. Graig Nettles	ATL	.206
9. Pedro Guerrero	LA	.333		128. Dave Parker	CIN	.208
10. Dion James	ATL	.328		127. Bob Melvin	SF	.210
11. Jose Uribe	SF	.324		126. Garry Templeton	SD	.210
12. Kal Daniels	CIN	.324		125. Tracy Woodson	LA	.215
13. Jerry Mumphrey	CHI	.318		124. Alan Ashby	HOU	.216
14. Ozzie Smith	STL	.317		123. Chris Speier	SF	.218
15. Terry Pendleton	STL	.316		122. Stan Jefferson	SD	.220
16. Dale Murphy	ATL	.314		121. Mariano Duncan	LA	.221
17. Will Clark	SF	.311		119. Tracy Jones	CIN	.221
18. Jose Oquendo	STL	.310		119. Phil Garner	LA	.221
19. Gerald Young	HOU	.308		118. Paul Noce	CHI	.221
20. Bob Dernier	CHI	.307		117. Tom Herr	STL	.223

Batting Average, Artificial Surfaces

American League

Top 20				Bottom 20		
1. Mike Greenwell	BOS	.466		162. Carlton Fisk	CHI	.098
2. Julio Franco	CLE	.422		161. Gary Pettis	CAL	.123
3. Larry Herndon	DET	.400		160. Mickey Tettleton	OAK	.150
4. Willie Randolph	NY	.392		159. Scott Fletcher	TEX	.152
5. Wally Joyner	CAL	.366		158. Matt Nokes	DET	.159
6. Don Mattingly	NY	.347		156. Fred Manrique	CHI	.167
7. Bill Schroeder	MIL	.333		156. Tom Brookens	DET	.167
7. Cecil Fielder	TOR	.333		155. Tim Laudner	MIN	.173
7. Wade Boggs	BOS	.333		154. Alan Wiggins	BAL	.173
10. Eddie Murray	BAL	.330		153. Doug DeCinces	CAL	.177
11. Brook Jacoby	CLE	.330		152. Argenis Salazar	KC	.184
11. Bill Buckner	CAL	.330		151. Brett Butler	CLE	.186
13. Kirby Puckett	MIN	.329		150. Larry Owen	KC	.186
14. Kevin Seitzer	KC	.325		149. Tom Nieto	MIN	.187
15. Oddibe McDowell	TEX	.319		148. Jim Rice	BOS	.189
16. Rance Mulliniks	TOR	.319		147. Gary Matthews	SEA	.193
17. Tony Fernandez	TOR	.318		146. Steve Balboni	KC	.196
18. Lee Lacy	BAL	.317		145. Ken Gerhart	BAL	.196
19. Phil Bradley	SEA	.315		144. Paul Molitor	MIL	.197
20. Dwight Evans	BOS	.313		141. Tony Phillips	OAK	.200
				141. Bob Boone	CAL	.200
				141. Mike Stanley	TEX	.200

National League

Top 20				Bottom 20		
1. Jerry Mumphrey	CHI	.372		136. Bob Melvin	SF	.171
2. Mickey Hatcher	LA	.372		134. Shane Mack	SD	.179
3. Mike Aldrete	SF	.365		134. Rafael Belliard	PIT	.179
4. Tony Gwynn	SD	.360		133. Andres Thomas	ATL	.179
5. Pedro Guerrero	LA	.354		132. Darren Daulton	PHI	.189
6. Tim Teufel	NY	.354		131. Phil Garner	LA	.192
7. John Kruk	SD	.345		130. Tim Flannery	SD	.195
8. Benito Santiago	SD	.342		129. Mariano Duncan	LA	.197
9. Rafael Palmeiro	CHI	.342		128. Terry Puhl	HOU	.200
10. Kal Daniels	CIN	.341		127. Luis Aguayo	PHI	.201
11. Dave Concepcion	CIN	.337		126. Jim Lindeman	STL	.209
12. Candy Maldonado	SF	.336		125. Jeff Reed	MTL	.213
13. Gerald Young	HOU	.328		124. Gary Carter	NY	.217
14. Tim Raines	MTL	.326		123. Keith Moreland	CHI	.220
15. Franklin Stubbs	LA	.326		122. Mike Diaz	PIT	.220
16. Jose Lind	PIT	.322		121. Steve Jeltz	PHI	.221
17. Tracy Jones	CIN	.321		120. Chili Davis	SF	.222
18. Milt Thompson	PHI	.318		119. Mike Scioscia	LA	.224
19. Mike Marshall	LA	.317		118. Jody Davis	CHI	.226
20. Alan Ashby	HOU	.313		117. Ron Oester	CIN	.226

Batting Average, Home Games

American League

Top 20				Bottom 20		
1. Wade Boggs	BOS	.411		162. Tim Hulett	CHI	.161
2. Paul Molitor	MIL	.394		161. Tim Laudner	MIN	.172
3. Robin Yount	MIL	.354		160. Dwayne Murphy	OAK	.178
4. Bill Schroeder	MIL	.350		159. Argenis Salazar	KC	.182
5. Alan Trammell	DET	.348		158. Rick Cerone	NY	.189
6. Scott Fletcher	TEX	.341		157. Steve Balboni	KC	.189
7. Brett Butler	CLE	.337		156. Garth Iorg	TOR	.209
8. Don Mattingly	NY	.336		155. Wayne Tolleson	NY	.211
9. Kevin Seitzer	KC	.335		154. Steve Lombardozzi	MIN	.211
10. Pat Tabler	CLE	.333		153. Terry Kennedy	BAL	.213
11. Rey Quinones	SEA	.330		152. Cory Snyder	CLE	.214
12. Mike Greenwell	BOS	.327		151. Mike Pagliarulo	NY	.214
13. Ken Williams	CHI	.326		150. Ken Gerhart	BAL	.216
14. Larry Sheets	BAL	.324		149. Jamie Quirk	KC	.218
15. Daryl Boston	CHI	.321		147. Reggie Jackson	OAK	.218
16. Mike Stanley	TEX	.321		147. Rick Burleson	BAL	.218
17. Mickey Brantley	SEA	.321		146. Mickey Tettleton	OAK	.219
18. Geno Petralli	TEX	.319		145. John Moses	SEA	.220
19. Rickey Henderson	NY	.317		144. Gary Pettis	CAL	.221
20. Ozzie Guillen	CHI	.316		143. Kelly Gruber	TOR	.222

National League

Top 20				Bottom 20		
1. Tony Gwynn	SD	.390		136. Jeff Reed	MTL	.163
2. Dave Magadan	NY	.382		135. Franklin Stubbs	LA	.167
3. Dion James	ATL	.376		134. Bob Melvin	SF	.175
4. Gerald Young	HOU	.359		133. Matt Williams	SF	.179
5. Manny Trillo	CHI	.348		132. Rafael Belliard	PIT	.187
6. Dale Murphy	ATL	.346		131. Jim Lindeman	STL	.196
7. Mike Schmidt	PHI	.342		130. Phil Garner	LA	.198
8. Will Clark	SF	.339		129. Garry Templeton	SD	.204
9. Randy Ready	SD	.339		128. Luis Aguayo	PHI	.207
10. Tim Raines	MTL	.337		127. Joey Cora	SD	.207
11. Mike Aldrete	SF	.335		126. Steve Jeltz	PHI	.209
12. Alan Ashby	HOU	.335		125. Stan Jefferson	SD	.211
13. Andre Dawson	CHI	.332		124. Chris Brown	SD	.219
14. Milt Thompson	PHI	.330		123. Shawon Dunston	CHI	.221
15. Tim Teufel	NY	.326		122. Tony Pena	STL	.225
16. Pedro Guerrero	LA	.324		121. Shane Mack	SD	.225
17. Darryl Strawberry	NY	.322		120. Chris Speier	SF	.226
18. Jose Uribe	SF	.316		118. Terry Francona	CIN	.227
19. Dave Concepcion	CIN	.316		118. Mariano Duncan	LA	.227
20. Andres Galarraga	MTL	.314		117. Gary Carter	NY	.231

Batting Average, Road Games

American League

Top 20				Bottom 20		
1. Kirby Puckett	MIN	.362		162. Mickey Tettleton	OAK	.170
2. Tony Fernandez	TOR	.344		161. Carmen Castillo	CLE	.176
3. Alan Trammell	DET	.339		160. Juan Castillo	MIL	.185
4. Larry Herndon	DET	.336		159. Bo Jackson	KC	.186
5. Mike Greenwell	BOS	.328		158. Don Slaught	TEX	.188
6. Julio Franco	CLE	.328		157. Larry Owen	KC	.189
7. Billy Ripken	BAL	.328		156. Doug DeCinces	CAL	.194
8. Danny Tartabull	KC	.327		155. Gary Pettis	CAL	.195
9. George Bell	TOR	.325		154. Daryl Boston	CHI	.195
10. Terry Steinbach	OAK	.324		153. Dan Pasqua	NY	.198
11. Brook Jacoby	CLE	.323		152. Rick Burleson	BAL	.198
12. Willie Randolph	NY	.321		151. Chris Bando	CLE	.204
13. Don Mattingly	NY	.318		150. Gary Gaetti	MIN	.205
14. Luis Polonia	OAK	.317		149. Al Newman	MIN	.208
15. George Brett	KC	.316		148. Garth Iorg	TOR	.210
16. Bill Schroeder	MIL	.315		147. Cecil Cooper	MIL	.211
17. Wally Joyner	CAL	.315		146. Tim Laudner	MIN	.212
18. Harold Reynolds	SEA	.315		145. Gary Ward	NY	.215
19. Wade Boggs	BOS	.312		144. Tom Brunansky	MIN	.216
20. Paul Molitor	MIL	.312		143. Fred Manrique	CHI	.217

National League

Top 20				Bottom 20		
1. Jerry Mumphrey	CHI	.379		136. Ken Landreaux	LA	.110
2. Kal Daniels	CIN	.358		135. Graig Nettles	ATL	.189
3. Pedro Guerrero	LA	.352		134. Matt Williams	SF	.195
4. Tony Gwynn	SD	.352		133. Andres Thomas	ATL	.200
5. Candy Maldonado	SF	.346		132. Tony Pena	STL	.203
6. Bobby Bonilla	PIT	.333		131. Herm Winningham	MTL	.204
7. John Kruk	SD	.328		130. Luis Aguayo	PHI	.205
8. Mookie Wilson	NY	.325		129. Mariano Duncan	LA	.205
9. Tim Raines	MTL	.323		128. Wally Backman	NY	.206
10. Dave Concepcion	CIN	.322		127. Phil Garner	LA	.213
11. Bob Dernier	CHI	.320		126. Tim Flannery	SD	.214
12. Benito Santiago	SD	.320		125. Dave Anderson	LA	.216
13. Ozzie Smith	STL	.318		124. Jose Cruz	HOU	.216
14. Brian Dayett	CHI	.316		123. Rick Schu	PHI	.219
15. Mike Aldrete	SF	.315		122. Bob Melvin	SF	.220
16. Marvell Wynne	SD	.315		121. Jim Lindeman	STL	.221
17. John Shelby	LA	.312		120. Rafael Belliard	PIT	.223
18. Andy Van Slyke	PIT	.311		119. Luis Salazar	SD	.223
19. Franklin Stubbs	LA	.311		118. Dave Parker	CIN	.225
20. Terry Pendleton	STL	.307		117. Jim Morrison	PIT	.225

Slugging Average, Home Games

American League

Top 20

1.	Wade Boggs	BOS	.638
2.	Larry Sheets	BAL	.627
3.	Carmen Castillo	CLE	.619
4.	Paul Molitor	MIL	.610
5.	Mickey Brantley	SEA	.604
6.	Kent Hrbek	MIN	.594
7.	Rickey Henderson	NY	.590
8.	Larry Herndon	DET	.583
9.	Bo Jackson	KC	.579
10.	Gary Gaetti	MIN	.575
11.	Tom Brunansky	MIN	.574
12.	Ivan Calderon	CHI	.573
13.	Don Mattingly	NY	.572
14.	Mark McGwire	OAK	.572
15.	Mike Greenwell	BOS	.571
16.	Alvin Davis	SEA	.570
17.	Dwight Evans	BOS	.567
18.	Brook Jacoby	CLE	.564
19.	Ken Phelps	SEA	.555
20.	Robin Yount	MIL	.550

Bottom 20

162.	Argenis Salazar	KC	.227
161.	Wayne Tolleson	NY	.230
160.	Alan Wiggins	BAL	.248
159.	Rick Cerone	NY	.250
158.	Garth Iorg	TOR	.264
157.	Tim Hulett	CHI	.268
156.	Gary Pettis	CAL	.284
155.	Jamie Quirk	KC	.293
154.	John Moses	SEA	.294
153.	Bob Boone	CAL	.296
152.	Dwayne Murphy	OAK	.297
151.	Billy Ripken	BAL	.313
150.	Steve Lombardozzi	MIN	.315
149.	Alfredo Griffin	OAK	.318
148.	Harold Reynolds	SEA	.319
147.	Mark McLemore	CAL	.319
146.	Chris Bando	CLE	.320
145.	Ed Romero	BOS	.324
144.	Tom Brookens	DET	.325
143.	Al Newman	MIN	.327

National League

Top 20

1.	Dale Murphy	ATL	.673
2.	Andre Dawson	CHI	.668
3.	Will Clark	SF	.657
4.	Darryl Strawberry	NY	.629
5.	Jack Clark	STL	.604
6.	Kal Daniels	CIN	.600
7.	Mike Schmidt	PHI	.585
8.	Randy Ready	SD	.579
9.	Tony Gwynn	SD	.574
10.	Dion James	ATL	.561
11.	Eric Davis	CIN	.560
12.	Juan Samuel	PHI	.559
13.	Manny Trillo	CHI	.554
14.	Chris James	PHI	.552
15.	Tim Wallach	MTL	.552
16.	Leon Durham	CHI	.551
17.	Keith Moreland	CHI	.548
18.	Dave Magadan	NY	.539
19.	Tim Teufel	NY	.538
20.	Bob Brenly	SF	.532

Bottom 20

136.	Rafael Belliard	PIT	.220
134.	Phil Garner	LA	.225
134.	Joey Cora	SD	.225
133.	Jeff Reed	MTL	.233
132.	Steve Jeltz	PHI	.270
131.	Tim Flannery	SD	.270
130.	Franklin Stubbs	LA	.287
129.	Garry Templeton	SD	.288
128.	Terry Francona	CIN	.291
127.	Ron Oester	CIN	.296
126.	Tony Pena	STL	.310
125.	Jim Lindeman	STL	.313
124.	Wally Backman	NY	.314
123.	Mike Scioscia	LA	.315
122.	Dave Anderson	LA	.321
121.	Craig Reynolds	HOU	.323
120.	Junior Ortiz	PIT	.323
119.	Mike Fitzgerald	MTL	.325
118.	Steve Sax	LA	.325
117.	Luis Salazar	SD	.326

Slugging Average, Road Games

American League

Top 20

1.	George Bell	TOR	.666
2.	Mark McGwire	OAK	.663
3.	Dwight Evans	BOS	.572
4.	Danny Tartabull	KC	.570
5.	Mike Greenwell	BOS	.569
6.	Alan Trammell	DET	.568
7.	Bill Schroeder	MIL	.562
8.	Jim Dwyer	BAL	.561
9.	Wally Joyner	CAL	.556
10.	Fred McGriff	TOR	.551
11.	Terry Steinbach	OAK	.546
12.	Don Mattingly	NY	.545
13.	Joe Carter	CLE	.544
14.	Pete Incaviglia	TEX	.543
15.	Ken Phelps	SEA	.542
16.	Wade Boggs	BOS	.535
17.	Matt Nokes	DET	.530
18.	Kirby Puckett	MIN	.530
19.	Paul Molitor	MIL	.521
20.	Carlton Fisk	CHI	.521

Bottom 20

162.	Gary Pettis	CAL	.232
161.	Juan Castillo	MIL	.242
160.	Wayne Tolleson	NY	.249
159.	Rick Burleson	BAL	.250
158.	Argenis Salazar	KC	.259
157.	Mickey Tettleton	OAK	.264
156.	Ed Romero	BOS	.268
155.	Al Newman	MIN	.279
154.	Alan Wiggins	BAL	.280
153.	Mark McLemore	CAL	.282
152.	Scott Fletcher	TEX	.289
151.	Jerry Browne	TEX	.292
150.	Fred Manrique	CHI	.293
149.	Mike Felder	MIL	.301
148.	Ozzie Guillen	CHI	.302
147.	Garth Iorg	TOR	.302
146.	Cecil Cooper	MIL	.303
145.	Thad Bosley	KC	.309
144.	Mike Heath	DET	.312
143.	Carmen Castillo	CLE	.314

National League

Top 20

1.	Kal Daniels	CIN	.632
2.	Eric Davis	CIN	.624
3.	Nick Esasky	CIN	.613
4.	Jack Clark	STL	.590
5.	Pedro Guerrero	LA	.585
6.	Jerry Mumphrey	CHI	.582
7.	Rafael Palmeiro	CHI	.571
8.	Franklin Stubbs	LA	.565
9.	Howard Johnson	NY	.555
10.	John Shelby	LA	.553
11.	Tim Teufel	NY	.551
12.	Candy Maldonado	SF	.547
13.	Andy Van Slyke	PIT	.538
14.	Darryl Strawberry	NY	.537
15.	John Kruk	SD	.534
16.	Tim Raines	MTL	.528
17.	Bobby Bonilla	PIT	.527
18.	Bob Dernier	CHI	.520
19.	Mike Schmidt	PHI	.511
20.	Mike Marshall	LA	.507

Bottom 20

136.	Ken Landreaux	LA	.187
135.	Tim Flannery	SD	.240
134.	Wally Backman	NY	.252
133.	Andres Thomas	ATL	.267
132.	Ken Caminiti	HOU	.292
131.	Mike Fitzgerald	MTL	.293
130.	Terry Francona	CIN	.299
129.	Garry Templeton	SD	.304
128.	Dave Anderson	LA	.304
127.	Tony Pena	STL	.305
126.	Johnny Ray	PIT	.307
125.	Gerald Young	HOU	.310
124.	Mariano Duncan	LA	.311
123.	Rafael Belliard	PIT	.313
122.	Jeff Reed	MTL	.314
121.	Tom Herr	STL	.322
120.	Matt Williams	SF	.323
119.	Manny Trillo	CHI	.324
118.	Graig Nettles	ATL	.326
117.	Jose Oquendo	STL	.328

Batting Average with Runners On Base

American League

Top 20

1.	Paul Molitor	MIL	.422
2.	Robin Yount	MIL	.376
3.	Mike Greenwell	BOS	.359
4.	Wade Boggs	BOS	.356
5.	Pat Tabler	CLE	.356
6.	Claudell Washington	NY	.352
7.	Bill Schroeder	MIL	.348
8.	Greg Brock	MIL	.347
9.	Marty Barrett	BOS	.345
10.	Harold Baines	CHI	.338
11.	Don Mattingly	NY	.337
12.	Bob Brower	TEX	.336
13.	B.J. Surhoff	MIL	.333
13.	Luis Polonia	OAK	.333
15.	Dwayne Murphy	OAK	.330
16.	Willie Randolph	NY	.326
17.	Larry Parrish	TEX	.326
18.	Dwight Evans	BOS	.324
19.	Tony Fernandez	TOR	.324
20.	Mickey Brantley	SEA	.323

Bottom 20

162.	Dave Henderson	BOS	.174
161.	Gary Pettis	CAL	.177
160.	Don Slaught	TEX	.186
159.	Rick Burleson	BAL	.188
158.	Jim Dwyer	BAL	.194
157.	Rick Cerone	NY	.198
156.	Argenis Salazar	KC	.200
155.	Lee Lacy	BAL	.200
154.	Ken Gerhart	BAL	.205
153.	Lou Whitaker	DET	.207
152.	Bo Jackson	KC	.207
151.	Dan Pasqua	NY	.210
150.	Juan Castillo	MIL	.211
149.	Daryl Boston	CHI	.213
148.	Carmen Castillo	CLE	.213
147.	Garth Iorg	TOR	.215
146.	Cory Snyder	CLE	.216
145.	Steve Balboni	KC	.216
144.	Reggie Jackson	OAK	.217
143.	Dan Gladden	MIN	.217

National League

Top 20

1.	Mike Aldrete	SF	.406
2.	Al Pedrique	PIT	.374
3.	Ted Simmons	ATL	.362
4.	Steve Lake	STL	.354
5.	Gerald Young	HOU	.346
6.	Dave Concepcion	CIN	.346
7.	Andres Galarraga	MTL	.344
8.	Randy Ready	SD	.342
9.	Tony Gwynn	SD	.339
10.	Will Clark	SF	.338
11.	Pedro Guerrero	LA	.337
12.	Jack Clark	STL	.330
13.	Mike Marshall	LA	.329
14.	Wally Backman	NY	.328
15.	Tim Raines	MTL	.325
16.	Terry Pendleton	STL	.320
17.	Kevin Mitchell	SF	.319
18.	Vince Coleman	STL	.318
19.	Dion James	ATL	.318
20.	Bill Doran	HOU	.316

Bottom 20

136.	Matt Williams	SF	.158
135.	Luis Aguayo	PHI	.163
134.	Stan Jefferson	SD	.168
133.	Steve Jeltz	PHI	.172
132.	Jim Lindeman	STL	.181
131.	Terry Francona	CIN	.202
130.	Jody Davis	CHI	.205
129.	Rafael Belliard	PIT	.207
128.	Garry Templeton	SD	.207
127.	Mariano Duncan	LA	.208
126.	Craig Reynolds	HOU	.209
125.	Tony Pena	STL	.210
124.	Phil Garner	LA	.211
123.	Albert Hall	ATL	.217
122.	Joey Cora	SD	.218
121.	Rick Schu	PHI	.221
120.	Kevin McReynolds	NY	.222
119.	Jeff Reed	MTL	.226
118.	Shawon Dunston	CHI	.229
117.	Jose Cruz	HOU	.230

Batting Average in Pressure Situations

American League						National League					
Top 20			**Bottom 20**			**Top 20**			**Bottom 20**		
1. Cecil Cooper	MIL	.452	164. Chet Lemon	DET	.130	1. Jerry Mumphrey	CHI	.409	138. Stan Jefferson	SD	.119
2. Bill Madlock	DET	.448	163. Ken Gerhart	BAL	.140	2. Tom Foley	MTL	.395	137. Tim Flannery	SD	.132
3. Rickey Henderson	NY	.431	162. Tim Hulett	CHI	.143	3. Tim Raines	MTL	.394	136. Andres Thomas	ATL	.133
4. Alan Trammell	DET	.431	161. Carmen Castillo	CLE	.146	4. Vince Coleman	STL	.389	135. Joey Cora	SD	.146
5. Paul Molitor	MIL	.426	159. Mike Heath	DET	.150	5. Bob Dernier	CHI	.389	134. Herm Winningham	MTL	.160
6. Ed Romero	BOS	.425	159. Greg Gagne	MIN	.150	6. Candy Maldonado	SF	.380	133. Luis Salazar	SD	.162
7. Bill Schroeder	MIL	.407	158. Roy Smalley	MIN	.152	7. Benito Santiago	SD	.379	132. Glenn Davis	HOU	.168
8. Larry Herndon	DET	.394	157. Tony Phillips	OAK	.161	8. Kal Daniels	CIN	.373	131. John Shelby	LA	.169
9. Mark McLemore	CAL	.380	156. Rick Burleson	BAL	.161	9. Dave Concepcion	CIN	.372	130. Franklin Stubbs	LA	.169
10. Julio Franco	CLE	.379	155. Bob Brower	TEX	.162	10. Dave Martinez	CHI	.371	129. Ken Landreaux	LA	.178
11. Willie Randolph	NY	.364	153. Dick Schofield	CAL	.167	11. Ken Caminiti	HOU	.368	128. Bo Diaz	CIN	.180
12. Tony Fernandez	TOR	.363	153. Ken Phelps	SEA	.167	12. Billy Hatcher	HOU	.358	127. Mickey Hatcher	LA	.188
13. Gene Larkin	MIN	.359	152. Dan Gladden	MIN	.170	13. Steve Sax	LA	.351	126. Shane Mack	SD	.190
14. Kent Hrbek	MIN	.358	151. Darrell Porter	TEX	.172	14. Rafael Palmeiro	CHI	.343	125. Alex Trevino	LA	.194
15. Jerry Royster	NY	.355	150. Ellis Burks	BOS	.176	15. Tim Teufel	NY	.341	124. Mike Marshall	LA	.196
16. Willie Wilson	KC	.347	149. Argenis Salazar	KC	.179	16. Tony Gwynn	SD	.337	123. Eric Davis	CIN	.203
17. Kevin Seitzer	KC	.342	148. Dwayne Murphy	OAK	.179	17. Jose Uribe	SF	.333	122. Rafael Ramirez	ATL	.206
18. Ivan Calderon	CHI	.342	146. Bob Boone	CAL	.182	17. Mike LaValliere	PIT	.333	121. Mike Diaz	PIT	.208
19. Wayne Tolleson	NY	.340	146. Pat Sheridan	DET	.182	19. Alan Ashby	HOU	.329	120. Carmelo Martinez	SD	.208
19. Mike Felder	MIL	.340	145. Frank White	KC	.185	20. Casey Candaele	MTL	.328	118. Chili Davis	SF	.211
									118. Lance Parrish	PHI	.211

Home Run Percentage in Pressure Situations

American League				National League			
Top 20		**Bottom 20**		**Top 20**		**Bottom 20**	
1. Bill Schroeder	MIL	11.11	46 players tied with .000	1. Jack Clark	STL	13.43	34 players tied with .000
2. Mike Pagliarulo	NY	10.14		2. Andre Dawson	CHI	10.71	
3. Steve Balboni	KC	9.84		3. Bob Brenly	SF	8.57	
4. Dan Pasqua	NY	9.09		4. Eric Davis	CIN	8.47	
5. Kirby Puckett	MIN	8.82		5. Tim Wallach	MTL	8.22	
6. Pete O'Brien	TEX	8.79		6. Howard Johnson	NY	7.59	
7. Mark McGwire	OAK	8.75		7. Ozzie Virgil	ATL	7.35	
8. Mark Ryal	CAL	8.33		8. Luis Aguayo	PHI	7.32	
9. Cory Snyder	CLE	7.78		9. Jody Davis	CHI	7.02	
10. Tom Brunansky	MIN	7.58		10. Andy Van Slyke	PIT	6.67	
11. Rey Quinones	SEA	7.46		11. Paul O'Neill	CIN	6.06	
11. Mike Greenwell	BOS	7.46		12. Manny Trillo	CHI	5.77	
13. Cecil Fielder	TOR	7.41		13. Alan Ashby	HOU	5.71	
13. Dave Bergman	DET	7.41		14. Barry Bonds	PIT	5.63	
13. Dale Sveum	MIL	7.41		15. Bob Dernier	CHI	5.56	
13. Paul Molitor	MIL	7.41		16. Chili Davis	SF	5.26	
17. Brook Jacoby	CLE	6.98		16. Lance Parrish	PHI	5.26	
18. Terry Kennedy	BAL	6.85		18. Dave Magadan	NY	5.13	
19. Mike Young	BAL	6.67		19. Franklin Stubbs	LA	5.08	
19. Ken Phelps	SEA	6.67		19. Sid Bream	PIT	5.08	
19. Jack Howell	CAL	6.67					
19. Kirk Gibson	DET	6.67					

% of Runners Driven in from Scoring Position, Pressure Situations

American League						National League					
Top 20			**Bottom 20**			**Top 20**			**Bottom 20**		
1. Ruppert Jones	CAL	.636	158. Henry Cotto	NY	.000	1. Marvell Wynne	SD	.588	140. Joey Cora	SD	.000
2. Brett Butler	CLE	.583	158. Bob Boone	CAL	.000	1. Tim Teufel	NY	.588	140. Darryl Strawberry	NY	.000
3. George Hendrick	CAL	.556	158. Roy Smalley	MIN	.000	3. Dave Engle	MTL	.556	140. Ron Roenicke	PHI	.000
4. Dave Winfield	NY	.550	158. Don Slaught	TEX	.000	4. Rob Thompson	SF	.538	140. Craig Reynolds	HOU	.000
5. Alfredo Griffin	OAK	.500	158. Argenis Salazar	KC	.000	5. Ron Oester	CIN	.500	140. Keith Moreland	CHI	.000
5. Matt Nokes	DET	.500	158. Ron Hassey	CHI	.000	6. Tom Herr	STL	.475	139. Chris James	PHI	.059
5. Chet Lemon	DET	.500	157. Brook Jacoby	CLE	.077	7. Pedro Guerrero	LA	.471	138. Dave Magadan	NY	.063
5. Wayne Tolleson	NY	.500	155. Pat Sheridan	DET	.091	7. Curt Ford	STL	.471	137. Danny Heep	LA	.067
9. Garth Iorg	TOR	.471	155. Andre Thornton	CLE	.091	9. Vance Law	MTL	.444	136. Tito Landrum	LA	.077
10. Juan Beniquez	TOR	.467	153. Butch Wynegar	CAL	.100	10. Graig Nettles	ATL	.429	135. Sid Bream	PIT	.083
11. Jose Canseco	OAK	.455	153. Dick Schofield	CAL	.100	10. Mike Scioscia	LA	.429	131. Gary Carter	NY	.091
11. Eddie Murray	BAL	.455	152. Mark McGwire	OAK	.105	12. Kevin Bass	HOU	.424	131. Barry Bonds	PIT	.091
13. Steve Lombardozzi	MIN	.444	147. Daryl Boston	CHI	.111	13. Lee Mazzilli	NY	.421	131. Garry Templeton	SD	.091
14. Willie Randolph	NY	.440	147. Tom O'Malley	TEX	.111	13. Carmelo Martinez	SD	.421	131. Jeff Stone	PHI	.091
15. Oddibe McDowell	TEX	.438	147. Stan Javier	OAK	.111	15. Von Hayes	PHI	.400	130. Dale Murphy	ATL	.095
16. Larry Sheets	BAL	.429	147. Jack Howell	CAL	.111	15. Phil Garner	LA	.400	129. Stan Jefferson	SD	.107
16. Darrell Porter	TEX	.429	147. Carmen Castillo	CLE	.111	15. Ozzie Virgil	ATL	.400	123. Leon Durham	CHI	.111
18. Rey Quinones	SEA	.421	146. Fred Lynn	BAL	.118	18. Candy Maldonado	SF	.393	123. Bill Almon	NY	.111
18. George Brett	KC	.421	144. Fred Manrique	CHI	.125	19. Andres Galarraga	MTL	.391	123. Eddie Milner	SF	.111
20. Bill Schroeder	MIL	.417	144. Dave Henderson	BOS	.125	20. Tim Raines	MTL	.389	123. Gary Matthews	CHI	.111
20. Mark Ryal	CAL	.417							123. Shane Mack	SD	.111
20. Dan Pasqua	NY	.417							123. Len Dykstra	NY	.111

On Base Average Leading Off the Inning

	American League						National League				
Top 20			**Bottom 20**			**Top 20**			**Bottom 20**		
1. Jim Dwyer	BAL	.468	162. Argenis Salazar	KC	.183	1. Ozzie Smith	STL	.469	137. Bob Melvin	SF	.176
2. Phil Bradley	SEA	.463	159. Garth Iorg	TOR	.200	2. Kal Daniels	CIN	.450	136. Herm Winningham	MTL	.186
3. Kirby Puckett	MIN	.462	159. Marc Sullivan	BOS	.200	3. Eric Davis	CIN	.442	135. Luis Salazar	SD	.204
4. Wade Boggs	BOS	.457	159. Fred Manrique	CHI	.200	4. Von Hayes	PHI	.435	134. Chris Brown	SD	.214
5. Geno Petralli	TEX	.448	158. Claudell Washington	NY	.206	5. Kevin McReynolds	NY	.432	133. Hubie Brooks	MTL	.231
6. Brian Downing	CAL	.433	157. Ken Williams	CHI	.211	6. Greg Gross	PHI	.431	132. Ken Landreaux	LA	.233
7. Alan Trammell	DET	.433	156. Tim Hulett	CHI	.213	7. Tim Raines	MTL	.431	131. Gary Carter	NY	.233
8. Paul Molitor	MIL	.421	155. Steve Balboni	KC	.216	8. Tim Teufel	NY	.429	130. Mariano Duncan	LA	.250
9. Jim Gantner	MIL	.419	154. Tony Bernazard	OAK	.231	9. Albert Hall	ATL	.423	129. Reid Nichols	MTL	.260
9. Jerry Royster	NY	.419	153. Alan Wiggins	BAL	.246	10. John Cangelosi	PIT	.422	128. Franklin Stubbs	LA	.261
11. Bill Madlock	DET	.414	152. Bob Boone	CAL	.248	11. Steve Jeltz	PHI	.415	127. Lance Parrish	PHI	.262
12. Brett Butler	CLE	.408	149. Willie Upshaw	TOR	.250	12. Dion James	ATL	.411	126. Rafael Santana	NY	.262
13. Rickey Henderson	NY	.408	149. Tim Laudner	MIN	.250	13. Alan Ashby	HOU	.402	125. Tony Pena	STL	.263
14. Lou Whitaker	DET	.406	149. Todd Benzinger	BOS	.250	14. Jose Oquendo	STL	.400	124. Joey Cora	SD	.267
15. Julio Franco	CLE	.406	148. Ray Knight	BAL	.252	15. Jack Clark	STL	.398	122. Marvell Wynne	SD	.269
16. Rick Cerone	NY	.403	147. Pat Tabler	CLE	.252	16. Tony Gwynn	SD	.397	122. Dave Anderson	LA	.269
17. Matt Nokes	DET	.394	146. Ernest Riles	MIL	.259	17. Pedro Guerrero	LA	.391	120. Matt Williams	SF	.273
18. Mike Greenwell	BOS	.392	145. Jim Presley	SEA	.260	17. Manny Trillo	CHI	.391	120. Junior Ortiz	PIT	.273
19. Doug DeCinces	CAL	.392	144. Steve Lyons	CHI	.260	19. Vince Coleman	STL	.390	119. Andres Thomas	ATL	.274
20. Gary Redus	CHI	.390	143. Kelly Gruber	TOR	.262	20. Tom Foley	MTL	.389	118. Jeff Reed	MTL	.275

Batting Average with Runners in Scoring Position

	American League						National League				
Top 20			**Bottom 20**			**Top 20**			**Bottom 20**		
1. Paul Molitor	MIL	.449	163. Andy Allanson	CLE	.098	1. Al Pedrique	PIT	.458	137. Steve Jeltz	PHI	.101
2. Rick Leach	TOR	.436	162. Mickey Tettleton	OAK	.137	2. Ted Simmons	ATL	.423	136. Luis Aguayo	PHI	.118
3. Pat Tabler	CLE	.383	161. Gary Pettis	CAL	.141	3. Mike Aldrete	SF	.419	135. Craig Reynolds	HOU	.131
4. Tony Fernandez	TOR	.377	160. Mike Young	BAL	.143	4. Dave Concepcion	CIN	.368	134. Rick Schu	PHI	.135
5. Mickey Brantley	SEA	.376	159. Dave Henderson	BOS	.154	4. Tim Teufel	NY	.368	133. Stan Jefferson	SD	.149
6. Claudell Washington	NY	.362	157. Tommy Hinzo	CLE	.161	6. Marvell Wynne	SD	.349	132. Barry Bonds	PIT	.159
7. Larry Parrish	TEX	.356	157. Don Slaught	TEX	.161	7. Pedro Guerrero	LA	.344	131. Matt Williams	SF	.159
8. Dave Winfield	NY	.355	156. Lou Whitaker	DET	.161	8. Tracy Jones	CIN	.338	130. Joey Cora	SD	.164
9. Bill Schroeder	MIL	.352	154. Stan Javier	OAK	.167	9. Tim Raines	MTL	.336	129. Mariano Duncan	LA	.170
10. Harold Baines	CHI	.346	154. Jim Dwyer	BAL	.167	10. Rob Thompson	SF	.333	128. Garry Templeton	SD	.187
11. Dwight Evans	BOS	.342	153. Reggie Jackson	OAK	.169	11. Andres Galarraga	MTL	.331	127. Terry Francona	CIN	.188
12. Scott Fletcher	TEX	.338	152. Jack Howell	CAL	.175	12. John Kruk	SD	.331	126. Jim Lindeman	STL	.190
13. Luis Polonia	OAK	.333	151. Daryl Boston	CHI	.185	13. Mike Marshall	LA	.328	125. Rafael Palmeiro	CHI	.196
13. Wade Boggs	BOS	.333	150. Steve Balboni	KC	.185	14. Andre Dawson	CHI	.328	124. Graig Nettles	ATL	.196
13. Carney Lansford	OAK	.333	149. Juan Castillo	MIL	.189	15. Randy Ready	SD	.326	121. Rafael Belliard	PIT	.200
13. Steve Lyons	CHI	.333	147. Fred McGriff	TOR	.191	16. Gerald Young	HOU	.326	121. Jody Davis	CHI	.200
13. Dwayne Murphy	OAK	.333	147. Cory Snyder	CLE	.191	17. Terry Pendleton	STL	.323	121. Dave Anderson	LA	.200
18. Wally Joyner	CAL	.329	146. Bo Jackson	KC	.194	18. Billy Hatcher	HOU	.321	120. Sid Bream	PIT	.204
19. Dave Valle	SEA	.326	145. Dan Pasqua	NY	.197	19. Juan Samuel	PHI	.321	119. Leon Durham	CHI	.204
20. Greg Brock	MIL	.325	144. Rickey Henderson	NY	.203	20. Rafael Ramirez	ATL	.321	118. Casey Candaele	MTL	.205

Batting Average with Runners in Scoring Position and Two Outs

	American League						National League				
Top 20			**Bottom 20**			**Top 20**			**Bottom 20**		
1. Pat Tabler	CLE	.440	162. Stan Javier	OAK	.000	1. Al Pedrique	PIT	.500	136. Steve Jeltz	PHI	.059
2. Paul Molitor	MIL	.400	161. Gary Pettis	CAL	.053	2. Rob Thompson	SF	.452	135. Rick Schu	PHI	.091
3. B.J. Surhoff	MIL	.396	160. Dan Pasqua	NY	.069	3. Marvell Wynne	SD	.450	134. Craig Reynolds	HOU	.093
4. Claudell Washington	NY	.390	159. Don Slaught	TEX	.071	4. Ted Simmons	ATL	.448	133. Dave Parker	CIN	.111
5. Tony Fernandez	TOR	.375	158. Tommy Hinzo	CLE	.077	5. Randy Ready	SD	.385	132. Matt Williams	SF	.114
6. Darrell Evans	DET	.368	157. Dave Henderson	BOS	.080	6. Terry Pendleton	STL	.384	130. Phil Garner	LA	.115
7. Kevin Seitzer	KC	.364	156. Mike Young	BAL	.086	7. Mike Aldrete	SF	.378	130. Terry Francona	CIN	.115
7. Lee Lacy	BAL	.364	155. Jim Dwyer	BAL	.087	8. Kevin Mitchell	SF	.373	129. Luis Aguayo	PHI	.120
7. Ernest Riles	MIL	.364	154. Cecil Fielder	TOR	.091	9. Andres Galarraga	MTL	.357	128. Jose Uribe	SF	.147
10. Bill Schroeder	MIL	.355	153. Jerry Hairston	CHI	.111	10. Andre Dawson	CHI	.356	127. Barry Bonds	PIT	.149
11. Bob Brower	TEX	.353	152. Ellis Burks	BOS	.129	11. Wally Backman	NY	.355	126. Stan Jefferson	SD	.151
11. Larry Parrish	TEX	.353	151. Tim Laudner	MIN	.130	12. Mike Schmidt	PHI	.350	125. Mariano Duncan	LA	.154
13. Scott Fletcher	TEX	.348	150. Reggie Jackson	OAK	.133	13. John Kruk	SD	.349	124. Tony Pena	STL	.156
14. Todd Benzinger	BOS	.346	149. Rickey Henderson	NY	.136	14. Herm Winningham	MTL	.343	123. Kal Daniels	CIN	.161
15. Mike Davis	OAK	.340	148. Lou Whitaker	DET	.141	15. Tim Teufel	NY	.325	122. Garry Templeton	SD	.169
16. Dave Winfield	NY	.333	147. Mike Pagliarulo	NY	.150	16. Benito Santiago	SD	.324	121. Leon Durham	CHI	.171
16. Harold Baines	CHI	.333	146. Daryl Boston	CHI	.156	17. Shawon Dunston	CHI	.323	120. Jeff Reed	MTL	.185
18. Dave Valle	SEA	.326	145. Brook Jacoby	CLE	.158	17. Mike Marshall	LA	.323	119. Keith Hernandez	NY	.188
19. Gary Gaetti	MIN	.326	144. Juan Castillo	MIL	.167	19. Bo Diaz	CIN	.322	116. Darren Daulton	PHI	.190
19. Mike Kingery	SEA	.326	143. Fred Lynn	BAL	.171	20. Hubie Brooks	MTL	.321	116. Barry Larkin	CIN	.190
									116. Carmelo Martinez	SD	.190

Batting Average with Runners On Base and Two Outs

American League

Top 20				Bottom 20		
1. Pat Tabler	CLE	.407		164. Jim Dwyer	BAL	.086
2. B.J. Surhoff	MIL	.397		163. Dave Henderson	BOS	.088
3. Bob Brower	TEX	.385		162. Don Slaught	TEX	.116
4. Paul Molitor	MIL	.384		161. Dan Pasqua	NY	.132
5. Claudell Washington	NY	.373		160. Daryl Boston	CHI	.146
6. Ernest Riles	MIL	.371		159. George Brett	KC	.160
7. Kevin Seitzer	KC	.368		158. Mike Young	BAL	.161
8. Julio Franco	CLE	.356		157. Fred Lynn	BAL	.164
9. Darrell Evans	DET	.344		156. Gary Pettis	CAL	.164
10. Robin Yount	MIL	.343		155. Tim Laudner	MIN	.167
11. Alfredo Griffin	OAK	.341		154. Kelly Gruber	TOR	.169
12. Willie Randolph	NY	.338		153. Darnell Coles	DET	.171
13. Alan Trammell	DET	.338		152. Wayne Tolleson	NY	.172
14. Alvin Davis	SEA	.336		151. Ivan Calderon	CHI	.175
15. Bill Schroeder	MIL	.333		150. Cory Snyder	CLE	.179
16. Gary Gaetti	MIN	.331		149. Tom Brunansky	MIN	.180
17. Dave Valle	SEA	.328		148. Reggie Jackson	OAK	.181
18. Jamie Quirk	KC	.328		147. Ellis Burks	BOS	.181
19. Kirby Puckett	MIN	.325		146. Dan Gladden	MIN	.182
20. Mike Davis	OAK	.325		145. Jim Gantner	MIL	.186

National League

Top 20				Bottom 20		
1. Al Pedrique	PIT	.426		136. Steve Jeltz	PHI	.089
2. Marvell Wynne	SD	.419		135. Luis Aguayo	PHI	.111
3. Mike Aldrete	SF	.417		134. Terry Francona	CIN	.122
4. Wally Backman	NY	.413		133. Matt Williams	SF	.122
5. Randy Ready	SD	.400		132. Darren Daulton	PHI	.133
6. Rob Thompson	SF	.386		131. Phil Garner	LA	.150
7. Andres Galarraga	MTL	.375		130. Jim Lindeman	STL	.163
8. Terry Pendleton	STL	.354		129. Jody Davis	CHI	.169
9. Shane Mack	SD	.352		128. Stan Jefferson	SD	.171
10. Benito Santiago	SD	.349		127. Craig Reynolds	HOU	.183
11. Mike Schmidt	PHI	.344		126. Garry Templeton	SD	.184
12. Ted Simmons	ATL	.333		125. Mariano Duncan	LA	.186
13. Andre Dawson	CHI	.328		123. Mike Diaz	PIT	.188
14. Dave Anderson	LA	.325		123. Mike Fitzgerald	MTL	.188
15. Steve Lake	STL	.324		122. Paul O'Neill	CIN	.189
16. Junior Ortiz	PIT	.324		121. Curt Ford	STL	.190
17. Bo Diaz	CIN	.318		120. Dave Parker	CIN	.193
18. Herm Winningham	MTL	.314		119. Mike Scioscia	LA	.194
19. Jack Clark	STL	.312		118. Kal Daniels	CIN	.196
20. John Kruk	SD	.311		117. Ozzie Virgil	ATL	.198

% of Runners Driven in from Scoring Position

American League

Top 20				Bottom 20		
1. Juan Beniquez	TOR	.415		163. Don Slaught	TEX	.076
2. Harold Baines	CHI	.412		162. Gary Pettis	CAL	.152
3. Paul Molitor	MIL	.388		161. Daryl Boston	CHI	.175
4. Tony Fernandez	TOR	.385		160. Steve Balboni	KC	.179
5. Larry Sheets	BAL	.377		159. Alan Wiggins	BAL	.188
6. Don Mattingly	NY	.376		158. Bo Jackson	KC	.194
7. Wally Joyner	CAL	.373		157. Rickey Henderson	NY	.200
8. Bill Buckner	CAL	.373		156. Reggie Jackson	OAK	.202
9. Claudell Washington	NY	.372		155. Jim Dwyer	BAL	.203
10. Mike Stanley	TEX	.371		154. Argenis Salazar	KC	.209
11. Mickey Brantley	SEA	.370		153. Fred McGriff	TOR	.212
12. Dave Winfield	NY	.368		152. Ed Romero	BOS	.217
13. Pat Tabler	CLE	.364		151. Mike Young	BAL	.220
14. Ernest Riles	MIL	.361		150. Jack Howell	CAL	.221
15. Bob Brower	TEX	.360		149. Cory Snyder	CLE	.223
16. Willie Randolph	NY	.360		148. Carmen Castillo	CLE	.227
17. Dwight Evans	BOS	.358		147. Ken Gerhart	BAL	.229
18. Cecil Cooper	MIL	.357		146. Wayne Tolleson	NY	.229
18. Jamie Quirk	KC	.357		145. Steve Lombardozzi	MIN	.230
20. B.J. Surhoff	MIL	.355		144. Willie Wilson	KC	.231

National League

Top 20				Bottom 20		
1. Mike Aldrete	SF	.384		136. Steve Jeltz	PHI	.122
2. Kal Daniels	CIN	.378		135. Dave Anderson	LA	.129
3. Tim Teufel	NY	.374		134. Luis Aguayo	PHI	.143
4. Terry Pendleton	STL	.368		133. Barry Bonds	PIT	.152
5. John Morris	STL	.367		132. Terry Francona	CIN	.155
6. Juan Samuel	PHI	.361		131. Matt Williams	SF	.165
7. Bo Diaz	CIN	.359		130. Mariano Duncan	LA	.175
8. Tom Herr	STL	.357		129. Joey Cora	SD	.176
9. John Kruk	SD	.355		128. Craig Reynolds	HOU	.183
10. Pedro Guerrero	LA	.354		127. Rafael Belliard	PIT	.186
11. Mike Diaz	PIT	.354		126. Stan Jefferson	SD	.188
12. Tim Wallach	MTL	.351		125. Luis Salazar	SD	.190
13. Candy Maldonado	SF	.350		124. Denny Walling	HOU	.204
14. Mickey Hatcher	LA	.349		123. Casey Candaele	MTL	.204
15. Alan Ashby	HOU	.346		122. Bob Melvin	SF	.205
16. Andres Galarraga	MTL	.346		121. Rick Schu	PHI	.210
17. Rafael Ramirez	ATL	.344		119. Ken Landreaux	LA	.211
18. Mike Marshall	LA	.343		119. Shawon Dunston	CHI	.211
19. Graig Nettles	ATL	.342		118. Alex Trevino	LA	.213
20. Jack Clark	STL	.337		117. Jose Uribe	SF	.224

% of Runners Driven in from Third with Less than Two Out

American League

Top 20				Bottom 20		
1. Jamie Quirk	KC	.900		162. Ray Knight	BAL	.273
2. Juan Beniquez	TOR	.833		161. Steve Balboni	KC	.320
3. Cecil Cooper	MIL	.800		159. Brook Jacoby	CLE	.333
4. George Brett	KC	.788		159. Roy Smalley	MIN	.333
5. Bill Buckner	CAL	.767		158. Bo Jackson	KC	.350
6. Bob Boone	CAL	.765		157. Rick Dempsey	CLE	.364
6. Ernest Riles	MIL	.765		156. Reggie Jackson	OAK	.368
8. Wally Joyner	CAL	.755		155. Jim Presley	SEA	.375
9. Jim Rice	BOS	.750		154. Ron Kittle	NY	.385
9. Mike Stanley	TEX	.750		153. Rickey Henderson	NY	.389
9. Wade Boggs	BOS	.750		152. Rob Deer	MIL	.400
9. Cecil Fielder	TOR	.750		151. Daryl Boston	CHI	.417
9. Mark McLemore	CAL	.750		150. Bill Schroeder	MIL	.429
9. Jim Morrison	DET	.750		149. Willie Upshaw	TOR	.435
15. Willie Randolph	NY	.742		145. Jesse Barfield	TOR	.444
16. Tony Phillips	OAK	.733		145. Doug DeCinces	CAL	.444
17. Marty Barrett	BOS	.731		145. Dave Henderson	BOS	.444
18. Mike Felder	MIL	.722		145. Gary Pettis	CAL	.444
19. Dwayne Murphy	OAK	.714		144. Jack Howell	CAL	.448
19. Harold Baines	CHI	.714		142. Fred McGriff	TOR	.450
19. Fred Manrique	CHI	.714		142. Terry Kennedy	BAL	.450

National League

Top 20				Bottom 20		
1. Lee Mazzilli	NY	.857		139. Shawon Dunston	CHI	.294
2. Herm Winningham	MTL	.833		137. Jeff Blauser	ATL	.300
2. Jose Oquendo	STL	.833		137. Barry Bonds	PIT	.300
4. Tony Gwynn	SD	.815		136. Dave Anderson	LA	.308
5. Kal Daniels	CIN	.810		135. Matt Williams	SF	.313
6. John Morris	STL	.786		133. Jim Lindeman	STL	.333
7. Juan Samuel	PHI	.771		133. Rob Thompson	SF	.333
8. Bo Diaz	CIN	.769		132. Luis Salazar	SD	.357
9. R.J. Reynolds	PIT	.762		130. Steve Jeltz	PHI	.364
10. Tom Herr	STL	.755		130. Mariano Duncan	LA	.364
11. Len Dykstra	NY	.750		129. Andy Van Slyke	PIT	.382
11. Phil Garner	LA	.750		128. Leon Durham	CHI	.385
11. Mike LaValliere	PIT	.750		127. Franklin Stubbs	LA	.389
11. Milt Thompson	PHI	.750		125. Joey Cora	SD	.400
15. Mickey Hatcher	LA	.727		125. Jim Sundberg	CHI	.400
16. Mike Aldrete	SF	.714		124. Bob Brenly	SF	.407
16. Bobby Bonilla	PIT	.714		122. Tom Foley	MTL	.417
16. Gary Roenicke	ATL	.714		122. Darnell Coles	PIT	.417
19. Glenn Hubbard	ATL	.700		120. Denny Walling	HOU	.421
20. Stan Jefferson	SD	.692		120. Kevin Mitchell	SF	.421
20. Chris Speier	SF	.692				

Opponents' Batting Average

American League

Top 20				Bottom 20			
1. Mitch Williams	TEX	.175		127. Jeff Ballard	BAL	.344	
2. Tom Henke	TOR	.188		126. Mark Knudson	MIL	.331	
3. Doyle Alexander	DET	.201		124. Mark Thurmond	DET	.331	
4. Dan Plesac	MIL	.213		124. Tom Bolton	BOS	.331	
5. Dewayne Buice	CAL	.213		123. Jerry Reuss	CAL	.327	
6. Bobby Witt	TEX	.219		122. Dennis Lamp	OAK	.326	
7. Jimmy Key	TOR	.221		121. Scott McGregor	BAL	.326	
8. Bill Wilkinson	SEA	.223		120. Neil Allen	NY	.326	
9. Charlie Hough	TEX	.223		119. Ed Vande Berg	CLE	.325	
10. Dave LaPoint	CHI	.224		118. Bob Stanley	BOS	.321	
11. Jack Morris	DET	.228		117. Steve Crawford	BOS	.314	
12. Dennis Eckersley	OAK	.228		116. Scott Nielsen	CHI	.307	
13. Dave Stewart	OAK	.229		115. Jay Aldrich	MIL	.306	
14. Jose DeLeon	CHI	.230		114. Jose Rijo	OAK	.305	
15. Jeff Reardon	MIN	.232		113. Pat Clements	NY	.299	
16. Mark Eichhorn	TOR	.234		112. Jeff Sellers	BOS	.299	
17. Roger Clemens	BOS	.235		111. Ken Schrom	CLE	.298	
18. Tim Stoddard	NY	.235		110. Edwin Correa	TEX	.297	
19. Jeff Musselman	TOR	.237		109. Mike Morgan	SEA	.296	
20. Mike Henneman	DET	.238		108. Scott Bailes	CLE	.296	

National League

Top 20				Bottom 20			
1. Scott Garrelts	SF	.192		112. Bob Knepper	HOU	.313	
2. Tim Burke	MTL	.196		111. Gene Garber	ATL	.311	
3. Nolan Ryan	HOU	.200		110. Lee Tunnell	STL	.307	
4. Pat Perry	CIN	.205		109. Randy O'Neal	STL	.302	
5. Pascual Perez	MTL	.206		108. Bruce Ruffin	PHI	.299	
6. Jeff Robinson	PIT	.209		107. Ed Lynch	CHI	.295	
7. Mike Scott	HOU	.217		106. Greg Maddux	CHI	.294	
8. Mike Jackson	PHI	.219		105. Bill Landrum	CIN	.292	
9. Bob Welch	LA	.221		104. Danny Cox	STL	.290	
10. Sid Fernandez	NY	.224		103. Jay Tibbs	MTL	.289	
11. Randy Myers	NY	.225		102. Mike Krukow	SF	.288	
12. Eric Nolte	SD	.226		101. Andy Hawkins	SD	.287	
13. Jeff Parrett	MTL	.229		100. Tim Leary	LA	.285	
14. Ron Darling	NY	.233		99. Tom Browning	CIN	.284	
15. Ken Dayley	STL	.234		98. Rick Mahler	ATL	.283	
16. Andy McGaffigan	MTL	.235		97. Mike LaCoss	SF	.283	
17. Steve Bedrosian	PHI	.237		96. David Palmer	ATL	.281	
18. Dickie Noles	CHI	.239		95. Storm Davis	SD	.280	
19. David Cone	NY	.239		94. Shane Rawley	PHI	.279	
20. Rob Murphy	CIN	.239		93. John Mitchell	NY	.279	

Opponents' Slugging Average

American League

Top 20				Bottom 20			
1. Doyle Alexander	DET	.262		127. Ken Dixon	BAL	.565	
2. Mitch Williams	TEX	.280		126. Jeff Ballard	BAL	.560	
3. Dan Plesac	MIL	.318		125. Edwin Correa	TEX	.552	
4. Bobby Witt	TEX	.325		124. Darrel Akerfelds	CLE	.530	
5. Tom Henke	TOR	.330		123. Scott Bankhead	SEA	.530	
6. Greg Minton	CAL	.333		122. Jerry Reuss	CAL	.525	
7. Dave LaPoint	CHI	.334		121. Steve Crawford	BOS	.524	
8. Jimmy Key	TOR	.344		120. Scott McGregor	BAL	.509	
9. Roger Clemens	BOS	.348		119. Ken Schrom	CLE	.508	
10. Dewayne Buice	CAL	.348		118. Dennis Rasmussen	NY	.504	
11. Bill Wilkinson	SEA	.350		117. Al Nipper	BOS	.498	
12. Mike Henneman	DET	.351		116. Eric Bell	BAL	.495	
13. Doug Jones	CLE	.353		115. Wes Gardner	BOS	.493	
14. Dave Stewart	OAK	.357		114. Joe Johnson	TOR	.489	
15. Dennis Eckersley	OAK	.362		113. Rich Yett	CLE	.488	
16. Dave Righetti	NY	.362		112. Phil Niekro	TOR	.487	
17. Danny Jackson	KC	.364		111. Mike Loynd	TEX	.486	
18. Jerry Reed	SEA	.365		110. Scott Bailes	CLE	.484	
19. Gary Lucas	CAL	.365		109. Neil Allen	NY	.477	
20. Eric Plunk	OAK	.368		108. John Cerutti	TOR	.476	
20. Dale Mohorcic	TEX	.368					

National League

Top 20				Bottom 20			
1. Tim Burke	MTL	.254		112. Bob Kipper	PIT	.516	
2. Nolan Ryan	HOU	.292		111. Bob Knepper	HOU	.502	
3. Pascual Perez	MTL	.298		110. Randy O'Neal	STL	.496	
4. Scott Garrelts	SF	.310		109. Ed Lynch	CHI	.488	
5. Jim Gott	PIT	.315		108. Bill Gullickson	CIN	.487	
6. Andy McGaffigan	MTL	.320		107. Tom Browning	CIN	.472	
7. Greg Booker	SD	.325		106. Scott Sanderson	CHI	.469	
8. Mike Scott	HOU	.331		105. Andy Hawkins	SD	.468	
9. Dickie Noles	CHI	.332		104. Mike Krukow	SF	.463	
10. Jeff Robinson	PIT	.336		103. Tim Leary	LA	.462	
11. Mike Dunne	PIT	.337		102. Brian Fisher	PIT	.458	
12. Eric Nolte	SD	.337		101. Bill Dawley	STL	.457	
13. Joe Magrane	STL	.338		100. John Tudor	STL	.455	
14. Ken Dayley	STL	.338		99. Greg Maddux	CHI	.452	
15. Steve Trout	CHI	.339		98. Tom Hume	CIN	.451	
16. Bob Welch	LA	.342		97. Gene Garber	ATL	.450	
17. Pat Perry	CIN	.342		96. Jay Tibbs	MTL	.450	
18. Shawn Hillegas	LA	.343		95. Guy Hoffman	CIN	.449	
19. Randy Myers	NY	.343		94. Paul Assenmacher	ATL	.448	
20. Dwight Gooden	NY	.344		93. Ricky Horton	STL	.443	

Opponents' Home Run Percentage

American League

Top 20				Bottom 20			
1. Doyle Alexander	DET	0.96		127. Ken Dixon	BAL	7.06	
2. Doug Jones	CLE	1.11		126. Edwin Correa	TEX	6.09	
3. Danny Jackson	KC	1.30		125. Darrel Akerfelds	CLE	6.08	
4. Pat Clements	NY	1.32		124. Scott Bankhead	SEA	5.90	
5. Greg Minton	CAL	1.45		123. Rich Yett	CLE	5.63	
6. Tommy John	NY	1.63		122. Dennis Rasmussen	NY	5.56	
7. Roger Clemens	BOS	1.80		121. John Cerutti	TOR	5.24	
8. Jeff Sellers	BOS	1.86		120. Jeff Ballard	BAL	5.15	
9. Bobby Witt	TEX	1.92		119. Don Sutton	CAL	5.14	
10. Chuck Finley	CAL	1.97		118. Eric Bell	BAL	4.98	
11. Tom Bolton	BOS	1.99		117. Curt Young	OAK	4.93	
11. Mark Thurmond	DET	1.99		116. Mike Loynd	TEX	4.90	
13. Mark Gubicza	KC	2.02		115. Wes Gardner	BOS	4.84	
14. Mike Flanagan	TOR	2.14		114. Calvin Schiraldi	BOS	4.79	
15. Dennis Lamp	OAK	2.15		113. Kirk McCaskill	CAL	4.76	
16. Mike Henneman	DET	2.21		112. Mike Trujillo	SEA	4.74	
17. Jeff Musselman	TOR	2.22		111. Joaquin Andujar	OAK	4.70	
18. Eric Plunk	OAK	2.23		110. Ken Schrom	CLE	4.68	
19. Jerry Reed	SEA	2.26		109. Jerry Reuss	CAL	4.66	
20. Dave LaPoint	CHI	2.27		108. Jeff Reardon	MIN	4.64	

National League

Top 20				Bottom 20			
1. Dickie Noles	CHI	0.40		112. Bob Kipper	PIT	5.79	
2. Ken Dayley	STL	0.90		111. Bill Gullickson	CIN	5.12	
3. Tim Burke	MTL	0.92		110. Doyle Alexander	ATL	4.69	
4. Steve Trout	CHI	1.08		109. Ed Whitson	SD	4.59	
5. Andy McGaffigan	MTL	1.12		108. Randy O'Neal	STL	4.48	
6. Jim Gott	PIT	1.19		107. Don Carman	PHI	4.27	
7. Lee Smith	CHI	1.23		106. Bill Dawley	STL	4.18	
8. Frank Williams	CIN	1.26		105. Scott Sanderson	CHI	4.04	
9. Bill Landrum	CIN	1.29		104. Mike Jackson	PHI	3.98	
10. John Mitchell	NY	1.35		103. Ed Lynch	CHI	3.85	
11. Joe Magrane	STL	1.41		102. Brian Fisher	PIT	3.83	
12. Rick Reuschel	SF	1.52		101. Tom Browning	CIN	3.81	
13. Doug Sisk	NY	1.63		100. Jim Deshaies	HOU	3.80	
14. Dennis Martinez	MTL	1.65		99. Mike Krukow	SF	3.79	
15. Dwight Gooden	NY	1.65		98. Jamie Moyer	CHI	3.61	
16. Mike Dunne	PIT	1.68		97. Bob Knepper	HOU	3.60	
17. Orel Hershiser	LA	1.70		96. Paul Assenmacher	ATL	3.59	
18. Jesse Orosco	NY	1.71		95. Tim Leary	LA	3.54	
18. Lee Tunnell	STL	1.71		94. Randy St. Claire	MTL	3.52	
20. Don Robinson	SF	1.71		93. Ted Power	CIN	3.51	

Opponents' Extra Base Hits per 100 At Bats

American League

Top 20				Bottom 20		
1. Doyle Alexander	DET	3.83		127. Edwin Correa	TEX	12.54
2. Greg Minton	CAL	4.71		126. Ken Dixon	BAL	12.53
3. Dave Righetti	NY	4.97		125. Dennis Rasmussen	NY	12.37
4. Mitch Williams	TEX	4.99		124. Al Nipper	BOS	11.87
5. Doug Jones	CLE	5.00		123. Eric Bell	BAL	11.82
6. Dan Plesac	MIL	5.07		122. Scott Bankhead	SEA	11.80
7. Bobby Thigpen	CHI	5.36		121. Steve Crawford	BOS	11.72
8. Dale Mohorcic	TEX	5.85		120. Wes Gardner	BOS	11.68
9. Mark Knudson	MIL	6.02		119. Joe Johnson	TOR	11.65
10. Jerry Reed	SEA	6.13		118. Darrel Akerfelds	CLE	11.49
11. Dave LaPoint	CHI	6.17		117. Jeff Ballard	BAL	11.34
12. Chuck Crim	MIL	6.20		116. Ken Schrom	CLE	11.13
13. Tommy John	NY	6.25		115. John Cerutti	TOR	10.99
14. Bobby Witt	TEX	6.35		114. Rich Yett	CLE	10.99
15. Mike Henneman	DET	6.35		113. Phil Niekro	TOR	10.81
16. Jimmy Key	TOR	6.41		111. Mike Griffin	BAL	10.00
17. Bill Wilkinson	SEA	6.57		111. Paul Kilgus	TEX	10.00
18. Jim Winn	CHI	6.57		110. Mike Smithson	MIN	9.98
19. Tom Bolton	BOS	6.77		109. Curt Young	OAK	9.86
20. Danny Jackson	KC	6.83		108. Ron Guidry	NY	9.82

National League

Top 20				Bottom 20		
1. Tim Burke	MTL	3.67		112. Bob Kipper	PIT	12.27
2. Greg Booker	SD	3.97		111. John Tudor	STL	11.17
3. Jim Gott	PIT	4.45		110. Bill Gullickson	CIN	11.16
4. Roger McDowell	NY	4.94		109. Bill Dawley	STL	10.86
5. Shawn Hillegas	LA	5.09		108. Guy Hoffman	CIN	10.80
6. Pascual Perez	MTL	5.16		107. Paul Assenmacher	ATL	10.76
7. Nolan Ryan	HOU	5.19		106. Tom Browning	CIN	10.73
8. Steve Bedrosian	PHI	5.39		105. Andy Hawkins	SD	10.72
9. Scott Garrelts	SF	5.49		104. Brian Fisher	PIT	10.64
10. Mike Dunne	PIT	5.54		103. Bob Knepper	HOU	10.24
11. Andy McGaffigan	MTL	5.59		102. Tom Hume	CIN	10.03
12. John Mitchell	NY	5.63		101. Scott Sanderson	CHI	10.02
13. Steve Trout	CHI	5.78		100. Ricky Horton	STL	9.98
14. Jesse Orosco	NY	5.80		99. Ed Lynch	CHI	9.98
15. Joe Magrane	STL	6.09		98. Tim Leary	LA	9.91
16. John Franco	CIN	6.13		97. Ted Power	CIN	9.90
17. Dwight Gooden	NY	6.17		96. Floyd Youmans	MTL	9.87
18. Jimmy Jones	SD	6.32		95. Randy O'Neal	STL	9.70
19. Kent Tekulve	PHI	6.33		94. Don Carman	PHI	9.55
20. Mike Scott	HOU	6.33		93. Ron Robinson	CIN	9.50

Opponents' Batting Average, Left-Handed Batters

American League

Top 20				Bottom 20		
1. Mitch Williams	TEX	.146		128. Len Barker	MIL	.360
2. Jeff Musselman	TOR	.165		127. Bob Stanley	BOS	.358
3. Tom Henke	TOR	.172		126. Steve Crawford	BOS	.333
4. Juan Nieves	MIL	.183		125. Tom Bolton	BOS	.330
5. Bill Wilkinson	SEA	.192		124. Mark Knudson	MIL	.324
6. Mark Langston	SEA	.197		123. Dan Quisenberry	KC	.320
7. Dave Leiper	OAK	.198		122. Mike Smithson	MIN	.320
8. Doyle Alexander	DET	.199		120. Ken Schrom	CLE	.316
9. Tommy John	NY	.203		120. Dennis Lamp	OAK	.316
10. Curt Young	OAK	.218		119. Jose Nunez	TOR	.315
11. Dewayne Buice	CAL	.219		118. Wes Gardner	BOS	.315
12. Jeff Robinson	DET	.227		117. Kirk McCaskill	CAL	.314
13. Bobby Witt	TEX	.229		116. Mike Loynd	TEX	.313
14. Bud Black	KC	.231		115. Dave Schmidt	BAL	.313
15. Charlie Leibrandt	KC	.232		114. Phil Niekro	TOR	.313
16. Dave Stewart	OAK	.233		113. Dennis Rasmussen	NY	.313
17. Don Sutton	CAL	.233		112. Moose Haas	OAK	.307
18. Bert Blyleven	MIN	.234		111. Tom Niedenfuer	BAL	.306
19. Roger Clemens	BOS	.235		110. Jeff Sellers	BOS	.304
20. Frank Tanana	DET	.236		109. Neil Allen	NY	.303

National League

Top 20				Bottom 20		
1. Dave Dravecky	SF	.142		112. Randy O'Neal	STL	.341
2. Atlee Hammaker	SF	.168		111. Tom Hume	CIN	.338
3. Randy Myers	NY	.175		110. Andy Hawkins	SD	.336
4. Scott Garrelts	SF	.180		109. Ed Lynch	CHI	.332
5. John Smiley	PIT	.195		108. Greg Maddux	CHI	.323
6. Dave Smith	HOU	.204		107. Les Lancaster	CHI	.318
7. Nolan Ryan	HOU	.211		106. Danny Cox	STL	.316
8. Tim Burke	MTL	.218		105. Storm Davis	SD	.315
9. Rick Honeycutt	LA	.218		104. Rick Mahler	ATL	.314
10. Mark Davis	SD	.221		103. Mike Krukow	SF	.313
11. Jeff Dedmon	ATL	.222		102. Don Carman	PHI	.312
12. Jamie Moyer	CHI	.222		101. Lary Sorensen	MTL	.311
13. Ron Darling	NY	.223		99. Greg Booker	SD	.309
13. Pascual Perez	MTL	.223		99. Kent Tekulve	PHI	.309
15. Ricky Horton	STL	.225		98. Guy Hoffman	CIN	.307
16. Joe Magrane	STL	.226		97. Rocky Childress	HOU	.306
17. Lance McCullers	SD	.226		96. Doyle Alexander	ATL	.303
18. Fernando Valenzuela	LA	.228		95. Mike LaCoss	SF	.302
19. Craig Lefferts	SF	.228		94. Rick Aguilera	NY	.301
20. Jeff Robinson	PIT	.232		93. John Mitchell	NY	.296

Opponents' Batting Average, Right-Handed Batters

American League

Top 20				Bottom 20		
1. Jeff Reardon	MIN	.158		127. Ed Vande Berg	CLE	.365
2. Mitch Williams	TEX	.189		126. Mark Thurmond	DET	.363
3. Juan Berenguer	MIN	.193		125. Neil Allen	NY	.353
4. Dennis Eckersley	OAK	.196		124. Pat Clements	NY	.350
5. Tom Henke	TOR	.204		123. Edwin Correa	TEX	.350
6. Doyle Alexander	DET	.204		122. Scott McGregor	BAL	.344
7. Jose DeLeon	CHI	.204		121. Jeff Ballard	BAL	.341
8. Calvin Schiraldi	BOS	.205		120. Dennis Lamp	OAK	.333
9. Bobby Witt	TEX	.206		119. Tom Bolton	BOS	.331
10. Dale Mohorcic	TEX	.207		118. Scott Nielsen	CHI	.320
10. Tim Stoddard	NY	.207		117. Tony Arnold	BAL	.319
12. Charlie Hough	TEX	.207		116. Jerry Reuss	CAL	.318
13. Dewayne Buice	CAL	.208		115. Jose Rijo	OAK	.308
14. Jose Nunez	TOR	.213		114. Tommy John	NY	.305
15. Jimmy Key	TOR	.215		113. Don Sutton	CAL	.305
16. Jack Lazorko	CAL	.216		112. Chuck Finley	CAL	.305
17. Charles Hudson	NY	.217		111. Greg Harris	TEX	.304
18. Jack Morris	DET	.218		110. Jeff Robinson	DET	.304
19. Mark Eichhorn	TOR	.219		109. Al Nipper	BOS	.303
20. Gary Lucas	CAL	.219		108. Ken Dixon	BAL	.302

National League

Top 20				Bottom 20		
1. Tim Burke	MTL	.172		112. Lee Tunnell	STL	.352
2. Mike Jackson	PHI	.178		111. Dave Meads	HOU	.344
3. Jeff Robinson	PIT	.180		110. Gene Garber	ATL	.338
4. Nolan Ryan	HOU	.187		109. Bob Knepper	HOU	.318
5. Pat Perry	CIN	.190		108. Bob Patterson	PIT	.315
6. Jim Gott	PIT	.193		107. Matt Young	LA	.311
7. Andy McGaffigan	MTL	.193		106. Roger McDowell	NY	.309
8. Mike Scott	HOU	.196		105. Bill Landrum	CIN	.308
9. Kent Tekulve	PHI	.196		104. Paul Assenmacher	ATL	.306
10. Greg Booker	SD	.197		103. Bruce Ruffin	PHI	.305
11. Mike Dunne	PIT	.199		102. Tim Conroy	STL	.304
12. Bob Welch	LA	.201		101. Bryn Smith	MTL	.295
13. Scott Garrelts	SF	.206		100. Rick Honeycutt	LA	.292
14. Floyd Youmans	MTL	.209		99. Bob Sebra	MTL	.288
15. Ed Whitson	SD	.210		98. Tom Browning	CIN	.287
16. Orel Hershiser	LA	.212		97. Bob Kipper	PIT	.286
17. Les Lancaster	CHI	.215		96. Mark Grant	SD	.285
18. Doyle Alexander	ATL	.215		95. Jay Tibbs	MTL	.283
19. Doug Drabek	PIT	.216		94. Bob Forsch	STL	.283
20. Steve Bedrosian	PHI	.220		93. Tom Glavine	ATL	.282

Opponents' Slugging Average, Left-Handed Batters

American League

Top 20			Bottom 20		
1. Mitch Williams	TEX	.244	128. Darrel Akerfelds	CLE	.613
2. Doyle Alexander	DET	.258	127. Tom Niedenfuer	BAL	.602
3. Tommy John	NY	.260	126. Mike Smithson	MIN	.593
4. Mike Flanagan	TOR	.270	125. Bob James	CHI	.560
5. Jeff Musselman	TOR	.275	124. Len Barker	MIL	.558
6. Juan Nieves	MIL	.286	123. Ken Dixon	BAL	.556
7. Tom Henke	TOR	.288	122. Jack Lazorko	CAL	.553
8. Mark Langston	SEA	.293	121. Wes Gardner	BOS	.549
9. Charlie Leibrandt	KC	.310	120. Ken Schrom	CLE	.548
10. Doug Jones	CLE	.319	119. Steve Crawford	BOS	.538
11. Ed Vande Berg	CLE	.324	118. Dennis Rasmussen	NY	.535
12. Roger Clemens	BOS	.332	116. Jeff Reardon	MIN	.532
13. Bobby Witt	TEX	.332	116. Kirk McCaskill	CAL	.532
14. Jim Winn	CHI	.336	115. Bill Gullickson	NY	.528
15. Danny Jackson	KC	.348	114. Mike Loynd	TEX	.522
16. Dewayne Buice	CAL	.349	113. Bob Stanley	BOS	.522
17. Dave Leiper	OAK	.354	112. Calvin Schiraldi	BOS	.514
18. Chuck Finley	CAL	.356	111. Phil Niekro	TOR	.507
19. Dave Stewart	OAK	.357	110. Scott Bankhead	SEA	.506
20. Jerry Reed	SEA	.358	109. Jose Nunez	TOR	.503

National League

Top 20			Bottom 20		
1. Atlee Hammaker	SF	.215	112. Doyle Alexander	ATL	.559
2. Dave Smith	HOU	.239	111. Ed Lynch	CHI	.534
3. Dave Dravecky	SF	.245	110. Andy Hawkins	SD	.515
4. Frank Williams	CIN	.271	109. Dorn Taylor	PIT	.515
5. Scott Garrelts	SF	.284	108. Lary Sorensen	MTL	.511
6. Tim Burke	MTL	.288	107. Rocky Childress	HOU	.506
7. Nolan Ryan	HOU	.289	106. Tom Hume	CIN	.490
8. Pascual Perez	MTL	.291	105. Randy O'Neal	STL	.489
9. John Smiley	PIT	.299	104. Greg Maddux	CHI	.487
10. Randy Myers	NY	.300	103. Mike Krukow	SF	.486
11. Lance McCullers	SD	.301	102. Les Lancaster	CHI	.481
12. Alejandro Pena	LA	.305	101. Bill Gullickson	CIN	.479
13. Rob Murphy	CIN	.308	100. Jay Tibbs	MTL	.479
14. Joe Magrane	STL	.312	99. Doug Drabek	PIT	.479
15. Zane Smith	ATL	.314	98. Scott Sanderson	CHI	.472
16. Todd Worrell	STL	.315	97. Shane Rawley	PHI	.471
17. Dwight Gooden	NY	.318	96. Rick Mahler	ATL	.469
18. Roger McDowell	NY	.320	95. Don Carman	PHI	.468
19. Jeff Dedmon	ATL	.323	94. Kent Tekulve	PHI	.467
20. Lee Tunnell	STL	.328	93. Mike LaCoss	SF	.466

Opponents' Slugging Average, Right-Handed Batters

American League

Top 20			Bottom 20		
1. Doyle Alexander	DET	.265	127. Edwin Correa	TEX	.692
2. Juan Berenguer	MIN	.274	126. Ed Vande Berg	CLE	.591
3. Jeff Reardon	MIN	.295	125. Rich Yett	CLE	.586
4. Greg Minton	CAL	.295	124. Ken Dixon	BAL	.573
5. Mike Henneman	DET	.297	123. Scott Bankhead	SEA	.558
6. Mitch Williams	TEX	.298	122. Jeff Ballard	BAL	.558
7. Mike Smithson	MIN	.303	121. Scott McGregor	BAL	.546
8. Dennis Eckersley	OAK	.312	120. Al Nipper	BOS	.530
9. Dale Mohorcic	TEX	.313	119. Mark Thurmond	DET	.525
10. Bobby Witt	TEX	.316	118. Jerry Reuss	CAL	.523
11. Gary Lucas	CAL	.320	117. Don Sutton	CAL	.518
12. Bill Wilkinson	SEA	.324	116. Steve Crawford	BOS	.513
13. Dan Plesac	MIL	.326	115. Greg Harris	TEX	.512
14. Jack Morris	DET	.333	114. Dennis Lamp	OAK	.507
15. Jerry Gleaton	KC	.333	113. Scott Bailes	CLE	.506
16. Jimmy Key	TOR	.336	112. Dennis Rasmussen	NY	.497
17. Calvin Schiraldi	BOS	.345	111. Scott Nielsen	CHI	.493
18. Jose DeLeon	CHI	.346	110. Dan Petry	DET	.491
19. Mark Clear	MIL	.346	109. Eric Bell	BAL	.490
20. Joe Niekro	MIN	.347	108. Mike Trujillo	SEA	.489
20. Dave LaPoint	CHI	.347			

National League

Top 20			Bottom 20		
1. Jim Gott	PIT	.216	112. Dave Meads	HOU	.588
2. Tim Burke	MTL	.217	111. Bob Kipper	PIT	.578
3. Andy McGaffigan	MTL	.237	110. Paul Assenmacher	ATL	.556
4. Mike Dunne	PIT	.254	109. Bob Knepper	HOU	.518
5. Greg Booker	SD	.261	108. Lee Tunnell	STL	.516
6. Kent Tekulve	PHI	.265	107. Bob Patterson	PIT	.512
7. Nolan Ryan	HOU	.295	106. Gene Garber	ATL	.510
8. Jeff Robinson	PIT	.296	105. Mark Grant	SD	.510
9. Rick Reuschel	SF	.297	104. Bill Dawley	STL	.502
10. Orel Hershiser	LA	.304	103. Bill Gullickson	CIN	.495
11. Lee Smith	CHI	.308	102. Brian Fisher	PIT	.482
12. Danny Darwin	HOU	.315	101. Tom Browning	CIN	.480
13. Charlie Puleo	ATL	.315	100. Ricky Horton	STL	.479
14. Steve Bedrosian	PHI	.319	99. Alejandro Pena	LA	.473
15. Eric Nolte	SD	.319	98. Tim Leary	LA	.473
16. Mike Scott	HOU	.325	97. Bob Forsch	STL	.465
17. Steve Trout	CHI	.327	96. Scott Sanderson	CHI	.465
18. Les Lancaster	CHI	.327	95. Bryn Smith	MTL	.462
19. Pat Perry	CIN	.330	94. Brian Holton	LA	.461
20. Doyle Alexander	ATL	.338	93. John Tudor	STL	.457

Opponents' Home Run Percentage, Left-Handed Batters

American League

Top 20			Bottom 20		
1. Mike Flanagan	TOR	0.00	128. Darrel Akerfelds	CLE	8.00
1. Ed Vande Berg	CLE	0.00	127. Tom Niedenfuer	BAL	7.41
3. Doug Jones	CLE	0.54	126. Mike Smithson	MIN	6.72
4. Danny Jackson	KC	0.62	125. Bill Gullickson	NY	6.60
5. Doyle Alexander	DET	0.66	124. Bob James	CHI	6.59
6. Chuck Finley	CAL	0.74	123. Ken Dixon	BAL	6.54
7. Tommy John	NY	0.81	122. Calvin Schiraldi	BOS	6.34
8. Roger Clemens	BOS	1.00	121. Jack Lazorko	CAL	6.32
9. Tom Bolton	BOS	1.03	120. Mike Loynd	TEX	5.97
10. Eric Plunk	OAK	1.04	117. Bill Wilkinson	SEA	5.77
11. Dennis Lamp	OAK	1.05	117. Kirk McCaskill	CAL	5.77
12. Mark Thurmond	DET	1.10	117. Jeff Reardon	MIN	5.77
13. Don Gordon	CLE	1.12	116. Bert Blyleven	MIN	5.77
14. Charlie Leibrandt	KC	1.29	115. Mark Portugal	MIN	5.66
15. Jim Winn	CHI	1.32	114. Ken Schrom	CLE	5.26
16. Jeff Sellers	BOS	1.38	113. Jack Morris	DET	5.25
17. Greg Harris	TEX	1.48	112. Edwin Nunez	SEA	5.10
18. Scott Nielsen	CHI	1.67	111. Dennis Rasmussen	NY	5.05
19. Gene Nelson	OAK	1.67	110. Les Straker	MIN	4.98
20. Steve Carlton	MIN	1.77	109. Wes Gardner	BOS	4.94

National League

Top 20			Bottom 20		
1. Doug Sisk	NY	0.00	112. Doyle Alexander	ATL	7.11
1. Dave Smith	HOU	0.00	111. Bill Gullickson	CIN	5.06
1. Lee Tunnell	STL	0.00	110. Dorn Taylor	PIT	5.05
1. Frank Williams	CIN	0.00	109. Jamie Moyer	CHI	4.63
5. Dickie Noles	CHI	0.79	108. Pat Pacillo	CIN	4.49
6. Ricky Horton	STL	0.83	107. Lary Sorensen	MTL	4.44
6. John Mitchell	NY	0.83	106. Craig Lefferts	SF	4.39
6. Rob Murphy	CIN	0.83	105. Doug Drabek	PIT	4.30
9. Lance McCullers	SD	0.84	104. Steve Bedrosian	PHI	4.15
10. Don Robinson	SF	0.90	103. Mike Krukow	SF	3.74
11. Atlee Hammaker	SF	0.93	102. Charlie Puleo	ATL	3.66
12. Zane Smith	ATL	0.95	101. Mario Soto	CIN	3.57
13. Ken Howell	LA	1.04	100. Jeff Parrett	MTL	3.57
14. Bob Forsch	STL	1.07	99. Rocky Childress	HOU	3.53
15. Joe Magrane	STL	1.08	98. Tom Browning	CIN	3.45
16. Pat Perry	CIN	1.09	97. Scott Sanderson	CHI	3.40
17. Alejandro Pena	LA	1.13	96. Ed Whitson	SD	3.28
18. John Smiley	PIT	1.15	95. Neal Heaton	MTL	3.25
19. Tim Burke	MTL	1.18	94. Mike Jackson	PHI	3.17
19. Kelly Downs	SF	1.18	93. Mike Bielecki	PIT	3.16

Opponents' Home Run Percentage, Right-Handed Batters

American League

Top 20			Bottom 20		
1. Mike Smithson	MIN	0.00	127. Scott Bankhead	SEA	8.68
2. Greg Minton	CAL	0.67	126. Edwin Correa	TEX	8.39
3. Neil Allen	NY	0.75	125. Rich Yett	CLE	8.08
4. Jeff Russell	TEX	1.00	124. Ken Dixon	BAL	7.56
5. Juan Berenguer	MIN	1.02	123. Don Sutton	CAL	5.93
6. Mike Henneman	DET	1.04	122. John Habyan	BAL	5.88
7. Bill Wilkinson	SEA	1.18	121. Dennis Rasmussen	NY	5.66
8. Doyle Alexander	DET	1.23	120. Ed Vande Berg	CLE	5.66
9. Pat Clements	NY	1.36	119. John Cerutti	TOR	5.50
10. Danny Jackson	KC	1.45	118. Curt Young	OAK	5.29
11. Joe Niekro	MIN	1.49	117. Mike Trujillo	SEA	5.26
12. Jack O'Connor	BAL	1.63	116. Jeff Ballard	BAL	5.22
13. Doug Jones	CLE	1.71	115. Jose Guzman	TEX	5.09
14. Bobby Witt	TEX	1.75	114. Dan Petry	DET	5.05
15. Tommy John	NY	1.79	113. Eric Bell	BAL	5.03
16. Dave Stieb	TOR	1.87	112. Greg Harris	TEX	4.84
17. Steve Trout	NY	1.95	110. Ray Searage	CHI	4.76
18. Mark Gubicza	KC	2.10	110. Wes Gardner	BOS	4.76
19. Tony Arnold	BAL	2.17	109. Jerry Reuss	CAL	4.69
20. Chris Bosio	MIL	2.18	108. Eric King	DET	4.67

National League

Top 20			Bottom 20		
1. Jim Gott	PIT	0.00	112. Bob Kipper	PIT	7.08
2. Tim Conroy	STL	0.00	111. Ed Whitson	SD	6.16
3. Andy McGaffigan	MTL	0.48	110. Mark Grant	SD	5.70
4. Tim Burke	MTL	0.64	109. Brian Fisher	PIT	5.49
5. Lee Smith	CHI	0.68	108. Bill Dawley	STL	5.24
6. Mike Dunne	PIT	0.74	107. Bill Gullickson	CIN	5.18
7. Bill Landrum	CIN	0.75	106. Scott Sanderson	CHI	4.90
8. Charlie Puleo	ATL	0.91	105. Paul Assenmacher	ATL	4.86
9. Steve Trout	CHI	1.21	104. Ed Lynch	CHI	4.72
10. Kent Tekulve	PHI	1.30	103. Mike Jackson	PHI	4.69
11. Matt Young	LA	1.32	102. Alejandro Pena	LA	4.67
12. Ken Dayley	STL	1.34	101. Dave Meads	HOU	4.58
13. Greg Booker	SD	1.41	100. Ted Power	CIN	4.56
14. Joe Magrane	STL	1.46	99. Tim Leary	LA	4.55
15. Danny Darwin	HOU	1.60	98. Don Carman	PHI	4.51
16. Rick Reuschel	SF	1.63	97. Brian Holton	LA	4.24
17. Orel Hershiser	LA	1.70	95. Tom Hume	CIN	4.17
18. Mike LaCoss	SF	1.76	95. Jim Deshaies	HOU	4.17
19. Eric Nolte	SD	1.85	94. Ron Darling	NY	4.12
20. John Mitchell	NY	1.96	93. Kevin Gross	PHI	4.08

Opponents' Batting Average, Day Games

American League

Top 20			Bottom 20		
1. Doyle Alexander	DET	.164	128. Dennis Lamp	OAK	.413
2. Dave Schmidt	BAL	.168	127. Tom Niedenfuer	BAL	.387
3. Dewayne Buice	CAL	.168	126. Jay Aldrich	MIL	.370
4. John Davis	KC	.173	125. Joe Johnson	TOR	.368
5. Tom Henke	TOR	.179	124. John Leister	BOS	.366
6. Dennis Eckersley	OAK	.179	123. Mike Moore	SEA	.357
7. Charles Hudson	NY	.183	122. Steve Crawford	BOS	.352
8. Floyd Bannister	CHI	.184	121. Ed Vande Berg	CLE	.350
9. Chuck Finley	CAL	.186	120. Mike Smithson	MIN	.349
10. Mark Clear	MIL	.188	119. Ken Schrom	CLE	.345
11. Jeff Reardon	MIN	.189	118. Phil Niekro	TOR	.344
12. Mitch Williams	TEX	.194	117. Neil Allen	NY	.343
13. Dan Plesac	MIL	.196	116. Jeff Sellers	BOS	.333
14. Jack Lazorko	CAL	.198	115. Jerry Reuss	CAL	.331
15. Eric Plunk	OAK	.200	114. Bob Stanley	BOS	.329
16. Rich Yett	CLE	.201	113. Jim Winn	CHI	.320
17. Jimmy Key	TOR	.202	112. Jeff Ballard	BAL	.317
18. Dave Righetti	NY	.206	111. Greg Harris	TEX	.312
19. Scott Nielsen	CHI	.210	110. Scott Bailes	CLE	.311
20. Mike Campbell	SEA	.212	109. Ken Dixon	BAL	.310

National League

Top 20			Bottom 20		
1. Tim Burke	MTL	.165	112. Jesse Orosco	NY	.362
2. Craig Lefferts	SF	.180	111. Ron Davis	LA	.354
3. Larry Andersen	HOU	.183	110. Matt Young	LA	.346
4. John Franco	CIN	.194	109. Tim Leary	LA	.336
5. Scott Garrelts	SF	.201	108. Jim Acker	ATL	.333
6. Todd Worrell	STL	.212	107. Bob Knepper	HOU	.332
7. Ron Darling	NY	.213	106. Lee Tunnell	STL	.328
8. Alejandro Pena	LA	.213	105. Drew Hall	CHI	.321
9. Brian Fisher	PIT	.213	103. Gene Garber	ATL	.315
10. Randy Myers	NY	.214	103. Roger McDowell	NY	.315
11. Kent Tekulve	PHI	.214	102. Jeff Dedmon	ATL	.315
12. Pat Perry	CIN	.214	101. Randy O'Neal	STL	.313
12. Ricky Horton	STL	.214	100. Mike Mason	CHI	.311
14. Mike Jackson	PHI	.218	99. Mike Bielecki	PIT	.309
15. Danny Darwin	HOU	.219	98. Shane Rawley	PHI	.308
16. Dennis Rasmussen	CIN	.220	97. Greg Maddux	CHI	.307
17. Mike Scott	HOU	.221	96. Dwight Gooden	NY	.303
18. Dave Dravecky	SF	.222	95. Jim Deshaies	HOU	.298
19. Eric Nolte	SD	.222	94. Charlie Puleo	ATL	.297
20. Paul Assenmacher	ATL	.224	93. Mark Grant	SD	.296

Opponents' Batting Average, Night Games

American League

Top 20			Bottom 20		
1. Mitch Williams	TEX	.170	127. Jeff Ballard	BAL	.354
2. Tom Henke	TOR	.193	126. Scott Nielsen	CHI	.349
3. Mark Eichhorn	TOR	.195	125. Mark Knudson	MIL	.341
4. Bobby Witt	TEX	.213	124. Scott McGregor	BAL	.338
5. Tom Candiotti	CLE	.217	123. Tony Arnold	BAL	.333
6. Charlie Hough	TEX	.218	122. Jerry Reuss	CAL	.324
7. Dave Stewart	OAK	.221	121. Jose Rijo	OAK	.322
8. Dan Plesac	MIL	.222	120. Dave Schmidt	BAL	.321
9. Dave LaPoint	CHI	.224	119. Neil Allen	NY	.316
10. Jack Morris	DET	.224	118. Bob Stanley	BOS	.316
11. Jose DeLeon	CHI	.226	117. Tommy John	NY	.314
12. Dewayne Buice	CAL	.227	116. Ed Vande Berg	CLE	.313
13. Juan Berenguer	MIN	.227	115. Chuck Finley	CAL	.312
14. Doyle Alexander	DET	.227	114. Kirk McCaskill	CAL	.311
15. Jeff Musselman	TOR	.228	113. Steve Carlton	MIN	.302
16. Bill Wilkinson	SEA	.231	112. Mike Morgan	SEA	.301
17. Dave Stieb	TOR	.232	111. Pat Clements	NY	.297
18. Mike Henneman	DET	.232	110. Rich Yett	CLE	.295
19. Bert Blyleven	MIN	.233	109. Don Gordon	CLE	.291
20. Jimmy Key	TOR	.235	108. John Candelaria	CAL	.290

National League

Top 20			Bottom 20		
1. Dave Smith	HOU	.175	112. Bill Landrum	CIN	.325
2. Nolan Ryan	HOU	.186	111. Barry Jones	PIT	.318
3. Scott Garrelts	SF	.187	110. David Palmer	ATL	.312
4. Jesse Orosco	NY	.193	109. Andy Hawkins	SD	.308
5. Jeff Robinson	PIT	.194	108. Gene Garber	ATL	.307
6. Pat Perry	CIN	.202	107. Bob Knepper	HOU	.306
7. Jeff Dedmon	ATL	.203	106. Jay Tibbs	MTL	.305
8. Tim Burke	MTL	.209	105. Bruce Ruffin	PHI	.305
9. Dwight Gooden	NY	.213	104. Tim Conroy	STL	.299
10. Sid Fernandez	NY	.213	103. Randy O'Neal	STL	.298
11. Bob Welch	LA	.214	102. Mike Krukow	SF	.297
12. Mike Scott	HOU	.216	101. Danny Cox	STL	.295
13. Mike Jackson	PHI	.219	100. Lee Tunnell	STL	.294
14. David Cone	NY	.223	99. Les Lancaster	CHI	.291
15. Steve Bedrosian	PHI	.225	98. Doug Sisk	NY	.291
16. Ken Dayley	STL	.225	97. Bob Kipper	PIT	.289
17. Eric Nolte	SD	.228	96. Rick Mahler	ATL	.287
18. Jim Acker	ATL	.229	95. Mike LaCoss	SF	.286
19. Floyd Youmans	MTL	.229	94. John Tudor	STL	.286
20. John Smiley	PIT	.231	93. Tom Hume	CIN	.284

Opponents' Batting Average, Grass Surfaces

American League

Top 20				Bottom 20			
1.	Mitch Williams	TEX	.176	127.	Jeff Ballard	BAL	.348
2.	Doyle Alexander	DET	.191	126.	Scott McGregor	BAL	.348
3.	Dewayne Buice	CAL	.197	125.	Tom Bolton	BOS	.338
4.	Dan Plesac	MIL	.203	124.	Mark Thurmond	DET	.337
5.	Charlie Hough	TEX	.219	123.	Neil Allen	NY	.332
6.	Bobby Witt	TEX	.222	122.	Mike Smithson	MIN	.331
7.	Jack Morris	DET	.222	121.	Mark Knudson	MIL	.331
8.	Dennis Eckersley	OAK	.226	120.	Bud Black	KC	.327
9.	Dave Stewart	OAK	.229	119.	Ed Vande Berg	CLE	.326
10.	Gary Lucas	CAL	.231	118.	Jerry Reuss	CAL	.325
11.	Dave Leiper	OAK	.231	117.	Scott Bankhead	SEA	.322
12.	Dave LaPoint	CHI	.232	116.	Edwin Correa	TEX	.321
13.	Calvin Schiraldi	BOS	.232	115.	Kirk McCaskill	CAL	.315
14.	Roger Clemens	BOS	.235	114.	Dennis Lamp	OAK	.314
15.	Jack O'Connor	BAL	.237	113.	Tony Arnold	BAL	.314
16.	Mark Langston	SEA	.238	112.	Ken Schrom	CLE	.312
17.	Frank Viola	MIN	.238	111.	Steve Crawford	BOS	.306
18.	Tim Stoddard	NY	.238	110.	Jeff Sellers	BOS	.306
19.	Mike Henneman	DET	.239	109.	Mike Moore	SEA	.306
20.	Rick Rhoden	NY	.241	108.	Bob Stanley	BOS	.305

National League

Top 20				Bottom 20			
1.	Joe Price	SF	.140	112.	Bob Knepper	HOU	.381
2.	Scott Garrelts	SF	.179	111.	Ron Davis	LA	.364
3.	Andy McGaffigan	MTL	.186	110.	Drew Hall	CHI	.330
4.	John Franco	CIN	.186	109.	Kevin Gross	PHI	.324
5.	Sid Fernandez	NY	.202	108.	Ed Lynch	CHI	.316
6.	Brian Fisher	PIT	.207	107.	Kevin Coffman	ATL	.313
7.	Eric Show	SD	.208	106.	Gene Garber	ATL	.311
8.	Nolan Ryan	HOU	.209	105.	Randy O'Neal	STL	.309
9.	Danny Darwin	HOU	.213	104.	Andy Hawkins	SD	.303
10.	Bob Welch	LA	.217	103.	Roger Mason	SF	.303
11.	Tim Belcher	LA	.217	102.	Bruce Ruffin	PHI	.303
12.	Rick Reuschel	SF	.217	101.	Mike Mason	CHI	.302
13.	Ron Robinson	CIN	.219	100.	Mike Jackson	PHI	.297
14.	Greg Mathews	STL	.221	99.	Neal Heaton	MTL	.296
15.	Craig Lefferts	SF	.221	98.	Terry Leach	NY	.292
16.	Jeff Robinson	PIT	.222	97.	Bob Sebra	MTL	.290
17.	Dickie Noles	CHI	.223	96.	Tom Glavine	ATL	.289
18.	Randy Myers	NY	.225	95.	Guy Hoffman	CIN	.289
19.	Jim Gott	PIT	.227	94.	Frank Williams	CIN	.288
20.	Doug Drabek	PIT	.227	93.	Pete Smith	ATL	.288

Opponents' Batting Average, Artificial Surfaces

American League

Top 20				Bottom 20			
1.	Mark Clear	MIL	.143	127.	Bob Stanley	BOS	.427
2.	Mitch Williams	TEX	.167	126.	Mike Birkbeck	MIL	.411
3.	Ken Schrom	CLE	.169	125.	Reggie Ritter	CLE	.409
4.	Steve Ontiveros	OAK	.170	124.	Mark Portugal	MIN	.402
5.	John Habyan	BAL	.171	123.	Rick Rodriguez	OAK	.390
6.	Jose DeLeon	CHI	.181	122.	Dan Schatzeder	MIN	.390
7.	Tom Henke	TOR	.182	121.	Allan Anderson	MIN	.385
8.	Mark Huismann	CLE	.188	120.	Melido Perez	KC	.375
9.	Kirk McCaskill	CAL	.200	119.	David Wells	TOR	.365
9.	Bobby Witt	TEX	.200	118.	Jose Rijo	OAK	.358
11.	Ted Higuera	MIL	.203	117.	Darrel Akerfelds	CLE	.357
12.	Jimmy Key	TOR	.203	116.	Rick Rhoden	NY	.354
13.	Edwin Correa	TEX	.207	114.	Pat Clements	NY	.348
14.	Jerry Gleaton	KC	.208	114.	Stan Clarke	SEA	.348
15.	Juan Berenguer	MIN	.211	113.	Steve Crawford	BOS	.345
16.	Mark Eichhorn	TOR	.212	112.	Steve Shields	SEA	.342
17.	Mike Boddicker	BAL	.213	111.	Bob Stoddard	KC	.342
18.	Bobby Thigpen	CHI	.213	110.	Greg Swindell	CLE	.339
19.	Charles Hudson	NY	.215	109.	Bill Long	CHI	.333
20.	Jeff Musselman	TOR	.218	108.	Don Sutton	CAL	.331

National League

Top 20				Bottom 20			
1.	Jeff Calhoun	PHI	.124	112.	Eric Show	SD	.376
2.	Dave Smith	HOU	.156	111.	Jerry Reuss	CIN	.354
3.	Jeff Robinson	PIT	.188	110.	Barry Jones	PIT	.349
4.	Mike Jackson	PHI	.189	109.	Storm Davis	SD	.330
5.	Nolan Ryan	HOU	.195	108.	Mark Grant	SD	.329
6.	Mike Scott	HOU	.195	107.	Lary Sorensen	MTL	.328
7.	Pat Perry	CIN	.198	106.	Rick Mahler	ATL	.323
8.	John Smiley	PIT	.204	105.	Scott Sanderson	CHI	.318
9.	Tim Burke	MTL	.208	104.	Rick Aguilera	NY	.315
10.	Terry Leach	NY	.208	103.	Les Lancaster	CHI	.314
11.	Jeff Parrett	MTL	.208	102.	Jimmy Jones	SD	.312
12.	Dennis Rasmussen	CIN	.212	101.	Greg Maddux	CHI	.311
13.	Lee Smith	CHI	.217	99.	Mike Krukow	SF	.308
14.	Mike Bielecki	PIT	.218	99.	Tim Conroy	STL	.308
15.	Scott Garrelts	SF	.220	98.	Fernando Valenzuela	LA	.307
16.	Pascual Perez	MTL	.226	97.	Tim Leary	LA	.302
17.	Rob Murphy	CIN	.230	95.	Craig Lefferts	SF	.300
18.	Todd Worrell	STL	.234	95.	Dave Dravecky	SF	.300
19.	Dwight Gooden	NY	.235	94.	Bill Landrum	CIN	.298
20.	Atlee Hammaker	SF	.236	93.	Bruce Ruffin	PHI	.297

Opponents' Batting Average, Home Games

American League

Top 20				Bottom 20			
1.	Dennis Eckersley	OAK	.154	127.	Mark Knudson	MIL	.401
2.	Tom Henke	TOR	.165	126.	Jeff Ballard	BAL	.351
3.	Dewayne Buice	CAL	.177	125.	Scott McGregor	BAL	.335
4.	Mike Henneman	DET	.178	124.	Jerry Reuss	CAL	.335
5.	Mitch Williams	TEX	.181	123.	Ed Vande Berg	CLE	.327
6.	Gary Lucas	CAL	.192	122.	Neil Allen	NY	.326
7.	Jimmy Key	TOR	.193	121.	Phil Niekro	TOR	.320
8.	Juan Berenguer	MIN	.204	120.	Scott Bailes	CLE	.319
9.	Calvin Schiraldi	BOS	.209	119.	Ken Schrom	CLE	.318
10.	Bobby Witt	TEX	.210	117.	Edwin Correa	TEX	.317
11.	Jeff Musselman	TOR	.213	117.	Jeff Russell	TEX	.317
12.	Dave Stewart	OAK	.215	116.	Darrel Akerfelds	CLE	.307
13.	Mark Eichhorn	TOR	.218	115.	Scott Nielsen	CHI	.306
14.	Dave Righetti	NY	.218	114.	Tommy John	NY	.304
15.	Roger Clemens	BOS	.219	113.	Jose Rijo	OAK	.304
16.	Dan Plesac	MIL	.219	112.	Steve Crawford	BOS	.301
17.	Jack Morris	DET	.220	111.	Ken Dixon	BAL	.301
18.	Doyle Alexander	DET	.221	110.	Bob Stanley	BOS	.299
19.	Jeff Robinson	DET	.223	109.	Pat Clements	NY	.297
20.	Ron Guidry	NY	.224	108.	Doug Jones	CLE	.296

National League

Top 20				Bottom 20			
1.	Mike Jackson	PHI	.151	112.	Jerry Reuss	CIN	.339
2.	John Smiley	PIT	.162	111.	Brian Fisher	PIT	.324
3.	Dave Smith	HOU	.172	110.	John Franco	CIN	.310
4.	Pat Perry	CIN	.190	109.	Lee Smith	CHI	.309
5.	Nolan Ryan	HOU	.192	108.	Zane Smith	ATL	.309
6.	Jeff Parrett	MTL	.195	106.	Andy Hawkins	SD	.308
7.	Mike Scott	HOU	.196	106.	Terry Leach	NY	.308
8.	Sid Fernandez	NY	.198	105.	David Palmer	ATL	.306
9.	Scott Garrelts	SF	.200	104.	Bruce Ruffin	PHI	.305
10.	Tim Burke	MTL	.201	103.	Doug Sisk	NY	.301
11.	Eric Show	SD	.201	102.	Gene Garber	ATL	.298
12.	Craig Lefferts	SF	.204	101.	Ed Lynch	CHI	.295
13.	Jeff Robinson	PIT	.209	100.	Bill Landrum	CIN	.292
14.	Frank DiPino	CHI	.214	99.	Scott Sanderson	CHI	.289
15.	Jim Deshaies	HOU	.215	98.	Danny Cox	STL	.287
16.	Atlee Hammaker	SF	.217	97.	Bob Knepper	HOU	.287
17.	Dennis Martinez	MTL	.217	96.	Ted Power	CIN	.287
18.	Dickie Noles	CHI	.218	95.	Tom Hume	CIN	.286
19.	Mark Davis	SD	.220	94.	Shane Rawley	PHI	.284
20.	Mike Dunne	PIT	.221	93.	Wally Ritchie	PHI	.284

Opponents' Batting Average, Road Games

American League

Top 20			Bottom 20		
1. Bill Wilkinson	SEA	.165	127. Dennis Lamp	OAK	.364
2. Mitch Williams	TEX	.168	126. Bob Stanley	BOS	.340
3. Dave LaPoint	CHI	.183	125. Mark Thurmond	DET	.336
4. Doyle Alexander	DET	.185	124. Jeff Ballard	BAL	.333
5. Charlie Hough	TEX	.205	123. Jay Howell	OAK	.330
6. Dan Plesac	MIL	.208	122. Steve Crawford	BOS	.326
7. Tom Henke	TOR	.213	121. Neil Allen	NY	.325
8. John Habyan	BAL	.217	120. Ed Vande Berg	CLE	.323
9. Eric King	DET	.221	119. Steve Trout	NY	.321
10. Jose DeLeon	CHI	.222	118. Jerry Reuss	CAL	.317
11. Floyd Bannister	CHI	.227	117. Scott McGregor	BAL	.316
12. Jack Lazorko	CAL	.228	116. Walt Terrell	DET	.315
13. John Farrell	CLE	.230	115. Dan Schatzeder	MIN	.311
14. Bobby Witt	TEX	.230	114. Scott Nielsen	CHI	.309
15. Charles Hudson	NY	.231	113. Mike Moore	SEA	.308
16. Bobby Thigpen	CHI	.234	112. Jose Rijo	OAK	.307
17. Frank Viola	MIN	.235	111. Scott Bankhead	SEA	.306
18. Tim Stoddard	NY	.236	110. Dave Righetti	NY	.306
19. Dale Mohorcic	TEX	.237	109. Greg Swindell	CLE	.306
20. Steve Ontiveros	OAK	.238	108. Gary Lucas	CAL	.305

National League

Top 20			Bottom 20		
1. Pascual Perez	MTL	.156	112. Lee Tunnell	STL	.369
2. Ken Dayley	STL	.161	111. John Smiley	PIT	.362
3. Shawn Hillegas	LA	.181	110. Dave Meads	HOU	.352
4. Scott Garrelts	SF	.187	109. Randy O'Neal	STL	.351
5. John Franco	CIN	.190	108. Bob Knepper	HOU	.342
6. Tim Burke	MTL	.190	107. Gene Garber	ATL	.330
7. Rob Murphy	CIN	.202	106. Greg Maddux	CHI	.313
8. Andy McGaffigan	MTL	.205	105. Storm Davis	SD	.308
9. Brian Fisher	PIT	.207	104. Tom Browning	CIN	.308
10. Nolan Ryan	HOU	.208	103. Mike LaCoss	SF	.305
11. Jeff Robinson	PIT	.209	102. Rick Mahler	ATL	.305
12. Lee Smith	CHI	.215	101. Roger McDowell	NY	.304
13. David Cone	NY	.216	100. Mark Grant	SD	.304
14. Bob Welch	LA	.217	99. Mike Krukow	SF	.301
15. Randy Myers	NY	.218	98. Jay Tibbs	MTL	.301
16. Steve Bedrosian	PHI	.222	97. Danny Cox	STL	.295
17. Pat Perry	CIN	.223	96. Jim Deshaies	HOU	.295
18. Zane Smith	ATL	.226	95. Ken Howell	LA	.295
19. Ron Robinson	CIN	.227	94. John Mitchell	NY	.294
20. Ron Darling	NY	.231	93. Ed Lynch	CHI	.294

Opponents' Batting Average with Runners On Base

American League

Top 20			Bottom 20		
1. Mitch Williams	TEX	.180	128. Scott Nielsen	CHI	.390
2. Dennis Eckersley	OAK	.198	127. Dennis Lamp	OAK	.362
3. Tom Henke	TOR	.201	126. Neil Allen	NY	.359
4. Dave LaPoint	CHI	.201	125. Jerry Reuss	CAL	.353
5. Charlie Hough	TEX	.205	124. Scott McGregor	BAL	.353
6. Roger Clemens	BOS	.205	123. Steve Crawford	BOS	.352
7. Mike Henneman	DET	.210	122. Jeff Robinson	DET	.350
8. Doyle Alexander	DET	.214	121. Mike Smithson	MIN	.346
9. Dennis Rasmussen	NY	.219	120. Dan Schatzeder	MIN	.342
10. Dale Mohorcic	TEX	.222	119. Jeff Ballard	BAL	.339
11. John Cerutti	TOR	.222	118. Ken Schrom	CLE	.333
12. Jeff Musselman	TOR	.223	117. John Candelaria	CAL	.331
13. Mark Clear	MIL	.225	116. Jay Aldrich	MIL	.327
14. Jack Morris	DET	.225	115. Scott Bankhead	SEA	.324
15. Bud Black	KC	.227	114. Bill Long	CHI	.323
16. Bobby Witt	TEX	.228	113. Ed Vande Berg	CLE	.319
17. Bobby Thigpen	CHI	.228	112. Ray Searage	CHI	.314
18. Paul Kilgus	TEX	.229	111. Mark Thurmond	DET	.314
19. Tim Stoddard	NY	.230	110. Doug Jones	CLE	.312
20. Dave Stewart	OAK	.231	109. Jeff Sellers	BOS	.311

National League

Top 20			Bottom 20		
1. Tim Burke	MTL	.180	113. Bob Knepper	HOU	.330
2. Eric Nolte	SD	.195	112. Doug Sisk	NY	.319
3. Todd Worrell	STL	.200	111. Jimmy Jones	SD	.317
4. Scott Garrelts	SF	.201	110. Paul Assenmacher	ATL	.317
5. Andy McGaffigan	MTL	.202	109. Jay Tibbs	MTL	.317
6. Dave Smith	HOU	.204	108. Tim Leary	LA	.313
7. Jeff Robinson	PIT	.209	107. Matt Young	LA	.312
8. Randy Myers	NY	.210	106. Neal Heaton	MTL	.306
9. Kent Tekulve	PHI	.212	105. Lee Tunnell	STL	.306
10. Nolan Ryan	HOU	.215	104. Bob Forsch	STL	.303
11. Steve Bedrosian	PHI	.220	103. Bob Sebra	MTL	.302
12. Mike Dunne	PIT	.221	102. Rick Mahler	ATL	.301
13. Ken Dayley	STL	.222	101. Mike Krukow	SF	.301
14. Wally Ritchie	PHI	.223	100. Greg Maddux	CHI	.301
15. Terry Leach	NY	.225	99. Doyle Alexander	ATL	.300
16. Mike Jackson	PHI	.226	98. Bill Landrum	CIN	.296
17. David Cone	NY	.227	97. Bryn Smith	MTL	.293
18. Rick Aguilera	NY	.227	96. Storm Davis	SD	.292
19. Eric Show	SD	.230	95. Rick Honeycutt	LA	.291
20. Pat Perry	CIN	.231	94. Bob Kipper	PIT	.288
20. Dwight Gooden	NY	.231			

Opponents' Batting Average with Bases Empty

American League

Top 20			Bottom 20		
1. Mitch Williams	TEX	.169	127. Bob Stanley	BOS	.354
2. Bill Wilkinson	SEA	.174	126. Mark Knudson	MIL	.350
3. Dan Plesac	MIL	.176	125. Jeff Ballard	BAL	.348
4. Tom Henke	TOR	.178	124. Ed Vande Berg	CLE	.333
5. Dewayne Buice	CAL	.185	123. Jose Rijo	OAK	.331
6. Doyle Alexander	DET	.195	122. Scott Bailes	CLE	.329
7. Jimmy Key	TOR	.198	121. Edwin Correa	TEX	.317
8. Jeff Robinson	DET	.205	120. Darrel Akerfelds	CLE	.311
9. Gary Lucas	CAL	.205	119. Jeff Russell	TEX	.311
10. Bobby Witt	TEX	.209	118. Mike Morgan	SEA	.310
11. Mike Campbell	SEA	.211	117. Jerry Reuss	CAL	.309
12. Jeff Reardon	MIN	.213	116. Paul Kilgus	TEX	.306
13. Dave Stieb	TOR	.217	115. Scott McGregor	BAL	.303
14. Juan Berenguer	MIN	.218	114. Pat Clements	NY	.301
15. Bill Gullickson	NY	.220	113. Joe Johnson	TOR	.300
16. Ted Higuera	MIL	.223	112. Mike Loynd	TEX	.299
17. Mark Langston	SEA	.225	111. Neil Allen	NY	.295
18. Dave Stewart	OAK	.227	110. Bud Black	KC	.295
19. Jose DeLeon	CHI	.227	109. Tommy John	NY	.291
20. Joel Davis	CHI	.228	108. Phil Niekro	TOR	.290

National League

Top 20			Bottom 20		
1. Scott Garrelts	SF	.185	112. Gene Garber	ATL	.345
2. Pascual Perez	MTL	.188	111. Randy O'Neal	STL	.340
3. Nolan Ryan	HOU	.190	110. Tom Hume	CIN	.323
4. Mike Scott	HOU	.191	109. Andy Hawkins	SD	.318
5. Pat Perry	CIN	.191	108. Rick Aguilera	NY	.315
6. Dorn Taylor	PIT	.197	107. Bruce Ruffin	PHI	.313
7. Bob Welch	LA	.207	106. Lee Tunnell	STL	.309
8. Tim Burke	MTL	.207	105. Ed Lynch	CHI	.303
9. Jeff Robinson	PIT	.209	104. Tom Browning	CIN	.302
10. Paul Assenmacher	ATL	.213	103. Danny Cox	STL	.302
11. Mike Jackson	PHI	.213	102. Bob Knepper	HOU	.300
12. Sid Fernandez	NY	.216	101. Brian Holton	LA	.298
13. John Smiley	PIT	.217	100. John Tudor	STL	.296
14. Shawn Hillegas	LA	.217	99. Mike LaCoss	SF	.292
15. Jeff Parrett	MTL	.218	98. Todd Worrell	STL	.291
16. Joe Magrane	STL	.221	97. Scott Sanderson	CHI	.290
17. Jim Gott	PIT	.221	96. Greg Maddux	CHI	.289
18. Don Carman	PHI	.223	95. Bill Landrum	CIN	.288
19. Jeff Dedmon	ATL	.224	94. Terry Leach	NY	.288
20. Doug Sisk	NY	.229	93. Shane Rawley	PHI	.287

Opponents' Home Run Percentage with Runners On Base

American League

Top 20			Bottom 20		
1. Tom Bolton	BOS	0.00	128. Calvin Schiraldi	BOS	7.65
2. Pat Clements	NY	0.62	127. Edwin Correa	TEX	7.63
3. Greg Minton	CAL	0.79	126. Jeff Reardon	MIN	7.04
4. John Farrell	CLE	0.92	125. Ken Dixon	BAL	6.90
5. Doyle Alexander	DET	0.97	124. Rich Yett	CLE	6.88
6. Chuck Finley	CAL	1.22	123. Steve Crawford	BOS	6.21
7. Mike Flanagan	TOR	1.27	122. Don Sutton	CAL	6.18
8. Jose DeLeon	CHI	1.28	121. John Candelaria	CAL	5.92
9. Tommy John	NY	1.30	120. Jerry Reuss	CAL	5.88
10. Dave Stieb	TOR	1.43	119. Jack Lazorko	CAL	5.81
11. Jim Winn	CHI	1.48	118. Scott McGregor	BAL	5.77
12. Ted Higuera	MIL	1.49	117. Kirk McCaskill	CAL	5.74
13. Bill Wilkinson	SEA	1.54	116. Ray Searage	CHI	5.71
14. Doug Jones	CLE	1.59	115. Greg Swindell	CLE	5.63
15. Jeff Sellers	BOS	1.64	114. John Cerutti	TOR	5.43
16. Charlie Leibrandt	KC	1.66	113. Curt Young	OAK	5.42
17. Ron Guidry	NY	1.70	112. Dan Schatzeder	MIN	5.41
17. Mike Henneman	DET	1.70	111. Mike Smithson	MIN	5.32
19. Bobby Witt	TEX	1.78	110. Wes Gardner	BOS	5.17
20. Danny Jackson	KC	1.80	109. Dan Petry	DET	5.04

National League

Top 20			Bottom 20		
1. Rob Murphy	CIN	0.00	113. Bob Kipper	PIT	6.21
1. Dave Smith	HOU	0.00	112. Doyle Alexander	ATL	6.00
1. Lee Smith	CHI	0.00	111. Mike Jackson	PHI	5.65
4. Terry Leach	NY	0.49	110. Neal Heaton	MTL	5.22
5. Andy McGaffigan	MTL	0.49	109. Mark Grant	SD	4.85
6. Jim Gott	PIT	0.57	108. Ed Whitson	SD	4.78
7. Frank Williams	CIN	0.62	107. Randy St. Claire	MTL	4.55
8. Lee Tunnell	STL	0.69	106. Bill Gullickson	CIN	4.53
9. John Franco	CIN	0.71	105. Jim Deshaies	HOU	4.52
10. Tim Burke	MTL	0.72	104. Doug Drabek	PIT	4.44
11. Dickie Noles	CHI	0.83	103. Guy Hoffman	CIN	4.31
12. Mike Dunne	PIT	0.83	102. Scott Garrelts	SF	4.27
13. Steve Trout	CHI	0.84	101. Don Carman	PHI	4.15
14. Kevin Gross	PHI	0.85	100. Jamie Moyer	CHI	4.11
15. Ken Dayley	STL	0.85	99. Tim Leary	LA	3.98
16. Bill Landrum	CIN	0.87	98. Paul Assenmacher	ATL	3.96
17. Roger McDowell	NY	1.09	97. Wally Ritchie	PHI	3.88
18. Dwight Gooden	NY	1.10	96. Pat Perry	CIN	3.85
19. Danny Darwin	HOU	1.32	95. Ed Lynch	CHI	3.81
20. Frank DiPino	CHI	1.39	94. Les Lancaster	CHI	3.64

Opponents' Home Run Percentage Bases Empty

American League

Top 20			Bottom 20		
1. Doug Jones	CLE	0.58	127. Darrel Akerfelds	CLE	7.19
2. Dan Plesac	MIL	0.65	126. Ken Dixon	BAL	7.17
3. Mark Knudson	MIL	0.71	125. Dennis Rasmussen	NY	7.00
4. Danny Jackson	KC	0.87	124. Mike Loynd	TEX	6.94
5. Doyle Alexander	DET	0.95	123. Scott Bankhead	SEA	6.48
6. Mark Gubicza	KC	1.36	122. Bill Gullickson	NY	5.51
7. Calvin Schiraldi	BOS	1.40	121. Jeff Ballard	BAL	5.49
8. George Frazier	MIN	1.42	120. Bert Blyleven	MIN	5.48
9. Gene Nelson	OAK	1.50	119. Scott Bailes	CLE	5.43
10. Tom Henke	TOR	1.57	118. Mike Campbell	SEA	5.26
11. Joel Davis	CHI	1.63	117. John Habyan	BAL	5.14
12. Roger Clemens	BOS	1.63	116. John Cerutti	TOR	5.11
13. Tommy John	NY	1.86	115. Edwin Correa	TEX	4.97
14. Jeff Musselman	TOR	2.00	114. Eric Bell	BAL	4.95
15. Greg Minton	CAL	2.01	113. Floyd Bannister	CHI	4.90
16. Jeff Sellers	BOS	2.03	112. Ken Schrom	CLE	4.89
17. Scott Nielsen	CHI	2.04	111. Jim Winn	CHI	4.76
18. Bobby Witt	TEX	2.09	110. Rich Yett	CLE	4.69
19. Pat Clements	NY	2.10	109. Al Nipper	BOS	4.67
20. Mitch Williams	TEX	2.25	108. Paul Kilgus	TEX	4.66

National League

Top 20			Bottom 20		
1. Doug Sisk	NY	0.00	112. Kevin Gross	PHI	5.57
1. Dickie Noles	CHI	0.00	111. Randy O'Neal	STL	5.56
3. John Mitchell	NY	0.82	110. Bob Kipper	PIT	5.49
4. Tim Burke	MTL	1.06	109. Bill Gullickson	CIN	5.47
5. Zane Smith	ATL	1.13	108. Bill Dawley	STL	5.26
6. Pascual Perez	MTL	1.18	107. Scott Sanderson	CHI	4.69
7. Steve Trout	CHI	1.27	106. Ed Whitson	SD	4.48
8. Joe Magrane	STL	1.30	105. Steve Bedrosian	PHI	4.35
9. Rick Reuschel	SF	1.35	104. Terry Leach	NY	4.35
10. Storm Davis	SD	1.46	103. Don Carman	PHI	4.34
11. Kelly Downs	SF	1.47	102. Brian Fisher	PIT	4.34
12. Nolan Ryan	HOU	1.50	101. Bob Knepper	HOU	4.32
13. Scott Garrelts	SF	1.50	100. Andy Hawkins	SD	4.31
14. Jesse Orosco	NY	1.50	99. Eric Show	SD	4.28
15. Dennis Martinez	MTL	1.52	98. Dorn Taylor	PIT	4.27
16. Pat Perry	CIN	1.60	97. Mike Krukow	SF	4.24
17. Andy McGaffigan	MTL	1.64	96. Brian Holton	LA	4.17
18. Bob Forsch	STL	1.64	95. Tom Browning	CIN	4.15
19. Bob Welch	LA	1.66	94. Doyle Alexander	ATL	4.03
20. Bill Landrum	CIN	1.69	92. Ricky Horton	STL	4.00
			92. Craig Lefferts	SF	4.00

Opponents' On Base Average Leading Off the Inning

American League

Top 20			Bottom 20		
1. Jeff Reardon	MIN	.200	127. Jeff Ballard	BAL	.456
2. Dan Plesac	MIL	.219	126. Bob Stanley	BOS	.445
3. Jeff Robinson	DET	.226	125. Bobby Witt	TEX	.427
4. Tim Stoddard	NY	.229	124. Scott McGregor	BAL	.424
5. Tom Henke	TOR	.231	123. Jose Nunez	TOR	.419
6. Dave Schmidt	BAL	.231	122. Kirk McCaskill	CAL	.407
7. Dewayne Buice	CAL	.237	121. Jim Winn	CHI	.405
8. Mark Eichhorn	TOR	.239	120. Joaquin Andujar	OAK	.400
9. Jimmy Key	TOR	.242	119. Steve Crawford	BOS	.397
10. Mark Williamson	BAL	.243	118. Jeff Musselman	TOR	.395
11. Dennis Eckersley	OAK	.245	117. Edwin Correa	TEX	.395
12. Bill Long	CHI	.253	116. Rich Yett	CLE	.394
13. John Candelaria	CAL	.262	115. Dennis Lamp	OAK	.393
13. Ron Guidry	NY	.262	114. Scott Bailes	CLE	.392
15. Doyle Alexander	DET	.264	113. Joe Johnson	TOR	.389
16. John Farrell	CLE	.264	112. Darrel Akerfelds	CLE	.388
17. Keith Atherton	MIN	.267	111. Ken Dixon	BAL	.387
18. Bill Wilkinson	SEA	.271	110. Dan Petry	DET	.380
19. Jack Morris	DET	.272	109. Bobby Thigpen	CHI	.380
20. Calvin Schiraldi	BOS	.273	108. Mitch Williams	TEX	.379

National League

Top 20			Bottom 20		
1. Randy St. Claire	MTL	.186	112. Ken Howell	LA	.474
2. Bryn Smith	MTL	.226	111. Tom Hume	CIN	.415
3. Mike Scott	HOU	.231	110. Randy O'Neal	STL	.406
4. Bob Welch	LA	.232	109. Lee Tunnell	STL	.395
5. Rob Murphy	CIN	.234	108. Storm Davis	SD	.394
6. Frank DiPino	CHI	.235	107. Bill Landrum	CIN	.393
7. Frank Williams	CIN	.243	106. Kevin Gross	PHI	.393
8. Neal Heaton	MTL	.248	105. Bruce Ruffin	PHI	.389
9. Doyle Alexander	ATL	.248	104. Andy Hawkins	SD	.385
10. Tim Burke	MTL	.250	103. Mike LaCoss	SF	.385
11. Nolan Ryan	HOU	.265	102. Mike Krukow	SF	.384
12. Jeff Parrett	MTL	.271	101. Jeff Dedmon	ATL	.381
13. Lee Smith	CHI	.275	100. Jesse Orosco	NY	.379
14. Lance McCullers	SD	.276	99. Shawn Hillegas	LA	.377
15. Danny Darwin	HOU	.277	98. Tom Browning	CIN	.370
16. Jim Deshaies	HOU	.281	97. Bill Dawley	STL	.370
17. Steve Bedrosian	PHI	.286	96. Rick Mahler	ATL	.369
18. Greg Maddux	CHI	.290	95. Roger McDowell	NY	.368
19. Greg Booker	SD	.290	94. Jamie Moyer	CHI	.367
20. Pascual Perez	MTL	.292	92. Rick Aguilera	NY	.364
			92. Danny Cox	STL	.364

Opponents' Batting Average with Runners in Scoring Position

American League

Top 20				Bottom 20		
1. Mitch Williams	TEX	.162		129. Scott Nielsen	CHI	.427
2. Mark Eichhorn	TOR	.172		128. Jeff Ballard	BAL	.397
3. Dennis Eckersley	OAK	.173		127. Dennis Lamp	OAK	.382
4. Jack Morris	DET	.176		126. Jerry Reuss	CAL	.373
5. John Cerutti	TOR	.178		125. Scott McGregor	BAL	.368
6. Mike Henneman	DET	.184		124. Jeff Robinson	DET	.366
7. Dave LaPoint	CHI	.185		123. Neil Allen	NY	.354
8. Charlie Hough	TEX	.188		122. Dan Quisenberry	KC	.353
9. Mark Clear	MIL	.193		121. Steve Crawford	BOS	.349
10. Greg Minton	CAL	.194		120. Ray Searage	CHI	.343
11. Dennis Rasmussen	NY	.198		119. Scott Bankhead	SEA	.340
12. Roger Clemens	BOS	.199		118. Ken Schrom	CLE	.335
13. Charlie Leibrandt	KC	.200		117. Jack Lazorko	CAL	.333
14. Lee Guetterman	SEA	.202		116. John Candelaria	CAL	.330
15. Tom Henke	TOR	.205		115. Pat Clements	NY	.324
16. Bob James	CHI	.205		114. Mike Loynd	TEX	.321
17. Bobby Witt	TEX	.208		113. Jeff Sellers	BOS	.318
18. Jerry Reed	SEA	.210		112. Jeff Russell	TEX	.316
19. George Frazier	MIN	.210		111. Doug Jones	CLE	.314
20. Mark Gubicza	KC	.211		109. Jay Aldrich	MIL	.313
				109. Don Gordon	CLE	.313

National League

Top 20				Bottom 20		
1. Steve Bedrosian	PHI	.156		112. Bill Landrum	CIN	.371
2. Eric Nolte	SD	.157		111. Doyle Alexander	ATL	.352
3. Jeff Robinson	PIT	.161		110. Paul Assenmacher	ATL	.343
4. Wally Ritchie	PHI	.176		109. Rob Murphy	CIN	.329
5. Kent Tekulve	PHI	.180		108. Jimmy Jones	SD	.324
6. Alejandro Pena	LA	.189		107. Lee Tunnell	STL	.315
7. Nolan Ryan	HOU	.191		106. Jay Tibbs	MTL	.314
8. Tim Burke	MTL	.195		105. Frank Williams	CIN	.311
9. John Franco	CIN	.198		104. John Smiley	PIT	.310
10. Mike Jackson	PHI	.200		103. Bruce Ruffin	PHI	.309
11. Randy Myers	NY	.203		102. Rick Mahler	ATL	.308
12. Rick Aguilera	NY	.204		101. Roger McDowell	NY	.306
13. Scott Garrelts	SF	.204		100. Neal Heaton	MTL	.305
14. Mike Dunne	PIT	.204		99. Greg Maddux	CHI	.305
15. David Cone	NY	.205		98. Tom Glavine	ATL	.304
16. Todd Worrell	STL	.207		97. Doug Sisk	NY	.303
17. Dave Smith	HOU	.209		96. Barry Jones	PIT	.303
18. Jesse Orosco	NY	.212		95. Bryn Smith	MTL	.301
19. Jim Gott	PIT	.215		94. Tim Leary	LA	.300
20. Fernando Valenzuela	LA	.216		93. Jamie Moyer	CHI	.299

Opponents' Batting Average in Pressure Situations

American League

Top 20				Bottom 20		
1. Dave Stieb	TOR	.056		127. Gary Lavelle	OAK	.484
2. Tom Henke	TOR	.174		126. Bob Stanley	BOS	.384
3. Eric Plunk	OAK	.176		125. Jim Clancy	TOR	.359
4. Mike Henneman	DET	.177		124. Les Straker	MIN	.359
5. Mitch Williams	TEX	.183		123. Jeff Sellers	BOS	.355
6. Jeff Robinson	DET	.189		122. Steve Shields	SEA	.351
7. Nate Snell	DET	.190		121. Steve Carlton	MIN	.350
8. Jack O'Connor	BAL	.191		120. Stan Clarke	SEA	.346
9. Rick Rhoden	NY	.192		119. Edwin Nunez	SEA	.345
10. Ted Higuera	MIL	.194		117. Scott Bailes	CLE	.333
11. Phil Niekro	TOR	.195		117. Pat Clements	NY	.333
12. Cecilio Guante	NY	.200		116. Steve Farr	KC	.327
13. Bill Wilkinson	SEA	.201		115. Greg Harris	TEX	.319
14. John Davis	KC	.203		114. Mark Williamson	BAL	.318
15. Jack Lazorko	CAL	.203		113. Don Gordon	CLE	.314
16. Sammy Stewart	CLE	.204		112. Dave Schmidt	BAL	.313
17. Eric Bell	BAL	.205		111. Mark Gubicza	KC	.312
18. Mike Griffin	BAL	.205		110. Dan Quisenberry	KC	.310
19. Doyle Alexander	DET	.207		109. Dale Mohorcic	TEX	.310
20. David Wells	TOR	.208		108. Jay Aldrich	MIL	.310

National League

Top 20				Bottom 20		
1. Floyd Youmans	MTL	.148		112. Doyle Alexander	ATL	.462
2. Jeff Calhoun	PHI	.156		111. Wally Ritchie	PHI	.409
3. Nolan Ryan	HOU	.175		110. Mark Grant	SD	.400
4. Sid Fernandez	NY	.182		109. Mike Krukow	SF	.388
5. Eric Show	SD	.188		108. Tom Hume	CIN	.385
6. Tim Burke	MTL	.189		107. Ed Lynch	CHI	.364
7. Pat Perry	CIN	.189		106. Tom Browning	CIN	.357
8. Bob Sebra	MTL	.189		105. Rick Mahler	ATL	.347
9. Dave Smith	HOU	.192		104. Neal Heaton	MTL	.347
10. Scott Garrelts	SF	.195		103. Ron Darling	NY	.343
11. Randy Myers	NY	.198		102. Ed Whitson	SD	.333
12. Aurelio Lopez	HOU	.200		101. Jamie Moyer	CHI	.325
13. Dennis Martinez	MTL	.206		100. Atlee Hammaker	SF	.317
14. Paul Assenmacher	ATL	.210		99. Matt Young	LA	.316
15. Jeff Robinson	PIT	.210		98. Orel Hershiser	LA	.315
16. Jay Baller	CHI	.211		97. Rick Aguilera	NY	.314
17. Alejandro Pena	LA	.211		96. Gene Garber	ATL	.314
18. Mark Davis	SD	.215		95. Bill Dawley	STL	.312
19. Jim Gott	PIT	.215		94. Zane Smith	ATL	.309
20. Kent Tekulve	PHI	.218		92. Terry Leach	NY	.308
				92. Bruce Ruffin	PHI	.308

Strikeout Percentage in Pressure Situations

American League

Top 20				Bottom 20		
1. Tom Henke	TOR	33.33		127. Tommy John	NY	2.50
2. Mitch Williams	TEX	28.50		126. Ken Schrom	CLE	3.85
3. Bill Wilkinson	SEA	27.27		125. Dennis Rasmussen	NY	5.00
4. Dennis Eckersley	OAK	26.74		124. Mark Thurmond	DET	6.00
5. David Wells	TOR	26.42		123. Dan Quisenberry	KC	6.52
6. Calvin Schiraldi	BOS	25.97		122. Les Straker	MIN	6.98
7. Jeff Reardon	MIN	25.21		121. Bill Wegman	MIL	7.32
8. Cecilio Guante	NY	25.00		119. Don Gordon	CLE	7.69
9. Dan Plesac	MIL	24.89		119. Mike Morgan	SEA	7.69
10. Eric Plunk	OAK	24.18		118. Bob Stanley	BOS	7.92
11. Jack O'Connor	BAL	24.07		117. Jim Winn	CHI	8.19
12. Ken Dixon	BAL	23.73		116. Dave Schmidt	BAL	8.24
13. Mark Eichhorn	TOR	23.59		115. Jack Lazorko	CAL	8.33
14. Dewayne Buice	CAL	23.19		114. Steve Carlton	MIN	8.45
15. Dave Stieb	TOR	23.08		113. Pat Clements	NY	8.89
16. Bobby Witt	TEX	23.08		112. Keith Atherton	MIN	8.92
17. Bert Blyleven	MIN	22.66		111. Greg Minton	CAL	9.20
18. Joe Sambito	BOS	22.50		110. Paul Mirabella	MIL	9.52
19. Doug Jones	CLE	22.41		109. Curt Young	OAK	9.72
20. Charlie Hough	TEX	22.39		108. Phil Niekro	TOR	9.80

National League

Top 20				Bottom 20		
1. Nolan Ryan	HOU	44.44		112. Gene Walter	NY	2.94
2. Scott Garrelts	SF	32.09		111. Juan Agosto	HOU	3.33
3. Mike Scott	HOU	30.69		110. Tom Hume	CIN	3.77
4. Joe Price	SF	28.57		109. Jamie Moyer	CHI	4.90
5. Randy Myers	NY	27.36		108. Les Lancaster	CHI	5.13
6. Dave Smith	HOU	27.11		107. Mark Grant	SD	6.00
7. Ken Dayley	STL	27.01		106. Doyle Alexander	ATL	6.45
8. Alejandro Pena	LA	26.42		105. Roger McDowell	NY	6.55
9. Lee Smith	CHI	26.20		104. Wally Ritchie	PHI	7.41
10. Todd Worrell	STL	24.74		103. Rick Mahler	ATL	8.14
11. Dave Meads	HOU	24.69		102. Lee Tunnell	STL	8.20
12. Sid Fernandez	NY	24.49		101. Bob Welch	LA	8.85
13. Guy Hoffman	CIN	24.24		100. Tom Browning	CIN	9.09
14. Jay Baller	CHI	24.00		99. Mike Dunne	PIT	9.21
15. Dave Dravecky	SF	24.00		97. Mike LaCoss	SF	9.52
16. Ken Howell	LA	23.91		97. Bruce Ruffin	PHI	9.52
17. Eric Show	SD	23.53		96. Zane Smith	ATL	9.86
18. Jesse Orosco	NY	23.36		95. Ed Lynch	CHI	10.00
19. Larry Andersen	HOU	21.93		94. Doug Sisk	NY	10.07
20. Terry Leach	NY	21.74		93. Pat Perry	CIN	10.34

VI
Single Season and Career Leaders

Single Season and Career Leaders

The Single Season and Career Leaders section lists, for a variety of batting and pitching categories, the top 25 performers since we began *The Player Analysis* in 1975.

When we began our analysis of play-by-play data from every game, we had a dual purpose: we recognized the value of the information for immediate use, and we knew we were accumulating and building a valuable resource for future study as well. This section gives us a chance to take stock of the results from our unparalleled files—files representing more than a million and a half plate appearances.

The leader categories for this section were chosen both for significance and for general interest (however quirky). The single season bests listed here provide an important context for evaluating the performances throughout this book. The career lists do considerably more; they combine twelve years' worth of statistics, and provide the definitive look at situational statistics since 1975.

Minimum qualifiers for most batting categories are expressed in hits rather than in the equivalent number of plate appearances. As a general rule, the number of hits is one third the number of at bats of the qualifying range, if you're more comfortable thinking about it in those terms.

In dealing with last season's statistics in the Ranking Section of this book, we used a more inclusive level for rankings qualification: the equivalent of 200 plate appearances. The levels used here are more stringent, corresponding more to everyday play than part-time or "semiregular" status.

In the pitching categories, it should not be too surprising that relievers dominate. They allow consistently lower batting averages than starters for a variety of reasons, not only in traditional statistics but in these situational statistics as well. We have tried to set qualifying levels that are meaningful for both starters and relievers; the levels are the equivalent of about one and a half seasons as a full-time starter, or three as a primary reliever.

Bear in mind that *The Player Analysis* began in 1975. For the vast majority of active players, this poses no obstacle to calling these "career" statistics. In some cases, the missing information is very minor (67 at bats out of Jim Rice's career; a little under 500 from George Brett's); in the case of a Pete Rose or Tony Perez, obviously, a larger chunk is missing. We'd love to be able to fill in the gaps; we'd also love to know how Lou Gehrig hit with runners in scoring position in late-inning pressure. Maybe someday . . .

CAREER BATTING AVERAGE VS. LEFT-HANDED PITCHERS		CAREER SLUGGING AVERAGE VS. LEFT-HANDED PITCHERS		CAREER HOME RUN PCT. VS. LEFT-HANDED PITCHERS		CAREER STRIKEOUT PCT. VS. LEFT-HANDED PITCHERS	
Min. 150 Hits		*Min. 200 Total Bases*		*Min. 20 Home Runs*		*Min. 500 PA*	
Kirby Puckett	.335	Pete Incaviglia	.617	Eric Davis	8.94	Ted Sizemore	2.90
Tony Gwynn	.318	Eric Davis	.612	Mike Diaz	7.59	Dave Cash	3.05
Bob Watson	.318	Mike Schmidt	.583	Dave Kingman	7.58	Tim Foli	3.08
Jim Rice	.317	Ellis Valentine	.562	Rob Deer	7.41	Marty Barrett	3.19
Julio Franco	.315	Jack Clark	.543	Pete Incaviglia	7.31	Bob Bailor	3.41
Wade Boggs	.314	Jose Canseco	.539	Mike Schmidt	7.05	Manny Sanguillen	3.48
Paul Molitor	.314	Dave Winfield	.535	Ron Cey	6.56	Felix Millan	3.49
Keith Moreland	.314	George Bell	.535	Bill Schroeder	6.50	Doug Flynn	4.69
Don Mattingly	.313	Dwight Evans	.535	Tom Brunansky	6.22	Rennie Stennett	4.72
Pedro Guerrero	.311	Dale Murphy	.532	Ron Kittle	6.14	Rich Dauer	4.96
Pat Tabler	.311	Jim Rice	.532	Gorman Thomas	6.12	Bob Boone	5.09
Rod Carew	.310	Johnny Bench	.531	Ellis Valentine	6.07	Bucky Dent	5.09
Hubie Brooks	.309	George Foster	.530	Johnny Bench	6.03	Mickey Hatcher	5.09
Mitch Webster	.309	Pedro Guerrero	.528	Steve Balboni	5.93	Bruce Benedict	5.17
Ron LeFlore	.309	Ron Cey	.523	George Foster	5.93	Pete Rose	5.21
Tim Raines	.309	Cliff Johnson	.518	Dale Murphy	5.92	Don Kessinger	5.30
Ellis Valentine	.307	Dave Kingman	.518	Gene Tenace	5.90	Bill Russell	5.34
Buddy Bell	.307	Tom Brunansky	.518	Glenn Davis	5.85	Mario Guerrero	5.46
John Castino	.307	Don Mattingly	.517	John Wockenfuss	5.85	Tony Gwynn	5.48
Marty Barrett	.307	Lance Parrish	.514	Jose Canseco	5.73	Rob Andrews	5.48
Rickey Henderson	.307	Cal Ripken	.514	Lance Parrish	5.70	Jerry Terrell	5.54
Hal McRae	.305	Bill Robinson	.513	Bob Horner	5.69	Willie Randolph	5.69
Bill Madlock	.305	Andre Dawson	.513	Dave Winfield	5.58	Steve Nicosia	5.71
Gary Matthews	.305	Hal McRae	.511	Cliff Johnson	5.57	Bill Buckner	5.86
Wayne Nordhagen	.304	Kirby Puckett	.509	George Bell	5.50	Eric Soderholm	6.03

CAREER BATTING AVERAGE VS. RIGHT-HANDED PITCHERS		CAREER SLUGGING AVERAGE VS. RIGHT-HANDED PITCHERS		CAREER HOME RUN PCT. VS. RIGHT-HANDED PITCHERS		CAREER STRIKEOUT PCT. VS. RIGHT-HANDED PITCHERS	
Min. 250 Hits		*Min. 300 Total Bases*		*Min. 40 Home Runs*		*Min. 750 PA*	
Wade Boggs	.371	Darryl Strawberry	.575	Ken Phelps	7.94	Felix Millan	3.29
Tony Gwynn	.343	Don Mattingly	.557	Darryl Strawberry	6.99	Bill Buckner	3.78
Rod Carew	.341	George Brett	.551	Mike Schmidt	6.91	Dave Cash	4.30
Don Mattingly	.340	Reggie Smith	.539	Ron Kittle	6.90	Johnny Ray	4.68
George Brett	.330	Mike Schmidt	.534	Mike Pagliarulo	6.44	Tony Gwynn	4.73
Al Oliver	.326	Will Clark	.533	Dave Kingman	6.35	Larry Bowa	5.04
Lyman Bostock	.325	Willie Stargell	.532	Willie Stargell	6.19	Ken Oberkfell	5.09
Pedro Guerrero	.309	Wally Joyner	.530	Cory Snyder	6.18	Mike Scioscia	5.10
Tim Raines	.308	Fred Lynn	.530	Bob Horner	6.14	Jack Brohamer	5.17
Mike Easler	.307	Danny Tartabull	.528	Reggie Jackson	6.10	Mike Squires	5.17
Jerry Mumphrey	.307	Ken Phelps	.525	Reggie Smith	5.99	Ozzie Smith	5.21
Ken Griffey	.306	Alvin Davis	.522	Rob Deer	5.94	Terry Francona	5.28
Phil Bradley	.306	Kent Hrbek	.518	Danny Tartabull	5.85	Rich Dauer	5.31
Thurman Munson	.306	Larry Sheets	.516	Larry Sheets	5.82	Greg Gross	5.35
Wally Backman	.306	Pedro Guerrero	.515	Gorman Thomas	5.80	Al Oliver	5.37
Bake'McBride	.306	Kirk Gibson	.514	Eric Davis	5.79	Rusty Staub	5.40
Tony Fernandez	.306	Greg Walker	.513	Steve Balboni	5.75	Don Mattingly	5.45
Cecil Cooper	.305	Wade Boggs	.512	Oscar Gamble	5.67	George Brett	5.60
Keith Hernandez	.305	Mike Pagliarulo	.509	Jesse Barfield	5.53	Wade Boggs	5.64
Milt Thompson	.305	Jim Rice	.508	Tony Armas	5.50	Tom Poquette	5.72
Jose Cruz	.305	Bob Horner	.507	Wally Joyner	5.50	Pete Rose	5.83
Mickey Rivers	.305	Eddie Murray	.505	Graig Nettles	5.43	Dan Meyer	5.95
Fred Lynn	.305	Reggie Jackson	.503	Dale Murphy	5.42	Bob Bailor	5.98
Bill Madlock	.302	Leon Durham	.503	Jason Thompson	5.29	Duane Kuiper	5.99
Dave Parker	.302	George Bell	.503	Franklin Stubbs	5.24	Mario Guerrero	6.01

SINGLE-SEASON BATTING AVERAGE VS. LEFT-HANDED PITCHERS

Min. 40 Hits

Rennie Stennett, 1977	.435
Sixto Lezcano, 1979	.411
Tim Raines, 1987	.396
Steve Henderson, 1979	.395
Mike Vail, 1979	.395
Ken Griffey, 1976	.393
Gerald Young, 1987	.390
Bill Buckner, 1978	.389
Paul Molitor, 1979	.387
Brian Downing, 1979	.386
Chet Lemon, 1984	.384
Keith Moreland, 1983	.382
Buddy Bell, 1977	.382
Rico Carty, 1975	.381
Don Baylor, 1975	.380
Jack Clark, 1980	.380
Jeffrey Leonard, 1984	.380
Jose Cardenal, 1975	.379
Ray Knight, 1986	.379
Lee Lacy, 1980	.379
Gary Carter, 1977	.378
Ken Singleton, 1977	.373
Larry Herndon, 1987	.373
Joe Charboneau, 1980	.373
Dwight Evans, 1975	.372

SINGLE-SEASON BATTING AVERAGE VS. RIGHT-HANDED PITCHERS

Min. 75 Hits

George Brett, 1980	.437
Wade Boggs, 1983	.398
Rod Carew, 1977	.398
Rod Carew, 1975	.379
Wade Boggs, 1985	.377
Wade Boggs, 1987	.377
Tony Gwynn, 1987	.376
Tony Gwynn, 1984	.371
Oscar Gamble, 1979	.370
Kal Daniels, 1987	.370
Cecil Cooper, 1980	.365
Fred Lynn, 1979	.364
Paul Molitor, 1987	.363
Willie Wilson, 1982	.360
Wade Boggs, 1986	.359
Rod Carew, 1983	.358
Bill Madlock, 1975	.357
Mike Easler, 1980	.357
Wade Boggs, 1982	.356
Wade Boggs, 1984	.356
Willie McGee, 1985	.356
Rod Carew, 1982	.355
Al Oliver, 1979	.353
Miguel Dilone, 1980	.353
Keith Hernandez, 1979	.353

SINGLE-SEASON BATTING AVERAGE IN HOME GAMES

Min. 75 Hits

Wade Boggs, 1985	.418
Wade Boggs, 1987	.411
Rod Carew, 1977	.401
Juan Beniquez, 1984	.399
Wade Boggs, 1983	.397
Paul Molitor, 1987	.394
George Brett, 1980	.391
Tony Gwynn, 1987	.390
Rod Carew, 1975	.387
Fred Lynn, 1979	.386
Al Oliver, 1980	.385
Hal McRae, 1976	.382
Miguel Dilone, 1980	.378
Tony Gwynn, 1984	.376
Dion James, 1987	.376
Mike Easler, 1984	.375
George Brett, 1979	.373
Bill Buckner, 1977	.372
Jim Rice, 1979	.369
Fred Lynn, 1975	.368
George Brett, 1985	.368
Dave Parker, 1977	.368
George Brett, 1976	.367
Kirby Puckett, 1986	.367
Dave Parker, 1978	.367

SINGLE-SEASON BATTING AVERAGE IN ROAD GAMES

Min. 75 Hits

George Brett, 1980	.388
Cecil Cooper, 1980	.386
Rod Carew, 1977	.374
Johnny Ray, 1984	.370
Rod Carew, 1983	.369
Don Mattingly, 1986	.367
Don Mattingly, 1984	.364
Kirby Puckett, 1987	.362
Brian Downing, 1979	.360
Bob Watson, 1975	.358
Mickey Rivers, 1977	.358
Bill Madlock, 1975	.357
Wade Boggs, 1986	.356
Ken Singleton, 1977	.354
Ben Oglivie, 1980	.353
Willie McGee, 1985	.353
Pedro Guerrero, 1987	.352
Tony Gwynn, 1987	.352
Steve Sax, 1986	.352
Keith Hernandez, 1979	.350
Dave Winfield, 1984	.349
Enos Cabell, 1984	.348
Al Oliver, 1978	.348
Robin Yount, 1982	.347
Rod Carew, 1980	.347

CAREER HOME RUN PCT. IN HOME GAMES

Min. 25 Home Runs

Ken Phelps	8.39
Bob Horner	7.92
Mike Schmidt	6.93
Rob Deer	6.54
Dave Kingman	6.52
Dale Murphy	6.36
Oscar Gamble	6.31
Cory Snyder	6.28
Ron Kittle	6.26
Willie Stargell	6.26
Greg Luzinski	6.25
Larry Sheets	6.02
Jesse Barfield	5.97
Eric Davis	5.95
Will Clark	5.87
Gorman Thomas	5.87
Reggie Jackson	5.80
George Foster	5.71
Mike Pagliarulo	5.59
Darryl Strawberry	5.59
Rick Monday	5.48
Gary Alexander	5.46
Graig Nettles	5.40
Andre Thornton	5.37
Reggie Smith	5.34

CAREER HOME RUN PCT. IN ROAD GAMES

Min. 25 Home Runs

Mark McGwire	9.65
Eric Davis	7.78
Steve Balboni	7.06
Mike Schmidt	6.95
Darryl Strawberry	6.91
Ron Kittle	6.91
Dave Kingman	6.90
Rob Deer	6.25
Bill Schroeder	6.18
Ken Phelps	6.18
Gorman Thomas	5.93
Pedro Guerrero	5.78
Larry Sheets	5.61
Pete Incaviglia	5.59
George Bell	5.56
Danny Tartabull	5.56
Reggie Jackson	5.51
Jack Clark	5.35
Willie Stargell	5.35
Glenn Davis	5.32
Willie Aikens	5.29
Cory Snyder	5.27
Tom Brunansky	5.21
Lance Parrish	5.18
Howard Johnson	5.14

CAREER BATTING AVERAGE IN HOME GAMES

Min. 200 Hits

Wade Boggs	.384
Tony Gwynn	.345
George Brett	.340
Rod Carew	.334
Kirby Puckett	.330
Don Mattingly	.328
Al Oliver	.326
Jim Rice	.325
Pat Tabler	.321
Lyman Bostock	.318
Dave Parker	.313
Phil Bradley	.313
Kent Hrbek	.312
Tim Raines	.311
Paul Molitor	.311
Thurman Munson	.311
Fred Lynn	.308
Carney Lansford	.308
Ryne Sandberg	.308
Mike Easler	.308
Lou Brock	.306
Hal McRae	.306
Bill Madlock	.306
Pedro Guerrero	.306
Julio Franco	.304

CAREER BATTING AVERAGE IN ROAD GAMES

Min. 200 Hits

Don Mattingly	.333
Rod Carew	.328
Tony Gwynn	.324
Wade Boggs	.324
Pedro Guerrero	.314
Mickey Rivers	.308
Tim Raines	.306
Lyman Bostock	.305
Bob Watson	.305
Tony Fernandez	.304
Manny Sanguillen	.303
Cecil Cooper	.301
Bill Madlock	.301
Keith Hernandez	.299
Mitch Webster	.299
Ken Griffey	.298
Thurman Munson	.297
Gene Richards	.297
Ken Singleton	.296
Dave Winfield	.295
Eddie Murray	.294
Brook Jacoby	.294
Rickey Henderson	.294
Steve Sax	.293
Glenn Adams	.293

CAREER BATTING AVERAGE WITH RUNNERS ON BASE

Min. 200 Hits

Wade Boggs	.361
Rod Carew	.348
Tony Gwynn	.339
Don Mattingly	.327
Lyman Bostock	.326
Kirby Puckett	.324
George Brett	.323
Dave Parker	.322
Thurman Munson	.321
Pete Rose	.319
Keith Hernandez	.317
Al Oliver	.316
Cecil Cooper	.315
Pat Tabler	.315
Bill Madlock	.313
Tim Raines	.312
Pedro Guerrero	.311
Jim Rice	.309
Bill Buckner	.308
Mike Easler	.307
Eddie Murray	.307
Manny Sanguillen	.307
Steve Garvey	.306
Bruce Bochte	.305
Kent Hrbek	.305

SINGLE-SEASON BATTING AVERAGE WITH RUNNERS ON BASE

Min. 75 Hits

Rod Carew, 1977	.422
Tony Gwynn, 1984	.406
George Brett, 1980	.400
Garry Templeton, 1979	.388
Wade Boggs, 1985	.387
Fred Lynn, 1979	.387
Keith Hernandez, 1979	.383
Dave Parker, 1978	.383
Wade Boggs, 1986	.379
Garry Templeton, 1977	.378
Rod Carew, 1975	.377
Robin Yount, 1987	.376
Mickey Rivers, 1977	.373
Bill Madlock, 1975	.370
Manny Sanguillen, 1975	.370
Bill Madlock, 1976	.368
Hal McRae, 1976	.368
George Brett, 1985	.367
Hal McRae, 1982	.366
Pete Rose, 1975	.366
Fred Lynn, 1975	.365
Ken Griffey, 1976	.362
Cecil Cooper, 1980	.362
Eddie Murray, 1985	.361
Dave Parker, 1976	.360

CAREER BATTING AVERAGE WITH RUNNERS IN SCORING POSITION

Min. 100 Hits

Wade Boggs	.361
Rod Carew	.345
Pat Tabler	.338
Tony Gwynn	.329
Thurman Munson	.329
Don Mattingly	.326
Lyman Bostock	.324
Pete Rose	.323
Al Oliver	.323
George Brett	.322
Broderick Perkins	.318
Rennie Stennett	.315
Cecil Cooper	.315
Jim Rice	.314
Lou Piniella	.314
Bill Madlock	.314
Scott Fletcher	.313
Dane Iorg	.313
Lamar Johnson	.312
Tony Fernandez	.310
Bake McBride	.309
Manny Sanguillen	.307
Larry Hisle	.307
Kirby Puckett	.307
Ted Simmons	.306

SINGLE-SEASON BATTING AVERAGE WITH RUNNERS IN SCORING POSITION

Min. 50 Hits

George Brett, 1980	.466
Cecil Cooper, 1980	.421
Tony Gwynn, 1984	.418
Bill Madlock, 1976	.414
Ken Griffey, 1976	.412
Pete Rose, 1975	.412
Don Mattingly, 1984	.405
Fred Lynn, 1975	.400
Mickey Rivers, 1977	.400
Kent Hrbek, 1982	.398
Wade Boggs, 1985	.392
Robin Yount, 1982	.392
Joe Morgan, 1976	.391
Willie McGee, 1985	.391
Hal McRae, 1982	.383
Pat Tabler, 1987	.383
Rod Carew, 1977	.382
Bake McBride, 1980	.380
Bill Robinson, 1977	.380
Garry Templeton, 1977	.379
Thurman Munson, 1975	.376
Rod Carew, 1978	.375
Ted Simmons, 1983	.375
Dave Winfield, 1979	.371
Eddie Murray, 1985	.370

CAREER BATTING AVERAGE WITH 2 OUTS AND RUNNERS ON BASE

Min. 75 Hits

Wade Boggs	.344
Kirby Puckett	.337
Larry Hisle	.321
Thurman Munson	.320
Tony Gwynn	.312
Al Oliver	.311
Wally Backman	.310
Dave Parker	.309
Don Mattingly	.309
Tony Fernandez	.308
Larry Biittner	.307
Cecil Cooper	.305
Jose Cardenal	.304
Rico Carty	.303
Bill Madlock	.302
Rod Carew	.301
Gene Richards	.301
Lyman Bostock	.301
Harold Baines	.301
Alan Trammell	.299
Donnie Hill	.299
Pete Rose	.298
Oscar Gamble	.297
Keith Hernandez	.297
Willie Montanez	.295

SINGLE-SEASON BATTING AVERAGE WITH 2 OUTS AND RUNNERS ON BASE

Min. 30 Hits

Barry Bonnell, 1977	.437
Lee Lacy, 1984	.432
Al Oliver, 1980	.424
Bruce Bochte, 1982	.418
Dave Parker, 1986	.412
Pat Tabler, 1987	.407
Ted Simmons, 1983	.404
Sixto Lezcano, 1979	.402
Garry Templeton, 1979	.400
Ray Knight, 1986	.400
Rod Carew, 1977	.398
Harold Baines, 1985	.391
Greg Gross, 1975	.390
Lee Mazzilli, 1979	.390
Larry Parrish, 1979	.388
Rod Carew, 1975	.388
Joe Rudi, 1976	.386
Frank Taveras, 1978	.386
Rennie Stennett, 1975	.383
Larry Hisle, 1978	.379
Steve Garvey, 1979	.377
Rod Carew, 1978	.376
Garry Templeton, 1977	.376
Steve Kemp, 1980	.375
Ozzie Guillen, 1986	.375

CAREER BATTING AVERAGE WITH 2 OUTS & RUNNERS IN SCORING POSITION

Min. 50 Hits

Wade Boggs	.344
Larry Hisle	.332
Tony Fernandez	.325
Thurman Munson	.325
Al Oliver	.320
Kirby Puckett	.316
Lamar Johnson	.307
Jose Canseco	.305
Lyman Bostock	.304
Gene Richards	.303
Pete Rose	.303
Lou Piniella	.303
John Castino	.302
Dane Iorg	.302
Terry Harper	.302
Bill Madlock	.302
Donnie Hill	.301
Jose Morales	.301
Pat Tabler	.300
George Brett	.299
Rod Carew	.299
Cecil Cooper	.297
Rudy Law	.297
Gary Ward	.297
Marty Barrett	.296

SINGLE-SEASON BATTING AVERAGE WITH 2 OUTS & RUNNERS IN SCORING POSITION

Min. 20 Hits

Kent Hrbek, 1982	.466
Bruce Bochte, 1982	.457
Al Oliver, 1980	.446
Rod Carew, 1975	.440
Pat Tabler, 1987	.440
Ted Simmons, 1983	.437
George Foster, 1981	.426
Chris Speier, 1978	.426
Dave Parker, 1986	.419
Rod Carew, 1978	.414
Cecil Cooper, 1980	.414
Rod Carew, 1977	.412
Lee Mazzilli, 1978	.412
Joe Rudi, 1976	.410
Lyman Bostock, 1978	.407
Dave Winfield, 1979	.407
Mike Ivie, 1979	.404
Tony Fernandez, 1986	.404
Larry Hisle, 1978	.403
Lee Lacy, 1984	.400
Paul Molitor, 1986	.400
Rusty Staub, 1976	.397
Ray Knight, 1986	.396
Pete Rose, 1975	.395
Barry Bonnell, 1977	.393

CAREER BATTING AVERAGE IN LATE-INNING PRESSURE SITUATIONS

Min. 50 Hits

Tim Raines	.352
Wade Boggs	.348
Tony Gwynn	.346
Ed Romero	.333
Will Clark	.331
Tony Fernandez	.329
George Brett	.324
Joe Lefebvre	.320
Ken Griffey	.319
Rickey Henderson	.318
Cecil Cooper	.318
Steve Sax	.318
Chris Brown	.315
Milt Thompson	.313
Eddie Murray	.312
Ron LeFlore	.312
Kirby Puckett	.312
Tom Paciorek	.309
Thurman Munson	.309
Mickey Rivers	.309
Jose Cardenal	.309
Mike Ivie	.308
Thad Bosley	.308
Mike Easler	.305
Eric Soderholm	.305

SINGLE-SEASON BATTING AVERAGE IN LATE-INNING PRESSURE SITUATIONS

Min. 25 Hits

Manny Trillo, 1981	.466
Bill Madlock, 1975	.464
Mickey Rivers, 1977	.439
Wade Boggs, 1986	.433
George Brett, 1976	.433
Alan Trammell, 1987	.431
Steve Kemp, 1979	.429
Ken Griffey, 1975	.423
Tom Paciorek, 1976	.419
Mike Easler, 1984	.416
Scot Thompson, 1979	.413
Cecil Cooper, 1982	.412
Lloyd Moseby, 1983	.410
Luis Salazar, 1981	.408
Bill Buckner, 1984	.403
Chris Chambliss, 1981	.403
Rick Manning, 1983	.402
Ken Griffey, 1986	.402
Cal Ripken, 1984	.398
Bill Buckner, 1978	.397
Will Clark, 1986	.397
Wade Boggs, 1985	.395
Tim Raines, 1987	.394
Rickey Henderson, 1983	.391
Dale Murphy, 1984	.391

CAREER HOME RUN PCT. IN LATE-INNING PRESSURE SITUATIONS

Min. 10 Home Runs

Gary Alexander	7.80
Ken Phelps	7.73
Steve Balboni	7.17
Dave Kingman	6.90
Craig Kusick	6.78
Cory Snyder	6.71
Eddie Murray	6.54
Mike Pagliarulo	6.37
Tony Armas	6.09
Andre Thornton	6.01
Mike Schmidt	5.85
Kirk Gibson	5.69
Graig Nettles	5.66
Howard Johnson	5.61
Pedro Guerrero	5.61
Jim Presley	5.58
Darryl Strawberry	5.57
Oscar Gamble	5.57
Reggie Smith	5.56
Bernie Carbo	5.41
Richie Zisk	5.32
Willie Stargell	5.25
Mel Hall	5.24
Cliff Johnson	5.24
Mike Young	5.24

CAREER BATTING AVG. IN LATE-INNING PRESSURE SITUATIONS WITH RUNNERS IN SCORING POSITION

Min. 25 Hits

Eric Soderholm	.429
Eddie Murray	.387
Wade Boggs	.373
Willie Montanez	.355
Lee May	.352
Cal Ripken	.351
Pete Rose	.346
George Bell	.343
Oscar Gamble	.343
Chili Davis	.342
Thurman Munson	.341
Rickey Henderson	.340
Mookie Wilson	.339
Bruce Bochte	.337
Mike Ivie	.333
Reggie Smith	.333
Don Mattingly	.333
Ozzie Virgil	.333
Joe Carter	.333
Dave Chalk	.333
Garth Iorg	.333
Ken Griffey	.332
Tim Raines	.331
Cesar Geronimo	.330
Rod Carew	.328

CAREER BATTING AVERAGE IN LATE-INNING PRESSURE SITUATIONS WITH RUNNERS ON BASE

Min. 25 Hits

Wade Boggs	.374
Jose Canseco	.372
Mike Ivie	.370
Ed Romero	.363
Eddie Murray	.362
Dickie Thon	.361
Eric Soderholm	.348
Garth Iorg	.342
Manny Mota	.342
Tim Raines	.340
Bill Buckner	.339
Chris Brown	.337
Jose Cardenal	.335
Reggie Smith	.333
Tony Gwynn	.333
Thad Bosley	.333
Phil Bradley	.333
Dave Rader	.333
Pete Rose	.332
George Bell	.331
Thurman Munson	.331
Vince Coleman	.331
Gerald Perry	.330
Rickey Henderson	.330
U.L. Washington	.329

SINGLE-SEASON BATTING AVERAGE IN LATE-INNING PRESSURE SITUATIONS WITH RUNNERS ON BASE

Min. 10 Hits

Rance Mulliniks, 1984	.684
Eddie Murray, 1985	.567
Bill Buckner, 1984	.563
Rey Quinones, 1987	.538
Rowland Office, 1975	.536
Rusty Staub, 1981	.536
Jack Clark, 1984	.526
Ron Oester, 1981	.524
Pedro Guerrero, 1980	.520
Manny Trillo, 1981	.520
Carl Yastrzemski, 1975	.500
Ken Griffey, 1975	.500
Bernie Carbo, 1976	.500
Mickey Rivers, 1977	.500
Ken Singleton, 1977	.500
Pete Rose, 1977	.500
Barry Foote, 1979	.500
Glenn Adams, 1979	.500
Dan Ford, 1983	.500
Paul Molitor, 1987	.500
Rob Deer, 1987	.500
Rick Manning, 1983	.486
Cesar Geronimo, 1976	.485
Mike Diaz, 1986	.483
Toby Harrah, 1985	.481

CAREER BATTING AVERAGE IN LATE-INNING PRESSURE SITUATIONS WITH 2 OUTS AND RUNNERS ON BASE

Min. 15 Hits

Garth Iorg	.446
Eric Soderholm	.429
Marty Perez	.405
Jose Canseco	.400
Mike Ivie	.387
Wade Boggs	.386
Dave Rader	.383
Phil Bradley	.366
Tim Raines	.365
Thurman Munson	.365
Eddie Murray	.361
Steve Henderson	.360
Oscar Gamble	.355
Jesse Barfield	.348
Vance Law	.346
Glenn Adams	.345
H. Pat Kelly	.344
Ed Ott	.343
Alan Trammell	.341
Manny Sanguillen	.341
U.L. Washington	.338
Dave Revering	.333
Rico Carty	.333
Pete Rose	.332
Rusty Staub	.325

CAREER BATTING AVG. IN LATE-INNING PRESSURE SITUATIONS WITH 2 OUTS AND RUNNERS IN SCORING POSITION

Min. 10 Hits

Jose Canseco	.464
Eric Soderholm	.444
Garth Iorg	.441
Marty Perez	.435
Jim Norris	.417
Rusty Staub	.405
Gary Pettis	.400
Cesar Geronimo	.391
Thurman Munson	.387
Chili Davis	.383
Vance Law	.382
Oscar Gamble	.381
Eddie Murray	.378
Jose Cruz	.376
Willie Horton	.373
Pete Rose	.372
Don Mattingly	.364
Dickie Thon	.364
Wade Boggs	.360
Kent Hrbek	.357
Ernie Whitt	.357
Steve Henderson	.356
Gerald Perry	.355
Bo Diaz	.354
Mike A. Marshall	.353

HIGHEST CAREER RATIO OF GROUND OUTS TO AIR OUTS

Min. 1,000 PA

Milt Thompson	2.69
Wally Backman	2.55
Steve Jeltz	2.31
Gary Pettis	2.25
Willie McGee	2.17
Juan Bonilla	2.10
Steve Henderson	2.04
Duane Kuiper	2.02
Billy North	2.02
Steve Carlton	1.99
Gene Richards	1.91
Rod Carew	1.89
Steve Sax	1.88
Tony Gwynn	1.88
Alan Wiggins	1.84
Ron LeFlore	1.82
Miguel Dilone	1.82
Phil Bradley	1.80
Pete Rose	1.79
Garry Templeton	1.77
Jerry Mumphrey	1.75
Lyman Bostock	1.73
Curtis Wilkerson	1.72
Mookie Wilson	1.71
Julio Cruz	1.70

LOWEST CAREER RATIO OF GROUND OUTS TO AIR OUTS

Min. 1,000 PA

Rob Deer	0.58
Franklin Stubbs	0.62
Jim Dwyer	0.63
Gene Tenace	0.63
Ken Phelps	0.65
Joe Morgan	0.65
Andre Thornton	0.65
Darrell Evans	0.65
Howard Johnson	0.66
Gary Redus	0.66
Don Baylor	0.66
Steve Balboni	0.69
Richie Hebner	0.70
Mike Schmidt	0.71
Buck Martinez	0.71
Dave Revering	0.72
Tom Brunansky	0.72
Tim Hulett	0.72
Ron Kittle	0.73
Bobby Murcer	0.73
Joe Carter	0.73
Jerry White	0.74
Dave Kingman	0.75
Tony Solaita	0.75
George Bell	0.75

CAREER BATTING AVERAGE IN DAY GAMES

Min. 100 Hits

Rod Carew	.347
Wade Boggs	.346
Don Mattingly	.332
Tony Gwynn	.326
Willie McGee	.325
Tim Raines	.323
George Brett	.318
Will Clark	.318
Bake McBride	.316
Al Oliver	.315
Ken Griffey	.315
Lyman Bostock	.313
Thad Bosley	.312
Jerry Grote	.312
Wayne Krenchicki	.312
Thurman Munson	.311
Jose Morales	.311
Reggie Smith	.310
Gene Richards	.309
Kirby Puckett	.309
Paul Molitor	.309
Carney Lansford	.307
Andre Dawson	.307
Mel Hall	.307
Steve Kemp	.306

CAREER BATTING AVERAGE IN NIGHT GAMES

Min. 100 Hits

Wade Boggs	.358
Tony Gwynn	.339
Don Mattingly	.330
Kal Daniels	.324
Rod Carew	.324
Mike Greenwell	.322
Dion James	.319
John Kruk	.318
Pedro Guerrero	.317
George Brett	.315
Mike Aldrete	.314
Kirby Puckett	.312
Lyman Bostock	.310
Mickey Rivers	.309
Kevin Seitzer	.308
Jim Rice	.306
Tony Fernandez	.306
Al Oliver	.306
Cecil Cooper	.304
Manny Sanguillen	.303
Bill Madlock	.302
Phil Bradley	.301
Tim Raines	.301
Mike Easler	.301
Rick Peters	.301

CAREER BATTING AVERAGE ON GRASS SURFACES

Min. 150 Hits

Wade Boggs	.357
Tony Gwynn	.339
Rod Carew	.331
Don Mattingly	.328
Al Oliver	.318
Lyman Bostock	.313
Will Clark	.313
Keith Hernandez	.310
Tim Raines	.309
Pedro Guerrero	.307
Jim Rice	.306
Thurman Munson	.306
Bob Watson	.305
Pat Tabler	.305
Bill Madlock	.303
Steve Garvey	.301
Andre Dawson	.301
Cecil Cooper	.301
Jose Cardenal	.300
Reggie Smith	.300
Paul Molitor	.300
Jerry Mumphrey	.300
Dion James	.300
Ryne Sandberg	.299
John Kruk	.299

CAREER BATTING AVERAGE ON ARTIFICIAL TURF

Min. 150 Hits

Don Mattingly	.346
Wade Boggs	.339
George Brett	.338
Kevin Seitzer	.337
Rod Carew	.333
Tony Gwynn	.323
Kirby Puckett	.321
Pedro Guerrero	.317
Al Bumbry	.314
Alan Trammell	.314
Mickey Rivers	.312
Cal Ripken	.312
Von Joshua	.311
Phil Bradley	.310
Tim Raines	.308
Jim Gantner	.308
Lee Lacy	.308
Mickey Hatcher	.307
Tony Fernandez	.307
Ken Griffey	.306
Mike Easler	.306
Steve Sax	.305
Jeff Stone	.304
Dave Parker	.304
Bill Madlock	.304

SINGLE-SEASON BATTING AVERAGE ON GRASS SURFACES

Min. 60 Hits

George Brett, 1980	.396
Rod Carew, 1977	.393
Paul Molitor, 1987	.376
Tony Gwynn, 1987	.374
Pete Rose, 1979	.373
Ray Knight, 1983	.370
Wade Boggs, 1987	.369
Ken Griffey, 1976	.368
Rod Carew, 1975	.367
Keith Hernandez, 1979	.366
Gary Gaetti, 1986	.364
Wade Boggs, 1983	.364
Wade Boggs, 1985	.363
Cecil Cooper, 1980	.363
Oscar Gamble, 1979	.362
Pat Sheridan, 1984	.358
Dan Gladden, 1984	.357
Wade Boggs, 1982	.354
Wade Boggs, 1986	.352
Juan Beniquez, 1984	.352
Alan Trammell, 1987	.352
Bill Buckner, 1978	.351
Fred Lynn, 1979	.350
Tony Gwynn, 1984	.349
Don Mattingly, 1984	.348

SINGLE-SEASON BATTING AVERAGE ON ARTIFICIAL TURF

Min. 60 Hits

Bill Madlock, 1975	.398
Steve Sax, 1986	.387
George Brett, 1980	.386
Hal McRae, 1976	.382
George Brett, 1979	.369
George Brett, 1976	.367
Keith Hernandez, 1985	.364
George Brett, 1978	.357
Lee Lacy, 1980	.356
Willie McGee, 1985	.356
George Brett, 1981	.356
Greg Gross, 1983	.356
Pete Rose, 1976	.354
Bake McBride, 1976	.354
George Brett, 1975	.352
Bill Madlock, 1981	.352
Kirby Puckett, 1986	.352
George Brett, 1985	.352
Mike Easler, 1980	.349
Kent Hrbek, 1984	.349
Willie Wilson, 1982	.349
Pete Rose, 1981	.348
Joe Morgan, 1975	.347
Pete LaCock, 1978	.347
Garry Maddox, 1976	.347

CAREER ON-BASE AVERAGE LEADING OFF INNINGS

Min. 200 PA

Kal Daniels	.444
Wade Boggs	.443
Tony Gwynn	.403
Rickey Henderson	.395
Rod Carew	.392
Willie Randolph	.392
Phil Bradley	.390
Tim Raines	.386
Mike Schmidt	.385
Pepe Mangual	.384
Greg Gross	.384
Mike Hargrove	.382
Tony Solaita	.382
Pedro Guerrero	.381
Bob Stinson	.377
Bobby Grich	.377
Jack Clark	.376
Gene Tenace	.375
Otto Velez	.375
Bernie Carbo	.374
Bobby Bonds	.374
Don Mattingly	.374
Joe Morgan	.372
Johnny Grubb	.372
Brian Downing	.371

SINGLE-SEASON ON-BASE AVERAGE LEADING OFF INNINGS

Min. 100 PA

Rod Carew, 1982	.523
Andre Thornton, 1975	.519
Carlton Fisk, 1977	.504
Wade Boggs, 1983	.494
Toby Harrah, 1981	.491
Joe Morgan, 1975	.470
Ozzie Smith, 1987	.469
Wade Boggs, 1985	.468
Ken Griffey, 1977	.466
Phil Bradley, 1987	.463
Kirby Puckett, 1987	.462
Willie Randolph, 1980	.457
Wade Boggs, 1987	.457
Hal McRae, 1977	.456
Mike Hargrove, 1977	.453
Mitchell Page, 1977	.452
Cal Ripken, 1984	.452
Kal Daniels, 1987	.450
Willie Randolph, 1985	.448
Jose Cruz, 1979	.448
Richie Zisk, 1981	.447
Von Hayes, 1986	.444
Johnny Grubb, 1976	.443
John Stearns, 1977	.442
Eric Davis, 1987	.442

CAREER WALK PCT. LEADING OFF INNINGS

Min. 25 Walks

Jim Wynn	19.71
Gene Tenace	15.78
Joe Morgan	15.34
Bernie Carbo	15.05
Pepe Mangual	14.76
Rob Deer	14.56
Otto Velez	14.55
Glenn Borgmann	14.35
John Cangelosi	14.33
Willie Randolph	14.26
Dwayne Murphy	14.26
Jerry Hairston	14.22
Rickey Henderson	14.16
Tommy Hutton	14.00
Joe Ferguson	13.84
Mike Hargrove	13.67
Lee Mazzilli	13.64
Billy North	13.62
Bud Harrelson	13.56
Ken Phelps	13.35
Merv Rettenmund	13.27
Toby Harrah	13.17
Tony Solaita	13.16
Rick Peters	13.13
Steve Jeltz	13.08

SINGLE-SEASON WALK PCT. LEADING OFF INNINGS

Min. 15 Walks

John Cangelosi, 1987	24.77
Jim Wynn, 1975	23.85
Jack Clark, 1987	23.39
Dwayne Murphy, 1987	23.08
Lee Mazzilli, 1982	22.97
Lee Mazzilli, 1983	22.50
Joe Morgan, 1975	22.00
Gene Tenace, 1977	21.43
Dwayne Murphy, 1981	21.43
Andre Thornton, 1975	21.30
Carlton Fisk, 1977	21.17
Bernie Carbo, 1975	21.05
Jerry Hairston, 1984	20.55
Mike Scioscia, 1985	20.54
Gary Matthews, 1984	19.82
Toby Harrah, 1981	19.81
Steve Kemp, 1981	19.74
Toby Harrah, 1985	19.71
Johnny Briggs, 1975	19.15
Gene Tenace, 1979	19.05
Mike Hargrove, 1977	18.95
Willie Randolph, 1980	18.78
Darrell Porter, 1975	18.75
Willie Randolph, 1981	18.75
Jose Oquendo, 1987	18.75

CAREER BATTING AVERAGE WITH BASES LOADED

Min. 15 Hits

Pat Tabler	.527
Rudy Law	.469
Miguel Dilone	.436
Biff Pocoroba	.435
Rick Bosetti	.429
Eddie Murray	.426
Lou Brock	.423
Ken Singleton	.417
Ellis Valentine	.417
Bill Madlock	.411
Rico Carty	.404
Lee May	.402
Jay Johnstone	.400
Denny Walling	.396
Oscar Gamble	.392
Tony Gwynn	.390
Larry Hisle	.389
Rod Carew	.388
Wade Boggs	.386
Dale Berra	.383
Richie Zisk	.382
Alan Trammell	.380
Johnny Grubb	.379
Lloyd Moseby	.376
Mike Young	.375

CAREER RRF RATIO (PER PA) WITH BASES LOADED

Min. 30 RRF

Darryl Motley	1.13
Eric Davis	1.12
Eddie Murray	1.12
John Milner	1.10
Larry Sheets	1.09
Pat Tabler	1.08
George Bell	1.07
Greg Walker	1.06
Biff Pocoroba	1.06
Terry Crowley	1.05
Mike Cubbage	1.04
Dane Iorg	1.03
Rico Carty	1.00
Lee Stanton	1.00
Roy Howell	0.99
Oscar Gamble	0.99
H. Pat Kelly	0.98
Jose Cruz	0.98
Dale Berra	0.98
Steve Garvey	0.98
Joe Rudi	0.98
Don Mattingly	0.96
John Wockenfuss	0.96
Rod Carew	0.96
Lee May	0.95

CAREER WALK PCT. WITH BASES LOADED

Min. 10 Walks

Oscar Gamble	17.65
Mike Hargrove	17.48
Sixto Lezcano	17.12
Alvin Davis	16.13
Gene Tenace	16.09
Leon Durham	15.71
Pete Rose	15.57
Darrell Porter	15.32
Gary Roenicke	15.29
Ken Oberkfell	14.63
Joe Morgan	14.55
Terry Puhl	13.16
Jeff Burroughs	12.90
Dwight Evans	12.43
Dan Driessen	12.40
Carl Yastrzemski	12.15
Jim Gantner	12.05
Rickey Henderson	11.83
Darrell Evans	11.80
Dave Winfield	11.63
Bobby Murcer	11.58
Ken Singleton	11.48
Dave Lopes	10.91
Brian Downing	10.81
Ruppert Jones	10.68

CAREER STRIKEOUT PCT. WITH BASES LOADED

Min. 50 PA

Rico Carty	1.43
Ozzie Smith	1.65
Jim Spencer	1.89
Biff Pocoroba	1.92
Jerry Morales	2.02
Craig Reynolds	2.13
Dave Cash	3.03
Mike Scioscia	3.57
Bruce Benedict	3.85
Lyman Bostock	3.92
Bill Buckner	3.98
Jose Cardenal	4.00
Ellis Valentine	4.00
Doug Flynn	4.08
Rich Dauer	4.35
Brett Butler	4.41
Bill Madlock	4.46
Frank Taveras	4.62
Lenny Randle	4.62
Larry Bowa	4.81
Jose Cruz	4.88
Ken Oberkfell	4.88
Bo Diaz	4.95
Toby Harrah	5.19
Lou Brock	5.36

CAREER PCT. OF RUNNERS DRIVEN IN FROM SCORING POSITION

Min. 100 RRF

Don Mattingly	.375
Wally Joyner	.356
Larry Sheets	.355
Wade Boggs	.355
Thurman Munson	.352
Dane Iorg	.352
Broderick Perkins	.349
Al Oliver	.349
Rusty Staub	.349
George Brett	.348
Cecil Cooper	.347
Rod Carew	.346
Kent Hrbek	.345
Ted Simmons	.345
Keith Hernandez	.341
Lou Piniella	.341
Pat Tabler	.340
Rico Carty	.340
Mike Hargrove	.340
Eddie Murray	.339
Rick Leach	.339
Dave Parker	.339
Dave Winfield	.338
Larry Hisle	.338
Bill Madlock	.335

SINGLE-SEASON PCT. OF RUNNERS DRIVEN IN FROM SCORING POSITION

Min. 50 RRF

George Brett, 1980	.507
Bill Buckner, 1981	.476
Cecil Cooper, 1980	.470
Bill Madlock, 1976	.448
Dave Parker, 1976	.430
Eddie Murray, 1985	.428
Bill Buckner, 1978	.427
Richie Hebner, 1980	.422
Cecil Cooper, 1976	.420
Bake McBride, 1980	.419
Buddy Bell, 1984	.418
Larry Parrish, 1986	.415
John Milner, 1976	.412
Harold Baines, 1987	.412
Rod Carew, 1977	.411
Ted Simmons, 1983	.410
Tommy Herr, 1985	.409
Rod Carew, 1975	.408
Joe Morgan, 1978	.408
Joe Morgan, 1976	.408
Pat Tabler, 1985	.407
Kent Hrbek, 1984	.405
Ray Knight, 1986	.403
Hal McRae, 1982	.402
Bill Madlock, 1979	.401

CAREER PCT. OF RUNNERS DRIVEN IN FROM SCORING POSITION IN LATE-INNING PRESSURE SITUATIONS

Min. 20 RRF

Jose Canseco	.444
Eric Soderholm	.427
Eddie Murray	.423
Jim Essian	.403
Jim Norris	.392
Pedro Guerrero	.384
Wade Boggs	.380
Pete LaCock	.379
Lenn Sakata	.377
Eddie Milner	.377
Gerald Perry	.375
Rick Leach	.373
Ozzie Virgil	.373
Don Mattingly	.372
Carmelo Martinez	.371
Mike Hargrove	.369
Rico Carty	.364
Bill Melton	.361
Rusty Staub	.357
Kevin Bass	.355
Reggie Smith	.354
Ellis Valentine	.352
Candy Maldonado	.351
Oscar Gamble	.349
Garth Iorg	.346

SINGLE-SEASON RDI OPPORTUNITIES FROM SCORING POSITION

Tony Perez, 1975	268
Willie McGee, 1987	260
Don Baylor, 1979	257
Jim Rice, 1986	250
Tim Wallach, 1987	247
Johnny Bench, 1975	246
George Foster, 1976	245
Julio Franco, 1985	244
George Foster, 1977	243
Bill Buckner, 1986	242
Keith Moreland, 1985	238
Jerry Morales, 1975	236
Bob Watson, 1976	236
Lance Parrish, 1983	235
Ruben Sierra, 1987	233
Tommy Herr, 1985	232
Joe Carter, 1987	232
Greg Luzinski, 1975	230
Thurman Munson, 1976	229
Cecil Cooper, 1983	229
Jim Rice, 1975	228
Jim Rice, 1984	228
Willie Montanez, 1975	227
Steve Garvey, 1978	227
Rusty Staub, 1978	227

CAREER PCT. OF RUNNERS DRIVEN IN FROM 3D BASE WITH LESS THAN 2 OUTS

Min. 40 RRF

Broderick Perkins	.753
Wally Joyner	.732
Don Mattingly	.730
Rico Carty	.722
Ed Kranepool	.720
Tony Solaita	.719
Rod Carew	.719
Wade Boggs	.713
Jerry Hairston	.699
Tony Gwynn	.697
Manny Sanguillen	.695
Pat Tabler	.693
Al Oliver	.692
Mike Hargrove	.689
Dave Winfield	.689
Rusty Staub	.686
Cal Ripken	.686
Wayne Krenchicki	.682
George Brett	.681
Bill Madlock	.680
Larry Sheets	.677
Pete Rose	.677
Hal McRae	.675
Toby Harrah	.674
Fred Lynn	.670

SINGLE-SEASON PCT. OF RUNNERS DRIVEN IN FROM 3D BASE WITH LESS THAN 2 OUTS

Min. 15 RRF

Ben Oglivie, 1986	.913
Rod Carew, 1983	.900
Toby Harrah, 1981	.889
Bill Madlock, 1986	.880
Elliott Maddox, 1978	.875
Bill Madlock, 1976	.868
Dave Revering, 1979	.857
Kevin McReynolds, 1984	.852
Al Oliver, 1983	.846
Jerry Mumphrey, 1985	.846
Sid Bream, 1986	.846
Paul Molitor, 1978	.842
Dave Bergman, 1984	.842
Pat Tabler, 1985	.840
George Brett, 1980	.838
Richie Hebner, 1976	.833
Rich Dauer, 1978	.833
Denny Walling, 1978	.833
Brian Downing, 1982	.833
Alan Wiggins, 1984	.833
Juan Beniquez, 1987	.833
Herm Winningham, 1987	.833
Jose Oquendo, 1987	.833
Buddy Bell, 1984	.829
Jerry Remy, 1982	.826

CAREER PCT. OF RUNNERS DRIVEN IN FROM 1ST BASE

Min. 30 RRF

Willie Stargell	.110
Eric Davis	.103
Darryl Strawberry	.102
Mike Schmidt	.099
Jose Canseco	.096
Danny Tartabull	.094
Alvin Davis	.094
Greg Luzinski	.092
Glenn Davis	.092
Larry Hisle	.091
Dave Kingman	.091
Hal McRae	.089
Dale Murphy	.089
Dave Parker	.088
Ken Phelps	.088
Greg Walker	.087
Steve Balboni	.087
Reggie Jackson	.087
Oscar Gamble	.086
Nick Esasky	.086
Fred Lynn	.086
Bill Robinson	.086
George Brett	.085
Lance Parrish	.085
Bob Horner	.084

SINGLE-SEASON RUNNERS DRIVEN IN FROM 1ST BASE

Hal McRae, 1982	36
George Foster, 1977	31
Jim Rice, 1978	29
Don Mattingly, 1985	29
Greg Luzinski, 1977	28
Alvin Davis, 1984	28
Keith Hernandez, 1979	27
Joe Carter, 1986	26
Jim Rice, 1983	25
Fred Lynn, 1979	24
Steve Garvey, 1979	24
Dave Kingman, 1984	24
Jose Canseco, 1986	24
Jeff Burroughs, 1977	23
Ron Cey, 1977	23
Jim Rice, 1979	23
Tony Armas, 1980	23
Tony Perez, 1980	23
Mike Schmidt, 1983	23
Eddie Murray, 1985	23
Darryl Strawberry, 1987	23
Fred Lynn, 1975	22
Johnny Bench, 1975	22
Bob Watson, 1977	22
Dave Parker, 1978	22

CAREER OPP. BATTING AVERAGE VS. LEFT-HANDED BATTERS

Min. 400 PA

Atlee Hammaker	.184
Jesse Orosco	.187
Mark Langston	.195
Rod Scurry	.199
Mark Davis	.200
Pat Underwood	.201
Bill Scherrer	.201
Bob Lacey	.201
Dave Dravecky	.207
Nolan Ryan	.208
Willie Hernandez	.209
John Candelaria	.213
Dave Smith	.213
Craig Lefferts	.214
Al Holland	.215
Mike Norris	.216
John Fulgham	.216
Bob McClure	.217
Bruce Sutter	.217
Dwight Gooden	.218
Joe Sambito	.218
Larry Gura	.218
Bob Shirley	.219
Frank DiPino	.219
John Tudor	.221

CAREER OPP. HOME RUN PCT. VS. LEFT-HANDED BATTERS

Min. 400 PA

Doug Sisk	0.43
Mickey Lolich	0.46
Bert Roberge	0.51
Frank Williams	0.56
Dave Smith	0.61
Jim Crawford	0.64
Paul Mirabella	0.68
Bruce Berenyi	0.69
Joe Sambito	0.69
Jeff Lahti	0.80
Gary Lavelle	0.82
Greg Minton	0.88
Jesse Orosco	0.91
Donnie Moore	0.93
Ricky Horton	0.94
Ken Howell	0.94
Pedro Borbon	0.94
Danny Jackson	0.95
Andy Hassler	0.95
Bob Shirley	0.99
Dwight Gooden	1.00
Jerry Reuss	1.03
Steve Trout	1.03
John Fulgham	1.03
Tippy Martinez	1.04

CAREER OPP. WALK PCT. VS. LEFT-HANDED BATTERS

Min. 400 PA

Steve Howe	3.06
Gary Nolan	3.23
Bill Long	4.18
Scott McGregor	4.18
Dick Bosman	4.75
Curt Young	4.79
Tom Burgmeier	4.80
Jim Kaat	5.13
Jon Matlack	5.14
Dan Quisenberry	5.20
Ted Higuera	5.25
Oil Can Boyd	5.31
Dave Tomlin	5.37
Will McEnaney	5.42
Bob Tewksbury	5.43
Bret Saberhagen	5.50
Frank Tanana	5.55
John Candelaria	5.59
John Tudor	5.59
Bob Knepper	5.60
Randy Jones	5.63
Rick Honeycutt	5.65
Pedro Borbon	5.69
Ron Guidry	5.77
Atlee Hammaker	5.79

CAREER OPP. STRIKEOUT PCT. VS. LEFT-HANDED BATTERS

Min. 100 Strikeouts

Tom Henke	29.54
Sid Fernandez	27.39
Mark Langston	25.29
Mark Davis	25.08
Nolan Ryan	24.85
Jesse Orosco	24.43
Dave Righetti	23.85
John Candelaria	23.50
Al Holland	23.35
Joe Sambito	23.22
John Tudor	23.17
Rod Scurry	22.59
Matt Young	21.94
Ted Higuera	21.85
Tippy Martinez	21.61
Steve Carlton	21.38
Frank DiPino	21.19
Gary Lavelle	21.08
Atlee Hammaker	20.96
Dave Dravecky	20.92
Dwight Gooden	20.91
Bill Caudill	20.84
John Hiller	20.42
Ken Howell	20.32
Willie Hernandez	20.31

CAREER OPP. BATTING AVERAGE VS. RIGHT-HANDED BATTERS

Min. 600 PA

Tim Burke	.184
Jose DeLeon	.186
Mark Eichhorn	.189
J.R. Richard	.190
Floyd Youmans	.194
Mitch Williams	.195
Bobby Witt	.199
Rich Gossage	.199
Luis DeLeon	.202
Mark Littell	.202
Lance McCullers	.203
Frank Williams	.204
Mario Soto	.205
Victor Cruz	.206
Dwight Gooden	.207
Jeff Reardon	.207
Andy Messersmith	.209
Eric Show	.209
Nolan Ryan	.210
Orel Hershiser	.210
Scott Garrelts	.211
Sid Fernandez	.212
Skip Lockwood	.213
Dan Warthen	.213
Steve Ontiveros	.213

CAREER OPP. HOME RUN PCT. VS. RIGHT-HANDED BATTERS

Min. 600 PA

Mark Fidrych	0.63
Rick Lysander	0.70
Steve Howe	0.80
Randy Niemann	0.93
Doug Sisk	0.94
J.R. Richard	0.98
Dave Heaverlo	1.00
Kent Tekulve	1.01
Pat Clements	1.02
Dave Frost	1.09
Mike Barlow	1.14
Greg Minton	1.19
Alejandro Pena	1.23
Pablo Torrealba	1.24
Ed Farmer	1.24
Mark Littell	1.26
Terry Forster	1.27
Jim Kern	1.28
Dale Murray	1.31
Frank Williams	1.31
Dave Tomlin	1.34
Steve Hargan	1.34
Carl Morton	1.35
John Urrea	1.36
Dave Smith	1.37

CAREER OPP. WALK PCT. VS. RIGHT-HANDED BATTERS

Min. 600 PA

Dan Quisenberry	2.18
LaMarr Hoyt	3.49
Gary Nolan	3.51
Bret Saberhagen	3.89
Bob Stanley	4.17
Bill Wegman	4.24
Lary Sorensen	4.47
Ferguson Jenkins	4.52
Dick Bosman	4.65
Jim Barr	4.73
Luis DeLeon	4.83
Fernando Arroyo	4.84
Dennis Leonard	4.95
Tom Hausman	4.96
Larry Andersen	4.99
Bill Gullickson	5.03
Roger Erickson	5.08
Moose Haas	5.10
Tim Leary	5.12
Rick Wise	5.12
Rick Reuschel	5.15
Scott Sanderson	5.17
Ed Lynch	5.19
Mike Caldwell	5.19
Doug Bird	5.20

CAREER OPP. STRIKEOUT PCT. VS. RIGHT-HANDED BATTERS

Min. 150 Strikeouts

Tom Henke	28.95
Ken Howell	28.59
Bobby Witt	28.37
Dwight Gooden	28.37
Jose DeLeon	26.39
Lee Smith	26.09
J.R. Richard	26.06
Roger Clemens	25.29
Mark Eichhorn	25.24
Jeff Reardon	25.05
Skip Lockwood	24.68
Cecilio Guante	24.55
Nolan Ryan	24.45
Victor Cruz	24.38
Mark Clear	24.32
Rich Gossage	23.74
Ron Robinson	23.73
Scott Garrelts	23.72
Mario Soto	23.45
Floyd Youmans	23.40
Luis DeLeon	23.00
Mark Littell	22.95
Bill Caudill	22.56
Steve Farr	22.44
Steve Bedrosian	22.13

SINGLE-SEASON OPP. BATTING AVERAGE VS. LEFT-HANDED BATTERS

Min. 125 PA

Bill Dawley, 1983	.142
Bob Lacey, 1977	.146
Mitch Williams, 1987	.146
Mark Clear, 1984	.147
Dave Smith, 1984	.152
Nolan Ryan, 1981	.153
Ron Guidry, 1978	.156
Bob Shirley, 1978	.156
Larry McWilliams, 1983	.156
Matt Young, 1983	.158
Gary Lavelle, 1984	.158
Bill Scherrer, 1983	.158
Rich Wortham, 1979	.159
Larry Gura, 1983	.159
Tom Burgmeier, 1980	.159
Mike Caldwell, 1978	.160
Sid Monge, 1979	.161
Andy Hassler, 1980	.162
Larry Gura, 1978	.164
Bob Knepper, 1981	.164
Gene Garber, 1978	.165
Jeff Musselman, 1987	.165
Mike Flanagan, 1982	.167
Tim Lollar, 1982	.170
Bruce Sutter, 1979	.170

SINGLE-SEASON OPP. BATTING AVERAGE VS. RIGHT-HANDED BATTERS

Min. 175 PA

J.R. Richard, 1980	.124
Mark Eichhorn, 1986	.135
Dave LaRoche, 1976	.139
Rich Gossage, 1977	.140
Mario Soto, 1980	.147
Lance McCullers, 1986	.154
Hank Webb, 1975	.156
Mike Scott, 1986	.156
Mark Clear, 1979	.157
Don Carman, 1985	.161
Jim Kern, 1979	.161
Jeff Reardon, 1984	.161
Aurelio Lopez, 1983	.162
Tom Niedenfuer, 1983	.162
Luis DeLeon, 1982	.163
Sid Monge, 1978	.164
Frank Williams, 1985	.164
Frank Williams, 1984	.166
Tim Burke, 1985	.166
Cecilio Guante, 1985	.166
Jose DeLeon, 1984	.168
Dwight Gooden, 1984	.170
Jose DeLeon, 1986	.171
J.R. Richard, 1978	.171
Rich Gossage, 1978	.171

CAREER OPP. BATTING AVERAGE IN HOME GAMES

Min. 500 PA

Sid Fernandez	.191
Nolan Ryan	.196
J.R. Richard	.197
Dwight Gooden	.200
Tom Henke	.202
Scott Garrelts	.205
Floyd Youmans	.207
Frank Williams	.208
Bobby Witt	.209
Bert Roberge	.212
Steve Ontiveros	.212
Jose DeLeon	.214
Mario Soto	.214
Mike Armstrong	.215
Joe Cowley	.215
Rich Gossage	.216
Skip Lockwood	.217
Eric King	.217
Al Holland	.218
Dave Righetti	.219
Orel Hershiser	.219
Craig Lefferts	.219
Mark Littell	.220
Bob Apodaca	.221
Roger McDowell	.221

CAREER OPP. BATTING AVERAGE IN ROAD GAMES

Min. 500 PA

Mark Littell	.203
John Fulgham	.208
Mark Eichhorn	.209
Jesse Orosco	.209
Floyd Youmans	.214
Brian Fisher	.215
Bruce Sutter	.216
Rich Gossage	.217
Lee Smith	.220
Jose DeLeon	.222
Mario Soto	.222
Steve Bedrosian	.222
Tim Burke	.222
John Martin	.222
Jeff Reardon	.223
J.R. Richard	.223
Dan Warthen	.224
Nolan Ryan	.224
Rod Scurry	.224
Tom Henke	.224
Joe Hesketh	.226
Andy Messersmith	.226
Tom Niedenfuer	.226
Dwight Gooden	.227
Don Gullett	.227

CAREER OPP. BATTING AVERAGE ON GRASS SURFACES

Min. 500 PA

Mitch Williams	.187
J.R. Richard	.195
Danny Frisella	.199
Sid Fernandez	.202
Dwight Gooden	.211
Mark Littell	.211
Nolan Ryan	.211
Dan Warthen	.213
Rod Scurry	.215
Scott Garrelts	.217
Mario Soto	.218
Rich Gossage	.220
Jeff Reardon	.221
Cecilio Guante	.221
Andy Messersmith	.221
Tom Henke	.221
Bill Laxton	.222
Joe Cowley	.223
Brent Strom	.223
Dan Plesac	.224
Craig Lefferts	.224
Bobby Witt	.225
Frank Williams	.225
Bob Apodaca	.226
Tom Seaver	.226

CAREER OPP. BATTING AVERAGE ON ARTIFICIAL TURF

Min. 500 PA

Jesse Orosco	.175
Mike Norris	.194
Floyd Youmans	.200
Tom Henke	.205
Nolan Ryan	.206
Rich Gossage	.206
Jose DeLeon	.211
Mark Littell	.212
Pat Perry	.215
J.R. Richard	.215
Mark Eichhorn	.216
Jim Kern	.216
Mario Soto	.217
Dennis Rasmussen	.218
Steve Bedrosian	.219
Lee Smith	.220
Al Holland	.220
Dwight Gooden	.220
Frank LaCorte	.222
Joe Sambito	.224
Dave Smith	.225
Bruce Sutter	.226
Len Barker	.226
Todd Worrell	.227
Bert Roberge	.227

CAREER OPP. BATTING AVERAGE IN DAY GAMES

Min. 250 PA

Nolan Ryan	.201
Mario Soto	.207
Scott Garrelts	.210
Sid Fernandez	.212
Dave Smith	.213
Mark Littell	.214
Joe Cowley	.214
Craig Lefferts	.216
Rich Gossage	.216
Al Hrabosky	.216
Bob James	.218
Tim Burke	.219
Frank Williams	.220
Andy Messersmith	.221
Jose DeLeon	.222
David Palmer	.222
Rollie Fingers	.222
Steve Busby	.222
Roger Clemens	.223
Bruce Berenyi	.223
Steve Bedrosian	.224
Floyd Youmans	.225
Tim Lollar	.225
Rod Scurry	.226
J.R. Richard	.226

CAREER OPP. BATTING AVERAGE IN NIGHT GAMES

Min. 250 PA

Mitch Williams	.181
Dwight Gooden	.195
Floyd Youmans	.202
J.R. Richard	.205
Mark Eichhorn	.206
Tom Henke	.209
Jesse Orosco	.210
Mark Littell	.210
Sid Fernandez	.210
Nolan Ryan	.211
Jeff Lahti	.215
Jose DeLeon	.215
Rich Gossage	.217
Mike Norris	.218
Joe Hesketh	.220
Luis DeLeon	.220
Lance McCullers	.221
Al Holland	.222
Cecilio Guante	.222
Mario Soto	.222
Dennis Rasmussen	.222
Bobby Witt	.222
Rod Scurry	.223
Jeff Reardon	.223
Bill Dawley	.223

CAREER OPP. BATTING AVERAGE IN LATE-INNING PRESSURE SITUATIONS

Min. 400 PA

Tom Henke	.192
Nolan Ryan	.199
Mark Davis	.202
Cecilio Guante	.205
Mitch Williams	.206
J.R. Richard	.209
Mark Eichhorn	.211
Scott Garrelts	.214
Mario Soto	.214
Mark Littell	.214
Rich Gossage	.216
Tim Burke	.218
Don Carman	.218
Steve Bedrosian	.220
Mike Boddicker	.220
Jesse Orosco	.221
Sid Monge	.221
Don Stanhouse	.222
John Candelaria	.223
Skip Lockwood	.224
Frank LaCorte	.224
Dwight Gooden	.225
Juan Berenguer	.225
Aurelio Lopez	.225
Dave Tobik	.226

SINGLE-SEASON OPP. BATTING AVERAGE IN LATE-INNING PRESSURE SITUATIONS

Min. 150 PA

Dave LaRoche, 1976	.142
Tom Niedenfuer, 1983	.146
Don Carman, 1985	.157
Tom Seaver, 1976	.163
Ron Davis, 1981	.166
Fernando Valenzuela, 1985	.167
Dennis Eckersley, 1977	.168
Bill Dawley, 1983	.169
Rich Gossage, 1977	.169
Tom Henke, 1986	.171
Aurelio Lopez, 1979	.173
Tom Henke, 1987	.174
Nolan Ryan, 1976	.174
Bill Caudill, 1982	.175
Manny Sarmiento, 1978	.176
Willie Hernandez, 1984	.176
Ed Farmer, 1979	.177
Skip Lockwood, 1976	.179
J.R. Richard, 1976	.179
Cecilio Guante, 1986	.180
Steve Bedrosian, 1982	.181
Frank Tanana, 1976	.181
Neil Allen, 1984	.182
Steve Carlton, 1979	.183
Mitch Williams, 1987	.183

CAREER OPP. HOME RUN PCT. IN LATE-INNING PRESSURE SITUATIONS

Min. 400 PA

Alejandro Pena	0.55
Steve Comer	0.61
Frank Williams	0.63
Jim Todd	0.71
Jeff Lahti	0.73
Dave A. Roberts	0.75
Fernando Valenzuela	0.76
Doug Sisk	0.78
Don Stanhouse	0.84
Dave J. Schmidt	0.85
Bill Gullickson	0.87
Dale Murray	0.96
Randy Jones	0.98
Don Carman	0.99
Clay Carroll	1.00
Steve Howe	1.00
Dave Giusti	1.04
Tommy John	1.05
Darold Knowles	1.09
Pete Vuckovich	1.12
Manny Sarmiento	1.14
Dickie Noles	1.18
Vern Ruhle	1.18
Woody Fryman	1.20
Gary Lavelle	1.22

CAREER OPP. STRIKEOUT PCT. IN LATE-INNING PRESSURE SITUATIONS

Min. 100 Strikeouts

Tom Henke	31.56
Dwight Gooden	26.14
Scott Garrelts	25.03
Mark Eichhorn	25.00
Ken Howell	24.69
Nolan Ryan	24.29
Mitch Williams	24.11
Mark Davis	24.05
Ken Dayley	23.67
Bill Caudill	22.94
Lee Smith	22.78
Mark Clear	22.69
Skip Lockwood	22.56
Jeff D. Robinson	22.56
Don Carman	22.48
Rich Gossage	22.46
Mark Littell	22.26
Dan Plesac	22.20
Rod Scurry	22.04
Steve Bedrosian	21.94
John Hiller	21.46
Victor Cruz	21.13
Jesse Orosco	20.86
Greg Harris	20.29
Bruce Sutter	20.05

CAREER OPP. BATTING AVERAGE IN LATE-INNING PRESSURE SITUATIONS WITH RUNNERS ON BASE

Min. 150 PA

Kevin Saucier	.160
Dave Tobik	.177
Cecilio Guante	.178
Mark Eichhorn	.189
Todd Worrell	.194
Steve McCatty	.197
Steve Bedrosian	.198
Don Carman	.200
Dave Dravecky	.200
Ron Darling	.203
Alejandro Pena	.205
Nolan Ryan	.206
Tom Henke	.208
Sid Monge	.209
Ricky Horton	.209
Danny Frisella	.210
Bud Black	.210
Dwight Gooden	.210
Jack Morris	.211
Dock Ellis	.211
Randy Lerch	.211
Tim Burke	.212
Bill Greif	.213
Mitch Williams	.213
Bill Caudill	.213

SINGLE-SEASON OPP. BATTING AVERAGE IN LATE-INNING PRESSURE SITUATIONS WITH RUNNERS ON BASE

Min. 60 PA

Frank Tanana, 1976	.116
Joe Sambito, 1981	.121
Dave LaRoche, 1976	.128
Jim Kern, 1976	.128
Bill Greif, 1976	.130
Dave Tobik, 1979	.130
Bud Black, 1986	.132
Joaquin Andujar, 1978	.133
Nolan Ryan, 1978	.134
Steve Bedrosian, 1982	.136
Kevin Saucier, 1981	.140
Tim Burke, 1987	.141
George Frazier, 1982	.143
Mike Torrez, 1975	.143
Tug McGraw, 1980	.146
Andy Hassler, 1980	.148
Dave Dravecky, 1984	.148
George Frazier, 1983	.149
Tom Niedenfuer, 1983	.150
Jeff Reardon, 1981	.151
Jesse Orosco, 1983	.152
Cecilio Guante, 1986	.153
Richard Dotson, 1984	.153
Dave Tobik, 1982	.154
Jon Matlack, 1978	.154

CAREER OPP. HOME RUN PCT. IN LATE-INNING PRESSURE SITUATIONS WITH RUNNERS ON BASE

Min. 150 PA

Bill Lee	0.00
Steve Comer	0.00
Frank Williams	0.00
Bob Ojeda	0.00
Charlie Williams	0.00
Andy McGaffigan	0.00
Mark Lee	0.00
Ken Kravec	0.00
Kevin Saucier	0.00
Dave J. Schmidt	0.31
Dave Tomlin	0.41
Steve Howe	0.43
Fernando Valenzuela	0.45
Dave A. Roberts	0.45
Vern Ruhle	0.47
Greg Minton	0.49
Bill Gullickson	0.53
Mark Eichhorn	0.56
Dwight Gooden	0.57
Rick Mahler	0.58
Orel Hershiser	0.58
Pat Clements	0.60
Alejandro Pena	0.60
Pete Vuckovich	0.62
Roy Thomas	0.69

CAREER OPP. STRIKEOUT PCT. IN LATE-INNING PRESSURE SITUATIONS WITH RUNNERS ON BASE

Min. 40 Strikeouts

Tom Henke	28.05
Dwight Gooden	25.74
Scott Garrelts	24.41
Jeff D. Robinson	24.12
Mark Clear	24.10
Mitch Williams	23.56
Bill Caudill	23.28
Ken Howell	21.98
Lee Smith	21.92
Cecilio Guante	21.91
Mark Eichhorn	21.89
Nolan Ryan	21.86
Skip Lockwood	21.50
Mark Littell	21.19
Rod Scurry	20.67
Ken Dayley	20.56
Alejandro Pena	20.40
Dan Plesac	20.08
John Hiller	20.00
Dave LaRoche	19.85
Tom Niedenfuer	19.84
Victor Cruz	19.80
Lance McCullers	19.76
Doug Bair	19.76
Steve Bedrosian	19.75

CAREER
OPP. BATTING AVERAGE
WITH RUNNERS ON BASE

Min. 500 PA

Todd Worrell	.192
Dwight Gooden	.206
Jesse Orosco	.208
Lance McCullers	.215
Sid Fernandez	.216
Tim Burke	.216
Mark Eichhorn	.219
Jeff Reardon	.220
Ron Darling	.220
Rod Scurry	.222
Mark Clear	.222
Bruce Sutter	.222
Bill Caudill	.223
Jose DeLeon	.223
Mario Soto	.223
Lee Smith	.224
J.R. Richard	.224
Nolan Ryan	.224
Roger Clemens	.225
Andy McGaffigan	.225
Cecilio Guante	.225
Mark Littell	.225
Steve Bedrosian	.226
Tom Henke	.227
Scott Garrelts	.227

SINGLE-SEASON
OPP. BATTING AVERAGE
WITH RUNNERS ON BASE

Min. 175 PA

John D'Acquisto, 1978	.155
Gene Garber, 1978	.160
Jesse Orosco, 1984	.167
Bill Caudill, 1980	.173
Jesse Orosco, 1983	.175
Jose DeLeon, 1986	.175
Rich Gossage, 1977	.175
Willie Hernandez, 1984	.176
Al Holland, 1983	.177
Charlie Hough, 1976	.177
Lee Smith, 1983	.178
Jim Deshaies, 1986	.180
Dwight Gooden, 1985	.180
Mitch Williams, 1987	.180
Doug Bair, 1978	.181
Mike Scott, 1986	.181
Tippy Martinez, 1983	.181
Sid Monge, 1979	.182
Bruce Sutter, 1977	.182
Jesse Orosco, 1986	.183
Mark Eichhorn, 1986	.183
Jose DeLeon, 1983	.185
Hal Dues, 1978	.185
Todd Worrell, 1986	.185
Rich Gossage, 1975	.186

CAREER
OPP. BATTING AVERAGE
WITH RUNNERS
IN SCORING POSITION

Min. 300 PA

Mitch Williams	.170
Dwight Gooden	.188
Tim Burke	.189
Mark Eichhorn	.189
Todd Worrell	.191
Steve Bedrosian	.193
Jesse Orosco	.198
Bob Apodaca	.199
Cecilio Guante	.201
Floyd Youmans	.202
Sid Fernandez	.205
Steve Busby	.206
Rich Gossage	.207
Lee Smith	.208
Mario Soto	.212
Jeff Lahti	.212
Ron Darling	.212
Stan Thomas	.213
Joe Cowley	.214
Roger Clemens	.214
Mark Clear	.214
Lance McCullers	.215
Bobby Witt	.215
Steve Ontiveros	.215
Tippy Martinez	.216

SINGLE-SEASON
OPP. BATTING AVERAGE
WITH RUNNERS
IN SCORING POSITION

Min. 125 PA

Jim Deshaies, 1986	.140
Rich Gossage, 1978	.143
Dwight Gooden, 1985	.144
Eric Show, 1986	.145
Tim Burke, 1985	.147
Joe Cowley, 1985	.148
Tom Hilgendorf, 1975	.149
John Candelaria, 1977	.149
Cecilio Guante, 1983	.151
Don Sutton, 1980	.153
Gene Garber, 1982	.156
Bob Lacey, 1977	.157
Tom Hausman, 1975	.159
Rich Gossage, 1977	.159
Mike Scott, 1986	.159
Steve McCatty, 1981	.161
Jeff D. Robinson, 1987	.161
Mitch Williams, 1987	.162
Tom Seaver, 1981	.163
Steve Bedrosian, 1986	.163
Bill Campbell, 1977	.165
Joaquin Andujar, 1978	.167
Mario Soto, 1980	.167
Dwight Gooden, 1986	.167
Steve McCatty, 1982	.169

CAREER
OPP. BATTING AVERAGE
WITH 2 OUTS
AND RUNNERS ON BASE

Min. 250 PA

Dwight Gooden	.178
Bill Caudill	.186
Dave Smith	.189
Victor Cruz	.190
Pete Ladd	.190
Cecilio Guante	.191
Sid Fernandez	.192
Jesse Orosco	.194
Pat Dobson	.196
Bobby Witt	.199
Craig Lefferts	.201
Eric Show	.202
Bruce Sutter	.202
J.R. Richard	.202
Jose DeLeon	.203
Lance McCullers	.203
Ted Higuera	.203
Rollie Fingers	.204
Mark Eichhorn	.204
Scott Garrelts	.205
Ed Glynn	.205
Bob Welch	.206
Dave Stewart	.206
Mark Littell	.207
Charlie Williams	.208

SINGLE-SEASON
OPP. BATTING AVERAGE
WITH 2 OUTS
AND RUNNERS ON BASE

Min. 100 PA

Bill Caudill, 1980	.103
Mike Scott, 1986	.109
Pat Dobson, 1976	.115
Jerry Ujdur, 1982	.122
Eric Show, 1986	.138
John Tudor, 1984	.143
Ed Whitson, 1984	.143
Ron Darling, 1986	.143
Jose DeLeon, 1985	.144
Bob Forsch, 1978	.147
Lance McCullers, 1986	.148
Eduardo Rodriguez, 1976	.149
Sparky Lyle, 1978	.149
Dan Warthen, 1975	.149
Bill Campbell, 1977	.149
Frank Tanana, 1977	.150
Fred Norman, 1978	.152
Scott Garrelts, 1985	.152
Tom Seaver, 1981	.153
Scott Sanderson, 1980	.154
Luis Tiant, 1978	.155
Britt Burns, 1981	.155
Steve Bedrosian, 1983	.156
Gene Nelson, 1985	.156
Rick Rhoden, 1984	.157

CAREER
OPP. BATTING AVERAGE
WITH 2 OUTS
AND RUNNERS
IN SCORING POSITION

Min. 150 PA

Tim Burke	.159
Todd Worrell	.163
Dwight Gooden	.165
Bob Apodaca	.165
Cecilio Guante	.166
Bobby Witt	.169
Mark Eichhorn	.171
Victor Cruz	.175
Craig Lefferts	.179
Dave Smith	.179
Mitch Williams	.180
Pete Ladd	.181
Dave Stewart	.182
J.R. Richard	.185
Lee Smith	.185
Eric Show	.185
Steve Busby	.186
Brian Fisher	.186
Floyd Youmans	.186
Mark Huismann	.188
Jesse Orosco	.189
Sid Fernandez	.190
Tippy Martinez	.190
Greg Harris	.191
Bill Caudill	.192

SINGLE-SEASON
OPP. BATTING AVERAGE
WITH 2 OUTS
AND RUNNERS
IN SCORING POSITION

Min. 75 PA

Jack Morris, 1987	.082
Dan Warthen, 1975	.100
John Tudor, 1984	.110
Bobby Witt, 1987	.111
Luis Tiant, 1978	.113
Bill Gullickson, 1982	.118
Mike Scott, 1986	.119
Rich Gossage, 1978	.119
Ed Whitson, 1984	.119
Mike Krukow, 1986	.123
Brian Fisher, 1987	.125
Doug Corbett, 1980	.127
Ron Darling, 1986	.129
Frank Tanana, 1977	.130
Fred Norman, 1978	.130
Dwight Gooden, 1985	.133
Pat Dobson, 1976	.133
Tim Burke, 1985	.134
Frank Tanana, 1976	.135
Bill Campbell, 1977	.136
Tom Seaver, 1981	.138
Dave Freisleben, 1976	.143
Doug Rau, 1977	.143
Rick Langford, 1977	.143
Eduardo Rodriguez, 1976	.145

SINGLE-SEASON DOUBLES ALLOWED

Dennis Leonard, 1978	62
Bruce Hurst, 1984	60
Rick Sutcliffe, 1983	58
Dennis Eckersley, 1986	58
Jim Barr, 1977	57
Jim Clancy, 1983	57
Bill Gullickson, 1983	56
Shane Rawley, 1987	56
Scott McGregor, 1983	55
John Montefusco, 1975	54
Dennis Leonard, 1980	54
Steve Rogers, 1983	54
Doyle Alexander, 1986	54
Mike Moore, 1987	54
Wilbur Wood, 1975	53
Mike Torrez, 1983	53
Ron Guidry, 1983	53
Doyle Alexander, 1984	53
Bob Knepper, 1985	53
Charlie Leibrandt, 1986	53
Ron Reed, 1975	52
Larry Christenson, 1977	52
Steve Carlton, 1977	52
Mike Flanagan, 1978	52
Jerry Koosman, 1980	52

SINGLE-SEASON TRIPLES ALLOWED

Larry Christenson, 1976	17
Paul Thormodsgard, 1977	16
Jim Barr, 1975	14
Jim Kaat, 1977	14
Jim Barr, 1977	14
Dave Goltz, 1977	14
Craig Swan, 1979	14
Randy Jones, 1979	14
Rick Sutcliffe, 1984	14
Ray Burris, 1976	13
Rick Reuschel, 1976	13
Luis Tiant, 1979	13
Dick Ruthven, 1980	13
Steve Carlton, 1980	13
Rich Gale, 1982	13
Tommy John, 1982	13
Mike Smithson, 1983	13
John Montefusco, 1975	12
Jim Kaat, 1976	12
Ken Holtzman, 1976	12
Ray Burris, 1978	12
Roger Erickson, 1979	12
Bob Forsch, 1979	12
Doc Medich, 1980	12
Mike Krukow, 1980	12

SINGLE-SEASON EXTRA-BASE HITS ALLOWED

Bert Blyleven, 1986	100
Phil Niekro, 1979	97
Dennis Leonard, 1978	94
Dennis Leonard, 1980	92
Rick Sutcliffe, 1983	92
Bert Blyleven, 1987	92
LaMarr Hoyt, 1984	91
Mike Witt, 1987	91
Jerry Garvin, 1977	90
Mike Moore, 1987	90
Wilbur Wood, 1975	89
Jim Barr, 1977	89
Dan Petry, 1983	89
Mark Langston, 1986	89
Jim Clancy, 1983	88
Bill Gullickson, 1987	88
Ferguson Jenkins, 1979	87
Frank Viola, 1986	87
Luis Tiant, 1975	86
Ferguson Jenkins, 1975	86
Scott McGregor, 1983	86
Bruce Hurst, 1984	86
Charlie Hough, 1984	86
Dennis Eckersley, 1986	86
Jack Morris, 1986	86

CAREER OPP. EXTRA-BASE HIT PCT.

Min. 1,000 PA

Steve Howe	4.04
Doug Sisk	4.99
Greg Minton	5.07
Scott Garrelts	5.13
Mark Fidrych	5.13
John Franco	5.21
Roger McDowell	5.22
Dwight Gooden	5.23
Gary Lavelle	5.24
Jesse Orosco	5.25
J.R. Richard	5.28
Nolan Ryan	5.34
Jim Kern	5.35
Mark Littell	5.40
Frank Williams	5.41
Orel Hershiser	5.42
Alejandro Pena	5.42
Dave Smith	5.43
Dave Righetti	5.44
Rich Gossage	5.50
Kent Tekulve	5.54
Clay Carroll	5.56
Jaime Cocanower	5.64
Lee Smith	5.68
Tim Burke	5.70

HIGHEST CAREER RATIO OF GROUND OUTS TO AIR OUTS

Min. 1,000 PA

Roger McDowell	3.16
Doug Corbett	2.96
Doug Sisk	2.85
Ray Fontenot	2.53
Tommy John	2.50
Bruce Ruffin	2.44
Jeff Dedmon	2.41
Greg Minton	2.39
Jim Todd	2.39
Dennis Lamp	2.34
Jaime Cocanower	2.34
Dan Quisenberry	2.31
Kent Tekulve	2.25
Bob Stanley	2.25
Orel Hershiser	2.24
Bill Swift	2.23
John Denny	2.21
Gene Garber	2.19
Bill Castro	2.17
Randy Jones	2.13
Jim Winn	2.11
David Palmer	2.10
Steve Trout	2.07
Terry Forster	2.06
Rick Lysander	2.05

LOWEST CAREER RATIO OF GROUND OUTS TO AIR OUTS

Min. 1,000 PA

Sid Fernandez	0.48
Keith Atherton	0.54
Mike Armstrong	0.55
Tom Niedenfuer	0.55
Don Carman	0.57
Jeff Reardon	0.57
Victor Cruz	0.59
Pete Ladd	0.60
Bill Caudill	0.60
Dave LaRoche	0.61
Juan Berenguer	0.62
Chris Knapp	0.62
Jim Deshaies	0.63
Al Hrabosky	0.63
Al Holland	0.65
Joe Price	0.65
Tom Henke	0.66
Skip Lockwood	0.66
Tom Browning	0.67
Aurelio Lopez	0.67
Tim Conroy	0.67
Cecilio Guante	0.67
Luis Tiant	0.67
Dennis Rasmussen	0.68
John Henry Johnson	0.68

CAREER GROUND OUT PCT. (PER 100 PA)

Min. 1,000 PA

Roger McDowell	43.8
Dan Quisenberry	43.0
Tommy John	41.4
Randy Jones	41.3
Doug Sisk	40.7
Bill Castro	40.0
Doug Corbett	39.9
Greg Minton	39.4
Ray Fontenot	39.2
Bob Stanley	39.0
Dennis Lamp	38.8
Kent Tekulve	38.7
Jim Todd	38.6
Bruce Ruffin	38.5
Paul Hartzell	38.2
Fernando Arroyo	38.0
Rob Dressler	37.8
Clay Carroll	37.5
Jaime Cocanower	37.4
Jeff Dedmon	37.3
Rick Matula	37.3
Dave Rozema	37.2
Mike Proly	37.1
John Denny	37.1
Jerry Reuss	36.9

CAREER AIR OUT PCT. (PER 100 PA)

Min. 1,000 PA

Gary Nolan	36.0
Catfish Hunter	35.8
John Martin	35.2
Keith Atherton	35.0
Mike Armstrong	34.8
Luis Tiant	34.3
Manny Sarmiento	34.2
Don Carman	34.2
Scott McGregor	34.1
Tom Browning	34.0
Tom Niedenfuer	33.6
Larry Gura	33.6
Chris Knapp	33.3
Pete Ladd	33.3
Grant Jackson	33.2
Steve McCatty	33.1
Sid Fernandez	33.0
Jeff Reardon	32.9
Brian Kingman	32.9
Craig Swan	32.9
Al Hrabosky	32.8
Ken Schrom	32.8
Pete Filson	32.8
Jim Palmer	32.7
Dennis Rasmussen	32.6

CAREER OPP. ON-BASE AVERAGE LEADING OFF INNINGS

Min. 250 PA

Dave J. Schmidt	.243
Dan Quisenberry	.248
Mike Armstrong	.252
Brad Havens	.257
Rich Gossage	.258
John Martin	.261
Dave Tobik	.262
Steve Howe	.266
Mark Eichhorn	.266
Tug McGraw	.269
Gary Nolan	.272
Darold Knowles	.273
Tom Niedenfuer	.275
Joe Hesketh	.276
Gene Garber	.277
Rod Scurry	.278
Don Sutton	.278
Pete Filson	.279
Marty Pattin	.279
Frank Tanana	.279
Jeff Reardon	.279
Ron Reed	.279
Rawly Eastwick	.280
Doug Corbett	.281
Rollie Fingers	.281

SINGLE-SEASON OPP. ON-BASE AVERAGE LEADING OFF INNINGS

Min. 100 PA

Greg Harris, 1985	.175
Dan Quisenberry, 1984	.188
Vern Ruhle, 1983	.191
Randy Martz, 1981	.202
Jeff D. Robinson, 1986	.212
Joe Price, 1983	.212
Dan Quisenberry, 1983	.215
Dave J. Schmidt, 1982	.217
John Tudor, 1985	.217
Rich Gossage, 1978	.219
Mike Armstrong, 1982	.220
Dan Schatzeder, 1984	.221
Don Sutton, 1975	.221
Dennis Eckersley, 1977	.223
Pat Underwood, 1982	.223
Ken Forsch, 1979	.223
Bob Forsch, 1977	.224
Marty Pattin, 1976	.224
Ron Guidry, 1981	.224
Vern Ruhle, 1981	.224
Rick Honeycutt, 1986	.225
Francisco Barrios, 1979	.225
Bryn Smith, 1987	.226
Jeff M. Robinson, 1987	.226
John Martin, 1981	.229

CAREER OPP. WALK PCT. LEADING OFF INNINGS

Min. 250 PA

Dan Quisenberry	2.31
Dave J. Schmidt	2.31
Scott Bankhead	2.48
Gary Nolan	2.49
Gene Garber	2.54
Kevin Kobel	3.02
Atlee Hammaker	3.41
Mark Eichhorn	3.50
Ron Reed	3.54
Mark Fidrych	3.55
Steve Howe	3.58
Gary Lucas	3.78
Gary Ross	3.88
Pedro Borbon	3.95
Bret Saberhagen	4.00
Dave Rozema	4.04
Tommy John	4.04
Jim Barr	4.05
Roger Erickson	4.16
LaMarr Hoyt	4.25
Ferguson Jenkins	4.27
Dennis Eckersley	4.28
Rick Reuschel	4.31
Kent Tekulve	4.38
Scott Sanderson	4.45

SINGLE-SEASON OPP. WALK PCT. LEADING OFF INNINGS

Min. 100 PA

Gene Garber, 1982	0.00
Dan Quisenberry, 1983	0.00
Dan Quisenberry, 1985	0.00
Rick Langford, 1982	0.41
Jim Barr, 1982	0.78
Tom Hausman, 1980	0.82
Bob Forsch, 1980	0.89
Dave J. Schmidt, 1982	0.94
Dennis Eckersley, 1987	0.94
Dennis Martinez, 1986	0.95
Jeff D. Robinson, 1986	0.96
Ron Reed, 1978	1.00
Mike Smithson, 1983	1.29
Gaylord Perry, 1981	1.29
Bryn Smith, 1987	1.29
Ferguson Jenkins, 1976	1.38
Glenn Abbott, 1983	1.45
Roger Clemens, 1984	1.45
Neal Heaton, 1987	1.48
Ron Guidry, 1981	1.49
Bob Shirley, 1980	1.50
Rick Rhoden, 1983	1.60
Atlee Hammaker, 1982	1.62
Gary Nolan, 1976	1.64
Roger Erickson, 1982	1.67

CAREER OPP. BATTING AVERAGE WITH BASES LOADED

Min. 50 PA

Eric Show	.138
Jesse Orosco	.140
Cecilio Guante	.143
Mitch Williams	.143
Ed Figueroa	.147
Doug Rau	.152
Mike Smithson	.153
Dave LaRoche	.159
Mark Gubicza	.160
Mark Eichhorn	.167
Dave Lemanczyk	.167
Dave J. Schmidt	.173
Ken Schrom	.175
Tippy Martinez	.178
Tom House	.179
John Franco	.184
Bruce Berenyi	.185
Ed Halicki	.185
Jeff D. Robinson	.186
Butch Metzger	.188
Jeff Dedmon	.188
Tom Griffin	.188
Craig Swan	.189
Mike Moore	.190
Keith Atherton	.190

CAREER MOST BATTERS FACED WITH BASES LOADED WITHOUT ALLOWING A GRAND-SLAM HOME RUN

Joaquin Andujar	149
Jim Kern	148
Mike Krukow	142
Pat Zachry	128
Bob Welch	110
Danny Darwin	109
Jim Palmer	105
Mike Moore	97
Al Hrabosky	96
Andy Hassler	93
Jesse Jefferson	91
Greg Harris	84
Bruce Berenyi	84
Juan Berenguer	82
Ed Figueroa	82
Doug Corbett	80
Frank DiPino	80
Gene Nelson	77
Joe Price	77
Roy Thomas	75
Eric Show	75
Don Hood	74
Rawly Eastwick	73
Mike Stanton	73
Roger Erickson	71

CAREER OPP. WALK PCT. WITH BASES LOADED

Min. 50 PA

Steve Crawford	0.00
Dave Heaverlo	0.81
Vern Ruhle	1.01
Rick Mahler	1.10
Steve McCatty	1.10
Matt Young	1.10
Ed Vande Berg	1.32
Ed Lynch	1.39
Craig Lefferts	1.39
Dave Tobik	1.43
Dennis Eckersley	1.63
Mike G. Marshall	1.64
Fred Breining	1.72
John Butcher	1.75
Larry Christenson	1.79
Jim Gott	1.79
Ferguson Jenkins	1.82
Mike Garman	1.82
Dave Dravecky	1.82
Butch Metzger	1.82
Jim Umbarger	1.82
Will McEnaney	1.89
Mike Parrott	1.89
Paul Reuschel	1.92
Tim Burke	1.96

CAREER OPP. STRIKEOUT PCT. WITH BASES LOADED

Min. 15 Strikeouts

Bobby Witt	34.78
Nolan Ryan	28.83
Dave Smith	28.81
John Hiller	28.13
Bruce Berenyi	27.38
Mark Littell	26.51
Dave LaRoche	25.20
Bill Caudill	25.00
Dwight Gooden	24.24
Al Holland	24.14
Steve Carlton	24.11
Rich Gossage	23.81
Sammy Stewart	23.61
Ron Guidry	23.47
Jeff Reardon	23.36
Mario Soto	23.28
Tippy Martinez	23.08
Orel Hershiser	22.89
Greg Harris	22.62
Bruce Hurst	22.35
Tom Seaver	22.29
Joe Sambito	22.12
Keith Atherton	21.79
Terry Forster	21.51
Dave Tobik	21.43

VII
Batter-Pitcher Matchups

Batter-Pitcher Matchups

The Batter-Pitcher Matchup section lists, for the selected players, their performances against every pitcher or batter they have faced for at least five at bats in their careers. These statistics include all regular season appearances since the beginning of their careers.

Earl Weaver used to keep them on index cards. Dave Johnson maintains his on a PC. But until the past few years the public was largely unaware of the importance many managers place on specific matchup statistics in setting a lineup. The stats do not even out over the long run, and the differences can be massive. In this section, we expand the "Loves to Face" and "Hates to Face" matchups listed in the Batter and Pitcher Sections to take a look at the career performances of some of the most extraordinary players in the game.

The seven players here are three pitchers and four batters, three National Leaguers and four American Leaguers. Now you can see in detail just how few pitchers really give Andre Dawson trouble. Or if anyone really has a book on George Bell yet. Here, at last, are the answers.

George Bell

Pitcher	AB	H	2B	3B	HR	BB	SO	BA	SA	OBA
Don Aase	6	1	0	0	0	1	0	.167	.167	.286
Doyle Alexander	8	1	0	0	0	0	3	.125	.125	.125
Neil Allen	17	5	0	0	0	0	1	.294	.294	.294
Allan Anderson	6	2	2	0	0	0	0	.333	.667	.333
Keith Atherton	16	4	2	0	0	1	3	.250	.375	.263
Scott Bailes	12	5	3	0	0	1	1	.417	.667	.462
Doug Bair	6	2	0	2	0	1	1	.333	1.000	.429
Scott Bankhead	15	8	1	0	4	0	1	.533	1.400	.533
Floyd Bannister	35	11	1	0	4	2	10	.314	.686	.368
Len Barker	6	1	0	0	0	0	0	.167	.167	.167
Jeff Barkley	5	0	0	0	0	0	3	.000	.000	.000
Salome Barojas	8	3	0	0	0	0	1	.375	.375	.375
Ross Baumgarten	5	1	0	0	0	0	0	.200	.200	.200
Jim Beattie	6	2	1	0	0	0	2	.333	.500	.333
Juan Berenguer	8	2	0	0	1	0	2	.250	.625	.250
Tim Birtsas	3	1	0	0	0	2	1	.333	.333	.600
Bud Black	31	11	1	1	2	1	3	.355	.645	.412
Bert Blyleven	34	15	2	1	3	3	2	.441	.824	.486
Mike Boddicker	39	5	1	0	0	3	8	.128	.154	.190
Rich Bordi	13	3	1	0	1	0	1	.231	.538	.214
Chris Bosio	7	3	3	0	0	1	1	.429	.857	.500
Oil Can Boyd	17	7	1	1	1	1	3	.412	.765	.474
Britt Burns	26	10	2	1	1	1	5	.385	.654	.407
Ray Burris	12	3	2	0	0	0	0	.250	.417	.250
John Butcher	9	3	1	0	1	0	0	.333	.778	.300
Mike Caldwell	12	3	1	0	0	0	0	.250	.333	.250
Ernie Camacho	6	1	0	0	0	0	0	.167	.167	.167
John Candelaria	8	4	0	1	2	0	1	.500	1.500	.500
Tom Candiotti	17	10	4	0	1	2	2	.588	1.000	.632
Steve Carlton	5	2	0	0	0	0	0	.400	.400	.400
Bryan Clark	6	0	0	0	0	0	0	.000	.000	.000
Mark Clear	14	1	0	0	0	2	3	.071	.071	.188
Roger Clemens	30	6	2	0	1	0	9	.200	.367	.200
Pat Clements	4	3	0	0	0	1	0	.750	.750	.800
Jaime Cocanower	8	1	0	0	0	3	1	.125	.125	.364
Chris Codiroli	9	1	0	0	0	0	2	.111	.111	.111
Tim Conroy	13	5	0	0	0	1	1	.385	.385	.429
Mike Cook	4	0	0	0	0	2	1	.000	.000	.333
Doug Corbett	5	1	0	0	0	0	0	.200	.200	.200
Ed Correa	12	4	0	0	2	0	1	.333	.833	.308
Joe Cowley	9	2	0	0	0	3	0	.222	.222	.417
Steve Crawford	12	2	2	0	0	1	1	.167	.333	.286
Keith Creel	4	0	0	0	0	1	0	.000	.000	.200
Danny Darwin	21	5	1	1	0	0	1	.238	.381	.238
Joel Davis	10	4	0	1	0	0	1	.400	.600	.400
Ron Davis	5	4	0	1	0	1	0	.800	1.200	.833
Storm Davis	10	3	0	0	1	1	1	.300	.600	.364
Jose DeLeon	10	2	0	0	1	3	2	.200	.500	.429
Ken Dixon	17	4	0	0	2	0	3	.235	.588	.235
Richard Dotson	26	7	2	0	0	1	1	.269	.346	.276
Doug Drabek	8	0	0	0	0	0	0	.000	.000	.000
Jamie Easterly	7	2	0	0	1	0	2	.286	.714	.286
Dennis Eckersley	6	2	0	0	2	0	2	.333	1.333	.333
Steve Farr	12	7	1	0	1	0	1	.583	.917	.538
Pete Filson	15	4	2	0	0	0	3	.267	.400	.267
Rollie Fingers	5	1	0	0	1	0	3	.200	.800	.200
Brian Fisher	6	1	0	0	0	0	0	.167	.167	.167
Mike Flanagan	26	5	0	0	2	0	2	.192	.423	.192
Ray Fontenot	8	3	3	0	0	0	0	.375	.750	.375
Ken Forsch	5	2	0	0	0	0	0	.400	.400	.400
George Frazier	7	0	0	0	0	1	1	.000	.000	.125
Rich Gale	6	3	1	0	0	0	0	.500	.667	.500
Wes Gardner	7	2	0	0	0	0	1	.286	.286	.250
Dave Geisel	5	3	0	1	0	1	1	.600	1.000	.667
Bob L. Gibson	8	5	0	0	0	1	1	.625	.625	.667
Mark Gubicza	17	5	2	0	1	1	1	.294	.588	.316
Lee Guetterman	6	1	1	0	0	1	0	.167	.333	.286
Ron Guidry	35	13	5	1	0	1	5	.371	.571	.389
Larry Gura	12	3	0	0	0	1	0	.250	.250	.308
Jose Guzman	11	7	0	0	0	0	2	.636	.636	.636
Moose Haas	27	8	2	0	1	0	3	.296	.481	.296
John Habyan	9	4	0	0	3	1	0	.444	1.444	.500
Greg Harris	13	6	2	0	2	0	2	.462	1.077	.462
Brad Havens	11	3	1	0	0	0	0	.273	.364	.273
Neal Heaton	22	9	3	0	3	0	0	.409	.955	.409
Mike Henneman	6	1	0	0	1	1	2	.167	.667	.375
Willie Hernandez	7	4	0	0	0	1	1	.571	.571	.625
Ted Higuera	26	5	0	0	2	0	6	.192	.423	.185
Ed Hodge	8	0	0	0	0	1	2	.000	.000	.111
Rick Honeycutt	8	2	0	1	0	0	0	.250	.500	.250
Charlie Hough	36	10	2	0	2	2	5	.278	.500	.316
Jay Howell	6	5	0	0	1	0	1	.833	1.667	.714
LaMarr Hoyt	13	2	0	0	0	0	2	.154	.154	.154
Mark Huismann	7	3	0	0	2	3	1	.429	1.286	.600
Bruce Hurst	32	6	3	0	2	1	6	.188	.469	.212
Danny Jackson	16	6	1	0	0	1	1	.375	.500	.412
Bob James	6	3	1	0	0	1	1	.500	1.167	.571
Tommy John	19	3	1	0	1	1	1	.158	.368	.200
John Henry Johnson	5	1	0	0	0	0	0	.200	.200	.200
Mike Jones	8	1	0	0	0	1	1	.125	.500	.111
Jim Kern	8	3	1	0	0	0	1	.375	.500	.375
Eric King	10	2	0	0	0	1	0	.200	.200	.273
Bruce Kison	3	1	0	0	0	0	0	.333	.333	.400
Bill Krueger	11	3	1	0	0	1	1	.273	.364	.308
Pete Ladd	12	4	1	0	0	0	1	.333	.417	.308
Dennis Lamp	7	3	0	0	1	1	1	.429	.857	.500
Rick Langford	5	1	0	0	0	0	1	.200	.200	.200
Mark Langston	29	8	1	0	3	3	8	.276	.621	.344
Dave LaPoint	5	3	1	0	0	0	1	.600	.800	.600
Jack Lazorko	7	0	0	0	0	0	0	.000	.000	.000
Tim Leary	7	4	0	1	0	1	1	.571	.857	.625
Charlie Leibrandt	35	10	1	0	2	0	2	.286	.486	.286
Dennis Leonard	10	2	0	0	0	0	0	.200	.200	.200
Aurelio Lopez	5	1	0	0	1	1	0	.200	.800	.333
Mike Loynd	7	1	0	0	0	1	1	.143	.143	.250
Urbano Lugo	6	0	0	0	0	0	1	.000	.000	.000
Dennis Martinez	14	4	2	0	0	0	1	.286	.429	.333
Tippy Martinez	7	2	0	0	1	0	1	.286	.714	.286
Mike Mason	15	6	0	0	1	5	1	.400	.600	.550
Kirk McCaskill	20	8	3	0	0	3	2	.400	.550	.478
Steve McCatty	7	2	0	0	2	1	2	.286	1.143	.375
Bob McClure	16	6	0	0	0	0	1	.375	.375	.375
Scott McGregor	37	13	1	0	2	1	4	.351	.541	.368
Dale Mohorcic	5	1	0	0	1	1	2	.200	.800	.333
Bill Mooneyham	6	2	0	0	1	0	0	.333	.833	.333
Donnie Moore	8	5	1	0	2	0	0	.625	1.500	.625
Mike Moore	41	10	3	0	1	1	7	.244	.390	.262
Mike Morgan	11	4	1	0	1	0	0	.364	.727	.333
Jack Morris	43	9	0	0	3	1	3	.209	.442	.244
Gene Nelson	15	4	2	0	0	1	2	.267	.400	.313
Joe Niekro	9	0	0	0	0	1	2	.000	.000	.182
Phil Niekro	24	6	2	1	0	0	5	.250	.417	.250
Juan Nieves	10	1	0	0	0	1	2	.100	.100	.182
Al Nipper	25	7	0	1	3	2	3	.280	.720	.333
Dickie Noles	10	1	0	0	0	1	2	.100	.400	.308
Edwin Nunez	7	2	1	0	0	0	3	.286	.429	.286
Bob Ojeda	15	4	0	0	1	0	1	.267	.467	.267
Randy O'Neal	7	2	0	0	0	0	1	.286	.286	.286
Steve Ontiveros	9	1	0	0	0	0	0	.111	.222	.111
Dan Petry	14	6	0	0	1	1	1	.429	.643	.467
Eric Plunk	12	2	0	0	0	2	2	.167	.167	.286
Mark Portugal	9	4	0	0	1	0	1	.444	.778	.444
Dan Quisenberry	16	2	0	0	1	0	3	.125	.313	.125
Dennis Rasmussen	16	6	1	0	2	2	2	.375	.813	.444
Shane Rawley	10	4	0	0	0	0	0	.400	.400	.400
Jerry Reed	5	1	0	1	0	0	0	.200	.600	.200
Rick Rhoden	5	3	0	1	1	0	1	.600	1.600	.600
Dave Righetti	17	6	1	1	1	0	4	.353	.706	.353
Jose Rijo	11	7	3	0	1	2	0	.636	1.182	.692
Reggie Ritter	6	3	0	0	1	0	0	.500	1.000	.500
Jeff M. Robinson	4	3	0	0	0	2	1	.750	.750	.833
Ron Romanick	13	3	1	0	0	0	2	.231	.308	.231
Dave Rozema	6	1	0	0	0	0	2	.167	.167	.167
Bret Saberhagen	14	3	0	0	1	0	1	.214	.429	.200
Luis Sanchez	7	1	0	0	0	0	0	.143	.143	.143
Bill Scherrer	6	2	0	0	0	1	1	.333	.333	.429
Calvin Schiraldi	5	1	0	0	0	0	1	.200	.200	.200
Dave J. Schmidt	10	1	0	0	0	0	0	.100	.100	.100
Ken Schrom	12	3	1	0	0	1	1	.250	.333	.308
Don Schulze	9	2	1	0	1	0	0	.222	.667	.222

George Bell continued

Pitcher	AB	H	2B	3B	HR	BB	SO	BA	SA	OBA
Ray Searage	5	0	0	0	0	2	1	.000	.000	.286
Tom Seaver	22	6	0	0	1	2	2	.273	.409	.333
Jeff Sellers	8	5	0	0	0	1	2	.625	.625	.667
Bob Shirley	10	2	0	0	0	2	1	.200	.200	.308
Jim Slaton	18	7	0	0	0	3	2	.389	.389	.476
Roy Smith	7	5	2	0	0	0	2	.714	1.000	.714
Mike Smithson	25	4	2	0	0	1	5	.160	.240	.222
Lary Sorensen	6	1	0	0	0	0	0	.167	.167	.167
Dan Spillner	4	2	1	0	0	1	0	.500	.750	.600
Paul Splittorff	5	1	0	0	0	0	1	.200	.200	.200
Bob Stanley	23	3	0	0	0	0	5	.130	.130	.125
Dave Stewart	27	6	3	0	2	1	2	.222	.556	.276
Sammy Stewart	8	2	0	0	0	2	2	.250	.250	.400
Tim Stoddard	5	1	0	0	0	0	1	.200	.200	.167
Rick Sutcliffe	4	2	0	0	1	1	1	.500	1.250	.667
Don Sutton	28	5	1	0	1	0	5	.179	.321	.179
Greg Swindell	10	4	1	0	1	0	1	.400	.800	.400
Frank Tanana	34	5	0	0	1	1	6	.147	.235	.216
Walt Terrell	25	10	4	0	1	1	3	.400	.680	.423
Bob Tewksbury	5	1	0	0	0	0	0	.200	.200	.167
Bobby Thigpen	7	2	1	0	1	0	0	.286	.857	.286
Steve Trout	12	4	0	0	0	0	0	.333	.333	.333
Tom Underwood	11	2	0	0	0	1	3	.182	.182	.250
Ed Vande Berg	7	3	2	0	1	0	2	.429	1.143	.429
Frank Viola	33	7	1	0	4	5	5	.212	.606	.316
Pete Vuckovich	8	3	0	1	1	0	0	.375	1.000	.375
Tom Waddell	13	6	0	0	2	2	3	.462	.923	.500
Rick Waits	8	3	0	0	0	1	0	.375	.375	.375
Curt Wardle	5	2	0	0	1	0	1	.400	1.000	.400
Bill Wegman	15	5	0	0	2	0	0	.333	.733	.353
Ed Whitson	12	4	1	0	1	0	1	.333	.667	.333
Milt Wilcox	11	1	0	0	0	0	3	.091	.364	.091
Al Williams	4	1	0	1	0	0	0	.250	.750	.400
Mitch Williams	5	1	1	0	0	1	1	.200	.400	.333
Mark Williamson	5	1	0	0	0	0	1	.200	.200	.200
Frank Wills	7	3	1	0	1	0	1	.429	1.000	.429
Bobby Witt	10	5	1	0	0	1	2	.500	.600	.500
Mike Witt	26	6	1	0	0	2	5	.231	.269	.286
Curt Young	15	8	0	1	0	3	2	.533	.667	.611
Matt Young	20	5	0	0	1	1	4	.250	.400	.286
Geoff Zahn	13	4	0	0	1	1	1	.308	.538	.357

Eric Davis

Pitcher	AB	H	2B	3B	HR	BB	SO	BA	SA	OBA
Jim Acker	5	0	0	0	0	1	1	.000	.000	.167
Rick Aguilera	13	2	1	0	1	1	6	.154	.462	.214
Doyle Alexander	6	0	0	0	0	0	2	.000	.000	.000
Larry Andersen	6	0	0	0	0	0	2	.000	.000	.000
Steve Bedrosian	6	0	0	0	0	0	0	.000	.000	.000
Bruce Berenyi	9	2	2	0	0	0	3	.222	.444	.222
Mike Bielecki	5	0	0	0	0	1	2	.000	.000	.167
Vida Blue	9	4	0	0	3	2	0	.444	1.444	.545
Tim Burke	8	2	1	0	0	2	2	.250	.375	.400
Rick Camp	4	1	0	0	1	1	1	.250	1.000	.400
John Candelaria	6	2	0	0	1	0	2	.333	.833	.333
Steve Carlton	10	1	0	0	1	2	3	.100	.400	.250
Don Carman	5	3	0	0	3	1	1	.600	2.400	.667
Tim Conroy	8	0	0	0	0	3	4	.000	.000	.250
Danny Cox	11	4	2	0	0	2	2	.364	.545	.462
Ron Darling	11	1	0	0	0	3	4	.091	.091	.333
Mark Davis	17	4	0	0	1	1	7	.235	.412	.278
Bill Dawley	4	1	1	0	0	0	0	.250	.500	.250
Jeff Dedmon	8	2	1	0	0	1	1	.250	.375	.333
Jim Deshaies	7	2	0	0	1	3	2	.286	.714	.500
Frank DiPino	6	3	1	0	1	5	1	.500	1.167	.727
Kelly Downs	9	1	0	0	0	2	3	.111	.111	.273
Doug Drabek	9	0	0	0	0	0	3	.000	.000	.000
Dave Dravecky	12	6	1	0	2	0	2	.500	1.083	.500
Mike Dunne	7	1	1	0	0	1	3	.143	.286	.250
Sid Fernandez	8	1	0	0	0	2	3	.125	.125	.300
Bob Forsch	13	3	0	0	1	1	4	.231	.462	.286
Gene Garber	6	2	0	0	2	0	1	.333	1.333	.333
Scott Garrelts	11	4	1	0	0	7	5	.364	.455	.611
Dwight Gooden	7	4	0	0	0	1	2	.571	.571	.625
Rich Gossage	7	2	0	0	1	0	2	.286	.714	.286
Jim Gott	6	0	0	0	0	3	4	.000	.000	.333
Mark Grant	7	3	1	0	0	3	2	.429	.571	.600
Kevin Gross	14	7	1	1	2	3	2	.500	1.143	.588
Bill Gullickson	5	1	1	0	0	0	2	.200	.400	.200
Atlee Hammaker	17	5	0	1	2	2	5	.294	.765	.368
Andy Hawkins	11	1	0	0	0	1	3	.091	.091	.167
Neal Heaton	8	2	0	0	2	0	4	.250	1.000	.250
Orel Hershiser	20	7	1	0	0	4	2	.350	.400	.440
Rick Honeycutt	15	3	0	0	1	5	1	.200	.400	.400
Ricky Horton	8	3	0	0	1	0	1	.375	.750	.375
Ken Howell	7	1	0	0	1	2	5	.143	.571	.333
Charles Hudson	7	3	1	0	2	1	2	.429	1.429	.500
Tom Hume	8	3	1	0	0	0	3	.375	.500	.375
Jimmy Jones	4	2	0	1	0	1	1	.500	1.000	.600
Bob Kipper	11	5	0	0	3	1	2	.455	1.273	.500
Bob Knepper	26	12	2	0	0	2	4	.462	.538	.500
Mike Krukow	24	7	0	0	4	1	7	.292	.792	.308
Mike LaCoss	13	2	0	0	0	1	2	.154	.154	.214
Dave LaPoint	18	4	0	1	1	0	5	.222	.500	.222
Bill Laskey	6	4	2	1	0	0	1	.667	1.333	.667
Tim Leary	10	1	1	0	0	0	5	.100	.200	.100
Craig Lefferts	5	1	1	0	0	2	1	.200	.400	.429
Aurelio Lopez	4	0	0	0	0	2	3	.000	.000	.333
Ed Lynch	7	0	0	0	0	0	2	.000	.000	.125
Mike Madden	2	1	1	0	0	3	0	.500	1.000	.800
Greg Maddux	5	0	0	0	0	1	2	.000	.000	.167
Rick Mahler	13	6	0	1	1	4	2	.462	.846	.588
Dennis Martinez	10	5	1	0	1	2	2	.500	.900	.583
Lance McCullers	6	0	0	0	0	2	2	.000	.000	.250
Roger McDowell	5	2	0	0	0	0	1	.400	.400	.400
Andy McGaffigan	8	2	1	0	0	2	3	.250	.375	.400
Craig McMurtry	7	3	0	0	2	1	2	.429	1.286	.500
Larry McWilliams	13	4	1	0	1	1	4	.308	.385	.357
Greg Minton	7	4	0	0	1	0	1	.571	1.000	.571
John Mitchell	5	2	0	0	1	0	0	.400	1.000	.400
Jamie Moyer	6	4	0	0	1	2	0	.667	1.167	.750
Terry Mulholland	7	2	1	0	0	1	0	.286	.429	.375
Tom Niedenfuer	5	2	0	0	0	0	2	.400	.400	.400
Bob Ojeda	7	1	0	0	0	0	2	.143	.143	.143
Jesse Orosco	3	1	0	0	0	2	0	.333	.333	.600
David Palmer	21	6	0	0	1	2	2	.286	.429	.348
Alejandro Pena	8	0	0	0	0	1	2	.000	.000	.111
Pat Perry	4	0	0	0	0	1	2	.000	.000	.200
Dennis Powell	5	2	0	0	1	1	3	.400	1.000	.500
Shane Rawley	20	3	1	0	2	2	8	.150	.500	.227
Jeff Reardon	6	1	0	0	0	0	4	.167	.167	.167
Rick Reuschel	6	1	0	0	0	0	3	.167	.167	.167
Jerry Reuss	8	4	0	0	1	1	1	.500	.875	.556
Rick Rhoden	5	2	0	0	2	0	1	.400	1.600	.400
Don Robinson	8	2	0	0	1	0	1	.250	.625	.222
Jeff D. Robinson	6	2	0	0	1	0	0	.333	.833	.333
Steve Rogers	11	3	2	0	0	0	1	.273	.455	.273
Bruce Ruffin	13	7	3	0	1	3	1	.538	1.000	.588
Nolan Ryan	12	1	0	0	1	2	10	.083	.333	.214
Scott Sanderson	14	3	1	0	1	2	4	.214	.500	.313
Mike Scott	21	2	0	0	1	2	9	.095	.238	.174
Bob Sebra	3	1	0	0	1	2	1	.333	1.333	.600
Eric Show	21	7	2	0	3	4	6	.333	.857	.462
Doug Sisk	6	2	1	0	0	1	2	.333	.500	.429
Bryn Smith	21	8	3	0	2	1	5	.381	.810	.409
Lee Smith	5	2	1	0	0	0	2	.400	.600	.400

Eric Davis continued

Pitcher	AB	H	2B	3B	HR	BB	SO	BA	SA	OBA
Zane Smith	22	5	2	0	0	3	3	.227	.318	.320
Rick Sutcliffe	6	4	0	0	0	4	0	.667	.667	.800
Kent Tekulve	7	1	0	0	0	1	2	.143	.143	.250
Jay Tibbs	13	5	0	0	0	1	4	.385	.385	.429
Steve Trout	4	2	0	1	0	1	0	.500	1.000	.600
John Tudor	14	1	0	0	0	1	3	.071	.071	.133
Lee Tunnell	4	0	0	0	0	1	1	.000	.000	.200
Fernando Valenzuela	20	3	0	0	1	6	8	.150	.300	.346
Ed Vande Berg	4	2	0	0	0	1	0	.500	.500	.600
Bob Walk	5	1	0	0	0	0	0	.200	.200	.200
Bob Welch	10	3	0	0	1	3	4	.300	.600	.462
Ed Whitson	14	7	0	0	1	0	3	.500	.714	.500
Frank Williams	3	1	0	0	0	2	1	.333	.333	.600
Todd Worrell	5	0	0	0	0	0	1	.000	.000	.000
Floyd Youmans	3	1	0	0	1	2	1	.333	1.333	.600

Andre Dawson

Pitcher	AB	H	2B	3B	HR	BB	SO	BA	SA	OBA
Jim Acker	6	2	0	0	0	0	1	.333	.333	.333
Rick Aguilera	21	6	1	0	2	2	3	.286	.619	.375
Doyle Alexander	16	4	1	0	0	0	2	.250	.313	.250
Neil Allen	24	7	1	0	2	2	6	.292	.583	.346
Porfi Altamirano	5	3	0	0	2	0	0	.600	1.800	.600
Larry Andersen	16	3	1	0	0	1	1	.188	.250	.235
Joaquin Andujar	80	18	6	2	4	3	9	.225	.500	.256
Bob Apodaca	8	1	0	0	0	0	6	.125	.125	.125
Doug Bair	21	8	3	0	1	1	7	.381	.667	.409
Rick Baldwin	5	0	0	0	0	0	0	.000	.000	.000
Jay Baller	8	1	1	0	0	0	2	.125	.250	.125
Floyd Bannister	13	3	2	0	0	1	5	.231	.385	.286
Len Barker	11	4	1	0	0	0	2	.364	.455	.364
Jim Barr	23	7	0	0	3	0	3	.304	.696	.292
Steve Bedrosian	38	9	0	0	1	1	6	.237	.316	.275
Juan Berenguer	6	3	1	0	0	0	0	.500	.667	.500
Bruce Berenyi	24	5	2	0	0	0	7	.208	.292	.208
Dwight Bernard	8	3	0	0	0	0	1	.375	.375	.375
Jim Bibby	35	11	1	1	2	1	4	.314	.571	.333
Mike Bielecki	8	2	1	0	0	1	3	.250	.375	.333
Jack Billingham	5	1	0	0	0	0	0	.200	.200	.200
Doug Bird	15	6	1	0	1	3	2	.400	.667	.500
Vida Blue	45	12	1	1	4	0	11	.267	.600	.267
Bert Blyleven	41	8	0	0	2	2	8	.195	.341	.233
Tommy Boggs	10	4	0	0	1	3	0	.400	.700	.538
Mark Bomback	11	1	0	0	0	0	3	.091	.091	.091
Bill Bonham	20	5	0	0	1	0	6	.250	.400	.250
Greg Booker	5	0	0	0	0	0	0	.000	.000	.000
Pedro Borbon	9	4	1	0	1	0	1	.444	.889	.444
Rich Bordi	5	1	0	0	1	0	1	.200	.800	.200
Fred Breining	11	0	0	0	0	0	4	.000	.000	.077
Tony Brizzolara	9	2	1	0	0	0	2	.222	.333	.222
Tom Browning	17	5	2	0	0	1	2	.294	.412	.333
Mike Bruhert	9	3	1	0	0	0	2	.333	.444	.333
Warren Brusstar	17	5	0	0	1	3	4	.294	.471	.429
Ray Burris	41	13	2	1	1	2	5	.317	.488	.364
Marty Bystrom	17	5	0	0	0	0	3	.294	.294	.333
Rick Camp	26	7	1	0	2	3	3	.269	.538	.345
Bill Campbell	16	7	2	1	1	0	2	.438	.875	.389
John Candelaria	41	12	0	1	1	2	1	.293	.415	.326
Doug Capilla	10	3	1	0	0	1	2	.300	.400	.364
Buzz Capra	7	1	0	0	1	0	1	.143	.571	.143
Steve Carlton	103	30	9	2	4	14	20	.291	.534	.381
Don Carman	13	3	0	0	1	0	5	.231	.462	.231
Bobby Castillo	11	3	1	0	1	1	2	.273	.636	.357
Bill Caudill	15	4	1	0	0	4	1	.267	.333	.421
Floyd Chiffer	8	1	0	0	0	0	2	.125	.125	.125
Larry Christenson	66	18	2	1	5	0	11	.273	.561	.290
Tim Conroy	7	1	0	0	0	1	0	.143	.143	.250
Mardie Cornejo	5	2	1	0	0	0	1	.400	.600	.400
Danny Cox	54	14	1	1	1	2	10	.259	.370	.286
John Curtis	15	4	0	0	2	2	0	.267	.667	.389
John D'Acquisto	8	4	0	1	2	1	1	.500	1.500	.556
Ron Darling	36	9	2	1	2	6	7	.250	.528	.357
Danny Darwin	6	2	0	0	1	1	2	.333	.833	.429
Mark Davis	14	4	1	0	0	1	3	.286	.357	.375
Bill Dawley	16	6	0	0	3	1	4	.375	.938	.412
Ken Dayley	17	7	0	0	2	0	0	.412	.765	.412
Jeff Dedmon	14	5	0	0	1	2	3	.357	.571	.438
Jose DeLeon	15	2	0	0	0	1	3	.133	.133	.188
Luis DeLeon	7	2	1	0	0	0	3	.286	.429	.286
John Denny	68	14	5	0	1	3	7	.206	.324	.239
Carlos Diaz	10	2	0	0	0	2	0	.200	.200	.333
Tom Dixon	3	2	0	1	1	1	1	.667	2.333	.750
Kelly Downs	7	2	0	0	0	2	2	.286	.286	.444
Doug Drabek	12	5	1	0	0	0	1	.417	.500	.417
Dave Dravecky	40	11	3	0	2	2	7	.275	.500	.302
Mike Dunne	7	1	0	0	0	0	1	.143	.143	.143
Jamie Easterly	7	2	0	0	0	0	0	.286	.286	.286
Rawly Eastwick	13	6	1	1	0	0	1	.462	.692	.462
Dennis Eckersley	38	6	2	1	1	0	4	.158	.342	.154
Juan Eichelberger	8	2	1	0	0	1	3	.250	.375	.400
Dock Ellis	7	1	0	0	0	2	2	.143	.143	.333
Nino Espinosa	39	11	1	0	1	1	5	.282	.385	.310
Pete Falcone	31	10	3	0	1	2	6	.323	.516	.364
Ed Farmer	5	1	0	0	0	1	0	.200	.200	.250
Sid Fernandez	14	3	3	0	0	1	4	.214	.429	.294
Tom Filer	7	2	0	0	0	0	1	.286	.286	.286
Rollie Fingers	11	3	0	0	1	0	1	.273	.545	.273
Brian Fisher	12	2	0	0	1	0	2	.167	.417	.231
Ray Fontenot	12	6	0	0	2	0	0	.500	1.000	.500
Bob Forsch	120	38	7	3	6	8	17	.317	.575	.359
Ken Forsch	14	3	1	0	0	1	2	.214	.286	.267
Terry Forster	8	3	1	0	1	1	1	.375	.875	.444
Alan Fowlkes	5	3	1	0	0	0	1	.600	.800	.500
John Franco	7	5	0	0	0	0	0	.714	.714	.714
George Frazier	18	9	2	0	1	1	2	.500	.778	.526
Dave Freisleben	7	2	0	0	0	0	3	.286	.286	.375
Woody Fryman	6	4	0	1	1	1	0	.667	1.500	.714
John Fulgham	12	2	0	0	0	2	3	.167	.167	.286
Brent Gaff	5	0	0	0	0	0	1	.000	.000	.000
Rich Gale	12	4	1	0	1	0	2	.333	.667	.308
Gene Garber	39	8	1	0	3	2	6	.205	.462	.279
Scott Garrelts	13	4	1	0	0	3	2	.308	.385	.438
Ed Glynn	5	0	0	0	0	0	1	.000	.000	.000
Dwight Gooden	38	11	1	0	1	0	9	.289	.395	.282
Tom Gorman	6	1	0	0	0	0	1	.167	.167	.167
Rich Gossage	10	1	1	0	0	1	1	.100	.200	.182
Jim Gott	15	3	0	0	0	1	5	.200	.200	.250
Mark Grant	11	8	1	0	3	0	0	.727	1.636	.727
Tom Griffin	14	2	0	0	0	0	1	.143	.143	.250
Kevin Gross	33	7	1	0	1	4	5	.212	.333	.316
Cecilio Guante	16	4	1	0	2	1	6	.250	.688	.278
Bill Gullickson	12	2	0	0	0	0	2	.167	.167	.154
Dave Gumpert	7	3	1	0	1	1	1	.429	1.000	.500
Ed Halicki	30	8	2	0	0	1	4	.267	.333	.290
Atlee Hammaker	23	3	0	0	0	0	3	.130	.130	.130
Preston Hanna	19	4	2	0	0	1	2	.211	.316	.250
Alan Hargesheimer	6	2	2	0	0	0	0	.333	.667	.333
Greg Harris	5	1	0	0	0	2	1	.200	.200	.429
Tom Hausman	15	7	0	0	3	0	3	.467	1.067	.467
Andy Hawkins	44	10	0	0	0	2	3	.227	.273	.217
Ben Hayes	4	0	0	0	0	1	0	.000	.000	.200
Neal Heaton	6	0	0	0	0	0	1	.000	.000	.000
Willie Hernandez	19	3	0	0	0	2	4	.158	.158	.238
Orel Hershiser	18	4	1	0	0	1	6	.222	.278	.300
Al Holland	12	1	0	0	0	0	1	.083	.083	.214
Brian Holton	6	1	0	0	0	0	1	.167	.167	.167

Andre Dawson continued

Pitcher	AB	H	2B	3B	HR	BB	SO	BA	SA	OBA
Rick Honeycutt	32	8	3	0	0	4	7	.250	.344	.333
Burt Hooton	50	16	3	1	2	3	7	.320	.540	.370
Ricky Horton	8	3	1	0	0	1	3	.375	.500	.444
Charlie Hough	13	2	0	0	1	0	3	.154	.385	.154
Steve Howe	8	3	0	0	0	1	0	.375	.375	.444
Ken Howell	11	2	0	0	0	0	5	.182	.182	.308
LaMarr Hoyt	7	2	1	0	0	1	0	.286	.429	.375
Al Hrabosky	8	5	1	0	1	1	0	.625	1.125	.667
Charles Hudson	22	4	0	0	1	0	5	.182	.318	.182
Tom Hume	30	7	1	1	2	1	6	.233	.533	.258
Grant Jackson	5	1	0	0	0	0	1	.200	.200	.200
Mike Jackson	4	1	0	0	1	1	0	.250	1.000	.400
Roy Lee Jackson	6	2	1	0	0	1	0	.333	.500	.429
Ferguson Jenkins	14	3	1	1	0	0	3	.214	.429	.200
Tommy John	12	3	0	0	0	0	3	.250	.250	.250
Barry Jones	6	1	0	0	0	0	2	.167	.167	.167
Odell Jones	10	4	3	0	0	1	2	.400	.700	.417
Randy Jones	31	13	1	0	1	3	2	.419	.548	.471
Jim Kaat	23	5	1	0	1	1	2	.217	.391	.250
Jeff Keener	4	1	0	0	0	1	0	.250	.250	.400
Kurt Kepshire	11	2	0	1	0	0	4	.182	.364	.182
Charlie Kerfeld	4	1	0	0	0	2	1	.250	.250	.429
Bob Kipper	9	0	0	0	0	0	3	.000	.000	.000
Bruce Kison	42	8	1	0	3	1	12	.190	.262	.244
Bob Knepper	56	21	3	0	7	7	6	.375	.804	.453
Kevin Kobel	8	5	1	1	0	1	1	.625	1.000	.600
Jerry Koosman	36	10	1	0	1	3	7	.278	.389	.333
Mike Krukow	76	23	5	1	4	3	15	.303	.553	.325
Frank LaCorte	9	3	0	0	1	1	2	.333	.667	.400
Mike LaCoss	50	22	1	1	2	2	3	.440	.620	.463
Lerrin LaGrow	5	0	0	0	0	1	2	.000	.000	.167
Jeff Lahti	13	3	0	0	0	2	1	.231	.231	.333
Dennis Lamp	28	10	1	0	1	2	8	.357	.500	.387
Dave LaPoint	29	5	0	1	2	4	7	.172	.448	.273
Dan Larson	4	0	0	0	0	1	0	.000	.000	.200
Bill Laskey	22	8	2	0	1	1	2	.364	.591	.391
Gary Lavelle	17	5	1	0	0	2	4	.294	.353	.368
Terry Leach	19	3	0	0	2	0	1	.158	.474	.158
Tim Leary	11	5	0	0	2	0	3	.455	1.000	.455
Mark Lee	12	2	2	0	0	1	1	.167	.333	.231
Craig Lefferts	7	4	1	0	1	2	1	.571	1.143	.667
Charlie Leibrandt	7	2	1	1	0	0	0	.286	.714	.286
Mark Lemongello	14	5	0	0	2	0	1	.357	.786	.333
Randy Lerch	31	12	1	0	2	1	2	.387	.613	.394
Brad Lesley	5	1	1	0	0	0	1	.200	.400	.200
Mark Littell	13	5	1	0	1	1	3	.385	.692	.429
John Littlefield	6	4	0	0	1	1	0	.667	1.167	.714
Skip Lockwood	11	1	1	0	0	2	5	.091	.182	.231
Mickey Lolich	5	1	1	0	0	0	0	.200	.400	.200
Tim Lollar	13	2	1	0	0	1	5	.154	.231	.214
Jim Lonborg	23	4	3	0	1	1	6	.174	.435	.200
Aurelio Lopez	8	2	0	1	1	0	1	.250	.875	.250
Gary Lucas	11	3	1	0	0	3	1	.273	.364	.400
Sparky Lyle	3	0	0	0	0	2	0	.000	.000	.400
Ed Lynch	31	4	1	0	1	0	4	.129	.258	.129
Mickey Mahler	6	4	0	0	1	0	0	.667	1.167	.714
Rick Mahler	57	17	2	1	1	3	4	.298	.421	.333
John Martin	12	3	1	1	0	0	2	.250	.500	.250
Renie Martin	11	4	1	0	2	0	1	.364	1.000	.364
Silvio Martinez	18	6	2	0	0	0	1	.333	.444	.333
Randy Martz	20	8	3	0	0	0	0	.400	.550	.400
Greg Mathews	8	2	2	0	0	1	0	.250	.500	.333
Ron Mathis	5	1	0	0	0	0	0	.200	.200	.200
Jon Matlack	9	1	1	0	0	0	1	.111	.222	.111
Rick Matula	8	2	0	0	0	0	1	.250	.250	.250
Lance McCullers	8	2	1	0	1	0	1	.250	.750	.333
Roger McDowell	15	3	0	0	0	0	2	.200	.200	.200
Andy McGaffigan	13	3	0	0	0	1	4	.231	.231	.286
Lynn McGlothen	29	9	0	0	2	4	4	.310	.517	.417
Tug McGraw	22	2	0	0	1	2	10	.091	.227	.167
Bo McLaughlin	5	1	0	1	0	0	2	.200	.600	.200
Craig McMurtry	13	0	0	0	0	1	2	.000	.000	.071
Larry McWilliams	47	18	5	1	2	6	7	.383	.660	.453
Butch Metzger	6	0	0	0	0	2	1	.000	.000	.250
Dyar Miller	8	1	0	0	0	0	2	.125	.125	.125
Greg Minton	27	7	0	0	2	4	3	.259	.481	.355
John Mitchell	7	2	1	0	0	0	1	.286	.429	.286
Randy Moffitt	11	5	1	0	1	0	0	.455	.818	.500
Sid Monge	7	1	0	0	0	0	2	.143	.143	.125
John Montefusco	29	6	3	0	0	0	6	.207	.310	.233
Donnie Moore	16	5	1	0	0	0	1	.313	.375	.313
Paul Moskau	12	6	0	0	3	0	1	.500	1.250	.500
Jamie Moyer	9	2	0	0	0	0	0	.222	.222	.222
Steve Mura	26	7	1	0	3	5	3	.269	.654	.375
Dale Murray	14	6	0	2	1	3	2	.429	.929	.500
Randy Myers	5	2	0	0	0	0	0	.400	.400	.400
Bob Myrick	9	3	0	0	1	0	1	.333	.667	.333
Phil Nastu	5	0	0	0	0	0	0	.000	.000	.000
Tom Niedenfuer	9	4	1	1	1	0	3	.444	1.111	.400
Joe Niekro	51	13	0	1	1	5	6	.255	.353	.321
Phil Niekro	55	23	2	1	0	4	4	.418	.491	.468
Dickie Noles	27	8	3	1	2	1	4	.296	.704	.345
Fred Norman	19	8	0	0	1	0	6	.421	.579	.421
Bob Ojeda	9	2	0	0	0	0	2	.222	.222	.222
Jesse Orosco	22	12	3	0	2	1	2	.545	.955	.565
Jim Otten	5	3	0	0	1	0	0	.600	1.200	.600
Bob Owchinko	11	5	0	1	2	0	0	.455	1.182	.455
Rick Ownbey	10	3	0	0	0	2	0	.300	.300	.300
David Palmer	8	0	0	0	0	1	5	.000	.000	.111
Frank Pastore	30	5	1	0	1	2	4	.167	.300	.257
Alejandro Pena	20	5	1	0	0	0	1	.250	.300	.286
Pascual Perez	27	8	3	0	1	2	6	.296	.519	.345
Gaylord Perry	13	4	0	0	0	0	2	.308	.308	.308
Ted Power	19	5	3	0	0	0	2	.263	.421	.263
Joe Price	20	2	1	0	0	2	4	.100	.150	.208
Mike Proly	13	3	1	0	0	1	2	.231	.308	.286
Charlie Puleo	19	2	0	0	0	2	3	.105	.105	.190
Chuck Rainey	8	2	0	0	1	0	1	.250	.625	.222
Dennis Rasmussen	6	2	0	0	1	0	1	.333	.833	.333
Eric Rasmussen	36	12	5	4	1	4	7	.333	.778	.429
Doug Rau	14	3	0	0	0	0	1	.214	.214	.214
Shane Rawley	36	16	3	1	5	4	3	.444	1.000	.488
Jeff Reardon	8	3	0	0	0	0	1	.375	.375	.375
Ron Reed	33	10	2	0	2	4	7	.303	.545	.378
Paul Reuschel	5	2	0	0	1	1	0	.400	1.000	.571
Rick Reuschel	102	34	9	2	2	3	12	.333	.520	.352
Jerry Reuss	58	17	3	1	1	0	5	.293	.431	.293
Rick Rhoden	82	21	5	1	2	5	13	.256	.415	.303
J.R. Richard	34	8	0	0	1	2	10	.235	.324	.289
Andy Rincon	6	3	1	1	1	0	1	.500	1.500	.500
Allen Ripley	3	1	0	0	0	1	0	.333	.333	.400
Bert Roberge	5	2	1	0	0	0	0	.400	.600	.400
Dave A. Roberts	7	3	1	0	0	0	0	.429	.571	.429
Don Robinson	48	9	1	0	2	1	12	.188	.333	.200
Jeff D. Robinson	13	1	0	0	0	0	4	.077	.077	.077
Ron Robinson	10	2	0	0	2	0	2	.200	.800	.200
Enrique Romo	10	4	1	0	1	1	2	.400	.800	.455
Vicente Romo	4	1	0	0	0	0	1	.250	.250	.400
Jim Rooker	13	6	1	1	0	0	0	.462	.692	.462
Dave Rucker	5	1	0	0	0	0	0	.200	.200	.200
Bruce Ruffin	10	2	1	0	0	0	1	.200	.300	.200
Vern Ruhle	29	8	2	0	1	0	2	.276	.448	.300
Jeff Russell	6	1	0	0	1	0	2	.167	.667	.167
Dick Ruthven	67	17	2	1	5	4	13	.254	.537	.301
Nolan Ryan	66	15	2	0	2	4	22	.227	.348	.288
Joe Sambito	6	2	0	0	1	0	1	.333	.833	.333
Scott Sanderson	10	2	2	0	0	1	1	.200	.400	.273
Manny Sarmiento	12	6	1	0	1	2	1	.500	.833	.600
Dan Schatzeder	4	2	0	0	0	2	0	.500	.500	.667
Buddy Schultz	5	1	0	0	0	0	1	.200	.200	.200
Mike Scott	33	9	1	0	1	0	8	.273	.394	.306
Rod Scurry	8	0	0	0	0	1	0	.000	.000	.111
Tom Seaver	58	13	2	3	1	3	15	.224	.414	.266
Bob Sebra	13	2	1	0	1	2	3	.154	.462	.267
Bob Shirley	21	6	0	0	1	2	3	.286	.429	.348
Eric Show	38	5	0	0	2	1	11	.132	.289	.175
Doug Sisk	13	2	0	0	1	2	2	.154	.385	.267
Craig Skok	5	1	0	0	1	0	0	.200	.800	.200
Bryn Smith	6	2	1	0	0	0	0	.333	.500	.333
Dave Smith	16	8	1	0	2	2	2	.500	.938	.556

Andre Dawson continued

Pitcher	AB	H	2B	3B	HR	BB	SO	BA	SA	OBA
Lee Smith	15	2	0	0	0	0	2	.133	.133	.133
Zane Smith	18	6	2	0	1	2	1	.333	.611	.400
Julio Solano	8	2	0	0	1	0	1	.250	.625	.250
Eddie Solomon	30	11	1	1	2	4	1	.367	.667	.457
Lary Sorensen	18	4	0	0	0	1	1	.222	.222	.300
Elias Sosa	4	2	1	0	0	1	1	.500	.750	.600
Mario Soto	52	18	3	2	4	2	11	.346	.712	.351
Dave Stewart	8	3	0	0	0	0	2	.375	.375	.375
Tim Stoddard	11	4	2	0	0	1	3	.364	.545	.417
John Stuper	20	10	2	0	1	1	2	.500	.750	.524
Rick Sutcliffe	33	10	1	0	1	3	5	.303	.424	.378
Bruce Sutter	46	8	2	0	0	5	12	.174	.217	.250
Don Sutton	32	11	3	1	4	2	7	.344	.875	.382
Craig Swan	58	15	3	1	1	3	7	.259	.397	.290
Kent Tekulve	59	12	1	0	0	1	11	.203	.220	.226
Walt Terrell	10	3	0	0	0	2	0	.300	.300	.385
Roy Thomas	6	6	1	0	0	0	0	1.000	1.167	.857
Mark Thurmond	9	4	0	0	1	4	2	.444	.778	.571
Luis Tiant	5	1	0	0	0	1	2	.200	.200	.333
Jay Tibbs	13	6	0	0	0	1	2	.462	.462	.500
Dick Tidrow	20	5	1	0	0	1	5	.250	.300	.304
Jackson Todd	10	4	2	0	2	0	2	.400	1.200	.400
Dave Tomlin	6	0	0	0	0	0	1	.000	.000	.000
Mike Torrez	10	2	1	0	0	0	1	.200	.300	.182
Steve Trout	35	9	1	0	3	3	4	.257	.543	.316
John Tudor	38	10	1	0	2	3	3	.263	.447	.326
Lee Tunnell	22	8	2	0	3	1	2	.364	.864	.440
Wayne Twitchell	6	2	1	0	1	1	1	.333	1.000	.429
John Urrea	28	9	1	1	0	1	4	.321	.429	.345
Fernando Valenzuela	50	10	1	2	3	1	8	.200	.480	.231
Pete Vuckovich	33	5	3	0	1	2	8	.152	.333	.200
Bob Walk	19	7	0	0	2	2	2	.368	.684	.455
Gene Walter	4	1	0	0	0	1	1	.250	.250	.400
Dave Wehrmeister	6	1	1	0	0	0	1	.167	.333	.167
Bob Welch	47	16	4	0	3	1	10	.340	.617	.367
Chris Welsh	19	6	2	0	0	0	0	.316	.421	.316
Ed Whitson	47	12	2	0	2	2	5	.255	.426	.286
Charlie Williams	5	3	0	1	0	2	0	.600	1.000	.714
Frank Williams	11	1	0	0	0	1	1	.091	.091	.167
Jim Winn	4	1	0	0	0	2	0	.250	.250	.500
Rick Wise	8	4	3	0	0	0	0	.500	.875	.500
Todd Worrell	12	3	0	0	1	0	3	.250	.500	.250
Pat Zachry	53	10	2	1	2	2	7	.189	.377	.218

Alan Trammell

Pitcher	AB	H	2B	3B	HR	BB	SO	BA	SA	OBA
Don Aase	31	8	0	0	1	2	4	.258	.355	.294
Glenn Abbott	12	6	2	0	0	1	0	.500	.667	.538
Jim Acker	8	2	1	0	0	1	1	.250	.375	.333
Juan Agosto	8	2	0	0	0	3	1	.250	.250	.455
Darrel Akerfelds	4	3	0	0	0	1	0	.750	.750	.800
Doyle Alexander	27	6	0	0	1	2	4	.222	.333	.267
Allan Anderson	8	2	0	0	0	2	0	.250	.250	.400
Bud Anderson	11	3	1	0	0	1	1	.273	.364	.333
Joaquin Andujar	9	2	0	0	0	2	1	.222	.222	.364
Luis Aponte	5	1	1	0	0	1	1	.200	.400	.333
Mike Armstrong	5	2	0	0	0	1	0	.400	.400	.500
Fernando Arroyo	7	2	1	0	0	1	0	.286	.429	.375
Keith Atherton	11	4	1	0	0	2	1	.364	.455	.462
Jerry Augustine	16	4	0	0	0	3	0	.250	.250	.368
Scott Bailes	8	3	0	0	1	1	0	.375	.750	.500
Scott Bankhead	12	2	1	0	1	1	1	.167	.500	.231
Floyd Bannister	51	17	4	1	0	5	4	.333	.451	.393
Len Barker	32	9	1	0	1	4	5	.281	.406	.361
Mike Barlow	5	3	0	0	0	0	0	.600	.600	.600
Salome Barojas	7	3	1	0	0	2	0	.429	.571	.556
Jim Barr	10	5	1	0	0	0	0	.500	.600	.500
Ross Baumgarten	18	4	1	1	0	2	3	.222	.389	.300
Dave Beard	5	1	0	0	0	1	2	.200	.200	.333
Jim Beattie	27	7	1	0	1	3	1	.259	.407	.355
Joe Beckwith	10	3	0	0	0	0	1	.300	.300	.300
Rick Behenna	7	2	1	0	0	2	0	.286	.429	.444
Eric Bell	8	3	1	0	1	0	2	.375	.875	.375
Juan Berenguer	4	0	0	0	0	1	1	.000	.000	.200
Jim Bibby	6	0	0	0	0	0	2	.000	.000	.000
Doug Bird	6	0	0	0	0	0	0	.000	.000	.000
Tim Birtsas	10	2	0	0	1	1	0	.200	.500	.273
Bud Black	24	5	0	0	2	5	1	.208	.458	.333
Vida Blue	7	3	0	0	1	2	0	.429	.857	.556
Bert Blyleven	47	11	1	0	0	3	7	.234	.255	.294
Mike Boddicker	23	11	2	1	0	3	5	.478	.652	.538
Mark Bomback	6	1	0	0	0	0	0	.167	.167	.286
Rich Bordi	9	2	0	0	0	1	2	.222	.222	.300
Chris Bosio	13	6	1	0	1	0	0	.462	.769	.462
Oil Can Boyd	37	11	2	0	2	3	2	.297	.514	.357
Tom Brennan	15	5	2	0	0	0	0	.333	.467	.333
Ken Brett	5	1	0	0	0	0	1	.200	.200	.200
Mike G. Brown	13	3	2	0	0	0	1	.231	.385	.231
Tom Burgmeier	12	3	0	1	0	2	0	.250	.417	.357
Britt Burns	29	10	3	0	0	9	1	.345	.448	.475
Ray Burris	11	6	0	0	3	1	0	.545	1.364	.538
Steve Busby	4	2	0	0	0	2	0	.500	.500	.667
Tom Buskey	6	2	0	0	0	0	0	.333	.333	.333
John Butcher	36	10	1	0	1	3	2	.278	.389	.333
Mike Caldwell	39	15	2	1	2	2	4	.385	.641	.415
Ernie Camacho	8	1	0	0	0	1	0	.125	.125	.222
Bill Campbell	7	3	0	0	0	0	0	.429	.429	.429
John Candelaria	9	3	1	0	0	1	0	.333	.444	.400
Tom Candiotti	8	1	0	0	0	3	2	.125	.125	.364
Steve Carlton	5	2	2	0	0	0	0	.400	.800	.400
Bobby Castillo	8	4	0	0	0	0	1	.500	.500	.444
Bill Castro	9	2	1	0	1	1	1	.222	.667	.300
Bill Caudill	8	2	0	0	1	2	1	.250	.625	.400
John Cerutti	9	3	1	0	0	0	0	.333	.444	.333
Clay Christiansen	6	4	0	0	0	0	1	.667	.667	.667
Jim Clancy	76	25	4	2	3	6	7	.329	.553	.386
Bryan Clark	9	2	0	0	0	4	1	.222	.222	.462
Ken Clay	5	0	0	0	0	0	2	.000	.000	.000
Mark Clear	15	3	2	0	0	6	4	.200	.333	.429
Roger Clemens	25	11	2	0	2	2	3	.440	.760	.481
Reggie Cleveland	12	2	0	0	0	0	1	.167	.167	.167
David Clyde	7	2	1	0	0	0	0	.286	.429	.286
Jaime Cocanower	13	5	0	0	0	1	0	.385	.385	.429
Chris Codiroli	22	10	2	1	0	5	1	.455	.636	.556
Steve Comer	15	7	0	0	0	1	1	.467	.467	.500
Tim Conroy	5	1	1	0	0	3	0	.200	.400	.500
Glenn Cook	4	2	0	1	0	2	0	.500	1.000	.667
Doug Corbett	18	9	0	0	2	1	1	.500	.833	.526
Ed Correa	11	4	2	0	1	0	3	.364	.818	.364
Joe Cowley	6	1	0	0	0	0	1	.167	.167	.167
Steve Crawford	9	4	0	0	1	1	1	.444	.778	.500
Victor Cruz	6	1	0	0	0	2	0	.167	.333	.375
John Curtis	8	3	1	1	0	0	1	.375	.750	.333
Danny Darwin	29	6	2	1	1	2	3	.207	.448	.258
Ron Davis	25	3	0	1	0	2	3	.120	.200	.185
Storm Davis	15	5	1	0	0	0	0	.333	.400	.313
John Denny	5	0	0	0	0	0	2	.000	.000	.143
Ken Dixon	9	2	1	0	0	2	3	.222	.333	.364
Richard Dotson	37	11	3	1	0	7	3	.297	.432	.409
Doug Drabek	4	1	0	0	0	0	2	.250	.250	.500
Dick Drago	7	0	0	0	0	0	1	.000	.000	.000
Rob Dressler	5	1	0	0	0	0	0	.200	.200	.167
Dennis Eckersley	49	13	5	1	0	2	7	.265	.408	.294
Mark Eichhorn	7	2	0	0	1	0	2	.286	.714	.286
Roger Erickson	16	7	0	1	0	2	0	.438	.563	.500
Ed Farmer	5	1	0	0	0	1	0	.200	.200	.333

Alan Trammell continued

Pitcher	AB	H	2B	3B	HR	BB	SO	BA	SA	OBA
Steve Farr	7	3	0	0	0	0	1	.429	.429	.375
Ed Figueroa	12	3	1	0	0	1	1	.250	.333	.308
Pete Filson	7	2	2	0	0	2	2	.286	.571	.400
Joel Finch	5	3	0	0	0	1	1	.600	.600	.667
Chuck Finley	5	1	0	0	0	2	0	.200	.200	.429
Brian Fisher	5	2	1	0	1	0	1	.400	1.200	.400
Mike Flanagan	84	28	5	2	2	6	6	.333	.512	.374
Ray Fontenot	11	3	0	0	0	1	1	.273	.273	.385
Ken Forsch	16	6	2	0	0	1	1	.375	.500	.412
Willie Fraser	5	0	0	0	0	1	0	.000	.000	.167
George Frazier	14	3	1	0	0	2	3	.214	.286	.333
Dave Frost	10	1	0	0	0	3	2	.100	.100	.308
Rich Gale	9	4	0	0	0	1	3	.444	.444	.500
Wayne Garland	11	2	0	0	0	1	3	.182	.182	.250
Jerry Garvin	14	4	1	0	0	0	0	.286	.357	.286
Dave Geisel	7	1	0	0	0	1	0	.143	.143	.250
Bob L. Gibson	10	2	0	1	0	3	1	.200	.400	.385
Jerry Don Gleaton	8	4	0	1	0	1	0	.500	1.000	.500
Dave Goltz	14	4	0	0	0	1	0	.286	.286	.333
Rich Gossage	17	2	0	0	0	1	5	.118	.118	.167
Jim Gott	19	7	1	2	1	1	5	.368	.789	.400
Mike Griffin	8	2	0	1	0	1	0	.250	.500	.333
Mark Gubicza	15	3	1	0	1	2	4	.200	.467	.333
Lee Guetterman	7	3	0	0	0	1	1	.429	.429	.500
Ron Guidry	75	21	3	1	0	8	13	.280	.347	.357
Don Gullett	7	0	0	0	0	0	0	.000	.000	.000
Larry Gura	42	11	3	0	0	7	1	.262	.333	.373
Jose Guzman	13	3	0	0	0	1	1	.231	.231	.313
Moose Haas	40	14	2	1	1	2	3	.350	.525	.381
John Habyan	11	3	1	0	0	1	1	.273	.364	.333
Greg Harris	11	4	2	0	0	2	1	.364	.545	.462
Paul Hartzell	6	0	0	0	0	1	1	.000	.000	.143
Andy Hassler	8	1	0	0	0	0	3	.125	.125	.125
Brad Havens	22	10	2	0	2	1	1	.455	.818	.478
Neal Heaton	24	7	2	0	0	2	3	.292	.375	.346
Dave Heaverlo	8	3	0	0	0	0	1	.375	.375	.444
Tom Henke	7	2	0	0	1	0	2	.286	.714	.286
Ted Higuera	21	6	1	0	1	5	6	.286	.476	.423
Guy Hoffman	3	0	0	0	0	2	1	.000	.000	.400
Rick Honeycutt	29	6	2	1	0	2	1	.207	.345	.258
Don Hood	14	5	0	0	0	2	1	.357	.357	.438
Burt Hooton	5	0	0	0	0	0	2	.000	.000	.000
Charlie Hough	39	13	1	0	2	7	6	.333	.513	.429
Tom House	6	1	0	0	0	0	0	.167	.167	.167
Jay Howell	8	1	0	0	0	2	1	.125	.125	.300
LaMarr Hoyt	28	9	1	0	0	2	6	.321	.357	.367
Charles Hudson	5	0	0	0	0	0	1	.000	.000	.000
Phil Huffman	7	4	0	0	0	0	2	.571	.571	.667
Mark Huismann	8	3	0	0	0	3	0	.375	.375	.545
Bruce Hurst	32	12	1	1	2	7	5	.375	.656	.487
Danny Jackson	27	4	0	1	1	1	4	.148	.333	.179
Darrell Jackson	25	7	0	2	0	5	2	.280	.440	.400
Roy Lee Jackson	12	5	1	0	0	1	2	.417	.500	.462
Bob James	7	3	1	0	0	0	1	.429	.571	.429
Jesse Jefferson	4	1	0	0	0	0	0	.250	.250	.250
Ferguson Jenkins	23	3	0	0	0	1	3	.130	.130	.167
Tommy John	50	13	1	0	0	1	2	.260	.280	.275
John Henry Johnson	12	3	0	0	0	1	2	.250	.250	.308
Jeff A. Jones	3	1	0	0	0	1	2	.333	.333	.500
Mike Jones	11	3	1	0	0	4	1	.273	.364	.467
Odell Jones	7	3	0	0	0	0	1	.429	.429	.429
Curt Kaufman	8	2	1	0	0	0	2	.250	.375	.250
Rickey Keeton	6	2	0	0	0	0	2	.333	.333	.333
Matt Keough	30	8	1	0	2	2	1	.267	.500	.313
Jim Kern	10	1	0	0	0	1	3	.100	.100	.182
Jimmy Key	28	7	2	1	0	3	1	.250	.393	.323
Brian Kingman	14	4	1	0	0	0	4	.286	.357	.286
Bruce Kison	18	3	0	1	0	2	8	.167	.278	.286
Chris Knapp	4	1	0	0	0	1	0	.250	.250	.400
Jerry Koosman	30	12	3	1	0	3	3	.400	.567	.441
Ken Kravec	10	0	0	0	0	2	0	.000	.000	.167
Bill Krueger	8	1	0	0	0	1	0	.125	.125	.222
Jack Kucek	5	1	1	0	0	0	0	.200	.400	.200
Bob Lacey	9	4	1	0	0	1	0	.444	.556	.500
Pete Ladd	10	3	1	0	0	0	0	.300	.400	.300
Dennis Lamp	32	6	0	0	0	1	6	.188	.188	.212
Rick Langford	35	10	2	0	2	2	1	.286	.514	.324
Mark Langston	34	11	1	0	2	2	6	.324	.529	.361
Dave LaRoche	13	4	0	0	1	1	1	.308	.538	.333
Jack Lazorko	7	1	0	0	0	1	1	.143	.143	.250
Luis Leal	39	11	4	2	0	6	5	.282	.487	.378
Charlie Leibrandt	20	10	2	0	2	1	0	.500	.900	.524
Dave Leiper	4	1	0	0	0	0	1	.250	.250	.200
Dave Lemanczyk	6	2	1	0	0	2	2	.333	.500	.500
Dennis Leonard	42	12	1	0	1	1	5	.286	.381	.302
Randy Lerch	15	1	0	0	0	4	2	.067	.067	.263
Paul Lindblad	4	2	0	0	0	1	1	.500	.500	.600
Tim Lollar	7	1	0	0	0	1	0	.143	.143	.250
Gary Lucas	9	1	0	0	0	1	1	.111	.111	.200
Sparky Lyle	8	0	0	0	0	1	0	.000	.000	.111
Rick Lysander	9	3	0	0	0	0	0	.333	.333	.300
Mike G. Marshall	5	1	0	0	0	0	0	.200	.200	.200
Dennis Martinez	49	15	2	0	0	4	4	.306	.347	.345
Tippy Martinez	23	7	1	0	0	3	4	.304	.348	.357
Mike Mason	15	1	1	0	0	0	3	.067	.133	.067
Jon Matlack	21	5	0	0	1	4	4	.238	.381	.360
Rudy May	25	10	4	0	0	0	4	.400	.560	.400
Kirk McCaskill	15	3	0	0	0	1	0	.200	.200	.250
Steve McCatty	27	7	0	0	3	2	4	.259	.593	.300
Bob McClure	17	5	2	0	0	3	1	.294	.412	.429
Scott McGregor	85	24	3	1	1	2	1	.282	.376	.295
Byron McLaughlin	7	0	0	0	0	0	0	.000	.000	.000
Joey McLaughlin	17	3	0	0	0	2	2	.176	.176	.263
Doc Medich	18	5	1	0	0	1	3	.278	.333	.286
Craig Minetto	11	2	0	0	0	0	1	.182	.182	.167
Paul Mirabella	12	4	1	0	0	1	1	.333	.417	.385
Paul Mitchell	9	2	1	0	0	0	2	.222	.333	.222
Sid Monge	15	0	0	0	0	0	3	.000	.000	.000
John Montague	2	1	0	0	0	2	0	.500	.500	.500
Balor Moore	13	5	0	0	0	1	2	.385	.385	.429
Donnie Moore	5	1	0	0	1	0	0	.200	.800	.200
Mike Moore	37	9	2	0	0	5	9	.243	.297	.333
Mike Morgan	11	3	0	0	2	1	0	.273	.818	.333
Dale Murray	12	4	1	0	1	0	0	.333	.667	.333
Ron Musselman	5	1	0	0	0	1	1	.200	.200	.333
Gene Nelson	13	2	1	0	0	3	2	.154	.231	.353
Joe Niekro	10	3	1	0	0	0	0	.300	.400	.300
Phil Niekro	27	6	0	0	1	3	7	.222	.333	.300
Scott Nielsen	5	2	0	0	1	0	0	.400	1.000	.400
Juan Nieves	13	5	1	0	1	5	1	.385	.692	.556
Al Nipper	23	11	3	1	1	0	0	.478	.826	.478
Dickie Noles	6	1	0	0	0	2	0	.167	.167	.375
Mike Norris	21	3	0	0	0	2	3	.143	.143	.217
Edwin Nunez	6	2	1	0	0	2	0	.333	.500	.500
Jack O'Connor	6	2	0	0	0	2	1	.333	.333	.556
Bob Ojeda	31	4	0	0	1	6	5	.129	.226	.270
Steve Ontiveros	9	2	0	0	0	0	1	.222	.222	.222
Bob Owchinko	12	4	1	0	0	4	1	.333	.417	.500
John Pacella	5	2	0	0	1	2	0	.400	1.000	.500
Jim Palmer	32	7	1	0	0	4	4	.219	.250	.306
Mike Parrott	15	4	2	0	0	0	3	.267	.400	.267
Mike Paxton	9	2	0	1	0	2	2	.222	.444	.364
Gaylord Perry	4	1	1	0	0	4	1	.250	.500	.625
Eric Plunk	8	1	0	0	0	1	3	.125	.125	.222
Chuck Porter	6	1	0	0	0	0	1	.167	.167	.167
Mike Proly	10	1	0	0	1	0	1	.100	.400	.100
Dan Quisenberry	33	9	4	0	1	2	2	.273	.485	.306
Chuck Rainey	7	4	0	1	0	0	1	.571	.857	.571
Dave Rajsich	5	2	0	0	0	1	0	.400	.400	.500
Dennis Rasmussen	26	10	2	1	2	3	3	.385	.769	.448
Shane Rawley	22	6	2	0	0	7	1	.273	.364	.448
Pete Redfern	13	4	1	0	0	2	0	.308	.385	.400
Jerry Reed	7	2	0	0	0	1	0	.286	.286	.375
Win Remmerswaal	4	1	0	0	0	1	1	.250	.250	.400
Steve Renko	15	4	0	0	1	2	3	.267	.467	.353
Andy Replogle	5	3	1	0	0	1	0	.600	.800	.667
Paul Reuschel	7	3	0	0	0	0	0	.429	.429	.429
Rick Rhoden	7	2	0	0	0	0	0	.286	.286	.286
Dave Righetti	29	8	0	0	0	9	3	.276	.276	.447
Jose Rijo	11	1	0	0	0	0	0	.091	.091	.091

Alan Trammell continued

Pitcher	AB	H	2B	3B	HR	BB	SO	BA	SA	OBA
Ron Romanick	6	1	0	0	0	0	0	.167	.167	.143
Vern Ruhle	6	1	1	0	0	0	1	.167	.333	.167
Jeff Russell	8	3	1	0	0	1	0	.375	.500	.444
Nolan Ryan	6	1	0	0	0	0	3	.167	.167	.167
Bret Saberhagen	42	15	2	1	0	1	6	.357	.452	.364
Joe Sambito	4	3	2	0	0	1	0	.750	1.250	.800
Luis Sanchez	10	3	2	0	0	0	0	.300	.500	.300
Calvin Schiraldi	7	2	0	0	0	0	1	.286	.286	.286
Dave J. Schmidt	12	4	1	0	1	3	1	.333	.667	.467
Ken Schrom	32	8	4	0	1	6	1	.250	.469	.368
Ron Schueler	7	1	0	0	0	0	1	.143	.143	.143
Don Schulze	8	4	1	0	1	0	1	.500	1.000	.500
Ray Searage	8	3	1	0	1	0	0	.375	.875	.375
Tom Seaver	26	5	0	0	0	0	6	.192	.192	.185
Jeff Sellers	5	3	1	0	1	0	0	.600	1.400	.600
Gary Serum	6	0	0	0	0	1	1	.000	.000	.143
Bob Shirley	19	6	0	0	1	2	1	.316	.474	.381
Jim Slaton	20	5	0	0	2	2	2	.250	.550	.318
Roy Smith	10	1	0	0	0	0	0	.100	.100	.100
Mike Smithson	21	8	2	0	1	3	1	.381	.619	.480
Nate Snell	7	2	0	0	0	0	0	.286	.286	.286
Lary Sorensen	33	10	2	0	0	1	2	.303	.364	.324
Dan Spillner	41	13	2	0	0	2	5	.317	.366	.349
Paul Splittorff	28	9	2	0	0	1	0	.321	.393	.345
Don Stanhouse	8	2	0	0	0	0	0	.250	.250	.250
Bob Stanley	30	11	2	0	1	1	5	.367	.533	.387
Mike Stanton	9	3	0	0	0	4	1	.333	.333	.538
Ricky Steirer	4	1	1	0	0	1	0	.250	.500	.400
Dave Stewart	12	3	1	0	0	1	0	.250	.333	.308
Sammy Stewart	38	11	1	0	0	3	1	.289	.316	.341
Dave Stieb	58	17	6	0	1	4	4	.293	.448	.349
Bob Stoddard	10	2	0	0	0	1	3	.200	.200	.273
Tim Stoddard	7	0	0	0	0	2	2	.000	.000	.222
Steve Stone	15	4	1	0	0	3	4	.267	.333	.389
Les Straker	4	1	0	0	0	1	0	.250	.250	.400
Rick Sutcliffe	10	4	0	0	1	2	0	.400	.700	.500
Don Sutton	29	5	0	0	0	0	4	.172	.172	.172
Bill Swaggerty	7	3	0	0	0	1	0	.429	.429	.500
Bill Swift	5	4	0	0	1	1	0	.800	1.400	.833
Frank Tanana	34	11	0	0	1	6	1	.324	.412	.439
Tom Tellmann	6	1	0	0	0	1	1	.167	.167	.286
Roy Thomas	13	4	0	0	1	3	3	.308	.538	.438
Luis Tiant	12	1	0	0	0	0	2	.083	.083	.083
Dick Tidrow	17	5	0	0	0	0	6	.294	.294	.294
Jackson Todd	8	4	0	0	2	0	0	.500	1.250	.500
Jim Todd	5	2	0	0	0	0	0	.400	.400	.400
Mike Torrez	39	15	1	0	1	3	3	.385	.487	.429
Bill Travers	15	2	0	0	0	2	3	.133	.133	.235
Steve Trout	16	5	0	1	0	0	0	.313	.438	.313
John Tudor	23	5	1	0	0	0	3	.217	.261	.217
Jim Umbarger	7	2	1	0	0	1	1	.286	.429	.375
Tom Underwood	26	8	2	0	0	1	1	.308	.385	.333
Ed Vande Berg	16	9	1	0	4	0	2	.563	1.375	.563
John Verhoeven	6	2	0	0	0	0	1	.333	.333	.333
Frank Viola	41	10	2	1	4	5	3	.244	.634	.326
Pete Vuckovich	25	11	1	0	1	5	4	.440	.600	.533
Tom Waddell	13	2	0	0	0	1	3	.154	.154	.214
Rick Waits	16	6	2	0	1	7	2	.375	.688	.565
Bill Wegman	18	4	1	0	1	2	1	.222	.444	.300
Sandy Wihtol	5	1	0	0	0	1	1	.200	.200	.333
Al Williams	17	4	1	0	0	1	4	.235	.294	.250
Mitch Williams	6	1	0	0	0	0	0	.167	.167	.286
Mark Williamson	5	0	0	0	0	0	0	.000	.000	.000
Mike Willis	7	3	0	0	0	0	1	.429	.429	.429
Frank Wills	6	0	0	0	0	2	1	.000	.000	.250
Rick Wise	6	4	0	0	0	1	1	.667	.667	.714
Bobby Witt	9	3	0	0	0	4	2	.333	.333	.538
Mike Witt	40	10	1	0	2	1	12	.250	.425	.268
Rob Woodward	7	0	0	0	0	0	0	.000	.000	.000
Rich Wortham	6	4	1	0	0	0	0	.667	.833	.667
Rich Yett	8	6	1	0	1	0	0	.750	1.250	.750
Curt Young	23	6	1	0	1	0	0	.261	.435	.261
Matt Young	24	9	4	1	0	3	1	.375	.625	.444
Geoff Zahn	37	8	1	0	0	2	3	.216	.243	.256

Steve Bedrosian

Batter	AB	H	2B	3B	HR	BB	SO	BA	SA	OBA
Bill Almon	5	3	2	0	0	0	2	.600	1.000	.600
Dave Anderson	14	2	0	0	0	2	3	.143	.143	.250
Joaquin Andujar	5	0	0	0	0	0	0	.000	.000	.000
Alan Ashby	18	5	0	0	1	2	2	.278	.444	.333
Wally Backman	18	3	0	0	0	3	5	.167	.167	.286
Mark Bailey	4	1	0	0	1	1	3	.250	1.000	.400
Bob Bailor	5	1	0	0	0	0	0	.200	.200	.333
Dusty Baker	16	4	0	0	1	3	3	.250	.438	.368
Kevin Bass	20	3	1	0	0	1	3	.150	.200	.190
Buddy Bell	7	1	0	0	0	0	2	.143	.143	.143
Johnny Bench	9	2	0	0	1	1	1	.222	.556	.300
Dave Bergman	4	2	0	0	0	1	0	.500	.500	.667
Dale Berra	9	0	0	0	0	0	3	.000	.000	.000
Larry Biittner	5	0	0	0	0	0	2	.000	.000	.000
Dann Bilardello	6	1	0	0	0	1	2	.167	.167	.286
Barry Bonds	5	2	1	0	0	3	1	.400	1.200	.625
Bobby Bonilla	5	3	1	0	1	0	0	.600	1.400	.600
Juan Bonilla	6	1	0	0	0	0	1	.167	.167	.167
Thad Bosley	4	1	0	0	0	1	0	.250	.250	.400
Larry Bowa	10	1	1	0	0	0	1	.100	.200	.100
Sid Bream	9	3	1	0	0	0	3	.333	.444	.333
Bob Brenly	21	5	1	0	0	1	5	.238	.286	.273
Greg Brock	18	3	0	0	2	0	3	.167	.500	.167
Hubie Brooks	28	3	0	0	0	0	14	.107	.107	.107
Bobby Brown	7	1	0	0	0	0	3	.143	.143	.143
Chris Brown	16	1	0	0	0	1	4	.063	.063	.167
Mike C. Brown	5	1	0	0	0	0	0	.200	.200	.200
Bill Buckner	10	0	0	0	0	0	0	.000	.000	.000
Enos Cabell	9	4	0	0	0	1	1	.444	.444	.500
Gary Carter	29	7	1	0	1	2	2	.241	.379	.290
Cesar Cedeno	13	4	0	0	0	0	3	.308	.308	.308
Ron Cey	22	5	0	0	1	2	7	.227	.364	.292
Jack Clark	21	4	1	0	1	1	2	.190	.381	.227
Will Clark	5	2	0	0	1	0	1	.400	1.000	.400
Vince Coleman	12	4	0	0	0	0	1	.333	.333	.333
Dave Concepcion	35	11	2	0	0	2	6	.314	.371	.351
Tim Corcoran	8	2	1	0	0	0	0	.250	.375	.250
Warren Cromartie	11	2	0	0	0	0	4	.182	.182	.182
Jose Cruz	26	5	0	0	1	3	5	.192	.308	.276
Chili Davis	24	8	1	0	2	4	4	.333	.625	.414
Eric Davis	6	0	0	0	0	0	0	.000	.000	.000
Glenn Davis	13	6	0	0	0	1	4	.462	.692	.500
Jody Davis	15	1	0	0	1	8	6	.067	.267	.391
Andre Dawson	38	9	0	0	1	1	6	.237	.316	.275
Rob Deer	4	1	0	1	0	1	1	.250	.750	.400
Ivan DeJesus	3	0	0	0	0	2	1	.000	.000	.400
Bob Dernier	10	4	0	0	0	1	1	.400	.400	.455
Bo Diaz	11	2	0	0	0	1	4	.182	.182	.308
Mike Diaz	5	2	0	0	0	0	1	.400	.400	.400
Bill Doran	21	6	1	0	0	3	3	.286	.333	.375
Dan Driessen	22	3	1	0	0	6	1	.136	.182	.345
Mariano Duncan	9	1	0	0	0	0	2	.111	.111	.100
Shawon Dunston	12	4	1	0	0	0	2	.333	.417	.333
Leon Durham	22	9	2	1	2	4	4	.409	.864	.500
Len Dykstra	6	2	0	0	0	4	0	.333	.333	.600
Mike Easler	5	1	0	0	0	1	2	.200	.800	.333
Nick Esasky	14	8	1	0	1	1	3	.571	.857	.625
Darrell Evans	10	3	1	0	0	0	3	.300	.400	.300

Steve Bedrosian continued

Batter	AB	H	2B	3B	HR	BB	SO	BA	SA	OBA
Jack Fimple	3	0	0	0	0	0	2	.000	.000	.000
Mike Fitzgerald	12	0	0	0	0	0	3	.000	.000	.000
Tim Flannery	18	4	1	0	0	1	5	.222	.278	.263
Doug Flynn	6	0	0	0	0	0	2	.000	.000	.000
Curt Ford	7	1	0	0	0	0	1	.143	.143	.143
George Foster	18	5	1	0	0	1	2	.278	.333	.316
Terry Francona	9	3	1	0	0	1	2	.333	.444	.400
Andres Galarraga	9	1	0	0	0	0	2	.111	.111	.111
Ron Gardenhire	6	3	1	0	0	0	1	.500	.667	.500
Phil Garner	17	6	3	0	0	2	5	.353	.529	.421
Steve Garvey	29	8	1	0	1	6	4	.276	.414	.400
Brian Giles	7	2	0	0	0	1	4	.286	.286	.375
Dan Gladden	11	3	0	0	0	1	1	.273	.273	.333
Denny Gonzalez	5	0	0	0	0	0	1	.000	.000	.000
David Green	5	2	0	0	0	2	0	.400	.400	.571
Greg Gross	6	2	0	0	0	4	0	.333	.333	.636
Pedro Guerrero	24	5	0	0	0	3	5	.208	.208	.296
Tony Gwynn	26	7	1	0	0	2	3	.269	.308	.321
Von Hayes	12	5	1	1	0	0	1	.417	.667	.385
Danny Heep	15	3	1	0	0	3	3	.200	.267	.333
George Hendrick	14	7	0	0	2	1	2	.500	.929	.533
Keith Hernandez	22	4	0	0	1	6	5	.182	.318	.357
Tommy Herr	21	6	0	0	1	1	7	.286	.429	.318
Ron Hodges	7	5	0	0	0	1	1	.714	.714	.750
Paul Householder	8	2	1	0	0	1	2	.250	.375	.333
Art Howe	3	1	0	0	0	2	0	.333	.333	.600
Dane Iorg	7	0	0	0	0	1	5	.000	.000	.125
Howard Johnson	12	4	0	0	2	0	3	.333	.833	.333
Jay Johnstone	5	1	0	0	1	0	3	.200	.800	.200
Ruppert Jones	7	0	0	0	0	0	4	.000	.000	.000
Mike Jorgensen	3	0	0	0	0	3	3	.000	.000	.500
Steve Kemp	4	1	0	0	0	4	2	.250	.250	.625
Terry Kennedy	28	8	1	0	1	3	1	.286	.429	.355
Dave Kingman	6	1	0	0	0	2	1	.167	.167	.375
Alan Knicely	6	0	0	0	0	0	2	.000	.000	.250
Ray Knight	23	11	1	0	2	1	2	.478	.783	.500
Wayne Krenchicki	12	5	1	0	1	2	2	.417	.750	.500
Ken Landreaux	24	8	2	0	1	6	5	.333	.542	.455
Dave LaPoint	4	1	0	0	0	1	1	.250	.250	.400
Mike LaValliere	5	0	0	0	0	0	0	.000	.000	.000
Vance Law	8	2	1	0	1	3	2	.250	.750	.455
Joe Lefebvre	7	1	0	0	0	1	1	.143	.143	.250
Johnnie LeMaster	10	2	0	0	1	2	4	.200	.500	.333
Jeffrey Leonard	24	6	0	0	1	2	13	.250	.375	.308
Sixto Lezcano	5	1	1	0	0	1	1	.200	.400	.333
Bryan Little	5	1	0	0	0	2	0	.200	.200	.429
Dave Lopes	4	0	0	0	0	3	0	.000	.000	.429
Garry Maddox	7	1	0	0	0	0	2	.143	.143	.143
Bill Madlock	21	7	3	0	0	1	2	.333	.476	.348
Mike A. Marshall	14	3	1	0	0	2	5	.214	.286	.313
Carmelo Martinez	11	1	1	0	0	0	3	.091	.182	.091
Dave Martinez	6	2	0	0	1	0	3	.333	.833	.333
Gary Matthews	12	3	0	0	0	4	5	.250	.250	.438
Len Matuszek	5	0	0	0	0	1	2	.000	.000	.143
Milt May	8	3	2	0	0	0	0	.375	.625	.375
Lee Mazzilli	9	2	1	0	1	8	2	.222	.667	.588
Andy McGaffigan	5	1	1	0	0	0	2	.200	.400	.200
Willie McGee	21	5	1	0	0	2	4	.238	.286	.304
Kevin McReynolds	23	3	0	0	0	2	5	.130	.130	.200
Eddie Milner	28	9	1	0	0	5	3	.321	.357	.424
Rick Monday	9	1	1	0	0	2	6	.111	.222	.273
Keith Moreland	25	5	1	0	0	1	4	.200	.240	.231
Omar Moreno	6	0	0	0	0	0	2	.000	.000	.000
Joe Morgan	6	1	0	0	0	3	2	.167	.167	.444
Jim Morrison	8	2	0	0	0	0	1	.250	.250	.250
Jerry Mumphrey	14	6	1	0	1	2	0	.429	.714	.500
Dale Murphy	3	2	0	0	0	2	0	.667	.667	.800
Graig Nettles	17	5	0	0	2	1	3	.294	.647	.333
Ken Oberkfell	11	2	1	0	0	0	1	.182	.273	.250
Ron Oester	32	6	1	0	1	4	8	.188	.313	.270
Al Oliver	11	5	3	0	0	4	1	.455	.727	.600
Tom O'Malley	5	1	0	0	0	1	1	.200	.200	.429
Jose Oquendo	8	3	0	0	0	1	2	.375	.375	.444
Joe Orsulak	8	2	0	0	0	0	2	.250	.250	.250
Dave Parker	27	7	1	0	0	3	1	.259	.296	.333
Tony Pena	21	4	1	0	0	1	3	.190	.238	.217
Terry Pendleton	16	3	0	0	0	1	3	.188	.188	.235
Tony Perez	5	0	0	0	0	1	1	.000	.000	.167
Darrell Porter	11	1	0	0	0	0	4	.091	.091	.091
Terry Puhl	12	1	0	0	1	0	2	.083	.333	.083
Tim Raines	26	9	1	1	0	3	6	.346	.462	.433
Gary Rajsich	4	1	0	0	0	2	2	.250	.250	.500
Mike Ramsey	5	0	0	0	0	0	1	.000	.000	.000
Johnny Ray	23	8	1	0	1	4	0	.348	.522	.444
Gary Redus	11	1	1	0	0	3	6	.091	.182	.286
Craig Reynolds	16	5	1	0	1	2	3	.313	.563	.389
R.J. Reynolds	9	4	2	0	0	3	1	.444	.667	.583
Gene Richards	7	1	0	0	0	0	1	.143	.143	.143
Ron Roenicke	8	0	0	0	0	3	4	.000	.000	.273
Pete Rose	22	6	2	0	0	6	2	.273	.364	.429
Bill Russell	12	4	0	0	0	3	2	.333	.333	.438
Luis Salazar	18	6	0	0	1	0	2	.333	.500	.333
Juan Samuel	7	1	0	1	0	2	2	.143	.429	.333
Ryne Sandberg	30	11	2	0	0	1	6	.367	.433	.387
Rafael Santana	7	0	0	0	0	0	1	.000	.000	.000
Steve Sax	39	9	3	0	0	1	8	.231	.308	.250
Mike Schmidt	12	3	1	0	1	3	5	.250	.583	.400
Mike Scioscia	20	6	1	0	1	5	3	.300	.500	.440
Tony Scott	7	1	0	0	0	0	1	.143	.143	.143
Lonnie Smith	8	2	1	0	0	1	2	.250	.375	.333
Ozzie Smith	17	5	0	0	0	4	1	.294	.294	.409
Mario Soto	5	1	0	0	0	0	2	.200	.200	.200
Chris Speier	16	5	1	0	0	0	0	.313	.375	.313
Harry Spilman	7	2	2	0	0	0	1	.286	.571	.286
Rusty Staub	8	3	1	0	0	0	0	.375	.500	.375
John Stearns	4	0	0	0	0	1	0	.000	.000	.200
Darryl Strawberry	15	2	0	0	1	5	5	.133	.333	.350
Franklin Stubbs	8	2	0	0	2	1	1	.250	1.000	.333
Jim Sundberg	5	0	0	0	0	0	1	.000	.000	.167
Garry Templeton	28	7	0	2	0	3	6	.250	.393	.313
Derrel Thomas	6	0	0	0	0	1	2	.000	.000	.143
Jason Thompson	10	2	0	0	1	5	4	.200	.500	.467
Scot Thompson	6	2	0	0	0	0	1	.333	.333	.333
Dickie Thon	8	2	0	0	0	1	2	.250	.250	.333
Alex Trevino	8	0	0	0	0	3	0	.000	.000	.273
Manny Trillo	21	4	0	0	2	1	4	.190	.476	.227
Jose Uribe	14	2	1	0	0	1	2	.143	.214	.200
Ellis Valentine	7	2	1	0	0	0	0	.286	.429	.286
Andy Van Slyke	10	3	0	0	1	3	1	.300	.600	.429
Max Venable	10	1	0	0	0	1	2	.100	.100	.182
Ozzie Virgil	11	3	1	0	0	2	3	.273	.364	.385
Duane Walker	11	2	0	0	0	4	4	.182	.182	.182
Tim Wallach	28	3	0	0	0	1	6	.107	.107	.138
Denny Walling	18	5	2	1	0	1	1	.278	.500	.316
Mitch Webster	7	1	0	0	1	2	0	.143	.571	.333
Alan Wiggins	17	6	0	0	0	2	1	.353	.353	.400
Bump Wills	5	0	0	0	0	0	1	.000	.000	.167
Glenn Wilson	8	1	0	0	0	0	3	.125	.125	.125
Mookie Wilson	22	7	1	0	0	0	6	.318	.364	.348
Herm Winningham	11	2	0	0	0	1	2	.182	.182	.250
Jim Wohlford	6	1	0	0	0	0	1	.167	.167	.167
Mike Woodard	4	2	0	0	0	1	0	.500	.500	.600
Gary Woods	5	0	0	0	0	0	0	.000	.000	.000
Marvell Wynne	13	5	1	0	0	1	2	.385	.462	.429
Joel Youngblood	13	1	1	0	0	1	5	.077	.154	.143

Roger Clemens

Batter	AB	H	2B	3B	HR	BB	SO	BA	SA	OBA	Batter	AB	H	2B	3B	HR	BB	SO	BA	SA	OBA
Willie Aikens	6	0	0	0	0	0	4	.000	.000	.000	Roy Howell	6	2	1	0	0	0	3	.333	.500	.333
Andy Allanson	5	2	1	0	0	1	1	.400	.600	.500	Kent Hrbek	30	8	2	0	1	4	4	.267	.433	.333
Harold Baines	28	8	1	0	1	2	5	.286	.429	.333	Tim Hulett	10	2	0	0	0	0	3	.200	.200	.200
Steve Balboni	19	2	0	0	2	1	10	.105	.421	.150	Dane Iorg	9	4	1	0	0	1	0	.444	.556	.500
Chris Bando	11	0	0	0	0	0	6	.000	.000	.000	Garth Iorg	8	1	0	0	0	1	0	.125	.500	.125
Jesse Barfield	22	4	0	0	0	3	6	.182	.182	.280	Bo Jackson	7	1	1	0	0	0	2	.143	.286	.143
Don Baylor	6	1	0	0	1	1	3	.167	.667	.286	Reggie Jackson	23	6	2	0	2	3	9	.261	.609	.346
George Bell	30	6	2	0	1	0	9	.200	.367	.200	Brook Jacoby	15	3	0	0	0	1	10	.200	.200	.250
Juan Beniquez	14	3	0	0	0	1	1	.214	.214	.267	Dion James	6	2	2	0	0	0	0	.333	.667	.333
Tony Bernazard	15	1	1	0	0	3	3	.067	.133	.263	Houston Jimenez	6	0	0	0	0	0	0	.000	.000	.000
Buddy Biancalana	6	1	0	0	0	0	3	.167	.167	.167	Cliff Johnson	6	0	0	0	0	0	1	.000	.000	.000
Bruce Bochte	14	4	0	0	0	3	2	.286	.286	.412	Ruppert Jones	19	4	2	0	0	2	4	.211	.316	.286
Juan Bonilla	6	2	0	0	0	0	0	.333	.333	.333	Wally Joyner	18	5	1	1	1	2	2	.278	.611	.350
Bob Boone	9	1	0	0	0	0	1	.111	.111	.111	Terry Kennedy	7	2	0	0	0	0	0	.286	.286	.286
Thad Bosley	8	1	1	0	0	0	1	.125	.250	.125	Mike Kingery	11	2	1	0	0	1	4	.182	.273	.250
Daryl Boston	10	2	0	0	0	1	1	.200	.200	.273	Dave Kingman	18	6	0	0	3	1	5	.333	.833	.368
Phil Bradley	24	4	1	1	0	0	11	.167	.292	.167	Ron Kittle	8	0	0	0	0	0	5	.000	.000	.000
Scott Bradley	14	3	1	1	0	0	2	.214	.429	.267	Ray Knight	7	1	0	0	0	0	3	.143	.143	.143
George Brett	18	3	1	0	0	3	2	.167	.222	.286	Lee Lacy	7	2	1	0	0	1	1	.286	.429	.375
Greg Brock	6	2	0	0	0	1	1	.333	.333	.429	Carney Lansford	23	6	3	0	0	0	5	.261	.391	.292
Tom Brookens	8	3	0	0	0	0	2	.375	.375	.375	Tim Laudner	5	1	0	0	0	1	4	.200	.800	.333
Bob Brower	7	1	0	0	0	2	3	.143	.143	.333	Rudy Law	14	3	1	0	0	2	4	.214	.286	.313
Jerry Browne	12	3	1	0	0	1	2	.250	.333	.308	Vance Law	7	2	1	0	0	0	1	.286	.429	.286
Tom Brunansky	33	9	2	0	2	4	5	.273	.515	.351	Rick Leach	7	3	0	0	0	1	1	.429	.429	.500
Steve Buechele	9	1	0	0	0	0	3	.111	.111	.111	Chet Lemon	16	5	1	0	0	1	5	.313	.375	.389
Randy Bush	32	5	1	0	1	2	8	.156	.281	.206	Steve Lombardozzi	19	0	0	0	0	3	8	.000	.000	.136
Brett Butler	29	10	2	0	0	0	3	.345	.414	.367	Greg Luzinski	5	2	0	0	0	0	2	.400	.400	.400
Ivan Calderon	6	0	0	0	0	0	4	.000	.000	.000	Fred Lynn	13	2	2	0	0	1	6	.154	.308	.267
John Cangelosi	10	3	0	0	0	2	0	.300	.300	.417	Steve Lyons	4	0	0	0	0	1	1	.000	.000	.167
Jose Canseco	17	4	0	0	2	0	5	.235	.588	.235	Bill Madlock	9	2	0	0	0	2	2	.222	.222	.364
Joe Carter	27	5	1	0	2	0	8	.185	.444	.185	Rick Manning	17	3	0	0	0	0	4	.176	.176	.176
Carmen Castillo	11	4	0	0	2	0	3	.364	.909	.364	Don Mattingly	22	8	0	0	0	0	2	.364	.364	.364
Darnell Coles	10	4	1	0	1	1	1	.400	.800	.455	Oddibe McDowell	13	4	1	0	0	1	4	.308	.385	.357
Dave Collins	20	6	0	0	0	1	3	.300	.300	.333	Fred McGriff	9	1	0	0	0	0	6	.111	.111	.111
Onix Concepcion	8	2	0	0	0	0	3	.250	.250	.250	Mark McGwire	5	0	0	0	0	1	2	.000	.000	.167
Cecil Cooper	18	3	1	0	0	0	3	.167	.278	.158	Mark McLemore	7	2	0	0	0	1	2	.286	.286	.375
Al Cowens	5	3	1	0	1	2	1	.600	1.400	.714	Hal McRae	8	1	0	0	0	2	2	.125	.125	.300
Julio Cruz	3	1	0	0	0	4	0	.333	.333	.625	Bobby Meacham	9	4	1	0	0	1	1	.444	.556	.500
Alvin Davis	19	10	4	0	2	2	2	.526	1.053	.571	Paul Molitor	18	6	2	0	0	0	6	.333	.444	.333
Mike Davis	22	7	2	0	1	1	8	.318	.545	.348	Charlie Moore	6	2	0	0	0	0	1	.333	.333	.286
Doug DeCinces	26	5	1	0	1	1	5	.192	.346	.222	Lloyd Moseby	26	3	2	0	0	4	11	.115	.192	.233
Rob Deer	8	1	0	0	0	0	6	.125	.125	.125	John Moses	12	3	0	0	0	0	3	.250	.250	.250
Rick Dempsey	5	0	0	0	0	0	4	.000	.000	.000	Darryl Motley	17	4	0	0	0	1	5	.235	.235	.278
Brian Downing	16	4	1	0	1	3	2	.250	.500	.409	Rance Mulliniks	30	10	4	0	1	2	6	.333	.567	.375
Jim Dwyer	9	1	0	0	0	1	3	.111	.111	.200	Dwayne Murphy	12	2	2	0	0	1	4	.167	.333	.231
Mike Easler	13	6	2	0	0	0	3	.462	.615	.462	Eddie Murray	20	7	1	0	2	4	1	.350	.700	.458
Darrell Evans	21	4	0	0	1	3	5	.190	.333	.292	Jerry Narron	11	4	1	0	0	1	3	.364	.455	.417
Mike Felder	10	2	2	0	0	0	2	.200	.400	.200	Al Newman	7	1	0	0	0	0	0	.143	.143	.143
Tony Fernandez	26	8	1	0	0	2	2	.308	.346	.367	Junior Noboa	4	1	0	0	0	0	0	.250	.250	.250
Carlton Fisk	21	6	0	0	5	2	3	.286	1.000	.375	Matt Nokes	8	2	0	0	0	1	1	.250	.250	.400
Scott Fletcher	14	1	0	0	0	4	3	.071	.071	.278	Pete O'Brien	17	8	1	0	0	5	1	.471	.529	.591
Julio Franco	28	5	1	0	0	0	5	.179	.214	.179	Ben Oglivie	14	6	0	0	0	0	1	.429	.429	.429
Gary Gaetti	32	8	2	0	2	4	3	.250	.500	.333	Tom O'Malley	13	3	2	0	0	2	2	.231	.385	.333
Greg Gagne	13	4	0	0	1	3	5	.308	.538	.438	Jorge Orta	11	4	1	0	0	1	1	.364	.455	.364
Jim Gantner	16	0	0	0	0	0	2	.000	.000	.000	Spike Owen	11	2	0	0	0	1	4	.182	.182	.250
Damaso Garcia	12	3	0	0	0	0	1	.250	.250	.250	Tom Paciorek	9	3	1	0	0	0	2	.333	.444	.333
Kirk Gibson	18	1	0	0	0	5	7	.056	.056	.250	Mike Pagliarulo	21	3	2	0	0	1	5	.143	.238	.182
Bobby Grich	5	0	0	0	0	3	3	.000	.000	.375	Lance Parrish	6	0	0	0	0	0	4	.000	.000	.000
Ken Griffey	9	5	0	0	0	2	1	.556	.556	.636	Larry Parrish	7	2	0	0	0	0	4	.286	.286	.286
Alfredo Griffin	16	7	3	0	0	1	2	.438	.625	.471	Dan Pasqua	9	2	0	0	0	1	4	.222	.222	.300
Johnny Grubb	10	3	2	0	0	1	1	.300	.500	.364	Jack Perconte	5	1	1	0	0	1	0	.200	.400	.333
Ozzie Guillen	18	4	0	0	0	0	3	.222	.222	.222	Rick Peters	5	0	0	0	0	0	2	.000	.000	.000
Jerry Hairston	12	1	1	0	0	0	1	.083	.167	.083	Geno Petralli	9	2	0	0	1	2	4	.222	.556	.364
Mel Hall	22	4	0	0	0	1	7	.182	.273	.217	Gary Pettis	18	2	0	0	0	4	8	.111	.111	.273
Mike Hargrove	11	3	0	0	0	0	1	.273	.273	.273	Ken Phelps	18	3	0	0	0	2	9	.167	.167	.286
Toby Harrah	5	0	0	0	0	2	3	.000	.000	.286	Tony Phillips	17	5	2	0	0	1	4	.294	.412	.333
Ron Hassey	11	3	1	0	0	1	1	.273	.364	.333	Luis Polonia	8	3	1	0	0	0	1	.375	.500	.375
Mickey Hatcher	12	3	0	0	0	1	1	.250	.250	.308	Darrell Porter	16	4	0	0	1	1	4	.250	.438	.333
Mike Heath	11	1	0	0	0	0	3	.091	.091	.091	Jim Presley	24	5	2	0	1	1	11	.208	.417	.240
Dave Henderson	9	3	1	0	0	0	4	.333	.444	.333	Kirby Puckett	36	9	1	1	0	1	9	.250	.333	.270
Rickey Henderson	18	4	1	0	0	1	6	.222	.278	.263	Rey Quinones	6	2	0	0	0	0	1	.333	.333	.286
Donnie Hill	13	2	1	0	0	0	2	.154	.231	.154	Domingo Ramos	5	1	0	0	0	0	1	.200	.200	.200
Marc Hill	5	2	0	0	0	0	0	.400	.400	.400	Willie Randolph	25	4	0	0	0	0	4	.160	.160	.160
Tommy Hinzo	7	2	0	0	0	0	4	.286	.286	.286	Floyd Rayford	4	1	0	0	0	2	0	.250	.250	.500
Jack Howell	17	1	0	0	0	2	3	.059	.059	.158	Jeff Reed	6	1	1	0	0	0	2	.167	.333	.167

Roger Clemens continued

Batter	AB	H	2B	3B	HR	BB	SO	BA	SA	OBA
Harold Reynolds	10	2	1	1	0	1	1	.200	.500	.333
Ernest Riles	19	5	0	0	0	0	3	.263	.263	.250
Cal Ripken	24	6	0	0	0	0	1	.250	.250	.250
Gary Roenicke	5	2	0	0	1	0	0	.400	1.000	.400
Mark Salas	22	9	1	0	0	2	1	.409	.455	.458
Argenis Salazar	6	1	0	0	0	0	0	.167	.167	.167
Dick Schofield	19	6	0	0	0	0	2	.316	.316	.350
Donnie Scott	6	1	0	0	0	0	3	.167	.167	.167
Kevin Seitzer	7	1	1	0	0	1	1	.143	.286	.250
Mike Sharperson	4	1	0	0	0	1	1	.250	.250	.400
Larry Sheets	16	5	2	0	0	2	2	.313	.438	.389
John Shelby	10	1	1	0	0	0	3	.100	.200	.100
Pat Sheridan	21	5	1	0	0	1	8	.238	.286	.273
Ruben Sierra	13	4	1	0	0	1	3	.308	.385	.357
Ted Simmons	10	2	0	0	0	1	1	.200	.200	.273
Roy Smalley	38	6	1	0	0	2	8	.158	.184	.200
Cory Snyder	9	0	0	0	0	0	9	.000	.000	.000
Jim Sundberg	15	5	0	1	0	0	4	.333	.467	.333
B.J. Surhoff	7	0	0	0	0	0	0	.000	.000	.000
Dale Sveum	9	1	1	0	0	1	3	.111	.222	.200
Pat Tabler	22	5	0	0	0	3	6	.227	.227	.320
Danny Tartabull	9	2	0	0	0	2	3	.222	.222	.364
Mickey Tettleton	7	2	0	0	1	1	2	.286	.714	.375

Batter	AB	H	2B	3B	HR	BB	SO	BA	SA	OBA
Tim Teufel	10	0	0	0	0	1	3	.000	.000	.083
Gorman Thomas	7	1	0	0	1	0	3	.143	.571	.143
Andre Thornton	5	2	0	0	0	4	2	.400	.400	.600
Wayne Tolleson	10	2	0	0	0	1	3	.200	.200	.273
Alan Trammell	25	11	2	0	2	2	3	.440	.760	.481
Willie Upshaw	31	8	0	1	1	0	6	.258	.419	.258
George Vukovich	12	4	1	0	0	0	5	.333	.417	.333
Greg Walker	21	5	2	0	0	2	4	.238	.333	.292
Gary Ward	14	4	0	0	1	3	6	.286	.500	.412
Claudell Washington	6	1	0	0	0	1	2	.167	.167	.286
John Wathan	5	1	0	0	0	0	0	.200	.200	.200
Lou Whitaker	24	9	1	0	0	2	4	.375	.417	.407
Devon White	12	1	0	0	0	0	2	.083	.083	.083
Frank White	24	3	0	0	0	2	6	.125	.125	.192
Ernie Whitt	21	1	1	0	0	2	3	.048	.095	.130
Rob Wilfong	9	2	0	0	0	0	4	.222	.222	.222
Curtis Wilkerson	14	6	0	1	0	0	2	.429	.571	.429
Jerry Willard	6	1	0	0	0	0	0	.167	.167	.167
Willie Wilson	30	6	0	1	0	0	4	.200	.267	.226
Dave Winfield	25	9	1	0	2	0	3	.360	.640	.360
George Wright	7	1	0	0	0	0	1	.143	.143	.143
Mike Young	13	1	0	0	0	0	3	.077	.077	.077
Robin Yount	24	7	0	0	2	1	5	.292	.542	.320

Frank Viola

Batter	AB	H	2B	3B	HR	BB	SO	BA	SA	OBA
Willie Aikens	9	1	0	0	0	0	2	.111	.111	.111
Andy Allanson	6	1	1	0	0	0	2	.167	.333	.167
Rod Allen	6	2	0	0	0	0	1	.333	.333	.333
Gary Allenson	6	1	0	0	1	1	1	.167	.667	.286
Bill Almon	20	7	2	0	0	2	1	.350	.450	.391
Tony Armas	39	14	1	1	3	0	2	.359	.667	.350
Benny Ayala	17	3	0	0	1	2	2	.176	.353	.263
Harold Baines	39	14	2	1	0	2	5	.359	.462	.390
Dusty Baker	18	5	0	0	0	1	2	.278	.278	.286
Steve Balboni	26	4	0	0	2	1	9	.154	.385	.185
Chris Bando	19	6	0	0	1	2	2	.316	.474	.381
Alan Bannister	10	3	1	1	0	3	1	.300	.600	.500
Jesse Barfield	40	10	2	0	1	6	13	.250	.375	.348
Marty Barrett	41	12	6	0	0	5	1	.293	.439	.370
Don Baylor	47	12	5	0	0	3	7	.255	.362	.352
Buddy Bell	21	5	1	0	0	3	0	.238	.286	.333
George Bell	33	7	1	0	4	5	5	.212	.606	.316
Juan Beniquez	36	11	0	1	1	1	2	.306	.444	.324
Tony Bernazard	42	13	4	0	1	4	7	.310	.476	.370
Dale Berra	7	1	0	0	0	0	1	.143	.143	.143
Buddy Biancalana	6	1	0	0	0	0	0	.167	.167	.167
Wade Boggs	45	15	0	0	0	5	3	.333	.333	.400
Juan Bonilla	12	3	0	0	1	1	1	.250	.500	.308
Barry Bonnell	24	6	0	0	0	2	4	.250	.250	.308
Bob Boone	29	5	0	0	0	2	3	.172	.172	.226
Phil Bradley	31	7	0	1	0	0	5	.226	.290	.226
Glenn Braggs	9	3	0	0	0	0	3	.333	.333	.333
George Brett	30	7	0	0	2	1	2	.233	.433	.258
Greg Brock	5	4	1	0	0	1	0	.800	1.000	.833
Tom Brookens	35	6	1	0	1	3	8	.171	.286	.237
Mark Brouhard	10	5	2	0	2	0	1	.500	1.300	.455
Mike C. Brown	6	0	0	0	0	1	2	.000	.000	.143
Jerry Browne	9	2	0	0	0	0	1	.222	.222	.222
Bill Buckner	37	11	1	0	0	1	3	.297	.324	.333
Steve Buechele	23	4	0	0	0	1	9	.174	.174	.208
Al Bumbry	5	1	0	0	0	1	0	.200	.200	.333
Ellis Burks	9	2	1	0	0	0	3	.222	.333	.200
Rick Burleson	13	1	0	0	0	2	3	.077	.077	.200
Jeff Burroughs	26	10	2	0	0	1	3	.385	.462	.407
Brett Butler	34	12	3	0	0	5	3	.353	.441	.436
Enos Cabell	11	4	0	0	1	1	1	.364	.636	.417
Ivan Calderon	25	8	4	0	1	1	6	.320	.600	.346
Bert Campaneris	5	1	0	0	0	2	0	.200	.200	.429

Batter	AB	H	2B	3B	HR	BB	SO	BA	SA	OBA
John Cangelosi	5	1	0	0	0	2	1	.200	.200	.429
Jose Canseco	20	5	1	0	1	3	5	.250	.450	.348
Rod Carew	21	8	0	0	0	3	2	.381	.381	.458
Joe Carter	30	9	0	0	2	0	6	.300	.500	.300
Carmen Castillo	23	7	2	0	2	5	4	.304	.652	.429
Marty Castillo	13	2	1	0	0	2	0	.154	.231	.267
Rick Cerone	24	2	2	0	0	3	5	.083	.167	.185
Ron Cey	5	1	0	0	0	2	3	.200	.200	.429
Bobby Clark	11	4	0	0	0	1	2	.364	.364	.417
Darnell Coles	9	2	1	0	0	0	0	.222	.333	.222
Dave Collins	10	1	0	0	0	0	1	.100	.100	.100
Onix Concepcion	13	0	0	0	0	0	1	.000	.000	.000
Cecil Cooper	20	7	0	0	0	1	6	.350	.350	.381
Henry Cotto	6	1	1	0	0	0	0	.167	.333	.167
Al Cowens	27	9	2	0	0	0	4	.333	.407	.333
Julio Cruz	33	10	3	0	1	2	5	.303	.485	.343
Todd Cruz	12	3	2	0	0	1	3	.250	.417	.308
Rich Dauer	18	1	1	0	0	2	1	.056	.111	.150
Alvin Davis	28	5	3	0	0	1	5	.179	.286	.233
Mike Davis	26	5	1	0	0	2	7	.192	.231	.250
Brian Dayett	7	1	0	0	0	1	0	.143	.143	.250
Doug DeCinces	48	11	1	0	2	1	7	.229	.375	.245
Rob Deer	15	3	1	1	1	1	5	.200	.600	.250
Rick Dempsey	33	10	2	0	0	4	3	.303	.364	.378
Bucky Dent	5	2	0	0	0	2	0	.400	.400	.571
Brian Downing	47	9	3	0	1	5	11	.191	.319	.264
Mike Easler	19	7	2	0	1	1	3	.368	.632	.429
Dave Edler	5	1	0	0	1	0	0	.200	.800	.333
Jim Essian	5	1	0	0	0	1	0	.200	.200	.333
Darrell Evans	14	2	0	0	1	0	3	.143	.357	.143
Dwight Evans	39	13	1	1	3	9	7	.333	.641	.458
Tony Fernandez	28	8	4	0	0	2	4	.286	.429	.355
Cecil Fielder	11	5	1	0	1	1	3	.455	.818	.500
Mike Fischlin	5	0	0	0	0	0	0	.000	.000	.000
Carlton Fisk	42	12	3	0	1	0	4	.286	.429	.286
Scott Fletcher	42	13	3	0	2	7	4	.310	.524	.408
Tim Foli	22	12	2	0	1	0	0	.545	.773	.545
Dan Ford	16	3	1	0	0	4	6	.188	.250	.350
Julio Franco	32	12	2	1	0	1	3	.375	.500	.394
Jim Gantner	23	10	2	1	1	0	0	.435	.739	.435
Barbaro Garbey	23	8	2	0	2	0	0	.348	.696	.348
Damaso Garcia	44	9	2	0	0	0	7	.205	.250	.205
Rich Gedman	17	3	0	0	1	0	3	.176	.353	.176

Frank Viola continued

Batter	AB	H	2B	3B	HR	BB	SO	BA	SA	OBA
Ken Gerhart	9	0	0	0	0	0	1	.000	.000	.000
Kirk Gibson	18	3	1	0	1	1	5	.167	.389	.250
Bobby Grich	32	9	1	0	3	5	3	.281	.594	.378
Ken Griffey	28	9	3	0	0	0	4	.321	.429	.321
Alfredo Griffin	49	13	2	0	0	0	4	.265	.306	.265
Kelly Gruber	8	2	0	0	0	1	3	.250	.250	.333
Ozzie Guillen	11	3	0	0	0	0	1	.273	.273	.273
Jackie Gutierrez	16	1	0	0	0	0	3	.063	.063	.063
Jerry Hairston	8	2	1	0	0	3	1	.250	.375	.455
Mel Hall	5	1	0	0	0	1	1	.200	.200	.333
Toby Harrah	16	4	1	0	0	2	4	.250	.313	.316
Ron Hassey	5	0	0	0	0	1	1	.000	.000	.167
Mike Heath	35	9	0	1	1	0	6	.257	.400	.257
Dave Henderson	33	11	1	0	2	3	7	.333	.545	.389
Rickey Henderson	36	10	1	0	1	7	9	.278	.389	.395
Steve Henderson	26	7	1	0	1	2	4	.269	.423	.321
George Hendrick	23	7	1	0	2	3	1	.304	.609	.385
Larry Herndon	43	13	4	0	1	2	5	.302	.465	.333
Donnie Hill	24	7	1	0	0	2	0	.292	.333	.346
Marc Hill	14	3	0	0	0	1	1	.214	.214	.267
Glenn Hoffman	13	3	0	0	0	1	3	.231	.231	.286
Dave Hostetler	12	3	0	0	0	2	4	.250	.250	.357
Tim Hulett	18	5	2	0	0	1	2	.278	.389	.316
Pete Incaviglia	23	4	1	0	1	1	12	.174	.348	.208
Garth Iorg	49	17	3	1	2	1	7	.347	.571	.360
Bo Jackson	9	1	1	0	0	0	4	.111	.222	.111
Reggie Jackson	14	1	0	0	1	0	5	.071	.286	.071
Ron Jackson	6	1	1	0	0	0	1	.167	.333	.167
Brook Jacoby	29	10	2	0	1	3	7	.345	.517	.406
Stan Javier	7	2	0	0	0	1	2	.286	.286	.375
Cliff Johnson	20	7	2	0	2	3	5	.350	.750	.440
Howard Johnson	7	1	1	0	0	0	3	.143	.286	.143
Lynn Jones	16	4	0	1	0	0	2	.250	.375	.250
Wally Joyner	19	6	0	0	1	1	2	.316	.474	.350
Ron Karkovice	4	0	0	0	0	1	3	.000	.000	.200
Bob Kearney	20	8	1	0	1	2	3	.400	.600	.478
Steve Kemp	14	3	0	0	0	1	4	.214	.214	.267
Dave Kingman	28	6	2	0	1	2	6	.214	.393	.267
Ron Kittle	33	7	1	0	3	3	12	.212	.515	.278
Ray Knight	10	2	0	0	1	0	2	.200	.500	.200
Rusty Kuntz	10	2	1	0	0	0	1	.200	.300	.200
Lee Lacy	27	9	1	0	2	1	4	.333	.593	.357
Carney Lansford	45	10	0	0	1	2	6	.222	.289	.271
Vance Law	22	5	1	0	0	2	1	.227	.273	.292
Ron LeFlore	5	2	0	0	0	0	2	.400	.400	.400
Chet Lemon	40	16	7	0	1	5	9	.400	.650	.467
Dave Lopes	21	8	1	0	2	2	4	.381	.714	.417
Greg Luzinski	19	8	4	0	1	1	1	.421	.789	.455
Fred Lynn	34	8	0	1	4	2	10	.235	.647	.278
Steve Lyons	7	0	0	0	0	0	3	.000	.000	.000
Scotti Madison	5	3	3	0	0	0	1	.600	1.200	.600
Rick Manning	10	1	0	0	0	0	2	.100	.100	.100
Fred Manrique	8	2	0	0	1	1	2	.250	.625	.333
Jerry Martin	7	2	0	0	0	0	4	.286	.286	.286
Buck Martinez	33	13	4	0	1	2	2	.394	.606	.429
Gary Matthews	7	3	0	0	0	0	0	.429	.429	.429
Don Mattingly	28	6	4	0	0	1	1	.214	.357	.241
Lee Mazzilli	5	0	0	0	0	1	3	.000	.000	.167
Oddibe McDowell	14	3	0	1	1	0	3	.214	.571	.214
Mark McGwire	10	2	0	0	0	3	6	.200	.200	.385
Mark McLemore	8	2	0	0	0	1	2	.250	.250	.333
Hal McRae	29	10	1	0	3	1	3	.345	.690	.367
Bobby Meacham	14	5	0	1	0	3	2	.357	.500	.500
Orlando Mercado	4	1	0	0	0	1	0	.250	1.000	.400
Larry Milbourne	4	1	0	0	0	1	0	.250	.250	.400
Darrell Miller	13	2	0	0	0	1	6	.154	.154	.214
Paul Molitor	26	7	1	1	1	2	4	.269	.500	.321
Don Money	7	2	0	0	1	2	0	.286	.714	.444
Charlie Moore	20	4	1	0	0	1	2	.200	.250	.273
Lloyd Moseby	37	14	1	0	3	2	3	.378	.649	.415
John Moses	11	2	0	0	0	0	2	.182	.182	.182
Darryl Motley	19	8	3	0	3	0	3	.421	1.053	.421
Jerry Mumphrey	7	1	0	0	0	1	2	.143	.143	.250
Dwayne Murphy	43	7	0	0	1	4	11	.163	.233	.234
Eddie Murray	49	13	1	0	1	4	9	.265	.347	.333

Batter	AB	H	2B	3B	HR	BB	SO	BA	SA	OBA
Graig Nettles	9	3	0	0	0	1	3	.333	.333	.400
Jeff Newman	11	2	0	0	0	1	2	.182	.182	.250
Reid Nichols	23	6	1	0	1	0	0	.261	.435	.261
Wayne Nordhagen	6	1	0	0	0	0	0	.167	.167	.167
Pete O'Brien	25	6	1	0	1	3	3	.240	.400	.321
Ben Oglivie	9	3	1	0	0	0	4	.333	.444	.333
Amos Otis	10	3	0	0	0	2	0	.300	.300	.417
Spike Owen	32	10	2	0	0	2	3	.313	.375	.353
Jim Paciorek	9	3	1	0	0	0	2	.333	.444	.333
Tom Paciorek	44	15	2	0	1	2	9	.341	.455	.370
Mike Pagliarulo	6	1	0	0	0	0	3	.167	.167	.167
Lance Parrish	29	6	1	0	2	3	4	.207	.448	.281
Larry Parrish	36	7	2	0	1	6	19	.194	.333	.310
Bill Pecota	4	1	1	0	0	2	0	.250	.500	.500
Jack Perconte	13	5	0	0	0	1	1	.385	.385	.429
Gary Pettis	30	7	1	0	0	2	9	.233	.267	.281
Tony Phillips	25	8	1	0	0	7	2	.320	.360	.469
Lou Piniella	20	8	2	0	0	1	2	.400	.500	.429
Jim Presley	30	5	0	0	1	2	9	.167	.267	.219
Greg Pryor	7	2	0	0	0	0	1	.286	.286	.286
Pat Putnam	11	2	0	0	1	0	2	.182	.455	.182
Rey Quinones	8	1	0	0	0	0	2	.125	.125	.125
Domingo Ramos	7	2	1	0	0	2	0	.286	.429	.444
Willie Randolph	36	14	0	0	0	2	1	.389	.556	.522
Floyd Rayford	18	4	0	0	1	3	4	.222	.389	.333
Randy Ready	6	2	0	0	1	2	1	.333	.833	.500
Gary Redus	13	3	0	0	2	0	1	.231	.692	.231
Jerry Remy	6	0	0	0	0	1	0	.000	.000	.143
Harold Reynolds	13	1	0	0	1	2	1	.077	.308	.200
Jim Rice	45	13	1	0	2	6	7	.289	.444	.373
Ernest Riles	9	2	0	0	1	0	1	.222	.556	.222
Cal Ripken	53	16	5	0	3	5	5	.302	.566	.356
Leon Roberts	10	3	0	0	0	1	1	.300	.300	.364
Andre Robertson	16	7	4	0	0	0	3	.438	.688	.412
Gary Roenicke	30	9	0	0	2	4	4	.300	.500	.382
Ron Roenicke	6	3	0	0	1	0	0	.500	1.000	.500
Ed Romero	24	3	0	0	0	0	3	.125	.125	.125
Joe Rudi	5	1	0	0	1	0	1	.200	.800	.200
Lenn Sakata	16	5	1	0	0	2	2	.313	.375	.389
Billy Sample	19	4	1	0	0	1	1	.211	.263	.250
Alejandro Sanchez	6	1	1	0	0	0	4	.167	.333	.167
Dick Schofield	27	5	1	0	1	2	7	.185	.333	.233
Bill Schroeder	21	4	0	0	3	3	6	.190	.619	.292
Kevin Seitzer	8	3	0	0	0	2	1	.375	.375	.500
John Shelby	27	5	1	0	1	0	6	.185	.333	.185
Ron Shepherd	4	1	0	0	0	1	2	.250	.250	.400
Ruben Sierra	26	7	2	0	0	0	4	.269	.346	.269
Nelson Simmons	5	2	0	0	0	0	0	.400	.400	.400
Ted Simmons	15	4	0	0	1	0	0	.267	.467	.313
Ken Singleton	7	5	0	0	1	2	1	.714	1.143	.778
Don Slaught	19	1	0	0	0	1	5	.053	.053	.095
Roy Smalley	10	1	0	0	1	3	1	.100	.400	.308
Lonnie Smith	15	2	1	0	0	0	2	.133	.200	.133
Cory Snyder	16	3	1	0	1	0	6	.188	.438	.188
Mike Stanley	12	5	2	0	1	1	3	.417	.833	.462
Dave Stapleton	14	2	1	0	0	1	0	.143	.214	.200
Dave Stegman	7	2	0	1	0	1	2	.286	.571	.375
Bill Stein	6	4	1	0	0	1	1	.667	.833	.714
Terry Steinbach	11	2	0	0	0	1	1	.182	.182	.308
Marc Sullivan	11	2	0	0	0	1	4	.182	.182	.250
Jim Sundberg	18	5	0	0	1	0	1	.278	.444	.278
Dale Sveum	11	3	2	0	0	1	3	.273	.455	.308
Pat Tabler	28	7	1	1	0	0	3	.250	.357	.250
Danny Tartabull	14	4	0	0	2	3	5	.286	.714	.412
Mickey Tettleton	9	0	0	0	0	2	2	.000	.000	.182
Gorman Thomas	26	5	0	0	4	4	3	.192	.654	.300
Andre Thornton	26	5	1	0	2	2	3	.192	.462	.250
Wayne Tolleson	13	1	0	0	0	1	4	.077	.077	.143
Alan Trammell	41	10	2	1	4	5	3	.244	.634	.326
Willie Upshaw	36	11	2	0	3	2	7	.306	.611	.342
Ellis Valentine	8	0	0	0	0	0	1	.000	.000	.000
Dave Valle	9	2	0	0	0	0	2	.222	.222	.222
Dave Van Gorder	4	3	0	0	1	2	1	.750	1.500	.833
Greg Walker	30	7	4	0	2	3	8	.233	.567	.303
Gary Ward	34	4	1	2	0	3	8	.118	.265	.189

Frank Viola continued

Batter	AB	H	2B	3B	HR	BB	SO	BA	SA	OBA	Batter	AB	H	2B	3B	HR	BB	SO	BA	SA	OBA
Claudell Washington	8	3	1	0	1	0	3	.375	.875	.375	Glenn Wilson	6	0	0	0	0	0	1	.000	.000	.000
U.L. Washington	6	1	1	0	0	1	2	.167	.333	.286	Willie Wilson	42	15	2	1	1	1	11	.357	.524	.372
John Wathan	13	2	0	0	0	3	3	.154	.154	.313	Dave Winfield	54	13	1	1	6	2	8	.241	.630	.268
Lou Whitaker	33	11	2	1	1	4	7	.333	.545	.405	John Wockenfuss	10	2	2	0	0	2	2	.200	.400	.333
Devon White	10	2	0	0	1	0	3	.200	.500	.200	George Wright	19	5	1	0	1	1	5	.263	.474	.333
Frank White	35	11	2	0	2	2	6	.314	.543	.351	Butch Wynegar	20	5	1	0	1	3	2	.250	.450	.348
Ernie Whitt	4	1	0	0	0	1	1	.250	.250	.400	Steve Yeager	6	1	0	0	0	0	0	.167	.167	.167
Alan Wiggins	20	9	2	0	0	0	1	.450	.550	.450	Ned Yost	9	3	1	0	0	0	2	.333	.444	.333
Curtis Wilkerson	14	3	1	0	0	1	2	.214	.286	.313	Mike Young	19	3	0	0	1	3	7	.158	.316	.261
Jerry Willard	7	1	0	0	0	1	3	.143	.143	.250	Robin Yount	28	8	2	0	1	5	2	.286	.464	.394
Ken Williams	15	3	0	0	0	0	4	.200	.200	.250	Richie Zisk	14	5	1	0	2	1	4	.357	.857	.400

VIII
Ballparks

Ballparks

The Ballparks section lists, for all 26 ballparks in use in the major leagues, a variety of statistics about the games played there over the past several years.

A ballpark's effect on performance has been a popular topic in recent years. Analysis that used to be limited to, "Gee, Fenway's a tough place for a lefty to pitch," has gotten increasingly sophisticated. Even the simplest conversation about an off-season trade now gets into such factors as the dimensions of a park, whether it has natural or artificial turf, the size of its foul territory, and how far it is above sea level. Our own analysis has led us to note in past editions those ballparks that promote doubles (like Fenway) or double plays (like Anaheim Stadium). But until last year we had not included anything systematic about the general effects of a given park.

A half page is devoted to each park. That half page is composed of two segments. The first is a box containing basic statistics for the games played there, as contrasted with that home team's games on the road. The totals listed are the complete statistics *for both teams* in those games. Totals and percentage differences are listed for the 1987 season, and for the five-year period from 1983 through 1987. Since the statistics represent performance by the same players in roughly the same number of games, the differences can be attributed to the peculiarities of the park. The significance or causes of these differences are "why" questions and are open to debate; the questions we're answering here are "what" and "how many."

The second set of tables highlights the performance of visiting players during the 1987 season. Listed are the top and bottom 10 in batting average, and the leaders in home runs and runs batted in. Qualifying for the batting average lists is based on a minimum of 3.1 plate appearances per game played by each player's team in that park.

Following the 13 pages of ballpark data is a new feature: tables that rank the stadiums according to their effects on various elements of play. To illustrate, let's say that you find that the Oakland Coliseum reduced scoring by 17.5 percent over the past five seasons. You'll no longer have to flip through the pages to check the corresponding figures for the 25 other stadiums to see where the Coliseum ranks. Just check the table at the end of the Ballparks section that ranks the 26 stadiums by their effect on scoring.

In addition to scoring, we've also included tables that rank the 26 parks by seven other categories. The fields with synthetic playing surfaces are indicated, giving you a quick read on what kind of impact plastic grass has on the category in question. For instance, if you check the table ranking the stadiums by their effect on stolen-base percentage, you'll see that the carpet has a nearly universal impact on base stealing.

Baltimore
Memorial Stadium

	1987 SEASON			1983 – 1987		
	Home Games	Road Games	Pct. Diff.	Home Games	Road Games	Pct. Diff.
G	82	80	2.5	404	405	– 0.2
AB	5627	5572	1.0	27474	27761	– 1.0
1B	958	1023	– 7.3	4962	5078	– 1.3
2B	265	245	7.1	1156	1283	– 9.0
3B	20	44	– 55.0	88	190	– 53.2
HR	235	202	15.2	900	852	6.7
R	807	802	– 1.8	3647	3811	– 4.1
BA	.263	.272	– 3.3	.259	.267	– 3.0
SLG	.442	.440	0.4	.405	.419	– 3.2
XB%	.229	.220	4.1	.200	.225	– 10.9
E	118	109	5.6	605	598	1.4
SHO	9	6	46.3	46	43	7.2

BATTING AVG. (Top 10)

Snyder, CLE	.556
Fernandez, TOR	.500
Barrett, BOS	.481
Valle, SEA	.476
Brunansky, MIN	.450
Seitzer, KC	.444
Evans, DET	.429
Owen, BOS	.421
Nokes, DET	.412
Calderon, CHI	.409

HOME RUNS

Carter, CLE	4
Snyder, CLE	4
Bell, TOR	3
Joyner, CAL	3
Nokes, DET	3
Presley, SEA	3
Sveum, MIL	3
Trammell, DET	3
Walker, CHI	3
22 players tied.	2

BATTING AVG. (Bottom 10)

O'Brien, TEX	.050
Pagliarulo, NY	.053
Redus, CHI	.091
Madlock, DET	.105
McLemore, CAL	.118
Upshaw, TOR	.130
Gladden, MIN	.143
Davis, SEA	.167
White, KC	.167
3 players tied.	.182

RUNS BATTED IN

Bell, TOR	11
Brunansky, MIN	9
Burks, BOS	9
Fisk, CHI	9
Joyner, CAL	8
Trammell, DET	8
Valle, SEA	8
5 players tied.	7

Boston
Fenway Park

	1987 SEASON			1983 – 1987		
	Home Games	Road Games	Pct. Diff.	Home Games	Road Games	Pct. Diff.
G	80	82	– 2.4	404	406	– 0.5
AB	5567	5627	– 1.1	28151	27913	0.9
1B	1081	1050	4.1	5470	5173	4.8
2B	322	265	22.8	1608	1249	27.7
3B	30	26	16.6	166	148	11.2
HR	161	203	– 19.8	755	834	– 10.2
R	819	848	– 1.0	3962	3788	5.1
BA	.286	.274	4.4	.284	.265	7.1
SLG	.442	.439	0.6	.434	.410	5.7
XB%	.246	.217	13.2	.245	.213	15.2
E	93	117	– 18.5	623	628	– 0.3
SHO	9	8	15.3	42	45	– 6.2

BATTING AVG. (Top 10)

Smalley, MIN	.529
Mulliniks, TOR	.500
White, CAL	.478
Carter, CLE	.455
Kennedy, BAL	.450
McGriff, TOR	.444
Winfield, NY	.440
Trammell, DET	.438
Davis, SEA	.435
Surhoff, MIL	.429

HOME RUNS

Carter, CLE	7
Brunansky, MIN	4
Fisk, CHI	4
Barfield, TOR	3
Gaetti, MIN	3
Hrbek, MIN	3
Pagliarulo, NY	3
5 players tied.	2

BATTING AVG. (Bottom 10)

Lombardozzi, MIN	.000
Tolleson, NY	.059
Howell, CAL	.111
Bernazard, OAK	.136
McGwire, OAK	.148
Wilson, KC	.148
Easler, NY	.150
McLemore, CAL	.150
Nokes, DET	.182
Gaetti, MIN	.190

RUNS BATTED IN

Carter, CLE	14
Barfield, TOR	8
Pagliarulo, NY	8
Baines, CHI	7
Gaetti, MIN	7
Hrbek, MIN	7
6 players tied.	6

California
Anaheim Stadium

	1987 SEASON			1983 – 1987		
	Home Games	Road Games	Pct. Diff.	Home Games	Road Games	Pct. Diff.
G	81	81	0.0	404	406	– 0.5
AB	5597	5573	0.4	27451	28102	– 2.3
1B	995	958	3.4	4944	5151	– 1.7
2B	211	289	– 27.3	1103	1333	– 15.3
3B	22	28	– 21.8	107	196	– 44.1
HR	204	180	12.8	859	746	17.9
R	782	791	– 1.1	3616	3756	– 3.3
BA	.256	.261	– 2.0	.255	.264	– 3.3
SLG	.411	.420	– 2.2	.397	.405	– 2.0
XB%	.190	.249	– 23.7	.197	.229	– 14.1
E	128	127	0.8	651	656	– 0.3
SHO	8	10	– 20.0	42	58	– 27.2

1987 Visiting Leaders

BATTING AVG. (Top 10)

Snyder, CLE	.522
Jacoby, CLE	.500
Nokes, DET	.500
Murphy, OAK	.458
Fisk, CHI	.440
Lemon, DET	.438
Tartabull, KC	.435
Valle, SEA	.412
Carter, CLE	.391
Boggs, BOS	.385

HOME RUNS

Nokes, DET	5
Boggs, BOS	4
Evans, BOS	4
Fisk, CHI	4
Lynn, BAL	4
7 players tied.	3

BATTING AVG. (Bottom 10)

Sveum, MIL	.050
Nixon, SEA	.105
Bush, MIN	.125
Sheridan, DET	.125
Upshaw, TOR	.158
Balboni, KC	.167
Baylor, MIN	.167
Calderon, CHI	.167
Evans, DET	.167
Lansford, OAK	.167

RUNS BATTED IN

Boggs, BOS	9
Murphy, OAK	9
Fisk, CHI	8
Gaetti, MIN	8
Nokes, DET	8
Bernazard, OAK	7
Braggs, MIL	7
White, KC	7
9 players tied.	6

Chicago
Comiskey Park

	1987 SEASON			1983 – 1987		
	Home Games	Road Games	Pct. Diff.	Home Games	Road Games	Pct. Diff.
G	81	81	0.0	405	406	– 0.2
AB	5570	5505	1.2	27315	27552	– 0.9
1B	1044	874	18.1	4769	4763	1.0
2B	265	244	7.3	1231	1215	2.2
3B	42	32	29.7	243	160	53.2
HR	162	200	– 19.9	761	784	– 2.1
R	808	686	17.8	3725	3433	8.8
BA	.272	.245	10.8	.256	.251	2.1
SLG	.422	.410	2.8	.403	.392	2.7
XB%	.227	.240	– 5.3	.236	.224	5.4
E	133	108	23.1	646	604	7.2
SHO	6	10	– 40.0	42	50	– 15.8

1987 Visiting Leaders

BATTING AVG. (Top 10)

Sheets, BAL	.565
Trammell, DET	.500
Fernandez, TOR	.423
Evans, BOS	.417
Pagliarulo, NY	.412
Brock, MIL	.391
Tabler, CLE	.389
Brantley, SEA	.375
Molitor, MIL	.375
3 players tied.	.368

HOME RUNS

Murray, BAL	4
Bell, TOR	3
Carter, CLE	3
Gerhart, BAL	3
White, KC	3
15 players tied.	2

BATTING AVG. (Bottom 10)

Fletcher, TEX	.105
Moseby, TOR	.125
Snyder, CLE	.125
Brunansky, MIN	.136
Kennedy, BAL	.160
Boggs, BOS	.167
Barfield, TOR	.174
Schofield, CAL	.188
5 players tied.	.200

RUNS BATTED IN

Davis, SEA	10
Murray, BAL	10
Sheets, BAL	9
Bell, TOR	8
Trammell, DET	8
Brock, MIL	7
Nokes, DET	7
White, KC	7
6 players tied.	6

Cleveland
Cleveland Stadium

1987 Visiting Leaders

BATTING AVG. (Top 10)		HOME RUNS	
Boggs, BOS	.571	McGwire, OAK	5
McGwire, OAK	.538	Canseco, OAK	4
Incaviglia, TEX	.500	Henderson, NY	4
Baines, CHI	.438	Winfield, NY	4
Polonia, OAK	.438	8 players tied.	3
Puckett, MIN	.429		
Molitor, MIL	.424		
McLemore, CAL	.412		
Downing, CAL	.409		
2 players tied.	.400		

BATTING AVG. (Bottom 10)		RUNS BATTED IN	
Owen, BOS	.136	Canseco, OAK	11
Murray, BAL	.143	Deer, MIL	11
Redus, CHI	.148	McGwire, OAK	10
Hill, CHI	.150	Sveum, MIL	10
Buechele, TEX	.158	Winfield, NY	10
Sierra, TEX	.160	Molitor, MIL	9
Phelps, SEA	.167	Parrish, TEX	9
White, KC	.174	Murray, BAL	8
Tartabull, KC	.176	C. Ripken, BAL	8
Burks, BOS	.179	3 players tied.	7

	1987 SEASON			1983 – 1987		
	Home Games	Road Games	Pct. Diff.	Home Games	Road Games	Pct. Diff.
G	81	81	0.0	405	407	– 0.5
AB	5722	5506	3.9	28101	27899	0.7
1B	1059	978	4.2	5611	5191	7.3
2B	276	262	1.4	1283	1316	– 3.2
3B	31	30	– 0.6	149	198	– 25.3
HR	212	194	5.2	757	729	3.1
R	892	807	10.5	4070	3907	4.7
BA	.276	.266	3.7	.278	.266	4.2
SLG	.446	.430	3.7	.415	.406	2.1
XB%	.225	.230	– 2.3	.203	.226	– 10.0
E	153	132	15.9	715	723	– 0.6
SHO	10	7	42.9	38	39	– 2.1

Detroit
Tiger Stadium

1987 Visiting Leaders

BATTING AVG. (Top 10)		HOME RUNS	
Polonia, OAK	.500	McGwire, OAK	7
McGwire, OAK	.480	Sierra, TEX	4
Surhoff, MIL	.476	Balboni, KC	3
Bernazard, OAK	.423	O'Brien, TEX	3
Seitzer, KC	.423	Ward, NY	3
Downing, CAL	.400	17 players tied.	2
Braggs, MIL	.391		
Franco, CLE	.370		
Davis, SEA	.364		
Fisk, CHI	.364		

BATTING AVG. (Bottom 10)		RUNS BATTED IN	
Deer, MIL	.053	McGwire, OAK	12
Beniquez, TOR	.059	Sierra, TEX	8
Jones, CAL	.059	Benzinger, BOS	7
• Brunansky, MIN	.100	Polonia, OAK	7
Snyder, CLE	.103	Surhoff, MIL	7
Jackson, OAK	.105	6 players tied.	6
Hall, CLE	.120		
Carter, CLE	.129		
White, KC	.136		
4 players tied.	.143		

	1987 SEASON			1983 – 1987		
	Home Games	Road Games	Pct. Diff.	Home Games	Road Games	Pct. Diff.
G	81	81	0.0	406	403	0.7
AB	5507	5730	– 3.9	27555	27914	– 1.3
1B	926	1060	– 9.1	4682	4972	– 4.6
2B	223	283	– 18.0	1080	1367	– 20.0
3B	20	48	– 56.6	168	206	– 17.4
HR	226	179	31.4	930	842	11.9
R	780	851	– 8.3	3639	3861	– 6.4
BA	.253	.274	– 7.5	.249	.265	– 5.9
SLG	.424	.434	– 2.2	.402	.419	– 4.1
XB%	.208	.238	– 12.6	.210	.240	– 12.4
E	122	136	– 10.3	621	648	– 4.9
SHO	11	3	266.7	49	29	67.7

Kansas City
Royals Stadium

1987 Visiting Leaders

BATTING AVG. (Top 10)		HOME RUNS	
Puckett, MIN	.481	M. Davis, OAK	3
Boggs, BOS	.478	Sierra, TEX	3
Joyner, CAL	.462	Canseco, OAK	2
Parrish, TEX	.455	Evans, BOS	2
McGwire, OAK	.444	Fielder, TOR	2
Bell, TOR	.435	Hall, CLE	2
Gagne, MIN	.409	McGwire, OAK	2
Jacoby, CLE	.409	O'Brien, TEX	2
Fernandez, TOR	.400	Parrish, TEX	2
Evans, BOS	.375	37 players tied.	1

BATTING AVG. (Bottom 10)		RUNS BATTED IN	
Rice, BOS	.048	Parrish, TEX	10
Brantley, SEA	.053	M. Davis, OAK	8
Sveum, MIL	.056	Mattingly, NY	7
Castillo, MIL	.087	McGwire, OAK	7
McDowell, TEX	.091	O'Brien, TEX	7
Wiggins, BAL	.125	Sierra, TEX	7
Calderon, CHI	.130	Knight, BAL	6
Fisk, CHI	.133	Morrison, DET	6
Redus, CHI	.150	Murray, BAL	6
Ward, NY	.154	6 players tied.	5

	1987 SEASON			1983 – 1987		
	Home Games	Road Games	Pct. Diff.	Home Games	Road Games	Pct. Diff.
G	81	81	0.0	407	404	0.7
AB	5471	5476	– 0.1	27902	27435	1.7
1B	958	1020	– 6.0	5078	5056	– 1.2
2B	293	212	38.3	1377	1174	15.3
3B	57	31	84.0	294	178	62.4
HR	130	166	– 21.6	569	737	– 24.1
R	724	682	6.2	3477	3404	1.4
BA	.263	.261	0.7	.262	.260	0.7
SLG	.409	.402	1.6	.394	.397	– 0.7
XB%	.268	.192	39.1	.248	.211	17.3
E	112	125	– 10.4	648	617	4.3
SHO	13	15	– 13.3	56	53	4.9

Milwaukee
County Stadium

1987 Visiting Leaders

BATTING AVG. (Top 10)		HOME RUNS	
Puckett, MIN	.571	Puckett, MIN	4
Randolph, NY	.560	14 players tied.	2
Steinbach, OAK	.522		
Moseby, TOR	.480		
Quirk, KC	.474		
Nokes, DET	.423		
Franco, CLE	.417		
Tartabull, KC	.417		
Fisk, CHI	.400		
Reynolds, SEA	.391		

BATTING AVG. (Bottom 10)		RUNS BATTED IN	
Parrish, TEX	.050	Moseby, TOR	10
Baines, CHI	.100	Quirk, KC	10
Whitt, TOR	.100	Randolph, NY	10
McDowell, TEX	.105	Steinbach, OAK	8
Whitaker, DET	.107	Incaviglia, TEX	7
Owen, BOS	.111	Puckett, MIN	7
White, KC	.125	7 players tied.	6
Snyder, CLE	.130		
White, CAL	.148		
DeCinces, CAL	.158		

	1987 SEASON			1983 – 1987		
	Home Games	Road Games	Pct. Diff.	Home Games	Road Games	Pct. Diff.
G	81	81	0.0	403	404	– 0.2
AB	5645	5682	– 0.7	27786	28000	– 0.8
1B	1141	1020	12.6	5341	5347	0.7
2B	279	257	9.3	1251	1287	– 2.0
3B	39	32	22.7	199	179	12.0
HR	151	181	– 16.0	660	731	– 9.0
R	860	819	5.0	3648	3771	– 3.0
BA	.285	.262	8.8	.268	.269	– 0.5
SLG	.429	.414	3.5	.399	.407	– 1.9
XB%	.218	.221	– 1.3	.214	.215	– 0.8
E	133	133	0.0	656	658	– 0.1
SHO	6	5	20.0	45	30	50.4

Minnesota
Metrodome

1987 Visiting Leaders

BATTING AVG. (Top 10)		HOME RUNS	
McDowell, TEX	.526	McDowell, TEX	5
Whitt, TOR	.500	Bernazard, OAK	3
Franco, CLE	.478	Boggs, BOS	3
Lemon, DET	.476	Joyner, CAL	3
Joyner, CAL	.458	Redus, CHI	3
Greenwell, BOS	.450	Tartabull, KC	3
O'Brien, TEX	.450	14 players tied.	2
Kingery, SEA	.429		
Fernandez, TOR	.391		
2 players tied.	.389		

	1987 SEASON			1983 – 1987		
	Home Games	Road Games	Pct. Diff.	Home Games	Road Games	Pct. Diff.
G	81	81	0.0	408	402	1.5
AB	5511	5444	1.2	28254	27072	4.4
1B	930	960	– 4.3	5059	4895	– 1.0
2B	269	264	0.7	1529	1222	19.9
3B	36	22	61.6	221	147	44.1
HR	198	208	– 6.0	862	822	0.5
R	759	833	– 8.9	3949	3589	8.4
BA	.260	.267	– 2.6	.272	.262	3.7
SLG	.430	.438	– 2.0	.433	.409	5.9
XB%	.247	.230	7.6	.257	.219	17.6
E	116	124	– 6.5	607	597	0.2
SHO	5	8	– 37.5	34	51	– 34.3

BATTING AVG. (Bottom 10)		RUNS BATTED IN	
Yount, MIL	.045	Greenwell, BOS	9
Fisk, CHI	.050	Lemon, DET	9
Parrish, TEX	.095	O'Brien, TEX	9
Browne, TEX	.105	Joyner, CAL	8
Kennedy, BAL	.105	Boggs, BOS	7
Presley, SEA	.111	Moseby, TOR	7
Molitor, MIL	.130	Fernandez, TOR	6
White, CAL	.138	Griffin, OAK	6
Pagliarulo, NY	.143	McDowell, TEX	6
2 players tied.	.150	Whitt, TOR	6

New York
Yankee Stadium

1987 Visiting Leaders

BATTING AVG. (Top 10)		HOME RUNS	
Jacoby, CLE	.526	Bell, TOR	4
Reynolds, SEA	.500	Jacoby, CLE	3
Steinbach, OAK	.478	Sveum, MIL	3
Fletcher, TEX	.455	15 players tied.	2
Moses, SEA	.412		
Guillen, CHI	.407		
Seitzer, KC	.400		
Baines, CHI	.385		
Gladden, MIN	.364		
2 players tied.	.360		

	1987 SEASON			1983 – 1987		
	Home Games	Road Games	Pct. Diff.	Home Games	Road Games	Pct. Diff.
G	81	81	0.0	403	406	– 0.7
AB	5474	5589	– 2.1	27486	28119	– 2.3
1B	1007	1007	2.1	5124	5171	1.4
2B	227	255	– 9.1	1182	1349	– 10.4
3B	23	26	– 9.7	163	174	– 4.2
HR	186	189	0.5	767	823	– 4.7
R	747	799	– 6.5	3611	3879	– 6.2
BA	.264	.264	– 0.2	.263	.267	– 1.5
SLG	.415	.421	– 1.2	.402	.415	– 3.3
XB%	.199	.218	– 8.8	.208	.228	– 8.6
E	110	106	3.8	641	632	2.2
SHO	10	11	– 9.1	53	45	18.7

BATTING AVG. (Bottom 10)		RUNS BATTED IN	
Fernandez, TOR	.087	Bell, TOR	12
Downing, CAL	.125	Barfield, TOR	7
Felder, MIL	.125	Parrish, TEX	7
Hrbek, MIN	.150	Brantley, SEA	6
Fisk, CHI	.158	Evans, BOS	6
Quinones, SEA	.158	Howell, CAL	6
Browne, TEX	.167	Rice, BOS	6
Gaetti, MIN	.167	Stanley, TEX	6
3 players tied.	.174	7 players tied.	5

Oakland
Oakland-Alameda County Coliseum

1987 Visiting Leaders

	1987 SEASON			1983 – 1987		
	Home Games	Road Games	Pct. Diff.	Home Games	Road Games	Pct. Diff.
G	81	81	0.0	405	405	0.0
AB	5431	5660	– 4.0	27470	27785	– 1.1
1B	902	1005	– 6.5	4950	5040	– 0.7
2B	239	286	– 12.9	1087	1363	– 19.3
3B	27	40	– 29.7	129	213	– 38.7
HR	163	212	– 19.9	719	881	– 17.5
R	714	881	– 19.0	3536	4118	– 14.1
BA	.245	.273	– 10.1	.251	.270	– 7.1
SLG	.389	.450	– 13.5	.378	.429	– 11.9
XB%	.228	.245	– 7.0	.197	.238	– 17.2
E	122	142	– 14.1	702	713	– 1.5
SHO	8	4	100.0	45	23	95.7

BATTING AVG. (Top 10)

Reynolds, SEA	.500
Newman, MIN	.412
White, CAL	.385
Sierra, TEX	.370
Mattingly, NY	.364
Butler, CLE	.353
Bell, TOR	.333
Brower, TEX	.333
Hrbek, MIN	.333
Tartabull, KC	.333

HOME RUNS

Parrish, TEX	4
Balboni, KC	3
Bell, TOR	3
Calderon, CHI	3
11 players tied.	2

BATTING AVG. (Bottom 10)

Baylor, MIN	.095
Lemon, DET	.105
Ward, NY	.105
Deer, MIL	.111
McLemore, CAL	.118
Nokes, DET	.120
C. Ripken, BAL	.125
Quinones, SEA	.130
Guillen, CHI	.138
Mulliniks, TOR	.143

RUNS BATTED IN

Parrish, TEX	11
Balboni, KC	9
Brower, TEX	8
Presley, SEA	8
Sierra, TEX	7
Sveum, MIL	7
White, CAL	7
Gaetti, MIN	6
Hrbek, MIN	6
Lacy, BAL	6

Seattle
Kingdome

1987 Visiting Leaders

	1987 SEASON			1983 – 1987		
	Home Games	Road Games	Pct. Diff.	Home Games	Road Games	Pct. Diff.
G	81	81	0.0	408	402	1.5
AB	5541	5500	0.7	27911	27120	2.9
1B	968	1047	– 8.2	4944	5014	– 4.2
2B	263	282	– 7.4	1346	1290	1.4
3B	43	39	9.4	187	193	– 5.9
HR	218	142	52.4	878	659	29.5
R	803	758	5.9	3790	3615	3.3
BA	.269	.275	– 1.9	.264	.264	– 0.1
SLG	.450	.417	7.9	.420	.399	5.3
XB%	.240	.235	2.4	.237	.228	3.7
E	122	125	– 2.4	620	672	– 9.1
SHO	9	10	– 10.0	39	51	– 24.7

BATTING AVG. (Top 10)

McDowell, TEX	.529
Evans, BOS	.500
Gantner, MIL	.500
Mattingly, NY	.500
Puckett, MIN	.500
Kennedy, BAL	.444
Bell, TOR	.429
Sveum, MIL	.429
Franco, CLE	.421
Lemon, DET	.412

HOME RUNS

Bell, TOR	5
Evans, BOS	4
Downing, CAL	3
Dwyer, BAL	3
Gruber, TOR	3
Jacoby, CLE	3
Pagliarulo, NY	3
Puckett, MIN	3
18 players tied.	2

BATTING AVG. (Bottom 10)

DeCinces, CAL	.087
Fletcher, TEX	.100
Brunansky, MIN	.105
M. Davis, OAK	.111
Hill, CHI	.111
Gladden, MIN	.118
Hrbek, MIN	.125
Barfield, TOR	.136
Brookens, DET	.136
2 players tied.	.150

RUNS BATTED IN

Bell, TOR	9
Jacoby, CLE	9
Mattingly, NY	9
Balboni, KC	8
Evans, BOS	8
Puckett, MIN	7
7 players tied.	6

Texas
Arlington Stadium

1987 Visiting Leaders

BATTING AVG. (Top 10)		HOME RUNS	
Surhoff, MIL	.524	Tartabull, KC	5
Walker, CHI	.524	Mattingly, NY	4
Tartabull, KC	.462	Walker, CHI	4
Bell, TOR	.458	Barfield, TOR	3
Yount, MIL	.423	Bell, TOR	3
Davis, SEA	.409	Davis, SEA	3
Joyner, CAL	.409	Evans, BOS	3
Lansford, OAK	.400	Evans, DET	3
Washington, NY	.400	McGwire, OAK	3
Hall, CLE	.391	Steinbach, OAK	3

BATTING AVG. (Bottom 10)		RUNS BATTED IN	
Ward, NY	.043	Tartabull, KC	12
Howell, CAL	.059	Walker, CHI	11
Winfield, NY	.059	Evans, DET	10
Rice, BOS	.067	Bell, TOR	9
Knight, BAL	.091	Mattingly, NY	9
B. Jackson, KC	.100	Yount, MIL	9
Gladden, MIN	.105	Carter, CLE	8
DeCinces, CAL	.111	Moseby, TOR	8
Phillips, OAK	.118	6 players tied.	7
Canseco, OAK	.130		

	1987 SEASON			1983 – 1987		
	Home Games	Road Games	Pct. Diff.	Home Games	Road Games	Pct. Diff.
G	81	81	0.0	403	406	– 0.7
AB	5594	5456	2.5	27679	27474	0.7
1B	1006	898	9.3	5160	4808	6.5
2B	252	261	– 5.8	1226	1222	– 0.4
3B	28	28	– 2.5	165	179	– 8.5
HR	204	189	5.3	733	762	– 4.5
R	873	799	9.3	3656	3550	3.8
BA	.266	.252	5.6	.263	.254	3.7
SLG	.431	.414	4.0	.399	.394	1.1
XB%	.218	.243	– 10.6	.212	.226	– 5.9
E	145	125	16.0	636	617	3.8
SHO	1	8	– 87.5	34	43	– 20.3

Toronto
Exhibition Stadium

1987 Visiting Leaders

BATTING AVG. (Top 10)		HOME RUNS	
Yount, MIL	.419	Deer, MIL	3
Baylor, MIN	.412	Incaviglia, TEX	3
P. Bradley, SEA	.409	Lansford, OAK	3
Trammell, DET	.400	Nokes, DET	3
Mattingly, NY	.385	Snyder, CLE	3
Lansford, OAK	.381	Winfield, NY	3
Sheets, BAL	.381	9 players tied.	2
Winfield, NY	.370		
C. Ripken, BAL	.364		
Puckett, MIN	.348		

BATTING AVG. (Bottom 10)		RUNS BATTED IN	
Boone, CAL	.059	Mattingly, NY	9
White, KC	.100	Snyder, CLE	9
DeCinces, CAL	.105	Lansford, OAK	8
Lemon, DET	.107	Winfield, NY	8
Fletcher, TEX	.115	Nokes, DET	7
Walker, CHI	.125	Yount, MIL	7
Bernazard, OAK	.129	Deer, MIL	6
Hill, CHI	.150	Gaetti, MIN	6
B. Jackson, KC	.150	6 players tied.	5
Young, BAL	.150		

	1987 SEASON			1983 – 1987		
	Home Games	Road Games	Pct. Diff.	Home Games	Road Games	Pct. Diff.
G	81	81	0.0	404	407	– 0.7
AB	5562	5499	1.1	27648	28037	– 1.4
1B	883	958	– 8.9	4719	5154	– 7.2
2B	283	262	6.8	1443	1232	18.8
3B	43	35	21.5	261	179	47.9
HR	184	189	– 3.7	835	783	8.1
R	744	756	– 1.6	3756	3600	5.1
BA	.250	.263	– 4.6	.263	.262	0.2
SLG	.416	.426	– 2.4	.424	.403	5.4
XB%	.270	.237	13.9	.265	.215	23.4
E	124	122	1.6	627	635	– 0.5
SHO	9	9	0.0	37	42	– 11.3

Atlanta
Atlanta-Fulton County Stadium

	1987 SEASON			1983 – 1987		
	Home Games	Road Games	Pct. Diff.	Home Games	Road Games	Pct. Diff.
G	81	80	1.2	404	404	0.0
AB	5546	5414	2.4	27660	26989	2.5
1B	1079	945	11.5	5365	4888	7.1
2B	279	258	5.6	1229	1127	6.4
3B	31	23	31.6	141	157	– 12.4
HR	170	145	14.5	725	600	17.9
R	871	705	22.0	3754	3242	15.8
BA	.281	.253	11.0	.270	.251	7.5
SLG	.435	.390	11.5	.403	.371	8.6
XB%	.223	.229	– 2.6	.203	.208	– 2.2
E	141	121	15.1	766	668	14.7
SHO	2	9	– 78.1	32	52	– 38.5

1987 Visiting Leaders

BATTING AVG. (Top 10)

Gwynn, SD	.459
Smith, STL	.458
McReynolds, NY	.429
Bass, HOU	.424
Hayes, PHI	.421
Davis, CIN	.417
Kruk, SD	.405
Daniels, CIN	.391
3 players tied.	.375

HOME RUNS

Kruk, SD	4
Bell, CIN	3
Brown, SD	3
Daniels, CIN	3
Davis, CIN	3
C. Davis, SF	3
Parker, CIN	3
Wallach, MTL	3
16 players tied.	2

BATTING AVG. (Bottom 10)

Flannery, SD	.103
Herr, STL	.125
Hatcher, HOU	.152
McGee, STL	.154
Anderson, LA	.172
Parrish, PHI	.176
Dawson, CHI	.208
Samuel, PHI	.217
Ray, PIT	.227
Bell, CIN	.235

RUNS BATTED IN

Kruk, SD	16
Maldonado, SF	12
Marshall, LA	11
Parker, CIN	11
Davis, CIN	10
Wallach, MTL	10
Bell, CIN	9
Doran, HOU	9
3 players tied.	8

Chicago
Wrigley Field

	1987 SEASON			1983 – 1987		
	Home Games	Road Games	Pct. Diff.	Home Games	Road Games	Pct. Diff.
G	80	81	– 1.2	402	404	– 0.5
AB	5568	5556	0.2	27760	27298	1.7
1B	1007	1037	– 3.1	5167	5029	1.0
2B	256	255	0.2	1281	1300	– 3.1
3B	41	35	16.9	212	195	6.9
HR	204	164	24.1	870	594	44.0
R	770	751	3.8	3884	3353	16.4
BA	.271	.268	0.9	.271	.261	4.0
SLG	.441	.415	6.3	.427	.388	10.0
XB%	.228	.219	4.2	.224	.229	– 2.2
E	133	122	10.4	644	624	3.7
SHO	7	5	41.7	39	47	– 16.6

1987 Visiting Leaders

BATTING AVG. (Top 10)

Johnson, NY	.429
Stubbs, LA	.429
Hatcher, HOU	.417
Gwynn, SD	.400
C. Davis, SF	.391
Shelby, LA	.389
Coleman, STL	.385
Dykstra, NY	.385
Carter, NY	.379
Doran, HOU	.375

HOME RUNS

Johnson, NY	4
Teufel, NY	4
Hernandez, NY	3
James, PHI	3
Murphy, ATL	3
Pendleton, STL	3
15 players tied.	2

BATTING AVG. (Bottom 10)

Virgil, ATL	.118
Pena, STL	.125
James, ATL	.158
Schmidt, PHI	.167
Esasky, CIN	.174
Duncan, LA	.182
Scioscia, LA	.188
Bass, HOU	.208
Bream, PIT	.208
Marshall, LA	.208

RUNS BATTED IN

Teufel, NY	11
Johnson, NY	10
Smith, STL	10
Hatcher, HOU	9
Hernandez, NY	9
Brown, SD	7
Doran, HOU	7
Herr, STL	7
4 players tied.	6

Cincinnati
Riverfront Stadium

1987 Visiting Leaders

BATTING AVG. (Top 10)		HOME RUNS	
Law, MTL	.500	Bonds, PIT	4
Smith, STL	.500	Clark, SF	4
Clark, SF	.464	Shelby, LA	4
Hayes, PHI	.458	Bonilla, PIT	3
Wallach, MTL	.458	Griffey, ATL	3
Guerrero, LA	.444	Law, MTL	3
Van Slyke, PIT	.421	Marshall, LA	3
Kruk, SD	.414	Mitchell, SF	3
Galarraga, MTL	.400	Parrish, PHI	3
Hatcher, HOU	.389	Wilson, PHI	3

	1987 SEASON			1983 – 1987		
	Home Games	Road Games	Pct. Diff.	Home Games	Road Games	Pct. Diff.
G	81	81	0.0	405	405	0.0
AB	5589	5529	1.1	27626	27244	1.4
1B	973	988	− 2.6	4906	4868	− 0.6
2B	316	257	21.6	1376	1127	20.4
3B	32	36	− 12.1	184	167	8.7
HR	191	171	10.5	709	654	6.9
R	797	738	8.0	3684	3350	10.0
BA	.271	.263	3.0	.260	.250	3.8
SLG	.441	.415	6.3	.400	.376	6.4
XB%	.263	.229	15.2	.241	.210	14.9
E	113	127	− 11.0	607	701	− 13.4
SHO	2	11	− 81.8	36	52	− 30.8

BATTING AVG. (Bottom 10)		RUNS BATTED IN	
Moreland, CHI	.125	Marshall, LA	13
Schmidt, PHI	.130	Clark, SF	12
Perry, ATL	.161	Bonilla, PIT	8
Davis, HOU	.167	Kruk, SD	8
Strawberry, NY	.182	Bonds, PIT	7
Doran, HOU	.189	Dawson, CHI	7
Carter, NY	.190	Herr, STL	7
Clark, STL	.190	Pendleton, STL	7
3 players tied.	.200	Perry, ATL	7
		Wallach, MTL	7

Houston
Astrodome

1987 Visiting Leaders

BATTING AVG. (Top 10)		HOME RUNS	
Pendleton, STL	.467	Johnson, NY	4
Clark, STL	.450	Clark, STL	3
Mumphrey, CHI	.444	McReynolds, NY	3
Law, MTL	.409	Mitchell, SF	3
Martinez, CHI	.381	Samuel, PHI	3
Johnson, NY	.368	6 players tied.	2
Stubbs, LA	.360		
Gwynn, SD	.357		
Thompson, PHI	.350		
Stillwell, CIN	.342		

	1987 SEASON			1983 – 1987		
	Home Games	Road Games	Pct. Diff.	Home Games	Road Games	Pct. Diff.
G	81	81	0.0	406	404	0.5
AB	5488	5449	0.7	27388	27283	0.4
1B	1016	931	8.4	5035	4860	3.2
2B	219	244	− 10.9	1098	1177	− 7.1
3B	27	49	− 45.3	218	200	8.6
HR	97	166	− 42.0	397	708	− 44.1
R	602	724	− 16.9	3062	3496	− 12.8
BA	.248	.255	− 2.9	.246	.255	− 3.2
SLG	.350	.409	− 14.4	.346	.390	− 11.4
XB%	.195	.239	− 18.6	.207	.221	− 6.1
E	123	125	− 1.6	642	692	− 7.7
SHO	13	8	62.5	69	41	67.5

BATTING AVG. (Bottom 10)		RUNS BATTED IN	
Coleman, STL	.043	Jones, CIN	11
Bream, PIT	.050	Clark, STL	9
Brenly, SF	.069	Concepcion, CIN	8
C. Davis, SF	.071	McReynolds, NY	7
Carter, NY	.095	Samuel, PHI	7
Webster, MTL	.111	Santiago, SD	7
Dawson, CHI	.136	Johnson, NY	6
Smith, STL	.136	Sax, LA	6
Flannery, SD	.143	Stillwell, CIN	6
Moreland, CHI	.143	6 players tied.	5

Los Angeles
Dodger Stadium

	1987 SEASON			1983 – 1987		
	Home Games	Road Games	Pct. Diff.	Home Games	Road Games	Pct. Diff.
G	81	81	0.0	404	407	– 0.7
AB	5517	5553	– 0.6	27450	27455	– 0.0
1B	1032	967	7.4	5242	4809	9.0
2B	200	300	– 32.9	944	1303	– 27.5
3B	12	38	– 68.2	82	178	– 53.9
HR	108	147	– 26.1	524	628	– 16.5
R	586	724	– 19.1	2990	3341	– 9.8
BA	.245	.261	– 6.3	.247	.252	– 1.8
SLG	.344	.409	– 15.7	.345	.381	– 9.4
XB%	.170	.259	– 34.2	.164	.235	– 30.5
E	141	159	– 11.3	757	762	0.1
SHO	16	8	100.0	72	57	27.3

1987 Visiting Leaders

BATTING AVG. (Top 10)

Raines, MTL	.458
Perry, ATL	.406
Mitchell, SF	.400
Smith, STL	.391
Bass, HOU	.389
Candaele, MTL	.389
Clark, STL	.381
Aldrete, SF	.370
Daniels, CIN	.346
3 players tied.	.333

HOME RUNS

Dawson, CHI	4
Murphy, ATL	4
Clark, STL	3
Davis, CIN	2
C. Davis, SF	2
Esasky, CIN	2
McReynolds, NY	2
Mitchell, SF	2
Perry, ATL	2
32 players tied.	1

BATTING AVG. (Bottom 10)

Thompson, PHI	.042
Strawberry, NY	.111
Parker, CIN	.139
Johnson, NY	.143
Van Slyke, PIT	.143
Moreland, CHI	.154
Brenly, SF	.160
McGee, STL	.200
Samuel, PHI	.200
Doran, HOU	.206

RUNS BATTED IN

Clark, STL	11
Murphy, ATL	11
Dawson, CHI	10
Davis, HOU	8
C. Davis, SF	8
Perry, ATL	7
Bass, HOU	6
5 players tied.	5

Montreal
Olympic Stadium

	1987 SEASON			1983 – 1987		
	Home Games	Road Games	Pct. Diff.	Home Games	Road Games	Pct. Diff.
G	81	81	0.0	404	404	0.0
AB	5580	5512	1.2	27272	27644	– 1.3
1B	987	997	– 2.2	4733	5045	– 4.9
2B	311	267	15.1	1343	1267	7.4
3B	41	27	50.0	202	189	8.3
HR	136	129	4.1	523	620	– 14.5
R	772	689	12.0	3203	3353	– 4.5
BA	.264	.258	2.6	.249	.258	– 3.2
SLG	.408	.386	5.7	.371	.384	– 3.5
XB%	.263	.228	15.4	.246	.224	9.9
E	136	136	0.0	617	668	– 7.6
SHO	7	12	– 41.7	58	53	9.4

1987 Visiting Leaders

BATTING AVG. (Top 10)

Gwynn, SD	.500
Sax, LA	.500
Bonilla, PIT	.429
C. Davis, SF	.421
Martinez, CHI	.407
Cruz, HOU	.400
Kruk, SD	.400
Smith, STL	.385
Hayes, PHI	.361
2 players tied.	.333

HOME RUNS

Durham, CHI	4
Schmidt, PHI	4
Strawberry, NY	4
Dawson, CHI	3
Leonard, SF	3
14 players tied.	2

BATTING AVG. (Bottom 10)

Murphy, ATL	.091
Carter, NY	.107
Virgil, ATL	.118
Flannery, SD	.125
Herr, STL	.147
Bass, HOU	.158
Clark, SF	.167
Dykstra, NY	.185
Parrish, PHI	.185
2 players tied.	.188

RUNS BATTED IN

Leonard, SF	10
Strawberry, NY	10
Dawson, CHI	9
Johnson, NY	9
Schmidt, PHI	9
Mumphrey, CHI	8
Parker, CIN	8
4 players tied.	7

New York
Shea Stadium

1987 Visiting Leaders

BATTING AVG. (Top 10)		HOME RUNS	
Kruk, SD	.450	Davis, HOU	3
Bonilla, PIT	.448	Dawson, CHI	3
Bream, PIT	.444	Guerrero, LA	3
Hubbard, ATL	.429	Murphy, ATL	3
Coleman, STL	.419	Raines, MTL	3
Raines, MTL	.400	Van Slyke, PIT	3
Hatcher, HOU	.391	Wilson, PHI	3
James, ATL	.391	5 players tied.	2
Guerrero, LA	.389		
Jefferson, SD	.385		

BATTING AVG. (Bottom 10)		RUNS BATTED IN	
Scioscia, LA	.125	Davis, HOU	8
Santiago, SD	.130	Murphy, ATL	8
Bonds, PIT	.135	Guerrero, LA	7
C. Davis, SF	.143	Raines, MTL	7
Webster, MTL	.143	Herr, STL	6
Mitchell, SF	.150	Martinez, SD	6
Templeton, SD	.167	Van Slyke, PIT	6
Parker, CIN	.174	7 players tied.	5
Clark, SF	.182		
Stubbs, LA	.188		

	1987 SEASON			1983 – 1987		
	Home Games	Road Games	Pct. Diff.	Home Games	Road Games	Pct. Diff.
G	81	81	0.0	406	404	0.5
AB	5506	5627	– 2.2	27286	27725	– 1.6
1B	1020	967	7.8	4946	5017	0.2
2B	257	266	– 1.3	1129	1220	– 6.0
3B	30	39	– 21.4	131	186	– 28.4
HR	156	171	– 6.8	615	628	– 0.5
R	742	779	– 4.7	3262	3466	– 6.3
BA	.266	.256	3.6	.250	.254	– 1.7
SLG	.408	.409	– 0.1	.369	.380	– 2.9
XB%	.220	.240	– 8.4	.203	.219	– 7.3
E	131	137	– 4.4	699	662	5.1
SHO	4	8	– 50.0	54	44	22.1

Philadelphia
Veterans Stadium

1987 Visiting Leaders

BATTING AVG. (Top 10)		HOME RUNS	
Davis, CIN	.500	Davis, CIN	5
Shelby, LA	.444	Bonilla, PIT	3
Bass, HOU	.435	Dernier, CHI	3
Thompson, SF	.400	Mumphrey, CHI	3
Bonilla, PIT	.394	Strawberry, NY	3
Gwynn, SD	.391	Virgil, ATL	3
Kruk, SD	.389	12 players tied.	2
Herr, STL	.371		
Doran, HOU	.370		
3 players tied.	.368		

BATTING AVG. (Bottom 10)		RUNS BATTED IN	
C. Davis, SF	.105	Davis, CIN	15
Thomas, ATL	.130	Brooks, MTL	11
Hernandez, NY	.133	Herr, STL	9
Law, MTL	.138	Moreland, CHI	9
Santana, NY	.148	Strawberry, NY	9
Sax, LA	.148	Bonilla, PIT	8
Oberkfell, ATL	.167	Kruk, SD	7
McReynolds, NY	.176	McGee, STL	7
Carter, NY	.182	4 players tied.	6
Maldonado, SF	.182		

	1987 SEASON			1983 – 1987		
	Home Games	Road Games	Pct. Diff.	Home Games	Road Games	Pct. Diff.
G	81	81	0.0	405	405	0.0
AB	5535	5463	1.3	27631	27608	0.1
1B	954	960	– 1.9	4868	5034	– 3.4
2B	271	234	14.3	1324	1126	17.5
3B	54	34	56.8	264	184	43.4
HR	158	178	– 12.4	668	692	– 3.5
R	758	693	9.4	3596	3388	6.1
BA	.260	.257	0.9	.258	.255	1.2
SLG	.414	.410	0.8	.397	.384	3.4
XB%	.254	.218	16.4	.246	.206	19.1
E	112	109	2.8	699	671	4.2
SHO	6	6	0.0	46	44	4.5

Pittsburgh
Three Rivers Stadium

1987 Visiting Leaders

1987 SEASON			1983 – 1987		
Home Games	Road Games	Pct. Diff.	Home Games	Road Games	Pct. Diff.
G	81	81	0.0	404	405	− 0.2
AB	5566	5407	2.9	27468	27394	0.3
1B	972	945	− 0.1	4923	4926	− 0.3
2B	272	268	− 1.4	1323	1230	7.3
3B	48	41	13.7	192	189	1.3
HR	155	140	7.6	586	575	1.6
R	767	700	9.6	3332	3263	2.4
BA	.260	.258	0.8	.256	.253	1.2
SLG	.410	.400	2.4	.382	.374	2.0
XB%	.248	.246	0.5	.235	.224	5.2
E	144	110	30.9	641	649	− 1.0
SHO	12	7	71.4	50	61	− 17.8

BATTING AVG. (Top 10)

Esasky, CIN	.500
Santiago, SD	.450
Webster, MTL	.429
McReynolds, NY	.400
Galarraga, MTL	.395
Pendleton, STL	.394
Oberkfell, ATL	.370
Teufel, NY	.364
Jefferson, SD	.357
Martinez, SD	.350

HOME RUNS

Lindeman, STL	4
Palmeiro, CHI	4
Raines, MTL	4
Carter, NY	3
Hernandez, NY	3
Strawberry, NY	3
Teufel, NY	3
Virgil, ATL	3
11 players tied.	2

BATTING AVG. (Bottom 10)

Diaz, CIN	.136
Larkin, CIN	.148
Johnson, NY	.152
Moreland, CHI	.154
Schmidt, PHI	.154
Dykstra, NY	.156
Hubbard, ATL	.158
Stillwell, CIN	.158
Brown, SD	.167
Winningham, MTL	.172

RUNS BATTED IN

Teufel, NY	14
Hernandez, NY	11
Carter, NY	10
Strawberry, NY	9
Davis, CIN	8
Raines, MTL	8
Galarraga, MTL	7
Thompson, PHI	7
Virgil, ATL	7
4 players tied.	6

St. Louis
Busch Stadium

1987 Visiting Leaders

1987 SEASON			1983 – 1987		
Home Games	Road Games	Pct. Diff.	Home Games	Road Games	Pct. Diff.
G	81	81	0.0	405	404	0.2
AB	5521	5568	− 0.8	27271	27555	− 1.0
1B	1024	1041	− 0.8	5025	5186	− 2.1
2B	290	261	12.1	1287	1197	8.6
3B	45	49	− 7.4	268	196	38.2
HR	102	121	− 15.0	434	534	− 17.9
R	726	765	− 5.1	3284	3424	− 4.3
BA	.265	.264	0.1	.257	.258	− 0.4
SLG	.389	.394	− 1.3	.372	.374	− 0.6
XB%	.247	.229	7.4	.236	.212	11.6
E	134	133	0.8	672	657	2.0
SHO	5	6	− 16.7	54	49	9.9

BATTING AVG. (Top 10)

Aldrete, SF	.529
Perry, ATL	.476
Guerrero, LA	.474
Templeton, SD	.450
Hatcher, LA	.435
Brenly, SF	.429
Leonard, SF	.423
Carter, NY	.407
Sax, LA	.400
Murphy, ATL	.391

HOME RUNS

Schmidt, PHI	5
C. Davis, SF	3
Johnson, NY	3
8 players tied.	2

BATTING AVG. (Bottom 10)

J. Davis, CHI	.148
Bonilla, PIT	.167
Parker, CIN	.167
Marshall, LA	.179
Bass, HOU	.190
Scioscia, LA	.190
Samuel, PHI	.205
C. Davis, SF	.207
Webster, MTL	.237
2 players tied.	.238

RUNS BATTED IN

Dawson, CHI	10
Wallach, MTL	10
Johnson, NY	9
C. Davis, SF	8
Schmidt, PHI	8
Carter, NY	7
Guerrero, LA	7
McReynolds, NY	7
Perry, ATL	7
Speier, SF	7

San Diego
San Diego/Jack Murphy Stadium

1987 Visiting Leaders

BATTING AVG. (Top 10)		HOME RUNS	
Bonds, PIT	.478	Aguayo, PHI	3
Johnson, NY	.474	Bonds, PIT	3
Wallach, MTL	.417	Clark, STL	3
Pendleton, STL	.391	Davis, HOU	3
Guerrero, LA	.371	Esasky, CIN	3
C. Davis, SF	.367	Hernandez, NY	3
Maldonado, SF	.367	Marshall, LA	3
Hayes, PHI	.333	Shelby, LA	3
Ray, PIT	.333	Stubbs, LA	3
Strawberry, NY	.313	16 players tied.	2

	1987 SEASON			1983 – 1987		
	Home Games	Road Games	Pct. Diff.	Home Games	Road Games	Pct. Diff.
G	81	81	0.0	406	405	0.2
AB	5426	5506	− 1.5	27276	27543	− 1.0
1B	923	1070	− 12.5	4937	5210	− 4.3
2B	216	246	− 10.9	1026	1213	− 14.6
3B	49	29	71.5	173	161	8.5
HR	157	131	21.6	712	566	27.0
R	695	736	− 5.6	3290	3418	− 4.0
BA	.248	.268	− 7.5	.251	.260	− 3.3
SLG	.393	.395	− 0.5	.380	.377	0.7
XB%	.223	.204	9.1	.195	.209	− 6.4
E	131	150	− 12.7	704	696	0.9
SHO	12	12	0.0	45	64	− 29.9

BATTING AVG. (Bottom 10)		RUNS BATTED IN	
Carter, NY	.143	Davis, HOU	10
Murphy, ATL	.147	Marshall, LA	10
Law, MTL	.150	Daniels, CIN	9
Lavalliere, PIT	.167	C. Davis, SF	8
Raines, MTL	.167	Guerrero, LA	8
Doran, HOU	.171	Hernandez, NY	7
Ford, STL	.182	Bream, PIT	6
McReynolds, NY	.182	Clark, STL	6
Sandberg, CHI	.182	Galarraga, MTL	6
Bass, HOU	.194	Shelby, LA	6

San Francisco
Candlestick Park

1987 Visiting Leaders

BATTING AVG. (Top 10)		HOME RUNS	
Moreland, CHI	.444	Martinez, SD	4
Scioscia, LA	.441	C. Reynolds, HOU	4
Santiago, SD	.419	Daniels, CIN	3
Coleman, STL	.400	Davis, CIN	3
Sandberg, CHI	.400	Davis, HOU	3
Hernandez, NY	.391	8 players tied.	2
Santana, NY	.389		
Webster, MTL	.381		
McGee, STL	.375		
Martinez, SD	.370		

	1987 SEASON			1983 – 1987		
	Home Games	Road Games	Pct. Diff.	Home Games	Road Games	Pct. Diff.
G	81	81	0.0	405	405	0.0
AB	5434	5692	− 4.5	27372	27722	− 1.3
1B	903	1042	− 9.2	4848	5123	− 4.2
2B	239	270	− 7.3	1141	1214	− 4.8
3B	25	35	− 25.2	127	192	− 33.0
HR	190	161	23.6	684	648	6.9
R	685	767	− 10.7	3312	3559	− 6.9
BA	.250	.265	− 5.7	.248	.259	− 4.0
SLG	.408	.410	− 0.4	.374	.387	− 3.2
XB%	.226	.226	− 0.1	.207	.215	− 3.7
E	127	137	− 7.3	750	748	0.3
SHO	12	6	100.0	50	41	22.0

BATTING AVG. (Bottom 10)		RUNS BATTED IN	
Reynolds, PIT	.095	Martinez, SD	10
Hayes, PHI	.118	Doran, HOU	8
J. Davis, CHI	.125	Davis, CIN	7
Clark, STL	.133	C. Reynolds, HOU	7
McReynolds, NY	.143	Wallach, MTL	7
Templeton, SD	.152	Carter, NY	6
Diaz, CIN	.160	Marshall, LA	6
Murphy, ATL	.161	Winningham, MTL	6
Parrish, PHI	.167	6 players tied.	5
Parker, CIN	.194		

Ranked by Effect on Runs

	1987 SEASON			1983 – 1987		
	Home Games	Road Games	Pct. Diff.	Home Games	Road Games	Pct. Diff.
Wrigley Field	770	751	3.8	3884	3353	16.4
Atlanta Stadium	871	705	22.0	3754	3242	15.8
*Riverfront Stadium	797	738	8.0	3684	3350	10.0
Comiskey Park	808	686	17.8	3725	3433	8.8
*Metrodome	759	833	− 8.9	3949	3589	8.4
*Veterans Stadium	758	693	9.4	3596	3388	6.1
Fenway Park	819	848	− 1.0	3962	3788	5.1
*Exhibition Stadium	744	756	− 1.6	3756	3600	5.1
Cleveland Stadium	892	807	10.5	4070	3907	4.7
Arlington Stadium	873	799	9.3	3656	3550	3.8
*Kingdome	803	758	5.9	3790	3615	3.3
*Three Rivers Stadium	767	700	9.6	3332	3263	2.4
*Royals Stadium	724	682	6.2	3477	3404	1.4
County Stadium	860	819	5.0	3648	3771	− 3.0
Anaheim Stadium	782	791	− 1.1	3616	3756	− 3.3
San Diego Stadium	695	736	− 5.6	3290	3418	− 4.0
Memorial Stadium	807	802	− 1.8	3647	3811	− 4.1
*Busch Stadium	726	765	− 5.1	3284	3424	− 4.3
*Olympic Stadium	772	689	12.0	3203	3353	− 4.5
Yankee Stadium	747	799	− 6.5	3611	3879	− 6.2
Shea Stadium	742	779	− 4.7	3262	3466	− 6.3
Tiger Stadium	780	851	− 8.3	3639	3861	− 6.4
Candlestick Park	685	767	− 10.7	3312	3559	− 6.9
Dodger Stadium	586	724	− 19.1	2990	3341	− 9.8
*Astrodome	602	724	− 16.9	3062	3496	− 12.8
Oakland Coliseum	714	881	− 19.0	3536	4118	− 14.1

Ranked by Effect on Home Runs

	1987 SEASON			1983 – 1987		
	Home Games	Road Games	Pct. Diff.	Home Games	Road Games	Pct. Diff.
Wrigley Field	204	164	24.1	870	594	44.0
*Kingdome	218	142	52.4	878	659	29.5
San Diego Stadium	157	131	21.6	712	566	27.0
Atlanta Stadium	170	145	14.5	725	600	17.9
Anaheim Stadium	204	180	12.8	859	746	17.9
Tiger Stadium	226	179	31.4	930	842	11.9
*Exhibition Stadium	184	189	− 3.7	835	783	8.1
*Riverfront Stadium	191	171	10.5	709	654	6.9
Candlestick Park	190	161	23.6	684	648	6.9
Memorial Stadium	235	202	15.2	900	852	6.7
Cleveland Stadium	212	194	5.2	757	729	3.1
*Three Rivers Stadium	155	140	7.6	586	575	1.6
*Metrodome	198	208	− 6.0	862	822	0.5
Shea Stadium	156	171	− 6.8	615	628	− 0.5
Comiskey Park	162	200	− 19.9	761	784	− 2.1
*Veterans Stadium	158	178	− 12.4	668	692	− 3.5
Arlington Stadium	204	189	5.3	733	762	− 4.5
Yankee Stadium	186	189	0.5	767	823	− 4.7
County Stadium	151	181	− 16.0	660	731	− 9.0
Fenway Park	161	203	− 19.8	755	834	− 10.2
*Olympic Stadium	136	129	4.1	523	620	− 14.5
Dodger Stadium	108	147	− 26.1	524	628	− 16.5
Oakland Coliseum	163	212	− 19.9	719	881	− 17.5
*Busch Stadium	102	121	− 15.0	434	534	− 17.9
*Royals Stadium	130	166	− 21.6	569	737	− 24.1
*Astrodome	97	166	− 42.0	397	708	− 44.1

*Playing surface is artificial turf.

Ranked by Effect on Batting Average

	1987 SEASON			1983 – 1987		
	Home Games	Road Games	Pct. Diff.	Home Games	Road Games	Pct. Diff.
Atlanta Stadium	.281	.253	11.0	.270	.251	7.5
Fenway Park	.286	.274	4.4	.284	.265	7.1
Cleveland Stadium	.276	.266	3.7	.278	.266	4.2
Wrigley Field	.271	.268	0.9	.271	.261	4.0
*Riverfront Stadium	.271	.263	3.0	.260	.250	3.8
*Metrodome	.260	.267	– 2.6	.272	.262	3.7
Arlington Stadium	.266	.252	5.6	.263	.254	3.7
Comiskey Park	.272	.245	10.8	.256	.251	2.1
*Three Rivers Stadium	.260	.258	0.8	.256	.253	1.2
*Veterans Stadium	.260	.257	0.9	.258	.255	1.2
*Royals Stadium	.263	.261	0.7	.262	.260	0.7
*Exhibition Stadium	.250	.263	– 4.6	.263	.262	0.2
*Kingdome	.269	.275	– 1.9	.264	.264	– 0.1
*Busch Stadium	.265	.264	0.1	.257	.258	– 0.4
County Stadium	.285	.262	8.8	.268	.269	– 0.5
Yankee Stadium	.264	.264	– 0.2	.263	.267	– 1.5
Shea Stadium	.266	.256	3.6	.250	.254	– 1.7
Dodger Stadium	.245	.261	– 6.3	.247	.252	– 1.8
Memorial Stadium	.263	.272	– 3.3	.259	.267	– 3.0
*Olympic Stadium	.264	.258	2.6	.249	.258	– 3.2
*Astrodome	.248	.255	– 2.9	.246	.255	– 3.2
San Diego Stadium	.248	.268	– 7.5	.251	.260	– 3.3
Anaheim Stadium	.256	.261	– 2.0	.255	.264	– 3.3
Candlestick Park	.250	.265	– 5.7	.248	.259	– 4.0
Tiger Stadium	.253	.274	– 7.5	.249	.265	– 5.9
Oakland Coliseum	.245	.273	– 10.1	.251	.270	– 7.1

Ranked by Effect on Slugging Percentage

	1987 SEASON			1983 – 1987		
	Home Games	Road Games	Pct. Diff.	Home Games	Road Games	Pct. Diff.
Wrigley Field	.441	.415	6.3	.427	.388	10.0
Atlanta Stadium	.435	.390	11.5	.403	.371	8.6
*Riverfront Stadium	.441	.415	6.3	.400	.376	6.4
*Metrodome	.430	.438	– 2.0	.433	.409	5.9
Fenway Park	.442	.439	0.6	.434	.410	5.7
*Exhibition Stadium	.416	.426	– 2.4	.424	.403	5.4
*Kingdome	.450	.417	7.9	.420	.399	5.3
*Veterans Stadium	.414	.410	0.8	.397	.384	3.4
Comiskey Park	.422	.410	2.8	.403	.392	2.7
Cleveland Stadium	.446	.430	3.7	.415	.406	2.1
*Three Rivers Stadium	.410	.400	2.4	.382	.374	2.0
Arlington Stadium	.431	.414	4.0	.399	.394	1.1
San Diego Stadium	.393	.395	– 0.5	.380	.377	0.7
*Busch Stadium	.389	.394	– 1.3	.372	.374	– 0.6
*Royals Stadium	.409	.402	1.6	.394	.397	– 0.7
County Stadium	.429	.414	3.5	.399	.407	– 1.9
Anaheim Stadium	.411	.420	– 2.2	.397	.405	– 2.0
Shea Stadium	.408	.409	– 0.1	.369	.380	– 2.9
Memorial Stadium	.442	.440	0.4	.405	.419	– 3.2
Candlestick Park	.408	.410	– 0.4	.374	.387	– 3.2
Yankee Stadium	.415	.421	– 1.2	.402	.415	– 3.3
*Olympic Stadium	.408	.386	5.7	.371	.384	– 3.5
Tiger Stadium	.424	.434	– 2.2	.402	.419	– 4.1
Dodger Stadium	.344	.409	– 15.7	.345	.381	– 9.4
*Astrodome	.350	.409	– 14.4	.346	.390	– 11.4
Oakland Coliseum	.389	.450	– 13.5	.378	.429	– 11.9

*Playing surface is artificial turf.

Ranked by Effect on Extra-Base Hit Percentage

	1987 SEASON			1983 – 1987		
	Home Games	Road Games	Pct. Diff.	Home Games	Road Games	Pct. Diff.
*Exhibition Stadium	.270	.237	13.9	.265	.215	23.4
*Veterans Stadium	.254	.218	16.4	.246	.206	19.1
*Metrodome	.247	.230	7.6	.257	.219	17.6
*Royals Stadium	.268	.192	39.1	.248	.211	17.3
Fenway Park	.246	.217	13.2	.245	.213	15.2
*Riverfront Stadium	.263	.229	15.2	.241	.210	14.9
*Busch Stadium	.247	.229	7.4	.236	.212	11.6
*Olympic Stadium	.263	.228	15.4	.246	.224	9.9
Comiskey Park	.227	.240	− 5.3	.236	.224	5.4
*Three Rivers Stadium	.248	.246	0.5	.235	.224	5.2
*Kingdome	.240	.235	2.4	.237	.228	3.7
County Stadium	.218	.221	− 1.3	.214	.215	− 0.8
Wrigley Field	.228	.219	4.2	.224	.229	− 2.2
Atlanta Stadium	.223	.229	− 2.6	.203	.208	− 2.2
Candlestick Park	.226	.226	− 0.1	.207	.215	− 3.7
Arlington Stadium	.218	.243	− 10.6	.212	.226	− 5.9
*Astrodome	.195	.239	− 18.6	.207	.221	− 6.1
San Diego Stadium	.223	.204	9.1	.195	.209	− 6.4
Shea Stadium	.220	.240	− 8.4	.203	.219	− 7.3
Yankee Stadium	.199	.218	− 8.8	.208	.228	− 8.6
Cleveland Stadium	.225	.230	− 2.3	.203	.226	− 10.0
Memorial Stadium	.229	.220	4.1	.200	.225	− 10.9
Tiger Stadium	.208	.238	− 12.6	.210	.240	− 12.4
Anaheim Stadium	.190	.249	− 23.7	.197	.229	− 14.1
Oakland Coliseum	.228	.245	− 7.0	.197	.238	− 17.2
Dodger Stadium	.170	.259	− 34.2	.164	.235	− 30.5

Ranked by Effect on Strikeout Percentage

	1987 SEASON			1983 – 1987		
	Home Games	Road Games	Pct. Diff.	Home Games	Road Games	Pct. Diff.
San Diego Stadium	.166	.140	18.6	.147	.131	12.0
*Metrodome	.160	.147	8.4	.140	.131	6.4
Shea Stadium	.165	.161	2.7	.163	.154	5.7
*Veterans Stadium	.160	.159	0.6	.164	.158	4.1
Memorial Stadium	.147	.144	2.3	.140	.135	4.1
*Exhibition Stadium	.164	.164	− 0.2	.146	.140	3.9
Arlington Stadium	.172	.174	− 0.9	.152	.148	3.2
*Kingdome	.149	.141	5.8	.152	.148	3.1
Tiger Stadium	.155	.143	8.6	.147	.144	2.1
*Astrodome	.179	.159	12.1	.156	.153	2.1
County Stadium	.168	.159	5.4	.136	.133	2.0
Wrigley Field	.168	.166	1.2	.152	.149	1.9
Fenway Park	.142	.153	− 6.9	.138	.137	1.3
*Olympic Stadium	.157	.157	− 0.3	.148	.146	1.1
Yankee Stadium	.149	.148	0.2	.138	.137	0.6
Candlestick Park	.169	.173	− 2.3	.159	.159	0.5
Comiskey Park	.136	.149	− 8.8	.146	.146	0.0
*Three Rivers Stadium	.145	.151	− 3.7	.150	.151	− 0.6
Oakland Coliseum	.178	.158	12.6	.141	.142	− 1.2
Anaheim Stadium	.150	.148	1.0	.135	.138	− 2.3
Dodger Stadium	.159	.168	− 5.3	.155	.159	− 2.4
*Riverfront Stadium	.142	.156	− 8.7	.146	.155	− 5.8
*Busch Stadium	.143	.145	− 1.1	.132	.142	− 7.2
Cleveland Stadium	.139	.151	− 8.1	.123	.135	− 8.9
Atlanta Stadium	.126	.142	− 11.8	.132	.147	− 10.3
*Royals Stadium	.146	.174	− 16.5	.126	.146	− 13.9

*Playing surface is artificial turf.

Ranked by Effect on Stolen Base Percentage

	1987 SEASON			1983 – 1987		
	Home Games	Road Games	Pct. Diff.	Home Games	Road Games	Pct. Diff.
*Royals Stadium	.764	.628	21.7	.718	.639	12.4
*Exhibition Stadium	.726	.668	8.6	.713	.638	11.8
*Metrodome	.782	.648	20.6	.689	.629	9.5
*Astrodome	.802	.765	4.8	.740	.689	7.3
*Kingdome	.705	.692	2.0	.676	.638	6.0
*Olympic Stadium	.723	.790	− 8.4	.741	.704	5.2
*Veterans Stadium	.773	.668	15.6	.733	.711	3.2
*Riverfront Stadium	.748	.691	8.3	.705	.687	2.7
*Busch Stadium	.759	.723	5.0	.729	.718	1.5
Tiger Stadium	.706	.711	− 0.7	.651	.643	1.2
Oakland Coliseum	.663	.716	− 7.3	.681	.679	0.2
Comiskey Park	.732	.661	10.8	.695	.694	0.1
Dodger Stadium	.646	.694	− 6.8	.648	.650	− 0.4
Candlestick Park	.571	.599	− 4.8	.642	.648	− 1.0
San Diego Stadium	.703	.683	2.9	.681	.690	− 1.3
*Three Rivers Stadium	.667	.651	2.4	.632	.640	− 1.3
County Stadium	.651	.730	− 10.9	.650	.669	− 2.8
Wrigley Field	.691	.716	− 3.6	.668	.692	− 3.4
Arlington Stadium	.689	.755	− 8.8	.671	.695	− 3.6
Memorial Stadium	.675	.680	− 0.7	.663	.689	− 3.8
Anaheim Stadium	.667	.649	2.7	.602	.637	− 5.5
Atlanta Stadium	.714	.727	− 1.7	.649	.690	− 5.9
Cleveland Stadium	.665	.744	− 10.7	.651	.701	− 7.2
Shea Stadium	.687	.814	− 15.6	.680	.749	− 9.2
Yankee Stadium	.639	.707	− 9.5	.650	.718	− 9.5
Fenway Park	.597	.673	− 11.3	.598	.665	− 10.0

Ranked by Effect on Errors

	1987 SEASON			1983 – 1987		
	Home Games	Road Games	Pct. Diff.	Home Games	Road Games	Pct. Diff.
Atlanta Stadium	141	121	15.1	766	668	14.7
Comiskey Park	133	108	23.1	646	604	7.2
Shea Stadium	131	137	− 4.4	699	662	5.1
*Royals Stadium	112	125	− 10.4	648	617	4.3
*Veterans Stadium	112	109	2.8	699	671	4.2
Arlington Stadium	145	125	16.0	636	617	3.8
Wrigley Field	133	122	10.4	644	624	3.7
Yankee Stadium	110	106	3.8	641	632	2.2
*Busch Stadium	134	133	0.8	672	657	2.0
Memorial Stadium	118	109	5.6	605	598	1.4
San Diego Stadium	131	150	− 12.7	704	696	0.9
Candlestick Park	127	137	− 7.3	750	748	0.3
*Metrodome	116	124	− 6.5	607	597	0.2
Dodger Stadium	141	159	− 11.3	757	762	0.1
County Stadium	133	133	0.0	656	658	− 0.1
Anaheim Stadium	128	127	0.8	651	656	− 0.3
Fenway Park	93	117	− 18.5	623	628	− 0.3
*Exhibition Stadium	124	122	1.6	627	635	− 0.5
Cleveland Stadium	153	132	15.9	715	723	− 0.6
*Three Rivers Stadium	144	110	30.9	641	649	− 1.0
Oakland Coliseum	122	142	− 14.1	702	713	− 1.5
Tiger Stadium	122	136	− 10.3	621	648	− 4.9
*Olympic Stadium	136	136	0.0	617	668	− 7.6
*Astrodome	123	125	− 1.6	642	692	− 7.7
*Kingdome	122	125	− 2.4	620	672	− 9.1
*Riverfront Stadium	113	127	− 11.0	607	701	− 13.4

*Playing surface is artificial turf.